A Comprehensive Guide to

Intellectual & Developmental Disabilities

A Comprehensive Guide to Intellectual & Developmental Disabilities

edited by

Ivan Brown, Ph.D.
Faculty of Social Work
University of Toronto

and

Maire Percy, Ph.D.
Surrey Place Centre
Toronto

Paul H. Brookes Publishing Co.

Baltimore • London • Sydney

·P A U L·H·
BROOKES
PUBLISHING Co.®

Paul H. Brookes Publishing Co.
Post Office Box 10624
Baltimore, Maryland 21285-0624

www.brookespublishing.com

Typeset by Integrated Publishing Solutions, Grand Rapids, Michigan.
Manufactured in the United States of America by
The Maple-Vail Book Manufacturing Group, York, Pennsylvania.

Photographs in Chapters 12 and 17 kindly provided by MukiBaum Treatment Centres,
Toronto, Canada (www.mukibaum.com).

Library of Congress Cataloging-in-Publication Data

A comprehensive guide to intellectual and developmental disabilities / edited by
Ivan Brown and Maire Percy.
p. cm.
Includes bibliographical references and index.
ISBN-13: 978-1-55766-700-7 (hardcover)
ISBN-10: 1-55766-700-4 (hardcover)
1. Developmentally disabled. 2. People with mental disabilities. 3. Developmental
disabilities. 4. Mental retardation. 5. Developmentally disabled—Services for.
6. People with mental disabilities—Services for. I. Brown, Ivan, 1947–
II. Percy, Maire Ede, 1939– III. Title.
HV1570.C66 2007
362.196′8—dc22 2006035713

British Library Cataloguing in Publication data are available from the British Library.

Contents

About the Editors

Ivan Brown, B.A., B.A. (Hons.), B.Ed., M.Ed., Ph.D., Associate Professor and Manager, Centre of Excellence for Child Welfare, Faculty of Social Work, University of Toronto, 246 Bloor Street West, Toronto, ON M5S 1A1, Canada

Ivan Brown has worked in, and contributed to, the field of disabilities for the past 25 years. He began his work life as an elementary school teacher for 8 years before taking a position with Community Living Toronto, where he worked as a vocational counselor and community living support worker while completing his graduate studies in counseling psychology (M.Ed.) and special education (Ph.D.). In 1991, he took a position as Senior Research Associate with the Centre for Health Promotion, Department of Public Health Sciences, University of Toronto, where he managed a number of large research projects. Several of these addressed quality of life of children with disabilities, adults with developmental disabilities, seniors, and adolescents. He held appointments during the 1990s as Assistant Professor in the Departments of Occupational Therapy and Public Health Sciences, both at the University of Toronto, and taught both in the graduate health promotion program in the Department of Public Health Sciences and in the School of Early Childhood Education at Ryerson University in Toronto, which has a special focus on young children with special needs. Ivan is manager of the Centre of Excellence for Child Welfare, a national body for research and policy development in child welfare, to which he brings an important disability focus. The Centre is housed within the graduate Faculty of Social Work at the University of Toronto, in which Ivan holds an appointment of Associate Professor. Research in disability has been, and continues to be, a critical part of his ongoing work.

Ivan has a strong history of community involvement in disability, serving on numerous government and community agency committees and boards, participating in research projects, and acting in leadership roles with several professional organizations. In particular, he was a longstanding member of the Board of Directors of the Ontario Association on Developmental Disabilities and served as its Chair for a 2-year period. In 2001, he was awarded this Association's highest honor, the Directors' Award of Excellence. He is a fellow of the International Association for the Scientific Study of Intellectual Disability and is a long-standing member of the American Association on Intellectual and Developmental Disabilities (formerly the American Association on Mental Retardation [AAMR]).

Ivan has contributed substantially to the Canadian and international literature, particularly in the areas of quality of life and intellectual disabilities. He has more than 100 peer-reviewed publications to his credit—in the form of books, book chapters, and journal articles—as well as numerous other articles, editorials, reviews, booklets, scales, and manuals. He has made 112 presentations at academic conferences in the past 10 years, including several keynote speeches. He serves on the review boards of seven academic journals and was co-editor with Maire Percy of the comprehensive text *Developmental Disabilities in Ontario, Second Edition* (Ontario Association on Developmental Disabilities, 2003). He was the founding editor of the *Journal on Developmental Disabilities* and still sits as a member of its Chief Editorial Board.

Ivan continues to be personally involved in disability issues, through sharing the lives of many friends with disabilities and through sharing his household with a man who has visual and cognitive impairments. He holds a strong belief that including disability as part of our daily life activities is an enriching experience for us all.

Maire Percy, B.Sc. (Hons.), M.A., A.R.C.T., Ph.D., Director, Neurogenetics Laboratory, Surrey Place Centre; Professor Emeritus of Physiology and Obstetrics & Gynaecology, University of Toronto, Surrey Place Centre, 2 Surrey Place, Toronto, Ontario, M5S 2C2, Canada

In addition to working at Surrey Place Centre (a Toronto agency providing coordinated service, education, and research in the intellectual disabilities field), Maire Percy is Professor Emeritus of Physiology and Obstetrics & Gynaecology at the University of Toronto. She holds a bachelor's degree in physiology and biochemistry, a master's degree in medical biophysics, and a doctoral degree in biochemistry, all from the University of Toronto; in addition, she is an Associate of the Royal Conservatory of Music of Toronto (A.R.C.T.). She did postdoctoral training as a Medical Research Council Fellow in immunology at the Agricultural Research Council Institute of Animal Physiology, Babraham, United Kingdom, and in immunology and genetics at the Hospital for Sick Children in Toronto. As National Health Research Scholar (Health Canada), Maire entered the field of intellectual and developmental disabilities after a meeting with Arthur Dalton, then Director of Behavior Research at Surrey Place Centre, who recognized the potential of her multidisciplinary background and creativity for research in intellectual disabilities. In collaboration with Arthur Dalton and Vera Markovic, cytogeneticist at Surrey Place, Maire initiated biochemical and genetic studies of aging and dementia in people with Down syndrome. Research in this field soon took precedence for her, and in 1989 she was invited to join the Department of Biomedical Services and Research at Surrey Place Centre, under the direction of Joseph M. Berg, eminent clinical geneticist and psychiatrist.

Maire's knowledge and expertise in the field of intellectual and developmental disabilities continued to expand as the result of her research; her role as Chair of the research ethics board at Surrey Place Centre; and her extensive professional activities in the intellectual disabilities field, which include cofounding the Research Special Interest Group of the Ontario Association on Developmental Disabilities and the Fragile X Research Foundation of Canada, being Chair of the Publication Committee of the Ontario Association on Developmental Disabilities, and being a member of the Chief Editorial Committee of the *Journal on Developmental Disabilities*. A dedicated teacher, Maire developed a graduate course entitled Neuroscience of the Developmental Disabilities, providing her with the inspiration and background material to produce *Developmental Disabilities in Ontario* (co-edited with Ivan Brown).

Author of more than 250 published papers, book chapters, and presentations and reviewer of publications and grants for numerous scientific journals and granting agencies, Maire is internationally known for her work on risk factors in serious human disorders and diseases and as an exemplary mentor of students at all levels. In 2004, in recognition for her lifetime contributions to the field of intellectual and developmental disabilities, she received the Research Excellence Award of the Ontario Association on Developmental Disabilities. The asteroid mairepercy is named in honor of her scientific and research contributions.

Maire currently is involved in collaborative studies of vitamin E in older persons with Down syndrome; in collaborative studies of the roles of iron, aluminum, and B vitamins in dementia; and in the development of screening tools to identify support needs of people with intellectual and developmental disabilities. She shares her home with her husband John (Professor of Astronomy) and two cats and is the mother of Carol (Professor of English).

Contributors

Marjorie Aunos, B.Sc., M.Ps., Ph.D.
Psychologist, Researcher-Clinician
West Montreal and Lisette-Dupras Readaptation Centres
University of Quebec in Montreal
8000 Notre Dame
Lachine, Quebec H8R 1H2
Canada

Michael Bach, B.A. (Hons.), M.E.S., Ph.D.
Executive Vice-President
Canadian Association for Community Living
Kinsmen Building
York University
4700 Keele Street
Toronto, Ontario M3J 1P3
Canada

Sivan Bega, B.Sc., M.Sc.
M.D. Candidate, University of Toronto
1507-77 Gerrard Street West
Toronto, Ontario M5G 2A1
Canada

Joseph M. Berg, M.B., B.Ch., B.Sc., M.Sc., FRCPsych, FCCMG
Professor Emeritus
Faculty of Medicine, University of Toronto
1 Admiral Road
Toronto, Ontario M5R 2L4
Canada

Christine Bigby, B.A. (Hons.), M.S.W., Ph.D.
Associate Professor and Reader
School of Social Work and Social Policy
LaTrobe University
Bundoora, Victoria 3086
Australia

Rivka Birkan, B.A., B.Sc. (Hons.)
LL.B Candidate 2009, Osgoode Hall Law School
120 Dell Park Avenue
Toronto, Ontario M6B 2V1
Canada

Anne Black, C.Y.W., B.A., M.Ed.
Coordinator, Child & Youth Worker Program
Centre for Community Services & Development
George Brown College
200 King Street East
Toronto, Ontario M5T 2T9
Canada

Elspeth A. Bradley, B.Sc., M.B.B.S., Ph.D., FRCPsych, FRCPC
Associate Professor, Post Graduate Education Coordinator, and Psychiatrist-in-Chief
Faculty of Medicine, University of Toronto
Surrey Place Centre
2 Surrey Place
Toronto, Ontario M5S 2C2
Canada

Avril V. Brereton, Dip. Ed., B.Ed., Ph.D.
Senior Research Fellow, Centre for Developmental Psychiatry and Psychology
School of Psychology, Psychiatry and Psychological Medicine
Monash University
Monash Medical Centre
246 Clayton Road
Clayton, Victoria 3168
Australia

Roy I. Brown, B.Sc. (Gen.), B.Sc.(Spec.), Dip Psych, Ph.D.
Emeritus Professor, University of Calgary, Canada, and Flinders University, South Australia
Adjunct Professor, School of Child and Youth Care
University of Victoria
Post Office Box 1700
Victoria, British Columbia STN CSC
Canada

M. Katherine Buell, B.Sc., M.A., Ph.D., CPsych
Coordinator, Psychological Services
Kingston Internship Consortium Director of Training
Ongwanada
191 Portsmouth Avenue
Kingston, Ontario K7M 8A6
Canada

Alison Burgess, B.Sc.
Ph.D. Candidate, Department of Laboratory Medicine and Pathobiology, University of Toronto
Neuroscience Research, Sunnybrook Health Sciences Centre
2075 Bayview Avenue
Room S-135
Toronto, Ontario M4N 3M5
Canada

Maureen Burke, M.Sc.
Education Audiologist
Toronto Catholic District School Board
270 Barton Avenue
Toronto, Ontario M4G 4R4
Canada

W. McIntyre Burnham, B.A., Ph.D.
Professor Emeritus, Department of Pharmacology
Faculty of Medicine, University of Toronto
Medical Sciences Building
1 King's College Circle
Toronto, Ontario M5S 1A8
Canada

Anne Carbert, B.A., LL.B.
Research Associate
Disability Rights Promotion International
HNES Building
York University
Toronto, Ontario M3J 1P3
Canada

Dionne Chambers, B.A., LL.B.
Legal Writer
Thomson Carswell
2075 Kennedy Road
Toronto, Ontario M1T 3V4
Canada

Tom Cheetham, B.A., M.D., CCFP
Assistant Professor
H.F. Frank Associate in Developmental Disabilities, Queen's University
Department of Family Medicine
Post Office Bag 8888, 220 Bagot Street
Kingston, Ontario K7L 5E9
Canada
Chief of Medical Staff, Rideau Regional Centre
Post Office Box 2000
3312 County Road 43 East
Smiths Falls, Ontario K7A 4T7
Canada

Rosemary A. Condillac, B.A. (Hons.), M.A., Ph.D., CPsych
Psychologist
ACK Consulting and Training
Box 84507
2336 Bloor Street West
Toronto, Ontario M6S 4Z7
Canada

Christina de Rivera, B.Sc., M.Sc.
Ph.D. Candidate, Department of Pharmacology, University of Toronto
Senior Project Manager, CanCog Technologies
120 Carlton Street, Suite 204
Toronto, Ontario M5A 4K2
Canada

Trish Domi, B.A., M.A.
Ph.D. Candidate, University of Toronto
Institute of Medical Science and Hospital for Sick Children
Children's Stroke Program
Child Health and Evaluative Sciences Department
77 Avenue Road, Unit 602
Toronto, Ontario M5R 3R8
Canada

Glen Dunlap, B.A, Ph.D.
Professor, Division of Applied Research and Educational Support
Department of Child and Family Studies
Louis de la Parte Florida Mental Health Institute
University of South Florida
2778 Mayberry Drive
Reno, Nevada 89509
United States of America

Stewart L. Einfeld, M.D., DCH, FRANZCP, MRACMA
Chair of Mental Health, Faculty of Health Sciences
Senior Scientist, Brain and Mind Research Institute
University of Sydney
100 Mallett Street
Camperdown, New South Wales 2050
Australia

Youssef El Hayek, B.Sc., M.Sc.
Ph.D. Candidate, Department of Physiology, University of Toronto
Toronto Western Research Institute, Fundamentals of Neurobiology Division
University of Toronto Health Network
40 Butterfield Drive
Toronto, Ontario M3A 2L8
Canada

Darcy Fehlings, M.D., M.Sc., FRCPC
Developmental Paediatrician, Associate Professor
Department of Paediatrics University of Toronto
Physician Director, Child Development Program
Scientist, Bloorview Research Institute
Bloorview Kids Rehab
150 Kilgour Road
Toronto, Ontario M4G 1R8
Canada

Maurice Feldman, B.A., Ph.D., C.Psych., BCBA
Department of Child and Youth Studies
Brock University
500 Glenridge Avenue
St. Catharines, Ontario L2S 3A1
Canada

Elaine B. Frankel, B.S., M.Ed., Ed.D.
Professor
School of Early Childhood Education
Ryerson University
350 Victoria Street
Toronto, Ontario M5B 2K3
Canada

Ann Fudge Schormans, B.P.E., B.A., B.S.W., M.S.W., RSW
Ph.D. Candidate, Faculty of Social Work
University of Toronto
81 Cambridge Avenue
Toronto, Ontario M4K 2L2
Canada

Diane Galambos, E.C.E., B.A., M.Ed., Ed.D.
Professor and Program Coordinator
Sheridan College Institute of Technology and Advanced Learning
1430 Trafalgar Road
Oakville, Ontario L6H 2L1
Canada

Shahar Gindi, B.A., M.A., Ph.D.
Research Unit
Beit Berl College
44905 Beit Berl Post Office
Israel

Maria Gitta, B.A. (Hons.), M.A.
Editor, Clinical Bulletin and Division Coordinator, University of Western Ontario
Coordinator, Developmental Disabilities Program
850 Highbury Avenue
Room E210
London, Ontario N6A 4H1
Canada

Susan Gold, B.Ed., M.Ed., Ed.D.
Associate Professor of Pediatrics and Education
Mailman Center for Child Development
University of Miami
1601 NW 12 Avenue
Miami, Florida 33136
United States of America

Robyn Salter Goldie, B.A., M.S.W.
Social Worker
The Hospital for Sick Children
555 University Avenue
Toronto, Ontario M5G 1X8
Canada

Everlyne Gomez, B.Sc., M.Sc.
Clinical Research Coordinator, Orthopaedic Surgery
The Hospital for Sick Children
S107-555 University Avenue
Toronto, Ontario M5G 1X8
Canada

Dorothy Griffiths, B.A. (Hons.), M.A., Ph.D.
Professor
Brock University
75 Shotwell Street
Welland, Ontario L3C 1P1
Canada

Susan M. Havercamp, B.A., M.A., Ph.D.
Developmental Disabilities Consulting and Psychological Services
Post Office Box 47104
Tampa, Florida 33647
United States of America

Amy Hayashi, B.Sc., M.Sc.
Toronto Western Research Institute
6 Palatin Court
Markham, Ontario L3S 4T2
Canada

John Heng, B.Sc., M.A.
Ph.D. Candidate
Lecturer, Department of Philosophy and Religious Studies
King's University College
University of Western Ontario, London
266 Epworth Avenue
London, Ontario N6A 2M3
Canada

Raquel Heskin-Sweezie, B.Sc.
Ph.D. Candidate, Department of Physiology
University of Toronto
801 King Street West, Suite #901
Toronto, Ontario M5V 3C9
Canada

Jeanette Jeltje Anne Holden, B.Sc., Ph.D., FCCMG
Professor, Departments of Psychiatry and Physiology, Queen's University
Director, Autism Research Program and DNA Research Laboratory
Ongwanada
c/o 191 Portsmouth Avenue
Kingston, Ontario K7M 8A6
Canada

Geraldine Holt, B.S., B.Sc. (Hons.), M.B., FRCPsych
Consultant Psychiatrist and Honorary Senior Lecturer
South London and Maudsley NHS Trust and King's College London
Institute of Psychiatry Estia Centre
York Clinic
Guy's Hospital
47 Westin Street, London SE1 3RR
United Kingdom

Tom Humphries, B.A. (Hons.), M.A., Ph.D.
Adjunct Associate Professor, School and Clinical Child Psychology Program
Department of Human Development and Applied Psychology
Ontario Institute for Studies in Education
University of Toronto
252 Bloor Street West
Toronto, Ontario M5S 1A1
Canada

Carolyn Hunt, B.Sc. (Hons.), M.D., FRCPC
Developmental Pediatrician
Grandview Children's Centre
600 Townline Road South
Oshawa, Ontario L1H 7K6
Canada

Abel Ickowicz, M.D., FRCPC
Associate Professor, Department of Psychiatry, University of Toronto
Psychiatrist-in-Chief, The Hospital for Sick Children
555 University Avenue
Toronto, Ontario M5G 1X8
Canada

Emoke Jozsvai, B.A. (Hons.), M.A., Ph.D., CPsych
Psychologist
Surrey Place Centre
2 Surrey Place
Toronto, Ontario M5S 2C2
Canada

Susan King, B.A., M.A., M.Sc., M.D., CM, FRCPC
Associate Professor, Department of Paediatrics, University of Toronto
Associate Scientist, Child Health Evaluative Sciences
The Hospital for Sick Children
555 University Avenue
Toronto, Ontario M5G 1X8
Canada

Dafna Knittel-Keren, B.A., M.A.
The Motherisk Program
Division of Clinical Pharmacology
The Hospital for Sick Children
555 University Avenue
Toronto, Ontario M5G 1X8
Canada

Gideon Koren, M.D., FRCPC, FACMT
Director, Motherisk Program
Professor of Pediatrics, Pharmacology, Pharmacy and Medical Genetics, University of Toronto
Ivey Chair in Molecular Toxicology, University of Western Ontario
Senior Scientist
The Hospital for Sick Children
555 University Avenue
Toronto, Ontario M5G 1X8
Canada

Anthony Lau, B.Sc.
Ph.D. Candidate, Department of Physiology
University of Toronto
Toronto Western Hospital, McL 11-416
399 Bathurst Street
Toronto, Ontario M5T 2S8
Canada

Andrew Levitas, B.S., M.D.
Associate Professor of Psychiatry
Medical Director, Division of Prevention and Treatment of Developmental Disorders
Department of Psychiatry
University of Medicine and Dentistry of New Jersey/School of Osteopathic Medicine
101 Laurel Road
Stratford, New Jersey 08084
United States of America

Sheldon Z. Lewkis, B.Sc. (Hons), M.A., Ph.D., RPsych
Private Practice
1128 Alberni Street, Suite 2807
Vancouver, British Columbia V6E 4R6
Canada

Bengt Lindqvist, M.A., Ph.D. H.C. Medicine, Ph.D., H.C. Social Science
Former M.P., Sweden
Former Minister for Social Services and Family Affairs
Former UN Special Rapporteur on Disability
Co-director at Disability Rights Promotion International, York University (Canada)
Lyktstigen 1
S149 92 Nynäshamn
Sweden

John S. Lovering, M.D., FRCPC
Developmental Pediatrician and Assistant Professor
Department of Pediatrics, University of Toronto
127 Lascelles Boulevard
Toronto, Ontario M5P 2E5
Canada

Karolina Machalek, B.Sc. (Hons.)
M.H.Sc. Candidate, Department of Public Health Sciences
Faculty of Medicine, University of Toronto
6th Floor, Health Sciences Building
155 College Street
Toronto, Ontario M5T 3M7
Canada

William A. MacKay, B.Sc., M.Sc., Ph.D.
Associate Professor
Department of Physiology
University of Toronto
1 King's College Circle
Toronto, Ontario M5S 1A8
Canada

Diana Mager, B.Sc. (Hons), R.D., M.Sc., Ph.D.
Assistant Professor, Clinical Nutrition
Department of Agricultural, Food and Nutritional Sciences
University of Alberta
318-A Agriculture/Forestry Centre
Edmonton, Alberta T6G 2P5
Canada

Michèle M.M. Mazzocco, B.S., M.Ed., Ph.D.
Associate Professor, The Johns Hopkins University School of Medicine
Associate Professor, The Johns Hopkins Bloomberg School of Public Health
Kennedy Krieger Institute
3825 Greenspring Avenue
Baltimore, Maryland 21211
United States of America

Anya McLaren, H.B.Sc., M.Sc.
Research Coordinator, St. Michael's Hospital
University of Toronto
201-17 Lascelles Boulevard
Toronto, Ontario M4V 2B6
Canada

Patricia Minnes, B.A. (Hons.), M.Phil., Ph.D., CPsych
Professor, Departments of Psychology and Psychiatry
Queen's University
62 Arch Street
Kingston, Ontario K7L 3N6
Canada

Bev Morrison, B.Sc. (Hons.), B.Ed.
Supply Teacher
Simcoe County and York Region District School Board
Utopia, Ontario L0M 1T0
Canada

J. Dale Munro, B.A., M.S.W., R.S.W., FAAIDD
Clinical Supervisor and Family Therapist
Regional Support Associates
125 Woodward Avenue
London, Ontario N6H 2H1
Canada

Ewa Niechwiej-Szwedo, B.Sc., M.Sc.
Graduate Department of Rehabilitation Science
University of Toronto
4321 Lee Drive
Mississauga, Ontario L4W 4A9
Canada

Irena Nulman M.D., Clinical Pharmacology Diploma
Ph.D. Candidate, Associate Professor of Pediatrics, University of Toronto
Program Director, Postgraduate Medical Training Program in Clinical Pharmacology, The Hospital for Sick Children
Associate Director Motherisk Program
Associate Scientist, Child Health Evaluative Sciences (CHES), Research Institute
Division of Clinical Pharmacology, The Hospital for Sick Children
555 University Avenue
Toronto, Ontario M5G 1X8
Canada

Leora M. Palace, B.A. (Hons.)
Speech-Language Pathologist
Private Practice
58 Katerina Avenue
Thornhill, Ontario L4J 8H4
Canada

Trevor R. Parmenter, A.M., B.A., Ph.D., FACE, FAAMR, FIASSID, FASSID
Professor of Developmental Disability
Director, Centre for Developmental Disability Studies
Faculty of Medicine, University of Sydney
Post Office Box 6
Ryde 1680
Australia

Paul B. Pencharz, M.D., Ch.B., Ph.D., FRCPC
Professor of Paediatrics and Nutritional Sciences, University of Toronto
The Hospital for Sick Children
555 University Avenue
Toronto, Ontario
M5G 1X8
Canada

Adrienne Perry, B.A., M.A., Ph.D., C.Psych., BCBA
Associate Professor
Department of Psychology
York University
4700 Keele Street, BSB 219
Toronto, Ontario M3J 1P3
Canada

Oma D.D. Persaud, B.Sc. (Hons.), M.Sc.
Department of Physiology, Faculty of Medicine, University of Toronto
Vision Science Research Program, Toronto Western Research Institute
45 Major Oak Terrace
Toronto, Ontario M1V 3E4
Canada

Nam Phan, B.Sc., M.Sc.
Toronto Western Research Institute
905-801 Bay Street
Toronto, Ontario M5S 1Y9

Denise J. Poston, B.A., M.S., Ph.D.
Research Associate
Beach Center on Disability
The University of Kansas
1200 Sunnyside Avenue
3111 Haworth Hall
Lawrence, Kansas 66045
United States of America

Vee Prasher, MBChB, MedSc, MRCPsych, M.D., Ph.D., FIASSID
Honorary Senior Research Fellow in Neuro-developmental Psychiatry
c/o The Greenfields
Monyhull Hall Road
Kings Norton, Birmingham B30 3QQ
United Kingdom

Evan Jon Propst, B.A., M.Sc., M.D.
Surgeon Scientist Program
Department of Otolaryngology-Head & Neck Surgery, University of Toronto
The Hospital for Sick Children
555 University Avenue
Toronto, Ontario, M5G 1X8
Canada

John P. Radford, B.A., M.A., Ph.D.
Professor
Department of Geography and Critical Studies in Disability Program
York University
4700 Keele Street
Toronto, Ontario M3J 1P3
Canada

Rebecca Renwick, Dip PT & OT, B.A., Ph.D., OT Reg (Ont), OT(C)
Professor and Director, Quality of Life Research Unit
Department of Occupational Science and Occupational Therapy
University of Toronto
500 University Avenue, Room #160
Toronto, Ontario M5G 1V7
Canada

Marcia H. Rioux, B.A., B.A. (Hons.), M.A., Ph.D.
Professor, School of Health Policy & Management
Graduate Director, M.A. (Critical Disability Studies)
Director, York Institute for Health Research
4th Floor HNES Building
York University
4700 Keele Street
Toronto, Ontario M3J 1P3
Canada

Peter Rosenbaum, B.Sc., M.D., C.M., D.Sc.(HC)
Professor of Pediatrics, McMaster University
Canada Research Chair in Childhood Disability
CanChild Centre for Childhood Disability Research
IAHS Building, Room 408
1400 Main Street West
Hamilton, Ontario L8S 1C7
Canada

Nora Rothschild, B.A., D.S.P., Reg CASLPO
Speech Language Pathologist
Bloorview Kids Rehab, Communication and Writing Aids Service
150 Kilgour Road
Toronto, Ontario M4G 1R8
Canada

Marcus Salvatori, B.Sc. (Hons.), M.Sc.
Marketing and Business Development
Aristex Health Solutions Inc.
Post Office Box 208
Station B
Toronto, Ontario M5T 2W1
Canada

Judith Sandys, B.A. (Hons), M.S.W., Ph.D.
Associate Professor
School of Disability Studies
Ryerson University
350 Victoria Street
Toronto, Ontario M5B 2K3
Canada

Robert L. Schalock, B.S., M.S., Ph.D.
Professor Emeritus
Hastings College
Post Office Box 285
Chewelah, Washington 99109
United States of America

Ralf W. Schlosser, B.S., B.S.W., M.A., Ph.D.
Co-Editor-in-Chief, *Evidence-based Communication Assessment and Intervention*
Professor and Interim Chair
Speech-Language Pathology and Audiology
Northeastern University
151C Forsyth
Boston, Massachusetts 02115
United States of America

Farrokh Sedighdeilami, B.A. (Hons.), M.A., Ph.D.
Registered Psychologist
Surrey Place Centre
Children & Youth Services Division
2 Surrey Place
Toronto, Ontario M5S 2C2
Canada

Jeff Sigafoos, B.A., M.A., Ph.D.
Professor and Associate Dean for Research
School of Education
The University of Tasmania
Private Bag 66
Hobart, Tasmania 7001
Australia

Dick Sobsey, B.S., M.Ed., Ed.D.
Professor & Director, JP Das Developmental Disabilities Centre
John Dossetor Health Ethics Centre
University of Alberta
Edmonton, Ontario T6G 2G5
Canada

Kevin P. Stoddart, B.A. (Hons.), M.S.W., ResDipSW, Ph.D, RSW
Consultant in Private Practice
180 Bloor Street West
Suite 601
Toronto, Ontario M5S 2V6
Canada

William F. Sullivan, B.A., B.Sc., M.A., M.D., CCFP, Ph.D.
Assistant Professor
Department of Family and Community Medicine, University of Toronto
Medical Services, Surrey Place Centre
2 Surrey Place
Toronto, Ontario M5S 2C2
Canada

Jane Summers, B.Sc., M.A., Ph.D., CPsych
Behaviour Therapy Consultation Service
McMaster Children's Hospital
Hamilton Health Sciences
Post Office Box 2000
Hamilton, Ontario L8N 3Z5
Canada

Jean Ann Summers, B.G.S., Ph.D.
Research Associate Professor and Director of Research
Beach Center on Disability
The University of Kansas
1200 Sunnyside, Room 3136
Lawrence, Kansas 66045
United States of America

Frances Telch, B.D.S., L.D.S., D.D.S., Dip Paediatric Dentistry
Pediatric Dentist
Canadian Academy of Pediatric Dentistry
2901 Bayview Avenue, #219
Willowdale, Ontario M2K 1E6
Canada

Joseph Telch, M.D., FRCPC, DCMT, M.Sc., FAAP
Paediatrician, Hospital for Sick Children
Lecturer, Department of Pediatrics, University of Toronto
548 Carlton Road, Suite 209
Unionville, Ontario L3R OC6
Canada

Bruce Tonge, M.B., B.S., M.D., DPM, MRCPsych, FRANZCP, Cert Child Psych, RANZCP
Head, Monash University
Centre for Developmental Psychiatry and Psychology
Monash Medical Centre
246 Clayton Road
Clayton, Victoria 3168
Australia

Ann P. Turnbull, B.Ed., M.Ed., Ed.D.
Co-Director, Beach Center on Disability
Professor, Department of Special Education
The University of Kansas
1200 Sunnyside Avenue
3111 Haworth Hall
Lawrence, Kansas 66045
United States of America

Patricia Noonan Walsh, B.A., M.Ed., M.Sc., Ph.D.
NDA Professor of Disability Studies
Centre for Disability Studies, School of Psychology
Newman Building D-005
University College Dublin
Belfield, Dublin 4
Ireland

Fiona Wong, B.Sc.
Department of Physiology, University of Toronto
Toronto Western Hospital
399 Bathurst Street, MC9-419
Toronto, Ontario M5T 2S8
Canada

Athena Ypsilanti, B.Sc. (Hons.), M.Sc.
Research Assistant, Pleiades Project
Centre for Molecular Medicine and Therapeutics
10832 Forbes Creek Drive, U306
Kirkland, Washington 98033
United States of America

Jennie Yum, B.Sc., M.Sc.
Toronto Western Research Institute
5304 Heritage Hills Boulevard
Mississauga, Ontario L5R 2K2
Canada

Foreword

Intellectual disabilities is a rapidly moving area of study. Recent years have seen important shifts in

- Fundamental conception of impairments and what is considered to be the nature and locus of disability
- Understanding societal response
- Hearing the aspirations of the people concerned
- Setting goals for service systems in line with those aspirations
- Gaining evidence on the relationship between the nature of program inputs and socially important outcomes
- Attempting to appreciate the lives of people with intellectual disabilities through a normative lifespan perspective, which might be applied to any or all sections of the population

Writing a comprehensive contemporary textbook is, therefore, a daunting challenge. Any such text requires far greater scope now than its equivalent of just a few decades ago.

In thinking how to justify the last sentence, I found myself drawing a comparison between this text and the third edition of *Mental Deficiency: The Changing Outlook* (Clarke & Clarke, 1974), which was published in the year after I first started work. Although rather U.K. oriented, it was a prestigious textbook in the *Methuen's Manuals of Psychology* series with contributions from leading U.K. academics such as Jack Tizard, Neil O'Connor, Peter Mittler, Albert Kushlick, Beate Hermelin, Janet Carr, and Chris Kiernan, as well as Anne and Alan Clarke themselves. The editors' preface to the third edition is interesting in that they begin by stating,

> Advances in research on mental retardation in all disciplines have been immense during the last decade. The outlook since the second edition of this book was prepared in the mid-1960s has changed so considerably that a complete restructuring and virtually complete rewriting of the volume has proved necessary, together with an extension of coverage. (p. xix)

They too saw themselves dealing with a rapidly moving area of study.

However, despite the extended coverage to which Clarke and Clarke referred, today's academic would probably emphasize their book's limited scope. Understanding of the condition was still framed predominantly in medical or psychological constructs. The more recent challenge that decouples disability from the functional impairment was still to be articulated. Coverage of support and intervention strategies, although present, was still limited. That people with severe intellectual disabilities could learn useful skills and be meaningfully employed is part of the legacy of these early researchers, but the world has moved on from the first experimental demonstrations to a concern for complete systems change in early years provision, schooling, adult employment, and occupation for older citizens. Many of the topics central to *A Comprehensive Guide to Intellectual and Developmental Disabilities* were not on the agenda 30 years ago. The burgeoning of our area of study has been remarkable.

Like Clarke and Clarke, I would attribute this expansion to an expanding contribution *by all disciplines.* Relevant issues for people with intellectual disabilities span the whole of the human condition. Any area of academic interest for the general population has a counterpart in how affairs are conducted by or in relation to people with intellectual disabilities. Part of the excitement in our field is the variety of perspectives which are becoming axiomatic. It is now natural, although a relatively recent development, to be concerned about such issues as human and legal rights, self-advocacy and empowerment, gender, sexuality, parenting, aging, palliative care, bereavement counseling, health promotion, healthy lifestyles, and quality of life. At the same time, more traditional perspectives such as genetics, medicine, psychology, and education have not just advanced knowledge but also have striven to accommodate their perspectives with others. I do not pretend that there are no internecine skirmishes as newer perspectives claim ascendancy over traditional ones or traditional ones reassert themselves. However, our area of study now has an appropriate complexity upon which to attempt to form a balanced and holistic appreciation.

This being so makes the writing or editing of a comprehensive contemporary textbook a considerable undertaking. It is to Ivan Brown and Maire Percy's great credit that they have embraced the challenge and produced a book that spans six major sections covering conceptual overview, etiology and particular conditions, support and intervention, development across the life cycle, health, and trends into the future. Forty-five erudite and well-referenced chapters are needed to cover the ground. Separately, each provides an excellent review of its respective topic. Collectively, they provide a mine of information, with a quite remarkable minimum of overlap and repetition. What is more, the aim has clearly been to give this textbook international validity. It does not provide a narrow national view. Understanding terminological differences, the ways service systems work, cultural attitudes and ambitions, and scientific evidence in or from different countries requires effort. The editors have made this effort and, as a result, the claim to have produced a comprehensive guide to intellectual and developmental disabilities can be fairly made. It is a very valuable resource for anyone interested in enthusing the next generation of students, workers, professionals, or researchers that doing the right things can make a real difference.

David Felce, Ph.D.
Professor
Director
Welsh Centre for Learning Disabilities
Cardiff University
Wales, United Kingdom

REFERENCE

Clark, A.M., & Clarke, A.D.B. (Eds.). (1974). *Mental deficiency: The changing outlook* (3rd ed.). London: Methuen.

Introduction

We are very pleased to bring you *A Comprehensive Guide to Intellectual and Developmental Disabilities.* This comprehensive text is intended to appeal to an international audience of people whose careers or personal lives include disability. The information presented is purposely designed to be useful to a broad audience, yet to reflect current trends, policies, and practices that are common across many areas of the world.

Students of disability in colleges and universities will find this text a valuable guide to their learning. We consider this to be particularly important, because these students are the future professionals and community leaders in the field of intellectual and developmental disabilities. This book is also intended for use by direct support staff, educators, health care workers, social workers, academics, policy makers, government leaders, those concerned with legal and ethical issues, and many others. Perhaps most important, the book provides one way for people with disabilities themselves and their family members to learn about a broad range of issues in the field of intellectual and developmental disabilities. At a time when many families want to have a stronger voice in determining support for their family members with disabilities, such information is needed. Finally, it is our hope that the material contained between these covers will help the general public to understand intellectual and developmental disabilities better and to include people with disabilities of all ages in the communities where they live.

In this book, we have attempted to capture cutting-edge core and practical information in the intellectual and developmental disabilities field and to present it in a format for learning and for day-to-day use. The main goal of the book is to promote the sharing of information, experience, solutions, and insights in order to help people with intellectual and developmental disabilities and their families improve their quality of life. By including extra resources at the end of the book that complement the chapter references, we also intend for *A Comprehensive Guide to Intellectual and Developmental Disabilities* to inspire self-directed learning, because information in this field is continually changing, and changing quickly.

We have assembled this book for three additional reasons. First, interest in a book of this nature arose from our collective experiences as researchers and teachers, as well as from networking through our activities with a number of international groups. We realized that service providers of all disciplines, service recipients, students, educators, researchers, policy makers, and others would benefit from a book about intellectual and developmental disabilities that presents core and practical information from a multidisciplinary perspective. Because the field is changing so quickly, and because most people do not have a broad understanding of all the issues in the field, much valuable information is not readily accessible to the people who need it at the very times they need it most. Second, this text brings together formal knowledge and informal knowledge—based on the extensive experiences of clinicians, educators, and researchers—in ways that have not been done before. Finally, new philosophical, policy direction, and service approaches have emerged in recent years, and good responses to these require solid knowledge of the field.

In many ways, the issues and challenges that are most important to the field of intellectual and developmental disabilities do not differ substantially from one country to another. For this reason, much of the information in *A Comprehensive Guide to Intellectual and Developmental Disabilities* will be very useful indeed to people in all countries. Still, there are obvious differences among countries—and among jurisdictions within countries—especially with respect to laws, policies, services, philosophies, and funding. In addition, people live within cultural and political environments that often have considerable influence on how disabilities are perceived and addressed. Thus, those who use this book will need to exercise judgment in linking the information presented for a more general audience to the specific situations in which they live and work.

One of the primary intents of this book is to capture as much as possible of the environment that influences the lives of people with intellectual and developmental disabilities. In doing so, our aim is to encourage readers to place the lives of such people—and the field of intellectual and developmental disabilities itself—within its environment and to explore, as much as possible, the interrelationship among people, the field, and the environment. As noted, an end-of-book appendix contains resources; that is, a list of "where to start" when confronted with a question about intellectual and developmental disabilities. This list is by no means intended to include all information available, but it provides a way for parents, family members, students, adults supporting people with disabilities, professionals in education and health care, and many others to explore additional knowledge and opinions and often to connect with other people and supports.

We have tried to capture a great deal of the complexity in the broad field of intellectual and developmental disabilities in the 45 chapters of this book. In doing so, we have not been able to include every aspect of life of people with disabilities, nor have we been able to raise every issue that is of importance to them, their families, and those who support them. We have brought to the readers, though, a comprehensive set of chapters under one cover about intellectual and developmental disabilities. We have endeavored to present much the material of these chapters within the context of real people's lives, and it is this unique feature of which we are most proud.

One of the interesting by-products of producing this book has been the opportunity for interaction with a wide variety of people whose lives are affected by intellectual and developmental disabilities, including people with disabilities, family members, professionals, policy makers, researchers, and those who provide numerous types of supports. This connecting with others and sharing of information about expert knowledge and life experiences has helped to shape the book's content.

It is our intent that *A Comprehensive Guide to Intellectual and Developmental Disabilities* will be informative and helpful to you in your understanding of intellectual and developmental disabilities. We hope that this book will encourage you to network with others in the field and to learn about intellectual and developmental disabilities in many different ways. Above all, we trust that your learning from the material will help to enhance your own lives and the lives of the people with intellectual and developmental disabilities whom you know.

For the Reader

Chapter 1 notes that terminology regarding intellectual and developmental disabilities varies by region and country. The term *mental retardation* has been used in the United States and some other countries recently but is being used with decreasing frequency worldwide. In 2006, the American Association on Mental Retardation (AAMR) voted to change its name to the American Association on Intellectual and Developmental Disabilities (AAIDD). This name change became official January 1, 2007 (see http://www.aamr.org/About_AAMR/new_name.shtml for more information). Because this name change was not official at the time *A Comprehensive Guide to Intellectual and Developmental Disabilities* was prepared for publication, the organization's name appears as "American Association on Mental Retardation" or "AAMR" throughout. This should not be confusing for readers, as AAMR will continue to be a recognized name for some time; however, we want to take this opportunity to provide readers with this important update regarding the field of intellectual and developmental disabilities.

We also want to explain a few special features of *A Comprehensive Guide to Intellectual and Developmental Disabilities.* Appendix A at the end of the book is a glossary of terms; glossary terms mentioned in chapter text appear in bold print at first mention in the book. Appendix B at the end of the book contains additional resources for particular topics that are not listed in the References sections of the chapters and that were available at the time the chapters were prepared for publication. In addition, chapter authors compiled a great deal of information to assemble concise background discussions for certain portions of Chapters 2, 7, 8, 10, 15, and 20; to improve readability, in-text references are provided in a "General source(s)" parenthetical note at the end of the relevant sections. As noted in the Chapter 15 introduction, the information on other syndromes is presented in a special table format; general references are given in an end-of-chapter reference list with headings for easy accessibility to the vast amount of information provided.

Acknowledgments

As editors, we must begin by acknowledging the outstanding contributions of the chapter authors. Without their expertise and wisdom, this book would simply not have been possible. In addition, their spirit of cooperation was evident throughout the writing and editing process, and we very much appreciate this. We thank all those who assisted them, as well as the organizations with which they are affiliated for supporting their participation. This has truly been a large team undertaking that has drawn broadly from the considerable international expertise in intellectual and developmental disabilities.

We are indebted to a number of other people who contributed to the content and production of *A Comprehensive Guide to Intellectual and Developmental Disabilities.* It is not possible to mention all by name, but a few merit special recognition. Our chief editorial assistant, Dionne Chambers, demonstrated strong organizational skills and persistence that enabled a great deal of material to be brought together and managed during the first year of the book's production in a relatively short period of time. Members of the editorial team—Rivka Birkan, Clara Choo, Sandeep Dhaliwal, Victoria Duda, Deborah Lightman, Karolina Machalek, Peter Schwarz, Mark Shumelda, and Rebecca Zener—provided valuable comments on the text, contributed to chapters, developed helpful tables and summaries, and assisted with the numerous tasks involved in compiling a book of this magnitude. All members of the editorial assistant team are students, potential future professionals in the field of disabilities, and through this opportunity they have gained valuable knowledge about both intellectual and developmental disabilities and the process of publication. Credit must be given to Jeff Orchard of Front Porch Publishing, producer of the first edition of *Developmental Disabilities in Ontario* in 1999—the prototype for this book—and the Ontario Association on Developmental Disabilities, which published the second edition in 2003. Their cooperation has simplified production of this book enormously. Tom Dearie, Director of Communications, ThreeSixtyCreative, provided many of the diagrams, often on short notice. We also acknowledge the helpful assistance and expert guidance of editorial staff at Paul H. Brookes Publishing Co., especially Nicole Schmidl, Rebecca Lazo, Steve Peterson, and Megan Calhoun, and the numerous anonymous individuals who provided critical, independent reviews of the chapters. All of these people worked with us to help create a quality product. Their good will and input are very much appreciated.

Editing a book the size of *A Comprehensive Guide to Intellectual and Developmental Disabilities* takes a great deal of time and effort, and, as editors, we are fully aware that we could not have completed the task without support. We wish to thank the Faculty of Social Work, University of Toronto, and Surrey Place Centre, Toronto, for providing us with the encouragement and infrastructure support to carry out the work of this book. Most important, we are grateful to all those with whom we have lived and worked during the book production for their ongoing patience, understanding, helpful comments, and support.

To our parents,
Austin and Edna Brown and Orval and Maire Robertson,
from whom we learned imagination,
the benefits of hard work and discipline,
and the important values of life

A Comprehensive Guide to Intellectual & Developmental Disabilities

I

Overview of Intellectual and Developmental Disabilities

1

What Is Meant by Intellectual and Developmental Disabilities

Ivan Brown

WHAT YOU WILL LEARN ABOUT IN THIS CHAPTER

- Literal, definitional, and social meanings of terms
- Terms used in other countries
- The need for disability terms
- Current usage of the terms *intellectual disabilities* and *developmental disabilities*

In this text, the terms *intellectual disabilities* and *developmental disabilities* are used to describe the characteristics of two somewhat different but overlapping groups of people. These people have existed throughout the world across human history, and they make up part of all cultures. They are part of the wide variety of people that exists in the human population at any one time. Although it is sometimes useful for us to describe them as groups for various positive purposes, they are not distinct groups of people at all; rather, they are individuals who each add one piece to the mosaic that illustrates the rich, interesting diversity that is characteristic of the human condition.

It has only been since the early 1900s that people with disabilities have been described and classified in any comprehensive way (see Chapters 2 and 4 for the historical and current contexts). This has been done primarily to identify those who need special learning and lifestyle support and to capture the ever-expanding knowledge of disability, but it has been done for a wide variety of other reasons as well. Numerous terms, now outdated, emerged over this period to help describe and classify people with disabilities. The use of specific terms—and sometimes the use of all terms—has been controversial at different periods of history, and misuse has no doubt occurred (Foreman, 2005). Still, it is important to know why such terms continue to be widely used and to understand the meaning that is ascribed to them.

LITERAL, DEFINITIONAL, AND SOCIAL MEANINGS OF TERMS

The term *intellectual disability* is widely used internationally. Other terms are also commonly used within some countries to mean almost the same thing: *mental retardation* (especially in the United States), *developmental disability* (especially in Canada), *learning disability* (especially in the United Kingdom), and *mental handicap* and *developmental handicap* (less common today, but still used in some countries). *Developmental disability* is sometimes used synonymously with *intellectual disability* and other terms, but at other times it is used to describe a slightly different group of people with somewhat different characteristics (especially in the United States, where *developmental disability* has its own definition).

The use of different terms, sometimes even within a country, to describe similar conditions may seem confusing. Yet, such difference in usage is important to recognize and understand. It represents the unique, and sometimes subtle, regional or national meanings of a similar condition (intellectual disability or developmental disability). These unique meanings derive from a blend of each term's literal meaning, definitional meaning (if available), and social meaning.

The literal meaning of a term refers to its semantics, or one's understanding of the words that make up a term. The literal meaning represents the simplest and broadest understanding of a term, because it goes no farther than an understanding of what the term's words mean. This literal meaning is the basic foundation for how a term is conceptualized, and, for this reason, it is a good place to begin to understand it. Thus, *intellectual disability* refers to some restriction or lack of ability having to do with the human intellect, and *de-*

The author is grateful to the following individuals for providing information on the use of terms in their countries: Mojdeh Bayat, Marco Bertelli, Chan Kum Leong, David Felce, Sonya Henderson, Geert Van Hove, Yves Lachapelle, Hasheem Mannan, Leena Matikka, Shimshon Neikrug, Trevor Parmenter, Dana Roth, Alice Schippers, Michael Shevlin, Balbir Singh, Ryo Takashiro, Miguel Verdugo, Patricia Noonan Walsh, and Mian Wang.

velopmental disability refers to some restriction or lack of ability having to do with human development.

There is often a need, however, to define the literal meaning of a term more specifically (and often more narrowly) for specific purposes, such as providing educational, medical, or social services. Thus, many professional organizations, government bodies, and other groups have built on the foundation provided by the literal meaning of a term to set out its formal definitional meaning. The definitional meaning shapes the more general, literal meaning to how a group envisions the term being interpreted and used for its purposes. Some specific examples of definitions of *intellectual disability, developmental disability,* and related terms (e.g., *mental retardation, mental handicap*) are provided in the following sections.

In addition, literal and definitional meanings of terms that are in use to describe groups of people are thought of, spoken about, and used differently by different groups of people. This is because the meanings of terms are subject, over time and place, to a wide variety of changing social values and attitudes, and by cultural, political, and economic trends. Such differences in attitude and use reflect the sometimes fluid social meaning of a term, or the particular and sometimes unique way the term is understood and used by people within their own social contexts. For example, the term *mental retardation* continues to be in wide use in the United States and some countries, but, due to regional social meaning, it is a derogatory term in the United Kingdom, Australia, Canada, and other countries—to different degrees and for a variety of reasons.

An understanding of the meaning of *intellectual disabilities, developmental disabilities,* and related terms requires an understanding of their literal, definitional, and social meanings. Moreover, it requires an understanding that these three meanings blend together in many different ways in countries around the world, and, indeed, in many different ways within individual countries.

Literal Meanings

As noted, understanding the literal meaning of a two-word term (e.g., *intellectual disability, developmental disability*) involves putting together the literal meanings of its two words. Literal meanings vary somewhat from one source to another, as shown in Table 1.1, which shows the slightly different literal meanings for the words *intellectual* and *disability* from two sources. According to *Webster's College Dictionary* (2001), *ability* means the "power or capacity to do or act physically, mentally, legally, morally, or financially," and *dis-*, as a prefix, has a "privative, negative, or reversing force relative to [a word]." The prefix *dis-* is used with *ability* in this way to mean not able, except that there is an implication that one is not able due to a specific reason or cause. Thus, *disability* means more than simply not able; it means not able because of something that deprives a person of performing or accomplishing something. The adjective *intellectual,* according to the *Oxford Advanced Learner's Dictionary of Current English, Sixth Edition* (2000), means "connected with or using a person's ability to think in a logical way or understand things." When the word *intellectual* is used as an adjective to qualify the noun *disability,* the separate meanings of the two words become enmeshed to form just one meaning. Thus, at the semantic (word meaning) level, *intellectual disability* refers to a person's ability to think in a logical way or understand things as the thing that deprives him or her of performing or accomplishing specific things.

Table 1.1. Sample literal meanings of *intellectual disability*

Intellectual

"Relating to your ability to think and understand things, especially complicated ideas"
Cambridge Advanced Learner's Dictionary
http://dictionary.cambridge.org/define.asp?key=41289&dict=CALD

"Of or associated with or requiring the use of the mind";
"Involving intelligence rather than emotions or instinct"
Webster's Online Dictionary
http://www.websters-online-dictionary.org/definition/intellectual

Disability

"An illness, injury or condition that makes it difficult for someone to do the things that other people do"
Cambridge Advanced Learner's Dictionary
http://dictionary.cambridge.org/define.asp?key=22009&dict=CALD

"The condition of being unable to perform as a consequence of physical or mental unfitness"
Webster's Online Dictionary
http://www.websters-online-dictionary.org/definition/disability

Similarly, the word *developmental,* as an adjective on its own, refers to "a state of developing or being developed" over time (*Oxford Advanced Learner's Dictionary,* 2000). When *developmental* is put together with *disability* and the two words are used as one term, *developmental disability* refers to something in the way a person develops over time that deprives him or her of being able to perform or accomplish specific things.

Obviously, there is overlap between these two terms—overlap that is apparent throughout this text. Lower intellectual functioning may be the "something" that affects the way an individual develops over time that deprives him or her of performing or accomplishing specific things. Conversely, delayed development may impede intellectual and related functioning. As a consequence, the two terms are sometimes used interchangeably in a number of countries. Especially in the

United States, however, the two terms (with *mental retardation* often utilized in place of *intellectual disability*) are sometimes used together and shortened to *MR/DD* to describe a broader group of people.

The literal meaning of a term that a person uses is the basic way that person, and others, understand it. An interesting question is whether the literal meaning of the terms *intellectual disability* and *developmental disability,* as they are used in 2007, adequately describe the area or field of inquiry that this book addresses. A related question is whether the meaning of the terms used adequately encompasses and reflects the values a person wants to promote about his or her area or field of inquiry.

Definitional Meanings

Definitional meanings of terms specify what the terms mean for particular groups, organizations, or purposes. There are many definitions of *intellectual disability* in use throughout the world. (Table 1.2 provides some sample definitions of terms from a variety of countries to illustrate.) These terms differ somewhat, because of their origin and purpose, but a great many of these are in keeping with the principal elements of the definitions of one or more of the following organizations: the American Association on Mental Retardation, the American Psychiatric Association, and the World Health Organization.

American Association on Mental Retardation[1]

The American Association on Mental Retardation (AAMR)'s definition of *mental retardation* has probably had the most international impact. In its 2002 definition, AAMR described mental retardation as "a disability characterized by significant limitations both in intellectual functioning and in adaptive behavior as expressed in conceptual, social, and practical adaptive skills. This disability originates before age 18" (2002, p. 8). (See Display 1.1 for more details.) AAMR's defi-

[1]In January 2007, AAMR became the American Association on Intellectual and Developmental Disabilities (AAIDD).

Table 1.2. Sample additional definitions of *intellectual disability* and related terms

Source	Quoted material offering definition
Law Reform Commission, 1995 New South Wales, Australia http://www.lawlink.nsw.gov.au/lrc.nsf/pages/R80CHP3	"Intellectual disability" means a significantly below average intellectual functioning, existing concurrently with two or more deficits in adaptive behaviour.
Canadian Association for Community Living http://www.cacl.ca/english/aboutus/definitions.html	An intellectual disability is an impaired ability to learn. It sometimes causes difficulty in coping with the demands of daily life. It is a condition which is usually present from birth, and it is not the same as mental or psychiatric illness.
Bedford County Public Schools: Special Education http:www.bedford.k12.va.us/specialed/page4.html	Developmental delay means a disability affecting a student ages two through eight: 1. Who is experiencing developmental delays, as measured by appropriate diagnostic instruments and procedures, in one or more of the following areas: physical development, cognitive development, communication development, social or emotional development, or adaptive development; and 2. Who, by reason, thereof, needs special education and related services.
British Institute of Learning Disabilities http://www.bild.org.uk/factsheets/what_is_learning_disability.htm	The term [learning disabilities] was widely adopted in England . . . in 1996. The World Health Organisation defines learning disabilities as • 'a state of arrested or incomplete development of mind' and somebody with a learning disability is said also to have • 'significant impairment of intellectual functioning' and • 'significant impairment of adaptive/social functioning'.
Costa Rica biblioteca virtual en Salud http://www.binasss.sa.cr/poblacion/pobla1.htm	El retardo mental consiste en un funcionamiento intelectual por debajo del promedio, que se presenta junto con deficiencias de adaptación y se manifiesta durante el período de desarrollo. [Mental retardation consists of below average intellectual functioning, that appears along with adaptive deficits and manifests during the developmental years.]
Disabled Persons' (Employment and Rehabilitation) Ordinance, 1981 (Pakistan) http://www.logos-net.net/ilo/159_base/pakistan/pak_rap/leg.htm	"[D]isabled person" means a person who, on account of injury, disease or congenital deformity, is handicapped for undertaking any gainful profession or employment in order to earn his livelihood, and includes a person who is blind, deaf, physically handicapped or mentally retarded.

Display 1.1

Definition of mental retardation by the American Association on Mental Retardation

Definition

Mental retardation is a disability characterized by significant limitations both in intellectual functioning and in adaptive behavior as expressed in conceptual, social, and practical adaptive skills. This disability originates before age 18.

The following five assumptions are essential to the application of this definition:

1. Limitations in present functioning must be considered within the context of community environments typical of the individual's age peers and culture.
2. Valid assessment considers cultural and linguistic diversity as well as differences in communication, sensory, motor, and behavioral factors.
3. Within an individual, limitations often coexist with strengths.
4. An important purpose of describing limitations is to develop a profile of needed supports.
5. With appropriate personalized supports over a sustained period, the life functioning of the person with mental retardation generally will improve.

Theoretical model

The theoretical model [of mental retardation] . . . denote[s] the relationship among individual functioning, supports, and five dimensions that encompass a multidimensional approach to mental retardation: . . . intellectual abilities; adaptive behavior (conceptual, social, practical skills); participation, interactions, and social roles; health (physical health, mental health, etiology); and context (environments, culture).

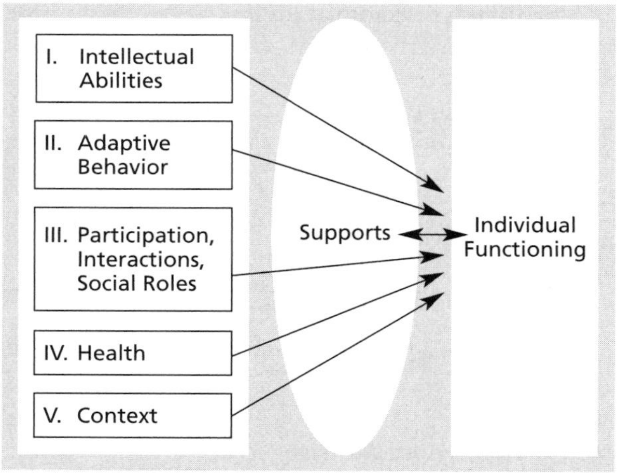

From MENTAL RETARDATION: DEFINITION, CLASSIFICATION, AND SYSTEMS OF SUPPORTS. 10TH EDITION (pp. 9, 10, & 13) by LUCKASSON, RUTH A. Copyright 2002 by AMERICAN ASSOCIATION ON MENTAL RETARDATION (AAMR). Reproduced with permission of AMERICAN ASSOCIATION ON MENTAL RETARDATION (AAMR) in the format Textbook via Copyright Clearance Center.

nition has evolved over the 20th century, and it reflects current thinking on the contributions of intelligence, the environment, support, and other interactions between a person and the context in which the person lives (see especially Schalock, 2002).

American Psychiatric Association The American Psychiatric Association (APA)'s *Diagnostic and Statistical Manual of Mental Disorders, Fourth Edition, Text Revision* (*DSM-IV-TR,* 2000) is more similar to AAMR's previous (Luckasson et al., 1992) definition. The *DSM-IV-TR* describes three characteristics of individuals with mental retardation (APA, 2000, p. 41):

1) sub-average intellectual functioning, IQ of 70 or below measured by an individually administered intelligence test;
2) concurrent limitations or alterations in adaptive functioning, lowered ability to cope with common life demands and to meet the standards of personal independence expected of them in at least two of the following domains: communication, self-care, domestic skills, social skills, self-direction, community, academic skills, work, leisure, and health and safety; and
3) onset before age 18

There are similarities and differences between the AAMR and *DSM-IV-TR* definitions of mental retardation (see AAMR, 2002, for a comparison of these and other definitions). Both are widely used in the United States and to varying degrees in many other countries. Because a great deal of the scholarly literature in the fields of intellectual disability and developmental disability is produced in the United States, those from other countries sometimes use the term *mental retardation* in some contexts to clarify the group of people to whom they are referring. As a result, the meanings associated with these terms have had considerable ongoing influence on the meaning of similar terms used in other parts of the world.

World Health Organization The World Health Organization (WHO) published a classification system in 2001 entitled *International Classification of Function-*

ing, Disability and Health (ICF). This is one of several classification systems developed by the WHO, and it is the current replacement of the *International Classification of Impairments, Disabilities, and Handicaps (ICIDH* and *ICIDH-2,* 1980 and 1997, respectively). It is considered to be complementary to that organization's *International Statistical Classification of Diseases and Related Health Problems* (*ICD-10*) (2003), a classification system that disability critics believe has too strong a medical focus. The ICF view of disability is quite broad, encompassing an impairment of body structure or function, a limitation in activities, or a restriction in participation, all of which are influenced by personal and environmental factors in a dynamic way.

Although the ICF is used to describe disability populations that are considerably broader than those described by intellectual disability or developmental disability, it serves two main functions for these fields: 1) it provides a way to understand disability in a more general way, avoiding the problems associated with specific terms taking on different meanings in different countries or the same condition being described by different terms in different countries and 2) it provides a framework for disabilities in general, within which intellectual and developmental disability have a legitimate place.

The term *developmental disability* is defined in many jurisdictions in a way that generally follows definitional meanings of intellectual disability or AAMR's definition of mental retardation. To give just one example, in Ontario, Canada, the Developmental Services Act (1990) and the Child and Family Services Act (1990) both use the term *developmental disability* to refer to "a condition of mental impairment present or occurring during a person's formative years, that is associated with limitations in adaptive behavior" (Brown, 2003). In the United States, there are a number of definitions of *developmental disability,* but the most influential is that of the Developmental Disabilities Assistance and Bill of Rights Act Amendments of 2000 (PL 106-402):

> The term 'developmental disability' means a severe, chronic disability of an individual 5 years of age or older that:
>
> A) is attributable to a mental or physical impairment or a combination of mental and physical impairments;
> B) is manifested before the individual attains age 22;
> C) is likely to continue indefinitely;
> D) results in substantial functional limitations in three or more of the following areas of major life activity: (i) self-care, (ii) receptive and expressive language, (iii) learning, (iv) mobility, (v) self-direction, (vi) capacity for independent learning, and (vii) economic self-sufficiency; and
> E) reflects the individual's need for a combination and sequence of special, interdisciplinary, or generic services, individualized supports, or other forms of assistance that are of lifelong or extended duration and are individually planned and coordinated.

Social Meanings

Literal and definitional understanding of the terms *intellectual disability* and *developmental disability* change, however, when they are used in real-life situations (Foreman, 2005). One important reason for this is that the interpretation of the word *abilities* varies. Perceptions of what abilities people "should" have, and thus the things that they "should" be able to perform and accomplish, differ considerably from one group of people to another and from one time period to another. Tolerance of people who have "too few" or "too many" abilities also differs among cultures and over time periods. Many interweaving factors are part of the emergence of such perceptions and levels of tolerance—social and political structures, economic conditions, cultural values and attitudes, and environmental demands—but somehow, in all social orders, a general understanding emerges about what constitutes typical development, and what things almost all people "should" be able to do. This general understanding forms the basis of what a person is expected to do in his or her social environment. Thus, the word *ability* takes on a particular meaning that is derived from social expectations.

People who do not have sufficient ability and cannot do the things that are socially expected of most people in their living environments are viewed as having disabilities. There are many reasons why people do not have ability or meet socially derived expectations in their particular environments. These include, among other things, genetic inheritance, chance occurrences both before and after conception, injury, lack of learning opportunities, poor family and social support, physical barriers (e.g., steps rather than ramps), systems that are too complex (e.g., electronic banking, complicated application procedures for services, use of written words rather than icons on signs), practices that are inappropriately difficult (e.g., sending letters to people who are visually impaired or who cannot read), unavailability of resources (e.g., money, housing, support personnel) in the immediate and broader environments, and very often a combination of several things.

People who, since childhood, have reduced intellectual capacity to do the things that are socially expected of most people in their particular living environments are considered to have intellectual disabilities. People who, during their childhood and adolescence, develop limited ability to do the things that are socially expected of most people in their particular living environments are those considered to have developmental disabilities. Thus, the terms *intellectual disability* and *developmental disability*, when applied, build on literal and definitional meanings to take on social meanings that may vary somewhat from one jurisdiction to another—meanings that are shaped by the perceptions and expectations of each of the social environments in which individuals live.

Other Factors to Consider

When considering the literal, definitional, and social meanings of terms, it is also important to consider two other factors: growing expectations of ability and growing acceptance of disability.

Growing Expectations of Ability Many of the expectations associated with carrying out the practical and social activities of everyday life are becoming increasingly complex. A large majority of the world's population now lives in urban areas, where it is typically necessary to use complicated transportation systems; shop in a large choice of venues; take specific action to maintain personal relationships; and deal with ever-changing technology (e.g., banking, public telephones, elevators), crowds, and many other challenges. Although many accommodations have been made in most cities to make daily life activities easier for people with disabilities, the very nature of urban life increases the expectations that people should be able to perform numerous everyday activities that are rather complex.

Whether or not people live in urban areas, daily life is becoming more complex. Technology used in the home—involving such things as telephones, televisions, equipment to play music and movies, and many adaptive devices—has been extremely helpful to many people with disabilities. At the same time, however, it changes at a rather rapid pace—a pace that is often bewildering even to those who eagerly embrace it. Literacy is a required skill in today's urban world. Computer literacy (the ability to use computer equipment to communicate with others and gather information) is very helpful to some people with disabilities and is quickly becoming a required skill; the "e-divide" is now a commonly understood term to describe those who are and are not computer literate. It is still too early to describe how much of an asset computer literacy will be to people with various types of disabilities (Davies, Stock, & Wehmeyer, 2004), but it is quite possible that it will be another way that they are separated from others in their environments (i.e., they are on the "wrong" side of the "e-divide").

As a result, an increasing number of people are not able to meet the expectations of daily life abilities, or they need help in meeting these expectations, and this expands the view of disability. When intellectual capacity appears to be the reason for not meeting these new expectations, the social meaning ascribed to intellectual disability expands accordingly. Similarly, when ability not developed during childhood and adolescence appears to be the reason for not meeting new expectations, the social meaning ascribed to developmental disability expands.

One problem that arises from an expanding view of disability due to new and increasing social expectations is that the definitional meanings of *intellectual disability* and *developmental disability* typically do not fully accommodate these changes. The five assumptions that are considered essential to application of the AAMR's 2002 definition (see Display 1.1) recognize the varying demands of individuals' environments; however, these assumptions do not explicitly accommodate expanding views of disability. For example, an adult who has lower-than-average intelligence but who does not meet all the criteria of the definition of mental retardation (or intellectual disability) may still find it impossible to cope independently with changing technological and social expectations. If community support agencies and other service organizations use strict definitional meanings of *intellectual disability* or *developmental disability* as eligibility criteria, as some of them do voluntarily or by requirement, many people who need some support—and for whom support might be warranted using the social meaning of their disability—do not get it. For service practice to respond effectively to the needs of people with intellectual and developmental disabilities, the literal, definitional, and social meanings of *disability* need to be considered in combination, and somewhat flexibly, when individuals are being considered for receiving support.

Growing Acceptance of Disability Paradoxically, in many parts of the world there is a trend toward altering the social view of intellectual and developmental disabilities so that people are more tolerant of them. It is increasingly recognized in many more affluent countries that people have a broad range of skills and lifestyles, and there is growing acceptance of people of varying skill levels and lifestyle choices. This view holds that not only should all people be free to live their lives in general accordance with the rules of society, but also they must be supported in doing so if help is required. Considerable effort has been made especially since approximately 1980 to remove some of the social and environmental barriers to inclusion so that all people—regardless of ability level, age, cultural background, and so forth—can live more ably in the general society. As a result, the social meaning of both *intellectual disability* and *developmental disability* has narrowed somewhat. Increasing numbers of people with these disabilities are included in society and are carrying out many socially expected life functions quite ably and independently.

Some definitional meanings do intrinsically accommodate a narrowing view of disability. The 2002 AAMR definition of *mental retardation* is given as an example because of its wide use. As noted, this definition sets out three requirements for determining that a person has mental retardation: 1) there are significant limitations in intellectual functioning; 2) there are significant limitations in adaptive behavior as expressed in conceptual, social, and practical adaptive skills; and 3) the condition originates before age 18. According to this definition, people who become independent and lead lives free of significant limitations in adaptive behavior might no longer be classified as having mental retardation.

TERMS USED IN OTHER COUNTRIES

Various terms are used to describe people around the world with approximately the same levels of cognition and other functioning as people who have intellectual disabilities or developmental disabilities. These terms have their own literal meanings related to the specific words and language used, may or may not be shaped both by formal definitions included in legislation or described by large organizations, and are influenced in a wide variety of ways by social meanings ascribed to them. Thus, similar terms can take on quite different meanings in different countries, even when they generally refer to the same populations.

There are also various degrees of acceptance of terms, even when they are used by people of the same language (see the footnote on the first page of this chapter). For example, the English term *mental retardation* has been widely used and accepted in the United States and elsewhere, long after it became unacceptable in Australia, Canada, Sweden, the United Kingdom, and elsewhere because it had taken on meanings that many people perceived as offensive. This tendency to move away from terms that have taken on negative connotations applies to other terms as well; therefore, the international usage of terms is quite fluid and sometimes confusing.

A number of countries use terms whose meanings are similar to the definition of the American term *mental retardation,* although the term *mental retardation* itself may or may not be used. Some countries use terms that are more accepted locally or internationally. In France, the birthplace of classification systems for individuals with developmental disabilities, the term *handicap mental* [mental handicap] is used to describe individuals with intellectual disabilities. By contrast, in Québec, the French-speaking part of Canada, the term *déficience* is used to refer to disability, and, when referring to people, the phrase typically used is *personne présentant une déficience intellectuelle* [person presenting with an intellectual deficiency], which is the literal translation, but the meaning is closer to intellectual disability. The Italian term *retardo mentale* is frequently used in the general population, although people who work in the human services field now use translations of "intellectual disability" or "cognitive impairment." In the Flemish-speaking part of Belgium, several terms are used: *mentale handicap* [mental retardation], *verstandelijke handicap* [intellectual handicap], and *verstandelijke beperking* [intellectual impairment/disability]. This is one of the language groups that uses the English-derived word *handicap,* even in legislative texts.

In The Netherlands, the Dutch terms *mensen met een verstandelijke beperking* [people with an intellectual restriction] or, somewhat less frequently, *mensen met een verstandelijke handicap* [people with an intellectual handicap] are used in formal settings (e.g., governmental, professional). The word *handicap* is taken from the English word, but its meaning differs—when it is translated into English, the word *disability* is used. These terms are literally translated from, and based on, the AAMR and ICD-10/ICF definitions. The main difference between the language used in formal settings and in services and daily life is that, in formal settings, people are said to have an (intellectual) disability, and, in commonly used language, people are said to be (intellectually) disabled. This illustrates clearly the different social contexts and the gap between policy and practice. In general language, the term *geestelijke handicap* [mentally disabled] is also used, but the equivalent of the Flemish *mentale handicap* is not common in Dutch.

An increasing number of countries have recently turned to using terms in their languages that are equivalent to *intellectual disability,* although other terms persist to some degree. The term mostly used in Spain, for example, is *discapacidad intelectual* [intellectual disability], which organizations, professionals, researchers, self-advocates, and government administrations tend to use as their first choice. Until about 2000, the term most frequently used was *retraso mental* [mental retardation], and it is still used by some people. Another term that is much less frequently used in Spain is *deficiencia mental* [mental deficiency], and the legal term in social policy is still *minusvalía psíquica* [psychological handicap].

In Israel, the term (in English letters) *pigur sichli* [mental retardation] is used and generally understood, although *nechut hitpatchutit* [developmental disabilities] is very often the term of choice by those who work in the human services field. The term *mefager* [retardate or retarded], depending on the context, is also in use in the general population. People-first language, as in the term *adam im pigur* [a person with mental retardation], has been used with increasing frequency since 1990. Two terms that are considered to be more politically correct and are increasingly being used are *yeled miuchad* [special child] and *adam em tzrachim miuchadim* [special needs person].

In Iran (currently known as Islamic Republic of Iran), the terms used to describe disabilities in children differ from those used to describe disabilities in adults. In the general culture, children whose disabilities are not physical are known to be *aqab oftadeh* [mentally retarded]. In governmental documents, children who have disabilities are referred to as *koodakan e estesnaii* [exceptional children]. This term encompasses all physical and mental (intellectual) disabilities. The term *natavan,* which is literally translated as "unable," is used as an adjective to describe a specific category, such as intellectual, behavioral, or physical disability. For example, *natavan e zehni* means "the person who is mentally unable." In the academic literature, the word *natavan,* which is the equivalent word to *disability* is used. In Persian literature, this word is usually used for "the poor" or "the elderly."

For the adults with disabilities, the term *ma'lool,* which is equivalent to the word *handicapped,* is used to refer to both physical and mental (intellectual) disabilities. Although the Iran Census of 1986 definition of this term does not formally include intellectual disabilities, the term is used in practice as an adjective to describe mental as well as physical disabilities. For example, *ma'lool e zehni or ma'lool e ravani* means "mentally handicapped." The census defined *ma'lool* as "any case of blindness, deafness and muteness, deafness, loss of arm, leg, or both, deformity of right or left hand/foot & full paralysis is known as disability." The English term *mental retardation* is frequently used within the medical and related professional documents in Iran to refer to individuals with intellectual disabilities.

Various terms are used throughout Asian countries. In Japan, the term *intellectual disability* was officially adopted in 1998. Singapore, which is a multilingual country, uses the English terms *intellectual disability* or *special needs,* although *mental retardation* is still occasionally used for some purposes. The Chinese term *zhi zhang* [intellectual disability], like its English counterpart, is typically used in people-first style: *zhi zhang ren shi* [persons with intellectual disability]. In China, *mental retardation* is the most commonly used term, but it does not mean the same thing as the AAMR definition. Instead, it refers to a variety of disabilities, usually including intellectual (cognitive) disabilities, learning disabilities, speech and language impairment, and autism. Not until about the year 2000 has *learning disability* been independently described in China.

Other countries have moved away from using similar terms. In Canada, *developmental disability* is commonly used as a synonym for *intellectual disability,* although *developmental disability* may also be used to describe conditions where there is not necessarily intellectual disability, such as cerebral palsy and Asperger syndrome. A number of countries use terminology in ways that are quite similar to the ways they are used in Canada. For example, Finland's accepted term is *kehitysvammainen,* which means "a person who has developmental disabilities." *Henkisesti jälkeenjäänyt,* the Finnish term for "mentally retarded," is no longer used. Finland does not typically use any formal definition for purposes of funding or access to education or social services, but sometimes employs terms or labels for such purposes as qualifying for a service or disability pension. In Finland, such labels are also used to excuse people with developmental disabilities from compulsory military service.

In the United Kingdom, the terms *learning disability* and *learning difficulty* have been in use for a number of years. The latter term tends to be used in the education system and sometimes in the health and social care systems. Some self-advocates prefer this latter term. People with disabilities and their advocates in the United Kingdom successfully lobbied to have lower intellectual functioning termed a learning disability rather than a mental handicap. The rationale was that these people are not different as human beings but simply have difficulty learning. On the one hand, the term *learning disability* has the same general meaning as the term *mental retardation* in the United States, but it appears to reflect more positive values for people with lower intellectual functioning. On the other hand, it can cause considerable confusion internationally because the term *learning disabilities,* as used in North America and elsewhere, refers to difficulties in learning but not lower intellectual functioning. Even in the United Kingdom, there is some confusion, particularly in the education field, where, for example, children with dyslexia may be said to have learning difficulties but not a learning disability. However, assessment of need within the education system is not based on labeling. A pupil may be identified as having special educational needs through possessing higher or lower intellectual functioning or a specific condition causing a difficulty in learning. An individual statement is then made regarding the need and the recommended response to it (this process is called *statementing*). The term *mental handicap* was historically used in the United Kingdom, and usage may still be common among the general population. Increasingly, academics are adopting the term *intellectual disabilities* in view of its international currency.

In Ireland, the term *mental handicap* was traditionally used and it persists in some quarters, but the Government's Review Group endorsed intellectual disability in its 1990 Report Needs and Abilities (P.N. Walsh, personal communication). There is no agreed-upon terminology, however, and a variety of terms are used, often interchangeably, including *intellectual disability, general learning disabilities, mild general learning disabilities, moderate general learning disabilities, severe/profound general learning disabilities,* and *learning difficulties.* Service provider agencies tend to use the term *learning disabilities.*

Sweden has led the way in introducing an interesting new concept to terminology. The view in Sweden, similar to that held throughout the Nordic countries, is that the use of terms is related to societal attitudes and that it is important to adopt terms that suggest desired attitudes and reflect those that are commonly held. Thus, it is also considered important to shift toward description of the function and away from a description of the impairment. The Swedes also have a language tradition of finding descriptive expressions (e.g., a cleaner is now called *an office caretaker*) and a general ideology that embraces the importance of reducing social inequities. For these reasons, Sweden uses the term *förstånds hinder* [understanding-inhibition]. It will be very interesting to track the international impact of this idea in future years as the social meanings of intellectual disability and developmental disability evolve.

A few countries have developed their own definitions and criteria that are used for service eligibility. For example, the term *intellectual disability,* not *mental retardation,* is used in Australia. Its meaning is set out in the Intellectually Disabled Persons' Services Act 1986, but it is close to the AAMR and APA definitions of mental retardation: intellectual disability in a person older than 5 years of age means a significant subaverage general intellectual functioning that co-occurs with deficits in adaptive behavior and is manifested during the developmental period. As in many other countries, the currently accepted way to address people with intellectual disabilities in Australia is to use people-first language, as in "person with an intellectual disability." Unlike some parts of the United States and Australia, most other developed countries do not have formal definitions of *developmental disabilities* or similar terms, at least not for use as criteria for access to services. This is generally the case, for example, in Belgium, Canada, Finland, Japan, Sweden, and the United Kingdom.

Overall, there is considerable overlap among the terms that are used around the world, but current usage in different countries also illustrates the importance of understanding that the precise meaning of the terms is a unique blending of the literal, definitional, and social meanings. Although the people being addressed may be very similar, the actual meanings of the words used to describe them across various languages differ in many, often subtle ways. The social contexts within which these terms are used vary considerably from region to region, and even the same word in the same language may be accompanied by values, attitudes, or connotations that render quite distinct meanings.

NEED FOR DISABILITY TERMS

Throughout history, people who have lower intellectual or developmental functioning have often been referred to through the use of special terminology. As of 2007, these individuals may be called "people with intellectual disabilities" or "people with developmental disabilities." An interesting question is whether other people, such as this book's editors, contributors, and readers, need to use such terms as *intellectual disability* and *developmental disability* at all.

Dangers of Using Disability Terms

Terms that are related to intellectual disability and developmental disability have been misused, both directly and indirectly, in numerous well-documented ways. These include isolating people from their families, friends, and communities; segregating people in schools, residences, and workplaces; denying personal freedoms and human rights; and preventing procreation (Roeher Institute, 1997; Zola, 1993). These misuses have had a significant negative impact on individuals' lives, and many of them continue in some form today. Misuse of terminology has caused some terms to become obsolete, a situation about which many disability advocacy groups have spoken (e.g., self-advocacy groups in some countries objected to individuals being called "retarded" after the term took on derogatory connotations). Some groups of people, such as those who have low hearing or vision, sometimes avoid the term *disability* altogether and instead describe their lifestyle as a subculture (e.g., Freebody & Power, 2001). For reasons such as these, the cautions about misuse of terms that are found throughout the literature on intellectual and developmental disabilities need to be clearly understood and assiduously applied.

Another danger more closely related to the meaning of terms is that terms used to describe those on the margins of society have a nasty habit of taking on negative connotations because of stereotyping (Blaska, 1993), even resulting at times in people with disabilities themselves not always wanting to be associated with the terms (Kaplan, 2005). It is almost impossible for individuals in the 21st century to believe those with lower intellectual functioning were once referred to as *idiots, morons, feeble-minded,* and *mentally deficient* by well-meaning and caring people. Throughout the last half of the 20th century, the term *mentally retarded* was quite respectable in most parts of the world, whereas many people now feel thoroughly insulted if they are called mentally retarded. In many countries, the term *devel-*

opmental handicap began to be commonly used around 1980 as a more acceptable alternative, but soon the word *handicap* was seen to have the wrong connotations, and *disability* quickly replaced it.

What are the chances of *intellectual disability* or *developmental disability* remaining respectable terms? Probably not good! In time, other more "appropriate" terms will replace them because the social meanings of the terms will change.

Why is there such a turnover of terms? Using special terms to refer to people whose lower abilities lead others to believe they are on the margins of society leads to a cycle of devaluation and degradation. The terms classify people, either formally or informally, as different. Classifying others as different carries with it perceptions that they are "not worthy" and "outsiders." Such perceptions lead others to treat those classified as different as if they really are different. Finally, treating people differently leads them to act differently. The irony is that because they act differently, those who classified them in the first place feel assured that their classification has been correct all along and it was therefore justified. Thus, the cycle may continue. This situation suggests that terms such as *intellectual disability* and *developmental disability* are harmful and perhaps best abandoned wherever possible.

Reasons for Using Disability Terms

The terms *intellectual disability, developmental disability,* and related terms are useful for several purposes. Six of the most important are highlighted in this section.

1. The principal argument that is used to support the use of terms such as *intellectual disability* and *developmental disability* is that they help to identify, and thus to assist, people who have special needs. Within the present context, it is often useful to classify people as having such disabilities so that they may receive the help they need to carry out the activities of daily living. This help may occur at any age and in many places, such as in family homes, in health services, in schools, in vocational and life skills development programs, or in the homes of adults with disabilities. Those who fund special assistance programs and those who provide them often want to be assured that their efforts are going to the intended recipients. Thus, classifying people as having intellectual disabilities or developmental disabilities can often lead to much-needed supports from those who fund programs. In practice, either formal or informal definitions may be used for such purposes, although there is often considerably more flexibility to respond to the needs of individuals when informal definitions influenced by the social meaning of intellectual disability or developmental disability are used.

2. People who are somewhat marginalized in society, such as those with intellectual and developmental disabilities, often need specific legal protection to express themselves personally and to participate fully in their communities. Terms that are identified with such groups can be used in legislation and legal documents to set out such protections. At the same time, including terms in legal documents demonstrates a commitment by the broader society to include identified marginalized groups. The material presented in Chapters 5 and 6 outlines rights and entitlements and illustrates the importance of such terms as *physical or mental handicap* for providing protection for people with disabilities. Many countries use terms similar to *intellectual disability* and *developmental disability* to such positive advantage. For example, Norway is often seen as having supportive laws regarding patient rights and child rights, and Canada and the United States are highly regarded by many countries for their legal recognition of minorities and other groups that may be marginalized.

3. Professionals who work in the intellectual and developmental disabilities fields, parents, and others sometimes need to use these terms to clarify to others what might be expected of a person with a disability. At times, people find it helpful to use other terms that have similar meanings to help others understand the nature of a disability. For example, a professional who is explaining, for the first time, the nature of delayed development in a young child to parents who have had no experience with disabilities might say something like, "Your child appears to have a developmental delay. Some people call this a developmental handicap, or developmentally challenged, or mental retardation, or mental handicap, but these all basically mean the same thing—that your child will be able to do many of the things that other children her age can typically do, but it will take her more time and effort to learn to do them. Some of those things she may not learn to do at all. However, she will learn other things that are important to her."

4. The terms *intellectual disability* and *developmental disability,* and their numerous subterms, are useful to classify various categories of disabilities. By allowing for precision, such classification helps to broaden knowledge of specific disabilities through research and practice and to understand better what services and treatments are required for people to live in the best possible ways.

5. Individual self-advocates and groups of self-advocates, such as People First and numerous others (see Chapter 6), take advantage of terms such as *intellectual disability* and *developmental disability* to make their cause known to others in ways that can be clearly understood. Parent and family groups, some of which play a strong advocacy role in various jurisdictions, often find it very helpful to draw attention to what it

means to have a child or family member with an intellectual or developmental disability and to show that this experience is different from that of having a child or family member without a disability.

6. Leaders in the fields of intellectual and developmental disabilities—such as academics, researchers, policy makers, and heads of organizations—need a term that describes their area of interest and that focuses attention on a specific set of issues. Having a field that is identified by the name of the disability adds a legitimacy to this area of interest and its set of issues and sets it apart as something that is worthwhile. In the same line of thinking, national and international organizations find it helpful to use these terms to describe their focus of interest. Some examples include the International Association for the Scientific Study of Intellectual Disabilities, the American Association on Mental Retardation, and the Australasian Society for the Study of Intellectual Disability.

CURRENT USAGE OF THE TERMS *INTELLECTUAL DISABILITIES* AND *DEVELOPMENTAL DISABILITIES*

For children, the term *developmental delay* is commonly used instead of *intellectual disability* or *developmental disability*. The reasoning is that all aspects of development are still in progress. It is possible that the delay is caused by a condition that will not persist over time and that there will not be an ongoing disability.

As of 2007, it is quite acceptable to talk about intellectual disabilities (or similar terms) as a group of disabilities, about the field of intellectual disabilities, or about people with intellectual disabilities as a whole population. (For a summary of acceptable terms, see Table 1.3.) When referring to a specific individual, however, the practice is to simply use the person's name. The reason for this was set out clearly by the Canadian Association for Community Living (2004), which noted that

> Intellectual disability, or mental handicap, was at one time called mental retardation. We have been informed by people who have an intellectual disability that they resent being labeled by this term. For this reason, we always refer to people for who they are, rather than by what they are (i.e., the "disabled").

Sometimes, for purposes of clarification, a term such as *intellectual disability* is added in people-first format, as in the following example: "Sarah, a woman with an intellectual disability." Alternatively, professionals who work in services for people with intellectual or developmental disabilities very often use the verb *support* when clarification is needed. Thus, they would say, "Sarah, a woman we support." This is thought to be more respectful of the person and to promote current thinking that the principal purpose of services is to support individuals in ways that will maximize their potential and their enjoyment of life.

Table 1.3. Acceptable use of *intellectual disabilities, developmental disabilities,* and related terms as of 2007

Term (applicable group)	Generally acceptable use	Example
Intellectual disabilities (adults or children)	A group of disabilities	"The disabilities related to intellectual and other abilities"
	A field of study or service	"Research in intellectual disabilities"
	Adjective for a group of people	"People with intellectual disabilities"
Intellectual disability (adults or children)	The term in general	"The meaning of *intellectual disability*"
	Adjective for an individual	"Sarina, a woman with an intellectual disability"
Developmental disabilities (adults or children)	A group of disabilities	"The disabilities related to the development of abilities"
	A field of study or service	"Supports for developmental disabilities"
	Adjective for a group of people	"Individuals with developmental disabilities"
Developmental disability (adults or children)	The term in general	"A definition of *developmental disability*"
	Adjective for an individual	"Jose, a man with a developmental disability"
Developmental delay (children only)	The field of study or service	"Study in developmental delay"
	Adjective for a group of children	"Education for children with developmental delay"
	Adjective for an individual child	"Kareem, a boy with a developmental delay"

People First, a large international organization that represents people with intellectual and developmental disabilities, suggests that people-first language should always be used. It is interesting to note that people with disabilities seldom refer to themselves by terminology at all in the course of carrying out their daily lives (Finlay & Lyons, 2005). The principal reason for this has been documented in many personal stories—it is simply that people with intellectual and developmental disabilities see themselves primarily as human beings, living in a world with other human beings. Like most of us, though, they recognize that they have more things in common with some people than others, and thus they often associate naturally with other people who have similar abilities and interests.

SUMMARY

The meanings of terms are a blend of their literal, definitional, and social meanings. For this reason, specific meanings vary somewhat among jurisdictions. The literal meaning of *intellectual disability*—a person's skill or power to know and understand, as the thing that deprives him or her of performing or accomplishing specific things—is tempered by widely accepted definitions of *intellectual disability* and similar terms (e.g., AAMR's definition of *mental retardation*) and by specific social contexts within which the term is used. Similarly, the literal meaning of *developmental disability*—something in the way a person grows and changes over time that deprives him or her of developing the abilities to perform or accomplish specific things—takes on specific meaning by those who use it in the jurisdictions where they live and work. A number of terms are used around the world to describe similar populations. There has been, and continues to be, misuse of terms, but there are also several advantages to using them. It is best to use people's names or people-first terminology when clarification is required.

FOR FURTHER THOUGHT AND DISCUSSION

1. Examine your own personal ideas and values around the term *intellectual disability,* and describe the social meaning you attach to the term.
2. To what degree should there be internationally understood meanings of the terms *intellectual disability* and *developmental disability*? What are the advantages and disadvantages to having such internationally understood meanings?
3. Do the terms *intellectual disability* and *developmental disability* encompass and reflect the values you hold for your field?
4. Examine the literal meaning of the term *intellectual disability* and the common definitional meanings for this term used in your country. What are some of the factors in your country that contribute to the social meaning of *intellectual disability*? How do these factors alter how people in your country think of the term's meaning?
5. The term *developmental delay* is often used for children, because they are still in their developmental years. Should different terms be used for children and adults? What are the advantages and disadvantages of using different terms for children and adults? When shaping your response, consider adolescents. If different terms are used for children and adults, at what age or stage of life is it best to change from using one term to using the other?
6. Is there a place for the term *mental retardation* in countries, or regions of countries, where this term has come to mean something derogatory?

REFERENCES

American Association on Mental Retardation. (2002). *Mental retardation: Definition, classification, and systems of supports* (10th ed.). Washington, DC: Author.

American Psychiatric Association. (2000). *Diagnostic and statistical manual of mental disorders* (4th ed., text rev.). Washington, DC: Author.

Blaska, J. (1993). The power of language: Speak and write using "person first." In M. Nager (Ed.), *Perspectives on disability* (2nd ed., pp. 25–32). Palo Alto, CA: Health Markets Research.

Brown, I. (2003). What do we mean by developmental disabilities in Ontario? In I. Brown & M. Percy (Eds.), *Developmental disabilities in Ontario* (2nd ed., pp. 19–30). Toronto: Ontario Association on Developmental Disabilities.

Canadian Association for Community Living. (2004). *Some definitions.* Retrieved November 24, 2004, from http://www.cacl.ca/english/aboutus/definitions.html

Davies, D.K., Stock, S.E., & Wehmeyer, M.L. (2004). Computer-mediated, self-directed computer training and skill assessment for individuals with mental retardation. *Journal of Developmental and Physical Disabilities, 16,* 95–105.

Developmental Disabilities Assistance and Bill of Rights Act Amendments of 2000, PL 106-402, 42 U.S.C. §§ 6000 *et seq.*

Finlay, W.M.L., & Lyons, E. (2005). Rejecting the label: A social constructionist analysis. *Mental Retardation, 43,* 120–134.

Foreman, P. (2005). Language and disability. *Journal of Intellectual & Developmental Disability, 30,* 57–59.

Freebody, P., & Power, D. (2001). Interviewing deaf adults in postsecondary educational settings: Stories, cultures, and life histories. *Journal of Deaf Studies and Deaf Education, 6,* 130–142.

Intellectually Disabled Persons' Services Act 1986, Act No. 53/1986: Version incorporating amendments as at 12 December 2005. Retrieved March 4, 2006, from http://www.dms.dpc.vic.gov.au/Domino/Web_Notes/LDMS/PubLawToday.nsf?OpenDatabase

Iran 1986 Population and Housing Census. (1986). Retrieved March 4, 2006 from http://www.ipums.umn.edu/international/CensusForms/Asia/Iran86.pdf

Kaplan, D. (2005). *The definition of disability.* Retrieved June 16, 2005, from http://www.accessiblesociety.org/topics/demographics-identity/dkaplanpaper.htm

Lin, J.-D. (2003a). The exploratory study of the definition and classification of disability. *Journal of Medical Science, 23,* 19–22.

Lin, J.-D. (2003b). Intellectual disability: Definition, diagnosis and classification. *Journal of Medical Science, 23,* 83–90.

Luckasson, R., Coulter, D.L., Polloway, E.A., Reiss, S., Schalock, R.L., Snell, M.E., et al. (1992). *Mental retardation: Definition, classification, and systems of supports* (9th ed.). Washington, DC: Author.

Ontario Developmental Services Act. (1990). R.S.O. 1990 Chapter D.11. Retrieved March 4, 2006, from http://www.mcss.gov.on.ca/CFCS/en/programs/SCS/DevelopmentalServices/Legislation/default.htm

Ontario Child and Family Services Act. (1990). R.S.O. 1990, CHAPTER C.11 Retrieved March 4, 2006, from http://72.14.207.104/search?q=cache:wiOPTBiFLXEJ:www.e-laws.gov.on.ca/DBLaws/Statutes/English/90c11_e.htm+cHILD+AND+FAMILY+SERVICES+ACT+1990+ONTARIO&hl=en&gl=ca&ct=clnk&cd=1

Oxford Advanced Learner's Dictionary of Current English (6th ed.). (2000). Oxford, United Kingdom: Oxford University Press.

Roeher Institute. (1997). *Disability, community and society: Exploring the links.* Toronto: Author.

Schalock, R.L. (2002). Definitional issues. In R.L. Schalock, P.C. Baker, & M.D. Croser (Eds.), *Embarking on a new century: Mental retardation at the end of the 20th century* (pp. 45–66). Washington, DC: American Association on Mental Retardation.

Webster's College Dictionary (4th ed.). (2001). New York: Random House.

World Health Organization. (1980). *International Classification of Impairments, Disabilities, and Handicaps.* Retrieved March 4, 2006, from http://www.alternatives.com/wow/who-old.htm

World Health Organization. (1997). *ICIDH-2: International Classification of Impairments, Activities, and Participation: A manual of dimensions of disablement and functioning.* Geneva: Author.

World Health Organization. (2001). *International Classification of Functioning, Disability and Health (ICF).* Geneva: Author.

World Health Organization. (2003). *International Statistical Classification of Diseases and Related Health Problems, 10th Revision (ICD-10).* Geneva: Author.

Zola, I.K. (1993). Self, identity and the naming question: Reflections on the language of disability. In M. Nager (Ed.), *Perspectives on disability* (2nd ed., pp. 15–23). Palo Alto, CA: Health Markets Research.

2

Historical Overview of Intellectual and Developmental Disabilities

IVAN BROWN AND JOHN P. RADFORD

WHAT YOU WILL LEARN ABOUT IN THIS CHAPTER

- Disability in antiquity
- Disability in the medieval era
- The expansion of disability as difference
- Inclusion in communities

Other chapters in this book primarily address recent and current issues in intellectual and developmental disabilities, although many ground their material in historical aspects that have influenced their specific topics. This chapter, however, provides an historical overview of intellectual and developmental disabilities. Understanding how these disabilities were perceived and treated in various ages gives some perspective on the way societies view disability today.

Perception and treatment of disability has differed considerably over time and across the regions of the world, and it is not possible in an overview to capture all of the known details. Rather, major trends that may influence current thinking are provided with accompanying examples. Of necessity, particular emphasis is given to the trends in areas that have become more affluent nations, where historical information is more readily and widely available to the authors.

Although disability has always been present, it has been perceived differently over time. Even since the early 1900s, thinking about disability has changed markedly. For this reason, it is essential to remember that when we speak of intellectual or developmental disability in an historical context, people at the time did not think of disability as we do today (Berkson, 2006; Goodey, 2001; Stainton, 2001). Also, people who lived in one era did not necessarily think of disabling conditions in the same way as people who lived in other eras or even in other parts of the world during the same era. Indeed, the word *disability* is very much a social concept (or social construct), because its meaning is not stable across time and place; rather, its very meaning and the connotations that accompany that meaning emerge from a variety of social and other environmental factors that are present in particular places and times (see also Chapter 1 for more information on the social meaning of terms). Thus, the terms *disability* and *intellectual disability* are used in this chapter purely for the sake of convenience, and it must be understood that many different descriptive terms have been used across time. Some such terms that are familiar are *fools, idiots, feeble-minded,* and *morons,* but there were many others. At the time of their use, such terms were sometimes used to describe groups of people or their development and thus were often value neutral. At other times (especially when terms had been in use for a while), they became derogatory or were used to categorize people in an unfair way—in the sense that today's "labels" are often considered overly restrictive, even if they are descriptive. The following section further explores these ideas.

DISABILITY IN ANTIQUITY

Detailed and relevant recorded documentation of disability in early history is a rare commodity. Consequently, investigation of disability in ancient times has necessarily spilled over into such disciplines as archaeology, anthropology, and genealogy. Evidence of disability in ancient cultures is sometimes categorized into two broad classes: natural (evidence from the remains of humans—e.g., bones, teeth) and cultural (evidence from cultural artifacts and recorded histories). Valuable clues to the existence of disability and treatment of people with disabilities may be drawn from each of these two sources. Natural evidence is almost invariably supplemented by cultural evidence—that is, written and graphic documentation, domestic relics, tools, art, architecture, and even spoken chronicles passed down through generations.

The authors are grateful to Peter Schwarz for research assistance and to Joseph M. Berg and Maire Percy for their comments on this chapter.

Archeological evidence shows that disability has existed since the dawn of humankind, and recent studies of Neanderthal specimens show that disability perhaps even predates that (Berkson, 2004). The extent of clear anthropological and other evidence about disabilities in early humans before recorded history leaves much to be desired for many reasons, including the following:

- Natural mortality was high among children with disabilities.
- Children and adults with disabilities were ostracized or killed in some societies.
- Milder disabilities may not have presented a major adaptive problem in some cultures and thus may have gone unrecorded.
- Humans, especially those not of high status, were not always buried after death (Papadopoulos, 2000).
- Evidence is naturally destroyed over the millennia.
- Writing only developed a little more than 5,000 years ago—and then only in some cultures—thus severely restricting before that time the way lasting information is available today.

Presence of Certain Disabilities

In spite of restrictions to historical knowledge, interesting evidence has been collected over the years from which some general conclusions can be drawn. Such evidence comes from a variety of times and places, but it was considerably mitigated by the emergence of artistic expression about 50,000 years ago, by people in what is now Europe and Western Asia changing from nomadic hunters and gatherers to settled agrarians approximately 10,000 years ago, and by the beginning of recorded history about 5,000 years ago. It seems clear from the available evidence that prehuman hominids, early Homo sapiens, and early civilizations lived with the following conditions (see Berkson, 2004, for a review; see also Display 2.1):

- A variety of physical malformations
- Anemia
- Blindness
- Broken limbs
- Down syndrome (and probably other **syndromes**)
- Head injuries
- Hydrocephaly (enlargement of the head caused by an abnormal accumulation of cerebrospinal fluid in the cranium)
- Microcephaly (smaller than normal circumference of the head because the brain had not developed properly or had stopped growing) and anencephaly (a congenital neural tube birth disorder that causes the absence of a major portion of the brain, skull, and scalp and is incompatible with life)
- Mobility impairments
- Osteoarthritis
- Paralysis

Somewhat paradoxically, advances in the human condition—notably a settled lifestyle that allowed agriculture, technology, and the arts to flourish—also contributed to the development of diseases and conditions that encouraged an increase in disabilities (e.g., overcrowding; diseases from cultivated plants and animals; polluted water; unclean environments; increase in rodents; increase in insects). For example, disabilities resulted from such things as malaria, smallpox, the plague, and measles—which spread rapidly throughout concentrated settlements—and from a variety of birth malformations (Centers for Disease Control and Prevention, 2004; Pangas, 2000; Warkany, 1959).

How Disabilities Were Viewed

Only scattered bits of archeological and written historical information are available about how people with disabilities were treated in very early human social groups (Berkson, 2004). Because there is evidence from a few parts of the world that some adults with these conditions lived into their adult years and were

Display 2.1

Ancient records of disability and its meaning

The oldest written records of disability are contained in the clay Tablet of Nineveh, found on the banks of the Tigris River and written by Chaldeans about 4,000 years ago. This tablet lists 62 deformities, along with the consequences they predicted. For example, if a newborn has no mouth, the mistress of the house will die; if his upper lip overrides the lower, the people of the world will rejoice; and if he has no right hand, an earthquake will shake the country (The Teratology Society, n.d.).

In ancient Egypt, physical deformity was recorded in art and iconography. Deformity was a manifestation of superhuman conflicts and cosmic forces, and disability was revered rather than feared.

The ancient Hebrews recognized disabilities, including being blind, deaf, mute, and lame and having skeletal deformities, muscle degeneration, various skin diseases, spinal deformities, genital loss, and leprosy. Disability was an impurity caused by sin and often resulted in people being excluded from social or religious activities (Stiker, 1999).

In Sparta, Athens, and early Rome, many disabilities were also known. Injuries and mild deformities were accepted, but children who could not perform daily tasks were subject to exposure (abandoned to the elements, placed in a hole, or drowned). Exposure resulted from tribal decisions to sacrifice the infants to the gods because of fear of what they might predict (Stiker, 1999).

buried after death, it seems reasonable to assume that they must have been treated by their families or wider social groups with a degree of care and, possibly, compassion.

There is somewhat more evidence from early civilizations that left pictorial and written records of their lives. Beliefs and superstitions associated with disabilities varied widely but probably had a strong impact on the social responses to disabilities; the following examples from Warkany (1959) and Edgerton (1968) illustrate that physical and mental disabilities were variously thought to be

- An indication that the person was possessed by demons
- Caused by sexual congress with animals or demons (see Displays 2.2 and 2.3)
- Caused by the sins or other misdeeds of the parents
- Caused by the stars and the moon
- Omens and warnings provided by the gods
- Predictions of the future
- Signs of displeasure of the god

From written or pictorial evidence, it appears that people with disabilities were sometimes protected, even esteemed at times. For example, people who were achondroplastic dwarfs (having the most common type of dwarfism, which is characterized by average-size trunk, short arms and legs, and a slightly enlarged head and prominent forehead) were held in high esteem in dynastic Egypt (e.g., Jeffreys & Tait, 2000). Humanitarian, equitable, and/or charitable treatment was also recorded in several ancient societies. The tendency to act with a degree of kindness and helpfulness toward those members of one's own social order who are in some distress may be not only a developed social value, but also an adaptive aspect of genetic heritage that is shared with other animals. Certainly, this trait can be widely observed in many higher-order species of the animal kingdom. However, Kanner's (1964) observation that there is no real evidence that the needs of early humans with the equivalent of intellectual or developmental disabilities were attended to in any *systematic* way appears to be still valid today.

Moreover, at the same time that people with disabilities were being helped in some ways in cultures that had recorded history, they were frequently maltreated or devalued in other ways. This duality has persisted in the treatment of people with intellectual and developmental disabilities, in a variety of ways, to modern times (Woodill & Velche, 1995). Some examples from early civilizations include the following:

- Caring for people with disabilities was set out as a moral obligation in the Bible and the Quran (Brown & Brown, 2003) as well as the Torah (Scheerenberger, 1983). For example, Mohammed advised, in the fourth verse of the fourth sura, "to

Display 2.2

Unusual explanations for children born with deformities

Throughout the ages, humans have provided explanations for children who were born with disabilities (e.g., disfigurations, deformities, unusual markings or proportions). Many of these explanations seem extremely unusual to us today.

Amusement of the gods or nature explained disability in some cultures. During Roman times, disability demonstrated the power of the gods but also showed the gods' humor and their "playing with" the human race. Pliny wrote, "Nature creates monsters [newborns with malformations] for the purpose of astonishing us and amusing herself" (The Teratology Society, n.d.). The *natural fool* of Medieval Europe, which spanned several centuries, also illustrates disability as amusement.

Offspring of evil spirits (devils, elves, fairies) were exchanged during the night for normal children, as it was widely believed throughout the Middle Ages in Europe and beyond, because the evil spirits wanted humans to raise their children. The resulting *changelings* were easily identified by their physical and behavioral characteristics, such as large head, ugly or wrinkled face, disproportionate body parts, lack of ability to walk or talk in the typical fashion, or poor ability to interact with other people. In some areas, such as Ireland, changelings were treated well, but it was more common for them to be treated cruelly because of a widespread belief that if they were treated badly enough (beating, neglecting, burning, torturing) the evil spirits would trade the changelings for their own children (Covey, 1998).

Sexual intercourse with the devil also produced changeling children, according to the Church's *Malleus Maleficarum* of 1487 (Covey, 1998). Because of this and other sins on the part of the parents, God allowed changeling children in the world. Mothers thought to have had sexual intercourse with the devil could be burned at the stake.

Hybridization was the belief that disabilities resulted from sexual relations between humans and animals. This extreme example, which existed in many cultures, illustrates a tendency to link disability with a behavior that was deemed highly unacceptable. For example, in the Judeo-Christian tradition, the scripture passage Leviticus 20:15–16 (New International Version) explains, "If a man has sexual relations with an animal, he must be put to death, and you must kill the animal. If a woman approaches an animal to have sexual relations with it, kill both the woman and the animal. They must be put to death; their blood will be on their own heads."

Display 2.3

Medieval punishments for hybridization

Punishments for hybridization, the belief that disability results from sexual relations between humans and animals, seem as unusual as the belief itself. In about 1200, a woman who reportedly gave birth to a cow with human features was sentenced to burn to death but was freed after her lawyer successfully argued that her child's deformities were caused by the positioning of the stars. A cyclopic pig, born in New Haven, Connecticut in 1641, was put to death along with a neighbor with only one good eye who was said to have sired it. A Copenhagen woman was burned at the stake for giving birth to a child who had a "cat's head" (The Teratology Society, n.d.), and a Danish woman was similarly burned for having a child who was "monkey-headed" (probably anencephalic or "incomplete brain, defective spinal cord, and or malformed skull"; Covey, 1998, p. 238).

feed and house those without reason and to give them kindly words" (Kanner, 1964, p. 3). Similarly, both the Old Testament and the New Testament of the Bible contain explicit instructions to treat disability with compassion (Berkson, 2006). Berkson also noted that in early Christianity, the notion emerged, especially in the writings of St. Augustine, of disability as a natural phenomenon rather than a punishment. At the same time, though, a man who was "blemished" was considered unfit to "offer the bread of his God" (Leviticus 22:17, as cited in Brown & Brown, 2003).

- In classical Greek culture, pensions were provided to people with disabilities, especially for people with physical disabilities that resulted from military service. Hippocrates demonstrated great concern for children with disabilities and attributed certain disabilities to "natural causes" rather than to possession by demons or wrath of the gods (Scheerenberger, 1983). Nonetheless, he lived in a civilization that generally believed that the birth of a child with a disability or other deformity was a show of anger by the gods, that held negative attitudes toward them, and that routinely ignored or rejected people with disabilities (Garland, 1995).
- Philip II of Macedon, father of Alexander the Great, raised a son named Arridaios who probably had an intellectual disability. It seems that Alexander treated this brother with kindness, having him accompany his great armies through Persia and India and ensuring that he lived in comfort throughout his life. After Alexander's death, Arridaios became Philip III for a brief period before he was murdered as a pawn in the political machinations of those vying for power. Yet, it seems from historical accounts that it was widely accepted at the time that Philip II would have been fully justified in having his son suffocated or otherwise disposed of at birth or in his early childhood (e.g., see Green, 1991).
- In Roman civilization, certain advanced medical procedures were intended to prevent or cure some disabilities (Berkson, 2006). At the same time, it was common practice to use people with various physical and mental disabilities as the source of amusement and entertainment (Brown & Brown, 2003). Moreover, Roman civilization, like classical Greek civilization, regarded individuals with disabilities as a scourge and ostracized or otherwise denigrated them accordingly (Berkson, 2004, 2006). According to the Teratology Society (n.d.), in the first century A.D., Roman society considered infants with physical disabilities to be a sign of a "god's power or a god at play, showing humor. Pliny was quoted as saying, 'Nature creates monsters [newborns with malformations] for the purpose of astonishing us and amusing herself.'" The Twelve Tables that emerged during the 5th century B.C.E. were highly influential throughout the Roman Empire and reflected both positive and negative perspectives of disabilities. For example, infanticide was reinforced, but ongoing care of people with disabilities was ensured by making males in the family legally responsible for them (Berkson, 2006).

It cannot be denied that, in ancient times, people with disabilities were subjected to various forms of discrimination, segregation, persecution, and attempted eradication (including infanticide, especially through the practice of exposure, whereby newborns were left outside to die; see Berkson, 2006, for a description). At the same time, though, certain stories and recorded actions appear to offer some evidence of interest in treating or curing disability. This interest might be interpreted in at least two ways: 1) as an attempt to eradicate disability and therefore an indication of the ongoing negative attitudes toward disability or 2) as an effort to demonstrate compassion and therefore an indication of a desire to help better the lives of people with disabilities. Whatever the intended meaning, some examples of treatments include the following (Berkson, 2004):

- Divine intervention (e.g., see John 9:1–7 of the Bible's New Testament for the story of Jesus curing a blind man)
- Herbal remedies
- Prosthetic devices (e.g., crutches; artificial limbs, eyes, and teeth)

- Surgery (e.g., amputating limbs, removing cataracts, drilling holes in the skull)

Overall, although disability existed and was recognized in antiquity, we do not know precisely how it was conceptualized. From the information that is available, it seems likely that disability was viewed more negatively than positively. Still, the beginnings of compassion toward people with disabilities, and the beginnings of positive action to care for and improve the lives of those people with disabilities, appears to have developed over this very long era.

DISABILITY IN THE MEDIEVAL ERA

Historians from a distinctly European perspective refer to the Medieval era, also sometimes called the Middle Ages, as the long period approximately spanning the years 500 to 1450. Although this is only one historical perspective, it is important because the rational and scientific principles that form the foundations of current thinking evolved to a very large extent from concepts that developed during this time.

References to something similar to an intellectual disability are scarce during this long period, and most historians only refer to evidence from the 11th century onward. From this evidence, two terms appear to have been in popular usage: *natural fool* and *idiot.* Although many people with intellectual impairment may have been thought of in this way, the terms referred more generally to people who did not accept the typical responsibilities of adult life for a whole variety of undefined reasons. Stainton (2001) wrote that these terms were unspecific and ambiguous, and that, although understood in a general way, they lacked any objective conceptual criteria.

Influences on the Way Disabilities Were Addressed

Four other interrelated characteristics of this era distinguish how conditions that might now be considered disabilities were addressed. These characteristics are discussed in the following sections.

Moral Perspective Disability was primarily viewed from a moral perspective. That is, people with disabilities were thought to illustrate that God made mankind as a species of imperfect beings; at the same time, they represented gifts from God toward which charity should be demonstrated by others. Small charitable institutions, supported by monasteries, were common by the 11th century. In England, for example, there were four main types of such institutions: almshouses, hospices for poor wayfarers and pilgrims, leper houses, and hospitals for the sick and infirm poor (Carlin, 1989). Of these, almshouses—places that cared for poor children and sometimes their parents, orphans, juvenile delinquents, and sometimes indigent adults who were elderly or mentally ill—were the most common. Although it seems that some people with intellectual impairments were cared for in these institutions, it was poverty rather than intellectual impairment that was the main criterion for care. In fact, some such institutions excluded those who were deemed incurable, including "idiots" (Stainton, 2001).

Probably of greater importance was the more general acceptance that charity toward those less fortunate was a religious and moral obligation. This trend became widely accepted because it was actively promoted by medieval religious institutions. This trend no doubt worked in favor of the well-being of people with intellectual impairment, yet it set them apart as well.

Lack of Distinction Between the Body and the Mind There was no generally understood distinction between the body and the mind. This is exemplified by the many historical accounts from the Middle Ages of the activities of "fools"—people whose appearance, characteristics, speech and actions were somewhat outside the accepted norm. Although fools were usually appreciated for their wit and for their representation of the full range of human characteristics, they typically had some physical and cognitive differences that were not particularly distinguished from one another. Thus, if a person acted and spoke like a fool, it was assumed that his cognitive skills were also deficient (Goodey, 2001).

Lack of Expectations for Large Segments of the Population Among large segments of the population, there typically were no specific expectations for learning or intellectual capacity. There was usually no reason, for example, for laborers and other members of the working poor or nonworking people of lower social status to show intellectual ability. Thus, people who would today be considered to have intellectual impairment might well not have been singled out conceptually because there was no need to do so and because they were capable of functioning alongside others of comparable socioeconomic status (Goodey, 2001).

Understanding Among People with Disabilities People with intellectual and other impairments sometimes shared a mutual understanding and communal bond. Although it is not clear how common this was, these individuals appeared to share resources and assist one another (Brown & Brown, 2003). For example, Woodill and Velche explained that

> Those who were intellectually or physically different were often found living . . . as poor beggars. Being a *disabled* beggar at that time was an advantage, in that it was easier to receive alms from the rich if disability were present. Or-

> ganized guilds of disabled beggars existed, sometimes sharing their "take" and helping each other. (1995, p. 2)

Woodill and Velche also cited the associations of blind people at Barcelona and Valencia, which had bylaws that were written in 1329 and "provided for the mutual loan of guides, visits to each other in case of sickness, and a fair division of alms received" (p. 9).

These and other characteristics contributed to tolerance and resulted in many people with intellectual impairment being able to live relatively well in their home communities. This was by no means the case for all individuals, however, and it would be hasty to conclude that the "fools" and "idiots" were well treated or well off. Many lived in their family homes, with varying degrees of care, while others lived in houses of refuge, were accommodated privately by charity, were homeless, or ended up in prison or institutions. There was poor access to medical help, and infant mortality was high and life expectancy short. In some places, tolerance and charity were the exception rather than the rule, and many individuals held fearful or derogatory attitudes toward people with intellectual and physical differences. Kanner (1964) quoted the French psychiatrist Jean Etienne Esquirol (1772–1840), who referred to the ongoing nature of this perspective: "[T]he idiot has always been in misfortune and misery. The state of . . . the idiot is always the same" (p. 102).

Summary of Influences On the whole, then, the Medieval era was a time when intellectual disability, or disability at all for that matter, was not conceptualized in any clear or separate way. Rather, it appears to be part of the broader and loosely defined terms *natural fool* and *idiot*. Perhaps for this reason, very little systematic policy or service provision was available for people with disabilities (Simmons, 1982). One important feature of this era was the rise of charity as a social and moral obligation. This resulted in the establishment of medieval charitable institutions supported by religious institutions and sometimes the state, although less formal charity was also actively promoted (Scheerenberger, 1983). Although the people chosen as recipients of charity did not necessarily have intellectual impairments, values related to caring for people on the margins of society were established that developed in a more formal, although uneven, way over the next centuries (see Display 2.4).

THE EXPANSION OF DISABILITY AS DIFFERENCE

The Industrial Revolution brought about huge social and personal changes, especially in the ways people earned their living (increasingly through industry rather than agriculture), in demographics (large numbers of people moving to towns and cities), and in the rapid growth of scientific thought as the basis for perceiving how all things function. These changes set the context for the growth of the view of disability as "difference" and the view that disability could be categorized separately from other human conditions. Several key knowledge trends that developed toward the end of the medieval period and throughout the rise of science and industrialization of the 18th and 19th centuries supported the growth of these views (*General sources:* Brown & Brown, 2003; Goodey, 2001; Stainton, 1994, 2001; Trent, 1994; Wolfensberger, 1972, 1976; Wright, 2001; Wright & Digby, 1996):

- *Descriptions of conditions:* Slowly over time, description of concepts related to what later was understood to be disability evolved and were recorded in printed documents. One often-cited example is the 1534 description by the English writer on legal matters, Anthony Fitz-Herbert: "[H]e who shall be found to be a sot and idiot from birth, is such a person who cannot accompt or number twenty pence, nor can tell who his Father, or Mother, nor how old he is etc."
- *Phenomenology:* This view held that a person has individual characteristics throughout the lifespan. This opened thinking to describe intellectual deficit as a characteristic that is placed within the individual person and persists throughout the person's lifespan.
- *Separation of the mind and body:* The view arose that the mind and body were two separate entities and functioned somewhat independently. This allowed for the mind and the intellect to be scientifically studied in isolation from the body.
- *Redefinition of nature:* Nature was understood to be governed by fixed, logical laws. This contrasted with earlier views that nature was precisely what one saw in the world, including the physical environment, culture, and social and political structures.
- *Theological debates:* Differences of opinion concerning the responsibility of humans for their own salvation resulted in the emergence of the view that individuals have to seek and work for the privilege of salvation. Yet, there were evidently some of God's own creation who did not appear to have the intellectual capacity to do this, so they needed to be thought of and treated separately.
- *Right of individuals to think and decide:* John Locke and others brought forth the view that individuals have not only the right, but also the moral obligation, to use their own intellectual capacity to reason and reach conclusions about virtually all aspects of human life and society. This included even how societies were governed (a perspective that was espe-

Display 2.4

Historical roles imposed on people with intellectual disabilities (Source: *Wolfensberger, 1972*)

A subhuman organism	Animal-like or a "vegetable"
A menace	An "alien" or a genetic threat to civilization
An object of dread	Sent as God's punishment; possibly a "changeling"
An object of pity	An unfortunate person, deserving charity
A holy innocent	Sent by God for some special purpose and incapable of sin
A diseased organism	Sick and probably incurable
An object of ridicule	The "village idiot" or "court fool" or "jester"
An eternal child	Persistently "subnormal," the victim of "arrested development"

Commentary:

These eight ways of seeing people with disability do not belong specifically to one historical period, although many of them appear to have their roots in the medieval era. It is important not to read any progression into these eight historical roles. They existed at various times, and, in fact, still exist to some degree and in some forms today. Moreover, they are often contradictory, even when they have often co-existed in the same society. Some are benevolent—if patronizing—whereas others are embedded in hostility. What they all share is the idea of a person with a disability as "the other," as different, and "not as one of us." These eight historical roles, then, illustrate that dominant social traditions toward people with disabilities over time have been characterized by exclusion.

A second important aspect of Wolfensberger's eight historical roles is that they illustrate that there is no intrinsic conceptualization of disability; rather, disability is a conceptualization constructed by people and by societies according to the contexts in which they live. All people are subject to the social role expectations of their times; role-expectations reflect the economic and social needs—as well as the values, traditions, and social norms—of the times (see also Chapter 1). When people, such as those with disabilities, do not have an obvious social role, one is sometimes partly or fully created. This process continues today. Current philosophical trends promote positive role-expectations for people with disabilities and encourage, among people without disabilities, the social value of including people with disabilities.

From Radford, J.P., & Park, D.C. (2003). Historical overview of developmental disabilities in Ontario. In I. Brown, &. M. Percy (Eds.), *Developmental disabilities in Ontario* (2nd ed., pp. 3–18). Toronto: Ontario Association on Developmental Disabilities; adapted by permission.

cially influential in the United States and France, but later throughout the developed world). Once this view was accepted, the group of people who did not appear to have the intellectual skills to think at a conceptual level and to make decisions for themselves became an obvious exception.

- *The Industrial Revolution:* The Industrial Revolution opened up an infinite number of possibilities for inventions and new ideas. It also resulted in the sudden rise of towns and cities, as well as the movement of large numbers of people from rural areas and their stable, agricultural way of life. The rise of towns and cities, and the industrial economy that supported them, brought numerous social problems with which the new industrial order was ill equipped to cope. Poverty, homelessness, and crime were considerably more important criteria for determining need than intellectual impairment. Still, it seems reasonable to assume that those with intellectual impairment might have found the complexities of living in the chaos of the newly formed industrial towns and cities difficult to manage and thus were more likely to be identified as being "different."
- *Legislation that addressed social problems:* Legislation in Britain, spanning a number of centuries, was particularly influential in the development of similar laws and other responses to social problems throughout the English-speaking world, although a series of laws also emerged in most other European countries. The United States developed its own complex series of laws to address social problems; these are well-documented in a number of books, articles and postings on the Internet (see also Scheerenberger, 1987; Trattner, 1999; Trent, 1994).

The Elizabethan Poor Law of 1601 amalgamated a number of previous English laws and established a compulsory "poor rate" to be levied on every parish; the creation of "Overseers" of relief; the "setting the poor on work"; and the collection of a poor relief from property owners (Bloy, 2002a). The Poor Law Amendment Act of 1834, however, is often seen as one of the most important pieces of legislation for setting the scene for the development of institutions for people of "difference." This Act established workhouses throughout England and Wales and later in Ireland (1838) and Scotland (1845). Once implemented, the Act established workhouses in every parish, or groups of parishes, that were overseen by Boards of Guardians; stopped outdoor relief (relief outside the workhouse); set in place the principle of "less eligibility" or making workhouse conditions sufficiently harsh that people would be discouraged from wanting to receive help; and established the principle of segregation of the workers (Bloy, 2002b). This law was later amended many times. Numerous other laws followed, laws that addressed the construction and governance of the many types of asylums and institutions that grew up over the ensuing decades, their reasons for being, and the "inmates" who were to live in them (e.g., see Bloy, 2002b, for documentation). See Figure 2.1 for an example.

Rise of Asylums

The previously described trends provide a great deal of the context that served as the catalyst in the 1800s for the emergence, in the more developed countries, of a mindset of social reform that was in keeping with the fast-developing reliance on scientific knowledge (see Display 2.5). Many jurisdictions began to move toward what was then thought of as a logical and progressive solution to the social problems that had arisen: establishing specialized institutions that were designed specifically to accommodate people who could not meet the daily living demands of their environments. In fact, this solution was so highly thought of that people—often described as dangerous and harmful to society—were moved into institutions for a variety of reasons that are considered horrifying at the beginning of the 21st century: being a fool or an idiot, receiving training or education (schools or industrial centers), not having parents (orphanages), being old, being poor (poorhouses), being in debt (debtor's prisons), having mental health problems (lunatic asylums), and others. Those with intellectual, physical, and other disabilities, or mental health problems, were especially moved to these institutions.

Figure 2.1. Southwell workhouse, established 1824. (From Bloy, M. [2002c]. *Southwell workhouse.* Retrieived November 2, 2005, from http://www.victorianweb.org/history/poorlaw/southwh.html; reprinted by permission.)

Display 2.5

Development of the asylum: Influence of industrial revolution and new scientific knowledge on asylums

With the coming of the Industrial Revolution, things changed quite dramatically in Europe, North America, and other parts of the world. The inquiry that had begun to become widespread amongst philosophers, scientists and others as part of a renaissance expanded to identifying and solving problems through exploration, logic and invention of specific tools. This was considered to be the way to progress, and such progress quickly became highly valued as a very good thing indeed, at least by those in positions of power. Science and technology increasingly became regarded as the best way to identify and solve all problems, including social problems. As a result, society itself came to be viewed over time, metaphorically, as a giant machine that was made up of many component parts. In this view, society could be manipulated and improved by inventing and developing new parts of it and fitting them together. The goal was to perfect and produce an ideal and efficiently run society.

Disability was one of the parts of the giant machine called society, and was perceived as one of the less effective parts. In the minds of the social industrialist, people with disabilities needed to be separated, but could be cared for, protected, and trained to lead productive lives in places of asylum. These could run efficiently and could provide, in their view, the best possible life for those who lived there.

From Brown, I., & Brown, R.I. (2003). *Quality of life and disability: An approach for community practitioners* (p. 61). London: Jessica Kingsley Publishers; reprinted by permission.

The institution was conceived by its founders and supporters as an instrument of reform by people whose intentions were honorable. It was a new way to express a tradition in Europe and elsewhere that people with disabilities and other "social" problems should be treated in humanitarian ways and taught to improve themselves. In some instances, this appeared to have worked very well (Woodill & Velche, 1995). For example, the institution in which the noted Italian composer Vivaldi worked and composed much of his music, the Ospedale della Pietà, was the home of children, mostly girls,

Display 2.6

Antonio Vivaldi and the Ospedale della Pietà

Antonio Vivaldi was employed for most of his working life by the Ospedale della Pietà. Often termed an orphanage, this Ospedale was in fact a home for the female offspring of noblemen and the numerous dalliances with their mistresses. The Ospedale was thus well endowed by the "anonymous" fathers; its furnishings bordered on the opulent, the young ladies were well looked after, and the musical standards were among the highest in Venice. Many of Vivaldi's concerti were indeed exercises which he would play with his many talented pupils. Though not Vivaldi's Ospedale della Pietà, this picture shows the interior "concert salon" of a typical Ospedale in Venice during Vivaldi's time. Note the elegant audience and opulent surroundings, and the Ladies performing well out of the Gentlemen's reach in the music gallery. Vivaldi maintained his long tenure at the Ospedale without, as he himself said, "a single scandal," something which appears to have been an exception.

Antonio Vivaldi

From Baroque Music Pages. (n.d.). *Baroque composers and musicians: Antonino Vivaldi.* Retrieved January 22, 2005, from http://www.baroquemusic.org/bqxvivaldi.html; reprinted by permission.

who were given over to care by being anonymously placed (usually at night) in a special hole in the wall of the building. Being female and illegitimate was the main "social disability" of these abandoned children. Under Vivaldi's tutelage, many became wonderful musicians (Baroque Music Pages, n.d.; see Display 2.6).

At the same time, there was growing pressure from prisons and overcrowded asylums. Managers of the asylums considered people with intellectual impairment to be unresponsive to their treatment programs, largely "incurable," and a waste of the energies of their staffs. Those who were considered "mentally defective" were often placed in separate annexes or wings of the asylums, where they often received nothing more than very basic custodial care. Specialized institutions for such people seemed to be the answer.

Thus, advocates for the early institutions saw a need for specialized training facilities that would prepare people with disabilities for a life in the world outside, or, if this were not possible, provide for their safety and comfort (Brown & Brown, 2003). This modern approach to addressing the specific needs of people with disabilities was characterized by considerable creative thought that was supported by medical, educational, religious, and other leaders in many countries. Schools for children with learning difficulties, hearing and visual impairments, and other disabilities were developed. Special health care facilities emerged to address such issues as hygiene, new and experimental physical therapies, and the treatment of conditions specific to the residents of institutions (e.g., epilepsy, vision and hearing problems). Buildings that functioned as places of care and training—both life skills and vocational—were set up in cities for children and adults with disabilities. Sites were established in the countryside that provided a clean fresh-air environment—a welcome relief from the polluted air and dirty streets of the cities—and a full range of life activities. Many of these, including several throughout the United Kingdom and North America in the late 1800s, functioned as model farms, with the residents working not only to provide for their own needs but also to produce quality products for sale to others. Typically, these institutions were designed and built to comprise a number of large buildings set on ample, well-groomed grounds that were designed to give a sense of tranquility (Edginton, 1995; Radford & Park, 1993). Normansfield Hospital, founded by John Langdon Down in 1868 (Figure 2.2), and Pennhurst (Figure 2.3) are shown as examples.

Early Focus on Education and Learning The initial focus in the growth of institutions was on children who had obvious disabilities. In the middle of the 19th century, educational thinkers suddenly claimed

Figure 2.2. Normansfield Hospital, founded by John Langdon Down in 1868. (From Bruinsma, M. [n.d.]. *Back to Normansfield hospital.* Retrieved November 1, 2005, from http://www.miriam-may.com; reprinted by permission.)

Figure 2.3. Pennhurst, an institution from the 1800s that was for people with intellectual and developmental disabilities. (From Abandoned Asylum. [n.d.]. *Pennhurst State School.* Retrieved July 7, 2006, from http://www.abandonedasylum.com/pss.html)

that these children could be intensively trained and educated within a controlled environment and prepared for a return to their home communities, where they would be able to adapt and contribute to community life (Woodill & Velche, 1995).

Germany adopted a fairly progressive approach toward disability for its time and was one of the leading pioneers in developing special schools for children deemed "idiots" in the early 19th century (Woodill & Velche, 1995). A document published in 1820 by educator Johann Traugott Weiss is thought to be the first concrete plan designed to provide instruction to children with disabilities (Kanner, 1964). A growing optimism toward the possibilities of education and training led to the belief that these "idiots" could develop skills that would allow them to function in the outside world, given proper conditioning and an environment conducive to drawing out their latent abilities. The expectation was to implement a vigorous and efficient program that would return the children to normal classrooms as quickly as possible so as not to alienate them any longer than necessary. France, England, the United States, and other countries were quick to follow suit and soon established their own institutions for special education. At the same time, an inclination toward investigating the physiological basis of "idiocy" was taking the scientific community by storm, and an understanding of disability that became the basis of the medical model (see Chapter 3) came to the forefront of science. Consequently, the approach toward what would later come to be known as intellectual and developmental disabilities moved away from a custodial nature and embraced methods of learning and causes of disability (Woodill & Velche, 1995).

The Supportive and Nonsupportive Role of Science The early "idiot asylums" of the mid-19th century represented the application of Enlightenment ideas to the "problem" of disability. As a result, the asylums were originally designed to provide healthy environments to prepare people (mainly children) for life in the outside world. Science, widely considered to be the way to progress, was mobilized to support these views. New methods of training and learning sprang up to support the work in the schools and training centers, and these and other positive interventions were supported by a growing knowledge of the neurological and environmental roots of disability.

At the same time, however, the quickly-expanding scientific knowledge of the 19th century also acted against the success of the asylums. Social Darwinism, a philosophy that viewed human social evolution as favoring those humans most "fit" to match the conditions and demands of their environments (Hawkins, 1997), suggested that people with disabilities were among the "unfit." A growing knowledge of genetics was used to reinforce this view and, further, to support the growth of eugenics, a movement that held that society could be improved by encouraging propagation among the more desirable portions of the general population and discouraging propagation among the less desirable portions. Intelligence testing was developed around the beginning of the 20th century, primarily to distinguish between those able and unable to learn in the school systems, but it was also used as an instrument to weed out those deemed incapable of learning, fit only for "training" at best. These applications of scientific knowledge justified the perpetuation of custodial asylums as warehouses for as many "hopeless cases" and "problem populations" as could be squeezed in.

Impact of Institutions

It is difficult for present-day readers to imagine the scale of the asylum movement. In 1914, there were 102 idiot asylums in the United Kingdom, housing 108,837 inmates (patients) (Cornwall, 2004). On top of this, there were lunatic asylums, workhouses, and many other types of institutions. An enormous social and economic investment—which was supported by political, scientific, religious, and other leaders of the time—had gone into establishing these settings as an integral part of society. This had a tremendous impact on the way people thought of the "unfortunates." They were seen as people unable, unworthy, or unfit to contribute to society and who were therefore best housed apart from society.

Early Attempts to Understand and Classify

Establishing institutions changed attitudes toward disability mostly by setting people apart and dictating to them a lifestyle that differed from that of most people of the times. One way this is illustrated is by the shifts in terms used to describe those for whom the institutions were designed. The most durable term to describe those people who would now be thought of as having intellectual disabilities was *idiot,* a word that was well-established in Medieval England as a descriptive term. Over the course of the asylum era, idiocy came to be understood as a "condition," called *feeble-mindedness,* with a single etiology. Kanner (1964) paraphrased Gertrude Stein in a somewhat tongue-in-cheek description of the prevailing attitude as "the feebleminded were the feebleminded were the feebleminded" (p. 102), signifying that this general group of people were seen as having ongoing undesirable characteristics.

To the extent that any differentiation was attempted for "idiots" or the "feeble-minded," medical and educational professionals, who were for the most part proponents of trying to understand disability in a scientific way, focused on quantifying degrees of "idiocy." A general, but not particularly clear, distinction was made between "imbeciles," who had mental deficiencies but could communicate verbally, and three classes of "idiots": 1) those who could use a few words and short sentences, 2) those who could utter monosyllables and grunts, and 3) those who had no language at all (Kanner, 1964). John Langdon Down (later known as John Langdon Haydon Down)—who was a physician to the Asylum for Idiots at Earlswood, served as founder of the Normansfield Hospital in 1868, and is now known for his identification of Down syndrome—put forward three categories of idiocy: 1) congenital idiocy (never had mental power), 2) developmental idiocy (deterioration after a satisfactory start), and 3) accidental idiocy (caused by illness or injury). Yet, it was Down's 1866 "clinical lecture and report" describing a condition that came to be known as mongolism (now known as Down syndrome) that precipitated a real interest in etiology and hence a move from thinking of feeble-mindedness in a homogeneous way toward thinking of it in terms of more comprehensive etiological classification systems (Kanner, 1964).

In the early years of the 20th century, a preoccupation among the middle class with "mental deficiency" and "feeble-mindedness" led educators and other professionals to identify the "moron" as a hidden group with "subnormal" intelligence apparently lurking within society's "problem populations." At the same time, advances in the testing and measurement of intelligence, particularly the work of the French psychologist Alfred Binet, allowed for what was believed to be a scientific method of describing categories of deficiency. This gave rise to the broad use of such terms as *moron, imbecile,* and *idiot.*

These terms were not originally intended to have negative connotations, but because they were brought forward to describe separate groups of people who were not socially valued, they quickly became derogatory. Similarly, later in the 20th century, sub-classifications and a growing understanding of the causes and contributing conditions of developmental and intellectual disabilities have contributed to a view that people with disabilities are "different." This has resulted in terms such as *mental retardation, mental handicap, developmental handicap,* and other terms that are considered to be derogatory in many countries (see Chapter 1).

It has become apparent that the institutional era was marked as much by attitudes as by buildings. Only a small proportion of people considered to be "mentally deficient" were actually institutionalized. This was not due to a belief that community living was superior; rather, it was mainly due to lack of space and resistance to the level of public spending that would have been required. It was widely believed that in a perfect society, all such people would be "put away"; it was often said that those who remained in the community "belonged in an institution." Opposition to such views existed but was a minority and not well documented (Woodill & Velche, 1995). The institutions created a sanctuary for mental deficiency within the social order, and it was widely believed that this place was both proper and beneficial, not only for society but also for those who were mentally deficient.

Decline of Institutions

If the institutions began as positive steps forward in the care and treatment of people with disabilities, why did they not succeed? As Brown and Brown (2003) put it, it is now well known that even though "many institutions started out as the benign well-oiled machines they were envisioned to be, they rusted out in time" (p. 61).

The optimism of the pioneers of institutionalization was, in fact, rather short-lived, and the institutions began to decline. Several interrelated factors contributed to this decline, and public attitudes gradually began to change. The most important factors associated with the decline of institutions included the following:

- *Lack of progress:* The reformers were unable to demonstrate noteworthy progress. The need to justify their existence as therapeutic facilities led, in some cases, to setting up demonstration projects in which education programs were applied only to children with the mildest disabilities. Gradually, the ideal of improved skills and health and successful return to community life faded, and the managers resigned themselves to a custodial, rather than an educational, role. The institutions became places in which people grew old, and this was a powerful social symbol that "mental deficiency" was both permanent and incurable.
- *Lack of knowledge:* The institutions were not only places of care and training for those who were housed in them. They were also places of experimentation and places of learning for those who ran them. Authorities and professionals of the time simply had little knowledge about how to handle the many types of disabilities and conditions they faced; although they experienced many successes, they also experienced a great many failures.
- *Stereotypes:* As noted, formerly held stereotypes of idiocy as an ongoing, permanent condition were not forgotten and proved durable, especially when the institutions lacked evidence of success. This led to a view that the residents of institutions were not capable of improving and that they "belonged" in places that were away from society.
- *Overcrowding:* More people with disabilities were institutionalized as it became increasingly accepted that such individuals were ideally housed in institutions. In addition, not as many people as anticipated developed sufficient independent living skills to move out of institutions. The growing number of residents increased demands on the institutions' available funds and staff, and many of the more capable people with disabilities were retained because of their value as workers, further contributing to the problem of overcrowding (Trent, 1994). Allocating time and other resources to individuals became increasingly more difficult, and attention was gradually shifted away from growth and development toward providing basic care. Living conditions deteriorated markedly in a great many institutions, such that family and service groups eventually began to advocate for change and closures. In some cases, such changes and closures were precipitated by disclosure of treatment and conditions that now seem quite shocking. One well-documented example was Pennhurst, a mental hospital and school for people with intellectual and developmental disabilities that was located in Pennsylvania (United States) and operated from the 1900s to the 1980s. An investigation of Pennhurst, prompted particularly by a series of unexplained deaths of residents, revealed the deteriorating level of treatment that residents received (El Peecho Productions, 2004). In addition, the investigation uncovered many cases of abuse and inhumane treatment that resulted in lawsuits, one of which resulted in a judgment by the U.S. Supreme Court. (For information on the court's judgment, see Legal Information Institute, 2005; for information on photographic documentation submitted in 1977 court proceedings, see El Peecho Productions, 2004.)
- *Use of drugs:* Medical advances, especially in the 20th century, increased the possibility that pharmacological treatment could alleviate immediate behavior issues and other problems. This made the institutions more manageable for overworked staff but shifted the emphasis away from developing health and independent living skills toward controlling behavior and maintaining care. This shift contributed to further overcrowding and lack of progress.
- *Reduced public interest and funding:* Moving people with disabilities to institutions segregated them from society at large, removing them from the public's attention. Somewhat ironically, the very institutions that were intended to function efficiently as the part of society that addressed the needs of people with disabilities lost the ability to function efficiently, in part because they were out of society's view. Reduced visibility led to reduced—and insufficient—funding for the large number of people who lived in institutions.
- *Improving community conditions:* With technological and social advances, living conditions, especially in cities, gradually improved. Cleaner water and air, broader sources of food, better working conditions, viable public transportation, and many other improvements made communities more attractive and viable places for people with disabilities to live. Thus, the need for people with disabilities to be housed in institutions was reduced.
- *Growth of interest in equality and human rights:* The growing trends toward acceptance of equality among people and valuing human rights (see Chapters 3 and 5) worked against isolating people—often without their consent—in institutions. These trends also strengthened the views that people with disabilities were equally entitled to all that society had to offer, which was not possible living within institutions, and, eventually, that fair treatment of people with disabilities is a social responsibility that requires inclusion.

- *Dramatic failure of eugenics:* Eugenics, the science of purposely influencing the genetic makeup of a society, had critics but was popular in many more developed countries (see Display 2.7). Eugenics sought to improve society by isolating and reducing reproduction among "the feeble-minded" or otherwise "unfit." For example, a note introducing an academic article entitled "The Control of Feeble-Mindedness" by E. Arthur Whitney read, "The author argues for the legalization of eugenic sterilization to achieve 'race betterment' by the elimination of the 'unfit'" (as cited in Rosen, Clark, & Kivitz, 1976, p. 198). These trends have been documented for several countries, including the United Kingdom, the United States, and Canada (Cavanaugh-O'Keefe, 2000; Kevles, 1985; McLaren, 1990; Tromblay, 1988). The application of eugenics escalated dramatically in Nazi Germany during the period 1933–1945, when a series of public policies were instituted to create a pure and able Aryan race. At first, this took the form of obviously favoring some types of people while persecuting and removing the personal rights of others; later, during the Second World War, great numbers of "undesirable" people were killed, in-

Display 2.7

Eugenics and its influence on disability

The theory of evolution that emerged in the middle of the 19th century gave rise to the concept of social evolution. This concept involved viewing society in an analogous way to plants and animals—as something that evolves over time and is selected because it suits a specific environment at a particular time.

Out of the concept of social evolution, the idea emerged that it should be possible to take action purposely to help society change and adapt in the best possible ways. Eugenics was the science and practice of purposely influencing the genetic makeup of a society in ways that seem to improve it. The thinking at that time was that by improving its overall genetic makeup, a society would be in a better position to make what was regarded as progress, because it would have more able members and would have fewer members who were thought to hamper development.

In the latter part of the 19th and the early part of the 20th centuries, eugenics was popular in the United States, many countries of Europe, and other countries that they influenced, including Canada and Australia. Its primary concern was to curb overprocreation among those of the lower social classes who were thought to be less socially desirable, and to promote higher levels of procreation among those who were considered to be of more worth to future society. To accomplish this, social and medical experts warned the lower classes against the moral and physical dangers of lust, especially the practice of masturbation and sexual relations outside wedlock. Industrial, religious, legal, academic, and social leaders supported the belief in eugenics in the wide variety of ways in which they carried out their functions. Dr. John Kellogg, for example, was an American physician with an interest in nutrition and eugenics, who is said to have believed that the new breakfast cereal he created in 1897, corn flakes, had a blandness that would help curb the sexual appetites of the patients in his mental hospital in Battle Creek, Michigan—people for whom such appetites would certainly have been considered undesirable (e.g., see Battle Creek Historical Society, 1998).

The effects of the eugenics movement were felt strongly by all groups of people who were considered to be socially undesirable but especially by people who were referred to as "feeble-minded." These were individuals we would think of today as having a variety of mental and intellectual disabilities and some physical disabilities (e.g., epilepsy), those who had fallen on 'hard times' or had been born into poor or abusive families, and also many people from native or aboriginal cultures because they were different. Those who were thought of as 'feeble-minded' were made particular targets of prohibition against procreation. Eugenicists believed that feeble-mindedness was largely hereditary and that if they could prevent feeble-minded people from having children, they would mostly eradicate this problem from their societies.

Many ways were found to put eugenics into practice. Isolation from the opposite sex, something that persists to this day in the care of people with disabilities, was widely practiced for the purpose of preventing pregnancy. Sterilizations, typically without consent, were also widely practiced, and persisted legally in some jurisdictions until well past the middle of the 1900s.

From Brown, I., & Brown, R.I. (2003). *Quality of life and disability: An approach for community practitioners* (p. 64–65). London: Jessica Kingsley Publishers; reprinted by permission.

cluding millions of Jews; approximately 5,000 children with disabilities; and thousands of other people with mental illness, other disabilities, and various differences (e.g., ethnic minorities, Romani or "gypsies," homosexuals). The discovery of these atrocities at the end of the war, coupled with other changing social attitudes and values, led to a quick decline of eugenics as a credible social philosophy.

INCLUSION IN COMMUNITIES

No single event marked the end of the institutional (asylum) era. Instead, the transition has extended over many decades. The pressure for change came from outside the asylum system and largely from outside the professions that had delivered services both within the asylums and in the wider community. Indeed, the professionals who believed they were providing a specialized and necessary set of services, along with some groups of parents who believed their sons and daughters to be safe and well cared for within the institutions, were often resistant to change. The impetus to end the institutional era was supported and sometimes led by academics, governments, staff and other professionals but mainly came from the voluntary sector, especially from parent and other advocacy groups that strongly criticized living conditions in the institutions. Sometimes the groups called for increased funding and improved asylum programs. Increasingly, though, they argued for resources to provide care in community settings as an alternative to large institutions.

Conceptual Basis for Community Living

An emerging body of theory, developed in close association with advocacy groups, shifted the trend away from institutions that were physically and psychologically separated from mainstream society. A movement that was primarily identified by its own interpretation of the term *normalization* set forth principles that endeavored to demolish the restricting constructs of disability by altering the environment of people with disabilities. Bengt Nirje, the movement's first pioneer, offered a conceptualization of disability with three interconnected components that raised the importance of environment. First, there is the primary medical or physical condition that is usually the most visible but is increasingly open to medical and other scientific advances. Second, there is the broader environment—the living conditions, daily routines, economic status, and prevailing social attitudes. The third component is the identity, or self-image, of the person with a disability. Such self-image is influenced by the physical condition, but this is not all-important. Rather, self-image develops as a reflection of the attitudes and values of those in the broader environment (Nirje, 1969).

In Nirje's view, the key to reform was to intervene in this complex interrelationship by altering the environment. Yet, what kind of environment is most suitable? The answer, quite simply, was the same rich variety of social niches within which everyone else creates their lifeworlds—in other words, a set of "normal" environments.

People with intellectual and developmental disabilities, Nirje argued, should be afforded normal daily, weekly, and yearly routines; ordinary housing; ordinary economic circumstances; and the usual life opportunities. Similar ideas were advanced by others, notably Wolf Wolfensberger, whose 1972 book *The Principle of Normalization in Human Services* is the classic and most comprehensive statement of the concept and its application. Normalization, it was claimed, was all about abandoning the stereotypes and ideologies of difference and substituting the principle of inclusion.

The implications were enormous. Numerous books and articles were published that described the reasons for deinstitutionalization and its implications for policy and practice. Policy had to be changed, funding mechanisms had to be altered from maintaining and expanding institutions to providing for community living, service delivery systems had to be reinvented to support more independent community living, and a whole new emphasis on professional training had to be developed (Casey et al., 1985; Paul, Stedman, & Neufeld, 1977; Scheerenberger, 1987; see also Chapters 3, 4, 5, 6, and 34 for additional details). For people with disabilities, the closing of institutions changed the opportunities that were available for participating in daily community life as they were introduced (not always willingly) to the new concept of normal living. As Wolfensberger forecasted, the effects of a movement that required the total inclusion of people with disabilities into the community were felt in every aspect of human services.

Reasons for Controversy Over Deinstitutionalization

For people with an early 21st-century perspective, it is perhaps difficult to appreciate why these proposals were so controversial. In the society of the early 1970s, though, people were still attuned to the difference of disability, and normalization was widely misunderstood or at least misrepresented. Some charged that to portray the person with an intellectual or developmental disability as normal was to deny reality. Here, it seemed to the critics, was another instance of unfounded optimism.

Some of the opposition stemmed from a sense of protectiveness. "Normal" environments can be hazardous, and it was considered by many that some people had needs that could only be met in the safety of the institution. Family members who had placed their relatives in closed institutions were often worried by the prospect of having to provide unaccustomed care in their homes. Many others were concerned—with some justification, as it turned out in many jurisdictions—that the money saved from institutional closure would not be fully reinvested in community services. The advocates of normalization responded to this by claiming that all individuals benefit from a degree of uncertainty. They grow through problem solving and should be allowed to experience the "dignity of risk," a term that became widespread to describe the view that protection and care need to be balanced with respecting and supporting the wishes and choices of people with disabilities, even if those wishes and choices involve some possible risk (see especially Wolfensberger, 1972).

Community Living

Despite these reservations, the principles of normalization, consolidated first in Scandinavia, began to be adopted in almost every jurisdiction in Western Europe, North America, Australia, New Zealand, and other countries during the 1970s and 1980s. Over a relatively short period of time, the principles were incorporated into official policy in many other countries as well, although the effects were felt more gradually in practice.

Closing the institutions and moving residents to communities was applied in uneven ways, both across and within countries. The main reasons for this were differences in political will, availability of financial resources to close institutions and support moves, local values and attitudes, traditional ways of housing people with disabilities, the presence or absence of local advocacy and conceptual leadership, the response by professionals and families, and the philosophies of funders of institutions (mostly governments). Among the many issues faced by those charged with closing institutions and establishing community living services were staffing problems; funding limitations; resistance by some professional groups and labor unions, who feared lower standards of care as well as loss of jobs; resistance by some parent groups, who feared loss of security and poorer care in the community; and municipal zoning bylaws that excluded group homes from residential neighborhoods. All of this resulted in the institutions proving to be more durable, and community homes much harder to find, than expected. Some countries (e.g., Norway) closed all of their institutions rather quickly, whereas most other countries have taken a more gradual approach that avoids many of the short-term challenges but delays community inclusion. In many countries (e.g., Italy, the Netherlands), there are still many institutions, although most of these have been modernized considerably so that they are more home-like. In still other countries, deinstitutionalization is an ideal that is only beginning to be realized, often because there is low funding or it is not a sociopolitical priority.

The concepts associated with community living are widely accepted throughout the world, turning idealism into reality for a great many people. Due to human rights awareness and closely linked legislation (see Chapters 5 and 6), it is gradually becoming more acceptable for people with disabilities to live in a broad array of neighborhoods and carry out all of their daily life activities in their home communities. Now the principles of normalization are questioned by those who believe they do not go far enough.

The "going farther" slogan that has been used in some quarters illustrates this objective (e.g., see Mercer, 1992), especially through the broader concepts of inclusion, quality of life, and self-determination (Brown & Brown, 2003). Since the early 1990s, ideas associated with these concepts have become paramount in more affluent countries and increasingly in less affluent countries as well. The focus is on trying to ensure that people who live in the community are able to have complete, fulfilling lives and that they can contribute to society in ways that are satisfying to themselves and others. The most hopeful indication of moving ahead into the future is that overt hostility towards people with disabilities is becoming the exception rather than the rule.

SUMMARY

It is essential to understand that disability was not always understood as it is today. Still, it is possible to learn valuable lessons from evidence of how people with various disabilities were treated. Disability existed since prehistoric times, and early civilizations often promoted compassion for disabling conditions, although there was overt discrimination as well. The Medieval era in Europe featured the growth of charity as a moral obligation and a broad public recognition of natural fools and idiots, although the conditions attached to these terms were not clearly conceptualized as disability. The rise of science and the influence of new thinking that came with industrialization encouraged more detailed descriptions of disability. Industrialization also brought on serious social problems that were eventually dealt with by building many large institutions for people who did not fit into the mainstream. These were not always built just for people with disabilities but often included them. Institutions were conceived of and built as progressive, positive solutions to social problems, but they eventually failed for a number of reasons. The decline and closure of institutions was precipitated by the growth of the philosophic view of normalization through community living. Although deinstitutionalization is still not the dominant policy of some countries, community living is now the norm in most. In many places, the current emphasis is on inclusion, individual ability, personal fulfillment, and enjoyment of life.

FOR FURTHER THOUGHT AND DISCUSSION

1. In early societies, there was evidence of compassion toward people with disabilities, but there was also discrimination. Think of the life of one person you know who has an intellectual or developmental disability. By describing a broad range of life activities for this person, show how compassion and discrimination are still being demonstrated.
2. In Medieval times, natural fools and idiots were some of the people to whom the rich were morally obliged to provide charity. Was this a good idea? Are there people today who "deserve" charity?
3. Place yourself in the early 1900s and ask, "Why were asylums espoused as a solution? What were the problems that needed solutions? Were asylums a good solution?"
4. Setting people with intellectual and developmental disabilities apart as "different" helped in understanding them but was also detrimental. Weigh the benefits against the detriments as you argue for what should have been done.
5. Despite deinstitutionalization and a community living approach, to what degree does society still think in terms of an "institutional" model of care?
6. What are the three most important lessons you have learned from the past? Write two or three paragraphs about each to describe your reasons.

REFERENCES

Abandoned Asylum. (n.d.). *Pennhurst State School.* Retrieved July 7, 2006, from http://www.abandonedasylum.com/pss.html

Baroque Music Pages. (n.d.). *Baroque composers and musicians: Antonino Vivaldi.* Retrieved January 22, 2005, from http://www.baroquemusic.org/bqxvivaldi.html

Battle Creek Historical Society. (1998). *Dr. John Harvey Kellogg, Battle Creek, Michigan.* Retrieved June 17, 2005, from http://www.geocities.com/Athens/Oracle/9840/kellogg.html

Berkson, G. (2004). Intellectual and physical disabilities in prehistory and early civilization. *Mental Retardation, 42,* 195–208.

Berkson, G. (2006). Mental disabilities in Western civilization from Ancient Rome to the Prerogativa Regis. *Mental Retardation, 44,* 28–40.

Bloy, M. (2002a). *The 1601 Elizabethan Poor Law.* Retrieved January 31, 2005, from http://www.victorianweb.org/history/poorlaw/elizpl.html

Bloy, M. (2002b). *The Poor Law: Introduction.* Retrieved January 31, 2005, from http://www.victorianweb.org/history/poorlaw/plintro.html

Bloy, M. (2002c). *Southwell workhouse.* Retrieved November 2, 2005, from http://www.victorianweb.org/history/poorlaw/southwh.html

Brown, I., & Brown, R.I. (2003). *Quality of life and disability: An approach for community practitioners.* London: Jessica Kingsley Publishers.

Bruinsma, M. (n.d.). *Back to Normansfield hospital.* Retrieved November 1, 2005, from http://www.miriam-may.com

Carlin, M. (1989). Medieval English hospitals. In L. Granshaw & R. Porter (Eds.), *The hospital in history* (pp. 21–40). London: Routledge.

Casey, K., McGee, J., Stark, J., et al. (1985). *A community-based system for the mentally retarded: The ENCOR experience.* Lincoln: University of Nebraska Press.

Cavanaugh-O'Keefe, J. (2000). *The roots of racism and abortion: An exploration of eugenics.* Retrieved February 20, 2005, from http://www.eugenics-watch.com/roots/index.html

Centers for Disease Control and Prevention. (2004). *The history of malaria: An ancient disease.* Retrieved January 22, 2005, from http://www.cdc.gov/malaria/history/index.htm#ancienthistory

Cornwall, S. (2004, October 4). *UK asylums.* Retrieved January 31, 2005, from http://www.simoncornwell.com/urbex/misc/asylums.htm

Covey, H.C. (1998). *Social perceptions of people with disabilities in history.* Springfield, IL: Charles C Thomas Publisher.

Fitz-Herbert, A. (1632). *The new Natura Brevium.* London. (Original Latin work published 1534)

Edgerton, R.B. (1968). Mental retardation in non-western societies: Toward a cross-cultural perspective on incompetence. In H.C. Haywood (Ed.), *Social-cultural aspects of mental retardation* (pp. 523–560). New York: Appleton-Century-Crofts.

Edginton, B. (1995). Architecture's quest for sanity. *Journal on Developmental Disabilities, 4*(1), 12–21.

El Peecho Productions. (2004). *Pennhurst information.* Retrieved May 2005 from http://www.elpeecho.com/pennhurst/pennhurst.htm

Garland, R. (1995). *The eye of the beholder: Deformity and disability in the Graeco-Roman world.* Ithaca, NY: Cornell University Press.

Goodey, C.F. (2001). What is developmental disability?: The origin and nature of our conceptual models. *Journal on Developmental Disability, 8*(2), 1–18.

Green, P. (1991). *Alexander of Macedon, 356–323 B.C.: A historical biography.* Berkeley: University of California Press.

Hawkins, M. (1997). *Social Darwinism in European and American thought 1860–1945: Nature as model and nature as truth.* Cambridge, United Kingdom: Cambridge University Press.

Jeffreys, D., & Tait, J. (2000). Disability, madness, and social exclusion in dynastic Egypt. In J. Humphrey (Ed.), *Madness, disability and social exclusion: The archaeology and anthropology of "difference"* (pp. 87–95). London: Routledge.

Kanner, L. (1964). *A history of the care and study of the mentally retarded.* Springfield, IL: Charles C Thomas.

Kevles, D.J. (1985). *In the name of eugenics: Genetics and the uses of human heredity.* Cambridge, MA: Harvard University Press.

Legal Information Institute. (2005). *Supreme Court collection: Pennhurst State School and Hospital v. Halderman.* Retrieved May 2005 from http://supct.law.cornell.edu/supct/html/historics/USSC_CR_0451_0001_ZO.html

McLaren, A. (1990). *Our own master race.* Toronto: McLelland and Stewart.

Mercer, J. (1992). The impact of changing paradigms of disability on mental retardation in the Year 2000. In L. Rowitz (Ed.), *Mental retardation in the Year 2000* (pp. 15–38). New York: Springer-Verlag.

Nirje, B. (1969). The normalization principle and its human management implications. In R. Kugel & W. Wolfensberger (Eds.), *Changing patterns in residential services for the mentally retarded* (pp. 179–195). Washington, DC: President's Committee on Mental Retardation.

Paul, J.L., Stedman, D.J., & Neufeld, G.R. (Eds.). (1977). *Deinstitutionalization: Program and policy development.* Syracuse, NY: Syracuse University Press.

Pangas, J.C. (2000). Birth malformations in Babyon and Assyria. *American Journal of Medical Genetics, 91,* 318–321.

Papadopoulos, J.K. (2000). Skeletons in wells: Toward the archaeology of social exclusion in the ancient Greek world. In J. Humphrey (Ed.), *Madness, disability and social exclusion: The archaeology and anthropology of "difference"* (pp. 96–118). London: Routledge.

Radford, J.P., & Park, D.C. (1993). The asylum as place: An historical geography of the Huronia Regional Centre. In J.R. Gibson (Ed.), *Canada: Geographical interpretations: Essays in honour of John Warkentin* (pp. 103–130). North York, ON, Canada: Geographical Monograph Series, York University, Atkinson College.

Radford, J.P., & Park, D.C. (2003). Historical overview of developmental disabilities in Ontario. In I. Brown, & M. Percy (Eds.), *Developmental disabilities in Ontario* (2nd ed., pp. 3–18). Toronto: Ontario Association on Developmental Disabilities.

Rosen, M., Clark, G.R., & Kivitz, M.S. (1976). *Habilitation of the handicapped: New dimensions in programs for the developmentally disabled.* Baltimore: University Park Press.

Scheerenberger, R.C. (1983). *A history of mental retardation.* Baltimore: Paul H. Brookes Publishing Co.

Scheerenberger, R.C. (1987). *A history of mental retardation: A quarter century of promise.* Baltimore: Paul H. Brookes Publishing Co.

Simmons, H.G. (1982). *From asylum to welfare.* Toronto: National Institute on Mental Retardation (now The Roeher Institute).

Stainton, T. (1994). *Autonomy and social policy: Rights, mental handicap and social care.* London: Avebury.

Stainton, T. (2001). Medieval charitable institutions and intellectual impairment c.1066–1600. *Journal on Developmental Disabilities, 8*(2), 19–29.

Stiker, H.-J. (1999). *A history of disability* [W. Sayers, Trans.]. Ann Arbor: University of Michigan Press.

The Teratology Society. (n.d.) *History of teratology.* Retrieved January 2005 from http://teratology.org/jfs/History.html

Trattner, W.I. (1999). *From poor law to welfare state: A history of social welfare in America* (6th ed.). New York: The Free Press.

Trent, J.W. (1994). *Inventing the feeble mind: A history of mental retardation in the United States.* Berkeley: University of California Press.

Tromblay, S. (1988). *The right to reproduce.* London: Weidenfeld and Nicholson.

Warkany, J. (1959). Congenital malformations in the past. *Journal of Chronic Diseases, 10,* 84–96.

Wolfensberger, W. (1972). *The principle of normalization in human services.* Toronto: National Institute on Mental Retardation (now The Roeher Institute).

Wolfensberger, W. (1976). The origins and nature of our institutional models. In R. Kugel & A. Shearer (Eds.), *Changing patterns in residential services for the mentally retarded.* Washington, DC: President's Committee on Mental Retardation.

Woodill, G., & Velche, D. (1995). From charity and exclusion to emerging independence: An introduction to the history of disabilities. *Journal on Developmental Disabilities, 4*(1), 1–11.

Wright, D. (2001). *Mental disability in Victorian England: The Earlswood Asylum 1847–1901.* Oxford, United Kingdom: Oxford University Press.

Wright, D., & Digby, A. (Eds.). (1996). *From idiocy to mental deficiency.* London: Routledge.

3

Changing Perspectives on Developmental Disabilities

Michael Bach

WHAT YOU WILL LEARN ABOUT IN THIS CHAPTER

- Developmental and intellectual disabilities
- Developmental disability as a legal status
- The biomedical view
- Toward a social and human rights model
- Challenges in making a social and human rights model a reality

This chapter looks at three different perspectives on developmental disability and how these have influenced supports to people with disabilities. Perspectives have shifted as the limitations of certain concepts of disability become apparent and alternatives are put forth. Underlying the shifting perspectives are different responses to the following questions: What is developmental disability? How should people who are labeled this way be identified? What are family, community, and state obligations to this group?

DEVELOPMENTAL AND INTELLECTUAL DISABILITIES

Developmental disability is one of a cluster of categories used to refer to people whose intellectual capacities, communication skills, and/or behavior are determined to be developing, or to have developed, at a slower rate or to a lesser extent than what is deemed to be normal. In defining developmental disability this way, the focus is on language, and on what scientific, legal, and service communities have determined to be "normal" paths of human development.

As noted in Chapter 1, in many places, *developmental disability* has replaced the term *mental retardation,* because this latter term was seen by people who were labeled this way as demeaning. In the North American context, *intellectual disability* is increasingly being used instead of developmental disability, because it is based on the notion that people face barriers and discrimination simply because of their intellectual differences. *Developmental* presumes there is a normal path of human development, an idea that is increasingly challenged in the psychological and sociological literature (Amundson, 2000). Elsewhere, as in the United Kingdom, *learning disability* is used instead of *developmental disability* or *intellectual disability.* In the North American context, however, *learning disability* refers to a different group of individuals, usually those whose intellectual difficulties are related to processing and expressing information. Dyslexia is a common example of what is referred to as a learning disability in the North American context.

There is another crucial difference between references to disability in the Americas (North, South, and Central America, including the Caribbean) and Europe. In the Americas, those who are challenging a biomedical view of disability tend to refer to "persons with disabilities" or a "person with" a developmental or intellectual disability, always placing the "person" or subject first in the grammar of the statement. This intentional placement of the "person" first is meant to communicate that the disability must always be considered secondary to the person, thereby adhering to a vision of fundamental human equality. In Europe, the same philosophical vision has led to a different grammatical position, so the reference is usually to "disabled persons," placing the "person" secondary to the process of disablement. The reasoning for this difference is that persons are seen to be "disabled" by the society and structures around them rather than by their particular impairments or developmental difficulties (Barnes, 1991; Barnes & Mercer, 1996). In this perspective, to refer to a "person *with* a disability" is to place the disability as an inherent feature of the individual, rather than as a result of the disabling aspects of society. This chapter uses the terminology *people with a developmental or intellectual disability,* still recognizing these debates and philosophical concerns.

Debates about terminology are not simply theoretical or symbolic. These debates matter because the creation and use of language comes to shape understandings about the world, about those who are in the position to assign the label of disability to others, and about those to whom the label is assigned. As Cocks and Allen (1996) wrote, intellectual disability is more about language and the value assigned to those who are different from a norm, than about a particular form of impairment: "A history of intellectual disability is, to a great degree, a history of language, knowledge, and power. It recalls the languages used to describe, classify and thus constitute certain members of society as 'disabled'" (p. 283).

Wolfensberger (1972) and Brennan (1995) made clear how the term *mental retardation* has become a part of the cultural landscape (as have *developmental disability* and *intellectual disability*) and has been used to divide and devalue a certain group of people through the discourses of law, public policy, and the professional fields. As Danforth and Navarro (1998) suggested, intellectual disability or mental retardation are not only categories of institutionalized legal and professional discourses. They also structure interpersonal interactions in everyday life. In a study of "speech acts" observed in everyday settings (e.g., hair salon, movie theatre), the researchers found that the label was used to "mark" others assumed to be mentally retarded. The term was used by the speaker to mark the other as abnormal, different, and distant. The speakers:

> Echoing words and phrases spoken by many through the years . . . quite casually accessed a well-known lexicon of human devaluation in order to perform common communicative functions. . . . In doing so, casual speakers simultaneously meet their own social purposes of communication and tragically contribute to the continuation of devalued identities for persons considered to have mental retardation. (Danforth & Navarro, 1998, p. 42)

A focus on developmental disability as first and foremost a linguistic reality, rather than an absolute feature of actual persons is consistent with a postmodern perspective in the social sciences. Lyotard (1984) argued that in the postmodern period, scientific knowledge that assumes linguistic categories (e.g., developmental disability) point to actual objects in the world has become delegitimized because there are competing perspectives and multiple truths about what actually exists. This is certainly true in the case of disability, as there are competing legal, biomedical, social, and human rights perspectives on disability. Fawcett (2000) showed how a postmodern perspective on the knowing of disability helps to unsettle the hold of "privileged knowledge frameworks" that pathologize some people on the basis of particular intellectual, physical, and genetic characteristics. A postmodern perspective highlights the professional discourses of disability that establish distinctions such as able/disabled, competent/incompetent, or normal/abnormal. It also values the diverse voices of people with disabilities as sources of legitimate knowledge. In separate analyses, McIntosh (2002) and Peters (2000) showed how the tools of a postmodern discourse analysis can reveal how people see those with intellectual and other disabilities as passive and in need of control and management. Postmodern legal perspectives show that when it comes to disability, the law is not neutral (Jones & Basser Marks, 1999). Carey (2003) suggested that a dominant legal narrative or story about what it means to be a citizen underlies the legal system. This is a narrative in which legal personhood has come to be defined solely by one's individual competence. The law is based on certain assumptions about what it means to be competent and to be a person, and it justifies differential legal, social, residential (e.g., institutional confinement), and other forms of status on these grounds. A postmodern approach to disability shows that these assumptions can always be challenged. Developmental disability is not a fixed and absolute fact or feature of a person. It is a human-made lens through which a person is seen.

The term *developmental disability* has come to shape the world perception of people labeled as such. This is evident, in part, in the differential legal, social, and economic status. The next sections explore three perspectives that help to understand how the meaning of *developmental disability* has evolved: legal, biomedical, and social and human rights. It examines the influence of these perspectives on public policy. The chapter also points to the importance of a postmodern approach to understanding disability, which recognizes that although one always views the world and others through a particular perspective or lens, one can critically evaluate our perspectives for the consequences they bring.

DEVELOPMENTAL DISABILITY AS A LEGAL STATUS

There are many legal and social histories to the term *developmental disability*. They evolve in tandem with the institution of legal personhood, which expresses what defines persons to whom rights and responsibilities apply in any particular legal context. Early Roman law established the legal category of "personne" and thus provided a legal norm from which those we now think of as having developmental disabilities begin to be marked as different. Carrithers, Collins, and Lukes (1985) reviewed the development of notions of personhood in different cultures over the centuries preceding and succeeding this early Roman innovation and showed how the category of person, just like the category of developmental disability, is subject to shifting perspectives and conflicts over what counts as a personhood.

This section picks up the threads of the legal history of personhood in English law in the 14th century, where the roots of the term *developmental disability* can be found in legal distinctions that still influence public policy and services today. The 14th-century English statute under Edward II, titled *De Prerogativa Regis* [the Royal prerogative] now referred to as the *parens patriae* jurisdiction, imposed an obligation on the state to provide for those deemed incompetent to manage their personal or financial affairs. Chapter IX of the law states, "The King shall have the Custody of the Lands of natural Fools, taking the Profits of them without Waste or Destruction, and shall find them their necessaries."

Determinations of incompetency to manage one's estate or person were made by jury trials at inquisitions called for the purpose. These determinations were the purview of the courts and juries exclusively, but they acted on the Royal prerogative—the *parens patriae* power (Neugebauer, 1996). As Foucault (1965) argued, it was from the 14th century on that reason and rationality became the defining feature of what it meant to be a person, and culture, science, and public policy since that time rest largely on this assumption. Development of statutory law during this period suggests that what reason comes to mean is constructed in tandem with the legal articulation of lunacy and idiocy.

As contracts between persons increasingly came to define both economic and social relationships, especially with industrialization beginning in the 18th century, a figure of "market man," a freely contracting agent, began to emerge. To protect the sanctity of contracts, parties had to be seen to fully understand their nature and consequences. Thus, industrialization and the infrastructure of contract law that supported it established requirements for what it meant to be a person at law and to be recognized as such in social and economic relationships (Cossman, 1990; Poole, 1985, 1991). People with intellectual or developmental disabilities thus came to be seen as a threat to the upholding of contract law—they were not seen as having the necessary reason and rationality to exercise responsibility in entering and fulfilling contracts. So a means other than providing them a right to enter contracts had to be found to ensure their basic needs were met. The Poor Law distinctions of the "worthy poor" provided the basis for state provision of basic supports, minimal as those were.

The 1890 English Lunacy Act was a successor to *De Prerogative Regis* and consolidated legal provisions related to lunacy and the *parens patriae* jurisdiction of the courts. The legislation was made effective under colonial law in many other countries under colonial rule. By conferring a differential legal status on people with a developmental disability, the *parens patriae* power helped to institutionalize the idea that what made a human being a person was the ability to meet certain tests of reason. Institutional care for people labeled as "idiots," "fools," or "lunatics" grew in succeeding years for those who were not considered to have the requisite "reason" to be recognized as a person and thus to enter contracts or take on other rights and responsibilities. Consequently, they were increasingly shut away from the mainstream of society.

State obligations to people with a developmental disability were consolidated in England with the passage of the Poor Law in 1601 (Hirst & Michael, 2003; King, 2000; Rushton, 1988). The statute established a distinction between the "worthy" and the "unworthy" poor and was later adopted in many of England's colonies. Adults with disabilities considered unable to work were, by this law, deemed worthy and entitled to state provision. The law contributed to both a marginalized economic and social status for people with disabilities that is still felt in the early 21st century. By linking disability and inability to work, the law institutionalized the idea that people with disabilities did not fit into the labor market, an assumption that still drives much employment-related policy. As well, by considering people with disabilities as "worthy poor," the state promised slightly better provision than for the "unworthy" poor—those who were deemed able-minded and able-bodied but unwilling to work. However, the cost of obtaining richer provision was the adoption of disability as a legally sanctioned charity status, one that people with disabilities are still trying to shake in favor of recognition as full citizens.

THE BIOMEDICAL VIEW

By the 18th century, a legal perspective on disability was being supplanted by a biomedical one. With the rise of institutional care, the need grew for regulation, licensing, and due process in committal to institutions. The growing medical profession was called upon to play this regulatory role and, over the 18th and 19th centuries, the powers to determine competence shifted from juries of inquisition under the courts to physicians. By the end of the 18th century, the Royal College of Physicians in England was responsible for the licensing of "madhouses." By the mid-19th century, resident physicians were required in madhouses of more than 100 persons. In the same period, the Association of Medical Officers of Hospitals for the Insane was established, and the organization published a diagnostic manual that included such categories as "mania," "melancholy," "monomania," "dementia," "moral insanity," "idiocy," "imbecility," "general paralysis," and "epilepsy" (Weistubb, 1990). The manual is one of the precursors of the *Diagnostic and Statistical Manual of Mental Disorders, Fourth Edition, Text Revision* (*DSM-IV-*

TR; American Psychiatric Association, 2000), which is widely used to diagnose developmental and other disabilities.

The idea that disability was not a status that was conferred but was in fact an individual deficit gained strength in the late 19th century, when Binet and Simon developed the first intelligence tests to identify children in France who were not progressing in school. The test was adapted and, in the early 20th century, became one of the common instruments for diagnosing what was labeled "mental retardation." Standardized intelligence tests were later developed for different age ranges, and normal deviations were constructed as a means of identifying those who fell below the normal range as "developmentally disabled." Developmental tests were later designed to measure how closely individuals met developmental targets at each age. The discrepancy in measures on language, motor, and behavioral development assisted in defining various categories of developmental disability.

These various strands in the evolution of the law and science of developmental disability converged with general research and public policy on disability. This led the World Health Organization (WHO) to suggest three elements of a definition within what came to be known as the *International Classification of Impairments, Disabilities, and Handicaps (ICIDH):*

- *Impairment:* In the context of health experience, an impairment is any loss or abnormality of psychological, physiological, or anatomical structure or function.
- *Disability:* In the context of health experience, a disability is any restriction or lack (resulting from an impairment) of ability to perform an activity in the manner or within the range considered normal for a human being.
- *Handicap:* In the context of health experience, a handicap is a disadvantage for a given individual, resulting from an impairment or disability, that limits or prevents the fulfillment of a role that is normal (depending on age, sex, social and cultural factors) for that individual. (WHO, 1980, pp. 27–29)

This definition, with its focus on abnormality and lack of ability in relation to a norm, is consistent with the language of developmental disability since its inception in law more than 600 years ago. It is also consistent with the definition of *mental retardation* by the American Association on Mental Retardation, even with its more recent reformulation to focus on "social competence" (Greenspan & Granfield, 1992) and associated definitions in which developmental or intellectual disability is related to "deficits" or "impairments" in conceptual, practical, and social intelligence (Greenspan & Driscoll, 1997) or lower than "normal" functioning in intellectual abilities (e.g., reasoning, acculturation knowledge, short- and long-term memory, visual and auditory processing, processing speed, quantitative knowledge) (Horn & Noll, 1997). Prescribed social competencies and roles are simply another norm, for which diagnostic and assessment tools are needed to measure the extent to which people demonstrate their fulfillment and the behaviors associated with them.

Although measurement and statistical analysis of a population can be conducted in ways to define certain norms of development, these norms remain just that—statistical constructions. Deviations from the norms do not signify "abnormal" development, they merely represent statistical deviations. However, normalcy has come to express a guiding assumption about human development. It means that if a child, youth, or adult does not proceed developmentally through a set of common functions, developmental stages, or critical developmental periods, then he or she is to be considered abnormal or to have deviations in skill development.

This assumption, which has framed much of the research in education, developmental psychology and social science research, is increasingly being called into question (Amundson, 2000; Skrtic, 1991). It has been suggested that rather than being scientific and objective, the concept of functional normality reflects the beliefs, preferences, and cultural expectations of a majority of the members of society. As Amundson (2000) suggested, if what it means to be normal is indeed a product of culture, then the yardsticks for measuring normalcy lack universal and scientific validity and "disadvantages experienced by people assessed as abnormal derive not from biology, but from implicit social judgments about the acceptability of certain kinds of biological variation" (p. 33). The definition of *normal* becomes arbitrary, relative, and specific to the limited context in which it occurs.

A critique of normalcy does not suggest that particular individuals do not have real limitations and difficulties, do not face barriers as a result, or do not require early intervention to help remediate limitations or address diseases and ill health. It simply means that each person must be considered as a unique person. His or her developmental progress will proceed like no other person's, even though at a population level one can look at trends in development across children and subgroups of children.

Mackelprang and Salsgiver (1999) pointed to some of the intellectual foundations of a broader view of developmental theory that begin to address the cultural biases of predominant approaches based on normalcy. This work stresses the need to shift the focus in developmental theory. There is a need to move from measuring the gap between age and expected developmental achievements and measuring the standard deviations of that gap to focusing on the conditions that enable children and adults with disabilities to carry out developmental tasks that are culturally shared and defined. To be able to communicate with others, for instance, is a developmental task whose achievement need not be measured by verbal language skills in the dominant language. Moving into adulthood need not be defined by the capacity for independence, which would exclude from successful adult achievement those who require ongoing personal supports. It can also be defined by the control one is given over one's supports; the development of mutually supportive, interdependent relationships; and the opportunity to develop and pursue a wider range of goals.

The WHO definition, its antecedents, and its contemporaries, all placed disability firmly within the individual while recognizing that it often brings needs for support from others, and social stigma for not measuring up to the norm. Yet, a biomedical view of disability is not inherently harming to people with intellectual disabilities. It can provide an understanding of a person's genetic differences and possible consequences. It can provide information (e.g., through a diagnosis) at an early stage of a person's life about the particular challenges to be faced in communication, motor, and behavioral development; thus, it can encourage access to early intervention programs and other developmental supports. Such information is vital to a child and family seeking to nurture as many life chances as possible.

The harm in a biomedical perspective comes from using it as the only way of viewing a person. This often leads to the assumption that all of the challenges to be faced arise from genetic or other differences. In order to address the challenges that arise from a devalued legal and social status, a broader perspective for viewing a person is needed—one that sheds light on how the legal system and economic, social, educational, and other environments in which people live can determine their life chances. A social and human rights perspective on developmental disability can help to shed this light.

TOWARD A SOCIAL AND HUMAN RIGHTS MODEL

An alternative social model of disability is being advanced by those who find in the WHO and other definitions a reductionist tendency—reducing the disability to individual characteristics (Barnes, 1991; Oliver, 1996; Rioux, 1996). In a social and human rights model, disability arises from the discrimination and disadvantage individuals experience in relation to others because of their particular differences and characteristics. This shift in thinking finds a primary source in feminist theories of difference, in which the challenge is to recognize such differences as gender, race, sexual orientation, and disability without assigning social or economic value on the basis of these differences (Minow, 1990).

In a social model of disability, the "pathology," to use Rioux's (1996) terminology, is not individual but rather social in nature. The unit of analysis shifts from the individual to the legal, social, economic, and political structures that calculate value and status on the basis of difference. The social model, which is informed by principles of human rights and an equality of outcomes that takes account of differences, does not reject biomedical knowledge of impairments and research on individual rehabilitation. Rather, it suggests that such a perspective should not exhaust the understanding of disability in society. In addition, the model suggests a reconstruction of the legal, social, and economic status of people with disabilities, starting with a recognition that first and foremost people are full, rights-bearing citizens. Their equality and citizenship rights bring into question the status that was first carved out for them under statutes such as *De Prerogativas Regis* and the forms of institutional and community care that have taken away their basic rights to self-determination, citizenship, and freedom from discrimination in employment.

There remains some question about the place of impairment within the social and human rights model of disability. In the response of Disabled Peoples' International (DPI) to the WHO definition, the term *handicap* was dropped, but *impairment* and *functional limitation* were kept as the foundation of the definition (DPI, 1982). Oliver (1996) suggested that this emphasis reinforces normalizing tendencies within the definition that need to be questioned. In keeping with Oliver's view, Shakespeare (1996) suggested that only by turning to the stories and experience of people with disabilities themselves can a legitimate place be given to their lived realities of impairment, as the meaning they give to their physical and intellectual differences. This approach acknowledges the reality of impairment while challenging the assumption that one person is given the status to define another as "impaired" from some so-called objective criteria of "normal" functioning. It is argued that by their very nature, such assessments reinforce a norm at the same time as they define someone as deficient in relation to the norm. Rather, impairment is a lived and subjective reality, given meaning within the individual and collective narratives expressed by people with disabilities themselves and those who are in personal relationship to them. Frazee (1997) stressed the importance of creating a culture of disability in which people's differences (or impairments, if they define them as such) can be named, given meaning, celebrated, and thereby transformed into a cultural and personal resource, even while people may experience limitations and needs for support.

The notions of a "social model of disability," "personal experience of impairment," and a "culture of disability" may not at first glance provide much hope to all individuals with a disability. Many who are labeled with a developmental disability have very challenging needs, are unable to communicate in ways that most others understand, sometimes act in ways that others find alarming, and sometimes demand attention from family and support workers. Those who advocate a social rather than biomedical perspective for understanding developmental disability argue that it is most important to bring this perspective to individuals who are in such a situation. It is they who are most at risk of being devalued in society for their differences, who are defined as being furthest from the norm, and who are perceived to be lacking a personal story or narrative that others value.

CHALLENGES IN MAKING A SOCIAL AND HUMAN RIGHTS MODEL A REALITY

If social, cultural, and political landscape of the times are shaped by competing perspectives on disability, how can society best move a human rights perspective forward? Through the 1980s and 1990s, much was accomplished in codifying in law human rights protections for people with disabilities and prohibitions against discrimination on this basis. Countries around the world are negotiating a United Nations Convention on Disability to establish a human rights standard to guide states in human rights legal developments and to provide a basis for global monitoring of human rights and disability. The dilemma now is to put those commitments into reality.

Although human rights laws have advanced, not as much has changed in the lives of people with disabilities in terms of poverty rates; unemployment; exclusion from general education; and rates of physical, psychological, and sexual abuse. Moreover, the inequities affecting people with disabilities within countries and between countries grows. The WHO, for example, estimated that in the majority of countries of the south, more than 95% of children with disabilities do not attend school at all. In North America and Europe, children with disabilities are much more likely to go to school, but there are challenges in moving from a segregated to an inclusive approach.

So, if there is legal change that significantly addresses the centuries of differential legal status imposed on people with disabilities, what are the next steps? A defining feature of today's global society is that it is knowledge driven. Innovation in policies, systems, and practices comes with creating, managing, and disseminating knowledge through processes that bring actors together in new ways (Homer-Dixon, 2001). As Fullen (2001) argued, innovation in social institutions such as education and grappling with growing diversity like disability requires leaders who build "relationships, relationships, relationships" and manage and broker knowledge for systems change.

This perspective can help to guide next steps in advancing the full inclusion of people with developmental disabilities. In sectors across society—education, recreation, employment, public services, health care, and others—there is a growing commitment to and belief in the equality of people with disabilities. Yet, often missing are the leadership, relationships, and knowledge required in these sectors to make full inclusion a reality. Closing the gap between exclusion and inclusion requires new roles and partnerships for actors who for many years advocated for legal change. With that now increasingly accomplished, advocacy groups, professionals, and governments must also engage in new ways to create, broker, and network the knowledge needed for teachers, health care professionals, government leaders, and others to change systems and practices to make them more inclusive of people with developmental and other disabilities. This also requires a new place for people with disabilities, their families, and their advocates in the process of knowledge creation about disability.

Just as Lyotard (1984) challenged the "metanarratives" that make scientific knowledge paramount in shaping society, so too it is time to challenge the metanarratives of disability. People with developmental disabilities are not simply deficits who need to be fixed by others. They bring voices and knowledge about what it means to create a more inclusive society. Their place in negotiating a new social order of inclusion should be central if knowledge is to be developed that shows the way to inclusive schools, workplaces, and communities.

SUMMARY

This chapter's brief overview of the term *developmental disability,* of public policy, and of their historical roots makes clear that there are different ways of making sense of the term *developmental disability.* The biomedical view, in which developmental disability tends to be seen primarily as a delay in normal human development, arose as the medical profession was increasingly called upon to determine to whom the category would be applied. Since the early 1980s, a broad perspective has begun to take shape that goes significantly beyond delineating norms to guide the assessment of developmental disability (e.g., intelligence, adaptive behaviors, social competencies, genetic structure), focusing instead on what needs to be done so that people, whatever their personal challenges and social and economic disadvantages, can exercise their human rights and full citizenship. A social and human rights model of disability has emerged to question the exclusive focus in a biomedical perspective on "deficits" and "delays." It aims to shed light on the social, economic, and political barriers to full citizenship that come when a person is labeled as intellectually delayed or deficient.

The discourse of human rights has not yet influenced thinking in the area of developmental disability as much as it has in other areas, such as gender, race, and religion. Nonetheless, with the recognition that the label has brought with it a devalued legal, social, and economic status, a human rights framework now has an irrevocable hold on understanding developmental disability. Since 1948, when the *Universal Declaration of Human Rights* was adopted, human rights provisions have been successively passed by national and state/provincial governments. The implications of these changes are being witnessed in the reform of federal and regional statutes—for the right to vote, for the right to participate on juries, for access to health care, for the right to education, and for other rights.

The adoption of a human rights perspective for understanding state obligations to its citizens is arguably the most profound conceptual advance for understanding developmental disability since terminology for it was first born in law hundreds of years ago. Human rights provisions have become the infrastructure for a social model of disability and indeed have made a social perspective on disability possible. They introduce a distinction into previous debates about the biomedical and behavioral nature of developmental disability, between an understanding of a person's competencies and what those competencies should mean for a person's legal, social, and economic status.

By stressing the value of human rights in understanding developmental disability, a social model needs not reject biomedical information. There is much to be learned and valued from an understanding of people's particular differences and the biomedical consequences and challenges they bring. A social model recognizes a biomedical view as one source of information for understanding developmental disability. Yet, it changes the vision and purpose of intervention from the concepts of *fixing, impairments,* and *abnormalities* to supporting people to exercise their human rights and thereby become full and valued members of society.

The legal, biomedical, and human rights perspectives on disability all underlie public policies for people with developmental disabilities. There has been a gradual shift in public policy from "care" for people with developmental disabilities to policies that enable greater social and economic inclusion of such people. However, concerns are growing that there is a "re-medicalization" of disability underway that will be used to distinguish between those who are deemed worthy of public support and those who are not. With human rights commitments now in place, the next step is to develop the knowledge needed for all sectors of society to build inclusive policies and practices that enable people with developmental disabilities to take their rightful place.

Although the implications of human rights obligations still need to be fully worked out, the vantage point they allow helps to reveal the inequalities in status between people with disabilities and the rest of the population, as well as among people with disabilities

FOR FURTHER THOUGHT AND DISCUSSION

1. Why do you think it is that a person with a disability has a right to health care and medical interventions in many countries (even if this right is not always fulfilled) but can only obtain disability-related supports as a matter of charity?
2. What arguments would you use to encourage a potential employer who would like to hire a person with a disability but who is concerned about the functional and behavioral assessments provided by a vocational counselor?
3. Imagine that you are supporting a young person with a developmental disability and her parents. The mother is 3 months pregnant and finds out that her second child will have Down syndrome. The mother turns to you for advice on whether she should abort her fetus. How do you counsel her?
4. Children have a right to education. Yet, some are excluded from attending their neighborhood school because they do not have the communication capacities or the needed augmentative communication systems are considered too expensive or cumbersome in the classroom. Should education be a matter of right or of capacity? Can functional and other biomedical assessments be used to help a child and a school to more fully exercise the right to education? In what ways might they undermine the possibility of full inclusion?
5. What is the difference between a physician's knowledge about the human rights of a person with a disability, about the provision of medical care to a person with a developmental disability, and about ways to ensure that a person with a developmental disability has access to the physician's office and can be supported to make health care decisions?

themselves. They provide a legitimate ground on which to restructure the institutions and policies that have brought inequality in the past and to consider what entitlements people require to fully exercise their citizenship and equality rights. As understandings of these inequalities in status inch further and farther into public consciousness, we can hope that genetic, behavioral, communicational, and intellectual differences will be seen for what they are—signs of diversity, horizons of human possibility, and a place to nurture support and foster reciprocity.

REFERENCES

American Psychiatric Association. (2000). *Diagnostic and statistical manual of mental disorders* (4th ed., text rev.). Washington, DC: Author.

Amundson, R. (2000). Against normal function. *Studies in History and Philosophy of Biomedical Science, 31,* 33–53.

Barnes, C. (1991). *Disabled people in Britain and discrimination.* London: Hurst & Co.

Barnes, C., & Mercer, G. (1996). *Exploring the divide: Illness and disability.* Leeds, United Kingdom: University of Leeds, The Disability Press.

Brennan, W. (1995). *Dehumanizing the vulnerable: When word games take lives.* Chicago: Loyola Press.

Carey, A. (2003). Beyond the medical model: A reconsideration of 'feeblemindedness,' citizenship, and eugenic restrictions. *Disability & Society, 18,* 411–430.

Carrithers, M., Collins, S., & Lukes, S. (1985). *The category of the person: Anthropology, philosophy, history.* New York: Cambridge University Press.

Cocks, E., & Allen, M. (1996). Discourses of disability. In E. Cocks, C. Fox, M. Brogan, & M. Lee (Eds.), *Under blue skies: The social construction of intellectual disability in Western Australia.* Perth, Australia: Centre for Disability Research and Development.

Cossman, B. (1990). A matter of difference: Domestic contracts and gender equality. *Osgoode Hall Law Journal, 28*(2), 303–377.

Danforth, S., & Navarro, V. (1998). Speech acts: Sampling the social construction of mental retardation in everyday life. *Mental Retardation, 36,* 31–43.

Disabled Persons International. (1982). *Proceedings of the First World Congress.* Singapore: Author.

Fawcett, B. (2000). *Feminist perspectives on disability.* Upper Saddle River, NJ: Prentice Hall.

Foucault, M. (1965). *Madness and civilization* (R. Howard, Trans.). New York: Random House.

Frazee, C. (1997). Prideful culture. *Entourage, 10,* 87–94.

Fullen, M. (2001). *Leading in a culture of change.* San Francisco: Jossey-Bass.

Greenspan, S., & Driscoll, J. (1997). The role of intelligence in a broad model of personal competence. In D. Flanagan, J. Genshaft, & P. Harrison (Eds.), *Contemporary intellectual assessment: Theories, tests, and issues.* New York: The Guilford Press.

Greenspan, S., & Granfield, J. (1992). Reconsidering the construct of mental retardation: Implications of a model of social competence. *American Journal on Mental Retardation, 96,* 442–453.

Hirst, D., & Michael, P. (2003). Family, community and the 'Idiot' in mid-nineteenth century North Wales. *Disability & Society, 18,* 145–163.

Horn, J., & Noll, J. (1997). Human Cognitive Capabilities: Gf-Gc Theory. In D. Flanagan, J. Genshaft & P. Harrison (Eds.), *Contemporary intellectual assessment: Theories, tests, and issues.* New York: The Guilford Press.

Homer-Dixon, T. (2001). *The ingenuity gap.* Toronto: Vintage.

Jones, M., & Basser Marks, L.A. (1999). Law and the social construction of disability. In M. Jones & L.A. Basser Marks (Eds.), *Disability: Divers-ability and legal change.* The Hague, Netherlands: Martinus Nijhoff Publishers.

King, S. (2000). *Poverty and welfare in England, 1700–1850.* Manchester, United Kingdom: Manchester University Press.

Lyotard, J.F. (1984). *The postmodern condition.* Minneapolis: University of Minnesota Press.

Mackelprang, R., & Salsgiver, R. (1999). *Disability: A diversity model approach in human service practice.* Belmont, CA: Wadsworth Publishing.

McIntosh, P. (2002). An archi-texture of learning disability services: The use of Michel Foucault. *Disability & Society, 17,* 65–79.

Minow, M. (1990). *Making all the difference: Inclusion, exclusion, and American law.* Ithaca, NY: Cornell University Press.

Neugebauer, R. (1996). Mental handicap in medieval and early modern England: Criteria, measurement and care. In D. Wright & A. Digby (Eds.), *From idiocy to mental deficiency: Historical perspectives on people with learning disabilities.* London: Routledge.

Oliver, M. (1996). Defining impairment and disability: Issues at stake. In C. Barnes & G. Mercer (Eds.), *Exploring the divide: Illness and disability.* Leeds, United Kingdom: University of Leeds, The Disability Press.

Peters, S. (2000). Is there a disability culture? A syncretisation of three possible world views. *Disability & Society, 15*(4), 583–601.

Poole, R. (1985). Morality, masculinity and the market. *Radical Philosophy, 39,* 16–23.

Poole, R. (1991). *Morality and modernity.* London: Routledge.

Ramcharan, P., Roberts, G., Grant, G., & Borland, J. (1997). *Empowerment in everyday life: Learning disability.* Philadelphia: Jessica Kingsley Publishers.

Rioux, M. (1996). Ethical and socio-political considerations on the development and use of classification. *Canadian Journal of Rehabilitation, 9*(2), 61–67.

Rushton, P. (1988). Lunatics and idiots: Mental disability, the community and poor law in North-East England, 1600–1800. *Medical History, 32,* 34–50.

Shakespeare, T. (1996). Disability, identity, difference. In C. Barnes & G. Mercer (Eds.), *Exploring the divide: Illness and disability.* Leeds, United Kingdom: University of Leeds, The Disability Press.

Skrtic, T.M. (1991). *Behind special education: A critical analysis of professional culture and school organization.* Denver, CO: Love Publishing Co.

United Nations General Assembly. (1948, December 10).

Universal declaration of human rights. General Assembly Res. 217A (III), UN Doc A/810 at 71. Retrieved August 2004 from http://www.un.org/Overview/rights.html

Weistubb, D. (1990). *Enquiry on mental competency: Final report.* Toronto: Osgoode Hall Law School.

Wolfensberger, W. (1972). *The principle of normalization in human services.* Toronto: National Institute on Mental Retardation.

World Health Organization. (1980). *International classification of impairments, disabilities, and handicaps (ICIDH).* Geneva: Author.

4

Trends and Issues in Intellectual and Developmental Disabilities

Ivan Brown, Trevor R. Parmenter, and Maire Percy

WHAT YOU WILL LEARN ABOUT IN THIS CHAPTER

- International socio-political trends
- International trends in disability
- Challenges for the field

The field of intellectual and developmental disabilities, like all others, has a set of core issues that do not change substantially over time. Such issues include providing needed care and support to individuals and families, ensuring that services are available and accessible, and promoting the dignity of people with disabilities as fully participating members of society.

Yet, this field has by no means remained static, either. The last half of the 20th century and beyond has been a time of tremendous change and growth, particularly in more economically developed countries. On the whole, these changes have resulted in many improvements in the lives of people with intellectual and developmental disabilities and their families, and they have drawn attention to many other changes that could lead to further improvements in the future.

Such changes have not occurred in isolation, however. The intellectual and developmental disabilities field has broadened and diversified or constricted and narrowed in response to numerous social, economic, political, and environmental factors that are both national and international in origin. Like other fields, interests and priorities have emerged and declined over time. Issues that were considered to be of utmost importance in one decade seemed less important the following decade and were replaced by others that were seen as more timely and urgent.

In this chapter, some of the main international trends and issues that are currently important to the field of intellectual and developmental disabilities are highlighted to provide a context for understanding disabilities in a more complete way. Such trends and issues are likely to become more important or less important over time. For the present and the near future, however, they are important for two reasons: 1) they guide thinking about the field and how to approach support for people with disabilities and 2) they provide the "top layer" of an everchanging groundwork, out of which future trends and issues will emerge.

INTERNATIONAL SOCIO-POLITICAL TRENDS

There have been a number of positive changes in the field of intellectual and developmental disabilities since the early 1980s. Some advances in public acceptance of disability have occurred since the United Nation (UN) declared 1981 the International Year of Disabled Persons, and efforts to include people with disabilities in society have progressed somewhat. There have also been some advances in disability entitlements in specific countries, such as the Americans with Disabilities Act (ADA) of 1990 (PL 101-336), the Individuals with Disabilities Education Improvement Act of 2004 (PL 108-446), and the Workforce Investment Act of 1998 (PL 105-220) in the United States (see Appendix B at the end of the book for more information; see Chapters 5 and 6 for additional details on entitlements in a variety of countries, Chapter 31 for additional details on education, and Chapter 33 for additional details on employment). On the whole, though, the advances for people with intellectual and developmental disabilities across the world during this time have been incremental rather than landmark. Such advances have been incremental, to a large extent, because changes in the field of intellectual and developmental disabilities have occurred within broader societal contexts that have curtailed bold advances.

Beginning in the 1980s, considerable shifts in thinking within most developed nations affected many aspects of the social order in an ongoing way, including, to some degree, how people with disabilities were perceived and treated. Key inter-related aspects of these shifts are explained in the following sections.

Toward a Global Economy

During the last decades of the 20th century, an increasingly global economy was creating pressure on countries, especially those that were strongest economically, to relax government regulations and restrictions on the ways the economy functioned nationally and internationally. The core element was a growing view that economic policies must allow freedom by businesses to choose which resources they could use and how such resources could be used. For example, this concept proposed that businesses should have considerable freedom to use raw materials, labor, and services from whatever countries of the world could provide them in the most cost-effective way. Critics of this view have pointed out that allowing businesses to "shop around the world" for cost-effective resources results in exploitation of weaker countries by stronger countries, especially in terms of worker wages.

At any rate, these views resulted in changes to the political discourse, and later to the public discourse, that were highly influential in many of the more developed countries by the early 1990s. Such changes were strongly influenced by the economic policies initiated by governments in the United Kingdom and the United States in the 1980s, and later by those of other developed countries such as Australia, where "economic rationalization" became a widely used description of a new set of policies and ways of thinking. These governments' policies supported the overall view that a strong economy would create a better environment within which all could prosper, including disadvantaged people. A strong economy, it was thought, could be created by reducing the tax burden on citizens and by reducing government restrictions on businesses. A strong economy also made maximum use of available resources, and there was considerable emphasis on what was referred to as "making do with less," "trimming the fat," or "utility maximization." The resulting booming economy, it was believed, would create money that would "trickle down" to those who were not able to benefit directly from the policies, including people with disabilities.

There were many benefits of these policies, but benefits for people with disabilities and other disadvantaged people did not occur on a widespread scale. For example, a first step was typically a strong emphasis on reducing or eliminating budget deficits. This was accomplished through budget cuts that resulted in a reduction or loss of numerous formerly funded social and other programs, including those for people with disabilities, and the stagnation of many others. Such moves did not help people with disabilities and in many cases actually acted as a barrier to maintaining the services that did exist and to expanding new ways of thinking. Thus, the degree to which these policies were beneficial for those with fewer advantages now seems to be in doubt, although this will be assessed and evaluated with the passage of time. Still, there is no doubt that the previously described overall changes in thinking represented a change that was highly influential internationally and continues to be influential into the early 21st century.

Perceived Need to Contain Public Spending

At about the same time, there developed a concern that the degree to which governments had been funding social and many other programs was not sustainable in the long term and that government overspending in these areas was depleting resources that were needed to restock the economy and to provide for people in the future. This trend appears to have arisen from some discontent in two areas. First, political parties that then formed governments considered the public to be unrealistically overreliant on them to resolve all social and economic problems. Second, the public came to believe that it was increasingly being asked to pay for more programs that were not necessarily useful or fully justified. As a consequence, government leaders and other policy makers in the most developed countries began to change the way their funds were generated (primarily through taxes) and redistributed by cutting or freezing taxes or reducing tax increases and reducing the number and scope of many of the programs and initiatives formerly funded, including some programs for people with intellectual and developmental disabilities.

The overall result of such moves was a stronger emphasis on economic investment and prosperity and on decreased government responsibility with a corresponding increased individual, community, and corporate responsibility. In shifting responsibility this way, the state began to play more of a supportive rather than a leadership role and to play a supportive role primarily for only those most in need. Within disability services, the thinking was that rather than commit to providing comprehensive secure care from cradle to grave, as was formerly (but imperfectly) the case, it was more economically viable to offer a "safety net" approach, by which support only would be offered to most individuals with disabilities and public money would only be used to offer fuller care to those most in need.

Many governments also adopted the theme of mutual obligation that requires people receiving financial or other support to contribute to their country's economy, especially by obtaining a job or attending training. Although this policy may have had some effect in removing people without disabilities from welfare support, the data on the numbers of people with disabilities without employment show that there are structural barriers preventing this population from obtaining meaningful work (e.g., see Eisenman, 2003; Yamaki & Fujiura, 2002). Indeed, data have shown that the only growth in employment for people with an intellectual disability is in the area of segregated (sheltered workshop) services (see Chapter 33 for a full discussion).

With all of these changes, there was a concomitant move to downsize government bureaucracies and to change the relationships between government institutions and the public into economic partnerships. This trend is outlined clearly and reflected in many policy documents for people with disabilities that shift more responsibility to individuals, families, and communities (e.g., Ministry of Community and Social Services, 1997). Accompanying such shifts in responsibility was encouragement to use existing community and family resources more. On the whole, though, such policy documents emphasize economic strength and show a reduced emphasis on social equity.

Growth of Individualism

An emphasis on the needs and wishes as well as the responsibilities of individuals has accompanied the previously described changes and constitutes what is referred to as *individualism.* The growth of individualism in society more generally influenced a similar emphasis with the field of intellectual and developmental disabilities. The concepts of freedom of individual choice, respect for the individual perspective, more control by individuals over their own lives, release from government regulation (e.g., direct funding to people with disabilities or their families), self-determination, and individual and family empowerment have all taken on increasing importance since the early 1990s. Person-centered approaches have been adopted by many service organizations, especially since approximately 1995, to respond to a perceived need to emphasize the individual (see this chapter's Person-Centered Approaches section for a fuller discussion). These are important trends for people with disabilities that have helped develop an understanding that people with disabilities have unique needs, wishes, life goals, and capabilities that need to be respected when providing support.

At the same time, however, the emphasis on individualism presents some threats to vulnerable groups of people such as those with intellectual and developmental disabilities. First, although individualism works to encourage as much independence as possible, many people in this population will, in many aspects of their lives, remain dependent upon supports. The thrust within individualism compromises the integrity of individuals with disabilities by expecting them to act on their own behalf in "normative" ways, which may not be characteristic of or realistic for them. It also contributes further to their being ascribed lower social status and being less valued than other human beings, precisely because they are not always able to act on their own behalf to improve their own lives. The individualistic view of the self militates against people with disabilities as dependents and contributes to dependence being viewed negatively. The challenge is for society to create environments where the interdependence of individuals is a central feature and where individuals perceive their identity and the conceptualization of self in the context of a mutually dependent society.

A second problem with individualism is that it seems to act contrary to those elements that build social cohesion and a sense of mutual obligation toward one's fellow citizens, especially people who are marginalized and relatively powerless. It is ironic that the focus on individualism does not sit comfortably with the call by many developed economies for a greater emphasis on the development of social capital and community capacity building. This call is a direct corollary to the policies of downloading responsibilities for care and solving problems from governments to communities, families, and individuals.

Finally, the growth of individualism also seems to have contributed rather significantly to the growing gap between the rich and the poor in both developed and developing countries. This gap constitutes a further impediment for social justice policies for disadvantaged groups in societies and is particularly relevant to people with disabilities, who are highly associated with poverty (Emerson, 2004).

Environmental Degradation

The assault on the world's ecosystems has had and continues to have profound negative effects on the health of the world's population. The rapid growth of the production of new chemicals has increased the risk for birth defects. It is estimated that there are approximately five million chemicals to which the population has significant exposure. Of these, Shephard (1986) reported that 1,600 had been tested in animals for teratogenicity, and there is little evidence that this gap has closed since that time. Occupational and environmental exposures to toxic solutions continue to contribute to birth defects worldwide (Schroeder, 2000). Lack of immunization programs (e.g., against rubella), and in some cases lack of commitment to them, continues to be a major problem in primary prevention of disability. The rampant spread of the human immunodeficiency virus (HIV), especially in Africa and Asia, is among the most common infectious causes of intellectual and developmental disability (see Chapter 16). Lead exposure and nutritional deficiencies also continue to be significant causes of birth defects in both developed and developing countries (Grantham-McGregor, Walker, & Chang, 2000). Iodine deficiency in parts of Europe and

Asia is still a major cause of intellectual disability (Hetzel, 1989). Effective nuclear waste disposal and the minimization of the risks of nuclear accidents, which could also lead to disabilities, continue to be challenges.

These are some examples of environmental degradation and the enormous problems that the human race faces in dealing with them. There are many others. Unfortunately, such problems are usually associated either directly or indirectly with disability and have strong impacts on both the breadth and nature of the work of the intellectual and developmental disability field.

INTERNATIONAL TRENDS IN DISABILITY

A number of important international trends have developed specifically in the field of intellectual and developmental disabilities that are influenced by the broader trends described in the previous section but also reflect the changing values, concepts, and knowledge that have emerged within the field. Trends that have greatly influenced current thinking about disability and the provision of supports to people with disabilities are highlighted in the following sections.

Pause in Funding Increases and Philosophical Approach

The previously described trends and policies, in general, have been accompanied by and resulted in a pause in both funding increases and philosophical approach. Funds of services for people with disabilities have been frozen, reduced, or increased only slightly in most countries. There have been exceptions to the funding pause, especially where funds are provided strategically (i.e., for specific programs, such as employment training, or for specific subpopulations, such as children with autism). On the whole, though, there have been no substantial increases in funding for people with disabilities in most countries for many years.

In keeping with this, the prevailing approach in disability philosophy since approximately 1985 has been to reflect on and scrutinize what services are for, how they are obtained, and what needs they are meeting. The time of philosophical pause has been a time of rethinking and reevaluating the efficiency and cost-effectiveness of services, rather than a time for generating new philosophical approaches. Although this philosophical pause has been countered to some degree by the expansion of new ideas associated with broad concepts such as inclusion, self-determination, and quality of life (see the following section for a more complete description), overall, there has been less emphasis on providing support that is based on principles and ideology and more emphasis on encouraging support that is responsive to such ideas as using alternative resources, financial accountability, and community and family involvement.

Emphasis on Inclusion, Quality, and Equality

In spite of the pause described in the preceding section—and, to some extent, in reaction to it—people with disabilities are probably more accepted in society now than at any time since the early 1900s. A number of interrelated clusters of concepts have contributed to this. The principles of normalization and community living have been strongly embraced and solidified within the field and to some degree within the general population (see Chapters 2 and 34). These principles, along with important developments in rights (see the discussion that follows), have helped to stress equality between people with and without disabilities. *Inclusion* has become the overall term for a strong international movement that seeks to improve the life circumstances of people with intellectual and other disabilities. As the name implies, inclusion strives to ensure that people with disabilities should not only live in communities but also be valued, accepted, respected, involved, and have the same life opportunities as people without disabilities. The concept *quality of life* emerged and expanded during the 1990s. It is an ideal that emphasizes the quality within individuals' lives and ways to bring maximum enjoyment of life for each individual. *Inclusion* and *quality of life* are companion terms, because both pursue similar general goals. Having accepted that people with disabilities can and must live in neighborhoods and communities alongside people without disabilities, these concepts seek to enhance the overall quality of people's living circumstances and life experiences. Since the 1990s, there has been considerable emphasis in many countries on promoting both inclusion and quality of life for children and adults with intellectual and developmental disabilities.

Underlying recent accomplishments in inclusion and quality of life is a belief in the equality of people with and without disabilities. This belief is being realized primarily through important developments in the rights of people with disabilities (see Chapters 5 and 6 for fuller details). The 1993 UN proclamation entitled *Standard Rules for the Equalization of Opportunities for People with a Disability* reinforced the notion of inclusion in all aspects of life of a person with a disability. The Rules reflect a strong moral and political commitment to governments taking action. Standard Rule 1 calls upon nations to raise awareness in society about the rights, needs, potential, and contribution of people with disabilities. Following the proclamation, a Special Rapporteur on Disability was appointed by the UN Commission for Social Development to monitor the implementation of the Standard Rules by member States. Other UN activities have included the 2003 *Bei-*

jing Declaration on the Elaboration of an International Convention to Promote and Protect the Rights and Dignity of Persons with Disabilities. The UN Ad Hoc Committee on a Comprehensive and Integral International Convention on the Protection and Promotion of the Rights and Dignity of Persons with Disabilities has established a Working Group, widely representative of UN regional groups, that is charged with the responsibility of preparing and presenting a draft text that would be the basis for negotiations by member states.

These UN developments had their origins in the 1971 *Declaration on the Rights of Mentally Retarded Persons,* the 1975 *Declaration of the Rights of Disabled Persons,* and the UN proclamation of the years 1983–1992 as the "Decade of Disabled Persons." In the eyes of major international nongovernment advocacy organizations, the realization of the rights of people with disabilities is a cardinal goal that is being achieved in a variety of ways. This includes the right of people with disabilities to have equal opportunities for access to education, employment, the physical environment, and information and communication. There is no denying the fact that special legislation enacted in most Western countries has underpinned the provision of a wide range of supports, which has enabled the fuller participation of people with a disability into regular community life. However, rights legislation may be seen as a necessary, but not sufficient, condition for people with disabilities to enjoy the acceptance of the community. Similarly, it is suggested that the moral language of rights may be necessary, but not sufficient, to ground moral responsibility for people with a disability. Nirje, a father of the normalization movement, commented:

> Laws and legislative work cannot provide total answers to problem solving and proper actions with regard to human rights. These can only come into existence in the full cultural and human context. Such problems are not only practical, but also ethical. (1985, p. 65)

As a universal approach, the rights movement may need to be adapted or reconceptualized. This may be especially the case for cultures that do not have a social system with a strong commitment to social welfare or social justice or in cultures that emphasize the notion of a person's obligations to the community or tribe more strongly than is the case in many Western cultures (see also Chapters 5 and 6). Notwithstanding, the emphasis on human rights and disability has led to some very positive steps forward in perceiving and treating people with intellectual and developmental disabilities as both valued and equal, and it has provided a strong philosophical foundation for other complementary concepts such as inclusion and quality of life.

Community Living and Community Supports

Changing approaches to intellectual and developmental disabilities led to an international trend to close institutions (see discussion in Chapter 2). In turn, closing institutions and moving people to community settings has had a tremendous impact on how society views intellectual and developmental disabilities. The philosophical significance of the shift from institutional to community living is that all people should be valued in society and that all people have a place within society, but at a very practical level, it has meant that people with intellectual and developmental disabilities now live in neighborhoods everywhere with a much higher degree of acceptance than would have been the case in the 1970s.

Some people still live in large government- and non–government-run facilities. The number of people in such settings is gradually being reduced in response to a firm commitment by governments in most countries to close them as soon as is feasible. In a number of countries, moving thousands of people from institutional living to community living has involved considerably more logistical problems than were anticipated when the initiative was first given consideration in the 1970s (see Chapters 2 and 34). As a result, at the time of this book's publication, there are still thousands of people living in congregate care facilities in Australia, Canada, France, Germany, Japan, the Netherlands, the United States, and elsewhere. In less developed countries, institutional care or living at home often remain the major ways to accommodate people with intellectual and developmental disabilities. In the growing economies of Asia, the move to more normalized environments has been slow; however, population density is a key factor in many of these countries, and Western-style residential models may not be appropriate. Contemporary Western philosophies have not always had a major impact on these countries, as many do not have similar social welfare and social justice histories.

With the possible exception of the Netherlands, where institutional living numbers have slowly increased, the large majority of the developed economies have made a commitment to close their large facilities. For instance, the United Kingdom, New Zealand, and Norway have closed all of their congregate care facilities (e.g., see Braddock et al., 2001). In other countries where this has not occurred, lack of the required commitment to developing community alternatives has been one of the major reasons for maintaining institutions, especially for people with very high support needs. The problem is usually that there is simply no place in the community that is adequately funded to provide needed supports to which these individuals can move.

Perhaps the biggest challenge in assisting people to move from congregate to community living is doing so in ways that respect the dignity of people; that provide them with personal choices and opportunities for self-expression; and that result in their leading happier, more fulfilled lives. There is ample evidence that people who have moved from congregate facilities to community-based living do have an improved lifestyle (Emerson et al., 2000; see also Chapter 34). However, there is also strong evidence that quality of life is still less than desirable for many of these people (Brown, Raphael, & Renwick, 1997). A move *into* a community setting does not guarantee they will become part *of* a community. There has possibly been too much emphasis on the physical environment to the detriment of deciding how people can be best supported to optimize their quality of life in community settings. This issue continues to be a challenge for policy planners and support providers.

Types and Range of Services and Supports Available A comprehensive set of community services and supports is available to most individuals with intellectual and developmental disabilities and their families, as described throughout this book. Although not available everywhere, these services are accessible in a great many countries and regions of countries by people who have demonstrated need. Yet, life in community settings—including adaptation to ongoing changes that occur, such as changes in transportation, communication, technology, and types of services—has produced new challenges for the types and range of supports that need to be made available. In addition, there are ongoing issues in obtaining and using the services and supports that are available, including unequal access to services and sources of funding, gaps in services (e.g., between school and adult community living), lack of continuity within and among services, services that do not respond to the specific needs of individuals, and difficulties in gaining access to needed services.

Loss of Advocates and Specialists Somewhat ironically, the move away from institutional care and toward community support has contributed to a sense in many jurisdictions that there is a loss of passionate spokespeople for intellectual and developmental disabilities (Dumeresq & Lawton, 2003). Perhaps the main factor that affects this is that there has been an increasing emphasis on using generic, rather than specialized, professionals and services (e.g., health care professionals, psychologists). In addition, a great many specialized professionals who worked within the institutional system now work elsewhere or have retired. Such professionals acted, in part, as strong advocates within the field, and the current use of less specialized professionals is such that this advocacy role is not being replenished.

Another difficulty that has been a problem for community support is the high turnover of frontline staff (Hatton et al., 2001). This results in a paucity of experienced support workers and also effective advocates at the level of the individual with disabilities. Ways to address shortages of trained personnel in the field of intellectual and developmental disabilities, and ways to encourage such personnel to have ongoing careers in the human services field, are concerns in many countries. Paradoxically, the loss of professionals as advocates may make this challenge all the more difficult.

Professional groups have not yet taken all of the necessary steps to ensure that there will be enough professionals with specialized training in intellectual and developmental disabilities. For some professions, although this differs among countries and regions of countries, there are experienced and trained professionals readily available to respond to the needs of people with disabilities. For many other professions, however, there is a scarcity of such professionals. For example, in many areas it is difficult to identify lawyers, psychiatrists, family physicians, therapists, nurses, home care staff, counselors, addictions workers, and many other professionals to address the needs of people with disabilities.

Increasing Knowledge About Disabilities

Another important trend is the continually increasing knowledge base about factors that cause or contribute to the occurrence of intellectual and developmental disabilities. Especially since 1990, there has been a dramatic increase in understanding of the roles of environmental hazards such as alcohol abuse, brain injury from accidents involving impaired driving and child maltreatment, low socioeconomic status, genetics, and many other factors (see Chapters 7 and 9 for complete details).

Such advances are positive in that they have added considerably to knowledge of the factors that cause or contribute to disabilities and, in some cases, to effective interventions (see also Chapter 21). In a number of cases, they are also beginning to have important implications for preventing and treating intellectual and developmental disabilities.

Implications of New Genetic and Clinical Knowledge The emphasis on genetics emerges from a burst of important medical and scientific advances that have occurred—advances that in all likelihood will escalate in coming years. Genetic and clinical advances have led to the identification of "new" intellectual and developmental disabilities (e.g., Asperger syndrome; see Chapters 7, 8, 9, and 13). In addition, changing environmental and health conditions have resulted in new disabilities emerging as the result of infectious disease (e.g., children with HIV; see Chapter 16). These present new challenges to professionals to develop effective interventions, which are often specific to the disability type. In addition, different disabilities compete with one another for professional attention, available services, and funding.

Until the mid-20th century, infectious diseases and malnutrition were major causes of sickness and death in the world. Because of advances in treatment of such problems, genetic disorders are now major health problems in industrialized countries. In the United States, for example, 3%–5% of babies are born with a birth defect of chromosomal, gene, or multifactorial origin, and the important role of genetics in pediatric illnesses is being increasingly recognized (McCandless, Brunger, & Cassidy, 2004). As many as 30%–71% of children admitted to the hospital have been found to have an underlying medical condition with a significant genetic component (Hall et al., 1978), and 10% of conditions for adult hospital admissions have a genetic component (Khalifa, 1999). Because genetic diseases are chronic, they require lifelong attention, as well as expensive support, therapy, and specialized care. Thus, genetic knowledge has also created some new problems for the intellectual and developmental disabilities field.

One way of addressing such problems is through prevention. Genetic disorders can be prevented by elective pregnancy termination, by not having children, or by using assisted reproductive technology to have only healthy children (see Chapters 21 and 28). For example, for some time it has been possible for parents to know during pregnancy if their child will have Down syndrome (see Chapters 10 and 28) or for parents to know before conception that there is a possibility that their child will have fragile X syndrome (see Chapter 11) and to choose not to have affected children. Such choices are not for everyone, however, and such knowledge can pose terrible ethical dilemmas such as having to decide whether to continue or initiate a pregnancy. It is clear that the prevalence of Down syndrome has decreased as the result of being able to diagnose it by serum analysis of the mother or by ultrasound (see Chapters 10 and 28), but it is not known if the ability to diagnose fragile X and other disorders by DNA analysis actually is resulting in decreased prevalence of such disorders. Any changes in the range and demographics of specific types of intellectual and developmental disabilities will affect the types of services required. Thus, it is important for us to understand such changes.

Genetic advances have raised broader ethical concerns in the field of intellectual and developmental disabilities that go beyond simple prevention. The possibility of genetic intervention as the key to preventing disabilities raises new and troubling questions about when and how to make decisions about whether to intervene genetically or medically. It also raises important questions especially for those who advocate the value placed on the lives of individuals with disabilities and about the value placed on disability as part of any social order (Brown & Brown, 2003). Without the possibility of genetic intervention, disability advocates often argue that disability adds to the richness of the human condition and has a legitimate and important place in any social order. With the possibility of genetic intervention, however, it is not clear that advocates—especially those who do not themselves have disabilities—would present the same views. These types of concerns stress a need for professionals and self-advocates in the field of disabilities to continuously assess their core values and to assume leadership in helping to shape and expand positive values for people with disabilities. They also stress a need to expand the role of ethical considerations in testing and carrying out interventions that will almost certainly result from a rapidly growing knowledge of genetic disabilities.

The need for disability professionals and self-advocates to take on this responsibility is especially important because new genetic knowledge gained through the Human Genome Project is increasing exponentially (see Chapters 7 and 45). It is anticipated that such new knowledge will have a particularly profound impact on the profession of nursing and that nurses will become more and more involved in referring people for genetic testing and for managing the genetic health aspects of individuals (Jenkins, Grady, & Collins, 2005). Health care systems will have to provide resources for meeting such training needs, for educating the public as well as professionals about genetic disorders, for meeting the demands for diagnosing new disorders, and for supporting individuals and families with newly diagnosed genetic disorders (National Human Genome Research Institute, 2005). Disability professionals and self-advocates will need to provide guidance and ethical leadership if these challenges are to be met adequately.

Self-Advocacy by People with Disabilities

The worldwide growth of self-advocacy groups is a potentially vital force for people with intellectual and developmental disabilities achieving equal citizenship with their peers who do not have disabilities. This force has been developing since approximately 1970, as Parmenter explained:

> The birth of the self-advocacy movement can be traced to a convention of people with disabilities held in Vancouver [Canada], in the early 1970s. A group known as People First was formally inaugurated in Oregon in the United States in 1973 by former residents of a state institution called Fairview Training Center. (2001, p. 285)

Since then, there has been considerable growth in self-advocacy (see the related resources in Appendix B at the end of the book). For example, the People First movement has spread to several countries, including some in the Middle East. A number of international self-advocacy conferences have been held in Canada, the United Kingdom, and the United States. At other conferences, self-advocacy has been one important aspect of the overall programs. For example, at the 10th World Congress of the International Association for the Scientific Study of Intellectual Disabilities (IASSID), which was held in Helsinki, Finland in 1996, one of the keynote presentations was made by self advocates.

There has been increasing recognition of the right of people with intellectual and other disabilities to have a voice in how they would like to live their lives. They are asserting their need to be consulted on a variety of policy and service issues, including involvement in setting the research agenda. The growth in the empowerment of these people to make their own decisions and choices is becoming one of the major forces of the early 21st century. Testimony to this development is the increasing number of people with an intellectual disability who are marrying or forming long-term relationships, having children, going to college, working in full-time jobs, and living more independently.

Person-Centered Approaches

Another important international trend, related to the growth of individualism, is the growing emphasis on person-centered approaches (see especially Chapter 22 for a more detailed discussion). This is resulting in community disability service agencies redefining their overall roles and the roles of their employees. Person-centered approaches refer to methods of providing support to individuals with intellectual and developmental disabilities and their families that place their wants and needs at the center of the supports they receive. Person-centered approaches imply that service organizations should neither predetermine what services are important to people with disabilities nor make the key decisions about the best ways to implement those services; rather, they should respond in individual ways to the needs and wishes of the people they support. For these approaches to be realized, service organizations need to be flexible in their organizational structure and have the capacity to respond to a wide variety of needs and wishes in ways that are sometimes new and that require creative solutions.

Person-centered approaches can lead to some interesting dilemmas for paid staff who support people with disabilities. Brown and Brown (2003) gave several examples where the needs and wishes of the person with disabilities conflict with the worker's own values, with what the worker thinks is the best course to pursue, with what the worker knows to be safe, or with the scope of services that the worker's agency is willing to offer. The point these authors made was that it is not always possible or advisable for support workers to respond to the needs and wishes expressed. Thus, although person-centered planning is generally considered to be useful because it responds better and more directly to the needs of the person with disabilities or the family, it also presents new challenges that service organizations and policy makers need to address.

A trend that is influencing services to people with intellectual and developmental disabilities and one that is related to person-centered approaches in many countries is the growth of direct funding—public money being dispersed by governments or government agents directly to individuals with disabilities or their families. Direct funding is based on the principle that services can be delivered in a more cost-efficient and effective way because many individuals and families are in the best position to know what supports they need most and are capable of using the money responsibly and effectively. One direct funding model makes an amount of money, typically up to a maximum, available to any individuals with intellectual disabilities or their families who apply for it. Another model assigns funding levels to individuals or families following an individual assessment. In some cases, money moves directly from government or other funding agents to individuals and families; in other cases, money is provided to community organizations who take responsibility for identifying, approving, and monitoring individuals or families who need funding and who use the method effectively. Models of direct funding have existed since the mid-1990s; many of these are still being amended, and new ideas are still being developed in this area.

Direct funding has important implications for both people with disabilities and their families. For families, it offers a degree of financial support and independence, but it is often only a portion of what they need. Furthermore, it places on them the ultimate responsibility for care of family members with disabilities, which some people with disabilities and families want but others do not. For adults with intellectual or developmental disabilities, it means that they are able to spend more years with their families, but it also often reduces or removes altogether the possibility of leading more independent lives. The trend toward providing funding directly to families has not yet been critically examined in any depth. It needs to be evaluated with a view to determining the degree to which it supports other current trends and values in the field of disabilities.

CHALLENGES FOR THE FIELD

The field of intellectual and developmental disabilities has faced challenges for many decades, and will continue to do so in the future. Nine important questions that emerge from the broader trends described in this chapter, and that challenge the field as of 2007, are presented here as examples (adapted from Brown & Percy, 2003).

1. What Is Meant by *Intellectual and Developmental Disabilities*?

The terms used, and the meanings we attach to those terms, change over time (see Chapter 1 for full details). For the allocation of special services and for access to generic community services and supports such as education, health care, and employment, it is helpful to know specifically what is meant by *intellectual and developmental disabilities.* It is especially important to know this if resources are scarce or if priorities are shifting. Two interesting questions are the degree to which those in the field need to understand the precise meaning of the terms *intellectual and developmental disabilities* for the purposes of supporting people with disabilities effectively and in cost-efficient ways, and whether this need differs according to the purpose for which the terms are being used.

2. How Can Useful Information and Tracking Systems Be Developed?

As of 2007, most countries have not implemented a systematic mechanism to track questions such as the following:

- How many people within a given population can be said to have intellectual or developmental disabilities?
- How many people can services systems identify as having needs?
- What kinds of services do these people need and use?
- Where do they live?
- What are their age ranges?
- What are their levels of need?
- What are their sources of financial support?
- What is the degree to which they have family and other social support?
- What are their living conditions?

The Australian Institute of Health and Welfare is an example of one initiative that has attempted to report much of these data in its biennial reports on Australian welfare services. Overall, though, it is difficult to find credible demographic information, especially information that is comparable among countries.

In addition, in most Western countries there are few mechanisms to track two groups of people who are important to disability services. First, those who will probably require support in the future are not being clearly identified in a great many areas by services for purposes of future planning. For example, although there are some exceptions, school systems do not typically plan in advance for ways to address the needs of students once they leave school, and community service organizations for adults with disabilities do not typically plan in advance for those who leave school and will probably need community support as adults (see Chapter 32 for a fuller discussion). Second, many people have been assisted by the service system in the past but no longer require support because they have learned independent living skills or are supported by family or others. For the most part, these people simply become lost to the service system. It would be helpful to track these people because valuable indicators of the success of the service system include successful independent living and the degree to which family and community support can be put in place.

Following these types of information over time and analyzing trends would result in interesting knowledge, but it is especially important for at least four reasons: 1) to help plan services and resources needed for what people will require in the future; 2) to identify those who are not receiving any support, but need it, because they are not known to the service system; 3) to develop a better understanding of how people with intellectual and developmental disabilities can be supported by other sectors outside the education and service systems; and 4) to provide a better measure of evaluation and accountability for public funds used in disability services.

3. What Are the Service Implications of People Living Longer?

There is a growing trend for people with intellectual and developmental disabilities to live much longer, due to improved living conditions and better medical treatment (see especially Chapter 39). Medical and technological advances also make it increasingly possible for older adults or those who are medically fragile to participate in community life much more than was possible even in the late 1980s. Sometimes, this requires special equipment or additional personnel. A challenge is to find ways to provide support to people who are living longer and to identify ways to balance the need for this support with the needs of others with disabilities.

4. What Are the Implications of New Genetic Knowledge?

Genetic knowledge has been increasing at a dramatic rate since the mid-1990s(see Chapters 7 and 45). Such knowledge has helped society to understand a number of disabilities and to shape medical and social support interventions, but it has opened up the need for new interventions and supports and has suggested numerous ethical challenges. It appears that there is a strong need for increased expertise within the field of intellectual and developmental disabilities especially to guide how new disability-related genetic knowledge should be generated; understand the utility of information generated for the field; help disseminate new genetic knowledge in ways that are understandable to people with disabilities, their families, and disability practitioners; and provide leadership in developing practical applications of new genetic knowledge.

5. How Effective Can Individualized Funding Be?

Although most countries have no comprehensive programs for individualized funding, a number of important shifts have tied funding closer to individual needs. The shift toward individualized funding may continue in the future, but major challenges will need to be faced if it is to be equitable (to respond fairly to the needs of individuals with intellectual and developmental disabilities and their families) and accountable (to ensure that the public's money is well spent). As a starting point, a method will have to be developed to assess needs and services in a standard way. This will involve determining what services should cost, who should receive them, and the extent to which public money should be used to fund them.

6. Are Services an Entitlement?

There is a growing sense, especially among parents, that services for their children with disabilities and services for families that support children with such disabilities should be an entitlement. Parents are often surprised to discover that in most countries, they are not entitled by law or policy to most services but rather that they may gain access to those that are provided and available, assuming that they meet the qualifying criteria. The difficulty is that the services that are available are not always those that are needed, there are long waits for services in some areas, and people with intellectual or developmental disabilities do not always meet the qualifying criteria (e.g., the ability to travel independently is sometimes a criterion for access to vocational support programs) (Brown et al., 2003) A discussion of entitlement to services is particularly timely in view of the shift toward shared responsibility among government, communities, and families. In practice, this has meant that families assume the primary responsibility for their children while they are still in school, with support services provided by various community agencies and government funding sources. Increasingly, families are continuing to assume the primary responsibility for young adults and even, in many cases, older adults with intellectual and developmental disabilities as well—usually without entitlement to services—and the degree to which families are willing or able to do this needs to be carefully monitored.

7. Does the Public Have a Right to Know How Service Funds Are Used?

A challenge that is related to individualized funding and increased responsibility for families is accountability for the specific ways public funds are used. On the one hand, it may also be important for planning purposes for funding sources to track how effective their funds are in helping individuals and families to reach identified goals. On the other hand, interesting ethical questions arise, such as whether individuals with disabilities who receive disability financial support, individuals or families who receive tax deductions, or families who receive funding under a government-funded program should choose how the money is used or if it should be used in ways specified by the funder. For example, Josef receives a government-sponsored disability pension, to which he is entitled by legislation, but he lives with his family and his family members support his daily living needs financially (i.e., they buy his food and clothing and do not charge him rent). He spends most of his money on his own entertainment and traveling with groups around the country. Should Josef be free to spend public money in this way, or should he only receive it if he needs it to pay for his basic needs?

8. Can Life-Span Planning Be Initiated?

It appears at the present time that it would be very helpful to develop a system of life-span (long-range) planning for people with intellectual and developmental disabilities. The emphasis now is more on providing services than on identifying children with disabilities and planning for their needs over their life-span. Making the shift to life-span planning will require considerable restructuring of services and current ways of thinking.

A shift toward life-span planning should spark considerable creativity in both policy and practice. For example, it should encourage creative and individualized solutions to planning for future financial needs (e.g., savings accounts, trust funds, property) and other personal support needs (e.g., designating family members who will assume responsibility at various stages of life, connecting individuals with needed community supports). Policy will need to set the environment for such activities, and the practical work will need to be done by community service organizations, self-advocacy, family advocacy, and other groups, as well as by individuals with disabilities and their family members.

9. What Are the Best Models of Care and Support?

At one time, it was assumed that a good model of care and support was for people with disabilities to live in large state-run institutions. As noted previously, this view has been in decline for many years.

At the beginning of the 21st century, the best model of care and support in Western countries is primarily to provide opportunities for adults with intellectual and developmental disabilities to live in community homes or supported independent living or to support families who have children or adults with disabilities living in the family home. However, this may not be the best model for all individuals (especially for individuals with severe disabilities who may benefit more from a higher-care residence, for older adults with disabilities, or for older parents or caregivers of people with disabilities), and it remains an ongoing challenge for the field to put into practice models that best enhance the lives of those it supports. In the meantime, it is important to assess current models in an ongoing way. For example, the field needs to examine whether shared homes for four people with disabilities are better than institutions for improving the lives of residents and whether adults are best serviced by living with their families.

In doing this, a challenge that must be addressed is how to take into account the views of people with intellectual and developmental disabilities themselves. An additional challenge for service providers and families in particular is how to react if the views of people with disabilities differ from the principles of current best models of care and support or if they contradict the wishes and values of supporting family members.

Alternative models of care and support need to extend beyond those traditionally provided by disability specific programs. These, too, will pose some interesting questions and challenges for the field. Some examples are provided next:

- People with disabilities have numerous health problems and needs associated with growing older (see Chapters 39, 41, and 44). To what degree should these needs be addressed by general health services rather than services funded by disability specific resources? For example, should older people with intellectual disabilities who need ongoing care live in group homes, nursing homes, or other facilities?
- Some types of disabilities do not typically meet criteria for access to the long-term care system. Should disability services deal with dementia and other mental health problems rather than incorporating dementia into generic services?
- In most developed countries at the beginning of the 21st century, it is not always clearly specified what services are funded by disability ministries or departments and which are funded by other ministries or departments, such as the department of health or the department of education. The general approach appears to be that if a problem that involves intellectual and developmental disability is not picked up by another ministry or department, then the disability service may address it.
- Various parts of government and various nongovernment bodies, both private and public, provide infrastructures for similar types of supports. The question of how to make the financial and human resources that are available do the most possible is an ongoing challenge.
- Disability service organizations could evolve to work in partnership with government, other community services and resources, and families in a variety of ways.

SUMMARY

The field of intellectual and developmental disabilities has a set of issues that have been relatively stable over time, but others have been influenced by current sociopolitical trends and trends with the disability field. Within developed countries, there has been an emphasis since the 1980s on economic prosperity and economic accountability at the cost of stressing social justice, although some progress has been made. There have been policy shifts toward governments supporting individuals, families, and communities and toward providing for those most in need and sharing responsibility with communities and families. The international field of intellectual and developmental disabilities itself has been experiencing a philosophical and funding pause but, at the same time, has generated important new knowledge and ideas, especially those that relate to community living, conceptual development, self-advocacy, and person-centered approaches. Overall, the field of intellectual and developmental disabilities looks better at the beginning of the 21st century than it has in past decades. Still, there are a number of long-standing challenges and a number of new challenges that have arisen due to recent trends.

FOR FURTHER THOUGHT AND DISCUSSION

1. To what degree should trends within the field of intellectual and developmental disabilities change in response to broader national and international trends?
2. How important is it for services for people with intellectual and developmental disabilities to be based on strong philosophical principles?
3. Have deinstitutionalization and other trends spread experts in intellectual and developmental disabilities within the community and lost them? If so, is this good or bad?
4. Debate the pros and cons of taking a person-centered approach. Illustrate your points by referring to people with intellectual and developmental disabilities or their families.
5. How feasible is it to implement a broad program of direct funding to families of people with intellectual and developmental disabilities? Illustrate by describing families you know.
6. Putting current models of care and support aside, create a fictional system of care and support that addresses the problems and challenges identified in this chapter. In doing so, be sure to develop ideas that are practical and that work in the best interests of people with intellectual and developmental disabilities.

REFERENCES

Americans with Disabilities Act (ADA) of 1990, PL 101-336, 42 U.S.C. §§ 12101 *et seq.*

Braddock, D., Emerson, E., Felce, D., et al. (2001). Living circumstances of children and adults with mental retardation or developmental disabilities in the United States, Canada, England and Wales, and Australia. *Mental Retardation and Developmental Disabilities Research Reviews, 7,* 115–121.

Brown, I., Anand, S., Fung, W.L.A., et al. (2003). Family quality of life: Canadian results from an international study. *Journal of Developmental and Physical Disabilities,* 15, 207–230.

Brown, I., & Brown, R.I. (2003). *Quality of life and disability: An approach for community practitioners.* London: Jessica Kingsley Publishers.

Brown, I., & Percy, M. (2003). Current trends and issues in developmental disabilities in Ontario. In I. Brown & M. Percy (Eds.), *Developmental disabilities in Ontario* (2nd ed., pp. 43–55). Toronto: Ontario Association on Developmental Disabilities.

Brown, I., Raphael, D., & Renwick, R. (1997). *Quality of life: Dream or reality? Life for people with developmental disabilities in Ontario.* Toronto: Centre for Health Promotion, Department of Public Health Sciences, University of Toronto.

Dumeresq, M., & Lawton, S. (2003). The role of the professional supporting people with developmental disabilities. In I. Brown & M. Percy (Eds.), *Developmental disabilities in Ontario* (2nd ed., pp. 493–507). Toronto: Ontario Association on Developmental Disabilities.

Eisenman, L.T. (2003). Theories in practice: School-to-work transitions for youth with mild disabilities. *Exceptionality, 11,* 89–102.

Emerson, E. (2004). Poverty and children with intellectual disabilities in the world's richer countries. *Journal of Intellectual & Developmental Disability, 29,* 319–338.

Emerson, E., Robertson, J., Gregory, N., et al. (2000). The quality and costs of community-based residential supports and residential campuses for people with severe and complex disabilities. *Journal of Intellectual & Developmental Disability, 25,* 263–279.

Grantham-McGregor, S.M., Walker, S.P., & Chang, S. (2000). Nutritional efficiencies and later behavioural development. *Proceedings of the Nutrition Society, 59,* 47–54.

Hall, J.G., Powers, E.K., McIlvaine, R.T., et al. (1978). The frequency and financial burden of genetic disease in a pediatric hospital. *American Journal of Medical Genetics, 1,* 17–36.

Hatton, C., Emerson, E., Rivers, M., et al. (2001). Factors associated with intended staff turnover and job search behaviour in services for people with intellectual disability. *Journal of Intellectual Disability Research, 45,* 258–270.

Hetzel, B.S. (1989). *The story of iodine deficiency: An international challenge in nutrition.* Oxford, United Kingdom: Oxford University Press.

Jenkins, J., Grady, P.A., & Collins, F.S. (2005). Nurses and the genomic revolution. *Journal of Nursing Scholarship, 37,* 98–101.

Khalifa, M.M. (1999). Preventive aspects of genetic morbidity: Experiences of the Canadian model. *East Mediterranean Health Journal, 5,* 1121–1128.

Individuals with Disabilities Education Improvement Act of 2004, PL 108-446, 20 U.S.C. §§ 1400 *et seq.*

McCandless, S.E., Brunger, J.W., & Cassidy, S.B. (2004). The burden of genetic disease on inpatient care in a children's hospital. *American Journal of Human Genetics, 74,* 121–127.

Ministry of Community and Social Services. (1997). *Making services work for people: A new framework for children and for people with developmental disabilities.* Toronto: Queen's Printer for Ontario.

National Human Genome Research Institute. (2005). *Genetics FAQ.* Retrieved July 13, 2005, from http://www.genome.gov/10001191

Nirje, B. (1985). The basis and logic of the Normalization Principle. *Australia & New Zealand Journal of Developmental Disabilities, 11,* 65–68.

Parmenter, T. (2001). Intellectual disabilities—quo vadis? In G.L. Albrecht, K.D. Seelman, & M. Bury (Eds.), *Handbook of disability studies* (pp. 267–296). Thousand Oaks, CA: Sage Publications.

Schroeder, S.R. (2000). Mental retardation and developmental disabilities influenced by environmental neurotoxic insults. *Environmental Health Perspectives, 108,* 47–54.

Shephard, Y.H. (1986). Human teratogens: How can we sort them out? In H.M. Wisniewski & D.A. Snider (Eds.), *Men-*

tal retardation: Research, education, and technology transfer (pp. 105–115). New York: New York Academy of Sciences.
United Nations. (1971). *Declaration on the rights of mentally retarded persons.* Retrieved October 27, 2005, from http://www.unhchr.ch/html/menu3/b/m_mental.htm
United Nations. (1975). *Declaration of the rights of disabled people.* Retrieved October 27, 2005, from http://daccessdds.un.org/doc/RESOLUTION/GEN/NR0/001/60/IMG/NR000160.pdf?OpenElement
United Nations. (1993). *Standard rules on the equalization of opportunities for persons with disabilities.* Retrieved September 26, 2005, from http://www.un.org/documents/ga/res/48/a48r096.htm
United Nations. (2003). *Beijing declaration on the elaboration of an international convention to promote and protect the rights and dignity of persons with disabilities.* Retrieved October 27, 2005, from http://www.worldenable.net/beijing2003/beijingdeclaration.htm
Workforce Investment Act of 1998, PL 105-220, 29 U.S.C. §2801 *et seq.*
Yamaki, K., & Fujiura, G.T. (2002). Employment and income status of adults with developmental disabilities living in the community. *Mental Retardation, 40,* 132–141.

5

International Human Rights and Intellectual Disability

MARCIA H. RIOUX, BENGT LINDQVIST, AND ANNE CARBERT

WHAT YOU WILL LEARN ABOUT IN THIS CHAPTER

- A human rights approach to disability
- Applying human rights in the context of intellectual disability
- Incorporating disability into the international human rights system

Human rights are principles that ensure that people are able to live in dignity, free from fear, harassment, or discrimination. They allow people to have choices and opportunities to fully participate in society as individuals and members of communities. All people have human rights simply because they are human. Values held and advanced throughout recorded human history and centuries of socio-political development show that human rights cover all areas of life. This includes, for example, the right to life; the right not to be subject to torture; legal rights such as equal protection of the law; political rights such as freedom of expression and the right to take part in government; and the rights to form a family, to own property, to work, to receive education and health care, and to participate in the cultural life of the community.

A HUMAN RIGHTS APPROACH TO DISABILITY

This chapter explains human rights, particularly in terms of disability. The discussion begins with this section's explanation of various human rights treaties and topics specific to disability.

International Human Rights Treaties

Human rights are set out in writing in legal documents that obligate governments to respect, protect, and fulfill basic standards. The legal human rights documents at the international level are international human rights treaties. At national and local levels, legal statements about human rights are found in constitutions, bills of rights, and human rights legislation. Human rights laws require governments to protect human rights in accordance with the law and also to create mechanisms for people to seek remedies if their rights have been violated.

The modern system of international human rights law began when the member nations of the United Nations (UN) proclaimed the *Universal Declaration of Human Rights* on December 10, 1948. This was negotiated after the end of World War II in response to the Holocaust. The Universal Declaration remains a powerful statement of the basic rights of all human beings. The Declaration is an enumeration of the rights and freedoms essential for life with dignity and well-being. In the decades following the adoption of the Declaration, the UN created more detailed human rights obligations by adopting international treaties. There are now seven treaties central to the UN human rights system:

1. *International Covenant on Economic, Social and Cultural Rights* (1976)
2. *International Covenant on Civil and Political Rights* (1976)
3. *International Convention on the Elimination of All Forms of Racial Discrimination* (1969)
4. *Convention on the Elimination of All Forms of Discrimination Against Women* (1981)
5. *Convention Against Torture and Other Cruel, Inhuman or Degrading Treatment or Punishment* (1987)
6. *Convention on the Rights of the Child* (1990)
7. *International Convention on the Protection of the Rights of All Migrant Workers and Members of Their Families* (2003)

See http://www.unhchr.ch/tbs/doc.nsf for additional information on these items.

Some of these treaties have supplementary optional agreements, called *Optional Protocols,* which create further obligations if governments agree to the Optional Protocols in addition to the central text of the treaty. By becoming parties to international human rights treaties, governments around the world have assumed legal obligations to uphold human rights and ensure that all of their citizens enjoy these rights without discrimination. Numerous international documents and declarations, some of which are referred to throughout this chapter (see Chapter 6 for other examples), reinforce these major international human rights treaties by emphasizing state responsibilities to guarantee human rights. In many instances these agreements highlight particular issues of concern such as the rights of women, children, and people with disabilities.

Human rights treaties are also supported by mechanisms to monitor the implementation of human rights. These mechanisms include committees that review government progress reports on the implementation of treaty rights. Some committees receive complaints from individuals or groups alleging that their human rights have been violated. The UN Commission on Human Rights also performs a monitoring role. Comprised of 53 of the countries that make up the UN, the Commission meets every year to consider global human rights issues. It has the power to create mechanisms and special procedures to promote the implementation of human rights, and it appoints independent experts to investigate important human rights themes such as health, food, education, adequate housing, torture, violence against women, internally displaced persons, and extreme poverty. (In 2005, the UN announced its intention to eliminate the Commission on Human Rights and reform the entire UN human rights system, but at the time of writing had not yet decided on concrete plans for new human rights mechanisms.)

How Disability Relates to Human Rights

Human rights for people with disabilities, sometimes referred to as *disability rights,* are not separate from the rights guaranteed through international human rights treaties. People with disabilities are people with the same rights as all others. This is the central principle behind a significant shift in the understanding of disability. Historically, people with disabilities have been seen as objects of deviance, disease, or charity, thus creating a focus on an individual's failure, or a family's failure, to attain standards of "normalcy" (see Chapter 2 for a fuller discussion of the history of disability). Since the 1980s in particular, it has become increasingly common to recognize people with disabilities as full citizens entitled to equal rights. The exclusion so often experienced by people with disabilities is now seen as the result of social and environmental failures to acknowledge and respond constructively to difference (see Chapter 3). People are realizing that the barriers faced by people with disabilities violate their human rights, perpetuate social isolation and exclusion, and place people with disabilities at greater risk of discrimination, abuse, and poverty (e.g., see Oliver, 1990).

Viewing people with disabilities as members of society with equal rights is a radical transformation in perspective. From this standpoint, it is no longer the responsibility of an individual with a disability to adapt or face exclusion. Societies and governments must embrace everyone and create policies, laws, programs, and services that acknowledge difference and respect each person's dignity. As a UN study on human rights and disability stated:

> Seeing people with disabilities as subjects rather than objects entails giving them access to the full benefits of basic freedoms that most people take for granted and doing so in a way that is respectful and accommodating of their difference. (Quinn & Degener, 2002, p. 13)

Governments are responsible for implementing the human rights of all citizens and must find ways to end widespread discrimination and to promote the full participation of people with disabilities.

It is now clear that many government practices and policies violate the human rights of people with disabilities by explicitly preventing them from exercising their rights or by failing to address their specific needs. In the context of increased human rights awareness, governments can no longer justify denying children with disabilities education, preventing people with disabilities from forming families, or prohibiting ownership of property or access to health care. A human rights approach presents the promise and challenge of creating a society that respects the dignity and equality of each person, regardless of differences among individuals. Internationally accepted human rights standards, as articulated in international treaties and declarations, become useful tools for disability advocacy and for responding to injustice.

The Emergence of a Human Rights Approach to Disability

In the late 1960s, organizations of people with disabilities began to articulate how the design and structure of societies, as well as the general attitudes toward people with disabilities, severely limited their opportunities. As this new perspective gathered support, the UN designated 1981 as the International Year of Disabled Persons. The International Year focused global attention on the situation of the estimated 600 million people with disabilities around the world and led to the adoption of the *World Programme of Action Concerning Disabled Persons* in 1982. The World Programme was a strategy document to promote the equalization of opportunities to achieve the full participation of people with disabilities in social life and national development.

The World Programme created momentum for many significant developments in the 1990s. First, more specific international commitments were adopted to promote and protect the rights of people with disabilities: the *Principles for the Protection of Persons with Mental Illness and the Improvement of Mental Health Care* in 1991 and the *Standard Rules on the Equalization of Opportunities for Persons with Disabilities* in 1993. These international documents drew attention to the rights and abuses experienced by people with disabilities and to the policies and actions needed to protect and promote their rights. The Standard Rules clearly stipulates that governments are responsible for taking steps to remove obstacles preventing the full participation of people with disabilities. Governments must act to empower people with disabilities and to create an accessible society. A special rapporteur was appointed to monitor and support the implementation of the Standard Rules and to report regularly to the UN. See Display 5.1 for more information on the Standard Rules.

In 1994, the Committee on Economic, Social and Cultural Rights—the body of experts responsible for monitoring the implementation of the *International Covenant on Economic, Social and Cultural Rights* (1976)—issued a detailed analysis of how the Covenant applies in the context of disability. The Committee's analysis, titled *General Comment 5: Persons with Disabilities,* explicitly stated that the Covenant applies fully to all members of society, including people with disabilities, and that discrimination on the basis of disability is prohibited. Furthermore, the Committee required States Parties to the Covenant to take appropriate measures to enable people with disabilities to overcome any disadvantages resulting from their disabilities that inhibit the enjoyment of Covenant rights. It recognized that this may involve the provision of supports, services and aids to enable social and economic inclusion, self-determination, and the realization of all rights in the treaty. The Committee's analysis was an historic recognition that people with disabilities are entitled to the equal effective enjoyment of treaty rights without discrimination and that governments have legal responsibilities to ensure the enjoyment of human rights for people with disabilities.

Another significant development in the emergence of the human rights approach to disabilities was the first legally binding international treaty specifically devoted to the rights of people with disabilities: the *Inter-American Convention on the Elimination of All Forms of Discrimination against People with Disabilities.* This treaty was adopted in 1999 by the Organization of American States and officially came into force in 2001. (At the time of writing, 15 countries were parties to the treaty.) Under the terms of the treaty, governments agree to adopt legislation and social, educational, or labor-related measures to fully include people with disabilities in society. The treaty calls for rehabilitation, education, job training, and other measures to promote the independence and quality of life of persons with disabilities.

Display 5.1

Standard Rules on the Equalization of Opportunities for Persons with Disabilities

With 22 rules on topics such awareness-raising, medical care, support services, employment, education, social security, and family life, the UN's *Standard Rules on the Equalization of Opportunities for Persons with Disabilities* (1993) outline a process for states to identify and remove obstacles to the full participation of people with disabilities. Paragraph 15 of the Standard Rules stated:

> The purpose of the Rules is to ensure that girls, boys, women and men with disabilities, as members of their societies, may exercise the same rights and obligations as others. In all societies of the world there are still obstacles preventing persons with disabilities from exercising their rights and freedoms and making it difficult for them to participate fully in the activities of their societies. It is the responsibility of States to take appropriate action to remove such obstacles. Persons with disabilities and their organizations should play an active role as partners in this process. The equalization of opportunities for persons with disabilities is an essential contribution in the general and worldwide effort to mobilize human resources. Special attention may need to be directed towards groups such as women, children, the elderly, the poor, migrant workers, persons with dual or multiple disabilities, indigenous people and ethnic minorities. In addition, there are a large number of refugees with disabilities who have special needs requiring attention.

The UN Commission on Human Rights passed two important resolutions specifically confirming the rights of people with disabilities. The Commission recognized that inequality or discrimination based on disability violates human rights (Resolution 1998/31). The Commission also called on the High Commissioner for Human Rights to strengthen the protection and monitoring of human rights of people with disabilities (Resolution 2000/51).

In December 2001, building on the support for a human rights approach to disability, the UN General Assembly created a committee to begin formal discussions on a thematic treaty on the rights and dignity of people with disabilities. In 2004, a working group prepared *Draft Comprehensive and Integral International Convention on the Protection and Promotion of the Rights and Dignity of Persons with Disabilities* and initiated negotiations to approve the text. Negotiations are ongoing.

All of these accomplishments at the international level are extremely important for improving the quality of life of people with disabilities and for achieving equality and justice. The activities at the international level have an impact at the national level in countries around the world. Awareness of the rights of people with disabilities has grown, strengthening disability organizations and their advocacy work in turn. Increased awareness and advocacy have encouraged national legislative reform as well as the creation of structures for participatory policy development and social planning. National human rights institutions are also increasingly addressing disability discrimination (Quinn & Degener, 2002). The trend toward a human rights approach to disability can only expand the possibilities for responding to and eliminating disability discrimination (see Display 5.2).

Display 5.2

Human rights and disability at the United Nations

The Office of the High Commissioner for Human Rights published a study on human rights and disability in 2001 (Quinn & Degener, 2002). The study had three aims: 1) to clarify the relevance of the major United Nations human rights treaties to disability; 2) to review how the system actually works in practice with respect to disability, by looking at how states parties report to the treaty monitoring bodies on human rights and disability and how the treaty monitoring bodies respond; and 3) to provide options for the future. To address this last aim, the study "provides observations, comments and recommendations as to how the various stakeholders might enhance the use of the six human rights instruments in the context of disability" (Quinn & Degener, 2002, p. 3).

The report's introduction places the human rights approach to disability in context:

> The disability rights debate is not so much about the enjoyment of specific rights as it is about ensuring the equal effective enjoyment of all human rights, without discrimination, by people with disabilities. The non-discrimination principle helps make human rights in general relevant in the specific context of disability, just as it does in the contexts of age, sex, and children. Non-discrimination, and the equal effective enjoyment of all human rights by people with disabilities, are therefore the dominant theme of the long-overdue reform in the way disability and the disabled are viewed throughout the world.
>
> The process of ensuring that people with disabilities enjoy their human rights is slow and uneven. But it is taking place, in all economic and social systems. It is inspired by the values that underpin human rights: the inestimable dignity of each and every human being, the concept of autonomy or self-determination that demands that the person be placed at the centre of all decisions affecting him/her, the inherent equality of all regardless of difference, and the ethic of solidarity that requires society to sustain the freedom of the person with appropriate social supports. (Quinn & Degener, 2002, p. 1)

APPLYING HUMAN RIGHTS IN THE CONTEXT OF INTELLECTUAL DISABILITY

To illustrate how human rights relate to the situation of people with intellectual disabilities, this section looks at selected rights: the right to education, the right to adequate housing, rights related to therapeutic treatment, and rights that are particularly relevant for women with intellectual disabilities. For each topic, common experiences of people with intellectual disabilities are connected to specific rights in UN human rights treaties, the *Standard Rules on the Equalization of Opportunities for Persons with Disabilities,* and other international documents.

Education

As of 2007, children with disabilities in many countries attend school and have full rights to an education. In most economically advanced countries, legislation requires schooling for children with disabilities and provides for effective teaching methods (see Chapters 6 and 31 for details). There are exceptions even in these countries, however, and in many other countries, large numbers of children with disabilities do not attend school and receive little or no education at all. Many of those who do go to school attend separate schools for children with disabilities or are in segregated classes in general education schools. Children with intellectual disabilities who are placed in classes with children who do not have disabilities often encounter teaching methods and curricula that do not respond to their particular learning needs. These problems differ markedly from country to country, because despite international foundations of the right to education, specific laws and policies that govern the implementation of education for children with disabilities are made by individual nations or states/provinces within nations. As a consequence, many of these problems are not being addressed well in some countries. In other countries, they are being addressed quite well, particularly in the more economically developed countries where laws and policies require schooling, promote effective teaching methods, and encourage inclusion (see Chapter 31 for full details).

Education is a human right and is very closely interconnected with the exercise of many other human rights. For example, education enhances enjoyment of the right to work, of rights to political participation, and of the right to take part freely in specific cultural activities (e.g., language, religion). Education supports greater individual participation in civil society. The right to education is found in several UN human rights treaties (see Chapters 6 and 31 for country-specific details):

- *International Covenant on Economic, Social and Cultural Rights,* Article 13 (1976)
- *Convention on the Rights of the Child,* Articles 28 and 29 (1990)
- *Convention for the Elimination of All Forms of Discrimination Against Women,* Article 10 (1981)
- *International Convention on the Elimination of All Forms of Racial Discrimination,* Article 5(e)(v) (1976)

These treaties address access to education as well as the aims and content of education. Human rights principles support accessible public education that includes people with disabilities in general education programs. In its role as monitor of the *International Covenant on Economic, Social and Cultural Rights,* the Committee on Economic, Social and Cultural Rights has noted that "[s]chool programmes in many countries today recognize that people with disabilities can best be educated within the general education system" (1994; General Comment 5, para. 35).

The Committee on Economic, Social and Cultural Rights emphasized some key components of accessible education: nondiscrimination, physical accessibility, and economic accessibility (1999; General Comment 13, para. 6). Other aspects of accessibility are highlighted by Rule 6 of the *Standard Rules on the Equalization of Opportunities for Persons with Disabilities.* At all levels of inclusive settings, students with disabilities sometimes require supports to ensure that they are able to participate fully. Rule 6 requires governments to provide support services to meet the needs of people with disabilities and to guarantee full accessibility. Among other responsibilities, governments must provide ongoing teacher training and also ensure that curricula are flexible and adaptable and that additions are made where necessary.

The Committee on the Rights of the Child also addressed the right to education for people with disabilities, specifically focusing on Article 29(1) of the *Convention on the Rights of the Child.* The Committee noted that any discrimination in relation to education is prohibited and specifically refers to discrimination experienced by children with disabilities:

> Discrimination against children with disabilities is also pervasive in many formal educational systems and in a great many informal educational settings, including in the home . . . All such discriminatory practices are in direct contradiction with the requirements in article 29 (1) (a) that education be directed to the development of the child's personality, talents and mental and physical abilities to their fullest potential. (2001; General Comment 1, para. 10)

People with intellectual disabilities are entitled to the full enjoyment of their human rights, including the right to education. For people with intellectual disabilities to enjoy this right, they must have access to education in an inclusive setting, with adequate support, and with teaching methods and content that respond to their particular learning needs and develop their individual potential. Notwithstanding, it is difficult for international law to address problems in education because implementation is carried out by nations or states/provinces (see Chapter 6 for full details). There have been numerous legal cases that have addressed the right to education. Details of the case of *Eaton v. Brant County Board of Education,* concluded in 1997, is provided in Display 5.3 as an example.

Adequate Housing

People with intellectual disabilities typically have little opportunity to freely choose their housing. Few, if any, options exist for affordable, supportive, and independent living, so people with intellectual disabilities often are dependent on family members or on full-service institutions. In many cases, government funding that is provided for housing and support services is completely inflexible and does not permit people with intellectual disabilities to choose a mix of services from different individuals or agencies. Instead, funds must be used to pay one agency to provide all services. As a result, people with intellectual disabilities are left with little choice in their living arrangements and often live in housing environments that isolate them from the community rather than promote independence and greater participation.

The human right to adequate housing is part of the right to an adequate standard of living (food, clothing, and housing). This right is found in the following documents:

- *International Covenant on Economic, Social and Cultural Rights,* Article 11(1) (1976)
- *Convention on the Elimination of All Forms of Discrimination Against Women,* Article 14 (1981)
- *Convention on the Rights of the Child,* Article 27 (1990)

Thus, adequate housing is a human right. Having a secure place to live is a central part of human dignity. An adequate housing environment is essential to quality of life and well-being. The Committee on Economic, Social and Cultural Rights elaborated on the content of

Display 5.3

Disability and the Right to Education: The Eaton *Case*

For 3 years, Emily Eaton regularly attended elementary school in Brant County, Ontario, Canada, with a full-time educational assistant—until an Identification, Placement and Review Committee (IPRC) found that her needs were not being met in the general education classroom. In accordance with procedures set out in legislation for children with disabilities, a Special Educational Tribunal considered an appeal and decided that Emily should be placed in a special class for students with disabilities. The Tribunal reasoned that because of her intellectual and physical disabilities Emily would not learn in a regular classroom. They challenged the way the School Board treated children with disabilities. The case went through several levels of appeal. At first, the Court agreed with the Tribunal, concluding the Emily needed to be in a special school to be able to learn. Next, the Appeal Court agreed with Emily's parents that placement in a segregated class without her parents' consent was a form of discrimination that violated Emily's rights under the Canadian Charter of Rights and Freedoms (1982). The Court of Appeal stated:

> Inclusion into the main school population is a benefit to Emily because without it, she would have fewer opportunities to learn how other children work and how they live. And they will not learn that she can live with them, and they with her.
>
> Thus, it seems to me that when analyzed in its social, historical and political context, the decision to educate Emily Eaton in a special classroom for disabled students is a burden or disadvantage for her and therefore discriminatory within the meaning of [the equality rights] of the Charter. When a measure is offered to a disabled person, allegedly in order to provide that person with her true equality entitlement, and that measure is one of exclusion, segregation and isolation from the mainstream, that measure in its broad social and historical context, is properly labelled [sic] a burden or a disadvantage. . . .

In the end, the case went to the Supreme Court of Canada, the highest court in the country. The judges of the Supreme Court concluded that a segregated school was in Emily's best interest. They decided that Emily's school could treat her differently because of her inability to learn in the same way as other children.

Although many people with disabilities and their family members were disappointed with how the judges interpreted the equality rights provisions of the *Canadian Charter of Rights and Freedoms* in this context, there were some positive messages in this decision. The court did say clearly that integrated education is preferable for students with disabilities because of the benefits it provides. Although the court made a particular decision in Emily's case, the court said that wherever possible, general education schools should accommodate students with different learning needs because the *Canadian Charter of Rights and Freedoms* guarantees equality rights without discrimination on the basis of disability.

On the international level, a statement on full inclusion in education was adopted by more than 300 participants representing 92 governments and 25 international organizations that met in Salamanca, Spain. *Salamanca Statement and Framework for Action on Special Needs in Education* was adopted by the World Conference on Special Needs Education: Access and Quality, which was sponsored by the Government of Spain and UNESCO (the United Nations Educational, Scientific and Cultural Organization) in June 1994.

the right to adequate housing, stating that "[a]dequate shelter means . . . adequate privacy, adequate space, adequate security, adequate lighting and ventilation, adequate basic infrastructure and adequate location with regard to work and basic facilities—all at a reasonable cost" (1991; General Comment 4, para. 7). The Committee also emphasized that the right to housing "cannot be viewed in isolation from other human rights." The full enjoyment of freedom of expression, freedom of association, freedom of residence, and the right to participate in public decision making are indispensable to the realization of the right to housing (para. 9). The Committee's emphasis on the interrelatedness of the right to housing and other rights recognizes that for people with disabilities, providing adequate housing is a necessary condition to equal participation in the political, social, economic, and cultural spheres of society.

States Parties to the *International Convention on Economic, Social and Cultural Rights* (1976) are required to take whatever steps are necessary to achieve the full realization of the right to adequate housing, which "will almost invariably require the adoption of a national housing strategy" (1991; General Comment 4, para. 12). A national strategy should "reflect extensive genuine consultation with, and participation by, all of those affected" (para. 12). Rule 5 of the Standard Rules also calls for the participation of people with disabilities in the development of policy related to access to the physical environment, including housing.

Therapeutic Treatment

Often people with intellectual disabilities are subject to inappropriate treatment: therapies that do not address actual needs, fail to enhance the enjoyment of individual rights, or in some cases violate rights. Therapies that punish behavior or focus on changing or "improving" the individual often contravene human rights principles. A human rights approach emphasizes the need to change the larger social context to create a nondiscriminatory society that accepts diversity and facilitates autonomy to the greatest extent possible.

For children subject to abusive treatment, the *Convention on the Rights of the Child* (1990) requires States Parties to

> Take all appropriate legislative, administrative, social and educational measures to protect the child from all forms of physical or mental violence, injury or abuse, neglect or negligent treatment, maltreatment or exploitation including sexual abuse, while in the care of parent(s), legal guardian(s) or any other person who has the care of the child. (Article 19(1)).

Article 23(1) clearly articulates that "a mentally or physically disabled child should enjoy a full and decent life, in conditions which ensure dignity, promote self-reliance and facilitate the child's active participation in the community."

Other than the overarching principle of human dignity, the major human rights treaties have few articles that apply directly to adults subject to abuse in the name of therapeutic treatment. The rights to liberty and security of the person that are found in international human rights treaties are interpreted somewhat narrowly to relate to situations of arrest, detention, or confinement. The early text of the *Draft Comprehensive and Integral International Convention on the Protection and Promotion of the Rights and Dignity of Persons with Disabilities* addressed issues of freedom from violence and abuse directly. The final text may address these issues as well. An express acknowledgment that people with disabilities are at greater risk of violence and abuse would require that States Parties to the Convention take measures to provide adequate protection.

Rule 3 of the Standard Rules (1993) addresses the content of rehabilitation programs. *Rehabilitation* is defined as a process aimed at enabling people with disabilities to reach and maintain their optimal physical, sensory, intellectual, psychiatric, and/or social functional levels, thus providing them with the tools to work toward a higher level of independence. Rule 3 stipulates that the accessibility, design and content of rehabilitation programs must meet the actual needs of people with disabilities. The right of people with disabilities and their families to participate in the design and organization of rehabilitation services, as well as in the evaluation of services, is also included in Rule 3. These international rights demonstrate the growing awareness of the vulnerability of people with disabilities and the need to develop laws, policies, services, and therapies that respect and enhance the equal effective enjoyment of human rights.

Rights of Women with Intellectual Disabilities

Women with intellectual disabilities experience double discrimination: discrimination on the basis of disability and on the basis of sex. This double discrimination affects many aspects of women's lives by limiting educational and employment opportunities and increasing their risk of poverty, social isolation, and dependence on others. Invisibility and isolation leave women with disabilities vulnerable to human rights abuses, including sexual violence.

Governments must actively ensure the enjoyment of all human rights to improve the quality of life of women with disabilities and reduce the risk factors for abuse. The Committee on the Elimination of Discrimination Against Women, which monitors the implementation of the *Convention on the Elimination of All Forms of Discrimination Against Women* (1981), recognized that women with disabilities "suffer from double discrimination" and are a "vulnerable group." The Committee recommended that States Parties to the Convention

> Provide information on disabled women in their periodic reports, and on measures taken to deal with their particular situation, including special measures to ensure that they have equal access to education and employment, health services and social security, and to ensure that they can participate in all areas of social and cultural life. (1991; General Recommendation 18)

Given the high incidence of sexual violence experienced by women with intellectual disabilities, governments must also take action to protect women with disabilities by encouraging them to report abuse and by instituting policies aimed at preventing and detecting abuse. Laws must treat the physical and sexual abuse of women with disabilities as serious crimes and bring those responsible for abuses to justice. Article 15 (1) of the *Convention on the Elimination of All Forms of Discrimination Against Women* (1981) guarantees women equality with men before the law, and this article should be understood to include equal protection of the law.

The rights of women with disabilities received minimal attention as international agreements and documents were developed with the emergence of the human rights approach to disability. It is important to respond to the unique experiences and vulnerabilities of women with disabilities to effectively ensure their equal enjoyment of all human rights.

INCORPORATING DISABILITY INTO THE INTERNATIONAL HUMAN RIGHTS SYSTEM

The previous examples demonstrate that international human rights laws can be interpreted to apply to the experiences of people with disabilities. Interpreting international treaty rights in this manner will encourage the protection and promotion of the rights of people with disabilities in practice. People with disabilities must continue to insist that they are entitled to the full protection of international human rights law.

The mechanisms to monitor the implementation of human rights treaties present two primary opportunities to advance the rights of people with disabilities within the UN human rights treaty system: 1) participating in the reporting process by which governments present information about the implementation of human rights in their countries and 2) filing individual complaints about the violation of treaty rights. Organizations of people with disabilities and others advocating for equal rights can potentially make use of these opportunities at the international level.

Few governments refer to people with disabilities in their reports on the implementation of treaty rights. Since the early 1990s, a growing number of nongovernmental organizations have provided information to treaty monitoring committees as part of the reporting process. This brings attention to discrimination and to rights that have not been implemented effectively. Participating in the state reporting process may be an effective way for disability advocates to raise awareness of human rights violations against people with disabilities. Advocates can find out whether their government is a party to the key international human rights treaties. If so, they can work to identify the specific responsibilities created by those treaties and instances in which the government has met or failed to meet these responsibilities as they relate to people with disabilities. States Parties must report to the treaty monitoring committees on a regular basis, usually every 4–5 years. When a government's next report is due, advocates can contact the department responsible for preparing the government report and offer to assist with information on the rights of people with disabilities or review the report and offer comments. Organizations may also send comments directly to the treaty monitoring committee for consideration before it reviews the government's report.

Filing complaints about human rights abuses may also be a way to use the international human rights system to advance the rights of people with disabilities. The *International Covenant on Civil and Political Rights* (1976), the *Convention on the Elimination of All Forms of Discrimination Against Women* (1981), the *Convention against Torture (1987), and the International Convention on the Elimination of All Forms of Racial Discrimination* (1969) all have complaint mechanisms. These mechanisms allow individuals, groups of individuals, and organizations representing individuals to file complaints of human rights violations if the government involved has accepted the complaint procedure as part of its treaty obligations. In general, before a complaint will be considered at the international level, efforts must have been made to resolve the issue through national courts or available human rights complaints mechanisms at the national level. Advocates can take steps to assert the rights of people with disabilities before their national courts and tribunals. If favorable results are not achieved and all opportunities for appeal have been exhausted, a complaint can be submitted to an international treaty committee, providing written details on the facts of the case and identifying the particular treaty rights that have been violated.

Detailed information on the discrimination faced by people with disabilities is essential to effective enforcement at international, national, or local levels. As part of the effort to gather data on the human rights situation of people with disabilities and to encourage change, a broad research and development project, Disability Rights Promotion International (DRPI) has been launched. DRPI is a collaborative initiative working with the support of disability groups, individuals, and the UN. DRPI will establish model monitoring projects in a number of countries in collaboration with established organizations of people with disabilities. The monitoring sites will develop the capacity to expose, report, and address disability rights violations. Training for monitors will include information on human rights and international human rights law. Local coordination of the projects will ensure that the monitoring activities, and resulting efforts to influence human rights standard setting, make a difference in the quality of life of people with disabilities. DRPI's implementation phase is underway with the support of the UN's Office of the High Commissioner for Human Rights and major international disability organizations.

SUMMARY

The human rights approach to disability that has emerged since the early 1980s is taking hold as of the early 21st century. People with disabilities are increasingly seen as full citizens entitled to equal rights. There is a growing understanding that the rights of the major international human rights treaties in the UN human rights system must apply equally to people with disabilities. Given the legal obligations that these treaties create, governments can no longer justify denying people with disabilities basic rights such as education, adequate housing, employment, equality before the law, and freedom from violence. Since the mid-1990s, international agreements on the rights of people with disabilities have informed more effective interpretations of treaty rights that recognize the experiences of people with disabilities. Governments and disability rights advocates can use achievements at the international level to promote change at national and local levels around the world. Ensuring the equal effective enjoyment of human rights for people with disabilities will improve these individuals' lives and create societies that respect the dignity and equality of each human being.

FOR FURTHER THOUGHT AND DISCUSSION

1. It appears to take decades for the equal rights of marginalized groups to be recognized. Women, indigenous peoples, people with disabilities, and others continue to strive for equality. What are some of the factors preventing the equal enjoyment of human rights by all?
2. How would you explain why people with intellectual disabilities are so often the last in line to have their rights recognized?
3. State reports to the UN bodies that monitor the implementation of human rights treaties include little information about the rights of people with disabilities. What are some of the reasons that might explain this?
4. Many people argue that people with intellectual disabilities can be excluded from schools and general education classrooms because they learn differently, even though basic education is accepted as a right for other children. How would you frame a rights argument to counter that exclusion?

REFERENCES

Canadian Charter of Rights and Freedoms. (1982). Retrieved April 19, 2006, from http://laws.justice.gc.ca/en/charter/index.html

Committee on Economic, Social and Cultural Rights. (1991, December 13). *General Comment 4: Right to Adequate Housing.* E/1992/23.

Committee on Economic, Social and Cultural Rights. (1994, December 9). *General Comment 5: Persons with Disabilities.* E/1995/22.

Committee on Economic, Social and Cultural Rights. (1999, December 8). *General Comment 13: The Right to Education.* E/C.12/1999/10.

Committee on the Elimination of Discrimination Against Women. (1991, January 4). *General Recommendation 18: Disabled Women.* A/46/38.

Committee on the Rights of the Child. (2001, April 17). *General Comment 1: The Aims of Education.* CRC/GC/2001/1.

Convention Against Torture and Other Cruel, Inhuman or Degrading Treatment or Punishment. General Assembly Res. 39/46, 39 UN GAOR Supp. (No. 51) at 197, entered into force June 26, 1987.

Convention on the Elimination of All Forms of Discrimination Against Women. General Assembly Res. 34/180, 34 U.N. GAOR Supp. (No. 46) at 193, entered into force Sept. 3, 1981.

Convention on the Rights of the Child. General Assembly Res. 44/25, Annex, 44 U.N. GAOR Supp. (No. 49) at 167, entered into force Sept. 2, 1990.

Eaton v. Brant County Board of Education. (1994). Court of Appeal of Ontario, C1214.

Inter-American Convention on the Elimination of All Forms of Discrimination Against Persons with Disabilities. Organization of American States, General Assembly AG/RES. 1608, entered into force Sept. 14, 2001. Retrieved August 2004, from http://www.oas.org/juridico/english/treaties/a-65.htm

International Covenant on Civil and Political Rights. General Assembly Res. 2200A (XXI), 999 U.N.T.S. 171, entered into force Mar. 23, 1976.

International Covenant on Economic, Social and Cultural Rights. General Assembly Res. 2200A (XXI), 993 U.N.T.S. 3, entered into force Jan. 3, 1976.

International Convention on the Elimination of All Forms of Racial Discrimination. General Assembly Res. 2106A (XX), 660 U.N.T.S. 195, entered into force Jan. 4, 1969.

International Convention on the Protection of the Rights of All Migrant Workers and Members of Their Families. General Assembly Res. 45/186, annex, 45 U.N. GAOR Supp. (No. 49A) at 262, entered into force Jul. 1, 2003.

Oliver, M. (1990). *Politics of disablement.* New York: Macmillan.

Quinn, G., & Degener, T. (2002). *Human rights and disability: The current use and future potential of United Nations human rights instruments in the context of disability.* Retrieved September 10, 2004, from http://www.unhchr.ch/html/menu6/2/disability.doc

Rioux, M. (2003). On second thought: Constructing knowledge, law, disability and inequality. In S.S. Herr, H.H. Kohl, & L.O. Gostin (Eds.), *Different but equal: The rights of persons with intellectual disabilities* (pp. 287–317). Oxford, United Kingdom: Oxford University Press.

United Nations. (2004, January 27). *Report of the Working Group to the Ad Hoc Committee on a Comprehensive and Integral International Convention on the Protection and Promotion of the Rights and Dignity of Persons with Disabilities, Annex I: Draft Comprehensive and Integral International Convention on the Protection and Promotion of the Rights and Dignity of Persons with Disabilities.* UN Doc. A/AC.265/2004/WG/1. Retrieved August 2004 from http://www.un.org/esa/socdev/enable/rights/ahcwgreportax1.htm

United Nations Commission on Human Rights. (1998, April 17). *C.H.R. res. 1998/31,* ESCOR Supp. (No. 3) at 117. Retrieved on September 10, 2004, from at http://www1.umn.edu/humanrts/UN/1998/Res031.html

United Nations Commission on Human Rights. (2000, April 25). *C.H.R. Res. 2000/51.* Retrieved on September 10, 2004, from http://www.unhchr.ch/Huridocda/Huridoca.nsf/(Symbol)/E.CN.4.RES.2000.51.En?Opendocument

United Nations Educational, Scientific and Cultural Organization. (1994, June 10). *Salamanca Statement and Framework for Action on Special Needs in Education.* E D-94/WS/18. Retrieved September 10, 2004, from http://inclusion.uwe.ac.uk/csie/slmca.htm

United Nations General Assembly. (1948, December 10). *Universal Declaration of Human Rights.* General Assembly Res. 217A (III), UN Doc A/810 at 71. Retrieved August 2004 from http://www.un.org/Overview/rights.html

United Nations General Assembly. (1982, December 3). *World Programme of Action Concerning Disabled Persons.* General Assembly Res. 37/52. Retrieved August 2004 from http://www.un.org/esa/socdev/enable/diswpa00.htm

United Nations General Assembly. (1991, December 17). *Principles for the Protection of Persons with Mental Illness and the Improvement of Mental Health Care.* General Assembly Res. 46/119. Retrieved August 2004 from http://www.unhchr.ch/html/menu3/b/68.htm

United Nations General Assembly. (1993, December 20). *Standard Rules for the Equalization of Opportunities for Persons with Disabilities.* General Assembly Res. 48/96, Annex. Retrieved August 2004 from http://www.un.org/esa/socdev/enable/dissre00.htm

6

Role of Advocacy in Ensuring Disability Rights and Entitlements

Dionne Chambers

WHAT YOU WILL LEARN ABOUT IN THIS CHAPTER

- The concepts of advocacy, rights, and entitlements
- The role of international law in ensuring disability rights and entitlements within countries
- The role of advocacy in promoting disability rights and entitlements

Chapter 5 addresses the questions "What does it mean to have disability rights?" and "What are the international bases of disability rights?" This chapter focuses more specifically on how international and other laws can be used to promote disability rights and entitlements and how disability groups can use laws to enhance the position of people with disabilities in international, regional, and national law. In particular, disability advocacy is highlighted as a key mechanism for ensuring rights and entitlements.

THE CONCEPTS OF ADVOCACY, RIGHTS, AND ENTITLEMENTS

To grasp how laws can be used to promote disability rights, it is necessary to have an understanding of certain core concepts. Advocacy, rights, and entitlements are described in the following sections.

Advocacy

The term *advocacy* literally means "speaking out." In the broadest sense, it means speaking out and standing up for what is important. In this chapter, *advocacy* refers specifically to speaking out and standing up for what is thought to be important for people with intellectual and developmental disabilities; their families; the professionals, paraprofessionals, and volunteers who work in the field; and the field in general. Sometimes advocacy involves lobbying. At other times, it means being involved in public policy, engaging in litigation, or standing up for the rights or entitlements of someone requiring a particular service.

The term *self-advocacy* refers to having the opportunity to know one's rights and entitlements as well as one's responsibilities, standing up for these rights and entitlements, and making choices about one's own life. In the intellectual and developmental disabilities field, *self-advocacy* refers to people with disabilities speaking for such things as their own values, life dreams, perspectives on inclusion, and needed supports. The concept of self-advocacy began in Sweden in the 1960s and spread to the United Kingdom, Canada, and elsewhere in the 1970s. In 1973, a group of Americans with disabilities from Oregon attended a conference that was supposed to be for people with mental retardation. Realizing that the conference was dominated by professionals, this group formed a self-advocacy group called People First. This organization has been highly successful in expressing a voice of people with intellectual and developmental disabilities; chapters now function in many countries. The concept and practice of self-advocacy has continued to gain momentum and recognition and has led to many positive advances for individuals and for the field. One simple example is the use of people-first language (e.g., saying "people with intellectual disabilities" rather than "intellectually disabled people"), which is widely accepted and practiced around the world. Self-advocacy is related to self-determination, which not only includes the concept of self-advocacy but also focuses on system changes, legislation, and policy.

Advocacy is essential in maintaining or improving the quality of life for people with various types of intellectual and developmental disabilities. In some cases (e.g., epilepsy), the disability is not so obvious to the casual observer; in others the disability is more apparent. Yet, people with any type of intellectual or developmental disability share life goals with those who do not have disabilities—to learn, live with dignity, contribute meaningfully to human life, have fulfilling social relationships, and be engaged in community activities. The particular needs of people with disabilities, and the particular ways they pursue life goals, varies vastly and often requires support from others. Disability advocacy gives an important voice to those people with mobility difficulties, health problems, lower cognitive and communicative abilities, and other limitations. It seeks to ensure that everyone with a disability receives the supports he or she needs in pursuit of his or her respective life goals.

Advocacy is important for ensuring the rights and entitlements of people with disabilities in two principal respects: 1) to get rights and entitlements on paper (i.e., through national or state/provincial legislation or other policy) and 2) to ensure that rights and entitlements are put into practice rather than ignored. Chapter 5 showed that under the provisions of various human and disability rights treaties at the international level, it is no longer permissible for governments around the world to deny people with disabilities their basic human rights, including an education, access to health care, and adequate housing. At the beginning of the 21st century, however, the reality is that many people with disabilities in many countries are being denied their basic human rights. Although many countries have agreed to or have adopted international, regional, or national legislation for people with disabilities, these individuals are frequently excluded from schools and work forces, do not have access to affordable health care, and do not have access to needed social services. For this reason, the role of advocacy in ensuring that rights and entitlements are put into practice rather than ignored is particularly important.

Table 6.1. Types of rights

Natural right	A right that belongs to every human being and that is conceived as part of natural law (legal and moral principles derived from a universalized conception of human nature) and that is therefore thought to exist independently of rights created by government or society. For example, freedom from slavery is a natural right, and children have a natural right to protection from harm from their parents. Where inequality or privilege exists, natural law demands its abolition.
Acquired right	A right that a person does not naturally enjoy but that is instead procured. Examples include the right to vote, the right to drive a car on public roads, or the right to own property.
Legal right	A right created or recognized by law.
Personal right	A right that forms part of a person's legal status or personal condition, as opposed to the person's estate.
Human right	Any of the freedoms, immunities, and benefits that according to modern values, all human beings should be able to claim as a matter of right in the society in which they live.
Public right	A right belonging to all citizens.
Constitutional right	A right enforceable in a court of law by virtue of the fact that it forms part of the constitution of a country. For example, in the United States the rights to life, liberty, and the pursuit of happiness are constitutional rights.
Inalienable right	A right that cannot be transferred or suspended.
Political right	The right to participate in the establishment or administration of government, such as the right to vote or the right to hold public office.
Sovereign right	Sovereignty is the exclusive right of a country to govern the affairs of its inhabitants and to be free from external control.

Sources: Garner (1999) and Slomanson (2003).

Rights and Entitlements

The term *right* means, at a semantic level, "that which is proper under law, morality, or ethics" (Garner, 1999, p. 1322). Rights are understood in a variety of ways, and some of the common types are described in Table 6.1. Often, rights are specified in constitutions (the supreme law within countries), laws, decrees, or other formal policy documents. At other times, though, rights are understood as moral or ethical principles that are widely accepted but may or may not be codified in law.

When rights have been conferred upon individuals or groups of individuals, and when those individuals or groups meet specified requirements, they are said to have entitlement to the benefits that accompany those rights. In other words, *right* refers to the concept or principle (which may or may not be backed by law) and *entitlement* refers to individuals having access to the benefits of rights.

In the field of intellectual and developmental disability, entitlements in four areas are particularly important (Peppin, Beatty, & Baker, 2003). These are outlined next, and readers are encouraged to seek local information that describes the specific entitlements in the areas where they live and work.

Consent and Substitute Decision Making Although subject to local laws and customs, it is generally assumed that adults are entitled to give their own consent and make decisions about their own care. A few people, including some with intellectual and developmental disabilities, are not able to do so, however. For this reason, many countries have laws that specify conditions under which giving consent or making decisions can be carried out by a substitute. Substitute consent or decision making might be required if an individual is 1) not capable of understanding what he or she is consenting to or deciding about or 2) unable to understand the consequences of consent or a decision.

Income Security, Housing, and Services Entitlements In most developed countries, people with intellectual or developmental disabilities who meet specified criteria are entitled to income from disability pension plans. Other forms of income security entitlement include tax benefits and special trust funds. Entitlement to housing varies greatly from one area to another. Adults with intellectual disabilities are entitled, in accordance with state law, to housing within a specified period of time in some areas, but in other areas similar adults have no entitlement to housing at all. Community living support is typically a public service rather than an entitlement. It is sometimes surprising to family members to learn that they are actually entitled to very few or no supports and services, thus making advocacy essential.

Health Care Entitlements Health care systems differ considerably from one country to another. In countries that have universal health care (cost-free access for approved health care services), such as the United Kingdom and Canada, people with disabilities are entitled to the same health care services as people without disabilities. In other countries, entitlements to health care are more complex (see, e.g., Green et al., 2004). Some important issues that affect health care entitlements for people with intellectual and developmental disabilities are

- The extent to which individuals can choose and consent to health care services
- What health care services are necessary, wanted, or in the individuals' best interest
- What decisions should be made regarding reproduction (e.g., contraception, sterilization, abortion, pregnancy, birth, infant care)
- Who makes end-of-life decisions
- The degree to which people with disabilities should be part of innovation and experimentation (e.g., be part of clinical trials for research)
- The use (and misuse) of pharmaceuticals and their effects on people with specific disabilities
- The degree to which health care professionals might be held responsible for negligence

Education Entitlements In the United States and some other countries, children who have been identified as having special education needs are entitled to a public education, an individualized education plan, and special supports (for details, see Chapter 31). Support for transition to adult living is also an entitlement in the United States and elsewhere, although this entitlement is applied to varying degrees. Adult education and training are available to people with disabilities in developed countries, but these are typically services rather than entitlements.

THE ROLE OF INTERNATIONAL LAW IN ENSURING DISABILITY RIGHTS AND ENTITLEMENTS WITHIN COUNTRIES

International laws that support the philosophy that respect for the human rights of people with disabilities is demonstrated by their full inclusion in community life are not always made effective within countries. There are two main reasons for this, and these reasons limit the role that international and regional law can play in the protection of disability rights. First, countries themselves have the main responsibility for ensuring disability rights; thus, in order for international and regional law to be binding upon a country's citizens, the government of that country must incorporate those provisions into its domestic legal system in some way. However, countries do this in a variety of ways. Second, international and regional monitoring and enforcement of disability rights are limited. These two reasons are explained in greater detail next.

Individual Countries Hold Primary Responsibility for Disability Rights

Individual countries have the primary responsibility for ensuring disability rights. They provide laws that describe how people with disabilities are treated and what their entitlements are, and they provide educational, health, and social services that support such laws. Regardless of a person's country of citizenship, it is possible for him or her to claim a disability right in a domestic court system if it is set out in an international treaty (and is not a part of the country's national disability legal framework). Yet, this is a claim only and not something that can be enforced.

Many countries recognize their domestic obligation for ensuring international disability and other rights by having in place legal mechanisms for directly incorporating international agreements into their domestic legal systems. In some countries, an international treaty signed by the appropriate person, such as a head of state, automatically becomes part of the country's body of laws upon ratification. This is the case, for example, in Belgium, Egypt, France, the Netherlands, and Switzerland. These countries have what is called a dual system of domestic incorporation.

Other countries have legal mechanisms that are not necessarily automatic. The approach most commonly taken by countries—including Germany, India, Thailand, and the United States—is the self-executing or non–self-executing distinction. Under this approach, treaties of a certain nature will require legislative implementation and others will not. In Germany, India, and Thailand, for example, treaties that would alter national boundaries are considered to be non-self-executing;

these require the passage of national legislation for the provisions of the treaty to be given effect domestically. In the United States and in Israel, any treaty that would require the passage of legislation that would create and/or alter new and/or existing rights and obligations is considered non-self-executing; it requires its legislature to pass a law incorporating the treaty provisions into the domestic system. Otherwise, in the United States, any other international treaty signed by the president is automatically incorporated into U.S. law.

International law may be used to assert a disability entitlement if

1. The country is a party to the international treaty: most countries acquire this status by the head of state (president, prime minister, or monarch) signing the treaty containing the entitlement
2. The country has ratified the international treaty, which is the process through which individual countries give effect to a signed treaty: some countries (e.g., Mexico, Russia, South Africa, the United States) require legislative approval to ratify an international treaty; other countries (e.g., Canada, Israel, the United Kingdom) do not require legislative approval for ratification of an international treaty
3. The country has incorporated, either expressly or implicitly, the relevant entitlement into domestic law: ratification of an international treaty does not necessarily automatically create rights or entitlements for people with disabilities in a domestic legal system; in many countries, the additional step of legislative enactment is required

Despite the preceding general principles, individual countries carry out their responsibilities for ensuring disability rights in a wide variety of ways. The four main reasons for this are that countries have unique national legal frameworks, some countries limit their national disability legal frameworks, and countries have unique ways of practicing and enhancing their national legal frameworks, and the relationship between international treaties and domestic laws differs. Each topic is explained next.

Countries Have Unique National Legal Frameworks A national legal framework for intellectual and developmental disabilities is a country's complex set of laws and policies that is designed to promote the full participation and equality of people with disabilities in society. Generally speaking, a legal framework comprises those national laws that promote entitlements of people with disabilities, prohibit discrimination against them, and specify constitutional provisions designed to promote the equal participation of people with disabilities in society. (For some of the principle statutory and constitutional provisions pertaining to disability rights in various countries, see Table 6.2.)

Promoting barrier-free access typically is the intent of a great variety of laws that exist. For example, the United States has numerous laws that promote barrier-free access. The Telecommunications Act of 1996 (PL 104-104) requires manufacturers of telecommunications equipment and providers of telecommunications services to ensure that such equipment and services are accessible to, and usable by, people with disabilities. The Individuals with Disabilities Education Improvement Act of 2004 (PL 108-446) requires public schools to make available to all eligible children with disabilities a free, appropriate public education that meets their individual needs. The Architectural Barriers Act of 1968 (PL 90-480) requires that buildings and facilities that are designed, constructed, or altered with federal funds or are leased by a federal agency comply with federal standards for physical accessibility. There are many other laws as well.

Anti-discrimination laws are in place in many countries around the world. In the United States, for example, the Americans with Disabilities Act (ADA) of 1990 (PL 101-336) prohibits discrimination on the basis of disability in employment, state, and local government; public accommodations; commercial facilities; transportation; and telecommunications. Similarly, in the United Kingdom, people with disabilities are protected by the Disability Discrimination Act (DDA) 1995, which prohibits discrimination against people with disabilities in the areas of employment; access to goods, facilities, and services; and property rental and ownership. The objectives of the Australian Disability Discrimination Act (DDA) of 1992 are as follows:

> To eliminate, as far as possible, discrimination against persons on the ground of disability in the areas of: work, accommodation, education, access to premises, clubs and sport; and the provision of goods, facilities, services and land; and existing laws; and the administration of Commonwealth laws and programs; and to ensure, as far as practicable, that persons with disabilities have the same rights to equality before the law as the rest of the community; and to promote recognition and acceptance within the community of the principle that persons with disabilities have the same fundamental rights as the rest of the community. (§3)

Many countries have constitutional provisions designed to promote the equal treatment of people with disabilities in society (e.g., Canada, Germany, South Africa, Switzerland, the United States). In the United States, for example, the Equal Protection and Due Process Clauses of the Amendment XIV to the U.S. Constitution provides equal protection for every American citizen under the law (s. 1). Similarly, in Canada, under s.15(1) of the Canadian Charter of Rights and Freedoms, every citizen is entitled to equal treatment under

Table 6.2. Sample national laws affecting disability rights and entitlements

Country	Federal statutes	Constitutional provisions
Australia	Disability Discrimination Act 1992 Human Rights and Equal Opportunity Commission Act 1986 Workplace Relations Act 1996	
Canada	Canadian Human Rights Act Employment Equity Act Education Act Ontario Human Rights Code	Canadian Charter of Rights and Freedoms, §15
China	Law of the People's Republic of China on the Protection of Disabled Persons	
Costa Rica	Ley no. 7600	
France	Code Penal Code de Travail Loi no. 91-633 Decree no. 98-543 Decree no. 99-756 Decree no. 99-757	
Germany	Neuntes Buch des Sozialgesetzbuches—SGB IX (Book 9 of the Social Code) Behindertengleichstellungsgesetz BGG (Equal Opportunities for Disabled People Act) Severely Handicapped Persons Act	Constitution, Article 3
Ghana	The Disabled Persons Act 1993	Constitution, Chapter V, Articles 17 and 29
Guatemala	Law of Attention to Persons with Disabilities	
Hungary	Equalization Opportunity Law (Act no. XXVI of 1998)	Constitution, Articles 70A and 70F
India	Persons with Disabilities (Equal Opportunities, Protection of Rights and Full Participation) Act, 1995	
Ireland	Employment Equality Act (No. 21 of 1998) Equal Status Act, 2000 National Disability Authority Act, 1999	
Israel	Equal Rights for People with Disabilities Law, 5758-1998	
Japan	Human Resources Development Promotion Law	
South Korea	Welfare Law for Persons with Disabilities (No. 4179, 1989) Act Relating to Employment Promotion, etc. of the Handicapped (No. 4129, 1990) The Special Education Promotion Law (amended 1994)	
Malawi	No. 48 of 1971	Constitution, Chapter IV, Article 20
Netherlands	Act on Equal Treatment on the Grounds of Handicap or Chronic Illness (2003)	
New Zealand	Human Rights Act, 1993 Human Rights Amendment Act of 2001	
Nigeria	Nigerians with Disability Decree 1993	
Paraguay	Labour Code of 1961	Political Constitution of 1992, Article 88
Scotland	Disability Discrimination Act 1995 (c. 50) Disability Discrimination Regulations 1996 Disability Rights Commission Act 1999 (chapter 17)	
South Africa		Constitution–Bill of Rights (1996), s. 9
Sri Lanka	1996 Protection of Persons with Disabilities Law	
Sweden	Act Concerning Support and Service for Persons with Certain Functional Impairments, SFS 1993 Law on a Ban Against Discrimination Disabled Persons in Working Life, 1999 Act Prohibiting Discrimination, SFS 2003	

(continued)

Table 6.2. *(continued)*

Country	Federal statutes	Constitutional provisions
Switzerland		Constitution, Article 8
Thailand	1991 Rehabilitation of Disabled Persons Act	
Uganda		Constitution, s. 21, 30, 35
United Kingdom	Disability Discrimination Act 1995 Disability Rights Act 1999 Northern Ireland, Disability Discrimination Regulations 1996	
United States of America	Americans with Disabilities Act (ADA) of 1990 (PL 101-336) Individuals with Disabilities Education Improvement Act of 2004 (PL 108-446)	Constitution, Equal Protection and Due Process Clauses of Amendment XIV to the U.S. Constitution
Zimbabwe	Disabled Persons Act 1992	

the law and to freedom from several specified types of discrimination.

Together, the laws promoting entitlements, prohibiting discrimination, and specifying constitutional rights form the national legal framework for intellectual and developmental disabilities. There are many similarities among countries but also many differences. Thus, the national legal frameworks are unique to each country.

Many Countries' National Legal Frameworks Are Limited in Important Ways Despite the fact that many countries—especially those in the Americas, Western Europe, and the continent of Australia—generally have comprehensive national disability legal frameworks, there are shortfalls. For instance, some countries that provide comprehensive constitutional protection for people with disabilities qualify that protection in important ways. In Canada, for example, s.15(1) of the Canadian Charter of Rights and Freedoms provides equal legal protection for every person and explicitly prohibits discrimination based on "mental or physical disability." However, this right is qualified by s.1, which provides that this right may be overridden if lawmakers can show that it is "demonstrably justified in a free and democratic society." Similarly, in Australia, the Disability Discrimination Act 1992 prohibits discrimination in a number of ways but qualifies this right in many instances by providing that it can be overridden if it would cause "unjustifiable hardship" (s. 11) to the individual or group responsible for proving the service or benefit.

Countries Exercise National Legal Frameworks in Unique Ways Countries put their national disability legal frameworks into practice in different ways. One important tool that many countries use is to have mechanisms within their legal systems that are designed specifically to enforce laws and constitutional provisions applicable to people with disabilities. If a disability entitlement or right has allegedly been denied to a person or groups of people with disabilities, that person or group and/or their advocates have legal recourse. For example, a school placement for a child with a disability can be appealed in several countries, providing that the required steps and procedures set out in legal documents are followed.

Countries also respond to the need to develop and update their national disability legal frameworks in different ways. One of the most commonly used ways is to respond to the activities of the legal and related systems. Lawsuits, and other quasi-legal procedures such as complaints and appeals, create a record of disability rights violations (Stephens & Ratner, 1996). Such a record can serve as an important marker of the degree of success in the broader disability rights movement, and it can also serve as a catalyst for the introduction of additional positive legislation by governments. In the United States, the shift in philosophy toward people with disabilities from paternalism to inclusion began with judicial opinions in the courts, and Congress followed suit with national legislation codifying these principles. For example, the Education for All Handicapped Children Act of 1975 (PL 94-142), which made public education available to all children with disabilities, was passed by Congress following two critical court decisions in the early 1970s. The decisions for *Pennsylvania Association for Retarded Children (PARC) v. Pennsylvania* (1971) and *Mills v. Board of Education* (1972) established that where a state provides education at public expense, it must do so on an equal basis for all children. In both cases, a child with an intellectual disability (mental retardation) was being denied access to public school education.

Relationship Between International Treaties and Domestic Laws Differs One factor that influences how a country responds to its responsibility to international law is the degree to which its international treaty obligations holds equal rank with its domestic laws. In some countries (e.g., Egypt, Russia, South Africa), the relationship between international treaties and domestic laws is decided by the latter-in-time rule, which provides that a treaty or legislation enacted subsequently will take the place of an existing treaty or legislation. In other countries, including Canada and Israel, such a conflict is decided in favor of the country's respective domestic law. In yet other countries, such as France, Mexico and Switzerland, a treaty provision prevails in the event of a conflict with a domestic law.

Federalism can cause complicating difficulties in ensuring international disability law within countries. For instance, the Canadian federation is unique in the sense that its federal government does not have the constitutional authority to force its provincial governments to implement international treaty provisions. In Canada, health, education, and social services all fall within the constitutional purview of provincial governments. If the federal government has ratified an international treaty containing provisions on disability entitlements that fall within these areas, the federal government is not only prohibited from passing such legislation to enforce the treaty, but it is also prohibited from forcing the provinces to do so. The Federal Republic of Germany differs from most other federal states in making treaty law in the sense that its states have a right to participate in the treaty-making process; that is, they are afforded a right to be heard when a proposed treaty would affect their boundaries or economic interests. This right, however, does not include a right to share in the decision-making process.

Monitoring and Enforcing International Disability Rights Is Limited

In addition to countries being primarily responsible for ensuring disability human rights, there are considerable limitations to how international laws and agreements can be monitored and enforced. First, international disability documents very often lack enforcement of domestic law. Second, international monitoring bodies are not strong. Third, international courts are not always a viable option for people with disabilities or their advocates.

International Disability Documents Often Lack the Force of Domestic Law The rights of people with disabilities are included under the umbrella of universal nondiscrimination principles such as the *Universal Declaration of Human Rights* (United Nations [UN], 1948) and the *International Covenant on Economic, Social and Cultural Rights* (1976). Existing disability-specific instruments include the *Declaration on the Rights of Disabled Persons* (UN, 1975) and the *Standard Rules on the Equalization of Opportunities for Persons with Disabilities* (often referred to as the Standard Rules; UN, 1993), but these documents are only guidelines that lack the force of law.

Since the 1990s, there has been an encouraging trend at the international, regional, and national levels to develop disability laws and policies that commit governments to including people with disabilities in society and providing access to necessary services. The Organization of American States's 1999 *Inter-American Convention on the Elimination of All Forms of Discrimination Against Persons with Disabilities* is a notable example of a supranational agreement regarding disability rights. The Americans with Disabilities Act (ADA) of 1990 provides a model for national and regional efforts and has served as an inspiration for reform, particularly in Europe.

Generally speaking, greater protection for people with disabilities is afforded by international, rather than domestic, disability rights law. Article 13(1) of the *International Covenant on Social, Economic, and Cultural Rights* recognizes the rights of every person to an education and to fully develop their human person and their sense of dignity. Article 3 of the *Declaration on the Rights of Disabled Persons* states that people with disabilities have the same fundamental rights as their fellow citizens of the same age. The persistent lack of legally enforceable global standards, however, remains a significant challenge in securing disability rights and entitlements to citizens of countries around the world (Center for International Rehabilitation, 2005).

Responding to increasing pressure from the international disability community, the U.N. General Assembly adopted a resolution on December 19, 2001, to create an ad hoc committee "to consider proposals for a comprehensive and integral international convention to protect and promote the rights and dignity of persons with disabilities" (UN, 2001). Progress toward achieving a convention has been somewhat slow and continues at the time of this book's publication.

International Monitoring Bodies Are Not Strong There are numerous universal human rights organizations (e.g., UN Human Rights Committee) and regional human rights organizations (e.g., the Inter-American Commission on Human Rights, the European Commission on Human Rights, the African Commission on Human and Peoples' Rights) that are mandated to monitor human rights at the national level. These organizations are known as commissions. Commissions have three primary responsibilities: 1) to receive petitions for compensation from individuals and organizations against whom a human rights violation has occurred; 2) to investigate complaints made by individuals or organizations of human rights abuses, including on-site investigations; and 3) to write reports pertaining to the state of human rights protections in specific countries.

The effectiveness of the monitoring function performed by universal and regional committees is limited. For example, the UN member states' monitoring system that is associated with the Standard Rules is based on government self-reporting—that is, member countries self-monitor their compliance with the Standard Rules under the guidance of a special rapporteur who reports to the Commission for Social Development. Also, action on petitions alleging human rights abuses in individual countries reviewed by a commission is rarely taken (Stephens, & Ratner, 1996). At best, therefore, reports of human rights violations may serve as an important opportunity to generate public debate about the human rights practices of a particular country.

Finally, some international treaties provide that signatory countries establish procedures to monitor implementation of national programs and services. For example, the Standard Rules provides that countries should periodically and systematically evaluate national disability programs and disseminate the results (Rule 20, UN, 1993). However, some countries opt out of certain clauses of international treaties for a variety of reasons; even where they do not opt out, the degree to which they implement the rights and entitlements and monitor their progress varies quite considerably, but is often not rigorous.

International Courts Are Not Always Viable

There are bodies whose job it is to monitor the human rights practices of countries, and there are also enforcement mechanisms available to people with disabilities and their advocates when an internationally recognized disability right has been denied at the national level.

Many universal and regional human rights treaties have established international human rights courts that hear cases on treaty-specific issues (e.g., the Inter-American Human Rights Court, the European Court on Human Rights, various UN bodies that act as enforcement bodies). These courts have the authority to order compensation or remedial measures to victims and offenders of human and disability rights violations. Although enforcement mechanisms by universal and regional human rights organizations are generally weak, a UN or regional human rights ruling can often have significant impact through negative publicity and diplomatic pressure.

Despite the existence of international courts with which recourse of human rights violations may be sought, the reality is that this is not a viable option for most people. This is the case for three main reasons. First, in order for a person with a disability or a disability advocate to have access to a universal or regional court, the country must be a signatory to, and must have incorporated the provisions of, the treaty establishing the court. Citizens of the United States, for example, do not have recourse to either the Inter-American Human Rights Court or the UN Committee on Economic, Social, and Cultural Rights because their country is not a party to either of the establishing treaties.

Second, if a person with a disability is a citizen of a country that has signed and incorporated a treaty alleged to have been violated, that person must first exhaust domestic legal remedies to gain access to international courts. This means that the case alleging a disability rights violation must pass through every level of the national legal system, including the highest appeal court in the country, before the case may be heard before an international court. This can be an extremely time-consuming and costly process.

Third, if a person with a disability, or his or her advocate, actually gets before an international court advocating for a particular right and/or entitlement, the individual's country is not bound by the decision taken by that court. In other words, a country may decide whether to follow the decision of the court.

Given this reality, domestic litigation of international disability rights/entitlements is the option most often taken by individuals with disabilities, their advocates, and disability organizations. There is, however, a considerable limitation to this approach as well: Courts in many countries afford very little weight to arguments based on international law. This is primarily because many courts are wary of accepting that disability rights under international law are binding unless the executive has made an express legislative statement to that effect. Although the United States has the most active court system in the world in the protection of human rights, to the author's knowledge, not one U.S. court has accepted international law claims to disability rights (Tolley Jr., 1991). More often, international law arguments are not even weighted heavily enough to be mentioned in the court's judgment (Tolley Jr.).

Thus, domestic and international litigation based on international law alone is insufficient to shape the disability rights movement both internationally and within individual countries. For this reason, in addition to the fact that many countries and regions of the world have failed to develop laws that reflect the principles and standards set forth in international treaties, disability advocacy organizations play a central role.

THE ROLE OF ADVOCACY IN PROMOTING DISABILITY RIGHTS AND ENTITLEMENTS

The previous section explained the ways that international law can be used to promote disability rights and entitlements and the degree to which its use is limited. In this section, disability advocacy is highlighted as a key mechanism for ensuring rights and entitlements. Litigation is one tool that organizations can use in promoting disability rights and entitlements. More specific types of organizations, for professionals and for self-advocates and family advocates, are discussed as well.

Overview of National Advocacy Organizations

Numerous national disability advocacy organizations exist all around the world. These can differ quite considerably in terms of membership base (e.g., membership constituted primarily by people with disabilities, professionals, or academics) and mandates (e.g., advocating for political support, legal rights, the rightful place of people with disabilities in communities, or services for people with disabilities). Whatever their memberships and mandates, the overall role of national disability advocacy organizations is to monitor the impact of the national legal framework on people with disabilities and to speak for the framework's improvement. Table 6.3 provides examples of disability advocacy organizations and their respective mandates. The table lists disability organizations in four countries and several international organizations whose role at least partly relates to advocacy. Readers are encouraged to supplement these examples with others they know of or may discover.

National disability advocacy organizations have more specific roles that are usually evident from their membership, mission statements, and statement of goals. Examples of particular goals include advocating for people with specific disabilities (e.g., Down syndrome, fragile X syndrome, neurofibromatosis) or advocating for rights and entitlements of families, equitable distribution of funds or services, employment opportunities, or greater application of disability public services (e.g., ramps, easy-to-read signs, accessible buses).

Legal Role of National Disability Advocacy Organizations Part of the role of many national disability advocacy organizations is to advance the legal rights and entitlements of people with disabilities. This is done in a variety of ways. One way is to provide forums for international collaboration within which countries from around the world can discuss law and policy entitlements pertaining to people with disabilities. For example, the Disability Rights Education and Defense Fund (DREDF), a U.S. disability advocacy organization, sponsored an international disability rights law and policy symposium entitled "From Principles to Practice," in which professionals from 57 countries participated. The participants discussed legal principles; shared ideas about laws and policies, enforcement mechanisms, and strategies for reform; and encouraged communication among lawyers and advocates around the world (DREDF, 2002).

Another way legal rights are advanced by some advocacy organizations is by encouraging the development of similar organizations in other countries. DREDF, for example, specializes in working with emerging leaders who have disabilities and parents who are developing strategies for change in their countries; the organization provides workshops, collaborative opportunities, and training.

One function of many national legal disability advocacy organizations is to assist in the complaint resolution process leading to judicial or tribunal outcomes that have a direct impact on the future rights and entitlements of people with disabilities, as well as on the disability movement in the country within which the complaint is brought. The extent to which disability advocacy organizations are willing and able to engage in litigation as a tool varies considerably from organization to organization and from country to country because mandates, levels of resources, and levels of expertise differ.

Legal action can be expensive, and for this reason disability advocacy organizations bring forward relatively few legal cases. Usually, these are "test cases"—that is, the litigation relates to issues that have not been previously considered by a court and have the potential to affect a large number of people in the disability community.

Yet, disability advocacy organizations play an essential role in improving the legal rights and entitlements of people with disabilities by litigating for necessary services. For example, DREDF has participated in much of the landmark U.S. and international litigation, and it has made a very substantial contribution to advancing national and international disability rights. In Canada, the ARCH Disability Law Centre initiated litigation on the adequacy of public transportation for people with disabilities. The organization is seeking to have the Canadian province of Ontario ordered to resume funding for special transit and to have appropriate service levels mandated. If these goals are achieved, they could have a profound impact on the delivery of special transit services across the province (Lyons, 2003). In the United Kingdom, the Disability Rights Commission took Ryanair to court for charging people with disabilities for the use of a wheelchair in British airports. In December 2004, the country's appeal court ruled that both Ryanair and all airports in Great Britain must provide a free wheelchair service to travelers with disabilities, ensuring that people with disabilities receive the same standard of service as travelers without disabilities (BBC News, 2004).

Table 6.3. Sample advocacy organizations for people with disabilities

Organization	Internet address	Main functions
Australia		
Self-advocacy/family advocacy		
Australian Federation of AIDS Organizations (AFAO)	http://www.afao.org.au	Provides advocacy, education, and policy services
Australian Federation of Disability Organisations (AFDO)	http://www.disfed.org.au	The primary national lobby group to the government for disability issues
Citizen Advocacy Eastside	http://www.citadv.asn.au	Seeks to promote, protect, and defend the rights and interests of people who have an intellectual disability in Sydney
Ethnic Disability Advocacy Centre (EDAC)	http://www.edac.org.au	Promotes and safeguards the rights of ethnic people with disabilities and their caregivers in Western Australia
National Council on Intellectual Disability (NCID)	http://www.dice.org.au	A recognized national organization on intellectual disabilities providing advocacy and lobbying services
National Peak Body for People from NESB with Disability	http://www.neda.org.au/index.html	A body for people from non–English-speaking backgrounds (NESBs) with disabilities that advocates at a federal level for the rights and interests of people with disabilities, their families, and caregivers
Physical Disability Council of NSW (PDCN)	http://www.pdcnsw.org.au	A body and a systematic disability advocacy organization that provides information about advocacy, including an advocacy knowledge base, tools, and articles about lobbying and the media
Legal advocacy		
Human Rights and Equal Opportunities Commission	http://www.humanrights.gov.au/disability_rights/index.html	Provides a range of resources and links on disability rights and discrimination issues
NSW Disability Discrimination Legal Centre	http://www.ddlcnsw.org.au/home.html	Organization that offers people with disabilities help in the complaint resolution process
Welfare Rights Legal Centre	http://www.welfarerightsact.org	Free community legal service for Australians with low incomes
Professional advocacy		
Association of Consultants in Access, Australia (ACAA)	http://www.access.asn.au	Association of professionals working toward access for people with disabilities
Disability Education Advocacy Australia	http://home.vicnet.net.au/~deaa/deaa.htm	Provides understanding to needs, rights, and concerns of people with disabilities by offering talks and workshops and training businesses in how to work with people with disabilities
Disability Studies and Research Institute	http://www.dsari.org.au	Provides research and education on disability issues
National Industry Association for Disability Services (ACROD)	http://www.acrod.org.au	Overarching organization, consisting of more than 550 disability organizations, that advocates for influence in public policy
People with Disability Australia Incorporated	http://www.pwd.org.au	A national disability rights and advocacy organization
Canada		
Organization	**Internet address**	**Main functions**
Self-advocacy/family advocacy		
Canadian Association for Community Living	http://www.cacl.ca	Association of family members who provide support to people with intellectual disabilities
Council of Canadians with Disabilities	http://wwww.ccdonline.ca	Advocates for disability rights at the federal and international level
Extend-A-Family	http://www.extendafamily.ca	Community-based organization made of families who advocate for inclusion of children with disabilities
Family Alliance Ontario	http://family-alliance.com	Network of families that promotes the inclusion of people with disabilities into all aspects of community life through a variety of programs
Learning Disabilities Association of Ontario	http://ldao.on.ca	Organization providing advocacy, educational, informational, and research services to people with disabilities

Organization	Internet address	Main functions
Canada *(continued)*		
Legal advocacy		
ARCH Disability Law Centre	http://www.archdisabilitylaw.ca	Legal aid clinic that goes to court to advance the rights of people with disabilities
Canadian Human Rights Commission	http://www.chrc-ccdp.ca	Dispute-resolution body that investigates and settles cases involving discrimination
Community Legal Education Ontario	http://www.cleo.on.ca/English/index.htm	Legal clinic that produces material in areas affecting people with disabilities who have low incomes
HIV and AIDS Legal Clinic of Ontario (HALCO)	http://www.halco.org/home.html	Community-based legal clinic providing legal services to people with HIV and AIDS who have low incomes
Professional advocacy		
Canadian Association of Independent Living Centres (CAILC)	http://www.cailc.ca	Organization devoted to policy, research, information, and promotion of independent living for people with disabilities
Canadian Centre on Disability Studies	http://www.disabilitystudies.ca	University-affiliated center dedicated to research, education, and information dissemination on disability issues
Canadian Council on Social Development, Disability Research	http://www.ccsd.ca/drip	Provides information about disability research
Ontario Association on Developmental Disabilities	http://www.oadd.org	Offers resources to professionals and students in the area of developmental disabilities
Persons with Disabilities Online	http://www.pwd-online.ca/pwdhome.jsp?lang=en	Provides information on disability-related programs and services in Canada
Roeher Institute	http://www.roeher.ca/english/about/about.htm	Professional organization providing policy research and development

Organization	Internet address	Main functions
United Kingdom		
Self-advocacy/family advocacy		
British Council of Disabled People (BCODP)	http://www.bcodp.org.uk	Umbrella organization representing more than 100 disability organizations advocating at the national and international level
Carers Association	http://www.carersireland.com	Provides family caregivers with support, and lobbying and advocacy services
Royal Association for Disability and Rehabilitation (RADAR)	http://www.radar.org.uk	Provides advocacy and information dissemination on disability issues
Professional advocacy		
Centre for Disability Studies	http://www.leeds.ac.uk/disability-studies	Interdisciplinary center for research and teaching in disability studies at the Leeds University in England
Disability Rights Commission (DRC)	http://www.drc-gb.org	Organization set up by the national government to provide litigation, investigation, and conciliation services
Employers' Forum on Disability	http://www.employers-forum.co.uk	Organization of employers working toward practices to best employ and serve people with disabilities

Organization	Internet address	Main functions
United States		
Self-advocacy/family advocacy		
American Association of People with Disabilities (AAPD)	http://www.aapd-dc.org	Organization working toward implementation and enforcement of disability rights laws
Disability Advocacy Work with Networking	http://home.earthlink.net/~dawwn	Provides information to help individuals advocate for themselves
National Association for Rights Protection and Advocacy (NARPA)	http://www.narpa.org	Provides advocacy on behalf of people with mental health disabilities
People First of New Hampshire	http://www.peoplefirstofnh.org	Organization made up of people with disabilities who advocate for themselves
The Arc of the United States	http://www.thearc.org	Organization providing support and services for people with developmental disabilities and their families

(continued)

Table 6.3. *(continued)*

Organization	Internet address	Main functions
	United States *(continued)*	
Legal advocacy		
Disability Rights Advocates	http://www.dralegal.org	Provides legal advocacy, research, and education for people with disabilities
Disability Rights Education and Defense Fund (DREDF)	http://www.dredf.org	National law and policy center seeking to protect rights of people with disabilities through legislation, litigation, advocacy, technical assistance, and education
Office of Protection and Advocacy for Persons with Disabilities	http://www.ct.gov/opapd	Provides litigation services as well as information, education, and investigations for the state of Connecticut
NYS Commission on Quality of Care for the Mentally Disabled	http://www.cqc.state.ny.us	Provides legal and non-legal advocacy services to people with disabilities in the state of New York
U.S. Equal Employment Opportunity Commission	http://www.eeoc.gov	Provides litigation on the various U.S. antidiscrimination acts
Professional advocacy		
American Association on Mental Retardation (AAMR)	http://www.aamr.org	Promotes policies and rights of people with intellectual disabilities through research and advocacy
Center for the Study and Advancement of Disability Policy (CSADP)	http://www.disabilitypolicycenter.org	Provides education, public policy research, information, and training to people with disabilities
Consortium for Citizens with Disabilities	http://www.c-c-d.org	Coalition of advocacy, professional, and provider organizations that advocate on behalf of people with disabilities
Institute for Community Inclusion (ICI)	http://www.communityinclusion.org	Advocacy organization made of practitioners, teachers, and researchers that provide community support for people with disabilities
Institute for Disabilities Research and Training	http://www.idrt.com	Professional organization that provides research and development, training, technical assistance, and advocacy
National Association for Down Syndrome	http://www.nads.org	Provides support and information to parents of children with Down syndrome, disseminates up-to-date information about Down syndrome, and promotes healthy environments for the development of children with Down syndrome
National Association for the Dually Diagnosed (NADD)	http://www.thenadd.org	Advances mental health wellness for people with developmental disabilities through the promotion of excellence in mental health care
National Center for Learning Disabilities (NCLD)	http://www.ncld.org	Provides public education, public policy analysis, and advocates for policies
Society for Disability Studies	http://www.uic.edu.orgs.sds	Publishes *Disability Studies Quarterly (DSQ)* and holds a yearly conference on disability issues

Organization	Internet address	Main functions
	International	
Self-advocacy/family advocacy		
Disabled Peoples' International	http://www.dpi.org	Organization made of a network of national organizations of people with disabilities
Inclusion International	http://www.inclusion-international.org	Global federation of family-based organizations advocating for people with disabilities worldwide
Professional advocacy		
Center for International Rehabilitation (CIR)	http://www.cirnetwork.org	Worldwide network of organizations providing education, advocacy, and innovation in form of prosthetic devices and wheelchairs for people with disabilities in low-income counties
Disability Rights Promotion International (DRPI)	http://www.yorku.ca/drpi	A project that aims to establish an international monitoring system to address disability discrimination worldwide
Independent Living Institute	http://www.independentliving.org	A foundation run and controlled by people with disabilities that offers resources including a virtual library

International *(continued)*		
Organization	Internet address	Main functions
International Association for the Scientific Study of Intellectual Disabilities	http://www.iassid.org	Promotes worldwide research and exchange of information on intellectual disabilities
International Center for Disability Resources on the Internet (ICDRI)	http:/www.icdri.org	Research institute organization run by and for people with disabilities providing education, outreach, and training
World Institute on Disability	http://www.wid.org	Nonprofit research, training, and public policy center

National Professional Advocacy Organizations The members of professional disability advocacy organizations are academics, researchers, and practitioners who work in the area of disability. These organizations address needs of people with disabilities from a professional point of view (e.g., practitioners see what types of services clients need society to offer, researchers' work yields findings that uphold certain issues), and they are often involved in advocacy initiatives for changes in the way services are funded and structured.

Self-Advocacy and Family-Advocacy Organizations As alluded to previously, self-advocacy involves people with intellectual and developmental disabilities speaking for themselves to advocate for their own needs, their quality of life, and their right to make decisions about their own lives. Self-advocacy is often thought of as a philosophy that encompasses the belief that people with disabilities should speak up for themselves and be listened to (e.g., see Shapiro, 2004). Self-advocacy disability organizations invariably advocate for such things as better services, funding, and laws, but the underlying function of most such organizations is to advance the perception that people with disabilities contribute to society in a valuable way. Inclusion International, one of the largest and most widely acknowledged disability advocacy organizations, emphasizes the philosophy that self-advocates all over the world have made it clear that the way to be valued is to be included in communities, schools, places of employment, religious organizations, and society overall (Inclusion International, 2005b).

Similar organizations with membership comprised primarily of family members are usually referred to as family-advocacy organizations. Most often, these organizations focus on promoting the family's importance for an individual with disabilities and on advocating for provision of necessary supports to enable the family to function successfully. Families invariably advocate for better supports and conditions for their family members who have disabilities, as well as for services and policies needed by the disability community in general. Sometimes people with disabilities are unable to speak for themselves and rely on family members to speak for them. One important role of family-advocacy groups is to act as spokespeople or supports for self-advocates who have difficulty expressing their views effectively.

Self-advocacy and family-advocacy sometimes take place as part of the work of national advocacy organizations, such as the National Association for Down Syndrome or The Arc of the United States. They also take place as part of the work of international advocacy groups, such as Inclusion International or Down Syndrome International.

One aspect of self-advocacy is the independent living movement, which emerged in the United States in the 1970s and, subsequently, has resulted in the establishment of Independent Living Centers in many countries around the world. The guiding philosophy of this movement is that people with disabilities have the right to live with dignity in barrier-free communities, participate in aspects of their lives, and be in control and make decisions about their own lives (Isaacson Kailes, 2005). According to Isaacson Kailes, Independent Living Centers provide two kinds of advocacy: 1) consumer advocacy, which involves center staff working with people with disabilities to obtain necessary support services from other agencies in the community and 2) community advocacy, which involves center staff, board members, and volunteers initiating activities to make changes in the community that make it easier for all people with disabilities to live more independently.

The Roles of Supranational/International Disability Advocacy Organizations

The goals of two influential international grassroots disability organizations, Disabled Peoples' International and Inclusion International, are similar to those of many national disability organizations—namely the equality and full inclusion of people with disabilities in society—except that they represent a global perspective and promote recognition of disability in developing countries. There are 600 million people with disabilities worldwide, 82% of whom live in developing countries (Inclusion International, 2005a). It is the broad goal of these global organizations to ensure comprehensive legislative protection for people with disabilities in every country around the world.

To further this broad goal, international organizations, in conjunction with national disability organizations, lobby national governments for the enactment or enforcement of comprehensive disability legislation in developing countries. There have been numerous significant advances in disability rights at the national level primarily in many developing countries as a result of such lobbying activities. In Romania, for example, the lobbying efforts of Inclusion International, in conjunction with the National Association of Persons with Mental Handicap in Romania, resulted in the coming together of nongovernmental organizations and representatives of the various relevant ministries in Romania. The purpose was to discuss a strategy of implementation of disability legislation, which the Romanian government adopted in October 2002.

Another important role played by international disability advocacy organizations is to provide support to individuals, and national disability advocacy organizations to engage in other advocacy techniques, such as protesting, toward the goal of advancing disability rights in that individual or organization's country. For example, Disabled Peoples' International provided support to two men in Trinidad and Tobago who launched a protest for the purpose of drawing public awareness to, and providing education about, their particular issue when they had been fired from their jobs for no reason other than their respective disabilities. Following 116 days of protesting, these men claimed success when the national government announced that the two men would be not only reinstated in their jobs but also promised the introduction of comprehensive disability legislation similar to the ADA in the United States (Reynolds, 2004).

A third role played by international disability advocacy organizations is to work with universal and regional bodies to promote inclusive approaches to international disability policy. Inclusion International, for example, has worked with many international agencies, including the World Health Organization (WHO), United Nations Economic and Social Council (ECOSOC), International Labour Organization (ILO), United Nations Children's Fund (UNICEF), and the International Disability Caucus on the UN Disability Convention.

A fourth role provided by international grassroots disability organizations is public awareness and information dissemination. Materials typically are aimed at policy makers and members of the public and concern issues affecting people with disabilities at both the national and international levels.

Fifth, due to the absence of a UN convention on disability rights and the lack of legally enforceable international standards, international disability advocacy organizations have collaborated in many advocacy initiatives. One such area is that of disability monitoring. The International Disability Rights Monitor (IDRM) project is an ongoing collaborative effort on the part of many international disability advocacy organizations—including the Center for International Rehabilitation, the International Disability Network, and Disabled Peoples' International—to document the rights and treatment of, as well as the challenges and barriers faced by, people with disabilities around the world. The impetus for the project grew from the realization that national and international policy makers and treaty-monitoring bodies have very little information pertaining to these issues.

SUMMARY

Individual countries are primarily responsible for protecting and enhancing disability rights and entitlements. Their respective legal systems are the primary venues by which remedies for abuses of disability rights and entitlements are pursued and new rights and entitlements are advanced. Rights and entitlements for people with disabilities have been set out in a number of international documents, although there are limitations to how well these can be enforced within countries. As a result, the reality is that many people with disabilities throughout the world are being denied their basic human rights. Disability advocacy organizations have played important roles in continuing to ensure disability rights and entitlements. International organizations focus primarily on global rights and entitlements, with a special emphasis on ensuring that developing countries are represented. National advocacy organizations focus on legal, professional, family, and individual issues. The value of self-advocacy is strongly held and is represented throughout all advocacy organizations.

FOR FURTHER THOUGHT AND DISCUSSION

1. Emily's two sons have the same disability, which can be disfiguring and is associated with significant intellectual disability. After her first son was found to have this disability, her medical insurance benefits continued; however, after her second son was born with the same condition, her medical benefits were discontinued. Her marriage broke up because her husband could not deal with the stress, and Emily incurred a large debt paying for her sons' medical treatments. When her first son reached the age of eligibility for a disability pension, he applied for and received the pension. When her second son reached this age, his application was denied. Ensuing applications were denied for years; when an application was finally successful, the government refused to pay the disability pension retroactively, despite documentation of medical and psychiatric problems and expenses for several surgeries. Emily herself is now in poor health, facing a terminal illness. She had to give up her job and is receiving a disability pension herself. What courses of action might Emily and her second son take to advocate for the retroactive disability pension?
2. Evidence shows that many young children with severe autism can benefit from intensive early behavior intervention (IBI). In some countries, programs delivering such intervention are provided as a service to children age 3–6 years. After age 6, children no longer are eligible for this program, and families must fend for themselves. Also, there are not enough placements for eligible children; waiting lists are long, and some children never are admitted. Elementary schools, which are already underfunded for IBI, are under pressure to provide this intervention to uphold acquired skills. What advocacy actions might be taken to address this situation?
3. For years, many people with intellectual and developmental disabilities lived in institutions. In most countries, these have been closed or will be closed soon, with the hope of a better quality of life when the individuals are included in the community. Some people living in institutions slated to be closed have realized that there are few community living choices for them. What actions might address this issue and, in particular, to ensure that people who have intellectual and developmental disabilities, as well as complex medical and psychiatric needs, have appropriate housing, adequate care, and the quality of life to which they are entitled?

REFERENCES

Amendment XIV to the U.S. Constitution.

Americans with Disabilities Act (ADA) of 1990, PL 101-336, 42 U.S.C. §§ 12101 *et seq.*

Architectural Barriers Act of 1968, PL 90-480, 42 U.S.C. §§ 4151 *et seq.*

Auton (Guardian ad litem of) v. British Columbia (Attorney General) (2004), S.C.J. No.71.

BBC News. (2004, January 30). *Ryanair loses disability ruling.* Retrieved January 4, 2006, from http://news.bbc.co.uk/1/hi/business/3443739.stm

Canadian Association of Independent Living Centres. (2005). *Regional report of the Americas.* Retrieved August 3, 2006, http://www.ideanet.org/cir/uploads/File/IDRM_Americas_2004.pdf

Canadian Charter of Rights and Freedoms. (1982). Retrieved April 19, 2006, from http://laws.justice.gc.ca/en/charter/index.html

Center for International Rehabilitation. (2005). *IDRM regional report of the Americas.* Retrieved November 20, 2005, from http://www.cirnetwork.org/idrm/reports/americas

Disability Discrimination Act 1995 (c. 50).

Disability Discrimination Act (DDA) 1992, Act No. 135 of 1992, as amended.

Disability Rights Commission. (2003). *DRC success stories.* Retrieved January, 30, 2005, from http://www.drc-gb.org/thelaw/newsdetails.asp?id=360&section=5

Disability Rights Education and Defense Fund. (2002). *From principles to practice: An international disability rights law and policy symposium page.* Retrieved December 22, 2005, from http://www.dredf.org/international/p2psymposium.html

Education for All Handicapped Children Act of 1975, PL 94-142, 20 U.S.C. §§ 1400 *et seq.*

Garner, B.A. (1999). *Black's law dictionary* (7th ed.). St. Paul, MN: West Group.

Green, C., Schultz, M., Corea, L., et al. (2004). Perceived barriers to healthcare: A survey of clients of the County Board of Mental Retardation and Developmental Disabilities in Cuyahoga County. *Clinical Pediatrics, 43,* 721–724

Inclusion International. (2005a). *Millennium development goals.* Retrieved April 28, 2005, from http://www.inclusion-international.org/en/ii_priority_areas/mdg/index.html

Inclusion International. (2005b). *Promoting inclusion, equality and opportunity for people with intellectual disabilities and their families worldwide.* Retrieved December 8, 2005, from http://www.inclusion-international.org/en/about_us/history_of_ii/index.html

Individuals with Disabilities Education Improvement Act of 2004, PL 108-446, 20 U.S.C. §§ 1400 *et seq.*

International Covenant on Economic, Social and Cultural Rights. General Assembly Res. 2200A (XXI), 993 U.N.T.S. 3, entered into force Jan. 3, 1976.

Isaacson Kailes, J. (2005). *An orientation to independent living centers.* Retrieved August 3, 2006, from http://www.jik.com/ilcorien.html

Lyons, C. (2003). *ARCH fights for equal transit services for persons with disabilities.* Retrieved January 4, 2006, from http://www.archdisabilitylaw.ca/publications/archAlert/2003/14_jun05/05_darts.asp

Mills v. Board of Education, 348 F. Supp. 886 (D.D.C. 1972).

Organization of American States. (1999). *Inter-American Convention for the Elimination of All Forms of Discrimination against Persons with Disabilities* [General Assembly AG/RES. 1608, entered into force September 14, 2001.] Retrieved August 2004, from http://www.oas.org/juridico/english/treaties/a-65.htm

Pennsylvania Association for Retarded Children (PARC) v. Pennsylvania, 334 F. Supp. 1257 (E.D. Pa. 1971).

Peppin, P., Beatty, H., & Baker, D. (2003). Entitlements for people with developmental disabilities. In I. Brown, & M. Percy (Eds.), *Developmental disabilities in Ontario* (2nd ed.; pp. 67–86). Toronto: Ontario Association on Developmental Disabilities.

Reynolds, D. (2004, September 4). Trinidad activists score victory with 15-week protest. *Inclusion Daily Express.* Retrieved October 23, 2005, from http://www.inclusiondaily.com/archives/03/09/04.htm#trinidad

Shapiro, J. (2004). *A Medicaid victory.* Retrieved February 2005 from http://www.npr.org/templates/story/story.php?storyId=974391

Slomanson, W.R. (2003). *Fundamental perspectives on international law* (4th ed.). Belmont, CA: Wadsworth/Thomson Learning.

Stephens, B., & Ratner, M. (1996). *International human rights litigation in U.S. courts.* New York: Transnational Publishers.

Telecommunications Act of 1996, PL 104-104, 47 U.S.C. §§ 225, 251(a)(2).

Tolley, H., Jr. (1991). Interest group litigation to enforce human rights: Confronting judicial restraint. In G.A. Lopez & M. Stohl (Eds.), *World Justice? U.S. courts and international human rights* (pp. 123–148). Boulder, CO: Westview Press.

United Nations. (2001). *Comprehensive and integral international convention to promote and protect the rights and dignity of persons with disabilities: Resolution adopted by the General Assembly [on the report of the Third Committee (A/56/583/Add.2)].* Retrieved January 8, 2006, from http://www.un.org/esa/socdev/enable/disA56168e1.htm

United Nations. (1975). *Declaration of the rights of disabled persons.* Retrieved October 27, 2005, from http://daccessdds.un.org/doc/RESOLUTION/GEN/NR0/001/60/IMG/NR000160.pdf?OpenElement

United Nations. (1993). *Standard rules on the equalization of opportunities for persons with disabilities.* Retrieved December 14, 2005 from http://www.un.org/esa/socdev/enable/dissre00.htm

United Nations. (1948, December 10). *Universal Declaration of Human Rights.* General Assembly Res. 217A (III), UN Doc A/810 at 71. Retrieved August 2004 from http://www.un.org/Overview/rights.html

United States Constitution.

Voting Accessibility for the Elderly and Handicapped Act of 1984, PL 98-435, 42 §§ U.S.C. 1973ee *et seq.*

II

Etiology and Conditions

7

Introduction to Genetics and Development

MAIRE PERCY, SHELDON Z. LEWKIS, AND IVAN BROWN

WHAT YOU WILL LEARN ABOUT IN THIS CHAPTER

- Introduction to genetics
- Basics of genetic disorders
- Introduction to development
- Future directions

This chapter provides an introduction to the basics of human genetics and development. It provides information that will help with the understanding of mechanisms that result in the intellectual and developmental disabilities highlighted in this book (e.g., Down syndrome) as well as other disorders that are discussed.

INTRODUCTION TO GENETICS

There are three reasons why an understanding of genetics is important. First, information and technology in the field of genetics is growing very rapidly. As explained in this chapter and in Chapters 9, 15, 28, and 45, genetics has the potential to affect the lives of everyone greatly and it should be of interest and of concern to everyone. More than 70% of intellectual and developmental disabilities already are known to have a genetic basis (see Chapter 9). As methods for detecting genetic abnormalities are becoming more sensitive, an increasing number of disabilities are being found to be genetic in origin.

Second, new knowledge about genetic causes of intellectual and developmental disabilities is leading to improved methods for their diagnosis and prevention and is spurring on searches for new treatments, preventions, and even cures. Thus, a fundamental understanding of genetics and development should be of interest and concern to everyone, particularly to those whose lives are affected by disabilities (Lazaridis & Petersen, 2005).

Finally, every individual carries, on average, genes for four to eight different hereditary diseases (Milunsky, 1977). Even if an individual is not personally affected, his or her children or other biological relatives may be. Familiarity with the basics of genetics and development enables people to think about the pros and cons of how new genetic knowledge might affect anyone, including people with genetic disorders. Furthermore, it is important for everyone to advocate for what they consider to be just. Such actions will help to guide policy makers to make wise decisions about the complex ethical, legal, and social concerns that are arising from the Human Genome Project (see Display 7.1). Fortunately, in addition to identifying genes, the Human Genome Project is providing funding to deal with these complex social ramifications (U.S. Department of Energy, Office of Science Human Genome Program, 2004).

Until the early 21st century, molecular biology enabled study of the characteristics of isolated parts of a cell or an organism. However, advances in experimental technologies that generate large quantities of data very quickly—such as DNA sequencing, mass spectrometry for identifying proteins, and microarray analysis for quantifying gene expression, along with breakthroughs in computer-assisted data analysis—are creating the potential to examine the characteristics of biological networks (i.e., clusters of processes in the body that work jointly, not independently of one another). Approaches for studying networks are evolving into a science that has been dubbed systems biology (Kitano, 2002; Medina, 2005). Systems biology will require collaboration between theoretical biologists who generate hypotheses, experimentalists who generate data, and computational experts who do modeling. It will not only enable better understanding but also prediction, for example, of how sets of genes communicate with

The authors gratefully acknowledge Rivka Birkan, Simon Wong, Tom Dearie, and Doug Biggarstaff for preparation of the diagrams.

Display 7.1

The Human Genome Project

In 1990, a huge international research endeavor called the Human Genome Project was officially launched. This project is involving many scientists and is equivalent in scope and cost to putting man on the moon. Its objective is to determine the sequence of all of the deoxyribonucleic acid (DNA) in the human **genome** and in the genome of selected model organisms such as the mouse, the fruit fly, and the small worm, *C. elegans.* This work will enable all of the genes in the human body, of which there are approximately 35,000, to be identified. It also will aid with the identification of defects causing virtually every known genetic disorder. As genes causing genetic disorders are identified, it will become possible to test individuals for increasing numbers of inherited disorders, including intellectual disabilities associated with brain malfunction. With the identification of genetic causes of specific intellectual disabilities will come the search for specific treatments, preventions, and cures. As the result of this project, new technologies for determining DNA sequences and for studying ribonucleic acid (RNA) and protein expression and function are being developed, and many new scientists are being trained for careers that will improve human health. The Human Genome Project also is examining the ethical, legal, and social implications of human genetic research and is developing guidelines to help society deal with such issues.

Sources: U.S. Department of Energy, Office of Science Human Genome Program, 2004; Watson, 1991, 2000.

one another, how drugs affect metabolic processes in people with particular genetic variants or **mutations,** how cells interact with one another and respond to environmental signals, and, ultimately, how organisms develop and function.

Basics of Molecular Biology

Children resemble their parents and their biological relatives. These resemblances are called traits or inherited characteristics. Genetics is the study of how traits are inherited and transmitted and what causes variations of traits, including atypical ones.

After the discovery was made about how genes code for proteins, there has been a growing tendency to try to explain many different human characteristics in terms of genes. Genes are important, because they contain the blueprint for life and people inherit half of their genes from their mothers and half from their fathers. However, it now is recognized that it is not only the genes per se that are important but whether the genes are active and how active they are. Furthermore, the activities of some genes are regulated by interaction with the environment. Genes are located in **chromosomes,** small structures which are in the **nucleus** of cells. It is the genes in chromosomes that determine traits—everything from the function of an individual cell (whether it is in the skin, brain, liver, kidney, or heart muscle) to physical, developmental, and probably even some behavior characteristics. Genes also determine traits considered to be abnormal or harmful. Genes are comprised of a chemical substance called deoxyribonucleic acid (DNA). DNA that is in the nucleus of cells is called genomic DNA. DNA is also located in **mitochondria,** the organelles that produce energy for cells, and is called mitochondrial DNA (mtDNA). As detailed later in the chapter, through a process called translation, the order of nucleotides in the DNA directs the production of ribonucleic acid (RNA) molecules that are complementary in sequence to the DNA. Through a process called *transcription,* the RNA molecules in turn produce molecules called *proteins,* which carry out much of the work that goes on in cells. Figure 7.1 shows the fundamental components of a cell.

The establishment of biology as a science goes back to 1859 with Charles Darwin's publication *On the Origin of Species by Means of Natural Selection* (see also Keynes, 1997). However, the story of DNA began in 1869, when the young Swiss physician Friedrich Miescher discovered a substance in white blood cells with properties different from those of proteins. This substance was DNA. Because it was located in the nucleus of cells, he named the novel substance *nuclein*—a term that is still retained today in the word *deoxyribonucleic acid* (Dahm, 2005). Since that time, many different people have contributed to the field that is now known as human genetics. The Human Genome Project's *Timeline* (n.d.) chronologically highlights many of the landmark discoveries made in the fields of biology and genetics since 1859 up to the present.

Gregor Mendel is considered to be the father of genetics, because he was the first person to trace the characteristics of successive generations of a living thing. Mendel was an Augustinian monk who taught natural science to high school students. His attraction to research came from his love of nature. His ideas about heredity came from observations that an atypical variety of an ornamental plant produced other plants like itself that were not affected by plants of the typical variety growing next to them. For the fun of it, Mendel

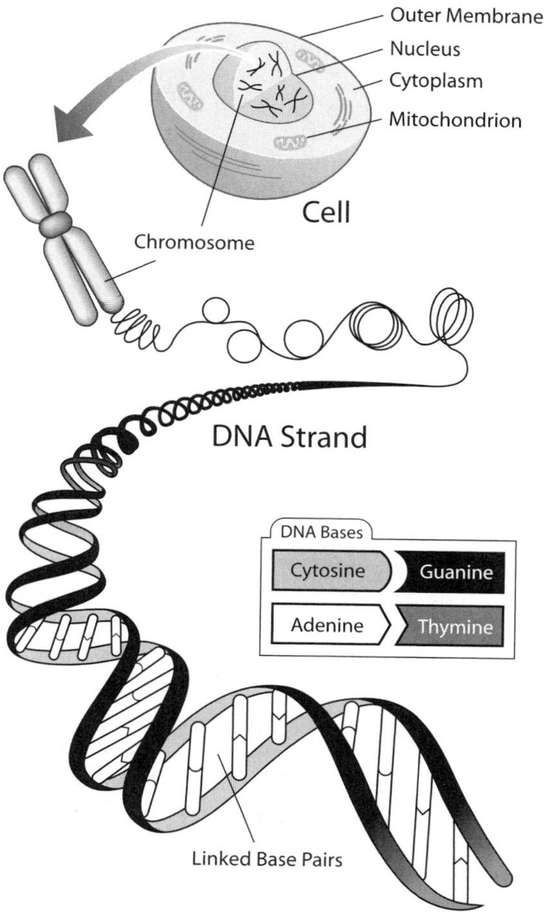

Figure 7.1. Fundamental components of a cell. Every cell has an outer membrane. The membrane helps the cell to hold its shape. The membrane also regulates what gets into and out of the cell and contains the cytoplasm. Cytoplasm is a gelatinous substance in which all cellular metabolism, including protein production, takes place. Within each cell is the nucleus, and within the nucleus are chromosomes that house the DNA that contains genes. The human body is comprised of 100 trillion cells. Thus, every organ in the body has an enormous number of cells. The brain is the most specialized of all the human organs. (*Source:* Percy, Lewkis, & Brown, 2003. *Illustration:* Copyright © 2007 by Tom Dearie, ThreeSixtyCreative; reprinted by permission.)

crossed peas and mice of different varieties and observed that certain traits were inherited in certain numerical ratios. He then tested these ideas in peas, an undertaking that he pursued between 1854 and 1867; his formal publication on the topic appeared in 1865. His studies resulted in discovery of the following basic laws of heredity:

- Hereditary factors do not combine but are passed intact
- Each member of the parental generation transmits only half of its hereditary factors to each offspring, and certain factors are **dominant** over others
- Different offspring of the same parents receive different sets of hereditary factors

Another milestone in genetics was reached in 1927, when Frederick Griffith, an army medical officer, discovered the process of hereditary bacterial transformation. He found that he could convert harmless bacteria to harmful ones by mixing live harmless ones with dead, heat-killed harmful ones that produced no infection on their own and then injecting the mixture of live and dead bacteria into mice. After more experimentation, it was concluded that the harmless bacteria used information from the hereditary material of the dead harmful bacteria and became harmful. Oswald Avery and colleagues pursued Griffith's findings to determine the nature of the hereditary material. In a landmark paper published in 1944, they showed that by treating bacteria with **enzymes** that digested protein or DNA, it was the DNA, not the protein, in the heat-killed bacteria that rendered the harmless bacteria harmful. The work of Avery and colleagues marked the beginning of the so-called "genetic revolution" by definitively establishing DNA as the fundamental unit of heredity. Another milestone establishing genetics as a discipline occurred in 1950 when Edwin Chargaff, a biochemist, first deduced the rule that predicted the relative proportions of adenine (A), thymine (T), guanine (G), and cytosine (C) in DNA. He concluded that the amount of A always equals the amount of T and that the amount of G equals the amount of C. Maurice Wilkins and Rosalind Franklin were the first to obtain very good X ray diffraction images of DNA fibers. Patterns in these images enabled James Watson and Francis Crick in 1951 to deduce the structure of the DNA molecule. In April of 1953, Watson and Crick published a landmark paper in which they proposed that DNA molecules assumed the form of a double **helix.** In 1966, the genetic code was cracked: Marshall Nirenberg, Har Khorana, and Severo Ochoa and colleagues showed how the order of four different nucleic acids in DNA molecules determines the order of the 20 kinds of amino acids in proteins. Other landmarks include determination of the number of chromosomes in a human cell in 1955, the discovery that Down syndrome was caused by having an extra chromosome 21 in 1959, and determination of the full DNA sequence of chromosome 21 in 2000. (*General sources:* Avery, Macleod, & McCarty, 2000; Casey, 1992; Chargaff, 1971; Dunn, 2003; Human Genome Project, n.d.; Maddox, 2003; Ochoa, 1959; National Library of Medicine, 2005; U.S. Department of Energy, Office of Science Human Genome Program, 2004; Watson & Crick, 1953a, 1953b.)

Since the late 20th century, there has been a profound shift in the understanding of genetics. It is recognized that a wide range of environmental factors—including nutrition, stress during fetal life and throughout all life stages, interpersonal interactions, and emotions—can function as signals that control the shaping (conformation) of regulatory proteins that are found in chromosomes and surround DNA. The specific environmentally influenced conformation of these regulatory proteins directly determines the specific portion of DNA that are transcribed by RNA and therefore which proteins are synthesized in the organism. The proteins that are synthesized in this way are the molecular building blocks for the structure and function of every cell of the organism. In this model, DNA remains what has been traditionally described as "the blueprint," but there is a very wide range of variation in the proteins that may possibly be synthesized from the same DNA code, and this variation depends on the particular environmental influences to which the organism is subjected. There is evidence too that these environmentally influenced changes in the activation of DNA can be passed on to offspring just as the DNA blueprint itself can. From this perspective, genes do not of themselves control biology.

The emphasis has been shifted to what activates the gene and how it is activated and, in turn, the dynamic interplay between the organism and the environment that follows. This contemporary view of genetics has been comprehensively described by Lipton (2005) and is based on published research. Although some disorders are caused by single gene defects that can be inherited, many human disorders are determined by multiple genes and in the previously described manner of dynamic interaction between genes activated in varying ways by regulatory proteins that have been influenced by the environment. This contemporary model of genetics is the broader context for understanding the remainder of this chapter.

DNA, RNA, and Proteins

Understanding how the information in genes codes for the synthesis of proteins in cells is necessary for understanding how changes in DNA (or RNA) result in intellectual disabilities. Proteins are the specialized molecules in cells that are required to build and maintain all components of the cell and to assist in regulating the many different metabolic processes in the cell throughout life. Proteins in a cell must function properly if the cell is to function normally. Different types of changes or errors in DNA can result in the underexpression, overexpression, malfunction, or complete absence of proteins. Dysfunctional proteins resulting from errors in DNA cause many genetic disorders, but errors in DNA and RNA that have no effect on protein sequence also can be problematic. **Mutations,** or errors in DNA sequence, occur as the result of the following: **deletions**; **duplications**; **translocations**; **inversions**; and single nucleotide changes, or **single nucleotide polymorphisms (SNPs)** (pronounced "snips"). SNPs occur when DNA sequence variations occur as the result of a difference in a single nucleotide, and such changes occur in at least 1% of the general population. SNPs are found in every 100–300 nucleotides throughout the genome. They can occur in both coding regions (i.e., genes) and noncoding regions of the genome. Many SNPs have no effect on cell function, but others may affect the function of a protein and predispose people to disease or influence their response to a drug. Scientists believe SNP maps will help them identify the multiple genes associated with such complex diseases as cancer, diabetes, vascular disease, and some forms of mental illness. Mutations also can occur in mtDNA.

If a protein does not function properly, and this protein is particularly important in brain cells, then brain cells will be particularly affected by the protein malfunction. Because cellular DNA is faithfully reproduced when a cell divides by **mitosis,** mistakes that are present in a DNA molecule usually also are reproduced. This is the basis of inheritance of genetic forms of intellectual and developmental disabilities. Generally, one gene produces one protein. However, some genes can produce more than one type of protein molecule because different species of RNA can be produced from the same gene. Intellectual and developmental disabilities that result from dysfunction or absence of only one protein are the ones for which the prospects of a cure are the most likely. (*General sources:* Human Genome Project, n.d.; Nussbaum, McInnis, & Willard, 2004.)

Basics of DNA

A DNA molecule is composed of two interconnected (hydrogen-bonded) helical chains consisting of a linear string of units called nucleotides. Each nucleotide contains a chemical substance called a *base.* There are four different bases in DNA: adenine (A), thymine (T), guanine (G), and cytosine (C). T and C groups are large, whereas A and G groups are small.

A nucleotide also contains a triphosphate group, and a deoxyribose group (a sugar). As shown in Figure 7.2, each base in a DNA molecule is linked to a deoxyribose group and the deoxyribose groups are linked to one another via the phosphate groups; the **linkages** between the deoxyribose and phosphate groups form the "string" or "backbone" to which the bases are attached.

DNA molecules are very long. In a chromosome, the DNA is very tightly wound up. A DNA molecule looks like a twisted ladder. The two sides of the ladder are connected by the rungs which are made up of pairs of bases. An A on one side of the ladder is always paired with a T on the other side, and a G with a C (Figure

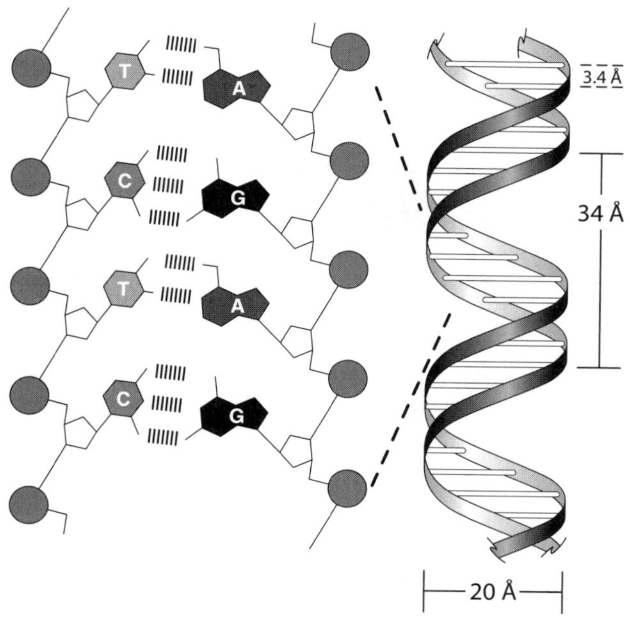

Figure 7.2. The structure of DNA. Left-hand panel: A two-dimensional representation of the two complementary strands of DNA, showing AT and GC base pairs. Right-hand panel: The double helix model of DNA proposed by Watson and Crick (1953a, b). The horizontal "rungs" represent the paired bases. The complementary nature of the two strands of the DNA molecule suggested that the two strands could separate from one another, each containing the complete information and act as a template for new strands. This hypothesis was confirmed by Meselson and Stahl in 1957 and is known as the *semi-conservative model of DNA replication,* with each new strand of DNA being composed of one previous strand and one newly formed strand. (*Source:* Percy, Lewkis, & Brown, 2003. *Illustration:* Copyright © 2007 by Tom Dearie, ThreeSixtyCreative; reprinted by permission.)

7.2). The four bases can create a code for something as complex as a human being because the base pairs can be repeated any number of times and in any sequence. Genomic DNA consists of approximately 300 billion base pairs.

DNA molecules in a single human chromosome range in size from 50×10^6 (50 million) nucleotide pairs in the smallest chromosome, up to 250×10^6 (250 million) nucleotide pairs in the largest. If these DNA molecules were stretched end to end, the DNA would extend 1.7 centimeters (cm) in the smallest chromosome) to 8.5 cm in the largest chromosome. In the intact chromosome, however, each DNA molecule is packed into a very compact structure. During mitosis, a typical chromosome is condensed into a structure about 5 micrometers (µm) long, which is a 10,000-fold reduction in length (a micrometer is equal to one millionth of a meter). If the DNA in a chromosome is unraveled (like a strand of wool from a ball of yarn), and if this DNA is enlarged to the thickness of a piece of string, it would be about 200 kilometers long. Approximately every 160 meters of a DNA strand that is stretched out in this way corresponds to a gene. There are approximately 35,000 genes in a cell. The function of each gene in the nucleus is to provide the cell with the information to construct a different protein.

DNA is present in small structures in the cytoplasm of cells, or mitochondria, as well as in the nucleus of cells. mtDNA is a circle of double-stranded DNA consisting of 16,569 nucleotide pairs—the exact normal sequence of which is already known for humans. mtDNA accounts for approximately 0.3% of total cellular DNA. Each cell has thousands of mitochondria. Each mitochondrion has 37 genes, including 13 protein (polypeptide)-coding, 2 **ribosomal RNA (rRNA),** and 22 **transfer RNA (tRNA)** genes. The polypeptides of the mtDNA are all subunits of the mitochondrial energy-generating pathway, or **oxidative phosphorylation.** Mitochondria replicate themselves in a cell independently of the processes that are necessary for mitosis. It is interesting to note that mitochondria present in sperm get eliminated during early cell divisions of the **embryo.** This means that the DNA in the mitochondria of cells in the body other than gametes are maternally derived. Mutations in mtDNA are thus maternally inherited; these result in quite a number of disorders, including **Leber's hereditary optic neuropathy.** (*General sources:* Human Genome Project 2005, n.d.; Lee & Wei, 2005; Nussbaum et al., 2004; The Report of the Committee on the Human Mitochondrial Genome, 1995; Watson & Crick, 1953a, 1953b.)

How DNA Produces RNA and Proteins

Information in the nucleus gets into the cell's cytoplasm (where **ribosomes,** the machinery to make proteins reside) via the production of a molecule called messenger RNA (mRNA). mRNA strands are working copies of the genetic code that correspond to the DNA sequences in the nucleus of the cell. Mature mRNA molecules are shorter than their corresponding DNA molecules because introns, or pieces of RNA not necessary for protein production, are removed by a process called splicing. Like DNA, RNA molecules are composed of a linear string of nucleotides. In RNA, the sugar group is ribose rather than deoxyribose, and thymine (T) residues are replaced by uracil (U) residues. In contrast to DNA molecules, mRNA molecules are single stranded. Different types of RNA molecules and different types of proteins can be produced from the same DNA sequence via RNA splicing. The process of RNA splicing explains in part why there are many more proteins than genes in the human body. Much of DNA does not code for genes; instead, it gets translated into RNA molecules that are thought to have regulatory functions. Determining the functions of such RNA molecules is a hot topic in molecular biology (Ying & Lin, 2005). (*General sources:* Human Genome Project, n.d.; Nussbaum et al., 2004.)

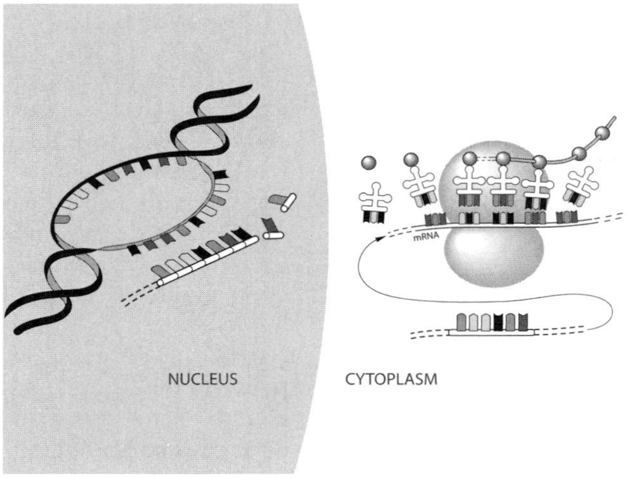

Figure 7.3. How protein is formed from DNA. Genetic information is contained in the chromosomes within the cell nucleus. Protein synthesis takes place in the cell cytoplasm using information encoded in the DNA. The molecular link between the DNA code of genes and the amino acid code of proteins is RNA. Then the following sequence occurs: DNA Transcription → RNA Translation → Protein. (*Source:* Percy, Lewkis, & Brown, 2003. *Illustration:* Copyright © 2007 by Tom Dearie, ThreeSixtyCreative; reprinted by permission.)

Genetic information is contained in DNA in the chromosomes within the cell nucleus. Protein synthesis takes place in the cell cytoplasm using information encoded in the DNA. The molecular link between the DNA code of genes and the amino acid code of proteins is RNA.

Figure 7.3 illustrates how protein is formed from DNA. Normally the sequence of events for the formation of protein from DNA is as follows. The two intertwined chains in DNA molecules separate in the cell's nucleus. The base sequence in the DNA is copied (transcribed) to form a mRNA chain. The mRNA molecule then moves out of the nucleus into the cytoplasm of the cell. There, the mRNA sequence is used as a template by ribosomes to form a protein chain. The mRNA is read by the process of translation. The key to translation is the order of sets of three adjacent bases in the mRNA molecules. Each set of three bases is called a *codon.* Each codon is specific for a particular amino acid. In translation of RNA, tRNA interacts with RNA that is bound to one or more ribosomes. Each tRNA molecule carries not only a set of three nucleotides that forms base pairs with a complementary set of three nucleotides in the mRNA but also a particular amino acid. In this way, the order of bases in DNA specifies the order of bases in mRNA and of amino acids in protein chains. Although many genes produce only one mRNA molecule and one protein, some genes produce more than one type of mRNA molecule (and more than one species of protein) through RNA splicing. After the protein chains are made, two or more chains may combine with the formation of disulfide bonds to form a single protein. Proteins also may be cleaved or modified chemically—for example, by adding carbohydrate or phosphate groups at certain sites.

Genetic Alleles and Protein Isoforms

Not all genes coding for one type of protein are identical. Genes that have different sequences but have the same biological function are called alleles. Alleles may or may not result in proteins that differ in structure, because alleles may differ in noncoding as well as in coding sequences. If alleles do result in proteins with a different amino acid sequence, then such protein variants are called isoforms. Well-known examples of protein isoforms are the three isoforms (E2, E3, and E4) encoded by the (2, (3 and (4 alleles of apolipoprotein E (ApoE; Kontula et al., 1990). The ApoE protein is involved in the transport of cholesterol. The E4 allele is a confirmed risk factor for Alzheimer's disease in Caucasians but it appears to confer an advantage during early development (see Chapter 44).

Meiosis and Mitosis

An introduction to genetics should involve an introduction to the processes involved in cell division and in production of sperm and ova. All cells in the body, except for the sperm and ova (eggs), are referred to as **somatic cells.** The number of chromosomes in somatic cells, or the **diploid** number (sometimes indicated by $2n$) is constant. Ova and sperm, or **gametes,** have only half of the diploid number of chromosomes and are said to be **haploid** (sometimes indicated by n). In order to maintain the same number of chromosomes in cells, two types of cell division occur. Mitosis occurs in cells in somatic tissues during growth and repair. It ensures constancy of chromosome number in cells and constancy of genetic material. **Meiosis** is a specialized form of cell division that results in the formation of four daughter cells, each with a haploid number of chromosomes. Meiosis occurs only in germ cells in genital tissue and results in formation of the gametes. In males, each spermatocyte forms four functional spermatids, which develop into sperm. The formation of sperm takes place on a continual basis from the time of sexual maturity. In females, each oocyte results in the formation of only one ovum; the other three daughter cells become nonfunctional polar bodies. In females, the formation of ova is largely complete at birth. Each gamete's chromosomes produced in meiosis has a unique combination of genes derived from both parents. During meiosis, each chromosome pair in a germ cell mixes the paternal and maternal genetic material in that cell by the process of **genetic recombination** (see Figure 7.4). Thus, each unpaired chromosome in a sperm or ovum has genetic material derived from both of the chromosomes that form a pair in the germ cell. Meiosis is fundamental to sexual reproduction and ensures genetic variability of species.

In humans, the diploid number is 46 and the haploid number 23. Twenty-two of the chromosome pairs, or **autosomes** are labeled 1–22 in decreasing order of their length. One of the 23 pairs is termed the *sex pair.* In females, the sex pair is comprised of two X chromosomes. Conversely, males have a sex pair comprised of an X and Y chromosome. (The X and Y chromosomes are not actually X or Y shaped.)

Figure 7.5 shows the process of meiosis. Sometimes, the process of meiosis is abnormal and not all the chromosomes come apart. The consequence is that one cell gets both sister **chromatids** that each become a chromosome, whereas the other cell does not get that chromosome. This abnormal process of meiosis is called **nondisjunction.** Nondisjunction can occur during particular stages of meiosis called meiosis I or meiosis II (see Figure 7.5). This results in an ovum or sperm having two copies of one particular chromosome or missing a copy of that chromosome. During meiosis, translocation sometimes occurs—that is, chromosomes sometimes get attached to one another and these do not separate properly. Figure 7.6 provides a photograph of chromosomes isolated from cultured white blood cells in a male child with Down syndrome, a common disorder resulting from nondisjunction of chromosome 21. See Chapter 10 for more information about Down syndrome.

Mosaicism and Lyonization

It is not always the case that all somatic cells in a **fetus** have identical chromosomes. For example, cells occa-

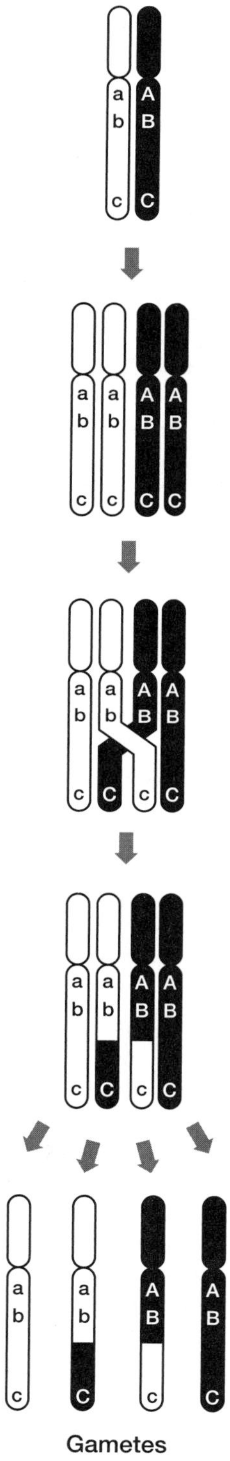

Figure 7.4. Crossing over and recombination during meiosis. During the early stages of cell division in meiosis, two chromosomes of a **homologous** pair may exchange segments in the manner shown, producing genetic variations in germ cells. This process ensures that each ovum and sperm produced will have a unique collection of alleles. This process is beneficial for survival. (*Illustration:* Copyright © 2007 by Tom Dearie, ThreeSixtyCreative; reprinted by permission.)

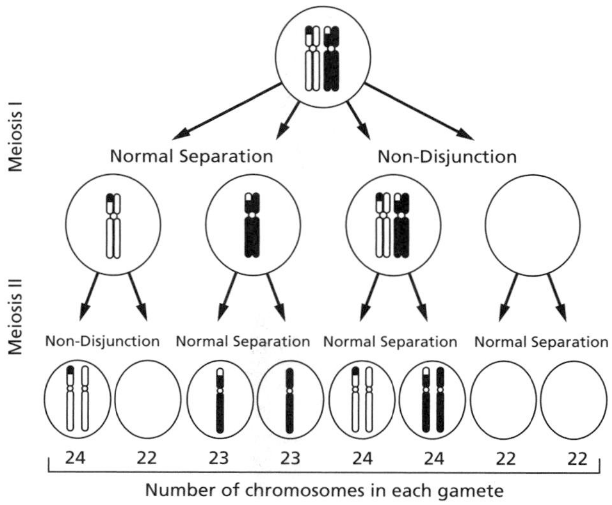

Figure 7.5. Diagram of normal and abnormal meiosis. (*Illustration:* Copyright © 2007 by Tom Dearie, ThreeSixtyCreative; reprinted by permission.)

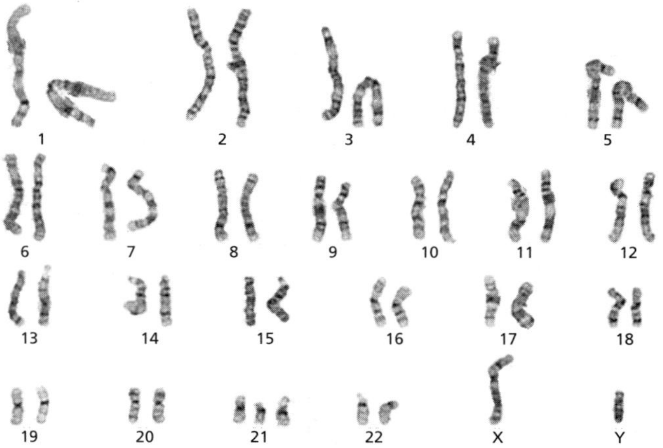

Figure 7.6. Photograph of chromosomes isolated from white blood cells of a male child with Down syndrome. Chromosomes are tightly coiled strands of DNA bound to proteins found in the cell nucleus. In this photograph, the chromosomes have been stained with Giemsa (G banding) and arranged in a standard fashion. They are numbered from 1–22 in order of decreasing length, with the X and Y chromosomes shown separately. This standard arrangement of an individual's chromosomes is known as a ***karyotype.*** Healthy, typically developing individuals have 22 pairs of chromosomes plus two sex chromosomes. The presence of three chromosome 21s in this photo indicates Down syndrome. (Karyotype courtesy of Dr. Kathy Chun, North York General Hospital, Toronto.)

sionally may gain or lose one or more chromosomes during mitosis. Individuals who carry somatic cells with the normal diploid number and cells that have one or more chromosomes missing or one or more extra chromosomes are said to carry more than one cell line. When individuals carry two or more different cell lines, they are said to have mosaicism. The development of mosaicism is not restricted to embryonic development; it can occur in any dividing tissue throughout one's life. There is evidence that mosaicism that normalizes the DNA content of a tissue or organ is beneficial. For example, as explained in Chapter 10, individuals who are **mosaic** for Down syndrome—that is, who have some normal cells in their tissues along with trisomy 21 cells—are less severely affected that individuals with complete trisomy 21. Errors sometimes occur in chromosomal segregation during mitosis after **zygote** formation in a process also resulting in mosaicism.

Another type of mosaicism occurs in all females. In females, one of the two X chromosomes in each somatic cell is inactivated, becoming the so-called "Barr body." This process has been called **lyonization** after Mary Lyon, the scientist who discovered it. Which X chromosome is inactivated, (i.e., the one that originally came from the sperm or the one from the ovum) is thought to be determined randomly. Inactivation of one of each ovum's X chromosomes starts to occur about three days after fertilization, when the developing embryo is comprised of approximately 32 cells. Should one of the X chromosomes be defective, the process of Lyonization ensures that some cells in the female always will have a normal X chromosome that is active. This process tends to spare females from the effects of defective genes on the X chromosome. In contrast, if the X chromosome in a male is defective, it will always be active in his cells. This normal female mosaicism explains why female carriers of an X-linked disorder are almost always spared from full effects of the disorder, whereas male carriers are strongly affected. **Fragile X syndrome, Duchenne muscular dystrophy,** and **Lesch-Nyhan syndrome** are examples of serious X-linked developmental disabilities in which females are significantly spared but males are severely affected. Figure 7.7 illustrates the process of lyonization in somatic cells of females. (*General source:* Nussbaum et al., 2004; see also Chapters 9, 10, 11, and 15.)

BASICS OF GENETIC DISORDERS

This section covers the causes of genetic disorders and approaches for identifying the causes, classification of genetic disorders, inheritance patterns of single-gene disorders, and unusual features of inheritance.

Causes of Genetic Disorders and Approaches for Identifying the Causes

Genetic disorders are caused by many different types of abnormalities in the DNA of an organism or by an abnormal number of chromosomes. Such changes

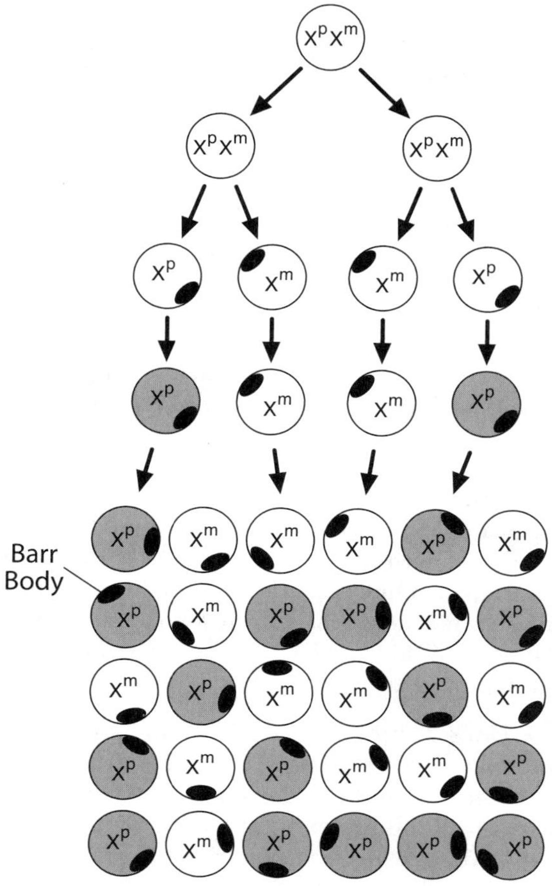

Figure 7.7. The process of lyonization, or random X chromosome inactivation, in female somatic cells. The ovals within the circles represent the Barr bodies that are formed from the inactivated paternal or maternal X chromosome. In any somatic cell in a female, either the paternally inherited X chromosome (X^p) or the maternally inherited X chromosome (X^m) may be active; which chromosome is active is entirely a matter of chance. Once one X chromosome has become inactivated in a cell, this X chromosome remains inactivated in all of the descendants of that cell. (*Source:* Percy, Lewkis, & Brown, 2003. *Illustration:* Copyright © 2007 by Tom Dearie, ThreeSixtyCreative; reprinted by permission.)

may arise without any family history, or they may be inherited. Previously undiscovered abnormalities that cause genetic disorders can be sought for in a number of different ways, which are discussed next.

Screenings for Altered Protein and/or RNA Expression In screenings for altered protein and/or RNA expression, researchers look for overexpression or underexpression of normal protein or RNA molecules or for expression of abnormal forms of protein or RNA. Further studies are then needed to determine the primary cause of the abnormality at the DNA level.

Chromosomal Analysis In chromosomal analysis approach, cells from tissues such as the blood or skin are grown in culture, stained in different ways, and then examined under the microscope to detect abnormalities of chromosome number or structure. Sometimes chromosomal analysis can reveal abnormalities even in single genes. Hybridization techniques in which labeled DNA molecules are applied to chromosomes on slides can detect not only errors of chromosome numbers but also regions of chromosomes that are missing or regions that are amplified.

Genetic Linkage Studies In genetic **linkage analysis,** DNA samples are obtained from blood samples of key individuals in large families in which the clinical disorder of interest has affected several individuals in at least two generations. Analyses are then carried out on the DNA samples to attempt to identify a DNA sequence that predicts occurrence of the clinical disorder. Genetic linkage studies are most fruitful for identifying causal mutations of single genes that result in intellectual disabilities. Causal mutations are ones that almost always result in the disorder if the mutant gene is present. Once the genetic cause of a particular disorder is known, procedures are developed to enable it to be readily diagnosed in the laboratory.

Twin Studies Identical (monozygotic) twins arise from a single fertilized egg that divides into two separate embryos within 14 days after fertilization. Fraternal or nonidentical (dizygotic) twins originate from the fertilization of two different eggs, usually at the same time. In contrast to nonidentical twins, identical twins share identical genes and should be subject to the same hereditary diseases. Twin studies can provide very important clues about whether a particular disorder is caused by genetic factors, environmental hazards, or a combination of both. (*General source:* Nussbaum et al., 2004.)

Measurements of Brain As explained in Chapter 8, there are a variety of methods for studying changes in the brain in people with intellectual and developmental disabilities. Quantitative studies that utilize brain tissue banked at autopsy and a variety of different methods for studying brain function, activity, and anatomy in living individuals are continually providing new insight about how genetic differences affect outcome at the level of brain structure and function. Quantitative studies of brain function and structure also are revealing that increasing numbers of intellectual and developmental disabilities have a biomedical basis.

Classification of Genetic Disorders

Genetic disorders are commonly classified into several types: chromosomal; single gene; and multifactorial, heterogeneous, and polygenic. Disorders caused by single genes are less frequent than disorders resulting from multiple genes acting on their own or in conjunction with environmental factors.

Chromosomal Disorders Chromosomal disorders are caused by a person having too many or too few chromosomes or by a change in the structure of a chromosome that disrupts its function. Approximately 60% of all first-trimester miscarriages (spontaneous abortions) occur as the result of a chromosomal abnormality. Many chromosomal disorders are not actually inherited even though they are considered to be genetic. Rather, they occur spontaneously. Examples of disorders that are considered to be chromosomal are Down syndrome, trisomy 13 (Patau syndrome), trisomy 18 (Edwards syndrome), **cri-du-chat syndrome, Turner syndrome, Klinefelter syndrome,** other disorders of **sex chromosome** number, **Prader-Willi syndrome, Angelman syndrome,** and **Williams syndrome.** See Chapters 9 and 15 for additional details about the different genetic changes that result in these disorders. See also the Genomic Imprinting Variation section for information relevant to Prader-Willi and Angelman syndromes.

Single-Gene Disorders If a chromosomal abnormality affects only one gene, it is called a single-gene disorder. Single-gene disorders are sometimes called Mendelian disorders or **inborn errors of metabolism.** Such disorders usually occur when cells cannot produce proteins or enzymes needed to convert certain chemicals into others or when cells cannot transport substances from one place to another. Single-gene disorders are the easiest to diagnose because they are caused by a change in a single gene. Approximately 1 in 1,500 children is born with a defective enzyme that results in an inborn error of metabolism. More than 350 inborn errors of metabolism have been identified, most of which impair the function of the brain. One example of a single-gene disorder resulting in intellectual disability is **phenylketonuria (PKU).** This disorder results from different types of mutations in the phenylalanine hydroxylase gene (see Chapters 9 and 15). See Chapter 15 for other examples of single-gene disorders.

Disorders that result from changes in single genes are inherited in one of three ways: dominant inheritance, **recessive** inheritance, and X-linked inheritance. Each is discussed next.

Dominant Inheritance In dominant inheritance, one affected parent of either sex has a defective gene that dominates its normal gene counterpart. Every child has a 50% chance of inheriting the defective gene (and the disease or disorder) or the normal gene from the affected parent. **Huntington disease, myotonic dystrophy, neurofibromatosis** and **tuberous sclerosis** are examples of intellectual/developmental disabilities that show autosomal dominant inheritance. The first two of these disorders are caused by amplifications of **trinucleotide repeat regions** within single genes on autosomes (see also Chapters 9, 11, and 15).

Recessive Inheritance In recessive inheritance, both parents carry a defective gene that by itself does not cause problems. Parents of children with autosomal recessive traits are sometimes called *carriers* because they each carry one copy of the abnormal trait but do not actually show it. The disorder or disease occurs when a person receives two copies of the recessive gene (i.e., one from each parent). There is a 25% chance that a person will inherit two copies of the defective gene and show the abnormality, a 50% chance that the person will be a carrier, and a 25% chance that the person will neither be a carrier nor be affected. Some examples of autosomal recessive intellectual disabilities are Smith-Lemli-Opitz syndrome, PKU, **homocystinuria, histidinemia, maple syrup urine disease, arginosuccinic aciduria, galactosemia, mucopolysaccharidoses (MPS)** I and III, and **Tay-Sachs disease.** (See also Chapters 9 and 15.)

X-Linked Inheritance In X-linked disorders (sometimes called sex-linked disorders), the defective gene is carried on the X chromosome of the mother, who usually shows few or no symptoms of the disorder. The disorder is expressed when a male receives the defective gene. Each male child has a 50% chance of being affected, whereas 50% of female children will carry the defective gene but usually will not be highly affected. Examples of X-linked disorders are Lesch-Nyhan syndrome, X-linked mental retardation, **adrenoleukodystrophy,** and fragile X syndrome. Fragile X syndrome also is an atypical X-linked disorder caused by amplification of a trinucleotide repeat region. (*General sources:* Milunsky, 1977; Nussbaum et al., 2004; Online Mendelian Inheritance in Man [OMIM], 2004; see also Chapters 9, 11, and 15.)

Multifactorial, Heterogeneous, and Polygenic Disorders One or several genes on different chromosomes in combination with environmental factors can result in an abnormal inheritance pattern of particular traits that is said to be **multifactorial.** Disorders with a multifactorial pattern of inheritance are inherited, but they do not share the characteristic inheritance patterns of single-gene disorders. The former should be distinguished from heterogeneous disorders, which have similar clinical features but different single-gene causes. Multifactorial disorders also should be distinguished from polygenic disorders, which result from a deleterious combination of two or more genes in the absence of environmental factors. One example of a multifactorial disability is spina bifida, a neural tube defect. Spina bifida results from failure of fusion of the caudal neural tube, and it is one of the most common malformations of human structure. Chromosomal abnormalities, single-gene disorders, and exposures to **teratogens** (see Embryonic and Fetal Development and Effects of Teratogens section) are associated with spina bifida. Up to 70% of spina bifida cases can be prevented by maternal, periconceptional folic acid supplementation. The mechanism underlying this protective effect is unknown, but it is likely to include genes that regulate folate transport and metabolism (Mitchell et al., 2004). One example of a disorder suspected of being polygenic is attention-deficit/hyperactivity disorder (Bobb et al., 2005; Comings, 2001). Other examples of disorders thought to be polygenic are schizophrenia, cancer, hypertension, heart disease, and type 2 diabetes; however, it is now recognized that environmental factors play an important role in development of these latter disorders, so their origin likely is multifactorial. (*General sources:* Belmont & Leal, 2005; Bobb et al., 2005; Kambouris, 2005; Matullo, Berwick, & Vineis, 2005; Milunsky, 1977; MindDisorders.com, 2006; Northup & Nimgaonkar, 2004; Nussbaum et al., 2004; OMIM, 2004.)

Unusual Features of Inheritance

Not all traits are inherited in the previously described ways. Some are now known to be the result of mtDNA variation, genomic **imprinting** variation, satellite sequence variation, and neurodegenerative **prion** disorders. Each is described next.

Mitochondrial DNA Variation Mitochondria play a key role in cellular metabolism and are vital determinants of embryonic development. Mitochondrial function and their replication rely on coordination of regulation and expression of both nuclear and mitochondrial genes. **Mitochondrial inheritance** is strictly maternal because paternally derived mitochondria normally are selectively eliminated during early embryonic cell divisions. However, there are reports on studies involving animals as well as human patients showing that paternal mitochondria can occasionally escape elimination, which in some cases leads to severe pathologies. The occurrence of maternal and paternal copies of mitochondrial genomes within the same cell is called mitochondrial heteroplasmy (Brenner, Kubisch, & Pierce, 2004). Examples of developmental disabilities resulting from mtDNA mutations are the **mitochondrial myopathies,** which can affect the nervous system in addition to muscle (OMIM, 2004). There is increasing concern that mitochondrial heteroplasmy may be an outcome of the use of invasive techniques in assisted reproduction in humans and in the cloning of animals. (*General sources:* Nussbaum et al., 2004; Taylor & Turnbull, 2005.)

Genomic Imprinting Variation It used to be thought that both paternally and maternally inherited copies of most genes are active and expressed (i.e., transcribed into mRNA, which is translated into protein). It now is known that for a small number of genes, only the paternal gene is active. In other cases, only the maternal gene is active. This selective form of gene expression is known as genomic imprinting. Rendering of one of the two inherited gene copies inactive or nonfunctional is associated with chemical modification of the inactive gene by the process of **methylation**—that is, the addition of a methyl group (-CH3) to certain bases (usually C) in the DNA. Methylation is thought to prevent mRNA from being formed from the modified gene (Paulsen & Ferguson-Smith, 2005). There are a number of conditions in which genomic imprinting effects are known to be associated with clinical disorders of importance in humans. Prader-Willi and Angelman syndromes are examples of very different disabilities associated with multiple anomalies and intellectual disability. However, they have a similar genetic basis in that they both involve genes located in a region of chromosome 15 that undergoes genomic imprinting. The genes that are involved in Prader-Willi syndrome are normally inactive in the maternally inherited chromosome 15. The genes that are involved in Angelman syndrome are normally inactive in the paternally inherited chromosome 15. Some cases of Prader-Willi syndrome result from deletions in the paternal chromosome 15 or duplication of the maternal chromosome 15. In contrast, some cases of Angelman syndrome result from deletions in maternal chromosome 15 or duplication of the paternal chromosome 15 (see Chapters 9 and 15). There is evidence that autism has a strong genetic basis, but as of 2007, scientists do not know which genes are involved. Curiously, a few cases of autism have been noted to be associated with having an extra chromosome that carries two copies of the genetic material that is missing in Prader-Willi or Angelman syndrome, resulting from a chromosome 15 deletion; this means that people with this extra chromosome actually have four copies of some genetic material in chromosome 15. This extra chromosome is called isodicentric chromosome 15 (Dykens, Sutcliffe, & Levitt, 2004). Genomic imprinting should be suspected in any disorder with overgrowth, undergrowth, or atypical behavior. (*General source:* Nussbaum et al., 2004; see also Chapter 9.)

Satellite Sequence Variation Only 10%–15% of the bases in DNA make up the genes. A large fraction of genomic DNA has no identified function and is said to be "silent." Some of the remaining base sequences perform crucial functions such as helping to turn genes on and off and holding chromosomes together. The DNA that does not have a specific, identified function has been referred to by some as "junk DNA." Part of this junk DNA includes unusual regions called DNA satellite sequences. These are repetitive sequences made of one or more of the four DNA bases (A, C, G, and T) that are repeated over and over. The repetitive nature of these satellite sequences makes them unstable. The term *microsatellite* is applied to very short repetitive sequences. Satellite sequence DNA occurs in the centromeric regions of chromosomes and at the ends of chromosomes in regions called telomeres. Variations of microsatellite sequences, or trinucleotide repeat regions, are now known to play an important role in numerous disorders that affect the central nervous system. Trinucleotide repeat regions consist of a repeated three-nucleotide sequence repeated over and over again—for example, CGG-CGG-CGG-CGG-CGG. It is suspected that microsatellites are involved in regulating the amount of protein produced by particular genes and that such regulation may be important in adaptation to environmental changes. Certain trinucleotide repeat regions are known to grow in length as they are transmitted. Trinucleotide repeat disorders can be categorized into two subclasses based on the relative location of the trinucleotide repeat to a gene. The first subclass, presently accounting for six disorders, has its repeats in noncoding sequences of certain genes, whereas the second subclass is characterized by (CAG)n repeats (which direct the formation of polyglutamine tracts) in the coding regions of certain genes. The latter group is referred to collectively as polyglutamine diseases. Some intellectual disabilities of the first subclass are fragile X syndrome (FRAXA), **fragile XE syndrome (FRAXE), Friedrich ataxia,** myotonic dystrophy, **spinocerebellar ataxia** type 8, and spinocerebellar ataxia type 12. Examples of the polyglutamine diseases are **spinobulbar muscular atrophy**; Huntington disease; dentatorubral-pallidoluysian atrophy; and spinocerebellar ataxia types 1, 2, 3, 6, and 7. Expansion of trinucleotide repeat regions actually causes particular disorders to become expressed at an age and/or more severely as they are transmitted through several generations in a family (e.g., fragile X syndrome); this process has been called genetic anticipation. (*General sources:* Costa Lima & Pimentel, 2004; Ellegren, 2004; Everett & Wood, 2004; Gorbunova et al., 2004; Nussbaum et al., 2004; OMIM, 2004; Richards, 2001; Tan & Lei, 2005; see also Chapters 9, 11, and 15.)

Neurodegenerative Prion Disorders A discussion of genetics would not be complete without mentioning the prion disorders that are associated with intellectual disability. The discovery of prions is attributed to Dr. Stanley Prusiner, who was awarded a Nobel Prize for his research in this field in 1997 (Prusiner, 1997, 2001). Prion disorders all are characterized by a spongy, Swiss-cheese appearance of the brain and a proliferation of nonneuronal cells. The relation between prion disorders and genetics is that some prion disorders are caused by inherited mutant prion genes. Others occur as new prion mutations in the absence of family history (i.e., they are sporadic). The acquiring of yet other prion disorders appears to depend on which normal prion alleles one has inherited. In all cases, an unusual infectious agent appears to be involved: rod-like particles consisting only of protein that is completely devoid of nucleic acid. The protein in prion particles is encoded by the prion gene on chromosome 20. Everyone has prion genes that make prion protein. The difference between normal prion protein and prion protein that causes disease is that the former, but not the latter, can be degraded by enzymes called proteases. There is evidence that protease resistant prion molecules (the dangerous prions) promote the conversion of protease sensitive protein into the protease resistant form by inducing changes in the three-dimensional structure of the protein when the two different types of molecules physically interact with one another; this process is similar to crystallization. In other words, infectious prion molecules may serve as templates to convert noninfectious molecules into infectious ones. The accumulation of protease resistant prion molecules is believed to cause disease. Prions are very distinct from other infectious agents such as bacteria, viruses, or parasites, which contain nucleic acid that specifies the formation of new organisms through the production of mRNA. See Display 7.2 for more information.

Examples of prion disorders are **scrapie** in sheep and mice; wasting disease of mule deer; transmissible mink **encephalopathy; bovine spongiform encephalopathy (BSE)**; and the human diseases **kuru, Creutzfeldt-Jakob disease (CJD), Gerstmann-Straussler disease,** and **fatal familial insomnia.** Prion disorders sometimes can mask as Alzheimer's disease or certain other disorders of the central nervous system. The reason for current interest in prions is that a new variant of CJD, discovered in 1990 and apparently related to BSE, has affected quite a number of young people in the United Kingdom and possibly in other countries as well. There is concern that the eating of beef infected with BSE has triggered this new epidemic of CJD. BSE, which first appeared in the United Kingdom in 1986, was nicknamed "mad cow disease" because it caused nervous, aggressive behavior in normally peaceful animals. Medical detective work has shown that BSE is caused by feeding cattle with meat and bone meal prepared from the tissue of sheep that are infected with scrapie. Scrapie has affected sheep in Britain for centuries, but it had

Display 7.2

The relationship between noninfectious and infectious prion molecules

As of 2007, the nature of the infectious agent responsible for prion diseases is not known with certainty. However, many pieces of evidence indicate that an abnormally folded form of the prion molecule is involved. Whereas the noninfectious (normal) prion molecule that is present in everyone has numerous helical or spiral-shaped stretches, the abnormally folded infectious molecule has several flat, sheet-like structures called beta sheets. The genetic mutations and polymorphisms identified in prion genes associated with different prion disorders, including bovine spongiform encephalopathy (BSE), are thought to affect the three-dimensional shape of the prion molecules; this, in turn, affects how the molecules clump up and damage the brain. Accumulation of abnormally folded prion molecules are characteristic of all humans or animals with prion disease. Refer to the web site of The Cohen Group (http://www.cmpharm.ucsf.edu/cohen) to see a three-dimensional diagram of noninfectious and infectious prion molecules.

not caused problems because the disease did not infect other animal species and people did not feed infected sheep to other animals. After the World War II, however, it became common practice to supplement cattle feed with meat and bone meal made from scrapie-infected sheep. Originally, this did not cause problems because a very high temperature was used to process the meat by-products. Evidently the problem resulted from taking short cuts in the process for fat rendering and from increasing the proportion of meat and bone meal in animal feed. A number of domestic pets, quite a number of zoo animals, and a cluster of more than 120 young people in the United Kingdom have succumbed to a disorder resembling mad cow disease. The disorder that affects humans is being called a new variant of CJD, or **vCJD** (Rhodes, 1998).

People have been cautioned not to handle scrapie-infected meat and bone meal with bare hands or to inhale it. Unfortunately, prions are very resistant to heat and cannot be completely destroyed by autoclaving, a process of sterilization involving treatment at high temperature and pressure that is often used to decontaminate biohazardous waste, as well as surgical and dental instruments (Fichet et al., 2004). One must ask what other animal products in addition to beef infected with BSE might be contaminated with prions—for example, gelatin, collagen, tallow, leather, and laboratory reagents such as calf serum, bovine serum albumin, and other bovine proteins.

Susceptibility to vCJD depends on one's genotype. The human prion gene has two common alleles that encode either methionine (M) or valine (V) at codon 129 (Tahiri-Alaoui et al., 2004). Because humans inherit two prion genes, one from each parent, there are three different genotypes: MM genotype, MV, and VV. To date, all persons with vCJD have been MM inheritors. It should be stressed that only a very small proportion of people with the MM variant are affected; the MM variant is a predisposing factor, not a cause. Livestock other than cattle—such as pigs, poultry, and sheep—also may be infected by BSE by the same means as cattle. BSE currently is not a major problem in the United States or Canada, but it could become one because isolated cases of BSE have recently been found in cattle in these countries.

As noted throughout this section, prions apparently cause prion disease. Nonetheless, some researchers have presented evidence that the primary agent resulting in overexpression of prions may be unusual forms of viruses or bacteria (Broxmeyer, 2005).

Section Summary The unusual genetic phenomena that have been described in this section are among the most profound biological discoveries of the 20th century. One wonders what Gregor Mendel, the monk who discovered the classical patterns of single-gene inheritance from his studies of pea plants, would think if he were to learn about how mitochondrial mutations, disorders of genomic imprinting, amplifications of DNA satellite sequences, and prions, as well as the emerging concept that interactions of genes with the environment can affect human development and function. (*General sources:* Broxmeyer, 2004; The Official Mad Cow Disease Home Page, n.d.; Rhodes, 1998.)

INTRODUCTION TO DEVELOPMENT

This section discusses embryonic and fetal development and effects of teratogens, developmental milestones, and approaches for identifying disorders resulting in intellectual and developmental disabilities.

Embryonic and Fetal Development and Effects of Teratogens

As noted in the previous section, genetic changes can cause intellectual and developmental disabilities. Yet, such disabilities also can arise from factors that interfere with typical development. In this section, stages of embryonic and fetal development are briefly reviewed and environmental agents or processes that interfere with development are highlighted.

The sperm fertilizes the ovum to form the zygote, which has 46 chromosomes, 23 from each parent. Sperm have only a single sex chromosome; some sperm have an X chromosome whereas others have a Y chromosome. All ova have one X chromosome. Females develop from zygotes with two X chromosomes, whereas males develop from zygotes with one X and one Y chromosome. To begin the formation of a multicelled embryo (referred to as a fetus starting week 12 in its development, when the main features of an adult can be recognized), the zygote divides by mitosis to form two cells that are referred to as daughter cells. In turn, each daughter cell then divides by mitosis and so forth. Through continuous mitotic division, all of the somatic cells of the fetus are formed. These somatic cells then move to different places in the zygote and begin to differentiate to form the various fetal tissues. The basic genetic information contained in the nucleus of the fetal somatic cells does not change during differentiation. During differentiation, however, cells make new proteins. It is these new proteins that cause cells in different tissues to have different shapes and membranes, as well as different structures and functions. The production of RNA that does not get translated into protein also plays a role in development. Understanding how the fertilized egg can develop into all the tissues in the body is one of the two great challenges in biology (the second is how the brain works; see Chapter 8). A particular challenge in early embryonic development is to identify and understand the mechanisms that regulate this development, some of which are intrinsic to the embryo whereas others are maternally derived (Leese, 2005).

Typical fetal development depends on the mother's good health and nutritional status. Because pregnancy is a period of rapid growth for both mother and fetus, both mother and fetus are vulnerable to disruptions in the supply of nutrients and micronutrients in the diet. Fetal growth and development can be adversely affected by many different factors, including teratogens. The word *teratogen* is derived from the Greek words *terato* ("monster") and *gen* ("to give rise to"). Teratogens are factors that interfere with normal embryonic and fetal differentiation, and teratology is the study of **congenital** anomalies and their causes, whether they are genetic or environmental in origin (Arndt, Stodgell, & Rodier, 2005). A large number of teratogenic materials have been identified. These include diethylstilbestrol (a drug used to prevent miscarriages and premature deliveries in the 1950s, 1960s, and early 1970s and also used in some countries as an emergency contraceptive or "morning after pill" to prevent implantation of a fertilized ovum in the womb), thalidomide (a drug used to treat morning sickness in the early 1960s in Canada), Agent Orange (a toxic agent used to defoliate trees, especially during the Vietnam war), valproic acid (an anticonvulsant), and misoprostol (a drug originally developed to prevent stomach ulcers in people who take certain arthritis or pain medications, including aspirin, but which also has been used in some countries to induce abortions. The rubella virus (which causes German measles) is also teratogenic. In addition, alcohol is a teratogen, and use of large amounts of alcohol during pregnancy can result in fetal alcohol syndrome and fetal alcohol spectrum disorders (see Chapter 14). Isotretinoin (13-cis-retinoic-acid, a vitamin A derivative), which is often used to treat severe acne, is a strong teratogen; a single dose taken by a pregnant woman may result in serious birth defects. Because of this effect, most countries have systems in place to ensure that isotretinoin is not given to pregnant women and that the patients are aware how important it is to prevent pregnancy during, and at least 1 month after, treatment.

Examples of effects caused by teratogens include some cases of cleft lip and/or palate, anencephaly, or ventricular septal defect, which are medically serious abnormalities present at birth. By interfering with the development of the brain and nervous system, teratogens also can result in intellectual and developmental disability. It is important to note that at least five teratogens are associated with an increased risk of autism; these include maternal rubella infection, ethanol, thalidomide, valproic acid, and misoprostol (Arndt et al., 2005). Fetal death, prematurity, growth retardation, and unexplained dysmorphology are all suggestive of teratogenic effects. The study of teratogens also is important because disorders resulting from them can be prevented by education of the community. Four factors that are important in teratogenicity are as follows:

1. Embryo/fetus age, or the gestational age of the fetus at the time of the exposure to the teratogen: Different organs of the body are forming at different times; therefore, the sensitivity to the teratogen and the affected organ will vary. Generally, the embryonic stage (i.e., the first trimester, or the period of 18 to 54–60 days of gestation) is more vulnerable than the fetal period (i.e., the second and third trimesters); see Chapter 14 for more information. For a period of approximately 2 weeks from the time of conception until implantation, teratogenic insults to the embryo are likely to result either in miscarriage (or resorption) or in intact survival. Because the embryo is undifferentiated at this stage, repair and recovery can occur through multiplication of totipotential cells. If the teratogen persists beyond this period, however, congenital malformations may result.
2. Dosage of the teratogen
3. Fetal genotype: This may make the fetus more or less resistant to the teratogen.
4. Maternal genotype: Pregnant women differ in their ability to detoxify teratogens.

(*General source:* Diav-Citrin & Koren, n.d.; see also Chapter 14.)

By considering the sequence of events involved in normal embryonic and fetal development, it is easy to see how teratogens may have different effects depending upon when they are encountered. The Visible Embryo web site (http://www.visembryo.com) enables one to navigate through the 40 weeks of pregnancy and see the unique changes in each stage of human development. Table 7.1 lists highlights of embryonic and fetal development.

Developmental Milestones

During the first year of life, a baby grows and develops rapidly. The child's weight doubles by age 5–6 months and triples by his or her first birthday. Some of the major achievements in the development of a baby are called developmental milestones. Many organizations have published developmental checklists. It must be emphasized that there is considerable variation among babies in their development rate; however, a substantial deviation from the norm, especially in walking or talking, sometimes may reflect a problem with brain development and the presence of intellectual disability. The time of onset of intellectual disability depends on its nature. Symptoms may be evident at birth or manifest later in childhood. Children who have illnesses such as **encephalitis** or **meningitis** (infections of the brain; see Chapter 15) may suddenly show signs of cognitive impairment or cognitive difficulties. Early intervention programs are very important in helping babies and young children to reach developmental milestones. (*General sources:* Carlson, 2001; Institute of Human Genetics, Newcastle, & MRC Human Genetics Unit, Edinburgh, 2004; Larsen, 2001; Matthews, 2001; Moore & Persaud, 1989; 1998; National Institute on Deafness and Other Communication Disorders, 2005; New York Medical College, n.d.; Sadler, 2004; Shore, 1997; Thompson, 2001; see also Chapters 9, 15, 28, and 29.)

Approaches for Identifying Disorders Resulting in Intellectual and Developmental Disabilities

There are a number of ways in which disorders resulting in developmental and/or intellectual disability can be detected before an infant is born. These include ultrasound scans and maternal serum screening, as well as amniocentesis, chorionic villus sampling, and percutaneous umbilical cord sampling.

Ultrasound Scans and Maternal Serum Screening As many as 9 in 10 pregnant women use some form of prenatal screening. The most common form of prenatal screening is to look directly at the fetus with ultrasound, or sound wave, scans. Ultrasound is usually done to determine an accurate gestational age, but the procedure also will pick up certain types of physical ab-

Table 7.1. Highlights of embryonic and fetal development

Conception	Conception takes place in one of the fallopian tubes midway through the menstrual cycle.
3 weeks	The blastocyst implants in the uterus; the primitive placenta produces the pregnancy hormone human chorionic gonadotrophin.
4 weeks	The embryo consists of two layers—the epiblast and hypoblast—from which all body parts develop. The primitive placenta also is made of two layers. Present at this time are the amniotic sac, the amniotic fluid, and the yolk sac. The future brain and nervous system are visible after approximately 4 weeks of gestation.
5 weeks	The embryo is approximately 1 millimeter (mm) across. It is made of three layers—the ectoderm, mesoderm, and endoderm. The ectoderm gives rise to the neural tube (which gives rise to brain, spinal cord, nerves, and backbone), skin, hair, nails, mammary and sweat glands, and tooth enamel. The mesoderm gives rise to the heart and circulatory system, muscles, cartilage, bone, and subcutaneous tissue. The endoderm gives rise to the lungs, intestine, rudimentary urinary system, thyroid, liver, and pancreas. The primitive placenta and umbilical cord already are delivering oxygen and nourishment.
6 weeks	The embryo is 4–5 mm across. The head appears large; dark spots mark where the eyes and nostrils will be; shallow pits on the sides of the head mark developing ears; arms and legs appears as protruding buds; hands and feet look like paddles with webbing between the digits. Below the opening that will be the mouth are small folds from where the neck and lower jaw develop. The heart is already beating 100–130 beats per minute. Blood is beginning to circulate. The intestines are developing. Tiny breathing passages appear where the lungs will be. Muscle fibers are beginning to form.
7 weeks	The embryo is approximately 0.5 inches (in.) long.
2 months	The embryo is the size of a lima bean. It moves and shifts constantly. It has distinct, slightly webbed fingers.
3 months	The fetus is approximately 2 in. long. The skin is transparent; the face is becoming humanlike.
4 months	The fetus is approximately 4.5 in. long. The heart pumps approximately 25 quarts of blood per day. The body is covered with downy hair.
5 months	The fetus is approximately 10 in. long from head to heel. A protective substance coats the skin.
6 months	The fetus is approximately 12 in. long and weighs approximately1 pound (lb). The skin is red, still transparent, and wrinkled. The lips, eyebrows and eyelids are distinct.
7 months	The fetus is approximately 15 inches long and weighs approximately 2.25 lbs. Body fat begins to form.
8 months	The fetus weighs approximately 4 lb. It may have "peach fuzz" on the head. It may have turned its head down in preparation for birth.
9 months	At birth, the baby is approximately 18 inches long and weighs approximately 6 lbs., but weight at birth is variable.

Sources: Harding and Bocking (2006); University of Maryland Medical Center (2002); The Visible Embryo (n.d.).

normalities such as a gross brain defect, a very large or very small head, poor fetal growth, and certain abnormal features that are characteristic of Down syndrome. It also will detect the presence of twins, triplets, or even more babies. Major improvement in ultrasound imaging resolution is taking place at the beginning of the 21st century.

Screening for Down syndrome and neural tube defects (e.g., spina bifida) can be done using a blood sample from a pregnant woman at 15–17 weeks of gestation for a process called maternal serum screening. As explained in Chapter 28, several substances can be measured in such blood samples in order to determine the risk that the woman may be carrying a baby with these conditions. Some prenatal clinics offer pregnant women screening for Down syndrome using both ultrasound and maternal serum testing. Because such testing is associated with false positive and false negative rates, some pregnant women choose to have diagnostic testing for Down syndrome using an invasive test that analyses cells from the fetus (see next section). (*General sources:* Filkins & Koos, 2005; Pearce & Easton, 2005; Ralston & Craigo, 2004.)

Amniocentesis, Chorionic Villus Sampling, and Percutaneous Umbilical Blood Sampling Women at risk of having a child with a birth defect, and women older than the age of 35 (who are at increased risk of having a child with Down syndrome), may choose to have amniocentesis (analysis of the fluid and or fetal cells gathered from the womb's amniotoic fluid), chorionic villus sampling (CVS; analysis of cells from the placenta), or percutaneous umbilical blood sampling (PUBS; analysis of blood from the umbilical cord) (see Figure 7.8). Tests that can be done on such samples include analysis for the presence of particular proteins, as well as analysis of cells under the microscope for the presence of extra or missing chromosomes or structurally altered chromosomes. Certain biochemical errors, such as a reduced level of a particular enzyme that results in a particular disorder, can be detected by measuring levels of certain metabolites or measuring the activity of particular enzymes in cells. To look for particular defects in DNA extracted from cells, long stretches of DNA along the chromosomes can now be copied billions of times in a procedure called the **polymerase chain reaction (PCR)** (Mullis, 1990). The PCR reaction is so sensitive that it can detect different types of genetic defects in single cells. (*General sources:* Brambati & Tului, 2005; Mullis, 1990; Ralston & Craigo, 2004.)

A new type of technical innovation, called a *microchip assay,* is making identification of genetic defects easier and faster. Microchips are pieces of material about the size of a thumbnail, which are imprinted with hundreds of different kinds of DNA probes corresponding to different genetic disorders. After exposing the microchips to DNA samples that have undergone PCR assay, scientists are able to scan the chips and to identify genetic errors in a way that is analogous to the scanning of barcodes for the prices of grocery items in a supermarket. A public-health genetic screening program aimed at early detection and treatment of presymptomatic newborns affected by specific disorders involves protein-based assays and PCR to confirm abnormal results. It has been proposed that DNA microarray technology might be an improvement over protein assays in the first stage of newborn screening. Although this approach would enable many disorders to be screened for at one time, it is associated with high initial cost and the analysis/storage of large data sets (Green & Pass, 2005).

Microarray analysis for quantifying levels of different RNA molecules in cells is an offshoot of DNA microchip analysis for rapidly identifying particular genetic mutations or variants (Kapranov, Sementchenko, & Gingeras, 2003). In this approach, RNA is isolated from cells and copied into complementary DNA (cDNA). (cDNA has a **complementary base pair sequence** that corresponds to the RNA from which it was produced.) cDNA from different cell types or cells that have been treated in different ways are spotted onto microchips that contain a few hundred to thousands of different types of DNA. The amounts of cDNA that hybridize to the different types of DNA can be readily quantitated. Researchers can then identify sets of genes whose expression is abnormal in particular diseases. The application of microarray analysis has revealed that the RNA production from genes involved in inflammation and in the response to ischemia are significantly altered in Alzheimer's disease (e.g., Lukiw, 2004). Similar approaches could be used to study changes in gene expression in the brain in many intellectual and developmental disabilities. Such information is key in the arenas of intervention and prevention. Microarray analysis also can be used to identify protein–protein interactions, to identify the substrates of protein kinases, or to identify the targets of biologically active small molecules. In this case, different molecules of protein are fixed to a piece of glass at separate locations in an ordered manner, thus forming a microscopic array.

Microarray analysis also promises to enable biotechnology and pharmaceutical companies to identify which RNA molecules are affected by treatment with particular drugs, thereby identifying drug targets. Because microarray analysis can identify individuals with similar biological patterns, this technique can assist drug companies in choosing the most appropriate candidates for participating in clinical trials of new drugs. In the future, microarray technology has the po-

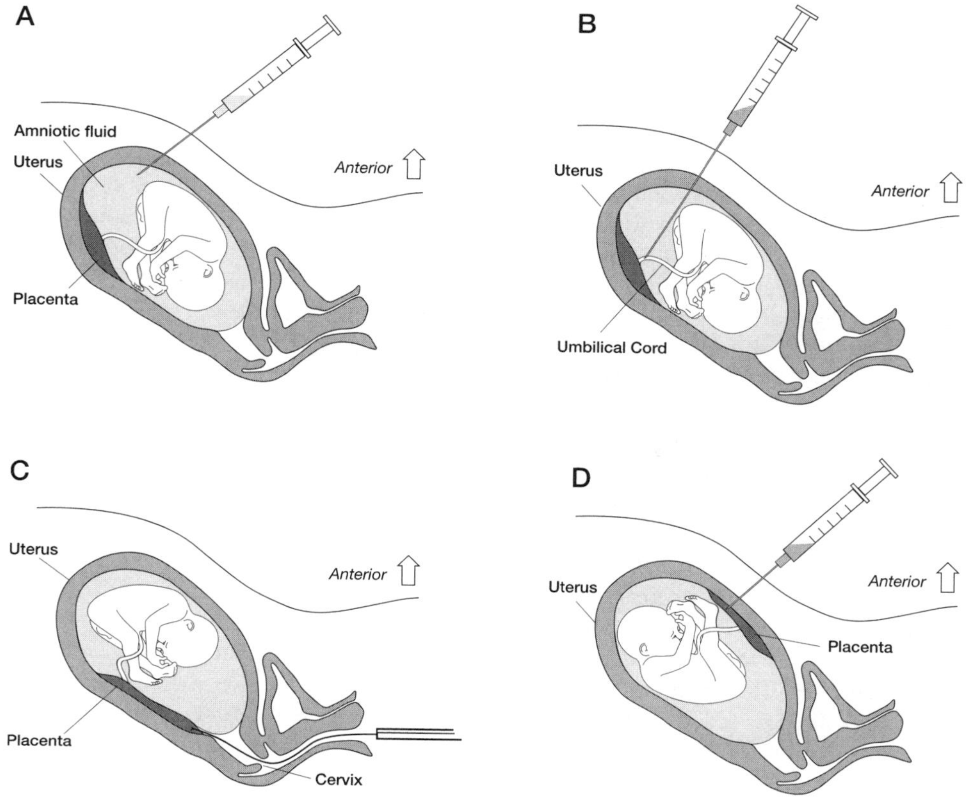

Figure 7.8. Amniocentesis (panel A), percutaneous umbilical cord sampling (panel B), and chorionic villus sampling (panels C and D). (*Illustration:* Copyright © 2007 by Tom Dearie, ThreeSixtyCreative; reprinted by permission.)

tential to help medical professionals select the most effective drugs, or those with the fewest side effects, for their patients. Such a scenario is possible because genetic variation may result in functional differences in the targets of drugs or in functional differences in enzymes that metabolize drugs. A difference in the target usually leads to differences in how well a drug works, whereas differences in metabolizing enzymes can result in differences in its effectiveness or toxicity. It also is possible that variants of genes not directly involved in a particular pathway may influence drug effectiveness and/or toxicity. The emerging field of pharmacogenetics studies how the actions of and reactions to drugs vary with a patient's genes. Those in the field of pharmacogenomics use human DNA sequence variability in the development and prescription of drugs (Chen, 2004). (*General sources:* Chen, 2004; Kapranov et al., 2003.)

FUTURE DIRECTIONS

Future issues in the area of genetics include the prevention and cure of genetic disorders as well as the use of cloning and **stem cells.** Inherent in these topics are various ethical and social issues, which are touched on within the next two sections. In addition, an overall section follows that summarizes broad issues regarding the ethical, legal, and social concerns arising from new genetics findings.

Prevention and Cure of Genetic Disorders

The availability of technology that can detect genetic defects causing intellectual and developmental disabilities is a blessing to many parents. Knowing the exact cause of the problem helps parents to understand the likely outcome for their child and to choose the best intervention. Such information is absolutely essential for researchers to develop rational treatments or even cures. It also provides people with choices for family planning. For example, after undergoing genetic counseling, parents may choose not to have a family or to have a therapeutic abortion if a life-threatening problem is identified in the fetus (Chapter 28).

Although there are many benefits that result from genetic diagnosis, there also are ethical concerns. Some women would never consider having a therapeutic abortion. Others feel great relief at receiving a genetic diagnosis. Yet, they must think carefully about whether they should tell other biological members of their family about the disorder and how they should communicate the information. Professionals should be sensitive to the attitudes of individuals and support the choices that they make. Another concern is whether it is really ethical to test children for genetic disorders (Campbell & Ross, 2003; Davis, 1998). Assigning a genetic diagnosis can have unexpected consequences in the sense that once this is made, the information is filed in the health records and can be made available to insurance agencies (Fogarty, 1999; see also Chapter 28). Although genetic information ultimately will lead to improvement in human health, many are concerned that genetic information will affect the availability of health insurance and lead to discrimination in the workplace. After years of negotiation, the Genetic Information Nondiscrimination Act of 2003 was finally passed in the United States (see also National Human Genome Research Institute, n.d.). Nevertheless, people with genetic disorders may still have problems obtaining health insurance (Children's Tumor Foundation, 2006). Although there is universal health care in some countries, the authors know of some families that have mortgaged their lives away to pay for cosmetic and dental surgery to repair their children's disfigurements from neurofibromatosis, which was considered not to be life threatening (see Chapter 15 for more information about neurofibromatosis).

A few conditions that are detected prenatally actually can be treated by experimental prenatal surgery (e.g., fetal airway obstruction: Rahbar et al., 2005). In addition, gene therapy in utero is being considered for certain conditions (Waddington et al., 2005). Sex-selection techniques based on in vitro fertilization can reduce the risk of giving birth to a baby with X-linked disorders. If couples know that they carry genes for life threatening illnesses that they do not want to pass on to their children, they can choose to have a procedure called preimplantation genetic diagnosis. This procedure begins with a process called in vitro fertilization. The term *in vitro* involves mixing sperm from the father with ova from the mother in a dish in the laboratory rather than having fertilization occur within the mother's body after intercourse. Single cells from the fertilized ova are then subjected to DNA analysis for a large number of disorders. Only those ova that have been found to have no screened-for genetic defects are implanted. A few thousand of these procedures have already been performed for couples who have genetic defects causing life-threatening conditions (Klipstein, 2005; Noah, 2004; see also Chapter 28). Screening for genetic defects also can be done on polar bodies in follicles that contain an ovum. In Europe and in a few centers in the United States, in vitro fertilization using washed sperm is being used to reduce the chance of HIV infection in a baby whose father is HIV positive (Sauer, 2005).

It is anticipated that future advancements in genetic technology known as gene therapy will actually be able to correct certain human genetic diseases, thereby improving the lives of children and their families. Strictly speaking, the term *gene therapy* refers to the correction of genetic diseases by modification of the somatic genome, in all cells of the body or in only diseased tissues and organs, by

- Replacement of the defective gene with normal DNA to reverse the genetic defect
- Transplantation of cells that have been genetically engineered to express molecules that are missing
- Transplantation of stem cells or of tissues produced from stem cells

Because it is believed that brain injury or stroke, other traumatic tissue injuries, and some neurodegenerative diseases also might be improved by genetic technology, the term *gene therapy* now is being used in a broader sense. (*General sources:* Karagiannis & El-Osta, 2005; Towns & Jones, 2004; Waddington et al., 2005.)

For different reasons, many people find some or all of the preceding concepts to be ethically and morally problematic, unacceptable, or completely wrong. The process of inclusion (the philosophy and practice of including all people who belong to a society in the functioning of the society) and prevention (the philosophy and practice of applying current knowledge about the causes of developmental disabilities to preventing them) are conflicting trends in the field of developmental disabilities. Because radical decisions have been made by some governments in the past, including involuntary sterilization during the **eugenics** movement and the practice of allowing infants born with Down syndrome to die from lack of medical treatment, it is imperative that the scientific and medical communities and governments hear the views of consumers and families about ethical issues that involve new genetic findings. Fortunately, as part of the Human Genome Project, research is now being conducted on such topics as

- Discrimination in insurance and employment
- Genetic testing screening and counseling
- Genetic therapies to cure intellectual disability

Use of Cloning and Stem Cells

A discussion of the new era of genomic medicine would not be complete without a discussion of cloning (Faber et al., 2004; Roslin Institute Edinburgh, 2000) and stem cells. As of 2007, the technology is available to create genetically identical animals from individuals by transferring the nucleus of a differentiated cell from a single animal into an unfertilized ovum from which the nucleus has been removed. **Clones** already have been made of sheep (Dolly is the most famous example), as well as numerous other animals including mice, cows, goats, and primates (Colman, 1999). Theoretically, it now is possible to reprogram human cells to differentiate into many different cell types, including entire human beings. Cloning technology will have many potentially important applications including bioagricultural needs and reprogramming cells for therapeutic purposes.

Bioagricultural Needs The ability to make identical copies of mammals is an important milestone in animal research as well as in agricultural and medical biotechnology. Animal cloning will provide genetically identical animals. Fewer animals will be needed for experimentation, and research efficiency will be greatly improved. Another advantage of animal cloning will be in the area of commercial production of pharmaceutically important proteins in transgenic goats, pigs, and cows. When combined, genetic manipulation and cloning will allow scientists to produce higher quality livestock. Engineered animal clones may also be used to provide organs for human transplantation. Cloning will also lead to the production of different types of human pharmaceuticals in, for example, cow's milk. (*General sources:* Colman, 1999; Niemann & Kues, 2003; Wheeler, 2003.)

Reprogramming Cells for Therapeutic Purposes Human adults or embryos, as well as animals, contain stem cells that have the ability to divide for indefinite periods in culture and to give rise to specialized cells (National Institutes of Health, 2005). The availability of cells that can differentiate into distinct cell types, tissue masses, or even whole organs has enormous potential for curing disorders associated with dysfunction or deterioration of particular tissues (Hassink et al., 2003). Studies with animals already provide hope that transplantation of stem cells will offer improved quality of life for people with neurological disorders such as **Parkinson's disease,** Huntington disease, and stroke (Kim, 2004; Levy et al., 2004; see also Chapter 15).

Since the new science of cloning brings with it the potential to clone human beings, there presently is large and widespread public debate about what should or should not be done with this technique. Complex social issues associated with cloning technology are arising very quickly. Different countries have different views about cloning for reproductive purposes and cloning for the purpose of generating stem cells for research (Pattinson & Caulfield, 2004). It is interesting to note that "Wharton's jelly," the jelly-like connective tissue surrounding the blood vessel walls of the human umbilical cord, has been found to be a rich source of embryonic stem cells (Mitchell et al., 2003). The availability of such cells should greatly facilitate all forms of stem cell research.

Ethical, Legal, and Social Concerns Arising from New Genetics Findings

As alluded to in the preceding sections, there are complex ethical, legal, and social ramifications resulting from the great strides that have been made in the field of genetics. Legal implications arising from new developments in genetics concern the degree to which interventions that use knowledge about genetics is carried out in ways that are in accordance with specific laws adopted by specific political jurisdictions. There are very few such laws currently, but since knowledge of genetics is increasing very rapidly, there is an urgent need to explore whether such laws are needed or wanted.

Ethics goes beyond legal concerns to consider what is the proper, best, and most appropriate course of action in particular circumstances. Ethical decisions are informed by both written and unwritten rules of human conduct. There is considerable debate about the rules of conduct and human values that guide practice with regard to knowledge about genetics. Once again, however, because such knowledge is increasing very rapidly, it appears that there is a strong need to encourage elaboration and clarification on these rules of conduct and human values so that ethical decisions regarding genetics can be made. As there are no absolute moral rules offering guidance, the public must guide policy makers regarding moral precepts applied to genetics. Two guiding principles are

- Acting to ensure respect for human life (Meininger, 2005)
- Protecting and promoting the human spirit (Polkinghorne, 2004).

(*General sources:* Godlovitch, 1998; Kim, 2004; Kimberly, 2002; Terry & Campbell, 2004; see also Chapter 40.)

SUMMARY

This chapter has provided a brief overview of the essentials of genetics and development, as well as the benefits and concerns that new genetic findings might have for people with intellectual and developmental disabilities and their families. The sciences of genetics and development are advancing very rapidly. Knowledge generated from the Human Genome Project will lead to identification of the genetic causes of many different disabilities; to the development of new tests for their detection; and to the discovery of specific treatments, cures, and methods for their prevention. It now is recognized that there are many ways in which genetic disorders, including those that affect the intellect and development, can result. The ability to address ethical issues of fairness and privacy that are related to new advances in genetics is lagging behind the scientific findings. It is very important to become familiar with fundamental genetic, biological, and neuroscience principles in order to understand how new genetics findings and technology might affect the lives of people with intellectual disabilities and their families. It is of utmost importance that any concerns, views, and possible solutions be communicated to policy makers to help them to formulate ethical and legal guidelines as needed before problems without solutions arise.

FOR FURTHER THOUGHT AND DISCUSSION

1. Should therapies for genetic conditions causing intellectual disability even be considered?
2. How can the public avoid stigmatizing those living with a genetic intellectual or developmental disability while trying to eliminate the condition in others?
3. Would you include your newborn child in experimental gene therapy research? Why or why not?
4. Is it wrong for the organs of a baby born with anencephaly (a severe neural tube defect that involves gross malformation of the head and is incompatible with life) to be used for transplant purposes even though the infant has not been declared legally dead?

REFERENCES

Arndt, T.L., Stodgell, C.J., & Rodier, P.M. (2005). The teratology of autism. *International Journal of Developmental Neuroscience, 23,* 189–199.

Avery, O.T., Macleod, C.M., & McCarty, M. (2000). Studies on the chemical nature of the substance inducing transformation of pneumococcal types: Induction of transformation by a desoxyribonucleic acid fraction isolated from Pneumococcus type III. Oswald Theodore Avery (1877–1955). *Clinical Orthopedics and Related Research, 379*(Suppl.), S3–S8.

Belmont, J.W., & Leal, S.M. (2005). Complex phenotypes and complex genetics: An introduction to genetic studies of complex traits. *Current Atherosclerosis Reports, 7,* 180–187.

Bobb, A.J., Castellanos, F.X., Addington, A.M., et al. (2005). Molecular genetic studies of ADHD: 1991 to 2004. *American Journal of Medical Genetics. B, Neuropsychiatric Genetics, 132,* 109–125.

Brambati, B., & Tului, L. (2005). Chorionic villus sampling and amniocentesis. *Current Opinion in Obstetrics and Gynecology, 17,* 197–201.

Brenner, C.A., Kubisch, H.M., & Pierce, K.E. (2004). Role of the mitochondrial genome in assisted reproductive technologies and embryonic stem cell-based therapeutic cloning. *Reproduction, Fertility and Development, 16,* 743–751.

Broxmeyer, L. (2005). Thinking the unthinkable: Alzheimer's, Creutzfeldt-Jakob and Mad Cow disease: The age-related reemergence of virulent, foodborne, bovine tuberculosis or losing your mind for the sake of a shake or burger. *Medical Hypotheses, 64,* 699–705.

Campbell, E., & Ross, L.F. (2003). Professional and personal attitudes about access and confidentiality in the genetic testing of children: A pilot study. *Genetic Testing, 7,* 123–130.

Carlson, B.M. (2001). *Human embryology and developmental biology* (2nd ed.). St. Louis: Mosby.

Casey, D. (1992). *Primer on molecular genetics.* Retrieved January 19, 2006, from http://www.ornl.gov/sci/techresources/Human_Genome/publicat/primer/toc.html

Chargaff, E. (1971). Preface to a grammar of biology. A hundred years of nucleic acid research. *Science, 172,* 637–642.

Chen, J.J. (2004). Microarrays in pharmacogenomics. *Journal of Biopharmaceutical Statistics, 14,* 535–537.

Children's Tumor Foundation. (2006). *Adults with NF1.* Retrieved July 10, 2006, from http://www.ctf.org/adults

Colman, A. (1999). Dolly, Polly and other 'ollys': Likely impact of cloning technology on biomedical uses of livestock. *Genetic Analysis: Biotechnical Engineering, 15,* 167–173.

Comings, D.E. (2001). Clinical and molecular genetics of ADHD and Tourette syndrome. Two related polygenic disorders. *Annals of the New York Academy of Sciences, 931,* 50–83.

Costa Lima, M.A., & Pimentel, M.M. (2004). Dynamic mutation and human disorders: The spinocerebellar ataxias. *International Journal of Molecular Medicine, 13,* 299–302.

Dahm, R. (2005). Friedrich Miescher and the discovery of DNA. *Developmental Biology, 278,* 274–288.

Darwin, C. (1859). *On the origin of species by means of natural selection.* London: John Murray.

Davis, D.S. (1998). Discovery of children's carrier status for recessive genetic disease: Some ethical issues. *Genetic Testing, 2,* 323–327.

Diav-Citrin, O., & Koren, G. (n.d.). *Human teratogens: A critical evaluation.* Retrieved July 10, 2006, from http://www.nvp-volumes.org/p2_4.htm

Dunn, P.M. (2003). Gregor Mendel, OSA (1822–1884), founder of scientific genetics. *Archives of Disease in Childhood. Fetal and Neonatal Edition, 88,* F537–F539.

Dykens, E.M., Sutcliffe, J.S., & Levitt, P. (2004). Autism and 15q11-q13 disorders: Behavioral, genetic, and pathophysiological issues. *Mental Retardation and Developmental Disabilities Research Reviews, 10,* 284–291.

Ellegren, H. (2004). Microsatellites: Simple sequences with complex evolution. *Nature Reviews in Genetics, 5,* 435–445.

Everett, C.M., & Wood, N.W. (2004). Trinucleotide repeats and neurodegenerative disease. *Brain, 127*(Pt. 11), 2385–2405. Epub 2004 Aug 25.

Faber, D.C., Ferre, L.B., Metzger, J., et al. (2004). Review: Agro-economic impact of cattle cloning. *Cloning Stem Cells, 6,* 198–207.

Fichet, G., Comoy, E., Duval, C., et al. (2004). Novel methods for disinfection of prion-contaminated medical devices. *The Lancet, 364,* 521–526.

Filkins, K., & Koos, B.J. (2005). Ultrasound and fetal diagnosis. *Current Opinion in Obstetrics and Gynecology, 17,* 185–195.

Fogarty, M. (1999). Genetic testing, Alzheimer disease, and long-term care insurance. *Genetic Testing, 3,* 133–137.

Genetic Information Nondiscrimination Act of 2003 (S. 1053). Retrieved August 18, 2006, from http://rpc.senate.gov/_files/L41HEALTHLABORdmkh100203.pdf

Godlovitch, G. (1998). Moral questions, legal answers, and biotechnological advances. *Victoria University of Wellington Law Review, 28,* 225–242.

Gorbunova, V., Seluanov, A., Mittelman, D., et al. (2004). Genome-wide demethylation destabilizes CTG.CAG trinucleotide repeats in mammalian cells. *Human Molecular Genetics, 13,* 2979–2989.

Green, N.S., & Pass, K.A. (2005). Neonatal screening by DNA microarray: Spots and chips. *Nature Reviews: Genetics, 6,* 147–151.

Gu, Y., & Nelson, D. L. (2003). FMR2 function: Insight from a mouse knockout model. *Cytogenetic and Genomic Research, 100*(1–4), 129–139.

Harding, R., & Bocking, A.D. (Eds.). (2006). *Fetal growth and development.* Cambridge, United Kingdom: Cambridge University Press.

Hassink, R.J., Brutel de la Riviere, A., Mummery, C.L., et al. (2003). Transplantation of cells for cardiac repair. *Journal of the American College of Cardiology, 41,* 711–717.

The Human Genome Project. (n.d.). *Timeline.* http://www.genome.gov/Pages/Education/Kit/main.cfm?pageid=1

Institute of Human Genetics, Newcastle, & MRC Human Genetics Unit, Edinburgh. (2004). *Electronic atlas of the developing human brain.* Retrieved January 19, 2006, from http://www.ncl.ac.uk/ihg/EADHB

Kambouris, M. (2005). Target gene discovery in extended families with type 2 diabetes mellitus. *Atherosclerosis(Suppl.), 6,* 31–36.

Kapranov, P., Sementchenko, V.I., & Gingeras, T.R. (2003). Beyond expression profiling: Next generation uses of high density oligonucleotide arrays. *Brief Functional Genomics and Proteomics, 2,* 47–56.

Karagiannis, T.C., & El-Osta, A. (2005). RNA interference and potential therapeutic applications of short interfering RNAs. *Cancer Gene Therapy, 12,* 787–795.

Keynes, R.D. (1997). Steps on the path to the origin of species. *Journal of Theoretical Biology, 187,* 461–471.

Kim, S.U. (2004). Human neural stem cells genetically modified for brain repair in neurological disorders. *Neuropathology, 24,* 159–171.

Kimberly, M. (2002). Reevaluating repugnance: A critical analysis of Leon Kass' writings on genetic reproductive technologies. *Princeton Journal of Bioethics, 5,* 8–24.

Kitano, H. (2002). Computational systems biology. *Nature, 420,* 206–210.

Klipstein, S. (2005). Preimplantation genetic diagnosis: Technological promise and ethical perils. *Fertility and Sterility, 83,* 1347–1353.

Kontula, K., Aalto-Setala, K., Kuusi, T., et al. (1990). Apolipoprotein E polymorphism determined by restriction enzyme analysis of DNA amplified by polymerase chain reaction: Convenient alternative to phenotyping by isoelectric focusing. *Clinical Chemistry, 36,* 2087–2092.

Larsen, W.J. (2001). *Human embryology* (3rd ed.). New York: Churchill Livingston.

Lazaridis, K.N., & Petersen, G.M. (2005). Genomics, genetic epidemiology, and genomic medicine. *Clinical Gastroenterology and Hepatology, 3,* 320–328.

Lee, H.C., & Wei, Y.H. (2005). Mitochondrial biogenesis and mitochondrial DNA maintenance of mammalian cells under oxidative stress. *The International Journal of Biochemistry & Cell Biology, 37,* 822–834.

Leese, H.J. (2005). Rewards and risks of human embryo creation: A personal view. *Reproduction, Fertility, and Development, 17,* 387–391.

Levy, Y.S., Stroomza, M., Melamed, E., et al. (2004). Embryonic and adult stem cells as a source for cell therapy in Parkinson's disease. *Journal of Molecular Neuroscience, 24,* 353–386.

Lipton, B.H. (2005). *Biology of belief: Unleashing the power of consciousness, matter and miracles.* Santa Rosa, CA: Mountain of Love/Elite Books.

Lukiw, W.J. (2004). Gene expression profiling in fetal, aged, and Alzheimer hippocampus: A continuum of stress-related signaling. *Neurochemical Research, 29,* 1287–1297.

Maddox, B. (2003). The double helix and the 'wronged heroine.' *Nature, 421,* 407–408.

Matthews, S.G. (2001). Antenatal glucocorticoids and programming of the developing CNS. *Pediatric Research, 47,* 291–300.

Matullo, G., Berwick, M., & Vineis, P. (2005). Gene-environment interactions: How many false positives? *Journal of the National Cancer Institute, 97,* 550–551.

Medina, M. (2005). Genomes, phylogeny, and evolutionary systems biology. *Proceedings of the National Academy of Sciences, U.S.A., 102*(Suppl. 1), 6630–6635.

Meininger, H.P. (2005). Narrative ethics in nursing for persons with intellectual disabilities. *Nursing Philosophy, 6,* 106–118.

Mendel, G. (1865). *Experiments in plant hybridization.* Retrieved November 8, 2005, from http://www.mendelweb.org/Mendel.html

Milunsky, A. (1977). *Know your genes.* Boston: Houghton Mifflin Company.

MindDisorders.com. (2006). *Encyclopedia of mental disorders: Genetic factors and mental disorders.* Retrieved April 3, 2006, from http://www.minddisorders.com/Flu-Inv/Genetic-factors-and-mental-disorders.html

Mitchell, K.E., Weiss, M.L., Mitchell, B.M., et al. (2003). Matrix cells from Wharton's jelly form neurons and glia. *Stem Cells, 21,* 50–60.

Mitchell, L.E., Adzick, N.S., Melchionne, J., et al. (2004). Spina bifida. *The Lancet, 364,* 1885–1895.

Moore, K.L., & Persaud, T.V.N. (1989). *Before we are born: Basic embryology and birth defects.* Philadelphia: W.B. Saunders Company.

Moore, K.L., & Persaud, T.V.N. (1998). *The developing human: Clinically oriented embryology* (6th ed.). Philadelphia. W.B. Saunders Company.

Mullis, K.B. (1990). The unusual origin of the polymerase chain reaction. *Scientific American, 262,* 56–61.

National Human Genome Research Institute. (n.d.). *Genetic discrimination in health insurance or employment.* Retrieved July 10, 2006, from http://www.genome.gov/11510227

National Institute on Deafness and Other Communication Disorders. (2005). *Speech and language: Developmental milestones.* Retrieved January 20, 2006, from http://www.nidcd.nih.gov/health/voice/speechandlanguage.asp

National Institutes of Health. (2005). *Stem cell basics.* Retrieved January 20, 2006, from http://stemcells.nih.gov/info/basics

National Library of Medicine. (2005). *Profiles in science.* Retrieved January 20, 2006, from http://profiles.nlm.nih.gov

New York Medical College. (n.d.). *Developmental milestones: Emerging patterns of behavior from 1 to 5 years of age.* Retrieved

January 19, 2006, from http://complab.nymc.edu/Pediatrics/DevelopmentalMilestones.htm

Niemann, H., & Kues, W.A. (2003). Application of transgenesis in livestock for agriculture and biomedicine. *Animal Reproduction Science, 79,* 291–317.

Noah, L. (2004). Trends in assisted reproductive technology. *New England Journal of Medicine 22, 351*(4), 398–389.

Northup, A., & Nimgaonkar, V.L. (2004). Genetics of schizophrenia: Implications for treatment. *Expert Review of Neurotherapeutics, 4,* 725–731.

Nussbaum, R.L., McInnis, R.R., & Willard, H.F. (2004). *Thompson & Thompson genetics in medicine* (6th ed.). Philadelphia: W.B. Saunders Co.

Ochoa, S. (1959). The structure and properties of synthetic and other polynucleotides. Introductory remarks. *Annals of the New York Academy of Sciences, 81,* 690–692.

The Official Mad Cow Disease Home Page. (n.d.). Retrieved November 8, 2005, from http://www.mad-cow.org

Online Mendelian Inheritance in Man (OMIM). (2004). *Home page.* Retrieved on March 11, 2005, from http://www.ncbi.nlm.nih.gov/entrez/query.fcgi?db=OMIM

Pattinson, S.D., & Caulfield, T. (2004). Variations and voids: The regulation of human cloning around the world. *BMC Medical Ethics, 5,* E9.

Paulsen, M., & Ferguson-Smith, A.C. (2005). DNA methylation in genomic imprinting, development, and disease. *The Journal of Pathology, 195,* 97–110.

Pearce, C., & Easton, K. (2005). Management of complications in early pregnancy. *Nursing Standard, 19*(34), 56–64, 66.

Percy, M., Lewkis, S., & Brown I. (2003). An introduction to genetics and development. In I. Brown & M. Percy (Eds.), *Developmental disabilities in Ontario* (pp. 89–116). Toronto, Ontario: Ontario Association on Developmental Disabilities.

Polkinghorne, J.C. (2004). The person, the soul, and genetic engineering. *Journal of Medical Ethics, 30,* 593–600.

Prusiner, S.B. (1997). Prion diseases and the BSE crisis. *Science, 278,* 245–251.

Prusiner, S.B. (2001). Shattuck lecture: Neurodegenerative diseases and prions. *New England Journal of Medicine, 344,* 1516–1526.

Rahbar, R., Vogel, A., Myers, L.B., et al. (2005). Fetal surgery in otolaryngology: A new era in the diagnosis and management of fetal airway obstruction because of advances in prenatal imaging. *Archives of Otolaryngology—Head & Neck Surgery, 131,* 393–398.

Ralston, S.J., & Craigo, S.D. (2004). Ultrasound-guided procedures for prenatal diagnosis and therapy. *Obstetrics and Gynecology Clinics of North America, 31,* 101–123.

The Report of the Committee on the Human Mitochondrial Genome. (1995). Retrieved November 8, 2005 from http://www.mitomap.org/report.html#function

Rhodes, R. (1998). *Deadly feasts: Tracking the secrets of a terrifying new plague.* New York: Simon & Schuster, Inc.

Richards, R.I. (2001). Dynamic mutations: A decade of unstable expanded repeats in human genetic disease. *Human Molecular Genetics, 10,* 2187–2194.

Roslin Institute Edinburgh. (2000). *Public interest.* Retrieved May 28, 2005, from http://www.roslin.ac.uk/public/cloning.html

Sadler, T.W. (2004). *Langman's medical embryology* (9th ed.). Philadelphia: Lippincott Williams & Wilkins

Sauer, M.V. (2005). Sperm washing techniques address the fertility needs of HIV-seropositive men: A clinical review. *Reproductive Biomedicine Online, 10,* 135–140.

Shore, R. (1997). *Rethinking the brain: New insights into early development.* New York: Families and Work Institute.

Tahiri-Alaoui, A., Gill, A.C., Disterer, P., et al. (2004). Methionine 129 variant of human prion protein oligomerizes more rapidly than the valine 129 variant: Implications for disease susceptibility to Creutzfeldt-Jakob disease. *Journal of Biological Chemistry, 279,* 31390–31397.

Tan, E.C., & Lai, P.S. (2005). Molecular diagnosis of neurogenetic disorders involving trinucleotide repeat expansions. *Expert Review of Molecular Diagnostics, 5,* 101–109.

Taylor, R.W., & Turnbull, D.M. (2005). Mitochondrial DNA mutations in human disease. *Nature Reviews: Genetics, 6,* 389–402.

Terry, L.M., & Campbell, A. (2004). Protecting the interests of the child bone marrow donor. *Medicine and Law, 23,* 805–819.

Thompson, R.A. (2001). Development in the first years of life. *The Future of Children, 11,* 20–33.

Towns, C.R., & Jones, D.G. (2004). Stem cells, embryos, and the environment: A context for both science and ethics. *Journal of Medical Ethics, 30,* 410–413.

University of Maryland Medical Center. (2002). *Fetal development.* Retrieved January 19, 2006, from http://www.umm.edu/ency/article/002398.htm

U.S. Department of Energy, Office of Science Human Genome Program. (2004). *Human Genome Project information.* Retrieved February 28, 2005, from http://www.ornl.gov/sci/techresources/Human_Genome/home.shtml

The Visible Embryo. (n.d.). Retrieved November 8, 2005 from http://www.visembryo.com

Waddington, S.N., Kramer, M.G., Hernandez-Alcoceba, et al. (2005). In utero gene therapy: Current challenges and perspectives. *Molecular Therapy, 11*(5), 661–676.

Watson, J. (2000, July 3). The double helix revisited: The man who launched the Human Genome Project celebrates its success. *Time, 156,* 30.

Watson, J.D. (1991). The human genome initiative: A statement of need. *Hospital Practice (Office Edition.), 26*(10), 69–73.

Watson, J.D., & Crick, F.H. (1953a). Genetical implications of the structure of deoxyribonucleic acid. *Nature, 171,* 964-967.

Watson, J.D., & Crick, F.H. (1953b). Molecular structure of nucleic acids: A structure for deoxyribose nucleic acid. *Nature, 171,* 737–738.

Wheeler, M.B. (2003). Production of transgenic livestock: Promise fulfilled. *Journal of Animal Science, 81*(Suppl. 3), 32–37.

Ying, S.Y., & Lin, S.L. (2005). Intronic microRNAs. *Biochemical and Biophysical Research Communications, 326,* 515–520.

8

Introduction to the Nervous Systems

William A. MacKay and Maire Percy

WHAT YOU WILL LEARN ABOUT IN THIS CHAPTER

- The nervous systems
- Brain function and structure
- Future directions in brain and neuroscience research

Human life is unique. This is, to a very large extent, the result of the way in which the human brain and sensory organs, collectively referred to as the *nervous systems,* have evolved. The search to understand how the human nervous systems work has resulted in an unprecedented explosion of knowledge. At the same time, researchers are beginning to understand the neurobiological basis of different intellectual and developmental disabilities and how factors in the environment and life experiences can affect brain development and function. In turn, such knowledge is leading to better interventions and treatments for intellectual and developmental disabilities, neurodegenerative disorders, and mental health problems, as well as better educational strategies, programs, practices, and policies. The purpose of this chapter is to provide a background for understanding the involvement of the nervous systems in the intellectual and developmental disabilities discussed in other chapters in this book.

THE NERVOUS SYSTEMS

As explained in other chapters in this book, many intellectual and developmental disabilities are now known to result from problems with, or insults to, the developing or mature brain or the sensory organs. In turn, such abnormalities result in deficits in many areas of day-to-day functioning, including communication, learning, behavior, and motor ability. Such problems may involve the central nervous system (CNS), the peripheral nervous system (PNS), or both. For any intellectual or developmental disability, it is important to conduct tests that determine which part of the nervous system is affected. With such knowledge, more effective interventions can be designed.

The authors thank Tom Dearie for rendering high-resolution reproductions of the artwork for certain figures in this chapter.

Central Nervous System

The CNS is divided into two parts: the brain and the spinal cord. In addition to the protection afforded by the skull and vertebrae of the spinal column, the meninges (the set of membranes covering the surface of the brain and spinal cord) protect and nourish the CNS. Fluid in the brain and spinal cord called cerebrospinal fluid (CSF) supports and cushions these tissues from trauma. CSF is made by the choroid plexus, a ribbon of tissue that is highly vascularized (i.e., contains a lot of blood vessels) and lines the ventricles (spaces) of the brain (see Figure 8.1 for an illustration of the ventricles). The volume of CSF is normally constant at about 215 milliliters (ml), although it is continually secreted at a rate of approximately 550 ml per day. To prevent buildup of intracranial pressure (pressure inside the skull), the CSF flows out of the fourth ventricle into the subarachnoid space (the area under the arachnoid mater, which is the middle membrane of the brain meninges) to eventually drain either into the venous or lymphatic system. CSF is made by filtration, diffusion, and active transport of substances from the blood. It washes away waste products of metabolism, drugs, and other substances that may gain access to the brain from the blood. CSF is clear and colorless; it contains only a few lymphocytes (white blood cells), small amounts of protein, glucose, potassium, and relatively large amounts of sodium chloride (salt). When the intracranial pressure is increased (e.g., as a result of brain injury, hydrocephalus, or a brain tumor), this can cause changes in behavior, agitation, confusion, decreased response, and coma.

Analysis of the CSF can give clues in cases of CNS disease. Total protein is increased in infections and viral diseases, and CSF cell counts increase in cases of meningitis (inflammation of the meninges) or encephalitis (infections of the brain) (see Chapter 15 for more information).

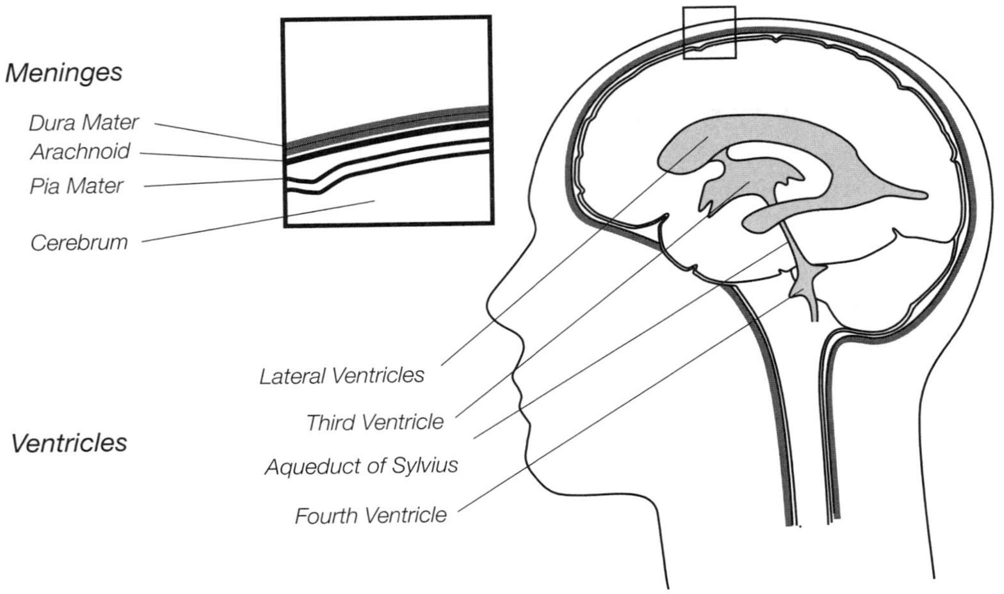

Figure 8.1. Meninges and ventricles of the brain. (*Illustration:* Copyright © 2007 by Tom Dearie, ThreeSixtyCreative; reprinted by permission.)

The brain is the highest or supervisory center of the nervous system. A vital organ, its survival depends on receiving (via the circulation of blood) an adequate supply of fuel (mainly glucose), other nutrients, and oxygen. It is supplied with blood anteriorly by the internal carotid arteries, which branch and become the anterior and middle cerebral arteries, and posteriorly by the vertebral arteries, which merge to become the basilar artery. These arteries are joined together by smaller connections to form the Circle of Willis (see Figure 8.2; see also the North Harris College Biology Department web site—http://science.nhmccd.edu/biol/cardio/circle.htm—for an animation of blood flow through the Circle of Willis). The small arteries of the Circle of Willis are a frequent site of infarction (area of coagulated tissue death due to a local obstruction of circulation). Reduced blood flow in the cerebral arteries radiating out from the Circle of Willis is a common cause of stroke (death of brain cells in a focal zone due to either infarction or hemorrhage). Venous drainage occurs via deep veins and sinuses that finally drain into the internal jugular veins. In a healthy brain, a homeostatic mechanism known as autoregulation allows blood flow to stay constant even when physiologic conditions change radically. However, seriously decreased cardiac output due to heart failure or decreased blood volume compromises cerebral blood flow—a factor that may contribute to the development of dementia, including Alzheimer's disease (see Chapter 44 for more information).

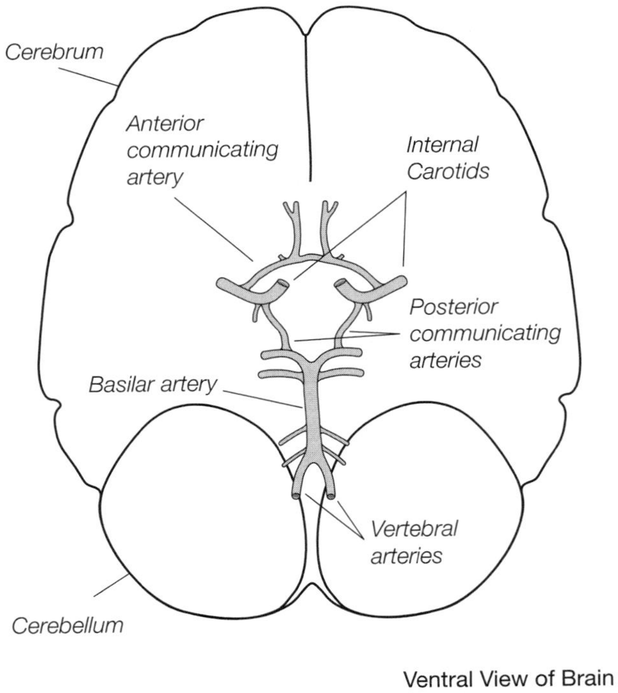

Figure 8.2. Circle of Willis. (*Illustration:* Copyright © 2007 by Tom Dearie, ThreeSixtyCreative; reprinted by permission.)

The average adult human brain weighs 1.3 kilograms (kg)–1.4 kg (approximately 3 pounds). It contains approximately 100 billion nerve cells (neurons) and trillions of three different types of nonneural support cells of ectodermal origin called glia. Microglia are the macrophages (phagocytic cells) of the brain. Astrocytes provide nutritional support to neurons, especially lactate and glutamine molecules. Moreover, they are thought to communicate with neurons and affect their ability to signal with each other. Oligodendrocytes encircle the axons of many neurons to form myelin sheaths in the white matter. With microglia, they form the perineuronal satellites in the gray matter.

Gray matter refers to brain tissue that is composed of the bodies of nerve cells (neurons) and the initial parts of the processes (axons and dendrites) that emerge from the neurons. Information processing takes place in the gray matter. The nerve impulses for information transmission throughout the nervous systems are initiated here and then are sent away to specific targets via axons that make up the white matter. White matter is thereby responsible for information transmission. Curiously, intelligence in males tends to correlate to the amount of gray matter in specific areas of the cerebral cortex, whereas intelligence in females correlates better to specific volumes of white matter (Haier et al., 2005).

The spinal cord is the main information pathway connecting the brain and PNS. It is comprised largely of white matter arranged in tracts of longitudinal fibers around a central core of gray matter; this central core of gray matter surrounds a small, longitudinal canal continuous with the ventricles of the brain that holds the CSF. The spinal cord is approximately 43 centimeters (cm) long in adult women and 45 cm long in adult men and weighs approximately 35 grams (g)–40 g (Gray, 1918). (*General sources:* Bear, Connors, & Paradiso, 2001; Matthews, 2001.)

Peripheral Nervous System

The PNS is divided into three parts: the somatic nervous system, the autonomic nervous system, and the enteric nervous system of the gut. The somatic nervous system is comprised of the afferent nerve network, which includes most sensory nerves leading to the spinal cord and brain, and the efferent nerve network, which includes all motor nerves leading from the brain and spinal cord to the muscles. (*Afferent* means carrying impulses toward the CNS; *efferent* means leading away.) In general, the somatic system mediates sensation and all body movement. The brain typically processes the information from the afferent network and responds through the efferent nerve network to elicit a response in the muscles. Sometimes, however, the brain does not fully process the information before a reflex arc within the spinal cord triggers a movement. Reflex arcs coordinate stereotyped reactions that are either protective in dangerous situations or regulatory. The term *regulatory* refers to the maintenance of a specific motoric function, be it postural balance, finger grip, or eye position. Certain stimuli, such as touching a hot surface, stimulate activity in a specific reflex arc. Nerve impulses travel up the afferent nerve, through several interneurons in the spinal cord, to eventually activate selected motor (efferent) neurons. (Interneurons are connector neurons that process signals from one or more sensory neurons and relay signals to motor neurons.) Finally, the reflex signal travels down the appropriate efferent nerves to jerk the hand away from the hot surface. This automatic response system results in reactions that are much quicker than is possible with consciously willed responses, and better scaled to the magnitude of the stimulus.

The autonomic nervous system controls smooth muscles, both in viscera (internal organs) and in blood vessels, and it controls the secretion of glands. It is involved in functions such as blood pressure, heart rate, breathing, digestion, excretion, body temperature, and copulation. The effector channels of the autonomic system are classified as either sympathetic or parasympathetic. The sympathetic system prepares the body for sudden stresses. The parasympathetic prepares the body for rest and helps the digestive tract to work. Efferents of the sympathetic nervous system originate in the thoracic segments of the spinal cord and are distributed to various parts of the body via the sympathetic chain of ganglia on either side of the vertebral column. (The term *ganglia* refers to PNS structures containing a collection of nerve cell bodies.) Sympathetic nerves also contain sensory afferents conveying metabolic information from internal organs to the CNS. Efferents of the parasympathetic nervous system originate in the brainstem and in the lowest segments of the spinal cord. The brainstem refers to the lower extension of the brain where it connects to the spinal cord. Neurological functions located here include those necessary for survival (e.g., breathing, digestion, heart rate, and blood pressure) and for arousal (being awake and alert). Again, sensory afferents mingle with efferents in parasympathetic nerves. For example, the large vagus nerve conveys information about blood pressure, levels of carbon dioxide in the blood, and the amount of food in the stomach. The sympathetic nervous system prepares the body for activities associated with fight or flight; it prepares for stressful events ranging from facing a violent confrontation to running from danger. In the fight-or-flight reaction, adrenalin and noradrenalin (hormones released by the medulla of the two adrenal glands) cause various parts of the body to respond in much the same way as the sympathetic nervous system. Because adrenalin and noradrenalin are released into the blood stream, they continue to exert effects after a stressful event has stopped. In the fight-or-flight reaction, blood sugar is increased, extra red blood cells are released from the spleen, peripheral blood vessels constrict, the pulse quickens, blood pressure elevates, and digestion stops. Parasympathetic function is largely nutritive, restorative, and restful; it will bring the body back from any emergency state that the sympathetic nervous system creates.

As noted previously, the sympathetic and parasympathetic systems are structurally distinct entities. Some functions of these two systems oppose one another—as in a push–pull balancing act—but other functions are complementary in nature (see Table 8.1).

Reflexes also operate within the autonomic nervous system, generally to regulate homeostatic functions such as blood pressure or body temperature. Moreover, many afferents within autonomic nerves transmit pain information. In the CNS, information about organ pain often converges with pain signals from surface areas of the body. As a result, the source of the information sometimes gets confused. This is called referred pain. One example is the referred pain that some people feel in the shoulders and arms when they are having a heart attack.

The autonomic nervous system influences all aspects of digestion including gut motility, ion transport associated with secretion and absorption, and gastrointestinal blood flow. Some of the control of the gastrointestinal system results from the feedback of digestive system hormones acting both on vagal afferents and directly on the CNS. However, the gastrointestinal tract also has its own, local nervous system referred to as the enteric nervous system (Grundy & Schemann, 2005).

The enteric nervous system contains as many neurons as the spinal cord. It is primarily composed of two networks of neurons extending from the esophagus to the anus, both of which are imbedded in the wall of the digestive tract and innervate the gastrointestinal muscles, pancreas, and gall bladder (i.e., viscera). Disorders of the gastrointestinal system, such as celiac disease and Helicobacter infection (see Chapter 10 for more information) or the intestinal inflammation that is common in people with autism, must involve the enteric nervous system. Feeling sick to the stomach or "having butterflies" when nervous are effects of a psychological disturbance to the enteric nervous system. (*General sources:* Bear et al., 2001; Matthews, 2001.)

Table 8.1. Some contrasting and complementary effects of sympathetic and parasympathetic arousal

Sympathetic nervous system	Parasympathetic nervous system
Pupil dilation and opening of the eyelids	Pupil constriction
Stimulation of the sweat glands	Activation of the salivary glands
Constriction of blood vessels in the skin and gut	Promotion of urination
Increase of the heart rate	Decrease of the heart rate
Dilation of the bronchial tubes	Constriction of the bronchial tubes
Inhibition of the secretions in the digestive system	Stimulation of intestinal movement and secretions of the stomach
Ejaculation of semen	Penile erection

BRAIN FUNCTION AND STRUCTURE

There are various elements of brain function and structure. These are explored in the following sections.

Cells of the Brain and Synapses

The brain is the most complex organ of the body. The various parts of the brain work together to enable perception and thoughts and to coordinate appropriate behaviors and body maintenance. The functional units of the brain are nerve cells or neurons (which carry electrochemical signals) and the neuroglia that perform other functions such as insulation; infection-fighting; and "housekeeping" duties such as maintaining ionic balance, and transfer of nutrients between brain capillaries and neurons. There are approximately 100 billion neurons in the human brain. The anatomical and biochemical connections between neurons are called synapses. There are two types of synapses: chemical and electrical. At chemical synapses, communication between two cells is mediated by specialized chemical molecules, or neurotransmitters (see the Neurotransmitters section later in this chapter). At electrical synapses, structures called gap junctions join cells, and signals are transmitted via ion currents without involvement of neurotransmitters. Specialized membranes of nerve cell axons enable them to conduct electrical impulses over long distances. The conduction of electrical impulses depends on the ability of axonal membranes to undergo rapid changes in permeability to small, positively charged ions. Conduction of impulses along axonal membranes consumes relatively little energy when compared with synaptic signal transmission. The needed energy is largely derived from the aerobic metabolism of lactate and glutamine, supplied to neurons by astroglia. In turn, the astroglia are ultimately dependent on glucose from the bloodstream. Consequently, the brain is very sensitive to disruption of a regular supply of glucose and of oxygen. Interference with any major metabolic system in the brain can deprive it of essential nutrients and other regulators that are required for its function (Restak, 1999). Therefore, it is not surprising that inborn errors of metabolism, or certain types of genetic disorders, very often result in intellectual or developmental disability associated with brain dysfunction. In an infant, the developing brain is continually forming and reforming synapses. A synaptic connection is preferentially made between neurons that are simultaneously active. When frequently stimulated, synapses become stronger. Signaling chemicals are sent out that make the connections stronger and more permanent. A diagram of a neuron and a chemical synapse is given in Figure 8.3. A cross-section of the human brain showing interconnections between neurons is shown in Figure 8.4.

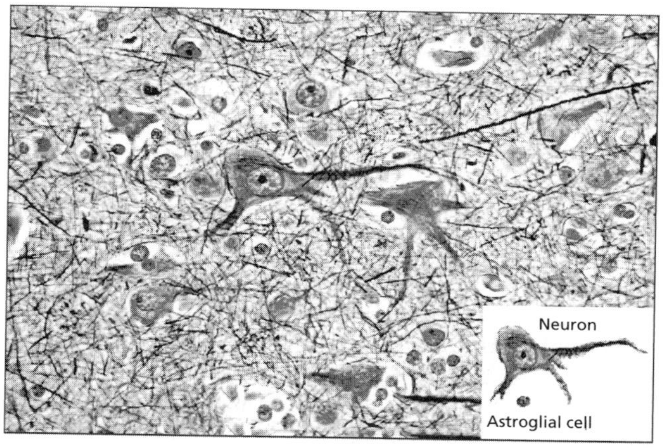

Figure 8.4. Cross-section of the cortex (outer region) of the human brain showing interconnections between neurons (the neuronal network). In this photograph, a small section of a normal human brain cortex has been fixed and stained with Bielschowsky silver stain. The large triangular cells with an oval nucleus are the neurons. The neurons are connected to one another by an intricate network of long processes (dendrites and axons, see Figure 8.3). Small nonneuronal cells are either astrocytes or microglia. (*Source:* Percy, Lewkis, & Brown, 2003. Photograph kindly provided by Dr. Catherine Bergeron, Centre for Research in Neurogenerative Disease, University of Toronto.)

Neurotransmitters

Neurotransmitters are classified into two broad categories depending on the effects that they trigger when they bind to specific receptors on the post-synaptic cell. First, at ionotropic synapses, transmitter–receptor binding causes the opening of diffusion channels through the postsynaptic membrane of a target neuron. Ion diffusion through the open channels then generates a postsynaptic potential, which may be either excitatory or inhibitory, depending on the properties of the channel. An electrical impulse is generated in the postsynaptic neuron if there is sufficient summation of the excitatory synaptic potentials. Ionotropic transmitters are glutamate, gamma aminobutyric acid (GABA), glycine, acetylcholine, and serotonin. Glutamate is the main excitatory neurotransmitter; GABA is the main inhibitory transmitter. Second, these same transmitters and many others—including catecholamines, peptides, and fatty acid amides—can bind to metabotropic receptors. In this case, transmitter–receptor binding initiates a cascade of enzyme activations or deactivations in the postsynaptic neuron that result in changes in the levels of 'second messenger' molecules and subsequently other signaling agents. The influence of the metabolic cascade lasts many minutes or longer. In general, this process has a modulatory effect, suppressing or enhancing adjacent ionotropic transmission. Some metabotropic transmitters are gases, such as nitric oxide, which cannot be stored in vesicles. Instead they are synthesized when an electrical impulse arrives at the end of the axon, and then they promptly diffuse everywhere in the vicinity. (*General sources:* Bear et al., 2001; Matthews, 2001.)

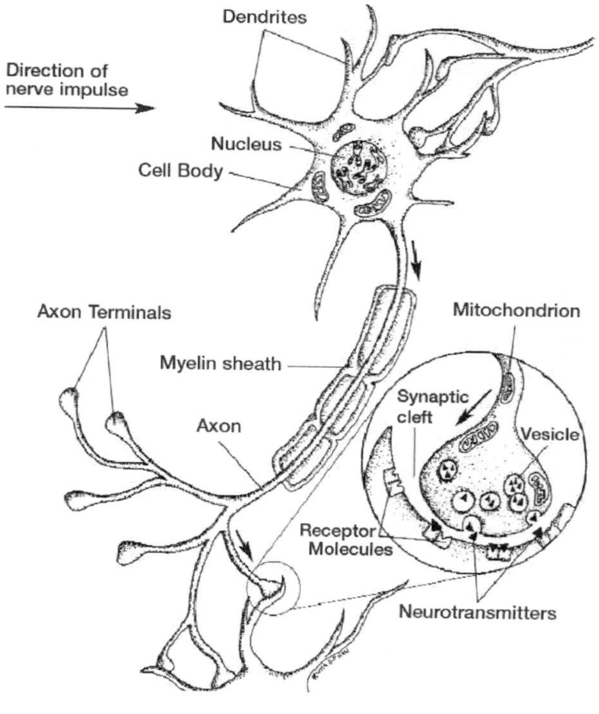

Figure 8.3. Diagrammatic representation of a neuron and a chemical synapse. Neurons are specialized cells in the brain. If a single neuron is magnified approximately 1,000 times, it looks like an uprooted tree. The "branches" at one end of the neuron are dendrites, and the long "trunk" is the axon. Dendrites and axons connect with neighboring cells. Dendrites receive signals from other cells. Axons pass signals on to other cells. The transfer of signals from axons to dendrites occurs at specialized junctions, or synapses. The narrow gap between an axon terminal and a dendrite is called the *synaptic cleft.* A neuron signals information by transmitting electrical impulses along its axon. When impulses reach the end of the axon, they trigger the release of neurotransmitters that are stored in pouches called vesicles. The neurotransmitters released from vesicles rapidly diffuse across the synaptic cleft and bind to receptor molecules in the postsynaptic membrane of the dendrite. (*Source:* Percy, Lewkis, & Brown, 2003. Diagram kindly provided by Rivka Birkan and Simon Wong.)

Parts of the Brain

The brain has both external and internal parts. These are described next.

External Structure The brainstem provides the connection between the brain and the spinal cord. It controls many vital and involuntary body functions such as blood pressure, breathing, and pulse; coordinates posture and locomotion; and regulates the level of consciousness. The cerebellum is a structure that greatly improves the fine temporal control of all body movements, from postural balance to speech and manual skills.

Figure 8.5 illustrates the lobes of the brain. These include the frontal lobes, parietal lobes, temporal lobes, occipital lobes, and the olfactory bulbs. The frontal lobes control personality and expression of emotion, motivation, and initiation, as well as inhibit an inappropriate or impulsive action. They store information and affect a person's ability to concentrate, plan strategically, and think in abstract terms. The parietal lobes control a person's awareness of his or her body parts and his or her position in space. In addition, they mediate physical sensations such as touch, kinesthesia (sense of body posture and movement), temperature, and pain. The temporal lobes embody memory, intellectual abilities, and impulse control. They also process visual and auditory input, making these lobes essential for object and color recognition, language comprehension, and music appreciation. The occipital lobes are the site of entry-level processing of visual information. This information is transmitted to the inferior temporal lobes for object recognition (ventral visual pathway) and to the parietal lobes for recognition of spatial relationships and direction (dorsal visual pathway). The olfactory bulbs (not shown in the diagram) are narrow extensions from the undersurface of the frontal lobes, one on each side of the mid-line. Neurogenesis (creation of new neurons) in the adult brain takes place continually in the olfactory bulbs. (*General source:* Bear et al., 2001.)

Inner Structure Figure 8.6 shows the brain's inner structure. The amygdala is intimately connected with the hypothalamus, the hippocampus, and the cingulated gyrus (on the medial surface of the cerebral cortex), structures that are part of the limbic system, which is primarily responsible for emotion. The amygdala plays an important role in motivation and emotional behavior. (For more information on the limbic system, see the Before Birth to the Second Year of Life section.)

The basal ganglia are large structures toward the center of the brain that surround the thalamus. The basal ganglia have both limbic and motor functions. They participate in making decisions, integrating feelings, forming habits, and linking motor elements into a habitual routine. They are involved with setting the body's idle or anxiety level. In addition, the basal gan-

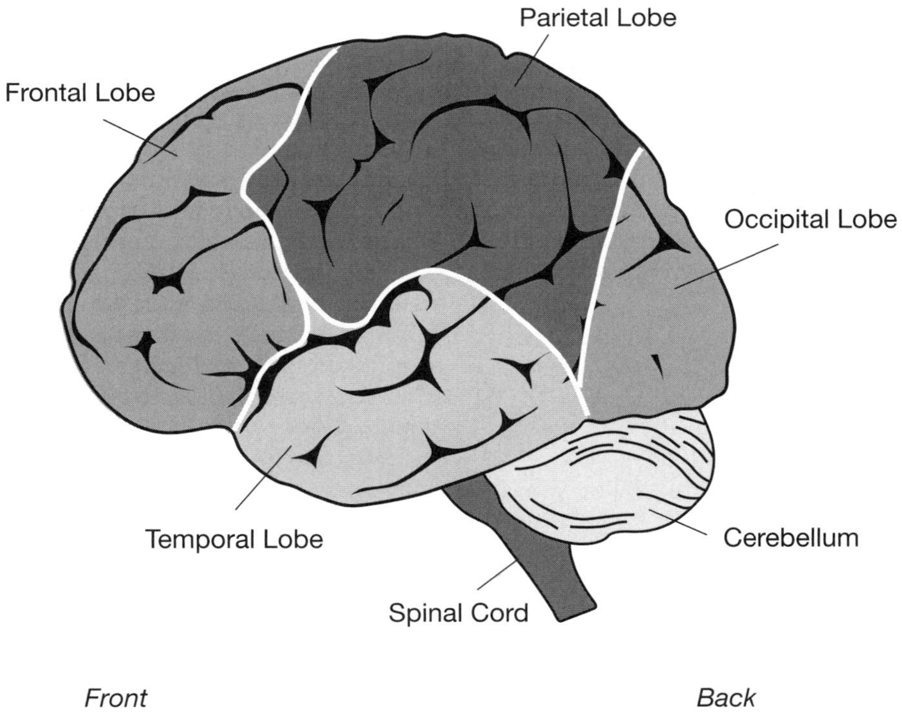

Figure 8.5. Major subdivisions of the cerebral cortex, p. 45, *Understanding the Brain—Towards a New Learning Science,* © OECD 2002 (available at http://www.oecd.org/dataoecd/50/25/15355617.gif); reprinted by permission.

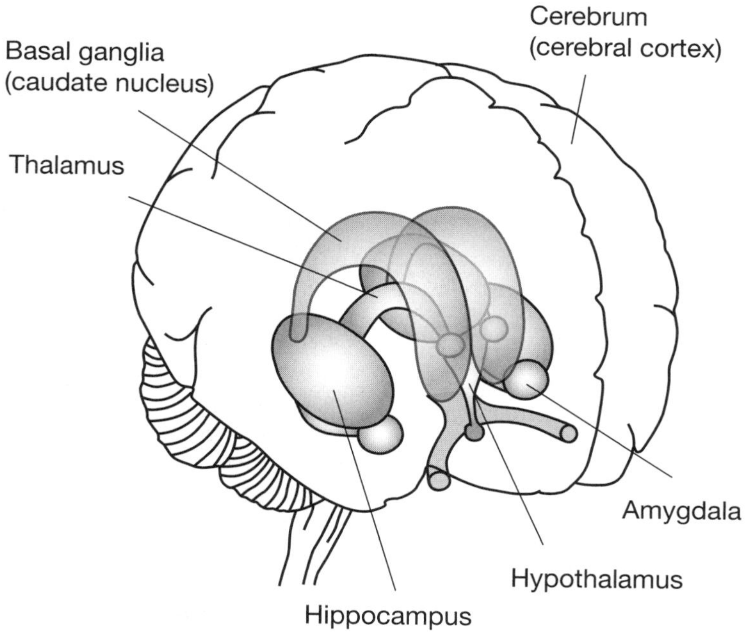

Figure 8.6. Inner structure of the human brain, including limbic system, p. 57, *Understanding the Brain—Towards a New Learning Science,* © OECD 2002 (available at http://www.oecd.org/dataoecd/50/26/15355602.gif); reprinted by permission.

glia help to modulate motivation and are likely involved with feelings of pleasure and ecstasy. Closely associated with the basal ganglia is a small region in the upper brain stem known as the substantia nigra ("black substance"). It contains neurons that produce and release dopamine, a neurotransmitter that acts within the basal ganglia to facilitate both movement-related and reward-related signals.

The cerebral cortex is the highest brain part in terms of abstraction and human-unique aspects. Phylogenetically, it is the most recent addition to the brain, and in human development, it is the last brain area to fully mature. It governs thoughts, senses, and skilled body motion. It consists of two (left and right) highly folded sheets of gray matter, called hemispheres. Each hemisphere is divided into four parts: the temporal, frontal, parietal, and occipital lobes.

The hippocampus forms the medial edge of the temporal lobe and is essential for memory and learning. Half is situated in the right hemisphere and half in the left. The hippocampus contains the dentate gyrus, one of two brain regions in which neurogenesis is known to take place in adults. The hippocampus is a component of the limbic system as well.

The hypothalamus is located just above the brainstem. It oversees the endocrine system to regulate thirst, hunger, body temperature, sleep, moods, sex drive, and the release of hormones from various glands. The hypothalamus controls the hypothalamic–pituitary–adrenal (HPA) axis (for more details, see the Hypothalamic–Pituitary–Adrenal Axis and Stress section). In general, the hypothalamus communicates with the body via the autonomic nervous system and the pituitary gland (or "master gland"), which produces hormones that are important in regulating growth and metabolism. The hypothalamus is also part of the limbic system, the network mediating emotional experience.

The thalamus is located in the center of the brain, beneath the cerebral hemispheres and next to the third ventricle. It is formed of gray matter and can be thought of as a processing station for nerve impulses being sent to the cerebral cortex or basal ganglia. (*General source:* Bear et al., 2001.)

Effects of Developmental Stage on Brain Structure and Function

Since the mid-1990s, evidence from genetic research and studies of the brain, especially brain imaging (see the Measuring Brain Activity and Structure section), has shown that many intellectual and developmental disabilities, including learning difficulties, have a neurobiological basis. This means that such disabilities result from changes in the structure or function of the brain or both. Compared with other organs, the human brain develops over a long period of time.

Before Birth to the Second Year of Life Development begins in the first weeks after conception, with most of the basic brain structure completed before birth. The brain is very vulnerable to environmental changes in early pregnancy and during the brain growth spurt that begins in the last trimester of pregnancy and extends to the end of the second year in life. Factors such as lack of oxygen, lack of essential fatty acids or folic acid and other vital nutrients, infections, drugs, toxins (including maternal use of alcohol), stress, and lack of stimulation can particularly affect normal development of the brain. Developing fetuses and babies are much more vulnerable to toxins than adults for the following reasons:

- Their brains are developing rapidly.
- Chemical exposures have a bigger effect on fetuses and babies than on adults simply because of body size difference.
- Their blood–brain barriers are not mature and allow substances to enter the CNS that adult brains would exclude.
- Their systems for detoxifying and excreting chemicals are not fully developed.
- They have more years than adults during which a problem caused by an exposure can develop.

(*General sources:* Environmental Working Group, 2005; Matthews, 2000; Restak, 1999; see also Center for Global Research and Education on Environment and Health [CGREEH], 2005, for additional information about chemical exposures hazardous to human health.)

A child's brain is characterized by plasticity. *Plasticity* means that connections between neurons can form, strengthen, weaken, or disappear, depending on the nature and duration of environmental and other experiences. Between 10 and 18 months, a baby's emotions begin to develop. Emotion involves the entire nervous system, but two parts of the nervous system are particularly important for emotion: the limbic system (see the Inner Structure section) and the autonomic nervous system (see the preceding Peripheral Nervous System section). The limbic system not only plays an important role in emotional life and how people respond to stress but it also is important in the formation of memories. Emotion and sensory perception (smelling, hearing, seeing, feeling, and tasting) are vital for survival, growth, development, and the experience of bodily pleasure. Learning between the ages of 3 and 10 years plays a key role in establishing connections in the child's brain. Positive experiences affect brain development in a positive way. Conversely, both acute and chronic stress can adversely affect brain development and function. Severe stress, particularly that which lasts a long time, can adversely affect a child's brain development and functioning when he or she becomes an adult. (*General sources:* Als et al., 2003; Bear et al., 2001; DeBord, 1997; Eisenberg, 1999; Greenspan, 1997; Ito, 2004; Lewis, 2004; Restak, 1999; Shore, 1997; Smith, 2004.)

Adolescence Puberty is said to be as critical a time for typical brain development as are the growth spurts in the fetal or baby brain. Puberty is marked by striking changes in neuroendocrine function. In particular, levels of steroidal gonadal hormones increase markedly. These steroidal hormones have profound effects on the structure and function of the maturing nervous system, and they influence the development of various steroid-dependent behaviors characteristic of adulthood (e.g., sexuality). They also affect stress reactivity. Changes in neuronal circuitry in adolescence involve steroid hormone-induced sculpting of certain synapses and the pruning of others. Because the areas of the brain involved in emotion mature earlier than those involved in judgment and reasoning, adolescents tend to make decisions more impulsively than adults, who balance emotion with reason and use both abilities to reach decisions. (*General sources:* Restak, 1999; Romeo, 2005; Sisk & Foster, 2004.)

Aging The brain in older individuals is characterized by challenges with memory, and more time is needed to learn new information. Yet, intelligence, abstract thinking, and verbal expression tend to remain the same with age. Life experiences provide older people with wisdom, making them more rational and flexible. Lifestyle is thought to be very important in the preservation of memory with aging. Mental and physical exercise promote increased blood circulation to the brain, stimulate the production of molecules that keep neurons healthy and disease resistant, and maintain important synaptic connections. Good nutrition also is extremely important, especially a rich and varied supply of antioxidants. (*General sources:* Allen, Bruss, & Damasio, 2005; Bengmark, 2006; Grady & Craik, 2000; Hess, 2005; Restak, 1999.)

The Right Brain and the Left Brain

The two hemispheres of the cerebral cortex are linked by the corpus callosum, the band of white matter through which the hemispheres communicate and coordinate. Generally, the right hemisphere controls the left side of the body and the left hemisphere controls the right side. When the left brain has been damaged, some of the lost functions can be taken over by the right brain (Gazzaniga, 2005). Nevertheless, the two hemispheres have some separate specializations. The left hemisphere predominates in reasoning ability (i.e., the detailed sequential thinking common in science and mathematics), and written and spoken language. In contrast, the right hemisphere predominates in spatial or integrative tasks, insight, imagination, and appreciation of art and music. Generally speaking, the left brain excels at information processing based on fine distinctions in temporal order and the right brain tends to ignore precise timing in favor of details regarding how information is grouped together.

The Male Brain and the Female Brain

There has been much controversy as to whether there are structural and functional differences between the brain in males and females. A few hypothalamic centers concerned with sex hormones are clearly different. Although there are no significant differences in general intelligence between males and females, there is evidence that women have more white matter and men more gray matter correlated to intellectual skill. It has been suggested that these differences may help to explain why men tend to be better in tasks requiring local processing and enhanced systemizing (e.g., mathematics), whereas women tend to excel at integrating and assimilating information as required for empathy and language proficiency. In a study by Haier et al. (2005), 84% of gray matter correlated to intelligence was found in the frontal region in women, as compared to 45% in men. In contrast, 86% of white matter correlated to intelligence was found in the frontal region in women, as compared with 0% in men. The more frontally focused basis of intelligence processing in women may explain why brain injuries affecting the frontal lobes tend to be more detrimental to cognitive performance in women than in men. (*General sources:* Haier et al., 2005; Legato, 2005.)

Relationship Between Brain Changes and Intellectual and Developmental Disabilities

Because the developing human brain is much more vulnerable to toxic insult than the mature brain, this insult affects not only those processes upon which development is dependent but also some processes that are programmed to start later. Research on the role of neurotoxicants as factors in intellectual and developmental disabilities is growing. In one study by the Environmental Working Group (2005), 285 environmental toxins were found in the blood of newborn babies. Of these, 217 were known neurotoxins. In order to develop properly, the brain must be well-fed and protected from neurotoxicants. Injury to the brain also may markedly affect brain development, or function, or both. For example, embryonic or fetal exposure to alcohol can result in injury to cells and, in turn, a markedly smaller brain and brain development that is affected in many different ways. Brain injury may result from traumatic injuries to tissue from an external impact to the head, from nontraumatic injuries caused by any change in the supply of blood or oxygen that the brain receives, or from tumors. Injury to the brain can affect function and development. See Chapters 15 and 20 for more information about traumatic brain injury.

Aberrations of development that affect brain morphology, circuitry, or both and that involve the serotonergic system (regions of the brain that release or respond to the neurotransmitter serotonin) may account for morphological changes in the frontal lobes, hippocampus, temporal lobes, amygdala, and cerebellum of children with autism (Whitaker-Azmitia, 2005). A theory has been proposed that autism represents an extreme of the male pattern of brain structure and function (impaired empathizing and enhanced systemizing). It has been proposed that high levels of testosterone present in the amniotic fluid—as the result of genetic or environmental factors or both—strengthen effects of maternal exposure to environmental mercury, which is present, for example, in certain types of fish (Baron-Cohen, Knickmeyer, & Belmonte, 2005; Geier & Geier, 2005).

Neurological aberrations of development may also account for changes in frontal–striatal circuitry and problems in executive functioning in people with attention-deficit/hyperactivity disorder (Willis & Weiler, 2005). They may also be responsible for brain changes that are characteristic of schizophrenia, Williams syndrome, fetal alcohol syndrome, and numerous other disorders (Smith, 2004; Thompson et al., 2005).

Systems and Processes Affecting Brain Development and Function

The blood–brain barrier, as well as the HPA axis and stress, affect brain development and function. Each topic is explored next.

Blood–Brain Barrier Typical brain function depends on the integrity of the so-called blood–brain barrier (BBB; Francis et al., 2003; see Figure 8.7). The BBB is made of the closely knit sheets of endothelial cells that form the walls of blood vessels in the brain. The BBB separates the brain and surrounding tissues that contain neurons, astrocytes, and microglia from circulating blood; tightly regulates the transport of nutrients and signaling molecules into the brain; and maintains proper biochemical conditions for normal brain function. It normally blocks circulating bacteria and viruses (pathogens) from entering the brain and thus acts as a sentry to defend against infection. If a pathogen gains entry to the endothelial cells, genes are activated that produce protein factors that recruit white blood cells to the brain to fight the infection. **Group B *Streptococcus*** (Doran, Liu, & Nizet, 2003) and HIV (McArthur, 2004) are two pathogens that manage

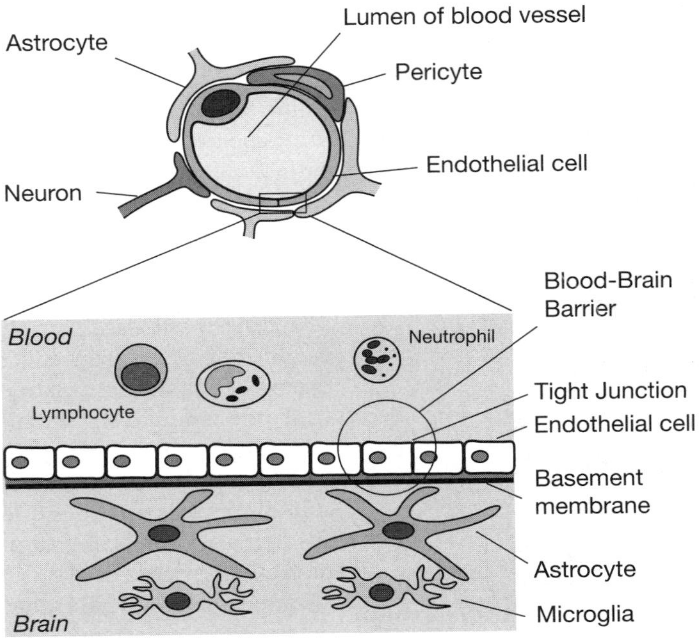

Figure 8.7. The blood–brain barrier. (From Francis, K., van Beek, J., Canova, C., et al. [2003, May 23]. Innate immunity and brain inflammation: The key role of complement. *Expert Reviews in Molecular Medicine,* 3. Reprinted with the permission of Cambridge University Press.

to gain access to the BBB. The former results in meningitis, which can result in intellectual disability; the latter can lead to dementia and different types of neuropathy. The BBB of fetuses and babies are not fully formed and may explain in part why their brains are so vulnerable to the effects of toxic substances. Some types of intellectual or developmental disability may result. See Matthews (2001) for more information on the BBB.

Hypothalamic–Pituitary–Adrenal Axis and Stress The HPA axis (see Figure 8.8) is a communication system between the hypothalamus and pituitary gland, which are in the brain, and the adrenal glands, which are located just above the kidneys. Various types of stress (psychological, emotional, and physical—including the tissue injury associated with infection, hypoglycemia, cold exposure, and pain) activate the HPA axis in the CNS and the sympathetic nervous system in the PNS. As explained at the end of this section, there is increasing evidence that abnormal functioning of the HPA axis, resulting from experiencing severe stress prenatally or postnatally, is involved in different types of intellectual and developmental disabilities, in challenging behavior, and in mental illnesses (which generally are more prevalent in people with intellectual disability), as well as in certain physical illnesses such as cardiovascular disease. Conversely, there also is evidence that in an appropriate environment, the HPA axis will develop typically or can be normalized (see also the Psychoneuroimmunology section).

It sometimes is said that chronic stress activates the CNS whereas acute stress activates the PNS, but this segregation is too simplistic. The two function in parallel as a double-barreled neural–endocrine defense system. Activation of the HPA axis may be involved in a complex way with the serotonergic system, which acts functionally as part of the sympathetic nervous system. Proper functioning of the HPA axis plays an important role in development, health, and resistance to stress (see Figure 8.8). Activation of the HPA axis ultimately results in the release of the hormone cortisol from the cortex of the two adrenal glands. Cortisol increases the level of blood sugar and increases the vascular tone, resulting in increased blood pressure. Blood sugar is increased because cortisol promotes the conversion of protein from muscle, glycogen from the liver, and fatty acids from fat tissue into intermediates that get converted into glucose. Cortisol also alters the balance of cells in the blood. It results in lowered numbers of lymphocytes (including T cells), eosinophils, basophils, monocytes, and macrophages but in increased numbers of neutrophils and red blood cells. It also increases the blood hemoglobin level. The paraventricular nucleus of the hypothalamus releases corticotropin-releasing hormone (CRH). In turn, CRH acts on the pituitary gland, which releases adrenocorticotropic hormone (ACTH). ACTH then causes the adrenal cor-

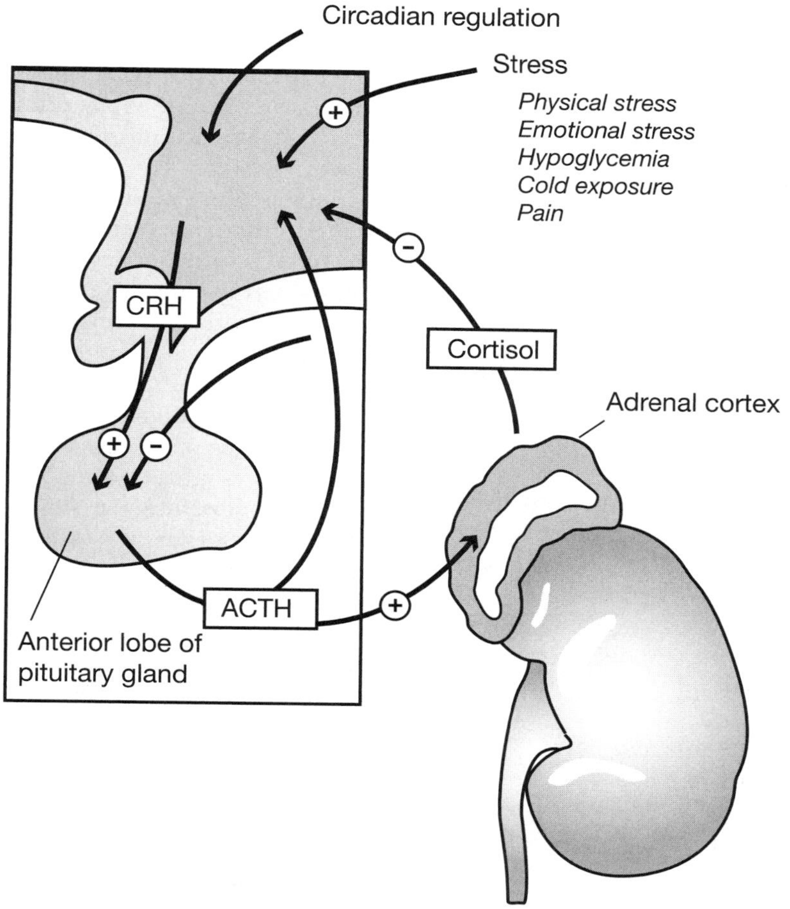

Figure 8.8. The hypothalamic-pituitary-adrenal axis. (From Kirk, L.F., Jr., Hash, R.B., Katner, H.P., et al. (2000). Cushing's disease: clinical manifestations and diagnostic evaluation. *American Family Physician, 62*(5), 1121. Original artwork © 2000 D. Klemm. Reprinted by permission.)

tex to release cortisol. It is this combined system of CRH–ACTH–cortisol release that is referred to as the *HPA axis*. Positive and negative feedback occurs at various sites in the brain to ensure that cortisol production stays within certain limits, depending on the body's requirements. Excessive cortisol production has a negative effect on the immune system, suppressing the production of cytokines (immunoregulatory proteins) such as IL-1, IL-2, IL-6, and TNF-alpha, which are produced by cells of the immune system (lymphocytes, macrophages, monocytes, neutrophils, and—within the CNS—microglia).

Appropriate responsiveness of the stress system to stressors is necessary for a sense of well-being, adequate performance of tasks, and positive social interactions. In contrast, inappropriate responsiveness of the stress system may impair growth and development and may account for a number of endocrine, metabolic, autoimmune, and psychiatric disorders that affect intellect, development, or both. Studies in rodents and nonhuman primates have shown that maternal stress during pregnancy can influence the developing fetus and can result in a delay of motor and cognitive development, impaired adaptation to stressful situations, small birth size, and an increased risk of cardiovascular disease in later life. It is thought that excessive cortisol production in the mother affects the way in which the HPA axis functions in the fetus. Understanding how maternal stress adversely affects fetal development and health outcomes later in life may hold the key to the development of therapeutic interventions aimed at reversing such adverse effects. There also is evidence that stress after birth can alter functioning of the HPA axis. For example, individuals with posttraumatic stress disorder as the result of sexual abuse have enhanced sensitization of the HPA axis (Duval et al., 2004). Furthermore, chronic excess cortisol secretion is believed to damage the hypothalamus and affect the normal sleep–wake cycle. (*General sources:* Andrews & Matthews, 2004; Buitelaar et al., 2003; Matthews, 2000; Matthews, 2001; Van den Bergh et al., 2005.)

FUTURE DIRECTIONS IN BRAIN AND NEUROSCIENCE RESEARCH

As explained in other chapters in this book, millions of people in all countries of the world are affected each year by different types of intellectual and developmental disabilities; impairments of speech, language, and hearing; spinal cord injuries; depressive disorders; and epileptic seizures, as well as by traumatic brain injury, strokes, and neurodegenerative brain diseases such as Alzheimer's disease. Researchers have come a long way in understanding how the brain works and what causes brain and nervous system malfunction and disease. Nonetheless, many mysteries still remain. New advances are being facilitated by the development of powerful microscopes, molecular genetics, brain imaging devices, animal models for human neurodevelopmental and neurological disorders, and the discovery of biological processes that respond to one's environment and affect brain development and function. These provide hope for future treatments and cures. The next sections highlight developments in four areas that promise to provide new insights into typical brain function and the neurodevelopmental or neurological basis of intellectual and developmental disabilities and related brain disorders.

Measuring Brain Activity and Structure

Three different approaches are providing quantitative information about functions of the brain and which areas are involved in different intellectual, developmental, and related disabilities. One very important approach involves the analysis of brain tissue donated to organizations called "brain banks" (International Brain Banking Network, n.d.; Perl et al., 2000). Many different histochemical, biochemical, molecular biological, and biophysical techniques can be applied to brain tissues collected at autopsy. Computer-assisted analysis of brain images taken with powerful microscopes (image analysis) enables the results to be expressed quantitatively.

The second approach involves the application of different neuroimaging techniques (and electrophysiological techniques to study the brain in living persons. One type of neuroimaging technique is a computed tomography (CT) scan, which involves passing a beam of X rays through the head. A computer then reconstructs an image of each slice or brain section, allowing structural abnormalities to be detected. Magnetic resonance imaging (MRI) is a technique that involves the application of a strong magnetic field, pulsed electromagnetic fields, and radiowaves to excite hydrogen nuclei (protons) to produce an image in the region of interest. Functional neuroimaging techniques—including positron emission tomography (PET), single photon emission computed tomography (SPECT), regional cerebral blood flow (rCBF), and functional magnetic resonance imaging (fMRI)—are used to measure brain activity while individuals are engaged in tasks such as reading. PET requires the injection of radioactive materials and involves the acquisition of physiologic images based on the detection of radiation from the emission of positrons. SPECT involves the injection of a radioactive chemical that emits gamma rays. The test differs from a PET scan in that the chemical stays in the blood stream rather than being absorbed by surrounding tissues, thereby limiting the images to areas where blood flows. SPECT scans are cheaper and more readily available than higher resolution PET scans. Similar to a PET scan, rCBF uses an inert radioactive element (usually the gas xenon), which is dissolved in the blood by being inhaled. As the blood flow increases or decreases, the radioactivity serves as a marker of the amount of the blood flow. fMRI is a variant of MRI that relies on the magnetic properties of blood to reveal images of blood flow as it is occurring. Electrophysiological techniques record electrical activity of the brain through electrodes or magnetometers. These techniques include electroencephalograms (EEGs), magnetoencephalograms (MEGs), event related potentials (ERPs), and averaged evoked potentials (AEPs).

The third approach to providing quantitative information involves quantitative neuropsychological assessments. These assessments include a variety of tests of cognitive/intellectual, language, visual-perceptual, scholastic, motor, sensory, and emotional/behavioral abilities and functions.

The coordinated application of all three approaches is proving to be key in identifying physiological, neurocognitive, and neurobehavioral consequences of single-gene mutations associated with intellectual disability. It also is key to identifying the neurobiological basis of cognitive and behavioral differences in males and females, of multifactorial intellectual or developmental disabilities, and of mental illnesses. As an example, Rett syndrome is a neurodevelopmental disorder that affects mainly girls. It results from a mutation in the methyl-CpG-binding protein (MECP2), which encodes a transcriptional repressor (a protein that suppresses the production of certain RNA molecules). Neuropsychological and neurobehavioral testing has shown that children with Rett syndrome have significant intellectual disability and behaviors frequently associated with autism. The application of PET imaging using radioactive fluorodeoxyglucose has shown that glucose uptake differs in specific regions of the brain of individuals with Rett syndrome compared with those in typically developing individuals, individuals with autism, individuals with Down syndrome, and individuals with Alzheimer's disease (Villemagne et al., 2002). Furthermore, studies of postmortem brain tissue from young adult females with Rett syndrome have revealed abnormalities in the density of excitatory (glutamate) and inhibitory (GABA) synaptic receptors (Johnston, Blue, & Naidu, 2005). This information thus supports the hypothesis that Rett syndrome is a genetic disorder associated with intellectual disability that affects the uptake of glucose in specific regions of the brain and the development of synapses, especially synapses that use glutamate and GABA as neurotransmitters. (See Chapter 15 for more information about Rett syndrome.) (*General sources:* Fiedorowicz et al., 2002; Mathias, 1996; Thompson et al., 2005.)

Neurogenesis

Another area of investigation that is attracting attention in the field of neuroscience is the idea that it might be possible to combat atypical brain development or brain damage by inducing the formation of new brain neurons. For many years it was thought that the formation of new neurons (neurogenesis) did not take place in the brain after birth. Altman's research dispelled this myth in the mid 1960s. It is now known that most neurogenesis occurs in two different regions of the adult brain: the dentate gyrus of the hippocampus and the olfactory bulb. Other regions such as the cortex or substantia nigra have not been excluded, but neurogenesis in these places would be on a smaller scale if it occurs. (See Figures 8.5 and 8.6 for the locations of these brain regions.) Many investigators are conducting studies to determine whether neurogenesis is affected by factors such as age, growth factors, hormones, environmental or pharmacological stimuli, physical activity, stress, and learning. These findings have considerable implications for neuroscience research, including the study of learning and memory, neural network plasticity, aging, neurodegeneration, and recovery from brain injury. It is thought that increased survival of cells in the dentate gyrus of the hippocampus may be the mechanism for the "use it or lose it" principle of memory function in aging. Impairment of adult neurogenesis may be involved in the pathophysiology of some brain conditions such as depression, epilepsy, ischemia, or neurodegenerative diseases. (*General sources:* Mackowiak et al., 2004; Matthews, 2001; Prickaerts et al., 2004.)

Nurturing Positive Brain Development

Animal studies have shown that environmental restriction or deprivation early in development can induce social, cognitive, affective, and motor deviations similar to those associated with autism. Conversely, rearing animals in larger, more complex environments results in enhanced brain structure and function, including increased brain weight, dendritic branching, neurogenesis, and gene expression, as well as improved learning and memory. The development of the human brain and ability to understand abstract concepts likewise is thought to be greatly influenced by interhuman interactions. An emerging research field is investigating ways to nurture the brain; this field integrates brain science, child care, and education and involves child neurology. It has emerged from the remarkable progress in brain science and strong social demands for improvements in child care, nutrition, and education. People (especially parents and other caregivers) are key features of an infant's environment, and their protection, nurturing behavior, and stimulation shape early development. Adults can undertake a number of different activities to help children's brains develop to the fullest potential. These can include giving consistent loving care, physically touching infants, paying attention to hearing and language, looking for teachable moments and using them to an advantage, using music to develop math skills, making emotional connections relaxed rather than stressful, and behaving in the ways that parents would like their children to behave (as behaviors of adults are mirrored in children). It is also key to remember that optimum development of the brain and nervous systems requires proper nutrition, avoidance of exposure to environmental toxins and avoidance of injury. (*General sources:* Als et al., 2003; Charmandari et al., 2003; DeBord, 1997; Eisenberg, 1999; Greenspan, 1997; Lewis, 2004; Shore, 1997; Thompson, 2001; see also Chapters 28 and 43.)

Psychoneuroimmunology

An introduction to future directions in neuroscience and intellectual disability research would not be complete without reference to psychoneuroimmunology. Psychoneuroimmunology arose as a discipline in the neurosciences in the late 1970s to early 1980s but is still in its infancy. This discipline is the study of interactions between a person's perception of the surrounding world and his or her stress level, behavior, brain functioning, and immune system (which is the body's defense against external infection and aberrant cell division). There is ample evidence that communication exists between the brain and other body systems, including different tissues in the body, the stress response system, and the immune system. Extensive communication among these different compartments is maintained by neurotransmitters; hormones; and various other signaling neurochemicals, such as peptides, endorphins, enkephalins, and cytokines. These molecules carry messages from cells in the brain to the immune system and to other tissues in the body and from the immune system and other tissues back to the brain. At both ends, the signaling molecules generate metabolic responses by binding to receptors in cell membranes. Chronic stress-related interactions between the brain and immune system is now thought to be very relevant to mental health disorders, to the effects of stress on adults' physical health, and to the effects of various stressors on premature babies and babies of low birth weight who are at high risk of developing an intellectual or developmental disability or both. The HPA axis (see Figure 8.8) is one component of this complex communication system. (*General sources:* Adamson-Macedo, 2004; Cohen, 2006; Fleshner & Laudenslager, 2004.)

SUMMARY

This chapter has provided background for a better understanding of the neurodevelopmental basis of the intellectual and developmental disabilities covered in other chapters of this book. It is hoped that the material also will stimulate the development of new research directions in the field of intellectual and developmental disability that will benefit from the combined expertise and insights of basic scientists, clinicians, and theoreticians in all relevant disciplines. In addition, this chapter's material should alert readers to their potential as concerned citizens to ensure that their food supplies and environment are conducive to having a healthy brain and nervous systems. For further information on involvement of the nervous systems in intellectual and developmental disability, the reader is referred to Smith (2004). See Institute of Human Genetics, Newcastle, & MRC Human Genetics Unit, Edinburgh (2004) for details about stages of development of the human brain.

FOR FURTHER THOUGHT AND DISCUSSION

1. List five ways in which parents can help their babies' brains develop and function typically. Explain why these approaches lead to good brain health and development.
2. What actions can concerned citizens take to ensure that neurotoxic substances are not a threat to daily living?
3. Why do environmental hazards place babies' brains more at risk than adults' brains?
4. How can the average citizen help researchers to better understand brain function and development?

REFERENCES

Adamson-Macedo, E.N. (2004). Neonatal health psychology [NNHP]: Theories and practice. *Neuroendocrinology Letters, 25*(Suppl. 1), 9–34.

Allen, J.S., Bruss, J., & Damasio, H. (2005). The aging brain: The cognitive reserve hypothesis and hominid evolution. *American Journal of Human Biology, 17*(6), 673–689.

Als, H., Gilkerson, L., Duffy, F.H., et al. (2003). A three-center, randomized, controlled trial of individualized developmental care for very low birth weight preterm infants: Medical, neurodevelopmental, parenting, and caregiving effects. *Journal of Developmental and Behavioral Pediatrics, 24,* 399–408.

Andrews, M.H., & Matthews, S.G. (2004). Programming of the hypothalamo-pituitary-adrenal axis: Serotonergic involvement. *Stress, 7,* 15–27.

Baron-Cohen, S., Knickmeyer, R.C., & Belmonte, M.K. (2005). Sex differences in the brain: Implications for explaining autism. *Science, 310*(5749), 819–823.

Bear, M.F., Connors, B.W., & Paradiso, M.A. (2001). *Neuroscience: Exploring the brain* (2nd ed.). Philadelphia: Lippincott Williams & Wilkins.

Bengmark, S. (2006). Impact of nutrition on ageing and disease. *Current Opinion in Clinical Nutrition and Metabolic Care, 9*(1), 2–7.

Buitelaar, J.K., Huizink, A.C., Mulder, E.J., et al. (2003). Prenatal stress and cognitive development and temperament in infants. *Neurobiology of Aging, 24*(Suppl. 1), S53–S60.

Center for Global Research and Education on Environment and Health. (2005). *Home page.* Retrieved December 22, 2005, from http://www.cgreeh.net

Charmandari, E., Kino, T., Souvatzoglou, E., et al. (2003). Pediatric stress: Hormonal mediators and human development. *Hormone Research, 59,* 161–179.

Cohen, N. (2006). The uses and abuses of psychoneuroimmunology: A global overview. *Brain, Behavior and Immunity, 20,* 99–112.

DeBord, K. (1997). *Brain development* [Extension Publication]. Raleigh: North Carolina Cooperative Extension Service.

Doran, K.S., Liu, G.Y., & Nizet, V. (2003). Group B streptococcal beta-hemolysin/cytolysin activates neutrophil signaling pathways in brain endothelium and contributes to development of meningitis. *Journal of Clinical Investigation, 112,* 736–744.

Duval, F., Crocq, M.A., Guillon, M.S., et al. (2004). Increased adrenocorticotropin suppression after dexamethasone administration in sexually abused adolescents with posttraumatic stress disorder. *Annals of the New York Academy of Sciences, 1032,* 273–275.

Eisenberg, L. (1999). Experience, brain, and behavior: The importance of a head start. *Pediatrics, 103*(5, Pt. 1), 1031–1035.

Environmental Working Group. (2005, July 14). *Body burden: The pollution in newborns.* Retrieved December 22, 2005, from http://www.ewg.org/reports/bodyburden2

Fiedorowicz, C., Benezra, E., MacDonald, W., et al. (2002). The neurobiological basis of learning disabilities: An update. *Learning Disabilities: A Multidisciplinary Focus, 11*(2), 61–73.

Fleshner, M., & Laudenslager, M.L. (2004). Psychoneuroimmunology: Then and now. *Behavioral and Cognitive Neuroscience Reviews, 3*(2), 114–130.

Francis, K., van Beek, J., Canova, C., et al. (2003, May 23). Innate immunity and brain inflammation: The key role of complement. *Expert Reviews in Molecular Medicine,* 1–19.

Gazzaniga, M.S. (2005). Forty-five years of split-brain research and still going strong. *Nature Reviews: Neuroscience, 6*(8), 53–59.

Geier, M.R., & Geier, D.A. (2005). The potential importance of steroids in the treatment of autistic spectrum disorders and other disorders involving mercury toxicity. *Medical Hypotheses, 64*(5), 946–954.

Grady, C.L., & Craik, F.I. (2000). Changes in memory processing with age. *Current Opinion in Neurobiology, 10*(2), 224–231.

Gray, H. (1918). The spinal cord or medulla spinalis. In *Anatomy of the human body.* Retrieved January 3, 2006, from http://www.bartleby.com/107/185.html

Greenspan, S. (1997). *Growth of the mind.* New York: Addison Wesley.

Grundy, D., & Schemann, M. (2005). Enteric nervous system. *Current Opinion in Gastroenterology, 21,* 176–182.

Haier, R.J., Jung, R.E., Yeo, R.A., et al. (2005). The neuroanatomy of general intelligence: Sex matters. *Neuroimage, 25*(1), 320–327.

Hess, T.M. (2005). Memory and aging in context. *Psychology Bulletin, 131*(3), 383–406.

Institute of Human Genetics, Newcastle, & MRC Human Genetics Unit, Edinburgh. (2004). *Electronic atlas of the developing human brain.* Retrieved January 19, 2006, from http://www.ncl.ac.uk/ihg/EADHB

International Brain Banking Network. (n.d.). *Registry of brain banks.* Retrieved March 31, 2006, from http://www.intbbn.org/html/registry_of_brain_banks.html

Ito, M. (2004). 'Nurturing the brain' as an emerging research field involving child neurology. *Brain & Development, 26,* 429–433.

Johnston, M.V., Blue, M.E., & Naidu, S. (2005). Rett syndrome and neuronal development. *Journal of Child Neurology, 20*(9), 759–763.

Kirk, L.F., Jr., Hash, R.B., Katner, H.P., et al. (2000). Cushing's disease: Clinical manifestations and diagnostic evaluation. *American Family Physician, 62*(5), 1119–1127, 1133–1134.

Legato, M.J. (2005). Men, women, and brains: What's hardwired, what's learned, and what's controversial. *Gender Medicine, 2,*(2), 59–61.

Lewis, M.H. (2004). Environmental complexity and central nervous system development and function. *Mental Retardation and Developmental Disabilities Research Reviews, 10,* 91–95.

Mackowiak, M., Chocyk, A., Markowicz-Kula, K., et al. (2004). Neurogenesis in the adult. *Polish Journal of Pharmacology, 56,* 673–687.

Mathias, R. (1996). The basics of brain imaging. *NIDA Notes, 11*(5). Retrieved December 22, 2005, from http://www.drugabuse.gov/NIDA_Notes/NNVol11N5/Basics.html

Matthews, G.G. (2001). *Neurobiology: Molecules, cells and systems* (2nd ed.). Cambridge, United Kingdom: Blackwell Science.

Matthews, S.G. (2000). Antenatal glucocorticoids and programming of the developing CNS. *Pediatric Research, 47,* 291–300.

McArthur, J.C. (2004). HIV dementia: An evolving disease. *Journal of Neuroimmunology, 157,* 3–10.

Organisation for Economic Co-operation and Development. (2002). *Understanding the brain—towards a new learning science.* Retrieved March 24, 2005, from http://www.oecd.org/dataoecd/50/25/15355617.gif

Percy, M., Lewkis, S., & Brown, I. (2003). An introduction to genetics and development. In I. Brown & M. Percy (Eds.), *Developmental disabilities in Ontario* (2nd ed, pp. 89–116). Toronto: Ontario Association on Developmental Disabilities.

Perl, D.P., Good, P.F., Bussiere, T., et al. (2000). Practical approaches to stereology in the setting of aging- and disease-related brain banks. *Journal of Chemical Neuroanatomy, 20*(1), 7–19.

Prickaerts, J., Koopmans, G., Blokland, A., et al. (2004). Learning and adult neurogenesis: Survival with or without proliferation? *Neurobiology of Learning and Memory, 81,* 1–11.

Restak, R.M. (1999). *The secret life of the brain.* New York: Canada Press.

Romeo, R.D. (2005). Neuroendocrine and behavioral development during puberty: A tale of two axes. *Vitamins and Hormones, 71,* 1–25.

Shore, R. (1997). *Rethinking the brain: New insights into early development.* New York: Families and Work Institute.

Sisk, C.L., & Foster, D.L. (2004). The neural basis of puberty and adolescence. *Nature Neuroscience, 7*(10), 1040–1047.

Smith, B. (2004.) *NICHCY connections to . . . learning and the brain.* (2005). Retrieved December 22, 2005, from http://nichcy.org/resources/brain101.asp

Thompson, R.A. (2001). Development in the first years of life. *Future Child, 11*(1), 20–33.

Thompson, P.M., Sowell, E.R., Gogtay, N., et al. (2005). Structural MRI and brain development. *International Review of Neurobiology, 67,* 285–323.

Van den Bergh, B.R., Mulder, E.J., Mennes, M., et al. (2005). Antenatal maternal anxiety and stress and the neurobehavioural development of the fetus and child: Links and possible mechanisms. A review. *Neuroscience and Biobehavioral Reviews, 29,* 237–258.

Villemagne, P.M., Naidu, S., Villemagne, V.L., et al. (2002). Brain glucose metabolism in Rett Syndrome. *Pediatric Neurology, 27*(2), 117–122.

Whitaker-Azmitia, P.M. (2005). Behavioral and cellular consequences of increasing serotonergic activity during brain development: A role in autism? *International Journal of Developmental Neuroscience, 23,* 75–83.

Willis, W.G., & Weiler, M.D. (2005). Neural substrates of childhood attention-deficit/hyperactivity disorder: Electroencephalographic and magnetic resonance imaging evidence. *Developmental Neuropsychology, 27,* 135–182.

9

Factors that Cause or Contribute to Intellectual and Developmental Disabilities

Maire Percy

> **WHAT YOU WILL LEARN ABOUT IN THIS CHAPTER**
>
> - The importance of understanding factors that cause or contribute to intellectual and developmental disability
> - The importance of education about causes of intellectual and developmental disabilities
> - Classification of factors causing or contributing to intellectual and developmental disabilities
> - Genetic and environmental factors resulting in specific intellectual and developmental disabilities
> - Factors causing or contributing to mental health disorders
> - Factors affecting the ability to identify the causes of intellectual and/or developmental disabilities

As explained in Chapter 7, the Human Genome Project is rapidly leading to the discovery of new genetic causes of intellectual and developmental disabilities. Understanding of environmental causes of intellectual and developmental disabilities is also expanding. These breakthroughs are, in part, the result of diagnostic advances in cytogenetics, molecular biology, and imaging. In turn, such advances are leading to the related field of bioethical research. Knowing the cause of a condition is fundamental to understanding its prevention, its potential complications, and prospective treatment strategies. Thus, there is a great need for better communication and cooperation between all professionals dedicated to the care of individuals with intellectual and developmental disabilities (Finucane, Haas-Givler, & Simon, 2003; Lewis, 2004). The information in this chapter provides readers with a background to help them better understand the wide spectrum of environmental and genetic factors that cause and/or contribute to intellectual and developmental disabilities and the reasons why such information is important. Chapters 7 and 15, as well as chapters dedicated to specific disorders, complement this chapter. See Appendix A at the end of the book for explanations of unusual terms that appear in bold print at first mention.

THE IMPORTANCE OF UNDERSTANDING FACTORS THAT CAUSE OR CONTRIBUTE TO INTELLECTUAL AND DEVELOPMENTAL DISABILITY

Everyone who works with children with intellectual disabilities knows the anxiety that a child's condition causes his or her parents. Thus, when a child's development is discovered to be delayed, the following questions are among the first that should be asked: What specifically is causing the problem? What can be done to enable the child to have the best possible quality of life and to develop to his or her potential? Can the problem be prevented in the future? For many people who have an intellectual disability, it is possible to identify a specific cause or contributing factor; however, for others these factors remain undetermined. Thus, it is crucial to try to understand what causes or contributes to intellectual and developmental disabilities (Curry, 2002; Curry et al., 1997; Moser, 2004; Poplawski, 2003). Several important reasons for doing so follow.

1. *Some intellectual disabilities resulting from certain genetic or hormone disorders can actually be prevented.* For example, intellectual impairment associated with certain genetic intellectual disabilities called **inborn errors of metabolism** can be prevented in large part by early dietary intervention (see Chapter 15). Phenylketonuria (PKU), a disorder in which the amino acid phenylalanine cannot be properly metabolized, is one example

The author is grateful to Joseph M. Berg and Marika Korossy for providing some key references and resource material for this chapter.

of such a disorder (see Chapter 15). Intellectual impairment resulting from **congenital** hypothyroidism, a common **endocrine** hormone disorder, can largely be prevented by treatment as soon as possible after birth; one form of congenital hypothyroidism results from iodine deficiency; the second form, which occurs in iodine-replete areas and affects approximately 1 in 4,000 newborns, is common in North America and is believed to be developmental and/or genetic in origin (Brown & Larsen, 2005; Glinoer & Delange, 2000; see also Chapter 15). In Canada, the United States, and other developed countries, newborns are screened for hypothyroidism and, if necessary, are given early thyroid replacement therapy to prevent severe intellectual disability.

2. *If the cause of an intellectual disability is inherited (e.g., fragile X syndrome), families have a right to know this information and to be able to plan their families in the most informed way.* For example, if parents are at risk of having a child with an inherited intellectual disability, they may choose not to have children, to adopt, to therapeutically abort an affected fetus, or to have an unaffected child through assisted reproductive technology (see Chapters 7 and 28).

3. *Some developmental disabilities resulting from certain environmental hazards can be prevented.* Some causes of intellectual disabilities that are inherently preventable include brain injury from avoidable car accidents incurred as the result of drunk driving, avoidable falls, and child battering, including shaken baby syndrome (see Chapter 15); maternal alcohol abuse during pregnancy (see Chapter 14); maternal smoking during pregnancy (see the Toxic Threats section in this chapter); maternal folic acid deficiency (see the Specific Environmental Factors section in this chapter), and hypothyroidism resulting from iodine deficiency in the soil (see Chapter 15 and the Specific Environmental Factors section in this chapter).

4. *In the absence of preventive measures, various approaches can improve the quality of life for individuals diagnosed with particular disabilities and can help them to develop to their maximum potential.* One example is intensive early behavioral intervention for severe autism (see Chapter 12). Some, although not all, children with severe autism who take part in this program experience less disruptive or obvious symptoms and can be included in general education classrooms. Other approaches for intervention include various strategies to improve concentration in attention-deficit/hyperactivity disorder (see Chapter 19). Particular educational strategies enable people with mild to moderate intellectual disabilities to complete secondary school and college or university and to have a rewarding career (see Chapter 31). Existing knowledge, gathered from research and experience, should be used in the management of specific disabilities. This will benefit the individuals who are affected and all of the people involved in their care and provision of services. Families—often highly motivated to find information, supports, and services—can both teach and learn from professionals.

5. *Knowledge about causes of intellectual disabilities will lead to the development of better interventions and treatments or, in some cases, prevention.* Effective interventions and treatments, including those that might prevent specific intellectual disabilities or lead to a cure, must be based on clear and complete information about the disability that is gathered from a broad range of disciplines and perspectives. Information can be obtained most effectively with the participation of affected individuals who have received a causal diagnosis and their families. Fragile X syndrome is one example of an intellectual disability caused by a mutation in a single **gene** for which research directed at treatment or cure is being aggressively promoted (see Chapter 11).

THE IMPORTANCE OF EDUCATION ABOUT CAUSES OF INTELLECTUAL AND DEVELOPMENTAL DISABILITIES

Professional, public, and governmental education about factors resulting in intellectual and developmental disabilities must go hand in hand with discoveries about such factors. Information about such factors and how they cause disabilities should be made generally accessible. Four important reasons for promoting education about causes of intellectual/developmental disabilities are detailed next.

1. *Deficiencies in education at the professional level can have adverse effects on supporting people with intellectual disabilities.* Many professionals and educators have had very little background or practical experience in the intellectual disabilities field. Educating professionals and the public about factors that cause or contribute to specific intellectual disabilities (e.g., excessive alcohol consumption resulting in fetal alcohol spectrum disorder, folic acid deficiency resulting in neural tube defects, iron-deficiency anemia in newborns and young children resulting in various delays and problems—see the Specific Environmental Factors section in this chapter) will increase awareness of how to prevent them. With specific knowledge, professionals can provide people with intellectual disabilities, their families, and their caregivers with the best advice for intervention and disability management. Family physicians, in particular, should receive basic training and clinical experience in developmental disabilities. In turn, professionals should listen to primary caregivers, who often

are the most knowledgeable about individuals, their disabilities, and the help that they need.

2. *There may be complex ethical, legal, and social issues associated with a primary diagnosis* that can interfere with obtaining medical or life insurance or with employment (see Chapter 28). People need to be educated about the pros and cons of finding out the cause of an intellectual or developmental disability. On the one hand, finding out the cause (e.g., fragile X syndrome) is key for obtaining educational supports (see Chapter 31) or disability pensions. On the other hand, finding out that an intellectual disability is caused by a genetic mutation associated with a characteristic prognosis that benefits from costly intervention (e.g., Hurler syndrome; see Chapter 15) may lead to difficulties in obtaining health insurance for the individual and/or his or her family. Knowledge that a person carries a genetic mutation that will cause a debilitating disorder at a later age (e.g., the individual is a paternal carrier of fragile X syndrome and at risk of developing Parkinson-like disease at a relatively early age; see Chapter 11) may lead to discrimination in the workplace. Input from people with disabilities and families to policy makers will help establish acceptable guidelines and laws.

3. *Policies about services and service delivery may not be realistic or driven by the needs of individuals.* One example is the closing of institutions. This is undeniably beneficial for many people, especially for those with mild disabilities. However, there are individuals with severe physical disabilities, with a mental illness in addition to intellectual disability, or with severe behavior problems for whom immediate community integration may pose a challenge. In regard to the closing of institutions, policy makers need to know how many people need to be moved, what their disabilities are, and what resources they need to have a good quality of life. Policy makers also need to be familiar with strategies that are working in other places to ensure that the best possible options for services and methods of service delivery become available.

4. *Health professionals are often reluctant to assess, diagnose, or treat people with intellectual disabilities because they are not paid adequately to do so.* For example, a serious problem in some health care systems (e.g., in Ontario, Canada) is the fixed rate with which physicians and certain other health care professionals are reimbursed that discounts the complexity of dealing with intellectual disabilities. This makes some professionals reluctant to assess, diagnose, and treat people with intellectual disabilities. Policy makers need to be educated about the importance of determining the primary cause of intellectual and developmental disabilities and ensure that health professionals are adequately compensated for this work.

CLASSIFICATION OF FACTORS CAUSING OR CONTRIBUTING TO INTELLECTUAL AND DEVELOPMENTAL DISABILITIES

This section describes etiology, its role in prenatal vulnerability, and a system for classifying etiological factors.

The Concept of Etiology

The term *etiology* is derived from the Greek word meaning "the study of cause." In this chapter, the term *etiology* refers to the study of factors that cause or contribute to the occurrence of different types of intellectual and developmental disability. Many factors that cause or contribute to intellectual disability have been identified. In cases of severe intellectual and developmental disability, a biomedical cause can be found in a high percentage of cases, but in 30%–50% of mild cases, the cause remains unknown (Curry et al., 1997; Daily, Ardinger, & Holmes, 2000; Moser, 2004). A full understanding of etiology requires more than knowing the causes or contributing factors. It is essential to understand when such factors have an effect on the developing **embryo, fetus,** or child; their severity; and the duration of time over which they act. Etiology is a first and crucial step in understanding intellectual disabilities. Many causes and contributing factors that result in disabilities are now known. The next step is discovering how the disabilities actually result. Etiology is also an important start in the process of understanding how children are likely to develop throughout their childhood years. Such information can be extremely helpful for parents, educators, caregivers, and professionals in developing realistic expectations for children with disabilities.

Etiology and Prenatal Vulnerability

The developing fetus is very susceptible to specific causes and contributing factors at certain developmental stages (Andersen, 2003; Brent, 2004; Dobbing, 1982; Gottesman & Hanson, 2005; Kimmel et al., 1993; Rodier, 2004). Substances and agents that induce the production of physical deformities in the fetus, including the central nervous system, are called *teratogens* (Guze, 2005; Polifka & Friedman, 2002). Table 9.1 shows the vulnerability of the fetus to different factors causing intellectual and/or developmental disabilities.

General Classification System of Etiological Factors

Intellectual disabilities result from genetic and environmental factors, alone or in combination. Genetic

Table 9.1. Fetal vulnerability at different stages of development

Developmental stage[a]	Developmental features	Possible outcome
Fertilization	Restoration of **diploid number** Establishment of sex Triggering of first **cleavage division**	
First week	Embryo is transported from site of fertilization to site of implantation in the uterus Formation of **blastula**	50%–70% of pregnancies end in spontaneous abortions within the first 2 weeks due to chromosomal abnormalities, which result in 60% of miscarriages; implantation failure; maternal immune response; and physical teratogens such as heat from a sauna, X-rays, and ionizing radiation
Second week	Embryo implants into lining of uterus **Amniotic** cavity and primitive **yolk sac** formed	See above
Third through eighth weeks	Organogenesis (beginning of the development of body form)	Chemical teratogens and metabolic upsets may produce major malformations
Second trimester	Multiplication of neurons	
Third trimester to 18–24 months after birth	Brain growth spurt **glial cell** multiplication **dendritic arborization** **synaptogenesis** **myelination**	Brain is very vulnerable to malnutrition, **endogenous** and environmental poisons, and hormonal imbalances In utero effects of teratogens may include minor malformations and neurobehavioral and/or neurocognitive function

Sources: Brent (2004), Dobbing (1981), Guze (2005), D. Laslo (personal communication, April 25, 1999), and Rice and Barone (2000); also Chapter 7.

[a]Pregnancy is measured from the start of a woman's last menstrual period. It usually lasts 40 weeks or approximately 9 calendar months. The first trimester runs from conception to 13 weeks, the second from 14 to 27 weeks, and the third from 28 to 40 weeks.

factors are related to changes in the sequence of **DNA** in the chromosomes of cells. Environmental factors include toxic (chemical) factors; nutritional factors; social factors related to social and family interaction, such as child stimulation and adult responsiveness; and behavioral factors related to harmful behaviors, such as maternal substance abuse. Educational factors, such as having or not having early intensive behavioral intervention in the case of autism, can positively or negatively influence mental development and the acquisition of adaptive skills; thus, these are also considered environmental risk factors for intellectual disability (see Chapter 31 for further details on this topic). Socioeconomic factors contribute to intellectual and/or developmental disability as well. For example, one study has indicated that poor socioeconomic status of parents is manifested in children's poorer health and a reduced capacity to benefit from the economic and social advances experienced by the rest of society (Najman et al., 2004). As a result, poor socioeconomic status may be 'transmitted' from one generation to another.

Factors that cause or contribute to intellectual disabilities may broadly be classified as being general or specific. Within each of these two classifications, causal and contributing factors may be genetic or environmental. Table 9.2 outlines this general classification system of factors that cause or contribute to intellectual disabilities.

Although the classification system in Table 9.2 suggests that intellectual disabilities can be neatly placed into one of four quadrants, it is important to stress that this is not necessarily the case. The nature and degree of disability in individuals may be the result of both genetic and environmental causes. For example, Prader-Willi syndrome (see Chapter 15) is a disorder with a genetic cause; however, if the affected person happens to live within an environment that does not promote good social development, his or her overall disability is the result of both the genetic factor causing the syndrome and the poor environment. Genetic factors also are thought to predispose an individual to developing depression or schizophrenia—disorders that an individual may have in addition to an intellectual or developmental disability. Factors such as stress may be involved in development or exacerbation of depression or schizophrenia (O'Dwyer, 1997; see also Chapters 7 and 20).

This general classification system in Table 9.2 is nevertheless useful for understanding the involvement of genetic and environmental factors in intellectual and developmental disability. The following section considers the relative importance of different etiological factors, and the section after this deals with factors resulting in specific intellectual and developmental disabilities.

Table 9.2. General classification of factors that cause or contribute to intellectual disabilities

Etiological classification	Specific causes	More general causes
Genetic	Harmful single genes and chromosomal aberrations that cause a particular type of intellectual disability	Common variants of one or more genes that affect the clinical expression of a disability
Environmental	Particular physical hazards (including malnutrition) or chemical teratogens that result in intellectual disability before, during, or after birth	Adverse domestic and social circumstances Poor educational experiences Adverse maternal behaviors (e.g., smoking, substance abuse) Complications of prematurity

Sources: American Association on Mental Retardation (2005), Berg (1985), and Curry et al. (1997).

Table 9.3. Relative importance of factors causing intellectual disabilities (mild to severe) in the United States

Etiological factor	Percent of people with intellectual impairment from this factor
Unknown	30–50
Structural central nervous system (CNS) abnormalities (cause not specified)	7–17
General, environmental	
Cultural–familial intellectual disability	3–12
Complications of prematurity	2–10
Specific, genetic	
Aberrant chromosomes	4–34
Known harmful single genes	3–9
Recognizable syndromes	3–7
Metabolic or endocrine causes	1–5
Provisionally unique syndromes	1–5
Specific, environmental	
Specific physical hazards or teratogens	5–13

From Curry, C.J. et al. (1997). Evaluation of mental retardation: Recommendations of a Consensus Conference: American College of Medical Genetics. *American Journal of Medical Genetics, 72,* 468–477; adapted by permission & *Source:* Shevell et al. (2003).

As explained in the Chapter 9 text, the relative importance of different factors causing intellectual disabilities varies markedly from one country to another. The data depicted above, derived from sources in the United States, do not capture the devastation resulting from iron deficiency, iodine deficiency, and malnutrition in some countries. Technological advances in genetics and in brain imaging are leading to a reduction in the percentage of people with an unknown cause of intellectual impairment and to relative increases in the percentage with structural CNS abnormalities or with specific genetic causes. Causes of almost all cases of global developmental delay can be determined using neuroimaging, genetic studies, and metabolic testing. Up to half of the causes of mild intellectual and developmental disability are not known.

Importance of Genetic and Environmental Etiological Factors

By identifying factors that cause or contribute to intellectual disabilities, strategies for counteracting their harmful effects can be developed. Table 9.3 shows the frequencies of different factors causing disabilities associated with intellectual impairment in the United States. As indicated in the table note, the frequencies in this table do not reflect the high rate of intellectual disability resulting from iodine deficiency or other types of malnutrition in certain regions of the world. The causes of a substantial proportion of intellectual disabilities are still unknown. More recent surveys suggest that geographical location, standard of living, and race may affect the proportion of intellectual disabilities that have a genetic basis and also the type of genetic disorder (Charrow, 2004; Heikura et al., 2005; Hofman et al., 1991).

Etiological factors have been easier to identify in people with severe intellectual disabilities than in people afflicted with milder levels of disability. For example, in a survey conducted by Bodensteiner and Schaefer (1995), a primary cause was identified in 85% of cases of a severe form of intellectual disability. Genetic abnormalities were found in 30% of cases; injury, including teratogens and pre-, peri- and postnatal injuries in 15%–29%; central nervous system abnormalities and malformations in 10%–25%; identifiable multiple congenital anomalies in 4%–5%; and endocrine and metabolic causes in 3%–5%. In Arvio and Sillanpaa's (2003) study of a Finnish population, a primary cause was found in an even higher percentage of people with severe intellectual disabilities.

GENETIC AND ENVIRONMENTAL FACTORS RESULTING IN SPECIFIC INTELLECTUAL AND DEVELOPMENTAL DISABILITIES

Table 9.2 showed that etiology can be classified according to genetic or environmental factors. This section further details these topics.

General Genetic Factors

In this text, the term *general genetic factors* is used to refer to genetic factors that predispose to intellectual and developmental disability (i.e., are risk factors for intellectual and developmental disability) as opposed to being specific genetic factors that actually cause them. General genetic factors are variants of single genes that are common in the general population. They sometimes are called "background" **genes.** An individual's background genes may contribute to development or health in a beneficial, harmful, or neutral way; furthermore, the effects of background genes may differ throughout life. A well-known example of a general genetic factor that affects health and cognitive function is the apolipoprotein E gene (see Chapter 7). Three forms of this gene are common in the general population: E2, E3 and E4. E3 is the most common variant. The E4 variant is thought to be protective during embryonic development (Zetterberg et al., 2002). However, people who carry one or two E4s have a greater chance of developing Alzheimer's disease when they get older than people who lack E4. Yet, many people with one or two E4s never develop Alzheimer's disease (see Chapter 44). The E2 variant may predispose people to longevity. Another general genetic factor affecting the **prevalence** of intellectual and developmental disability is sex. Sex is determined by the presence of two X chromosomes in females and by the presence of one X and one Y in males. Boys are more likely than girls to have an intellectual or developmental disability (Drews et al., 1995). One probable reason for this observation is that the X chromosome carries a peculiarly large number of genes concerned with mental functions (Skuse, 2005). As explained in Chapter 7, if genes on one X chromosome harbor mutations, then these mutations will affect males more than females, because males have only one X chromosome whereas females have two. Ethnic background also affects the frequency of certain intellectual and developmental disabilities. Although this may be in part the result of background genes, the mutation that causes intellectual and developmental disability when present in two copies sometimes is known to confer a survival advantage when one copy is present. Thus, effects of ethnic background are discussed in the Specific Genetic Factors section.

General Environmental Factors

There are a number of general environmental factors that cause or contribute to intellectual disabilities. These may result from a wide variety of adverse domestic and social circumstances. One such set of circumstances that has been studied, and thus may serve as an example, is low socioeconomic status (Stromme & Magnus, 2000). It is important to stress that although low socioeconomic status is associated with intellectual and developmental disability, numerous factors associated with this condition may be involved. *Socioeconomic status* is a broad term that is widely used as a construct in the social sciences. Different ways of measuring it have been proposed, but most include some quantification of family income, parental education, and occupational status (Bradley & Corwyn, 2002). People with different socioeconomic status may have different access to medical care, healthy food, physical activities, and so forth. In one U.S. study, a strong relationship between low socioeconomic status and the presence of mild intellectual impairment was identified (Murphy et al., 1998). In one Norwegian study, parents of children with severe intellectual disability had a higher socioeconomic status than parents of children with mild intellectual disability (Stromme & Magnus, 2000). Although specific factors resulting in intellectual impairment are not known, they may include poor nutrition (prior to conception, during pregnancy, during birth, or after birth), substance abuse, lack of intellectual stimulation, poor medical care, psychosocial stress (including abuse), and poor parenting. Another general factor that affects intellectual disability is maternal age (Williams & Decouflé, 1999). One study found that older mothers are more likely than younger mothers to have a child with intellectual disability accompanied by another neurological condition (Drews et al., 1995).

Specific Genetic Factors

This section breaks down specific genetic factors into two categories: specific genetic factors that cause intellectual disabilities and conditions caused by specific genetic disorders. The section also discusses some factors that affect the prevalence of specific genetic disabilities.

Specific Genetic Factors that Cause Intellectual Disabilities The term *specific genetic factors* refers to abnormalities of genes or chromosomes that have significant effects on cellular function and actually *cause* particular intellectual disabilities. The term *specific genetic factors* includes alterations in the usual number of chromosomes that cause an intellectual and developmental disability such as Down syndrome or Klinefelter syndrome (see Chapters 10 and 15). Table 9.4 lists the most common, specific genetic causes of intellectual disabilities and their approximate prevalences. It should be stressed that genetic disabilities may be inherited or arise spontaneously through the occurrence of new mutations in genes (i.e., sporadically). Disabilities arising sporadically from new mutations are far more common than inherited ones. Males contribute more mutations than females to their offspring because their sperm are formed from cells that have gone through many more cell divisions than the oocytes of females. More than 7,000 different genetic disorders have been discovered, and they continue to be discovered at the rate of four or five each year. Of these, approximately 1,200 are known to be associated with cognitive disability (Moser, 2004). Some genetic disorders are called syndromes. As explained in Chapter 15, the

Table 9.4. The most common specific genetic intellectual disabilities

Diagnosis	Type of disorder	Genetic basis	Incidence per 1,000 live births
Down syndrome	Chromosomal	Extra chromosome 21	1.7
Fragile X syndrome	Single gene (FMR1 is involved most commonly)	Triplet repeat disorder, X-linked	0.5 (males) 0.2 (females)
Turner syndrome	Chromosomal	Missing X or part of an X in females	0.2–0.4
Trisomy 18 (Edwards syndrome)	Chromosomal	Extra chromosome 18	0.13–0.17
Duchenne muscular dystrophy	Single gene (dystrophin)	X-linked recessive	0.5–1
Trisomy 13 (Patau syndrome)	Chromosomal	Extra chromosome 13	0.08–0.13
Tuberous sclerosis	Single gene (tuberin)	Autosomal dominant	0.033–0.17
Klinefelter syndrome	Chromosomal	Extra X in males	1–2
Phenylketonuria	Single gene (phenylalanine hydroxylase, and other enzymes and cofactors involved in phenylalanine metabolism)	Autosomal recessive	0.067
Cri-du-chat syndrome	Chromosomal deletion	Small deletion on chromosome 5	0.02–0.067
Williams syndrome	Chromosomal deletion (elastin is one gene involved)	Small deletion on chromosome 7	0.02–0.05
Galactosemia	Single gene (**GALT, GALK,** or epimerase)	Autosomal recessive	0.05
Hunter syndrome	Single gene (lysosomal hydroxylase)	X-linked	0.003–0.015
Lesch-Nyhan	Single gene (**HPRT**)	X-linked recessive	0.0026
Prader-Willi syndrome	Genomic imprinting syndrome defect (involves **SNRPN**)	Chromosome 15	0.04–0.13
Angelman syndrome	Genomic imprinting defect (involves **UBE3A**)	Chromosome 15	0.05–0.10

Sources: Harris (1995) and Moser (1995, 2004); also Chapters 10, 11, and 15.

The reported birth incidences are for North America. As explained in the Chapter 9 text, the prevalences of intellectual disability resulting from fetal alcohol spectrum disorder, autism spectrum disorders, iron and iodine deficiencies, and malnutrition are far more common than for specific genetic disabilities.

term *syndrome* indicates a set of symptoms that occur together. The term *symptom* means any subjective evidence of disease or of a patient's condition indicative of some bodily or mental state. Within given syndromes, there may be considerable variability of expression of the disorder. This is because a syndrome is not always caused by exactly the same type of genetic abnormality. Different individuals have different background genes, people are exposed to different environmental effects, and genetic abnormalities sometimes are expressed differently in males and females. Genetic factors that result in syndromes may have consequences that are behavioral, physical, or a combination thereof. As noted in Chapter 7's explanation of how genetic abnormalities arise and how they are transmitted from parent to offspring, mutations affecting genes on most of the autosomes (chromosomes 1 to 22) are said to be **autosomal**; usually they are expressed when inherited from both the mother and father. In some cases, however, it matters whether the mutation comes from the mother or father; in these cases, the genes involved are said to be imprinted (Butler, 2002; see also Chapters 7 and 15). Imprinted genes likely have evolved over time in mammals to fine-tune the growth of the fetus. Imprinted genes inherited from the father tend to enhance growth, whereas imprinted genes inherited from the mother appear to suppress growth (Butler, 2002). Mutations affecting genes on the X chromosome are said to be **X-linked.** As noted, males carry only one X chromosome whereas females have two. If there is a mutation in a gene on one X chromosome, males will be affected more severely than females, because the normal X chromosome in the female will compensate for the mutation on the other one.

Conditions Caused by Specific Genetic Disorders This section briefly describes several of the common genetic forms of intellectual disabilities presented in Table 9.4. Others are explained in Chapter 15 and other chapters in this book.

Down syndrome is the most common intellectual disability resulting from an aberration of chromosome number (see Chapter 10). It is usually caused by the presence of an additional chromosome 21 and is referred to as trisomy 21 (i.e., having three copies of chromosome 21). Most cases are not inherited and occur spontaneously without a family history. The birth incidence of Down syndrome increases markedly after the age of 35; both increased maternal age and increased paternal age are now known to increase the risk of having a child with Down syndrome (Fisch et al., 2003). Trisomy 18, or Edwards syndrome, and trisomy 13, or Patau syndrome, are other common autosomal trisomies. Many babies with the latter two syndromes are stillborn or die in the perinatal period.

Fragile X syndrome is the most common inherited intellectual disability (see Chapter 11). (Down syndrome occurs more frequently, but this disorder is not usually inherited; see Chapter 10.) Fragile X is caused by inherited mutations on the X chromosome that result in the absence of a protein called FMR1. It is an extraordinary disability, because it is caused by unstable mutations in a single gene that tend to become larger and larger when they are passed on by females. Many people carry fragile X mutations but are unaware that this is the case. Numerous other disabilities associated with neurodegeneration are known to be caused by similar unstable mutations (Everett & Wood, 2004; Hagerman, 1997; Mandel & Biancalana, 2004; see also Chapter 7).

Inherited **genetic metabolic disorders** include PKU, galactosemia, Hunter syndrome, and Lesch-Nyhan syndrome; these are caused by defects in single genes regulating the **metabolism** of an **amino acid,** a sugar, a **mucopolysaccharide,** and a **purine nucleotide,** respectively. Abnormalities in the number of sex chromosomes (Turner syndrome and Klinefelter syndrome) tend to result in mild disabilities. Two **genomic imprinting** disorders, Prader-Willi and Angelman syndromes, are very different disabilities caused by **small deletions** in exactly the same region of chromosome 15, or by duplication of one chromosome 15 and loss of the other. Prader-Willi syndrome is often caused by deletions in the paternal chromosome 15 or by duplication of the maternal chromosome 15. Angelman syndrome is often caused by deletions in the maternal chromosome 15 or by duplication of the paternal chromosome 15 (Nussbaum, McInnes, & Willard, 2004; see also Chapter 15). Not shown in Table 9.4 is congenital hypothyroidism that does not result from iodine deficiency and is primarily genetic in origin; this affects approximately 1 in 4,000 newborns in North America.

New genetic causes of intellectual disabilities continue to be reported (Gecz, 2004). **Mutations** in the MECP2 gene on the X chromosome result in Rett syndrome, an autism spectrum disorder (ASD) that affects mainly females (Percy & Lane, 2004). Mutations in a gene called ARX have been found to cause X-linked West syndrome (a form of epilepsy), X-linked myoclonic epilepsy with spasticity and intellectual disability, Partington syndrome (intellectual disability with **ataxia** and **dystonia**), nonsyndromic forms of intellectual disability, and another group of disabilities that include malformation of the cerebral cortex. The exact prevalence of ARX mutations is not known with certainty, but it is suspected that they may be as common as those causing fragile X syndrome (Sherr, 2003). Remarkable progress has been made in finding genetic causes of the different types of epilepsies (Gutierrez-Delicado & Serratosa, 2004).

Progress also has been made in finding causes of intellectual disability termed *idiopathic* (no known cause). In one composite summary of 21 studies of idiopathic intellectual disability (Xu & Chen, 2003), 4.6% of cases were found to be associated with subtle chromosomal defects, including deletions and rearrangements near the ends of chromosomes, which tend to be very rich in genes. Over time, the Human Genome Project will lead to identification of the genes that are in these altered regions and their functions. Thus, the prospects of understanding the basis of many more intellectual disabilities with previously unknown cause is on the horizon.

Some Factors that Affect the Prevalence of Specific Genetic Disabilities Ethnic origin may influence the chances of a child being affected by, or being a carrier of, a genetic disability. For example, there is a high frequency of Tay-Sachs disease (a fatal genetic disorder in which harmful quantities of a fatty substance, **ganglioside** GM2, accumulate in the nerve cells of the brain) among Jewish people of Ashkenazic (central, northern, or eastern European) descent but not among Jewish people of Sephardic (Spanish, Portuguese, or Middle Eastern) descent (Charrow, 2004), whereas PKU is mostly found in Caucasians and is rare in people of African descent and in Asians (Hofman et al., 1991; Milunsky, 1977; see also Chapter 15). Fragile X syndrome is reported to be particularly common in Finland and in Quebec (Matilainen et al., 1995; Rousseau et al., 1995). Disorders that have a high prevalence in certain ethnic groups, regardless of where they live now, result from probable common ancestry, which explains why there are many more people in these groups who carry a gene for the disorder than in the general population.

Survival advantage is a consequence of traits for some genetic disabilities. In some, **recessive** mutant genes that are harmful when present in two copies have some advantage when they are singularly expressed. Sickle cell anemia (a condition in which red blood cells are sickle shaped rather than round) and beta-thalassemia (a condition in which the body cannot make the beta chains of hemoglobin) are two recessive genetic disorders that are sometimes associated with intellectual disability in which being the carrier of one mutant gene has an advantage. The trait for sickle-cell anemia, found in many people of African descent, is connected with a resistance to malaria; two sickle cell genes result in the expression of anemia and resistance to malaria while a carrier possessing a single sickle cell gene is resistant to malaria and lacks the anemia (Steen et al., 2003; Ther & Kazzi, 2004). The traits of beta-thalassemia (Takeshita, 2005), found in people of Mediterranean origin, similarly are connected with a resistance to malaria. Treatment for the anemia in both disorders requires blood transfusions, which leads to iron overload and organ failure if the body iron load is not normalized by treatment with drugs that remove iron from the body (Monastero et al., 2000; Steen et al., 2003).

Specific Environmental Factors

Numerous specific environmental factors can cause or contribute to intellectual disabilities. The main ones that cause intellectual and/or developmental disabilities are listed in Table 9.5 according to three stages of fetal/child development: prenatal (before birth), perinatal (encompassing a certain period of time before and after birth, as well as the time period during birth), and postnatal (after birth). The following sections elaborate on some common environmental causes of intellectual and developmental disability, of which some should be largely preventable.

Malnutrition Malnutrition is suspected of being a cause or contributing factor of intellectual disability in a large proportion of affected individuals. Preconceptual malnutrition may be the largest culprit (see Chapter 28). Although adults are remarkably resistant to the effects of malnutrition, the developing fetal brain is very susceptible. Protein calorie malnutrition and deficiencies of certain vitamins (e.g., folic acid, B_{12}, vitamin A) and minerals (e.g., iodide, iron) are problems not only in underdeveloped countries but also in developed countries, including Canada and the United States. In 1990, more than a third of the world's population younger than 5 years of age was malnourished. This number of approximately 174 million people was reduced to about 154 million by 2000 (UNICEF, 2000). There are still some countries (especially in South Asia and sub-Saharan Africa) in which the prevalence of malnutrition is shockingly high. Malnutrition is still common among lower-income groups in all countries. For example, over the time period 1988–1994, 1.4% of U.S. children from birth to 59 months of age were found to be moderately to severely underweight; that is, their weights fell below minus 2 standard deviations of the median of the reference population (UNICEF, 2000). (Being underweight is a reflection of malnutrition which can affect intellectual function, but it is not a cause of intellectual impairment per se.) The importance of these dietary factors and consequences of their deficiencies are detailed next. The amounts of dietary factors necessary for good health were previously known as Recommended Dietary Allowances (RDAs). The United States and Canada are making a collaborative effort to revise RDAs, which will be renamed as Dietary Reference Intakes (DRIs) (see National Institutes of Health Office of Dietary Supplements, 2004).

Protein Calorie Malnutrition Dietary protein is key for proper nerve and muscle function. Protein calorie malnutrition (a reduced protein to total calorie intake over an extended period of time) eventually leads to depletion of the tissue reserve, or decreased proteins in the body, and then to lowering of blood protein levels. Intellectual function is compromised. This may be irreversible if protein deprivation occurs during periods of brain development. Economic, social, and cultural factors (e.g., poor feeding habits, superstitions, misinformation) all contribute to protein malnutrition in many countries. Infants and young children are very vulnerable. There are two disorders of protein calorie malnutrition: kwashiorkor (Krawindel, 2003; Williams, 1935) and marasmus (Gehri, Stettler, & Di Paolo, 2003). The term *kwashiorkor* is derived from an African word meaning "first child-second child," because a first-born child often develops kwashiorkor when the second child is born and replaces the first-born child at the mother's breast. Children with kwashiorkor have an odd reddish orange color of the hair, as well as a characteristic red skin rash. In kwashiorkor, the total calorie intake may be adequate, but there is a deficiency of protein in the diet. Kwashiorkor often is associated with a maize-based diet (Williams, 1935). The Greek term *marasmus* means "wasting away." In marasmus, there is severe deficiency of calories in the diet, including calories from protein. In the 19th century, more than half of infants' deaths were said to be due to marasmus, but the causes of marasmus differed among different age groups. In the early 21st century, this term is used to describe a type of protein calorie malnutrition that results in severe growth failure and emaciation in infants and young children. Protein calorie malnutrition results in more severe infections than would occur in a state of adequate nutrition (Keusch, 2003). Many programs have been implemented worldwide to address this problem. Such programs include public awareness, education of students and professionals, and prevention (see United Nations System, Standing Committee on Nutrition, n.d., for examples of how malnutrition is being addressed worldwide). In the United States, there are many programs to help people get healthy foods (Grigsby, 2005). In other countries, organizations such

Table 9.5. The most common specific environmental causes of intellectual or developmental disabilities

Classification	Contribution to intellectual or developmental disability
Prenatal causes	
Preconceptual and prenatal malnutrition, including iodine deficiency	Suspected of being the major factor, but impact varies from one population to another
Folic acid deficiency	Neural tube defects are caused in large part by folic acid deficiency
Maternal behaviors and exposures	
Alcohol abuse	Possibly up to 1% of children are affected; impact varies from one population to another
Maternal metabolic effects (obesity, diabetes, hypothyroidism, and phenylketonuria)	Metabolic and hormonal imbalances in pregnant women should be controlled to avoid adverse effects on fetal development
Preterm delivery from any cause	Majority of babies born prematurely die shortly after birth; the survivors are at high risk for cerebral palsy, blindness, deafness, and intellectual impairment; premature delivery causes 2%–10% of intellectual impairment
Parental age	The risk of having a child with certain intellectual or developmental disabilities increases with increasing parental (especially maternal) age (e.g., Down syndrome)
Perinatal causes	
Asphyxia	5% of all intellectual impairment
Intrauterine infections	3%–5% of all intellectual impairment
Premature cutting of the umbilical cord	Longitudinal studies of infants with immediate or delayed cord clamping are needed to determine if immediate cord clamping results in intellectual or developmental disability
Postnatal causes	3%–15% of all intellectual impairment
Head trauma due to child battering, motor vehicle accidents, and falls	52% of postnatal intellectual impairment
Near drownings	4% of postnatal intellectual impairment
Stroke (mainly from sickle cell anemia)	7% of postnatal intellectual impairment
Brain tumors	1% of postnatal intellectual impairment
Infections (congenital cytomegalovirus infection affects 40,000 newborns/year in the U.S.)	33% of postnatal intellectual impairment
Toxins (e.g., lead, methylmercury)	Effects vary from one population to another
Vitamin and mineral deficiencies (e.g., vitamin A, iron)	Effects vary from one population to another
Malnutrition	Effects vary from one population to another

Sources: Brent (2004); Cannon and Davis (2005); Mendola et al. (2002); Mercer, 2001; Morley (n.d.); and Murphy et al. (1998).

Although the term *intellectual or developmental disability* is used here, data for this table are drawn primarily from U.S.-based studies in which the term *mental retardation* has been used. See Chapter 15 for more details about asphyxia, brain injury, stroke, and infections (e.g., meningitis).

as the Red Cross should be contacted about addressing malnutrition.

Folic Acid Deficiency Folate, or folacin, is a water-soluble vitamin that is present in grains such as whole wheat bread, dark green vegetables such as spinach and broccoli, organ meat such as liver, and beans such as lentils and kidney beans; it is also present in mushrooms and cantaloupe. Folate is essential for the synthesis of adenine and thymine, two of the four nucleic acids that make up human genes and DNA. It is also required for the body to use the essential amino acid methionine that is found primarily in animal proteins. A folic acid deficiency may result from low dietary intake of folic acid (eating the wrong foods) and/or as the result of one's genetic background. Folic acid deficiency is known to result in an elevated level of homocysteine, a sulfur-containing amino acid (Beers & Berkow, 2005). High homocysteine levels, in turn, have been associated with cardiovascular disease and other undesirable conditions including Alzheimer's disease (see Chapter 44). Research has shown that folic acid deficiency is a risk factor for a **neural tube defect,** and that women who take vitamins that contain folic acid may lower the risk that their baby will be born with this birth defect (Mitchell, 2005). **Spina bifida** (a birth defect in the bony encasement of the spinal cord) and **anencephaly** (a birth defect characterized by missing or very reduced brain tissue) are two conditions caused by neural tube defects. These defects occur 25 to 29 days after a woman gets pregnant, a time when many are still unaware that they are pregnant. It is suggested that women who have diabetes, epilepsy, or a genetic predisposition for neural tube defects (i.e., have family members—brothers, sisters, parents, or cousins—with conditions caused by neural tube defects) take 5 milligrams (mg) of folic acid daily before and during pregnancy (Motherisk, 1996). To ensure that women of reproductive age receive the recommended daily intake of folic acid, in some countries it has become mandatory to fortify enriched grain products, such as bread, with folic acid. There is also evidence that vitamin B_{12} (cobalamin) deficiency may be a risk factor for neural tube defects (Steen et al., 1998). Vitamin B_{12} and folate deficiency also may contribute to the development of Alzheimer's disease.

Vitamin A Deficiency and Excess Vitamin A (retinol) is a fat-soluble vitamin that is found mainly in fish liver oils, liver, egg yolks, butter, and cream. Carotene and carotenoids, the substances that the body converts to vitamin A, are found in green leafy and yellow vegetables. Vitamin A is particularly important for proper function of the immune system (Beers & Berkow, 2005). Although the literature does not reveal an involvement of vitamin A deficiency (VAD) in human cognitive functioning, this deficiency results in spatial-learning and memory impairment in rats (Cocco et al., 2002). VAD is a public health problem in 118 countries, especially those in Africa and Southern and Eastern Asia (Beers & Berkow, 2005). Primary VAD is usually caused by prolonged dietary deprivation. It is endemic in areas, such as southern and eastern Asia, that have a rice-based diet (rice does not contain any carotene) (Potrykus, 2003). Secondary VAD may be due to inadequate conversion of carotene to vitamin A or interference with absorption, storage, or transport of vitamin A (e.g., as in celiac disease, cystic fibrosis, giardiasis, and other disorders affecting intestinal function). VAD is common in protein-energy malnutrition because the diet is deficient but also because vitamin A storage and transport are defective. VAD is the leading cause of preventable blindness in children and raises the risk of disease and death from severe infections accompanied by diarrhea and measles. Approximately 500,000 children per year die from VAD in developing countries (Farhang & Nikoopour, 2004; Underwood, 2004). In pregnant women, VAD causes night blindness and may increase the risk of maternal mortality.

For pregnant women in high-risk areas, VAD occurs especially during the last trimester, when demand by both the unborn child and the mother is highest. VAD may also be associated with elevated mother-to-child human immunodeficiency virus (HIV) transmission (Underwood, 2004). In developing countries where VAD is the major cause of blindness in children, prophylactic doses of vitamin A palmitate are provided orally 2 to 4 times per year. To prevent VAD, the diet should include dark green leafy vegetables and yellow fruits, such as mangoes and papaws (papayas). For secondary deficiency, vitamin A supplements should be given routinely. Infants suspected of being allergic to milk should be given adequate vitamin A in substitute formula. In some countries, flour, bread, sugar, and monosodium glutamate are fortified with vitamin A (Beers & Berkow, 2005). Genetically modified rice that produces carotenes is also being evaluated as a solution to VAD (Potrykus, 2003).

More of vitamin A is not necessarily better, however. Too much vitamin A is toxic and may lead to death. Women of childbearing age need to be particularly careful when supplementing vitamin A. Even taking 10 mg of vitamin A daily (the amount in some multivitamins) during the first 3 months of pregnancy has been linked to a high risk of birth defects. A dose of 2.5 times this amount is known to cause spontaneous abortions when taken early in pregnancy. For these reasons, women who are pregnant should consult with their doctor about how much vitamin A to take and should carefully check the amount of vitamin A in their multivitamin to make sure the dose is safe (Beers & Berkow, 2005; Higgins, 1999).

Iodine Deficiency Iodide is a trace mineral used by the thyroid gland to produce the important thyroid hormone called thyroxine. Thyroxine helps regulate blood cell production, body temperature, growth reproduction, metabolic rate, and nerve and muscle function. Iodide occurs in soil and seawater and is oxidized to iodine in the body. Good sources of iodine include bread, iodized salt, lobster, marine fish, milk, oysters (cooked), and shrimp (Beers & Berkow, 2005). Iodine deficiency usually results in an enlargement of the thyroid gland that is known as a *goiter.* This is visible as a swelling in the front of the throat. Iodine deficiency disorder is the single most common cause of preventable intellectual disability and brain damage in the world. Globally 2.2 billion people (38% of the world's population) have iodine deficiency (Hetzel, 2005; International Council for the Control of Iodine Deficiency Disorder, 2005). In North America, iodine deficiency is not usually a problem because salt is usually iodized. In developing countries that have low levels of iodide in the soil, such as China and Mexico, hypothyroidism resulting from iodine deficiency is a serious problem (Hauser, McMillin, & Bhatara, 1998; see also Chapter 15). Surprisingly, iodine deficiency still is a problem in some developed countries such as Switzerland and Germany. Iodine deficiency in children can cause stunted growth; apathy; difficulty with movement, speech, and hearing (see Chapter 25); and intellectual impairment. Iodine deficiency in pregnant women causes miscarriages and stillbirths; if the fetus survives, severe maternal iodine deficiency retards fetal growth and brain development (Sethi & Kapil, 2004). Infants with iodine deficiency are given L-thyroxine for a week plus iodide to quickly restore a euthyroid state. Iodide supplementation is then continued. More iodide is not necessarily better. Chronic iodine toxicity results when iodide intake is 20 times greater than the daily requirement. Paradoxically, although the introduction of salt iodinization reduces the prevalence of goiter, it also has been associated with increased hyperthyroidism and autoimmune thyroid disease as well as changes in the histologic type of thyroid cancer (Beers & Berkow, 2005; Lind et al., 2002). On the basis of the latter observations, diets which are too high in salt should be a concern not only because of harmful effects of excessive sodium but also of excessive iodide. Due to the overall benefits associated with iodide supplementation, iodized salt programs and iodized oil supplements are being implemented worldwide to prevent iodine deficiency disorder (Hetzel, 2005; International Council for the Control of Iodine Deficiency Disorder, 2005; World Health Organization, 2002; see also Chapter 15).

Iron Deficiency Iron, a trace metal that is essential for life, is absorbed in the intestines. It comes in two forms: heme iron (found in meats), which is well absorbed, and nonheme iron (found in leafy vegetables such as spinach), which is not as well absorbed. The body uses most of the iron that is consumed to form hemoglobin, the substance that helps red blood cells transport oxygen from the lungs to the rest of the body. The rest of the iron is stored for future needs and mobilized when dietary intake is inadequate. Because iron also plays a key role in helping to prepare the immune system to do its job, a deficiency may lead to colds. Low iron levels can also cause fatigue, pallor, and listlessness—hallmarks of anemia (Beers & Berkow, 2005).

Not all countries have a good system for diagnosing, treating, and preventing iron deficiency; thus, an international effort is needed to eliminate iron deficiency, the world's leading nutritional problem. In developing countries, 66% of children and women, ages 15–44 years, have this problem. In developed countries, 10%–20% of women of childbearing age are anemic (Scrimshaw, 1991; Zlotkin, 2004). Complications of iron deficiency anemia in infants and children include: developmental delays; behavior disturbances such as decreased motor activity, social interaction, and attention to tasks; compulsive eating of non-food items (pica) and ice; and irreversible impairment of learning ability. In adults, iron deficiency anemia can result in a low capacity to perform physically demanding labor. Metabolic consequences include impairment of the immune system, and a lowered metabolic rate and body temperature when exposed to cold. It is not known why iron-deficiency anemia affects physical work, but it is suspected that low blood hemogloblin levels may impair the oxygen content of blood enough to impair aerobic metabolism, which depends on oxygen availability. Iron-deficiency anemia also contributes to lead poisoning in children by increasing the gastrointestinal tract's ability to absorb heavy metals, including lead. Iron-deficiency anemia is associated with conditions that may independently affect infant and child development (e.g., low birth weight, generalized malnutrition, poverty, high blood level of lead). Iron deficiency during pregnancy contributes to maternal mortality and fetus/infant mortality in the perinatal period. During the first two trimesters of pregnancy, it is associated with a twofold-increased risk for preterm delivery and a threefold increased risk for delivering a low birth weight baby (Centers for Disease Control and Prevention [CDC], 1998). Iron deficiency can result from any of the following: poor diet, parasitic diseases (especially worm and malaria infections), and abnormal uterine bleeding. In many developing countries, vegetarian diets contribute to high rates of iron deficiency. Iron therapy in anemic children can often, but not always, improve behavior and cognitive performance, lead to normal growth, and hinder infections.

However, excessive iron can be damaging. Too much supplemental iron in a malnourished child or in people from certain ethnic backgrounds promotes fatal infections because the excess iron is available for the pathogen's use (Moalem, Weinberg, & Percy, 2004). In addition, excess iron is toxic, causing vomiting, diarrhea, and damage to the intestines. Iron may accumulate in the body when a person is given iron therapy in excessive amounts or for too long, receives repeated blood transfusions, or has chronic alcoholism. Iron overload disease (hemochromatosis) is a potentially fatal but treatable hereditary disorder in which too much iron accumulates in the body. People with chronic fatigue, diabetes, arthritis, or a family history of hemochromatosis should not take extra iron unless tests are done by a physician to determine if they are really iron deficient (Moalem et al., 2004).

Toxic Threats Toxic threats to a child's environment and development can have adverse outcomes. Depending on timing and dose of the toxic threat, the effects range from severe intellectual disability to more subtle changes such as problems with attention, memory, learning, social behavior, and IQ scores (Stein et al., 2002). Toxic threats that may result in intellectual and developmental disability include exposures to lead, mercury, and polychlorinated biphenyls (commonly know as PCBs), dioxins, pesticides, ionizing radiation, and environmental tobacco smoke, as well as maternal use of alcohol, tobacco, marijuana, and cocaine. Asbestos is a well-documented toxic threat in terms of cancers and respiratory diseases, but as yet there is no association with intellectual and developmental disability. Many chemicals produced in large amounts may have some effect on neurodevelopment, but very few (nine pesticides and three solvents) of among 3,000 have been adequately tested as of 1998 (Makris et al., 1998; Stein et al., 2002). The pesticide DEET—an effective mosquito repellant—and isopropanol—the main component of rubbing alcohol, which is used as an antiseptic—are two of the twelve substances that have been examined. These two substances are potentially poisonous as the result of excessive ingestion, inhalation, or dermal application. Infants and children have unique patterns of exposure and special vulnerabilities to pesticides (Landrigan et al., 2004). However, the benefits of pesticides and other potentially hazardous substances must be considered along with the risks (Kendrick, 2006; Koren, Matsui, & Bailey, 2003; Stremski & Hennes, 2000).

Exposures not previously considered to be a threat include maternal consumption of antidepressants (Kallen, 2004) and antianxiety drugs (Bercovici, 2004; "Neonatal complications after intrauterine exposure to SSRI antidepressants," 2004), as well as maternal exposure to dental X rays (Hujoel et al., 2004).

In both the United States and Canada, initiatives are being undertaken to identify toxic threats that are compromising the health and intellect of children (Centre for Global Research and Education on the Environment and Health, n.d.; National Institute of Environmental Health Sciences: Children's Environmental Health, 2003). By learning about different types of toxic threats and their sources—and by taking efforts to avoid them by promoting handwashing (this removes toxins from hands, prevents people from putting toxins into their mouths, and lessens absorption of toxins through the skin) and good dietary habits (e.g., not eating fish contaminated with mercury, washing fruits and vegetables or peeling them to remove pesticides and preservatives from the surface)—caregivers and parents can play an important role in reducing exposures to toxicants present in consumer products (Stein et al., 2002). These activities will not help to reduce the sources of toxic substances that are in the air, however (Health Canada, 2004; Motta et al., 2004).

Lead Humans may be exposed to lead through the air, drinking water, food, contaminated soil, deteriorating lead-based paint, dust, traditional or folk medications, certain types of candy or pottery, certain cosmetics, and lead-based crystal. Lead used to be used in paint, gasoline, water pipes, and many other products before it was known to be harmful. Old lead-based paint is the most significant source of lead exposure in the United States at the beginning of the 21st century. Harmful exposures from this source arise when lead-based paint is removed from surfaces by dry scraping, sanding, or open-flame burning. High concentrations of airborne lead particles in homes can also result from lead dust from outdoor sources, including contaminated soil that is tracked inside and use of lead in certain indoor activities such as soldering and stained-glass making (National Safety Council, 2004; U.S. Environmental Protection Agency, 2005). Children's costume jewelry may contain lead (Health Canada, 2003). Perinatal exposures to high doses of lead result in encephalopathy and convulsions. Lower dose lead exposures are associated with impairment in intellectual function and attention. Remedies for lead poisoning include eliminating lead in the environment; changing children's behavior (e.g., by training them to wash their hands and not to play in areas known to be contaminated with lead); and obtaining adequate dietary intake of calcium and iron intake, which reduces the uptake of lead (Kegler & Malcoe, 2004). Follow-up testing for elevated levels of lead in screening tests is key to prevention of chronic poisoning (Kemper et al., 2005). Once lead overload is identified, it can be readily treated by a form of treatment known as chelation (Markowitz, 2000).

Mercury Mercury is widespread in the environment. Human exposure to methylmercury comes largely through ingestion of contaminated food as follows. Much of the mercury that ends up on dinner tables comes from smokestacks of power plants (especially ones that are coal-fired), waste incinerators, and other industrial sources. Power plants are responsible for nearly one-third of man-made mercury emissions and are the largest industrial source of mercury entering the air (Trubey, 2005). There also is concern worldwide about the use of mercury amalgam in dental fillings (Spencer, 2000).

Methylmercury is a organic form of mercury that can accumulate up the aquatic food chain and lead to high concentrations in predatory fish (U.S. Department of Health and Human Services and U.S. Environmental Protection Agency, 2004; U.S. Environmental Protection Agency, 2005). Contaminated fish represent a public health risk when they are consumed by humans, particularly women of childbearing age and children. Because many types of fish are also a source of essential omega-3 fatty acids, which promote good health, the public should refer to dietary guidelines about eating fish (Mahaffey, 2004). Although such guidelines exist (U.S. Department of Health and Human Services and U.S. Environmental Protection Agency, 2004), they are not readily available to the public; there is great need for different groups to make these available.

At high level of prenatal exposure, methylmercury produces intellectual disability, cerebral palsy, and visual and auditory deficits in children of exposed mothers (Davidson, Myers, & Weiss, 2004; Mendola et al., 2002). As with lead overload, methylmercury overload can be readily treated, once identified, by chelation (George et al., 2004).

Alcohol Alcohol is a legal teratogen (factor that causes fetal malformations) and is the most widely used agent that can damage the developing fetus. As explained in Chapter 14, the birth incidence of intellectual and developmental disabilities resulting from maternal use of alcohol surpasses that of Down syndrome, fragile X syndrome, and neural tube defects. Women should not drink alcoholic beverages during pregnancy because of the demonstrated risk of birth defects. For the sake of our children, a zero-tolerance policy should be instated worldwide regarding pregnancy and alcohol use.

Prenatal Maternal Smoking Prenatal maternal smoking is a statistically significant risk factor for a number of problems in offspring. These include antisocial outcomes (Maughan et al., 2004), lower intelligence in males (Mortesen et al., 2005), higher risks of criminal arrest and hospitalization for substance abuse in male and female adults (Brennan et al., 2002), and attention-deficit/hyperactivity disorder (ADHD; Rowland, Lesesne, & Abramowitz, 2002). Unfortunately, secondhand smoke may result in similar risks in nonsmokers. It is possible that apparent adverse effects of prenatal maternal smoking may signal a causal association. Conversely, this association may be the result, at least in part, of other confounding factors such as genetics, low socioeconomic status or poor nutrition. As there is evidence that smokers have a tendency to abuse other drugs, apparent adverse effects of smoking may include consequences of exposure to other recreational drugs (Merrill et al., 1999). Paternal smoking also may have harmful neurocognitive outcomes, although it is not clear whether this is a primary or secondary effect or the result of confounding factors (Ozmert et al., 2005). The public needs to be better educated about the harmful effects of smoking on fetal development.

Other Toxic Threats It is well recognized that antiepileptic medications may have adverse effects on fetal development (Adab et al., 2004). In utero exposure to valproate, phenobarbitol, and polytherapy may all be teratogenic, with valproate having the highest risk (Motamedi & Meador, 2006). Pregnant women who must take valproate should balance the risk of teratogenicity with seizure control.

Street drugs such as cocaine and marijuana are also problematic for fetal development. In one U.S. study, children who were exposed to cocaine in utero were found to have significant cognitive deficits and a doubling of the rate of developmental delay during the first 2 years of life. Because 2-year outcomes are predictive of later cognitive outcomes, affected children may continue to have learning difficulties at school age (Singer et al., 2001). Another study found that heavy cocaine use by pregnant women was associated with poor motor performance in offspring (Miller-Loncar et al., 2005). In addition, cocaine use in pregnancy has been found to be associated with **acculturation** (reasons for this association are not clear but may be related to lack of self-esteem), lack of prenatal care, and significant social and obstetric complications resulting in increased neonatal morbidity secondary to prematurity, congenital infection and withdrawal syndrome (Ogunyemi & Hernandez-Loera, 2004). Despite the extensive use of marijuana by the general public and as a medicine, very limited information exists as to the consequences of prenatal cannabis exposure on the developing human brain. Studies of such effects in fetuses that have been aborted suggest that maternal marijuana use may affect growth at mid-gestation (Hurd et al., 2005) and impair certain distinct regions of the brain that regulate emotional behavior (Wang et al., 2004).

In addition, solvents such as toluene pose toxic threats to fetal development. Many women of reproductive age are exposed to organic solvents in the workplace. There is evidence that in utero exposure to organic solvents is associated with poorer performance on some specific subtle measures of neurocognitive function, language, and behavior (Laslo-Baker et al., 2004).

Maternal Metabolic Effects Certain metabolic abnormalities in the mother may have harmful effects on the developing fetus during **gestation.** Such effects are called gestational programming (Ross & Desai, 2005). Such effects include maternal obesity, diabetes, abnormal thyroid function, and maternal PKU.

Obesity is becoming a worldwide epidemic. Associated with obesity is the occurrence of type 2 diabetes, a disorder in which the level of blood sugar is excessively high. Some women have diabetes before they become pregnant. Others develop it during pregnancy, a form called gestational diabetes. Approximately 3% of pregnant women have problems with their blood sugar, and it is important that pregnant women control their blood sugar levels. (See Bo et al., 2003; Hampton,

2004; Sesma & Georgieff, 2003; & Watkins et al., 2003.) Babies born to mothers with diabetes tend to be very large. This poses risks to their health and to the mothers who may require delivery by cesarean section. Furthermore, babies born to mothers with diabetes may have cognitive dysfunction and may develop diabetes themselves (Persaud, in press). In addition, maternal obesity during pregnancy is associated with a greatly increased risk of neural tube defects such as spina bifida and anencephaly, although it presently is unclear whether it is obesity or high blood sugar that results in the neural tube defects.

Abnormal thyroid function in a pregnant mother has repercussions on neurobehavioral and neurocognitive development. Hypothyroidism in pregnant women, whether resulting from iodine deficiency or another cause, is associated with an increased risk of miscarriage, **hypertension, preeclampsia, abruptio placentae, low birth weight** infants, still births, and fetal distress in labor. Children born to mothers with untreated hypothyroidism during pregnancy score lower on IQ tests than children of healthy mothers. Thus, it is important for pregnant mothers with hypothyroidism to be adequately treated during their pregnancy (Poppe & Glinoer, 2003; see also Chapter 15 and the discussion in this chapter on iodine deficiency disorder).

As explained in Chapter 15, women with PKU are likely to give birth to infants with congenital abnormalities and cognitive disability if the fetus is exposed to high levels of phenylalanine while in the uterus. Thus, it is important for affected women to stay on a low phenylalanine diet before conception through delivery.

Infection Intrauterine and perinatal TORCH (i.e., **toxoplasmosis,** other [**syphilis, varicella-zoster virus, parvovirus B19**], **rubella, cytomegalovirus [CMV],** and **herpes simplex virus**) infections used to cause a larger percentage of intellectual disabilities in children than they do in the early 21st century (Stegmann & Carey, 2002). With the availability of prevention methods; early identification; and, in some cases, vaccination, these infections in many instances can be prevented or treated early enough to prevent damage to the central nervous system of the fetus. Nevertheless, blindness, deafness, and intellectual disability from intrauterine and/or perinatal CMV infection affect approximately 40,000 young children per year in the United States (Canon & Davis, 2005). The application of antibiotics to cut umbilical cords prevents many cases of newborn infection (Mullany, Darmstadt, & Tielsch, 2003). As of 2007, however, there is a resurgence of some vaccine-preventable diseases in North America due to the presence of immigrants from countries that do not promote vaccination. New challenges also include pediatric HIV and perinatal bacterial infections related to Group B *Streptococcus* and ***Listeria monocytogenes.*** In addition, there is concern that unidentified multiple organisms causing maternal bacterial vaginal infections may be causing intellectual impairment in some children (Murphy et al., 1998).

Preterm Delivery Preterm delivery (birth occurring before 36 weeks of gestation) is associated with increased risk for intellectual disability. Prematurity is more likely in cases of multiple births regardless of the cause; placental failure; and excess amniotic fluid. The more premature or underweight the newborn, the greater the risks of illness (infection, respiratory distress, or other problems), disabilities such as cerebral palsy and learning problems, hearing and vision problems, and death (Haas et al., 2005; McGregor & French, 1997; Monset-Couchard, de Bethmann, & Relier, 2004). Preterm delivery is known to place the immature brain at risk of hemorrhage and thus tissue damage. One study reported that infants born before 33 weeks of gestation have a high prevalence of structural brain abnormalities and that more than half have an abnormal **magnetic resonance imaging (MRI)** brain scan. In adolescence, these abnormalities were correlated more often with behavioral abnormalities than with neurological impairments (Stewart et al., 1999).

Premature Cutting of the Umbilical Cord The umbilical cord is the tube that leads from the placenta to the unborn child and carries blood, oxygen, and nutrients to the baby. For more than 200 years, there has been an awareness that the umbilical cord should not be cut before the baby has drawn its first breath and before the cord stops pulsating. Since 1980, however, this practice has changed, and the umbilical cord is frequently clamped before the baby has drawn its first breath; in some cases doctors cut the cord following delivery of the fetal head. The practice of early clamping of the umbilical cord has increased in response to requests from neonatologists for cord blood samples for diagnosis of asphyxia as soon as possible after birth in order to protect doctors from lawsuits (Iffy, Varadi, & Papp, 2001). Although this practice is saving some lives as the result of early diagnosis of asphyxia, it is believed to be causing brain damage in many infants not suffering from asphyxia, and there is concern that this practice may be resulting in intellectual disability later in life. Longitudinal studies of infants who have had immediate or delayed cord clamping are needed (Mercer, 2000; Morley, n.d).

Postnatal Brain Injury Postnatal brain injury (injury after birth) is the most identifiable, and should be the most preventable, cause of intellectual impairment (see Chapter 20). In the United States, traumatic brain injury is the leading cause of death in people younger than age 45 (BrainInjury.com, 2006); motor vehicle accidents are a leading cause of brain injury (BrainInjury.com, 2006), and drunk driving accounts for approximately 40% of motor vehicle accidents (Centers for Disease Control and Prevention, 2002). Leading causes in children include meningitis and child battering (CDC, 1996). Brain injury also is incurred in falls, shaken baby syndrome, bicycle and scooter accidents, sports accidents, and accidents with guns. Surveillance and intervention activities could prevent many cases of brain injury. (See Chapters 15 and 20 for more information about brain injury, including traumatic brain injury and shaken baby syndrome, and Chapter 15 for more information about meningitis.)

FACTORS CAUSING OR CONTRIBUTING TO MENTAL HEALTH DISORDERS

There is a complex relationship among intellectual and developmental disabilities, psychiatric illnesses, and behavior disturbances (see Chapters 20 and 42). As explained elsewhere in this book, some intellectual and developmental disabilities (e.g., ASDs, ADHD) are classified as mental health disorders. Also, psychiatric illnesses and behavior disturbances (otherwise known as mental health disorders) have been consistently found to affect a much higher proportion of people with intellectual and developmental disabilities than in the general population (Deb, Thomas, & Bright, 2001a, 2001b). It is thus appropriate for a section on factors and causes underlying mental health disorders to be included in this chapter. It should be stressed that psychiatric illnesses, difficult behaviors, and mental health disorders are functional classifications and not etiological diagnoses.

Life stresses play a significant role in triggering psychiatric illnesses, but there is increasing evidence for genetic predisposition in certain psychiatric conditions. These include alcoholism, anorexia nervosa, ASDs, bipolar disorder, depression, dyslexia, **enuresis nocturna,** epilepsy, obsessive-compulsive disorder, schizophrenia, Alzheimer's disease, and frontal lobe dementia (Abdolmaleky, Thiagalingam, & Wilcox, 2005; Shibayama et al., 2004) . However, it does appear that the vast majority of psychiatric illnesses result from more than one genetic and/or environmental factor. In contrast to the dementias that are characterized by neurodegeneration later in life, there is evidence that schizophrenia is a disorder associated with abnormal development of the brain (Woods, 1998).

As outlined in Chapter 20, some of the most common psychiatric disorders that affect both the general population and people with intellectual and developmental disabilities are as follows: ADHD, anxiety disorders such as phobias, bipolar disorder (formerly known as manic-depression), eating disorders such as anorexia nervosa and bulimia nervosa, major depression (unipolar disorder), schizophrenia, seizure disorders (epileptic disorders), and Alzheimer's disease. (See also Chapters 18, 19, and 44.) People who have a psychiatric illness or behavior disturbance in addition to another intellectual disability are said to have a *dual diagnosis* and are most in need of help and service (Kessler, 2004). It is particularly complicated to identify the causes of severe behavior disturbances associated with certain intellectual and developmental disabilities. Problems arise because of the considerable difficulty identifying mental illness in individuals unable to communicate their mental experiences. As a consequence, behaviors that are part of the intellectual disability are often misunderstood as being symptoms of psychiatric illness. Inappropriate treatments, often with serious long-term side effects (e.g., **antipsychotic medications**) may be initiated (Bradley & Bryson, 1998; Holden & Gitlesen, 2004). Likewise, psychiatric symptoms, such as the withdrawal and agitation of a depressive illness, may be misinterpreted as being part of the developmental disorder, and a treatable condition may go unrecognized as a result. This latter phenomenon is referred to as diagnostic overshadowing (Rush et al., 2004).

ASDs include autism, Asperger syndrome, Rett syndrome, and pervasive developmental disorder-not otherwise specified (PDD-NOS) (see also Chapters 12 and 13). ASDs are part of the larger diagnostic family of pervasive developmental disorders (PDDs). These disorders are included in the mental health section because protocols for their diagnosis are provided in the *Diagnostic and Statistical Manual of Mental Disorders* (*DSM-IV-TR*; American Psychiatric Association, 2000) and the International Statistical Classification of Diseases and Related Health Problems (ICD-10; World Health Organization, 1990) manuals. Research studies have determined that the ASDs have an extremely strong genetic basis, although complex interaction between genetic and environmental factors is suspected. A survey conducted in 2004 pointed out that as many as 15 different genetic loci may be involved in the ASDs (Muhle, Trentacoste, & Rapin, 2004). With the exception of Rett syndrome, which results from mutations of the MECP2 gene, and some syndromes that manifest as ASDs, the specific genetic factors that may be involved in the ASDs are not yet known. Disorders that may manifest clinically as ASD or PDD include epilepsy, Prader-Willi, Angelman, fragile X, and tuberous sclerosis, among others; surveys indicate that these may account for up to 12%–25% of ASD cases (Muhle et al., 2004). Children with ASDs who have dysmorphic features, congenital anomalies, intellectual disability, or family members with intellectual disabilities are those most likely to benefit from extensive medical testing and genetic consultation, because they are most likely to have a genetic form of epilepsy or one of the aforementioned genetic syndromes that can mask as ASDs. It is interesting to note that environmental factors such as rubella and cytomegalovirus infection account for a small percentage of ASDs (Libbey et al., 2005; Muhle et al., 2004). The prevalence of the ASDs has clearly been increasing since the 1980s, but it is not known if more cases really are being caused or if past ASD rates were underestimates. One controversy surrounds the potential role of childhood vaccinations (especially those containing aluminum and mercury additives) in causing ASDs (Geier & Geier, 2005; Libbey et al., 2005; Rutter, 2005). Concerns about increases in ASDs, their causes, and the high costs of intervention have highlighted the need for systematic public health monitoring. The CDC and Metropolitan Atlanta Developmental Disabilities Surveillance Program (MADDSP) have established a model program for population monitoring of ASDs and developmental disabilities that has been implemented in other states (Rice et al., 2004). Such monitoring will establish databases that will be of enormous benefit to discovering the causes of ASDs as well as to facilitating research, service, and education in the ASD and intellectual disability fields.

FACTORS AFFECTING THE ABILITY TO IDENTIFY THE CAUSES OF INTELLECTUAL AND/OR DEVELOPMENTAL DISABILITIES

A number of factors affect the ability to identify the specific genetic or environmental causes of an intellectual or developmental disability. These include the following:

1. *The severity of intellectual impairment associated with the disability:* The ability to find a cause for an intellectual or developmental disability depends on the severity of the intellectual impairment—the greater the severity, the more likely it will be that a cause can be identified and also the more likely it will be that the cause is genetic (Durkin, 2002; Moser, 2004; Raynham et al., 1996; Yeargin-Allsopp & Boyle, 2002). Data compiled from a number of surveys indicate that mild intellectual impairment is considerably more prevalent than moderate to profound impairment (e.g., see Kabra & Gulati, 2003). Thus, having severe intellectual disability should prompt attempts to find a primary cause.

2. *The severity of sensory impairments associated with the disability:* The ability to find a cause of a disability not only depends on the severity of intellectual impairment, but also on the severity of the sensory impairments that accompany it. Children with known causes of intellectual disability often have hearing, speech, and language impairment, as well as seizures, unusual behaviors such as those associated with autism, and the presence of cerebral palsy (e.g., see Carvill, 2001). Thus, detection of a significant sensory impairment in a child with an intellectual or developmental disability should prompt attempts to find a primary cause.

3. *Sex:* More boys than girls are found to have intellectual disability (particularly mild intellectual disability), with a ratio of approximately 1.4:1. The reason for this is not clear, but it may be due in part to the contribution of genetic X-linked disabilities that primarily affect males (Gecz, 2004; Nussbaum et al., 2004). In etiological studies, it is important to consider the sex of the participants.

4. *Scientific technology:* The capacity to identify causes of intellectual and developmental disabilities is increasing because of advancements in molecular biology techniques and new brain imaging techniques that can detect structural and functional abnormalities in the brain of living individuals. As cytogenetic, molecular biological, and imaging techniques continue to become more sensitive, it is anticipated that an increasing number of intellectual and developmental disabilities will be found to have a genetic basis (Battaglia, 2003; Battaglia & Carey, 2003; Shevell et al., 2003).

Importance of Identifying the Primary Cause of an Intellectual or Developmental Disability

It is crucial that the primary cause (or etiological diagnosis) of an intellectual or developmental disability be made carefully and correctly to enable the best possible intervention and to provide relief from uncertainty. Providing an incorrect explanation, conversely, can lead to inappropriate counseling, stigmatization, and labeling that may continue for years—even if the cause of the disability is changed.

How to Increase the Chances of Finding the Primary Cause of an Intellectual or Developmental Disability

Certain conditions that are associated with characteristic physical features, such as Down syndrome and neural tube defects (e.g., spina bifida, anencephaly) are readily identifiable at birth. Prenatal screening for these conditions is routinely available in some countries for women older than the age of 35. Neonatal screening is done routinely on newborns to detect PKU, galactosemia, and congenital hypothyroidism in Canada, the United States, and many other countries. Other intellectual and developmental disabilities may require ongoing evaluation, often over a period of several years, in order to find the primary cause.

Currently, there is no agreement on the exact procedure for finding the cause for an intellectual or developmental disability. Finding the primary cause of a disability that is not obvious must be guided by a clinician's experience and common sense. Examining the family history should be an essential component. It is important to find out if the condition has been inherited or if it is sporadic (i.e., has occurred in the absence of family history). Furthermore, mild to major complications that may accompany disability—such as plugged ears, ear infections, bad eyesight, toothaches, abuse (emotional, physical, or sexual), and psychiatric illnesses—must always be checked for and appropriately addressed (see Chapter 41). A multidisciplinary assessment involving many different health care specialists may be necessary before the cause is identified. Wilska and Kaski (2001) developed an etiological classification based on timing and type of injury to the central nervous system. Since 1979, it has been adopted by 40–50 physicians in Finland and has been proven to enhance the diagnostic activity and genetic counseling of physicians. Because new cytogenetic, molecular biology, and imaging techniques are so costly, use of these techniques to attempt to identify the primary cause of a disability should be applied only when there is a strong rationale for doing so. Thus, finding the primary cause of a disability may involve activities that take place over a number of years.

Resources for Assessment

Health professionals, families, educators, caregivers, friends, and relatives all have the potential to help identify the primary cause of an intellectual or developmental disability. Having knowledge of factors known to cause or contribute to developmental disabilities is essential for correctly finding the cause in individuals.

How the primary causes of intellectual and developmental disabilities are found varies from one region to another and from one country to another. People who have access to large hospitals will benefit from prenatal and neonatal screening and the expertise of developmental pediatricians who examine babies when they are born, as well as geneticists, developmental neurologists, psychiatrists, and other health professionals with vast collective experience who can intervene at any stage.

When a child has a relatively mild intellectual disability, parents or astute teachers—who often know the child best—can guide health care professionals. Referrals for specialized workgroups are done through a family doctor. Some agencies that specialize in intellectual disabilities have developed assessment protocols that have helped to find causes of disabilities in children or adults who have "fallen through the cracks" in other settings. Research that involves parents and people with intellectual and developmental disabilities has proven helpful in gaining insight into ways to improve the search for causes and interventions.

SUMMARY

Intellectual and developmental disabilities can be caused by genetic and environmental factors, alone or in combination. Finding the primary cause of an intellectual or developmental disability sometimes can be done quickly, but more often this process requires investigation over a number of years. Approximately 1,200 of 7,000 genetic disorders are already known to be associated with significant cognitive disability. As the result of technological advances in cytogenetics, molecular biology, and brain imaging, it is believed that more intellectual and developmental disabilities will be found to have a genetic basis.

The causes of as many as 50%–70% of intellectual and developmental disabilities presently are known. Disabilities associated with mild cognitive impairment are more common, and pose more difficulty in determining a cause, than those associated with moderate to profound impairment. A much higher proportion of intellectual disabilities associated with severe cognitive impairment are caused by genetic factors than those associated with mild cognitive impairment.

The most common genetic forms of intellectual disability are Down syndrome and fragile X syndrome. Recent genetic advances include identification of mutations of the MECP2 gene that causes Rett syndrome, mutations of the ARX gene that cause a spectrum of different disorders, genetic mutations that cause certain types of epilepsy, and the discovery of regions on several different chromosomes that are linked to autism. The complications of certain genetic forms of intellectual disability (especially congenital hypothyroidism) and certain inborn errors of metabolism (e.g., PKU, galactosemia) can essentially be prevented by dietary management or supplementation if they are diagnosed and treated in time.

A large proportion of intellectual disabilities are caused by environmental factors that should be preventable; three such conditions very commonly expressed, are fetal alcohol spectrum disorder, iron deficiency anemia, and thyroid malfunction resulting from iodine deficiency. Brain injury due to accidents caused by drunk driving, certain types of falls, and repeated child battering also should be completely preventable. Other causal environmental factors include maternal use of antidepressant and antianxiety medications and maternal exposure to dental X rays. The medical practice of clamping newborns' umbilical cords before they draw their first breath may be harming children's brains.

People with intellectual and developmental disabilities may also have mental health problems. It is important to correctly distinguish psychiatric illness from underlying disability, each of which may require a different treatment.

Professionals involved in determining the primary cause of an intellectual or developmental disability should proceed cautiously, as complex ethical issues may arise. Gaps between professionals in the biomedical and psychosocial fields need to be bridged so that people with intellectual and developmental disabilities, their caregivers, and their families receive the best care to which they are entitled in order to maximize quality of life. The establishing of public health databases is a key component of finding causes of intellectual and developmental disabilities; this fosters not only education but also prevention, better treatment and service provision, and research endeavors that will lead to new treatments and cures. Thus, it is impossible to overemphasize the importance of education at all levels in the intellectual and developmental disabilities field, as well as the ramifications—such as prevention—that this education will have in the field.

FOR FURTHER THOUGHT AND DISCUSSION

1. What can be done to target and educate prospective mothers about the dangers of folic acid deficiency, drinking and smoking during pregnancy, and other preventable causes of developmental disabilities?
2. What actions might be taken to curb brain injury due to drunk driving accidents, accidental falls, and child battering?
3. What actions might policy makers take to ensure that health professionals are appropriately paid for providing services to people with intellectual and developmental disabilities?
4. Given that advancements for effective interventions, treatments, or even prevention depend on research, what action might be taken by grass roots organizations, families of people with disabilities, members of the general public, and researchers and other health professionals to increase the level of funding for research on intellectual and developmental disabilities? (Hints: lobby politicians, become involved in fund-raising activities, promote establishment of public health monitoring systems, participate in the research)

REFERENCES

Abdolmaleky, H.M., Thiagalingam, S., & Wilcox, M. (2005). Genetics and epigenetics in major psychiatric disorders: Dilemmas, achievements, applications, and future scope. *American Journal of Pharmacogenomics, 5*(3), 149-160.

Adab, N., Tudur, S.C., Vinten, J., et al. (2004). Common antiepileptic drugs in pregnancy in women with epilepsy. *Cochrane Database of Systematic Reviews* [On line]. http://www.cochrane.org/reviews/en/ab004848.html

American Association on Mental Retardation. (2005). *Definition of mental retardation.* Retrieved September 12, 2006, from http://www.aamr.org/Policies/faq_mental_retardation.shtml

American Psychiatric Association. (2000). *Diagnostic and statistical manual of mental disorders* (4th ed., text rev.). Washington, DC: Author.

Andersen, S.L. (2003). Trajectories of brain development: Point of vulnerability or window of opportunity? *Neuroscience and Biobehavioral Reviews, 27,* 3–18.

Arvio, M., & Sillanpaa, M. (2003). Prevalence, aetiology and comorbidity of severe and profound intellectual disability in Finland. *Journal of Intellectual Disabilities Research, 47*(Pt. 2), 108–112.

Battaglia, A. (2003). Neuroimaging studies in the evaluation of developmental delay/mental retardation. *American Journal of Medical Genetics. Part C: Seminars in Medical Genetics, 117,* 25–30.

Battaglia, A., & Carey, J.C. (2003). Diagnostic evaluation of developmental delay/mental retardation: An overview. *American Journal of Medical Genetics. Part C, Seminars in Medical Genetics, 117,* 3–14.

Beers, M.H., & Berkow, R. (Eds.). (2005). Section 1: Nutritional disorders. In *The Merck manual of diagnosis and therapy* (17th ed.). Retrieved September 8, 2005, from http://www.merck.com/mrkshared/mmanual/section1/chapter3/3b.jsp

Bercovici, E. (2004). Prenatal and perinatal effects of psychotropic drugs on neurocognitive development in the fetus. *Journal on Developmental Disabilities, 11*(2), 1–26.

Berg, J.M. (1985). Physical determinants of environmental origin. In A.M. Clarke, A.D.B. Clarke & J.M. Berg (Eds.), *Mental deficiency: The changing outlook* (pp. 99–143). London: Methuen and Co.

Bo, S., Menato, G., Signorile, A., et al. (2003). Obesity or diabetes: What is worse for the mother and for the baby? *Diabetes & Metabolism,* 29(2, Pt. 1), 175–178.

Bodensteiner, J.B., & Schaefer G.B. (1995). Evaluation of the patient with idiopathic mental retardation. *Journal of Neuropsychiatry, 7,* 361–370.

Bradley, E., & Bryson, S. (1998). Psychiatric illness in mentally handicapped adolescents (and young adults) with autistic disability. *Final report to NHRDP* (Project Number 6606-4919-63).

Bradley, R.H., & Corwyn, R.F. (2002). Socioeconomic status and child development. *Annual Review of Psychology, 53,* 371–399.

BrainInjury.com. (2006). *Traumatic brain injury (TBI).* Retrieved May 16, 2006, from http://braininjury.com/injured.html

Brennan, P.A., Grekin, E.R., Mortensen, E.L., et al. (2002). Relationship of maternal smoking during pregnancy with criminal arrest and hospitalization for substance abuse in male and female adult offspring. *American Journal of Psychiatry, 159,* 48–54.

Brent, R.L. (2004). Environmental causes of human congenital malformations: The pediatrician's role in dealing with these complex clinical problems caused by a multiplicity of environmental and genetic factors. *Pediatrics, 113*(Suppl. 4), 957–968.

Brown, R., & Larsen, P.R. (2005). Chapter 15: Thyroid gland development and disease in infants and children. In *The thyroid and its diseases.* Retrieved September 7, 2005, from http://www.thyroidmanager.org

Butler, M.G. (2002). Imprinting disorders: Non-Mendelian mechanisms affecting growth. *Journal of Pediatric Endocrinology & Metabolism, 15*(Suppl. 5), 1279–1288.

Cannon, M.J., & Davis, K.F. (2005). Washing our hands of the congenital cytomegalovirus disease epidemic. *BMC Public Health, 5,* 70.

Carvill, S. (2001). Sensory impairments, intellectual disability and psychiatry. *Journal of Intellectual Disabilities Research, 45*(Pt. 6), 467–483.

Centers for Disease Control and Prevention (CDC). (1996). Postnatal causes of developmental disabilities in children aged 3–10 years: Atlanta, Georgia, 1991. *Morbidity and Mortality Weekly Report, 45*(6), 130–134.

Centers for Disease Control and Prevention (CDC). (1998). *Recommendations to prevent and control iron deficiency in the United States.* Retrieved July 15, 2005, from http://www.cdc.gov/mmwr/preview/mmwrhtml/00051880.htm

Centers for Disease Control and Prevention (CDC). (2002). Involvement by young drivers in fatal alcohol-related motor-vehicle crashes: United States, 1982–2001. *Morbidity and Mortality Weekly Report, 51*(48), 1089–1091.

Centre for Global Research and Education on the Environment and Health. (n.d.). *Research and education on the environment and health.* Retrieved May 15, 2006, from http://cgreeh.org

Charrow, J. (2004). Ashkenazi Jewish genetic disorders. *Familial Cancer, 3,* 201–206.

Cocco, S., Diaz, G., Stancampiano, R., et al. (2002). Vitamin A deficiency produces spatial learning and memory impairment in rats. *Neuroscience, 115,* 475–482.

Conrad, M.E. (2006). Iron deficiency anemia. In *E-Medicine.* Retrieved May 15, 2006, from http://www.emedicine.com/med/topic1188.htm

Curry, C.J. (2002). Rational evaluation of the adolescent with mental retardation. *Adolescent Medicine, 13,* vii, 331–343.

Curry, C.J., Stevenson, R.E., Aughton, D., et al. (1997). Evaluation of mental retardation: Recommendations of a Consensus Conference: American College of Medical Genetics. *American Journal of Medical Genetics, 72,* 468–477.

Daily, D.K., Ardinger, H.H., & Holmes, G.E. (2000). Identification and evaluation of mental retardation. *American Family Physician, 61,* 1059–1067.

Davidson, P.W., Myers, G.J., & Weiss, B. (2004). Mercury exposure and child development outcomes. *Pediatrics, 113* (4, Suppl.), 1023–1029.

Deb, S., Thomas, M., & Bright, C. (2001a). Mental disorder in adults with intellectual disability. 1: Prevalence of functional psychiatric illness among a community-based population aged between 16 and 64 years. *Journal of Intellectual Disability Research, 45*(Pt. 6), 495–505.

Deb, S., Thomas, M., & Bright, C. (2001b). Mental disorder in adults with intellectual disability. 2: The rate of behaviour disorders among a community-based population aged between 16 and 64 years. *Journal of Intellectual Disability Research, 45*(Pt. 6), 506–514.

Dobbing, J. (1981). The later development of the brain and its vulnerability. *Journal of Inherited Metabolic Disease, 5*(2), 88.

Drews, C.D., Yeargin-Allsopp, M., Decouflé, P., et al. (1995). Variation in the influence of selected sociodemographic risk factors for mental retardation. *American Journal of Public Health, 85,* 329–334.

Durkin, M. (2002). The epidemiology of developmental disabilities in low-income countries. *Mental Retardation and Developmental Disabilities Research Reviews, 8,* 206–211.

Everett, C.M., & Wood, N.W. (2004). Trinucleotide repeats and neurodegenerative disease. *Brain, 127*(Pt. 11), 2385–2405.

Farhang, B., & Nikoopour, H. (2004). The effect of light and temperature on stability of vitamin A in the fortified vegetable oils (hydrogenated and nonhydrogenated). *Asia Pacific Journal of Clinical Nutrition, 13*(Suppl.), S161.

Finucane, B., Haas-Givler, B., & Simon, E.W. (2003). Genetics, mental retardation, and the forging of new alliances. *American Journal of Medical Genetics. Part C, Seminars in Medical Genetics, 117,* 66–72.

Fisch, H., Hyun, G., Golden, R., et al. (2003). The influence of paternal age on Down syndrome. *Journal of Urology, 169,* 2275–2278.

Gecz, J. (2004). The molecular basis of intellectual disability: Novel genes with naturally occurring mutations causing altered gene expression in the brain. *Frontiers in Bioscience, 9,* 1–7.

Gehri, M., Stettler, N., & Di Paolo, E.R. (2004). *Marasmus.* Retrieved January 12, 2005, from http://www.emedicine.com/ped/topic164.htm

Geier, D.A., & Geier, M.R. (2005). A two-phased population epidemiological study of the safety of thimerosal-containing vaccines: A follow-up analysis. *Medical Science Monitor, 11,* CR160–170.

George, G.N., Prince, R.C., Gailer, J., et al. (2004). Mercury binding to the chelation therapy agents DMSA and DMPS and the rational design of custom chelators for mercury. *Chemical Research in Toxicology, 17,* 999–1006.

Glinoer, D., & Delange, F. (2000). The potential repercussions of maternal, fetal, and neonatal hypothyroxinemia on the progeny. *Thyroid, 10,* 871–887.

Gottesman, I.I., & Hanson, D.R. (2005). Human development: Biological and genetic processes. *Annual Review of Psychology, 56,* 263–286.

Grigsby, D.G. (2005). *Protein-energy malnutrition.* Retrieved May 6, 2005, from http://www.chclibrary.org/micromed/00062340.html

Gutierrez-Delicado, E., & Serratosa, J.M. (2004). Genetics of the epilepsies. 1. *Current Opinions in Neurology, 17,* 147–153.

Guze, C. (2005). *Teratogens.* Retrieved July 15, 2005, from http://www.carolguze.com/text/442-13-teratogens.shtml

Haas, J.S., Fuentes-Afflick, E., Stewart, A.L., et al. (2005). Prepregnancy health status and the risk of preterm delivery. *Archives of Pediatric & Adolescent Medicine, 159,* 58–63.

Hagerman, R.J. (1997). Fragile X syndrome: Molecular and clinical insights and treatment issues. *Western Journal of Medicine, 166,* 129–137.

Hampton, T. (2004). Maternal diabetes and obesity may have lifelong impact on health of offspring. *Journal of the American Medical Association, 292,* 789–790.

Harris, J.C. (1995). *Developmental neuropsychiatry, Volume II: Assessment, diagnosis and treatment of developmental disorders.* Oxford, United Kingdom: Oxford University Press.

Hauser, P., McMillin, J.M., & Bhatara, V.S. (1998). Resistance to thyroid hormone: Implications for neurodevelopmental research on the effects of thyroid hormone disruptors. *Toxicology and Industrial Health, 14,* 85–101.

Health Canada. (2003). *Health Canada warns Canadians about potential child's lead exposure.* Retrieved July 15, 2005, from http://www.hc-sc.gc.ca/english/protection/warnings/2003/2003_82.htm

Health Canada. (2004). *Health and air quality: Canada–United States border air quality strategy.* Retrieved July 15, 2005, from http://www.hc-sc.gc.ca/ewh-semt/air/out-ext/border_air_e.html

Heikura, U., Linna, S.L., Olsen, P., et al. (2005). Etiological survey on intellectual disability in the northern Finland birth cohort 1986. *American Journal on Mental Retardation, 110,* 171–180.

Hetzel, B.S. (2005). Towards the global elimination of brain damage due to iodine deficiency: The role of the International Council for Control of Iodine Deficiency Disorders. *International Journal of Epidemiology, 34* (4), 762–764.

Higgins, M.L.M. (1999). *Carotenoid (vitamin A) food sources: Fruits and vegetables "best buys."* Retrieved July 11, 2006, from http://www.oznet.ksu.edu/humannutrition/_timely/Atbl.htm

Hofman, K.J., Steel, G., Kazazian, H.H., et al. (1991). Phenylketonuria in U.S. blacks: Molecular analysis of the phenylalanine hydroxylase gene. *American Journal of Human Genetics, 48,* 791–798.

Holden, B., & Gitlesen, J.P. (2004). Psychotropic medication in adults with mental retardation: Prevalence, and prescription practices. *Research in Developmental Disabilities, 25,* 509–521.

Hujoel, P.P., Bollen, A.M., Noonan, C.J., et al. (2003). Antepartum dental radiography and infant low birth weight. *Journal of the American Medical Association, 291,* 1987–1993.

Hurd, Y.L., Wang, X., Anderson, V., et al. (2005). Marijuana impairs growth in mid-gestation fetuses. *Neurotoxicology and Teratology, 27,* 221–229.

Iffy, L., Varadi, V., & Papp E. (2001). Untoward neonatal sequelae deriving from cutting of the umbilical cord before delivery. *Medicine and the Law, 20,* 627–634.

International Council for the Control of Iodine Deficiency Disorder. (2005). *Iodine deficiency disorder (IDD).* Retrieved May 16, 2006, from http://indorgs.virginia.edu/iccidd/aboutidd.htm

Kabra, M., & Gulati, S. (2003). Mental retardation. *Indian Journal of Pediatrics, 70,* 153–158.

Kallen, B. (2004). Neonate characteristics after maternal use of antidepressants in late pregnancy. *Archives of Pediatric and Adolescent Medicine, 158,* 312–316.

Kegler, M.C., & Malcoe, L.H. (2004). Results from a lay health advisor intervention to prevent lead poisoning among rural Native American children. *American Journal of Public Health, 94,* 1730–1735.

Kemper, A.R., Cohn, L.M., Fant, K.E., et al. (2005). Follow-up testing among children with elevated screening blood lead levels. *Journal of the American Medical Association, 293,* 2232–2237.

Kendrick, D.B. (2006). Mosquito repellents and superwarfarin rodenticides: Are they really toxic in children? *Current Opinion in Pediatrics, 18*(2), 180–183.

Kessler, R.C. (2004). The epidemiology of dual diagnosis. *Biological Psychiatry, 56,* 730–737.

Keusch G.T. (2003). The history of nutrition: Malnutrition, infection and immunity. *Journal of Nutrition, 133,* 336S–340S.

Kimmel, C.A., Generoso, W.M., Thomas, R.D., et al. (1993). A new frontier in understanding the mechanisms of developmental abnormalities. *Toxicology and Applied Pharmacology, 1991,* 159–165.

Koren, G., Matsui, D., & Bailey, B. (2003). DEET-based insect repellents: Safety implications for children and pregnant and lactating women. *Canadian Medical Association Journal, 169*(3), 209–212.

Krawindel, M. (2003). Kwashiorkor is still not fully understood. *Bull World Health Organ, 81*(12), 910–911.

Landrigan, P.J., Kimmel, C.A., Correa, A., et al. (2004). Children's health and the environment: Public health issues and challenges for risk assessment. *Environmental Health Perspectives, 112,* 257–265.

Laslo-Baker, D., Barrera, M., Knittel-Keren, D., et al. (2004). Child neurodevelopmental outcome and maternal occupational exposure to solvents. *Archives of Pediatrics & Adolescent Medicine, 158,* 956–961.

Lewis, M.E.S. (2004). Genes, screens, and means for advancing the diagnosis and anticipatory care of individuals with congenital intellectual disability. *Clinical Genetics, 65*(1), 1.

Libbey, J.E., Sweeten, T.L., McMahon, W.M., et al. (2005). Autistic disorder and viral infections. *Journal of Neurovirology, 11,* 1–10.

Lind, P., Kumnig, G., Heinisch, M., et al. (2002). Iodine supplementation in Austria: Methods and results. *Thyroid, 12*(10), 903–907.

Mahaffey, K.R. (2004). Fish and shellfish as dietary sources of methylmercury and the omega-3 fatty acids, eicosahexaenoic acid and docosahexaenoic acid: Risks and benefits. *Environmental Research, 95,* 414–428.

Makris, S., Raffaele, K., Sette, W., et al. (1998). *Retrospective analysis of twelve developmental neurotoxicity studies submitted to the FIFRA Scientific Advisory Panel (SAP).* Retrieved May 16, 2006, from http://www.epa.gov/scipoly/sap/1998/december/neuro.pdf, December 1998.

Mandel, J.L., & Biancalana, V. (2004). Fragile X mental retardation syndrome: From pathogenesis to diagnostic issues. *Growth Hormone & IGF Research, 14*(Suppl. A), S158–S165.

Markowitz, M. (2000). Lead poisoning: A disease for the next millennium. *Current Problems in Pediatrics, 30*(3), 62–70.

Matilainen, R., Airaksinen, E., Mononen, T., et al. (1995). A population-based study on the causes of mild and severe mental retardation. *Acta Paediatrica, 84,* 261–266.

Maughan, B., Taylor, A., Caspi, A., et al. (2004). Prenatal smoking and early childhood conduct problems: Testing genetic and environmental explanations of the association. *Archives of General Psychiatry, 61,* 836–843.

McGregor, J.A., & French, J.I. (1997). Preterm birth: The role of infection and inflammation. *Medscape Womens Health, 2,* 1.

Mendola, P., Selevan, S.G., Gutter, S., et al. (2002). Environmental factors associated with a spectrum of neurodevelopmental deficits. *Mental Retardation and Developmental Disabilities Research Reviews, 8*(3), 188–197.

Mercer, J.S. (2001). Current best evidence: A review of the literature on umbilical cord clamping. *Journal of Midwifery & Women's Health, 46*(6), 402–414.

Merrill, J.C., Kleber, H.D., Shwartz, M., et al. (1999). Cigarettes, alcohol, marijuana, other risk behaviors, and American youth. *Drug and Alcohol Dependence, 56*(3), 205–212.

Miller-Loncar, C., Lester, B.M., Seifer, R., et al. (2005). Predictors of motor development in children prenatally exposed to cocaine. *Neurotoxicology and Teratology, 27*(2), 213–220.

Milunsky, A. (1977). *Know your genes.* Boston: Houghton Mifflin Company.

Mitchell, L.E. (2005). Epidemiology of neural tube defects. *American Journal of Medical Genetics. Part C, Seminars in Medical Genetics, 135,* 88–94.

Moalem, S., Weinberg, E.D., & Percy, M.E. (2004). Hemochromatosis and the enigma of misplaced iron: Implications for infectious disease and survival. *Biometals, 17,* 135–139.

Monastero, R., Monastero, G., Ciaccio, C., et al. (2000). Cognitive deficits in beta-thalassemia major. *Acta Neurologica Scandinavica, 102,* 162–168.

Monset-Couchard, M., de Bethmann, O., & Relier, J.P. (2004). Long term outcome of small versus appropriate size for gestational age co-twins/triplets. *Archives of Disease in Childhood. Fetal and Neonatal Edition, 89*(4), F310–F314.

Morley, G.M. (n.d.). *How the cord clamp injures your baby's brain.* Retrieved May 16, 2006, from http://www.whale.to/a/morley1.html

Mortensen, E.L., Michaelsen, K.F., Sanders, S.A., et al. (2005). A dose–response relationship between maternal smoking during late pregnancy and adult intelligence in male offspring. *Paediatric and Perinatal Epidemiology, 19,* 4–11.

Moser, H.G. (1995). A role for gene therapy in mental retardation. *Mental Retardation and Developmental Disability Research Reviews (Gene Therapy), 1,* 4–6.

Moser, H.W. (2004). Genetic causes of mental retardation. *Annals of the New York Academy of Sciences, 1038,* 44–48.

Motamedi, G.K., & Meador, K.J. (2006). Antiepileptic drugs and neurodevelopment. *Current Neurobiology and Neuroscience Reports, 6*(4), 341–346.

Motherisk. (1996). *Treating the mother: Protecting the unborn: Taking folic acid before you get pregnant.* Toronto: The Hospital for Sick Children.

Motta, S., Federico, C., Saccone, S., et al. (2004). Cytogenetic evaluation of extractable agents from airborne particulate matter generated in the city of Catania (Italy). *Mutation Research, 561,* 45–52.

Muhle, R., Trentacoste, S.V., & Rapin, I. (2004). The genetics of autism. *Pediatrics, 113,* e472–486. Retrieved May 16, 2006, from http://pediatrics.aappublications.org/cgi/eletters/113/5/e472

Mullany, L.C., Darmstadt, G.L., & Tielsch, J.M. (2003). Role of antimicrobial applications to the umbilical cord in neonates to prevent bacterial colonization and infection: A review of the evidence. *The Pediatric Infectious Disease Journal, 22,* 996–1002.

Murphy, C.C., Boyle, C., Schendel, D., et al. (1998). Epidemiology of mental retardation in children. *Mental Retardation and Developmental Disabilities Research Reviews, 4,* 6–13.

Najman, J.M., Aird, R., Bor, W., et al. (2004). The generational transmission of socioeconomic inequalities in child cognitive development and emotional health. *Social Science and Medicine, 58,* 1147–1158.

National Institute of Environmental Health Sciences: Children's Environmental Health. (2003). *Environmental contaminants and their relation to learning, behavioral and developmental disorders.* Retrieved July 15, 2005, from http://www.niehs.nih.gov/oc/factsheets/ceh/contamin.htm

National Institutes of Health Office of Dietary Supplements. (2004). *Nutrient recommendations: Dietary reference intakes (DRI) and recommended dietary allowances (RDA).* Retrieved May 9, 2005, from http://ods.od.nih.gov/health_information/Dietary_Reference_Intakes.aspx

National Safety Council. (2004). *Lead poisoning.* Retrieved July 15, 2005, from http://www.nsc.org/library/facts/lead.htm

Neonatal complications after intrauterine exposure to SSRI antidepressants. (2004). *Prescrire International, 13,* 103–104.

Nussbaum, R.L., McInnes, R.R., & Willard, H.F. (2004). *Thompson & Thompson genetics in medicine* (6th ed.). Philadelphia: W.B. Saunders.

O'Dwyer, J.M. (1997). Schizophrenia in people with intellectual disability: The role of pregnancy and birth complications. *Journal of Intellectual Disability Research, 41*(Pt. 3), 238–251.

Ogunyemi, D., & Hernandez-Loera, G.E. (2004). The impact of antenatal cocaine use on maternal characteristics and neonatal outcomes. *The Journal of Maternal-Fetal Neonatal Medicine, 15,* 253–259.

Ozmert, E.N., Yurdakok, K., Soysal, S., et al. (2005). Relationship between physical, environmental and sociodemographic factors and school performance in primary schoolchildren. *Journal of Tropical Pediatrics, 51,* 25–32.

Percy, A.K., & Lane, J.B. (2004). Rett syndrome: Clinical and molecular update. *Current Opinion in Pediatrics, 16,* 670–677.

Persaud, O. (in press). Maternal diabetes and the consequences for her offspring. *Journal on Developmental Disabilities, 12*(2).

Polifka, J.E., & Friedman, J.M. (2002). Medical genetics: 1. Clinical teratology in the age of genomics. *Canadian Medical Association Journal, 167,* 265–273.

Poplawski, N.K. (2003). Investigating intellectual disability: A genetic perspective. *Journal of Paediatrics and Child Health, 39,* 492–506.

Poppe, K., & Glinoer, D. (2003). Thyroid autoimmunity and hypothyroidism before and during pregnancy. *Human Reproduction Update, 9,* 149–161.

Potrykus, I. (2003). Nutritionally enhanced rice to combat malnutrition disorders of the poor. *Nutrition Reviews, 61*(6, Pt. 2), S101–S104.

Raynham, H., Gibbons, R., Flint, J., et al. (1996). Review: The genetic basis for mental retardation. *Quarterly Journal of Medicine, 89,* 169–175.

Rice, D., & Barone, S., Jr. (2000). Critical periods of vulnerability for the developing nervous system: Evidence from humans and animal models. *Environmental Health Perspectives, 108*(Suppl. 3), 511–533.

Rice, C., Schendel, D., Cunniff, C., et al. (2004). Public health monitoring of developmental disabilities with a focus on the autism spectrum disorders. *American Journal of Medical Genetics, 125C,* 22–27.

Rodier, P.M. (2004). Environmental causes of central nervous system maldevelopment. *Pediatrics, 113*(Suppl. 4), 1076–1083.

Ross, M.G., & Desai, M. (2005). Gestational programming: Population survival effects of drought and famine during pregnancy. *American Journal of Physiology. Regulatory, Integrative and Comparative Physiology, 288,* R25–R33.

Rousseau, F., Rouillard, P., Morel, M.L., et al. (1995). Prevalence of carriers of premutation-size alleles of the FMR1 gene—and implications for the population genetics of fragile X syndrome. *American Journal of Human Genetics, 57,* 1006–1018.

Rowland, A.S., Lesesne, C.A., & Abramowitz, A.J. (2002). The epidemiology of attention-deficit/hyperactivity disorder (ADHD): A public health view. *Mental Retardation and Developmental Disabilities Research Reviews, 8,* 162–170.

Rush, K.S., Bowman, L.G., Eidman, S.L., et al. (2004). Assessing psychopathology in individuals with developmental disabilities. *Behavior Modification, 28,* 621–637.

Rutter, M. (2005). Incidence of autism spectrum disorders: Changes over time and their meaning. *Acta Paediatrica, 94,* 2–15.

Scrimshaw N.S. (1991). Iron deficiency. *Scientific American, 265, 4,* 46–52.

Sesma, H.W., & Georgieff, M.K. (2003). The effect of adverse intrauterine and newborn environments on cognitive development: The experiences of premature delivery and diabetes during pregnancy. *Development and Psychopathology, 5,* 991–1015.

Sethi, V., & Kapil, U. (2004). Iodine deficiency and development of brain. *Indian Journal of Pediatrics, 71,* 325–329.

Sherr, E.H. (2003). The ARX story (epilepsy, mental retardation, autism, and cerebral malformations): One gene leads to many phenotypes. *Current Opinions in Pediatrics, 15,* 567–571.

Shevell, M., Ashwal, S., Donley, D., et al. (2003). Quality Standards Subcommittee of the American Academy of Neurology; Practice Committee of the Child Neurology Society. Practice parameter: evaluation of the child with global developmental delay: Report of the Quality Standards Subcommittee of the American Academy of Neurology and the Practice Committee of the Child Neurology Society. *Neurology, 60,* 367–380.

Shibayama, A., Cook, E.H., Jr., Feng, J., et al. (2004). MECP2 structural and 3'-UTR variants in schizophrenia, autism and other psychiatric diseases: A possible association with autism. *American Journal of Medical Genetics, 128B,* 50–53.

Singer, L.T., Hawkins, S., Huang, J., et al. (2001). Developmental outcomes and environmental correlates of very low birthweight, cocaine-exposed infants. *Early Human Development, 64,* 91–103.

Skuse, D.H. (2005). X-linked genes and mental functioning. *Human Molecular Genetics, 14*(Spec. No. 1), R27–R32.

Spencer, A.J. (2000). Dental amalgam and mercury in dentistry. *Australian Dental Journal, 45,* 224–234.

Steen, M.T., Boddie, A.M., Fisher, A.J., et al. (1998). Neural-tube defects are associated with low concentrations of cobalamin (vitamin B12) in amniotic fluid. *Prenatal Diagnosis, 18,* 545–555.

Steen, R.G., Miles, M.A., Helton, K.J., et al. (2003). Cognitive impairment in children with hemoglobin SS sickle cell disease: Relationship to MR imaging findings and hematocrit. *American Journal of Neuroradiology, 24,* 382–389.

Stegmann, B.J., & Carey, J.C. (2002). TORCH Infections. Toxoplasmosis, Other (syphilis, varicella-zoster, parvovirus B19), Rubella, Cytomegalovirus (CMV), and Herpes infections. *Current Women's Health Reports, 2,* 253–258.

Stein, J., Schettler, T., Wallinga, D., et al. (2002). In harm's way: Toxic threats to child development. *Journal of Developmental and Behavioral Pediatrics, 23*(Suppl. 1), S13–S22.

Stremski, E., & Hennes, H. (2000). Accidental isopropanol ingestion in children. *Pediatric Emergency Care, 16*(4), 238–240.

Stewart, A.L., Rifkin, L., Amess, P.N., et al. (1999). Brain structure and neurocognitive and behavioural function in adolescents who were born very preterm. *The Lancet, 353,* 1653–1657.

Stromme, P., & Magnus, P. (2000). Correlations between socioeconomic status, IQ and aetiology in mental retardation: A population-based study of Norwegian children. *Social Psychiatry and Psychiatric Epidemiology, 35,* 12–18.

Takeshita, K. (2005). *Beta-thalassemia.* Retrieved September 8, 2005, from http://www.emedicine.com/med/topic2260.htm

Ther, A., & Kazzi, A. (2004). *Anemia, sickle cell.* Retrieved October 4, 2004, from http://www.emedicine.com/emerg/topic26.htm

Trubey, R.N. (2005). The impact of mercury on human health. *Alternative Therapies in Health and Medicine, 11,* 19.

Underwood, B.A. (2004). Vitamin A deficiency disorders: International efforts to control a preventable "pox." *Journal of Nutrition, 134,* 231S–236S.

UNICEF. (2000). *UNICEF statistics: Malnutrition.* Retrieved September 8, 2005, from http://www.childinfo.org/eddb/malnutrition/index.htm

United Nations System, Standing Committee on Nutrition. (n.d.). *Reports on the world nutrition situation (RWNS).* Retrieved July 15, 2005, from http://www.unsystem.org/scn/Publications/html/RWNS.html

U.S. Department of Health and Human Services and U.S. Environmental Protection Agency. (2004). *FDA and EPA announce the revised consumer advisory on methylmercury in fish.* Retrieved July 15, 2005, from http://www.fda.gov/bbs/topics/news/2004/NEW01038.html

U.S. Environmental Protection Agency. (2005). *Sources of indoor air pollution.* Retrieved July 15, 2005, from http://www.epa.gov/iaq/lead.html

Wang, X., Dow-Edwards, D., Anderson, V., et al. (2004). In utero marijuana exposure associated with abnormal amygdala dopamine D2 gene expression in the human fetus. *Biological Psychiatry, 56,* 909–915.

Watkins, M.L., Rasmussen, S.A., Honein, M.A., et al. (2003). Maternal obesity and risk for birth defects. *Pediatrics, 111*(5, Pt. 2), 1152–1158.

Williams, C.D. (1935) Kwashiorkor: A nutritional disease of children associated with a maize diet. *The Lancet, 229* 1151–1152.

Williams, L.O., & Decouflé, P. (1999). Is maternal age a risk factor for mental retardation among children? *American Journal of Epidemiology, 149,* 814–823.

Wilska, M.L., & Kaski, M.K. (2001). Why and how to assess the aetiological diagnosis of children with intellectual disability/mental retardation and other neurodevelopmental disorders: Description of the Finnish approach. *European Journal of Paediatric Neurology, 5,* 7–13.

Woods, B.T. (1998). Is schizophrenia a progressive neurodevelopmental disorder? Towards a unitary pathogenetic mechanism. *American Journal of Psychiatry, 155,* 1661–1670.

World Health Organization. (1990). *International Statistical Classification of Diseases and Related Health Problems (ICD-10).* Geneva: World Health Organization.

World Health Organization. (2002). Eliminating iodine deficiency disorders: The role of the International Council in the global partnership. *Bulletin of the World Health Organization, 80,* 410–413, 413–417.

Xu, J., & Chen, Z. (2003) Advances in molecular cytogenetics for the evaluation of mental retardation. *American Journal of Medical Genetics, 117C,* 15–24.

Yeargin-Allsopp, M., & Boyle, C. (2002). Overview: The epidemiology of neurodevelopmental disorders. *Mental Retardation and Developmental Disabilities Research Reviews, 8,* 113–116.

Zetterberg, H., Palmer, M., Ricksten, A., et al. (2002). Influence of the apolipoprotein E epsilon4 allele on human embryonic development. *Neuroscience Letters, 324,* 189–192.

Zlotkin, S. (2004). A new approach to control of anemia in "at risk" infants and children around the world. Ryley-Jeffs memorial lecture. *Canadian Journal of Dietetic and Practical Research, 65,* 136–138.

10

Down Syndrome

John S. Lovering and Maire Percy

WHAT YOU WILL LEARN ABOUT IN THIS CHAPTER

- Causes of Down syndrome
- Diagnosis of Down syndrome
- Characteristics of Down syndrome
- Communication issues
- Physical health concerns
- Mental health issues
- Assessment and management of health conditions
- Research developments and future directions
- Achievements

Down syndrome is the most common genetic cause of moderate intellectual or developmental disability. It is considered to be a genetic disorder because most cases result from having an extra chromosome 21; however, in contrast to fragile X syndrome, which is the most common inherited cause of intellectual disability, most cases of Down syndrome are not inherited (see below and Chapter 7 for additional details). In North America, the prevalence is approximately 1 per 800–1,000 live births. Although its existence may have been documented throughout the ages, including possible depictions in classical art, it was first formally described by John Langdon Down in 1866 (Berg, 2003; Berg & Korossy, 2001; Down, 1866; see Display 10.1). This advance reflected the growing recognition that mental health conditions and cognitive disabilities are different and that each requires different types of care and interventions. Since that time, there has been an increasing awareness of the many causes of intellectual and developmental disability and a vast expansion of knowledge about Down syndrome. The purpose of this chapter is to familiarize readers about the complexities of Down syndrome and to highlight the importance of health care, health promotion, and disease prevention so that quality of life can be enhanced for people with Down syndrome. (The term *health promotion* refers to one or more actions taken to maximize physical or mental health and well-being. The term *disease prevention* refers to intervention before the onset of a disorder to prevent its development.)

CAUSES OF DOWN SYNDROME

The chromosomal basis of Down syndrome was established independently by groups headed by Patricia Jacobs and Jerome Lejeune (Jacobs et al., 1959; Lejeune, Gauthier, & Turpin, 1959a, 1959b; see also Chapter 7). Approximately 95% of individuals with Down syndrome have an extra chromosome 21 (trisomy 21), for a total of three instead of the normal two. The extra chromosome 21 usually results from an error that occurs during meiosis (cell division in an ovary or in the testicles) called *nondisjunction;* this causes an ovum in a female or a sperm in a male to have a second chromosome 21 instead of the usual one (see Chapter 7 for details about meiosis and nondisjunction). The risk of nondisjunction that results in a child having trisomy 21 has been shown to increase with advancing maternal age (see Figure 10.1) and significantly increases after the age of 35 years. Advancing paternal age, especially when the maternal age is greater than 40 years, also appears to increase the risk of trisomy 21 (Fisch et al., 2003). Yet, approximately 80% of babies with Down syndrome are born to mothers younger than 35. This is because fertility is much greater under the age of 35 than over it. Approximately 85% of cases of trisomy 21 result from an extra maternal chromosome 21; approximately 15% result from an extra paternal chromosome 21 (Antonarakis et al., 2004). Although most cases of Down syndrome are caused by trisomy 21, approximately 4% are caused by a critical extra part of chromosome 21 being attached to another chromosome (usually to a chromosome 14 or a chromosome 22 but sometimes to 13 or 15 or another 21); in this

We are grateful to Benjamin Tan (Malaysia) for providing web site information. We thank Tom Dearie for rendering high-resolution reproductions of the artwork for certain figures in this chapter.

Display 10.1

John Langdon Haydon Down

John Langdon Haydon Down was born in Cornwall, United Kingdom. He began a scientific career at the age of 13½ by assisting his father, who was a pharmacist. At 18, Down moved to London and worked as an assistant to a surgeon in private practice. In 1847, he began work at the laboratory of The Pharmaceutical Society in Bloomsbury Square, London, focusing on organic chemistry. He then became research assistant to Michael Faraday (1791–1867), one of the greatest scientists of all time. At age 25, Down entered medical school in the London Hospital, where he excelled scholastically. In 1858, he became resident physician at the university hospital and then medical superintendent at the Earlswood Asylum for Idiots in Surrey. (At the time, people with intellectual and developmental disabilities were said to have "idiocy.") After becoming doctor of medicine in London in 1859, Down worked with children with mental retardation. Until 1868, he worked at both the Earlswood Asylum and his London practice. He supervised the organization and development of Earlswood and turned it into a model for the care of people with mental illnesses in the United Kingdom. In 1868, he set up consultant practice in London, and the next year established an institution at Teddington for training children with intellectual and developmental disabilities who came from wealthier families. This institution was named Normansfield after Down's friend Norman Wilkinson. Down was the first to distinguish people with the condition that now bears his name from those with cretinism, a severe form of congenital hypothyroidism.

Sources: Enerson (2001); Percy and Prasher (2006).

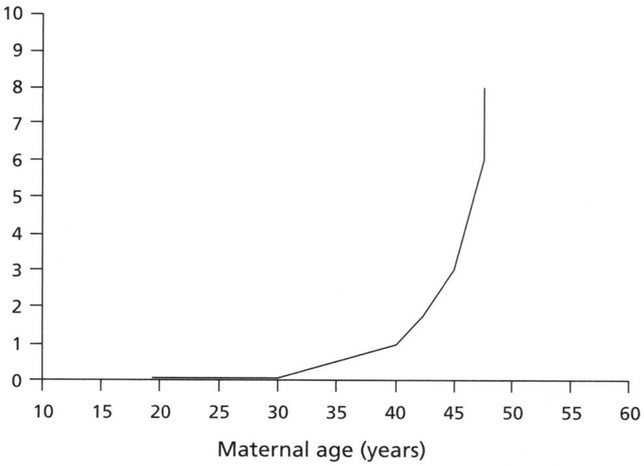

Figure 10.1. Percentage of live births with Down syndrome and mother's age in years. (From Behrman, R.E. [Ed.]. [1992]. *Nelson textbook of pediatrics* [14th ed., p. 284]. Philadelphia: W.B. Saunders Company; reprinted with permission from Elsevier.)

case the hybrid chromosome is called a *translocation chromosome.* For female or male carriers with such a translocation chromosome, the risk of having a child with Down syndrome is 10%–15% and 3%–8%, respectively, even when they are young adults. A third cause of Down syndrome is an internal duplication of some critical genes on one chromosome 21. A fourth cause is mosaicism for chromosome 21. Individuals affected by mosaicism have two cell lines—some cells have three chromosome 21s, while other cells have two. The proportion of these two kinds of cells may vary from one tissue to another (e.g., be different in white blood cells and in skin cells). Only approximately 1% of identified individuals with Down syndrome have mosaicism. Mosaicism for Down syndrome is difficult to diagnose, and people with this disorder tend to be less severely affected than those with trisomy 21 (Fishler & Koch, 1991). (For more details, see Chapter 7, as well as Antonarakis et al., 2004; Devlin & Morrison, 2004; and Mutton, Alberman, & Hook, 1996.) As discussed later in the chapter, people with Down syndrome have certain physical characteristics in common that collectively distinguish them from people in the general population. They also have certain brain changes; changes in development, language and intellectual function, hearing, vision, fine and gross motor coordination, personality, and behavior; and increased susceptibility to numerous neurological conditions, including early onset dementia of the Alzheimer type (DAT), stroke, and calcification of the basal ganglia (Lev & Melamed, 2002; see also Chapter 44). People with Down syndrome have an increased susceptibility to numerous medical disorders as well.

DIAGNOSIS OF DOWN SYNDROME

Down syndrome often is diagnosed during pregnancy on the basis of fetal ultrasound analysis and/or the maternal triple or quad screen test (DeVore & Romero, 2003). Fetal ultrasound analysis (see Chapter 7) looks for fetal abnormalities that are characteristic of Down syndrome; this approach continues to become increasingly sensitive in detecting fetuses with Down syndrome (Nicolaides, 2004). The maternal triple screen test measures levels of **alpha-fetoprotein, human chorionic gonadotropin,** and **unconjugated estriol** in maternal serum samples (Summers, Farrell, Huang, et al., 2003). In the maternal quad test, the level of **inhibin-A** is measured as well. If an accurate diagnosis of Down syndrome is desired, then it is possible to examine fetal chromosomes, or to study the fetal DNA, using the **polymerase chain reaction** (El Mouatassim et al., 2004; see also Chapter 7). Both of these procedures can be applied to tissue samples obtained by **chorionic villus sampling** or by **amniocentesis** (see Chapter 7 for more information about these procedures). Because there is a slight risk of miscarriage or of causing damage to the fetus, chronionic villus sampling and amniocentesis usually are recommended only if the mother is older than age 35, has had another child with Down syndrome, has had an abnormal ultrasound or triple screen test, or has a family history of Down syndrome. All prenatal testing should require informed consent.

Diagnosis of Down syndrome also can be done shortly after birth by chromosomal analysis. It may take 2–3 weeks to get the complete results of this test. In addition, a health professional is able to provide an opinion about the likelihood that a baby has Down syndrome without chromosomal or DNA analysis. This opinion is based on the baby's appearance, the results of a physical exam, family history, and results of ultrasound and the maternal triple screen test (if done during the pregnancy).

CHARACTERISTICS OF DOWN SYNDROME

The following sections discuss the physical characteristics, some brain changes, growth, and life expectancy of people with Down syndrome.

Physical Characteristics

There is considerable variability in the appearance of individuals with Down syndrome; not all of the features described next are always present, and some may disappear over time. Many of these features are also seen in the general population but at a lower frequency than in people with Down syndrome; in addition, fewer of these characteristics occur in any one person who does not have Down syndrome. Hereditary factors also influence the physical appearance of children and adults with Down syndrome.

Physical features that are commonly present in individuals with Down syndrome include the following:

- Brachycephaly (short, broad head)
- Brachydactyly (short fingers)
- Broad hands
- Duodenal atresia (complete obliteration of the **duodenal lumen**)
- Epicanthal folds (the skin fold of the upper eyelid that covers the inner corner of the eye)
- Fifth-finger clinodactyly (curving in of the little finger)
- Flat nasal bridge
- Hypotonia (reduced muscle tone or resistance to passive movement)
- Intellectual disability
- Lax ligaments
- Mouth that is often open
- Short stature
- Wide gap between the first and second toes

Other features may include gray-white raised Brushfield spots on the surface of the iris that have no clinical significance and require no treatment; small ears, often with a low and oblique placement on the face; narrowing of the ear canals and absent or incompletely attached ear lobes; lips that may gradually become more prominent with fissuring and thickening (in cold weather the lips are prone to chapping); a protruding tongue; a short and widened neck (extra folds of skin at the back of the neck are sometimes seen in newborn babies, but these gradually disappear); umbilical hernias; and a single transverse palmar crease on at least one hand. (*General sources*: Korenberg et al., 1994; Roizen & Patterson, 2003.)

Some Brain Changes

The brains of individuals with Down syndrome tend to be smaller than normal and have an abnormal shape. They have fewer neurons, smaller axons, fewer dendritic ramifications, structural abnormalities of the synapses, altered cortical lamination, and delayed myelination (Wisniewski & Kida, 1997). Such abnormalities begin early in gestation. With increasing age, brains of individuals with Down syndrome develop characteristic features of Alzheimer's disease that are visible under a microscope: amyloid plaques and neurofibrillary tangles (see Chapter 44). Almost all individuals older than age 40 who have come to autopsy have such hallmarks of Alzheimer's disease. Not everyone with Down syndrome develops clinical manifestations of Alzheimer's disease, however, although this is common particularly after the age of 50 (see Chapter 44).

Growth

Children with Down syndrome usually grow less quickly than other children. This seems to hold from before birth to adolescence, but the differences in growth velocity are most evident in the first few years of life. Growth velocity during middle childhood tends to more closely parallel growth changes in children who do not have Down syndrome. The cause of short stature in children with Down syndrome is unclear but may result from a number of causes, including having the extra chromosome 21, having a resulting deficiency of growth hormone, or having celiac disease or significant hypothyroidism. Environment and heredity may be factors as well. Children living in institutional settings tend to be shorter than those living at home, probably as the result of poorer nutrition.

In view of the consistent findings in the growth patterns of children with Down syndrome, special growth charts have been constructed (Cronk et al., 1988; Myrelid et al., 2002; Richards, 2001). These help in following the physical development of children with Down syndrome. If concerns arise around a child's pattern of growth or weight, the use of standard charts for typically developing children helps identify and follow unusual trends in height and weight.

Life Expectancy

Life expectancy for people with Down syndrome in North America has shown dramatic increases since the 1950s as the result of improved medical care, such as the use of antibiotics (because people with Down syndrome are unusually prone to infections), the correction of congenital heart disease (CHD), and treatment of leukemia (see the Physical Health Concerns section later in this chapter). Data from a variety of studies have been summarized in graphic form in Figure 10.2 to demonstrate this change through the first 10 years of life (Berg, Karlinsky, & Holland, 1993). In British Columbia, Canada, where accurate figures have been maintained since 1952 from numerous sources, the survival rate for individuals with Down syndrome at 30 years of age has been estimated to be 72% (Baird & Sadovnick, 1987). Because CHD is a leading cause of sickness and death among people with Down syndrome, particularly during the first year of life, the survival rate is somewhat higher when one considers those who do not have CHD. Baird and Sadovnick pointed out that the survival rate in the general population at age 30 is 97%. In moderate developmental disability other than Down syndrome, it is 92%. In Down syndrome the survival rate appears to plateau from about the age of 5–40 years. After age 40, the rate decreases. In the United States, a substantial improvement in the median age of death in individuals with Down syndrome has been noted since the 1980s. In one large U.S. survey, the median age of death was found to increase from 25 years in 1983 to 49 years in 1997 ($p < 0.0001$). The median age of death was significantly higher in Caucasians than in African Americans or people of other races, presumably the result of inequality in medical care (Racial Disparities in Median Age at Death, 2001). Factors predicting longevity in people with Down syndrome did not differ from those for people with intellectual disability who did not have Down syndrome. For children younger than 11 years of age, the main factor predicting poor survival rates was being nonmobile or fed by tube; in contrast, for those ages 11–39 years, being able to walk about was the main predictor of survival. No comparable data are available for other countries. The importance of a physically active lifestyle to prevent deterioration of health cannot be overemphasized (Carmeli et al., 2004; Rimmer et al., 2004). Physical activity is encouraged through participation in the Special Olympics, in which many people with Down syndrome take part.

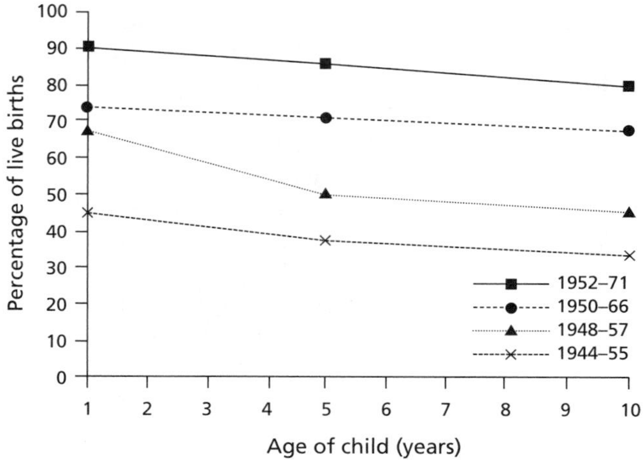

Figure 10.2. Percentage of live births with Down syndrome surviving through childhood. (From Fryers, T. [1986]. Survival in Down syndrome. *Journal of Mental Deficiency Research, 30*[2], 101–110; published by Blackwell Publishing, Oxford, United Kingdom; reprinted by permission.)

COMMUNICATION ISSUES

Compared with most other syndromes associated with intellectual and developmental disabilities, communication issues have been well-studied in individuals with Down syndrome (Blackstone, 1992; Chapman & Hesketh, 2000, 2001; Miller, Leddy, & Leavitt, 1999). In particular, Chapman and Hesketh (2001) characterized and compared communication issues in children, adolescents, and adults with Down syndrome, but only a few key features are highlighted in this section. Hearing and vision problems are very common in people with Down syndrome and should be corrected at the earliest possible age so that they do not interfere with development of communication skills (see Chapter 25 for more information about hearing and vision). Relative to typically developing children of the same mental age, people with Down syndrome have a delay in nonverbal cognitive development, specific deficits in speech and language production, and deficits in short-term auditory memory; however, they have fewer adaptive behavior problems than individuals with other cognitive disabilities. There is no critical period for the acquisition of communication in Down syndrome. Speech and language skills continue to develop even into adulthood, although at a slower pace than in typically developing individuals. Language skills are less well developed than visuo-spatial skills. The next sections discuss issues related to speech, expressive and receptive language, and intervention, as well as overall achievements.

Speech

Speech intelligibility in Down syndrome is adversely affected by two neurological factors:

1. Dysarthria (difficulty with the strength and precision of muscle movements, leading to thick and imprecise articulation)
2. Apraxia (the inability to program, combine, organize, and sequence muscle movements)

Other conditions common in Down syndrome affect intelligibility and clarity of speech. These include mouth breathing (breathing through the mouth rather than through the nose), enlargement of the tonsils and adenoids (which block the nasal airways), velopharyngeal incompetence (difficulty forming a seal between the pharynx and nasal passages), and relative macroglossia (a tongue that is too large for the size of the oral cavity). Mid-facial hypoplasia, hypotonicity of the oral cavity, high arched palate, and dental problems (including delayed eruption, crowding, and malformations of teeth) also play a role. In addition, phonological processes may be substantially delayed. All children make errors and inconsistencies in pronouncing words, but in children with Down syndrome, these errors are more common and persist into adolescence and adulthood.

Expressive and Receptive Language

The expressive language skills in children with Down syndrome do not keep pace with cognitive skill development (Chapman & Hesketh, 2001), a finding that is evident in most children with Down syndrome by 3 years of age. In addition to having syntactic difficulties (difficulties with the grammatical arrangement of words—i.e., showing their connection and relation), problems with short-term memory and auditory processing impair the development of expressive language. In contrast, the onset of babbling, with its patterns of syllables; the time period for emergence of first words (8–45 months of age); and the content of the first 50 words (a preponderance of nouns over verbs) are similar to those of typically developing children matched for mental age. Signing can be taught through the second cognitive year and is a particularly helpful intervention in improving vocabulary development and language skills. Children 2–3 years of age who can sign may learn to read a large number of words. At 20–24 months of age, children with or without Down syndrome use two-word utterances similarly. After that, expressive **syntax** differs significantly; in particular, children with Down syndrome have more difficulties with verb agreement and use pronouns less frequently than children without Down syndrome.

Vocabulary comprehension is a relative strength in adolescents with Down syndrome, and the acquisition of skills in this area is similar to that of typically developing children matched for mental age. Adults with Down syndrome have more difficulty with syntax comprehension, a problem that begins in adolescence (Kernan, 1990).

Communication Interventions

Early intervention is extremely important in the first 6 years of life, as cognitive and communication skills lag behind personal-social and adaptive skills (see Chapters 21 and 29). Intervention also improves the style of mothers' interactions with their children, which in turn benefits the children's receptive language.

The majority of individuals with Down syndrome read at some level (Cupples & Iacono, 2000), and reading skills can develop beyond mental age abilities. Because sign, picture communication, and reading fall into the visual domain and are relative strengths, it is often helpful if they form the primary focus of communication intervention. Group therapy has proven to be a valuable form of intervention in improving language in childhood and early adulthood.

PHYSICAL HEALTH CONCERNS

The medical conditions found in people with Down syndrome are, for the most part, no different than those found in individuals without Down syndrome. There is, however, clear evidence of increased risk for a variety of health concerns. These altered risks are thought to result, in part, from the chromosomal nature of the condition and the effect it has on developmental processes. One can anticipate these problems before they have an opportunity to produce significant illness. Individuals with Down syndrome should be followed on a regular basis by a physician who is experienced in the care of individuals with Down syndrome. The following are the most common considerations in the health care of individuals with Down syndrome. The content is not exhaustive and the reader is referred to additional resources and books on the subject (Bosch, 2003; Chicoine et al., 1994; Pueschel, 1990, 2006; Pueschel & Pueschel, 1992; Roizen & Patterson, 2003; Smith, 2001; Wallace & Dalton, 2005).

Congenital Heart Disease

Children with Down syndrome have a significant increase in risk of CHD; as many as 40%–50% are affected, compared to approximately 3% of the general population. Improvements in the treatment of CHD have had a dramatic impact on the life expectancy of children with Down syndrome.

Understanding CHD benefits from a review of normal heart structure and function (a cross-section of the normal heart is provided in Figure 10.3). The heart has four chambers: two atria (the upper, low pressure chambers) and two ventricles (the lower, high pressure chambers). With each heartbeat, the atria contract first, pumping blood into the ventricles. Then both ventricles contract, pumping blood out of the heart into the arteries. One-way valves in the heart ensure that the blood flows in the correct direction. The muscular wall called the septum ensures that blood does not leak from one side of the heart to the other. Normally, oxygen-poor blood returns to the right atrium from the body, travels to the right ventricle, and then is pumped into the lungs where it receives oxygen. Oxygen-rich blood returns to the left atrium from the lungs, passes into the left ventricle, and then is pumped out to the body through the aorta.

Table 10.1 lists different forms of CHD in infants with Down syndrome and their frequencies. Atrioventricular (AV) canal defect is a complex heart problem that involves several abnormalities of structures inside the heart, including an atrial septal defect, a ventricular septal defect, and improperly formed mitral and/or tricuspid valves; in this defect there is a lack of separation of the four chambers of the heart. AV canal is sometimes referred to as "endocardial cushion defect" or "atrioventricular septal defect," a newer term. During the first 8 weeks of pregnancy, a structure called the endocardial cushion does not fuse with the septum, resulting in this defect. Atrial septal defect (ASD) is an opening in the atrial septum; this defect allows blood flow between the left and right atria. Ventricular septal defect (VSD) is an opening in the ventricular septum; this defect allows blood flow between the left and right ventricles. Patent ductus arteriosus (PDA) is a connection between the aorta and the pulmonary artery which allows oxygen-rich blood that should go to the body to recirculate through the lungs. Tetralogy of Fallot is a complex of four specific defects that lead to a reduced blood flow to the lungs and a mixing of oxygen-rich and oxygen-poor blood in the heart. Because the body does not receive enough oxygen-rich blood, the skin, lips, fingernails, and tongue often have a bluish tint (cyanosis). Babies with this condition are sometimes called "blue babies."

Table 10.1. Different forms of congenital heart disease in infants with Down syndrome

Form	Approximate frequency of occurrence
Any heart defect	56.0%
Tetralogy of Fallot	2.5%
Atrioventricular canal	17.1%
Ventricular septal defect	6.4%
Atrial septal defect	6.3%
Aortic abnormalities	5.5%
Mitral valve abnormalities	4.9%
Patent ductus arteriosus (isolated)	3.4%
Pulmonary artery abnormalities	2.4%
Abnormalities of great veins	1.3%
Single umbilical artery	0.8%

From California Birth Defects Monitoring Program. (n.d.). *Down syndrome: Associated birth defects.* Retrieved March 26, 2006, from http://www.cbdmp.org/bd_down_defects.htm; adapted by permission.

These data are based on 2,984 infants.

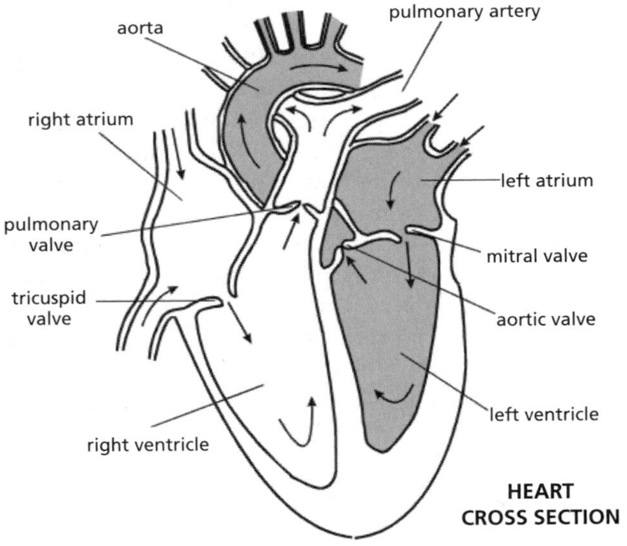

Figure 10.3. Cross section of a normal heart. From Patient UK. (2006). *Heart—cross section (diagram).* http://www.patient.co.uk/showdoc/21692435; reprinted by permission.

If CHD is not corrected, then it may later manifest as Eisenmenger syndrome, which basically is end-stage CHD. Many adolescents and adults with Down syndrome whose CHD was not treated in infancy have this condition (Wallace & Dalton, 2005). Eisenmenger syndrome most commonly results from VSD. The abnormal circulation in VSD causes elevated pressure in the lung arteries (pulmonary hypertension). Pulmonary hypertension eventually pushes low oxygen blood from the right side of the circulation back into the high oxygen, left-sided circulation, bypassing the lungs and often resulting in cyanosis. Once this syndrome develops, surgery to repair the defect is not possible. It is managed by medication. (*General sources:* British Heart Foundation, 2006; Mayo Clinic, 2006; MedLine Plus, 2006b; Patient UK, 2006; Wallace & Dalton, 2005).

An infant with Down syndrome must have a cardiovascular examination because of the high risk of

CHD. The examination usually includes an **electrocardiogram,** a chest X ray, and an **echocardiogram.** Early diagnosis and surgery, when necessary, are important for the prevention of complications. CHD in people with Down syndrome can be surgically repaired, with limited risk of death as the result of complications from the operation, and with significant improvement in quality of life and life expectancy (Stos et al., 2004).

In adults with Down syndrome, there is high prevalence of **aortic regurgitation** and **mitral valve prolapse,** presumably related to connective tissue abnormalities. Prophylactic treatment with antibiotics should be given to individuals with valvular heart disease prior to dental work in order to prevent development of endocarditis (infection of damaged heart valves or heart tissue with certain bacteria dislodged from other sites of the body; Wallace & Dalton, 2005). It is not clear if the prevalence of atherosclerosis (lesions of medium-sized arteries that contain fatty deposits, including cholesterol) is lower in people with Down syndrome than in the general population or whether it is lower than in people with other forms of intellectual disability. On the one hand, a lower prevalence of hypertension and smoking may be protective against atherosclerosis. On the other hand, obesity associated with a sedentary lifestyle and elevated levels of fasting insulin could be predisposing factors (Wallace & Dalton, 2005).

Gastrointestinal Obstructions and Conditions

The following sections describe the most common gastrointestinal obstructions, as well as other gastrointestinal conditions experienced by many people with Down syndrome.

Gastrointestinal Obstructions

Gastrointestinal obstructions affect many individuals with Down syndrome (Langman, 1963), including approximately 10% of children. Approximately 70% of children with gastrointestinal defects also have some form of CHD. Gastrointestinal obstructions are second only to CHD as causes of infant mortality. An understanding of these disorders requires a short discussion of embryology. During fetal development, the lumen of the bowel is patent (open) and then is obliterated as tissue forms. During the 4th to 6th weeks of gestation, a process of recanalization (reopening of the lumen) of the gastrointestinal tract takes place. If this process fails at any point, an obstruction remains. There may be associated interference in the separation between the trachea and esophagus, leading to a persistent opening between the two that is known as a tracheoesophageal fistula. The finding of an imperforate anus is also related to defects in the process of recanalization.

Esophageal Atresia and Tracheoesophageal Fistula The trachea, or windpipe, carries air to the lungs. The esophagus carries food to the stomach. The term *esophageal atresia* means that the esophagus is blocked to a greater or lesser degree. The term *tracheoesophageal fistula* means that the trachea and esophagus are connected. Sometimes during development, these two tubes do not separate completely but remain connected by a short passage. When this happens, air enters the gastrointestinal system, causing the bowels to distend, and mucus is breathed into the lungs, causing aspiration pneumonia and breathing problems. Figure 10.4 contains diagrams depicting the most common forms of tracheoesophageal fistula. Diagram A represents approximately 87% of these anomalies, whereas Diagrams B and C represent 8% and 4%, respectively (Behrman, 1992). The most common signs of this condition include respiratory distress and drooling. Early diagnosis is important, and appropriate treatment limits the degree of respiratory compromise. An attempt to pass a firm feeding tube into the stomach will meet resistance when an esophageal atresia or obstruction is present. X rays will establish the level of the atresia and the most likely location of the fistula. Blockages and fistulas are treated by surgical correction. Sometimes a number of surgeries are required over time. The most common complications from surgery include leaks around the repair sites, which may result in chronic lung disease and reflux or regurgitation.

Gastroesophageal Reflux Gastroesophageal reflux is the movement of stomach contents up the esophagus toward the mouth, rather than down through the digestive system. Problems such as choking and difficulty swallowing often occur with these strictures. It may be difficult to move from a fluid to a solid diet, and failure to thrive may occur if the problem persists. Up to one half of children with this condition will require dilatation (stretching of the narrowed area or stricture using a dilator or a balloon) to gradually improve the

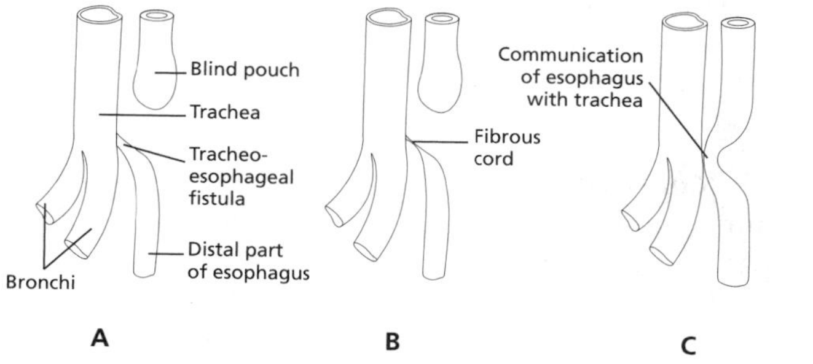

Figure 10.4. The most common forms of tracheoesophageal fistula. (From Langman, J. [1963]. *Medical embryology* [p. 218]. Philadelphia: Lippincott, Williams & Wilkins Company.)

patency of the esophagus. Reflux can usually be managed medically with small feedings, antacids, and other newer medications (e.g., cimetidine).

Duodenal Atresia and Duodenal Stenosis *Duodenal atresia* refers to complete blockage of the duodenal lumen. *Duodenal stenosis* refers to an incomplete blockage. These intestinal obstructions cause symptoms such as vomiting and, depending on the level of the blockage, abdominal distention, and bile-stained vomit. X rays are often helpful in diagnosing this condition, and the treatment is surgical. Feeding difficulties are common after the surgery but gradually abate.

Hirschsprung Disease Hirschsprung disease (also known as aganglionic megacolon) is commonly associated with Down syndrome. In this condition, there is an absence of ganglion cells (absence of nerve endings) in a portion of the large intestine (bowel). The result is an inability of the bowel muscle to relax and produce normal peristaltic movement; the bowel enlarges, and severe constipation results. Newborn babies with this condition do not pass meconium (the dark green mucilaginous substance present in the intestine of the full-term baby) in the first 24 hours as expected, and they develop vomiting and abdominal distention. Some babies also develop bloody diarrhea and generalized infection. Treatment for this disorder is removal of the segment of colon that lacks the nerve endings. In the past, the surgery was often performed in two stages: The first surgery attached the ending of the colon to a specially made opening (colostomy); then, the rectum was reattached months later. As of 2007, however, many surgeons remove the affected segment of colon and reattach it to the rectum in one procedure (Leshin, 2003). Before surgery, intravenous feeding may be necessary to boost a child's weight. Such surgery is not done before the child is 1 year old. Patience is required for the child to eventually achieve normal bowel function and to eradicate bowel accidents.

Gastrointestinal Conditions

Celiac disease (CD) and *Helicobacter pylori* infection are two particular gastrointestinal problems common among people with Down syndrome. Each is described next.

Celiac Disease CD, an autoimmune disorder, is much more common in the general population than previously believed, and it is more common in Down syndrome than in the general population. In the general population, the prevalence of CD is 0.5%–1%. In Down syndrome, the prevalence is reported to be 3%–7% in the United States and 7%–16% in Europe (Cogulu et al., 2003; Roizen & Patterson, 2003; Zachor, 2000). CD is often diagnosed in the general population between 6 months and 2 years of age, whereas the diagnosis often occurs much later in children and adults with Down syndrome. It is important to diagnose CD as early as possible. This is done by testing for the presence of certain antibodies in the serum and, if possible, by also examining a biopsy of the small intestine for the presence of features characteristic of CD (Wallace & Dalton, 2005). One laboratory now tests for CD by analysis of a stool sample (EnteroLab, 2006).

As shown in Table 10.2, CD often is associated with intestinal symptoms. However, sometimes the symptoms are more subtle, or it is associated with nonintestinal symptoms including dermatitis herpetiformis, a chronic benign skin disorder associated with a burning, itching rash. Unfortunately, CD frequently is not recognized because the symptoms are similar to those of other problems. An intestinal infection with *Giardia lamblia,* for example, may produce symptoms that are similar to those of CD.

People with CD have a sensitivity to gluten, a protein found in wheat, barley, and rye. In many cases, virtually all of the symptoms of CD can be alleviated by appropriate treatment, which is adherence to a gluten-free diet (Hill et al., 2005). Because bread, cookies, other baked products, and many packaged or proc-

Table 10.2. Symptoms of celiac disease

Intestinal	Nonintestinal
Abdominal pain	Anemia
Abdominal distention (from excessive gas production)	Bone and joint pain
Diarrhea	Bone disease (e.g., osteoporosis, fractures)
Lactose intolerance	Breathlessness
Nausea and vomiting	Bruising
Stools that float	Dental enamel discoloration
Weight loss	Depression
	Dermatitis herpetiformis (a skin condition)
	Fatigue
	Growth delay (in children)
	Hair loss
	Hypoglycemia
	Irritability and behavior changes
	Malnutrition
	Mouth ulcers
	Muscle cramps
	Nosebleeds
	Seizures and other neurological abnormalities
	Swelling (general or abdominal)
	Vitamin or mineral deficiency

Source: Medline Plus (2006a).
Symptoms of celiac disease vary from one person to another. This table is not all inclusive. See the cited source for additional information.

essed foods contain gluten, maintaining a gluten-free diet can be difficult without cooperation and commitment, and it can be especially challenging for children. However, gluten-free products are available. Once CD is diagnosed, a gluten-free diet must be adhered to, because severe long-term complications of untreated CD can include growth failure, additional gastrointestinal symptoms, behavior problems, intestinal lymphomas, severe malnutrition, or even death. Vitamin supplementation and the help of support groups are additional aspects of intervention.

Helicobacter Pylori Infection Infection with the microorganism *Helicobacter pylori* is common in the general population, but it occurs twice as frequently in people with various forms of intellectual disability, including Down syndrome (Wallace & Dalton, 2005; Wallace, Webb, & Schluter, 2002). As with celiac disease, this problem is underdiagnosed in people with Down syndrome. It is a cause of gastritis, ulcers, and some types of gastrointestinal cancer. Symptoms associated with this infection are listed in Table 10.3. Diagnosis of helicobacter infection includes blood tests for antibodies, breath tests, stool tests, and sometimes endoscopy. Treatment involves administration of 1 or 2 antibiotics and antacids for 10–14 days.

Ear, Nose, and Throat Problems

Individuals with Down syndrome have underdeveloped midfacial structures and a reduced distance from the back to the front of the skull. Anatomic variations are often present in association with these findings. The oral cavity is often relatively small, and this may cause the tongue to protrude. It is common to find dysfunction of the middle ear and eustachian tube, the connection between the middle ear and the nasopharynx. (See Figure 10.5 for a cross-section of the human ear and Chapter 25 for further details about hearing and correction of hearing deficits.)

For people with Down syndrome, infections are common—much more so than in the general population—and these affect the chest as well as structures of the ear, nose, and throat. In Down syndrome, the external ear canal is often narrow and can be easily impacted with cerumen (earwax). Hearing loss also occurs frequently (Shott, Joseph, & Heithaus, 2001). Otitis media (middle-ear infection) with effusion (accumulation of sticky thick fluid in the middle ear) is the most common cause. This results in what is called a *conductive hearing loss* and affects 60%–90% of individuals with Down syndrome. In conductive hearing loss, the transmission of sound through the ear canal to the tiny bones in the middle ear and then to the nerve connections of the inner ear is in some way impeded. Less commonly, the neural pathway is affected, producing what is known as *sensorineural hearing loss*. Some individuals have a combination of both types of hearing problems.

For people with Down syndrome, monitoring by an audiologist every 6–12 months and by an ear, nose, and throat specialist is advisable. Routine hearing screenings (audiometry) and aggressive treatment are important to maintain optimal language and cognitive development. Removal of earwax is a simple but often very important procedure that can be done in the family doctor's office. The placement of ventilating tubes through the eardrum may be required when standard treatment of middle ear infection and effusion is unsuccessful. Many individuals with Down syndrome benefit from hearing aids or some form of amplification (e.g., desktop and personal frequency modulated systems), and experts recognize the role for a team of health care professionals in these circumstances. People with Down syndrome are at risk for velopharyngeal incompetence following surgical removal of adenoids and/or tonsils; thus the decision to have such surgery should be made carefully (Biavati & Rocha-Worley, 2003). (Velopharyngeal incompetence is a condition in which the velopharyngeal sphincter, or soft palate muscle, does not close properly during speech; it is characterized by an acute nasal quality of the voice.)

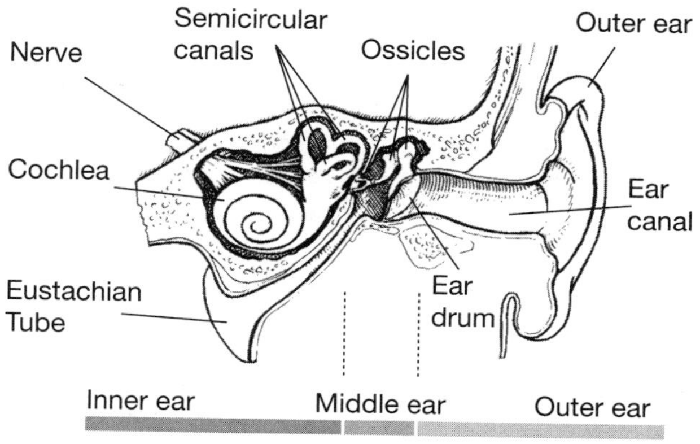

Figure 10.5. Cross-section of the human ear. (From *Medical Illustration Library* [Page/Image GA2_6001]. [1994]. Philadelphia: Lippincott, Williams & Wilkins.)

Table 10.3. Symptoms of *Helicobacter pylori* infection

Young children	Older children and adults
Nausea Vomiting Abdominal pain	Gnawing or burning pain in abdomen below ribs and above navel that is relieved by eating, drinking milk, and taking antacid

Oral Health

The oral cavity is typically small in people with Down syndrome, and relative macroglossia is common. This may lead to protrusion of the tongue and a tendency to keep the mouth open. Occasionally, surgical intervention is used to reduce the size of the tongue.

Malocclusion of teeth is very common and occurs in most individuals with Down syndrome. *Occlusion* refers to the alignment of teeth and the way that the upper and lower teeth fit together (bite), so *malocclusion* means the teeth are not aligned properly. Types of malocclusion include cross bite, crowded teeth, misaligned teeth, open bite, overbite and underbite. Malocclusion is the most common reason for referral to an orthodontist. Most malocclusion is mild enough not to require treatment. If a severe misalignment is present, orthodontics and/or oral surgery may be required.

Caries (dental cavities) have been found in some studies to occur less frequently in people with Down syndrome than in others with or without other forms of intellectual disabilities. However, when other factors are taken into consideration—such as diet, number of teeth, and spacing of teeth—these differences are not characteristic of Down syndrome.

In people with Down syndrome, both primary and permanent teeth often erupt 1–2 years later than expected. Because of this, permanent teeth often erupt in front of, or behind the primary teeth. Teeth are often missing, particularly the upper lateral incisors, and less frequently, second bicuspids and lower incisors.

Marked, rapid, and early onset of periodontal (gum) disease is a concern in the dental care of individuals with Down syndrome. Periodontal disease may result in the teeth losing their attachment to alveolar bone, leading to a loss of teeth. Gingivitis and gingival bleeding are common in children with Down syndrome, and there is often more plaque and calculus than in children with other forms of intellectual disability. Diet, oral hygiene, and immunodeficiency are all factors in the evolution of these dental problems. Thus, good oral hygiene is very important. Routine tooth brushing combined with dental visits every 6 months can prevent periodontal disease and associated tooth loss. (See Fiske & Shafik, 2001, & Hennequin et al., 1999, for reviews of this topic.)

Skin Conditions

A number of skin conditions are common in people with Down syndrome (Schepis et al., 2002). Syringomas (benign tumors of the sweat glands), milia-like calcinosis cutis (grain-like, white deposits of calcium in the skin), folliculitis (inflammation of the hair follicles) and elastosis perforans serpiginosa (a rare disorder occurring more frequently in males than females in which abnormal elastic fibers are expelled through the dermis) tend to occur in people with Down syndrome (Schepis et al., 2002). Other common skin conditions are explained next.

Alopecia Areata Alopecia areata is a condition in which round patches of hair loss (from the scalp, beard area, eyebrows, or eyelashes) appear suddenly. The hair-growing tissue is attacked by the patient's own immune cells for unknown reasons. There is a tendency for spontaneous recovery.

Atopic Dermatitis Atopic dermatitis, commonly referred to as eczema, is a chronic skin disorder categorized by scaly and itching rashes. Red scaly patches can occur on the flexor surfaces of the arm, creases of the elbow, backs of the knee, the ankles, wrists, and cheeks. The skin is itchy and becomes thickened. Oilated oatmeal (e.g., Aveeno) in the bath and hydrophilic lotions are often helpful. Medications such as antihistamines, antibiotics, and topical corticosteroids may be necessary to deal with inflammation and infection.

Cheilitis Cheilitis is an inflammation and cracking of the lips that involves red scaling and crusting. Among people with Down syndrome, it is more common in males than females. Zinc oxide or white petrolatum may be used to treat the condition.

Xerosis *Xerosis* is the term for dry skin. There is often a gradual change in the skin of individuals with Down syndrome. The skin is soft and velvety in infancy, but by mid-adolescence it becomes dry and scaly in approximately 70% of individuals. Symptoms of itching develop and, because of thickening and cracking, the skin becomes prone to infections and may heal slowly. Moisturizers and emollients are helpful, oilated oatmeal can be added to bath water, and soaps that dry the skin should be avoided.

Scrotal Tongue Scrotal tongue is a benign condition that is characterized by numerous shallow or deep grooves or furrows (fissures) on the back (dorsal) surface of the tongue. The surface furrows may differ in size and depth, radiate outward, and cause the tongue to have a wrinkled appearance. This condition is present in 3%–5% of the general population, but it occurs in nearly all persons with Down syndrome.

Eye Conditions

Several conditions related to the eyes are common in people with Down syndrome (Davis, 1996; van Splunder et al., 2004). The following sections discuss these conditions.

Brushfield Spots Brushfield spots are white to light yellow nodules or speckles at the periphery of the iris. They are common in people with Down syndrome, particularly those who have blue or hazel eyes. Brushfield spots are benign and require no treatment.

Blepharitis Blepharitis is an inflammation of the eyelid. This condition occurs in up to half of individuals with Down syndrome. Daily cleansing of lid margins helps to reduce the likelihood of blepharitis.

Keratoconus A cone-shaped cornea occurs in 5%–8% of individuals with Down syndrome, and this condition may occur acutely. Keratoconus is a frequent cause of blindness in Down syndrome, second only to complications related to cataract surgery. Nonpenetrating corneal grafting is recommended as the procedure of choice to correct this disorder (Haugen et al., 2001).

Cataracts Cataracts are an opacity of the lens of the eye. In people with Down syndrome, cataracts may occur in the form of gray flaky opacities near the surface of the lens. Children with Down syndrome can have cataracts, and cataracts become more common as individuals with Down syndrome age. Some investigators believe that virtually all older adults with Down syndrome have some degree of cataract formation. When visual acuity decreases substantially, cataracts are surgically removed.

Strabismus Strabismus is a deviation (crossing inward) of one or both eyes that cannot be voluntarily overcome. The presence of epicanthic folds sometimes gives the appearance of the eyes converging inwards; as the bridge of the nose develops and the epicanthic folds become less prominent or disappear altogether, strabismus may disappear. However, true strabismus also is common in Down syndrome. The condition is treated by using patching, eyeglasses, or—if these interventions are unsuccessful—surgery. Treatment is important, particularly in cases when only one eye is affected: Reduced visual acuity may develop in the normal eye if its vision is involuntarily suppressed to avoid double vision.

Nystagmus In nystagmus, the eye beats back and forth involuntarily, usually in a horizontal direction in a fine rapid pendular fashion. These oscillating movements often first occur in the first year of life and may improve over time. No definitive treatment is available.

Refractive Errors Refractive errors are common, affecting more than one half of people with Down syndrome. Myopia, or shortsightedness, is the most common cause of the higher degrees of refractive errors. This occurs when the distance between the front and back of the eyeball is increased. As a result, the focused image lies in front of the retina. An individual with this condition is able to see well at close range but must use corrective lenses to clearly see objects far away. The prescribed lenses are concave in shape. The reverse is true in hyperopia, or farsightedness, for which a convex lens is required to see objects close to the eye. Astigmatism is another cause of refractive errors; in this condition, the cornea is misshapen or uneven. Corrective lenses compensate for astigmatism.

Thyroid Abnormalities

Thyroid abnormalities are common in Down syndrome (Prasher, 1999). The thyroid gland (see Figure 10.6) is responsible for the production and secretion of thyroid hormones (triiodothyronine [T3] and thyroxine [T4]—the most active thyroid hormone). Thyroid hormones are essential for every cell in the body and help regulate a variety of functions, including heart rate, blood pressure, body temperature, and the rate at which food is converted into energy. Thyroid hormones also help children grow and develop. Falling levels of thyroxine cause the pituitary gland to produce increasing levels of thyrotropin or thyroid stimulating hormone (TSH). The thyroid gland responds by producing more thyroxine. (See also Chapter 9 for further information about the role of the thyroid in the body.)

Some children are born with hypothyroidism. This is known as congenital hypothyroidism, and it can be an inherited or transient condition. Congenital hypothyroidism can cause intellectual disability, so newborns with the condition must be treated. In the U.S. and Canada, congenital hypothyroidism is not usually the result of iodine deficiency, and treatment involves administration of a thyroid hormone supplement. In some other countries, congenital hypothyroidism is the result of iodine deficiency (see Chapter 9), and treat-

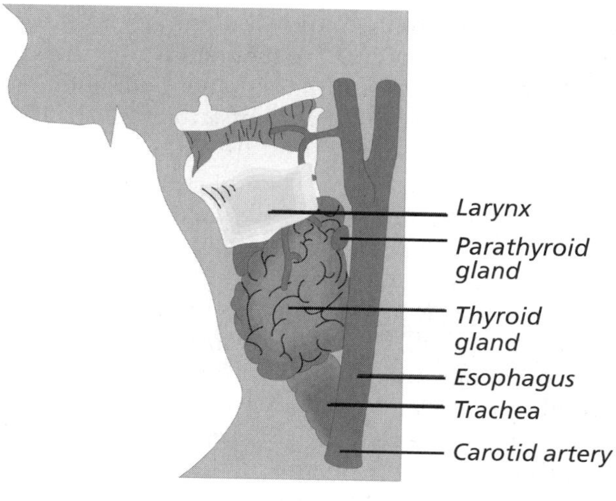

Figure 10.6. Cross-section of the neck. (From *Corel Gallery 2.* [1995]. Ottawa, ON, Canada: Corel Corporation; reprinted by permission. Copyright © 2007 John Lovering and Corel and its licensors. All rights reserved.)

ment involves provision of an iodine supplement and a thyroid hormone supplement.

In most developed countries, newborns are screened for congenital hypothyroidism. The January 2004 U.S. Preventive Services Task Force guidelines do not recommend routine screening for thyroid disease in asymptomatic children or adults, regardless of age or sex (Felz, 2005). Health guidelines for people with Down syndrome are different, however. The guidelines recommend reviewing results of the newborn thyroid function screen, then repeating thyroid function tests at the 6 months of age, 12 months of age, and then annually (Hardy et al., 2004; Roizen & Patterson, 2003). If the TSH value is high or low, then T4 or T3 should be measured; if either of the latter are abnormal, then autoantibodies to the thyroid gland should be measured. Some guidelines recommend that treatment for hypothyroidism should be started only 1) if the TSH is high and the T4 and/or T3 is low or 2) if the TSH is high, the T4 or T3 is normal, and autoantibodies to the thyroid gland are present. Treatment for hyperthyroidism (overactive thyroid) should be started if the TSH is low and T4 and/or T3 are high.

The most common form of acquired hypothyroidism in people with Down syndrome, as in the general population, is called *hypothyroid autoimmune thyroiditis* (also known as lymphocytic thyroiditis or Hashimoto's thyroiditis). In this disorder, autoimmunity causes the body to fail to recognize its own tissue, and it mounts an autoimmune response that destroys cells in the thyroid gland. Circulating autoantibodies to the thyroid gland may be found to support this diagnosis. Autoimmune thyroiditis is frequently associated with normal thyroid function, at least in the early stages of the disease.

Compensated hypothyroidism is a condition that is associated with normal or only slightly reduced levels of T3 and/or T4 and elevated TSH. An individual with compensated hypothyroidism is usually asymptomatic. Although some studies have suggested lower than normal rates of growth and development among people with this condition (see van Trotsenburg et al., 2005), many physicians refrain from treatment with thyroid hormone supplements until there is clinical and laboratory evidence of hypothyroidism.

Newborn screening tests indicate that congenital hypothyroidism is approximately 28 times more common in Down syndrome than in the general population (McCoy, n.d.). Past the newborn stage, as many as 85% of infants with Down syndrome younger than 12 months of age have elevated TSH, but after this age, the prevalence of elevated TSH decreases. Levels of T3 and T4 tend to decrease with advancing age. Hypothyroid autoimmune thyroiditis affects 13%–63% of adults with Down syndrome. Overt hyperthyroidism also can occur in people with Down syndrome, but this disorder is not common. Prasher and Haque (2005) pointed out that the prevalence of hypothyroidism possibly may be overrepresented in Down syndrome because reference levels used to interpret test results are obtained from data on people without Down syndrome.

Table 10.4 shows the signs and symptoms of abnormally low thyroid function The presence or absence of symptoms does not always predict thyroid status. People with Down syndrome whose laboratory tests are indicative of hypothyroidism often do not show the classic symptoms. In part, this is because some of the physical features that suggest hypothyroidism may already be present in people with Down syndrome.

Curiously, there may be a connection between thyroiditis and hepatitis B virus (HBV) infection, at least in adults with Down syndrome. In one study, the frequency of hypothyroid autoimmune thyroiditis in individuals with Down syndrome who were also carriers of the HBV surface antigen, HbsAg, was found to be threefold higher than the frequency of thyroid disease in those with Down syndrome who were not carriers of HBsAg (65% versus 23%) (May & Kawanishi, 1996). Vaccinations against hepatitis viruses A, B, and C are greatly reducing the prevalence of infectious hepatitis generally and specifically in people with Down syndrome.

Diabetes Mellitus

Diabetes appears to be more prevalent in people with Down syndrome than in the general population, although data are limited and the relative prevalences of type 1 and type 2 diabetes in individuals with Down syndrome are not known (Anwar, Walker, & Frier, 1998; Shield et al., 1999; Wallace & Dalton, 2005). In an epidemiological study in Scotland, Anwar, Walker, and Frier (1998) calculated the prevalence of type 1

Table 10.4. Symptoms of hypothyroidism

Weakness, lethargy, and fatigue
Dry skin
Coarse hair, hair loss
Intolerance to cold temperatures
Constipation
Weight gain
Muscle cramps and aches
Edema (swelling from fluid accumulation) of eyelids, face, and legs
Hoarseness
Hearing loss, memory loss
Menorrhagia (heavy menstrual flow)
Slowing of return phase of reflexes (e.g., knee jerk)
Bradycardia (abnormally slow heartbeat)

Note: Physical symptoms of hypothyroidism are not often evident in people with Down syndrome because certain physical features suggestive of hypothyroidism are also related to Down syndrome.

diabetes in Down syndrome to fall between 1.4% and 10.6%, which was higher than expected; they also observed the prevalence to increase with age. Differences in glycemic control between participants with and without Down syndrome were not significant, despite less stringent insulin regimens in the participants with Down syndrome. Individuals with one type of autoimmune disorder (e.g., celiac disease, autoimmune thyroiditis) may be at increased risk of having diabetes (Wallace & Dalton, 2005).

Hematological Abnormalities

Hematology is the study of the blood. The types of hematological abnormalities among individuals with Down syndrome do not differ substantially from those of the general population. However, some of these problems are much more common in people with Down syndrome.

Red Blood Cell Abnormalities The numbers and size of red blood cells in newborns with Down syndrome are often increased; these conditions are called *erythrocytosis* and *macrocytosis,* respectively. The mechanisms that cause these conditions are unknown. In most infants, the number and size of red blood cells returns to normal at approximately 1 month of age, but in infants with Down syndrome, this time may be reduced to approximately 3 weeks. Macrocytosis also occurs in adults with Down syndrome.

White Blood Cell Abnormalities People with Down syndrome tend to have a normal response to infectious processes, but they often have an increased number of circulating white blood cells, especially in the neutrophils, the most common form of granulocytes. Granulocytes are white blood cells that help to protect the body from infection. They are able to envelop microorganisms such as bacteria, draw them into the cell, and surround them by the cell membrane (phagocytosis). The "captured" bacteria are then killed by an enzymatic process.

Platelet Abnormalities Platelets are blood cells that play a role in the blood clotting process. A reduction in the platelet count (thrombocytopenia) may be found in newborns with Down syndrome as a mild and insignificant occurrence that resolves spontaneously. In cases of platelet abnormalities, however, the physicians must consider the possibility of less benign conditions, including transient myelodysplasia or leukemia (see next section). Transient elevated platelet counts may also be seen in infants with or without Down syndrome.

Leukemia Leukemia is a type of cancer in which white blood cells displace normal blood. This leads to infection, shortage of red blood cells (anemia), bleeding, and other disorders; the condition is often fatal. Children with Down syndrome have a higher likelihood of developing leukemia than children without Down syndrome. Myeloid leukemia is especially common in children with Down syndrome; studies suggest that there is a 10%–30% increase in risk (Webb, 2005). Infants and young children with Down syndrome are also much more likely to have acute non-lymphoblastic leukemia (ANLL) and, in particular, acute megakaryoblastic leukemia (AMKL), which affects precursor cells of platelets. In fact, AMKL is several hundred times more common in children with Down syndrome than in the general population (Zipursky, 1996). The reason for this is unclear, but it may have something to do with the increase in gene dosage from the extra chromosomal material. Immature "blast" cells are not normally present in circulating blood. Myelodysplasia is a condition in which these immature cells appear in the blood but in smaller numbers than in cases of true leukemia. In the first few months of life, infants with or without Down syndrome sometimes develop transient myelodysplasia, which resolves between 1–3 months without treatment. There is, however, a 20% chance that this condition will later reappear as AMKL, so follow-up is important. Many hematologists/oncologists begin treatment before the threshold of 30% immature cells appears in a blood smear. Part of the initial evaluation for leukemia includes a bone marrow biopsy. A condition known as *myelofibrosis* commonly accompanies AMKL and increases the amount of fibrous tissue in the bone marrow. This interferes with the aspiration of a sample for microscopic analysis.

Traditional treatment of leukemia involves alkylating agents, such as methotrexate. People with Down syndrome are particularly sensitive to alkylating agents, so these individuals frequently experience negative side effects such as sores in the mouth and gastrointestinal tract and the suppression of bone marrow function. Newer treatment regimens have been modified to avoid these drugs and often include administration of cytosine arabinoside (ARA-C) and daunorubricin instead. Although patients with Down syndrome are unusually sensitive to traditional forms of treatment, those with acute myeloid leukemia who are treated with ARA-C have significantly higher, event-free survival rates compared with children without Down syndrome (Gamis, 2005; Hitzler & Zipursky, 2005).

Testicular Cancer

Evidence for a suspected association of Down syndrome and testicular cancer continues to accumulate. Along with genetically determined malformations in many other organs in trisomy 21, the gonads also undergo maldevelopment, thus creating the conditions for the first step of germ cell tumor oncogenesis in utero. Physicians caring for patients with Down syndrome should be aware of the possible association with testicular neoplasms (Goldacre et al., 2004). Various other types of solid tumors may occur less frequently in Down syndrome than in the general population (Hasle, 2001).

Obesity

Prevention of obesity is an important goal for people with Down syndrome (Roizen & Patterson, 2003). Infants with Down syndrome tend to be light for their height, but by age 3–4 years, these children are often overweight. A study by Patel et al. (2004) supported the hypothesis that higher estrogen levels in obese women with Down syndrome are associated with better performance on verbal memory tests. Nevertheless, efforts to prevent such weight gain should begin by the age of 2 years and should include the following:

- A total calorie intake that is less than the recommended daily allowance
- Sensible food choices—that is, foods that are high in nutrients and fiber and low in calories and fat
- Supplementary vitamins and minerals, especially calcium and vitamin D
- Participation in physical and social activities

Arthritis and Problems with Walking

People with Down syndrome are susceptible to arthritis, carpal tunnel syndrome, and other disorders that lead to problems with walking (Roizen & Patterson, 2003; Wallace & Dalton, 2005). These include the following:

- A rheumatoid arthritis-like disorder in 1.2% of children and adolescents; this is associated with joint subluxations and with dislocations of the cervical spine, patella, and other joints. *Subluxation* refers to a bone in a joint or a vertebra that has lost its juxtaposition with the one above or below it and impinges on nerves and interferes with the transmission of impulses over or through the affected nerve.
- Unusual waddling gait (sometimes referred to as "Chaplinesque" because it resembles the shuffling gait used by the comedian Charlie Chaplin) resulting from hips externally rotated, knees in flexion and valgus (twisted away from the center of the body), and tibias (shin bones) externally rotated
- Pes planovalgus (flat feet) with marked pronation of the foot (turning in of the foot so that the inner edge bears too much weight)
- Severe bunions and hammer toe deformities
- Plantar fasciitis (inflammation of the plantar fascia, a tight band of tissue on the bottom of the foot extending from the heel bone to the back of the toes)
- Pedal (foot) arthritis associated with severe flat feet

Management of these conditions may include consultation with an orthopedic specialist or a podiatrist.

Atlantoaxial Instability

The first description of atlantoaxial instability dates back to 3,500 B.C.–4,000 B.C., although it was first reported in the medical literature in 1961 as an abnormality associated with Down syndrome (Roche, Seward, & Sunderland, 1961). The prevalence varies, but it is approximately 15%. Atlantoaxial instability became much more visible in 1983, when the Special Olympics required cervical spine X-rays of all entrants with Down syndrome. In 1995, however, the Committee on Sports Medicine and Fitness of the American Academy of Pediatrics published a position paper on this topic that included several arguments that disfavors such screening. Nevertheless, screening for atlantoaxial instability is considered prudent (Pueschel, 1990, 1998).

The second cervical vertebra, the axis, has a fingerlike extension on its upper and front surface called the odontoid process, or dens (see Figure 10.7). A transverse ligament holds the odontoid process against the front inner surface of the atlas, or the first cervical ver-

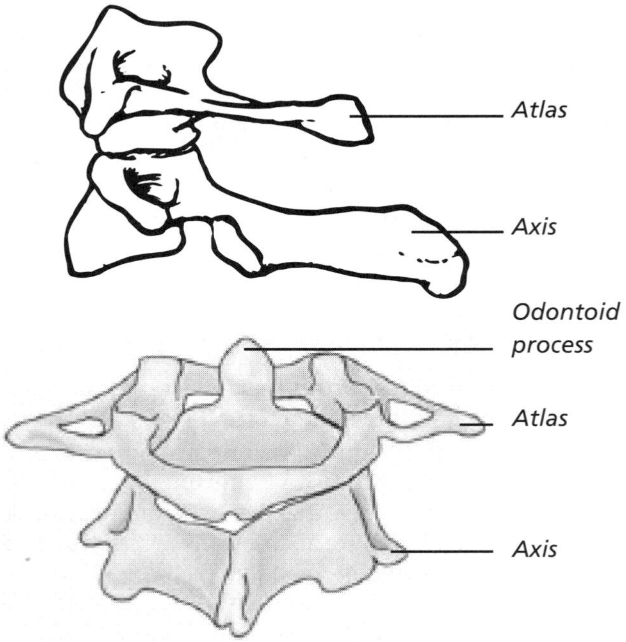

Figure 10.7. Lateral and posterior views of the articulated atlas and axis. (From *Corel Gallery 2.* [1995]. Ottawa, ON, Canada: Corel Corporation; reprinted by permission. Copyright © 2007 John Lovering and Corel and its licensors. All rights reserved.)

tebra above it. Presumably, as the result of laxity of this ligament in Down syndrome, the odontoid process is able to rock and/or slide backwards when the neck moves, especially when the head flexes forwards. The odontoid process in this circumstance impinges to some extent on the spinal canal that lies directly behind it and therefore on the spinal cord and on the various nerve roots that emerge from it in this area.

Most children with atlantoaxial instability have no symptoms or signs, but there are reports of catastrophic neurological events that affect the spinal cord. Approximately 1% of individuals with Down syndrome have neurological signs, such as stiff neck, problems with walking, numbness, tingling, or weakness.

X rays of the cervical spine in three positions—neutral, flexion, and extension—are typically carried out to measure the distance between the odontoid process and the atlas. An interval or space of <5 millimeters is usually considered the acceptable threshold, although higher values are sometimes used. When instability is found, the individual is advised—as a precaution—not to engage in activities in which there is a high risk of extreme neck flexion. Activities to avoid if atlantoaxial instability is diagnosed include the following:

- Gymnastics
- Diving (including a diving start for swimming competitions)
- Pentathlon activities, which consist of five contests (discus, javelin, long jump, wrestling, and foot race)
- Butterfly stroke in swimming
- High jump
- Soccer
- Alpine skiing

As noted, screening for atlantoaxial instability is recommended by most authorities. It should be initiated when a child with Down syndrome enters an educational or child care program, in which organized physical activities often are first introduced. The screening includes a history to assess any symptoms of atlantoaxial instability; a neurological examination; laboratory investigations; and neck X rays in neutral, flexion, and extension. In appropriate circumstances, **computed tomography (CT)** or magnetic resonance imaging (MRI) scans aid in the diagnosis. Nerve conduction studies (or somatosensory evoked potentials) may be helpful in the assessment as well. Evaluation is also recommended prior to surgery requiring general anesthesia, as the anesthetist may need to flex the patient's neck to ensure a patent airway and to prepare for intubation. At 9–10 years of age, if the child is introduced to the Special Olympics or other sports programs, another evaluation is recommended. As of 2007, people with Down syndrome are allowed to take part in the previously noted high-risk sports provided that a thorough physical examination shows no evidence of atlantoaxial stability, appropriate documentation is provided by a physician, and a signed consent is provided by the participant and/or his or her caregiver (Special Olympics, n.d.).

The presence of atlantoaxial instability requires monitoring over time. In most instances, no intervention is required other than avoidance of activities that are likely to produce undue stress on the neck. Sometimes, the interval distance gradually changes: It may normalize, or it may even increase. The presence of any neurological symptoms, however, requires immediate reassessment to evaluate the need for further intervention. This may require a stabilizing surgical procedure in which the two vertebrae are fused together to avoid serious damage to the spinal cord.

Hypotonia

Almost all children with Down syndrome have central hypotonia, or reduced muscle tone or resistance to passive movement. This is apparent in early infancy, affecting certain physiological reflexes (i.e., **Moro response** and **parachute reflex**), but gradually improves over time. However, it is commonly found in young children with Down syndrome. Although hypotonia itself is not dangerous (Wisniewki & Kida, 1997), it has a variety of consequences in early development. Children with Down syndrome with hypotonia have a reduced capacity for producing muscle force. Such children have been found to exhibit significantly higher levels of stiffness and forcing (angular impulse) when walking on a treadmill and higher forcing, but not stiffness overground, than children with typical development. It is suspected that such stiffness is a form of compensation for hypotonia and laxity of joints (Ulrich et al., 2004).

Seizures

Although there was once controversy in medical literature over the prevalence of seizures among people with Down syndrome, many experts agree that non-Asian individuals with Down syndrome are more prone to seizures than those in the general population (Romano et al., 1990; Thiel and Fowkes, 2004). It should be noted that the term *seizures* includes febrile seizures (those that occur during a high fever) and afebrile seizures (those that occur in the absence of fever). The term *epilepsy* refers to having two or more episodes of afebrile seizures. In the field of Down syndrome, researchers and clinicians tend to use the term *seizures* without distinguishing among febrile, afebrile, and epileptic. Approximately 6%–8% of individuals with

Down syndrome suffer from recurrent afebrile seizures (i.e., epilepsy). This is particularly true of adults, although infants and children are also affected.

There appear to be two or three peak age ranges for the onset of seizures (i.e., a bimodal or trimodal distribution). The first occurs in infancy during the first year of life. Infantile **spasms** and **tonic-clonic seizures,** often with **myoclonus,** are the most common seizure types. Pueschel and Pueschel (1992) reported that 40% of seizures in people with Down syndrome occur during this time period. Approximately 40% of individuals with Down syndrome who have seizures are first affected in the second peak age range: late adolescence or early adulthood. Seizures in this age range are more often tonic-clonic or partial in nature. However, these seizures also may be complex—that is, accompanied by altered consciousness (i.e., impairment, distortion, or loss of consciousness).

The third age range for onset of seizures occurs later in life. This timing is associated with DAT. Some authors have reported that up to 75%–84% of individuals with this type of dementia have associated seizure disorders (Menendez, 2005; Pueschel & Pueschel, 1992; see also Chapter 44).

Thiel and Fowkes (2004) hypothesized that nutritional factors may be at least partially responsible for seizures in people with or without Down syndrome. If this hypothesis is supported empirically, then it may be possible to ward off or control seizure frequency by nutritional and metabolic treatments. Traditional treatment approaches depend on the nature of the seizures and is as successful in Down syndrome as in the general population. However, Tsiouris et al. (2002) cautioned that phenytoin should not be used for control of late-onset seizures in people with Down syndrome and dementia because of adverse side effects.

Reproductive Health

There are a number of important medical issues that are related to reproductive health for people with Down syndrome. These are discussed next.

Puberty and Fertility The physical features of and age of onset for puberty in adolescent girls and boys with Down syndrome are similar to those of other adolescents. Fertility is reduced in both men and women with Down syndrome, but more so in men. With rare exceptions, men with Down syndrome cannot father a child. In any pregnancy, women with Down syndrome have a 50% chance of having a child with Down syndrome, but many affected fetuses are miscarried (Bovicelli et al., 1982).

Need for Sexual Education Programs Some people with Down syndrome marry. Even if they do not, they may wish to be sexually active. Responsibility within any sexual relationship includes mutual consent, contraception, and prevention of sexually transmitted diseases, including HIV. All of these topics need to be the subject of sexual education programs for both men and women with Down syndrome.

Earlier Menopause The onset of menopause typically occurs earlier for women with Down syndrome than for other women. The average age of onset is 47.1 years, whereas it is 49.3 years for women with intellectual disability who do not have Down syndrome (and 51 years for women without intellectual disability (Schupf et al., 1997).

Menstrual Problems As for all women, pelvic examinations are recommended for those with Down syndrome who are sexually active or who have menstrual problems. Family skill training (to outline procedures that improve general and personal hygiene), behavioral support (to reinforce routines for maintaining hygiene), and hormone treatment (oral contraceptives to reduce the severity of menstrual flow) may be successful in helping with menstrual hygiene (Kaur, Butler, & Trumble, 2003). Many women, including women with Down syndrome, may experience premenstrual syndrome (PMS). This may manifest in difficult behaviors such as temper tantrums, social withdrawal, or even seizures at (or just before) the time of menstruation (catamenial epilepsy). It has been recognized for centuries that seizure frequency increases in a high percentage of women affected with epilepsy at the time of menstruation (Reddy, 2004). Fortunately, progress is being made about its causes and treatments. Women with Down syndrome who experience PMS may benefit from typical treatments for this condition that include vitamin supplements, diet changes, drug therapy, education, and psychological counseling (Kaur et al., 2003; Rapkin, 2003).

Susceptibility to Anesthetics

Down syndrome is one of numerous genetic conditions that makes individuals unusually susceptible to the adverse side effects of anesthetics or difficult to sedate or anesthetize because of potential airway obstruction or neck instability (Butler et al., 2000; Meitzner & Skurnowicz, 2005; Procedural Sedation Resource Center, 2006). Furthermore, in the experience of the chapter authors, seizures resulting in aspiration and aspiration pneumonia have been encountered as an unexpected consequence of general anesthetic administration. Physicians and dental anesthetists should review the topic of anesthetic susceptibility before anesthetics or sedatives are administered to persons with Down syndrome for any reason (see also Wallace & Dalton, 2005).

MENTAL HEALTH ISSUES

Mental health issues with particular relevance to individuals with Down syndrome include behavioral issues and dual diagnosis, as well as sleep disorders. A discussion of the level of intellectual functioning also is included in this section because it is reflective of brain function and may be affected by the same factors that cause mental illnesses.

Level of Intellectual Functioning

Although many individuals with Down syndrome have intellectual and developmental disabilities, there is a wide range of functioning in all areas of development, including intellectual functioning. The degree of intellectual impairment ranges from mild to moderate. Among people with Down syndrome, a high level of cognitive functioning has been reported to be associated with fewer cases of dementia (Temple et al., 2001). It has been recommended that any study of aging take cognitive ability into account (Burt et al., 1995). In addition, low intellectual functioning in people with Down syndrome is reported to be associated with certain types of sleep abnormalities (Diomedi et al., 1999).

Table 10.5. Reported frequencies of certain mental health issues among people with Down syndrome

Mental health issue	Frequency
Children	
Autism (this disorder is expected to also affect adults, but the frequency has only been reported for children)	7%
Aggressive behavior	6.5% (in individuals younger than 20 years)
Attention-deficit/hyperactivity disorder	6.1%
Oppositional defiant or conduct disorder	5.4%
Adults	
Major depressive disorder	6.1%
Aggressive behavior	6.1% (This value differs from that in children because studies in children and adults were done independently.)
Dementia	Up to 50% of individuals age 50 years and older

Source: Roizen & Patterson (2003).

Note: Mental health issues have not been comprehensively studied across the age range in Down syndrome. Entries for mental health issues in this table reflect published data in the literature. Conversely, lack of representation of certain mental health issues (e.g., autism in adults) means that there are no data in the literature about this condition.

Behavioral Issues and Dual Diagnosis

People with Down syndrome are often believed to have a friendly, affectionate, and outgoing personality or a stubborn obsessional temperament with resistance to change. These views oversimplify reality, however. Individuals with Down syndrome have more behavior and psychiatric problems than other children but fewer than other individuals with intellectual and developmental disabilities (Roizen & Patterson, 2003). Among people with Down syndrome, these difficulties affect approximately 18% of individuals younger than 20 years of age and approximately 26% of adults. Psychiatric disorders in children with Down syndrome (i.e., a dual diagnosis) most frequently include autism (7%), a disruptive behavior disorder resembling attention-deficit/hyperactivity disorder (6.1%), oppositional defiant or conduct disorder (5.4%), or aggressive behavior (6.5%). A positive family history of autism in first degree relatives, infantile spasms with **hypsarrythmia,** and early hypothyroidism have been considered as possible medical factors in the development of autism in Down syndrome (Ghazluddin, 1997; Gillberg et al., 1986). Psychiatric disorders of adults with Down syndrome most frequently include major depressive disorder (6.1%) or aggressive behavior (6.1%) (Roizen & Patterson, 2003; see also Table 10.5).

People with Down syndrome also are at increased risk of developing DAT much earlier than people in the general population. As in the general population, the frequency of dementia in Down syndrome increases with advancing age, but not everyone with Down syndrome develops dementia. Chicoine, McGuire, and Rubin (1999) reported that decline in function does not always signify the development of DAT (see Table 10.6), particularly in those younger than 40 years of age. It is crucial to attempt to determine if a decline in function has a reversible cause. See Chapter 44 for additional information on Alzheimer's disease.

Sleep Disorders

Good sleep is very important for everyone's physical and mental health. Sleep is a complex process with phases and stages that conform to a pattern of progressive slowing of the brain's electrical wave activity:

- Stage 1 and Stage 2 represent light sleep (sleep spindles and K-complexes).
- Stage 3 and Stage 4 represent deep sleep (high amplitude, low frequency waves that are concentrated in the first third of the night).
- REM, or rapid eye movement, sleep occurs in a cyclic fashion throughout the night, the first episode typically approximately 70 minutes after the onset of sleep. It is implicated in cognitive well-being, information processing, and memory.
- Non-REM sleep is associated with physical well-being and tissue restoration.

The concept that sleep might also be involved in brain plasticity and or brain maturation has been studied for years; this hypothesis, in fact, is supported by recent research data (Dang-Vu et al., 2006). Disruption of sleep architecture and of sleep–wake rhythms appears to be common in many individuals with developmental and intellectual disabilities. Furthermore, people with Down syndrome are unusually susceptible to certain sleep disorders (Erler & Paditz, 2004). The term *sleep apnea* refers to disruption of breathing that interferes with normal sleep. There are two main types of sleep apnea. Obstructive sleep apnea (OSA) may represent cessation of breathing due to mechanical blockage of the airway. Central sleep apnea appears to be related to a malfunction of the brain's normal signal to breathe. Symptoms of sleep apnea include restless sleep; loud, heavy snoring (often interrupted by silence and then gasps); falling asleep during the day (e.g., while in the car, at work, or watching television); morning headaches; loss of energy; trouble concentrating; and mood or behavior changes. There are a variety of treatments available for those that suffer from sleep apnea, including medications, behavior therapy, weight reduction, and, in extreme cases, surgery. Sleep apnea is diagnosed by an overnight sleep test. This generally includes monitoring airflow through the nose and mouth; blood pressure, heartbeat, and blood oxygen level; brain wave patterns and eye movements; and movements of respiratory muscles and limbs. As of 2006, a low-cost, disposable device called a SleepStrip is being used to screen for sleep apnea at home (for more information, go to http://www.sleepstripcanada.ca/links.asp).

Table 10.6. Diagnosed disorders for 148 adults with Down syndrome who presented with a decline in function

Condition	Frequency	Percent (%) of diagnosed disorders
Mood disorder	76	31
Anxiety disorder	31	13
Obsessive-compulsive disorder	29	12
Behavior disorder	23	9
Hypothyroidism	22	9
Adjustment disorder	12	5
Alzheimer's disease	11	4
B_{12} deficiency	7	3
Menopause	7	3
Attention deficit/hyperactivity disorder	6	2
Gastrointestinal or urinary disorder	6	2
Sensory impairment	6	2
Psychotic disorder	4	2
Other medical conditions[a]	4	2
Cardiac conditions	3	1
Total	247	100

[a]Includes Parkinson's disease, hyperthyroidism, and seizure disorder.

OSA is reported to be common in Down syndrome, with the prevalence varying from 30%–50%. Levanon, Tarasiuk, and Tal (1999), however, found significant sleep fragmentation in a study of 23 children with Down syndrome (mean age 4.8 years) that was only partially related to OSA. Sleep was considered fragmented when a subject experienced an abnormal number of arousals, awakenings, periodic limb movements, shortening of sleep continuity, and frequent shifts from deeper to lighter sleep stages. Espie et al. (1998) previously questioned the suitability of conventional sleep stages for individuals with intellectual disabilities, because typical electroencephalographic patterns of sleep are often difficult to identify. In their study, 32% of individuals with intellectual disabilities had evidence of a sleep disorder based on calculations of sleep efficiency. There also was evidence of high levels of light and deep sleep rhythms intruding during daytime hours. These patterns might lead to a tendency to fall asleep while passively engaged, become irritable, or experience mood changes. A person with such sleep patterns would be prone to drowsiness or behavior problems.

People with Down syndrome may be at increased risk of OSA because of anatomical abnormalities. The upper airway is anatomically narrow because of midfacial and mandibular hypoplasia (undergrowth of tissue). In addition, glossoptosis (abnormal downward or back placement of the tongue) and adenoidal and tonsillar hypertrophy (enlargement) are common. Other predisposing factors include generalized hypotonia with malfunction of the upper airway muscles. Obesity also can also lead to interrupted sleep in people with Down syndrome (Ng & Chan, 2004).

Removal of the tonsils and adenoids (Donnelly et al., 2004) or losing weight, if relevant, may improve sleep for some people with Down syndrome. The use of devices that provide continuous positive airway pressure is sometimes not practicable in people with intellectual disabilities because these devices are cumbersome and uncomfortable. Because access to sleep laboratories normally is limited and because it is known that breathing devices are not likely used, routine screening for sleep disorders in Down syndrome is often not feasible.

In addition to the previously mentioned strategies, sleep problems in people with Down syndrome have been successfully treated with

- Niaprazine, a histamine H1-receptor antagonist that has marked sedative properties and is considered to be not addictive

- The pineal gland hormone, melatonin
- Behavioral interventions

Sedatives that are addictive and hypnotics are not advised.

ASSESSMENT AND MANAGEMENT OF HEALTH CONDITIONS

Table 10.7 summarizes the range of physical and mental health issues that are relevant to the quality of health for people with Down syndrome The importance of health promotion and disease prevention across the lifespan cannot be overemphasized. Care providers can help people with Down syndrome achieve a high quality of life by being aware of the different conditions and disorders that affect them, by helping to communicate their needs to professionals, and by advocating for their health needs.

Table 10.7. Scope of physical and mental health issues in people with Down syndrome

Actions	Relevant health issues
Newborn screening for	Congenital heart disease
	Congenital hypothyroidism
	Gastrointestinal obstructions and fistulas
Regular monitoring for	Cardiovascular disease (valvular heart disease, pulmonary hypertension, and Eisenmenger syndrome)
	Leukemia
	Atlantoaxial instability
	Hearing and vision problems
	Other issues (breast cancer, dental health, exercise, immunizations, concurrent medications, nutrition, obesity, prostate cancer, environmental safety, sexual education, sexual health, skin problems, and testicular cancer)
Watch for symptoms of	Cardiovascular disease (valvular heart disease, endocarditis, pulmonary hypertension, and Eisenmenger syndrome)
	Thyroid dysfunction and diabetes
	Gastrointestinal problems (bowel dysfunction, gastroesophageal reflux disease, hepatitis infections, *Helicobacter pylori* infection, and celiac disease)
	Musculoskeletal problems (atlantoaxial instability, arthritis, osteoporosis, carpal tunnel syndrome, walking problems, and falls)
	Pneumonia
	Hearing and vision problems
	Other problems (tooth decay and gum disease)
	Mental health issues (dementia, depression, other behavioral issues, seizures, and sleep apnea)
Take action to prevent	Cardiovascular disease (endocarditis, pulmonary hypertension, and Eisenmenger syndrome)
	Gastrointestinal disorders (hepatitis virus infections and celiac disease)
	Falls and accidents
	Complications of anesthetics and sedatives
	Other (cavities and gum disease, medication interactions, unwanted pregnancies, sexually transmitted diseases, and seizures)

RESEARCH DEVELOPMENTS AND FUTURE DIRECTIONS

A review of Down syndrome would not be complete without reference to some ground-breaking advances in basic research that have been made since 1999. The Human Genome Project (see Chapters 7, 8, and 9) has been a highlight of the early 21st century. This has resulted in determining the DNA sequence of the entire chromosome 21; identifying 225 genes; and predicting that 329 more exist (Hattori et al., 2000; Reeves, 2000; Roizen & Patterson, 2003). One surprising finding was that much of the DNA of chromosome 21 is not found in genes; although this DNA does not code for proteins as most genes do, it does result in the production of RNA molecules whose specific functions are not yet known. Of the known genes, 16 have a role in energy and reactive oxygen species metabolism; 9 may affect brain development, neuronal loss and Alzheimer-type neuropathology; and 6 have a role in folate and methyl group metabolism (Roizen & Patterson, 2003).

Researchers have already realized that it is a mistake to assume that the clinical features of Down syndrome are only due to a few chromosome 21 genes that are overexpressed (Olson et al., 2004). Furthermore, the gene products that are overexpressed in Down syndrome are not the same for everyone because many chromosome 21 genes have a number of different allelic variants (see Chapters 7 and 8). Such allelic variation may explain why some but not all people with Down syndrome are born with congenital heart disease and gastrointestinal abnormalities or develop autoimmune thyroiditis. How the overexpressed gene products of chromosome 21 interact with normally expressed gene products on other chromosomes is a key issue already under intensive investigation.

Using a variety of methods, scientists are able to produce mice that mimic the human condition of Down syndrome or enable the functions of specific chromosome 21 genes to be determined (Antonarakis et al., 2004). For example, in addition to their own genome, some mice carry various additional regions of mouse chromosome 16, which is the homologue of human chromosome 21, and they have different types of brain and behavior abnormalities. Furthermore, it is possible to create genetically engineered mice that lack particular chromosome 16 genes or that have excess normal or mutant human chromosome 21 genes. From such mouse models, it will be possible to identify functions of the genes on human chromosome 21 that are important regarding

- Cognition and behavior
- Immunity
- Predisposition to and protection against certain cancers
- Functions of chromosome 21 RNA that does not get translated into protein
- The way chromosome 21 genes "talk" to one another and to genes on other chromosomes
- The causes of the nondisjunction that result in trisomy 21

In addition, such mouse models will aid enormously in the identification of genes and molecular processes affecting the development of DAT, as well as with the testing of new drugs and medicines for treatment of DAT and any characteristics of the Down syndrome phenotype resulting from extra chromosome 21 genes.

Last but not least, as of 2007, two large clinical trials have relevance for individuals with Down syndrome. These are designed to determine treatment outcomes and thereby improve health and quality of life for people with Down syndrome. The first trial, for which recruitment already is complete, involves a study of antioxidants and folinic acid in babies (Antioxidants and folinic research project; Down's Syndrome Research Foundation Ltd., 2005). A second study, in which recruitment is anticipated until at least 2008, involves a study of the ability of high doses of vitamin E to slow deterioration of neurocognitive and neurobehavioral function in aging individuals with Down syndrome (National Institutes of Health, 2005). Thus, these studies may lead to the development of new strategies that will increase longevity, that will at least ameliorate the development of intellectual disability and various aspects of the Down syndrome phenotype in children, and that will even possibly prevent DAT in older persons with Down syndrome.

ACHIEVEMENTS

Despite the numerous challenges and health problems that can be associated with Down syndrome, some people with Down syndrome have made remarkable achievements. Chris Burke and Cathy Lemon (see Displays 10.2 and 10.3) are exemplary role models for people with intellectual and developmental disabilities. The support of family and many people in the community was key to making Cathy's dream a reality.

Display 10.2

Chris Burke's story

Chris Burke is a well known actor and singer with Down syndrome. He always aspired to becoming an actor, singer, and writer and to helping other people like himself, and he has never let prejudices get in his way. As an actor, featured television roles have included playing "Corky" in *Life Goes On* and "Taylor," the angel of faith, in *Touched by an Angel.* As singer with his band, together with Joe and John DeMasi, with whom he has been friends for over 25 years, Chris already has recorded four uptlifing albums. In addition to acting and singing, Chris works for the National Down Syndrome Society and serves as editor-in-chief of its magazine *Upbeat,* which is written by and for people with Down syndrome. He also has coauthored a book about his life called *A Special Kind of Hero,* published in 1992 by Bantam Doubleday Dell. Last but not least, Chris also has a reputation for being an inspirational speaker and for always referring to Down syndrome as "UP Syndrome." For further information about Chris Burke, how his band developed, and how his family and education influenced his life, refer to the official web site of Chris Burke with Joe and John DeMasi (http://www.chrisburke.org).

Display 10.3

Cathy Lemon's story

A young woman with Down syndrome, Cathy Lemon loved to bake, and she dreamed of starting her own company. In 1998, Cathy's parents, Carolyn and Jim, applied on behalf of Cathy for a grant from the Ontario Government to start up a catering company called Lemon & Allspice Cookery. Community Living Toronto provided free use of its kitchen, and the company expanded into a thriving business that sells its products wholesale and retail. In 2000, the Cookery created Common Ground Cooperative, Inc. This is a nonprofit service organization, with a membership of over 100 individuals from the community, that promotes the establishment of initiatives for people with intellectual and developmental disabilities to use their talents to provide employment for themselves. As of 2005, there were 16 partners with intellectual and/or developmental disabilities in the Cookery who were helped by job coaches and held the equivalent of 3.5 full-time positions. The Cooperative also manages three "Coffee Sheds" that sell baked goods, sandwiches, and organic "fair trade" coffee and other beverages at three different organizations. This model has been so successful that it is worth duplicating in other communities.

Sources: Common Ground Cooperative, Inc. (n.d.); Lemon and Lemon (2003).

SUMMARY

People with Down syndrome are at risk for numerous medical complications that can, to a large extent, be treated or prevented to lead to high quality of life. Health professionals have played a more extensive and energetic role in the overall care and support for individuals with Down syndrome as they have become more familiar with the individuals' medical and nonmedical needs. This awareness has led to a more anticipatory and preventative approach. Medical conditions are now treated earlier, and there is the potential for a shorter course of treatment and fewer complications. The hope for the future lies in the emergence of new interventions as more is learned about Down syndrome and its etiology. This process will develop partly through research efforts focused on these same conditions that are found in the general population. The information provided in this chapter provides optimism that the quality of life for people with Down syndrome and their potential for achievement will continue to increase in the future.

FOR FURTHER THOUGHT AND DISCUSSION

1. What preventive strategies should be undertaken to improve the quality of life for people with Down syndrome? Who should take the initiative for preventive care?
2. What medical conditions are most likely to cause serious or life-threatening problems for individuals with Down syndrome?
3. There has been a gradual increase in the longevity of individuals with Down syndrome since the mid-1980s in some countries. What changes in the provision of health care are responsible for this?

REFERENCES

Antonarakis, S.E., Lyle, R., Dermitzakis, E.T., et al. (2004). Chromosome 21 and Down syndrome: From genomics to pathophysiology. *Nature Reviews: Genetics, 5,* 725–738.

Anwar, A.J., Walker, J.D., & Frier, B.M. (1998). Type 1 diabetes mellitus and Down's syndrome: Prevalence, management and diabetic complications. *Diabetic Medicine, 15,* 160–163.

Baird, P.A., & Sadovnick, A.D. (1987). Life expectancy in Down syndrome. *Journal of Pediatrics, 110,* 849–854.

Behrman, R.E. (Ed.). (1992). *Nelson textbook of pediatrics* (14th ed.). Philadelphia: W.B. Saunders Company.

Berg, J.M. (2003). Down syndrome before Down: A postscript. *American Journal of Medical Genetics, Part A, 116,* 97–98.

Berg, J.M., Karlinsky, H., & Holland, A.J. (1993). *Alzheimer disease, Down syndrome, and their relationship.* Oxford, United Kingdom: Oxford University Press.

Berg, J.M., & Korossy, M. (2001). Down syndrome before Down: A retrospect. *American Journal of Medical Genetics, 102,* 205–211.

Biavati, M.J., & Rocha-Worley, G. (2003). *Palatopharyngeal incompetence.* Retrieved January 26, 2006, from http://www.emedicine.com/ped/topic1707.htm.

Blackstone, S.W. (1992). People with Down syndrome: Characteristics affecting the development of communication skills. *Augmentative Communication News, 5*(2). Retrieved March 21, 2006, from http://www.augcominc.com/articles/5_2_1.html

Bosch, J.J. (2003). Health maintenance throughout the life span for individuals with Down syndrome. *Journal of the American Academy of Nurse Practitioners, 15,* 5–17.

Bovicelli, L., Orsini, L.F., Rizzo, N., et al. (1982). Reproduction in Down syndrome. *Obstetrics & Gynecology, 59*(6, Suppl.), 13S–17S.

British Heart Foundation. (2006). *Heart health.* Retrieved March 11, 2006, from http://www.bhf.org.uk/hearthealth/index_home.asp?SecID=1

Burt, D.B., Loveland, K.A., Chen, Y.W., et al. (1995). Aging in adults with Down syndrome: Report from a longitudinal study. *American Journal on Mental Retardation, 100*(3), 262–270.

Butler, M.G., Hayes, B.G., Hathaway, M.M., et al. (2000). Specific genetic diseases at risk for sedation/anesthesia complications. *Anesthesia and Analgesia, 91,* 837–855.

California Birth Defects Monitoring Program. (n.d.). *Down syndrome: Associated birth defects.* Retrieved March 26, 2006, from http://www.cbdmp.org/bd_down_defects.htm

Carmeli, E., Kessel, S., Bar-Chad, S., et al. (2004). A comparison between older persons with Down syndrome and a control group: Clinical characteristics, functional status and sensorimotor function. *Down's Syndrome, Research and Practice, 9,* 17–24.

Chapman, R.S., & Hesketh, L.J. (2000). Behavioral phenotype of individuals with Down syndrome. *Mental Retardation and Developmental Disabilities Research Reviews, 6*(2), 84–95.

Chapman, R.S., & Hesketh, L.J. (2001). Language, cognition, and short-term memory in individuals with Down syndrome. *Down's Syndrome, Research and Practice, 7,* 1–7.

Chicoine, B., McGuire, D., Hebein, S., et al. (1994). Development of a clinic for adults with Down syndrome. *Mental Retardation, 32,* 100–106.

Chicoine, B., McGuire, D., & Rubin, S. (1999). Adults with Down syndrome: Specialty clinic perspectives. In M. Janicki, & A. Dalton (Eds.), *Dementia, aging and intellectual disabilities. A handbook* (pp. 278–291). London: Taylor and Francis. (Retrieved September 8, 2005, from http://www.ds-health.com/adults.htm)

Club NDSS. (2002). *About Chris Burke.* Retrieved March 21, 2006, from http://www.clubndss.org/clubndss.cfm?fuseaction=cbStory

Cogulu, O., Ozkinay, F., Gunduz, C., et al. (2003). Celiac disease in children with Down syndrome: Importance of follow-up and serologic screening. *Pediatrics International, 45,* 395–399.

Common Ground Cooperative, Inc. (n.d.). *Home page.* Retrieved March 21, 2006, from http://www.commonground co-op.ca

Corel Gallery 2. (1995). Ottawa, ON, Canada: Corel Corporation.

Cronk, C.E., Crocker A.C., Pueschel, S.M., et al. (1988). Growth charts for children with Down syndrome: 1 month to 18 years of age. *Pediatrics, 81,* 102–110.

Cupples, L., & Iacono, T. (2000). Phonological awareness and oral reading skill in children with Down syndrome. *Journal of Speech, Language, and Hearing Research, 43,* 595–608.

Dang-Vu, T.T., Desseilles, M., Peigneux, P., et al. (2006). A role for sleep in brain plasticity. *Pediatric Rehabilitation, 9*(2), 98–118.

Davis, J.S. (1996, March). Ocular manifestations in Down syndrome. *Pennsylvania Medicine 99*(Suppl.), 67–70.

Devlin, L., & Morrison, P.J. (2004). Accuracy of the clinical diagnosis of Down syndrome. *Ulster Medical Journal, 73,* 4–12.

DeVore, G.R., & Romero, R. (2003). Genetic sonography: An option for women of advanced maternal age with negative triple-marker maternal serum screening results. *Journal of Ultrasound Medicine, 22,* 1191–1199.

Diomedi, M., Curatolo, P., Scalise, A., et al. (1999). Sleep abnormalities in mentally retarded autistic subjects: Down's syndrome with mental retardation and normal subjects. *Brain and Development, 21*(8), 548–553.

Donnelly, L.F., Shott, S.R., LaRose, C.R., et al. (2004). Causes of persistent obstructive sleep apnea despite previous tonsillectomy and adenoidectomy in children with Down syndrome as depicted on static and dynamic cine MRI. *American Journal of Roentgenology, 183,* 175–181.

Down, J.L.H. (1866). Observations on an ethnic classification of idiots. *London Hospital Reports, 3,* 259.

Down's Syndrome Research Foundation Ltd. (2005, March). *Antioxidants and folinic research project: Vitamins & Minerals for children with Down's syndrome.* Retrieved February 26, 2005, from http://www.dsrf.co.uk (Click on http://cddg-downs.org.uk/index.html for information about the clinical trial).

El Mouatassim, S., Becker, M., Kuzio, S., et al. (2004). Prenatal diagnosis of common aneuploidies using multiplex quantitative fluorescent polymerase chain reaction. *Fetal Diagnosis and Therapy, 19*(6), 496–503.

Enersen, O.D. (2001). John Langdon Haydon Down. *Who named it?* Retrieved March 24, 2006, from http://www.whonamedit.com/doctor.cfm/335.html

EnteroLab. (2006). Retrieved January 23, 2006, from http://68.178.214.220

Erler, T., & Paditz, E. (2004). Obstructive sleep apnea syndrome in children: A state-of-the-art review. *Treatments in Respiratory Medicine, 3,* 107–122.

Espie, C.A., Paul A., McFie, J., et al. (1998). Sleep studies of adults with severe or profound mental retardation and epilepsy. *American Journal on Mental Retardation, 103,* 47–59.

Felz, M.W. (2005). Who should be screened for thyroid disease? *Postgraduate Medicine, 118*(3), 9–10.

Fisch, H., Hyun, G., Golden, R., et al. (2003). The influence of paternal age on Down syndrome. *Journal of Urology, 169,* 2275–2278.

Fishler, K., & Koch, R. (1991). Mental development in Down syndrome mosaicism. *American Journal on Mental Retardation, 96,* 345–351.

Fiske, J., & Shafik, H.H. (2001). Down's syndrome and oral care. *Dental Update, 28,* 148–156.

Fryers, T. (1986). Survival in Down syndrome. *Journal of Mental Deficiency Research, 30*(2), 101–110.

Gamis, A.S. (2005). Acute myeloid leukemia and Down syndrome evolution of modern therapy: State of the art review. *Pediatric Blood and Cancer, 44,* 13–20.

Ghazluddin, M. (1997). Autism in Down's syndrome: Family history correlates. *Journal of Intellectual Disability Research, 41*(1), 87–91.

Gillberg, C., Persson, E., Grufman, N., et al. (1986). Psychiatric disorders in mildly and severely mentally retarded urban children and adolescents: Epidemiological aspects. *British Journal of Psychiatry, 149,* 68–74.

Goldacre, M.J., Wotton, C.J., Seagroatt, V., et al. (2004). Cancers and immune related diseases associated with Down's syndrome: A record linkage study. *Archives of Disease in Childhood, 89,* 1014–1017.

Hardy, O., Worley, G., Lee, M.M., et al. (2004). Hypothyroidism in Down syndrome: Screening guidelines and testing methodology. *American Journal of Medical Genetics, 124A,* 436–437.

Hasle, H. (2001). Pattern of malignant disorders in individuals with Down's syndrome. *The Lancet Oncology, 2*(7), 429–436 (Review).

Hattori, M., Fujiyama, A., Taylor, T.D., et al. (2000). Chromosome 21 mapping and sequencing consortium. The DNA sequence of human chromosome 21. *Nature, 405*(6784), 311–319.

Haugen, O.H., Hovding, G., Eide, G.E., et al. (2001). Corneal grafting for keratoconus in mentally retarded patients. *Acta Ophthalmologica Scandinavica, 79,* 609–615.

Hennequin, M., Faulks, D., Veyrune, J.L., et al. (1999). Significance of oral health in persons with Down syndrome: A literature review. *Developmental Medicine and Child Neurology, 41,* 275–283.

Hill, I.D., Dirks, M.H., Liptak, G.S., et al. (2005). Guideline for the diagnosis and treatment of celiac disease in children: Recommendations of the North American Society for Pediatric Gastroenterology, Hepatology and Nutrition. *Journal of Pediatric Gastroenterology and Nutrition, 40,* 1–19.

Hitzler, J.K., & Zipursky, A. (2005). Origins of leukaemia in children with Down syndrome. *Nature Reviews: Cancer, 5,* 11–20.

Jacobs, P.A., Baikie, A.G., Court Brown, W.M., et al. (1959). The somatic chromosomes in mongolism. *The Lancet, 1,* 710.

Kaur, H., Butler, J., & Trumble, S. (2003). *Options for menstrual management.* Retrieved January 28, 2006, from http://www.nas.com/downsyn/staff.html

Kernan, K.T. (1990). Comprehension of syntactically indicated sequence by Down's syndrome and other mentally retarded adults. *Journal of Mental Deficiency Research, 34*(Pt. 2), 169–178.

Korenberg, J.R., Chen, X.N., Schipper, R., et al. (1994). Down syndrome phenotypes: The consequences of chromosomal imbalance. *Proceedings of the National Academy of Sciences, 91,* 4997–5001.

Langman, J. (1963). *Medical embryology.* Philadelphia: Lippincott, Williams & Wilkins.

Lejeune, J., Gauthier, M., & Turpin, R. (1959a). Les chromosomes humains en culture de tissus. *Comptes Rendus*

Hebdomadaires Des Seances De L'Academie Des Sciences, 248, 602–603.

Lejeune, J., Gauthier, M., & Turpin, R. (1959b). Etude des chromosomes somatiques de neuf enfants mongoliens. *Comptes Rendus Hebdomadaires Des Seances De L'Académie Des Sciences, 248,* 1721–1722.

Lemon, C., & Lemon, J. (2003). Community-based cooperative ventures for adults with intellectual disabilities. *The Canadian Geographer, 47*(4), 414–428.

Leshin, L. (2003). *Constipation and Down syndrome.* Retrieved January 23, 2005, from http://www.ds-health.com/constip.htm

Lev, N., & Melamed, E. (2002). [Neurological complications in Down's syndrome] *Harefuah, 141*(9), 820–823, 857.

Levanon, A., Tarasiuk, A., & Tal, A. (1999). Sleep characteristics in children with Down syndrome. *Journal of Pediatrics, 134,* 755–760.

Lovering, J. (2003). Down syndrome: Characteristics and health issues. In I. Brown, & M. Percy (Eds.), *Developmental disabilities in Ontario* (pp. 171–193), Toronto: Ontario Association on Developmental Disabilities.

May, P., & Kawanishi, H. (1996). Chronic hepatitis B infection and autoimmune thyroiditis in Down syndrome. *Journal of Clinical Gastroenterology, 23*(3), 181–184.

Mayo Clinic. (2006). *Treatment of Eisenmenger's syndrome at Mayo Clinic.* Retrieved January 28, 2006, from http://www.mayoclinic.org/eisenmengers-syndrome

McCoy, E. (n.d.). *Clinical info: Endocrine conditions in Down syndrome.* Retrieved January 24, 2006, from http://www.ndss.org/content.cfm?fuseaction=InfoRes.HlthArticle&article=36

Medline Plus. (2006a). *Celiac disease—sprue.* Retrieved March 11, 2006, from http://www.nlm.nih.gov/medlineplus/ency/article/000233.htm

MedLine Plus. (2006b). *Congenital heart disease.* Retrieved March 11, 2006, from http://www.nlm.nih.gov/medlineplus/ency/article/001114.htm

Medical Illustration Library. (1994). Philadelphia: Lippincott, Williams & Wilkins.

Meitzner, M.C., & Skurnowicz, J.A. (2005). Anesthetic considerations for patients with Down syndrome. *AANA Journal, 73,* 103–107.

Menendez, M. (2005). Down syndrome, Alzheimer's disease and seizures. *Brain Development, 27,* 246–252.

Miller, J.F., Leddy, M., & Leavitt, L.A. (Eds.). (1999). *Improving the communication of people with Down syndrome.* Baltimore: Paul H. Brookes Publishing Co.

Mutton, D., Alberman, E., & Hook, E.B. (1996). Cytogenetic and epidemiological findings in Down syndrome, England and Wales 1989 to 1993. National Down Syndrome Cytogenetic Register and the Association of Clinical Cytogeneticists. *Journal of Medical Genetics, 33,* 387–394.

Myrelid, A., Gustafsson, J., Ollars, B., et al. (2002). Growth charts for Down's syndrome from birth to 18 years of age. *Archives of Disease in Childhood, 87,* 97–103.

National Institutes of Health. (2005). *Vitamin E in aging persons with Down syndrome.* Retrieved February 28, 2005, from http://clinicaltrials.gov/ct/show/NCT00056329?order=123

Ng, D.K., & Chan, C.H. (2004). Obesity is an important risk factor for sleep disordered breathing in children with Down syndrome. *Sleep, 27,* 1023–1024.

Nicolaides, K.H. (2004). Nuchal translucency and other first-trimester sonographic markers of obstructive sleep apnea despite previous tonsillectomy and adenoidectomy in children with Down syndrome as depicted on static and dynamic cine MRI. *American Journal of Roentgenology, 183,* 175–181.

Olson, L.E., Richtsmeier, J.T., Lesz, J., et al. (2004). A chromosome 21 critical region does not cause specific Down syndrome phenotypes. *Science, 306*(5696), 687–690.

Patel, B.N., Pang, D., Stern, Y., et al. (2004). Obesity enhances verbal memory in postmenopausal women with Down syndrome. *Neurobiology of Aging, 25,* 159–166.

Patient UK. (2006). *Heart—cross section (diagram).* Retrieved March 21, 2006, from http://www.patient.co.uk

Percy, M.E., & Prasher, V.P. (2006). Thyroid abnormalities and dementia of the Alzheimer type in Down syndrome. In V. Prasher & M. Janicki (Eds.), *Down syndrome, Alzheimer's disease: Biological correlates* (pp. 99–139). Oxford, United Kingdom: Radcliffe Medical Press.

Prasher, V.P. (1999). Down syndrome and thyroid disorders: A review. *Down's Syndrome, Research and Practice, 6,* 25–42 [Review].

Prasher, V., & Haque M.S. (2005). Misdiagnosis of thyroid disorders in Down syndrome: Time to re-examine the myth? *American Journal of Mental Retardation, 110*(1), 23–27.

Procedural Sedation Resource Center. (2006). Retrieved January 24, 2006, from http://anesthesia.uihc.uiowa.edu/proceduralsedation3/peds/downs.asp

Pueschel, S.M. (1990). Clinical aspects of Down syndrome from infancy to adulthood. *American Journal of Medical Genetics, 7*(Suppl.), 52–56.

Pueschel, S.M. (1998). Should children with Down syndrome be screened for atlantoaxial instability? *Archives of Pediatric & Adolescent Medicine, 152,* 123–125.

Pueschel, S.M. (Ed.). (2006). *Adults with Down syndrome.* Baltimore: Paul H. Brookes Publishing Co.

Pueschel, S.M., & Pueschel, J.K. (Eds.). (1992). *Biomedical concerns in persons with Down syndrome.* Baltimore: Paul H. Brookes Publishing Co.

Racial Disparities in Median Age at Death of Persons With Down Syndrome—United States, 1968–1997. (2001, June 8). *MMWR: Morbidity and Mortality Weekly Report, 50*(22), 463–465.

Rapkin, A. (2003). A review of treatment of premenstrual syndrome and premenstrual dysphoric disorder. *Psychoneuroendocrinology, 28*(Suppl. 3), 39–53.

Reddy, D.S. (2004). Pharmacology of catamenial epilepsy. *Methods and Findings in Experimental and Clinical Pharmacology, 26*(7), 547–561.

Reeves, R.H. (2000). Recounting a genetic story. *Nature, 405*(6784), 283–284.

Richards, G. (2001). *Growth charts for children with Down syndrome.* Retrieved January 23, 2005, from http://www.growthcharts.com

Rimmer, J.H., Heller, T., Wang, E., et al. (2004). Improvements in physical fitness in adults with Down syndrome. *American Journal on Mental Retardation, 109,* 165–174.

Roche, A.F., Seward, F.S., & Sunderland, S. (1961). Nonmetrical observations on cranial roentgenograms in mongolism. *American Journal of Roentgenology, Radium Therapy and Nuclear Medicine, 84,* 659–662.

Roizen, N.J., & Patterson, D. (2003). Down's syndrome. *The Lancet, 361,* 1281–1291.

Romano, C., Tine, A., Fazio, G., et al. (1990). Seizures in patients with trisomy 21. *American Journal of Medical Genetics, 7*(Suppl.), 298–300.

Schepis, C., Barone, C., Siragusa, M., et al. (2002). An updated survey on skin conditions in Down syndrome. *Dermatology, 205,* 234–238.

Schupf, N., Zigman, W., Kapell, D., et al. (1997). Early menopause in women with Down's syndrome. *Journal of Intellectual Disability Research, 41*(Pt. 3), 264–267.

Shield, J.P., Wadsworth, E.J., Hassold, T.J., et al. (1999). Is disomic homozygosity at the APECED locus the cause of increased autoimmunity in Down's syndrome? *Archives of Disease in Childhood, 81*(2), 147–150.

Shott, S.R., Joseph, A., & Heithaus, D. (2001). Hearing loss in children with Down syndrome. *International Journal of Pediatric Otorhinolaryngology, 61,* 199–205.

Smith, D.S. (2001). Health care management of adults with Down syndrome. *American Family Physician, 64,* 1031–1038.

Special Olympics. (n.d.). *Special Olympics guidelines. Participation by individuals with Down syndrome who have atlantoaxial instability.* Retrieved January 24, 2006, from http://www.specialolympics.org/Special+Olympics+Public+Website/English/Coach/Coaching_Guides/Basics+of+Special+Olympics/Down+Syndrome+and+Restrictions+Based+on+Atlantoaxial+Instability.htm

Stos, B., Dembour, G., Ovaert, C., et al. (2004). [Risks and benefits of cardiac surgery in Down's syndrome with congenital heart disease]. *Archives de Pediatrie, 11*(10), 1197–1201.

Summers, A.M., Farrell, S.A., Huang, T., et al. (2003). Maternal serum screening in Ontario using the triple marker test. *Journal of Medical Screening, 10,* 107–111.

Temple, V., Jozsvai, E., Konstantareas, M.M., et al. (2001). Alzheimer dementia in Down's syndrome: The relevance of cognitive ability. *Journal of Intellectual Disability Research, 45*(Pt. 1), 47–55.

Thiel, R.J., & Fowkes, S.W. (2004). Down syndrome and epilepsy: A nutritional connection? *Medical Hypotheses, 62,* 35–44.

Tsiouris, J.A., Patti, P.J., Tipu, O., et al. (2002). Adverse effects of phenytoin given for late-onset seizures in adults with Down syndrome. *Neurology, 59,* 779–780.

Ulrich, B.D., Haehl, V., Buzzi, U.H., et al. (2004). Modeling dynamic resource utilization in populations with unique constraints: Preadolescents with and without Down syndrome. *Human Movement Science, 23,* 133–156.

van Splunder, J., Stilma, J.S., Bernsen, R.M., et al. (2004). Prevalence of ocular diagnoses found on screening 1539 adults with intellectual disabilities. *Ophthalmology, 111,* 1457–1463.

van Trotsenburg, A.S., Vulsma, T., van Rozenburg-Marres, S.L., et al. (2005). The effect of thyroxine treatment started in the neonatal period on development and growth of two-year-old Down syndrome children: A randomized clinical trial. *The Journal of Clinical Endocrinology and Metabolism, 90*(6), 3304–3311.

Wallace, R.A., & Dalton, A.J. (2005). Clinicians' guide to physical health problems of older adults with Down syndrome. *Journal of Developmental Disabilities, 12*(1, Suppl.).

Wallace, R.A., Webb, P.M., & Schluter, P.J. (2002). Environmental, medical, behavioural and disability factors associated with Helicobacter pylori infection in adults with intellectual disability. *Journal of Intellectual Disability Research, 46*(Pt. 1), 51–60.

Webb, D.K. (2005). Optimizing therapy for myeloid disorders of Down syndrome. *British Journal of Haematology, 131*(1), 3–7.

Wisniewski, K.E., & Kida, E. (1997). *Neurological and neuropathlogical aspects of children with Down syndrome* [Abstract]. Retrieved May 30, 2005, from http://www.altonweb.com/cs/downsyndrome/index.htm?page=madridneuro.html

Zachor, D.A. (2000). Down syndrome and celiac disease: A review. *Down Syndrome Quarterly, 5*(4), 1–5.

Zipursky, A. (1996). The treatment of children with acute megakaryoblastic leukemia who have Down syndrome [Editorial comment]. *Journal of Pediatric and Hematological Oncology, 18,* 10–12.

11

Fragile X Syndrome

Michèle M.M. Mazzocco and Jeanette Jeltje Anne Holden

WHAT YOU WILL LEARN ABOUT IN THIS CHAPTER

- The genetics of fragile X syndrome
- Genetic testing for fragile X syndrome
- How the full mutation affects individuals
- Special needs of children with fragile X syndrome
- How the premutation affects individuals

Fragile X syndrome is the most common known inherited form of intellectual disability worldwide. Some effects of this syndrome include intellectual and developmental disabilities, characteristic physical features and atypical behaviors, and other health effects as discussed later in this chapter.

THE GENETICS OF FRAGILE X SYNDROME

The term *fragile X syndrome* comes from the observation of a fragile site (a small break) at the tip of the X chromosome in some individuals who have this disorder (see Figure 11.1). The gene at site Xq27.3 (i.e., near the end [27.3] of the long [q] arm of the X chromosome [X]) is the **Fragile X Mental Retardation 1 (FMR1) gene.** When that gene is mutated, the consequent events result in fragile X syndrome.

The most common mutations in the FMR1 gene that result in fragile X syndrome involve extensive expansion of a CGG trinucleotide repeat in the FMR1 gene (see Figure 11.2) This type of mutation, often called a triplet repeat expansion, is described in more detail in the Trinucleotide Repeats and the Fragile X Syndrome: Defining the FMR1 Mutation section of this chapter. The mutation is referred to as dynamic because, in contrast to most mutations, which are inherited without change from one generation to the next, the number of copies of the CGG repeat in people with a mutation generally increases when it is transmitted from one generation to the next. It is important to note that this expansion occurs across generations rather than in a given individual during the course of that person's life.

The link between the FMR1 gene mutation and the fragile X syndrome lies in the role of the typical (nonmutated) FMR1 gene in producing proteins important for brain development and function. Specifically, the FMR1 gene contains genetic information for production of the Fragile X Mental Retardation protein (FMRP). When the number of copies of the CGG repeat exceeds a threshold, there is an interruption in the typical production of the protein, leading to reduced levels of FMRP. This, in turn, results in the characteristic features of the fragile X syndrome.

It is believed that the degree to which children are affected by fragile X is related, at least in part, to the degree to which FMRP is reduced (Bailey, Hatton, et al., 2001). Animal models allow researchers to assess the role of gene function in a way that cannot be attempted with humans. Mice with the fragile X gene mutation have been developed and are being used to explore the function of FMRP and other aspects of fragile X. A review of animal models for fragile X syndrome, including mice and fruit flies, shows how such animal models aid our understanding of the range of phenotypes in individuals with fragile X syndrome (Bakker & Oostra, 2003; McBride et al., 2005; Zhang & Broadie, 2005).

In order to discuss how the fragile X mutation affects the development of an individual, it is necessary to review some of the complexities that underlie the genetics of the fragile X syndrome. As evident in later sections of this chapter, information about the genetics of fragile X influences how the effects of the gene, and even its prevalence, are discussed.

Fragile X Gene

Everyone has one copy of the FMR1 gene on each X chromosome. Most individuals have the typical FMR1 gene, whereas people with the fragile X syndrome have the FMR1 mutation. In 1991, Verkerk et al. found that people with the fragile X syndrome actually have a

The chapter authors thank the following agencies for support of their research on the fragile X syndrome: the Medical Research Council of Canada, the Canadian Institutes of Health Research (#43820), the Ontario Mental Health Foundation, and the National Institutes of Health (#RO1 HD 034061).

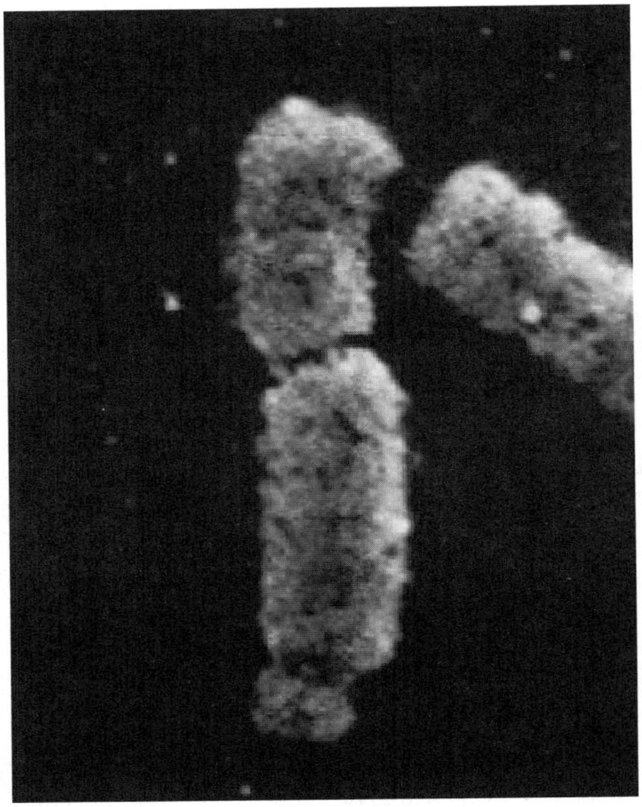

Figure 11.1. A fragile X chromosome. The FMR1 gene is located in the constricted region near the bottom end of the chromosome. (This scanning EM image was kindly provided by Dr. G.Y. Wen and Dr. E.C. Jenkins of the New York State Institute for Basic Research in Developmental Disabilities [IBR].)

larger FMR1 gene than people in the general population. The increased size is the result of a large expansion in the CGG trinucleotide repeat region of FMR1. The following genetic information is included to provide a more in-depth understanding of the nature of the fragile X gene mutation and an appreciation for the complexity of information that fragile X families encounter when they receive a diagnosis of fragile X in a family member.

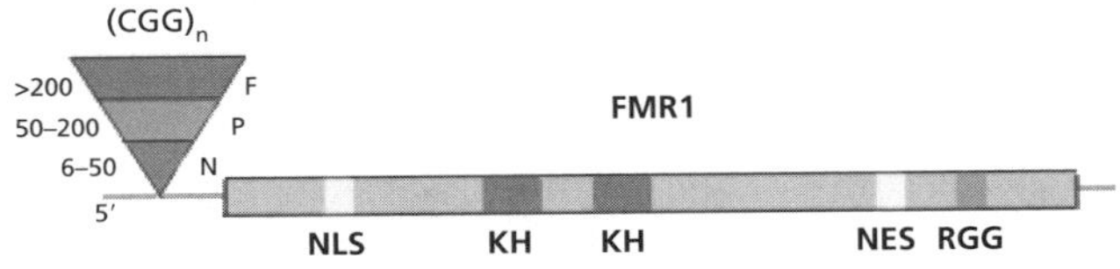

Figure 11.2. Schematic representation of the FMR1 gene. The coding region of the FMR1 that specifies FMR1 RNA and protein is depicted by the gray bar. Noncoding regions of the gene called untranslated regions (UTRs) are depicted by lines. The CGG repeat region that is expanded in fragile X syndrome is located in the 5′ UTR. The relative sizes of the CGG repeat region are shown for healthy individuals that do not have fragile X (N), for people who have a premutation (P) and for people who have a full mutation (F). The terms *NLS, KH, NES,* and *RGG* refer to regions of FMR1 DNA that affect important functions of FMR1 protein. The KH and RGG regions of FMR1 protein are involved in RNA binding. The NES region helps the protein to move from the cell nucleus to the cytoplasm. The NLS region helps the protein to move from the cytoplasm to the cell nucleus. (From Oostra, B.A., Hoogeveen, A.T., & Willemsen, R. [n.d.]. *Fragile X syndrome and FMR1.* Retrieved September 13, 2006, from http://www2.eur.nl/fgg/kgen/research/fmr1.html; reprinted by permission.)

Trinucleotide Repeats and the Fragile X Syndrome: Defining the FMR1 Mutation

DNA is the genetic material that determines many human characteristics. (Although many characteristics result from an interaction between genetics and environmental factors, the discussion here is limited to the role of genetics.) Information about these characteristics, such as potential height, eye and hair color, and the genetic disorders to which one is susceptible is encoded in one's DNA. This information is in distinct segments; these distinct segments of DNA—called *genes*—appear in long strands that make chromosomes. Genes code for the different proteins in all cells, including those that make up the outer walls of cells and all of the different proteins that give each cell a specific function. For example, some proteins are made only in blood cells and other proteins are made only in muscle cells. Yet in all cases, DNA is made up of two strands comprising four different bases (molecules) called *A-T-C-G* (see Chapter 7 for additional details), which are attached together much like a zipper. Thus, like a zipper, the two strands appear alongside one another, and each has an individual mate. These pairs of bases, or DNA base pairs, vary in number and order across different genes. In the case of the fragile X gene mutation, the change in the gene results in the presence of extra base pairs. The extra bases in this gene come in sets of three (e.g., CGG CGG CGG), or in triplet repeats.

Categories of the FMR1 Mutation

There is much variation in the number of CGG repeats in different people in the general population (see Figure 11.2). This variation has led to the use of the following terms to classify the size of the triplet repeat region in the FMR1 gene. These categories reflect not only the size of the genes but also the characteristics with which they are associated. The first category refers to the normal FMR1 gene present in the majority of individuals. The "premutation" and "full mutation" categories refer to distinctly different forms of the FMR1 mutation.

Normal FMR1 Repeats Everyone in the general population has an FMR1 gene on each X chromosome. When the number of CGG repeats within the FMR1 gene is between 6 and 54, individuals are said to have a normal FMR1 gene. There is no evidence that the number of CGG repeats, within this normal range, is associated with variation in intelligence in the general population (Daniels et al., 1994; Mazzocco & Reiss, 1997). In general, FMR1 genes that have a CGG repeat region in the normal size range do not change in size (i.e., they are stable genes) and remain the same from one generation to the next. Yet, some limited instability is seen in repeat sizes above 40 or so repeats (see the Gray Zone section).

Premutation Genes Individuals with an FMR1 gene having between approximately 55 and 200 triplet repeats are said to have a premutation. If a female carrier of a premutation passes this gene to her sons, there is an ~80% risk that the premutation expands to a full mutation rather than remaining within the premutation range. In fact, premutations in the 55–65 repeat range rarely expand to full mutations, but those that are greater than approximately 80 repeats almost always do. Thus, the chance of a mother passing a full mutation to her son is based on the number of the mother's CGG repeats (Fu et al., 1991). The term *premutation* is confusing because the *pre* erroneously suggests that the change in the gene is, in itself, not a mutation. Despite the term *premutation,* this category of mutation size is indeed a type of FMR1 mutation. One of the more recent controversies in fragile X research is whether the premutation leads to any effects. This is discussed later in the chapter.

Full Mutation Genes When the number of copies of the CGG repeat exceeds 200, the mutation is considered a full mutation. In most cases, the full mutation essentially silences the gene so that it does not produce its protein (or produces insufficient amounts of protein), and this results in the clinical features associated with the fragile X syndrome. Thus, genes with 200 or 2,000 repeats are basically equivalent in terms of the effects to which they lead, because each silences the FMR1 gene and the FMR1 protein is deficient in both cases. This point is important, because it means that it is not necessarily "worse" to have a full mutation of 2,000 repeats relative to 500. Thus, the size category (i.e., normal, premutation, or full mutation), not the exact size, determines how fragile X is expressed.

Gray Zone The size ranges used to define the three primary categories of FMR1 genes are only approximations. This is particularly true when differentiating premutation versus normal FMR1 genes. Some individuals have an FMR1 gene with a slightly larger than average number of CGG repeats. In these cases, it is unclear whether that gene is a large normal gene or a small premutation. When faced with such challenges, it is useful to remember that a defining feature of the FMR1 mutation is gene instability—meaning that the mutation changes in size over generations. Therefore, one way to distinguish whether a gray zone allele (an FMR1 gene ranging in size from 40–54 repeats) is a premutation is to examine the size of that gene across family members. Constant size over many generations is evidence for a normal, stable gene. The significance of the distinction between normal and premutation genes lies primarily in the risk for future offspring. There is no evidence that the size of the FMR1 gene among carriers of either a normal or gray zone gene has any influence on cognitive development (Allen et al., 2005; Mazzocco & Reiss, 1997).

Gene Stability and Instability: Mosaicism

Most gene mutations do not change when passed from one generation to the next. They, like other normal genes, are considered stable. The fragile X mutation is very different from most gene mutations. As mentioned previously, the fragile X mutation is dynamic, or unstable, because the size of the mutation changes from one generation to another. The number of triplet repeats usually increases when passed from parent to child (see Figure 11.3). This instability can also be seen at the level of the individual, such that the size of the CGG repeat region varies within an individual. Sometimes this change is within the previously described categories of the mutation, such as when a woman has genes with different sizes of the premutation or when a child has different sizes of the full mutation in different cells. These are examples of mosaicism (see Chapter 7 for more information).

Several ongoing studies are designed to assess the prevalence of the fragile X full mutation, premutation, and grey zone alleles in different populations, as well as to shed light on how the normal fragile X gene becomes a premutation. Large-scale prevalence studies among males from the general population identified 13 premutations in 10,572 males tested from Quebec, Canada (Dombrowski et al., 2002); 7 gray zone alleles and 4 premutations in 5,000 males from the Catalan population in Spain (Rife et al., 2003); and 70 males with a gray zone gene (45–54 repeats) and 6 males with a premutation in 10,046 males in Taiwan (Tzeng et al., 2005). The Quebec study did identify 36 males with gray zone alleles, but their procedure was optimized for identifying CGG repeats greater than 50 repeats. Additional large-scale studies are needed to determine whether differences in the prevalence of grey zone and premutation FMR1 genes in the different regions are statistically significant.

Inheritance of Fragile X Syndrome

Although the factors influencing gene instability are largely unknown, one that has been identified is the sex of the parent carrying the fragile X mutation. Gene expansion occurs with maternal transmission but not with paternal transmission. Thousands of families with the fragile X syndrome have been studied to determine

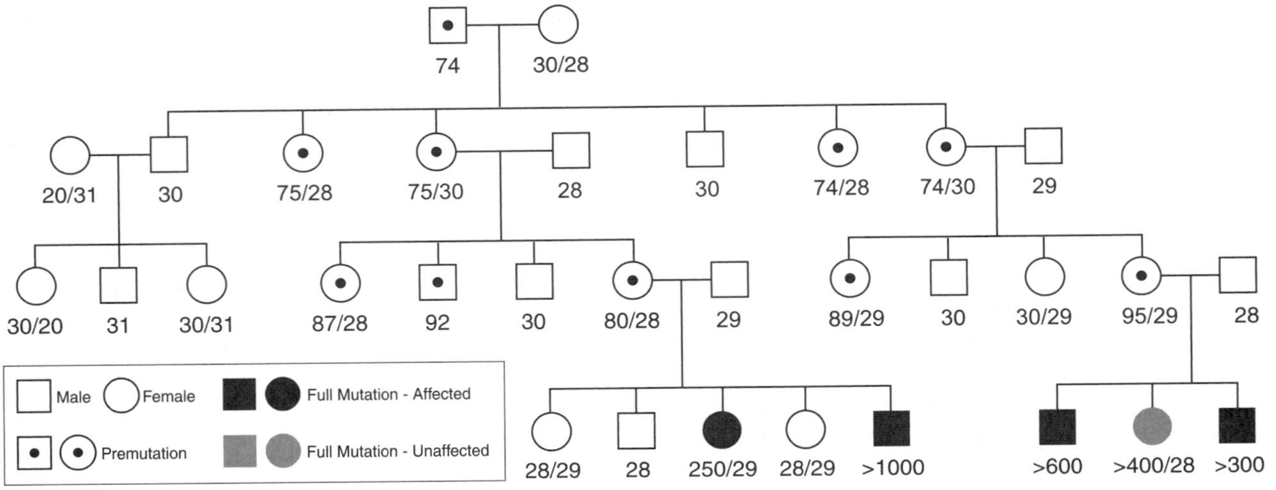

Figure 11.3. Pedigree of a family with the fragile X syndrome, showing inheritance of the FMR1 gene. The numbers under the pedigree symbols indicate the number of CGG repeats in the FMR1 gene on each chromosome of that particular individual. Females have two X chromosomes and hence have two FMR1 genes; males have a single X chromosome and hence a single FMR1 gene. (*Source:* Lee, et al., 2003.)

the likelihood of premutation and full mutation carriers having affected offspring.

The findings indicate that when the FMR1 premutation is passed from fathers to daughters, the premutation almost never expands to a full mutation. Zeesman et al. (2004) reported a case in which a daughter with fragile X syndrome received her mutated FMR1 gene from her father, who had a premutation. In this case, however, there was expansion of the premutation to a full mutation postzygotically, because the daughter was a mosaic for premutation and full mutation FMR1 genes. In contrast, when the same size premutation is passed from a mother to her sons or daughters, it typically expands. Whether the premutation expands to a full mutation is highly (but not exclusively) influenced by the size of the premutation. If the mother has a fragile X full mutation, then the children who inherit the mutation are nearly certain to have the full mutation. Only rarely does the premutation contract to a gray zone or normal size FMR1 gene when passed from one generation to the next. Nolin et al. (2003) summarized the findings in four cases of contraction in which the FMR1 mutations decreased from premutation sizes to intermediate or normal size CGG repeats (from 95 repeats to 35; from 145 repeats to 43; from 130 repeats to 10; and from 70 repeats to 54 repeats).

Consistent with all X-linked disorders, males with an FMR1 mutation will pass the mutation on to all of their daughters (who inherit their father's one X chromosome) and to none of their sons (who inherit their father's Y chromosome). Females who have an FMR1 mutation (and who also have a second, normal chromosome) have a 50% chance of transmitting their fragile X mutation with each pregnancy, regardless of whether the offspring is male or female.

Why the Sex of the Individual Affects Expression of Fragile X Syndrome

Both males and females can inherit the fragile X full mutation. So why are males, as a group, affected more significantly than females? Indeed, males with a full mutation almost always have intellectual disability, and many have significant behavior difficulties. It is more difficult to predict outcome for females, because not all females with a full mutation are affected. There are case reports of females with the full mutation who show no apparent effects. Of those females who are affected, many are less affected than males. Still, it should not be overlooked that a significant number of females with fragile X may experience moderate impairment in learning and social functioning. Finally, some females are as affected by their FMR1 mutation as are males with the disorder and have moderate to significant intellectual disability.

A primary reason for this phenotypic variation that is typical of X-linked disorders results from the simple fact that males have only one X chromosome and females have two X chromosomes. In all typically developing females, two X chromosomes are present in each cell, but in each cell one of the two X chromosomes is inactivated. For a female with the FMR1 mutation, the mutation is present on one of her two X chromosomes. Whether and the degree to which she is affected depends to a large extent on whether the X chromosome with the normal or mutated FMR1 gene is active in cells that rely on FMR1 protein to function properly (Abrams et al., 1994). For example, if the majority of cells in the brain of a female have the mutant FMR1 gene on the active X-chromosome, this increases the female's likelihood of being affected. The reverse is also true: if the majority of cells in her brain have the normal FMR1 gene on the active X chromosome, the female may appear to be unaffected. (For additional information about X inactivation, see Chapter 7.) Theoretically, if a female has the FMR1 full mutation on both of her two X chromosomes, the severity of her symptoms of fragile X will be comparable to the severity observed among males with the full mutation.

Prevalence of Fragile X Syndrome

The number of people reported to be affected by fragile X syndrome varies depending on whether the prevalence is specific to people with only the full mutation (versus the premutation), whether the effects examined are limited to intellectual disability, and whether less prominent effects—such as learning disabilities—are included. Still, the reported prevalence rates of fragile X syndrome are comparable across most studies worldwide and for both Caucasian and African American samples in the United States (Crawford et al., 2002). In a report from the Centers for Disease Control in the United States prevalence figures for people with the full mutation were cited as approximately 1 in 4,000 for males and 1 in 9,000 for females (Crawford, Acuna, & Sherman, 2001). It is important to note that most prevalence studies are based on screening for the fragile X full mutation in populations that are of interest to researchers or clinicians serving families with intellectual disabilities, such as populations of children receiving special education services. This ascertainment differs from that used in studies based on general population screening and thus may overestimate or underestimate actual prevalence rates.

In contrast to prevalence rates for the full mutation, the prevalence of the premutation is much higher. Studies in Quebec, Canada, suggest that the frequency of females with the premutation is approximately 1 in 259 (Rousseau et al., 1995). A study of 14,334 Israeli women of child-bearing age who did not have a family history of intellectual disability found a carrier frequency of 1 in 113, indicating that the carrier frequency is extremely high (Toledano-Alhadef et al., 2001).

Individuals carrying an FMR1 premutation or full mutation are sometimes referred to as carriers regardless of whether they are affected. This use of the term *carrier* differs from the more common use of the term, which often refers to asymptomatic carriers of a gene associated with a recessive disorder, such as sickle cell disease. Although the term *carrier female* or *carrier male* is sometimes used to refer to individuals with the premutation, this selective use is inconsistent across studies and across clinical reports. To clarify the presence of the full mutation or premutation, it is necessary to look for these specific terms in descriptions of research participants or in reports of genetic testing. Whether this distinction is indicated depends on the type of genetic testing carried out, as discussed in the following section.

GENETIC TESTING FOR FRAGILE X SYNDROME

Chromosome testing and gene testing can be used to detect fragile X syndrome. These two topics, as well as the issues of who is eligible for testing and when it should occur, are discussed next.

Chromosome Testing

Until 1991, genetic testing for fragile X syndrome relied on the examination of chromosomes to search for the small break or fragile site at the end of the X chromosome. Although this test was important for distinguishing fragile X from other causes of developmental delay, the test was not always reliable and sometimes resulted in misdiagnoses. For example, a diet high in folic acid (found in many vitamin supplements) possibly may suppress the fragile site in cultured cells and lead to false-negative reports. In addition, the premutation does not usually result in a fragile site, so people with the premutation were not detected by this method, making genetic counseling for people with the premutation very difficult. Indeed, the existence of the premutation was not known until 1991, more than 20 years after the fragile site was identified (Lubs, 1969).

Gene Testing

Since the discovery of the FMR1 gene in 1991, two diagnostic tests have been developed: polymerase chain reaction (PCR) and **Southern blotting** (see Appendix A at the end of the book). Both gene tests are used to examine the number of repeats in the FMR1 genes from individuals, using a small sample of blood or even a swab of cells from the inside of the cheek. The PCR test is more accurate for determining the precise number of repeats, especially when the number is less than approximately 200, because it provides somewhat of a close-up view of the mutation. Therefore, the PCR test is preferable for ruling out the fragile X premutation. The Southern blot provides a broader picture of the gene, somewhat more of an aerial view, and is therefore more accurate for establishing the presence of the larger, full mutation; this is because very large mutations may not be detected by the PCR test. It is difficult to accurately determine the number of repeats when the mutation exceeds 200, although some methods can give reasonably accurate counts. However, because it is the size category (beyond 200) and not the size per se that determines full mutation status, it is not clinically necessary to accurately determine the number of CGG repeats for full mutations. A simple method for accurately determining the number of repeats in the FMR1 gene using only a small spot of blood has been used for both clinical and large population studies (Holden et al., 1996).

The DNA tests are precise procedures that approach 100% accuracy. If a result is based on cytogenetics alone, there is a substantial chance that the test result could be a false-negative. Therefore, DNA testing for fragile X is the gold standard to date and has been since 1991.

Who Is Eligible for Testing

Fragile X is the most common known inherited cause of intellectual disability. Therefore, anyone with a family history of fragile X syndrome should be offered testing for the FMR1 mutation, unless it can be determined by pedigree that the identified carrier in the family could not have passed an X chromosome to the individual in question. Not all individuals with fragile X have intellectual disability, so anyone with an undiagnosed intellectual or developmental disability or behaviors similar to those of autism, or with a family history of these conditions, is eligible for testing. The lack of several cases of intellectual disability in a family should not be used to rule out testing for fragile X because there is always a first case in a given family, and it is important to identify that case as early as possible. Thus, even a single case of intellectual disability in a family should be investigated.

The family pedigree in Figure 11.3 illustrates no instances of intellectual or developmental disability prior to the youngest generation. Genetic testing of other family members revealed the FMR1 premutation in several family members and that expansion had occurred in each generation until it reached the full mutation in five members of the last generation. Four of the five are affected with fragile X syndrome, with one daughter being unaffected. Because all individuals with the fragile X syndrome inherit an abnormal FMR1 gene from a parent, all relatives of an affected individual are eligible for testing and should be offered testing.

Despite the seemingly predictable odds described previously in this chapter, fragile X syndrome often appears in a family unexpectedly. This is because small premutations, which have been present in the family for several generations, expand in size, finally reaching a size that is clinically significant (i.e., produces symptoms in the person having the mutation), without having presented any clinical warning signs. Until newborn screening or prenatal testing is offered routinely, there will be cases of fragile X syndrome that remain undiagnosed until the emergence of a new proband, or an affected individual who comes to clinical attention, in a given family. This means that until widespread screening is offered via routine prenatal care, additional families will join the prevalence figures of families with the fragile X mutation.

There is considerable interest in newborn screening for the fragile X syndrome. Current guidelines for any newborn screening indicate that the following conditions be met: 1) the disorder must be a significant public health problem that has major consequences for affected individuals; 2) there is an accurate and cost-effective screening procedure; and 3) there is means for treating the disorder, which results in significantly better outcome for the individual. Although there is no cure for fragile X syndrome, there are several treatments that can lead to better outcomes for affected individuals, particularly when started early in life. Several studies have addressed the issue of newborn screening for fragile X syndrome, but despite the interest and availability of accurate screening methods, there remains controversy over implementing screening. Bailey (2004) reviewed the situation and argued that providing earlier identification will enable optimal development for people with this syndrome. He is leading a large-scale population-based screening study, the first of its kind in the United States.

When to Provide Testing

Until newborn screening for fragile X syndrome is routine, clinicians need to make decisions regarding when to recommend genetic testing. Genetic testing can be performed for individuals at any age; it can also be performed prenatally or for a developing fetus. The decision to have genetic testing for oneself, for a child, or for a relative is a personal choice and can evoke a variety of emotions. Professional assistance can be helpful when dealing with such challenging choices.

Researchers have found that many parents of a child with fragile X syndrome have concerns about their child by 9 months of age, although there is much variability in the child's age at the time of a parent's first concern and in the age at which the diagnosis of fragile X syndrome is made. Families have reported that clinicians had initially discounted their concerns (Bailey et al., 2000). These findings point to a need to attend to parental report about developmental delay. Other frustrations reported by parents include delay in getting the diagnosis, especially if another child is born during that time period (Bailey, Skinner, & Sparkman, 2003). Indeed, Crawford et al. (2002) reported that most children with fragile X syndrome were not diagnosed until the age of 10 years. It is important to understand that while testing may be specific to a child, it has implications for, and effects on, the child's immediate and extended family.

HOW THE FULL MUTATION AFFECTS INDIVIDUALS

The fragile X gene mutation affects the physical, cognitive, and behavioral phenotype of individuals with fragile X syndrome. (The term *phenotype* refers to the characteristics that are common to a particular genetic disorder.) For the many complex reasons previously discussed in this chapter, the effects are highly variable across males and females, across children and adults, and from person to person with the syndrome. It is important to be aware of both the reported "typical" effects and the variability of these effects in order to avoid unnecessarily ruling out fragile X and to avoid basing inappropriate expectations on the diagnosis alone. Awareness of the qualitative and quantitative differences of the features is the most important means by which to avoid these potential responses to an individual with fragile X syndrome.

Physical Features of Fragile X Syndrome

The physical features of fragile X may be noticeable, but they are not evident in all individuals with the syndrome. The features, when present, are most likely to include a long face; prominent jaw and ears; high, arched palate; flat feet; and loose joints. Strabismus (sometimes referred to as "lazy eye" or a "cross-eyed" appearance) may be observed in childhood, and it results from the connective tissue abnormalities that also underlie the hyperflexibility and loose joints. It is difficult to use these features alone to determine likelihood of fragile X syndrome in an individual, because many of these features are seen with some regularity among people without the disorder as well (as reviewed in detail by Hagerman, 2002). For example, Hatton and colleagues reported that strabismus occurs with approximately the same frequency in children with fragile X as in the general population (Hatton et al., 1998). Selection bias may result in elevated reports of medical difficulties in children with fragile X syndrome. Another challenge in relying on physical features to identify or screen for fragile X results from the fact that many children with fragile X, particularly girls, lack some or all of these features (see Figure 11.4). Among children with physical features of fragile X syndrome, the features become more prominent with age. Therefore, the lack of physical features—particularly in young children, when diagnosis is critical—is not reason enough to dismiss fragile X as a possible diagnosis. For this reason, awareness of cognitive or behavioral features may enhance identification of fragile X in a child with developmental delay.

Figure 11.4. A girl with fragile X full mutation, at infancy, preschool age, and adolescence.

Cognitive and Behavioral Features of Fragile X Syndrome

Additional characteristics of fragile X syndrome are cognitive or behavioral in nature. These, too, are highly variable, even if they occur with greater frequency than the physical features. The cognitive features range from mild to severe intellectual disability, learning disabilities, or subtle cognitive difficulties. Behavioral features may include eye gaze aversion, hyperactivity or hyperarousal, intense shyness or social anxiety, and autism or behaviors similar to those found in people with autism.

Many males with the fragile X syndrome have intellectual disability by the age of 4 years (Bailey et al., 1998). Many also have behavioral problems, such as hyperactivity, aggression, social problems, and behaviors similar to those that accompany autism (Hatton et al., 1999). There is some controversy regarding the mechanisms that underlie social problems, particularly with respect to whether arousal difficulties are specifically social in nature (Murphy & Abbeduto, 2005). Approximately half of boys with fragile X syndrome have self-injurious behaviors, most commonly manifested as hand-biting (Symons et al., 2003). Some of the behavior characteristics observed in children with fragile X are associated with hyperarousal (i.e., they are overstimulated by factors that do not affect other people). For both boys (Roberts, Boccia, et al., 2001) and girls (Keysor et al., 2002; Roberts et al., 2006) with fragile X syndrome, physiological arousal is higher at baseline levels relative to children without fragile X. One important issue that needs to be researched is how intervention affects arousal levels and associated behaviors, such as attention levels and motor activity. In addition, problems in language and communication are evident in a significant number of boys with fragile X syndrome, to varying degrees (Roberts, Mirrett, & Burchinal, 2001), and in girls as well (Abbeduto & Hagerman, 1997). This is often manifested as speech delay, perseverative speech (repetition of others' words), and speech in rapid bursts (or "cluttered" speech).

Difficulties in cognitive skills have been observed among both boys and girls with fragile X syndrome and also in adults with the full mutation. To different degrees, these difficulties are evident even among the relatively high-functioning females with the disorder (i.e., females with IQ scores above 70), despite the lack of intellectual disability. In females, working memory, or executive function difficulties, appear in the form of difficulty with goal-oriented tasks that require deliberate, effortful cognitive flexibility, such as learning complicated rules (e.g., Kirk, Mazzocco, & Kover, 2005) or planning a sequence of steps (Mazzocco, Hagerman, & Pennington, 1992). Such inhibitory control difficulties may underlie other aspects of the phenotype observed in females, such as difficulty with language comprehension when discourse is not straightforward (Simon et al., 2001). In males, executive function deficits are more significant and include difficulty with impulse control. Cornish and colleagues (2001) proposed that difficulty in inhibitory control underlies the perseverative behaviors often observed in boys with the full mutation. Among both males and females, additional cognitive difficulties are noted in aspects of attention and visuospatial reasoning (e.g., Cornish et al., 2001; Mazzocco, Bhatia, & Lesniak-Karpiak, 2006, respectively). Difficulties in mathematics have also been reported for females (Mazzocco, 2001), although it is unclear what specific aspects of mathematics or related cognitive skills are the cause of these math difficulties (as reviewed elsewhere in detail; see Mazzocco & McCloskey, 2005).

When assessing phenotypes, it is helpful to recognize individual strengths and weaknesses associated with specific disorders. Fragile X syndrome is no exception. Although the degree of strengths varies as much as the deficits, one commonly reported strength in children with fragile X syndrome is in some aspects of memory, particularly as reflected in rote-like skills. For example, Murphy, Mazzocco, Gerner, and Henry (2006) found that young girls with the fragile X full mutation are as accurate as their peers at rote (memorized) skills such as counting aloud. However, this does not necessarily translate to accurate application of memory-based skills; indeed, Murphy and colleagues found that applied counting skills were weaker among girls with the full mutation, relative to their age-matched peers, despite strong rote counting skills.

Because of these highly variable features, it is difficult—indeed, inaccurate—to attest to any "typical" fragile X profile. For this reason, fragile X can be incorrectly dismissed as a possible diagnosis in a person with a developmental disability when hallmark features, such as large ears or eye aversion, are absent. Quick dismissal of the possibility of fragile X without genetic testing may result in missed diagnoses. Awareness of the full range of behavioral features or developmental delay in the absence of intellectual disability or physical features is therefore critical to ensure this diagnosis is not missed. For example, children whose fragile X syndrome is diagnosed by DNA screening typically engage in atypical behavior (Bailey, Roberts, et al., 2001), even if this behavior itself did not lead to the DNA testing. In a screening study of 18 toddlers with a confirmed diagnosis of fragile X, Mirrett et al. (2004) found that approximately 75% had developmental delay detected by three routine developmental screening tests by the age of 9–12 months. On the basis of evidence from this study and others, the authors of that study concluded that fragile X testing in children with developmental delay is well justified. The Quality Assurance Committee of the Laboratory Practice Committee of the American College of Medical Genetics (Maddalena et al., 2005) prepared an educational resource for medical geneticists and other health care providers to help them provide quality medical services to families undergoing screening for fragile X syndrome.

Another source of difficulty in identifying fragile X syndrome stems from the overlap observed between some individuals with fragile X and individuals with another genetic disorder. Some examples of such overlap are reviewed next.

Variation in Fragile X Phenotypes

Although the following specific phenotypes have not yet been documented in large numbers of studies, it is important to recognize these overlaps because genetic testing for the other conditions, such as Prader-Willi syndrome or Sotos syndrome, would eliminate only those syndromes as the cause of the disability. Tests for these latter syndromes would not identify fragile X syndrome as the cause because diagnosis for fragile X is based on a completely different genetic test.

Obesity Phenotype Males with fragile X syndrome who also have truncal obesity, short broad hands and feet, hyperpigmentation, and small genitals are often referred to as having a "Prader-Willi-like phenotype" because these characteristics resemble a different genetic disorder called Prader-Willi syndrome. Classic Prader-Willi syndrome is not X-linked, however, and is not associated with fragile X syndrome.

Overgrowth Phenotype Some males with fragile X syndrome have above average birth weight, increased head circumference, and extreme overall body overgrowth, with increased height in childhood and adulthood. This phenotype resembles Sotos syndrome and has thus been referred to as "Sotos-like."

Autism Children with fragile X can be intensely shy and may exhibit **stereotypies** such as hand flapping. These are traits that resemble behaviors seen in children with autism (see Chapter 12). Approximately 25% of boys with fragile X meet criteria for autism, and many more have features of autism without meeting the full criteria for autism disorder per se. Among those who do meet the criteria for autism, few have severe autism (Bailey et al., 1998). Although the majority of children with autism (more than 90%) do not have fragile X, and although the majority of children (approximately 66%) with fragile X do not have autism, fragile X is the most common known genetic disorder associated with autism. In her statement before the United States House of Representatives Subcommittee on Health and Environment, Dr. Hagerman (1999) recommended that "all children with autism . . . should be tested for fragile X."

Awareness of Fragile X Syndrome

Despite the significant consequences and high prevalence, public awareness about fragile X is low in many areas. Even health care professionals, educators, and other service providers often have little information about this syndrome, creating additional difficulties for families of individuals with fragile X. Among special educators, familiarity with autism and Down syndrome is greater than familiarity with fragile X syndrome (Wilson & Mazzocco, 1993; York et al., 1999). It is important for a wide range of professionals to be familiar with fragile X, because the effects of this condition on a family extend beyond the individual with the syndrome. Fragile X in a family influences family planning; education; health care; financial planning; and life planning for siblings, other family members, and future descendants. Indeed, Bailey (2004) proposed that public health professionals will benefit from awareness of the issues surrounding a genetic basis of developmental disorders and that fragile X syndrome provides a model for such issues.

SPECIAL NEEDS OF CHILDREN WITH FRAGILE X SYNDROME

There is no known cure for fragile X syndrome. Currently, treating the symptoms of fragile X is the only option available to help people affected by the full mutation. Available interventions such as medication, special education, and psychological counseling provide some, albeit limited, assistance (Berry-Kravis & Potanos, 2004). Specifically, general health care needs, educational needs, and family support needs are summarized next, and suggestions are provided regarding interventions in the future.

Health Care Needs

Family physicians provide the health care needs of most individuals with fragile X syndrome, along with referrals for specialized services as required. Interventions may include behavior or medical therapies to modify sleep disturbances, hyperactivity, short attention span, and other concerns. Specialized services include assessment of fine motor or gross motor functioning, speech and language development, learning abilities, and behaviors, as well as occupational therapy or physiotherapy. Not all children with fragile X syndrome have medical complications, but it is important to recognize that such children are at higher risk for some problems than unaffected children of the same age.

Educational Needs

In the United States and many other countries, students with developmental disabilities are eligible for inclusion in general classrooms but are likely to require special education services. There is a wide range of recommended interventions because of the wide range of effects of fragile X syndrome on development. However, very few practices have been studied with children who have fragile X syndrome, so recommendations may not be empirically based.

General guidelines that can facilitate positive classroom experiences are similar to guidelines that apply to any child with hyperarousal or distractibility. These include limiting distractions and sources of overarousal, maintaining predictable routines, and not forcing eye contact. Children with fragile X syndrome resemble children with autism in that both may be dismayed by change; thus, changes in routine may result in behavioral outbursts. Loud noises and bright lights can be distracting and cause problems in a learning environment, so control over these factors can promote a positive learning environment. Table 11.1 gives some examples of common behavior disturbances and potentially effective responses. In view of the fact that

Table 11.1. Causes of common behavior disturbances in individuals with fragile X syndrome and potentially effective strategies

Cause	Strategies to try
Change in routine	
Has the routine suddenly changed?	Keep the routine as predictable as possible.
Is there a new teacher?	Introduce changes gradually.
Have seating arrangements been changed?	Give appropriate notice of change. (*Note:* Excessive amount of notice may cause anxiety.)
Loud noises	
Are there loud or unpredictable noises?	Keep unpredictable sounds (e.g., from alarms and pagers) to a minimum.
Did an alarm go off?	Avoid loud or abrupt noises.
Does someone have a beeper?	Use soothing, uninterrupted sounds, such as quiet steady hums, classical music, and tapes of nature.
	Preface loud noises with a warning (e.g., "This pencil sharpener will be loud, so let's cover our ears before I use it").
	Consider the possibility that noises that may not be too loud for most people may be too loud for individuals with hyperarousal.
Lights	
Is the lighting too bright?	Remember that natural daylight is preferable to fluorescent lighting.
Are there flashing lights?	Reduce brightness by using pink or other soft tone light bulbs.
	Install dimmer switches when possible.
Crowds and social discomfort	
Are there too many people around?	Maintain a sense of spaciousness; avoid crowds.
Are people too close together?	Choose aisle seats or back sections for more space and an easy exit.
Is eye contact being forced?	When working one to one with a child, sit next to the child instead of across from child, so as to not force eye contact.
	Allow the child to look away, and recognize that it is not necessary for the child to look at others during assessment, instruction, or other interactions.

Source: Lee et al. (2003).

symptoms of fragile X vary from child to child (particularly between boys and girls), it is important to assess each child individually rather than assuming that a particular strategy will be successful for all children with fragile X syndrome.

Students with fragile X syndrome sometimes benefit from short periods away from regular classroom activity. Others may benefit from being in a smaller classroom throughout the school day. Most children with fragile X syndrome benefit from an individualized education program (IEP) to identify specific goals, which is required in some jurisdictions. Successful creation of an IEP requires support from teachers and others (e.g., an educational psychologist, family members, disability professionals) and periodic reassessment inside and outside of the classroom. The IEP may specify the need for speech-language therapy and/or occupational therapy. Parents of children with fragile X report that these services are useful but that more services are needed, or at least desired, for their children (Hatton et al., 2000; see also Chapter 31).

In view of evidence regarding the benefits of early intervention, early intervention programs provide an important service for children with fragile X and their families. These include infant development or stimulation programs, such as those that provide in-home support with suggestions for parents on how to address the needs of a child with a developmental disability or that provide parents with training on enhancing their child's development or communication skills. In Canada, this type of program is generally available through the local health unit or hospital; in the United States, it may be available through a mental health clinic or through the public school system. For 3- to 5-year-olds in the United States, preschool development services provide activities to stimulate development that can be carried out in the home or child care setting. During the school years, programs may be available in schools for children meeting eligibility criteria for special education services.

Indeed, in the United States, special services are required for children who meet the criteria outlined in the Individuals with Disabilities Education Improvement Act (IDEA) of 2004 (PL 108-446). In some parts of Canada, the Ministry of Health–supported programs in the schools provide occupational therapy and physiotherapy, as well as support for speech and language development. In adolescence and adulthood, sheltered work environments and group homes provide support for individuals who are significantly impaired, socially or cognitively. Many women with fragile X will not need such services, given the milder impairment typically observed in females. Indeed, many women with the fragile X full mutation graduate from college and lead independent lives.

Family Support Needs

It is important to understand how families cope with the stress of raising children with fragile X syndrome. However, there is very little research on this topic. One such study explored parents' experiences in obtaining health care services for their children with fragile X syndrome (Minnes, Lauckner, & Recoskie, 2004). The parents reported challenges in negotiating the health care system, including entering into the system through referrals, dealing with waiting lists, facing a lack of needed services, and living at a distance from services. The parents also expressed concern regarding physicians' lack of education about intellectual disabilities and the inability for parents' needs to be met during abbreviated appointments. These observations may be related to the aforementioned studies that report how parents' concerns about their child's developmental delays were initially discounted by clinicians (Bailey et al., 2000) and to the delay parents experience obtaining the diagnosis of fragile X (Bailey et al., 2003).

Looking Ahead: Interventions in the Future

Returning to our discussion of the genetics of fragile X syndrome, it is important to recall the role of FMRP in the development of an individual with the full mutation. FMRP seems to play a crucial role, but not the only role, in this development. Several different approaches are being investigated in order to develop better treatments and interventions for fragile X. These include, but are not limited to identifying the nature of synaptic protein synthesis in fragile X syndrome (e.g., Bear, Huber, & Warren, 2004) so that researchers can understand how FMRP influences brain development and function; designing gene therapy that could deliver a new, working copy of the fragile X gene to brain cells so that the gene will function normally, producing normal protein levels (Rattazzi, LaFauci, & Brown, 2004); and discovering ways to provide cells and tissues with substitutes for the function of the FMR1 protein. Clearly, these are not easy solutions, but work towards these efforts is underway. In addition, through the use of animal models of fragile X syndrome, it is possible to study how certain forms of behavior therapy or drugs alter the shape of neurons, their sizes and their connections, and behavioral consequences.

HOW THE PREMUTATION AFFECTS INDIVIDUALS

All of the information presented in the previous sections concerned effects of the fragile X full mutation. As was discussed in the Genetics of Fragile X Syndrome section, there is an important distinction between the fragile X full mutation (more than 200 CGG repeats) and the fragile X premutation. There have been reports of psychological and mental health issues in premutation carriers of fragile X, but in many ways this is not surprising in view of the number of individuals who have the premutation. With a prevalence of 1 in 259 (Rousseau et al., 1995), it is important to determine whether reported prevalence rates of psychological difficulties exceed the prevalence of such difficulties in the general population. Research participants in studies of the premutation may be limited to those who come to clinical attention, in which case the participants are no longer representative of premutation carriers in general. It is essential that ascertainment bias be addressed and acknowledged in studies of the premutation, in view of the high prevalence of this mutation (as reviewed in this chapter's Prevalence of Fragile X Syndrome section).

When research participants are clinically ascertained, it is important to consider appropriate research comparison groups. For example, Reiss and his colleagues reported an increased level of depression among women with the premutation (who had children with fragile X syndrome), but depression was as common among women without fragile X who had a child with developmental delay (Reiss et al., 1993). One of the questions stemming from these observations is whether psychological factors associated with the premutation are due to the genetics of fragile X or due to the consequences of living with the fragile X mutation and raising a child with fragile X.

In the few controlled studies of cognitive effects of the premutation, no evidence of impaired cognitive or behavior impairment has been noted (Mazzocco & Holden, 1996; Myers et al., 2001). For psychological effects, there is insufficient evidence that such difficulties are indeed related to the premutation. Studies that do support some effect of the premutation on cognition show minimal effects. Allen and colleagues (2005) found slight lowering of verbal IQ scores among females with the premutation, but the effects associated with the premutation were minor relative to other factors and these effects may be due to the confound of a more well-substantiated characteristic of the premutation, which is early menopause.

In contrast to research on psychological consequences of the premutation, findings related to premature ovarian failure (i.e., early menopause) in women with the premutation are empirically well-supported. Whereas less than 1% of women in the general population experience menopause before the age of 40 years, approximately 20%–28% of women with a premutation have early menopause, some even in their early 20s (Allingham-Hawkins et al., 1999; Kenneson & Warren, 2001; Vianna-Morgante & Holden, 2003). In a study of 507 women with a premutation, Sullivan et al. (2005) found that when the FMR1 repeat size is more than 80 repeats, ovarian dysfunction is clinically significant. The explanation for this relationship is unclear, but Welt et al. (2004) measured various hormone levels in carriers of the premutation and women without the premutation, all 22–41 years of age, and found that despite regular ovulatory cycles in the women with the premutation, there were differences in the levels of follicle stimulating hormone in the two groups of women. These findings are relevant to the health care of women with premutations, who may be concerned about family planning and general health issues, such as the need for hormone replacement therapy or related alternatives and the increased risk of osteoporosis that results from decreased levels of estrogen.

Finally, another physical consequence has been reported for older males with the premutation. It was once thought that males with the premutation were spared clinical involvement. However, it is thought that approximately 33% of middle-age males with a premutation develop progressive intention tremor, gait ataxia (an inability to coordinate voluntary muscle movements, or unsteady movements and staggering gait), features similar to those of Parkinson's disease, and memory loss. This combination of characteristics is referred to as *fragile-X-associated tremor/ataxia syndrome (FXTAS)* (Berry-Kravis et al., 2003; Hagerman & Hagerman, 2004). Having been identified only in 2001, knowledge about this proposed syndrome is limited to the outcomes of research in its very early stages (e.g., Berry-Kravis et al., 2003; Hagerman & Hagerman 2004; Jacquemont et al., 2004; Loesch et al., 2005). Although ascertainment bias in these studies is of potential concern, research efforts are expanding.

It is challenging to identify effects of the premutation given its high prevalence in the general population. When considering ascertainment bias and appropriate comparison groups, findings regarding a cognitive or behavior phenotype of the premutation are inconclusive. In contrast, the physical consequence of early menopause is well substantiated. Together, these findings indicate that when effects of the premutation are observed, the phenotype differs from those seen with the full mutation. For example, there is no clear evidence that boys or girls with a premutation have cognitive impairment (Franke et al., 1999; Myers et al., 2001) in the way that the full mutation affects individuals. Also, the premature menopause that occurs in many women with the premutation is not observed in women with a full mutation. The symptoms of FXTAS are also not observed in individuals with the full mutation.

FOR FURTHER THOUGHT AND DISCUSSION

1. Parents of students with fragile X do not always inform teachers and other students about the fragile X diagnosis. Discuss possible advantages and disadvantages of sharing or not sharing this information.
2. When a woman is identified as a **fragile X carrier**, she may be offered the option of prenatal diagnosis and pregnancy termination. Offspring of carrier males would have different risks. Should carrier screening be conducted among adults? For whom should screening be made available (e.g., newborn females, teenagers, pregnant women)?
3. Family members of a person with fragile X syndrome have a high probability of carrying the mutation. Genetic counselors recommend that family members tell their relatives about fragile X so that they too can avail themselves of genetic counseling and testing for the mutation if they wish. For a variety of reasons, some family members choose to not inform relatives about fragile X. Should this task be left to the family member who received the diagnosis? If clinicians know the names of the extended family members, do they have an obligation to tell these potential carriers about the fragile X diagnosis? Would this be a violation of confidentiality? How can one protect an individual's right not to know?
4. Several research initiatives are looking at the possibility of gene therapy for fragile X syndrome. This involves the delivery of a working copy of the fragile X gene into the cells of the brain in the hope that the gene would make the needed protein and reverse the cognitive disabilities associated with this syndrome. Discuss arguments for and/or against such therapy.
5. It is possible to address many of the remaining questions about the evolution of the fragile X full mutation, and questions about the mutation's impact on brain development, in post mortem studies of brain tissue. There are no benefits of this research for the family of the deceased person, but the benefits to the field can be significant. How and when should the importance of this research be addressed? Also consider that many answers about the evolution of the FMR1 premutation and the full mutation can be made by examining unfertilized eggs. How and when should this type of research be considered, if at all?
6. The increasingly common reliance on in vitro fertilization and alternative methods of pregnancy has led to cases of the fragile X mutation appearing in products of donor eggs and donor sperm. What are the implications for screening and genetic counseling?

SUMMARY

Fragile X syndrome is one of many causes of intellectual disability. Among syndromes that are hereditary, fragile X is the most common, based on current knowledge. Although it is X-linked, both males and females are affected by fragile X. The term *fragile X syndrome* generally refers to the outward manifestation—physical or psychological—of the fragile X full mutation. This manifestation, or phenotype, is highly variable across individuals, making it impossible to paint a picture of the "typical" person with fragile X. The severity of effects differs remarkably between males and females, with males being more strongly affected as a group. However, some females can be affected as severely affected as males with the syndrome.

People affected by fragile X generally have good health, but may require specialized services or treatment. Health care services are provided through family physicians, and additional services are offered by speech-language therapists, occupational therapists, educational psychologists, and other professionals. General public education for individuals with fragile X syndrome is available in many countries, but affected individuals often require special education assistance. There is no single empirically-based educational program specific for children with fragile X. As for every child with special needs, educational modifications and accommodations should be made on the basis of the individual child's needs and strengths. Idea sharing among support groups is one way that families work towards the goal of having their child's needs met.

Families of individuals affected with fragile X syndrome frequently experience challenges in raising a child with a developmental disability and finding information, services, and support. There is a need for families to adapt to having fragile X in the family. Family members generally encounter a lack of awareness of fragile X in the community and among professionals. More research, public awareness, and support for fragile X syndrome is needed worldwide.

Unaffected family members can also carry the fragile X mutation, and this often affects their family planning decisions. Among these "unaffected" carriers of the fragile X premutation, a significant minority of women will experience premature ovarian failure, leading to health concerns. A significant minority of men may experience ataxia and tremors (FXTAS) in middle age. There is much information still to be uncovered regarding how individuals with fragile X develop and function, despite vast increases in knowledge about the gene and its function since its discovery in 1991.

Research in the fragile X syndrome field continues to gain momentum. In addition to regularly held local family meetings and international scientific meetings, the National Fragile X Foundation of the United States has sponsored a biennial meeting since 1990. Conference proceedings from some of the previous meetings are available from the Foundation (e.g., see http://www.fragileX.org/html/2004_proceedings.htm). These organized meetings provide a forum for researchers and family members to communicate about research gains and the questions in need of answers. Conferences and local meetings provide a means by which family members share experiences and support each other. Together, the large and small scale meetings provide a mechanism by which to enhance awareness of fragile X syndrome. Increased awareness in turn serves to maximize the number of children readily identified and to increase the likelihood that needs of individuals with fragile X syndrome will be addressed.

REFERENCES

Abbeduto, L., & Hagerman, R. (1997). Language and communication in fragile X syndrome. *Mental Retardation and Developmental Disabilities Research Review, 3,* 313–322.

Abrams, M.T., Reiss, A.L., Freund, L.S., et al. (1994). Molecular-neurobehavioral associations in females with the fragile X full mutation. *American Journal of Medical Genetics, 51,* 317–327.

Allen, E.G., Sherman, S., Abramowitz, A., et al. (2005). Examination of the effect of the polymorphic CGG repeat in the FMR1 gene on cognitive performance. *Behavior Genetics, 35,* 435–445.

Allingham-Hawkins, D.J., Babul-Hirji, R., Chitayat, D., et al. (1999). Fragile X premutation is a significant risk factor for premature ovarian failure: The International Collaborative POF in Fragile X study—preliminary data. *American Journal of Medical Genetics, 83,* 322–325.

Bailey, D.B., Roberts, J.E., Mirrett, P., et al. (2001). Identifying infants and toddlers with fragile X syndrome: Issues and recommendations. *Infants and Young Children, 14,* 24–33.

Bailey, D.B., Skinner, D., Hatton, D., et al. (2000). Family experiences and factors associated with the diagnosis of fragile X syndrome. *Journal of Developmental and Behavioral Pediatrics, 21,* 315–321.

Bailey, D.B., Jr. (2004). Newborn screening for fragile X syndrome. *Mental Retardation and Developmental Disabilities Research Review, 10,* 3–10.

Bailey, D.B., Jr., Hatton, D.D., Tassone, F., et al. (2001). Variability in FMRP and early development in males with fragile X syndrome. *American Journal of Mental Retardation, 106,* 16–27.

Bailey, D.B., Jr., Mesibov, G.B., Hatton, D.D., et al. (1998). Autistic behavior in young boys with fragile X syndrome. *Journal of Autism and Developmental Disorders, 28,* 499–508.

Bailey, D.B., Jr., Skinner, D., & Sparkman, K.L. (2003). Discovering fragile X syndrome: Family experiences and perceptions. *Pediatrics, 111,* 407–416.

Bakker, C.E., & Oostra, B.A. (2003). Understanding fragile X syndrome: Insights from animal models. *Cytogenetic and Genome Research, 100,* 111–123.

Bear, M.F., Huber, K.K., & Warren, S.T. (2004). The mGluR theory of fragile X mental retardation. *Trends in Neuroscience, 27,* 370–377.

Berry-Kravis, E., Lewin, F., Wuu, J., et al. (2003). Tremor and ataxia in fragile X premutation carriers: Blinded videotape study. *Annals of Neurology, 53,* 616–623.

Berry-Kravis, E., & Potanos, K. (2004). Psychopharmacology in fragile X syndrome—present and future. *Mental Retardation and Developmental Disabilities Research Review, 10,* 42–48.

Cornish, K.M., Munir, F., & Cross, G. (1998). The nature of the spatial deficit in young females with fragile-X syndrome: A neuropsychological and molecular perspective. *Neuropsychologia, 11*(36), 1239–1246.

Cornish, K.M., Munir, F., & Cross, G. (1999). Spatial cognition in males with fragile-x syndrome: Evidence for a neuropsychological phenotype. *Cortex, 2*(35), 263–271.

Cornish, K.M., Munir, F., & Cross, G. (2001). Differential impact of the FMR-1 full mutation on memory and attention functioning: A neuropsychological perspective. *Journal of Cognitive Neuroscience, 13,* 144–150.

Crawford, D.C., Acuna, J.M., & Sherman, S.L. (2001). FMR1 and the fragile X syndrome: Human genome epidemiology review. *Genetic Medicine, 3,* 359–371.

Crawford, D.C., Meadows, K.L., Newman, J.L., et al. (2002). Prevalence of the fragile X syndrome in African-Americans. *American Journal of Medical Genetics, 110,* 226–233.

Daniels, J.K., Owen, M.J., McGuffin, P., et al. (1994). IQ and variation in the number of fragile X CGG repeats: No association in a normal sample. *Intelligence, 19,* 45–50.

Dombrowski, D., Levesque, S., Morel, M.L., et al. (2002). Premutation and intermediate-size FMR alleles in 10,572 males from the general population: Loss of an AGG interruption is a late event in the generation of fragile X syndrome alleles. *Human Molecular Genetics, 11,* 371–378.

Franke, P., Leboyer, M., Hardt, J., et al. (1999). Neuropsychological profiles of FMR-1 premutation and full-mutation carrier females. *Psychiatry Research, 87,* 223–231.

Fu, Y.-H., Kuhl, D.P.A., Pizzuti, A., et al. (1991) Variation of the CGG repeat at the fragile X site results in genetic instability: Resolution of the Sherman paradox. *Cell, 67,* 1047–1058.

Hagerman, P.J., & Hagerman, R.J. (2004). The Fragile X premutation: A maturing phenotype. *American Journal of Human Genetics, 74,* 805–816.

Hagerman, R. (1999, Fall). Statement of Dr. Randi Hagerman to the House Subcommittee on Health and Environment. *The National Fragile X Foundation Quarterly Newsletter,* 9–10.

Hagerman, R.J. (2002). The physical and behavioral phenotype. In Hagerman, R.J., & Hagerman P.J. (Eds.), *Fragile X syndrome: Diagnosis, treatment, and research* (3rd ed., pp. 3–109). Baltimore: The Johns Hopkins University Press.

Hagerman, R.J., & Hagerman P.J. (Eds.). (2002). *Fragile X syndrome: Diagnosis, treatment, and research* (3rd ed.). Baltimore: The Johns Hopkins University Press.

Hatton, D.D., Bailey, D.B., Roberts, J.P., et al. (2000). Early intervention services for young boys with fragile X syndrome. *Journal of Early Intervention, 23,* 23–27.

Hatton, D.D., Buckley, E., Lachiewicz, A., et al. (1998). Ocular status of boys with fragile X syndrome: A prospective study. *Journal of AAPOS, 2,* 298–302.

Hatton, D.D., Hooper, S.R., Bailey, D.B., et al. (1999). Problem behavior in young boys with fragile X syndrome. *American Journal of Medical Genetics, 108,* 105–116.

Holden, J.J., Chalifoux, M., Wing, M., et al. (1996). The Fragile X syndrome: Current understanding and testing procedures. *Journal of Developmental Disabilities, 2,* 82–90.

Individuals with Disabilities Education Improvement Act (IDEA) of 2004, PL 108-446, 20 U.S.C. §§ 1400 *et seq.*

Jacquemont, S., Hagerman, R.J., Leehey, M.A., et al. (2004). Penetrance of the fragile X-associated tremor/ataxia syndrome in a premutation carrier population. *Journal of the American Medical Association, 291,* 460–469.

Kenneson, A., & Warren, S.T. (2001). The female and the fragile X reviewed. *Seminars in Reproductive Medicine, 19,* 159–165.

Keysor, C.S., Mazzocco, M.M.M., McLeod, D.R., et al. (2002). Physiological arousal in females with fragile X or Turner syndrome. *Developmental Psychobiology, 41,* 133–146.

Kirk, J., Mazzocco, M.M.M., & Kover, S.T., (2005). Assessing executive dysfunction in girls with fragile X or Turner syndrome using the Contingency Naming Test. *Developmental Neuropsychology, 28*(3), 755–777.

Lee, B.A., MacKenzie, J.J., & Holden, J.J.A. (2003). Fragile X syndrome. In I. Brown & M. Percy (Eds.) *Developmental disabilities in Ontario* (pp. 229–244). Toronto: Ontario Association on Developmental Disabilities.

Loesch, D.Z., Churchyard, A., Brotchie, P., (2005). Evidence for, and a spectrum of, neurological involvement in carriers of the fragile X pre-mutation: FXTAS and beyond. *Clinical Genetics, 67,* 412–417.

Lubs, H.A. (1969). A marker X chromosome. *American Journal of Human Genetics, 21,* 231–244.

Maddalena, A., Richards, C.S., McGinniss, M.J., et al. (2005). *Quality Assurance Subcommittee of the Laboratory Practice Committee, American College of Medical Genetics. Technical standards and guidelines for fragile X, 2005 edition.* Retrieved on April 20, 2005, from http://www.acmg.net/Pages/ACMG_Activities/stds-2002/fx.htm

Mazzocco, M.M.M. (2001). Math learning disability and math LD subtypes: Evidence from studies of Turner syndrome, fragile X syndrome, and neurofibromatosis type 1. *Journal of Learning Disabilities, 34*(6), 520–533.

Mazzocco, M.M.M., Bhatia, N.S., & Lesniak-Karpiak, K (2006). Visuospatial skills and their association with math performance in girls with fragile X or Turner syndrome. *Child Neuropsychology, 12,* 87–110.

Mazzocco, M.M.M., Hagerman, R.J., & Pennington, B.F. (1992). Problem solving limitations among cytogenetically expressing fragile X women. *American Journal of Medical Genetics, 43* (1) 78–86.

Mazzocco, M.M.M., & Holden, J.A. (1996). Neuropsychological profiles of three sisters homozygous for the fragile X premutation. *American Journal of Medical Genetics, 64*(2), 323–328.

Mazzocco, M.M.M., & McCloskey, M. (2005). Math performance in girls with Turner or fragile X syndrome. In J. Campbell (Ed.), *Handbook of mathematical cognition* (pp. 269–297). New York: Psychology Press.

Mazzocco, M.M.M., & Reiss, A.L. (1997). Normal variation in size of the FMR1 gene is not associated with variation in intellectual performance. *Intelligence, 24,* 355–366.

McBride, S.M., Choi, C.H., Wang, Y., et al. (2005). Pharmacological rescue of synaptic plasticity, courtship behavior, and mushroom body defects in a Drosophila model of fragile X syndrome. *Neuron, 45,* 753–764.

Minnes, P., Lauckner, H., & Recoskie, K. (2004, April). *Healthcare concerns of parents of individuals with ID: Results from qualitative data analyses.* Paper presented at the Ontario Association on Developmental Disabilities Conference Research Day. Barrie, ON, Canada.

Mirrett, P.L., Bailey, D.B., Jr., Roberts, J.E., et al. (2004). Developmental screening and detection of developmental delays in infants and toddlers with fragile X syndrome. *Journal of Developmental and Behavioral Pediatrics, 25,* 21–27.

Murphy, M.M., & Abbeduto, L. (2005). Indirect genetic effects and the early language development of children with genetic mental retardation syndromes: The role of joint attention. *Infants and Young Children, 18,* 47–59.

Murphy, M.M., Mazzocco, M.M.M., Gerner, G., et al. (2006). Mathematics learning disability in girls with Turner syndrome or fragile X syndrome. *Brain and Cognition, 6,* 195–210.

Myers, G.F., Mazzocco, M.M.M., Maddalena, A., et al. (2001). No widespread psychological effect of the fragile X premutation in childhood: Evidence from a preliminary controlled study. *Journal of Developmental Behavioral Pediatrics, 22,* 353–359.

Nolin, S.L., Brown, W.T., Glicksman, A., et al. (2003). Expansion of the fragile X CGG repeat in females with premutation or intermediate alleles. *American Journal of Human Genetics, 72,* 454–464.

Oostra, B.A., Hoogeveen, A.T., & Willemsen, R. (n.d.). *Fragile X syndrome and FMR1.* Retrieved September 13, 2006, from http://www2.eur.nl/fgg/kgen/research/fmr1.html

Rattazzi, M.C., LaFauci, G., & Brown, W.T. (2004). Prospects for gene therapy in the fragile X syndrome. *Mental Retardation and Developmental Disabilities Research Reviews, 10,* 75–81.

Reiss, A.L., Freund, L., Abrams, M.T., et al. (1993). Neurobehavioral effects of the fragile X premutation in adult women: A controlled study. *American Journal of Human Genetics, 52,* 884–894.

Rife, M., Badenas, C., Mallolas, J., et al. (2003). Incidence of fragile X in 5,000 consecutive newborn males. *Genetic Testing, 7,* 339–343.

Roberts, J.E., Boccia, M.L., Bailey, D.B., Jr., et al. (2001). Cardiovascular indices of physiological arousal in boys with fragile X syndrome. *Developmental Psychobiology, 39,* 107–123.

Roberts, J.E., Mirrett, P., & Burchinal, M. (2001). Receptive and expressive communication development of young males with fragile X syndrome. *American Journal of Mental Retardation, 106,* 216–230.

Roberts, J., Mazzocco, M.M.M., Murphy, M.M., et al. (2006). *Arousal modulation and cognitive task performance in females with fragile X or Turner syndrome.* Manuscript submitted for publication.

Rousseau, F., Rouillard, P., Morel, M.L., et al. (1995). Prevalence of carriers of premutation-size alleles of the FMR1 gene—and implications for the population genetics of the fragile X syndrome. *American Journal of Human Genetics, 57,* 1006–1018.

Simon, J.A., Keenan, J.M., Pennington, B.F., et al. (2001). Discourse processing in women with fragile X syndrome: Evidence for a deficit establishing coherence. *Cognitive Neuropsychology, 18,* 1–18.

Sullivan, A.K., Marcus, M., Epstein, M.P., et al. (2005). Association of FMR1 repeat size with ovarian dysfunction. *Human Reproduction, 20,* 402–412.

Symons, F.J., Clark, R.D., Hatton, D.D., et al. (2003). Self-injurious behavior in young boys with fragile X syndrome. *American Journal of Medical Genetics A, 118,* 115–121.

Toledano-Alhadef, H., Basel-Vanagaite, L., Magal, N., et al. (2001). Fragile-X carrier screening and the prevalence of premutation and full-mutation carriers in Israel. *American Journal of Human Genetics, 69*(2), 351–360.

Tzeng, C.C., Tsai, L.P., Hwu, W.L., et al. (2005). Prevalence of the FMR1 mutation in Taiwan assessed by large-scale screening of newborn boys and analysis of DXS548-FRAXAC1 haplotype. *American Journal of Medical Genetics A, 133,* 37–43.

Verkerk, A.J., Pieretti, M., Sutcliffe, J.S., et al. (1991). Identification of a gene (FMR-1) containing a CGG repeat coincident with a breakpoint cluster region exhibiting length variation in fragile X syndrome. *Cell, 65,* 905–914.

Vianna-Morgante, A.M., & Holden, J.J. (2003, July). *Premature menopause.* Paper presented at the 8th International Fragile X Conference, Chicago.

Welt, C.K., Smith, P.C., & Taylor, A.E. (2004). Evidence of early ovarian aging in fragile X premutation carriers. *Journal of Clinical and Endocrinological Metabolism, 89,* 4569–4574.

Wilson, P.G., & Mazzocco, M.M.M. (1993). Awareness and knowledge of fragile X syndrome among special educators. *Mental Retardation, 31,* 221–227.

York, A., von Fraunhofer, N., Turk, J., et al. (1999). Fragile-X syndrome, Down's syndrome and autism: Awareness and knowledge amongst special educators. *Journal of Intellectual Disability Research, 43*(Pt. 4), 314–324.

Zeesman, S., Zwaigenbaum, L., Whelan, D.T., et al. (2004). Paternal transmission of fragile X syndrome. *American Journal of Medical Genetics A, 129,* 184–189.

Zhang, Y.Q., & Broadie, K. (2005). Fathoming fragile X in fruit flies. *Trends in Genetics, 21,* 37–45.

12

Autism and Related Disabilities

Adrienne Perry, Glen Dunlap, and Anne Black

WHAT YOU WILL LEARN ABOUT IN THIS CHAPTER

- Overview of autism and pervasive developmental disorders
- Intervention
- Large systems challenges

It is often said that no two people with autism are alike. The three examples in Display 12.1 demonstrate a number of important things about autism from the outset. First, autism may seem very different from one person to another, depending on the person's age, level of cognitive functioning, personality, and particular pattern of symptoms and behavior. Second, children and adults with autism can be found in a variety of environments, including school programs (both segregated and inclusive), children's mental health and treatment agencies, residential settings, and generic community settings. Third, having a child with autism has far-reaching effects on parents and other family members, with different issues arising at different stages in the family life cycle.

OVERVIEW OF AUTISM AND PERVASIVE DEVELOPMENTAL DISORDERS

Autism was first described by Leo Kanner in 1943; since that time, understanding of autism has changed and grown. Autism is not an illness or disease; it is a behaviorally defined syndrome, which means that its definition is based on a pattern of symptoms, not on a blood test or certain physical features. There have been many different definitions of autism and sets of diagnostic criteria; as of 2007, however, most professionals have adopted the same definition, which comes from the *Diagnostic and Statistical Manual of Mental Disorders, Fourth Edition, Text Revision* (*DSM-IV-TR;* American Psychiatric Association [APA], 2000). Autistic Disorder (usually just called *autism*) is the most well known of the five disorders that *DSM-IV-TR* describes under the general category of pervasive developmental disorders (or PDDs). All of the PDDs involve pervasive difficulties (i.e., severe impairments across many areas of development). The three broad areas of particular difficulty for autism are 1) reciprocal social interaction and play, 2) verbal and nonverbal communication, and 3) repetitive and unusual behavior and/or interests.

Definition and Description of Autism

Display 12.2 shows a brief summary of the *DSM-IV-TR* definition of Autistic Disorder. This section first describes how each of the three areas of difficulty is expressed in autism and then briefly mentions the other PDDs and related terms.

Display 12.2 notes that autism involves, first and foremost, pervasive difficulties in reciprocal social interaction. This social deficit does not necessarily involve withdrawing from social contact, but there is difficulty developing and sustaining relationships with other people. Children with autism may prefer isolation and ignore other people, may be unresponsive or aloof when others try to interact with them, often show no interest in playing with other children, and rarely initiate social contact. People with autism often have multiple deficits in nonverbal behaviors. These include such things as eye contact that may be very brief, odd, or almost nonexistent; infrequent smiling or other facial expression; and great difficulty with the use of gestures and behaviors to establish joint attention—that is, to engage the attention of another person in a social context. Individuals tend not to display spontaneous social sharing such as showing others something they have made or pointing out things of interest. Even high-functioning people with autism have great difficulty thinking about the feelings and thoughts of other people (this is sometimes described as lacking "theory of mind"). For example, they may appear not to notice if another person is hurt or upset, and they do not seem to have empathy for others. This makes true mutual friendships extremely difficult for people with autism. In fact, having very poor or no peer relationships is one of the defining features of the disorder.

As noted in Display 12.2, the second area of difficulty is pervasive impairments in verbal and nonverbal

Display 12.1

Three profiles of autism

Ben is 2½ and he loves trains. He is content to play alone with them for hours. Yet, Ben does not seem to really understand that they *are* trains. He does not pretend to make them go on the track or have crashes, imagine what the cars are carrying, or talk as he plays. He just lines up the trains in the same way every time and gets very upset if anyone rearranges his trains. Sometimes Ben carries a train around with him and rubs it against his chin or waves it in front of his eyes. He never brings a train to show his father and never points to the trains to show his sister. In fact, Ben completely ignores his sister. He does not talk to her or look at her, no matter how hard she tries to be a good big sister. Ben does not talk at all, rarely looks at other people, and rarely smiles. His mother suspects something is wrong, but the doctor told her Ben is probably just slow talking and will outgrow the other odd behavior. Ben will be starting nursery school soon and his mother hopes that will lead to improvements.

Carolyn is 12 and is great at doing puzzles quickly, even if they are upside down. She struggles with her school work, especially language arts and social studies, but is quite good at spelling and math and has an excellent memory. Carolyn was in special education classes when she was younger but is now in a general education class. She seems very friendly and talkative, though a bit immature. Carolyn asks questions of everyone she comes in contact with, even if they are not interested in talking to her. She does not know how to relate to her peers but really wants to be friends. She is enrolled in a social skills group at a local treatment agency. Her mother worries about what is in store for Carolyn as a teenager and adult. Although Carolyn has come so far from the 3-year-old who used to repeat nursery rhymes and television commercials, she still has some very pervasive difficulties.

Jeff is 23 and has lived, for the past 2 years, in a group home with four other young men who have developmental disabilities. Jeff just got a job in a warehouse. Although he has the skills needed to do the actual work, Jeff still needs a lot of support and his employer insists a staff person is with him at all times. One reason is that Jeff sometimes has seizures at work. Also, Jeff has a hard time when asked to do new things or when tasks are changed slightly from what he is used to; he will bang his head and scream when he gets frustrated in such situations. At the group home, three staff members work with Jeff and his housemates to teach them how to cook, clean their rooms, and do their laundry. Jeff's parents are pleased with how well he has adjusted to the group home and his new job. It was very hard for them to place their son out of their home, but Jeff's father has some serious health problems and his mother was not able to look after both of them.

Source: Perry and Black (2003).

communication. Approximately 1 in 3 people with autism are completely nonverbal. Others do speak, at least to some extent, and many use a variety of other communication systems such as pictures or signs to communicate their wants and needs. Even people with good speech have difficulty using it in socially appropriate ways, such as having a real two-way conversation. Some children exhibit echolalia, or repeat the words of others, either right away (immediate echolalia) or some time later (delayed echolalia). Although this may seem strange, it can be quite meaningful if the function of the echoed speech is understood. For example, people with autism may repeat a question when they do not understand it or do not know the answer. Other people with autism may use gibberish or made-up words. They often seem to confuse pronouns (e.g., saying "you" instead of "I").

The play of children with autism is also very problematic. In addition to the previously mentioned social difficulties, children with autism often have difficulty with imitation and usually do not engage in symbolic or pretend play (e.g., pretending to give a doll a drink). They may have a good memory but seem to have little imagination. For example, a child with autism may repeatedly open and close the window of a playhouse, whereas another child might pretend to sell ice cream cones in the playhouse.

A pattern of restricted, repetitive, and unusual behaviors and interests is the third area of difficulty seen in Display 12.2. People with autism may show obsessive preoccupations (e.g., arranging the books on the coffee table a certain way) or intense interest in one topic (e.g., the call letters of radio stations). They frequently have great difficulty coping with change and transi-

Display 12.2

Diagnostic Criteria for 299.00 Autistic Disorder

A. A total of six (or more) items from (1), (2), and (3), with at least two from (1), and one each from (2) and (3):

(1) qualitative impairment in social interaction, as manifested by at least two of the following:

(a) marked impairment in the use of multiple nonverbal behaviors such as eye-to-eye gaze, facial expression, body postures, and gestures to regulate social interaction

(b) failure to develop peer relationships appropriate to developmental level

(c) a lack of spontaneous seeking to share enjoyment, interests, or achievements with other people (e.g., by a lack of showing, bringing, or pointing out objects of interest)

(d) lack of social or emotional reciprocity

(2) qualitative impairments in communication, as manifested by at least one of the following:

(a) delay in, or total lack of, the development of spoken language (not accompanied by an attempt to compensate through alternative modes of communication such as gesture or mime)

(b) in individuals with adequate speech, marked impairment in the ability to initiate or sustain a conversation with others

(c) stereotyped and repetitive use of language or idiosyncratic language

(d) lack of varied, spontaneous make-believe play or social imitative play appropriate to developmental level

(3) restricted, repetitive, and stereotyped patterns of behavior, interests, and activities, as manifested by at least one of the following:

(a) encompassing preoccupation with one or more stereotyped and restricted patterns of interest that is abnormal either in intensity or focus

(b) apparently inflexible adherence to specific, nonfunctional routines or rituals

(c) stereotyped and repetitive motor mannerisms (e.g., hand or finger flapping or twisting, or complex whole-body movements)

(d) persistent preoccupation with parts of objects

B. Delays or abnormal functioning in at least one of the following areas, with onset prior to age 3 years: (1) social interaction, (2) language as used in social communication, or (3) symbolic or imaginative play.

C. The disturbance is not better accounted for by Rett's Disorder or Childhood Disintegrative Disorder.

tions, and they like things in their environment to stay the same. For example, an altered school bus route or a new picture on the wall may be upsetting enough to precipitate a tantrum in some children. Repetitive or stereotyped behaviors (often assumed to be self-stimulatory) are common. These are often the most noticeable odd things seen in people with autism, although the behaviors may not be obvious in very young children. Stereotyped behaviors include rocking, hand flapping, and other unusual body movements. The behaviors may also involve unusual manipulation of objects, such as jiggling, spinning, tapping, or rubbing certain things constantly. Individuals with autism may not use toys and objects as intended and sometimes get fixated on one small part of a toy, such as spinning the wheels of a toy car.

As seen in the top of Display 12.2, there are many different combinations of characteristics that could meet the definition of autism. It is important to understand that not all people with a diagnosis of autism will have all of the symptoms listed. Individuals with autism vary widely in ability, behavior, activity level, and personality. Furthermore, someone who does not have a particular symptom on the list may still have autism. For example, absent or disordered eye contact is often characteristic of children with autism, but some people with autism have relatively good eye contact. In addition, some children with autism enjoy activities such as rough-and-tumble play; if children enjoy this type of social interaction but have other symptoms, autism cannot be ruled out. Conversely, simply exhibiting one or two of the symptoms on the list does not mean that a person has autism. The whole pattern of symptoms must be considered. Furthermore, each of the characteristics listed has to be judged atypical relative to the person's developmental level. That is, it is not just that children with autism have delayed development; rather, their development is disordered. For example, their speech is not just immature, but is unusual; their play is not just delayed, it is different.

Part of the definition for autism is onset before 3 years of age. In fact, most children with autism have probably had the condition from birth. Peculiarities can be seen on early home videos, even if neither parents nor professionals initially recognized them. In such videos, children later diagnosed with autism may not respond to their names, may not point to draw another person's attention, may show unusual or absent facial expression, may not look at people, may not talk or form two-word combinations by age 2, and may show minor attentional and motor difficulties. However, some children do have a typical early infancy and then regress as toddlers—for example, losing the ability to say words they had learned. Early screening is very important, and parents should be respected and believed when they suspect something is wrong. Many parents have been told to "wait and see" or that their child "will likely grow out of it," but this is bad advice. Children should be referred as soon as possible for a comprehensive diagnostic assessment and, in locations where there is a long waiting list for that assessment, it may be wise to begin intervention even before a formal diagnosis is obtained. (Ideas for getting started are discussed in the Early Intervention section.)

Making the diagnosis of autism is a complex task and should only be done by an experienced professional (usually a psychologist, developmental pediatrician, neurologist, or child psychiatrist) or multidisciplinary team, based on some combination of the following: direct observation of the child, the child's history, diagnostic interviews with parents, completion of rating scales designed to measure autism, and assessment of the child's developmental level. A proper diagnostic assessment can be useful to answer the family's questions and may be necessary to obtain services or funding, but it should also help promote a better understanding of the child and guide intervention efforts. For more in-depth information about best practices in the assessment and diagnosis of autism, see clinical practice parameters described in Filipek et al. (1999); New York State Department of Health (1999); Perry, Condillac, and Freeman (2002); and Sattler (2002).

Prevalence

Autism is not a rare disorder. Autism occurs in all cultures and all social classes, and it is much more common in boys than in girls (approximately 4:1). The prevalence of autism is at least 1 in every 1,000 children. For the whole PDD category, it is at least 3 in every 1,000 (Fombonne, 2003). Some studies have suggested even higher numbers, perhaps double. The frequency of PDDs seems to be increasing, and certainly the demand for services and educational resources is increasing significantly. However, it is not known whether this is a real increase in prevalence or whether it is due to the different definitions of autism being used, the narrowness or breadth of diagnoses examined in the studies (i.e., Did they include related PDDs or only autism? Did they include intellectual and/or developmental disabilities?), the recognition of earlier diagnosis, increased awareness of autism among community professionals and the public, or the increased resources (in some jurisdictions) for intervention (Fombonne, 2003; Wing & Potter, 2002).

Connection Between Autism and Intellectual Disabilities

Autism often co-occurs with other disorders and diagnoses. The most common is intellectual disability (or mental retardation, developmental handicap, or cognitive/intellectual impairment—which, as described in Chapter 1, all have similar meanings). Approximately three quarters of people with autism also have some degree of cognitive impairment (APA, 2000; National Research Council [NRC], 2001) but level of functioning is not necessarily impaired for all people with PDDs (see the Related Disorders section). When providing support or intervention, it is important to understand that autism can be more or less severe, as can be the degree of cognitive impairment. That is, one person could have a severe intellectual disability and mild autism, another could have high intellectual functioning but have severe autism, and yet another could have severe difficulties in both respects.

Although there may be overall delays, the cognitive profiles of people with autism are somewhat different from those of other individuals with intellectual and developmental disabilities. (This is related to the "not just delayed, but disordered" idea.) In general, people with autism show an uneven pattern of skills. A lot of people with autism have peak skills (also called *splinter skills* or *islets of ability*), which are characteristic strengths in their cognitive profiles. These individuals are better at nonverbal reasoning tasks such as doing puzzles, copying designs, and using rote memory than they are at tasks requiring abstract verbal reasoning and comprehension of social situations. Some people with autism are very good at spelling and reading decoding (pronouncing words), even scoring well above their expected age or grade levels. This is called *hyperlexia*. It is important to recognize that understanding or comprehension is usually very poor in these individuals and that hyperlexia does not indicate a high level of intelligence. Also, a small number (probably less than 1%) of people are autistic savants who have amazing abilities in music, arithmetic calculations, or drawing. Having savant skills also does not indicate a high level of intelligence. In fact, savants may be quite low functioning in most other areas of life.

Causes

A great deal of research has been done and continues to be done to determine the cause(s) of autism. Although many questions remain unanswered, the following is known: 1) Autism is not caused by bad parenting (this is an old idea that has been totally discredited), and 2) autism is a neurological disorder, but there is probably no single, straightforward cause. A variety of sources (see Fombonne, 2003; Gillberg & Coleman, 2000; Glidden, 2001; Tanguay, 2000) indicate that there are probably multiple causes resulting in a similar pattern of behavior or perhaps different subgroups with different causes. Several lines of reasoning support this idea:

- Some people with autism (but probably only 10% or less) also have a genetic disorder known to cause other developmental disabilities, such as fragile X syndrome or tuberous sclerosis. It is important to diagnose such genetic disorders in individuals with autism to increase potential options for treatment and prevention. (It is also important to note that people with these other disorders do not necessarily have autism.)
- Family studies show that there is a genetic component to at least some cases of autism (this is an active research area). Studies suggest that a family that has one child with autism has a higher than average chance of having another child with difficulties. These could be related to autism (approximately 2%–3%), some form of PDD (approximately 5%–8%), or some language disorder or learning disability (approximately 25%).
- Twin studies show that identical twins, who have identical genes, are much more likely to be concordant—that is, both have autism than are fraternal twins. The fact that this does not always happen, however, indicates that other, nongenetic factors must be involved.
- People with autism have a higher than average rate of seizures (approximately 1 in 3), indicating abnormal electrical activity in the brain. Some children have early onset (sometimes called *infantile spasms*) and some have onset during adolescence.
- There is a somewhat higher than usual incidence of birth and pregnancy complications in mothers of children with autism. These are fairly general complications (e.g., late-stage bleeding), however, and probably are not the cause of the autism.
- Researchers are trying to pinpoint which area(s) of the brain may be malfunctioning or not typically developed. This research is very complex and hard to interpret because of slightly different research methods, slightly different definitions of autism, and so on. It is likely that whatever goes wrong in the developing brain happens quite early in fetal development and affects a number of different brain areas.
- The neurochemicals that the brain uses to pass messages along various pathways are also being investigated. These studies have not yet reached clear conclusions because of problems with the methods used and the groups of people studied.
- Several theories about vaccines causing autism, or environmental factors such as pollution or toxic waste causing autism, remain controversial and are not supported by any firm evidence to date.

In summary, there may be a number of different subgroups of autism with different causes, some of which are genetic, some of which are associated with other known disorders, some of which involve a combination of the previously listed factors, and a number of which are not yet well understood. Funding for basic research into the causes of autism has increased significantly since the 1990s and this will result in improved knowledge about autism over time. Unfortunately, for parents who, understandably, want to know why autism occurred in their child, the current reality is that a particular cause may never be identified.

Related Disorders

As noted previously, autism is the most well-known PDD and is the focus of this chapter. To give the reader an overview, however, this chapter briefly mentions the other PDDs according to the terminology and descriptions provided in the *DSM-IV-TR* (APA, 2000).

Rett's Disorder Rett's Disorder is quite rare (Fombonne, 2003), and it appears to affect females only. Typically, girls with Rett's Disorder (also called Rett syndrome) experience a regression at 6–24 months of age, after a period of apparently typical development. They generally cease making social contact and develop characteristic hand-wringing mannerisms in place of typical hand skills. Severe cognitive disabilities and some physical complications are also associated with the disorder (see Perry, 1991).

Childhood Disintegrative Disorder Children with Childhood Disintegrative Disorder look similar to children with severe autism. This disorder has much later onset, however, with a period of typical development until 3 or 4 years of age (or even later) that is followed by a regression and loss of skills. It is very rare and not well understood (Fombonne, 2003).

Asperger's Disorder People with Asperger's Disorder (also called Asperger syndrome) have many characteristics similar to those of people with autism, but they have relatively intact language and cognitive abilities (i.e., they are higher functioning). The *DSM-IV-TR* criteria specify there must be qualitative impairment in reciprocal social interaction (the same four social criteria that are included in the criteria for Autistic Disorder) and restricted and repetitive interests (also the same four criteria) but no clinically significant difficulties with cognition or language; nonetheless, people with Asperger's Disorder may have great difficulty using their knowledge and speech appropriately in social situations. Asperger's Disorder is fairly uncommon relative to autism, occurring in approximately 2.5 per 10,000 children (Fombonne, 2003). It is often not diagnosed until the child is school-age and the social difficulties become more apparent. There is some controversy among experts about whether people with Asperger's Disorder really differ from those with high-functioning autism (i.e., autism with higher cognitive levels; see Klin, Volkmar, & Sparrow, 2000, for further information). Asperger's Disorder may co-occur with nonverbal learning disabilities, as well as psychiatric diagnoses such as obsessive-compulsive disorder, Tourette's disorder, depression, and anxiety. (See Chapter 13 for more information on Asperger syndrome.)

Pervasive Developmental Disorder-Not Otherwise Specified The term Pervasive Developmental Disorder-Not Otherwise Specified (PDD-NOS) is a rather confusing term that is meant to be used for individuals who are within the overall PDD category but do not meet the criteria for any of the other four disorders (as shown in Figure 12.1, PDD-NOS falls in the space in between the four specific disorders that have already been discussed). In practice, this term is most often used to describe milder or atypical disorders and basically means "mild autism." Sometimes, however, clinicians use the term *PDD-NOS* when the age of onset is late or unclear, when a child is very low functioning and it is difficult to differentially diagnose the autism symptoms relative to developmental level, or when the child is very young (younger than 2 years of age) and a professional is reluctant to give the label of autism. Note that the term *PDD* is not really a diagnosis (it is the general category), but it is sometimes used to mean "PDD-NOS."

There are no official criteria for a diagnosis of PDD-NOS; it is used when the criteria for Autistic Disorder are not quite fulfilled. Sometimes children with PDD-NOS are described as "having autistic-like symptoms," "being developmentally delayed with autistic features," "having autism/PDD," "having autistic tendencies," and so forth. The lack of specific diagnostic criteria is unfortunate, because PDD-NOS seems to be quite common—in fact, more common than Autistic Disorder (Fombonne, 2003). For most practical purposes (e.g., the selection of accommodations or behavior support), however, the distinction between Autistic Disorder and PDD-NOS is not very meaningful. Interventions should be individualized for each person, taking into account his or her particular abilities and disabilities.

Autism Spectrum Disorder To date, the term *Autism Spectrum Disorder (ASD)* does not have *DSM* criteria, but it is being used more frequently to express the idea of a spectrum, or continuum, of symptoms (Wing, 1988). Some people use the term *ASD* to mean all the PDDs, but *ASD* usually means a continuum with Autistic Disorder at the more severe end, PDD-NOS in the middle, and Asperger's Disorder at the milder end. Instead of a group of related disorders within a cate-

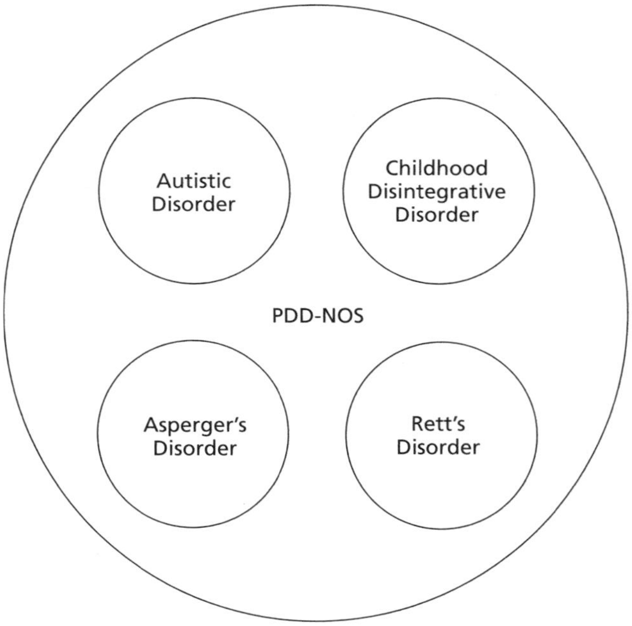

Figure 12.1. Graphic overview of pervasive developmental disorders. (*Key:* PDD-NOS = Pervasive Developmental Disorder-Not Otherwise Specified).

gory (i.e., the *DSM* concept of the PDDs), this spectrum idea suggests there is a continuum of severity regarding symptoms, as well as a range of developmental level. It is important to realize that *ASD* is a much broader concept than *autism*.

INTERVENTION

Autism is generally considered a lifelong disorder. However, better diagnosis, better intervention, and better education programs make a real difference. The future for children with autism in the early 21st century is much more optimistic than was the case in the past. Still, many individuals with autism will continue to need significant supports throughout their lives.

Early Intervention

Behavioral early intervention programs (some of which have been in operation for approximately four decades) have been shown to produce significant improvements in children's cognitive level, language, and ability to function in school. In fact, a significant minority of these children improve so much that they would no longer be said to have autism or a developmental delay (Green, 1996). These children are sometimes described as "recovered" although this term is quite controversial. Other children, especially those who are initially lower functioning, can be expected to improve significantly but not to the same extent.

The most well-known of these behavioral early intervention programs was developed by Lovaas in California in the 1960s. It was the first one established; as of 2007, the first children treated have been followed well into adulthood. The results are very impressive (42% "recovered" or with best outcome). This intervention has been well researched and shown to have good efficacy (although some people have criticized the research). Since the mid-1980s, a number of other programs have been developed along the same lines, and some of these have also carried out research to demonstrate their effectiveness. These programs differ regarding the settings where the intervention takes place (e.g., home-based, clinic-based, school-based), the specific methods used, the specific type of children selected (e.g., certain age, developmental level), and so forth. There is not enough evidence yet to say whether any specific variation is better than any other, but there are certain basic similarities among the effective ones. Common features of these successful programs include the following (based partly on Powers, 1992):

- They begin in the preschool years, usually at age 2–4 years (considerable evidence suggests best outcomes are much more likely if children begin very young).
- They are intensive (often 20–40 hours per week for 1 to 2 years).
- They use structured behavioral teaching principles (reinforcement, task analysis, shaping, repetition, and practice). See Martin & Pear (1999) for a good basic text on these methods.
- They are comprehensive (i.e., they provide teaching in all areas of development including language, play, social skills, academics, self-help skills, and so forth).
- They are individualized (specific goals and methods are individualized based on thorough developmental assessment, as well as the child's strengths and weaknesses and preferences).
- They use highly trained staff and also usually involve parents in the treatment.
- They involve some inclusion with typically developing peers.

Table 12.1 gives some idea of the early stages of a developmentally based curriculum that might provide the sequence of early skills to be taught, even if a child is not yet formally diagnosed with autism. For more specific details and programs, see Koegel and LaZebnik

Table 12.1. Early intervention strategies for parents and therapists

Intervene in social aloofness and self-stimulatory behavior
Work on motivation
Learn to learn
Find effective means of reinforcement (primary at first, if needed)
Teach attending and cooperating
Sitting, looking, following instructions, trying
Teach imitation
Gross motor, fine motor
Oral-motor, vocal
Social, parallel play
Teach pointing
Receptive (pointing response for teaching receptive vocabulary)
Requesting—(shape "autistic leading" into pointing to ask for things)
Pointing to show (joint attention)—(practice with prompts and commenting)
Teach toy play
Means-end toys
Functional use
Symbolic use of toys (i.e., pretend play)
Teach social play
Turn taking
Social interaction games
Practice greetings and routines
Parallel play
Sharing

(2004), Maurice, Green, and Foxx (2001), and Maurice, Green, and Luce (1996).

There has been debate among professionals about the best theoretical background for preschool autism programs. Some have characterized this debate as behavioral versus developmental (NRC, 2001), but clearly both are important. Since the mid-1990s, there has been a gradual coming together and recognition of the similarities across approaches rather than a focus on the differences. Dunlap (1999) suggested four main messages about the current state of the field. First, although there are differences among approaches, there is a growing consensus on critical ingredients in early intervention (e.g., all promote or teach active engagement of the child with other people). Second, very few studies involve direct comparisons of one approach to another with similar children, so it is difficult to say that one theory, approach, or program is better than another in any overall sense. However, it is likely that future research will help establish that certain approaches may be better for certain individual children and families. Third, having acknowledged the lack of comparison studies, it is important to point out that the vast majority of the early intervention programs that have documented evidence of effectiveness are based on principles of applied behavior analysis (ABA). There is great variation, however, in where and how the principles are implemented (e.g., discrete trial training, incidental teaching, pivotal response training, verbal behavior approach). Fourth, it is crucial to consider the family perspective, not only in assessment and goal selection, but also in terms of finding the intervention approach that best suits the family's beliefs, values, and culture and does not inadvertently damage the family by adding stress or undermining parenting.

Even with the best early intervention, however, the majority of children with autism will not improve enough to function without supports in school and in adult life. Older children and adults can still continue to benefit from a similar approach involving structured teaching and individualized goals in a comprehensive range of areas of functioning (Howlin, 1997; Smith 1990). Teaching vocational skills and life skills becomes more important as individuals with autism get older. These skills need to be learned and applied in a variety of environments. In addition, some other characteristics of autism have implications for intervention with older children and adults. The next sections briefly examine some of these characteristics.

Educational Intervention

Children and adolescents with autism have a right to an "appropriate" education in many places. However, there is considerable variability in different countries, states, and provinces regarding the resources and expertise available, the philosophical approaches among and within different school districts, the legislative and appeals processes, and so forth. Children with autism certainly present a challenge to educational systems, but it is important to remember that they are, first and foremost, students who need to be taught. All of the specialized interventions and treatments that may be needed are really just specialized ways of teaching children what they need to know to grow and develop.

As with the other forms of intervention discussed in this chapter, educational programming should be evidence-based and effective. Compared with the early intervention literature, there is not the same body of research literature and consensus panels to guide educators and others working with school-age individuals with autism. However, hundreds of small studies have looked at specific intervention approaches to teach specific skills to individuals or small groups of children and adolescents. Iovannone, Dunlap, Huber, et al. (2003) reviewed the literature regarding effective educational practices for children with ASD older than age 5 and formulated six core elements that are evidence-based and that should be included in a comprehensive educational intervention program for any student with autism. Programs should 1) be individualized, 2) be systematic, 3) be structured, 4) have specific autism-related curriculum goals, 5) use positive behavior support, and 6) involve families. Each of these is discussed next.

Individualized Effective supports should be individualized. Given the individual differences among students with autism in terms of the previously described symptoms and characteristics, as well as behaviors and functioning level, it stands to reason that educational programs need to be individually tailored to suit each child, not the label of autism. Furthermore, individualization needs to take into account the student's likes and dislikes, strengths and weaknesses, and motivation. In part, this means instructional materials and tasks should be interesting to the student, perhaps tapping into his or her particular interests or strengths (e.g., for a child who loves puzzles, use a map puzzle to learn geography).

Appropriate individualized motivational systems (i.e., reinforcement) are crucial to help children with autism learn. Reinforcement does not just mean using candies to reward correct responses. It could include check marks or stickers for correct answers in written work, frequent praise for working quietly without disruptive behavior, hugs and tickles for a spontaneous social initiative, and effective use of activity reinforcers and treats. Also, giving students certain choices among activities, or choices of reinforcers to work for, assists

Photo courtesy of MukiBaum Treatment Centres (http://www.mukibaum.com).

with motivation for task-related behavior and minimizes problem behavior.

People with autism may have difficulty paying attention or paying attention to the things that others find relevant (e.g., they may pay attention to a small, irrelevant detail in a picture and "miss the big picture"). They may have difficulty processing multiple cues at the same time (e.g., the shape of puzzle pieces and the pattern on the pieces). They may have trouble shifting their attention from one thing to another. It sometimes helps to have a child with autism point to what he or she is expected to look at or to move the child's whole body to get the child to attend to something new. It is often necessary to remind an individual with autism to look at what he or she is doing (e.g., during dressing tasks).

In some cases, "sensory issues" need to be taken into account in planning intervention programs. People with autism may be unusually over- or undersensitive to sensory input, such as certain sounds or textures. Individuals with autism also may have trouble processing two senses at the same time. They may use sensations to soothe themselves, decrease anxiety, or gain a sense of control of their world. Working effectively with a person with autism requires knowing the person well and taking into account potential sensory preferences and sensitivities.

Systematic Effective educational intervention is systematic—that is, carefully planned and structured, as well as constantly evaluated and modified based on data. Most of the published literature reviewed by Iovannone et al. (2003) is based on principles derived from ABA, but these studies can be very different from each other in terms of specific methodologies. They include such diverse approaches as self-management training to promote independent academic work, in vivo training to teach grocery shopping skills, and discrete trial training to teach academic skills. All involve data collection and analysis. It may be difficult to collect certain kinds of data in school settings (e.g., the trial-by-trial data that are often used in preschool programs), but it is important that there are adequate data on the child's skills to answer questions such as, "How do you know he has learned *blue?*" "When do we move on to the next set of reading words?" and "Has she mastered appropriate greetings?" There should be enough data to make data-based decisions.

Structured Children with autism need a structured environment. That means the structure of the day (or of a task or lesson) is predictable and understandable for the student. A number of supportive strategies may be helpful, such as providing pictorial schedules, visual cues for a task sequence, warnings before transitions to new tasks or environments, and so forth. Many—but not all—people with autism respond well to visual cues and teaching aids. Pictures are especially useful because they can be used to prompt an activity (e.g., matching cutlery to an outline on the table to teach how to set the table), to provide helpful structure and predictability (e.g., having a picture activity schedule of the tasks expected of the person over the day), and to help break a task down into easier to understand steps (e.g., following pictures of the sequence for making a sandwich). Pictures can also help people be more independent if they can use the pictures to cue themselves rather than waiting for someone to remind them verbally what to do next.

Specific Autism-Related Curriculum Goals Within the individualized approach, there should be a functional curriculum that addresses the specific characteristics of autism. This means there should be explicit teaching of social and communication skills that are meaningful and useful for the child's life. Social abilities are crucial in all aspects of life, so a child with autism is at a particular disadvantage. Sometimes very basic social skills (e.g., taking turns) and specific social skills (e.g., asking other children to join in a game) must be taught and practiced in real-life settings, including in school and at home. The nature of the specific instructional targets may vary a great deal depending on the child.

Improving communication skills is likely to be a goal for all people with autism, regardless of their age or functioning level. For people with good verbal skills, intervention focuses on reciprocal conversation skills and social routines to help the person use his or her speech for social communication purposes. For individuals with few or no verbal abilities, there are various other means of communication, known collectively as augmentative and alternative communication (AAC). AAC approaches include nonsymbolic gestures (e.g., leading someone by the hand to obtain a desired object), learned cultural gestures (e.g., waving), and formal systems of symbolic gestures (i.e., sign language). Sign language can be helpful at times, as long as people in the environment understand what the person with autism is signing. There are also various graphic systems including miniature objects, photographs, drawings, symbols, and printed words. These are classified as low-technology (e.g., carrying a wallet of pictures to use for requesting desired objects) or high-technology (e.g., using a computerized speech synthesizer that says words when certain keys are pressed). Different communication systems have different advantages and disadvantages for different people with autism (in terms of their portability, flexibility, appeal to the child, cost, effectiveness, understandability to unfamiliar others, and so forth). Parents sometimes worry that learning one of these other systems will discourage their children's development of speech. In fact, the opposite is true—the Picture Exchange Communication System (PECS; Bondy & Frost, 1994) and sign language not only help children communicate their needs at the time but also may help children to speak later as well (Mirenda & Erickson, 2000). See also Chapter 25.

It is important to remember, however, that finding the one best system is not likely to suddenly make a nonverbal person with autism able to communicate at a sophisticated level. The real goal is not so much to increase vocabulary or teach the rules of grammar; rather, it is for people with autism to learn to communicate about things that are relevant in their lives and in ways that are effective in their environments. For example, it is more important (and more functional) for a child to be able to request a drink when thirsty (using a sign or picture) than to be able to name 100 flash cards of obscure objects.

Positive Behavior Support Effective school-based intervention includes a functional approach to understanding a child's problem behavior. Some people with autism may exhibit severe problem behaviors, such as tantrums, aggression, destruction, and self-injurious behavior. These behaviors are not part of the definition of autism, but they may be related to level of functioning and difficulties with communicating, adapting to change, and understanding social situations. Thus, helping students with these problems is a crucial part of their educational program. Some methods for addressing these behaviors have been quite controversial. It was once believed best to try to eliminate such behavior by using punishment, extinction, or medication. Fortunately, methods of assessment and intervention for problem behaviors have improved considerably since the mid-1980s, a great deal of research has accumulated, and practices and even policies and legislation have changed in some places.

The overall approach that is now recommended is known as *positive behavior support* (PBS; see Jackson & Panyan, 2002; Koegel, Koegel, & Dunlap, 1996). First, it is important to rule out any medical issues (e.g., a child who is biting his hand may have a toothache, an adolescent who bangs the side of her head may have an earache). Also, the environment and the nature of the schoolwork that is being asked of a child need to be examined. Is the classroom too loud and distracting? Are the tasks too boring or too difficult for the student? Sometimes, it is quite easy to prevent the problem behavior by attending to these environmental factors. If the behavior persists, a behavior support plan may need to be developed and it should be based on the concept of a functional assessment (or functional behavioral assessment). Note that the term *functional* is used here in a slightly different way than it was previously used in the chapter. In this case, it refers to the function of the behavior or why the behavior is happening. Challenging behaviors do not happen "out of the blue"; it is the responsibility of professionals and support providers to figure out the reason(s) why they occur. For example, is it the only way the person has of getting something that he or she wants? Is it an effective way for the person to avoid an activity that he or she does not like? Has the behavior been reinforced by other people's attention? Once the function of the behavior is determined, an intervention plan to reduce or change it can be designed. Many classroom-based strategies can be used, but one of the most important principles is to teach the person alternative behaviors and skills to use instead of the problem behavior (e.g., teaching a person to sign BREAK, teaching a person to raise his or her hand to get the teacher's attention). Also, there are a variety of positive reinforcement-based approaches that involve differentially reinforcing the absence of the problem behavior (i.e., paying attention to a person when he or she is behaving appropriately), reinforcing the presence of the new replacement skill (e.g., "Oh, good, you raised your hand—I'll be right there"), reinforcing other incompatible behaviors (e.g., putting hands in pockets instead of flapping hands), and so forth. Ultimately, the goal is for the natural environment (peers, school personnel) to take over reinforcing appropriate behavior so that it becomes natural. See Chapter 24 and Martin and Pear (1999) for more detail.

Family Involvement Active family involvement is crucial to the effectiveness of educational intervention. Parents should be involved in assessing and determining goals for a child's individual learning plan, should have input into the methods and motivational strategies used (they have often discovered the best strategies already), and could help determine progress (e.g., by reporting how well skills are generalized to the home setting). There should be frequent communication between home and school. In some cases, parents can supplement the teaching at home by either helping the child practice specific skills or by doing informal generalization (e.g., helping the child use a skill in a different setting and with different people). The transitions of going to school for the first time, progressing to a new school, and moving from school to postschool adult life are often very stressful for families, and everyone involved needs to work together respectfully. Having a child with autism is one of the hardest things that can happen to a family, and even families that generally cope well struggle at times. For a summary of family needs and issues at different family life cycle stages, see Perry and Condillac (2003); see also Chapter 35 in this book. For more information about families and positive behavior support, see Lucyshyn, Dunlap, and Albin (2002), a book written about and with parents.

New and Controversial Approaches

In the autism field, new treatment methods tend to spring up regularly. Valid new treatments and techniques may be found, and it is necessary to keep an open mind, as well as maintain an appropriate level of hope about the futures of people with autism. It is important, however, for parents and professionals to be both optimistic and realistic. Parents and others who care about children and adults with autism naturally wish that a cure would be found; as a result, they are tempted to try these new approaches and are vulnerable to being disappointed when they turn out to be ineffective or even harmful in some cases.

The previously described early intervention programs and educational programs require considerable effort, time, and money. They do not offer quick fixes but have been proven over time. It is important to learn how to check out the next "miracle cure" that comes along. The following are points to keep in mind and questions to ask regarding controversial or unproven treatment techniques (based partly on Freeman, 1997, and on Green, 1996):

- Be open minded but skeptical; do not rush to try every new approach.
- Ask about the theory behind the approach and decide whether it makes sense based on what is known about autism.
- Ask what research has been done to demonstrate its effectiveness.
- Beware if the approach is being promoted as a miracle, a "cure," or a breakthrough.
- Beware if the approach is claimed to work for everyone and/or is implemented the same way for everyone (rather than being based on an individualized assessment).
- Ask whether the approach is monitored and changed regularly based on some form of data.
- Ask what harm the approach could do, and what side effects or risks might be possible.
- Ask who is qualified to provide the treatment and/or what training and supervision the person receives.
- Consider the costs in money, time, and energy to the person with autism, his or her family, and any professionals or paraprofessionals who work with the person.
- Do a risk–benefit analysis taking all of the preceding points into consideration.
- Do not discontinue other approaches known to be beneficial if a new approach is tried as well, and try to evaluate the new approach's effectiveness systematically.

Some of the approaches that have gone through this cycle and been discredited include facilitated communication, patterning, Gentle Teaching, and secretin injections. Other current approaches that have caused excitement but do not yet have enough evidence regarding effectiveness include the Miller method, floor time, auditory training, sensory integration, and the gluten- and casein-free diet. For a review of the scientific evidence on a number of therapies, see Perry and Condillac (2003) and the New York State Department of Health's guidelines (1999).

LARGE SYSTEMS CHALLENGES

Autism presents a conspicuous challenge to educational, social service, and health care systems. Families, professionals, and policy makers alike struggle with several issues (Dunlap & Fox, 2004). First, the increasing prevalence and broader understanding of ASDs is putting tremendous pressure on the whole service system. Second, there is a heightened level of parental advocacy, litigation, and demand for services that are appropriate and effective. Third, in many jurisdictions there are new regulations or policies that begin to address these issues, and even considerable new financial resources in some cases, but the capacity building required is slow to happen (i.e., large-scale recruiting and training, spreading of knowledge about autism throughout the system, and so forth). Systems need to address several very important issues in the near future; these are discussed in the remainder of this section.

Assessment and Diagnosis

Assessment and diagnosis of autism (and related disorders) often happens late and is approached inconsistently in different places. There are excellent centers in some locations (usually in large urban hospitals) and very limited resources in others. Some professionals are not well informed about autism and may hesitate to label young children with the disorder. Families may travel long distances, go through misdiagnoses, receive apparently contradictory diagnoses, and long waiting periods. Even when a correct diagnosis of autism is given in a timely fashion, the child's developmental assessment is often inadequate. Given the progress that has been made in articulating best practices for assessment and diagnosis of autism (Filipek et al., 1999; NRC, 2001; Perry et al., 2002), systems must be adequately funded and organized to conduct comprehensive multidisciplinary assessments that result in early and accurate diagnoses, and these assessments should feed directly into early intervention programs. In some locales, this will require greater cooperation across professions and across funding sources (e.g., funding for health, funding for education) than exists as of 2007.

Intervention

In terms of intervention, systems must be structured to be both comprehensive and flexible. They must allow for the wide range of needs of children, adolescents, and adults with autism and their families. No one particular model (e.g., a certain specialized autism classroom) is going to be appropriate for all children with autism because they differ so much from one another. Rather, a range of evidence-based approaches, individually tailored to each child, is needed, and systems have to be suitably organized to deliver interventions with this in mind.

Cooperation, Collaboration, and Continuity

There needs to be greater cooperation, collaboration, and continuity across systems and agencies, and there should be less debate about whose responsibility it is to deliver services. From the family's point of view, the arbitrary divisions among services by diagnostic label, age, or particular symptom are often nonsensical and inefficient. Because a family must deal with many different services, agencies, and schools, there are many transition points in the lives of children with autism and their families; the number and difficulty of these transitions should be reduced whenever possible. Given that not all changes can be avoided, transition planning must be addressed more systematically and at an earlier time.

Shortage of Services for Adults

In many jurisdictions, services for adults with autism are in particularly short supply. There is a shortage of appropriate day programs, vocational programs, and meaningful work for these adults in most communities. Parents of these individuals are often exhausted from fighting the system for years to receive adequate services. Adults with autism (as well as some adolescents and children) may require residential placement outside the family home at some point. There are shortages of spaces and long wait lists for these placements in many cases.

Information

Information about autism, interventions, local service systems, and supports for families is crucial. Since the mid-1990s or so, great progress has been made in some locations. In many areas, however, families flounder with misinformation or lack of information. The Internet can be both a blessing and a curse in this respect. It is important to help families (and staff) critically evaluate such information.

Family Support Services

Some family support services, particularly service coordination (sometimes called case management) and respite care, are in short supply. Service coordination, which is important to help families navigate the system, is complex and poorly integrated in many locales. Respite offers parents a reprieve, as those qualified to work with people who have disabilities such as autism are able to provide temporary care. There is a need for greater funding for in-home respite and more out-of-home respite spaces that accept children with autism.

Integration of Intervention for Challenging Behavior and Skill Development

Intervention for challenging behavior must be integrated with a skill development focus into the overall program for a person with autism. The differences among treatment, education, therapy, intervention, and rehabilitation are purely semantic. For example, if a child engages in problem behavior (e.g., aggression) when frustrated while doing difficult school work, the "treatment" of the problem behavior cannot be divorced from the "teaching" of appropriate communication skills. Terminology is not as important as action.

Well-Trained Personnel

Well-trained personnel are needed at all levels of the service system. Even a hundred-fold multiplication of existing financial resources would not overcome the reality that there is a critical shortage of trained professionals. (See the NRC, 2001, recommendations regarding training of teachers and support staff in the education system.) Senior-level clinicians who can offer supervision of early intervention programs and consultation to school and adult programs are also in short supply. Greater numbers of such individuals are needed as soon as possible, because it takes at least a decade to train and mentor these professionals.

Professional Organizations

To fill the gap provided by the large service demand, some positions are filled by people with less than optimal training. This has resulted, in part, in professional organizations proposing standards for consumers to use in choosing professionals (e.g., see Autism Special Interest Group, 2004). Other organizations are promoting a formal certification process that ensures consumers and employers that at least core behavioral content has been mastered (e.g., http://www.bacb.com), although it may not be specific to autism.

SUMMARY

Autism is a PDD involving severe difficulties in social relationships, severe difficulties in communication, and unusual repetitive behaviors. In addition, most people with autism also have an intellectual and/or developmental disability. People with autism differ from one another a great deal depending on their age, level of functioning, and particular symptoms. Autism is a biological disorder, but there is probably no single cause. Rather, there may be different subgroups with different causes.

For young children, intensive behavioral early intervention programs can make a significant difference. Older children may continue to need comprehensive, structured intervention and education. It is important to give people with autism functional communication systems and to take their attention and sensory difficulties into account when designing intervention. Problem behaviors need to be well understood and addressed carefully, based on a functional approach. New and controversial treatments should be approached with a healthy skepticism. Families of people with autism have many challenges to face and may

FOR FURTHER THOUGHT AND DISCUSSION

1. Select one of the treatment approaches currently being used in the field of autism. Explain this approach and evaluate its effectiveness.
2. Tim is 3 years old. His mother says he was "a good baby." In fact, he seemed more contented when left alone. Tim's mother recalls that he neither smiled nor seemed to recognize her when he was a young infant. He walked at 9 months of age and has always been very agile, rarely falling or hurting himself. He has not yet begun to speak and does not yet dress or feed himself. Both of Tim's parents report that he does not seem to be interested in their love and affection. His lack of speech and responsiveness continue along with an increase in unusual behaviors. He spends much of the day fascinated with lint, which he throws in the air and then watches intently as it falls to the floor. He also licks the back of his hands and stares at the saliva. The family doctor is concerned about Tim's developmental delays and has referred Tim to an early intervention program. Assume that you are the early intervention worker who has been assigned to work with Tim and his family and consider the following:
   - Which aspects of Tim's behavior are consistent with the diagnosis of Autistic Disorder? What steps would you take to ensure he gets a complete and accurate diagnosis?
   - What issues do you think the family might face as they receive a diagnosis of Tim's disorder? What supports would you provide for the family in response to the issues identified? Be specific.
   - Would you begin to work with Tim before he had received a formal diagnosis? Explain your answer.
   - Which areas of Tim's functioning would you work on? Detail some specific strategies that might be used to enhance Tim's functioning in each of these areas.
3. For many individuals diagnosed with Autistic Disorder, the prognosis is poor. Many families initially raise their children with autism at home. Others, however, seek out-of-home placement for their children. What factors do you think might prevent a family seeking out-of-home care for their children and why? What supports and services do you think families require to continue raising their children at home and why?
4. Some people view autism as an illness from which people can recover. Yet, intellectual disability tends to be seen as an unchanging characteristic. Do you agree with these positions? Why or why not? Is it justified to spend more money treating children with autism than providing intervention for children with other intellectual or developmental disabilities?

need a variety of supports. In addition, autism presents a number of significant challenges to large systems.

No doubt, these are formidable challenges. Yet, the early 21st century is also a time of exciting opportunities—opportunities to make a very real difference in the lives of individuals with autism and their families; students, paraprofessionals, and professionals in the human services field; and with policy makers and legislators. The autism field has come a long way, but there is still a long way to go.

REFERENCES

American Psychiatric Association. (2000). *Diagnostic and statistical manual of mental disorders* (4th ed., text rev.). Washington, DC: Author.

Autism Special Interest Group, Association for Behavior Analysis. (2004). *Revised Guidelines for consumers of applied behavior analysis services to individuals with autism and related disorders.* Retrieved April 20, 2006, from http://www.abainternational.org/sub/membersvcs/sig/contactinfo/Autism.asp

Bondy, A., & Frost, L. (1994). The Picture Exchange Communication System. *Focus on Autistic Behavior, 9,* 1–19.

Dunlap, G. (1999). Consensus, engagement, and family involvement for young children with autism. *Journal of The Association for People with Severe Handicaps, 24,* 222–225.

Dunlap, G., & Fox, L. (2004). *The challenge of autism from a large systems perspective.* Manuscript submitted for publication.

Filipek, P.A., Accardo, P.J., Baranek, G.T., et al. (1999). The screening and diagnosis of autism spectrum disorders. *Journal of Autism and Developmental Disorders, 29,* 439–484.

Fombonne, E. (2003). Epidemiological surveys of autism and other pervasive developmental disorders: An update. *Journal of Autism and Developmental Disorders, 33,* 365–382.

Freeman, B.J. (1997). Guidelines for evaluating intervention programs for children with autism. *Journal of Autism and Developmental Disorders, 27,* 641–651.

Gillberg, C., & Coleman, M. (2000). *The biology of the autistic syndromes* (3rd ed.). London: Mac Keith Press.

Glidden, L.M. (Ed.). (2001). *International Review of Research in Mental Retardation: Vol. 23. Autism.* San Diego: Academic Press.

Green, G. (1996). Early behavioral intervention for autism: What does the research tell us? In C. Maurice, G. Green & S.C. Luce (Eds.), *Behavioral intervention for young children with autism: A manual for parents and professionals* (pp. 29–44). Austin, TX: PRO-ED.

Howlin, P. (1997). *Autism: Preparing for adulthood.* London: Routledge.

Iovannone, R., Dunlap, G., Huber, H., et al. (2003). Effective educational practices for students with autism spectrum disorders. *Focus on Autism and Other Developmental Disabilities, 18,* 150–165.

Jackson, L., & Panyan, M.V. (2002). *Positive behavioral support in the classroom: Principles and practices.* Baltimore: Paul H. Brookes Publishing Co.

Kanner, L. (1943). Autistic disturbances of affective contact. *Nervous Child, 2,* 217–250.

Klin, A., Volkmar, F.R., & Sparrow, S.S. (Eds.). (2000). *Asperger syndrome.* New York: The Guilford Press.

Koegel, L.K., Koegel, R.L., & Dunlap, G. (Eds.). (1996). *Positive behavioral support: Including people with difficult behavior in the community.* Baltimore: Paul H. Brookes Publishing Co.

Koegel, L.K., & LaZebnik, C. (2004). *Overcoming autism: Finding the answers, strategies, and hope that can transform a child's life.* New York: Viking.

Lucyshyn, J.M., Dunlap, G., & Albin, R.W. (Eds.). (2002). *Families and positive behavior support: Addressing problem behaviors in family contexts.* Baltimore: Paul H. Brookes Publishing Co.

Martin, G., & Pear, J. (1999). *Behavior modification: What it is and how to do it* (6th ed.). Upper Saddle River, NJ: Prentice Hall.

Maurice, C., Green, G., & Foxx, R.M. (Eds.). (2001). *Making a difference: Behavioral intervention for autism.* Austin, TX: PRO-ED.

Maurice, C., Green, G., & Luce, S.C. (Eds.). (1996). *Behavioral intervention for young children with autism: A manual for parents and professionals.* Austin, TX: PRO-ED.

Mirenda, P., & Erickson, K.A. (2000). Augmentative communication and literacy. In Warren & J. Reichle (Series Eds.) & A.M. Wetherby & B.M. Prizant (Vol. Eds.), *Communication and Language Intervention Series: Vol. 9. Autism spectrum disorders: A transactional developmental approach* (pp. 333–367). Baltimore: Paul H. Brookes Publishing Co.

National Research Council. (2001). *Educating children with autism.* Washington, DC: National Academies Press.

New York State Department of Health. (1999). *Autism/pervasive developmental disorders: Clinical practice guideline technical report.* New York: Author.

Perry, A. (1991). Rett syndrome: A comprehensive review of the literature. *American Journal on Mental Retardation, 96,* 275–290.

Perry, A., & Black, A. (2003). Autism. In I. Brown & M. Percy (Eds.), *Developmental disabilities in Ontario* (pp. 281–293). Toronto: Ontario Association on Developmental Disabilities.

Perry, A., & Condillac, R.A. (2003). *Evidence-based practices for children and adolescents with autism spectrum disorders: Review of the literature and practice guide.* Toronto: Children's Mental Health Ontario.

Perry, A., Condillac, R.A., & Freeman, N.L. (2002). Best practices and practical strategies for assessment and diagnosis of autism. *Journal on Developmental Disabilities, 9*(2), 61–75.

Powers, M.D. (1992). Early intervention for children with autism. In D.E. Berkell (Ed.), *Autism: Identification, education, and treatment* (pp. 225–252). Mahwah, NJ: Lawrence Erlbaum Associates.

Sattler, J.M. (2002). *Assessment of children: Behavioral and clinical applications* (4th ed.). San Diego: Author.

Smith, M.D. (1990). *Autism and life in the community: Successful interventions for behavioral challenges.* Baltimore: Paul H. Brookes Publishing Co.

Tanguay, P.E. (2000). Pervasive developmental disorders: A 10-year review. *Journal of the American Academy of Child and Adolescent Psychiatry, 39,* 1079–1095.

Wing, L. (1988). The continuum of autistic disorders. In E. Schopler & G.B. Mesibov (Eds.), *Diagnosis and assessment in autism* (pp. 91–110). New York: Kluwer Academic/ Plenum Publishers.

Wing, L., & Potter, D. (2002). The epidemiology of autistic spectrum disorders: Is the prevalence rising? *Mental Retardation and Developmental Disabilities Research Reviews, 8,* 151–161.

13

Asperger Syndrome

Kevin P. Stoddart

> **WHAT YOU WILL LEARN ABOUT IN THIS CHAPTER**
>
> - Traits of Asperger syndrome
> - Assessment
> - Prevalence and etiology
> - Asperger syndrome across the life span
> - Areas for future consideration

Asperger syndrome is a relatively new diagnosis in the field of developmental disabilities. Because it was not included until the fourth edition of the *Diagnostic and Statistical Manual of Mental Disorders* (*DSM-IV;* American Psychiatric Association [APA], 1994), information sharing with students, parents and professionals is a primary task of those working with affected individuals. This chapter provides an introduction to the syndrome's cluster of symptoms. First, the traits of Asperger syndrome are summarized; then, discussions of assessment, prevalence, and etiology are provided. The chapter also provides information about Asperger syndrome across the life span and notes areas for future consideration.

TRAITS OF ASPERGER SYNDROME

Interest in Asperger syndrome grew throughout the 1980s following the publication of a paper by Wing (1981) in the United Kingdom. Subsequently, Frith (1991) published a book on the topic, which included the English translation of Hans Asperger's seminal 1944 paper "'Autistic Psychopathy' in Childhood." In the 1990s, Szatmari and colleagues further suggested that key characteristics of Asperger syndrome included solitary behavior, impaired social interaction, impaired nonverbal communication, and odd speech (Szatmari, 1991, 1992; Szatmari, Bremner, & Nagy, 1989).

In the *DSM-IV* (APA, 1994), diagnostic criteria for Asperger's Disorder[1] were first included in the section on Pervasive Developmental Disorders (PDDs). As noted in Chapter 12, other PDDs include Autistic Disorder, Rett's Disorder, Childhood Disintegrative Disorder, and Pervasive Developmental Disorder-Not Otherwise Specified. (See Display 13.1 for the Asperger's Disorder criteria as they appear in the *Diagnostic and Statistical Manual of Men-tal Disorders, Fourth Edition, Text Revision*; APA, 2000). Debate and research continue regarding which characteristics should be included, and how they should be articulated, in the diagnostic criteria for Asperger syndrome. One question is whether Asperger syndrome is different from high-functioning autism. Two characteristics distinguish the two disorders: 1) delayed language development in people with autism but not in people with Asperger syndrome and 2) average or above-average intellectual abilities in individuals with Asperger syndrome.

ASSESSMENT

The method of assessment and diagnosis of Asperger syndrome depends on the age of the individual being assessed, the assessor's experience with the diagnosis, and the assessor's profession. This section focuses on the age of the individual to provide a general overview of the assessment process.

When conducting a diagnostic assessment of a school-age child, a clinician will inquire about the presence of key features that suggest Asperger syndrome, as defined in the *DSM-IV-TR* (APA, 2000). It is important to note that some symptoms are not included in diagnostic criteria for Asperger syndrome, and these symptoms overlap considerably with other disorders (see Table 13.1).

The foundation for all good assessments is a thorough clinical interview with the person being assessed and with others familiar with the individual. The format and style of the interview with a child depends on his or her willingness to engage with the clinician, the child's age, and the time allotted for the interview. The observational skills of the assessor are important, especially if the child is young or tends not to respond to direct questioning. The most revealing aspects are the child's ability to interact socially, the child's use of

[1] The APA uses the term *Asperger's Disorder;* however, the more commonly used term *Asperger syndrome* appears throughout this chapter.

Display 13.1

Diagnostic Criteria for 299.80 Asperger's Disorder

A. Qualitative impairment in social interaction, as manifested by at least two of the following:
   (1) marked impairment in the use of multiple nonverbal behaviors such as eye-to-eye gaze, facial expression, body postures, and gestures to regulate social interaction
   (2) failure to develop peer relationships appropriate to developmental level
   (3) a lack of spontaneous seeking to share enjoyment, interests, or achievements with other people (e.g., by a lack of showing, bringing, or pointing out objects of interest to other people)
   (4) lack of social or emotional reciprocity

B. Restricted, repetitive, and stereotyped patterns of behavior, interests, and activities, as manifested by at least one of the following:
   (1) encompassing preoccupation with one or more stereotyped and restricted patterns of interest that is abnormal either in intensity or focus
   (2) apparently inflexible adherence to specific, non-functional routines or rituals
   (3) stereotyped and repetitive motor mannerisms (e.g., hand or finger flapping or twisting, or complex whole-body movements)
   (4) persistent preoccupation with parts of objects

C. The disturbance causes clinically significant impairment in social, occupational, or other important areas of functioning.

D. There is no clinically significant general delay in language (e.g., single words used by age 2 years, communicative phrases used by age 3 years).

E. There is no clinically significant delay in cognitive development or in the development of age-appropriate self-help skills, adaptive behavior (other than in social interaction), and curiosity about the environment in childhood.

F. Criteria are not met for another specific Pervasive Developmental Disorder or Schizophrenia.

Table 13.1. Symptoms that may coexist with Asperger syndrome

Attentional problems
Depression
Anxiety
Tics or Tourette syndrome
Fine and gross motor problems
Sensory sensitivities
Speech and language differences (poor pragmatic communication)
Eating problems
Poor sleep patterns
Non-verbal learning disability

play materials, the content and style of the child's language and communication, and his or her behavior. For example, a child with Asperger syndrome may engage in repetitive and unusual play patterns (e.g., he or she lines up all the toy cars and resists the assessor's attempts to use them creatively). Assessment of an older child or adolescent suspected of having Asperger syndrome is based more on verbal interview. Often, youth with Asperger syndrome are expressive and well spoken, which facilitates this method of assessment. Youth with Asperger syndrome may present deceivingly well in a structured interview, however, causing assessors to mistakenly believe these individuals do not meet diagnostic criteria. Their problems with the use of language and social interaction may not be revealed unless an informal and less structured exchange with the assessor or an in-depth interview with the parents occurs.

Schnurr (2004a, 2004b) recommended that 11 major areas of content be addressed in the parent interview when engaging in a diagnostic assessment of a child:

1. Transitions and changes
2. Friends
3. Social behavior
4. Sensory sensitivities
5. Routines
6. Special interests and exceptional skills
7. School
8. Communication skills
9. Early developmental history
10. Motor skills
11. Family history

The family interview is often complemented by discussion with others such as teachers or other school personnel. Review of any past assessments is also helpful. Psychological testing, which may include an assessment of intellectual abilities, may be a part of some assessments.

Diagnostic assessment of adults is most commonly carried out with the individual suspected of having Asperger syndrome as the main informant. Obtaining additional information from family members or friends is also helpful, as the adult may not be aware of the problems he or she exhibits in social interactions or relationships. Features associated with Asperger syndrome are explored in detail; however, the features seen in adults may be more apparent and longstanding. In addition, experience with identifying this syndrome is still in its formative stages, and the symptoms in adults have not yet been fully articulated. For these reasons, even clinicians who are familiar with the diagnostic criteria may not recognize symptoms of Asperger syndrome in adults.

Specific instruments have been developed that target the features of Asperger syndrome. This approach is an emerging area of research, however, so some of the tools developed to assess other PDDs may be helpful in assessing a child for Asperger syndrome. These tools need to be used as an adjunct to the clinical interview and clinician judgment, and should not be used alone for assessment. Campbell (2005); Goodlin-Jones and Solomon (2003); O'Brien, Pearson, Berney, and Barnard (2001); and Howlin (2000) provided summaries and critiques of assessment tools for autism spectrum disorders (ASDs) and Asperger syndrome.

PREVALENCE AND ETIOLOGY

The rate of diagnosis of PDDs, including Asperger syndrome, has been increasing since the 1990s. This is because there is greater recognition of PDDs. Due to advances in professional and public education and greater amounts of information in the media, clinicians and the public are beginning to develop a greater awareness of Asperger syndrome. In turn, people who once would have been considered "eccentric" are recognized as having higher-functioning presentations of PDDs, such as Asperger syndrome. Much work remains to be done in raising awareness of this syndrome, however. Unfortunately, individuals of all ages may have difficulty obtaining the correct diagnosis. When they do, they may have difficulty obtaining the services that they require, as service providers may not be abreast of these individuals' need for intervention and supports.

Given that the importance of Asperger syndrome has only recently been identified, little prevalence research has been conducted. In Göteborg, Sweden, a screening of children between the ages of 7 and 16 suggested a minimum prevalence rate of 3.6 per 1,000 children and a male to female ratio of 4:1. When suspected and possible cases were included, the prevalence rose to 7.1 per 1,000 children, and the male to female ratio dropped to 2.3:1 (Ehlers & Gillberg, 1993). Fombonne (2003) reviewed 32 epidemiological surveys of PDDs published between 1966 and 2001. He suggested that for all PDDs, the prevalence rate is from 30 per 10,000 to 60 per 10,000 children and that a conservative rate for Asperger syndrome is 2.5 per 10,000. This figure is based on rates of Asperger syndrome identified in six epidemiological studies of PDDs.

As early as 1944, Hans Asperger noted that the parents and children he observed shared certain characteristics. Asperger's contributions were precedent setting because he suggested that the syndrome was genetic rather than psychogenic in origin. Scientific evidence since the late 20th century supports the view of a complex genetic role in PDDs, with at least several susceptibility genes acting together. (The International Molecular Genetic Study of Autism, 1998, 2001). In a genome-wide scan for loci of Asperger syndrome, linkage was observed on nine chromosomal regions (Ylisaukko-oja et al., 2004). Exploration of a genetic etiology does not, however, rule out the possibility of biological and/or environmental contributions.

Other theories have been proposed to account for some of the deficits seen in individuals with Asperger syndrome and other PDDs. For example, Ellis and Gunter (1999) proposed that in Asperger syndrome there is a right-hemisphere brain dysfunction, as is nonverbal learning disability. As support for their argument, Ellis and Gunter pointed out that many people with Asperger syndrome have deficits recognizing faces, understanding humor, and carrying out motor functions—all of which are right hemisphere functions. Deficits in theory of mind (the ability to imagine and understand the thoughts, perspectives, and feelings of others; Baron-Cohen, 1995), central coherence (the ability to derive meaning from seeing the parts and understand how they relate to the whole; Frith, 1989), and executive function (the ability to maintain an appropriate problem-solving set to meet a goal; Ozonoff, 1995) have also been presented as explanations for the traits seen in individuals with Asperger syndrome.

ASPERGER SYNDROME ACROSS THE LIFE SPAN

Asperger syndrome may be diagnosed as early as the preschool years. The following sections discuss characteristics of the syndrome throughout the various stages of life.

Preschoolers

Preschoolers with Asperger syndrome may appear odd in their behavior or seem like "little professors." However, these characteristics may be thought to be too mild for a diagnosis of autism, the most familiar of the PDDs. This mild presentation of symptoms may delay a diagnosis of Asperger syndrome, as some professionals may be unfamiliar with the entire range of functioning in this spectrum of disorders (see Display 13.2). Screening tests for young children with Asperger syndrome are still in developmental stages.

Preschoolers with Asperger syndrome may exhibit unusual language development. For example, parents often report that the first words their children say are related to their particular interests rather than to people. These children may learn language in rote ways, such as continually repeating verbatim dialogues from their favorite cartoons. If there is interaction with other children, it tends to be parallel rather than cooperative in nature. That is, children with Asperger syndrome often play alongside other children rather than engaging in the give and take of play. Children with Asperger syndrome may also play with another child by directing the child in their own interests, not taking into consideration the interests of their playmate.

It is most important to ensure that a preschooler who has been identified as having Asperger syndrome is involved with typically developing peers as much as possible. This may involve participation in a preschool program with support from a developmental specialist. It is helpful if parents understand the implications of the diagnosis for their child's behavior. For example, because people with Asperger syndrome tend to have problems with transitions, a preschooler with Asperger syndrome may have difficulties with moving to a new activity. In addition, they focus intensely on an activity they enjoy, making it difficult for them to shift attention and move to another task. Sensory sensitivities seen in children with Asperger syndrome are another often overlooked cause of behavior problems. Thus, it is critical for caregivers to realize that various factors, specific to the syndrome, can influence the behavior of children with Asperger syndrome early in their development.

Display 13.2

Jacob's story

Four-year-old Jacob had an older brother who had been diagnosed with autism. Generally, Jacob was a well-behaved toddler; in fact, he could occupy himself for hours if left alone. Most of the time, he was fascinated by certain cartoons and repeatedly played the videos that his parents bought him. His speech developed early, and much of the time he recited parts of his videos. Most of the behavior problems with Jacob occurred when he was not allowed to watch a video or when routines changed. He also showed extreme discomfort when wearing some types of clothing and with the labels in his shirt collars. His mother was startled one day to notice that he did not play interactively with other children; instead, she realized, he was always "outside" of the play. She worried that he was showing signs of autism. Jacob's mother took him to the family doctor, who believed there was probably no cause for concern but referred Jacob to a developmental pediatrician for an assessment. After a period of assessment, it was determined that Jacob had Asperger syndrome. He was enrolled in the local preschool for half days to provide him with greater exposure to typically developing peers.

School-Age Children

Although increasing numbers of children are being recognized as having Asperger syndrome in early childhood, many are still overlooked until they reach elementary school. A study in the United Kingdom reported that children with Asperger syndrome received a diagnosis at an average age of 11 years, even though parents began to have concerns about their children as early as 30 months of age (Howlin & Asgharian, 1999).

The good academic achievement and expressive communication skills of children with Asperger syndrome may be misleading. In the context of the classroom, however, odd social or behavioral mannerisms of a child with Asperger syndrome may be more apparent because of increased demands to comply with a teacher's agenda, increased sensory input and distractions, and the demands to play cooperatively and perform academically. Following even simple rules, such as lining up or sitting in a circle for story time, may be difficult. Transitional periods at school—such as the times before and after school, lunchtime, and recess—are often the most difficult times of the day for school-age children with Asperger syndrome. These children may also be subject to teasing and ridicule by the other children because of their odd mannerisms. This problem needs careful monitoring by parents and school personnel.

Finding a suitable school and classroom for school-age children with Asperger syndrome is sometimes difficult for parents, especially as their children reach second or third grade. At this time, the children may begin struggling with both academic and social demands. Children with Asperger syndrome need to be identified, and teachers may have to familiarize themselves with how this exceptionality affects the student's individualized education program (IEP) or similar plan. Most often, students with Asperger syndrome benefit from inclusion as much as possible, with necessary supports (e.g., a teaching assistant, assistive computer technology, sensory accommodations) or pull-out services in some cases.

A variety of professional supports and interventions can be helpful for the school-age child with Asperger syndrome. School-age children with Asperger syndrome need continual exposure to other peers outside school time through involvement in recreational activities. An individual support person may need to be present in such settings for some children with Asperger syndrome. This person can ensure that a child receives sufficient opportunities for socialization and is effectively included. In addition, this person can help explain the child's unusual behaviors to peers. Other interventions include social skills training in groups, in which the child is taught cooperative play and social interaction skills. A speech-language pathologist who is experienced in working with children who have PDDs may also provide assessment and recommendations about ways that parents and teachers can address deficiencies in pragmatic language skills. Psychoeducational assessments play an important role in addressing the unique learning profile of students with Asperger syndrome. Table 13.2 provides strategies for helping students with Asperger syndrome.

Adolescents

Individuals with Asperger syndrome may be first diagnosed in adolescence. By this time, the main characteristics of Asperger syndrome, such as a restricted range of interests and poor social skills, are clearly evident. They may also have extraordinary skills in some areas. This uneven skill profile can be puzzling to parents and clinicians.

Teenagers may have previously been diagnosed with other disorders that mimic criteria for Asperger syndrome, such as attention-deficit/hyperactivity disorder or non-verbal learning disability. However, a diagnosis of Asperger syndrome is usually more inclusive of all of their symptoms. Mental health problems may be seen in adolescents with Asperger syndrome (Stoddart, 1999). The tendency to display mental health problems may be worsened by these adolescents' emerging awareness that they are different from their peers in many ways. By adolescence, individuals with Asperger syndrome may have gravitated towards interests that are solitary in nature (especially if the syndrome has gone unidentified); as a result, they may be more socially isolated. Social interactions may cause or increase preexisting anxiety.

Medication may be used to address mental health symptoms. Individual therapy can be helpful for adolescents with Asperger syndrome, as it gives them the opportunity to discuss their diagnosis and social experiences with peers. There are several age-appropriate books designed to assist parents, teachers, or therapists to explain Asperger syndrome to children as well as adolescents. Although parents may fear having to tell their children about the diagnosis, such knowledge usually comes as a relief to those with the syndrome. Understandably, deciding when and how to tell children about their diagnosis is a difficult decision, and parents may need to seek professional support to discuss this concern. Social skills groups may be used to teach adolescents to interact properly with their peers, but more significantly these groups give the adolescents an opportunity to meet others who are similarly affected (Mishna & Muskat, 1998). (See Display 13.3 for an illustration of some of the issues involved in providing a diagnosis and intervention for adolescents with Asperger syndrome.)

Table 13.2. Strategies for helping students with Asperger syndrome

Provide a structured and predictable teaching environment.
Provide gradual exposure to new activities.
Use interests to teach new topics and reinforce positive behaviors.
Reduce assignment and homework demands.
Avoid dependence on gross or fine motor skills.
Provide a longer period for completion of assignments or tests.
Attend to sensory distractions or sensory overload.
Ensure that instruction is visual and concrete.
Be aware of anxiety-provoking situations and provide an escape.
Promote positive peer interaction, models, and supports.

Adults

Many individuals first receive the diagnosis of Asperger syndrome in adulthood. Some adults with Asperger syndrome find out about the symptoms through the Internet or the media and come to diagnosticians seeking a confirmation of their suspicions. These adults are often found in vocations that rely on a circumscribed area of knowledge, such as computer programming, engineering, or accounting. Most often, adults with Asperger syndrome are comforted to finally have an explanation for their puzzling characteristics. Such information is also helpful to family members in understanding their relative's behaviors and poor abilities to function successfully in relationships.

A key problem for younger adults with Asperger syndrome, once they have received a diagnosis, is finding assessment and treatment services. Children's services often end at age 18, and there may be little help for making the transition to the adult services sector. This lack of transitional services is especially critical,

Display 13.3

Michael's story

Fourteen-year-old Michael's parents were increasingly concerned about his social anxiety, lack of friends, and overall poor performance in school. All of his teachers believed he was bright but not achieving to his full potential. He was extremely interested in science, particularly astronomy, and spent much of his time looking at astronomy books or going to the local planetarium. His unusually fervent interest in this topic further alienated him from his peers. He was anxious in social situations, in part because he was the brunt of teasing from peers who saw that he was socially awkward and odd.

Michael's parents decided to take him to the local children's family counseling center. Assessment by a clinician revealed that Michael had Asperger syndrome. Michael's parents were relieved to finally have an explanation for his poor social skills, restricted range of interests, and social isolation. Michael began attending the center's social skills group for teenagers with Asperger syndrome. His parents worked with the clinician to monitor Michael's progress in the group and at school. The clinician met with school personnel and explained Asperger syndrome to them. Proper academic accommodations were made, and the teaching staff were more vigilant about stopping the teasing to which Michael was subjected. Short-term use of medication helped to reduce Michael's anxiety.

given that many young adults with Asperger syndrome often have great difficulty making the shift to an independent adult lifestyle. They are faced with making decisions about their career, involvement in postsecondary education, or living arrangements.

Another pressing service concern is the gap between mental health services and developmental services. It is difficult for both service providers and adults with Asperger syndrome to decide where they are best served. By definition, adults with Asperger syndrome do not have an overall cognitive delay (although there may be significant delays in day-to-day functioning and certain aspects of cognition); as a result, they form a unique population in the developmental services sector. To further complicate matters, they may have mental health issues that may not be sufficiently addressed.

The characterization of adults with Asperger syndrome often points to a high degree of social isolation and inability to form significant, long-term relationships. However, this is not always the case. Many adults with Asperger syndrome do enter long-term relationships, marry, and have children. In fact, adults are often diagnosed after a child or other family member receives a diagnosis of Asperger syndrome or another PDD. Clinicians and researchers have yet to fully understand the variables that lead to successful long-term relationships among adults with Asperger syndrome. In addition, further study is required for clinical work with adults who are in relationships and seek marital or family counseling. Most of the current literature on relationships and Asperger syndrome comes from first-hand accounts (e.g., Slater-Walker & Slater-Walker, 2002).

Older Adults

The topic of autism and Asperger syndrome in older people has received little attention in the literature. It is probable, however, that many in the aging population who have displayed lifelong problems in social functioning, experience long-standing mental health problems, and have a restricted range of interests have Asperger syndrome that has gone unrecognized (see Display 13.4). Thus, clinicians who support older people need to consider the symptoms of this syndrome. Grandparents of children with PDDs are sometimes called "loners," "eccentric," or "odd" by family members, although there has been no formal explanation for these characteristics until their grandchildren's diagnosis. Realization that a grandparent may have traits of Asperger syndrome leads to a better understanding of that individual's behavior.

Much has yet to be learned about older adults with Asperger syndrome. Helping them cope with one of the major developmental transitions in older life, retirement, needs to be explored. Unfortunately, retirement can mean reduced social contacts and less daily structure and routine, which is important for people with Asperger syndrome. As of 2007, little information is available about the medical needs of older adults with PDDs. It is important to remember that the medical needs of older adults with Asperger syndrome may also be complicated by their inability to organize medical appointments, by mental health problems (including anxiety and depression), and by lack of social supports.

AREAS FOR FUTURE CONSIDERATION

Many areas of research in Asperger syndrome are needed. First, the nature of the Asperger syndrome must be explored in greater detail. Some significant questions include "Is Asperger syndrome qualitatively different from high-functioning autism?" and "What are the neurological, genetic, psychological, or sensory differences that lead to this cluster of symptoms?" Second, effective interventions for Asperger syndrome

Display 13.4

Harvey's story

Harvey, a 63-year-old, saw a television news story on Asperger syndrome. The story discussed symptoms at various life stages and he immediately identified with the middle-age man with Asperger syndrome in the report. Harvey, too, was without any significant relationships in his life and considered himself a loner. He contacted the television station that ran the piece, which led to him contacting the clinician who had been interviewed for the report. In his first session with the clinician, Harvey disclosed a lifetime of loneliness, social isolation, depression, insomnia, and problems with anger management and change. He worked as a pipe fitter for most of his life. He was known in the industry for his attention to detail and precision. He had received both inpatient and outpatient services from many local psychiatric programs. In-depth history and psychological assessment revealed that Harvey's intelligence was in the typical range; however, he had severe deficits in some areas of functioning, such as understanding the thoughts and feelings of others and knowing how to function socially. In addition to his struggles with chronic depression and insomnia, Harvey was obsessive about the cleanliness of food, was upset when others broke rules (e.g., another bus passenger resting his feet on a bus seat), and struggled with repetitive thoughts. His overriding interest was his garden. When the assessment verified that Harvey did have Asperger syndrome, he was relieved to find that his suspicions were correct.

need to be identified and assessed. Key questions for this topic are "Are social skills groups useful for teaching interactional abilities to people with Asperger syndrome?" and "What are the outcomes of other interventions such as medication (e.g., selective serotonin reuptake inhibitors, or SSRIs), individual psychotherapy, dietary restrictions, social inclusion, or attention to sensory problems?"

Since the early 1990s, awareness of the symptoms of Asperger syndrome has increased considerably, yet much remains to be done. Unquestionably, it is becoming increasingly recognized in children, adolescents, and adults because of public education, better assessment approaches, published literature, and inclusion of Asperger syndrome in the *DSM-IV* and *DSM-IV-TR*. Although increased recognition has meant relief for many, the resulting strain on services has been enormous. Through strong parent advocacy, the profile of this syndrome is being raised, and these efforts, along with others from professionals, may well result in more effective recognition, assessment, and intervention for people with Asperger syndrome.

SUMMARY

According to the *DSM-IV-TR*, Asperger syndrome is characterized by a qualitative impairment in social interaction; restricted repetitive and stereotyped patterns of behavior, interests, and activities; and no clinically significant delay in language or cognitive development. Although the specific etiology is not known, there is good evidence to suggest, as with other ASDs, that genetics play an important role. The process of assessment for a diagnosis of Asperger syndrome may vary according to the clinician's discipline and his or her experience with the syndrome. Determination of whether an individual meets diagnostic criteria can be ascertained through observation, interview of the person and his or her teachers and family members, and the use of psychological measures or interview guides.

The diagnosis of Asperger syndrome may be made at any point in an individual's life; however, suitable coping strategies and understanding of an individual's traits are promoted by an early and accurate diagnosis. Intervention for a child suspected of having Asperger syndrome can begin as early as the preschool years, although most children are not diagnosed at this young age. In a school-age child, a diagnosis may mean a greater understanding of the child's needs and provision of the necessary accommodations in school. An adolescent with Asperger syndrome may struggle with social isolation, anxiety and depression if his or her traits are not understood. Although some adults with Asperger syndrome continue to experience psychosocial problems, others have long-term relationships and have children. In this latter group, many recognize symptoms in themselves subsequent to their children receiving a diagnosis of a PDD. Even a diagnosis in later life can bring relief to individuals with Asperger syndrome, as it provides an explanation for their problems throughout life. Nonetheless, the most common psychosocial issues that older adults with Asperger syndrome experience are not yet fully understood. Intervention at all stages in the life span may include counseling for individuals or their families, exposure to typically developing peers, education about the syndrome, attention to sensory issues, assessment and intervention related to cognitive strengths and weaknesses and learning styles, social skills training, and pharmacological intervention. Much work remains regarding research related to this syndrome and educating professionals and the public.

FOR FURTHER THOUGHT AND DISCUSSION

1. What are the key characteristics of Asperger syndrome?
2. Why is it important to have agreement on the diagnostic criteria for Asperger syndrome?
3. What is an argument against including Asperger syndrome in the *DSM-IV-TR?*
4. What are the problems encountered in epidemiological studies of PDDs?
5. Why is diagnosis important at each life stage?
6. What are other psychosocial problems that may exist for individuals with Asperger syndrome at each life stage?

REFERENCES

American Psychiatric Association. (1994). *Diagnostic and statistical manual of mental disorders* (4th ed.). Washington, DC: Author.

American Psychiatric Association. (2000). *Diagnostic and statistical manual of mental disorders* (4th ed, text rev.). Washington, DC: Author.

Asperger, H. (1944). Die "autistischen psychopathen" im kindeslater ["Autistic psychopathy" in childhood]. *Archive fur Psychiatrie un Nervenkrankheiten, 117,* 76–136.

Baron-Cohen, S. (1995). *Mindblindness: An essay on autism and theory of mind.* Cambridge, MA: The MIT Press.

Campbell, J.M. (2005). Diagnostic assessment of Asperger's Disorder: A review of five third-party rating scales. *Journal of Autism and Developmental Disorders, 35*(1), 25–35.

Ehlers, S., & Gillberg, C. (1993). The epidemiology of Asperger syndrome: A total population study. *Journal of Child Psychology and Psychiatry and Allied Disciplines, 34*(8), 1327–1350.

Ellis, H.D., & Gunter, H.L. (1999). Asperger syndrome: A simple matter of white matter? *Trends in Cognitive Sciences, 3*(5), 192–200.

Fombonne, E. (2003). Epidemiological surveys of autism and other pervasive developmental disorders. *Journal of Autism and Developmental Disorders, 33*(4), 365–382.

Frith, U. (1989). *Autism, explaining the enigma.* Oxford, United Kingdom: Blackwell Publishing.

Frith, U. (Ed.). (1991). *Autism and Asperger syndrome.* Cambridge, United Kingdom: Cambridge University Press.

Goodlin-Jones, B.L., & Solomon, M. (2003). Contributions of psychology. In S. Ozonoff, S.J. Rogers, & R.L. Hendren (Eds.), *Autism spectrum disorders: A research review for practitioners.* Washington, DC: American Psychiatric Publishing.

Howlin, P. (2000). Assessment instruments for Asperger syndrome. *Child Psychology and Psychiatry Review, 5*(3), 120–129.

Howlin, P., & Asgharian, A. (1999). The diagnosis of autism and Asperger syndrome: Findings from a survey of 770 families. *Developmental Medicine and Child Neurology, 41,* 834–839.

International Molecular Genetics Study of Autism Consortium. (1998). A full genome screen for autism with evidence for linkage to a region on chromosome 7q. *Human Molecular Genetics, 7,* 571–578.

International Molecular Genetics Study of Autism Consortium. (2001). A genome wide screen for autism: Strong evidence for linkage to chromosomes 2q, 7q, and 16p. *American Journal of Human Genetics, 69,* 570–581.

Mishna, F., & Muskat, B. (1998). Group therapy for boys with features of Asperger syndrome and concurrent learning disabilities: Finding a peer group. *Journal of Child and Adolescent Group Therapy, 8*(3), 97–114.

O'Brien, G., Pearson, J., Berney, T., et al. (2001). Measuring behavior in developmental disability: A review of existing schedules. *Developmental Medicine and Child Neurology, Supplemental, 87,* 5–18.

Ozonoff, S. (1995). Executive functions in autism. In E. Schopler & G.B. Mesibov (Eds.), *Learning and cognition in autism.* New York: Kluwer Academic/Plenum Publishers.

Schnurr, R.G. (2004a). Clinical assessment of children and adolescents with Asperger syndrome. In K.P. Stoddart (Ed.), *Children, youth and adults with Asperger syndrome: Integrating multiple perspectives.* London: Jessica Kingsley Publishers.

Schnurr, R.G. (2004b). *Schnurr interview guidelines for Asperger's disorder in children and adolescents (SIGADCA).* Ottawa, ON, Canada: Anisor Publishing.

Slater-Walker, C., & Slater-Walker, G. (2002). *An Asperger marriage.* London: Jessica Kingsley Publishers.

Stoddart, K.P. (1999). Adolescents with Asperger syndrome: Three case studies of individual and family therapy. *Autism: The International Journal of Research and Practice, 3*(3), 225–271.

Szatmari, P. (1991). Asperger's syndrome: Diagnosis, treatment, and outcome. *Psychiatric Clinics of North America, 14* (1), 81–93.

Szatmari, P. (1992). Asperger's syndrome. *Current Opinion in Pediatrics, 4,* 616–622.

Szatmari, P., Bremner, R., & Nagy, J. (1989). Asperger's syndrome: A review of clinical features. *Canadian Journal of Psychiatry, 34*(6), 554–560.

Wing, L. (1981). Asperger's syndrome: A clinical account. *Psychological Medicine, 11,* 115–129.

Ylisaukko-oja, T., Nieminen-von Wendt, T., Kempas, E., et al. (2004). Genome-wide scan for loci of Asperger syndrome. *Molecular Psychiatry, 9*(2), 161–168.

14

Fetal Alcohol Spectrum Disorder

Irena Nulman, Abel Ickowicz, Gideon Koren, and Dafna Knittel-Keren

WHAT YOU WILL LEARN ABOUT IN THIS CHAPTER

- Prevalence, incidence, and costs
- Alcohol use by women
- Effect of alcohol on the developing fetus
- Key factors for developing fetal alcohol spectrum disorder
- Screenings in pregnant women, neonates, and children
- The challenges of diagnosing fetal alcohol spectrum disorder
- Secondary disabilities associated with in utero alcohol exposure
- Mental health and behavioral issues
- In utero alcohol exposure and attachment disorders
- Intervention and prevention

Fetal alcohol spectrum disorder (FASD) is an umbrella term used to describe the range of physical, cognitive, behavioral and/or learning disabilities with possible lifelong implications that are caused by prenatal exposure to **alcohol.** It has been officially endorsed as an umbrella term by the National Organization on Fetal Alcohol Syndrome (NOFAS; 2004b), the National Institute on Alcohol Abuse and Alcoholism (NIAAA; 1993), the Centers for Disease Control and Prevention (CDC), and Health Canada (NOFAS Newsroom, 2004). FASDs are caused entirely by a woman drinking alcohol at any time during her pregnancy.

The term *spectrum* is used because each individual with FASD may have some or all of a spectrum of mental and physical challenges. In addition, each individual with FASD may have these challenges to a degree, or across a spectrum from mild to very severe. Fetal alcohol syndrome (FAS), partial FAS, alcohol-related birth defects (ARBD), and alcohol-related neurological disorders (ARND) are the diagnostic categories used to refer to the various forms of impact, resulting from exposure to prenatal alcohol (Chudley et al., 2005; Institute of Medicine, 1996):

- The term *FAS* refers to the most severe presentation of FASD. It is the leading nongenetic cause of intellectual and developmental disabilities in the Western world. This syndrome refers to the set of physical and mental birth defects that can result when a woman abuses alcohol during pregnancy, and it is characterized by brain damage, facial anomalies, and growth deficits. Vision and hearing problems are also are common. Individuals with FAS have difficulties with behavior, temperament, learning, attention, memory, and problem solving.
- The term *partial FAS* includes evidence of a complex pattern of behavior or cognitive abnormalities that are inconsistent with developmental level and cannot be explained by familial background or environment alone, as well as some unique facial dysmorphic features and growth impairment (Institute of Medicine, 1996).
- The term *ARND* was officially recommended by the Institute of Medicine Report in 1996, after studying the topic for more than a year. It is reserved for individuals with functional or cognitive impairments linked to prenatal alcohol exposure, which may include decreased head size at birth, structural brain abnormalities, and a pattern of behavioral and mental abnormalities.
- The term *ARBD* describes the physical defects linked to prenatal alcohol exposure, including heart, skeletal, kidney, ear, and eye malformations.
- The term *FAE* has been popularly used to describe alcohol-exposed individuals whose condition does not meet the full morphological criteria for an FAS diagnosis. It was originally developed for use in animal studies, which caused considerable confusion. Various investigators believe that the term *FAE MO* should be used only in the research, not the clinical, domain (Aase, Jones, & Clarren, 1995). Thus, the term *ARND* has replaced the term *FAE* in clinical settings (Institute of Medicine, 1996).

Maternal alcohol use—specifically the drinking of beverages containing ethanol—is the most common

The authors are grateful to Olivia Tischler for her contribution to the content of this chapter.

preventable cause of intellectual disability worldwide. Because ethanol use may result in miscarriages, fetal malformations, impaired growth and central nervous system (CNS) dysfunction, it is classified as a teratogen. Knowledge of alcohol teratogenicity and alcohol-related birth defects dates back to Biblical times, and there is evidence that people in a number of different regions of the world have been aware of the consequences of maternal drinking for centuries (Tuormaa, 1994). In more recent times, little formal attention was given to the potential toxic effects of alcohol until 1968, when Lemoine, Harousseau, Borteyru, et al. (1968) first described the relationship between alcohol intake during pregnancy and fetal development. In 1973, Jones, Smith, Ulleland, et al. described a distinct group of abnormalities associated with alcohol exposure during pregnancy. Six months later, the term *fetal alcohol syndrome* was coined by Jones and Smith to refer to this spectrum of abnormalities (Jones & Smith, 1973).

Alcohol crosses the placenta, enters the fetal blood circulatory system, and can adversely affect the developing fetus in a number of ways. These include miscarriage, growth, CNS development, **craniofacial,** and internal organ abnormalities. Jones and colleagues noted in 1973 that children exposed in utero to alcohol had a similar pattern of craniofacial defects associated with growth and neurodevelopmental delays that began before birth. Since that time, the criteria for diagnosis of FAS has been based on the presence of all of the following three features, worded per the original text (Jones, Smith, Ulleland, et al., 1973):

1. Growth retardation prior to and/or following birth
2. CNS involvement (signs of neurobehavioral abnormalities and mental retardation)
3. Characteristic facial anomalies (e.g., flat mid-face; indistinct, flat *philtrum*; short eye openings, and thin upper lip; see Figure 14.1)

PREVALENCE, INCIDENCE, AND COSTS

The term *prevalence* is used to describe the presence of a particular incident (in this case, usually FAS and/or ARND) among a particular study population. It includes all new and existing cases identified at that time period. The term *incidence* refers to new cases occurring at birth or within a defined time period. The literature on incidence and prevalence of FAS and related problems reflects variables known as "epidemiological inconsistencies." Discrepancies result from variation in study design, failure to estimate the amount and pattern of drinking, precise time of exposure during gestation, failure to include confounding factors, inclusion of different populations, and different reporting practices.

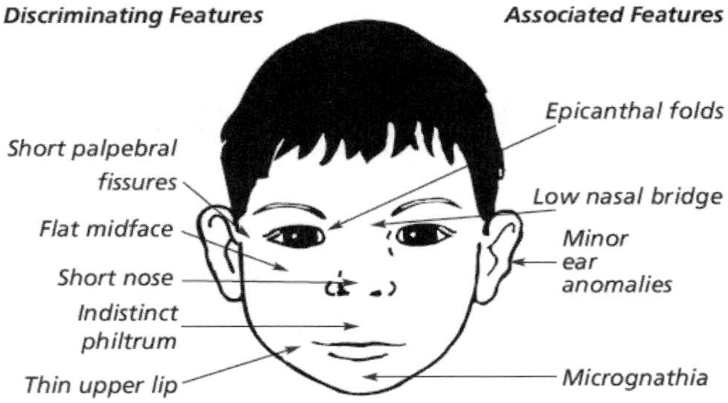

Figure 14.1. Facial features in fetal alcohol syndrome in the young child. (From Streissguth, A.P., & Little, R.E. [1994]. *Unit 5: Alcohol, pregnancy, and the fetal alcohol syndrome: Second edition. Project Cork Institute Medical School Curriculum; Slide lecture series on Biomedical education: Alcohol use and its medical consequences.* Produced by Dartmouth Medical School, Hanover, NH.)

Prevalence varies both among and within countries. The prevalence of FAS (the full expression) found in the United States ranges from 0.6 to 3 per 1,000 in most populations, with some communities having higher rates. Subpopulation analysis within the United States showed that in selected subpopulations in inner cities, the rates were 2.29 cases per 1,000, compared with 0.26 cases per 1,000 at sites where the population is middle class (Institute of Medicine, 1996). Combined rates of FAS and ARND are estimated to be at least 9.1–10 per 1,000. This higher figure underscores the importance of considering clinically the whole spectrum of severity. What is important to keep in mind is that nearly 1% of live births in North America are children born with problems related to prenatal alcohol use, clearly a preventable condition, representing a public health problem of appalling dimensions (NOFAS, 2004a; Sampson et al., 1997). Because about 4 million babies are born annually in the United States, each year, FAS affects as many as 12,000 babies and FASD affects approximately 40,000 (NOFAS, 2004a).

Outside the United States, Harris and Bucens (2003) found the prevalence of FAS in the northern territory of Australia to be 0.68 per 1,000. In indigenous children, the prevalence was calculated to be between 1.87 and 4.7 per 1,000 live births, which is comparable to the high rates in indigenous populations worldwide. The high-risk populations in Western Cape Province of South Africa were found to have a prevalence of 48.2 per 1,000. In Moscow, Russia, 14.1% of assessed subjects were diagnosed with FAS (Warren et al., 2001). Accurate estimates of incidence are hampered by differences in research methodology, even among populations and locations that are quite similar. A seminal paper in FAS epidemiology has attempted to establish a universal FAS rate incorporating systematic analysis of various prospective studies. Abel (1998) reviewed the available epidemiological studies on FAS and calculated the prevalence of FAS based on geographical, ethnic, and socioeconomic variables. He estimated, after an analysis of 29 prospective studies, a mean incidence of 0.97 cases per 1,000 live births in the general obstetric population. In a study based in New Mexico, May et al. (2005) found that rates were close to Abel's (1998) estimate of 0.97 per 1,000.

Costs

The costs of FAS and related conditions are extremely high for the individual, the family, the education and health care system, and society at large. Just as it is difficult to assess the incidences or prevalence of FAS and ARND, it is also challenging to make a competent estimate of the costs associated with fetal alcohol toxicity. Cost information usually falls into two categories: 1) total annual cost of FAS to the nation and 2) lifetime cost of each child born with FAS. Factors that affect such costs include the incidence or prevalence rate that is used, health impacts and associated care/services, and the time period over which the estimate is based (Lupton, Burd, & Harwood, 2004).

The 10th Special Report to the U.S. Congress on Alcohol and Health estimated the annual cost of FAS in 1998 to be $2.8 billion U.S. dollars (CDC, 2005). Other estimates for the annual economic impact have ranged as high as $9.7 billion (Klug & Burd, 2003). Lupton et al. (2004) reported that the lifetime health cost in 2002 for one person with FAS was $2 million. This is an average for all persons with FAS. People with severe problems, such as profound intellectual disability, have much higher costs. Klug and Burd (2003) estimated the mean annual cost of health care for children with FAS from birth through 21 years of age from records in North Dakota. This was found to be $2,842 dollars ($n = 45$). In contrast, the annual average cost of care for children who did not have FAS was $500. Prevention of one case of FAS per year in North Dakota would result in a cost savings of $128,810 after 10 years and $491,820 after 20 years. After 10 years of prevention, the annual savings in health care costs alone for one case of FAS would be $23,420.

ALCOHOL USE BY WOMEN

Alcohol is a legal, socially and culturally acceptable drug that is a part of the lifestyles of many women throughout the world. The statistics supporting alcohol use by women are disparate, but they are sufficient to document why FASD is a serious problem worldwide. In one U.S. national survey, 61.5% of all women reported consuming alcohol in the previous year. Moreover, 75% of women ages 18–34 reported using alcohol in the preceding year, making alcohol the most widely used agent that can affect fetal development (Koren & Nulman, 1994). In England, in 2000, 46% of 15-year-old girls were noted to have used alcohol. Over the years, the general tendency to drink is increasing: There has been an increase in the average weekly consumption of spirits from 0.8 units in 1992 to 1.9 units in 2000 (Office for National Statistics, 2004). According to Abel (1998), 49% of women drink some alcohol during pregnancy. The 2004 CDC report addressed the overall prevalence of alcohol use during the last 3 months of pregnancy by women in eight U.S. states during 2000 and 2001. This prevalence ranged from 3.4% in Nebraska to 9.9% in Colorado. Women who were more than 35 years of age, non-Hispanic women, women with more than a high school education, and women with higher incomes reported the highest prevalence of alcohol use during pregnancy (Phares et al., 2004).

One of the problems with alcohol consumption and the risk of FASD is that many women are not aware of their pregnancies for the first 4 to 6 weeks—in fact, a large number of pregnancies are unplanned. There is currently no evidence of a "risk-free" drinking level. Thus, women who are actively seeking to become pregnant should stop using alcohol (and other substances), and women who are not seeking to become pregnant should stop using alcohol (and other substances) as soon as they become aware of their pregnancies.

EFFECT OF ALCOHOL ON THE DEVELOPING FETUS

It is crucial to understand how alcohol affects the developing fetus in order to develop effective prevention and intervention strategies. CNS abnormalities resulting from in utero exposure to alcohol are mediated by a number of factors. Alcohol can affect most areas of brain development and, although it is not yet possible to detail precisely how alcohol affects each stage of development, it is likely that several factors act together.

As alcohol crosses the placenta and blood brain barrier (the cells that line the walls of blood vessels in the brain), it can be directly toxic to the developing fetal CNS cells, affecting cell structure, organization, and migration and triggering programmed cell death (Bearer, 2001; Ikonomidou et al., 2000). As a result, the brain of an exposed fetus may be reduced in size. In addition, the range of other abnormalities seen in children affected by alcohol (e.g., **cerebral dysgenesis,** enlarged **ventricles,** atypical neural/glial migration) indicate that brain structure and function differ from children with developmental delay not caused by alcohol (Mattson et al., 1994). Some specific brain anomalies can be attributed to prenatal alcohol exposure. Bookstein, Streissguth, Sampson, et al. (2001) found that individuals exposed in utero to alcohol showed abnormal corpus callosum development, which was related to impaired executive and motor functions. Alcohol can also adversely affect brain growth and the neurotransmitter systems (Luo & Miller, 1998; Ma et al., 2001; Miller & Luo, 2002).

The major metabolite of alcohol (the substance into which alcohol is converted), **acetaldehyde,** is also toxic to the fetus (Hard, Raha, Spino, et al., 2001). In addition, alcohol can affect the fetus indirectly through its secondary effects, such as insufficient oxygen supply due to constriction of vessels in the **umbilical cord** (Fisher, Duffy, & Atkinson, 1986; Ugarte & Valenzuela, 1971; Yang, Shum, & Ng, 1986). Alcohol induced alterations in DNA may be responsible for the atypical physical and behavioral development observed in FASD. Factors such as increased **prostaglandin** levels (Collier, McDonald-Gibson, & Saeed, 1975) may lead to a reduction in the rate of cell division and a possible decrease in the weight of the fetal brain. The metabolism of alcohol increases the liver's demand for oxygen, resulting in oxygen deprivation (Lieber, 1991). This may be intensified by alcohol-induced contraction of umbilical arteries and veins and by impaired oxygen unloading from **hemoglobin** by acidification of the blood. In addition, numerous other factors—such as **free radical** damage (Davis et al., 1990), **long-term potentiation** disruption (Broun, 1996), and the inhibition of the enzyme **aldehyde dehydrogenase**—can contribute to alcohol's devastating effects on a fetus (Henderson, Chen, & Schenker, 1999). Although current knowledge is not complete, it is clear that alcohol affects the developing fetus in numerous adverse ways.

KEY FACTORS FOR DEVELOPING FETAL ALCOHOL SPECTRUM DISORDER

The fact that not all children exposed to gestational alcohol consumption develop FASD suggests that a variety of factors may be interacting with the maternal alcohol exposure to influence their development. Abel (1995) proposed two categorical types of maternal risk factors that increase fetal vulnerability to alcohol at the cellular level:

1. Permissive factors: predisposing behavioral, social, or environmental factors, such as alcohol consumption pattern or socioeconomic status (SES)
2. Provocative factors: biological conditions, such as high blood alcohol concentration or decreased antioxidant status

This categorization appears to be a useful way to think of the key factors involved in developing FASD. A complicating factor, however, is that risk factors may cluster in women, especially in those who have heavy use of alcohol. For example, in one Canadian study, Gladstone, Levy, Nulman, et al. (1997) found that pregnant women who report binge alcohol consumption often report use of cigarettes and illicit drugs such as cocaine and marijuana, all of which represent a significant risk to the fetus.

Risk Factors

The following sections discuss potential risk factors for FASD.

Alcoholism in First-Degree Relatives The most powerful predictor of alcohol abuse in any individual is the occurrence of alcoholism in first-degree relatives. For those with a family history of alcohol abuse, the risk of developing an alcohol use disorder increases two- or three-fold (Bierut et. al., 1998). In turn, a woman with such a propensity for alcohol misuse may be more likely to drink during pregnancy.

Psychiatric Disorders The presence of a psychiatric disorder is one of the most significant risk factors for alcohol misuse. The risk is particularly high in individuals affected by schizophrenia, major depression, bipolar disorders, anxiety disorders, and personality disorders (Kessler et al., 1994). The risk of alcohol use during pregnancy is also higher in women with psychiatric disorders. Thus, in addition to the potential damage by the alcohol alone, there may be other genetic and environmental adverse effects on the development of the fetus. As already discussed, the spectrum of severity of these abnormalities varies considerably.

Low Socioeconomic Status Low SES is often related to poor maternal nutrition and health, decreased access to prenatal care, and increased stress. Each of these factors can theoretically adversely affect pregnancy outcome and could interact with the effects of alcohol on the developing fetus (Abel & Hannigan, 1996).

Genetic factors Clinical reports on monozygotic and dizygotic twins have provided evidence for the involvement of genetic factors in risk vulnerability for FAS (Warren & Li, 2005). Theoretically, genetic factors in the mother and genetic factors in the fetus might affect the risk for FAS and other alcohol effects. Factors responsible for differences in alcohol metabolism, rates of transport of nutrients across the placenta, and alteration in uterine blood flow could influence the severity of fetal alcohol-induced damage. Ethanol is metabolized by two enzymes in the liver, alcohol dehydrogenase (ADH) and cytochrome P4502E1 (CYP2E1), to acetaldehyde; acetaldehyde is then oxidized to acetate by **aldehyde dehydrogenase** (ALDH). Genetic variants of each of these enzymes occur. A high activity variant of ADH, ADH2*2, and a low activity variant of mitochondrial ALDH, ALDH2*2, have been conclusively associated with reduced risk of alcoholism (Higuchi et al., 2004). Research to identify specific **polymorphisms** contributing to FASD is still at an early stage. To date, polymorphisms of only one of the genes for the alcohol dehydrogenase enzyme family, the ADH1B, have been demonstrated to contribute to FASD vulnerability. In comparison with ADH1B*1, both maternal and fetal ADH1B*2 have been shown to reduce risk for FAS in a mixed ancestry South African population. ADH1B*3 appears to afford protection for FASD outcomes in African American populations (Warren & Li, 2005).

Use of Other Drugs Women who abuse alcohol also tend to abuse illicit drugs (Gladstone et al., 1997). Cocaine used in combination with alcohol produces cocethylene, an exceptionally toxic substance. The combination of maternal alcohol consumption and cigarette smoking increases the risk of low birth weight, **microcephaly,** and hearing difficulties (Olsen, Pereira, Da, et al., 1991).

Other Factors Poor maternal health, poor nutrition, poor prenatal care, and other factors may influence the development and presentation of FASD.

The Role of Timing

From a consideration of the stages of human fetal development (see Chapters 7 and 9), it is clear that the timing of alcohol exposure is an important factor in fetal outcome. Alcohol is a low molecular substance and is able to cross the placental barrier and enter the fetus. In the first 21 days of the fetal development, the preliminary cellular organization of the embryo begins to take place. If an excessive amount of alcohol is consumed before the blastocyst is embedded in the uterus, the impact can be so severe that the fetus is miscarried. In fact, both male and female alcohol intakes during the week of conception increase the risk of early pregnancy loss (Henriksen et al., 2004). By the end of the 36th day, often long before the woman even realizes that she is pregnant, the neural tube is clearly present and open, and most of the rudimentary organs have already been formed, such as limbs, heart, brain, eyes, mouth, and digestive tract. It is therefore obvious that if alcohol is consumed during this critical period of rapid growth, malformations such as heart defects, musculoskeletal abnormalities, cognitive disabilities, and so forth can occur without any specific outward signs of FAS. Because there is a brain growth spurt toward the end of the last trimester (see Chapters 7 and 8), alcohol exposure at this later stage may affect brain development and function particularly. Of particular concern to the human situation is that approximately half of pregnancies are unplanned, and women often do not know they are pregnant for the first few weeks of this critical period.

Research with animal models has resulted in valuable insights into clarifying the importance of timing of prenatal alcohol exposure with respect to outcome and the teratogenic mechanisms of prenatal alcohol **toxicity** of possible relevance to humans. For example, animal studies on FAS strongly suggest that the facial dysmorphology (short palpebral fissures, flat mid-face, and indistinct philtrum; see Figure 14.1) that is characteristic of FAS results from exposure during the first 2 months of gestation (Sulik et al., 1986; Sulik et al., 1981). However, the relationship becomes less clear in the examination of growth retardation. It appears that both early exposure (during the first 2 months of pregnancy) and exposure during the third trimester affect growth (Maier, Chen, Miller, et al., 1997; Middaugh & Boggan, 1991). Effects on head circumference—and, by extension, brain growth—appear to be the most consistent and permanent outcomes of exposure during these two periods. It is more difficult to examine behavioral effects than physical anomalies using a trimester approach, due to the nature of behavior development. Correlational studies suggest that early exposure may be more damaging to behavior than is later exposure, but some animal studies indicate that exposure in the third trimester may specifically affect the hippocampus and the cerebellum, leading to deficits in learning and motor skills (Coles, 1991). In rats, a single exposure to high blood alcohol concentrations (BACs) can produce a severe loss of brain cells in the fetus (Goodlett, Marcussen, & West, 1990). Microcephaly is associated with alcohol consumption throughout pregnancy (all three trimesters). Animal studies have shown that although many areas of the brain are affected by maternal alcohol exposure, its effects seem to be particularly detrimental on the dorsal hippocampus (Sakata-Haga et al., 2003), possibly accounting for deficits in spatial memory of children born to mothers using alcohol during pregnancy.

Effects Associated with Drinking Patterns

Drinking patterns are typically characterized by average daily, weekly, or monthly alcohol intake levels. However, the definitions of *mild, moderate,* and *heavy* use vary considerably among studies, making generalizations and comparisons difficult. It is now evident that the pattern of drinking plays a crucial role in predicting the effects that alcohol has on the fetus. The critical variable appears to be the woman's blood alcohol level. Research indicates that binge alcohol consumption with high BACs during a critical time in pregnancy is harmful to the embryo or fetus, and is sufficient to produce a wide spectrum of physical and neurodevelopmental deficits (Streissguth, Bookstein, & Barr, 1996). This is particularly important for women who are alcoholics. Most such women decrease their consumption of alcohol during pregnancy, but when they do drink, they tend to binge (Alvik, Haldorsen, & Lindemann 2005; May et al., 2005).

Peak BACs are a function of both the dose and rate of alcohol consumption. Alcohol consumed in a binge pattern can rapidly produce higher BACs than daily amounts consumed in a slower or more spread out manner. A very different pattern of BACs might be achieved by two different types of women: those who spread 10 drinks throughout the day from morning to evening and those who binge on 10 drinks in the evening (Gladstone, Nulman, & Koren, 1996). This may explain some of the large variability in the prevalence of FASD in children of alcohol users.

As to specific effects on children, one to five binges by women who were not alcohol dependent, have been associated with a greater degree of disinhibited behavior in exposed children (Nulman et al., 2004). A prospective, longitudinal study by Streissguth, Bookstein, and Barr (1996) investigated children exposed in utero to a moderate amount of alcohol, characteristic of social drinking, and examined three types of teratogenic outcomes: deficits in growth, morphology, and function—all of which were evident in children with FAS. They reported that neurobehavioral functioning, observed from the first day of life through 14 years, showed the most reliably persistent effects of prenatal alcohol exposure. These effects were dose dependent and, in the school-age years, more salient in the children of mothers with binge-type drinking patterns. Learning problems were observed from 7 through 14 years of age, but problems with attention and speed of information processing were observable over the entire 14-year period. In the dose-response analysis, there was no evidence of a risk-free drinking level or any threshold level of prenatal alcohol exposure.

The high association between alcohol intoxication and unplanned or unprotected sexual activity is another area of concern. Unfortunately, women who engage in binge-style alcohol consumption may increase their likelihood of engaging in unprotected sex and unplanned pregnancy and, consequently, may unknowingly expose their fetus to alcohol. This is particularly alarming among teenagers, given their high rate of binge drinking, the rising rate of teenage pregnancy, and the tendency for adolescents to recognize their pregnancies later than adults (Cornelius et al., 1994; Dunn, Bartee, & Perko, 2003; Windle, 2003). Taken together, these variables make the offspring of teenagers significantly more susceptible to FASD (Gladstone et al., 1996).

SCREENINGS IN PREGNANT WOMEN, NEONATES, AND CHILDREN

The accuracy of a screening or diagnostic test depends on a number of factors, including the sensitivity and specificity of the test and its false-negative and false-positive rates. The term *sensitivity* refers to the ability of the test to detect true positives (i.e., individuals who really have the FASD). The term *specificity* refers to the ability of the test to detect negatives (i.e., individuals who really do not have FASD). A *false-positive test result* refers to a positive test result in an individual who does not have the disorder. A *false-negative test result* refers to a negative test result in an individual who does have FASD. When considering the use of screening tests, clinicians and participants should make sure that they understand the information that the test is likely to yield, as well as the further confirmative testing and appropriate management that are available to them after the testing has been done, particularly if the test is positive.

Screening for Prenatal Alcohol Abuse by Pregnant Women

Screenings for alcohol abuse by pregnant women include questionnaires and blood tests. Each method is described next.

Questionnaires Alcohol use disorders may be formally diagnosed using *Diagnostic and Statistical Manual of Mental Disorders, Fourth Edition, Text Revision* (*DSM IV-TR;* American Psychiatric Association, 2000), and *International Statistical Classification of Diseases and Related Health Problems* (ICD-10; World Health Organization, 2003) criteria. However, there is much interest in developing and using brief screening questionnaires and blood tests to aid with their diagnosis. Brief screening questionnaires for alcohol use disorders that have been validated include the Alcohol Use Disorders Identification Test (AUDIT), the CAGE (Cut Down, Annoyed, Guilty, Eye Opener) questions, the CRAFFT (Car, Relax, Alone, Forget, Friends, Trouble) questions, the Rapid Alcohol Problems Screen with Quantity Frequency (RAPS-QF) questions, the RUFT-Cut (composed of questions from the other tests) (Kelly, Donovan, Chung, et al., 2004); the Tolerance, Worry, Eye Opener, Amnesia, Cut-Down (TWEAK) questions (Gareri et al., 2005); and others. There is considerable disparity regarding their sensitivities and specificities in different populations and different settings.

Blood Tests Blood tests are often used as biological markers to screen for alcohol abuse. Measuring alcohol in the blood or in exhaled air reflects only recent drinking, so these approaches are of limited use. To detect significant chronic alcohol exposure in pregnant women, Stoler et al. (1998) suggested the following as the most sensitive combination of laboratory test results predicting maternal alcohol dependence:

1. Elevated levels of glutamyl transpeptidase: > 45 units per liter (U/L), reflecting liver damage
2. Lowered mean red cell volume (< 98 femtoliter)
3. High carbohydrate-deficient transferrin level: positive result is above 99th percentile (differs from lab to lab)
4. High whole blood-associated acetaldehyde (WBAA) level: > 9.0 μmol/L (micromole per liter)

Stoler et al. found that women who drink one or more ounces of absolute alcohol per day have at least one positive blood marker. They also found that the presence of two or more positive markers was predictive of smaller birth weight, length, and head circumference than self-reporting measures.

Usually the body's load of alcohol is eliminated from the body after conversion to acetaldehyde and water. Studies in adults have shown that circulating alcohol complexes combine with fatty acids to form fatty acid esters (FAEE). FAEE have been found to be produced by the fetus due to continuous exposure to alcohol in utero. A study from Cleveland (Bearer et al., 1999) showed accumulation of FAEE in meconium (first neonatal stool). The presence of FAEE in meconium reflects alcohol exposure during the last 4 months of pregnancy. FAEE belong to a group of nonoxidative alcohol metabolites with emerging clinical significance in screening for chronic alcohol exposure (Klein, Karaskov, & Koren, 1999; Moore & Lewis, 2001).

Screening of Neonates to Identify Heavy Maternal Drinking During Pregnancy

Determination of the amount and schedule of alcohol exposures in pregnancy is often unreliable. Ethanol cannot be measured in hair or meconium; however, its FAEE derivatives accumulate in meconium during the last 4 months of pregnancy (Koren, Chan, Klein, et al., 2002). As noted, measurement of FAEEs in meconium has emerged as a promising test for heavy maternal drinking in the second half of pregnancy (Chan, Klein, Karaskov, et al., 2004). To determine if a pregnant woman is drinking during pregnancy, the Motherisk Clinic at the Hospital for Sick Children in Toronto, Canada, uses the TWEAK test to screen for problem drinking. Following birth, the infant's meconium is tested for FAEEs to determine chronic exposure to ethanol (Gareri et al., 2005).

Screening of Children for Fetal Alcohol Spectrum Disorder

Early identification of children affected by prenatal alcohol use can help provide needed supports, with the hope of decreasing the costly and debilitating secondary disabilities (Streissguth, Bookstein, Sampson, et al., 1996). Some studies have shown that screening can be useful to identify children at high risk of being affected by prenatal alcohol use before a formal diagnosis is made using the facial features, growth parameters, and impaired neurobehavioral function (Clarren et al., 2001; Koren & Nulman, 2002). For example, Poitra and colleagues (2003) reported results of effective screening using Burd's rapid screening tool for FAS (Burd, Klug, Martsolf, et al., 2003). These studies showed that screening the female at-risk population may be efficient in identifying children for future formal testing of FASD.

THE CHALLENGES OF DIAGNOSING FETAL ALCOHOL SPECTRUM DISORDER

The spectrum of alcohol's harmful effects on the fetus spans a wide continuum. As a result, there are several difficulties associated with making the diagnosis of FASD. Especially when the phenotype is "incomplete" or the clinician is inexperienced in making this diagnosis, FASD may be misdiagnosed.

Factors that Complicate Diagnosis

Many problems associated with fetal alcohol exposure may be subtle and even go undetected. The phenotype of FAS varies with age and may alter or normalize as an person moves through childhood into adolescence and adulthood. An affected individual may have an IQ score ranging from normal to very low and may have physical features that range from normal appearance to evident anomalies. Likewise, a child exposed to alcohol prenatally may have typical growth and physical features but have slight or significant behavioral and/or cognitive problems. The behavior problems may represent increased genetic susceptibility transmitted by affected parents who may be using alcohol as self-medication for anxiety, mood and personality disorders, or specific learning and attention problems. Evidence of a complex pattern of behavioral or cognitive impairment that is inconsistent with an individual's developmental level and that cannot be explained by familial or genetic background or environment alone may reflect ethanol toxicity in utero.

Many individual deficits seen in FASD do not specifically reflect the in utero alcohol toxicity and may similarly be observed in isolation or in combination in children not exposed to alcohol prenatally. A wide range of atypical neurobehavioral features with low specificities have been found by a large number of investigators. These include the following:

- Intellectual impairment with low-average IQ scores and lower scores on arithmetic and memory tests (Streissguth & Little, 1994)
- A deficit in different components of attention and executive control functioning (Noland et al., 2003)
- Impaired information processing, visual-spatial reasoning, visual memory, and verbal learning and memory function (Kaemingk, Mulvaney, & Halverson, 2003; Mattson, Riley, Delis, et al., 1996; Willford, Richardson, Leech, et al., 2004)
- Impaired motor functioning, speech and hearing performance, practical reasoning, and eye–hand coordination (Adnams et al., 2001)
- Behavior and emotional difficulties (Steinhausen & Spohr, 1998), and behavior regulation disorders (in children with ARND)
- Impaired judgment and poor adaptability (Streissguth, Barr, Kogan, et al., 1996; Streissguth, Bookstein, Sampson, et al., 1996)

Diagnoses Similar to FAS

Some other conditions are sometimes confused with FAS or FASD because the features are similar. One such condition is fetal solvent syndrome (FSS). FSS results from exposure to toluene, a chemical to which some women are exposed in their workplaces (e.g., working around gasoline, kerosene, heating oil, paints, lacquers, or automobile exhaust) or through use as a recreational drug (by sniffing) (Costa & Guizzetti, 2002). Neonates who were exposed to toluene have phenotypic characteristics similar to those of FAS.

Another condition with similar features is **phenylketonuria (PKU),** which is caused by a genetic defect in an enzyme that converts phenylalanine (Phe) to tyrosine. Women with uncontrolled high plasma levels of Phe or its metabolites may have children with maternal PKU (mPKU) syndrome. (Whether Phe itself or one of its metabolites is responsible for the CNS dysfunction associated with mPKU is unclear; Costa & Guizzetti, 2002.) Children with mPKU have severe CNS dysfunction, microcephaly, unusual structural facial features, congenital heart disease, and growth retardation. In fact, there is very close resemblance between the facial features of children with mPKU and those of FAS. It is not clear why there is so much overlap of physical phenotype between FAS, FSS, and PKU. It is suspected that different toxic substances may act on similar developmental pathways (Vorhees, 1986).

Various other conditions can be confused with FAS or FASD. Children with **Aarskog-Scott syndrome, Bloom syndrome, Dubowitz syndrome, fetal hydantoin syndrome,** fragile X syndrome, **Noonan syndrome,** Opitz syndrome, **Turner syndrome, velocardiofacial syndrome,** or **Williams syndrome** may display similar physical and neurodevelopmental features (Institute of Medicine, 1996).

SECONDARY DISABILITIES ASSOCIATED WITH IN UTERO ALCOHOL EXPOSURE

FASD has lifelong physical, mental, and behavioral consequences (Streissguth et al., 1991). Streissguth defined *primary disabilities* as those that are congenital and reflect a diagnosis of FAS or ARND. They refer to physical anomalies and brain damage that results in cognitive impairment in people with FASD. Primary disabilities are measured by general intelligence, mastery of reading, spelling, math, and level of adaptive functioning, representing the CNS manifestations of FASD. *Secondary disabilities* are those that are not present at birth but occur as a result of the primary disabilities and can presumably be prevented or lessened by better understanding and appropriate interventions. They tend to result from relatively good cognition but poor social adaptability and judgment. Streissguth carried out a study of 473 individuals to determine secondary disabilities associated with in utero alcohol exposure (Streissguth, Barr, et al., 1996; Streissguth, Bookstein, & Barr, 1996; Streissguth, Bookstein, Sampson, et al., 1996). The sample of 473 individuals included 178 with FAS and 295 with FAE (which is now considered ARND). The range of IQ scores of individuals with FAS was from 29 to 120, with mean score of 79. The range of IQ scores of individuals with FAE (ARND) was from 42 to 142, with a mean score of 90. Only 16% of all individuals in this study legally qualified as having mental retardation. This means that 86% of the individuals with FAS or FAE (ARND) in this study had an IQ score in the "normal" range and did not qualify for services for developmental disabilities. They nevertheless had impaired mental functioning caused by brain damage that is permanent and incurable. **Adaptive behavior** scores were low in both the FAS and FAE (ARND) subgroups (61 and 67, respectively). Up to 94% of participants had symptoms of one or more psychiatric conditions. Disrupted school experience and trouble with the law were reported in 60% of assessed individuals. Among the participants, criminal and inappropriate sexual behavior were reported in 50%, alcohol or drug problems in 30%, and dependent living and problems with employment in 80%. Rates of secondary disabilities were nearly equal for males and females.

Streissguth and colleagues (Streissguth, Barr, et al., 1996; Streissguth, Bookstein, & Barr, 1996; Streissguth, Bookstein, Sampson, et al., 1996) pointed out that strong protective factors for secondary disabilities (except for mental health) include receiving a diagnosis before 6 years of age and receiving a diagnosis of FAS rather than FAE (ARND). These factors point to the importance of early diagnoses of ARND so that treatment and intervention can be started at the earliest possible age. They also suggest that individuals with ARND have a greater chance of developing serious secondary disabilities than do individuals with FAS.

MENTAL HEALTH AND BEHAVIORAL ISSUES

In the study by Streissguth, Barr, et al. (1996), mental health problems were the most prevalent secondary disability, experienced by 94% of the full sample. The mental health disorders that seem most likely to accompany FASD are **attention-deficit/hyperactivity disorder (ADHD), conduct disorder,** depression, alcohol or drug dependence, or psychotic episodes. Other psychiatric problems—such as anxiety disorders, eating disorders, and posttraumatic stress disorder—have also been reported for some people with FASD.

Medical complications, developmental delays, and psychiatric symptoms are often evident in children with FASD from birth. In the preschool period, eating disorders, bedwetting, speech delay, stereotypies, and ADHD have been reported. In the early school age years, problems such as speech delay and stereotypies, and anxiety or sleep disorders, may occur. Steinhausen, Nestler, and Huth (1982) reported among children with FASD a prevalence rate of 63% for either a single psychiatric disorder or psychiatric disorders that occur together (or are **comorbid**). In the study by Streissguth, Barr, et al. (1996), during childhood, 60% of children with FASD had ADHD. In another study by O'Connor, Shah, et al. (2002), 87% of children evaluated because of heavy exposure to alcohol met the criteria for a psychiatric disorder. The majority (61%) were assigned a mood disorder diagnosis, 26% were diagnosed with major depressive or adjustment disorders, and 35% met criteria for bipolar disorder. Factors such as increased severity of morphological (structural) damage, psychopathology, and cognitive delay often cluster together in children who are severely affected by FASD. These children tend to come from extremely deprived backgrounds that include chronic parental alcoholism and mental health disorders. No study has yet disentangled the effects of alcohol from other environmental and genetic factors associated with poor neurocognitive and behavioral achievement in children. Longitudinal studies have shown that even a stimulating environment with sensitive parents or a good institution only partially compensates for prenatally damaged CNS functioning.

Although cognitive deficits are overrepresented among children with FASD, cognitive functioning varies widely, and some of these children may function at satisfactory academic levels at school, even though they may display behavior problems (Mattson, Riley, Gramling, et al.,1997). Steinhausen, Willms, Metzke, et al. (2004) studied the behavioral phenotype in children with FAS, children with FAE (ARND), and children with intellectual disability of unknown cause. They found significant differences in the behavior profile between the two groups of children exposed to alcohol and the control group but not between the FAS and FAE (ARND) groups.

Most adolescents and young adults with FASD must learn to cope with persisting cognitive impairment and psychiatric disorders that can cause serious problems throughout life. In addition, a substantial proportion of these individuals remain dependent on support from others such as mental health and developmental disability professionals. There is evidence that adults with FASD are at substantial risk of developing, in particular, alcohol and substance abuse, depression, psychotic disorders, and personality disorders (Famy, Streissguth, & Unis, 1998). In the study by Streissguth, Barr, et al. (1996), most adults with FASD had clinical depression, 23% of the adults had attempted suicide, and 43% had threatened to commit suicide.

IN UTERO ALCOHOL EXPOSURE AND ATTACHMENT DISORDERS

Attachment disorders are the psychological result of negative experiences with caregivers, usually since infancy, that disrupt the exclusive and unique relationship between children and their primary caregiver(s). Though oppositional and defiant behaviors may be a manifestation of conduct disorder, they also may be the expression of disruptions in the mother–child relationship (i.e., attachment). Several models describe the mother–child relationship. The interactive model, which suggests that child development results from a combination of factors, is one of the most salient for understanding attachment (Coles & Platzman, 1993). The neonatal symptoms of CNS dysfunction in infants born to mothers who report drinking large quantities of alcohol during pregnancy include irritability, **autonomic instability,** decreased sucking response, **motor immaturity,** slow habituation, low levels of arousal, and distorted sleep patterns. High-pitched crying, disturbed sleep, and feeding difficulties often follow withdrawal symptoms and may persist for days or weeks (Coles & Platzman, 1993). Behavior difficulties may continue into the preschool period and may be coupled with problems in cognitive functioning and sustained attention, emotional instability, increased activity level, **rigidity,** and irritability. These neurobehavioral effects may, in turn, affect attachment and mother-infant relationships.

O'Connor, Kogan, and Findlay (2002) proposed that alcohol consumption following pregnancy was directly related to the mother's interaction with her child, resulting in a **negative affective response** in the child and an insecure attachment. One of their models tested the hypothesis that independent and direct paths could be drawn between prenatal drinking and infant negative affect, maternal behavior, and attachment behavior. The model was based on the possibility that alcohol consumption affected the mother and infant independently. The results showed that children exposed in utero to maternal drinking were more likely to be associated with insecure attachments than their controls (80% versus 36%). The authors also reported that prenatal alcohol exposure predicted child's negative affect, which improved with higher levels of emotional support from the mother (O'Connor, Kogan, & Findlay, 2002). Thus, the supportive presence of a mother may mediate the association between prenatal alcohol exposure and a child's security of attachment.

Streissguth et al. (2004) showed that there are major problems with adaptive behavior for adolescents and adults with FASD, highlighting the need to examine pathways for later **maladaptation** and therapy for the child at as early an age as possible. Impaired attachment in early childhood is associated with maladaptive behaviour later in life. Future research might focus on studying the mechanisms of secure attachment and a positive mother–child relationship, as a better understanding of this complex process would lead to early intervention before the primary attachment relationship becomes disturbed.

INTERVENTION AND PREVENTION

Table 14.1 highlights the difficulties associated with FASD. It is clearly evident that alcohol exposure is associated with long-term physical, cognitive and behavioral disabilities as well as with verbal and visual deficits (Kaemingk et al., 2003). Strategies to alleviate the effects of FASD must include interventions targeting society at large and cultural and community groups, as well as medical and public health professionals. Pediatrician and family doctor involvement should focus on prevention, early diagnosis, and multidisciplinary treatment of this disorder once diagnosed. Providing physicians with tools to diagnose and manage FASD can increase changes for correct diagnosis and, in turn, early intervention. Educating school nurses about FASD also is critical, because they are positioned within the community and have links to children, families, and health care systems (Caley, Kramer, & Robinson, 2005).

Because FASD is the most preventable form of neurodevelopmental disability, prevention is intervention at its earliest form. The most effective prevention of FASD is optimally approached from a multifaceted perspective. Publicity about the dangers of maternal drinking can intensify a woman's despair over the damage she may have done to the fetus and her inability to stop drinking. Campaigns must therefore be mounted that motivate at-risk women to reduce alcohol consumption, stress the potential for success in overcoming alcohol addiction, and encourage these women to seek prenatal care. The various specialties involved in treating pregnant women with alcohol addictions must be coordinated to deal with the accompanying complex medical and social issues. Approaches for prevention are typically classified as primary, secondary, and tertiary.

Primary prevention efforts target the universal level, striving to ensure that society as a whole is aware of the hazards associated with using alcohol, particularly during pregnancy. The choice to refrain from alcohol use prior to and during pregnancy is the goal of primary prevention. Prevention and treatment of maternal alcohol abuse are difficult and often unsuccessful, so effective contraception is a more discernible focus for primary prevention efforts.

Secondary prevention efforts are initiated after the diagnosis of heavy alcohol consumption in early pregnancy is recognized. At this stage, a woman's physician should inform her about the risks posed to her fetus to date, potential risks if alcohol use is continued, and the possibility for termination of pregnancy. Realistic discussion about the lifelong risks to the fetus should be conveyed to the mother. Cessation of alcohol use should be strongly encouraged if the woman chooses to continue the pregnancy, and suitable follow-up for postdelivery should be arranged.

Tertiary prevention efforts focus on early intervention and screening of children with FAS and ARND in an attempt to prevent the development of secondary disabilities. Maternal and fetal biological markers are effective screening methods for identifying maternal alcohol abuse and extent of fetal exposure.

A variety of programs have been developed to prevent drinking during pregnancy and the resulting health problems (Hankin, 2002). Some of these efforts include public service announcements and beverage warning labels to increase the public's knowledge about FAS. In selective prevention, women of reproductive age who drink alcohol are targeted by selective prevention or by indicated prevention. Approaches for selective prevention may involve screening of pregnant women at risk for alcohol consumption and counseling those women who do drink. In indicated prevention, high-risk women (e.g., women who have previously abused alcohol or have had a child with FAS or other

Table 14.1. Fetal alcohol spectrum disorder (FASD) at a glance

Overview of facts	Includes growth, physical, behavioral, and cognitive problems caused by heavy drinking during pregnancy Is a leading preventable cause of developmental delay in children May affect 1% of fetuses Is completely preventable Is a marker of alcohol abuse during gestation
How alcohol affects the fetus	Is toxic to the embryo and the fetus Is converted to acetaldehyde, which is toxic to the embryo and fetus Deprives the fetus of oxygen; it constricts the umbilical cord vessels Has deleterious effects on fetal metabolism Causes an increase in complexes of alcohol with fatty acids in the meconium (first neonatal stool)
Main effects of FASD by age	Early childhood Physical and neurodevelopmental delay Medical complications and psychiatric symptoms Attachment insecurity Low adaptability and impaired judgment Childhood and adolescence Physical abnormalities and cognitive impairments Behavior and learning problems Secondary disabilities, such as disruptive school experiences, trouble with the law, confinement (inpatient treatment for mental health problems or alcohol/drug problems, or incarceration for a crime), inappropriate sexual behavior, alcohol and drug problems, dependent living, and unemployment Significant psychiatric comorbidity Low adaptability and impaired judgment Adulthood Mental health issues Major problems with adaptive behavior
Key risk factors for FASD	Maternal heavy drinking and binge drinking Maternal high blood alcohol levels Maternal high alcohol consumption and unplanned pregnancy Genetic factors that affect embryologic and/or fetal development in conjunction with maternal alcohol consumption
Intervention	Focus on early diagnosis Use a multidisciplinary approach Focus on early intervention to address the development of secondary disabilities
Prevention	Refrain from alcohol abuse Increase societal awareness of fetal alcohol related abnormalities Educate women about the consequences of drinking alcohol while pregnant Encourage women to stop drinking alcohol while trying to get pregnant or during pregnancy Consider alternatives to continuing pregnancy Use effective contraception if educational and treatment efforts are unsuccessful

Source: Nulman et al. (2003).

alcohol-related effects) are targeted and typically offered repeated counseling over several years. Both selective and indicated prevention efforts can reduce maternal alcohol consumption and improve children's outcomes. Furthermore, many excellent programs exist for treatment of alcohol abuse. (For examples and further details, see the web sites listed in Appendix B at the end of the book.)

SUMMARY

Because alcohol is in most cases legal and socially acceptable, it is used on a much larger scale than any other known noxious substance. Alcohol is currently the most widely used substance resulting in fetal malformation and intellectual disability. FASD in a child reflects maternal alcohol abuse, and it is a permanent condition for which there is no specific treatment. Prenatal exposure to alcohol, even when used in moderate doses, can create a variety of extensive problems.

In utero exposure to alcohol is among the most common causes of congenital brain injury and neurobehavioral problems in children. The cognitive and neurobehavioral impairment in FASD has a wide range of clinical presentations that also can occur with numerous other disorders. Potential secondary disabilities include various social, behavior, and learning problems. FASD also is closely associated with mental health disorders. Screening for maternal alcohol abuse and fetal exposure can lead to early diagnosis and early intervention.

There have been significant advances in understanding alcohol's harmful effects, but it is not yet fully clear how the timing of alcohol exposure, SES, prenatal care, maternal health, genetic susceptibility, and other factors contribute to FASD. What is known is that the economic costs of FASD are extraordinarily high for society as a whole, for the education and health care systems, and for those individuals affected and their families.

FOR FURTHER THOUGHT AND DISCUSSION

1. To what degree are the criteria for diagnosing FAS, ARBD, and ARND useful?
2. What methods can support the confirmation of alcohol abuse in pregnancy?
3. Review the several risk factors for developing FASD. What preventive measures could be initiated for each?
4. Can a stimulating environment compensate for prenatal damage due to alcohol exposure? What intervention program might you suggest for a child with FAS or ARND?
5. What might constitute an effective public health prevention program for FASD? Whom should such a program target?
6. What should the direction be for future research?

REFERENCES

Aase, J.M., Jones, K.L., & Clarren, S.K. (1995). Do we need the term FAE? *Pediatrics, 95,* 428–430.

Abel, E.L. (1995). An update on incidence of FAS: FAS is not an equal opportunity birth defect. *Neurotoxicology and Teratology, 17,* 437–443.

Abel, E.L. (1998). Why fetal alcohol abuse syndrome? In E.L. Abel (Ed.), *Fetal alcohol abuse syndrome* (pp. 7–8). New York: Plenum Press.

Abel, E.L., & Hannigan, J.N. (1996). Risk factors pathogenesis. In H.L. Sopohr & H. Steinhausen (Eds.), *Alcohol pregnancy and the developing child* (pp. 63–75). Cambridge, United Kingdom: Cambridge University Press.

Adnams, C.M., Kodituwakku, P.W., Hay, A., et al. (2001). Patterns of cognitive-motor development in children with fetal alcohol syndrome from a community in South Africa. *Alcoholism: Clinical and Experimental Research, 24,* 557–562.

Alvik, A., Haldorsen T., & Lindemann, R. (2005). Consistency of reported alcohol use by pregnant women: Anonymous versus confidential questionnaires with item nonresponse differences. *Alcoholism: Clinical and Experimental Research, 29,* 1444–1449.

American Psychiatric Association. (2000). *Diagnostic and statistical manual of mental disorders* (4th ed., text rev.). Washington, DC: Author.

Bearer, C.F. (2001). L1 cell adhesion molecule signal cascades: Targets for ethanol developmental neurotoxicity. *Neurotoxicology, 22,* 625–633.

Bearer, C.F., Lee, S., Salvator, A.E., et al. (1999). Ethyl linoleate in meconium: A biomarker for prenatal ethanol exposure. *Alcoholism: Clinical and Experimental Research, 23,* 487–493.

Bierut, L.J., Dinwiddie, S.H., Begleiter, H., et al. (1998). Familial transmission of substance dependence: Alcohol, marihuana, cocaine and habitual smoking. *Archives of General Psychology, 55,* 982–988.

Bookstein, F.L., Streissguth, A.P., Sampson, P.D., et al. (2001). Corpus, callosum, shape and neuropsychological deficits in adult males with heavy fetal alcohol exposure. *NeuroImage, 15,* 233–251.

Broun, S. (1996). New experiments underscore warnings on maternal drinking. *Science, 273,* 738–739.

Burd, L., Klug, M.G., Martsolf, J.T., et al. (2003). Fetal alcohol syndrome: Neuropsychiatric phenomics. *Neurotoxicology and Teratology, 25,* 697–705.

Caley, L.M., Kramer, C., & Robinson, L.K. (2005). Fetal alcohol spectrum disorder. *The Journal of School Nursing, 21,* 139–146.

Centers for Disease Control and Prevention. (2005). *Fetal alcohol syndrome: Frequently asked questions.* Retrieved November 16, 2005, from http://www.cdc.gov/ncbddd/fas/faqs.htm

Chan, D., Klein, J., Karaskov, T., et al. (2004). Fetal exposure to alcohol as evidenced by fatty acid ethyl esters in meconium in the absence of maternal drinking history in pregnancy. *Therapeutic Drug Monitoring, 26,* 474–481.

Chudley, A.E., Conry, J., Cook, J.L., et al. (2005). Fetal alcohol spectrum disorder: Canadian guidelines for diagnosis. *Canadian Medical Association Journal, 172*(5, Suppl.), S1–S21.

Clarren, S.K., Randels, S.P., Sanderson, M., et al. (2001). Screening for Fetal Alcohol Syndrome in primary schools: A feasibility study. *Teratology, 63,* 3–10.

Coles, C.D. (1991). *Critical periods for prenatal alcohol exposure: Evidence from animal and human studies.* Retrieved September 8, 2005, from http://www.fas-region3.com/files/critperiod.pdf

Coles, C.D., & Platzman, K.A. (1993). Behavioral development in children prenatally exposed to drugs and alcohol. *International Journal of Addiction, 28,* 1393–1433.

Collier, H.O.J., McDonald-Gibson, W.J., & Saeed, S.A. (1975). Letter: Stimulation of prostaglandin biosynthesis by capsaicin, ethanol, and tyramine. *The Lancet, 1,* 702–712.

Cornelius, M.D., Richardson, G.A., Day, N.L., et al. (1994). A comparison of prenatal drinking in two recent samples of adolescents and adults. *Journal of Studies in Alcohol, 55,* 412–419.

Costa, L.G., & Guizzetti, B.M. (2002). Developmental neurotoxicity: Do similar phenotypes indicate a common mode of action? A comparison of fetal alcohol syndrome, toluene embryopathy and maternal phenylketonuria. *Toxicology Letters, 127,* 197–205.

Davis, W.L., Crawford, L.A., Cooper, O.J., et al. (1990). Ethanol induces the generation of reactive free radicals by neural crest cells in vitro. *Journal of Craniofacial Genetics & Developmental Biology, 10,* 277–293.

Dunn, M.S., Bartee, R.T., & Perko, M.A. (2003). Self-reported alcohol use and sexual behaviors of adolescents. *Psychological Reports, 92,* 339–348.

Famy, C., Streissguth, A.P., & Unis, A.S. (1998). Mental illness in adults with fetal alcohol syndrome or fetal alcohol effects. *American Journal of Psychiatry, 155,* 522–554.

Fisher, S.E., Duffy, L., & Atkinson, M. (1986). Selective fetal malnutrition: Effect of acute and chronic ethanol exposure upon rat placental Na,K-ATPase activity. *Alcoholism: Clinical and Experimental Research, 10,* 150–153.

Gareri, J., Chan, D., Klein, J., et al. (2005). Screening for fetal alcohol spectrum disorder. *Canadian Family Physician, 51,* 33–34.

Gladstone, J., Levy, M., Nulman, I., et al. (1997). Characteristics of pregnant women who engage in binge alcohol consumption. *Canadian Medical Association Journal, 156,* 789–794.

Gladstone, J., Nulman, I., & Koren, G. (1996). Reproductive risks of binge drinking during pregnancy. *Reproductive Toxicology, 10,* 3–13.

Goodlett, C.R., Marcussen, B.L., & West, J.R. (1990). A single day of alcohol exposure during the brain growth spurt induces brain weight restriction and cerebellar Purkinje cell loss. *Alcohol, 7,* 107–114.

Hankin, J.R. (2002). Fetal alcohol syndrome prevention research. *Alcohol Research and Health, 26,* 58–65.

Hard, M.L., Raha, S., Spino, M., et al. (2001). Impairment of pyruvate dehydrogenase activity by acetaldehyde. *Alcohol, 25,* 1–8.

Harris, K.R., & Bucens, I.K. (2003). Prevalence of fetal alcohol syndrome in the top end of the northern territory. *Journal of Pediatrics and Child Health, 39,* 528–533.

Henderson, G., Chen, J., & Schenker, S. (1999). Ethanol, oxidative stress, reactive aldehydes, and the fetus. *Frontiers in Bioscience, 4,* 541–550.

Henriksen, T.B., Hjollund, N.H., Jensen, T.K., et al. (2004). Alcohol consumption at the time of conception and spontaneous abortion. *American Journal of Epidemiology, 160,* 661–667.

Higuchi, S., Matsushita, S., Masaki, T., et al. (2004). Influence of genetic variations of ethanol-metabolizing enzymes on phenotypes of alcohol-related disorders. *Annals of the New York Academy of Sciences, 1025,* 472–480.

Ikonomidou, C., Bittigau, P., Ishimura, M., et al. (2000). Ethanol-induced apoptotic neurodegeneration and fetal alcohol syndrome. *Science, 287,* 1056–1060.

Institute of Medicine of the National Academy of Sciences Committee to Study Fetal Alcohol Syndrome. (1996). Introduction. In K. Stratton, C. Howe, & F. Battaglia (Eds.), *Fetal alcohol syndrome* (pp. 17–32). Washington, DC: National Academies Press.

Jones, K.L., & Smith, D.W. (1973). Recognition of the fetal alcohol syndrome in early infancy. *The Lancet, 2,* 999–1001.

Jones, K.L., Smith, D.W., Ulleland, C.H., et al. (1973). Pattern of malformation in offspring of chronic alcohol mothers. *The Lancet, 1,* 1267–1271.

Kaemingk, K.L., Mulvaney, S., & Halverson, P.T. (2003). Learning following prenatal alcohol exposure: Performance on verbal and visual multitrial tasks. *Archives of Clinical Neuropsychology, 18,* 33–47.

Kelly, T.M., Donovan, J.E., Chung, T., et al. (2004). Alcohol use disorders among emergency department-treated older adolescents: A new brief screen (RUFT-Cut) using the AUDIT, CAGE, CRAFFT, and RAPS-QF. *Alcoholism: Clinical and Experimental Research, 28,* 746–753.

Kessler, R.C., MacGonagle, K.A., Zhao, S., et al. (1994). Lifetime and 12-month prevalence of DSM-II-R psychiatric disorders in the United States. *Archives of General Psychology, 51,* 8–19.

Klein, J., Karaskov, T., & Koren, G. (1999). Fatty acid ethyl esters—a novel biological marker for heavy in utero ethanol exposure: A case report. *The Drug Monitor, 21,* 644–646.

Klug, M.G., & Burd, L. (2003). Fetal alcohol syndrome prevention: Annual and cumulative cost savings. *Neurotoxicology and Teratology, 25,* 763–765.

Koren, G., Chan, D., Klein, J., et al. (2002). Estimation of fetal exposure to drugs of abuse, environmental tobacco smoke, and ethanol. *The Drug Monitor, 24,* 23–25.

Koren, G., & Nulman, I. (1994). Teratogenic drugs and chemicals in humans. In G. Koren (Ed.), *Maternal-fetal toxicology* (pp. 33–48). New York: Marcel Dekker.

Koren, G., & Nulman, I. (2002). *The Motherisk guide to diagnosing fetal alcohol spectrum disorder.* Toronto: The Hospital For Sick Children.

Lemoine, P., Harousseau, H., Borteyru, J.P. (1968). Children of alcoholic parents—observed anomalies: Discussion of 127 cases. *Ouest Medical (Paris), 21,* 476–482.

Lieber, C.S. (1991). Alcohol, liver, and nutrition. *Journal of the American College of Nutrition, 10,* 602–632.

Luo, J., & Miller, M. (1998). Growth factor-mediated neural proliferation: Target of ethanol toxicity. *Brain Research Review, 27,* 157–167.

Lupton, C., Burd, L., & Harwood, R. (2004). Cost of fetal alcohol spectrum disorders. *American Journal of Medical Genetics. Part C, Seminars in Medical Genetics, 127,* 42–50.

Ma, W., Pancrazio, J.J., Andreadis, J.D., et al. (2001). Ethanol blocks cytosolic Ca2+ responses triggered by activation of GABA (A) receptor/Cl-channels in cultured proliferating rat neuroepithelial cells. *Neuroscience, 104,* 913–922.

Maier, S.E., Chen, W.J., Miller, J.A,. et al. (1997). Fetal alcohol exposure and temporal vulnerability regional differences in alcohol-induced microencephaly as a function of the timing of binge-like alcohol exposure during rat brain development. *Alcoholism: Clinical and Experimental Research, 21,* 1418–1428.

Mattson, S.N., Riley, E.P., Delis, D.C., et al. (1996). Verbal learning and memory in children with fetal alcohol syndrome. *Alcoholism: Clinical and Experimental Research, 20,* 810–816.

Mattson, S.N., Riley, E.P., Gramling, L., et al. (1997). Heavy prenatal alcohol exposure with or without physical features of fetal alcohol syndrome leads to IQ deficits. *Journal of Pediatrics, 131,* 718–721.

Mattson, S.N., Riley, E.P., Jernigan, T.L., et al. (1994). A decrease in the size of the basal ganglia following prenatal alcohol exposure: A preliminary report. *Neurotoxicology, 16,* 283–297.

May, P.A., Gossage J.P., Brooke L.E., et al. (2005). Maternal risk factors for fetal alcohol syndrome in the Western cape province of South Africa: A population-based study. *American Journal of Public Health, 95,* 1190–1199.

Middaugh, L.D., & Boggan, W.O. (1991). Postnatal growth deficits in prenatal ethanol-exposed mice: Characteristics and critical periods. *Alcoholism: Clinical and Experimental Research, 15,* 919–926.

Miller, M., & Luo, J. (2002). Effects of ethanol and basic fibroblast growth factor on the transforming growth factor beta 1 regulated proliferation of cortical astrocytes and C6 Astrocytoma cells. *Alcoholism: Clinical and Experimental Research, 26,* 671–676.

Moore, C.M., & Lewis, D. (2001). Fatty acid ethyl esters in meconium: Biomarkers for the detection of alcohol exposure in neonates. *Clinica Chimica Acta, 312,* 235–237.

National Institute of Alcohol Abuse and Alcoholism. (1993). *Eighth special report to the U.S. Congress on alcohol and health.* Washington, DC: U.S. Department of Health and Human Services.

National Organization on Fetal Alcohol Syndrome. (2004a). *What are the statistics and facts about FAS and FASD?* Retrieved September 12, 2005, from http://www.nofas.org/faqs.aspx?id=12

National Organization on Fetal Alcohol Syndrome. (2004b). *What is FAS/FASD?* Retrieved September 12, 2005, from http://www.nofas.org/faqs.aspx?id=9

NOFAS Newsroom. (2004, April 15). *Historic agreement heralds new era for prevention and treatment of fetal alcohol spectrum disorders.* Retrieved September 12, 2005, from http://www.nofas.org/news/04152004.aspx

Noland, J.S., Singer, L.T., Arendt, R.E., et al. (2003). Executive functioning in preschool-age children prenatally exposed to alcohol, cocaine, and marijuana. *Alcoholism: Clinical and Experimental Research, 27,* 647–656.

Nulman, I., Laslo, D., & Koren, G. (2003). Fetal alcohol syndrome. In I. Brown & M. Percy (Eds.), *Developmental disabilities in Ontario* (pp. 245–259). Toronto: Ontario Association on Developmental Disabilities.

Nulman, I., Rovet, J., Kennedy, D., et al. (2004). Binge alcohol consumption by non-alcohol-dependent women during pregnancy affects child behavior, but not general intellectual functioning: A prospective controlled study. *Archives of Women's Mental Health, 7,* 173–181.

O'Connor, M.J., Kogan, N., & Findlay, R. (2002). Prenatal alcohol exposure and attachment behavior in children. *Alcoholism: Clinical and Experimental Research, 26,* 1592–1602.

O'Connor, M.J., Shah, B., Whaley, S., et al. (2002). Psychiatric illness in a clinical sample of children with prenatal alcohol exposure. *The American Journal of Drug and Alcohol Abuse, 28,* 743–754.

Office for National Statistics. (2004). *The health of children and young people.* Retrieved June 14, 2005, from http://www.statistics.gov.uk/pdfdir/health0304.pdf

Olney, J.W., Wozniak, D.F., Farber, N.B., et al. (2002). The enigma of fetal alcohol neurotoxicity. *Annals of Medicine, 34,* 109–119.

Olsen, J., Pereira, A., Da, C., et al. (1991). Does maternal tobacco smoking modify the effect of alcohol on fetal growth? *American Journal of Public Health, 81,* 69–73.

Phares, T.M., Morrow, B., Lansky, A., et al. (2004). *Surveillance for disparities in maternal health-related behaviors—selected states, Pregnancy Risk Assessment Monitoring System (PRAMS), 2000–2001.* Retrieved September 20, 2004, from http://www.cdc.gov/mmwr/preview/mmwrhtml/ss5304a1.htm

Poitra, B.A., Marioin, S., Dionne, M., et al. (2003). A school-based screening program for fetal alcohol syndrome. *Neurotoxicology and Teratology, 25,* 725–729.

Sakata-Haga, H., Sawada, K., Ohta, K., et al. (2003). Adverse effects of maternal ethanol consumption on development of dorsal hippocampus in rat offspring. *Acta Neuropathologica (Berl), 105,* 30–36.

Sampson, P.D., Streissguth, A.P., Bookstein, F.L., et al. (1997). Incidence of fetal alcohol syndrome and prevalence of alcohol-related neurodevelopmental disorder. *Teratology, 56,* 317–326.

Sokol, R.J., Delaney-Black, B., & Nordstrom, B. (2003). Fetal alcohol spectrum disorder. *Journal of the American Medical Association, 290,* 2996–2999.

Steinhausen, H.C., Nestler, V., & Huth, H. (1982). Psychopathology and mental functions in the offspring of alcoholic and epileptic mothers. *Journal of the American Academy of Child and Adolescent Psychology, 21,* 268–273.

Steinhausen, H.C., & Spohr, H.L. (1998). Long-term outcome of children with fetal alcohol syndrome: Psychopathology, behavior, and intelligence. *Alcoholism: Clinical and Experimental Research, 22,* 334–338.

Steinhausen, H.C., Willms, J., Metzke, C.W., et al. (2004). Behavioural phenotype in foetal alcohol syndrome and foetal alcohol effects. *Developmental Medicine and Child Neurology, 45,* 179–182.

Stoler, J.M., Huntington, K.S., Peterson, C.M., et al. (1998). The prenatal detection of significant alcohol exposure with maternal blood markers. *Journal of Pediatrics, 133,* 346–352.

Streissguth, A.P., Aase, I.M., Clarren, S.K., et al. (1991). Fetal alcohol syndrome in adolescents and adults. *Journal of the American Medical Association, 265,* 1961–1967.

Streissguth, A.P., Barr, H.M., Kogan, J., et al. (1996). *Understanding the occurrence of secondary disabilities in clients with fetal alcohol syndrome (FAS) and fetal alcohol effects (FAE), Final report to the Centers for Disease Control and Prevention (CDC), August, 1996.* Seattle: University of Washington, Fetal Alcohol & Drug Unit (Tech. Rep. No. 96-06).

Streissguth, A.P., Bookstein, F.L., & Barr, H.M. (1996). A dose-response study of the enduring effects of prenatal alcohol exposure: Birth to 14 years. In H. Spohn & H. Steinhausen (Eds.), *Alcohol, pregnancy and the developing child* (pp. 141–168). Cambridge, United Kingdom: Cambridge University Press.

Streissguth, A.P., Bookstein, F.L., Sampson, P.D., et al. (1996). *The enduring effects of prenatal alcohol exposure on child development.* Ann Arbor: University of Michigan Press.

Streissguth, A.P., Bookstein, F.L., Barr, H.M., et al. (2004). Risk factors for adverse life outcomes in fetal alcohol syndrome and fetal alcohol effects. *Journal of Developmental and Behavioral Pediatrics, 25,* 228–238.

Streissguth, A.P., & Little, R.E. (1994). *Unit 5: Alcohol, pregnancy, and the fetal alcohol syndrome: Second edition. Project Cork Institute Medical School Curriculum; Slide lecture series on Biomedical education: Alcohol use and its medical consequences.* Produced by Dartmouth Medical School, Hanover, NH.

Substance Abuse and Mental Health Service Administration. (1996). *National household survey on drug abuse.* Rockville, MD: U.S. Department of Health and Human Services.

Sulik, K.K., Johnston, M.C., Draft, P.A., et al. (1986). Fetal alcohol syndrome and DiGeorge anomaly: Critical ethanol exposure periods for craniofacial malformations as illustrated in an animal model. *American Journal of Medical Genetics, 2,* 97–112.

Sulik, K.K., Johnston, M.C., & Webb, M.A. (1981). Fetal alcohol syndrome: Embryogenesis in a mouse model. *Science, 214,* 936–938.

Tuormaa, T.E. (1994). *The adverse effects of alcohol on reproduction: Foresight literature summaries.* Retrieved September 12, 2005, from http://www.foresight-preconception.org.uk/summaries/frames/alcohol-nf.html

Ugarte, G., & Valenzuela, J. (1971). Mechanisms of liver and pancreas damage in man. In Y. Israel & J. Mardones (Eds.), *Biological basis of alcoholism* (pp. 133–161). Hoboken, NJ: John Wiley & Sons.

Vorhees, C.V. (1986). Principles of behavioral teratology. In E.P. Riley & C.V. Vorhees (Eds.), *Handbook of behavioral teratology* (pp. 23–48). New York: Kluwer Academic/Plenum Publishers.

Warren, K.R., Calhoun, F.J., May, P.A., et al. (2001). Fetal alcohol syndrome: An international perspective. *Alcoholism: Clinical and Experimental Research, 25,* 202S–206S.

Warren, K.R., & Li, T.K. (2005). Genetic polymorphisms: Impact on the risk of fetal alcohol spectrum disorders. Birth defects research. *Clinical and Molecular Teratology, Part A, 73,* 195–203.

Willford, J.A., Richardson, G.A., Leech, S.L., et al. (2004). Verbal and visuospatial learning and memory function in children with moderate prenatal alcohol exposure. *Alcoholism: Clinical and Experimental Research, 28,* 497–507.

Windle, M. (2003). Alcohol use among adolescents and young adults. *Alcohol Research and Health, 27,* 79–85.

World Health Organization. (2003). *International Statistical Classification of Diseases and Related Health Problems, 10th Revision (ICD-10)—version for 2003.* Retrieved January 24, 2006, from http://www3.who.int/icd/vol1htm2003/fr-icd.htm

Yang, H.Y., Shum, A.Y.C., & Ng, H.T. (1986). Effect of ethanol on human umbilical artery and vein in vitro. *Gynecologic and Obstetric Investigation, 22,* 131–135.

15

Other Syndromes and Disorders Associated with Intellectual and Developmental Disabilities

MAIRE PERCY, TOM CHEETHAM, MARIA GITTA, BEV MORRISON, KAROLINA MACHALEK, SIVAN BEGA, ALISON BURGESS, CHRISTINA DE RIVERA, TRISH DOMI, YOUSSEF EL HAYEK, EVERLYNE GOMEZ, AMY HAYASHI, RAQUEL HESKIN SWEEZIE, ANTHONY LAU, ANYA MCLAREN, EWA NIECHWIEJ-SZWEDO, OMA D.D. PERSAUD, NAM PHAN, EVAN JON PROPST, MARCUS SALVATORI, FIONA WONG, ATHENA YPSILANTI, AND JENNIE YUM

WHAT YOU WILL LEARN ABOUT IN THIS CHAPTER

- Syndromes and disorders commonly associated with intellectual and developmental disabilities that are not presented in separate chapters in this book
- Physical and behavior characteristics, causes, prevalence, diagnosis, and intervention issues applicable to each disorder
- Relevant resources that will provide more information about the disorders described and promote independent learning

The word *syndrome* is derived from the Greek words *syn* (meaning "together with") and *drome* (meaning "to run"), which, taken together, mean "a running together" or "a complex of concurrent things." In the early 21st century, the term is understood to mean a group of signs and symptoms that are characteristic of a particular disease or disorder. This chapter focuses on more than 30 of the most common syndromes and disorders that are associated with intellectual or developmental disabilities, or both, and are not emphasized in other chapters. Many, although not all, of the conditions covered in this chapter have a genetic basis. Surveys indicate that parents and professionals, including teachers and pediatricians, have limited knowledge about genetic syndromes and disorders associated with intellectual and developmental disabilities—particularly their physical, cognitive, and behavioral aspects (e.g., Fidler, 2002; Lee et al., 2005). Professionals are in a position to make a diagnosis or to provide a referral for a diagnosis and also to make critical treatment and education decisions for individuals with intellectual and developmental disabilities. Furthermore, as behavioral information becomes better known, more targeted treatments and educational accommodations can be developed for children with specific genetic intellectual or developmental disabilities. Because of general lack of awareness in the field, it is important that basic information about syndromes and disorders, as well as approaches for their intervention and treatment, be readily available for both laypeople and professionals. Chapter 9 outlined different categories of factors that result in intellectual and developmental disabilities. Chapter 15 provides insights into processes and mechanisms that cause specific syndromes and disorders in addition to those highlighted in other chapters of this book. The material in this chapter and its organization enables readers to quickly compare different features of different syndromes and disorders and to focus, for example, on the behavioral features.

There are many other known syndromes that are not covered in this chapter, and still others will no doubt become known or come to greater prominence in coming years. Knowledge about syndromes and disorders is changing very rapidly. Thus, the organization of material in this chapter is intended to promote curiosity and a passion for knowledge that will form the basis for lifelong learning in this area.

Due to the comprehensive nature of this chapter, references have been styled differently to streamline text and improve readability. Each section provides an overview of a genetic syndrome not detailed elsewhere in this book. Basic information was synthesized from general sources to create these overviews; the sources are grouped by syndrome in the references list at the end of the chapter.

The chapter authors are grateful to Marika Korossy, Surrey Place Centre, for providing some key references for this chapter, and to Victoria Duda and Rivka Birkan for their helpful comments.

This chapter's information on syndromes and disorders is presented in special table format, for easy reference. Tables are divided into sections that cover different aspects of each syndrome or disorder. The topics covered include physical and health characteristics, prevalence, genotype (the genetic basis) or cause, functional and behavioral phenotype (observable characteristics), diagnosis, and intervention approaches and issues. Unless otherwise stated, the prevalence of the syndrome or disorder is internationally recognized and is based on a number of studies from around the world.

The term *best practice* is often used in the field of intellectual and developmental disabilities. This term refers to techniques or methodologies that, through experience and research, have proven to reliably lead to a desired result—for example, in diagnosis and treatment. A commitment to using the best practices in any field is a commitment to using all of the reliable knowledge and technology at one's disposal to ensure success. The information in this chapter goes beyond best practice, and in some instances it describes approaches that are still experimental. Such information may not only promote multidisciplinary collaboration in research but may also save lives. (An example of experimental treatment is of Hunter syndrome with enzyme replacement therapy.)

Although not specifically highlighted in the sections on treatment and intervention, genetic counseling should always be considered in the case of syndromes and disorders that have a genetic basis (whether inherited or not) and thus a chance of recurring. Issues that are discussed in genetic counseling include the following: the risk for a genetic condition to occur or recur; the meaning of a diagnosis and its range of severity; the way in which the condition is inherited so that informed decisions can be made about who in a family should be tested for the disorder; and options for family planning, including prenatal diagnosis, egg/sperm donation, or adoption. Each option has risks and benefits that individuals need to understand in order to choose the option that is appropriate for them. (See Chapter 28 for more details about genetic counseling.) The reader is reminded that assessment, diagnosis, treatment, and other applications should be based on more in-depth information than is given in this chapter and should be carried out by qualified professionals.

Various methods are used for the diagnosis of the syndromes and disorders presented in this chapter. Some tests include enzyme assays, electron microscopy of tissue samples, brain imaging techniques, electroencephalograms (EEG), ultrasounds, echocardiograms, electrical studies of the eyes, various forms of chromosomal analysis, and genetic testing. Enzyme assays identify specific missing enzymes. Electron microscopy of tissue samples can detect various types of deposits in tissues. Brain imaging techniques include computed tomography (CT) scans, magnetic resonance imaging (MRI), and magnetic resonance spectroscopy (MRS). A CT scan uses X rays and a computer to create a sophisticated picture of the brain's tissues and structures. MRI uses a combination of magnetic fields and radio waves, instead of radiation, to create a picture of the brain. MRS is a type of imaging that reveals levels of particular substances. EEG uses special patches placed on the scalp to record patterns of electrical activity inside the brain, which may indicate that an individual has seizures. Ultrasounds use high frequency sound waves to produce images of organs and of the fetus. Echocardiography (ECHO, ultrasound of the heart) enables examination of the size, shape, and motion of the heart. Electrical studies of the eyes include visual-evoked potentials (VEP), electro-retinograms (ERG), and retinal angiography, which can detect various eye problems. Electron microscopy of tissue samples can detect various deposits found in tissues. (*General source:* U.S. National Library of Medicine & the National Institutes of Health, 2003.)

Chromosomal analysis (the analysis of genetic material which is packaged into chromosomes) and genetic testing can be done both prenatally and postnatally. Three common prenatal diagnostic techniques include amniocentesis, chorionic villus sampling (CVS), and percutaneous umbilical blood sampling (PUBS). Amniocentesis involves the surgical insertion of a hollow needle through the abdominal wall and into the uterus of a pregnant female; amniotic fluid is obtained and examined for fetal chromosomal abnormalities. CVS is a removal of fetal cells through the abdominal wall or by way of the vagina and uterine cervix for analysis; it is performed at nine to twelve weeks of gestation. PUBS involves removal of a sample of fetal blood from the umbilical cord. It is important to note that there are certain risks associated with these procedures (see Chapters 7 and 28 for more information on amniocentesis, CVS, and PUBS). Chromosomal analysis includes the use of fluorescence in situ hybridization (FISH) and karyotyping. Changes in DNA extracted from cells can be detected by polymerase chain reaction (PCR) analysis, Southern blotting, and other techniques. FISH is a process which vividly paints chromosomes or portions of chromosomes with fluorescent molecules. A karyotype is the chromosomal component of an individual, including the number of chromosomes and any visible abnormalities. This term also refers to a photograph of an individual's chromosomes, and karyotyping is the process of taking a photograph of an individual's chromosomes and examining them for abnormalities. Each chromosome has a p (for *petit*) arm and q (next letter in the alphabet) arm.

Chromosomes 13, 14, and 15 have very small p arms. When a karyotype is made, the chromosomes are oriented so that the q arms are always on the bottom and the p arms on the top. The arms are separated by a region known as the centromere—a pinched area of the chromosome. Regions of chromosomes that contain abnormalities are designated with three identifiers. For example, in an abnormality identified as 15q11, the 15 refers to chromosome 15, the q to the q arm, and the 11 to band 11 on the q arm. PCR is a technique for making an unlimited number of copies of any piece of DNA. The copied DNA can be analyzed using a variety of techniques that can detect changes in the nucleotide sequence or in the patterns of the addition of methyl groups to specific parts of the DNA. A common approach used in genetic testing involves cleaving the DNA (cutting at a specific site) with a specific restriction endonuclease enzyme and determining the sizes of the fragments using gel electrophoresis. Southern blotting is a process of identifying and locating DNA sequences that are complementary to another piece of DNA called a probe. Distinct segments of DNA form genes. Attempts are being made to give every gene in the human body a unique and meaningful name and guidelines exist for this process (Wain et al., 2002). (*General sources:* National Human Genome Research Institute, 2004; U.S. National Library of Medicine & the National Institutes of Health, 2003; see also Chapters 7 and 9.)

In addition to the information presented on each syndrome and disorder in table format, the chapter gives background information; this includes historical aspects of the syndrome and disorder, such as the origin of its name, when it was discovered, and its mode of genetic inheritance, if applicable. (As explained in Chapter 7, common modes of inheritance include autosomal dominant, autosomal recessive, X-linked dominant, and X-linked recessive.) Because genes are distinct segments of DNA, the inheritance of genetic disorders, abnormalities, or traits is described by both the type of chromosome on which the abnormal gene resides (autosomal or sex chromosome) and by whether the trait itself is dominant or recessive. Autosomal disorders are inherited through the non–sex chromosomes (pairs 1 through 22). Sex-linked disorders are inherited through the X chromosome, one of the sex chromosomes (disorders are not thought to be inherited through the Y chromosome). Because females have two X chromosomes and males have only one, males usually are severely affected by X-linked disorders, whereas females often are spared. Dominant inheritance occurs when an abnormal gene from one parent is capable of causing a disorder even though the matching gene from the other parent is normal; in this case, expression from the abnormal gene dominates the outcome of the gene pair. Recessive inheritance occurs when both genes of a pair must be abnormal to produce a disorder; if only one gene in the pair is abnormal, the disorder does not occur or is only mildly present. For X-linked recessive inheritance, any male with one copy of an X-linked recessive disorder gene is affected, because males only have one X chromosome. Many syndromes and disorders are sporadic in nature, meaning that they occur in individuals with no history of the disorder in their family; they are often due to a de novo chromosomal mutation, a permanent alteration of the chromosomes that is not inherited but that can be transmitted. (*General source:* Human Genome Project Information, 2004; see also Chapter 7.)

Chapters 7, 8, and 9 contain background information that complements specific information in this chapter, and Appendix A at the end of the book defines certain technical terms. The chapter resources that appear at the end of this book are excellent starting points for finding additional information. Although the Internet is not always a reliable source of information, it has revolutionized the way that information about any topic can be obtained. Information about almost any syndrome or disorder can now be quickly obtained from specific and general web sites. University library and other electronic databases (e.g., PubMed, PsycINFO) include a wide range of theoretical, research, and descriptive articles on syndromes and disorders.

ANGELMAN SYNDROME

Background

Angelman syndrome was first described in 1965 by Harry Angelman, an English physician. He described three children with a stiff and jerky gait, absent speech, excessive laughter, and seizures. Angelman syndrome is sometimes referred to as "happy puppet" syndrome (although this is not the preferred term) because of paroxysmal (convulsive or fitful) laughter and an ataxic, "puppet-like" gait. The same chromosomal region is involved in both Angelman syndrome and Prader-Willi syndrome, but the two syndromes are clinically distinct. Angelman syndrome usually occurs sporadically, but some cases are inherited in an autosomal dominant fashion.

BATTEN DISEASE/ NEURONAL CEROID LIPOFUSCINOSIS

Background

Batten disease is the juvenile, and the most common, form of a group of disorders called the neuronal ceroid lipofuscinoses (NCLs). The term *Batten disease* is sometimes used interchangeably with *NCL*. Batten disease is named after the English neurologist and pedia-

Table 15.1. Aspects of Angelman syndrome

PHYSICAL AND HEALTH CHARACTERISTICS
- Dysmorphic or atypical facial features that develop by the age of 2 years, including a wide and smiling mouth, a pointed chin, a prominent tongue, wide-spaced teeth, a large jaw, and deep-set eyes.
- Approximately one half of all affected individuals have fair-colored hair and skin, and most have blue eyes.
- Head circumference is usually below the 50th percentile; approximately one fourth of affected individuals have microcephaly (a small head).

PREVALENCE
- 1 in 10,000 to 1 in 20,000 live births but the condition is underdiagnosed.

GENOTYPE OR CAUSE
- A variety of genetic abnormalities involving chromosome 15 and the 15q11-13 region account for 80%–90% of cases. These abnormalities interfere with expression of the UBE3A gene, which encodes a protein called E6-AP ubiquitin protein ligase (or ubiquitin ligase 3)—an enzyme that is necessary for normal protein turnover within cells.
- Genetic abnormalities include deletions on chromosome 15 inherited from the mother, duplication of chromosome 15 inherited from the father, imprinting defects (defects in expression of a gene), and point mutations (mutations involving a single nucleotide) or small deletions within the UBE3A gene in this region.
- The UBE3A gene demonstrates tissue specific imprinting—it is expressed from maternal and paternal alleles in all tissues except specific parts of the central nervous system. In the brain, the paternal copy of UBE3A is naturally silenced, and UBE3A is expressed only from the maternal copy of the gene.
- If the protein coded by UBE3A is not made, then certain proteins in the brain are not degraded.

FUNCTIONAL AND BEHAVIORAL PHENOTYPE
- Severe to profound developmental delay is evident in 100% of cases by 6–12 months of age.
- Individuals laugh frequently and inappropriately; hand flapping may occur.
- Individuals walk with a wide-base gait and stiff legs ("puppet-like" gait).
- Grabbing and hair pulling is frequently seen.
- Affected individuals tend to love water.
- Sleep disturbances are common.
- Affected individuals have a happy, sociable disposition.
- Speech is profoundly impaired in 98% of cases and absent in 88%; the ability to comprehend language is stronger than the ability to express it.
- Affected individuals may exhibit alternating strabismus (squinting caused by inability of one eye to attain binocular vision with the other eye because of an imbalance of the muscles of the eyeball).
- Seizure disorder with a characteristic EEG occurs in approximately 80% of affected individuals.

DIAGNOSIS
- A clinical diagnosis can be confirmed by laboratory testing in approximately 80% of cases.
- A chromosome study and a molecular analysis by FISH, polymorphism analysis, or methylation testing are employed to look for alterations in 15q11-q13.
- A positive genetic test may confirm the diagnosis, but a normal result does not exclude the diagnosis; about 20% of individuals whose clinical presentation is characteristic of Angelman syndrome will have normal results after genetic laboratory studies of chromosome 15.

INTERVENTION APPROACHES AND ISSUES
- Seizure management is the main focus of the primary care physician; seizure control sometimes requires trials with more than one anticonvulsant medication.
- Pharmacotherapy (drug therapy) and behavior management may help with sleep disturbances.
- Sign language may be required for communication.
- Identifying behavior problems and providing appropriate intervention can improve adaptive functioning.

trician, Frederick Eustace Batten, who first described it in 1903. It is a severe form of lysosomal storage disease. Lysosomes are organelles in cells that are sometimes referred to as the "garbage disposal units." They contain a large variety of enzymes that are capable of breaking down most biological macromolecules including proteins, lipids, nucleic acids, and carbohydrates. NCLs are caused by neuronal cell death linked to the buildup of lipopigments. Lipopigments are made up of fats and proteins and, when viewed under a microscope, they appear yellowish-green. Lipoprotein deposits come in various forms: osmophilic (resembling sand or gravel), curvilinear (resembling half-moons), rectilinear (characterized by straight as opposed to curved lines), or fingerprint (resembling fingerprints).

The different forms of NCL are classified by age of onset: infantile NCL, late infantile NCL, juvenile NCL, and adult NCL; all forms have a similar progression and outcome, but they are all genetically different. The mode of inheritance of NCL is usually autosomal recessive, except for adult NCL, which can occasionally be autosomal dominant. Refer also to the Lafora Disease/Lafora Progressive Myoclonus Epilepsy section for more information on NCL and related disorders.

CATCH 22/22q11.2 DELETION SYNDROME

Background

Chromosome 22q11.2 deletion syndrome (22q11DS), previously referred to as CATCH 22 syndrome, denotes a group of phenotypically similar syndromes caused by a deletion on the long arm of chromosome 22. 22q11.2 DS includes syndromes such as DiGeorge syndrome (DGS), velocardiofacial (Shprintzen) syndrome (VCFS), velofacial hypoplasia (Sedlackova syndrome), conotruncal anomaly face syndrome (CTAF), Caylor cardiofacial syndrome, and autosomal dominant Opitz G/BBB syndrome. Individuals affected with DiGeorge syndrome, named after American pediatrician Angelo Mari DiGeorge, have a collection of findings which include a congenital heart defect, hypocalcemia (low serum calcium), increased susceptibility to infections (due to abnormalities of the thymus gland), and occasionally a cleft palate (roof of the mouth). In 1955, a pattern of velofacial hypoplasia (undergrowth) causing hypernasal speech and associated facial dysmorphism was observed in children of Czech origin by Dr. Eva Sedlackova. In 1976, Dr. Kinouchi, a Japanese

Table 15.2. Aspects of Batten disease/neuronal ceroid lipofuscinosis (NCL)

PHYSICAL AND HEALTH CHARACTERISTICS
- Over time, affected individuals experience cognitive impairment, worsening seizures, and progressive loss of sight and motor skills. Eventually, individuals with Batten disease/NCL become blind, confined to bed, and unable to communicate.
- As of 2007, the disorder is fatal.

PREVALENCE
- Overall: 1 in 20,000 to 1 in 100,000 births internationally, except for 1 in 12,500 in Finland.
- Infantile NCL: 11%–23% of all cases.
- Late infantile NCL: 35% of all cases.
- Juvenile NCL: 35%–50% of all cases.
- Adult NCL: 1%–10% of all cases.

GENOTYPE OR CAUSE
- Infantile NCL: A mutation of the CLN1 gene on chromosome 1. The CLN1 gene encodes a lysosomal enzyme called palmitoyl-protein thioesterase (PPT), which removes fatty acids, such as palmitate, that are linked to proteins by thioester bonds.
- Late infantile NCL: A mutation of the CLN2 gene on chromosome 11. The CLN2 gene encodes a lysosomal enzyme called tripeptidyl-peptidase 1 (TTP1), which cleaves protein chains at serine residues.
- Juvenile NCL: A mutation of the CLN3 gene on chromosome 16. The CLN3 gene encodes a 438-amino-acid lysosomal membrane protein.
- Adult NCL: A mutation of the CLN4 gene, which has yet to be localized and identified.

FUNCTIONAL AND BEHAVIORAL PHENOTYPE

Infantile NCL
- Onset occurs between the ages of 6 months and 2 years.
- Early signs include a very small head, myoclonic jerks (sudden increases in muscle tone), loss of motor function, seizures, and cognitive impairment.
- There is a very rapid progression to complete vision loss and a vegetative state.
- Usually fatal before 5 years of age.

Late infantile NCL
- Onset occurs between the ages of 2 and 4 years.
- Early signs include loss of motor function, seizures, and cognitive impairment.
- Rapid progression to complete vision loss and a vegetative state.
- Usually fatal between 8 and 12 years of age.

Juvenile NCL
- Onset occurs between the ages of 5 and 10 years.
- Early signs include loss of vision, loss of motor function, seizures, and mental impairment.
- Moderate progression to complete vision loss and a vegetative state.
- Usually fatal by late teens or early 20s.

Adult NCL
- Onset usually before the age of 40 years.
- Early signs are similar to those of childhood NCLs but are much milder.
- Complete vision loss occurs in the autosomal recessive form but not in the autosomal dominant form.
- Very slow progression to vegetative state.
- Life expectancy is shortened, but the age of fatality is variable.

DIAGNOSIS

The following tests are used to diagnose NCLs:
- Enzyme assays: Identify specific missing lysosomal enzymes for infantile and late infantile forms only.
- Brain imaging: CT scan reveals affected brain areas; MRI reveals generalized brain atrophy (shrinkage of the brain); and MRS application detects loss of certain substances in neurons, altered levels of certain substances in glia (nonneuronal cells that support neuronal function), and increased levels of lactate (a substance used to produce energy) in the gray and white matter of the brain.
- EEGs detect seizures.
- Electrical studies are conducted for the eyes: VEP, ERG, and retinal angiography detect various eye problems, such as retinal cell death and shrinkage of the optic nerve.
- Electron microscopy is conducted for tissue samples: granular osmophilic deposits are found in most tissue types in infantile NCL; lipoprotein deposits of different shapes (curvilinear, rectilinear, and fingerprint) are found in most tissue types in late infantile NCL; and lipoprotein deposits in the form of fingerprint bodies found in most tissue types in juvenile NCL. Findings are unspecified for adult NCL.

INTERVENTION APPROACHES AND ISSUES
- Currently, no treatment can stop or reverse progression.
- Anticonvulsant drugs to control seizures.
- Physical and occupational therapy to help prolong retention of motor and mental function.
- Increased intake of vitamins C and E in combination with reduced intake of vitamin A to slow progression.
- In October 2005, the U.S. Food and Drug Administration approved the transplantation of fetal neuronal cells into the brains of children with infantile and late infantile versions of Batten disease.

physician, reported a typical facial appearance specifically seen in patients with conotruncal anomalies and called it conotruncal anomaly face syndrome (CTAF). In 1978, Robert Shprintzen, an American speech pathologist, described a disorder running in families where the patients had a combination of cleft palate or velopharyngeal-incompetence (VPI; the failure of the back of the palate and the throat to close the space connecting the mouth and the nose during normal speech, causing the patient to sound like he or she has a cold), heart defects, learning disabilities, and a characteristic facial appearance. Shprintzen called this condition velocardiofacial syndrome (*velo* for palate or roof of the mouth, *cardio* for heart, and *facial* for the typical facial characteristics seen in patients). In 1980 in Japan, Dr. Shimizu noticed that there were similarities between individuals who were diagnosed with CTAF and those who were diagnosed with DiGeorge syndrome. In 1981, Shprintzen reviewed the patients reported to have CTAF and suggested that they had velocardiofacial syndrome. Opitz G/BBB syndrome was first described by John Opitz, a German-American human geneticist and physician; the hallmark features include hypertelorism (widely-spaced eyes), hypospadias (the opening of the penis is not at the tip), swallowing problems, and noisy breathing. These findings were extremely variable, from severe to mild, in affected family members. All of these syndromes were found to have the same underlying cause—a deletion on the long arm of chromosome 22; hence, are all known as 22q11.2 deletion syndrome.

Table 15.3. Aspects of CATCH 22/22q11.2 deletion syndrome

PHYSICAL AND HEALTH CHARACTERISTICS

- Variable dysmorphic features that include abnormalities of the palate, particularly velopharyngeal incompetence and a cleft palate, as well as characteristic facial features such as a round face, almond-shaped eyes, bulbous nose, and posteriorly rotated and malformed large ears.
- Physical features are present at birth and do not increase in severity with age.
- Congenital heart disease in 74% of individuals, particularly conotruncal malformations (tetralogy of Fallot, interrupted aortic arch, ventricular septal defect, and truncus arteriosus; see Chapter 10 for more information about these malformations).
- Immune deficiency occurs in 77% of individuals.
- Other health risks include hypocalcemia, hypoparathyroidism (underactivity of the parathyroid gland); hypotonia and weak muscles; significant feeding problems; renal (kidney) anomalies; recurrent ear infections, including otitis media (middle ear infection), which may lead to hearing loss; growth hormone deficiency leading to short stature; skeletal abnormalities such as scoliosis (curvature of the spine); vision problems; autoimmune disorder; and seizures (in absence of hypocalcemia).

PREVALENCE

- 1 in 4,000 to 1 in 6,395 live births.

GENOTYPE OR CAUSE

- A microdeletion on the long arm of chromosome 22, specifically 22q11.2.
- The chance of inheriting the syndrome is only 10%–15% when one parent possesses the deletion.

FUNCTIONAL AND BEHAVIORAL PHENOTYPE

- There is a wide phenotypic spectrum.
- Apraxia of speech (difficulty planning and executing speech that is not the result of muscular disturbance) occurs, as well as developmental delays.
- Learning disabilities are present, with verbal skills typically being much better preserved than nonverbal skills. There is a pronounced deficit in visual–spatial memory.
- Psychiatric illnesses can occur. The most common is schizophrenia, of which the prevalence is approximately 25%. Other psychiatric problems reported in adults who have 22q11.2 deletion syndrome include major depression, bipolar disorder, obsessive-compulsive disorder, and alcoholism.

DIAGNOSIS

- In most cases, the deletion is too small to be detected by routine chromosomal analysis, so a more sensitive chromosome test (FISH) is used.

INTERVENTION APPROACHES AND ISSUES

- In the case of inherited 22q11.2 deletion syndrome, the parent possessing the deletion often displays mild features and is not diagnosed until after the child is diagnosed.
- It is necessary to manage congenital heart disease, immune deficiency, and the other previously noted health risks.

Approximately 3% of people with congenital heart problems have 22q11.2 deletion syndrome. Most forms of 22q11.2 deletion syndrome are sporadic and some are inherited in an autosomal dominant manner.

CONGENITAL HYPOTHYROIDISM

Background

The thyroid is a gland situated at the front of the neck just below the Adam's apple. It takes iodine from foods and uses this in the production of thyroid hormones, triiodothyronine (T3) or thyroxine (T4). The thyroid stimulating hormone (TSH) is released from the pituitary gland following stimulation by low levels of T3, T4, or both, and it stimulates the production of T3 and T4 by the thyroid. Thyroid hormones control metabolism (conversion of oxygen and calories to energy). Every cell in the body depends on thyroid hormones for regulation of their metabolism. Thyroxine affects the function and development of many body systems and is essential for normal growth and development; it is especially necessary in the first 3 years of life when it plays an important role in ensuring normal brain growth and nervous system development.

As explained in Chapter 9, congenital hypothyroidism can result from a deficiency of iodine and sometimes from a deficiency of other micronutrients; hypothyroidism resulting from iodine deficiency is sometimes referred to as "cretinism" and is most common in developing nations and areas of the world in which available food is low in iodine. In the absence of iodine deficiency, congenital hypothyroidism is associated with thyroid gland agenesis (inadequate or absence of development) or dysgenesis (faulty development) or with deficient production of thyroid hormones. In North America, congenital hypothyroidism due to iodine deficiency is rare and it is associated with three different types of thyroid abnormalities: 40% of affected infants have underdeveloped or absent thyroid glands, 40% have thyroid glands that are in the wrong place (e.g., under the tongue, at the far side of the neck), and the remaining 20% of infants have a deficient production of thyroid hormones. The deficiency in thyroid hormones can result from either a deficiency in TSH or a deficiency in T3, T4, or both. In most cases that are not due to iodine deficiency, hypothyroidism arises from an underfunctioning thyroid gland. In rare instances, there can be a normally functioning gland that does not make enough thyroid hormone because of insufficient TSH from the pituitary.

Congenital hypothyroidism can be transient or permanent; an estimated 15%–20% of infants with hypothyroidism have a temporary form of the disorder and will only require treatment for a limited number of years. In cases with a genetic basis, some defects are sporadic, whereas others are known to be inherited in an autosomal recessive manner.

Table 15.4. Aspects of congenital hypothyroidism

PHYSICAL AND HEALTH CHARACTERISTICS
Features may include
- Arrested physical growth
- Thick neck due to goiter (enlargement of the thyroid gland)
- Puffy face
- Dry, swollen skin
- Large abdomen
- Possible umbilical hernia
- Prolonged jaundice
- Feeding difficulties
- Respiratory difficulties aggravated by a large tongue
- Cold, mottled arms and legs

PREVALENCE
- Iodine deficiency is the leading cause of intellectual and developmental disability worldwide; up to 10% of some populations (e.g., in China) are affected by iodine deficiency that affects thyroid function.
- Too much iodine can also result in hypothyroidism.
- In iodine-replete areas in North America, 1 in 3,000 to 1 in 4,000 newborns are affected.
- More females than males are affected by congenital hypothyroidism not involving iodine deficiency. No sex predominance is apparent in congenital hypothyroidism resulting from iodine deficiency.

GENOTYPE OR CAUSE
- In China, the E4 allele of apolipoprotein E is a risk factor for fetal iodine deficiency spectrum. (Negative effects of iodine deficiency in a population can be prevented by ensuring that the population has an adequate intake of iodine.)
- In the absence of iodine deficiency, many different genetic factors result in congenital hypothyroidism, such as mutations in the TSH receptor gene or thyroid transcription factors PAX 8, TTF 1, TTF 2, Pit 1, and Prop 1 (transcription factors are regulatory proteins that initiate or influence the copying of DNA into RNA—i.e., production of RNA—upon binding with DNA).

FUNCTIONAL AND BEHAVIORAL PHENOTYPE
- Lower cognitive functioning that becomes apparent with age.
- Sluggishness, sleepiness, poor cry.

DIAGNOSIS
- In North America, congenital hypothyroidism is assessed by the "heel stick" procedure, in which a few drops of blood are collected on filter paper by pricking the heel before an infant is discharged from the hospital or birthing center. The dried blood specimens are tested for the amount of T3, T4, or both, and for the amount of TSH.
- A low level of T3, T4, or both, and an elevated level of TSH indicate that an infant lacks normal thyroid function.
- Although an elevated level of TSH is a more sensitive and specific marker of hypothyroidism, the majority of North American screening programs check levels of T3, T4, or both at the initial test and confirm the diagnosis with the measurement of TSH.

INTERVENTION APPROACHES AND ISSUES
- Early detection and treatment is vital to impede the progress of this syndrome; newborns should be screened for iodine deficiency or thyroid hormone deficiency.
- Treatment should be given for iodine deficiency, if relevant.
- Treatment should be given for thyroid hormone deficiency if the level of TSH is high and the levels of T3, T4, or both are low.

CONGENITAL RUBELLA SYNDROME

Background

Rubella is a viral infection that affects the fetus but causes only a minor fever and rash in the mother. Much of the earlier work on rubella was done by German and French scientists, and hence it is also known as German measles and French measles. In 1941, Normann Gregg, an Australian opthalmologist, observed that large numbers of cataracts and other birth defects in children occurred right after rubella outbreaks. He suggested that if pregnant women caught rubella, the virus could be devastating to the fetus. Between 1964 and 1965, there was a worldwide epidemic of rubella. Pregnant women who contracted rubella in the first trimester of their pregnancy passed the rubella virus to their developing fetus, causing the child to be born with intellectual or developmental disability, or both, and other health problems. In the United States alone, approximately

Table 15.5. Aspects of congenital rubella syndrome (CRS)

PHYSICAL AND HEALTH CHARACTERISTICS
- Central nervous system disorders, specifically microcephaly (small head) and developmental disabilities, are apparent.
- Hearing impairment occurs.
- Visual impairment is involved, typically cataracts (clouding of the eye lens), glaucoma (increased pressure within the eyeball), or chorioretinitis (inflammation of the choroid and the retina, two layers of the eye).
- Congenital heart disease and patent ductus arteriosus (abnormal, persistent opening of a blood vessel between the outflow of the heart and the lungs after birth) can occur.
- Affected children can develop additional medical problems as they get older; glaucoma (an eye disease associated with increased pressure within the eyeball, resulting in damage to the retina) and diabetes (high blood sugar) are two of the most common late-onset manifestations.

PREVALENCE
- CRS is a serious problem in some countries but is rare in vaccinated areas.
- 100,000 cases per year appear worldwide.

GENOTYPE OR CAUSE
- An immature blood–brain barrier and the absence of antibodies to rubella may predispose to rubella infection of the central nervous system.

(continued)

Table 15.5. *(continued)*

FUNCTIONAL AND BEHAVIORAL PHENOTYPE
- Developmental disabilities occur.
- In one study of 243 children with CRS, 15% had "reactive" behavior disorder and 7% had autism (Chess, Fernandez, & Korn, 1978).

DIAGNOSIS
- If the testing is done in the first year of life, CRS can be diagnosed with blood tests by isolating the rubella virus and demonstrating rubella-specific immunoglobulin M (IgM) antibody or by detecting an infant rubella antibody level that persists at a higher level and for a longer period than expected from passive transfer of maternal antibody. The rubella virus can also be detected using PCR.
- Following 1 year, it is difficult to ascertain whether CRS is the cause of symptoms, although certain clinical findings make a diagnosis of CRS more likely than others. The most common congenital defects associated with CRS are cataracts, heart disease, sensorineural deafness, and mental retardation.

INTERVENTION APPROACHES AND ISSUES
- Primary preventive action is immunization of all children, usually between 12 and 15 months of age, but immunization can occur as young as at the age of 9 months. Immunity against rubella tends to be long-lasting, but the effects of vaccination do wear off. Women of child-bearing age should be vaccinated and should refrain from becoming pregnant for at least 28 days after immunization.
- There are a number of rubella vaccines available, either as single antigen vaccines or in combination with either a measles vaccine (MR), mumps vaccine, or a measles and mumps vaccine (MMR). In most countries, the vaccine is given as MR or MMR.
- There is controversy about the safety of the MMR vaccine. It contains aluminum (a potent neurotoxin that is added to increase the body's immune response to the vaccine) and attenuated live viruses (live virus that is weakened through chemical or physical processes in order to produce an immune response without causing the severe effects of the disease). Some batches of the vaccine contain thimerosal (a methylmercury compound that is highly toxic). The bulk of the evidence suggests, however, that the benefits of the vaccine far outweigh any risks, preventing disability and many deaths worldwide.

20,000 children were born with two or more symptoms; this grouping of symptoms came to be known as congenital rubella syndrome (CRS).

CORNELIA DE LANGE SYNDROME

Background

Cornelia de Lange syndrome (CdLS), sometimes called Lange syndrome, was named after a Dutch pediatrician who described the syndrome in two children in 1933. This syndrome is also known as Brachmann-de Lange syndrome because German physician Winfried Brachmann wrote about a similar syndrome that he discovered in a child in 1916. CdLS is a congenital syndrome (i.e., is present from birth). Most of the physical and behavior characteristics may be recognized at birth or shortly thereafter, but a child need not demonstrate all of them for the diagnosis to be made. This

Table 15.6. Aspects of Cornelia de Lange syndrome (CdLS)

PHYSICAL AND HEALTH CHARACTERISTICS
- Most frequently observed facial characteristics include thin, down-turned lips, low-set ears, long eyelashes, bushy eyebrows that meet in the middle, ptosis (drooping of upper eyelid), hypertelorism (abnormal width between the eyes), and excessive body hair.
- Brachycephaly (disproportionately short head), small hands and feet, and syndactylism (webbing or fusing) of the toes are apparent.
- There is swallowing difficulty in infants, with an associated risk of aspiration pneumonia.
- Feeding problems and gastroesophageal reflux (GER; reverse flow of stomach contents into the esophagus) occur.
- Congenital heart problems and hearing impairment are present.
- In almost all cases, the skin on the arms and legs of affected individuals has an unusual marbled (bluish, mottled) appearance, particularly when cold.

PREVALENCE
- 1 in 10,000 to 1 in 30,000 live births.
- Males and females are affected equally.

GENOTYPE OR CAUSE
- Mutations in a gene called NIPBL ("Nipped B-like") on chromosome 5 occur in approximately 50% of affected individuals; this gene regulates biological signals that have wide-ranging effects on a variety of organ systems during development. The protein product of this gene has been called delangin.
- Duplication of part of chromosome 3 can produce a phenotype similar to CdLS.

FUNCTIONAL AND BEHAVIORAL PHENOTYPE
- Delays in cognition and communication are present.
- CdLS may be associated with features similar to those associated with autism, including seizures, self-injury, hyperactivity, daily aggression, and sleep disturbances.
- Despite the previously noted challenging features, parents frequently report their children are happy and charming, love to laugh and giggle, and enjoy interacting with others.
- Strengths include perceptual organization, visuo-spatial memory, and fine motor skills.

DIAGNOSIS
- CdLS is indicated primarily by a clinical diagnosis based on observable characteristics.
- Mutations in the NIPBL gene are being found in approximately 50% of individuals with CdLS. A positive test confirms a diagnosis of CdLS, but not finding a mutation does not rule out the diagnosis.

(continued)

Table 15.6. *(continued)*

INTERVENTION APPROACHES AND ISSUES • Speech-language therapy, sign language, or both may be required for communication. • Anticonvulsant medication may be needed for seizures. • Pharmacotherapy and behavior management may help with sleep disturbances, hyperactivity, and aggression.	• Gastroesophageal reflux disease (GERD) is managed through special diets, medications, and elevation of the child after eating. A surgical procedure such as a gastrostomy (provides a hole in the stomach for feeding through a gastronomy tube) may be required.

syndrome is usually sporadic in nature, but rare cases of autosomal dominant disorder have been reported.

CRI-DU-CHAT SYNDROME

Background

Cri-du-chat syndrome was first described in 1964 by Dr. Jerome Lejeune, a French geneticist who also discovered the chromosomal abnormality characteristic of Down syndrome. Cri-du-chat syndrome is also known as 5p-syndrome because of a defect on the short (p) arm of chromosome 5. The name *cri-du-chat* comes from the characteristic high-pitched, cat-like cry made by infants with the syndrome. This syndrome is usually sporadic in nature, but 10%–15% of cases are familial, with the majority resulting from parental translocations.

DEVELOPMENTAL COORDINATION DISORDER

Background

The term *developmental coordination disorder (DCD)* is used to describe children who exhibit difficulties in activities that require motor coordination, such as playing ball, writing, or tying shoelaces. DCD first appeared in the *Diagnostic and Statistical Manual of Mental Disorders, Third Edition, Revised (DSM-III-R)* in 1987. Previous terminology was not consistent, so DCD has also been referred to as developmental dyspraxia, sensorimotor dysfunction, perceptual-motor problem, minor neurological dysfunction, minimal brain dysfunction, and clumsiness. Inheritance patterns in DCD have not been fully researched.

HUNTER SYNDROME/ MUCOPOLYSACCHARIDOSIS TYPE II

Background

Mucopolysaccharidosis (MPS) syndromes are characterized by excessive storage of mucopolysaccharides (complex carbohydrates) in various tissues and organs. The newest term for mucopolysaccharide is *glycosaminoglycan.*

Hunter syndrome is a mucopolysaccharidosis type II (MPS II) lysosomal storage disorder. Hunter syndrome was first described in 1917 by Charles Hunter, a Scottish-Canadian physician. There are two forms of this disorder: a severe, early-onset form (Type A) and a mild, late-onset form (Type B). The severe form of Hunter syndrome is typically diagnosed in children ages 18–36 months. The mild form causes later and less severe symptoms and often is not diagnosed until adulthood. This syndrome has an X-linked recessive mode of inheritance; consequently, it is usually only seen in males, but rare cases in females have been re-

Table 15.7. Aspects of cri-du-chat syndrome

PHYSICAL AND HEALTH CHARACTERISTICS • Early hypotonia occurs. • Prominent epicanthic folds (skin fold from the root of the nose extending to the inner end of the eyebrow), microcephaly (small head), and low-set ears may be observed. PREVALENCE • 1 in 15,000 to 1 in 50,000 live births. GENOTYPE OR CAUSE • There is a 5p deletion—that is, a deletion of variable size on the p arm of chromosome 5. FUNCTIONAL AND BEHAVIORAL PHENOTYPE • Infants have a characteristic high-pitched, cat-like cry. • There are severe motor, language, and developmental delays. • Stereotypic (repetitive) behavior has been observed, and hyperactivity is common.	• Occasionally, aggressive and self-injurious behaviors are seen, but more typically, individuals have a friendly and happy demeanor. • More than 75% of affected individuals are easily distracted, restless, and excessively active. DIAGNOSIS • Clinical features such as the physical characteristics and cat-like cry suggest diagnosis from birth. • The deletion on chromosome 5 can be confirmed by chromosomal analysis techniques such as FISH. INTERVENTION APPROACHES AND ISSUES • Intensive early intervention is needed to improve speech, as well as motor and self-help skills. • Clinicians may consider medication to address hyperactivity.

Table 15.8. Aspects of developmental coordination disorder (DCD)

PHYSICAL AND HEALTH CHARACTERISTICS
- Characteristics of DCD include motor coordination during performance that is below that expected on the basis of age or measured intelligence, as well as impairments in motor coordination that interfere with academic achievement and activities of daily living and are not due to other neurological disorders such as cerebral palsy, hemiplegia, or muscular dystrophy.

PREVALENCE
- Occurs in 5%–6% of school-age children.
- DCD is more frequent in males than females.

GENOTYPE OR CAUSE
- The cause is unknown; hypotheses include atypical brain development or abnormal fatty acid metabolism.

FUNCTIONAL AND BEHAVIORAL PHENOTYPE
- There is variability of expression in perceptual and motor impairments, and children may have any or all of the following:
  —Poor control of distal movements during fine and gross motor tasks, including writing, dressing, catching, or kicking a ball (timing and accuracy affected)
  —Slowness and clumsiness when performing motor tasks
  —Delayed motor development (e.g., sitting, crawling, walking)
  —Difficulty learning new skills
  —Difficulty maintaining balance, particularly when performing another challenging task
  —Increased reliance on visual information
  —Difficulties with motor imagery and visual memory
  —Poor academic skills, such as writing, reading, spelling, and mathematics, compared with other children of same age
  —Decreased social skills and lack of confidence
  —Attention-deficit disorder (ADD) and attention-deficit/hyperactivity disorder (ADHD) occur in 41% of affected individuals.
  —Learning disabilities, such as dyslexia, occur in 38% of individuals.

DIAGNOSIS
- Clinical diagnosis is based on a combination of the previously listed physical and behavioral characteristics.

INTERVENTION APPROACHES AND ISSUES
- As a consequence of the great variability in clinical presentation of this disorder, the intervention must be tailored individually to each child.
- The following interventions have been used with limited success due to the fact that the training does not generalize to tasks other than the ones used during the intervention: sensory integration intervention, process-oriented treatment, perceptual motor training, and task-specific training.
- Cognitive approaches have been developed based on a problem-solving framework; further research is needed to assess the efficacy and validity of this new approach.

Table 15.9. Aspects of Hunter syndrome/mucopolysaccharidosis type II (MPS II)

PHYSICAL AND HEALTH CHARACTERISTICS
Severe, early-onset form (Type A)
- Appearance is generally typical at birth, although noisy breathing, umbilical or inguinal hernias (bulging at the belly button or bulging of a portion of the bowel through the inguinal canal into the groin), or both may be present.
- Features of Hunter syndrome are very variable. These begin to develop at approximately age 2. Classical features include the following:
  —Characteristic skin features: papular skin lesions that are ivory in color and located on the upper back and on the sides of the upper arms and thighs excessive body hair, and excessive Mongolian spots (flat birthmarks with wavy borders and irregular shape that sometimes resemble bruises)
  —Coarse facial features, large head, frontal bossing (protuberance of frontal skull), and enlarged tongue
  —Hydrocephaly (enlargement of ventricles of the brain due to an accumulation of cerebrospinal fluid in the brain; typically associated with an enlarged head)
  —Slowed growth rate and stiffening of joints
  —Clouding of corneas
  —Wide spaces between erupting teeth
  —Hepatosplenomegaly (enlargement of liver and spleen)
- Other features may include
  —Thickened heart valves
  —Carpal tunnel syndrome (disorder caused by compression, or squeezing, of a nerve in the wrist that causes a prickling or numbness in the hand)
  —Upper airway obstruction due to thickened walls of the airways
  —Flexed hands and skeletal changes, referred to as dysostosis multiplex (e.g., wide medial clavicle [collar bone], flat ribs)
  —Susceptibility to ear infections, colds, and meningitis; the latter frequently leads to deafness
- Death usually occurs in the second or third decades of life, often from cardiac or respiratory failure.
- There may be an unusual sensitivity to anesthesia.

Mild, late-onset form (Type B)
- This form often is difficult to diagnose until adulthood; it resembles Scheie syndrome (see section on Hurler syndrome).
- There may be airway obstruction secondary to accumulation of mucopolysaccharide in the trachea and bronchi.
- Affected individuals survive well into adulthood and may live into the seventh decade of life.

PREVALENCE
- 1 in 16,000 to 1 in 30,000 live births for all MPS disorders.
- 1 in 65,000 to 1 in 320,000 live births for MPS II.
- Birth incidence is increased among Jewish population of Israel.
- Usually only affects males. Females may be affected, however. Most of those who inherit a mutant iduronate-2-sulphatase (IDS) gene inherit it from their mother. The nonmutant allele inherited from the father is preferentially inactivated. Females tend to express the severe form.

GENOTYPE OR CAUSE
- MPS II is an X-linked disorder resulting from heterogeneous mutations in the IDS gene, which results in lack of the enzyme iduronate sulfatase; in its absence, mucopolysaccharides collect in various body tissues, causing damage.

FUNCTIONAL OR BEHAVIORAL PHENOTYPE
- The severe, early-onset form of the syndrome is characterized by cognitive deterioration, severe cognitive delay, aggressive behavior and hyperactivity.
- The mild, late-onset form is characterized by mild to no cognitive impairment.

(continued)

Table 15.9. *(continued)*

DIAGNOSIS
- Urine tests are conducted for increased excretion of heparan sulfate and dermatan sulfate (these tests measure the amount of mucopolysaccharides excreted in the urine over a 24-hour period).
- Enzyme assays are conducted for decreased iduronate sulfatase activity.
- Genetic testing may show mutation in the iduronate sulfatase gene.

INTERVENTION APPROACHES AND ISSUES
- For MPS disorders in general, there is no consensus on effective interventions.
- Current intervention is primarily supportive: hearing aids, physical therapy, and selected surgical procedures may be helpful for some individuals.
- There has been variable success in lessening the effects of the MPS disorders with bone marrow transplantation, but the procedure is not generally recommended.
- In the future, gene therapy may be possible.

ported. (Refer to the Hurler Syndrome/Mucopolysaccharidosis Type I and Sanfilippo Syndrome/Mucopolysaccharidosis Type III sections for more information on MPS disorders.)

HURLER SYNDROME/ MUCOPOLYSACCHARIDOSIS TYPE I

Background

Hurler syndrome is one of the MPS syndromes. This syndrome is named after the German pediatrician Gertrude Hurler, who described it in 1919. It is also known as "gargoylism" (although this term is not preferred), mucopolysaccharidosis type I (MPS I), and Hurler-Scheie or Scheie syndrome—after Harold Glendon Scheie, an American physician and opthalmologist who, in 1962, described a less severe form of Hurler syndrome. Hurler-Scheie syndrome is less severe than Hurler syndrome but more severe than Scheie syndrome. All three syndromes are due to a defect in the same enzyme. Hurler syndrome has an autosomal recessive mode of inheritance. (Refer to the Hunter Syndrome/Mucopolysaccharidosis Type II section and Sanfilippo Syndrome/Mucopolysaccharidosis Type III sections for more information on MPS disorders.)

Table 15.10. Hurler syndrome/mucopolysaccharidosis type I

PHYSICAL AND HEALTH CHARACTERISTICS
- There is a characteristic pattern of facial features, including coarseness of facial features, thick coarse hair, and bushy eyebrows.
- Skeletal abnormalities include dwarfism, kyphosis (an abnormal degree of forward curvature of part of the spine), a broad hand with short fingers, joint contractures, and radiological features of dysostosis multiplex.
- Hepatosplenomegaly, or enlargement of liver and spleen, is present.
- Structural abnormalities of the heart are present.
- Clouding of corneas occurs.
- Umbilical and inguinal hernias (see Hunter syndrome) occur.
- Most individuals have conductive hearing loss.
- Severe respiratory tract infections are likely.
- Patients with MPS may have unusual sensitivity to anesthesia.
- Death often occurs by the second decade of life due to heart failure and severe respiratory tract infections.

PREVALENCE
- 1 in 16,000 to 1 in 30,000 live births for all MPS disorders.
- 1 in 76,000 to 1 in 150,000 live births for MPS I.

GENOTYPE OR CAUSE
- The syndrome results from mutations in the alpha-L-iduronidase gene located on chromosome 4 (4p16.3). Mutations in this gene are responsible for alpha-L-iduronidase enzyme deficiency, which leads to the accumulation of partially degraded mucopolysaccharides in the lysosomes of cells.

FUNCTIONAL AND BEHAVIORAL PHENOTYPE
- Cognitive development is usually typical in the first few years of childhood.
- Severe, progressive learning disorders are evident by later childhood.

DIAGNOSIS
- Urine tests are conducted for increased excretion of dermatan sulfate and heparan sulfate (these tests measure the amount of mucopolysaccharides excreted in the urine over a 24-hour period).
- Enzyme assays are conducted for decreased alpha-L-iduronidase activity.
- Genetic testing may show mutation in the alpha-L-iduronidase gene.
- X rays of the skeleton are conducted to detect skeletal abnormalities.
- ECHOs are conducted to detect structural abnormalities of the heart.

INTERVENTION APPROACHES AND ISSUES
- Complications should be supported and treated by means such as supplemental oxygen for breathing difficulties, continuous positive airway pressure (CPAP) machines for interrupted breathing during sleep (sleep apnea), surgery (tracheotomy) for difficulties in breathing, physical therapy for joint stiffness, and heart valve replacement therapy for heart problems.
- Severe MPS I is being treated with transplantation of bone marrow cells from a healthy adult and transplantation of stem cells from the umbilical cord blood of an unrelated healthy baby. This is in contrast to Hunter syndrome, in which beneficial effects of such treatments have been rarely observed.
- Severe MPS I also is being treated by enzyme replacement therapy with laronidase (Aldurazyme). Laronidase is a polymorphic variant of the human enzyme deficient in MPS I.

HYPOXIC-ISCHEMIC ENCEPHALOPATHY/ NEONATAL ENCEPHALOPATHY

Background

Hypoxic-ischemic encephalopathy (HIE), also known as neonatal encephalopathy (NE), is an acquired clinical neurologic syndrome that involves acute brain injury due to asphyxia (impaired oxygen intake). HIE is usually caused by hypoxia (subnormal oxygen concentration) of the brain, as well as ischemia (inadequate blood supply) to the brain resulting from systemic hypoxia and reduced cerebral blood flow. The implications of HIE are severe; it accounts for 25% of full-term neonatal mortality, and in cases of severe HIE, 50% of affected infants die. A considerable fraction of infants who survive develop permanent neurological impairments. HIE is the most common cause of cerebral palsy, intellectual disability, learning disability, epilepsy, and behavior problems.

The outcome of HIE is not always predictable from the severity of the injury. The tissue damage associated with HIE takes the form of neuronal death (necrosis) in the affected region (the infarct) or the death of all cellular elements in and around the infarct. Death occurs because HIE initiates a series of biochemical events that result in a shifting of metabolism from an aerobic (involving oxygen consumption) to an anaerobic (not involving oxygen consumption) state. Anaerobic metabolism cannot meet cellular energy demands and causes an accumulation of toxins (e.g., ethanol, lactate, carbon dioxide), resulting in cell death.

Table 15.11. Aspects of hypoxic-ischemic encephalopathy (HIE)/neonatal encephalopathy (NE)

PHYSICAL AND HEALTH CHARACTERISTICS

The following must be present for diagnosis of HIE in a newborn:

- Umbilical artery blood shows evidence of acidosis—a high hydrogen ion concentration (i.e., has a low pH: pH <7; pH is the log to base 10 of the reciprocal of the hydrogen ion concentration.)
- The **Apgar** score is 0 to 3 for more than 5 minutes.
- Neurological symptoms such as seizures, coma, and hypotonia are present.
- Multiple organs are involved (e.g., kidney, lungs, liver, heart).

PREVALENCE

- 6 in 1,000 live births in industrialized countries.
- Prevalence is much higher in developing countries.
- Affects males and females equally.

GENOTYPE OR CAUSE

- Prolonged partial asphyxia due to disturbances in cerebral blood flow.
- Brief intrapartum events leading to asphyxia, such as placental abruption.

FUNCTIONAL OR BEHAVIORAL PHENOTYPE

Mild HIE

- Muscle tone increases slightly and deep tendon reflexes are brisk.
- Behavior problems (e.g., poor feeding, irritability) present transiently.
- By 3–4 days of age, central nervous system examination findings are normal.

Moderately severe HIE

- Lethargia (drowsiness) occurs, with significant hypotonia and diminished deep tendon reflexes.
- Grasping, sucking, and Moro (or "startle") reflexes are sluggish or absent.
- There are occasional periods of apnea (temporary respiratory arrest).
- Seizures may occur within the first 24 hours of life.
- An initial period of well-being may be followed by sudden deterioration; during this period of deterioration, there may be seizures or the seizure intensity might increase.

Severe HIE

- Stupor or coma is typical.
- Irregular breathing—ventilatory support may be needed.
- There is generalized hypotonia and depressed deep tendon reflexes.
- Neonatal reflexes are absent.
- Problems such as disturbances of eye motion or dilated, fixed, or poor reaction of pupils may be apparent.
- Seizures increase in frequency 2–3 days after their onset.
- Heartbeat and blood pressure are irregular.

DIAGNOSIS

- Diagnosis is based on the presence of the preceding physical characteristics.

INTERVENTION APPROACHES AND ISSUES

- The time frame for therapeutic intervention is very small: 1–2 hours.
- Success depends on identification of HIE as soon as possible after birth.
- There is no uniform standard of care.
- Treatment of seizures is an essential initial step.
- Maintenance of ventilation, perfusion, and metabolic status is critical.
- Prevention of hypoxia and hypercapnia (too much carbon dioxide in the blood) and hypocapnia (too little carbon dioxide in the blood) is important.
- Maintenance of blood gases (by intubation and artificial ventilation) and acid–base status is necessary. In some cases, compensation by the lungs or kidneys is adequate to bring the pH imbalance under control, but in many cases, treatment of an underlying medical condition is necessary. For example, in neonatal diabetic ketoacidosis, elevated blood glucose levels are treated with insulin, fluids lost through excessive urination are replaced, and electrolyte imbalances are corrected. If the cause of the acidosis is an infection, this is treated. In acidosis associated with kidney failure, dialysis may be required, whereas in respiratory acidosis, mechanical ventilation may be sufficient
- Mean arterial blood pressure above 35 millimeters (mm) of mercury (Hg) is maintained with medications. (Blood pressure is read as the number of mm of Hg above atmospheric pressure, which is used as the zero reference.)
- Focal cooling of brain by 3°–6° Celsius reduces extent of tissue injury.
- It is necessary to evaluate neurological functioning.
- The use of imaging technologies to assess HIE is becoming increasingly accepted; however, there is concern that CT scans may result in damage to the brain.

The process of cellular destruction in infants is faster than in adults: 1 to 2 hours versus 1 to 2 days, respectively. Thus, immediate identification of HIE is paramount, especially in infants, because the therapeutic window is small. In severe cases of HIE, mortality can be as high as 50%; 80% of infants who survive severe HIE suffer serious complications, and 10% will have typical development, the remainder being affected to some degree.

INTRAVENTRICULAR HEMORRHAGE

Background

Intraventricular hemorrhage (IVH) refers to bleeding from fragile blood vessels in the brain into the brain ventricles. Bleeding in the brain puts pressure on nerve cells and can damage them. Severe damage to nerve cells results in brain injury. IVH is most common in premature infants; the smaller and more premature the infant, the greater the risk of IVH. Most cases of IVH occur within the first 3 days of life, but cases in adults have been reported.

KLINEFELTER SYNDROME

Background

Klinefelter syndrome is also known as Klinefelter-Reifenstein-Albright syndrome, after the three men who described it. In 1942, Harry Klinefelter, an American physician, and his colleagues Edward Reifenstein and Fuller Albright, published a report on nine men who had gynecomastia (enlarged breasts), sparse facial and body hair, small testes, and the inability to produce sperm. In 1959, these men were discovered to have an extra sex chromosome (genotype XXY) instead of the usual male sex complement (genotype XY). The mode of inheritance of this syndrome is usually sporadic. There is a trend for chromosomal errors to be transmitted to the offspring of men with this syndrome.

Table 15.12. Aspects of intraventricular hemorrhage (IVH)

PHYSICAL AND HEALTH CHARACTERISTICS
- Apnea (temporary stoppage of breathing) and bradycardia (slow heart rate) are present.
- Paleness or blue coloring (cyanosis) is visible.
- Infants have a weak suck.
- Infants have a high-pitched cry.
- Seizures occur.
- In infants, there is swelling or bulging of the fontanelles (the "soft spots" between the bones of the baby's head).
- Anemia (low number of red blood cells in peripheral circulation) is present.
- IVH is graded from 1 to 4 according to the severity of the bleeding; small amounts of bleeding are given grades of 1 to 2 and do not usually cause any long-term damage. Larger amounts of bleeding are given grades 3 to 4 and cause long-term problems. Bleeding associated with grades 3 and 4 causes hydrocephalus, or a blockage of the circulation system for cerebrospinal fluid.

PREVALENCE
- IVH accounts for 3%–10% of all intracerebral hemorrhages in the United States.
- Prevalence in the United States is as high as 50% in infants with very low birth weight (less than 1,500 g) or less than 35 weeks of gestation.
- There is no evidence that prevalence is different in males and females.

GENOTYPE OR CAUSE
- No genetic link has been proven.
- Primary causes can be spontaneous, but notable causes include head trauma, insertion or removal of a ventricular catheter (a tube used to drain fluid from the ventricles), intraventricular vascular malformation, aneurysm (bulging in the wall of a blood vessel), tumor, hypertension (high blood pressure), or conditions that predispose to excessive bleeding.
- Other causes of IVH in infants include rapid ventricle volume expansion; with ventilator use, asynchrony between mechanically delivered and spontaneous breaths; hypertension or beat-to-beat variability of blood pressure; blood clotting disorders; deficiency of oxygen and/or poor blood flow to the brain; respiratory disturbances; acidosis (too much acid in the body); infusions of hypertonic solution (e.g., sodium bicarbonate); anemia; vacuum-assisted delivery; frequent handling; and tracheal suctioning (a procedure used to remove mucus in the airways).

FUNCTIONAL AND BEHAVIORAL PHENOTYPE
- Grade 1 and Grade 2 hemorrhages: Prognosis is good. Neurodevelopment is slightly hindered compared with infants born without complications.
- Grade 3 hemorrhage without white matter disease (disease characterized by demyelination, or the loss of myelin): Mortality rate is less than 10%. Cognitive or motor disorder is present in 30%–40% of cases.
- Grade 4: Mortality approaches 80%–90%. Severe neurological sequelae, including cognitive and motor disturbances, are present.

DIAGNOSIS
- In prenatal and neonatal cases, cranial ultrasounds (also known as cranial sonograms) are used to image the brain via the fontanelles and thereby evaluate the level of bleeding.
- In adult cases, CT scans can be employed.

INTERVENTION APPROACHES AND ISSUES
- For adults, treatment involves ventricular drainage and administration of recombinant tissue plasminogen activator (rtPA) to remove the blood clots.
- For infants, treatment involves supportive care for cardiovascular, respiratory, or neurological complications, including treatment of lung conditions and infections, assistance with breathing, blood transfusions, seizure treatment, and treatment for hydrocephalus by spinal taps (placement of a needle into the spinal canal to remove fluid) or surgical placement of tubes into the ventricles for draining of excess fluid. In cases of severe hydrocephalus, a permanent ventricular-peritoneal shunt is inserted to drain fluid from the ventricle to the abdominal cavity, where it is absorbed, or to the heart, so it can join circulating blood.
- If a premature delivery is expected, giving the mother corticosteroids before birth reduces the risk of IVH in the baby.

Table 15.13. Aspects of Klinefelter syndrome

PHYSICAL AND HEALTH CHARACTERISTICS
- The physical phenotype is variable; affected individuals may or may not have
  —Hypogonadism (small testes, small penis, inadequate testosterone production)
  —Gynecomastia in approximately half of individuals
  —Above average height (often), or tall with slim stature, long legs, and a tendency for truncal obesity
  —Female distribution of body fat in adults, sparse facial and body hair
  —Hypotonia (low muscle tone), motor skill difficulties
- The syndrome is most common cause of infertility in males.
- Hypothyroidism, breast cancer, osteoporosis, leg ulcers, depression, dental problems, varicose veins, and mitral valve prolapse are possible.
- There is an increased risk for autoimmune disorders, including type 2 diabetes and autoimmune thyroiditis.

PREVALENCE
- 1 in 500 to 1 in 1,000 live male births.
- One fifth of males who seek services from infertility clinics have Klinefelter syndrome.

GENOTYPE OR CAUSE
- Most commonly, males with this syndrome have three sex chromosomes (X,X,Y) instead of two (X,Y). Some are mosaic for this abnormality. (In genetic mosaicism, some cells have the typical 46 chromosomes, whereas others will have the extra X; see Chapter 7.)
- Klinefelter syndrome results from nondisjunction during meiosis I and may have a paternal (50%–60%) or maternal (40%–50%) origin. This contrasts with Down syndrome, in which the extra chromosome 21 is maternal in approximately 85% of cases. (The chromosomes fail to detach and pass to opposite poles of the nucleus during meiosis I; see Chapter 7 for an explanation of nondisjunction and meiosis.)

FUNCTIONAL AND BEHAVIORAL PHENOTYPE
- Most males with genotype XXY have average to superior intelligence, with only approximately 20% scoring below average on standardized intelligence tests.
- Cognitive impairment is rare; when this occurs, the IQ score is lower by only 10–15 points.
- There is a tendency for problems with expressive language, and learning to speak, read, and write. Dyslexia is common.
- Individuals have an increased risk of psychiatric disorders, including depression.
- There is a tendency for social skills deficits, anxiety, and self-esteem issues.

DIAGNOSIS
- Karyotyping may be used to detect an extra sex chromosome (genotype XXY).
- A low semen count and low serum testosterone levels are present.
- High levels of serum luteinizing hormone, serum follicle stimulating hormone, and serum estradiol (estrogen) are present.

INTERVENTION APPROACHES AND ISSUE
- Testosterone replacement corrects symptoms of androgen deficiency (e.g., loss of libido, decreased energy, increased abdominal fat) and may have positive effects on language or behavior problems, but it has no positive effect on infertility. Hormone treatment during adolescence may encourage a more typical puberty.
- Some individuals require help in school for learning difficulties and behavior problems, and some need to participate in special education programs. A substantial number go on to postsecondary education.
- Intracytoplasmic sperm injection (injection of a single sperm into the cytoplasms of a mature oocyte using a glass needle; see Chapter 28) offers an opportunity for procreation even when there are no spermatozoa in the ejaculate. In a substantial number of azoospermic individuals, spermatozoa can be extracted from testicular biopsy samples, and pregnancies and live births have been achieved through this method.

LAFORA DISEASE/LAFORA PROGRESSIVE MYOCLONUS EPILEPSY

Background

Lafora disease is the most common form of teenage-onset progressive myoclonus epilepsy. The disorder is named after Spanish neuropathologist Gonzalo Lafora, who in 1911 described findings of distinct spherical inclusions in the brains of patients that had myoclonus epilepsy. This disorder has an autosomal recessive mode of inheritance. Lafora disease is a member of the family of progressive myoclonus epilepsies; refer to the Progressive Myoclonus Epilepsy section for more information (see also Chapter 18).

LESCH-NYHAN SYNDROME

Background

Lesch-Nyhan syndrome is an inheritable disorder that affects how the body builds and breaks down purines (compounds in RNA and DNA). Lesch-Nyhan syndrome was first discovered by Michael Lesch and William Nyhan (an American cardiologist and an American pediatrician, respectively) in 1964, when they described two affected brothers. The underlying enzyme defect was discovered in 1967, and the responsible gene was discovered in 1985.

Lesch-Nyhan syndrome is characterized by diffuse effects throughout the central nervous system and specific effects in the basal ganglia (see Chapter 8 for more information about the regions of the brain). It has an X-linked recessive mode of inheritance; therefore, the syndrome is seen mainly in males.

MENINGITIS

Background

Meningitis is an infection of the meninges (membranes surrounding the brain) and the fluid surrounding the brain and spinal cord. There are two types of this disease: viral meningitis and bacterial meningitis. In general, viral meningitis is less severe and can resolve without treatment, whereas bacterial meningitis can be

Table 15.14. Aspects of Lafora disease/Lafora progressive myoclonus epilepsy

PHYSICAL AND HEALTH CHARACTERISTICS
- Lafora disease is a severe, progressive form of epilepsy that is characterized by seizures and progressive neurological degeneration. It begins in late childhood or early adolescence; death usually occurs within 10 years of the first symptoms.
- The condition is characterized by the presence of inclusions called polyglucosan bodies (polymers of glucose) in one or more of the following: the cells of the nervous system (brain, spinal cord, or nerves), muscle (or muscle fibers), or skin.

PREVALENCE
- Lafora disease occurs worldwide but is most common in the Mediterranean countries of Southern Europe and Northern Africa, in the Middle East, and in Southern India. It is rare in the United States and Canada, except in ethnically isolated populations in the Southern United States and Quebec, Canada.

GENOTYPE OR CAUSE
- The condition is caused by mutations in one of three genes that result in abnormal carbohydrate metabolism.
- Among affected individuals, 80% have mutations in the EPM2A (laforin) gene, found at the 6q24 locus. These mutations include missense and frameshift mutations, insertions, and deletions.
- Mutations in the EPM2B (malin) gene have also been found.
- A third locus is postulated.

FUNCTIONAL AND BEHAVIORAL PHENOTYPE
- The first signs are generalized tonic-clonic seizures (epileptic seizures associated with loss of consciousness), with some cases of occipital seizures.
- Individuals may exhibit rapid, isolated, asynchronous jerks of the mouth and hand as disorder progresses.
- Progressive dementia and cognitive dysfunction can be observed in individuals who have had the conditon for 2–6 years.
- Behavioral problems, such as violent behavior, can also be observed.
- Death occurs within 10 years after onset and can occur as early as 2 years after onset.

DIAGNOSIS
- EEGs show loss in alpha-rhythm (the most prominent rhythm of brain activity), generalized epileptiform discharges and photosensitivity (triggering of seizures by a flashing light). The generalized epileptiform discharges are typically activated by sleep.
- Postmortem, considerable neuronal loss is observed in the brain, but inflammation or demyelination of nerves is not seen.

INTERVENTION APPROACHES AND ISSUES
- Intervention is based on support, and no definite therapy has been discovered.
- Certain drugs, such as valproic acid and benzodiazepine, may help control myoclonic jerks and seizures.

Table 15.15. Aspects of Lesch-Nyhan syndrome

PHYSICAL AND HEALTH CHARACTERISTICS
- Development is typical in the prenatal period and in the first 2–3 months of the neonatal period.
- The first symptom is likely to be presence of urate crystals (orange-colored, crystal-like deposits resembling orange sand) in the child's diaper or urine.
- There is an increased urate to creatinine ratio in the blood or urine; a ratio of more than 2:1 indicates dysfunction. (Urate is the breakdown product of dietary purines formed by action of the enzyme xanthine oxidase; creatinine is a by-product of muscular exertion and a marker of kidney function.)
- Reflex sensitivity is increased.

PREVALENCE
- 1 in 380,000 live births.
- Affects males almost exclusively.

GENOTYPE OR CAUSE
- The cause is a severe mutation in the gene encoding the hypoxanthine-guanine phosphoribosyltransferase (HPRT) enzyme, which is a catalyst necessary for prevention of uric acid buildup in the body.
- HPRT mutation leads to elevated uric acid levels in the blood (hyperuricemia).
- Uric acid buildup is toxic to the body and causes most of the syndrome's symptoms.
- The HPRT chromosomal locus is Xq26-q27.2.

FUNCTIONAL AND BEHAVIORAL PHENOTYPE
- Symptoms first present by 3–6 months after birth and include unusual irritability and nervous system impairment (e.g., the inability to lift the head or to sit up).
- By the end of the first year, atypical motor development is evident, including writhing motions (athetosis) and spasmodic movements of limbs and facial muscles (chorea).
- The majority of children affected never develop the ability to walk.
- There is a tendency toward compulsive self-injury that intensifies as syndrome progresses, including biting of the lips, tongue, and fingers and head banging.
- Kidney stones develop and cause kidney damage.
- Joints are swollen and tender (gout).
- There is the presence of neurological dysfunction resembling athetoid cerebral palsy (i.e., that resulting from damage to the cerebellum or basal ganglia).

DIAGNOSIS
- HPRT enzyme activity is decreased.
- Levels of uric acid in the serum are increased.
- Levels of uric acid in the urine are increased.

INTERVENTION APPROACHES AND ISSUES
- There are no known interventions for the neurological effects.
- Allopurinol (an inhibitor of the enzyme xanthine oxidase that slows down formation of urate) can lower blood uric-acid levels but does not reduce many of the syndrome's symptoms.
- Lithotripsy (a nonsurgical procedure that uses high-energy shock waves to break up stones in the kidneys and ureters) reduces kidney stone formation.
- Parkinson's disease medication and tranquilizers are prescribed to control involuntary movements.
- Individuals' teeth are often removed to limit self-injury.
- Restraints are often used to reduce self-injurious behaviors.
- If the condition is properly managed, individuals can survive until their twenties or thirties.

Table 15.16. Aspects of meningitis

PHYSICAL AND HEALTH CHARACTERISTICS
- Symptoms include high fever, headache, stiff neck, nausea, and vomiting. Approximately one third of individuals have seizure activity. A red or purple rash caused by meningococcal bacteria is present in 75% of cases.
- Symptoms persist for hours to days and worsen with time.

PREVALENCE
- In industrialized countries, as many as 13 in 100,000 people are affected each year.
- In developing countries, meningitis outbreaks are more common.

GENOTYPE OR CAUSE
- There is no genetic predisposition to meningitis; however, certain congenital immunodeficiencies (e.g., complement deficiencies, immunoglobulin deficiencies, asplenia) or acquired immunodeficiencies (e.g., from HIV infection) predispose one to the disease.
- Meningitis often occurs secondary to a bacterial infection in another part of the body such as the respiratory tract, urinary tract, or the ear. The disease is contagious and can be spread by contact, particularly through body fluids from an infected person such as discharges from the nose and throat.

FUNCTIONAL AND BEHAVIORAL PHENOTYPE
- Infants show increasing distress when held and rocked.
- Individuals appear disoriented and drowsy.
- If the disease is not treated directly, serious complications may result, including intellectual impairment; epilepsy; visual, speech, and hearing impairments (including deafness from damage to the cochlea or auditory nerve); and death.

DIAGNOSIS
- A lumbar puncture procedure (an invasive test in which cerebrospinal fluid surrounding the spinal cord is extracted with a needle for examination and the pressure of the fluid in the spinal column is measured) is performed to confirm a diagnosis and to identify the causal bacteria.

INTERVENTION APPROACHES AND ISSUES
- Many forms of meningitis can be prevented by vaccination.
- Antibiotics are used to treat bacterial meningitis, but their effectiveness is dependent on early diagnosis.
- Interventions for any ensuing complications are varied and specific to each case (e.g., anticonvulsants for seizure activity).
- There is controversy about the safety of the *Haemophilus influenzae* B vaccine. Some, although not all, studies have reported that exposure to immunization against this bacteria is associated with an increased risk of type 1 diabetes. The bulk of the evidence suggests that the benefits of the vaccine far outweigh any risks, preventing disability and many deaths worldwide.

quite serious and may result in brain damage, cognitive impairment, and even death. More than 50 types of bacteria can cause meningitis, and the causative agent changes with age. The bacteria responsible for the majority of meningitis cases are *Nisseria meningicoccus, Haemophilus influenzae* type B, and *Streptococcus pneumoniae*. The information presented in Table 15.16 pertains, for the most part, to bacterial meningitis.

NEUROFIBROMATOSIS

Background

Neurofibromatosis is a genetic syndrome also known as von Recklinghausen disease. It sometimes is called "elephant man disease," although this term is not preferred; indeed, it is misleading, as it is now believed that "the elephant man" had Proteus syndrome. Neurofibromatosis was first described in 1768 by Mark Akenside, but it is named after the German pathologist Friedrich Daniel von Recklinghausen, who provided a detailed description in 1882 based on the autopsy findings in a female and a male.

There are two types of neurofibromatosis. Neurofibromatosis type 1 (NF1), or von Recklinghausen disease, is responsible for 85% of cases. Neurofibromatosis type 2 (NF2) is responsible for 15% of cases. Neurofibromatosis occurs sporadically in approximately 50% of cases, and is inherited in an autosomal dominant manner in the remainder. Refer to the sections in this chapter entitled Sturge-Weber Syndrome and Tuberous Sclerosis Complex/Syndrome for information on related disorders.

NEURONAL MIGRATION DISORDERS

Background

Neuronal migration from the ventricular zone of the brain during embryonic development is an essential step in the proper formation and organization of the cerebral cortex. This process is particularly important in the layer formation of the neocortex, the most recently evolved part of the cerebral cortex that is believed to be required for higher motor, sensory, and cognitive functions. As of 2007, many disorders of neuronal migration have been described. By far, the most common are the lissencephalies. Lissencephaly (LIS) literally means "smooth brain" and has traditionally been separated into two classes: classical (previously type I LIS) and cobblestone complex (previously type II LIS). Classical LIS is the more prevalent and presents itself clinically in two common ways: isolated lissencephaly sequence (ILS) and Miller-Dieker syndrome (MDS). Other manifestations of classical LIS include X-linked lissencephaly (XLIS)/subcortical band heterotopia (SBH), and X-linked lissencephaly with abnormal genitalia (XLAG). For a review of other classical LIS syndromes and the genes causing them in humans see Kato and Dobyns (2003), and for a comprehensive

Table 15.17. Aspects of neurofibromatosis

PHYSICAL AND HEALTH CHARACTERISTICS

NF1 is characterized by two or more of the following:

- Six or more café-au-lait (coffee-with-cream/light brown) skin spots
- Two or more neurofibromas (tumors that grow on a nerve or nerve tissue, under the skin) or one plexiform neurofibroma (involving many nerves)
- Multiple freckles in the axiliary (armpit) or inguinal (groin) region
- Osseous lesion (lesion on the bone)
- Optic glioma (tumor of the optic nerve)
- Two or more iris hamartomas (clumps of pigment in the pigmented part of the eye)
- Severe scoliosis (curvature of the spine)
- Enlargement or deformation of certain bones other than those in the spine
- First-degree relative (parent, child, or sibling) with NF1

NF2 is characterized by either of the following:

- Bilateral (occurring on both sides of the body) acoustic neuromas, benign (noncancerous) tumors that originate from the nerves of hearing (cochlear nerve) and balance (vestibular nerve)
- First-degree relative (parent, child, or sibling) with NF2 plus one of the following: unilateral acoustic neuroma at younger than 30 years of age; any two of meningioma (a benign tumor that arises from the cells in the meninges, coverings of the brain and spine), glioma (tumor that arises from the glia, the support cells of the central nervous system), schwannoma (a usually benign tumor that originates in peripheral nerve fibers and is composed chiefly of Schwann cells), or juvenile cortical cataract (cataract that begins in the cortex of the lens)

Neurofibromatosis predisposes to pediatric stroke.

PREVALENCE

- NF1: 1 in 3,000 to 1 in 4,000 live births.
- NF2: 1 in 30,000 to 1 in 40,000 live births.

GENOTYPE OR CAUSE

- NF1 is caused by a mutation in the neurofibromin gene on chromosome 17. Familial NF1 has 100% penetrance (the frequency, under given environmental conditions, with which a specific phenotype is expressed by those with a specific genotype) and variable expressivity (the degree to which an expressed gene produces its effects in an organism). One known function of neurofibromin is to inhibit another gene called Ras from sending signals to other genes and proteins. Mutations of the NF1 gene disrupt neurofibromin function, impairing its ability to inhibit Ras.
- NF2 is caused by a mutation in the merlin tumor suppressor gene on chromosome 22, specifically 22q12. Merlin normally controls the way cells communicate with each other; merlin-deficient cells cannot "sense" each other and continue to divide when there is no more room.

FUNCTIONAL AND BEHAVIORAL PHENOTYPE

NF1

- Phenotype depends on the system affected.
- Signs may include seizures; cognitive, visual, or hearing impairment; movement disorders; dislocations; endocrine abnormalities; autonomic involvement; bowel irregularities; and hypertension.

NF2

- Phenotype depends on the system affected.
- There may be acoustic neuromas (occurring with high frequency), sensorineural hearing loss, vertigo (dizziness), tinnitus (ringing of the ears), and facial paralysis.
- Cataracts lead to blindness.
- Spinal tumors cause pain and paraplegia or quadriplegia.

DIAGNOSIS

- A clinical diagnosis is made based on the previously listed physical characteristics.
- MRI can be done of the affected site to determine presence of neurofibromas and other tumors.
- Genetic analysis can confirm clinical diagnosis if the condition results from familial inheritance; sporadic mutations cannot be confirmed genetically.
- Prenatal diagnosis of familial NF1 or NF2 can be made through amniocentesis or CVS.

INTERVENTION APPROACHES AND ISSUES

- Interventions for NF1 depend on the organ being investigated.
- Interventions for NF2 include surgical removal or radiotherapy for acoustic neuromas.

review of neuronal migration disorders, including those without lissencephaly, see Ross and Walsh (2001).

Miller-Dieker syndrome (MDS) was the first LIS syndrome delineated, and the gene causing it was the first human neuronal migration gene to be cloned. MDS generally exhibits a sporadic mode of inheritance due to a de novo chromosomal deletion (a chromosomal deletion that has not been inherited); however, in rare cases, the deletion is the result of a chromosomal translocation (an interchange of genetic material on two different chromosomes). In the latter case, the risk of recurrence may be as high as 33%. The inheritance of LIS also appears to be sporadic, and in some cases autosomal recessive. Both disorders primarily affect the cortex, whereas MDS also affects the cranium and facial tissues. Table 15.18 focuses on MDS and LIS because these are the most common LIS syndromes and because they share a common genetic pathway and exhibit similar symptoms.

NOONAN SYNDROME

Background

Noonan syndrome (NS) is a genetic disorder characterized by short stature, minor facial anomalies, and congenital heart defects. Many features of NS are similar to those of Turner syndrome, except that NS has no apparent chromosomal abnormality and occurs in both sexes. A male with webbing of the neck, incomplete folding of the ears, and a low posterior hair line was first reported in 1883 by Koblinsky, a medical student at the Russian/Estonian University of Dorpat. Further characteristics of the syndrome were described by Jacqueline Noonan and Dorothy Ehmke (an American cardiologist and an American pediatrician, respectively) in 1963. The syndrome occurs sporadically and is inherited in an autosomal dominant manner.

Table 15.18. Aspects of neuronal migration disorders

PHYSICAL AND HEALTH CHARACTERISTICS

- The most important characteristics, as indicated by MRI, are a very thick cortex (10–20 millimeters), malformations of the gyri (ridges on the surface of the cerebellum) that are more severe in posterior than anterior brain regions, and a prominent cell-sparse zone in the cortex. These features are more severe in MDS than in LIS. A grading system has been established to distinguish various classes of LIS.
- Individuals with MDS have characteristic craniofacial features, the most consistent of which include a broad and often high forehead, a subtle indentation of the temples, a slightly upturned tip of the nose, a thin upper lip, and a small jaw.
- Individuals are at high risk of recurrent pneumonia, a problem related to associated feeding problems.

PREVALENCE

- The only published data on the prevalence of classical LIS comes from a 1991 Dutch study, which reported 11.7 in 1,000,000 live births; however, this statistic is probably an underestimation. The increasing use of MRI technology and more widespread recognition of neuronal migration disorders will likely lead to better estimates in the future.

GENOTYPE OR CAUSE

- Virtually 100% of MDS cases, and 40% of LIS cases, are caused by a heterozygous mutation in the LIS1 gene on chromosome 17, specifically 17p13.3. The deletion in MDS extends further toward the 17p telomere and includes the genes CRK and 14-3-3-epsilon.
- LIS1 is a highly conserved protein and has two main functions: 1) It is a noncatalytic subunit of platelet-activating-factor acetylhydrolase isoform 1B (PAFAH1B), and 2) it associates with microtubules and regulates a protein called dynein in the cytoplasm. The second function is likely involved in neuronal migration.

FUNCTIONAL AND BEHAVIORAL PHENOTYPE

- Individuals have severe intellectual and developmental delay, have epilepsy, and usually die early in childhood; these symptoms are much more severe in MDS. Furthermore, there is a gradient of severity in LIS, which correlates with the mutation type and intragenic location.
- Feeding problems are common in both cases and include gagging while feeding, refusal of feeding, spitting up, and weight loss. These problems are usually the result of aspiration and reflux.

DIAGNOSIS

- MRI is conducted to determine physical characteristics of the brain.
- It is possible to make a rapid diagnosis using PCR and molecular markers known to be deleted in all patients with MDS but not in patients with LIS.
- CVS or amniocentesis, followed by fetal chromosome analysis (by FISH or karyotyping), has been used for prenatal diagnosis. The cerebral gyri normally develop after 28 weeks of pregnancy; consequently, imaging cannot be used to diagnose lissencephaly until this time.

INTERVENTION APPROACHES AND ISSUES

- There is no cure, and management is for symptoms. Nasogastric tubes (feeding tubes inserted through the nose to the stomach) and gastrostomies (openings made through the abdominal wall into the stomach, usually for inserting a feeding tube) may be helpful to reduce the complications that arise due to feeding problems (see Chapters 41 and 43). Medication is required to control seizures. Taken together, these approaches may increase life expectancy to adolescence.

Table 15.19. Aspects of Noonan syndrome (NS)

PHYSICAL AND HEALTH CHARACTERISTICS

- Individuals with NS tend to be of short stature.
- Facial characteristics include: hypertelorism (extra width between the eyes); ptosis (drooping) of eyelids; palpebral (eyelid) slant; epicanthal folds (skin fold from root of nose to inner termination of eyebrow); micrognathia (small jaw); low-set, prominent, and atypically rotated ears; and neck webbing.
- Skeletal abnormalities include cubitus valgus (increased carrying angle of the elbow) and hemivertebrae (a condition often apparent before the age of 6 months in which one or more of the vertebrae are half-formed; the defective vertebrae can lead to lateral curvature of the spine or scoliosis).
- Congenital heart disease, usually valvular pulmonary stenosis, may be present. In this disorder, outflow of blood from the right ventricle of the heart is obstructed at the level of the pulmonic valve (valve which separates the heart from the pulmonary artery).
- Gonadal defects vary from severe deficiency to apparently normal sexual development; defects include cryptorchidism (undescended testes) in males.
- Other features include hepatosplenomegaly (enlargement of liver and spleen) and abnormal bleeding.
- Individuals with NS with specific mutations in PTPN11 are at risk of developing mild juvenile myelomonocytic leukemia.

PREVALENCE

- 1 in 1,000 to 1 in 2,500 live births.

GENOTYPE OR CAUSE

- In approximately 50% of cases, the condition is caused by a missense mutation (a nucleotide substitution that changes a codon so that it codes for a different amino acid in the protein) in the PTPN11 gene on chromosome 12, resulting in a gain of function of the protein SHP-2—a protein tyrosine phosphatase produced by PTPN11.

FUNCTIONAL AND BEHAVIORAL PHENOTYPE

- There is no specific behavioral phenotype.
- Cognitive delay or impairment is present in up to 50%–60% of affected individuals (full-scale IQ scores range from 48 to 130, with a mean of 86.1); these effects are mild to moderate in 33% of affected individuals.
- The prevalence of progressive high-frequency sensorineural hearing loss (hearing loss caused by a problem in the inner ear or auditory nerve affecting a person's ability to hear some frequencies more than others) in NS may be as high as 50%.
- Children with NS may exhibit stubbornness, clumsiness, mood problems, and communication problems and be fussy eaters.
- Some individuals have features that resemble those of autism.

DIAGNOSIS

- Clinical diagnosis is based on physical characteristics and the functional and behavioral phenotype, as previously detailed.
- No testing is available to confirm a diagnosis.

(continued)

Table 15.19. *(continued)*

DIAGNOSIS *(continued)*
- A child suspected of having NS should receive a detailed cardiac workup, including an electrocardiogram (ECG), an ECHO, and consultation with a pediatric cardiologist.

INTERVENTION APPROACHES AND ISSUES
- If no serious heart problem exists, life expectancy is normal.
- Assessment of development is necessary to identify any delays and allow for intervention.
- Mildly affected individuals should respond well to traditional educational methods.
- Audiological evaluation is needed to determine if there is high-frequency sensorineural hearing loss.

PEDIATRIC STROKE

Background

The pediatric age range includes neonates, infants, and adolescents. *Stroke* is defined as the sudden occlusion or rupture of cerebral arteries or veins resulting in focal cerebral damage and clinical neurological deficits. There are two types of stroke: hemorrhagic stroke and ischemic stroke. Hemorrhagic stroke occurs when a blood vessel bursts inside the brain; the brain is very sensitive to bleeding and damage can occur very rapidly, either because of the presence of the blood itself or because the fluid increases pressure on the brain and harms it by pressing it against the skull. Ischemic stroke occurs when blood supply is reduced to a part of the brain, due to occlusion of a blood vessel. In arterial ischemic stroke (AIS), occlusion in the artery is usually due to thromboembolism (a blood clot that forms, breaks off, and travels through the bloodstream to another part of the body), which results in an infarct (localized area of ischemic necrosis usually caused by vascular blockage). Neonates (infants younger than 28

Table 15.20. Aspects of pediatric stroke

PHYSICAL AND HEALTH CHARACTERISTICS
- In neonates, characteristics include the presence of seizures, lethargy, or decreased consciousness.
- In older infants and children, characteristics include acute focal neurological impairment (usually motor, speech, or visual), as well as one or more of the following:
  —Weakness or inability to move a body part
  —Numbness or loss of sensation
  —Decreased or lost vision (may be partial)
  —Speech difficulties
  —Inability to recognize or identify familiar things
  —Sudden headache
  —Vertigo (sensation of one's surroundings spinning around)
  —Dizziness
  —Loss of coordination
  —Swallowing difficulties
  —State of being sleepy, stuporous, lethargic, comatose, or unconscious

PREVALENCE
- 2.3 cases in 100,000 per year (1.2 for ischemic stroke and 1.1 for hemorrhagic stroke).
- In one study, the prevalence was more than 8 cases in 100,000 per year (deVeber, 2003).
- Males are affected more frequently.

GENOTYPE OR CAUSE
There are numerous causes of pediatric stroke, and approximately half the children with first-ever AIS have a known predisposing cause; the following genetic disorders predispose to stroke:
- Sickle cell anemia: an autosomal recessive disorder of red blood cells that confers resistance to malaria.
- Homocystinuria: an autosomal recessive amino acid disorder caused primarily by a deficiency in cystathionine.
- Fabry disease: one of several inherited disorders called lysosomal storage disorders.
- Progeria: a rare genetic disorder that accelerates the aging process approximately seven-fold.
- Neurofibromatosis: see this chapter's Neurofibromatosis section.
- Coagulation disorders: Factor V Leiden is the most common inherited blood abnormality that results in blood clots. This disorder results in activated protein C resistance (a condition that occurs in patients with the Factor V mutation).

Other risk factors for pediatric stroke include the following:
- Congenital heart disease, such as ventricular or atrial septal defect (incomplete closure between walls of the heart), patent ductus arteriosus (failure of the ductus arteriosus to close), and aortic or mitral stenosis (closure or narrowing of the valve openings); see Chapter 10 for more details.
- Acquired heart disease (e.g., rheumatic heart disease, infection from a prosthetic heart valve, bacterial endocarditis, infection of a heart valve, arrhythmia).
- Systemic vascular disease (e.g., systemic hypertension, volume depletion or systemic hypotension) and diabetes.
- Vasculitis (e.g., inflammation of blood vessels due to meningitis; systemic infection; systemic lupus erythematosus, or a chronic inflammatory disorder of the connective tissue).
- Vasculopathies (abnormalities in the content of the vessels or vessel walls).
- Vasospastic disorders resulting from ergot (fungal parasite in the heads of grains) poisoning or nitrous oxide poisoning (nitrous oxide is used as an anesthetic).
- Hematologic disorders and coagulopathies (e.g., leukemia, vitamin K deficiency, congenital coagulation defects).
- Structural abnormalities of the cerebrovascular system.
- Trauma (e.g., child abuse; obstruction of a blood vessel by a blood clot, air bubble, fat deposit, or other substance; penetrating intracranial trauma).
- Pediatric HIV/AIDS.

(continued)

Table 15.20. *(continued)*

FUNCTIONAL AND BEHAVIORAL PHENOTYPE

- After stroke, a wide range of behaviors and functional problems are possible, depending on the location of the infarct in the brain.
- Long-term neurological impairment occurs after childhood AIS in 60%–85% of cases.
- The most frequently reported neurological impairment is hemiparesis (one-sided weakness), but less obvious residual deficits—including speech, learning, and behavior problems—also occur.

DIAGNOSIS

- As many as 48–72 hours often elapse between the onset of symptoms of arterial occlusion and a child's diagnosis.
- A CT scan or MRI can detect infarct or hemorrhage.
- Eye examination may show abnormal eye movements.

INTERVENTION APPROACHES AND ISSUES

- As of 2007, aside from trials with individuals who have sickle cell anemia, treatment is experimental.
- Initial strategies for AIS aim to reduce the size of the infarct.
- For older children, antithrombotic agents—such as antiplatelet drugs (e.g., aspirin), which prevent platelets from clumping, and anticoagulants (e.g., heparin or warfarin), which prevent new blood clots from forming or existing clots from enlarging—are given to reduce the 20%–30% risk of recurrence of AIS.
- Rehabilitative services (e.g., neuropsychological assessments to determine the relationship between behavior and brain functioning, speech and language therapy, occupational therapy and physiotherapy) are often necessary. Help with inclusion back into school may be needed.
- Prophylactic blood transfusions prevent strokes in children with sickle cell anemia who have abnormalities on transcranial Doppler ultrasonographic examination, but it is not known how long transfusion should be continued.
- More research is needed to develop strategies for the treatment and prevention of strokes in children. Large, multicenter networks are being formed in pursuit of evidence-based treatments for improvement of outcome from childhood stroke.

days of age) make up 25% of pediatric AIS patients. Hemorrhagic stroke is somewhat less common but more frequently fatal than ischemic stroke. The majority of information presented in Table 15.20 pertains to AIS because survivors of AIS are more likely to be encountered clinically than survivors of hemorrhagic stroke. Pediatric stroke is largely an understudied condition, with no clinical trials completed to date. However, this condition is being increasingly recognized. As explained in Table 15.20, numerous genetic disorders predispose to pediatric stroke, especially sickle cell anemia.

PHENYLKETONURIA

Background

Phenylketonuria (PKU) is a rare hereditary disorder in which the amino acid phenylalanine is not properly metabolized. Phenylalanine is one of eight essential amino acids found in protein-containing foods. In PKU, phenylalanine cannot be normally metabolized because of a deficiency in an enzyme necessary for its breakdown. As a result, high levels of phenylalanine and its derivatives build up in the body; these compounds are toxic to the central nervous system and cause brain damage.

PKU was first described by Norwegian physiologist Ivar Asbjorn Folling in 1934. It was characterized by paleness of skin, eyes, and hair; eczema; cognitive delay; and a characteristic odor of the urine due to high levels of the amino acid phenylalanine in the blood and excretion of the metabolite phenylketone in the urine. Within several years the name *phenylketonuria* was coined by Lionel Penrose, a British geneticist. In Norway, the syndrome is still known as Folling's disease, after the person who discovered it.

By 1951, dietary treatment, involving restriction of phenylalanine from the diet, had begun. Most developed countries have been screening newborns for PKU since 1969. In the past, 600 micromoles/liter (micromol/L) was accepted as the upper limit of phenylalanine in blood plasma, but since 1998, the recommended preschool level has been revised downward to 360 micromol/L.

This disorder has an autosomal recessive mode of inheritance. Women with PKU are likely to give birth to infants with congenital abnormalities and cognitive disability if the fetus is exposed to high levels of phenylalanine while in the uterus. Thus, it is important for affected women to stay on a low phenylalanine diet before conception through to delivery.

PRADER-WILLI SYNDROME/ PRADER-LABHART-WILLI SYNDROME

Background

Prader-Willi syndrome (PWS), or Prader-Labhart-Willi syndrome, was first described in 1956 by Andrea Prader, Alexis Labhardt, and Heinrich Willi (a Swiss pediatrician and endocrinologist, a Swiss internist, and a Swiss pediatrician, respectively). The description was made on the basis of nine children with small stature, small hands and feet, obesity after early infancy, and mental retardation. Prader and Willi reviewed the condition in 1961, expanded the phenotype, and drew attention to the presence of hypotonia in infancy and the development of diabetes mellitus in later childhood. Most cases of PWS arise sporadically, but some have an autosomal dominant mode of inheritance.

Table 15.21. Aspects of phenylketonuria (PKU)

PHYSICAL AND HEALTH CHARACTERISTICS
Affected individuals usually have
- Fair skin, blond hair, and blue eyes.
- Eczema (skin rash).
- Typical physical development and nutritional state (i.e., no characteristic nutritional deficiencies).
- No dysmorphic features, although mild microcephaly (small head) is possible.
- Characteristic odor of the urine due to high levels of the amino acid phenylalanine in the blood and excretion of the metabolite phenylketone in the urine.

PREVALENCE
- 1 in 15,000 live births in the United States.
- Prevalence varies internationally: Turkey has the highest incidence in the world, with approximately 1 in 2,600 live births; a high incidence is also reported in the Yemenite Jewish population, as well as in regions of northern and eastern Europe, Italy, and China.

GENOTYPE OR CAUSE
- The amino acid phenylalanine cannot be converted to tyrosine because the enzyme phenylalanine hydroxylase is absent or nonfunctional.
- A deficiency of tetrahydrobiopterin also causes some cases of the disorder; this form of PKU is not responsive to dietary restriction of phenylalanine, but some affected individuals respond to treatment with tetrahydrobiopterin.

FUNCTIONAL AND BEHAVIORAL PHENOTYPE
- The main feature is developmental delay, observable by mid-infancy, if the condition is left untreated.
- Severe behavior disturbances may include hyperactivity, destructiveness, impulsiveness, uncontrolled rage, and self-injury.
- Symptoms similar to those of autism and schizophrenia are possible.
- Tonic-clonic seizures (epileptic seizures associated with loss of consciousness) occur in approximately 25% of affected children.
- Hyperreflexia (exaggerated reflexes) in about 50% of affected individuals.
- Spastic cerebral palsy may also appear.
- Athetosis (involuntary twisting of upper extremities), hand posturing, and behavioral stereotypies (frequent repetition of the same posture, movement, or form of speech) may be present.

DIAGNOSIS
- PKU screening in infants involves the Guthrie heel prick test (blood sample taken from heel of infant before 4 days of age).
- CVS can detect fetal PKU.
- An enzyme assay can be conducted to detect the genetic carrier state of parents.

INTERVENTION APPROACHES AND ISSUES
- If treatment involving a low phenylalanine diet is started before 3 weeks of age, there are usually no apparent effects. If treatment is started between 3 and 6 weeks of age, there are mild effects. After 6 months of age, there appears to be little beneficial effect of treatment.
- Individuals who receive early treatment can usually expect a typical life in adulthood, although slightly lower intellectual functioning may occur.
- The duration of treatment remains somewhat controversial. Dietary restriction until at least 10 years of age is usual; problems of untreated adults with PKU include intellectual disabilities and numerous behavioral and psychological problems; dietary restriction for life is recommended.
- A potent source of phenylalanine is the artificial sweetener aspartame; this should be avoided.
- Guidelines or recommendations for management of PKU vary from one country to another.

Table 15.22. Aspects of Prader-Willi syndrome (PWS)/Prader-Labhart-Willi syndrome

PHYSICAL AND HEALTH CHARACTERISTICS
- Affected individuals commonly possess blond to light brown hair, blue eyes, and sun-sensitive, fair skin.
- Newborns have poor muscle tone and a weak cry, as well as a poor sucking response and feeding difficulty. The latter changes to overeating between 6 months and 2 years of age.
- Without intervention, obesity occurs after infancy.
- Individuals have short stature, as well as small hands and feet.
- Cryptorchidism (undescended testicle[s]) and hypogonadism (small testes, small penis, and inadequate testosterone production).
- Hypotonia is present.
- There is the presence of dysmorphic facies (unusual facial features).
- Excessive daytime sleepiness is possible.
- There is an increased occurrence of scoliosis (curvature of the spine) and other orthopedic problems.
- Some individuals affected by PWS suffer "Pickwickian syndrome," in which severe obesity impairs breathing, leading to drowsiness, cyanosis (bluish discoloration due to decreased oxygen in the blood), and possible heart failure.
- People with PWS are likely to have a hypothalamic growth hormone deficiency.
- Obesity may cause other complications, such as heart failure and diabetes.

PREVALENCE
- 1 in 8,000 to 1 in 25,000 live births.
- Frequency is the same in males and females.

GENOTYPE OR CAUSE
- PWS is the first human disorder attributed to genomic imprinting; in disorders attributed to genomic imprinting, genes are expressed differentially based on the parent of origin.
- An imprinting center has been identified on chromosome 15, within 15q11-13; gene expression may be regulated by DNA methylation at cytosine bases.
- PWS results from the loss of imprinted genomic material (normally active genetic material) within the paternal 15q11.2-13 locus (the loss of maternal genomic material at the 15q11.2-13 locus results in Angelman syndrome).
- This loss of paternal genetic material may occur in three different ways: 1) a deletion on the paternal chromosome 15, 2) a mutation on the paternal chromosome 15, and 3) maternal uniparental disomy (i.e., two copies of chromosome 15 from the mother and none from the father).

(continued)

Table 15.22. *(continued)*

FUNCTIONAL AND BEHAVIORAL PHENOTYPE • The majority of individuals with PWS exhibit mild to moderate developmental delay. • Typical behavior patterns include irritability, anger, temper tantrums, stubbornness, low frustration tolerance, anxiety, compulsive eating (hyperphagia), and self-injurious behavior (skin picking is the most common). • More than 70% of individuals display serious behavior problems, with anger and hostility being the most common features. • Rates of obsessive compulsive disorder may be 20 to 40 times more common than in the general population, including non–food-related obsessive compulsive behavior. • Food-related problem behaviors include food seeking, overeating, and hoarding. • Other maladaptive behavior includes argumentativeness and aggression. • Some individuals with PWS have difficulty in sequential processing and visual and motor short-term memory. • Relative strengths include expressive vocabulary, long-term memory, visual memory, and visual–spatial integration. • Some individuals with PWS have an unusually intense interest in jigsaw puzzles.	DIAGNOSIS • Clinical diagnosis is made by assessing physical characteristics and the functional and behavioral phenotype, as previously detailed. • Genetic testing includes chromosome analysis and assessment for methylation patterns in the PWS region (methylation patterns can be determined by Southern blot hybridization or by PCR using DNA primers that can detect methylated cytosine). • When a deletion in the 15q region is suspected, a prenatal diagnosis can be made using CVS or amniocentesis; the prenatal diagnosis can be confirmed using FISH. INTERVENTION APPROACHES AND ISSUES • Length of life depends on successful weight management; individuals with PWS have survived into their fifties. • Recommended intervention involves a combination of dietary management; behavior management; family intervention; physiotherapy, with passive exercises and frequent change in position to prevent disuse atrophy and joint contractures; and medications for treating challenging behaviors (e.g., aggression, obsessive-compulsive behavior). • Growth hormone use is being tried on an experimental basis.

PROGRESSIVE MYOCLONUS EPILEPSY

Background

Progressive myoclonus epilepsy (PME) is a group of rare catastrophic epilepsies, which include Unverricht-Lundborg disease, Lafora disease, five forms of neuronal ceroid lipofuscinosis, myoclonic epilepsy with ragged red fibers (MERRF), and sialidosis (a disorder in which a lysosomal enzyme called neuraminidase is missing; this enzyme is involved in the first stage of breakdown of large carbohydrate groups, removing sialic acid residues). PME is associated with myoclonus (sudden, brief, jerky, shock-like, involuntary movements), tonic-clonic seizures (formerly called grand-mal seizures, these involve contraction of all skeletal muscles and loss of consciousness), and neurological decline. This group of disorders affects young children and adolescents. All types of PME are genetic. Most have an autosomal recessive mode of inheritance, and one affects mitochondrial DNA. Refer to the Batten Disease/Neuronal Ceroid Lipofuscinosis and Lafora Disease/Lafora Progressive Myoclonus Epilepsy sections in this chapter for more information.

RETT SYNDROME

Background

Rett syndrome was originally described in 1966 by Andreas Rett, an Austrian pediatrician. Nonetheless, the syndrome was not known worldwide until two decades later, following a report by Bengt Hagberg and colleagues that described 35 affected girls from Sweden, Portugal, and France. More than 99% of Rett syndrome cases are sporadic. However, the disorder can be inherited in an X-linked dominant (lethal) mode. Females have two X chromosomes, so even when one has a significant mutation, as in Rett syndrome, the other X chromosome provides enough normal protein for the child to survive. Males conceived with this mutation do not have a second X chromosome to compensate for the problem. Therefore, the mutation in males is usually lethal, leading to miscarriage, stillbirth, or very early death. A small number of males with Rett syndrome mutations survive. Some have classic features of Rett syndrome and others are variably affected. Those with features of Rett syndrome have an extra X chromosome in many or all of the cells in their body. The presence of this extra X chromosome compensates for effects of the mutation and enables the boys to survive. Other cases result from mutations that occur after conception and are present in only a fraction of the body's cells.

SANFILIPPO SYNDROME/ MUCOPOLYSACCHARIDOSIS TYPE III

Background

Sanfilippo syndrome was recognized by American physician Sylvester Sanfilippo and colleagues in 1963. The syndrome, which is also called mucopolysaccharidosis

Table 15.23. Aspects of progressive myoclonus epilepsy (PME)

PHYSICAL CHARACTERISTICS
- Generalized or multifocal myoclonus (stimulus sensitive) occurs.
- Tonic-clonic seizures occur.
- Cognitive abilities deteriorate.
- There are EEG abnormalities.

PREVALENCE
- PME accounts for 1% of all epilepsy cases in childhood and adolescence.

GENOTYPE OR CAUSE

Disorder	*Locus*	*Chromosome*	*Gene*
• Unverricht-Lundborg disease	EPM1	21q22.3	Cystatin B
• Lafora disease	EPM2A EPM2B	6q24 6p22	Laforin Malin
• Infantile NCL	CLN1	1p32	Palmitoyl-protein thioesterase 1
• Late infantile NCL	CLN2	11p15	Tripeptidyl peptidase 1
• Finnish variant of NCL	CLN5	13q22	Novel membrane protein
• Juvenile NCL	CLN3	16p12	Novel membrane protein
• Northern epilepsy variation of NCL	CLN8	8p23	Novel membrane protein
• MERRF	MTTK	mtDNA	$tRNA^{Lys}$
• Sialidosis	NEU1	6p21	Neuraminidase 1

FUNCTIONAL AND BEHAVIORAL PHENOTYPE
- Cognitive abilities deteriorate, and dementia develops.
- Cerebellar ataxia (impaired ability to coordinate voluntary movements resulting from damage to the cerebellum) occurs.
- Sensory-neural impairments (hearing and vision impairments) occur.
- Optic atrophy (damage to the optic nerve resulting in a degeneration or destruction of the optic nerve) and macular spots (blind spots in the macula, the part of the retina needed for sharp, central vision) occur.

DIAGNOSIS
- Enzyme assays, brain imaging techniques, and EEGs can be used for diagnosis.

INTERVENTION APPROACHES AND ISSUES
- Antiepileptic medication useful in controlling myoclonus and seizures.
- Intervention approaches for mitochondrial disease include vitamins (B, C, E), enzyme cofactors (co-enzyme Q10), and antioxidants.

Table 15.24. Aspects of Rett syndrome

PHYSICAL AND HEALTH CHARACTERISTICS
- Children develop typically for the first 6 to 18 months after birth.
- Hypotonia is frequently the first sign.
- At approximately 2–6 months of age, head growth slows, along with gray matter atrophy that leads to acquired microcephaly (small head).
- Affected individuals have
  —A shaky, unsteady, or stiff gait
  —Scoliosis
  —Poor circulation that can lead to cold and bluish arms and legs
  —Small feet
  —Excessive saliva and drooling
- The syndrome progresses through four stages (see Schneider, 2005, for more information).

PREVALENCE
- 1 in 23,000 live births in United States.
- 1 in 10,000 to 1 in 45,000 live births internationally.

GENOTYPE OR CAUSE
- Rett syndrome is caused by a mutation of the gene encoding methyl-CpG-binding protein 2 (MeCP2) on the X chromosome, specifically Xq27-qter; MeCP2 normally binds methylated DNA regulating gene expression and chromatin structure.
- Mutations in MeCP2 have also been found in males with cognitive delays and children with autism.

FUNCTIONAL AND BEHAVIORAL PHENOTYPE
- Development regresses along with slowing of head growth.
- Language skills regress and there is eventual loss of communication skills.
- Affected individuals have
  —Intellectual disabilities and learning difficulties
  —Apraxia
  —Seizures
  —Breathing abnormalities
  —Loss of normal sleep patterns and sleep disturbances
- Gastrointestinal complaints (including ongoing, severe constipation and gastroesophageal reflux disease

DIAGNOSIS
- Chromosomal analysis may be used to search for mutations of the MeCP2 gene; studies have shown that mutations can be found in 75% of girls with Rett syndrome.
- Because the mutation is not identified in everyone with the syndrome, the diagnosis is still based on physical characteristics and functional and behavioral phenotype, as previously detailed.

INTERVENTION APPROACHES AND ISSUES
- Physical and occupational therapy slow the progression of motor deterioration.
- Speech-language therapy improves communication skills.
- Music therapy is sometimes used to prompt and provide motivation for communication and learning.

type III (MPS III), is the most common of seven MPS disorders that fall into a broader class of disorders (lysosomal storage disorders) caused by the deficiency of specific lysosomal enzymes and the lysosomal accumulation of glycosaminoglycans, or mucopolysaccharides. Each type of MPS is associated with a particular enzymatic deficiency, although the various disorders share many clinical features. The MPSs are ubiquitous; therefore, multiple organ systems can be involved. Severe cognitive delay can also occur and is usually associated with Sanfilippo syndrome, as well as Hurler syndrome (MPS-I) and Hunter syndrome (MPS-II). (Refer to the Hunter Syndrome/Mucopolysaccharidosis Type II and Hurler Syndrome/Mucopolysaccharidosis Type I sections for more information on MPS disorders.)

There are four different enzyme deficiencies that cause Sanfilippo syndrome, resulting in types A, B, C, and D. The mode of inheritance is autosomal recessive.

SHAKEN BABY SYNDROME

Background

Brain injuries are the leading cause of traumatic death and the leading cause of child abuse fatalities. The term *whiplash shaken baby syndrome* was made popular in 1972 by pediatric radiologist John Caffey. Caffey used this phrase to label a cluster of clinical findings in infants, which included retinal hemorrhages, subdural and subarachnoid hemorrhages, and little or no evidence of external cranial trauma; these findings have since become known as *shaken baby syndrome (SBS).*

The type of shaking that causes SBS is easily recognized as violent and likely to inflict serious injury or death. These shaking events usually result from tension and frustration in parents or caregivers that are generated by a child's crying. Because the infant is un-

Table 15.25. Aspects of Sanfilippo syndrome/mucopolysaccharidosis type III (MPS III)

PHYSICAL AND HEALTH CHARACTERISTICS
- Children appear typical at birth and seem to develop typically for the first 1–2 years. As increasing numbers of cells become damaged, symptoms begin to appear.
- Mild coarsening of facial features is apparent, and changes in bones and skeletal structures occurs with age.
- Other problems can include narrowing or the airway passage in the throat, enlargement of tonsils and adenoids (making it difficult to swallow), vomiting and diarrhea, and recurring respiratory infections (including pneunomia).
- The syndrome is difficult to diagnose due to mild dysmorphic features and the lack of mucopolysaccharides in the urine.
- Other features include
  —Hairiness
  —Minimal signs of dysostosis multiplex (incomplete/defective bone formation)
  —Corneal clouding and hepatosplenomegaly (enlargement of the liver and spleen) in rare cases
  —Diarrhea
- Individuals tend to have short life spans. Many die between 10 and 20 years of age as a result of pneumonia. Some people with a mild form of type B live well into adulthood.
- Individuals with MPS may have unusual sensitivity to anesthesia.

GENOTYPE OR CAUSE
- The syndrome results from a deficiency of one of four enzymes that are necessary to degrade heparan sulfate (a sulfated polysaccharide that consists of alternating hexuronate and glucosamine units).
- Type A results from deficiency of the enzyme heparan sulfatase.
- Type B results from deficiency of the enzyme N-acetyl-alpha-D-glucosaminidase (NAG).
- Type C is caused by a deficiency of the enzyme acetyl coA-alpha-glucose N-acetyl transferase.
- Type D is caused by a deficiency of the enzyme N-acetyl glucosamine 6-sulfate sulfatase.
- In each case, a partially broken-down sugar, or mucopolysaccharide, accumulates in the brain and the body's cells and tissues, causing progressive damage; the storage process affects an individual's appearance, bodily functions, and development.

PREVALENCE
- 1 in 16,000 to 1 in 30,000 live births for all MPS disorders.
- Sanfilippo syndrome accounts for approximately 50% of all cases of MPS and has a prevalence of 1 in 53,000 to 1 in 280,000 live births.
- The prevalence of type A is 1 in 24,000 to 1 in 89,000; this type is the most severe and the most common. Type B is the second most common type.

FUNCTIONAL AND BEHAVIORAL PHENOTYPE
- There is severe cognitive disability in the form of cognitive deterioration and dementia.
- Symptoms can mimic those of autism.
- Severe behavior disturbance is a common feature of the syndrome and can include hyperactivity, aggression, and sleep disturbances; some affected children like to chew on anything.
- There is a loss of language, vision, and hearing.
- Joint stiffness is possible.

DIAGNOSIS
- Enzyme assays are conducted to determine specific enzymatic activity.
- Prenatal diagnosis by measurement of the specific enzyme is also possible through amniocentesis or CVS.
- Urinary excretion of heparan sulfate is increased.
- Imaging studies may be useful for defining mild cases of dysostosis multiplex and other skeletal abnormalities.
- CT scans show mild to moderate cortical atrophy.

INTERVENTION APPROACHES AND ISSUES
- Intervention is needed for associated health and behavior problems, the latter being one of the more difficult aspects of the disorder to address.
- Bone marrow transplants and gene therapy may be attempted. (See the Hunter Syndrome/Mucopolysaccharidosis Type II and Hurler Syndrome/Mucopolysaccharidosis Type I sections for information.)

Table 15.26. Aspects of shaken baby syndrome (SBS)

PHYSICAL AND HEALTH CHARACTERISTICS

- Retinal hemorrhage is the first clue and a classic marker of SBS.
- Subdural hematoma (bleeding between the arachnoid and dura mater of the brain) and subarachnoid hemorrhage (bleeding between the pia mater and the arachnoid of the brain) may occur (see also Chapter 8).
- There is an absence of any external trauma to the head, face, and neck.
- The caregiver may provide an inadequate history or report.

PREVALENCE

- An estimated 50,000 cases occur each year in the United States.
- The victims of SBS range in age from a few days to 5 years, with an average of 6–8 months.
- SBS is reported as the leading cause of death in children younger than 4 years in the United States.

GENOTYPE OR CAUSE

- SBS results from vigorous shaking of a child by the arms, legs, chest, or shoulders, such that his or her brain rotates more than the surrounding skull and dura.
- SBS involves angular deceleration forces that exceed those pertaining to routine play, infant swings, or falls from a low height.
- Males tend to predominate as the perpetrators (i.e., in 65%–90% of cases); the mothers are the least likely to be the abusers.

FUNCTIONAL AND BEHAVIORAL PHENOTYPE

- In less severe cases, vomiting, poor feeding, lethargy or irritability, hypothermia, increased sleeping, difficulty arousing, and failure to vocalize may occur.
- In more severe cases, seizures, apnea (transient cessation of respiration), bradycardia (relatively slow heart action), and complete cardiovascular collapse occur.

DIAGNOSIS

- A CT scan of the brain is sufficient to diagnose one or more of the following: subdural hemorrhage, cerebral edema, or subarachnoid hemorrhage.
- MRI as a follow-up study can determine the extent of the neurological injury and may be helpful for continued management and prognosis.
- An ophthalmologic evaluation and retinal examination is helpful in diagnosis; papilledema (swelling of the optic disc) indicates presence of increased intracranial pressure, and retinal hemorrhage strongly points to the diagnosis of SBS.

INTERVENTION APPROACHES AND ISSUES

- To treat a child with SBS, interdisciplinary intervention by clinical teams and community programs is imperative, yet costly.
- Effective prevention strategies include increasing public awareness regarding the consequences of shaking a child and educating health care professionals to identify infants at high risk for abuse.

able to give a history at the time of examination by a medical professional and the caregiver may be unwilling to be truthful or may not know the truth, there is often delayed diagnosis. Advances in neuroimaging, CT scans, and MRI have been helpful in detailing the extent of intracranial injury, directing neurosurgical intervention, and determining when injuries occurred.

SMITH-LEMLI-OPITZ SYNDROME

Background

In 1964, Smith-Lemli-Opitz syndrome (SLOS) was first described in three unrelated boys by David Weyhe Smith, Luc Lemli, and John Marius Opitz (American pediatrician and dysmorphologist, Belgian pediatrician, and German-American human geneticist, respectively). The authors later called the disorder RHS syndrome, from the initial letters of the family names of the patients who were described, but the syndrome is also known as SLOS, after the three men who discovered it. Smith-Lemli-Opitz syndrome is caused by a deficiency in the enzyme 7-dehydrocholesterol reductase (DHCR7), which acts in the sterol synthetic metabolic pathway to convert 7-dehydrocholesterol (7DHC) into cholesterol. The syndrome is thus caused by a lack of plasma cholesterol as well as the presence of high levels of the precursor 7DHC, which is toxic at high concentrations. Severity generally correlates with plasma sterol concentration. Very severe cases involve multiple congenital malformations, miscarriages, or death within the first few weeks of life.

Cholesterol is required by practically all cells in the body to function effectively; therefore, SLOS potentially affects all organs. However, morphogenic abnormalities are predominantly located in the craniofacial, limb, skeletal, and urogenital systems, as well as internal organs such as the heart. It is linked with a high rate of mortality due to multiorgan system failure, congenital heart disease, and hepatic failure. The syndrome has an autosomal recessive mode of inheritance.

SMITH-MAGENIS SYNDROME

Background

The first group of children with this syndrome was described in the 1980s by Ann Smith, a genetic counselor, and Ellen Magenis, a physician and chromosome expert. Currently, more than 100 people with Smith-Magenis syndrome (SMS) have been reported in the medical literature. A variety of unusual physical and behavior characteristics have been found in people with SMS. This syndrome is usually sporadic in nature. Rarely, the microdeletion causing SMS may arise in a child because one of the parents carried a "balanced" chromosomal rearrangement involving chromosome 17.

Table 15.27. Aspects of Smith-Lemli-Opitz syndrome (SLOS)

PHYSICAL AND HEALTH CHARACTERISTICS
- Individuals with mild cases have subtle facial dysmorphia.
- Individuals with severe cases often have these characteristics:
  —Intrauterine growth retardation and slow growth after birth
  —Cleft palate
  —Anteverted nostrils
  —Microcephaly
  —Genital anomalies
  —Syndactyly (joining or webbing of two or more fingers or toes) or polydactyly (having more than the normal number of fingers or toes)
  —Cardiac malformation

PREVALENCE
- Incidence of diagnosed SLOS in 3 different countries (United States, United Kingdom, and Canada) is 1 in 20,000 to 1 in 60,000 live births.
- As many as 1 in 30 people carry one mutant gene, which suggests true birth incidence of 1 in 5,000 to 1 in 18,000. The lower observed incidence may be the result of miscarriage of fetuses with SLOS, the failure of these fetuses to survive to term, and/or underdiagnosis of SLOS.
- SLOS occurs most frequently in Caucasians of Eastern European descent and occurs least frequently among those of Asian or African descent.
- The syndrome is equally prevalent among males and females.

GENOTYPE OR CAUSE
- SLOS is caused by diverse mutations in the DHCR7 gene located on chromosome 11, specifically 11q12.13.
- Possession of mutations on both alleles of the gene leads to expression of a more or less pronounced phenotype, depending on the specific mutations carried; possession of a mutation on one allele leads to a healthy carrier phenotype.

FUNCTIONAL AND BEHAVIORAL PHENOTYPE
- Neuropsychiatric and neurodevelopmental problems are frequent.
- One or more of the following is present: antisocial, self-destructive, hyperactive, aggressive behavior, or withdrawn behavior.
- Withdrawal or autism-like behavior, or both
- Intellectual function ranges from profound cognitive delay to borderline typical intelligence.
- Language and hearing impairments occur.

DIAGNOSIS
- Prenatal diagnosis includes measuring 7DHC levels through amniocentesis or CVS.
- Postnatal diagnosis includes measurement of plasma cholesterol and 7DHC, as well as enzyme analysis for ambiguous cases.

INTERVENTION APPROACHES AND ISSUES
- Cholesterol supplementation helps by raising plasma cholesterol levels and lowering 7DHC levels. Otherwise, there is no medication or treatment for this syndrome.
- Medical treatment is available for some of the physical characteristics, such as surgery for congenital heart failure, surgery to repair of polydactyly, and hearing aids.
- In the future, fetal therapy, including cholesterol supplementation, might decrease the severity of the syndrome.

STURGE-WEBER SYNDROME

Background

A certain type of birthmark called a "port wine stain" often signifies the neurodevelopmental disorder Sturge-Weber syndrome (SWS). Visible birthmarks have been singled out in babies from ancient times and were thought to be caused by some adverse event experienced by the mother. The presence of neurological problems in individuals with certain types of visible birthmarks often caused lack of acceptance by society. The link between birthmarks and other features was made in 1860 by German opthalmologist Rudolf Schirmer. In 1879, English physician William Allen Sturge clearly described the main clinical manifestations in a young girl and deduced that they resulted from a vascular lesion. In 1922, English physician Frederick Parkes Weber described the radiographic features of the syndrome for the first time. This syndrome occurs sporadically and rarely more than once in a family. It is included with the neurocutaneous (or phacomatoses) syndromes; refer to the Neurofibromatosis and Tuberous Sclerosis Complex/Syndrome sections for more information on related disorders.

TOURETTE SYNDROME

Background

Tourette syndrome was recognized as early as 1825 by French physician Jean Marc Gaspard Itard. The condition is named after French neurologist Georges Albert Édouard Brutus Gilles de la Tourette, who in 1885 described a condition involving multiple tics, involuntary movements, echolalia (involuntary repetition of a word or sentence just spoken by another person), and coprolalia (involuntary utterance of vulgar or obscene words). Tourette syndrome is a childhood-onset neurological disorder characterized by motor and vocal tics. The mode of inheritance is difficult to determine because of the variability of clinical presentation.

TRAUMATIC BRAIN INJURY

Background

Traumatic brain injury (TBI) occurs as a result of either direct or indirect forces to the brain matter and is divided into two phases of injury. The primary phase includes all damage to the brain and its structures as a direct result of the force of the injury. The secondary

Table 15.28. Aspects of Smith-Magenis syndrome (SMS)

PHYSICAL AND HEALTH CHARACTERISTICS
- Brachycephaly (a disproportionately short head); broad face; broad nasal bridge; flat mid-face; posteriorly rotated or low-set ears; short, broad hands; atypical upper limb formation; and eye problems, including strabismus (one or both eyes are not correctly aligned and are pointing in different directions) and high myopia (nearsightedness), are present.
- Low muscle tone and feeding problems occur in infancy.
- Short stature is evident.
- Older children and adults have a prominent jaw.
- There are abnormalities of the palate, with or without cleft lip.
- Individuals have a down-turned mouth.
- Chronic ear infections and hearing impairments can occur.
- Fingers and toes are short.
- Heart defects and murmurs can occur.
- Urinary system problems are present.
- Scoliosis (curvature of the spine) can occur.
- Individuals have an unusual gait (walking pattern).

PREVALENCE
- 1 in 25,000 live births in the United States, but the condition is underrecognized and underdiagnosed.

GENOTYPE OR CAUSE
- SMS is associated with a microdeletion involving chromosome 17, specifically 17p11.2.
- Frameshift and missence mutations leading to protein truncation in the retinoic acid induced 1 gene (RAI1) have been observed in individuals who exhibit SMS characteristics but do not have a 17p11.2 deletion.

FUNCTIONAL AND BEHAVIORAL PHENOTYPE
- There is moderate cognitive impairment (IQ score is typically in the 50–60 range), with speech and language delays.
- Some individuals never show significant behavior problems.
- Some show maladaptive behaviors, including hyperactivity, sleep problems (frequent awakenings), and features similar to those of autism.
- A "self-hugging" posture involving a spasmatic upper body squeeze is characteristic of SMS.
- Indivduals with SMS tend to ask the same questions over and over—for example, "Where are you from?" or "What's your name?"
- There may be aggression, self-injury, head banging, hand biting, pulling out of fingernails and toenails, and polyembolokoilamania (insertion of foreign bodies or objects into bodily orifices, observed in up to 70% of individuals with SMS).
- There may be a relative insensitivity to pain.
- Individuals are at risk of stereotypic (repetitive) movement disorders.

DIAGNOSIS
- Clinical diagnosis is based on physical characteristics and functional and behavioral phenotype, as previously detailed.
- PCR and DNA sequencing strategies are used to assess RAI1 mutations.
- FISH staining is used to look for an 17p11.2 deletion containing the RAI1 gene.

INTERVENTION APPROACHES AND ISSUES
- Family services must include behavioral intervention planning.
- Psychotropic drugs are used for modifying problem behaviors and addressing sleep disorders.
- Speech-language therapy, occupational therapy, physical therapy, and orthopedic intervention are needed.
- Support is needed from schools, workplaces, and residential service providers, as well as from individuals' family members (especially for managing behavior disorders).
- Early intervention programs are very important.
- A strong international network of families has formed to exchange experiences and information about SMS, to sponsor regular national meetings where professionals and parents learn from one another, and to promote and fund research in the field.

Table 15.29. Aspects of Sturge-Weber syndrome (SWS)

PHYSICAL AND HEALTH CHARACTERISTICS
- SWS is a neurodevelopmental disorder characterized by an angiomatous, "port-wine stain" facial malformation. This is caused by overgrowth of capillaries beneath the skin surface and excessive growth of blood vessels on the surface of the brain (usually the back) on the same side as the birthmark. Brain tissue underneath the abnormal vessel growth may not receive adequate perfusion.
- Hemiparesis (a weakening or loss of the use of one side of the body) may develop opposite to the port-wine stain.
- Buphthalmos (an enlarging of the eye) can occur as a result of the stain.
- Glaucoma, a disease of the eye marked by increased pressure within the eyeball that can result in damage to the optic disk and gradual loss of vision, may also occur.

PREVALENCE
- SWS is sporadic, and the prevalence has not been estimated.
- Males and females are affected equally.

GENOTYPE OR CAUSE
- SWS is caused by the persistence of residual embryonal blood vessels and their secondary effects on surrounding brain tissue.

FUNCTIONAL AND BEHAVIORAL PHENOTYPE
- Seizures often occur, usually beginning between 2 and 7 months of age.
- Varying degrees of developmental delay in motor and cognitive skills may also occur.

DIAGNOSIS
- Diagnosis can be made following examination by plain skull radiography, CT scan, MRI, and angiography.

INTERVENTION APPROACHES AND ISSUES
- Laser treatment may be used to lighten or to remove port-wine stains in children as young as 1 month of age.
- Diagnosis of glaucoma and intracranial involvement, even if asymptomatic, is fundamental.
- Intervention focuses on treating associated neurologic and ocular abnormalities.
- Anticonvulsants are used to control seizures. Vagus nerve stimulation (VNS) implants (which electrically stimulate the vagus nerve, leading to an antiepileptic effect) can be used in children older than 12 years of age. Brain surgery can also be utilized for seizure management.
- Physical and occupational therapy may be needed.
- Special education services may be necessary.

Table 15.30. Aspects of Tourette syndrome

PHYSICAL AND HEALTH CHARACTERISTICS
- There are no associated physical characteristics aside from the associated tics and unusual behaviors.

PREVALENCE
- 1 in 2,000 live births is generally accepted as the prevalence rate in the United States.
- The incidence is higher in special groups, such as children who receive special education services.
- Tourette syndrome is three to four times more common in males than females.

GENOTYPE OR CAUSE
- The syndrome has a significant genetic component. Inheritance may involve several mechanisms, including autosomal dominant, bilinear, or polygenic transmission.
- The pathophysiology is still unknown, although this is thought to involve striatocortical circuits (nerves that link the basal ganglia to frontal cortical areas of the brain).

FUNCTIONAL AND BEHAVIORAL PHENOTYPE
- Symptoms begin between the ages of 2 and 15 years, but most people have symptoms by the age of 11.
- Tourette syndrome often is not recognized in individuals with severe or profound intellectual or developmental disability.
- Affected individuals exhibit head and facial tics, as well as vocalizations (e.g., throat clearing, barking, snorting, grunting, coughing, word accentuation).
- Other symptoms are frequently present and include touching, hitting, jumping, and smelling objects; saying involuntary and inappropriate obscene remarks, as well as engaging in obsessive-compulsive behaviors, hyperactivity, self-injury, inappropriate sexual activity, exhibitionism, and antisocial behavior.
- ADHD and learning disabilities can occur.
- Sleep disorders are common.

DIAGNOSIS
- There is no test to make a definitive diagnosis.
- Diagnosis is made by clinical examination and history.
- Diagnostic criteria, even if applied systematically, cannot be confirmed.

INTERVENTION APPROACHES AND ISSUES
- It is critical to work with the individual's family.
- Traditional neuroleptics (antipsychotic drugs) are the standard treatment, but there is increasing interest in nonneuroleptic drugs, behavior therapies, and surgical approaches.
- Treatment begins with modification of the work and home environments.
- Treatment of tics with specific drugs needs to be carefully considered, as these may result in more disability than the tics themselves.
- Tourette syndrome was once believed to be a lifelong condition, but noticeable improvement or remissions may occur without the use of medication; 30%–40% of children may have total remission, and another 30% exhibit substantial reduction of symptoms.

Table 15.31. Aspects of traumatic brain injury (TBI)

PHYSICAL AND HEALTH CHARACTERISTICS
- Abnormalities in brain anatomy following a TBI include edema (swelling of the brain), hematomas (bruising of the tissue), diffuse axonal injury lesions, and various types of hemorrhages, as well as neuronal death in deep areas of the brain from lack of oxygen.

PREVALENCE
- Each year, more than 1.6 million people in North America sustain TBIs, resulting in 80,000 permanent, severe neurological disabilities and 52,000 deaths.

GENOTYPE OR CAUSE
- TBIs can result from falls and bicycle, sports, and motor vehicle accidents.
- TBIs also can result from direct or indirect forces that cause direct or indirect injury, respectively. Direct injury is immediate and results from the force of an object striking or penetrating the head. Indirect injury results from acceleration or deceleration forces generated by the variable movements of areas of the brain against one another, as well as by the impact of the brain against the skull.

FUNCTIONAL AND BEHAVIORAL PHENOTYPE
- Individuals with TBIs can have symptoms that mimic those of psychiatric disorders. These include amnesia, headaches, confusion, dizziness, blurred vision, fatigue or lethargy, a change in sleep patterns, a change in behavior and mood, and difficulties concentrating and being attentive.
- Moderate or severe TBI causes repeated vomiting or nausea, convulsions, slurred speech, weakness or numbness in the extremities, and loss of coordination.
- TBIs can lead to permanent disabilities associated with cognition, communication, sensory processing, and behavior or mental health. Long-term complications are associated with Alzheimer's disease and Parkinson's disease, posttraumatic dementia, epilepsy, stroke, and dysfunction of the autonomic nervous system.

DIAGNOSIS
- Physical characteristics are most often diagnosed by medical history and neuroimaging.
- CT scans are used most often; MRI tests are also employed, being more sensitive in the detection of most types of lesions caused by TBI.
- Neurological assessment examinations, such as those employed in the Glasgow Coma Scale (GCS), are also used in TBI diagnoses. The GCS scores represent a rating of the quality of eye-opening response, motor response, and verbal response. Based on GCS scores, TBI is categorized according to severity (mild, moderate, or severe).
- Neuropsychological assessments are also carried out.

INTERVENTION APPROACHES AND ISSUES
- In addition to rehabilitation programs, successful intervention approaches for individuals with TBI require the support and patience of family members, society, and clinicians.
- For children with TBI, approaches are more extensive, ranging from providing school-based behavioral intervention to teaching and reinforcing metacognitive thinking strategies.

phase consists of a cascade of physiological, cellular, and molecular events that exacerbate the primary injury to neurons and worsen the neurological outcome of patients suffering from TBI. Structures of the brain that may become damaged during the primary phase of injury include the skull, the frontal and temporal lobes, nerve cells in the brain's connecting nerve fibers, and the cerebral vasculature. The tissues and cells that are affected by the secondary phase can include all the cells and tissue types in the brain.

TUBEROUS SCLEROSIS COMPLEX/SYNDROME

Background

Tuberous sclerosis (TS) complex/syndrome is one of the neurocutaneous syndromes, also referred to as *phacomatoses* (a group of congenital and hereditary diseases characterized by the development of hamartomas, or benign tumor-like malformations, in various tissues). The phacomatoses include neurofibromatosis, tuberous sclerosis, Sturge-Weber syndrome and ataxia-telangiectasia. Refer to the Neurofibromatosis and Sturge-Weber Syndrome sections for more information on neurocutaneous syndromes.

Tuberous sclerosis was probably first described by German pathologist Friedrich Daniel von Recklinghausen in 1862, and French neurologist Désiré-Magloire Bourneville formally labeled the condition as *tuberous sclerosis* in 1880. The onset of TS occurs in the first decade of life. It is characterized by the classic triad of epilepsy, low cognitive functioning, and adenoma sebaceum (benign tumors of the sebaceous glands, the small glands associated with hair follicles that secrete oily substances or sebum to lubricate the skin and hair). TS occurs sporadically and may be inherited in an autosomal dominant fashion.

TURNER SYNDROME

Background

Turner syndrome was first described by American endocrinologist Henry Hubert Turner in 1938. Previously named XO syndrome, it is now known to be caused by the total or partial absence of, or by structural abnor-

Table 15.32. Aspects of tuberous sclerosis (TS) complex/syndrome

PHYSICAL AND HEALTH CHARACTERISTICS
- Benign tumors or growths develop on the brain and other organs (especially the kidneys, heart, liver, spleen, and lungs) and on the face.
- Facial growths typically appear as small, bright red or brownish nodules occurring in a butterfly distribution on nose and cheeks; these facial growths become evident between 2 and 5 years of age.
- Areas of hypopigmentation (decreased pigmentation) on the arms, trunk, and legs are often exhibited at birth.
- There are tooth enamel defects.
- Periungual fibromas (tumors under fingernails) occur in approximately half of affected individuals.
- Shagreen patches (irregularly thickened, slightly elevated soft plaques that are usually noted over lumbosacral area) occur in approximately 70% of those affected.
- One or more cardiac rhabdomyomas (benign tumors composed of striated muscle fibers) may be present.

PREVALENCE
- 1 in 5,800 to 1 in 30,000 live births.

GENOTYPE OR CAUSE
- Two genetic loci have been identified so far, resulting in mutations to the TSC1 and TSC2 genes, encoding the proteins hamartin and tuberin, respectively.
- TSC1 maps to chromosome 9, specifically 9q34; TSC2 maps to chromosome 16, specifically 16p13.
- Tuberin, the protein gene product of TSC2, shows a small region of homologic identity to the Rap 1 guanosine triphosphatase activity protein (Rap 1 GAP). Rap 1 is a member of a group of proteins involved in the regulation of cell proliferation and differentiation. Loss of tuberin activity is thought to lead to activation of Rap 1 in tumors.
- Hamartin, the TSC1 gene product, has been isolated and may function as a tumor suppressor.

FUNCTIONAL AND BEHAVIORAL PHENOTYPE
- Convulsions occur in approximately 80% of affected individuals.
- Mild to severe developmental disabilities are apparent in approximately 70% of affected individuals.
- TS sometimes involves behavior disturbances, including socially unacceptable behaviors (e.g., hyperactivity, screaming, destructiveness, temper tantrums, aggression, self-mutilation) and those associated with autism and Asperger syndrome.
- Sleep disorders have been documented for some affected individuals (e.g., night walking, early morning waking).

DIAGNOSIS
- Clinical diagnosis is based on physical characteristics and a functional and behavioral phenotype, as previously detailed.
- CT scans and MRI are used to detect tumors.
- EEG is used when presentation includes epileptic seizures.
- Renal ultrasonography is used to evaluate presence of renal tumors.
- Molecular diagnosis using DNA testing is not yet routinely available, but could be developed in the future.

INTERVENTION APPROACHES AND ISSUES
- Medication is given for seizures.
- Surgery or plastic surgery can be done to address skin conditions.
- Psychoeducational and behavior therapy are needed to address behavior problems.
- Pharmacological interventions are provided for behavior problems.
- Individuals with mild cases may live productive lives.
- Individuals with severe cognitive impairments and seizure problems require extensive medical and psychosocial intervention.

Table 15.33. Aspects of Turner syndrome

PHYSICAL AND HEALTH CHARACTERISTICS
- Early characteristics include low birth weight, edema (fluid retention) on the dorsum (back) of hands and feet, and loose skin folds at the nape of the neck.
- Later-developing characteristics include short stature, webbing of the neck, low posterior hairline, small mandible (lower jaw), prominent ears, epicanthic folds, high-arched palate, broad chest and wide-spaced nipples, cubitus valgus, hyperconvex fingernails, ovarian dysgenesis (atypical embryonic development) that results in amenorrhea (absence of menstrual periods) and infertility, and sensorineural hearing loss.
- A high rate of colorblindness, short stature, chronic middle-ear infections, kidney and urinary tract abnormalities, and coarctation of the aorta (malformation causing narrowing of the main outflow artery of the heart) may be present.
- Abnormalities of the ear lobes are associated with progressive sensorineural hearing loss that often does not begin until the second decade of life.

PREVALENCE
- 1 in 2,500 to 1 in 5,000 live female births.
- Turner syndrome is thought to be a common cause of miscarriages.

GENOTYPE OR CAUSE
- Turner syndrome results when a female's cells have one normal X chromosome and the other sex chromosome is missing or altered. The syndrome is associated with the SHOX gene (short homeobox gene) located on each of the sex (X and Y) chromosomes. Approximately 40% of individuals with this syndrome have Y chromosome material in their DNA.

FUNCTIONAL AND BEHAVIORAL PHENOTYPE
- Intelligence is usually in the typical to low range, with developmental disability occurring in fewer than 10% of those affected.
- Affected individuals may have ADHD, poor right–left directionality, impaired social cognition, low self-esteem, increased risk of depression and anorexia nervosa, dysgraphia (inability to write properly), dyscalculia (math inability), problems with visual-spatial organization (e.g., impaired shape copying), and psychomotor delays or disabilities.

DIAGNOSIS
- Diagnosis is confirmed by chromosomal karyotyping.
- Renal (kidney) and cardiovascular imaging studies are conducted to detect abnormalities of the kidney and of the heart.

INTERVENTION APPROACHES AND ISSUES
- Administration of a growth hormone, either alone or with a low dose of androgen, will increase growth velocity and probably final adult height.
- Estrogen replacement therapy can promote the development of secondary sexual characteristics and maintain good tissue and bone integrity; it should be noted that estrogen replacement therapy has been associated with an increased risk of breast cancer and blood clots, among other complications.
- Modern reproductive technologies have also been used to help women with Turner syndrome become pregnant if they desire; for example, a donor egg can be used to create an embryo, which is carried by the woman with Turner syndrome.
- Hypertension in adulthood may need treatment.
- Psychiatric symptoms may be decreased by providing appropriate medical treatment.
- Psychological treatment may help boost self-esteem and address eating disorders.
- Affected individuals process information best when it is presented verbally.
- Life expectancy is typical.

malities in, one sex chromosome. The disorder is specific to females. Its most common characteristics include short stature and lack of ovarian development. A number of other physical features, such as webbed neck, arms that turn out slightly at the elbow (cubitus valgus), and a low hairline in the back of the head, are sometimes seen in people with Turner syndrome. Individuals with Turner syndrome are also prone to cardiovascular problems, kidney and thyroid problems, skeletal disorders such as scoliosis (curvature of the spine) or dislocated hips, and hearing and ear disturbances. Turner syndrome usually occurs sporadically.

WILLIAMS SYNDROME

Background

Williams syndrome was first identified by New Zealand cardiologist J.C.P. Williams and colleagues in 1961 on the basis of a pattern of cardiovascular anomalies. In 1978, the multisystem nature of the syndrome was recognized to include specific heart defects (which occur in approximately 80% of cases), developmental disabilities, and unusual facial features. Williams syndrome usually occurs sporadically, but an autosomal dominant mode of inheritance has been reported.

SUMMARY

Professionals in the field of intellectual and developmental disabilities have limited knowledge about specific syndromes and disorders. This chapter is a guide to basic information about some of these syndromes and disorders. The chapter also offers sources of further information for individuals who are interested in learning more about particular conditions.

REFERENCES

Introduction

Fidler, D. (2002, Summer). Behavioral phenotypes and special education: Parent report of educational issues for children with Down syndrome, Prader-Willi syndrome, and Williams syndrome. *Journal of Special Education*. Retrieved March 6, 2006, from http://www.wsf.org/behavior/research/phenotypes.htm

Human Genome Project Information. (2004). *What are genetic disorders?* Retrieved June 27, 2005, from http://www

Table 15.34. Aspects of Williams syndrome

PHYSICAL AND HEALTH CHARACTERISTICS
- Facial features include a broad forehead, medial eyebrow flare, depressed nasal bridge, star-like pattern in the iris, wide-spaced teeth, and full lips. The face is frequently described as "elfin like."
- Growth is delayed.
- Birth weight is low.
- Mild microcephaly (small head) is present.
- Renal and cardiovascular irregularities occur.
- Difficulties in feeding, digestive disorders, constipation, and failure to thrive usually present in infancy.
- Hypertension, supravalvular aortic stenosis (narrowing or stricture above the aortic heart valve), pulmonary stenosis (narrowing or stricture of the pulmonary heart valve), and hypercalcemia (elevated calcium in the blood) with increased urination and water intake can occur. There may be urethral stenosis (narrowing of the ureter, the canal through which urine is carried out of the body from the bladder) and bladder diverticula (pouch).
- Contractures in the legs are common.
- There can be a high frequency of middle-ear infections.

PREVALENCE
- 1 in 20,000 to 1 in 50,000 live births.

GENOTYPE OR CAUSE
- Williams syndrome is caused by microdeletions on chromosome 7, including approximately 20 genes.
- A submicroscopic deletion of variable size on chromosome band 7q11.23, which includes the elastin gene, is present in 95–98% of affected individuals.

FUNCTIONAL AND BEHAVIORAL PHENOTYPE
- Developmental delays occur; cognitive abilities range from severe disability to average ability.
- Auditory sensitivity is present.
- There is an increased risk of anxiety disorders and ADHD.
- Despite lower overall mental age and visuospatial functioning, higher-level language abilities are evident. For example, individuals with Williams syndrome often display "cocktail party speech."
- Emotional and behavior difficulties can include irritability, poor concentration, temper tantrums, overactivity, eating difficulties, poor peer relationships, and sleep disturbances.
- Individuals may display inappropriate attention-seeking behavior.
- Affected children show lack of social constraints (e.g., friendliness toward adults, including strangers).

DIAGNOSIS
- Clinical diagnosis is based on physical and behavior characteristics.
- FISH may be used to confirm a diagnosis.
- Serum calcium measurement may be conducted to detect hypercalcemia and blood urea nitrogen (BUN) and serum creatinine levels to screen for associated renal disorders.
- ECHO may be conducted to detect cardiovascular problems; approximately one half of all children with Williams syndrome have a significant cardiac lesion.

INTERVENTION APPROACHES AND ISSUES
- Children with Williams syndrome respond better to verbal teaching methods.
- Early intervention programs for speech-language therapy and occupational therapy may benefit affected children.
- Sociability needs to be appropriately directed (affected individuals may be at risk for exploitation due to their friendly nature).
- Many individuals and their families may require help from mental health professionals.
- Most affected adults live and work in supervised settings.
- Life expectancy may be lessened if congenital heart disease is present.

.ornl.gov/sci/techresources/Human_Genome/medicine/assist.shtml

Lee, T.H., Blasey, C.M., Dyer-Friedman, J., et al. (2005). From research to practice: Teacher and pediatrician awareness of phenotypic traits in neurogenetic syndromes. *American Journal of Mental Retardation, 110,* 100–106.

National Human Genome Research Institute. (2004). *Talking glossary of genetic terms.* Retrieved June 24, 2005, from http://www.genome.gov/glossary.cfm?search=

U.S. National Library of Medicine & the National Institutes of Health. (2003). *Medline plus medical encyclopedia.* Retrieved June 14, 2005, from http://www.nlm.nih.gov/medlineplus/encyclopedia.html

Wain, H.M., Bruford, E.A., Lovering, R.C., et al. (2002). Guidelines for human gene nomenclature. *Genomics, 79* (4), 464–470.

Angelman Syndrome

Angelman syndrome: Information for families & professionals. (n.d.). Retrieved February 28, 2005, from http://www.asclepius.com/angel

Clayton-Smith, J., & Laan, L. (2003). Angelman syndrome: A review of the clinical and genetic aspects. *Journal of Medical Genetics, 40,* 87–95.

Enersen, O.D. (2001). Harry Angelman. *Who named it?* Retrieved July 3, 2005, from http://www.whonamedit.com/doctor.cfm/242.html

Hitchins, M.P., Rickard, S., Dhalla, F., et al. (2004). Investigation of UBE3A and MECP2 in Angelman syndrome (AS) and patients with features of AS. *American Journal of Medical Genetics A, 125,* 167–172.

Williams, C. (2003). *Incidence statistics: How common is Angelman syndrome?* Retrieved June 13, 2005, from http://www.angelman.org/angel/index.php?id=104

Williams, C.A., Angelman, H., Clayton-Smith, J., et al. (2004). *Angelman syndrome: Consensus for diagnostic criteria.* Retrieved June 13, 2005, from http://www.angelman.org/angel/index.php?id=65

Williams, C.A., Dong, H-J., & Driscoll, D.J. (2004, September 3). Angelman syndrome. *Gene Reviews.* Retrieved June 9, 2005, from http://www.geneclinics.org/profiles/angelman/details.html

Batten Disease/ Neuronal Ceroid Lipofuscinosis

Chang, C.H. (2002, February 20). Neuronal ceroid lipofuscinoses. *eMedicine.* Retrieved January 31, 2005, from http://www.emedicine.com/neuro/topic498.htm

Cooper, J.D. (2003). Progress towards understanding the

neurobiology of Batten disease or neuronal ceroid lipofuscinosis. *Current Opinions in Neurology, 16,* 121–128.
Enersen, O.D. (2001). Frederick Eustace Batten. *Who named it?* Retrieved July 3, 2005, from http://www.whonamedit.com/doctor.cfm/7.html
Ezaki, J., & Kominami, E. (2004). The intracellular location and function of proteins of neuronal ceroid lipofuscinoses. *Brain Pathology, 14,* 77–85.

CATCH 22/22q11.2 Deletion Syndrome

Bassett, A.S., Chow, E.W., Weksberg, R., et al. (2002). Schizophrenia and genetics: New insights. *Current Psychiatry Reports, 4,* 307–314.
Enersen, O.D. (2001a). Angelo Mari DiGeorge. *Who named it?* Retrieved July 3, 2005, from http://213.236.152.40/www-whonamedit-com/doctor.cfm/2047.html
Enersen, O.D. (2001b). John Marius Opitz. *Who named it?* Retrieved July 3, 2005, from http://213.236.152.40/www-whonamedit-com/doctor.cfm/854.html
Fokstuen, S., Vrticka, K., Riegel, M., et al. (2001). Velofacial hypoplasia (Sedlackova syndrome): A variant of velocardiofacial (Shprintzen) syndrome and part of the phenotypical spectrum of del 22q11.2. *European Journal of Pediatrics, 160,* 54–57.
Guduri, S., & Hussain, I. (2002, May 28). DiGeorge syndrome. *eMedicine.* Retrieved June 21, 2005, from http://www.emedicine.com/med/topic567.htm
Manning, M.A., Cassidy, S.B., Clericuzio, C., et al. (2004). Terminal 22q deletion syndrome: A newly recognized cause of speech and language disability in the autism spectrum. *Pediatrics, 114,* 451–457.
McDonald-McGinn, D.M., Emanuel, B.S., & Zackai, E.H. (2003, July 23). 22q11.2 deletion syndrome. *Gene Reviews.* Retrieved June 13, 2005, from http://www.geneclinics.org/profiles/22q11deletion/details.html
McDonald-McGinn, D.M., & Zackai, E.H. (2005). *The history of the 22q11.2 deletion.* Retrieved June 13, 2005, from http://www.cbil.upenn.edu/VCFS/22qandyou/history.html
McKusick, V.A., Tiller, G.E., Stone, D.L., et al. (2003). DiGeorge syndrome. *OMIM: Online Mendelian Inheritance in Man.* Retrieved April 29, 2005, from http://www.ncbi.nlm.nih.gov/entrez/dispomim.cgi?id=188400
Minier, F., Carles, D., Pelluard, F., et al. (2005). Syndrome de Di George, étude rétrospective de 52 cas [DiGeorge syndrome, a review of 52 patients.] *Archives de Pediatrie, 3,* 254–257.
Murphy, K.C. (2002). Schizophrenia and velocardiofacial syndrome. *The Lancet, 359,* 426–430.
National Institute on Deafness and Other Communication Disorders. (2005). *Velocardiofacial syndrome.* Retrieved February 3, 2005, from http://www.nidcd.nih.gov/health/voice/velocario.asp
Oskarsdottir, S., Vujic, M., & Fasth, A. (2004). Incidence and prevalence of the 22q11 deletion syndrome: A population-based study in Western Sweden. *Archives of Disease in Childhood, 89,* 148–151.
Velo-Cardio-Facial Syndrome Educational Foundation. (2005). *Home page.* Retrieved February 3, 2005, from http://www.vcfsef.org

Congenital Hypothyroidism

American Academy of Pediatrics. (2003). Newborn screening for congenital hypothyroidism: Recommended guidelines. *Pediatrics, 91,* 1203–1209. Retrieved April 29, 2005, from http://aappolicy.aappublications.org/cgi/content/abstract/pediatrics;91/6/1203
Gruters, A., Krude, H., & Biebermann, H. (2004). Molecular genetic defects in congenital hypothyroidism. *European Journal of Endocrinology, 151,* U39–U44.
Lazarus, J.H. (2005). Congenital hypothyroidism. *Archives of Disease in Childhood, 90,* 112–113.
New England Newborn Screening Program. (n.d.). *Congenital hypothyroidism.* Retrieved June 14, 2005, from http://www.umassmed.edu/nbs/screenings/disorders/hypothyroidism.cfm
Park, S.M., & Chatterjee, V.K. (2005). Genetics of congenital hypothyroidism. *Journal of Medical Genetics, 42*(5), 379–389.
Rovet, J.F. (2004). In search of the optimal therapy for congenital hypothyroidism. *Journal of Pediatrics, 144,* 698–700.
Skordis, N., Toumba, M., Savva, S.C., (2005). High prevalence of congenital hypothyroidism in the Greek Cypriot population: Results of the neonatal screening program 1990–2000. *Journal of Pediatric Endocrinology & Metabolism, 18,* 453–461.
Thyroid Disease Manager. (n.d.). *Home page.* Retrieved April 29, 2005, from http://www.thyroidmanager.org
Thyroid Foundation of America. (2004). *Congenital hypothyroidism.* Retrieved June 14, 2005, from http://www.tsh.org/disorders/pregnancy/newborns.html
Wang, H.Y., Zhang, F.C., Gao, J.J., et al. (2000). Apolipoprotein E is a genetic risk factor for fetal iodine deficiency disorder in China. *Molecular Psychiatry, 5,* 363–368.

Congenital Rubella Syndrome

Atkins, G.J., & Cosby, S.L. (2003). Is an improved measles-mumps-rubella vaccine necessary or feasible? *Critical Reviews in Immunology, 23,* 323–338.
Centers for Disease Control and Prevention. (2005). Elimination of rubella and congenital rubella syndrome: United States, 1969–2004. *MMWR: Morbidity and Mortality Weekly Report, 54,* 279–282.
Centers for Disease Control and Prevention. (2005). Progress toward elimination of measles and prevention of congenital rubella infection: European region, 1990–2004. *MMWR: Morbidity and Mortality Weekly Report, 54,* 175–178.
Chess, S., Fernandez, P., & Korn, S. (1978). Behavioral consequences of congenital rubella. *Journal of Pediatrics, 93,* 699–703.
Chow, J. (1999). *History and timeline.* Retrieved June 14, 2005, from http://www.stanford.edu/group/virus/1999/jchow/histtime.html
Greene, A. (2003). *Rubella.* Retrieved June 14, 2005, from http://www.drgreene.com/21_1176.html
Libbey, J.E., Sweeten, T.L., McMahon, W.M., et al. (2005). Autistic disorder and viral infections. *Journal of Neurovirology, 11,* 1–10.

Reef, S., & Coronado, V. (n.d.). Chapter 12: Congenital rubella syndrome. *A–Z deafblindness.* Retrieved April 29, 2005, from http://www.deafblind.com/crs.html

World Health Organization. (2003). *Rubella vaccines.* Retrieved June 14, 2005, from http://www.who.int/vaccines/en/rubella.shtml#vaccines

World Health Organization. (2005). Progress towards elimination of measles and prevention of congenital rubella infection in the WHO European Region, 1990–2004. *Weekly Epidemiological Record/Health Section of the Secretariat of the League of Nations, 80,* 66–71.

Cornelia de Lange or de Lange Syndrome

Cornelia de Lange Syndrome (CdLS) Foundation. (2005). *Home page.* Retrieved April 29, 2005, from http://www.cdlsusa.org

Enersen, O.D. (2001a). Cornelia Catharina de Lange. *Who named it?* Retrieved July 5, 2005, from http://213.236.152.40/www-whonamedit-com/doctor.cfm/1059.html

Enersen, O.D. (2001b). Winfried Robert Clemens Brachmann. *Who named it?* Retrieved July 5, 2005, from http://213.236.152.40/www-whonamedit-com/doctor.cfm/1060.html

Krantz, I.D., McCallum, J., DeScipio, C., et al. (2004). Cornelia de Lange syndrome is caused by mutations in NIPBL, the human homolog of Drosophila melanogaster Nipped-B. *Nature Genetics, 36,* 631–635.

McKusick, V.A., O'Neill, M.J.F., Dolan, S.M., et al. (2005). Cornelia de Lange syndrome. *OMIM: Online Mendelian Inheritance in Man.* Retrieved April 29, 2005, from http://www.ncbi.nlm.nih.gov/entrez/dispomim.cgi?id=122470

Cri-du-Chat Syndrome

Cerruti Mainardi, P. (2003). Cri du chat syndrome. *Orphanet Encyclopedia.* Retrieved June 14, 2005, from http://www.orpha.net/data/patho/GB/uk-criduchat.pdf

DiseaseDirectory.net. (2005). *Cri du chat syndrome.* Retrieved April 29, 2005, from http://www.diseasedirectory.net/Neurological_Disorders/Chromosomal/Cri_du_Chat_Syndrome/default.aspx

Family Village: A Global Community of Disability-Related Resources. (2003). *Cri du chat syndrome.* Retrieved April 29, 2005, from http://www.familyvillage.wisc.edu/lib_cric.htm

McKusick, V.A., Wright, M.J., Lurie, I.W., et al. (2005). Cri-du-chat syndrome. *OMIM: Online Mendelian Inheritance in Man.* Retrieved April 29, 2005, from http://www3.ncbi.nlm.nih.gov/entrez/dispomim.cgi?id=123450

Van Buggenhout, G.J., Pijkels, E., Holvoet, M., et al. (2000). Cri du chat syndrome: Changing phenotype in older patients. *American Journal of Medical Genetics, 90,* 203–215.

Zhang, X., Snijders, A., Segraves, R., et al. (2005). High-resolution mapping of genotype-phenotype relationships in cri du chat syndrome using array comparative genomic hybridization. *American Journal of Human Genetics, 76,* 312–326.

Developmental Coordination Disorder

American Psychiatric Association. (1987). *Diagnostic and statistical manual of mental disorders* (3rd ed., rev. ed.). Washington, DC: Author.

American Psychiatric Association. (1994). *Diagnostic and statistical manual of mental disorders* (4th ed.). Washington, DC: Author.

CanChild: Centre for Childhood Disability Research. (n.d.). *Developmental coordination disorder.* Retrieved April 29, 2005, from http://www.fhs.mcmaster.ca/canchild

Dewey, D., & Wilson, B.N. (2001). Developmental Coordination Disorder: What is it? *Physical & Occupational Therapy in Pediatrics, 20,* 5–27.

Dyspraxia Foundation. (2005). *Home page.* Retrieved April 29, 2005, from http://www.dyspraxiafoundation.org.uk

Mandich, A.D., Polatajko, H.J., Macnab, J.J., et al. (2001). Treatment of children with Developmental Coordination Disorders: What is the evidence? *Physical & Occupational Therapy in Pediatrics, 20,* 51–68.

Miller, L., Missiuna, C., Macnab, J., et al. (2001). Clinical description of children with developmental disorder. *Canadian Journal of Occupational Therapy, 68,* 5–15.

Richardson, A.J., & Ross, M.A. (2000). Fatty acid metabolism in neurodevelopmental disorder: A new perspective on associations between attention-deficit/hyperactivity disorder, dyslexia, dyspraxia and the autistic spectrum. *Prostaglandins, Leukotrienes and Essential Fatty Acids, 63,* 1–9.

Visser, J. (2003). Developmental coordination disorder: A review of research on subtypes and comorbidities. *Human Movement Science, 22,* 479–493.

Hunter Syndrome/ Mucopolysaccharidosis Type II

Bax, M.C., & Colville, G.A. (1995). Behaviour in mucopolysaccharide disorders. *Archives of Diseases in Childhood, 73,* 77–81.

Bittar, T. (2004, September 16). Mucopolysaccharidosis. *eMedicine.* Retrieved June 16, 2005, from http://www.emedicine.com/orthoped/topic203.htm

The Canadian Society for Mucopolysaccharide and Related Diseases, Inc. (n.d.). *Links to MPS and related websites.* Retrieved March 25, 2005, from http://www.mpssociety.ca/support/links.html

Enersen, O.D. (2001). Charles A. Hunter. *Who named it?* Retrieved June 14, 2005, from http://www.whonamedit.com/doctor.cfm/1094.html

Family Village: A Global Community of Disability-Related Resources. (2004). *Mucopolysaccharidosis.* Retrieved April 30, 2005, from http://www.familyvillage.wisc.edu/lib_muco.htm

Fenton, C.L. (2002, December 11). Mucopolysaccharidosis type II. *eMedicine.* Retrieved June 16, 2005, from http://www.emedicine.com/ped/topic1029.htm

Filocamo, M., Bonuccelli, G. Corsolini, F., et al. (2001). Molecular analysis of 40 Italian patients with mucopolysaccharidosis type II: New mutations in the iduronate-2-sulfatase (IDS) gene. *Human Mutation, 18,* 164–165.

Hong, Y., Yu, S.S., Kim, J.M., et al. (2003). Construction of a high efficiency retroviral vector for gene therapy of Hunter's syndrome. *The Journal of Gene Medicine, 5,* 18–29.

Li, P., Bellows, A.B., & Thompson, J.N. (1999). Molecular basis of iduronate-2-sulphatase gene mutations in patients with mucopolysaccharidosis type II (Hunter syndrome). *Journal of Medical Genetics, 36,* 21–27.

The National MPS Society. (2003). *MPS II.* Retrieved March 25, 2005, from http://www.mpssociety.org/mps2.html

U.S. National Library of Medicine & the National Institutes of Health. (2004). Hunter syndrome. *Medline Plus Medical Encyclopedia.* Retrieved June 14, 2005, from http://www.nlm.nih.gov/medlineplus/ency/article/001203.htm

Hurler Syndrome/ Mucopolysaccharidosis Type I

Beck, M. (2003, September). Mucopolysccharidosis I. *Orphanet encyclopedia.* Retrieved June 14, 2005, from http://www.orpha.net/data/patho/GB/uk-MPS1.pdf

Bittar, T. (2004, September 16). Mucopolysaccharidosis. *eMedicine.* Retrieved June 16, 2005, from http://www.emedicine.com/orthoped/topic203.htm

Enersen, O.D. (2001a). Gertrud Hurler. *Who named it?* Retrieved June 14, 2005, from http://www.whonamedit.com/doctor.cfm/1090.html

Enersen, O.D. (2001b). Harold Glendon Scheie. *Who named it?* Retrieved June 14, 2005, from http://www.whonamedit.com/doctor.cfm/563.html

Enersen, O.D. (2001c). Hurler-Scheie syndrome. *Who named it?* Retrieved June 14, 2005, from http://www.whonamedit.com/synd.cfm/1115.html

Enersen, O.D. (2001d). Hurler's syndrome. *Who named it?* Retrieved June 14, 2005, from http://www.whonamedit.com/synd.cfm/1111.html

Genzyme Corporation. (2005). *Treatment options.* Retrieved March 29, 2005, from http://www.aldurazyme.com/pt/treat/az_us_pt_treat_options.asp

Hein, L.K., Bawden, M., Muller, V.J., et al. (2004). Alpha-L-iduronidase premature stop codons and potential read-through in mucopolysaccharidosis type I patients. *Journal of Molecular Biology, 30,* 453–462.

Krivit, W. (2004). Allogeneic stem cell transplantation for the treatment of lysosomal and peroxisomal metabolic diseases. *Springer Seminars in Immunopathology, 26,* 119–32.

Nash, D. (2003, December 16). Mucopolysaccharidosis type IH. *eMedicine.* Retrieved June 16, 2005, from http://www.emedicine.com/ped/topic1031.htm

U.S. National Library of Medicine & the National Institutes of Health. (2003). Hurler syndrome. *Medline Plus Medical Encyclopedia.* Retrieved June 14, 2005, from http://www.nlm.nih.gov/medlineplus/ency/article/001204.htm

Wraith, E.J., Hopwood, J.J., Fuller, M., et al. (2005). Laronidase treatment of mucopolysaccharidosis I. *BioDrugs, 19,* 1–7.

Hypoxic-Ischemic Encephalopathy/Neonatal Encephalopathy

Auckland District Health Board. (2005). *Neonatal encephalopathy (NE).* Retrieved June 14, 2005, from http://www.adhb.govt.nz/newborn/Guidelines/Neurology/NE.htm

Belet, N., Belet, U., Incesu, L., et al. (2004). Hypoxic-ischemic encephalopathy correlation of serial MRI and outcome. *Pediatric Neurology, 31,* 267–274.

Ferriero, D.M. (2004). Neonatal brain injury. *The New England Journal of Medicine, 351,* 1985–1995.

Hallioglu, O., Topaloglu, A.K., Zenciroglu, A., et al. (2001). Denver developmental screening test II for early identification of the infants who will develop major neurological deficits as a sequalea of hypoxic-ischeminc encephalopathy. *Pediatrics International, 43,* 400–404.

Higgins, R.D. (2005). Hypoxic ischemic encephalopathy and hypothermia: A critical look. *Obstetrics & Gynecology, 106*(6), 1385–1387.

Perlman, J.M. (1997). Intrapartum hypoxic-ischmic cerebral injury and subsequent cerebral palsy: Medicolegal issues. *Pediatrics, 99,* 851–859.

Raju, T. (2003, December 16). Hypoxic-ischemic encephalpathy. *eMedicine.* Retrieved April 29, 2005, from http://www.emedicine.com/ped/topic149.htm

Sargent, M.A., Poskitt, K.J., Roland, E.H., et al. (2004). Cerebellar vermian atrophy after neonatal hypoxic-ischemic encephalopathy. *American Journal of Neuroradiology, 25,* 1008–1015.

Vannucci, R.C., & Perlman, J.M. (1997). Interventions for perinatal hypoxic-ischemic encephalopathy. *Pediatrics, 100,* 1004–1014.

Intraventricular Hemorrhage

Annibale, D.J., & Hill, J. (2003, May 14). Periventricular hemorrhage-intraventricular hemorrhage. *eMedicine.* Retrieved February 2, 2005, from http://www.emedicine.com/ped/topic2595.htm

Engelhard, H.H., Andrews, C.O., Slavin, K.V., et al. (2003). Current management of intraventricular hemorrhage. *Surgical Neurology, 60,* 15–22.

Longatti, P.L., Martinuzzi, A., Fiorindi, A., et al. (2004). Neuroendoscopic management of intraventricular hemorrhage. *Stroke, 35,* 35–38.

Lucille Packard Children's Hospital at Stanford, Lucile Packard Foundation for Children's Health. (n.d.). *High-risk newborn: Intraventricular hemorrhage.* Retrieved January 4, 2006, from http://www.lpch.org/DiseaseHealthInfo/HealthLibrary/hrnewborn/ivh.html

Klinefelter Syndrome

American Association for Klinefelter Syndrome Information & Support (AAKSIS). (n.d.). *Home page.* Retrieved May 1, 2005, from http://www.aaksis.org

Enersen, O.D. (2001). Klinefelter's syndrome. *Who named it?* Retrieved June 14, 2005, from http://www.whonamedit.com/synd.cfm/1633.html

Klinefelter Syndrome and Associates. (n.d.). *Home page.* Retrieved May 1, 2005, from http://www.genetic.org/ks

Klinefelter Syndrome Support Group. (2005). *Home page.* Retrieved May 1, 2005, from http://www.klinefeltersyndrome.org

Lanfranco, F., Kamischke, A., Zitzmann, M., et al. (2004). Klinefelter's syndrome. *The Lancet, 364,* 273–283.

Tyler, C., & Edman, J.C. (2004). Down syndrome, Turner syndrome, and Klinefelter syndrome: Primary care throughout the life span. *Primare Care, 31,* 627–648, x–xi.

U.S. National Library of Medicine & the National Institutes of Health. (2004). Klinefelter syndrome. *Medline Plus Medical Encyclopedia.* Retrieved June 14, 2005, from http://www.nlm.nih.gov/medlineplus/ency/article/000382.htm

Lafora Disease/ Lafora Progressive Myoclonus Epilepsy

Chan, E.M., Andrade, D.M., Franceschetti, S., et al. (2005). Progressive myoclonus epilepsies: EPM1, EPM2A, EPM2B. *Advances in Neurology, 95,* 47–57.

Chan, E.M., Omer, S., Ahmed, M., et al. (2004). Progressive myoclonus epilepsy with polyglucosans (Lafora disease): Evidence for a third locus. *Neurology, 63,* 565–567.

Enersen, O.D. (2001). Gonzalo Rodriguez Lafora. *Who named it?* Retrieved July 4, 2006, from http://213.236.152.40/www-whonamedit-com/doctor.cfm/2730.html

Erbay, H., Balci, C., Tomatir, E., et al. (2003). Refractory status epilepticus in intensive care unit: A case of Lafora body disease. *The Internet Journal of Emergency and Intensive Care Medicine, 6.* Retrieved February 3, 2004, from http://www.ispub.com/ostia/index.php?xmlFilePath=journals/ijeicm/vol6n2/epi.xml

Ganesh, S., Delgado-Escueta, A.V., Suzuki, T., et al. (2002). Genotype–phenotype correlations for EPM2A mutations in Lafora's progressive myoclonus epilepsy: Exon 1 mutations associate with an early-onset cognitive deficit subphenotype. *Human Molecular Genetics, 11,* 1263–1271.

Minasian, B. (2001). Lafora's disease: Towards a clinical, pathologic, and molecular synthesis. *Pediatric Neurology, 25,* 21–29.

Worldwide Education and Awareness for Movement Disorders (WEMOVE). (2005). *Etiologic classification.* Retrieved February 3, 2004, from http://www.wemove.org/myo/myo_ec.html

Zupanc, M., & Legros, B. (2004). Progressive myoclonic epilepsy. *The Cerebellum, 3,* 156–171.

Lesch-Nyhan Syndrome

Enersen, O.D. (2001a). Michael Lesch. *Who named it?* Retrieved July 4, 2005, from http://213.236.152.40/www-whonamedit-com/doctor.cfm/1955.html

Enersen, O.D. (2001b). William Leo Nyhan. *Who named it?* Retrieved July 4, 2005, from http://213.236.152.40/www-whonamedit-com/doctor.cfm/1957.html

Jinnah, H.A., & Friedman, T. (2001). Lesch-Nyhan disease and its variants. In C.R. Scriver, A.L. Beaudet, W.S. Sly, et al. (Eds.), *The metabolic and molecular bases of inherited diseases* (8th ed., pp. 2571–2584). New York: McGraw-Hill.

Jinnah, H.A., Harris, J.C., Nyhan, W.L., et al. (2004). The spectrum of mutations causing HPRT deficiency: An update. *Nucleosides, Nucleotides & Nucleic Acids, 23,* 1153–1160.

Lesch, M., & Nyhan, W.L. (1964). A familial disorder of uric acid metabolism and central nervous system function. *American Journal of Medicine, 36,* 561–570.

National Institute of Neurological Disorders and Stroke. (2005). *Lesch-Nyhan syndrome information page.* Retrieved March 15, 2005, from http://www.ninds.nih.gov/disorders/lesch_nyhan/lesch_nyhan.htm

Nicklas, J.A., O'Neill, J.P., Jinnah, H.A., et al. (2005). *Lesch-Nyhan syndrome.* Retrieved March 9, 2006, from http://www.geneclinics.org/profiles/lns/details.html

Nyhan, W.L. (2005). Disorders of purine and pyrimidine metabolism. *Molecular Genetics and Metabolism, 86*(1–2), 25–33.

U.S. National Library of Medicine & the National Institutes of Health. (2004). Lesch-Nyhan syndrome. *Medline Plus Medical Encyclopedia.* Retrieved June 15, 2005, from http://www.nlm.nih.gov/medlineplus/ency/article/001655.htm

U.S. National Library of Medicine & the National Institutes of Health. (2005). Lesch-Nyhan syndrome. *Genetics home reference.* Retrieved March 15, 2005, from http://ghr.nlm.nih.gov/condition=leschnyhansyndrome

Visser, J.E., Bar P.R., & Jinnah, H.A. (2000) Lesch-Nyhan disease and the basal ganglia. *Brain Research Review, 32,* 449–75.

Meningitis

Classen, J.B., & Classen, D.C. (2002). Clustering of cases of insulin dependent diabetes (IDDM) occurring three years after hemophilus influenza B (HiB) immunization support causal relationship between immunization and IDDM. *Autoimmunity, 35*(4), 247–253.

Fellick, J.M., & Thomson, A.P. (2002). Long-term outcomes of childhood meningitis. *Hospital Medicine, 63,* 274–277.

Meningitis Research Foundation of Canada. (n.d.). *Home page.* Retrieved March 15, 2005, from http://www.meningitis.ca

Saez-Llorens, X., & McCracken, G. (2003). Bacterial meningitis in children. *The Lancet, 361,* 2139–2148.

Swartz, M.N. (2004). Bacterial meningitis: A review of the past 90 years. *The New England Journal of Medicine, 351,* 1826–1828.

World Health Organization. (2005). *Meningitis.* Retrieved March 15, 2005, from http://www.who.int/topics/meningitis/en

Neurofibromatosis

Enersen, O.D. (2001). Recklinghausen's disease. *Who named it?* Retrieved June 15, 2005 from http://www.whonamedit.com/synd.cfm/1207.html

Hussein, M., & Smith, R.J.H. (2005). Genetic sensorineural hearing loss. In C.W. Cummings, P.W. Flint, L.A. Harker, et al. (Eds.), *Cummings otolaryngology head and neck surgery* (4th ed., pp. 4473). Philadelphia, PA: Mosby.

Khan, A.N., Turnbull, I., Macdonald, S., et al. (2004, February 10). Neurofibromatosis type 1. *eMedicine.* Retrieved January 29, 2005, from http://www.emedicine.com/radio/topic474.htm#target1

National Institute of Neurological Disorders and Stroke. (2005). *Neurofibromatosis fact sheet.* Retrieved June 14, 2005, from http://www.ninds.nih.gov/disorders/neurofibromatosis/detail_neurofibromatosis.htm

Post, J.C. (2003). Molecular biology in pediatric otolaryngology. In C.D. Bluestone, S.E. Stool, C.M. Alper, et al.

(Eds.), *Pediatric otolaryngology* (4th ed., pp. 66–81). Philadelphia: W.B. Saunders.

Wagner, A.L. (2003, March 13). Neurofibromatosis type 2. *eMedicine.* Retrieved January 29, 2005, from http://www.emedicine.com/RADIO/topic475.htm

Neuronal Migration Disorders

Kato, M., & Dobyns, W.B. (2003). Lissencephaly and the molecular basis of neuronal migration. *Human Molecular Genetics, 12,* R89–R96.

The Lissencephaly Network. (2004). *Home page.* Retrieved May 2, 2005, from http://www.lissencephaly.org

McKusick, V.A., Hamosh, A., Wright, M.J., et al. (2003). Miller-Dieker lissencephaly syndrome. *OMIM: Online Mendelian Inheritance in Man.* Retrieved May 2, 2005, from http://www.ncbi.nlm.nih.gov/entrez/dispomim.cgi?id=247200

Ross, M.E., & Walsh, C.A. (2001). Human brain malformations and their lessons for neuronal migration. *Annual Review of Neuroscience, 24,* 1041–1070.

Noonan Syndrome

Disease Directory.net. (2005). *Diseases: Genetic disorders.* Retrieved March 29, 2005, from http://www.diseasedirectory.net/Genetic_Disorders/default.aspx

Enersen, O.D. (2001). Noonan's syndrome. *Who named it?* Retrieved June 15, 2005, from http://www.whonamedit.com/synd.cfm/1920.html

Ibrahim, J. (2002, October 30). Noonan syndrome. *eMedicine.* Retrieved June 15, 2005, from http://www.emedicine.com/ped/topic1616.htm

Jongmans, M., Sistermans, E.A., Rikken, A., et al. (2005). Genotypic and phenotypic characterization of Noonan syndrome: New data and review of the literature. *American Journal of Medical Genetics A, 134,* 165–170.

Lee, D.A., Portnoy, S., Hill, P., et al. (2005). Psychological profile of children with Noonan syndrome. *Developmental Medicine and Child Neurology, 47,* 35–38.

The Noonan Syndrome Support Group, Inc. (n.d.). *Home page.* Retrieved March 29, 2005, from http://www.noonansyndrome.org/home.html

National Organization for Rare Disorders (NORD). (2000). *Noonan syndrome.* Retrieved May 2, 2005, from http://www.rarediseases.org/search/rdbdetail_abstract.html?disname=Noonan%20Syndrome

Pediatric Stroke

Adams, R.J., & Brambilla, D. (2005). Optimizing primary stroke prevention in sickle cell anemia (STOP 2) trial investigators: Discontinuing prophylactic transfusions used to prevent stroke in sickle cell disease. *New England Journal of Medicine, 353*(26), 2769–2778.

Children's Hemiplegia and Stroke Association. (2005). *Home page.* Retrieved March 29, 2005, from http://www.chasa.org

deVeber, G. (2003). Arterial ischemic strokes in infants and children: An overview of current approaches. *Seminars in Thrombosis and Hemostasis, 29,* 567–573.

deVeber, G. (2005). In pursuit of evidence-based treatments for paediatric stroke: The UK and Chest guidelines. *The Lancet Neurology, 4*(>7), 432–436.

deVeber, G.A., MacGregor, D., Curtis, R., et al. (2000). Neurologic outcome in survivors of childhood ischemic stroke and sinovenous thrombosis. *Journal of Child Neurology, 15,* 316–324.

Fullerton, H.J., Wu, Y.W., Zhao, S., et al. (2003). Risk of stroke in children: Ethnic and gender disparities. *Neurology, 61,* 189–194.

Ganesan, V., Prengler, M., McShane, M.A., et al. (2003). Investigation of risk factors in children with arterial ischemic stroke. *Annals of Neurology, 53,* 167–173.

Kids Have Strokes. (2005). *Home page.* Retrieved March 29, 2005, from http://www.KidsHaveStrokes.org

Kirkham, F.J. (2003). Is there a genetic basis for pediatric stroke? *Current Opinion in Pediatrics, 15,* 547–558.

Roach, E.S., deVeber, G., Riela, A.R., et al. (2005). *Recognition and treatment of stroke in children: Child Neurology Society Ad Hoc Committee on Stroke in Children, National Institute of Neurological Disorders and Stroke.* Retrieved March 9, 2006, from http://www.ninds.nih.gov/news_and_events/proceedings/stroke_proceedings/childneurology.htm

Swaiman, K.F., Ashwal, S., & Ferreiro, D. (2006). *Pediatric neurology: Principles and practice* (4th ed.). Philadelphia: Mosby.

U.S. National Library of Medicine & the National Institutes of Health. (2004). Hemorrhagic stroke. *Medline Plus Medical Encyclopedia.* Retrieved June 15, 2005, from http://www.nlm.nih.gov/medlineplus/ency/article/000761.htm

Phenylketonuria

The Arc of the United States. (n.d.). *Phenylketonuria (PKU).* Retrieved March 29, 2005, from http://www.thearc.org/faqs/pku

Arnold, G.L. (2003, May 20). Phenylketonuria. *eMedicine.* Retrieved June 15, 2005, from http://www.emedicine.com/ped/topic1787.htm

Brumm, V.L., Azen, C., Moats, R.A., et al. (2004). Neuropsychological outcome of subjects participating in the PKU adult collaborative study: A preliminary review. *Journal of Inherited Metabolic Disease, 27,* 549–566.

Centerwall, S.A., & Centerwall, W.R. (2000). The discovery of phenylketonuria: The story of a young couple, two retarded children, and a scientist. *Pediatrics, 105,* 89–103.

Enersen, O.D. (2001). Ivar Asbjorn Folling. *Who named it?* Retrieved June 15, 2005 from http://www.whonamedit.com/doctor.cfm/2400.html

Lee, P.J., Ridout, D., Walter, J.H., et al. (2005). Maternal phenylketonuria: Report from the United Kingdom Registry 1978-97. *Archives of Disease in Childhood, 90,* 143–146.

National PKU News. (2005). *Home page.* Retrieved on March 29, 2005, from http://www.pkunews.org

Thony, B., Ding, Z., & Martinez, A. (2004). Tetrahydrobiopterin protects phenylalanine hydroxylase activity in vivo: Implications for tetrahydrobiopterin-responsive hyperphenylalaninemia. *FEBS Letters, 577,* 507–511.

U.S. National Library of Medicine & the National Institutes of Health. (2004). Phenylketonuria. *Medline Plus Medical*

Encyclopedia. Retrieved June 15, 2005, from http://www.nlm.nih.gov/medlineplus/ency/article/001166.htm

Prader-Willi Syndrome/Prader-Labhart-Willi Syndrome

Dykens, E.M., Sutcliffe, J.S., Levitt, P. (2004). Autism and 15q11-q13 disorders: Behavioral, genetic, and pathophysiological issues. *Mental Retardation and Developmental Disabilities Research Reviews, 10,* 284–291.

Eiholzer, U., & Whitman, B.Y. (2004). A comprehensive team approach to the management of patients with Prader-Willi syndrome. *Journal of Pediatric Endocrinology and Metabolism, 17,* 1153–1175.

Enersen, O.D. (2001a). Alexis Labhart. *Who named it?* Retrieved July 5, 2005, from http://213.236.152.40/www-whonamedit-com/doctor.cfm/521.html

Enersen, O.D. (2001b). Andrea Prader. *Who named it?* Retrieved July 5, 2005, from http://213.236.152.40/www-whonamedit-com/doctor.cfm/90.html

Enersen, O.D. (2001c). Heinrich Willi. *Who named it?* Retrieved July 5, 2005, from http://213.236.152.40/www-whonamedit-com/doctor.cfm/1718.html

Ontario Prader-Willi Syndrome Association. (2005). *Home page.* Retrieved January 4, 2006, from http://members.allstream.net/~opwsa

Prader-Willi Syndrome Association. (n.d.). *Home page.* Retrieved May 2, 2005, from http://www.pwsausa.org

Scheimann, A. (2003, July 10). Prader-Willi Syndrome. *eMedicine.* Retrieved June 15, 2005, from http://www.emedicine.com/ped/topic1880.htm

Progressive Myoclonus Epilepsy

Delgado-Escueta, A.V., Ganesh, S., & Yamakawa, K. (2001). Advances in the genetics of progressive myoclonus epilepsy. *American Journal of Medical Genetics, 106,* 129–138.

Epilepsy Ontario. (n.d.). *Home page.* Retrieved May 2, 2005, from http://www.epilepsyontario.org

National Institute of Neurological Disorders and Stroke. (2005). *Seizures and epilepsy: Hope through research.* Retrieved May 2, 2005, from http://www.ninds.nih.gov/disorders/epilepsy/detail_epilepsy.htm

Zupanc, M.L., & Legros, B. (2004). Progressive myoclonic epilepsy. *Cerebellum, 3,* 156–71.

Rett Syndrome

Enersen, O.D. (2001). Andreas Rett. *Who named it?* Retrieved July 5, 2005, from http://213.236.152.40/www-whonamedit-com/doctor.cfm/1972.html

International Rett Syndrome Association. (n.d.). *Home page.* Retrieved May 2, 2005, from http://www.rettsyndrome.org

Johnston, M.V., Mullaney, B., & Blue, M.E. (2003). Neurobiology of Rett syndrome. *Journal of Child Neurology, 18,* 688–692.

Neul, L.J., & Zoghbi, H.Y. (2004). Rett syndrome: A prototypical neurodevelopmental disorder. *The Neuroscientist, 10,* 118–128.

Rett Syndrome Research Foundation. (2004). *Home page.* Retrieved May 2, 2005, from http://www.rsrf.org

Schneider, J.H. (2005, May 23). Pervasive developmental disorder: Rett syndrome. *eMedicine.* Retrieved June 16, 2005, from http://www.emedicine.com/ped/topic2653.htm

U.S. National Library of Medicine & the National Institutes of Health. (2004). Rett syndrome. *Medline Plus Medical Encyclopedia.* Retrieved June 15, 2005, from http://www.nlm.nih.gov/medlineplus/ency/article/001536.htm

Sanfilippo Syndrome/Mucopolysaccharidosis Type III

Ben's Dream Sanfilippo Research Foundation. (n.d.). *Home page.* Retrieved May 3, 2005, from http://www.bensdream.org/link.html#moreman

Bittar, T. (2004, September 16). Mucopolysaccharidosis. *eMedicine.* Retrieved June 16, 2005, from http://www.emedicine.com/orthoped/topic203.htm

The Canadian Society for Mucopolysaccharide and Related Diseases. (2004). *Home page.* Retrieved May 3, 2005, from http://www.mpssociety.ca

Nash, D. (2003, June 19). Mucopolysaccharidosis type III. *eMedicine.* Retrieved June 16, 2005, from http://www.emedicine.com/ped/topic2040.htm

The National MPS Society. (2003). *Home page.* Retrieved May 3, 2005, from http://www.mpssociety.org/mps3.html

The Sanfilippo Children's Research Foundation. (2005). *A life for Elisa.* Retrieved June 16, 2005, from http://www.alifeforelisa.org

Society for Mucopolysaccharide Diseases. (2005). *Home page.* Retrieved May 3, 2005, from http://www.mpssociety.co.uk

Yogalingam, G., & Hopwood, J.J. (2001). Molecular genetics of mucopolysaccharidosis type IIIA and IIIB: Diagnostic, clinical, and biological implications. *Human Mutation, 18,* 264–281.

Shaken Baby Syndrome

Committee on Child Abuse and Neglect. (2001). Shaken baby syndrome: Rotational cranial injuries: Technical report. *Pediatrics, 108,* 206–210.

Moorjani, B. (2004, September 16). Neonatal injuries in child abuse. *eMedicine.* Retrieved June 16, 2005, from http://www.emedicine.com/neuro/topic238.htm

National Center on Shaken Baby Syndrome. (n.d.). *Home page.* Retrieved May 3, 2005, from http://www.dontshake.com

Smith, J. (2003). Shaken baby syndrome. *Orthopaedic Nursing, 22,* 196–203.

Wrong Diagnosis Disease Center. (2005). *Information on shaken baby syndrome.* Retrieved May 3, 2005, from http://www.wrongdiagnosis.com/s/shaken_baby_syndrome

Smith-Lemli-Opitz Syndrome

Enersen, O.D. (2001a). David Weyhe Smith. *Who named it?* Retrieved July 5, 2005, from http://213.236.152.40/www-whonamedit-com/doctor.cfm/1219.html

Enersen, O.D. (2001b). John Marius Opitz. *Who named it?* Retrieved July 5, 2005, from http://213.236.152.40/www-whonamedit-com/doctor.cfm/854.html

Enersen, O.D. (2001c). Luc Lemli. *Who named it?* Retrieved July 5, 2005, from http://213.236.152.40/www-whonamedit-com/doctor.cfm/1592.html

Jira, P.E., Waterham, H.R., Wanders R.J., et al. (2003). Smith-Lemli-Opitz syndrome and the DHCR7 gene. *Annals of Human Genetics, 67,* 269–280.

Nowaczyk, M.J.M., Whelan, D.T., Heshka, T.W., et al. (1999). Smith-Lemli-Opitz syndrome: A treatable inherited error of metabolism causing mental retardation. *Canadian Medical Association Journal, 161,* 165–170.

Smith-Lemli-Opitz/RSH Syndrome Advocacy & Exchange. (n.d.). SLO/RSH. Retrieved February 1, 2005, from http://www.members.aol.com/slo97/index.html

Steiner, R.D., Martin, L.S, & Hume, R.F. (2005, April 25). Smith-Lemli-Opitz syndrome. *eMedicine.* Retrieved June 16, 2005, from http://www.emedicine.com/ped/topic2117.htm

Smith-Magenis Syndrome

Cohen, D., Pichard, N., Tordjman, S., et al. (2005). Specific genetic disorders and autism: Clinical contribution towards their identification. *Journal of Autism and Developmental Disorders, 35,* 103–116.

Collins, D. (2004). *Smith-Magenis syndrome.* Retrieved April 29, 2005, from http://www.kumc.edu/gec/support/smith-ma.html

Girirajan, S., Elsas, L.J., Devriendt, K.H., et al. (2005). RAI1 variations in Smith-Magenis syndrome patients without 17p11.2 deletions. *Journal of Medical Genetics, 42*(11), 820–828.

Parents and Researchers Interested in Smith-Magenis Syndrome (PRISMS). (n.d.). *Home page.* Retrieved April 29, 2005, from http://www.prisms.org/start.htm

Shelley, B.P., & Robertson, M.M. (2005). The neuropsychiatry and multisystem features of the Smith-Magenis syndrome: A review. *The Journal of Neuropsychiatry and Clinical Neurosciences, 17,* 91–97.

Spadoni, E., Colapietro, P., Bozzola, M. (2004). Smith-Magenis syndrome and growth hormone deficiency. *European Journal of Pediatrics, 163,* 353–358.

Spilsbury, J., & Mohanty, K. (2003). The orthopaedic manifestations of Smith-Magenis syndrome. *Journal of Pediatric Orthopedics Part B, 12,* 22–26.

Vlangos, C.N., Wilson, M., Blancato, J., et al. (2005). Diagnostic FISH probes for del(17)(p11.2p11.2) associated with Smith-Magenis syndrome should contain the RAI1 gene. *American Journal of Medical Genetics, 132,* 278–282.

Sturge-Weber Syndrome

Baselga, E. (2004). Sturge-Weber syndrome. *Seminars in Cutaneous Medicine and Surgery, 23,* 87–98.

British Epilepsy Association. (2005). *Sturge-Weber syndrome.* Retrieved January 4, 2006, from http://www.epilepsy.org.uk/info/sturge.html

Comi, A.M. (2003). Pathophysiology of Sturge-Weber syndrome. *Journal of Child Neurology, 18,* 509–516.

Enersen, O.D. (2001a). Frederick Parkes Weber. *Who named it?* Retrieved July 5, 2005, from http://213.236.152.40/www-whonamedit-com/doctor.cfm/413.html

Enersen, O.D. (2001b). William Allen Sturge. *Who named it?* Retrieved July 5, 2005, from http://213.236.152.40/www-whonamedit-com/doctor.cfm/1661.html

Khan, A.N. (2003, March 17). Sturge-Weber syndrome. *eMedicine.* Retrieved June 16, 2005, from http://www.emedicine.com/radio/topic660.htm

Sturge-Webber Foundation [Canada]. (n.d.). *Home page.* Retrieved May 3, 2005, from http://www2.vpl.ca/dbs/redbook/orgpgs/2/2124.html

Sturge-Weber Foundation [U.K.]. (n.d.). *Home page.* Retrieved May 3, 2005, from http://www.sturgeweber.org.uk

The Sturge-Weber Foundation [U.S.]. (n.d.). *Home page.* Retrieved May 3, 2005, from http://www.sturge-weber.com

Sujansky, E., & Conradi, S. (1995). Outcome of Sturge-Weber syndrome in 52 adults. *American Journal of Medical Genetics, 57,* 35–45.

University Hospitals of Cleveland Comprehensive Epilepsy Program. (n.d.). *Vagus nerve stimulator (VNS).* Retrieved June 16, 2005, from http://epilepsyuhc.uhhs.com/vns.htm

Tourette Syndrome

Enersen, O.D. (2001a). Georges Albert Édouard Brutus Gilles de la Tourette. *Who named it?* Retrieved June 16, 2005, from http://www.whonamedit.com/doctor.cfm/357.html

Enersen, O.D. (2001b). Jean Marc Gaspard Itard. *Who named it?* Retrieved June 16, 2005, from http://www.whonamedit.com/doctor.cfm/1168.html

Faridi, K., & Suchowersky, O. (2003). Gilles de la Tourette's syndrome. *Canadian Journal of Neurological Sciences, 30* (Suppl. 1), S64–S71.

Singer, H.S. (2005). Tourette's syndrome: From behaviour to biology. *The Lancet Neurology, 4,* 149–159.

Soliman, E. (2004, June 20). Tourette Syndrome. *eMedicine.* Retrieved June 16, 2005, from http://www.emedicine.com/med/topic3107.htm

Tourette Syndrome Association. (2005). *Home page.* Retrieved March 28, 2005, from http://www.tsa-usa.org

Tourette Syndrome Foundation of Canada. (2005). *Home page.* Retrieved March 28, 2005, from http://www.tourette.ca

Traumatic Brain Injury

American Speech-Language-Hearing Association. (n.d.). *Traumatic brain injury.* Retrieved February 4, 2005, from http://www.asha.org/public/speech/disorders/Traumatic-Brain-Injury.htm

Gottesman, R.F., Komotar, R., & Hillis, A.E. (2003). Neurologic aspects of traumatic brain injury. *International Review of Psychiatry, 15,* 302–309.

Kreutzer, J.S., Kolakowsky-Hayner, S.A., Demm, S.R., et al. (2002). A structured approach to family intervention after brain injury. *Journal of Head Trauma and Rehabilitation, 17,* 349–367.

Marlowe, W.B. (2000). An intervention for children with disorders of executive functions. *Developmental Neuropsychology, 18,* 445–454.

National Institute of Neurological Disorders and Stroke. (2005). *Traumatic brain injury: Hope through research.* Retrieved February 4, 2005, from http://www.ninds.nih.gov/disorders/tbi/detail_tbi.htm#What%20is%20a%20Traumatic%20Brain%20Injury?

Sosin, D.M., Sniezek, J.E., & Thurman D.J. (1996). Incidence of mild and moderate brain injury in the United States, 1991. *Brain Injury, 10,* 47–54.

Stelmasiak, Z., Dudkowska-Konopa, A., & Rejdak, K. (2000). Head trauma and neuroprotection. *Medical Science Monitor, 6,* 426–432.

Tintinalli, J.E., Kelen, G.B., & Stapczynski, S.J. (2004). *Emergency medicine: A comprehensive study guide* (6th ed.). Ontario: McGraw-Hill.

Tuberous Sclerosis Complex

Au, K.S., Williams, A.T., Gambello, M.J., et al. (2004). Molecular genetic basis of tuberous sclerosis complex: From bench to bedside. *Journal of Childhood Neurology,* 19, 699–709.

Enersen, O.D. (2001a). Désiré-Magloire Bourneville. *Who named it?* Retrieved June 23, 2005, from http://www.whonamedit.com/doctor.cfm/2408.html

Enersen, O.D. (2001b). Friedrich Daniel von Recklinghausen. *Who named it?* Retrieved June 23, 2005, from http://www.whonamedit.com/doctor.cfm/2408.html

Mak, B.C., & Yeung, R.S. (2004). The tuberous sclerosis complex genes in tumor development. *Cancer Investigation, 22,* 588–603.

Maria. B.L., Deidrick, K.M., Roach, E.S., et al. (2004). Tuberous sclerosis complex: Pathogenesis, diagnosis, strategies, therapies, and future research directions. *Journal of Childhood Neurology, 19,* 632–642.

Nambi, R. (2004, February 20). Tuberous sclerosis. *eMedicine.* Retrieved June 16, 2005, from http://www.emedicine.com/derm/topic438.htm

Tuberous Sclerosis Alliance. (2005). *Home page.* Retrieved March 28, 2005, from http://www.tsalliance.org

The Tuberous Sclerosis Association. (n.d.). *Home page.* Retrieved March 28, 2005, from http://www.tuberous-sclerosis.org

Tuberous Sclerosis Canada. (n.d.). *Home page.* Retrieved March 28, 2005, from http://www.tscst.org

Turner Syndrome

Enersen, O.D. (2001). Henry Hubert Turner. *Who named it?* Retrieved June 23, 2005, from http://www.whonamedit.com/doctor.cfm/1048.html

Postellon, D. (2005, May 13). Turner syndrome. *eMedicine.* Retrieved June 23, 2005, from http://www.emedicine.com/ped/topic2330.htm

Rovet, J. (2004). Turner syndrome: A review of genetic and hormonal influences on neuropsychological functioning. *Neuropsychology, Development, and Cognition. Section C, Child Neuropsychology: A Journal on Normal and Abnormal Development in Childhood and Adolescence, 10,* 262–279.

Sybert, V.P., & McCauley, E. (2004). Turner's syndrome. *The New England Journal of Medicine, 351,* 1227–1238.

Turner's Syndrome Society of Canada. (n.d.). *Home page.* Retrieved March 28, 2005, from http://www.turnersyndrome.ca

Turner's Syndrome Society of the United States. (n.d.). *Home page.* Retrieved March 28, 2005, from http://www.turner-syndrome-us.org

U.S. National Library of Medicine & the National Institutes of Health. (2004). Hormone replacement therapy (HRT). *Medline Plus Medical Encyclopedia.* Retrieved June 15, 2005, from http://www.nlm.nih.gov/medlineplus/ency/article/007111.htm

Williams Syndrome

Canadian Association for Williams Syndrome. (2003). *Home page.* Retrieved March 29, 2005, from http://www.caws-can.org

Enersen, O.D. (2001). J.C.P. Williams. *Who named it?* Retrieved July 5, 2005, from http://213.236.152.40/www-whonamedit-com/doctor.cfm/56.html

Huang, L., & Robin, N. (2003, October 15). Williams syndrome. *eMedicine.* Retrieved June 23, 2005, from http://www.emedicine.com/ped/topic2439.htm

Laws, G., & Bishop, D. (2004). Pragmatic language impairment and social deficits in Williams syndrome: A comparison with Down's syndrome and specific language impairment. *International Journal of Language and Communication Disorders, 39,* 45–64.

Mervis, C.B. (2003). Williams syndrome: 15 years of psychological research. *Developmental Neuropsychology, 23,* 1–12.

Tassabehji, M. (2003). Williams-Beuren syndrome: A challenge for genotype-phenotype correlations. *Human Molecular Genetics, 15,* R229–R237.

The Williams Syndrome Association. (2004). *Home page.* Retrieved March 29, 2005, from http://www.williams-syndrome.org

Williams Syndrome Foundation. (2005). *The Williams syndrome comprehensive web site.* Retrieved March 29, 2005, from http://www.wsf.org

16

Children, Families, and HIV Infection

Rebecca Renwick, Robyn Salter Goldie, and Susan King

WHAT YOU WILL LEARN ABOUT IN THIS CHAPTER

- The basics
- Assessment
- Intervention
- Family issues
- Stigma of HIV infection: Social and community issues
- Confidentiality and disclosure
- Help for children and their families

The first few children known to have HIV (human immunodeficiency virus), which causes chronic infection and affects the central nervous system, were identified in1982 (King, Lindegren, & Rogers, 2003). Since then, there has been a remarkable increase in the reported number of children with HIV. There continues to be increasing numbers of children with HIV worldwide. In resource-rich countries, where HIV therapy is affordable, programs to decrease mother-to-child transmission of HIV have successfully reduced the number of new HIV infections in children. For children who have HIV infection, however, one of the most significant symptoms is developmental delay (American Academy of Pediatrics, 2003; Brouwers, Walters, & Civitello, 1998). Without proper treatment, between 75% and 90% of children with HIV will have developmental delays or disabilities. In fact, the first signs of HIV infection in children may be those that affect the child's central nervous system (i.e., the brain and spinal cord).

When a child has HIV, important family issues—as well as social, community, and societal issues—can dramatically affect the child's health, well-being, and quality of life. For example, families are faced with decisions about whether they should share their child's diagnosis with anyone (e.g., the child's siblings, their own friends, their relatives, the child's child care provider, the parent's employer). Some service providers may be fearful about working with a child who has HIV. Many people in the family's community (e.g., their landlords, their children's schoolmates), and in society in general, may have misinformation about the causes of HIV and how it is transmitted. They may behave in ways that show fear and negative attitudes toward children with HIV and their families. For these reasons, children who have HIV infection and their families are likely to encounter difficult and complex problems in the course of their daily lives. Vignettes about one family illustrate such issues throughout the chapter.

THE BASICS

HIV is a chronic disease that affects a person's immune system. When the immune system is healthy, it can usually fight off infections and diseases. HIV weakens the immune system so that it becomes less capable of doing so (American Academy of Pediatrics, 2003; Kaiser & Rasminsky, 1995). The person's immune system may deteriorate quickly or over a much longer period. As the immune system deteriorates, he or she becomes more susceptible to other health problems. For example, the person may more easily get opportunistic infections—that is, other infections made possible by a weakened immune system—and some forms of cancer.

The later and final stages of HIV disease have been referred to as AIDS (acquired immunodeficiency syndrome) (Kaiser & Rasminsky, 1995). The term *AIDS* is not as commonly used among health professionals now. Instead, they distinguish between differences in the disease process mainly by referring to the CD4 levels present in the person's immune system and by measuring the viral load, or the amount of virus in the blood.

After the HIV infection has entered a person's blood system, it becomes attached to CD4 cells (cells that usually fight infection). Then, the virus reproduces and starts to destroy the CD4 cells. As more CD4 cells are destroyed, the immune system becomes weaker. Levels of CD4 cells in the blood can be measured, and

The authors greatly appreciate the assistance of Ari Bitnun in obtaining some of the information for this chapter.

Throughout this chapter, the statistical information presented about HIV was current at the time of publication. However, research on HIV and treatment for people with HIV are changing rapidly as new approaches and insights are discovered and the incidence of HIV worldwide is constantly changing. Thus, this statistical information will also continue to change as well.

these levels indicate the strength or weakness of the immune system. If a child's CD4 levels (or counts) become low, he or she typically begins to have certain symptoms (e.g., delayed walking, delayed speech development) (American Academy of Pediatrics, 2003). The child is then said to be symptomatic for HIV. When a child tests positive for HIV but does not have a very low CD4 count or any medical problems caused by HIV, he or she is said to be asymptomatic. That is, the child does not have evident HIV symptoms.

Associated Symptoms and Problems

Table 16.1 lists the most common symptoms of HIV disease among children. Feeding may be a problem due to swallowing difficulties, nausea, or loss of appetite. Recurring diarrhea may also lead to poor absorption of food. These feeding problems may contribute to malnutrition and poor growth. Problems with the respiratory (breathing) system can include recurring sinus and ear infections, thrush (yeast infection of the mouth), or pneumonia. Recurring fevers due to infections are common. There may also be pain (e.g., in bones or joints) that is due to inflammation or infection and ranges from mild to severe (American Academy of Pediatrics, 2003; Burchett & Pizzo, 2003).

Before good antiretroviral medications (drugs that control symptoms of HIV but do not cure it) were available, 50%–90% of children with HIV infection eventually developed problems with their neurological systems (see Table 16.2). Once these medications became available, this rate dropped. Neurological system problems can become obvious as early as 2 months after birth or as late as 10 to 15 years of age (American Academy of Pediatrics, 2003; Burchett & Pizzo, 2003).

Miriam, age 4, lives with her mother (Deborah), father (Michael), 9-year-old brother (Peter), and 15-month-old sister (Sarah). One year ago, Miriam received a diagnosis of HIV with symptoms. When she was diagnosed at nearly 3 years of age, she had been having frequent fevers and diarrhea. Miriam was short for her age and underweight. In addition, she had just started walking and could say very few words.

Table 16.1. Major symptoms of HIV in children

A child with HIV may have symptoms that include the following:
- Recurring diarrhea
- Recurring fevers
- Thrush
- Feeding problems
- Poor growth
- Respiratory problems
- Pain
- Neurological problems

Sources: American Academy of Pediatrics (2003); Health Canada (1998); and Renwick, Goldie, and King (2003).

Ways that HIV Is Transmitted to Children

The most common way children contract HIV infection is through perinatal, or mother-to-baby, transmission. In the United States, 91% of children with HIV infection and nearly all children who are newly infected have acquired the disease in this way (American Academy of Pediatrics, 2003; Burchett & Pizzo, 2003; Centers for Disease Control and Prevention [CDC], 2002; King et al., 2003). Children may acquire the virus during their mother's pregnancy, during delivery, or from their mother's breast milk. In contrast, for adults, the most common forms of HIV transmission are through 1) exchange of body fluids during intimate sexual contact with another person who has the virus and 2) sharing needles for intravenous drug use (Health Canada, 2003; King et al., 2003).

In the 1990s, a significant proportion of the children with HIV had been infected through transfusion. At the beginning of the 21st century, however, now transfusion is unlikely to be a source of transmission in resource-rich countries (i.e., approximately a 1 in 1 million chance); since 1985, all blood products have been screened for the presence of HIV-infection in North America (King et al., 2003). Almost all individuals in North America who were infected by transfusion are adults. Thus, transfusion is now rarely the cause of HIV transmission to children. Sexual abuse by a person who already has HIV infection is also a possible, but much less commonly reported, form of transmission to children (King et al., 2003; CDC, 2002; National Institutes of Health, 2004; World Health Organization [WHO], 2004). See Table 16.3 for a summary of the ways that HIV is transmitted to children.

All babies born to mothers with HIV receive antibodies from their mothers, and these antibodies may be present in the baby for up to 18 months. During this time, these babies will test positive for HIV but most will not actually have the virus itself. Without preventive

Table 16.2. Brain and spinal cord symptoms of HIV in children

Symptoms often affecting a child's brain and spinal cord include the following:
- Delayed development
- Loss of previously attained developmental milestones
- Cognitive delays
- Memory problems
- Problems with attention (e.g., distractibility)
- Language impairment (i.e., problems producing or comprehending language)
- Motor problems (e.g., problems with muscle tone, walking, mobility, and coordination)
- Behavior problems (e.g., depressed mood, irritability, impulsiveness)
- Problems with social skills

Sources: Health Canada (1998) and Renwick, Goldie, and King (2003).

Table 16.3. Ways HIV is transmitted to infants and preadolescent children

Mother-to-child transmission
During pregnancy
During birth
Through breastfeeding
Sexual abuse by someone who is HIV positive
Contaminated shared medical equipment
Infected blood and blood products

Sources: King, Lindegren, and Rogers (2003); National Institutes of Health (2004); Renwick, Goldie, and King (2003); and World Health Organization (2004).

therapy, approximately 14%–25% of babies exposed to HIV will be infected. With therapy, this rate may now be reduced to as low as 1%. A clear HIV diagnosis can be made 3–6 months after birth (King & the Committee on Pediatric AIDS, 2004) by means of repeated special blood tests to detect the presence of the virus itself. Therefore, HIV testing should be routinely offered during pregnancy so that all women who test HIV-positive can have access to HIV therapy to improve their own health and reduce the risk of transmission of HIV to their babies. Table 16.4 shows important ways to reduce the risk of mother-to-baby transmission.

HIV changed Michael's and Deborah's lives in many important ways. During Deborah's pregnancy with Sarah, her doctor learned of a new policy of recommending HIV testing for all pregnant women. (If a woman is pregnant, it means she has had unprotected sex, which is a potential source of HIV infection and other sexually transmitted infections.) As a result, the doctor suggested HIV testing. Deborah consented, although she had not previously thought that she could be HIV-positive. When she did test positive, the doctor arranged for all other members of the family to be tested, too. Miriam and her father, Michael, tested positive. The presence of HIV infection explained Miriam's physical symptoms and developmental delay. Miriam had become infected through mother-to-child transmission.

Deborah's HIV diagnosis during the pregnancy with Sarah was cause for concern, not only for herself but also her unborn baby. She accepted her doctor's recommendation to begin taking anti-HIV medications to reduce the chances of Sarah getting HIV from her. The medications and other precautions reduced the risk of Sarah contracting HIV infection from 25% to 1%. Sarah tested negative for HIV by the time she was 6 months old.

It was obvious that Miriam had become infected with HIV through mother-to-child transmission during pregnancy, through delivery, or from her mother's breast milk. Yet, Deborah and Michael wondered how they become HIV-positive. Neither had experienced any symptoms. They had never had a blood transfusion or used street drugs requiring needles. They discussed this question and thought that Michael had probably been infected first, through sexual contact with a previous partner, and that Deborah became infected through sexual contact with Michael. Deborah did not know if she was HIV-positive while pregnant with her oldest child, Peter. Fortunately, Peter's HIV test results were negative.

Table 16.4. Ways to reduce risk of HIV transmission from mothers to babies

Selective use of cesarean sections for delivering babies
Avoidance of breastfeeding in countries where clean water is not available for preparation of baby formula
Use of antiretroviral treatment during pregnancy and delivery and for the newborn baby

Sources: American Academy of Pediatrics (2003); King, Lindegren, and Rogers (2003); and Renwick, Goldie, and King (2003).

Some people have misinformation or not enough information about how HIV infection is transmitted. Table 16.5 indicates ways in which some people erroneously believe HIV may be transmitted but in fact, are *not* ways in which the virus is passed from the child to another person or vice versa. See Table 16.3 for a review of ways that HIV is transmitted to children; see Table 16.6 for a summary of ways that HIV is transmitted to adolescents and adults.

Prevalence of HIV in Children

Numbers of people with HIV infection vary from one country to another. For example, as of December 2000 in the United States, 774,467 individuals were reported to the CDC as infected, with 8,908 (1.2%) being children younger than 13 years (King et al., 2003). As of June 2003 in Canada, 53,887 individuals have been reported to be HIV-positive, with 675 (1.25%) being children younger than15 years (Health Canada, 2003).

Despite these statistics, the actual number of children with HIV infection in the United States and Canada is not really known. Available statistics give only numbers of children identified as having the virus. These statistics also constitute an underestimate because some women of childbearing age and children who have the virus may have never been tested for HIV infection and, thus, would not be included.

At the beginning of the early 21st century, HIV infection is considered to be a global pandemic. The WHO web site (http://www.who.int) provides regularly updated estimates of the epidemic's magnitude. As of December 2003, these estimates indicate that between

Table 16.5. Ways that HIV is NOT transmitted

Hugging, touching, bathing, and kissing a child with HIV
Sharing household activities, facilities, and objects with a child who has HIV
Having contact with a child with HIV during normal living, school/child care, or play activities

Sources: American Academy of Pediatrics (1999); Chanock (1999); and Renwick, Goldie, and King (2003).

Table 16.6. Ways HIV can be transmitted to adolescents and adults

Sexual intercourse
Needle sharing
Blood and blood products

Sources: Health Canada (2003); King, Lindegren, and Rogers (2003); Renwick, Goldie, and King (2003); and Samples, Goodman, and Woods (1998).

34 and 46 million people worldwide have HIV infection or AIDS, including between 2.1 and 2.9 million children younger than 15 years. The largest numbers of these children are living in countries of sub-Saharan Africa (King et al., 2003). There are effective prevention and treatment programs for pregnant women and for children in economically well-developed countries (e.g., Australia, the United States, Canada, most European countries). In resource-poor countries, however, the lack of such programs is critical, and HIV continues to be a major cause of children's deaths (De Cock, Fowler, Mercier, et al., 2000, as cited in King et al., 2003).

ASSESSMENT

Assessment is particularly important because it can identify areas of difficulty and strength related to the child's and his or her family's health and quality of life. Repeated medical assessments are necessary for children who are HIV-positive, even if they do not have symptoms, in order to detect and address any health problems as early as possible. Early treatment is most effective for treating and preventing symptoms of HIV or reducing their severity (American Academy of Pediatrics, 2003). However, early treatment depends on frequent assessment to identify any opportunistic infections or other health problems.

Repeated psychological assessment is also needed because of the high risk of developmental delay and disability for children with HIV. This kind of assessment focuses on psychological functions (e.g., intelligence, language, memory and learning, attention, concept formation, perception), motor functions, behavior, and personality (Blanchette et al., 2001; Brouwers et al., 1998).

Other kinds of interdisciplinary assessments are important for many children with HIV, especially those who have developmental disabilities. For example, occupational therapy assessment can identify specific daily or regular life activities (e.g., personal care, play, learning, attending school, social activities) that are difficult for a child and his or her family or caregivers. Any difficulties identified can then be addressed to help improve both the child's ability to participate in usual daily activities and his or her quality of life. Physical and social aspects of the environment can also be identified and then modified to make life activities easier for the child. Physical obstacles to getting around and insufficient practical help or emotional support from others exemplify aspects of the child's environment that could be improved. Physical therapy assessment can pinpoint specific needs related to muscular strength, coordination, and exercise. Nutritional assessment can indicate the child's specific dietary needs (e.g., particular foods that are easily swallowed or readily absorbed, frequency of eating, getting adequate calories) (American Dietetic Association & Dietitians of Canada, 2000; Health Canada, 1998).

Psychosocial assessment for the family is also important (Wiener, Septimus, & Grady, 1998). It can highlight the family's strengths as well as areas in which supports, resources, and services could help the family cope better and improve quality of life.

When Miriam was diagnosed with HIV infection, her family doctor referred her to the HIV program at a large, regional children's hospital. Miriam and her parents met with the program's pediatric specialist doctor, a nurse, and a social worker. They also met the other members of the team: a nutritionist, an occupational therapist, a physical therapist, and a psychologist. The team members assessed Miriam and her family's situation so that they could recommend the most helpful interventions. They focused on Miriam's health but also worked with both parents to ensure that infected family members received the best available health care and that emotional and social needs were met for all family members. For example, they discussed Peter's emotional situation and how his parents could support him. They also assessed Sarah, the youngest child, and enrolled her in a program that would follow her growth and development to determine whether there were any effects of exposure to the anti-HIV medications Deborah took during her pregnancy with Sarah.

INTERVENTION

Several kinds of interventions are available for children with HIV. Table 16.7 provides a summary of these interventions; a more complete discussion follows.

Drug therapy (treatment with prescribed medications) is an area in which some rapid developments are taking place. Most children receive a combination of medications that are effective in controlling HIV infection but cannot cure it (Mueller, Kline, & Pizzo, 1998). Immunizations are also given to prevent other infections (e.g., flu vaccine to prevent influenza).

Interventions that are carried out by therapists and other professionals include treatments and services that address physical and cognitive functioning, as well as educational, psychological, social, and community issues. For example, sensory stimulation strategies (e.g., use of textured materials, sounds, and moving toys for stimulating and activating a child's senses of touch, hearing, and vision) can be helpful for chil-

Table 16.7. Interventions for children with HIV and their families

Several or all of the following may be used as interventions for children with HIV and their families:
Medications
Nutritional counseling/therapy
Feeding/swallowing strategies
Exercise/activities (to increase/enhance mobility and physical strength, endurance, and coordination)
Equipment and assistive devices
Accommodations to facilitate activities of daily life
Environmental modification (physical and social aspects)
Education for child and family
Counseling (psychological, spiritual, legal, financial, issues in living with HIV)
Connection to community supports/resources
Future care planning for children whose parents have HIV

Sources: American Dietetic Association and Dietitians of Canada (2000); Antle, Wells, Salter Goldie, De Matteo, and King (2001); Health Canada (1998); and Renwick, Goldie, and King (2003).

dren who are slow to reach developmental milestones (Health Canada, 1998).

Helpful equipment and environmental modifications (e.g., ramps, wheelchair, adapted seating, bath seat, aide to assist a child) can also be provided so that the child can participate in daily activities. Children with muscle weakness and coordination problems can receive help to do specific exercises and use positioning to improve their motor functioning (e.g., strength, endurance, coordination). Strategies for making swallowing food easier and/or special foods or diets are also recommended for some children (American Dietetic Association & Dietitians of Canada, 2000; Health Canada, 1998).

Children and families often need more information and education about HIV and ways to cope with it. In addition to general information about HIV, they can receive information that is tailored to their own particular needs and ways of coping with HIV and its impact on their lives (Salter Goldie et al., 2000; Wiener et al., 1998). They can also be linked with helpful community resources and supports, such as support groups and professionals and organizations that will provide practical help, information, and emotional support. Counseling is also a common intervention for these families, who are struggling with a variety of serious, and often sensitive, issues. (See the next two sections, which outline some of these issues.) One or more types of counseling may be appropriate for a particular child and his or her family (e.g., psychological, spiritual, legal, financial).

If one or both parents also have HIV, future planning for their child's care, with the help of a professional or self-help group, can be very important. For example, parents who have HIV themselves may want to have information about how to choose a guardian who will assume responsibility for their children should the parents become very ill or die (Antle et al., 2001). They may also want advice, assistance, and emotional support as they go through the process of selecting a guardian and making the appropriate legal arrangements. However, the need to engage in future planning may become more salient for people living in resource-poor countries than for those living in countries where there is ready access to treatment.

Based on the results of the team's assessments, Miriam began to take antiretroviral medications for HIV. These medications helped alleviate her symptoms. Miriam also started to follow a diet consisting of foods that her body could absorb more easily, so she began to develop and grow at a much better rate. However, she still had developmental delay.

FAMILY ISSUES

Families of children with HIV are likely to be faced with some complex issues and difficulties. These families may be experiencing extreme stress that results from several problems (e.g., health, finances, coping with their circumstances, refugee and immigration issues, drug abuse). The parents often experience guilt, regardless of how HIV was transmitted to their child, as well as anger and depression (Shandor Miles, Gillespie, & Holditch-Davis, 2001; Wiener et al., 1998). In addition, they are trying to cope with their child's illness and the uncertainty about their future.

Furthermore, one or both parents may have HIV infection and, thus, may have medical problems. In some cases, they may be terminally ill or already deceased. As noted, for parents who are ill themselves, the ability to provide for their children in the future may be a serious concern. In some families, one or both parents also may be misusing drugs. These problems are often accompanied by employment and financial difficulties. Furthermore, many people with HIV are living in countries with high rates of HIV or they are refugees or immigrants from these countries. According to the WHO web site, people in this situation are most likely to have become infected with HIV from sexual contact or through use of shared medical equipment contaminated by blood or body secretions of a person infected with HIV.

Parents are also faced with the dilemma of whether, how much, and when to tell their children, close relatives, friends, and others (Gerson et al., 2001; Nehring, Lashley, & Malm, 2000). Because they often do not do so, or delay telling others, they may become socially isolated (Wiener et al., 1998). This lack of disclosure to those who could offer help and support often means that parents take total responsibility for the care of their child while bearing "the additional burden of keeping the truth to themselves" (Wiener & Septimus,

1994, p. 813). In addition, children with HIV infection often know, at some level, that something is worrying their parents and think that they are responsible for causing that worry. This perception can be tremendously stressful for children with HIV infection. Professional assessment of children's understandings of their illness may be useful, because such understandings may be influenced by developmental level more than by age. This kind of assessment can be helpful to parents in that they can be more informed about what and when to tell their child (Wiener & Figueroa, 1998).

Children are almost always emotionally affected when their sibling(s) or parent(s) are HIV-positive. Not telling others within or outside of the family about their family member's illness may be stressful. They are also usually frightened about the possibility of their affected family member's death (Wiener & Figueroa, 1998).

In countries where medical treatment is available, family members (including siblings) benefit from information about the hope for good health that these medications bring. Even if children who have HIV infection and their uninfected siblings have not been told that HIV is the cause of the illness, they can be told about the effectiveness of the medications to help keep family members well. In resource-poor countries, lack of access to health care and medications for HIV infection is associated with ill health and early death. Thus, the experiences of people living there will be very different from those of people in countries where treatment is available and accessible.

Miriam's parents were devastated about their own HIV diagnoses, as well as by Miriam's diagnosis. They were very worried about getting ill themselves and about what would happen to all of them, including Peter and Sarah, their children who were not infected. They also felt guilty about getting HIV and passing it on to Miriam.

They had to cope with strong emotional reactions, as well as getting medical treatment for themselves and for Miriam. They also had to learn about how the virus and treatment works and how to deal with all of these changes in their lives. On top of it all, they had to decide whom to tell and whom not to tell. At first, they decided not to tell anyone except their health care providers. Although Peter was mature enough to be told, they were not ready to tell him. However, Peter knew something was wrong and often worried about it.

When Deborah was pregnant with Miriam, Deborah, Michael, and Peter came to Canada as refugees from a country where there are very high rates of HIV. During a war in their country of origin, they had been through very difficult experiences which still affected them. They had been accepted as refugees and were applying for permanent resident status, but they still worried that their HIV status could affect their immigration application. They knew that if they had to return to their country of origin, HIV medications would not be available. They also feared the discrimination that could result if anyone found out about their diagnoses. The social worker in the HIV program referred them to a special immigration lawyer who was aware of these difficult issues and would help them through the immigration process.

Deborah and Michael were also afraid to tell any of their family members in their country of origin about their HIV. First, they did not want to bring shame on themselves and their families. Second, they were afraid of being rejected by their families or being discriminated against because of the terrible prognosis associated with the disease in resource-poor countries, including their own country of origin. These were very real concerns for Deborah and Michael because they knew the consequences of how society in their country of origin deals with such issues.

STIGMA OF HIV INFECTION: SOCIAL AND COMMUNITY ISSUES

One of the most damaging aspects of HIV for individuals and families is the stigma that others in their community and society associate with the illness. When stigma is attributed to someone, that person is seen as unworthy, disgraced, or discredited due to some characteristics that make him or her noticeably different from others (Letteney & Heft LaPorte, 2004). Historically, certain diseases and disorders (e.g., epilepsy, mental illness, leprosy, syphilis) and visible physical disabilities have resulted in stigmatization. Even now, people tend to actively avoid, devalue, and discriminate against others who are stigmatized due to their disease, disorder, or disability. Recently, some people in early 21st-century society have begun to understand HIV and accept those who have it, but others remain fearful and consider HIV to be a "punishment from God" or something a person "deserves" because of his or her (or a parent's) behavior or lifestyle. Such misconceptions, combined with a lack of knowledge about HIV and its transmission, may help to promote negative attitudes and behaviors toward people with HIV, including children (Letteney & Heft LaPorte, 2004).

Children with HIV and their families often fear negative consequences because of the stigma attached to the infection (Antle et al., 2001; Lee & Rotheram-Borus, 2002; Letteney & Heft LaPorte, 2004). Their fear may make them want to hide the real nature of their child's illness. It may also cause them to isolate themselves from others from whom they want to hide the truth, even when those others could potentially offer help and support (Burr & Emery, 1994; Salter Goldie et al., 2000; Wiener & Figueroa, 1998; Wiener et al.,1998).

Education of the Public

At a community or societal level, public education campaigns about HIV can be a form of intervention. Information to the public is usually promoted in various ways (e.g., public service announcements on television, in newspapers, or on billboards; education through brochures, videos, and classroom sessions). The purposes of such interventions are to help prevent HIV transmission, to encourage people to be tested and receive early treatment if they test positive, and to reduce the stigma associated with HIV.

Standard Practices to Prevent Infection Transmission

The adoption of routine or standard practices to prevent infection transmission represents another approach to reducing stigma and discrimination toward people with HIV. Standard, or routine, practices are guided by the principle that taking precautions to prevent HIV transmission only with those who are known to have HIV or are potentially infected is inappropriate and discriminatory. These standard practices represent a more inclusive approach because procedures and practices to prevent *any* kind of communicable disease—not just HIV infection—are used with everyone in a particular setting (e.g., school, child care facility, community clinic, hospital) (American Academy of Pediatrics, 1999; Chanock, 1999; Health Canada, 1999) Table 16.8 summarizes some standard or routine prevention and infection control procedures that are commonly used.

Table 16.8. Standard/routine practices for preventing transmission of infection for use with children in out-of-home care

Situations requiring precautions:
Diapering
Contact with bodily fluids (e.g., urine, feces, vomit, exudate from wounds)
Contact with blood
Contact with bodily fluids containing visible blood
Contact with broken skin
Practices:
Wash hands
Before contact with each person
Immediately after exposure
After removing latex gloves
With warm, running water
With soap or waterless antiseptic hand rinse
Use gloves when indicated:
Use disposable latex gloves for larger exposures to blood and body fluids with visible blood
Change gloves before and after contact with each person
Dispose of gloves and blood-stained materials (e.g., linens) in separate, waterproof bag (e.g., plastic bag)
Clean blood and other fluids from surfaces using a bleach solution

Sources: American Academy of Pediatrics (1999, 2003); Centers for Disease Control and Prevention (2002); Chanock (1999); Health Canada (1999); and Renwick, Goldie, and King (2003).

Children with HIV should be able to attend any school or child care setting and participate in all activities there, as permitted by the setting's health and treatment procedures (American Academy of Pediatrics, 1999). The kinds of contact that typically take place in school and child care settings do not result in transmission of HIV infection when there is no exposure to blood (King & the Committee on Pediatric AIDS, 2004).The use of routine or standard prevention and infection control practices noted in Table 16.8 further reduces the risk of transmission.

Deborah and Michael decided to enroll Miriam in an inclusive child care program for 3 days each week. The program, attended by children with and without developmental delay, used standard practices with all participating children. All of the program's staff were thoroughly educated in these practices, and the use of these practices was monitored on an ongoing basis.

CONFIDENTIALITY AND DISCLOSURE

Because the stigma associated with being HIV-positive can result in serious consequences for both children with HIV and their families (e.g., prejudice, discrimination, exclusion), their decisions about disclosure of this diagnosis are often difficult to make. Similarly, these families are often concerned about keeping information about their diagnosis confidential.

Confidentiality Issues

Confidentiality is essential for the development of trust between a child, his or her parents, and his or her service providers. *Confidentiality* refers to the responsibility a professional has not to disclose information that has been obtained as a result of the client–professional relationship. However, this kind of information is often shared with others at the same institution or agency who are providing services to the same child and family. If an agency or institution has this approach or policy with respect to confidentiality, then parents should be told during their first meeting with a service provider. In order for a service provider to be able to offer support, the parents, child, and family must perceive that their confidentiality is respected. Thus, when a service provider shares information with others outside the agency or institution who are also currently providing services to the family, the parents' formal permission must be obtained first.

Miriam's parents were very concerned about keeping their daughter's diagnosis confidential. As they became more familiar with the professionals providing services to Miriam and their family, they developed more trust as well as a deeper understanding of confidentiality. They began to realize that staff members communicated with professionals such as the family's doctor so that Miriam could get the best health care. They learned that no information could be shared with their doctor or other professionals outside the hospital without their permission. This is a good time to mention that Miriam's family is not an actual story. However, their story consists of aspects of several families' experiences. We could not use real names and details because, to preserve confidentiality, this kind of information cannot be published.

An exception to this practice concerning confidentiality occurs when there are laws about reporting on HIV to public health authorities. Laws and public policies concerning public health vary by jurisdiction (e.g., by country, state, or province). In some places, there is an obligation to report occurrences of communicable diseases, including HIV infection, to public health staff. The purpose of such a policy regarding HIV is to ensure that everyone in the family is tested and receives education about how to prevent transmission of HIV.

Guidelines for Disclosure

The important issue of disclosure has been referred to several times in this chapter. Whether, whom, when, what, and how much to tell are extremely difficult decisions for families to make. Telling children with HIV infection and their siblings about the HIV diagnosis is an especially sensitive area of communication within families. These decisions are often influenced by the family's circumstances, level of acceptance of HIV, coping styles among family members, parental need to protect their child with HIV infection and his or her uninfected siblings, and the child's age and cognitive functioning (Gerson et al., 2001; Lee & Rotheram-Borus, 2002; Letteney & Heft LaPorte, 2004; Nehring et al., 2000). In addition, the degree of trust shared by family members is an important factor (De Matteo et al., 2002). Parents frequently worry that if their children know about HIV in the family, they may tell someone else—resulting in problems for the family (Antle et al., 2001).

In order to assist children with HIV and their families in dealing with these issues, some service providers and facilities have developed formal policies concerning disclosure. Good policies are based on ideas such as the following:

- Disclosure is a process that unfolds over time rather than occurring as a single conversation (Nehring et al., 2000).
- Professionals and parents are partners in the children's care. They can work together to assess children's needs for health information, to decide the best way and time to tell children, and to help children understand and cope with this information.
- Parents' and children's needs may sometimes differ. For example, a child may want to talk to his grandmother about his diagnosis. His parents may not agree because they fear that his grandmother may react with disapproval or rejection of her grandson and them.
- People's cultural backgrounds may affect the beliefs and values that guide their behaviors and decisions about disclosure.

If a child learns about his or her own diagnosis in an unplanned way, it is recommended that professional team members assess the needs of the family (including the child; the parents; and, as appropriate, the siblings). Then, the team can address family members' questions, concerns, and needs (DeMatteo et al., 2002). Table 16.9 lists DOs and DON'Ts for child service providers concerning disclosure.

Deborah and Michael decided to talk with Peter and Miriam about Miriam's illness. They said that Miriam had a problem with her blood and this is why she had to take pills and see her doctor every month. Deborah and Michael decided not to tell the children about their own health and medical treatment.

Deborah and Michael want to prevent the stigma associated with HIV from hurting their children, so they decided not to tell any of their friends or neighbors. They knew they had the right not to tell anyone, and the HIV program staff gave them support while and after they made this decision. The staff knew that there was almost no risk of anyone getting HIV from Miriam at school or anywhere else. As Peter, Miriam, and Sarah get older, they will need more information about health and family issues related to HIV. Deborah and Michael will decide what their children will be told and when. The HIV program staff members will work with the parents and help them with these decisions, if Michael and Deborah would like such help. Miriam's parents and health service providers will be able to form a partnership based on respect and support for the family and the family's coping style.

HELP FOR CHILDREN AND THEIR FAMILIES

In the United States, Canada, and some other resource-rich countries, information about HIV testing, referrals for treatment and support services, and many other topics are available from HIV/AIDS service or-

Table 16.9. DOs and DON'Ts for child care service providers regarding disclosure

DO respect the parents' right to tell or not tell others about their child's HIV.
DO respect the family's values and choices about whom to tell or not to tell about the child's HIV.
DO show understanding and support for parents and families.
DON'T tell anyone about the child's HIV without permission of the child's parents.
DON'T talk to children about HIV without their parents' permission.

Source: Renwick, Goldie, and King (2003).

ganizations. Staff at these organizations are very knowledgeable about local medical and support services. They are also very aware of confidentiality issues.

Children and parents can be tested for HIV by their family doctors and in other places (e.g., clinics, hospitals). If children test positive, they can be referred to specialized programs and to pediatricians who specialize in the care of children with HIV.

The Internet offers worldwide access to many other resources and organizations. Some web sites providing such lists and links appear in Appendix B at the end of the book.

SUMMARY

This chapter has provided a broad overview of a very complex topic. It has discussed HIV as a leading cause of developmental delay and disability in children. Some basic information was provided about HIV in children, how common it is in children, and how it is usually transmitted. Common forms of assessment and intervention were outlined as well. The chapter emphasized the reasons for adopting standard procedures to prevent transmission of infection in settings such as schools, child care facilities, and hospitals.

For several reasons, a diagnosis of HIV for children also seriously affects family members and their relationships with each other. For example, the mother of a child with HIV is likely to be HIV-positive and possibly the father, too. In addition, the child's siblings are usually aware that their parents are very worried about something, even if they have not yet been told about the diagnosis.

HIV is very stigmatizing to individuals and their families, so they often do not want to tell others anything about it. Thus, the chapter outlined some relevant family, community, and societal issues, as well as several important issues about confidentiality and disclosure. The chapter concluded with some general information about testing, treatment, services, and sources of help and support for children with HIV and their families.

FOR FURTHER THOUGHT AND DISCUSSION

1. Imagine that you are a service provider who works at Miriam's child care center and you suspect that she has HIV. What would you do?
2. If you were Miriam's parents, would you tell anyone about HIV infection in the family? Whom would you feel comfortable telling? If you decide to tell anyone, how would you determine whether they would support you and whether they would tell anyone else?
3. Have you ever tried to keep an important secret? What do you think it would be like living with the secret of HIV in the family? How would you explain why you were taking your child to the doctor so often? How would you explain why you are so concerned about taking universal precautions to prevent communicable diseases? How would you explain why you might be so worried or tired much of the time?
4. How do you think the HIV diagnosis changed the lives of Deborah, Michael, Peter, Sarah, and Miriam?

REFERENCES

American Academy of Pediatrics. (2003). Human Immunodeficiency Virus infection. In L.K. Pickering, C.J. Baker, G.D. Overturf, et al. (Eds.), *Redbook: 2003 report of the committee on infectious diseases* (26th ed., pp. 360–382). Elk Grove Village, IL: Author.

American Academy of Pediatrics, Committee on Pediatric AIDS and Committee on Infectious Diseases. (1999). Issues related to Human Immunodeficiency Virus transmission in schools, medical settings, the home, and community. *Pediatrics, 104*(2), 318–324.

American Dietetic Association & Dietitians of Canada. (2000). Position of the American Dietetic Association and Dietitians of Canada: Nutrition intervention in the care of persons with human immunodeficiency virus infection. *American Journal of the Dietetic Association, 100,* 708–717.

Antle, B., Wells, L., Salter Goldie, R., et al. (2001). Challenges of parenting for families living with HIV/AIDS. *Social Work, 46*(2),159–169.

Blanchette, N., Smith, M.L., Fernandez-Penney, A., et al. (2001). Cognitive and motor development in children with vertically transmitted HIV infection. *Brain & Cognition, 46,* 50–53.

Brouwers, P., Walters, P., & Civitello, L. (1998). Central nervous system manifestations, and assessment. In P.A. Pizzo & C.A. Wilfert (Eds.), *Pediatric AIDS: The challenge of HIV infection in infants, children, and adolescents* (3rd ed., pp. 293–308). Philadelphia: Lippincott, Williams & Wilkins.

Burchett, S.K., & Pizzo, P.A. (2003). HIV infection in infants, children, and adolescents. *Pediatric Review, 24,* 186–194.

Burr, C.K., & Emery, L.J. (1994). Speaking with children and families about HIV infection. In P.A. Pizzo & C.A. Wilfert (Eds.), *Pediatric AIDS: The challenge of HIV infection in infants, children, and adolescents* (2nd ed., pp. 923–935). Philadelphia: Lippincott, Williams & Wilkins.

Centers for Disease Control and Prevention. (2002). *Department of health and human services. Public health services. HIV surveillance report: 2002.* Retrieved from http://www.cdc.gov/hiv/stats/hasr/402/2002SurveillanceReport.pdf

Chanock, S.J. (1999). Medical issues in the home, day care, school, and community. In S.L. Zeichner & J.S. Read (Eds.), *Handbook of pediatric HIV care* (pp. 557–571). Philadelphia: Lippincott, Williams & Wilkins.

De Matteo, D., Harrison, C., Arneson, C., et al. (2002). Disclosing HIV/AIDS to children: The paths families take to truth telling. *Psychology, Health & Medicine, 7,* 341–356.

Gerson, A.C., Joyner, M., Fosarelli, P., et al. (2001). Disclosure of HIV diagnosis to children: When, where, why, and how. *Journal of Pediatric Health Care, 15*(4), 161–167.

Health Canada. (1998). *Rehabilitation services: A comprehensive guide for the care of persons with HIV disease.* Toronto: The Wellesley Central Hospital.

Health Canada. (1999). *Routine practices and additional precautions for preventing the transmission of infection in health care (Canada Communicable Disease Report).* Ottawa, ON, Canada: Author.

Health Canada. (2003). *HIV and AIDS in Canada: Surveillance report to June 30, 2003.* Ottawa, ON, Canada: Ministry of Health, Division of HIV/AIDS Epidemiology and Surveillance, Centre for Infectious Disease Prevention and Control.

Kaiser, B., & Rasminsky, J.S. (1995). *HIV/AIDS and child care: Fact book.* Ottawa, ON, Canada: Canadian Child Care Foundation and Health Canada.

King, S.M. (2004). Sexually transmitted diseases. In R.A. Haslam & P.J. Vallletutti (Eds.), *Medical problems in the classroom: The teacher's role in diagnosis and management* (4th ed., pp. 609–616). Austin, TX: PRO-ED.

King, S.M., & the Committee on Pediatric AIDS. (2004). Evaluation and treatment of the human immuno deficiency virus-1-exposed infant. *Pediatrics, 114*(2), 497–505.

King, S.M., Lindegren, M.L., & Rogers, M.F. (2003). Epidemiology of Pediatric HIV infection. In G. Wormser (Ed.), *AIDS and other manifestations of HIV infections* (4th ed., pp. 29–39). Amsterdam: Elsevier Science.

Lee, M.B., & Rotheram-Borus, M.J. (2002). Parents' disclosure of HIV to their children. *AIDS, 16*(16), 2201–2207.

Letteney, S., & Heft LaPorte, H. (2004). Deconstructing stigma: Perceptions of HIV-seropositive mothers and their disclosure to children. *Social Work in Health Care, 38*(3), 105–123.

Mueller, B.U., Kline, M.W., & Pizzo, P.A. (1998). Antiretroviral treatment. In P.A. Pizzo & C.A. Wilfert (Eds.), *Pediatric AIDS: The challenge of HIV infection in infants, children, and adolescents* (3rd ed., pp. 463–486). Philadelphia: Lippincott, Williams & Wilkins.

National Institutes of Health. (2004). *Mother-to-infant transmission-Statistical graphs.* Retrieved September 12, 2005, from http://www.niaid.nih.gov/daids/prevention/text/infant.htm

Nehring, W.M., Lashley, F.R., & Malm, K. (2000). Disclosing the diagnosis of pediatric HIV infection: Mothers' views. *Journal of the Society of Pediatric Nurses, 5*(1), 5–14.

Renwick, R., Goldie, R.S., & King, S. (2003). Children who have HIV and their families. In I. Brown & M. Percy (Eds.), *Developmental disabilities in Ontario* (pp. 261–275). Toronto: Ontario Association on Developmental Disabilities.

Salter Goldie, R.L., De Matteo, D.J., Wells, L.M., et al. (2000). Social planning in Canada for children with HIV infection. *Canadian Journal of Public Health, 91,* 353–356.

Samples, C.L., Goodman, E., & Woods, E.R. (1998). Epidemiology and medical management of Adolescents. In P.A. Pizzo & C.A. Wilfert (Eds.), *Pediatric AIDS: The challenge of HIV infection in infants, children, and adolescents* (3rd ed., pp. 615–643). Philadelphia: Lippincott, Williams & Wilkins.

Shandor Miles, M., Gillespie, J.V., & Holditch-Davis, D. (2001). Physical and mental health in African American mothers with HIV. *Journal of the Association of Nurses in AIDS Care, 12*(4), 42–50.

Wiener, L., & Figueroa, A. (1998). Children speaking with families and children about HIV infection. In P.A. Pizzo & C.A. Wilfert (Eds.), *Pediatric AIDS: The challenge of HIV infection in infants, children, and adolescents* (3rd ed., pp. 729–758). Philadelphia: Lippincott, Williams & Wilkins.

Wiener, L., & Septimus, A. (1994). Psychosocial support for child and family. In P.A. Pizzo & C.A. Wilfert (Eds.), *Pediatric AIDS: The challenge of HIV infection in infants, children, and adolescents* (2nd ed., pp. 809–828). Philadelphia: Lippincott, Williams & Wilkins.

Wiener, L., Septimus, A., & Grady, C. (1998). Psychosocial support for child and family. In P.A. Pizzo & C.A. Wilfert (Eds.), *Pediatric AIDS: The challenge of HIV infection in infants, children, and adolescents* (3rd ed., pp. 703–728). Philadelphia: Lippincott, Williams & Wilkins.

World Health Organization. (2004). *AIDS epidemic update: December 2003.* Retrieved September 12, 2005, from http://www.who.int/hiv/pub/epidemiology/epi2003/en/index.html

17

Cerebral Palsy

DARCY FEHLINGS, CAROLYN HUNT, AND PETER ROSENBAUM

WHAT YOU WILL LEARN ABOUT IN THIS CHAPTER

- Causes and prevalence
- Types of cerebral palsy
- Associated medical problems
- Psychosocial issues
- Intervention
- Innovative treatments

Cerebral palsy (CP) is a commonly used term that refers to a group of motor disorders. The main features of CP are as follows:

- Onset is before, during, or after birth and involves the developing brain.
- There are motor difficulties that are secondary to brain impairment.
- There is abnormal muscle tone and impaired control of movements, with poor motor coordination and balance or abnormal movements and postures (or a combination of these features).
- The disorder is permanent but nonprogressive, although it often changes in its manifestations over time.
- The disorder is often accompanied by disturbances of sensation, cognition, communication, perception, and/or behavior and/or by a seizure disorder.

A child is often first suspected of having CP in the first year of life when his or her motor milestones are delayed. For example, the child might be late in sitting, crawling, and walking. Parents may also notice that their baby has an atypical way of moving, such as commando crawling (crawling by pulling the body forward with the arms and dragging the legs behind) or that their child always stands or walks on his or her toes. The child may also appear to have "advanced" development—for example, being left-handed or "wanting to stand all the time." Clear evidence of handedness before 2 years of age is unusual and actually suggests impairment in the limb that is not used, whereas a child who seems "too strong" is probably showing evidence of increased stiffness in their muscles due to spasticity.

Diagnoses of CP are typically made by pediatricians. Pediatricians who suspect CP begin with conducting a careful review of a child's history, including any potential risk factors for CP (e.g., premature birth), and of a child's developmental progress. Pediatricians will do a physical examination, concentrating on a neurological examination (checking the child's muscle tone by moving the child's arms and legs and assessing reflexes), watching how the child is moving, and observing and assessing abnormalities in muscle tone and motor function (Rosenbaum, 2003). Signs can include stiff muscles (hypertonia) when arms or legs are moved or muscles that are floppy (hypotonia). Pediatricians may order a special picture of the brain (by **computerized axial tomography [CAT] scan** or magnetic resonance imaging [MRI]) to help evaluate the underlying brain structure problems that can sometimes provide information about the causes of CP. It is important to note, however, that there is no specific test or X ray that can prove that a child has CP. Often a diagnosis is not made in the first year because parents and doctors may think that a child's delay is simply a variation of typical development. The differences in the quality of a child's motor function (e.g., being too stiff or too loose) can be helpful in suspecting a variation outside of the usual range of function.

CAUSES AND PREVALENCE

CP is associated with multiple risk factors that are categorized by the prenatal (before birth), perinatal (during birth), and postnatal (after birth) periods (see Table 17.1). An important risk factor is premature birth, which predisposes an infant to periventricular leukomalacia, an injury to the white matter of the brain close to the ventricles. The motor messages to the legs pass through this area. An important risk factor for both premature and full-term babies is the presence of chorioamnionitis (intrauterine infection) (Wu & Colford, 2000). It is postulated that the infection leads to a fetal inflammatory response that puts the infant at risk for a brain injury. It is often assumed that children who develop CP have had a difficult birth. As more studies are done, however, it is becoming evident that

Table 17.1. Possible risk factors for cerebral palsy

Prenatal	Perinatal	Postnatal
Abnormal placenta (small; inflammation or infarction) Antenatal stroke Chorioamnionitis Congenital malformations of the brain Congenital infections (e.g., rubella [German measles], cytomegalovirus) Exposure to chemicals/toxins (for example alcohol, cocaine, and crack) Low birth weight Prematurity Toxemia (high blood pressure) Twins/multiple births/death of a twin	Cord prolapse Intracranial hemorrhage/infarction/leukomalacia Neonatal encephalopathy Premature separation of the placenta (abruption) or severe placental bleeding Uterine rupture	Asphyxia (secondary to choking, or near drowning) Brain injury Brain infections such as meningitis and encephalitis

only a small percentage of children with CP have difficulties related to their delivery (Cummins et al., 1993; Nelson, 1996; Stanley, Blair, & Alberman, 2000). Birth asphyxia is a condition in which the newborn is felt to have a low oxygen level during delivery (sometimes resulting in delayed crying and poor respiratory effort at birth), and it is associated with the subsequent development of CP. Yet, birth asphyxia often appears to be a secondary symptom of an otherwise sick baby; thus, it is not the primary cause of CP in the majority of cases. One study of children with CP found that 78% did not have birth asphyxia (Torfs et al., 1990). Of the 22% who did have birth asphyxia, all had prenatal risk factors as well, which might have been the reason they had difficulty during the delivery. In fact, due to this type of research, the term *birth asphyxia* has been replaced with the term *neonatal encephalopathy* because this latter term does not imply a causal relationship.

CP is very common. In developed countries, the mean prevalence rate is estimated to be between 2 and 2.5 for every 1,000 children (Kuban & Leviton, 1994; Murphy et al., 1993; Stanley et al., 2000). There is also evidence that CP is more prevalent in more deprived socioeconomic groups (Odding, Roebroeck, & Stam, 2006).

TYPES OF CEREBRAL PALSY

There are several different types of CP (Cans, 2000; see Table 17.2). They can be broadly divided into two main categories: spastic and **extrapyramidal.** *Spasticity* refers to extra stiffness in the muscles. This category can be further divided by describing which parts of the body have extra stiffness. For example, *hemiplegia* refers to stiffness on one side of the body, *diplegia* to stiffness predominantly in both legs, and *quadriplegia* to stiffness in both arms and legs. The *extrapyramidal* category (sometimes called *dyskinetic CP*) is associated with a marked variability in tone in which the individual's muscles can go from having low tone to being very stiff. It can also be associated with involuntary movements. Some individuals can have a mixed type, with features of both spasticity and dyskinesia. Different types of CP are associated with different risk factors and possible causes. For example, children who have had a prenatal or antenatal stroke usually have hemiplegia.

In addition to the different types of CP, there is wide variability in the extent of motor abilities and limitations among individuals with the same subtype. Researchers from the CanChild Centre for Childhood Disability Research at McMaster University in Hamilton, Ontario, Canada, created a new classification system, which categorizes CP according to function and divides CP into five ability levels. The classification system is outlined in Table 17.3 (Palisano et al., 1997). Subsequent research has produced natural history "motor development curves" for the five levels of function. These allow evidence-based prognostication about future gross motor potential, based on the level of mobility that is present (Rosenbaum et al., 2002).

IMPACT ON DEVELOPMENT

CP has the potential to affect various aspects of development. These are discussed in the following sections.

Movement

The defining feature of CP is difficulty controlling and planning motor movements in the parts of the body that are affected. Most individuals with hemiplegia, and many with spastic diplegia, are able to walk. Some people with spastic diplegia use canes or walkers to help with walking.

Table 17.2. Types of cerebral palsy

Spastic
Hemiplegia (one side)
Diplegia (predominantly leg involvement)
Quadriplegia (whole body movement)
Extrapyramidal
Choreoathetotic
Dystonic
Ataxic
Mixed

Source: Fehlings & Hunt (2003).

Table 17.3. Gross Motor Function Classification System (describing children's function at age 6–12 years)

Level I	Walks without restrictions; limitations in more advanced gross motor skill
Level II	Walks without assistive devices; limitations walking outdoors and in the community
Level III	Walks with assistive mobility devices; limitations walking outdoors and in the community
Level IV	Self-mobility with limitations; children are transported or use power mobility outdoors and in the community
Level V	Self-mobility is extremely limited even with the use of assistive technology

Source: Rosenbaum et al. (2002).

Individuals who are able to walk for short distances can use a wheelchair for longer distances (e.g., for mobility in the community). A higher percentage of individuals with spastic quadriplegia or dyskinetic CP use a wheelchair for mobility. Note, however, that the type of CP in itself does not allow categorical certainty about the functional abilities of people with CP (Gorter et al., 2004).

Hand Control and Activities of Daily Living

People with CP vary from being completely independent in their activities of daily living (ADLs) to being significantly dependent. Their degree of independence often relates to the motor control they have in their hands. Individuals with hemiplegia can become very good at doing tasks with one hand and can achieve independence. People with spastic diplegia can have some overflow tone into their hands, but many can also achieve independence in their ADLs. They can have more subtle difficulties with hand control, such as slower written output. Compared with the other types of CP, there are higher rates of dependence in ADLs in individuals with spastic quadriplegia or dyskinetic CP.

Learning and Intellectual Disabilities

People with CP can have typical intelligence levels, but they are at significantly greater risk to have slowed learning, or a learning disability. Reported rates of slower intellectual development associated with CP vary from 30% to 60% (Evans, Evans, & Alberman, 1990), depending on where the study was done and how abilities are measured. Individuals with CP can have both an intellectual disability as well as a physical disability, although this certainly is not always the case.

Speech/Language

Many people with CP are able to speak fluently and clearly. Some have difficulty with articulation, which can make speech difficult for a listener to understand. Others may be unable to speak because of motor problems and require alternate strategies, such as picture or symbol displays to communicate. This is more likely to be the case for people with extrapyramidal CP. Some people with CP have language learning disabilities.

ASSOCIATED MEDICAL PROBLEMS

People with CP are at risk for medical complications. The main medical complications include the following:

- Seizures (seen in approximately 20%–30% of people with CP)
- Visual impairment
- Strabismus (turning in or out of the eye, commonly known as "lazy eye")
- Hearing loss
- Dental cavities
- Drooling
- Swallowing difficulties
- Poor growth/nutrition
- Aspiration pneumonia
- Gastroesophageal reflux
- Constipation
- Orthopedic complications

The medical complications associated with CP are not inevitable; they require careful monitoring and active treatment. Seizures occur when there is an episodic excess of electrical activity in the brain (often arising from an area of the brain that has been injured). This can lead to shaking of the arms and legs and a loss of consciousness. However, seizures can have much more subtle signs, such as eye deviation or staring spells. Seizures are usually treated with anticonvulsants that help to prevent or decrease their frequency and severity. Strabismus is usually treated with eye surgery that helps to align both eyes. Hearing loss can often be helped with a hearing aid and occasionally with cochlear implants. If there is persisting fluid in the middle ear secondary to recurrent ear infections, the fluid can be drained with a small tube inserted into the eardrum. Drooling often improves with age and training. If it persists past 5 years of age, a surgical procedure can be done that moves the saliva ducts farther back in the mouth. Medications can also be used to decrease the saliva production.

Feeding difficulties, especially difficulties with swallowing, are commonly seen in people with spastic quadriplegia and extrapyramidal CP. It takes good muscle coordination to swallow food, particularly thin liquids such as juice. When swallowing is poor, food can go into the lungs and create aspiration pneumonia. It can also decrease the total amount of food and caloric intake, which can cause poor nutrition and delayed growth. Thickening liquids and watching the physical position of the individual when he or she is eating can

Photo courtesy of the MukiBaum Treatment Centres (http://www.mukibaum.com).

help (sitting up in a comfortable supported seat is best). Sometimes a feeding tube (a gastrostomy tube placed in the stomach) is required to ensure adequate nutrition over the growing years.

Orthopedic (bone) complications are frequently seen in CP. They can require surgical intervention by an orthopedic surgeon. The extra stiffness in the muscle decreases the muscle growth. This can lead to joint contractures that can affect an individual's gait (walking pattern). The surgeon can do an operation that lengthens the tendon of the muscle to help to increase flexibility. For instance, with a heel cord lengthening, a child can go from always standing on his or her toes to being able to bring the heel down to the floor. A significant complication of the extra stiffness can be subluxation (a partial sliding out) of the hip joint. The surgeon can lengthen the muscles around the hip and do a procedure to reshape the pelvis and try to prevent a complete dislocation of the hip. Scoliosis (curve of the spine) can occur. Children with CP are also at risk for osteopenia (low bone density) if they are nonambulatory. This in turn increases the risk of fractures of "thin" bones.

Life expectancy can be reduced in individuals with CP. However, the majority of individuals will survive long into adulthood. Factors that are associated with a shortened life expectancy include having severe deficits in cognitive function, being immobile, having seizures, and not being able to eat independently (Crichton, Mackinnon, & White, 1995; Eyman et al., 1990). Hutton, Cooke, and Pharoah (1994) published a study on life expectancy in children with CP based on a population registry of 1,258 children with CP born between 1966 and 1984. The 20-year survival rate was 89.3% for the whole cohort, and for children with severe disabilities, the survival rate was 50%.

PSYCHOSOCIAL ISSUES

Many challenges face children with CP, including fitting in with friends and at school. Children with disabilities often feel left out and have difficulty finding role models and mentors. In many places, there are physical barriers, such as lack of ramps and accessible restrooms, that make it impossible for children with disabilities such as CP to participate in activities. Many children with CP have difficulties with speech production and language. Developing communication and social skills is a critical factor for successful inclusion. Children and teenagers can feel isolated and alone. Often their peer group cannot relate well to their experience with disability. Since the 1980s, inclusion in the classroom setting has starting to improve some of these relationships. Parents and educators need to be aware of how bullying and exclusion can affect children with disabilities and then take steps to minimize it.

The transitions from childhood to adolescence and from adolescence to adulthood are difficult for all families, but this stage of development can become particularly challenging when a child has a disability. The first challenge begins with learning to cope independently from one's parents. Other important issues include development of friendships, career planning, emotional and sexual relationships, and marriage. It is known that individuals with disabilities such as CP have more difficulty finding satisfying relationships and making career plans. Only 51% of youth with disabilities have plans for postsecondary education, compared with 74% of same-age peers (Stevens et al., 1996).

INTERVENTION

Intervention (sometimes called rehabilitation) for CP focuses on health, wellness, functioning, and participation (Rosenbaum & Stewart, 2004; World Health Organization, 2001). The aim is to help people with CP achieve their developmental potential. Many professionals can be involved: nurses, occupational therapists, orthopedic surgeons, orthotists who make splints, pediatricians, physiotherapists, psychologists, recreation consultants, social workers, speech therapists, and teachers. Having so many service providers can be confusing. Families have told health researchers that it is very important to coordinate services, to provide long-term continuity of care, and to focus on the whole individual and his or her family (rather than just on problems or medical issues). In the rehabilitation field, this is called family-centered care (Rosenbaum, King, & Cadman, 1992; Rosenbaum et al., 1998).

Many different interventions are available for people with CP. Increasingly, it is recognized that intervention needs to be evidence based (has data showing that it does some good and that this outweighs any possible harmful side effects). This applies to standard therapy as well as alternative therapy. Table 17.4 lists some types of commonly used interventions.

Children with CP have lifelong challenges with movement and motor coordination and often with other aspects of development. Related intervention, or rehabilitation therapies, can offer improvement in some cases but do not offer a cure. When individuals are faced with this situation, they frequently turn to alternative and complementary therapies. Alternative and complementary therapies are defined as a group of diverse medical and health care systems, practices, and products that are not presently considered to be part of conventional medicine. Alternative therapies are not supported by scientific evidence and are generally provided outside conventional intervention programs. Complementary therapies are offered in conjunction with conventional therapies and supported by some scientific evidence. In general, it is helpful to support parents when they are exploring these options and to help families make informed decisions. Some therapies that are commonly used as alternative and

Table 17.4. Types of intervention for cerebral palsy

Developmental area	Example of intervention	Health professionals involved
Gross motor function	Physiotherapy to teach stretching to maintain flexibility, improve muscle strength, and work on functional movements (i.e., walking, sitting, rolling) Special equipment such as walkers to help promote independence in walking Wheelchairs (manual and electric) to help promote mobility Splints/braces (e.g., an ankle-foot orthosis that helps the individual put his or her heel on the floor)	Physiotherapists Orthotists
Fine motor function/ activities of daily living	Stretching, strengthening, activities to promote hand control, and splinting (e.g., a neoprene splint that helps to keep a stiff thumb out of the palm to make grasping objects easier) Assessment for equipment to make activities of daily living easier (e.g., handlebars near toilets and bathtubs, commode chairs, seating trays to create a stable work or play area, lifting systems) Home renovations to promote wheelchair accessibility Computer-assisted writing aids	Occupational therapists Writing aids clinic staff (typically occupational therapists)
Speech and language	Parent education to teach parents of young children how to encourage language development (e.g., by use of the Hanen Program) Speech and language therapy to improve articulation and promote language development Augmentative and alternative communication (AAC) systems used for individuals who are not able to speak effectively (e.g., a communication book with picture symbols that the individual can look at or point to, voice output computer systems)	Speech-language pathologists AAC clinic staff (typically speech-language pathologists and occupational therapists)
Learning/cognitive development	Infant stimulation programs for children younger than 2 years of age Nursery school programs for children ages 2–4 years that include therapy consultation Special education Psychological assessment to evaluate learning strengths and weaknesses and thereby assist with school and vocational planning Vocational programs to provide training and support individuals with disabilities to enter the workplace	Early childhood educators School board members Teachers Psychologists Specialized program staff (typically teachers, occupational therapists, and psychologists)
Psychosocial development/ wellness	Support to family and siblings Participation in recreational and extracurricular activities Promotion of peer interactions	Social workers Recreational therapists

Source: Fehlings & Hunt (2003).

complementary therapies in CP include acupuncture, chiropractics, craniosacral therapy, conductive education, electrical stimulation, patterning, and therapeutic touch. Parents are most likely to consider alternative and complementary therapies when their child has quadriplegia, is young, and is nonambulatory (Hurvitz et al., 2003). There are several concerns regarding these therapies, including safety, cost, and parents' ability to cope with and move forward with their child's diagnosis. One example that illustrates some of these pitfalls is hyperbaric oxygen therapy (HBO).

HBO is used to relieve decompression sickness in deep-sea divers. It involves placing the individual in a pressurized container with 100% oxygen. Since the mid-1990s, HBO has become very popular for treating neurological conditions. There was hope that delivering oxygen under this pressurized mechanism would allow oxygen to get to affected areas of the brain and promote brain development and subsequent improvement in motor function. Many families were seeking this type of therapy and paying large sums of money to receive it. In such situations, the concern was that parents were focusing their financial resources, hope, and energy into something with little scientific evidence of effectiveness. When a scientific study involving a random assignment of patients, placebo group, and "blinding" of the raters was completed, no evidence was found that HBO was better than a placebo (Collet et al., 2001; Rosenbaum, Fehlings, & Iliffe, 2001). This illustrates the need to be careful when helping individuals navigate the alternative and complementary therapy market and make appropriate and meaningful decisions.

INNOVATIVE TREATMENTS

Spasticity management (reducing the stiffness in muscles) has advanced significantly since the 1990s. The intramuscular injection of botulinum toxin into spastic muscles has become an important tool. When injected into a muscle, clostridium botulinum toxin type A (BTA) produces a local, temporary weakness that is associated with a decrease in spasticity (De Paiva et al., 1999; Jankovic & Brin, 1991). It is thought that decreased muscle stiffness allows for better stretching of shortened muscles, increased range of motion, and opportunities to strengthen muscles that work opposite to the muscle that has been injected. These changes should allow the person to learn better control of movement and to improve his or her motor function. Within 2–3 days of the injection, the treated muscles become weak with a reduction in tone, reaching a maximum effect at 2 weeks. The reduction in tone lasts an average of 3 months, with a gradual increase in tone and gains in muscle strength occurring after this time. Effects from BTA can still be noted up to 6 months postinjection. There is increasing evidence for BTA's effectiveness in CP (Fehlings et al., 2000; Ubhi et al., 2000).

Intrathecal baclofen (ITB) is a new method of controlling severe generalized hypertonia. ITB consists of a system whereby a continuous infusion pump is implanted subcutaneously (underneath the skin) in the lower abdomen and is attached to a catheter that is inserted into the fluid surrounding the spinal cord. Baclofen is delivered via continuous infusion into the fluid and binds to receptors in the spinal cord to reduce muscle tone. This leads to a significant and long-standing reduction in hypertonia. Individuals using ITB have noted a positive impact on their quality of life. Reports include less pain from muscle spasms, improved ease of caregiving, better seating tolerance, and improved sleeping comfort (Butler & Campbell, 2000; Gilmartin et al., 2000; Middel et al., 1997; Van Schaeybroeck et al., 2000). Nonetheless, ITB is an expensive and complex management strategy to maintain over many years; thus, its efficacy is still being assessed.

SUMMARY

People with CP have motor difficulties secondary to brain injury or atypical brain development. There are various types of CP, and these are common conditions with mean prevalence rates of 2.0–2.5 for every 1,000 children. Having CP can affect many areas of an individual's development and function. There is a high association with a coexisting intellectual disability (30%–60%) and medical complications. Intervention often requires the teamwork of many different social service and health professionals working together over many years with individuals with CP and their families to maximize developmental potential and promote quality of life. People with CP can lead active lives and make a valuable contribution to society.

FOR FURTHER THOUGHT AND DISCUSSION

1. What are best types of service delivery models for people with CP?
2. Discuss the importance of providing interventions that are evidenced based and family centered. How can such interventions be promoted in service organizations?
3. A new drug used to improve a pregnancy-related health issue in pregnant women is considered by some to have the potential to be associated with the baby developing CP. How would you evaluate this drug as a potential risk factor?
4. What can you do personally to promote universal accessibility for people with disabilities?

REFERENCES

Butler, C., & Campbell, S. (2000). Evidence of the effects of intrathecal baclofen for spastic and dystonic cerebral palsy. *Developmental Medicine and Child Neurology, 42,* 634–645.

Cans, C. (2000). Surveillance of cerebral palsy in Europe: A collaboration of cerebral palsy surveys and registers. *Developmental Medicine and Child Neurology, 42,* 816–824.

Collet, J.P., Vanasse, M., Marois, P., et al. (2001). Hyperbaric oxygen for children with cerebral palsy: A randomised multicentre trial. HBO-CP Research Group. *The Lancet, 357*(9256), 582–586.

Crichton, J., Mackinnon, M., & White, C. (1995). The life expectancy of persons with cerebral palsy. *Developmental Medicine and Child Neurology, 37,* 567–576.

Cummins, S.K., Nelson, K.B., Grether, J.K., et al. (1993). Cerebral palsy in four northern California counties, births 1983 through 1985. *The Journal of Pediatrics, 123,* 230–237.

De Paiva, A., Meunier, F.A., Molgo, J., et al. (1999). Functional repair of motor endplates after botulinum neurotoxin type A poisoning: Biphasic switch of synaptic activity between nerve sprouts and their parent terminals. *Proceedings of the National Academy of Sciences of the United States of America, 96,* 3200–3205.

Evans, P.M., Evans, S.J.W., & Alberman, E. (1990). Cerebral palsy: Why we must plan for survival. *Archives of Disease in Childhood, 65,* 1329–1333.

Eyman, R., Grossman, H.J., Chaney, R.H., et al. (1990). The life expectancy of profoundly handicapped people with mental retardation. *New England Journal of Medicine, 323,* 584–589.

Fehlings, D., & Hunt, C.I. (2003). Cerebral palsy. In I. Brown & M. Percy (Eds.), *Developmental disabilities in Ontario* (pp. 195–204). Toronto: Ontario Association on Developmental Disabilities.

Fehlings, D., Rang, M., Glazier, J., et al. (2000). An evaluation of botulinum A toxin injections to improve upper extremity function in children with hemiplegia cerebral palsy. *The Journal of Pediatrics, 137,* 331–337.

Gilmartin, R., Bruce, D., Storrs, B.B., et al. (2000). Intrathecal baclofen for management of spastic cerebral palsy: Multicenter trial. *Journal of Child Neurology, 15*(2), 71–77.

Gorter, J.W., Rosenbaum, P.L., Hanna, S.E., et al. (2004). Limb distribution, type of motor disorder and functional classification of cerebral palsy: How do they relate? *Developmental Medicine and Child Neurology, 46*(7), 461–467.

Hurvitz, E.A., Leonard, C., Ayyangar, R., et al. (2003). Complementary and alternative medicine use in families of children with cerebral palsy. *Developmental Medicine and Child Neurology, 45,* 364–370.

Hutton, J., Cooke, T., & Pharoah, P. (1994). Life expectancy in children with cerebral palsy. *British Medical Journal, 309,* 431–435.

Jankovic, J., & Brin, M.F. (1991). Therapeutic uses of botulinum toxin. *New England Journal of Medicine, 324,* 1186–1194.

Kuban, K., & Leviton, A. (1994). Cerebral palsy. *New England Journal of Medicine, 330*(3), 188–195.

Middel, B., Kuipers-Upmeijer, H., Bouma, J., et al. (1997). Effect of intrathecal baclofen delivered by an implanted programmable pump on health related quality of life in patients with severe spasticity. *Journal of Neurology, Neurosurgery, and Psychiatry, 63*(2), 204–209.

Murphy, C.C., Yeargin-Allsopp, M., Decouflé, P., et al. (1993). Prevalence of cerebral palsy among ten-year-old children in metropolitan Atlanta, 1985 through 1987. *The Journal of Pediatrics, 123*(5), S13–20.

Nelson, K.B. (1996). Epidemiology and etiology of cerebral palsy. In A.J. Capute & P.J. Accardo (Eds.), *Developmental disabilities in infancy and childhood: Vol. II. The spectrum of developmental disabilities* (pp. 73–79). Baltimore: Paul H. Brookes Publishing Co.

Odding, E., Roebroeck, M., & Stam, H. (2006). The epidemiology of cerebral palsy: Incidence, impairments, and risk factors. *Disability and Rehabilitation, 28*(4), 183–191.

Palisano, R., Rosenbaum, P., Walter, S., et al. (1997). Development and reliability of a system to classify gross motor function in children with cerebral palsy. *Developmental Medicine and Child Neurology, 39*(4), 214–223.

Rosenbaum, P.L. (2003). An overview of cerebral palsy: What do parents and practitioners want to know? *British Medical Journal, 326,* 970–974.

Rosenbaum, P., Fehlings, D., & Iliffe, C. (2001). *Hyperbaric oxygen therapy: Hot or not?* Hamilton, ON, Canada: CanChild Centre for Childhood Disability Research. Retrieved July 5, 2004, from http://www.fhs.mcmaster.ca/canchild/

Rosenbaum P., King, S., & Cadman, D. (1992). Measuring processes of caregiving to physically disabled children and their families. 1: Identifying relevant components of care. *Developmental Medicine and Child Neurology, 34,* 103–114.

Rosenbaum, P., King, S., Law, M., et al. (1998). Family-centred services: A conceptual framework and research review. *Physical and Occupational Therapy in Pediatrics, 18*(1), 1–20.

Rosenbaum, P., & Stewart, D. (2004). The WHO International Classification of Functioning, Disability and Health. A model to guide clinical thinking, practice and research in the field of cerebral palsy. *Seminars in Pediatric Neurology, 11*(1), 5–10.

Rosenbaum, P., Walter, S., Hanna, S., et al. (2002). Prognosis for gross motor function in cerebral palsy, creation of motor development curves. *The Journal of the American Medical Association, 288,* 1357–1363.

Stanley, F.J., Blair, E., & Alberman, E. (2000). *Cerebral palsies: Epidemiology and causal pathways.* London: Mac Keith Press.

Stevens, S.E., Steele, C.A., Jutai, J.W., et al. (1996). Adolescents with physical disabilities: Some psychosocial aspects of health. *Journal of Adolescent Health, 19,* 157–164.

Torfs, C.P., van den Berg, B.J., Oechsli, F.W., et al. (1990). Prenatal and perinatal factors in the etiology of cerebral palsy. *The Journal of Pediatrics, 116,* 615–619.

Ubhi, T., Bhakta, B.B., Ives, H.L., et al. (2000). Randomized double blind placebo controlled trial of the effect of botulinum toxin on walking in cerebral palsy. *Archives of Disease in Childhood, 83,* 481–487.

Van Schaeybroeck, P., Nuttin, B., Lagae, L., et al. (2000). Intrathecal baclofen for intractable cerebral spasticity: A prospective placebo-controlled, double-blind study. *Neurosurgery, 46*(3), 603–609.

World Health Organization. (2001). *International Classification of Functioning, Disability and Health (ICF).* Geneva: Author.

Wu, W., & Colford J. (2000). Chorioamnionitis as a risk factor for cerebral palsy: A meta-analysis. *Journal of the American Medical Association, 284*(11), 1417–1424.

18

Epilepsy

W. McIntyre Burnham

> **WHAT YOU WILL LEARN ABOUT IN THIS CHAPTER**
>
> - The nature of epilepsy
> - Intractable epilepsy
> - Comorbidities of epilepsy

The **epilepsies** are a group of neurological disorders, characterized by spontaneous, recurring **seizures.** Except for headache, epilepsy (as the epilepsies are often called) is the most common condition treated by neurologists. About 4% of the population will have epilepsy at some time during their lives. Approximately 1% of the population in North America has epilepsy at any given time.

Because epilepsy is sometimes called a seizure disorder, it is important to define seizures. Seizures are periods of neural hyperactivity, caused by an imbalance between excitation and inhibition in the central nervous system. During a seizure, the neurons in the brain cease their normal activities and fire in massive, synchronized bursts. After a few seconds or minutes, the inhibitory mechanisms of the brain regain control, and the seizure ends. Seizures are also called attacks, which is an acceptable word at the time of this book's publication. The term *fit* is acceptable in some places, such as the United Kingdom, but not in North America and some other regions. (For a more detailed discussion, see Burnham, 2002, Engel & Pedley, 1997, and Guberman & Bruni, 1999.)

During a seizure, the epileptic activity in the brain can be seen as a series of spikes or spikes and waves in electroencephalographic (EEG) recordings. These spikes or spikes and waves are called the electrographic seizure. The behavior of an individual during the epileptic attack—which may or may not involve convulsions—is called the clinical seizure. If the clinical seizure involves muscle spasms, it is called a convulsion.

The author thanks Paul Hwang, Irene Elliott, and the staffs of Epilepsy Ontario and Epilepsy Toronto for help in preparing this chapter.

THE NATURE OF EPILEPSY

The onset of epilepsy may occur at any time during life. In many individuals, however, seizure onset occurs in childhood, before the age of 15 years. During young adulthood or in middle age, seizure onset is less likely. There is an increased frequency of seizure onsets after the age of 60. These late-onset epilepsies may be the result of small strokes (Guberman & Bruni, 1999).

The frequency of seizures varies enormously. Some individuals experience only a few seizures during their whole lives. Other people experience many seizures every day.

Classes of Epileptic Seizure

There are a number of different types of epileptic seizure, some of which occur primarily in children. A description of all of the seizure types is beyond the scope of this chapter. Some of the more common types are described in Table 18.1.

Epileptic Syndromes

Since the late 1990s, there has been an attempt to fit epileptic seizures into larger entities called epileptic syndromes. An epileptic syndrome consists of a seizure type (or types), a prediction about the time of seizure onset and (possibly) offset, a possible cause, a prognosis, and a likely response to medication.

Well known—and very serious—epileptic syndromes include West syndrome and Lennox-Gastaut syndrome. West syndrome usually has its onset during the first year of life, whereas Lennox-Gastaut syndrome usually begins between ages 1 and 8. Both syndromes involve drug-resistant seizures, an abnormal EEG between seizures, and, in most cases, mild to severe developmental delay (see Guberman & Bruni, 1999).

Causes of Epilepsy

In some individuals with seizures (approximately 40%), there is a clear-cut abnormality in the brain, such as a scar or a tumor, that causes the seizures. These people are said to have "symptomatic" epilepsy. In other indi-

Table 18.1. Common seizure types (old names in parentheses)

Type	Description
Generalized seizures (involve the whole brain)	
Absence seizures (petit mal)	These are nonconvulsive seizures that consist only of a few seconds of unconsciousness, blank staring, and immobility. The eyelids may flutter. Electroencephalographic (EEG) reading shows 3-second spike and wave activity all over the brain. The individual has no memory for the period of the attack.
Tonic-clonic seizures (grand mal)	These are dramatic seizures that involve a loss of consciousness plus whole-body convulsions, which consist first of stiffening (tonus) and then of jerking (clonus). EEG reading shows constant spiking all over the brain. The individual has no memory for the period of the attack.
Partial seizures (involve only part of the brain)	
Simple partial seizures (focal cortical)	These include sensory or emotional experiences or contralateral jerking on one side of the body. Sensory experiences relate to the part of the brain involved and may be auditory, visual, and so forth. The EEG reading shows spiking limited to one part of the brain. The individual is conscious and will remember the period of the attack.
Complex partial seizures (psychomotor)	The individual is conscious but is out of touch with the surrounding world. There may be automatic movements, such as lip smacking and fumbling with the clothes. The EEG reading shows spiking in the temporal lobe. The individual has no memory for the period of the attack.

From Burnham, W.M. (1998). Antiseizure drugs. In H. Kalant & W. Roschlau (Eds.), *Principles of medical pharmacology* (p. 253). Oxford, United Kingdom: Oxford University Press. By permission of Oxford University Press, Inc.

viduals with seizures (approximately 60%), the brain appears to be completely normal. These people are said to have "idiopathic" epilepsy. In those with idiopathic epilepsy, the seizures are thought to be caused by genetic factors.

In some types of idiopathic epilepsy, the genetic factor is strong, and inheritance follows simple Mendelian rules. In most cases of idiopathic epilepsy, however, inheritance is multifactorial—meaning that several genes are involved. In these cases, inheritance does not follow simple Mendelian rules (see Burnham, 2002; Guberman & Bruni, 1999).

Actually, there is probably a genetic contribution to most cases of epilepsy. Some people with a scar or tumor on the brain develop seizures (i.e., develop symptomatic epilepsy), whereas others do not, suggesting a genetic predisposition in those who do.

Relationship to Other Disabilities

A number of common disabilities are caused by brain damage or dysfunction. People with these disabilities often also have seizures as well. Table 18.2 presents a list of common disabilities and indicates the percentage of individuals who also have epilepsy.

Drug Therapy

The most common therapy for epilepsy is the administration of **anticonvulsant drugs.** The anticonvulsant medications are also called antiepileptic drugs, AEDs, or antiseizure drugs. A wide variety of anticonvulsant drugs are available. Among those commonly prescribed are 1) ethosuximide, which is used for absence seizures; 2) phenytoin and carbamazepine, which are used for tonic-clonic and partial seizures; and 3) valproic acid, which is a wide-spectrum anticonvulsant that is effective against many types of seizures. Phenobarbital is an older drug that is still in use, most often in children. A number of new drugs have been introduced since 1990. These include gabapentin, lamotrigine, levetiracetam, tiagabine, topiramate, vigabatrin, and zonisamide. The new drugs are generally thought to have fewer side effects than the older drugs. It is not clear, however, that they are better at stopping seizures, and they are considerably more expensive. Felbamate is another new drug, but it is rarely prescribed due to its rare, but possibly fatal, side effects.

Anticonvulsant medications do not cure epilepsy. They simply suppress seizures on a temporary basis. People with seizures must continue to take their medications, once, twice or three times daily, sometimes for the rest of their lives. (For more discussion, see Bialer et al., 2002; Burnham, 1998; and Guberman & Bruni, 1999.)

Table 18.2. Disabilities often associated with seizures (percent of affected individuals likely to have seizures indicated in parentheses)

Genetic syndromes	Nongenetic syndromes
Tuberous sclerosis (>80%)	Cerebral palsy (frequent, varies with type)
Sturge Weber syndrome (70%–90%)	AIDS (acquired immunodeficiency syndrome) (13%)
Fragile X syndrome (20%–40%)	Multiple sclerosis (5%–10%)
Rett syndrome (70%–80%)	Stroke (5%–10% embolic, 2.5%–25% hemorrhagic)
Down syndrome (2%–15%)	Alzheimer's disease (15%)
Huntington's disease (5%–10%)	

From Guberman, A., & Bruni, J. (1999). *Essentials of clinical epilepsy* (p. 35). Woburn, MA: Butterworth-Heinemann.

INTRACTABLE EPILEPSY

People who have seizures in public experience both social and economic discrimination. The impact that seizures have on life, therefore, really relates to whether they can be controlled with anticonvulsant medications. If the seizures are responsive to medication—as they are in approximately 60% of cases—the individual may never have another seizure. He or she will have to take medication regularly, but epilepsy will not prevent a full, productive life.

If the seizures are only partly responsive to medications—as they are in approximately 20% of cases—the individual will continue to have some attacks. If the attacks occur in public, he or she may experience negative consequences. Moreover, if an individual has even one seizure per year, he or she may never be able to legally drive again (see next paragraph). Partially resistant seizures, therefore, have a clear, negative effect on life. Still, many people with partially resistant seizures also live productive, successful lives.

If seizures are fully drug resistant—as they are in approximately 20% of cases—the individual will continue to experience seizures, which may be frequent, despite use of the best medications available. Drug-resistant seizures are called **intractable seizures** or refractory seizures. Patients with intractable seizures cannot legally drive and often have major problems at home, at school, and at work (see also Burnham, Carlen, & Hwang, 2002; Johannessen et al., 1995). Patients with intractable epilepsy frequently take two or three anticonvulsants at the same time. Even such polypharmacy, however, does not stop the attacks. These people are referred for nonpharmacological interventions, such as surgery, the ketogenic diet, or vagus nerve stimulation.

Nondrug Therapies

If seizures prove intractable to drug therapy, or if drug side effects cannot be tolerated, several sorts of nondrug therapy are available. If the individual experiences partial seizures, and the seizures always arise from the same part of the brain (the "focus"), he or she may be a candidate for **seizure surgery.** In adults, the most common sort of seizure surgery involves removal of the part of the brain that contains the focus, most often the anterior part of one of the temporal lobes. Surgery may stop the seizures or make them more controllable with medication (see Luders, 1992). Side effects of surgery are rare.

Another nondrug therapy is the **ketogenic diet.** This is a high-fat diet, with adequate protein and very little carbohydrate. Many people find the diet unpalatable, and it is hard to maintain because all of the food must be weighed and measured. The ketogenic diet, however, stops seizures in approximately one third of people who have failed drug therapy, and it decreases seizures in another third. Traditionally, the diet has been used only in children. Newer reports, however, suggest that it is effective in adults as well. Unfortunately, due to the unbalanced nature of the diet, individuals can only stay on it for 2–3 years. (For additional discussion, see Wheless, 1995, 2001.)

A third treatment for drug-resistant seizures is **vagus nerve stimulation (VNS).** A device similar to a cardiac pacemaker is implanted into the chest muscle, and a wire is connected to the vagus nerve, the tenth cranial nerve. Intermittent stimulation is used to control seizures. VNS is not as effective as surgery or the ketogenic diet, but it is an alternative to consider when the other therapies fail. VNS is the second most common type of nondrug therapy used in the United States (see McLachlan, 1997).

Unfortunately, many people with intractable seizures are not good candidates for seizure surgery. The ketogenic diet does not offer long-term control, and less than half the people who try vagal stimulation show significant benefits. Many individuals with intractable epilepsy face a life of uncontrolled seizures, despite the best attempts at therapeutic intervention.

Intractable Epilepsy as a Disability

Epilepsy is sometimes called the "invisible disability." Is this a reasonable assessment? If one thinks in terms of people with drug-responsive seizures, the term *disability* is probably too strong. These people usually lead normal lives and reach their full potential for accomplishment.

Intractable epilepsy, however, is clearly a disability. Part of the problem is the seizures themselves. Public, and even private, seizures can lead to stigma, embarrassment, loss of self-confidence, and sometimes loss of friends. Many people with intractable seizures have difficulty going to school or work, and most face considerable barriers to their education and careers. There is also the possibility of physical harm, such as head injury due to the falls. People with uncontrolled seizures have to be careful about performing many activities, such as climbing ladders or standing near the edge of subway platforms. They are warned against swimming alone and advised to take showers rather than baths. They cannot drive. Life becomes limited and circumscribed.

The seizures themselves, however, are only part of the problem. In addition to seizures, many people with epilepsy have related nonphysical disabilities. These are called the comorbidities of epilepsy.

COMORBIDITIES OF EPILEPSY

Comorbidities are less well known than seizures and less understood. Yet, many family members and educators agree that the comorbidities of epilepsy are often more serious than the seizures themselves. Some common comorbidities are listed in Table 18.3.

In some cases, the comorbidities seem to be the result of repeated seizures. In other cases, the comorbidities have their onset before the seizures begin and seem to be the result of the brain abnormalities that later cause seizure activity. In either case, strategies for dealing with the comorbidities must be developed. Unfortunately, they are seldom addressed.

Most of the following sections focus on children, in whom the comorbidities often first occur. Later sections also deal with adult problems, such as reproduction, work, and driving.

Cognitive Impairment

Epilepsy, and particularly intractable epilepsy, is often associated with cognitive impairment. As noted, severe impairments are seen in children with West and Lennox-Gastaut syndromes; however, cognitive impairment may be associated with many forms of intractable seizures. In children, this often becomes evident during the school years. Children with intractable seizures have lower IQ scores, often in the "low-normal" range of 80–85. Studies have also found a significant correlation between low IQ scores and the longer duration of the child's seizure disorder.

Even when their IQ scores are in the normal range, children with uncontrolled seizures tend not to do as well in school as children without epilepsy. A number of factors may contribute to this.

Table 18.3. Comorbidities of epilepsy

Cognitive
Lowered IQ scores
Developmental delay (in West and Lennox-Gastaut syndromes)
Selective cognitive deficits (related to partial seizures)
Global memory problems due to seizures
Global memory problems due to the sedative side effects of anticonvulsant drugs
Psychosocial
Low self-esteem
Psychiatric disturbances (found in at least 30% of cases)
Attention-deficit/hyperactivity disorder (in 20%–30% of children)
Personality changes due to the side effects of anticonvulsant drugs
Reproductive (in adults)
Lowered fertility
Lessened desire and responsiveness

Source: Burnham (2003).

All of these vary from individual to individual. They will be sometimes present and sometimes absent.

1. *Frequent absence attacks:* One cause of learning problems is frequent absence seizures. These mild, nonconvulsive attacks consist only of brief lapses of consciousness. Some children have hundreds per day, however, and clusters of dozens may occur within a few minutes. During these periods, children cannot follow what is going on around them. Children with absence epilepsy, therefore, may give the appearance of being "slow learners" when their intelligence may very well be normal or even higher.
2. *Aftereffects of seizures:* Severe seizures, such as tonic-clonic attacks, cause a major perturbation in the brain. The after effects of such seizures last for hours. Children who have had one or more seizures during the night may show excessive fatigue during the following day and may appear to have forgotten things learned the day before.
3. *Interictal spikes:* Some children, particularly those with complex partial seizures, have isolated epileptic spikes in their EEG between seizures. These are called *interictal spikes.* Interictal spikes produce no outward manifestation, but they slow the children's ability to process and retrieve information, causing transient cognitive impairments.
4. *Site-related deficits:* Children with an epileptic focus in particular parts of the brain may show selective deficits related to that area. Children with a focus in the left hemisphere (dominant for language), for example, often have trouble with finding and remembering words. Children with a focus in the right hemisphere may have problems with visual memory.
5. *General memory defects:* One of the most common complaints in people with epilepsy is a general defect in memory. Children complain that they have to have their lessons repeated over and over before they can remember them. They know that their classmates do not have this problem. The reasons for memory impairment are not completely clear. In some cases, it may relate to the side effects of anticonvulsant drugs. In others, it may relate to changes in the brain. Individuals with long-standing intractable seizures arising in the temporal lobes begin to lose neurons in the hippocampus, a subcortical forebrain structure. This loss of neurons is called *hippocampal sclerosis* or *mesial temporal sclerosis.* The hippocampus is involved in memory formation, and hippocampal sclerosis, when severe, is associated with memory problems.
6. *Side effects of medication:* In addition to the cognitive impairments associated with seizures, there are impairments associated with the sedative (sleep-inducing) side effects of anticonvulsant drugs. These side effects are most serious at the start of therapy.

They improve as tolerance develops, but they do not entirely disappear. They are worst with the older drugs, such as phenobarbital, but they may be seen with almost any of the anticonvulsants. They are more of a problem in children taking multiple drugs. Table 18.4 presents the commonly used anticonvulsants and indicates whether they are likely to significantly impair cognition.

7. *Sleep disorders/daytime drowsiness:* As noted, people with seizures often experience sleep disturbances. These are believed to be caused both by their seizures and by some of the anticonvulsant drugs. This disturbed sleep leads to daytime drowsiness and poor cognitive performance (see Bazil, 2003; Foldvary-Schaefer, 2002).

As children grow, the comorbidities of epilepsy grow with them. The focus of trouble simply shifts from the school to the workplace. Cognitive deficits, once acquired, are likely to remain. The after effects of seizures still occur in adults, as do the sedative side effects of anticonvulsant medications. (For further discussion, see Bortz, 2003; Motamedi & Meador, 2003; Viskontas, McAndrews, & Moscovitch, 2000; and Williams, 2003.)

Psychosocial Impairment

Emotional and psychosocial difficulties are disproportionately high in people with epilepsy, particularly in people with intractable epilepsy. In one large study (Alving, Sahlholdt, & Uldall, 1992), approximately 50% of the children with intractable epilepsy were identified as having serious psychosocial problems. In another study, clear-cut psychiatric disorders were identified in 33% of children with epilepsy, as compared with 7% in the general population and 2% in children with other chronic illnesses. A later study on adults admitted to the hospital for long-term monitoring indicated that more than half had psychiatric problems, many of them having a mixture of psychiatric symptoms that Blumer termed "interictal dysphoric dysorder" (Blumer, 2002).

Some of the most common problems include anxiety, depression, irritability, aggression, and irrational periods of rage. In children at risk for suicide, there is a fifteen-fold overrepresentation of children with epilepsy.

Table 18.4. Anticonvulsant drugs that are more and less likely to have sedative side effects and cause cognitive impairment (brand names in parentheses)

More likely	Less likely
Clonazepam (Rivotril)	Carbamazepine (Tegretol)
Phenobarbital (Luminal)	Clobazam (Frisium)
Phenytoin (high doses) (Dilantin)	Gabapentin (Neurontin)
Primidone (Mysoline)	Lamotrigine (Lamictal)
Topiramate (Topamax)	Valproate (Depakene, Epival)

Source: Guberman and Bruni (1999).
Note: Effects vary from individual to individual.

Emotional disturbances, especially anxiety and depression, are also common in adults with uncontrolled epilepsy. Self-confidence is low. Often there is social isolation and withdrawal. Adults may continue to live with their parents. The suicide rate is five times higher than in the general adult population. People with seizures are also overrepresented in the prison population (Guberman & Bruni, 1999).

In addition to anxiety and depression, about 5%–10% of people with intractable seizures develop a schizophreniform psychosis. Usually, a person with this condition has complex partial seizures with a focus in one of the temporal lobes, and he or she typically has had uncontrolled epilepsy for at least 10 years. Occasionally, the psychosis clears after a seizure and then gradually reappears.

In both children and adults, these psychiatric problems are responsive to therapy—including therapy with antidepressant medications. Unfortunately, these psychiatric problems are seldom diagnosed or treated. Intervention for epilepsy focuses on seizure control, and emotional problems are neglected. (For further discussion, see Blumer, 2002; Boro & Haut, 2003; Bortz, 2003; Gilliam, Hecimovic, & Sheline, 2003; Harden & Goldstein, 2002; Jahnukainen, 1995; Leonard & George, 1999; Sahlholdt, 1995; and Vazquez & Devinsky, 2003.)

Attention-Deficit/Hyperactivity Disorder

In addition to having emotional problems, children with seizures may have problems with hyperactivity. It is estimated that 20%–30% of children with epilepsy have concurrent attention-deficit/hyperactivity disorder (ADHD). A still larger number of children with seizures show deficits in attention or in impulse control without showing the full ADHD syndrome.

The emotional and behavior problems associated with ADHD may be compounded by the effects of the anticonvulsant drugs. ADHD is exacerbated by sedatives, and many of the anticonvulsants have sedative side effects. Children taking anticonvulsants, therefore, may experience a change of personality. They may become impulsive, hyperactive and irritable, and they may engage in both verbal and physical aggression. These problems usually disappear when anticonvulsant drugs are stopped.

Neurologists report that most of the anticonvulsants can produce these behavioral side effects. The worst problems, however, are probably associated with clonazepam (Rivotril). A related drug, clobazam (Frisium), causes fewer problems. In children, phenobarbital also sometimes causes hyperactivity. One of the new drugs, vigabatrin (Sabril), is associated with depression or outright psychosis in a small number of individuals (2%–4%). Vigabatrin is infrequently prescribed because it also tends to cause visual field defects. Such "paradoxical excitability" is less likely to occur in adults, but it may be seen in older adults.

The connection between anticonvulsants and behavior problems is often overlooked. If a person has a change in behavior after the initiation of a new drug, the possibility of behavioral side effects should be considered. Someone with severe behavior problems while taking one drug may not have these problems at all when taking another. (For more discussion, see Sanchez-Carpintero, & Neville, 2003, and Williams, 2003.)

Reproductive Problems

Reproductive and hormonal disorders are common in both men and women with epilepsy and, especially those with intractable epilepsy. This is particularly true if the epilepsy is of temporal-lobe origin. In women, menstrual disorders are seen, such as irregular or missed menstrual cycles or cycles in which there is no ovulation. Fertility is reduced to 70%–80% of typical rates. Hormonal disorders include hypogonadism (too little estrogen) and polycystic ovaries (too much estrogen and testosterone). Anticonvulsant drugs, particularly valproate, may contribute to these disorders. In men with intractable epilepsy, there is an increased risk of erectile dysfunction. More than 90% of men with epilepsy have abnormal semen analyses, including decreased sperm count and impaired sperm motility. In both sexes, diminished sexual desire and responsiveness have been described (Boro & Haut, 2003; Edwards, MacLusky, & Burnham, 2000; Isojarvi, 2003; Morrell, 1991, 1998, 2003).

Effects on the Family Unit

Uncontrolled seizures—and the emotional, cognitive, and behavior problems that accompany them—are difficult not only for a child but also for his or her family. Parents, and particularly mothers, often blame themselves for their child's epilepsy. In some cases, shame is added to guilt as such people as grandparents blame the parents for the child's condition. Many parents go through the stages of denial, anger, and depression that are typical of the grieving process (e.g., when a child dies). Some parents develop psychosomatic reactions, such as sleep disturbances, headaches, and loss of appetite. It appears that the episodic, unpredictable nature of epilepsy makes it harder to live with than other childhood disabilities. Both mothers and fathers live in fear of the next attack. It is common in newly diagnosed cases that one parent will stay up all night for fear that the child will die during sleep.

Eventually, most parents come to terms with their child's epilepsy. Some, however, remain stuck in a state of constant crisis. Many parents of children with chronic epilepsy would benefit from short-term psychotherapy. They seldom seek it or receive it, however. Support groups consisting of other parents living with childhood epilepsy are of considerable help as well. These are usually organized by the regional epilepsy associations. In the absence of therapy or support, divorce is a very real possibility.

Siblings of epileptic children suffer as well. They may develop both emotional complaints (e.g., fear of becoming sick or dying, nightmares) and physical complaints (e.g., headache, vomiting). There may be sibling rivalry, as parents are perceived as favoring the child with seizures. A large study found that approximately 25% of the siblings of children with chronic epilepsy were perceived as "disturbed" by their teachers. Siblings may also require therapy, in addition to children with seizures and their parents. (For discussion, see Ellis, Upton, & Thompson, 2000, and Wada et al., 2001.)

School

Children with intractable epilepsy often have major problems at school. These may be due in part to the cognitive problems associated with seizures. Because the children often have selective learning difficulties, it is important that they undergo psychological or psychoeducational assessments to identify areas of weakness and strength. Once it is established that a child has specific learning difficulties, an education plan can be identified to improve academic performance in that area.

From the school's point of view, however, most difficulties typically relate not to cognitive problems but to behavior problems. Most teachers receive little or no training in epilepsy and often do not understand the connection between uncontrolled seizures and behavior problems. When behavior problems occur, the children are often simply perceived as "bad." Children with epilepsy are frequently sent to the principal, and are often suspended from school. The children themselves sometimes express hatred of their teachers, and their families often end up at war with the school system.

The stigma of epilepsy and the insensitivity of other children—and sometimes teachers—negatively affect the emotional and behavioral status of children with epilepsy. Many children with seizures are excluded from school and recreational activities by teachers and are teased and bullied by their peers.

The school situation would be much improved if both the schools and the parents understood the comorbidities associated with intractable epilepsy. What is needed is a partnership among a child's health care providers, parents, and school. It is important that 1) parents and health care providers tell the school about the child's seizures and how they are to be managed; 2) the comorbidities of intractable epilepsy are explained and addressed; 3) an education plan to improve academic success is developed and implemented; 4) supports, such as an educational assistant, are put in place; 5) the importance of the child's participation in recreational and class activities is accepted, and 6) social interactions with peers are encouraged. (For discussion, see Hightower, Carmon, & Minick, 2002, and Tidman, Saravanan, & Gibbs, 2003.)

Work and Driving

Perhaps the biggest problems for adults center around work. The majority of adults with uncontrolled seizures are unemployed or underemployed—that is, employed in jobs well below their level of competence.

Part of the problem is driving. In most countries, driver's licenses are revoked after the first seizure. They can be reinstated if the driver is seizure free for a period of time, often a year. People with intractable epilepsy, however, are seldom seizure free for a period as long as a year. Most of them will never legally drive again; therefore, they cannot take any job that requires driving or that can only be reached by car.

A second part of the problem is public seizures. People are often fired if they experience seizures at work. Even when the laws in many countries forbid firing for conditions such as epilepsy, employers terminate employees with public seizures by using some other pretext.

A final problem is disclosure. People with seizures fear that they will not be hired if they disclose their problem to potential employers. They also fear that they will be fired later if they do not.

There are no simple solutions to these problems. Being able to work—and earn a stable income—are major concerns for adults with intractable epilepsy. (For a discussion, see Bishop & Allen, 2001, & Wada et al., 2001.)

SUMMARY

Epilepsy occurs frequently in children and adults with intellectual and developmental disabilities. Many seizures can be controlled, and there may or may not be problems associated with learning and memory, behavior, emotional health, social interaction, and life activities. Some of these problems are related to anticonvulsant drugs. Children with uncontrolled epilepsy especially experience such problems, and people who work with these children must learn patience and try to develop effective compensatory strategies. Adults with uncontrollable seizures also have cognitive and psychosocial problems. They cannot legally drive, and they may develop reproductive disorders. They face discrimination in the workplace and are frequently unemployed or underemployed. Work and a stable income are major concerns. Such adults need understanding and support. Intractable epilepsy is a true—if invisible—disability.

FOR FURTHER THOUGHT AND DISCUSSION

1. Much of the stigma associated with epilepsy arises from the fact that seizures are frightening to watch. Should the public be shown what seizures look like? Should they become accustomed to seizures? Should they be taught first aid for seizures?
2. People with seizures who continue to drive have more accidents than people in the general population. They do not have more accidents than people with diabetes or heart disease, however, and people with diabetes and heart disease are allowed to drive. None of these disease groups has as many accidents as young adult males without any disability or health condition. Should people with seizures be allowed to drive?
3. What are the economic and social costs of intractable epilepsy, a disorder that often starts in childhood, often lasts through life, and is found in 1 in every 250 people?
4. Many teachers receive little or no training related to the disabilities they will meet in the classroom. Should education in disabilities be a part of teacher training? If so, what should teachers know?

REFERENCES

Alving, J., Sahlholdt, L. & Uldall, P. (1992). Evaluation of the Danish Epilepsy Center: Children (Abstract). *Seizure, 1*(Suppl. A), P9/01.

Bazil, C.W. (2003). Epilepsy and sleep disturbance. *Epilepsy & Behavior, 4,* 39–45.

Bialer, M., Johannessen, S.I., Kupferberg, H.J., et al. (2002). Progress report on new antiepileptic drugs: A summary of the Sixth Eilat Conference (EILAT VI). *Epilepsy Research, 51,* 31–71.

Bishop, M.L., & Allen, C. (2001). Employment concerns of people with epilepsy and the question of disclosure: Report of a survey of the Epilepsy Foundation. *Epilepsy & Behavior, 2,* 490–495.

Blumer, D. (2002). Psychiatric aspects of intractable epilepsy. In W.M. Burnham, P.L. Carlen & P.A. Hwang (Eds.),

Intractable seizures (pp. 133–147). New York: Kluwer Academic/Plenum Publishers.

Boro, A., & Haut, S. (2003). Medical comorbidities in the treatment of epilepsy. *Epilepsy & Behavior, 4,* 2–12.

Bortz, J. (2003). Neuropsychiatric and memory issues in epilepsy. *Mayo Clinic Proceedings, 78,* 781–787.

Burnham, W.M. (1998). Antiseizure drugs. In H. Kalant & W. Roschlau (Eds.), *Principles of medical pharmacology.* Oxford, United Kingdom: Oxford University Press.

Burnham, W.M. (2002). Epilepsy. In L. Nadel (Ed.), *Encyclopedia of cognitive neuroscience.* London: Nature Publishing Group.

Burnham, W.M. (2003). Intractable epilepsy. In I. Brown & M. Percy (Eds.), *Developmental disabilities in Ontario* (pp. 351–364). Toronto: Ontario Association on Developmental Disabilities.

Burnham, W.M., Carlen, P.L., & Hwang, P.A. (Eds.). (2002). *Intractable seizures: Diagnosis, treatment and prevention.* New York: Kluwer Academic/Plenum Publishers.

Edwards, H.E., MacLusky, N.J., & Burnham, W.M. (2000). The effect of seizures and kindling on reproductive hormones in the rat. *Neuroscience & Biobehavioral Reviews, 24* (7), 753–762.

Ellis, N., Upton, D., & Thompson, P. (2000). Epilepsy and the family: A review of current literature. *Seizure, 9,* 22–30.

Engel, J., & Pedley, T.A. (Eds.). (1997). *Epilepsy: A comprehensive textbook.* Philadelphia: Lippincott, Williams & Wilkins.

Foldvary-Schaefer, N. (2002). Sleep complaints and epilepsy: The role of seizures, antiepileptic drugs and sleep disorders. *Journal of Clinical Neurophysiology, 19*(6), 514–521.

Gilliam, F., Hecimovic, H., & Sheline, Y. (2003). Psychiatric comorbidity, health, and function in epilepsy. *Epilepsy & Behavior, 4,* 26–30.

Guberman, A., & Bruni, J. (1999). *Essentials of clinical epilepsy.* Woburn, MA: Butterworth-Heinemann.

Harden, C.L., & Goldstein, M.A. (2002). Mood disorders in patients with epilepsy. *CNS Drugs, 16*(5), 291–302.

Hightower, S., Carmon, M., & Minick, P. (2002). A qualitative descriptive study of the lived experiences of school-aged children with epilepsy. *Journal of Pediatric Health Care, 16,* 131–137.

Isojarvi, J.I.T. (2003). Reproductive dysfunction in women with epilepsy. *Neurology, 61*(2), 27–34.

Jahnukainen, H. (1995). Psychosocial consequences of intractable epilepsy in adults. In S. Jhannessen, L. Gram, M. Sillanpaa, et al. (Eds.), *Intractable epilepsy* (pp. 165–169). Bristol, PA: Wrightson Biomedical Publishing Ltd.

Johannessen, S., Gram, L., Sillanpaa, M., et al. (Eds.). (1995). *Intractable epilepsy.* Bristol, PA: Wrightson Biomedical Publishing Ltd.

Leonard, E.L., & George, M.R.M. (1999). Psychosocial and neuropsychological function in children with epilepsy. *Pediatric Rehabilitation, 3*(3), 73–80.

Luders, H.O. (Ed.). (1992). *Epilepsy surgery.* New York: Raven Press.

McLachlan, R. (1997). Vagus nerve stimulation for intractable epilepsy: A review. *Journal of Clinical Neurophysiology, 14,* 358–368.

Morrell, M.J. (1991). Sexual dysfunction in epilepsy. *Epilepsia, 32*(6), 38–45.

Morrell, M.J. (1998). Effects of epilepsy on women's reproductive health. *Epilepsia, 39*(8), 32–37.

Morrell, M.J. (2003). Reproductive and metabolic disorders in women with epilepsy. *Epilepsia, 44*(4), 11–20.

Motamedi, G., & Meador, K. (2003). Epilepsy and cognition. *Epilepsy & Behavior, 4,* 25–38.

Salholdt, L. (1995). Psychosocial consequences of intractable epilepsy in children. In S. Johannessen, L. Gram, M. Sillanpaa, et al. (Eds.), *Intractable epilepsy* (pp. 153–163). Bristol, PA: Wrightson Biomedical Publishing Ltd.

Sanchez-Carpintero, R., & Neville, B.G.R. (2003). Attentional ability in children with epilepsy. *Epilepsia, 44*(10), 1340–1349.

Tidman, L., Saravanan, K., & Gibbs, J. (2003). Epilepsy in mainstream and special educational primary school settings. *Seizure, 12,* 47–51.

Vazquez, B., & Devinsky, O. (2003). Epilepsy and anxiety. *Epilepsy & Behavior, 4,* 20–25.

Viskontas, I., McAndrews, M.P., & Moscovitch, M. (2000). Remote episodic memory deficits in patients with unilateral temporal lobe epilepsy and excisions. *Journal of Neuroscience, 20*(15), 5853–5857.

Wada, K., Kawata, Y., Murakami, T., et al. (2001). Sociomedical aspects of epileptic patients: Their employment and marital status. *Psychiatry and Clinical Neurosciences, 55,* 141–146.

Wheless, J.W. (1995). The ketogenic diet: Fa(c)t or fiction. *Journal of Child Neurology, 10*(6), 419–423.

Wheless, J.W. (2001). The ketogenic diet: An effective medical therapy with side effects. *Journal of Child Neurology, 16*(9), 633–635.

Williams, J. (2003). Learning and behavior in children with epilepsy. *Epilepsy & Behavior, 4,* 107–111.

19

Attention-Deficit/Hyperactivity Disorder

Tom Humphries

WHAT YOU WILL LEARN ABOUT IN THIS CHAPTER

- The nature of attention-deficit/hyperactivity disorder
- A brief history of the field of attention-deficit/hyperactivity disorder
- Attention-deficit/hyperactivity disorder in individuals with intellectual disabilities
- Approaches to diagnosis, assessment, and intervention

People with attention-deficit/hyperactivity disorder (ADHD) have traditionally been regarded as possessing the abilities to learn but often not using them successfully due to inattention, hyperactivity, and/or impulsivity. ADHD, then, results in an interference with the availability for learning (Silver, 1990). This behavioral view of ADHD focuses mainly on the disruptive effect that the symptoms of the disorder can have on engaging in learning. Consideration of underlying neurocognitive weaknesses (e.g., in working memory) can also contribute to the understanding of the disorder and have important implications for the development of programming strategies (Martinussen et al., 2005; McInnes et al., 2003; see also Chapter 21).

THE NATURE OF ATTENTION-DEFICIT/HYPERACTIVITY DISORDER

The following section discusses ADHD in terms of prevalence, identifying features at various ages, causes, and relationship to learning disabilities.

Prevalence

A conservative estimate of prevalence is that 3%–7% of school-age children have ADHD (American Psychiatric Association, 2000). This estimate may rise as high as 6%–8% to account for children who are primarily inattentive and, as a result, remain undiagnosed because their behavior is less disruptive (Shea & Baren, 1996).

Estimates of the ratio of boys to girls with ADHD range from 9 to 1 in clinical samples to 4 to 1 in epidemiological samples (Cantwell, 1996). However, there may be a referral bias—girls with ADHD tend to exhibit problems with inattention and cognition, which are less likely to result in a referral, whereas boys often present impulsive and aggressive behaviors, which are more likely to result in a referral (Cantwell, 1996; Wolraich et al., 1996).

Identifying Features at Various Ages

Symptoms of the disorder are manifested in different ways depending on the age of the individual. Contrary to earlier beliefs, ADHD does not begin to wane in adolescence and adulthood.

Preschool Years During the preschool years, the greatest challenge can be distinguishing between ADHD and the natural exuberance of a young child. Among preschoolers who receive a clinical diagnosis of ADHD, approximately 48% continue to demonstrate such difficulties in later childhood and adolescence (Barkley, 1998b). In addition to the presence of the primary symptoms of the disorder, especially hyperactivity-impulsivity (Barkley, 1996), a diagnosis of ADHD at the preschool level may result from perceived noncompliance (e.g., temper tantrums, argumentative and aggressive behaviors) and sleep disturbance (Campbell, 1990).

Elementary School Years At school age, both hyperactivity-impulsivity and greater inattention are characterized as primary symptoms (Barkley, 1996; Loeber et al., 1992). Key marker signs during these years include problems socializing with peers, low productivity, and difficulty starting and completing academic work independently. These and other problems may lead to oppositional disorder in approximately one half or more of children with ADHD (Barkley et al., 1990; Loeber et al., 1992; Taylor et al., 1991). Mother–child discord and family problems are most prevalent when ADHD co-occurs with oppositional difficulties (Barkley et al., 1992; Barkley et al., 1990). Display 19.1 provides an illustration of ADHD in the elementary childhood years.

Display 19.1

Kevin's story

Kevin was having difficulty adjusting to the routine of his first year of school. Kevin's mother told his teacher that Kevin had been active as a preschooler but that the family had always regarded his behavior as fairly typical for a young boy. By the end of the school year, Kevin was even more restless and impulsive, especially when there was an increased need for him to fit into classroom routines. Kevin's behavior was not only making it difficult for him to follow instructions but also disrupting the rest of the class. It seemed clear that Kevin was having more than a temporary problem adjusting to school. Kevin was diagnosed as having attention-deficit/hyperactivity disosrder (predominantly hyperactive-impulsive subtype). By the next school year, Kevin was responding well to the methylphenidate that was prescribed by his pediatrician. He could sit still in the classroom for longer periods without fidgeting and interfering with his classmates.

Adolescence Adolescents may exhibit fewer of the core symptoms and overt hyperactivity may give way to more subtle, fidgety behavior, and feelings of restlessness (Barkley, 1990; Cantwell, 1996). However, 50%–80% of children with ADHD may continue to exhibit the core symptoms of the disorder into adolescence (Barkley et al., 1990). An estimated 24% of children with ADHD drop out of school by the 11th grade due to poor grades and academic failure (Mannuzza et al., 1993). More frequent motor vehicle accidents may also characterize the adolescent ADHD profile, especially when ADHD is accompanied by oppositional or conduct problems (Weiss & Hechtman, 1994).

Adulthood It has been estimated that as many as 30%–50% of individuals with an earlier diagnosis of the disorder may still exhibit ADHD in adulthood (Barkley, 1996). Problems experienced by adults with ADHD can include difficulty in adhering to tasks and activities, completing projects, and keeping a job, as well as possible lability of mood (Wender, 1994).

Causes

Although ADHD is identified and diagnosed almost solely on the basis of its behavioral presentation, there has been some interesting work that addresses possible causes of ADHD.

Impaired Response Inhibition One theoretical explanation of the cause of the disorder is neurocognitive. Barkley (1998a) suggested that impaired response inhibition is the central deficit in ADHD. Failure to inhibit a response is regarded as a major impediment to performing a task. Without response inhibition, there is impairment of the executive functions by which one plans, organizes, shifts strategies, engages in reflection and verbal mediation, and controls emotions in interacting and performing tasks. A deficit in executive function manifests itself as the hyperactive and impulsive symptoms of ADHD or the combination of inattention and hyperactivity/impulsivity. Barkley's (1998a) theory does not attempt to account for symptoms of inattention alone. Although compelling, Barkley's theory requires further empirical support. Evidence indicates that poor response inhibition using a stop signal paradigm (Logan, 1994) also occurs in children with reading disability (Purvis & Tannock, 2000) and specific language impairment (Oram, Johnson, & Tannock, 2001) and therefore is not unique to ADHD.

Poor Self-Regulatory Control Douglas (1999) proposed that poor self-regulatory control is at the core of ADHD. The view is that due to regulatory problems, individuals with ADHD have difficulty both with activating and with inhibiting responses when needed.

Different Brain Functioning Brain imaging studies implicate the prefrontal cortex, the vermis region of the cerebellum, and clusters of nerve cells in the caudate nucleus as areas of the brain that function differently in individuals with ADHD (Barkley, 1996; 1998a). Figure 19.1 is a diagram showing regions of the human brain thought to be affected in ADHD.

Genetics The possibility that changes in genes associated with these brain regions may contribute to their inadequate functioning has stimulated a whole body of research that investigates the genetic basis of ADHD. Family, twin, and adoption studies have provided strong evidence for a genetic etiology of the disorder. Studies suggest that at least six different genes might play a causal role in ADHD (Shastry, 2004). Barr and colleagues have found evidence of an association between symptoms of ADHD and variations in the dopamine genes (D4 receptor gene, dopamine transporter gene) that are responsible for controlling the transmission of neural impulses by the biochemical dopamine (Barr et al., 2000).

Relationship to Learning Disabilities

The term *learning disability (LD)* is used in most parts of the world outside the United Kingdom (see Chapter 1) to mean that a person of average or higher intelligence has impaired ability to learn in only certain academic areas (e.g., reading, mathematics, writing) due to specific deficits in underlying neurocognitive functioning (e.g., perception, memory, language). Some individuals

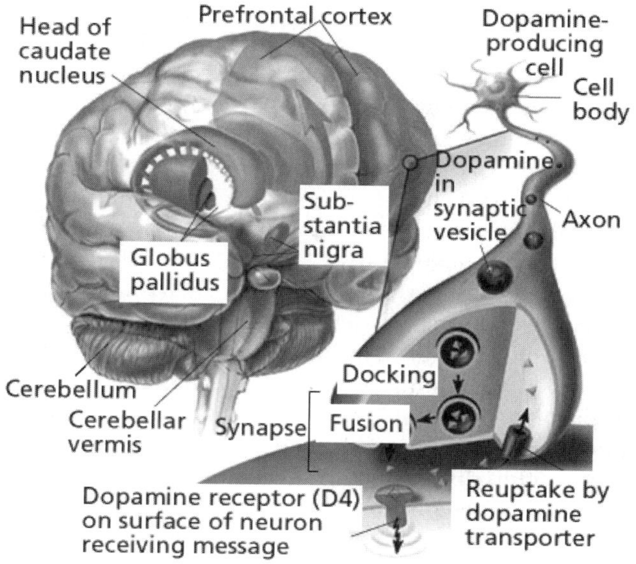

Figure 19.1. A diagram of the human brain showing regions thought to be affected in attention-deficit/hyperactivity disorder (ADHD). Brain structures affected in ADHD use dopamine to communicate with one another (see large arrows, top center). Genetic studies suggest that people with ADHD might have alterations in genes encoding either the D4 dopamine receptor, which receives incoming signals, or the dopamine transporter, which scavenges released dopamine for reuse. The substantia nigra, where the death of dopamine-producing neurons causes Parkinson's disease, is not affected in ADHD. (From Barkley, R.A., [1998a]. Attention-deficit hyperactivity disorder. *Scientific American, 279* [3], 69; reprinted by permission. Copyright © 1998 Terese Winslow.)

have both ADHD and LD, showing specific difficulties in learning as well as problems in controlling their attention and responding that warrant a diagnosis of both disorders. Four hypotheses have been proposed to explain this comorbidity from research on the relationship between ADHD and specific reading disability, a type of LD:

1. ADHD and reading disability represent two primary, pure disorders in the same individual (Douglas & Benezra, 1990; Narhi & Ahonen, 1995).
2. Both disorders are present, but one causes the other.
3. One of the disorders is primary and, although the symptoms of the other disorder are present, the symptoms do not actually represent that disorder (i.e., the other disorder is secondary or a phenocopy); for example, symptoms of ADHD may be secondary to reading disability (Pennington, Groisser, & Welsh, 1993).
4. Because individuals with ADHD and reading disability have sometimes been found to exhibit unique cognitive problems that are not characteristic of either group; a third factor causes both disorders (Korkman & Pesonen, 1994).

Approximately 26% of children with ADHD also have LD (Barkley, 1990). Regarding more specific learning disabilities, Oram et al. (1999) found that approximately 20% of children with ADHD had receptive language impairments, 33% had expressive impairments, 30% had word retrieval problems, and 25% had weak phonological awareness. Among children with LD, estimates of those who also have ADHD range from 17%–40%. Estimated rates of comorbidity of ADHD with more specific types of LD are as follows:

- Reading disability: 15%–30%
- Mathematics disability: 10%–60%
- Language disorders: 8%–90% (for reviews, see Brown, 2000; Tannock & Brown, 2000)

ADHD has also been found to be comorbid with mental health and behavior disorders (see also Chapter 20) such as the following:

- Oppositional defiant disorder: 54%–67% of children and adolescents with ADHD (Barkley & Biederman, 1997)
- Conduct disorder: 20%–56% of children with ADHD, 44%–50% of adolescents with ADHD (Barkley, 1998b)
- Anxiety disorder: approximately 25% of children and adolescents with ADHD (Tannock, 1998)

A BRIEF HISTORY OF THE FIELD OF ATTENTION-DEFICIT/HYPERACTIVITY DISORDER

Attention-deficit/hyperactivity disorder (ADHD) is the diagnostic label currently in use to refer to an identified disorder associated with problems in attention, impulsivity and/or motoric restlessness. Prior to 1987, when ADHD was first presented in the *Diagnostic and Statistical Manual of Mental Disorders, Third Edition, Revised* (*DSM-III-R*; APA, 1987), many other labels were used to describe some or many of the symptoms of the disorder. In the early 1900s, Still (1902), an English physician, was one of the first individuals to describe behavior difficulties in children that are very similar to the features associated with ADHD. Among other symptoms, Still described some of the children in his clinical practice as being aggressive, lacking in inhibitory control, and resisting discipline. These symptoms could appear in children with both lower and close-to-average intelligence. The children were described as showing behavior that was atypical compared with other children their age. Still also considered that the problems of these children were not due to a poor upbringing but, rather, to a mild form of prenatal, perinatal, or postnatal brain insult or to heredity. Further support for Still's description of the symptoms, and for brain insult as their cause, came from observations of similar behaviors in children who were known to have experienced brain injury from the encephalitis epidemic of 1917.

In the 1930s and 1940s, other types of brain insult were investigated as an explanation of behavior problems in children. At this time, the first reports began to appear about the effectiveness of stimulant medication in reducing behavior difficulties and hyperactivity. Also during this period, children who would be diagnosed as having ADHD in 2006 were assumed to have had a brain injury if they exhibited the same behavioral symptoms as individuals with known brain damage (Barkley, 1996). In the 1940s, investigators such as Werner and Strauss (1940, 1941) described symptoms within the same child that are now associated with both ADHD and LD, including perceptual and conceptual difficulties, hyperactivity, and distractibility. Eventually, labels such as "minimal brain damage" and "minimal brain dysfunction" (Clements, 1966), under which all these characteristics were grouped, were regarded as too all-encompassing and were ultimately abandoned. It was the abandonment of these overinclusive labels that ushered in more specific terms to describe ADHD and LD, a trend that has continued into the early 21st century in descriptions of different subtypes of each disorder and possible core types of information-processing deficits to account for them. Early labels that were more specific to ADHD, such as "hyperactive" or "hyperkinetic child syndrome" (Laufer & Denhoff, 1957), gradually gave way to terms that are more recognizable today. Table 19.1 lists some more recent advances regarding the disorder.

ATTENTION-DEFICIT/HYPERACTIVITY DISORDER IN INDIVIDUALS WITH INTELLECTUAL DISABILITIES

Compared with the extensive research conducted on ADHD among people with typical cognitive functioning, relatively few studies have investigated the characteristics of ADHD that are associated with intellectual disabilities. This is surprising in light of longstanding recognition of the fact that children with developmental delay are four to six times more likely to have behavior or emotional disorders than typically developing children (Rutter et al., 1976). Indeed, the prevalence of ADHD among children and adolescents with developmental delay is between 10% and 21% (Benson & Aman, 1999), with 10% representing a conservative estimate (Hunt & Cohen, 1988). This is considerably higher than the 3%–7% usually reported for ADHD in the general school-age population. The number of children and adolescents with developmental delay who are described as having ADHD climbs even higher in clinically referred samples. An important caution with regard to these figures, however, is that some studies refer to an actual diagnosis of ADHD, whereas others only report prevalence for particular symptoms of ADHD without a diagnosis.

Table 19.1. Some promising advances in the field of attention-deficit/hyperactivity disorder (ADHD)

Study of the genetic and neurocognitive basis of the disorder
The use of multimodal assessment and treatment
Better understanding of the specific subtypes of the disorder
Recognition that ADHD may be comorbid with other disorders that also have to be addressed in a management plan

Any attempt to describe the characteristics of ADHD in children with developmental delay, or in adults with intellectual disabilities, is limited by difficulty in identifying inattention, impulsivity, and hyperactivity as problems associated with ADHD as a disorder separate from the cause of the intellectual disability. That is, it is often difficult to know whether a specific behavior should be considered to be "typical" of the cause of the disability or whether it should be considered to be a symptom of ADHD unrelated to the cause of the disability.

Johnson, Lubetsky, and Sacco (1995) found that among symptoms of ADHD, noncompliance and aggression were more prevalent in higher-, rather than lower-functioning preschoolers with developmental delay. Autism and pervasive developmental disorder-not otherwise specified were more evident in preschoolers with moderate, severe, or profound delays. In a broader age range (3.2–19.4 years) of participants with developmental delay that included school-age children, Hardan and Sahl (1997) also reported that ADHD and oppositional defiant disorder were the most common psychiatric diagnoses. Impulsivity was the most frequent symptom. Compared with the usually reported estimate of a 4–9:1 greater prevalence of ADHD in boys than girls, the male/female ratio among children with developmental delay seems to be lower, at 1.25–2:1 (Pearson, Yaffee, et al., 1996; Tizard, 1968a, 1968b).

Among the few studies that have investigated specific aspects of attentional functioning, Pearson, Santos, et al. (1996) found that children with developmental delay and ADHD showed no evidence of an actual deficit in sustained attention compared with children who also had delays but no symptoms of ADHD. However, the children with delay and ADHD had weaker visual selective attention, especially when sorting stimuli in an accelerated classification task that required greater processing effort in order to ignore highly salient distractors. This study also suggested that ADHD might be more of a problem for girls with developmental delay than typically developing girls.

One explanation that has been offered to account for the apparently better performance of children with developmental delay and ADHD in sustaining their attention is cognitive inertia. Rather than demonstrating the ability to sustain attention per se, it has been proposed that these children may instead be exhibiting more of a failure to lose interest, or persistence in an automatic response when it is no longer appropriate. Evidence for this proposal has come from studies that have shown that compared with children without developmental delay, those with delay do not appear to be as efficient in exploring stimuli or as flexible in their response style (Krakow & Kopp, 1982, 1983; Loveland, 1987), and they fail to habituate to repetitive auditory stimuli when children without developmental delay do so quickly (Schafer & Peeke, 1982). Thus, due to cognitive inertia, children with both developmental delay and ADHD may not appear to have a problem with sustained attention.

APPROACHES TO DIAGNOSIS, ASSESSMENT, AND INTERVENTION

The diagnosis, assessment, and treatment of ADHD have each evolved over time.

Diagnosis

Over the years, the American Psychiatric Association (APA) has published different diagnostic criteria and labels for ADHD in its *Diagnostic and Statistical Manual of Mental Disorders (DSM)*. The various versions of the disorder that have been published in the *DSM* reflect changing views on the importance of inattention, impulsivity, and hyperactivity in diagnosis. The most recent revision, the *Diagnostic and Statistical Manual of Mental Disorders, Fourth Edition, Text Revision* (*DSM-IV-TR;* APA, 2000), provides the newest diagnostic and classification criteria.

The *DSM-IV-TR* sets out symptom descriptions and criteria for a predominately inattentive type of the disorder that has also been referred to as attention-deficit disorder (ADD) (e.g., poor listening, lack of focused and sustained attention, incomplete work), a predominately hyperactive-impulsive type (e.g., fidgety, disruptive of others), and a combined type that includes symptoms of both these types. In addition to being both excessive for developmental age and not due to other psychiatric disorders, the symptoms must show some persistence and be pervasive, or they must occur across different settings. A complete description of ADHD symptoms, subtypes, and diagnostic criteria can be found in the *DSM-IV-TR* (APA, 2000).

In clinical settings with children who have been diagnosed with ADHD, the combined type (inattentive and hyperactive-impulsive symptoms) occurs most commonly, in 45%–62% of children (Eiraldi, Power, & Nezu, 1997; Faraone et al., 1998; Paternite, Loney, & Roberts, 1995). In community samples, the inattentive type is the most prevalent; it occurs in approximately 4.5%–9.0% of the general population of children, with the hyperactive-impulsive type at 1.7%–3.9% and the combined type at 1.9%–4.8% (Baumgaertel, Wolraich, & Dietrich, 1995; Gaub & Carlson, 1997; Wolraich et al., 1996).

Several studies have indicated that the symptoms of inattention tend to persist longer into adolescence and adulthood than do symptoms of hyperactivity-impulsivity (Achenbach et al., 1995; Hart et al., 1995; Levy et al., 1997). In addition to discovering this evidence, which suggests the two main subtypes of ADHD differ developmentally, Barkley, Murphy, and Kwasnik (1996), Barkley (1997), and Quay (1997) also suggested that the inattentive, hyperactive-impulsive, and combined types may have different etiologies. There is much debate about whether the inattentive subtype should even be included under the diagnosis of ADHD or whether it instead represents a different type of unique disorder (Milich, Balentine, & Lynam, 2001). There is a suggestion that the symptoms of inattention in the inattentive subtype may be most clearly distinguished by a "sluggish cognitive tempo" consisting of lethargy, drowsiness, and behavioral passivity that is a qualitatively different kind of inattention from that seen in the ADHD combined subtype (e.g., distractability, poor persistence). The inattentive subtype is also associated with poorer academic achievement than the combined ADHD subtype, particularly in mathematics. This finding has led to speculation that the inattentive subtype may be characterized by different cognitive processing deficits than the combined subtype and that the problems of the inattentive subtype may be more typical of LD. Despite these interesting research results, there is currently not enough evidence to warrant identifying the inattentive subtype as a distinct disorder and the debate continues. Display 19.2 is an example of a case that demonstrates the inattentive subtype.

A diagnosis of ADHD is made on the basis of *DSM-IV-TR* (APA, 2000) criteria and on behavioral symptoms that are judged as excessive in relation to developmental or mental age, regardless of intelligence level. Several studies have found that children with ADHD score an average of 7–15 IQ points lower than children without ADHD (Faraone et al., 1993; Fischer et al., 1990; McGee et al., 1989), although the results of another study indicated that the IQ scores of the majority of children with ADHD were average or higher, based on a short-form estimate (Kaplan et al., 2000). It is when intelligence is very low that it can be difficult to distinguish ADHD from the inattention, hyperactivity, and impulsivity that may reflect overall lower cognitive ability. Barkley (1990, 1998b) suggested that adding a diagnosis of ADHD to developmental delay when the degree of delay falls in the severe or profound range may not be helpful because it contributes little to clin-

Display 19.2

Jessica's story

Jessica cooperated well with others in her third-grade classroom, and her behavior posed no problem for her teacher. In fact, if anything, Jessica was somewhat quiet. However, she had trouble following instructions, worked slowly, and was not very successful in completing her school work. Mathematics was particularly difficult for her. Jessica's confusion and academic underachievement were severe enough to warrant a referral to her pediatrician and to the school psychologist for consideration of a learning disability and attention-deficit/hyperactivity disorder (ADHD). Jessica was diagnosed as having both, and her ADHD was the predominantly inattentive subtype. It was important to explain to Jessica and her parents that even though ADHD is often associated with excessive motor activity, people who are less restless but more inattentive and distractible can also have the disorder. Jessica has responded well to behavior modification techniques that have helped her to complete more of her work. She is also is being taught specific strategies to assist her in following instructions and improve her mathematics assignments.

ical decision making. At the other extreme, for the individual of higher intelligence, it is important to be able to separate ADHD from secondary symptoms of inattention, impulsivity, and hyperactivity that may be due to boredom associated with understimulation (Shea & Baren, 1996).

Notwithstanding the possibility of a core deficit in response inhibition or self-regulation, there is no single, definitive cognitive or medical test that can be used clinically to make a diagnosis of ADHD. Furthermore, a positive response to stimulant medication is not diagnostic of ADHD, because the attention of typical children without any symptoms of the disorder can also improve on medication (Shea & Baren, 1996).

The criterion that ADHD symptoms be persistent means that inattention, impulsivity, and hyperactivity that are a reaction to temporary stress or crisis do not constitute ADHD. By the same token, the requirement that symptoms be pervasive across different situations reflects the view that ADHD is inherent to the individual and should not be diagnosed on the basis of factors that are primarily situation specific. Neither of these criteria means that the symptoms of ADHD are without variability. For example, although symptoms have to be pervasive, their severity and frequency can differ across settings such as home and school. Factors such as differences in tolerance for symptoms or ability to manage symptoms between parent and teacher may contribute to such variability. In addition, an accumulation of multiple environmental stressors (e.g., large family size, lower socioeconomic status) can aggravate symptoms (Biederman et al., 1995). Finally, there is some evidence that individuals with lower intelligence may be more likely to exhibit pervasive rather than situational hyperactivity (Schachar, 1991).

Assessment and Intervention for the General Population

Assessment and treatment of ADHD in the general population has developed to the point where there is currently a well-recognized clinical approach to the problem.

Assessment In current practice, there is widespread support for a multimodal method of assessing and treating ADHD. This has not always been the case. At times, the approach to diagnosis and management has been reductionist—that is, the focus has been mainly on prescribing medication based on the impressions gained from a brief office visit. Such an approach has come to be regarded as too narrow to capture the complexity of the factors that both contribute to and result from the disorder, not to mention being potentially dangerous to a person's health. A multimodal approach to assessment entails gathering information through many methods (e.g., interview, rating scales, observation, standardized cognitive and academic tasks) and from many sources (e.g., from parents and teachers, in a variety of social situations). This information is in turn evaluated in light of the *DSM-IV-TR* criteria to reach a clinical decision.

Rating scales, such as the Conners' Rating Scales–Revised (Conners, 1997), that are based on observations of the child by parents and teachers provide information about the presence of symptoms of ADHD. They also shed light on comorbid disorders and on the pervasiveness of symptoms across home and school. These ratings yield norm-referenced scores but cannot be used alone to make a diagnosis. In assessing children, it is important also to complete a history documenting the chronology of the symptoms. Semistructured interviews done with both the parent (Schachar, Ickowicz, & Wachsmuth, 1994) and teacher (Schachar & Tannock, 1994) should be carried out. Such interviews are designed to give much needed clarification of the ratings.

Intervention Among the more popular forms of intervention for ADHD are the use of medication, behavior therapy, or a combination of both. These approaches have been the focus of much research.

Stimulant medication is the most frequently used intervention for ADHD. Estimates of the number of youth with a clinical diagnosis of ADHD who are given stimulants range from 52%–71% (Barkley et al., 1992; Bosco & Robin, 1980; Copeland et al., 1987; Cullinan, Gadow, & Epstein, 1987). Methylphenidate (Ritalin) is the most commonly administered stimulant. Stimulants act on the areas of the central nervous system that are responsible for the self-regulation of behavior. They increase the amount of biochemicals (e.g., the neurotransmitters dopamine and norepinephrine) that are available to facilitate the transmission of neural impulses associated with controlling behavior. The result of this stimulation of the central nervous system, which is sometimes described as an increase in central nervous system arousal, is better behavioral control over attention, impulses, and the level of motor activity.

Approximately 70%–80% of individuals with ADHD have a favorable response to stimulants (Shea & Baren, 1996). Frequently cited positive effects include improvements in attention and impulsivity, socialization, aggression levels, conduct, and handwriting, as well as in the quantity, accuracy, and rate of completed schoolwork (Cantwell, 1996; Shea & Baren, 1996). Stimulants do not give individuals specific academic skills that they are missing, but they can help people to engage better with instruction in order to acquire and apply the skills that they lack due to their symptoms of ADHD (Brown, 2000).

It is not possible to know in advance which stimulant will result in the best response for any given individual. The level of responsiveness and the appropriate dose have to be determined by a trial run of the medication. Sometimes an individual will respond better to one stimulant than to another. It is important to be aware that in some individuals, higher doses that create positive behavioral effects may have negative effects on aspects of cognition (Cantwell & Swanson, 1992). The preferred dose level is one that calms behavior without diminishing cognitive functioning.

The main side effects of stimulants for an individual with ADHD include loss of appetite, difficulty sleeping, headaches, stomachaches, and irritability, but these effects are usually not long lasting (Shea & Baren, 1996). Stimulants continue to be effective well into adolescence and adulthood, and approximately 80% of adults with ADHD respond favorably to them (Smith et al., 1998; Spencer et al., 1995). In addition to stimulants, other nonstimulant medications (e.g., antidepressants, antianxiety drugs, anticonvulsants) may also be administered in an attempt to address behaviors associated with ADHD. Other medications may be tried either when there is a poor response to stimulants or when there are too many side effects. In addition, other medications may be tried to control the symptoms of comorbid disorders that accompany ADHD, such as oppositional defiant disorder, conduct disorder, and anxiety (see Chapter 20).

The Multimodal Treatment Study of Children with ADHD (MTA; MTA Cooperative Group, 1999) was a large-scale investigation of the effectiveness of using both medication and behavioral techniques in intervention for ADHD. This study compared the long-term efficacy (longer than 14 months) of medication, intensive behavioral intervention, a combined approach of medication and behavioral intervention, and intervention as provided to a community comparison group. The interventions were designed to improve the symptoms of ADHD in a sample of 579 children who were 7 to 9.9 years old, had average intelligence, and had the combined type of ADHD. The effect of the interventions on other functioning outcomes (e.g., social skills, oppositional aggressive symptoms, academic performance) was also examined. Medication consisted of both stimulant and nonstimulant drugs, depending on the responsiveness of the particular participant, but methylphenidate was the most frequently administered medication. Behavioral intervention included parent education, child-focused intervention, and school-based intervention. Combined treatment incorporated elements from both approaches. The community comparison group permitted comparison of the benefits provided by MTA's intensively, closely monitored interventions and the benefits of interventions usually provided by community providers. Community interventions consisted of those agreed on by the children's parents and that were available in their communities. Two thirds of the children in the community group received stimulant medication, but community treatments were much less intensive than MTA-delivered interventions (e.g., medication was received less often, generally in lower doses, and/or monitored less frequently).

The medication treatment and the combined treatment were each superior to the behavioral intervention and community outcomes in reducing children's symptoms of inattention and hyperactivity-impulsivity as rated by parents and teachers. There was no significant difference in efficacy between the medication and combined interventions for the ADHD symptom outcomes. However, preliminary analyses indicated that the combined intervention outcomes were ultimately achieved with lower total daily doses of medication than those used in the medication-only approach. For the other functioning outcomes, there were few differences between the MTA-delivered interventions and only the combined treatment showed some consistent superiority over the community outcomes.

In a follow-up study (MTA Cooperative Group, 2004) conducted after 24 months, greater deterioration in the effectiveness of controlling ADHD symptoms was found in the two groups that initially had shown the most benefits of intervention (medication and combined treatment groups) than in the groups that had shown the smallest benefits (behavior and community comparisons groups). This change in results seemed to be related to use of medication. During the follow-up period, a greater number of children stopped taking medication and a smaller number started taking it in the medication and combined groups than in the behavior and community comparison groups. These results—including the finding that in addition to medication compliance, there are a variety of variables (e.g., presence of comorbid anxiety and/or disruptive behavior) that can effect intervention outcomes—reinforce the importance of considering multiple options and needs when providing intervention for ADHD.

Individual responsiveness and circumstances may warrant selecting one approach over another or changing the approach being used. For example, if medication side effects seem too great from a medication-only approach, a combined approach could be used, whereby it may be possible to administer the medication at a lower dose. Because of its behavioral component, the use of a combined approach may be beneficial for the child to learn about behavioral control. These interventions can also be combined with other effective options such as social skills training (Pelham & Bender, 1982; Swanson, 1992), education and counseling of both the child and the family about ADHD, and use of a structured classroom environment (Cantwell, 1996). If medication is beneficial but there is not compliance, it may be necessary to explore, in a sensitive way, both child and parent views on longer-term medication use.

Assessment and Intervention for People with Intellectual Disability

In contrast to the general population, assessment and treatment of ADHD among people with intellectual disability is less well developed.

Assessment Regardless of assessment method (rating scales, interviews, or observations), the suitability of using these approaches for children with developmental delay requires much improvement. Most diagnostic instruments that assess ADHD-associated behaviors implicitly presume intelligence that is above the intellectual disability range. Instrumentation and other assessment techniques need to be designed that capture differences between the behavior of individuals with typical functioning and those with intellectual disabilities, as well as between people with intellectual disabilities of relatively higher and lower intellectual functioning. For example, a number of investigators have noted that ADHD may be expressed more as cognitive symptoms (e.g., inattention) in individuals with mild-to-moderate intellectual disability; in individuals with more severe disabilities, motoric/organic features may be more useful in diagnosis (Pearson, 1993).

Clinical observation, observation of play, and assessment of academic performance are useful techniques to use in assessing ADHD in children with developmental delay. Handen et al. (1998) found that children with developmental delay and ADHD made more toy changes than their peers without ADHD. These children also exhibited more toy touches and off-task behaviors during an academic task. In another study, Handen et al. (1994) found that children with developmental delay and ADHD could be distinguished from their peers without developmental delay and ADHD only by classroom observations of more frequent off-task behavior and fidgeting, especially when there was little teacher supervision or feedback.

Intervention Regarding intervention for both developmental delay and ADHD, antecedent exercise has been found to reduce both overactivity and off-task behavior (Bachman & Sluyter, 1988; McGimsey & Favell, 1988), whereas physical restraint has not been shown to be successful in controlling hyperactivity (Singh, Winton, & Ball, 1984). Research reports indicate that the use of both behavior modification techniques and stimulant medication are quite common in addressing ADHD in individuals with intellectual disability. Stimulant medication has been estimated to be prescribed in close to 15% of children with mild developmental delay and ADHD (Cullinan et al., 1987) and 3.4% of children with moderate delay and ADHD (Gadow, 1985), although the actual figures may well be higher.

Handen et al. (1992) and Handen, McAuliffe, and Caro-Martinez (1996) found that 64%–66% of students with developmental delay and ADHD responded favorably to stimulant medication. In the earlier of these two studies, improvements were noted in on-task behavior and attentional skills but not in learning or social interactions. In the second study, the students showed gains in both their work output and, to a lesser degree, work accuracy, but it was concluded that teaching of specific learning strategies and behavioral interventions was also necessary to allow them to take full advantage of the benefits of medication. In a small sample of children with both developmental delay and ADHD, Johnson et al. (1994) also reported similar positive effects for stimulants, as well as improvement in work accuracy, when a behavioral intervention specifically targeted accuracy instead of on-task behavior in a general sense. Further support for the efficacy of behavioral intervention was reported by DeWitt, Aman, and Rojahn (1997), who found that partial reinforcement was as effective as continuous reinforcement in shaping and maintaining the adaptive behavior of children with developmental delay and ADHD. The differential reinforcement of other behavior has also been shown to be successful in decreasing activity and increasing toy play of children with delay and ADHD (Twardosz & Sajwaj, 1972).

The overall impression of a favorable response to stimulants among children with developmental delay and ADHD has been qualified by several reports. Despite the findings of Handen et al. (1992) and Handen et al. (1996) that approximately two thirds of children with delay and ADHD show a favorable stimulant response, a **meta-analysis** of studies using stimulants suggested that the response rate for such individuals may be closer to 54% (Aman, 1996). Regardless of which figures are used from these various studies, the stimulant response rate for individuals with developmental delay and ADHD seems to be lower than that of typically functioning individuals with ADHD. Furthermore, although Handen, Janosky, and McAuliffe (1997) found that 72% of children with delay and ADHD who took stimulants showed behavior improvement, more than two thirds continued to be rated at or above the 98th percentile on the Hyperactivity Index of the Conners' Parent Rating Scale (Conners, 1990). In addition, those children who had initially received high ratings on the Conners' Parent Rating Scale Conduct Problem Scale were more likely to have continuing behavioral problems upon follow-up. Similarly, in a 4-year follow-up of participants with developmental delay and ADHD who had been taking stimulants, Aman et al. (1996) found a significant decrease in parents' ratings of disruptive behavior disorders, but these behaviors still remained atypically high compared with norms. The children also failed to make lasting friendships or had only one or two weak friendships, and their rated irritability at initial contact rather than their hyperactivity predicted both externalizing and internalizing problems at follow-up.

Aman et al. (1993) and Aman et al. (1991) also found that the lower the measured intelligence of children with developmental delay and ADHD (i.e., IQ score of less than 45), the poorer the response to stimulants. Dose level may also make a difference with regard to responsiveness. In a study of 13 school-age children with delay and ADHD, Pearson, Santos, et al. (1996) reported that it was only at a higher dose that teachers rated the students as showing a significant decline in ADHD symptoms. Furthermore, even though Handen et al. (1999) obtained results that suggested preschool children with both developmental delay and ADHD responded favorably to stimulants at rates that are comparable to school-age children with the same conditions, preschoolers were more susceptible to adverse medication effects.

SUMMARY

ADHD is characterized by symptoms of inattention, hyperactivity-impulsivity, or a combination of both; by virtue of their frequency, severity, and pervasiveness, these symptoms constitute a distinct syndrome. Since the early 1990s, research has begun investigating ADHD's neurobiological, cognitive, and genetic basis—thereby moving beyond an understanding only in terms of behavioral symptoms.

ADHD sometimes exists along with learning disabilities and other disorders in the same person. In contrast to LD, however, ADHD is diagnosed in individuals who have below-average as well as average and above-average IQ scores. It has been reported that when IQ scores are very low, it is more difficult to separate symptoms of the disorder from the effects of generally lower intellectual functioning. The fact that there is much less research on the occurrence of ADHD in individuals with intellectual disability than on the occurrence of ADHD in the general population suggests the need for caution in interpreting research results. A conservative estimate is that ADHD may be diagnosed twice as frequently in individuals with intellectual disability than in the general population. Although many ADHD symptoms are common across populations, especially oppositionality, there is some evidence that impulsivity may be more characteristic of people with intellectual disability, whereas inattention is less characteristic. In both populations, oppositional behavior seems to be the most common behavioral comorbidity. Among individuals with developmental delay, greater noncompliance and aggression may be associated with somewhat higher cognitive functioning. Research on effective assessment and intervention is helping in the understanding of ADHD in people with intellectual disability, although considerably more work is needed in this area.

FOR FURTHER THOUGHT AND DISCUSSION

1. What might be some of the challenges in treating an individual who has both LD and ADHD, as compared with treating an individual who only has ADHD?
2. Is ADHD still an appropriate diagnostic label if its subtypes (e.g., inattentive type, hyperactive-impulsive type) differentiate the disorder more specifically?
3. What are some reasons why ADHD may not be recognized or diagnosed in children, youth, and adults with intellectual disability?

REFERENCES

Achenbach, T.M., Howell, C.T., McConaughty, S., et al. (1995). Six-year predictors of problems in a national sample. III: Transitions to young adult syndromes. *Journal of the American Academy of Child and Adolescent Psychiatry, 34,* 658–669.

Aman, M.G. (1996). Stimulant drugs in the developmental disabilities revised. *Journal of Developmental and Physical Disabilities, 8,* 347–365.

Aman, M.G., Kern, R.A., McGee, D.E., et al. (1993). Fenfluramine and methylphenidate in children with mental retardation and ADHD: Clinical and side effects. *Journal of the American Academy of Child and Adolescent Psychiatry, 32,* 851–859.

Aman, M.G., Marks, R.E., Turbott, S.H., et al. (1991). Clinical effects of methylphenidate and thioridazine in intellectually subaverage children. *Journal of the American Academy of Child and Adolescent Psychiatry, 30,* 246–256.

Aman, M.G., Pejeau, C., Osborne, P., et al. (1996). Four-year follow-up of children with low intelligence and ADHD. *Research in Developmental Disabilities, 17,* 417–432.

American Psychiatric Association. (1987). *Diagnostic and statistical manual of mental disorders* (3rd ed., rev). Washington, DC: Author.

American Psychiatric Association. (2000). *Diagnostic and statistical manual of mental disorders* (4th ed., text rev). Washington, DC: Author.

Bachman, J.E., & Sluyter, D. (1988). Reducing inappropriate behaviors of developmentally disabled adults using antecedent aerobic dance exercises. *Research in Developmental Disabilities, 9,* 73–83.

Barkley, R.A. (1990). *Attention-deficit/hyperactivity disorder: A handbook for diagnosis and treatment.* New York: The Guilford Press.

Barkley, R.A. (1996). Attention-deficit/hyperactivity disorder. In E.J. Mash & R.A. Barkley (Eds.), *Child psychopathology* (pp. 63–112). New York: The Guilford Press.

Barkley, R.A. (1997). *ADHD and the nature of self-control.* New York: The Guilford Press.

Barkley, R.A. (1998a). Attention-deficit hyperactivity disorder. *Scientific American, 279*(3), 66–71.

Barkley, R.A. (1998b). *Attention deficit hyperactivity disorder: A handbook for diagnosis and treatment* (2nd ed.). New York: The Guilford Press.

Barkley, R.A., Anastopoulos, A.D., Guevremont, D.G., et al. (1992). Adolescents with attention deficit hyperactivity disorder: Mother-adolescent interactions, family beliefs and conflicts, and maternal psychopathology. *Journal of Abnormal and Child Psychology, 20,* 263–288.

Barkley, R.A., & Biederman, J. (1997). Towards a broader definition of the age of onset of criterion for attention deficit hyperactivity disorder. *Journal of the American Academy of Child and Adolescent Psychiatry, 36,* 1204–1210.

Barkley, R.A., Fischer, M., Edelbrock, C.S., et al. (1990). The adolescent outcome of hyperactive children diagnosed by research criteria—I: An 8 year prospective follow-up study. *Journal of the American Academy of Child and Adolescent Psychiatry, 29,* 546–557.

Barkley, R.A., Murphy, K., & Kwasnik, D. (1996). Psychological adjustment and adaptive impairments in young adults with ADHD. *Journal of Attention Disorders, 1,* 41–54.

Barr, C.L., Wigg, K.G., Bloom, S., et al. (2000). Further evidence from haplotype analysis for linkage of the dopamine D4 receptor gene and attention-deficit hyperactivity disorder. *American Journal of Medical Genetics, 96,* 262–267.

Baumgaertel, A., Wolraich, M.L., & Dietrich, M. (1995). Comparison of diagnostic criteria for attention deficit disorders in a German elementary school sample. *Journal of the American Academy of Child and Adolescent Psychiatry, 34,* 629–638.

Benson, B.A., & Aman, M.G. (1999). Disruptive behavior disorders in children with mental retardation. In H.C. Quay & A.E. Hogan (Eds.), *Handbook of disruptive behavior disorders* (pp. 559–578). New York: Kluwer Academic/Plenum Publishers.

Biederman, J., Millberger, S., Faraone, S.V., et al. (1995). Family environment risk factors for attention-deficit hyperactivity disorder: A test of Rutter's indicators of adversity. *Archives of General Psychiatry, 52,* 464–470.

Bosco, J.J., & Robin, S.S. (1980). Hyperkensis: Prevalence and treatment. In C.K. Whalen & B. Henker (Eds.), *Hyperactive children: The social ecology of identification and treatment* (pp. 173–187). New York: Academy Press.

Brown, T.E. (2000). Emerging understandings of attention deficit disorders and comorbidities. In T.E. Brown (Ed.), *Attention-deficit disorders and comorbidities in children, adolescents and adults* (pp. 3–55). Washington, DC: American Psychiatric Press.

Campbell, S.B. (1990). *Psychiatric disorder in preschool children.* New York: The Guilford Press.

Cantwell, D.P. (1996). Attention deficit disorder: A review of the past 10 years. *Journal of the American Academy of Child and Adolescent Psychiatry, 35*(8), 978–987.

Cantwell, D.P., & Swanson, J. (1992, October). *Cognitive toxicity in ADHD children treated with stimulant medication.* Paper presented at the American Academy of Child and Adolescent Psychiatry Annual Meeting, San Francisco.

Clements, S.D. (1966). *Minimal brain dysfunction in children: Terminology and identification phase one of a three-phase project.* Washington, DC: U.S. Department of Health, Education, and Welfare.

Conners, C.K. (1990). *Manual for Conners' Rating Scales.* Toronto: Multi-Health Systems.

Conners, C.K. (1997). *Conners' Rating Scales–Revised Technical Manual.* Toronto: Multi Health Systems, Inc.

Copeland, L., Wolraich, M., Lindgren, S., et al. (1987). Pediatrician's reported practices in the assessment and treatment of attention deficit disorders. *Journal of Developmental and Behavioral Pediatrics, 8,* 191–197.

Cullinan, D., Gadow, K.D., & Epstein, M.H. (1987). Psychotropic drug treatment among learning-disabled, educable mentally retarded, and seriously emotionally disturbed students. *Journal of Abnormal Child Psychology, 15,* 469–477.

DeWitt, M.B., Aman, M.G., & Rojahn, J. (1997). Effects of reinforcement contingencies on performance of children with mental retardation and attention problems. *Journal of Developmental and Physical Disabilities, 9,* 101–115.

Douglas, V.I. (1999). Cognitive control processes in attention-deficit hyperactivity disorder. In H.C. Quay & A.E. Hogan (Eds.), *Handbook of disruptive behavior disorders* (pp. 105–138). New York: Kluwer Academic/Plenum Publishers.

Douglas, V.I., & Benezra, E. (1990). Supraspan verbal memory in attention deficit disorder with hyperactivity, normal and reading disabled boys. *Journal of Abnormal Child Psychology, 18,* 617–638.

Eiraldi, R.B., Power, T.J., & Nezu, C.M. (1997). Patterns of comorbidity associated with sub-types of attention-deficit/hyperactivity disorder among 6- to 12-year-old children. *Journal of the American Academy of Child and Adolescent Psychiatry, 36,* 503–514.

Faraone, S.V., Biederman, J., Lehman, B.K., et al. (1993). Evidence for the independent familial transmission of attention-deficit/hyperactivity disorder and learning disabilities: Results from a family genetic study. *American Journal of Psychiatry, 150,* 891–895.

Faraone, S.V., Biederman, J., Weber, W., et al. (1998). Psychiatric, neuropsychological, and psychosocial features of DSM-IV subtypes of attention-deficit/hyperactivity disorder: Results from a clinically referred sample. *Journal of the American Academy of Child and Adolescent Psychiatry, 37,* 185–193.

Fischer, M., Barkley, R.A., Fletcher, K., et al. (1990). The adolescent outcome of adolescent children diagnosed by research criteria, II: Academic, attentional, and neuropsychological status. *Journal of Consulting and Clinical Psychology, 58,* 580–588.

Gadow, K.D. (1985). Prevalence and efficacy of stimulant drug use with mentally retarded children and youth. *Psychopharmacology Bulletin, 21,* 291–303.

Gaub, M., & Carlson, C.L. (1997). Gender differences in ADHD: A meta-analysis and critical review. *Journal of the American Academy of Child and Adolescent Psychiatry, 36,* 1036–1045.

Handen, B.L., Breaux, A.M., Janosky, J., et al. (1992). Effects and non-effects on methylphenidate in children with mental retardation and ADHD. *Journal of the American Academy of Child and Adolescent Psychiatry, 31,* 455–461.

Handen, B.L., Feldman, H.M., Lurier, A., et al. (1999). Efficacy of methylphenidate among preschool children with developmental disabilities and ADHD. *Journal of the American Academy of Child and Adolescent Psychiatry, 38,* 805–812.

Handen, B.L., Janosky, J., & McAuliffe, S. (1997). Long-term follow-up of children with mental retardation, borderline intellectual functioning and ADHD. *Journal of Abnormal Psychology, 25,* 287–295.

Handen, B.L., McAuliffe, S., & Caro-Martinez, L. (1996). Stimulant medication effects on learning in children with mental retardation and ADHD. *Journal of Developmental and Physical Disabilities, 8,* 335–346.

Handen, B.L., McAuliffe, S., Janosky, J., et al. (1994). Classroom behavior and children with mental retardation: Comparison of children with and without ADHD. *Journal of Abnormal Child Psychology, 22,* 267–280.

Handen, B.L., McAuliffe, S., Janosky, J., et al. (1998). A playroom observation procedure to assess children with mental retardation and ADHD. *Journal of Abnormal Child Psychology, 26,* 269–277.

Hardan, A., & Sahl, R. (1997). Psychopathology in children and adolescents with developmental disorders. *Research in Developmental Disabilities, 18,* 369–382.

Hart, E.L., Lahey, B.B., Loeber, R., et al. (1995). Developmental change in attention-deficit hyperactivity disorder in boys: A four-year longitudinal study. *Journal of Abnormal Child Psychology, 23,* 729–749.

Hunt, R.D., & Cohen, D.J. (1988). Attentional and neurochemical components of MR: New methods for an old problem. In J.A. Stark, F.J. Menolascino, M.H. Albarelli, et al. (Eds.), *MR and mental health: Classification, diagnosis, treatment, services* (pp. 90–97). New York: Springer-Verlag.

Johnson, C.R., Handan, B.L., Lubetsky, M.J., et al. (1994). Efficacy of methylphenidate and behavioral intervention in children with ADHD and mental retardation. *Behavior Modification, 18,* 470–487.

Johnson, C.R., Lubetsky, M.J., & Sacco, K.A. (1995). Psychiatric and behavioral disorders in hospitalized preschoolers with developmental disabilities. *Journal of Autism and Developmental Disorders, 25,* 169–182.

Kaplan, B.J., Crawford, S.G., Dewey, D.M., et al. (2000). The IQ's of children with ADHD are normally distributed. *Journal of Learning Disabilities, 33,* 425–432.

Korkman, M., & Pesonen, A.E. (1994). A comparison of neuropsychological test profiles of children with attention-deficit/hyperactivity disorder and/or learning disability. *Journal of Learning Disabilities, 27,* 383–392.

Krakow, J.B., & Kopp, C.B. (1982). Sustained attention in young Down syndrome children. *Topics in Early Childhood Special Education, 2,* 32–34.

Krakow, J.B., & Kopp, C.B. (1983). The effects of developmental delay on sustained attention in young children. *Child Development, 54,* 1143–1155.

Laufer, M., & Denhoff, E. (1957). Hyperkinetic behavior syndrome in children. *Journal of Pediatrics, 50,* 463–474.

Levy, F., Hay, D.A., McStephen, M., et al. (1997). Attention-deficit/hyperactivity disorder: A category or a continuum? Genetic analysis of a large-scale twin study. *Journal of the American Academy of Child and Adolescent Psychiatry, 36,* 737–744.

Loeber, R., Green, S., Lahey, B.B., et al., (1992). Developmental sequences in the age of onset of disruptive child behaviors. *Journal of Child and Family Studies, 1,* 21–41.

Logan, G. (1994). On the ability to inhibit thought or action: A users' guide to the stop signal paradigm. In D. Dagenbach & T.H. Carr (Eds.), *Inhibitory processes in attention, memory and language* (pp. 189–239). San Diego, CA: Academic Press.

Loveland, K.A. (1987). Behavior of young children with down syndrome before the mirror: Exploration. *Child Development, 58,* 768–778.

Mannuzza, S., Gittelman-Klein, R.G., Bessler, A., et al. (1993). Adult outcome of hyperactive boys: Educational achievement, occupational rank, and psychiatric status. *Archives of General Psychiatry, 50,* 565–576.

Martinussen, R., Hayden, J., Hogg-Johnson, S., et al. (2005). A meta-analysis of working memory impairments in children with attention-deficit/hyperactivity disorder. *Journal of the American Academy of Child and Adolescent Psychiatry, 44,* 377–384.

McGee, R., Williams, S., Moffitt, T., et al. (1989). A comparison of 13-year-old boys with attention deficit and/or reading disorder on neuropsychological measures. *Journal of Abnormal Child Psychology, 17,* 37–53.

McGimsey, J.F., & Favell, J.E. (1988). The effects of increased physical exercise on disruptive behavior in retarded persons. *Journal of Autism and Developmental Disorders, 18,* 167–179.

McInnes, A., Humphries, T., Hogg-Johnson, S., et al. (2003). Listening comprehension and working memory are impaired in attention-deficit hyperactivity disorder irrespective of language impairment. *Journal of Abnormal Child Psychology, 31,* 427–443.

Milich, R., Balentine, A.C., & Lynam, D.R. (2001). ADHD combined type and ADHD predominantly inattentive type are distinct and unrelated disorders. *Clinical Psychology: Science and Practice, 8*(4), 463–488.

MTA Cooperative Group. (1999). A 14-month randomized clinical trial of treatment strategies for Attention-Deficit/Hyperactivity Disorder. *Archives of General Psychiatry, 56,* 1073–1086.

MTA Cooperative Group. (2004). National Institute of Mental Health multimodal treatment study of ADHD follow-up: Changes in effectiveness and growth after the end of treatment. *Paediatrics, 113*(4), 762–769.

Narhi, V., & Ahonen, T. (1995). Reading disability with and without attention-deficit/hyperactivity disorder: Do attentional problems make a difference? *Developmental Neuropsychology, 11,* 337–350.

Oram, J., Fine, J., Okamoto, C., et al. (1999). Assessing the language of children with attention-deficit/hyperactivity disorder: Role of executive function. *American Journal of Speech-language Pathology, 8,* 72–89.

Oram, J., Johnson, C.J., & Tannock, R. (2001, June). *Towards discriminating SLI and ADHD: A basic processes approach.* Paper presented at the 22nd Annual Symposium on Research in Child Language Disorders, Madison, WI.

Paternite, C.E., Loney, J., & Roberts, M.A. (1995). External validation of oppositional disorder and attention deficit disorder with hyperactivity. *Journal of Abnormal Child Psychology, 23,* 453–471.

Pearson, D.A. (1993). Dual diagnosis in children: Attention deficit hyperactivity disorder. *Southwest Quarterly Review, 1,* 1–3.

Pearson, D.A., Santos, C.W., Roache, J.D., et al. (1996). Effects of methylphenidate on behavioral adjustment in children with mental retardation and ADHD: Preliminary findings from a study in progress. *Journal of Developmental and Physical Disabilities, 8,* 313–333.

Pearson, D.A., Yaffee, L.S., Loveland, K.A., et al. (1996). Comparison of sustained and selective attention in children who have mental retardation with and without attention deficit hyperactivity disorder. *American Journal on Mental Retardation, 100,* 592–607.

Pelham, W.E., & Bender, M.E. (1982). Peer relationships in hyperactive children: Description and treatment. In K. Gadow & I. Bailer (Eds.), *Advances in learning and behavioral disabilities* (pp. 365–436). Greenwich, CT: JAI Press.

Pennington, B.F., Groisser, D., & Welsh, M.C. (1993). Contrasting cognitive deficits in attention-deficit/hyperactivity disorder versus reading disability. *Developmental Psychology, 29,* 511–552.

Purvis, K.L., & Tannock, R. (2000). Phonological processing, not inhibitory control, differentiates ADHD and reading disability. *Journal of the American Academy of Child and Adolescent Psychiatry, 39,* 485–494.

Quay, H.C. (1997). Inhibition and attention-deficit/hyperactivity disorder. *Journal of Abnormal Child Psychology, 25,* 7–13.

Rutter, M., Tizard, J., Yule, W., et al. (1976). Isle of Wight studies, 1964-74. *Psychological Medicine, 6,* 313–332.

Schachar, R. (1991). Childhood hyperactivity. *Journal of Child Psychology and Psychiatry, 32,* 155–191.

Schachar, R., Ickowicz, A., & Wachsmuth, R. (1994). *Parent interview for child symptoms, revised.* Unpublished manuscript, Hospital for Sick Children, Toronto.

Schachar, R., & Tannock, R. (1994). *Teacher telephone interview for disruptive behavior disorders (DSM-III-R).* Unpublished manuscript, Hospital for Sick Children, Toronto.

Schafer, E.W.P., & Peeke, H.V.S. (1982). Down syndrome individuals fail to habituate to cortical evoked potentials. *American Journal of Mental Deficiency, 87,* 332–337.

Shastry, B.S. (2004). Molecular genetics of attention-deficit hyperactivity disorder (ADHD): An update. *Neurochemistry International, 44*(7), 469–474.

Shea, S., & Baren, M. (1996). What ADHD is and isn't . . . and what to do. *Patient Care Canada, 7,* 26–51.

Silver, L.B. (1990). Attention deficit/hyperactivity disorder: Is it a learning disability or a related disorder? *Journal of Learning Disabilities, 23,* 394–397.

Singh, N.N., Winton, A.S., & Ball, P.M. (1984). Effects of physical restraint on the behavior of hyperactive mentally retarded persons. *American Journal on Mental Deficiency, 89,* 16–22.

Smith, B.H., Pelham, W.E., Gnagy, E., et al. (1998). Equivalent effects of stimulant treatment for attention-deficit hyperactivity disorder during childhood and adolescence. *Journal of the American Academy of Child and Adolescent Psychiatry, 37,* 314–321.

Spencer, T., Wilens, T.E., Biederman, J., et al. (1995). A double-blind, crossover comparison of methylphenidate and placebo in adults with childhood-onset of attention-deficit/hyperactivity disorder. *Archives of General Psychiatry, 52,* 434–443.

Still, G.F. (1902). Some abnormal psychical conditions in children. *The Lancet, 1,* 1008–1012, 1077–1082, 1163–1168.

Swanson, J.M. (1992). *School-based assessment and intervention for ADD students.* Irvine, CA: KC Publications.

Tannock, R. (1998). Attention deficit hyperactivity disorder: Advances in cognitive, neurobiological, and genetic research. *Journal of Child Psychology and Psychiatry, 39,* 65–99.

Tannock, R., & Brown, T.E. (2000). Attention-deficit disorders with learning disorders in children and adolescents. In T.E. Brown (Ed.), *Attention-deficit disorders and comorbidities in children, adolescents, and adults* (pp. 231–295). Washington, DC: American Psychiatric Press.

Taylor, E., Sandberg, S., Thorley, G., et al. (1991). *The epidemiology of childhood hyperactivity.* Oxford, United Kingdom: Oxford University Press.

Tizard, B. (1968a). Observations of over-active imbecile children in controlled and uncontrolled environments-I: Classroom studies. *American Journal of Mental Deficiency, 72,* 540–547.

Tizard, B. (1968b). Observations of over-active imbecile children in controlled and uncontrolled environments-II: Experimental studies. *American Journal of Mental Deficiency, 72,* 548–553.

Twardosz, S., & Sajwaj, T. (1972). Multiple effects of a procedure to increase sitting in a hyperactive, retarded boy. *Journal of Applied Behavior Analysis, 5,* 73–78.

Weiss, G., & Hechtman, L.T. (1994). *Hyperactive children grown up* (2nd ed.). New York: The Guilford Press.

Wender, P. (1994). *Attention deficit disorder in adults.* Oxford, United Kingdom: Oxford University Press.

Werner, H., & Strauss, A.A. (1940). Causal factors in low performance. *American Journal of Mental Deficiency, 45,* 213–218.

Werner, H., & Strauss, A.A. (1941). Pathology of figure background relation in the child. *Journal of Abnormal and Social Psychology, 36,* 236–248.

Wolraich, M.L., Hannah, J.N., Pinnock, T.Y., et al. (1996). Comparison of diagnostic criteria for attention-deficit/hyperactivity disorder in a countrywide sample. *Journal of the American Academy of Child and Adolescent Psychiatry, 50,* 333–340.

20

Abnormal Behavior

MAIRE PERCY, IVAN BROWN, AND SHELDON Z. LEWKIS

WHAT YOU WILL LEARN ABOUT IN THIS CHAPTER

- Descriptions of normal and abnormal behavior
- Behavior in people with intellectual and developmental disabilities
- Abnormal behavior related to disabilities
- Abnormal behavior related to brain injury
- Abnormal behavior related to mental and physical health
- Abnormal behavior in the school system
- Seeking help

We all do hundreds of things every day, from the moment we wake up to the time we go to sleep, and even while we are sleeping. All these things we do constitute our behavior. Behavior is what other people see us doing; thus, it is a principal way others form their understanding of us and their views on who we are as people.

Behavior can take many forms and can be described in many ways. For example, it can be described as actions or reactions, conscious or unconscious, intentional or unintentional, or overt (obvious) or covert (secretive). Behavior occurs on the "outside" but is a result of internal functions—the body's endocrine system (the network of tissues and organs that secrete hormones) and the nervous systems (see Chapter 8). The complexity of human behavior is related to the complexity of the human nervous systems. For many years, there was a debate over whether behavior was the consequence of nature or nurture. At the beginning of the 21st century, it is accepted that one's behaviors, both normal and abnormal, reflect a blend of both genetic inheritance and learning that has occurred throughout life. Such learning results from a person's unique life experiences, abilities and disabilities, and interactions with the numerous aspects of changing environments (Gottesman & Hanson, 2005; Rutter, 2006; Tselis & Booss, 2003).

DESCRIPTIONS OF NORMAL AND ABNORMAL BEHAVIOR

Behavior is expected to conform to certain patterns that are acceptable to most people. In the sociology field, acceptable patterns of behavior are called behavioral norms, although society in general usually thinks of these patterns as "normal" behavior. Behavioral norms differ from one culture to another and from one time period to another, but they serve an important purpose. When almost everybody conforms to them, behavior is largely predictable. Predictable behavior exhibited by others alleviates stress and encourages trust.

At the same time, there is considerable variation in normal behavior at the personal level. Each person, while behaving generally in accordance with behavioral norms, also does things that are unique. In fact, people are often described in terms of the unique aspects of their behavior because that is what distinguishes them as individuals. One of the things most intriguing about other people is how their behavior is different from one's own, even if both people follow the same general behavioral norms.

Having some degree of unique behavior is also beneficial to humans as a species, because it allows people to explore and experiment with new ideas independently. The human race would not have developed to where it is today had each person held fast to the same behavioral norms. Still, the unique behaviors of individuals need to be acceptable to others and to fit into the broader rules set for behavioral norms. Thus, it is considered "normal" for humans to show a range of individual behaviors while conforming to a general set of behavior rules.

The authors acknowledge Rivka Birkan and Tina Crockford, co-authors of "Abnormal Behaviour" (Percy et al., 2003), for their valuable contribution to this chapter.

The amount of detail in this chapter may initially seem overwhelming. It is not to be memorized but to be browsed, used as a reference and guide for problem solving, and used as a stepping stone to self-directed and lifelong learning.

Abnormal behavior, in a literal sense, means "away from" normal behavior. It is a behavior that seems too far from the behavioral norm, too odd, or too unusual to be acceptable. It usually means rare in the statistical sense. For example, a person walking down the street shouting angrily at unseen people is exhibiting a behavior that is usually considered to be abnormal. Abnormal behaviors are by no means exclusively related to mental illness, however, and are present to some degree in all people. A few less serious abnormal behaviors in any one person are typically acceptable, especially if they are counterbalanced by many more normal behaviors. If a person has a number of abnormal behaviors, however, these may outweigh the normal behaviors such that the behavior pattern as a whole deviates too far from acceptable norms.

Abnormal behavior is not only overly unusual but also troublesome—either to the people who exhibit the behavior or to others who experience it. It is unpredictable and creates stress and uncertainty. It can lead to great personal distress and interfere with daily functioning. It can result in the breakdown of relationships with other people, and sometimes it even leads to the need for institutional care. In a broader sense, abnormal behavior can threaten the well-being of family and community. The troublesome aspects of abnormal behavior can take many forms. It might, for example, be amoral, dangerous, compulsive, counterproductive to well-being, distressful, incomprehensible, irrational, maladaptive, uncomfortable or painful, unconventional, or unwanted. Because of the difficulties it creates, abnormal behavior is considered undesirable, and, if possible, something to be improved through intervention. The goal of intervention is to reduce the number or degree of abnormal behaviors so that day-to-day life can be more enjoyable and less troublesome for people who are affected and others who interact with them. In some cases, appropriate intervention can actually result in a cure. For example, adhering to a diet which is low in phenylalanine eliminates autistic-like behavior in individuals affected with phenylketonuria (PKU) and also enables typical development (see also Chapter 15).

This chapter focuses on a spectrum of behaviors that are not normal. Some are associated with particular intellectual and/or developmental disabilities. Others are not and constitute disabilities in their own right and can occur in people with or without intellectual disabilities. While reviewing this chapter, the reader should note that the term *abnormal* is not considered appropriate in some fields, and behaviors that are not normal are sometimes called atypical, challenging and/or difficult. Also intervention that results in a cure is sometimes referred to as a treatment rather than an intervention.

BEHAVIOR IN PEOPLE WITH INTELLECTUAL AND DEVELOPMENTAL DISABILITIES

People with intellectual and developmental disabilities, like those without disabilities, have a wide range of behaviors. Most of their behavior, both normal and abnormal, is similar to that of people without disabilities, although the range of what is accepted as normal behavior for people with intellectual and developmental disabilities can be broader because some of their behavior is understood to be a result of their disabilities. At the same time, they can exhibit any of the abnormal behaviors described in this chapter. In fact, abnormal behaviors occur more frequently in people with intellectual and developmental disabilities than in people without disabilities.

In spite of this broader understanding and acceptance, some people with intellectual and developmental disabilities do behave in ways that are particularly troublesome, as described in the next section.

Two Troublesome Forms of Abnormal Behavior

Two forms of particularly troublesome behavior are somewhat common. They can be quite serious, and they typically result from any one of a number of causes or a combination of causes.

Stereotypic or Self-Stimulatory Behaviors Stereotypic behavior is a repetitive, invariant behavior pattern with no obvious goal or function. It sometimes is referred to as self-stimulatory, or "stimming" behavior. This can involve any of the senses or a combination of them (Edelson, 2005a). Stereotypic behavior in humans can be categorized in these ways:

- Visual: staring at lights, blinking repetitively, moving one's fingers in front of one's eyes, flapping one's hands
- Auditory: tapping ears, snapping fingers, making vocal sounds
- Tactile: rubbing the skin with one's hands or with another object, scratching
- Vestibular: rocking front to back, rocking side to side
- Taste: placing body parts or objects in one's mouth, licking objects
- Smell: smelling objects, sniffing people

Although such behaviors are seemingly purposeless, they may excite or arouse the nervous system and provide pleasure. Conversely, they may be calming. They interfere with attention and learning but can be a positive reinforcer if a person is allowed to do them after finishing a task. It is possible to reduce the frequency of stereotypic behaviors by providing alternative, more socially appropriate forms of stimulation such as chewing on a piece of rubber or silicone tubing, stimulation in a Snoezelen room (a room that excites the senses through provision of different lights, smells and touch sensations and helps to reduce anxiety and promote relaxation), or exercise (Cuvo, May, & Post, 2001; Edelson, 2005a). Drugs (e.g., risperidone) can be used to address such behaviors, but it is not known if these reduce the behaviors directly or indirectly by slowing down overall motor movement (McDougle et al., 2005). As outlined in Chapter 12, intensive early behavioral intervention is reported to "normalize" some children with severe autism by reducing and/or eliminating stereotypical and other problem behaviors. (See also Shea, 2004.)

Self-Injurious Behavior Self-injurious behavior (SIB) is one of the most devastating behaviors exhibited by people with intellectual and/or developmental disabilities. SIB often refers to any behavior that causes tissue damage such as bruises, redness, and open wounds. The most common forms of these behaviors include head banging, hand biting, and excessive self-rubbing and scratching (Edelson, 2005b). SIB has an unusually high frequency in a number of disorders, including pervasive developmental disorders (Chapters 12 and 13), Tourette syndrome (National Institute of Neurological Disorders and Stroke, 2005; Chapter 15), intellectual and/or developmental disabilities (e.g., Lesch-Nyhan syndrome, Chapter 15; Cornelia de Lange syndrome, Chapter 15; fragile X syndrome, Chapter 11; Smith-Magenis syndrome, Chapter 15), schizophrenia, borderline personality disorder, and stereotypic movement disorder. It also may occur as the result of abuse or incest. SIB does not include suicidal behavior, but in people with schizophrenia, deliberate self-harm is a strong predictor of suicide. The causes and purposes of SIBs are not known, though physiological and social factors play a role as for stereotypic behaviors (Edelson, 2005b).

A variety of approaches are used in managing SIB, including psychotropic medication (e.g., antidepressants, anxiolytics, risperidone), mechanical restraint, cognitive-behavioral therapy, behavioral intervention, massage and/or sensory integration therapy, and group and family therapy. Deep brain stimulation and psychosurgery have been used in severe, refractory cases of Tourette syndrome. (*General sources:* Anandan et al., 2004; Dellinge-Ness & Handler, 2006; Edelson, 2005b; Haw et al., 2005; Jaffe, 2004; Lovell, 2004; Moss et al., 2005; Symons et al., 2003; Weiss, 2002; see also Chapters 11, 12, 13, 23, and 41.)

Causes

Some of the abnormal behavior seen in people with disabilities is related to the cause of their disability, some is related to brain injury, and some is related to other mental or physical health problems. It is essential to determine whether disability, brain injury, or mental or physical health (or a combination) is the underlying reason for abnormal behavior to ensure that an appropriate intervention can be undertaken. The main sections that follow describe these three major underlying reasons for abnormal behavior in people with intellectual and developmental disabilities.

ABNORMAL BEHAVIOR RELATED TO DISABILITIES

Some abnormal behaviors that are assumed to be related to disabilities are not well understood, but others are. In addition, some abnormal behaviors appear to be unique to individuals, whereas others are common to many people because of the particular type of disability they have. These abnormal behaviors are part of a larger pattern of behaviors that are "typical" of the disability and that are referred to as *behavioral phenotypes.*

Abnormal Behavior that Is Part of Behavioral Phenotypes

Behavioral phenotypes are patterns of behavior that are characteristic of particular types of intellectual or developmental disabilities. These emerge primarily from biological, genetic, or emotional disorders, but they are influenced by other environmental and developmental factors (O'Brien & Yule, 1995). Some behavioral phenotypes are directly related to genetic anomalies, and there is considerable work underway to explore the role of genes in certain behavior. It is believed that different networks of genes—possibly even hundreds to thousands—work in concert with environmental factors to influence brain development and function, which in turn influence behavior (Hamer, 2002).

Behavioral phenotypes that are perhaps best understood are those evident for people with certain genetic disorders (Dykens, 1995; Dykens, Hodapp, & Finucane, 2000; Gillberg & O'Brien, 2000; Moldavsky, Lev, & Lerman-Sagie, 2001; Ruggieri & Arberas, 2003; Steinhausen et al., 2002). Numerous disorders with a genetic basis have come to be recognized as syndromes; that is, they have a characteristic set of associated symptoms. Each syndrome has a distinct pattern of physical and neurological features, sometimes with a characteristic facial appearance or other physical feature. Furthermore, distinct patterns of behavior and personality, cognitive profiles, and patterns of learning difficulties have been found to be associated with some of these syndromes. Collectively, these latter patterns constitute the behavioral phenotype. It should be noted, however, that behavioral phenotypes are not necessarily unique to each syndrome. Moreover, not all individuals with a given syndrome necessarily show all of the patterns of the behavioral phenotype.

Some behaviors within behavioral phenotypes are not considered to be particularly problematic or abnormal, but others are. For example, in Prader-Willi syndrome, the desire for enormous amounts of food, and the lengths that people with this disorder go to obtain and hoard food, is part of a behavioral phenotype that is considered abnormal because it is detrimental to the person's health and it often creates enormous problems within the family, school, and other social settings (see Chapter 15).

Other examples of disorders with characteristic behavioral phenotypes include Angelman syndrome (Chapter 15), pervasive developmental disorders (Chapters 12 and 13), certain epilepsies with a genetic basis such as Lafora disease (Chapter 15), Tourette syndrome (Chapter 15), and Williams syndrome (Chapter 15).

In some cases, the characteristic behavioral phenotype results from metabolic abnormalities that can be treated and prevented. People with PKU cannot metabolize the amino acid phenylalanine. In this disorder, damage to the central nervous system (CNS) is minimized if dietary management in the form of phenylalanine restriction is begun shortly after birth and maintained over the period of most rapid development. Dietary management also should be maintained during pregnancy to promote typical fetal development. (See the PKU section in Chapter 15 for more detail.)

People with galactosemia are missing an enzyme that converts the sugar galactose into glucose (Tyfield et al., 1999). In this disorder, some nervous system damage can be prevented by strict exclusion of lactose and galactose from the diet. Treatment for galactosemia is life long, but unfortunately this does not reduce numerous long-term complications (Thompson, Arrowsmith, & Allen, 2003).

Smith-Lemli-Opitz syndrome is the first example of an intellectual disability that is associated with severe cholesterol deficiency (Tierney, Nwokoro, & Kelley, 2000; see also Chapter 15). People with this syndrome have a deficiency in an enzyme that is involved in cholesterol metabolism. Clinical trials are underway to determine the extent to which oral cholesterol supplements will correct this deficiency (Merkens et al., 2004). It appears that cholesterol supplementation should be provided at as young an age as possible, even when babies are breast feeding.

ABNORMAL BEHAVIOR RELATED TO BRAIN INJURY

The physical properties of brain tissue render it very vulnerable to damage by physical forces. Although the skull is protective, the inner surface contains many sharp and rough features that can lacerate brain tissue and its blood vessels when sudden acceleration–deceleration forces (e.g., impact in a car accident) cause the brain to collide with these inner skull features. The brain is also very vulnerable to injury by virtue of its constant high and finely tuned metabolic needs (e.g., oxygen supply), so that disruption for a relatively short period of time causes damage. The brain is also vulnerable to damage because of its relatively poor intrinsic healing properties, although some neuroplastic changes can take place.

At this time, there is little to offer people with brain injury in terms of medications that can help heal the brain or protect it from the chain of events leading to damage soon after injury (Bruce, 1995). However, there is much progress in research in this area (Arciniegas & Silver, 2006). In particular, much progress is being made in the development and/or identification of compounds that improve the functional plasticity of the human central nervous system; such compounds are referred to as *nootropics* (i.e., "acting on the mind").

Causes of Brain Injury

The major causes of brain injury are physical impact (e.g., motor vehicle accidents, falls, bicycle accidents, sports injuries, assaults, bullet wounds), exposure to neurotoxic agents (e.g., lead poisoning, excessive alcohol use), disruption of cerebral blood supply (e.g., stroke), violent shaking of an infant's head, and hypoxia (lack of oxygen—e.g., from drowning or disruption of breathing at birth). Any of the preceding events may result in mild to severe brain injury and death (Gaetz, 2004; Povlishock, 1993; see also Chapter 15 for more information on shaken baby syndrome and traumatic brain injury).

Results of Brain Injury

Brain injury can result in a broad range of abnormal behaviors. It can affect both neurocognitive functions (e.g., ability to think, understand, reason, remember, learn) and neurobehavioral functions (e.g., speech, mobility, dexterity) in numerous ways. Brain injury also may result in emotional and personality changes. It is interesting to note that neonatal temporal lobe lesions in monkeys result in behavioral changes strikingly similar to those characteristic of autism (Bachevalier, Malkova, & Mishkin, 2001). Typically, emotional problems resulting from brain injury take the form of depression, anxiety, emotional blunting, and irritability.

There are a number of rare disorders resulting from brain injury (Miller, 1994); a few examples follow:

- Factitious disorder: Intentionally created or exaggerated physical or psychological symptoms; used

for obtaining care rather than avoiding work; may also be conceptualized with an emphasis on preconscious, rather than fully intentional, origin
- Confabulation: Fictitious or distorted narrative accounts of events
- Reduplicative paramnesia: Belief that people and places are duplicates of the originals
- Capgrass syndrome: Strong belief that one's family and friends are impostors who only look like family and friends
- Ganser syndrome: Seemingly nondeliberate distortions and exaggerations of symptoms with psychometrically severe deficits disproportional to the injury
- Episodic/autobiographical amnesia: Impaired memory for events in one's own life
- Transient global amnesia: Loss of ability to form new memories for all types of information
- Prosopagnosia: Loss of ability to recognize faces
- Anosognosia: Denial or inability to realize that one has acquired physical or psychological impairments

Diagnosis

The *Diagnostic and Statistical Manual of Mental Disorders, Fourth Edition, Text Revision* (*DSM-IV-TR;* APA, 2000), sets out diagnostic criteria for a number of disorders that are relevant to the impact of brain injury. Among these disorders are dementias due to head trauma, substance-induced persisting dementia, amnestic disorder due to a general medical condition, substance-induced persisting amnestic disorder, and cognitive disorder not otherwise specified. Various learning and emotional disorders may also pertain.

The terms *concussion* and *mild brain injury* are often used interchangeably. A widely utilized North American set of diagnostic criteria for mild brain injury (Mild Traumatic Brain Injury Committee of the Head Injury Interdisciplinary Special Interest Group of the American Congress of Rehabilitation Medicine, 1993) does not require the loss of consciousness; alteration of mental state such as feeling dazed, disoriented, or confused can be sufficient in terms of alteration in state of consciousness (Levin, Benton, & Grossman, 1982; Levin, Eisenberg, & Benton, 1991). There is growing recognition of postconcussional disorder or syndrome as a legitimate and relatively common clinical disorder with potential long-term or permanent effects that can be significantly disrupting to an individual's normal mode of cognitive and emotional function (Parker, 2001; Ryan & Warden, 2003). This type of problem is particularly relevant to car accidents and sports injuries. Post-traumatic stress disorder can produce symptoms similar to mild brain injury. The extent to which brain injury has lasting effects cannot be generalized. Certainly, brain injury in childhood, particularly in infancy and early childhood, can affect the acquisition of fundamental cognitive and socioemotional skills of children with a "snowballing" effect.

The extent of brain injury is typically underimaged by conventional **computed tomography (CT)** and **magnetic resonance imaging (MRI)** scans (Bigler, 1999). These techniques are particularly deficient for the imaging of diffuse microscopic damage to neurons, the most prevalent form being diffuse axonal injury. More sophisticated forms of MRI (e.g., **anistrophy** of water diffusion by diffusion-weighted imaging) are proving to be very effective for imaging microscopic damage to neurons. Techniques such as **positron emission tomography (PET)**, **functional (fMRI)**, and quantitative electroencephalography (EEG) are effective for imaging neuropathophysiological alterations following brain injury (e.g., likely derangements in cerebral metabolism and usual patterns of neuronal transmission). Of important note is the fact that low doses of ionizing radiation to the brain in infancy have been found to influence cognitive abilities in adulthood (Hall et al., 2004). Thus, brain CT scans should be used in young children only with careful consideration of the risks and likely benefits.

Neuropsychological assessment may be used to assist in the determination of whether brain injury has in fact occurred and to specify likely changes in cognition and emotional function. In such assessment, the clinician chooses psychometric tests that he or she believes may be helpful for elucidating possible change in mental function; interviews the patient; and, in more comprehensive assessments, interviews family members and friends and investigates other sources of premorbid mental status (e.g., report cards, occupational achievements). Typically, a single neuropsychological test measures the integration of a number of cognitive functions such as working memory, resistance to distraction, sustained attention response inhibition, and processing speed. Psychometric testing utilizes normative data and cutoff scores that act as landmarks for judging level of impairment (e.g., the 16th percentile rank is typically used as a marker for mild impairment). However, estimating degree of change in a given individual following brain injury is more complex; it involves a sensitive estimation of comprehensive premorbid mental function and measurement of current function. In neuropsychological evaluation, diagnosis is derived from the consideration of both results on individual tests and the overall pattern of results.

Features of mental function and symptoms typically considered in neuropsychological evaluation are as follows: various forms of attention and ability to concentrate; various forms of working memory (e.g., verbal, spatial); executive function (e.g., planning, mental flexibility, inductive reasoning/concept formation, response inhibition, mental switching); mental processing speed; various forms of memory (verbal, visual, long term, short term); hand dexterity; ability to differentiate common odors; visual–spatial perception and construction; receptive and expressive language function; affect regulation; psychopathology, including posttraumatic stress disorder; apathy; initiation of activity and sustaining of motivation; social judgment; sensory abnormality; tendency to perseverate; ability to sustain mental energy; dizziness; and headache.

ABNORMAL BEHAVIOR RELATED TO MENTAL AND PHYSICAL HEALTH

People with intellectual and developmental disabilities are at higher risk than people in the general population of developing mental health problems associated with abnormal behavior. The reasons for this are not clearly understood. People who have intellectual or developmental disability and who have also been diagnosed with mental health or severe behavior problems are said to have a dual diagnosis. As noted, not all behaviors associated with mental health problems are abnormal, but some are. At times, it is challenging to distinguish abnormal behaviors associated with the disability from those associated with the mental health condition (Deb et al., 2001; Rush & Frances, 2002; Summers et al., 2005; Trestman, Sevarino, & Kelly, 2004).

There are many causes of, and contributing conditions for, abnormal behavior associated with mental and physical health problems. For the most part, these are the same for people with or without disabilities. These are described in the following two subsections about neurological disorders and mental health disorders.

Neurological Disorders

The serious neurological disorders described in this section can affect people with or without intellectual and/or developmental disability. In some cases, they can cause intellectual and/or developmental disability.

Neurobiological Deterioration Numerous disorders associated with unusual and abnormal behaviors are known, from studies of the brain using imaging techniques in vivo or investigation post mortem, to be the result of neurobiological deterioration in specific regions of the brain or other components of the nervous systems. There are many causes for such deterioration, both genetic and environmental (e.g., toxins, infections).

Alzheimer's Disease Alzheimer's disease occurs especially in older people. It is characterized by progressive brain malfunction and results in abnormal behaviors that typically change as the disease progresses. Problems are related to cognition (memory, language, and reasoning skills), ability to function (activities of daily living), and mental health (anxiety, delusions, and agitation). See Chapter 44 for further detail on this topic.

Aphasia Aphasia is a language disorder that results from damage to the temporal lobe or the higher region of the frontal lobe. It impairs comprehension and the structuring of words into language. In turn, this results in difficulties with reading, writing, and expression. Not being able to use language or to use it properly is considered an atypical behavior because these difficulties interfere with communication, which is a component of normal behavior.

Bell's Palsy Bell's palsy is a form of one-sided facial paralysis that often is temporary. It is caused by damage to the seventh (facial) cranial nerve, most commonly resulting from the herpes simplex virus, and has a number of neurobehavioral consequences. It may include significant facial distortion, twitching, drooling, an inability to close the eye, pain, a dulled sense of taste, hearing trouble, and heightened sensitivity to sound in one ear.

Cerebrovascular Disease Cerebrovascular disease affects the blood vessels of the brain and can cause aneurysms and strokes. An aneurysm—the swelling of a blood vessel, usually as a result of atherosclerosis and hypertension—can lead to stroke. Stroke (also called *cerebrovascular accident [CVA]*) can result when blood movement to a region of the brain is interrupted by a break in a blood vessel or a clot, which blocks a blood vessel or artery. Thus, cerebrovascular disease often results in an unequal distribution of deficits in cognitive function (e.g., impaired executive function, memory, or speech but relatively intact thinking, reasoning, and information processing), partial paralysis, and/or visual field defects. See Chapter 15 for more information.

Creutzfeldt-Jakob Disease Creutzfeldt-Jakob disease is a progressive neurological disorder that involves dementia, as well as difficulty walking and talking. See Chapter 7 for additional details on this and related prion disorders.

Epilepsy Epilepsy is a brain disorder characterized by seizures that are caused by signal malfunctions of nerve cell bundles or single neurons in the brain. This leads to unusual sensations, emotions, and behavior and sometimes convulsions, muscle spasms, and loss of consciousness. Epilepsy may be caused by brain damage, brain injury, or impaired brain development. It is crucial that seizures be controlled, as they may actually lead to impaired brain development and intellectual impairment. See Chapter 18 for further details on this topic.

Huntington Disease Huntington disease is a severe degenerative brain disorder that progressively impairs an individual's cognition, speech, and mobility. Primary symptoms may include depression, mood swings, memory lapses, clumsiness, involuntary twitching, and lack of coordination. Eventually, walking, speaking, and swallowing abilities deteriorate; concentration and short-term memory is decreased; and movements of the head, trunk, and limbs increase. Complications such as choking, infection, or heart failure are often the cause of death. As of 2007, there is no available cure. (*General sources:* APA, 2000; Beers & Berkow, 2005.)

Neuroimmunological Disorders The most common **neuroimmunological disorder** is multiple sclerosis (MS). MS is a progressive disease caused by the demyelination (loss of the myelin sheaths) of nerve fibers in the CNS. Early symptoms include numbness, strange sensations in the limbs or on one side of the face, muscle weakness, and vision impairments. These may progress to mood swings, loss of muscle control, defective reflexes, and difficulty urinating. There can be cycles where symptoms are either alleviated or are more severe (Beers & Berkow, 2005).

Neuromuscular Disorders **Neuromuscular disorders** include Guillain-Barré syndrome, Charcot-Marie-Tooth Disease, and the muscular dystrophies.

Guillain-Barré Syndrome Guillain-Barré syndrome is a rare disorder involving inflammation of the peripheral nerves. The body produces antibodies against them; this results in loss of the nerves' myelin sheath, which slows down the conduction of impulses through the nerves. It is characterized by rapid onset of weakness and often paralysis of the legs, arms, breathing muscles, and face.

Charcot-Marie-Tooth Disease Charcot-Marie-Tooth disease is an hereditary motor and sensory neuropathy that causes damage to the peripheral nerves—that is, the tracts of nerve fibers that connect the brain and spinal cord to muscles and sensory organs. The nerve damage can lead to weakness, wasting, and some loss of sensation in the extremities of the body (feet, lower legs, hands, and forearms).

Muscular Dystrophies The muscular dystrophies are a group of genetic disorders characterized by weakness and degeneration of the skeletal or voluntary muscles that control movement. The muscles of the heart and some other involuntary muscles also may be affected. A few forms involve other organs as well. The major forms of muscular dystrophy are Duchenne, Becker, limb-girdle, facioscapulohumeral, congenital, oculopharyngeal, distal, and Emery-Dreifuss. Duchenne muscular dystrophy is the most common form affecting children and is associated with intellectual and/or developmental disability. Myotonic dystrophy is the most common form affecting adults (*General source:* Beers & Berkow, 2005.)

Neurooncological Disorders **Neurooncological disorders** include neurofibromatosis, cerebroretinal angiomatosis, and brain tumors. Neurofibromatosis is an inherited condition classified by neurofibromas (fibrous extensions) of the nerves and skin and light-brown patches on the skin and in other tissues. There are two different types of neurofibromatosis. Neurofibromatosis type 1 is associated with peer problems, hyperactivity, emotional symptoms, conduct disorder, sleepwalking, and sleep terrors (Johnson et al., 2005). It is interesting to note that type 1 is approximately 150 times more frequent in people with autistic disorder (Mbarek et al., 1999). Neurofibromatosis type 2 is associated with tinnitus (ringing in the ears, which some individuals find intolerable) and balance problems resulting from vestibular nerve lesions (see Chapter 15 for additional details). Cerebroretinal angiomatosis, or von Hippel-Lindau disease, is a hereditary disease marked by tumorous growths in the retina and cerebellum and often on the spinal cord, pancreas, kidneys, and other organs. This may result in seizures and developmental disability (Friedrich, 2001). Brain tumors, regardless of the cause, can result in symptoms that include headaches, seizures, nausea and vomiting, vision or hearing problems, behavior and cognitive problems, motor problems, and balance problems. Spinal cord tumor symptoms include pain, sensory changes, and motor problems (National Institute of Neurological Disorders and Stroke, 2006).

Neurootological Disorders The best-known **neurootological disorder** is Meniere's disease. This is a disorder characterized by periodic episodes of dizziness, sensed fullness or pressure in the ear, progressive low-frequency hearing loss, tinnitus (ringing in the ear[s]), and acoustic neuroma (a benign tumor of the acoustic nerve) (Beers & Berkow, 2005).

Pain Disorders Pain disorders form a category of neurobiological disorders that includes migraines, sinus headaches, backaches, toothaches, sprains, strains, and central pain syndrome. Central pain syndrome results from CNS damage by stroke, brain and spinal cord injury, MS, reaction to medications, cancer, and any condition that can cause myelin-sheath destruction or other damage to the nerves or brain. Severe or prolonged pain can result in reactions that appear abnormal to observers who do not understand the distress that it causes (Beers & Berkow, 2005).

Parkinson's Disease **Parkinson's disease** is caused by damaged brain cells. Symptoms worsen over time and include tremors while at rest, weakness in a limb, a hand tremor, stooped posture, a shuffling gait that may cause falls, bradykinesia (difficulty making voluntary movements), rigidity from increased muscle tone, and decreased facial expression. In response, patients may develop progressive depression and anxiety (Clarke & Moore, 2004).

Pediatric Neurological Disorders Neurological disorders designated as "pediatric" manifest at an early age in contrast to others, such as Alzheimer's disease and Parkinson's disease, which manifest later in life. Common pediatric neurological disorders include dyslexia, a reading disorder (Shaywitz & Shaywitz, 2005), cerebral palsy, a motor nerve disorder caused by a permanent brain defect or brain damage at or shortly after birth (see Chapter 17), as well as epilepsy (see Chapter 18), brain tumors, and muscular dystrophies.

Mental Health Disorders

Abnormal behaviors that are unique to individuals cannot be classified. Those that are common to numbers of people, however, can be classified and are referred to as behavior disorders. Guidelines used by the majority of clinicians to classify disorders associated with abnormal behavior(s) are contained in the *DSM-IV-TR* (APA, 2000), and the *International Statistical Classification of Diseases and Related Health Problems, Tenth Revision* (ICD-10; World Health Organization [WHO], 1992). These and other sources, such as *The Merck Manual of Diagnosis and Therapy, Seventeenth Edition* (Beers & Berkow, 2005), list an exhaustive array of disorders that are associated with abnormal behavior. Next, some of the most common of these are described briefly.

Stress The term *stress* is common in everyday language, and everyone experiences it at some time or another. Stress is an internal process that occurs when a person is faced with a demand that is perceived to exceed the resources available to effectively respond to it and where failure to effectively deal with the demand has important and undesirable consequences. In other words, stress causes the effects that individuals feel when people or events in their environment are too demanding for them to cope with easily. These factors are called stressors.

Stress can result from many different things (e.g., infection, childbirth, psychological factors), and it may be temporary or long lasting. Individuals vary greatly in the degree to which they can tolerate stress, and most people tolerate one kind of stress more than other kinds. Some stress in life is usually seen as a good thing, because it motivates people to do new things and to adapt their behavior to the conditions that exist around them. The process of stress leads to arousal and selection of a coping response. If the coping response is effective, the coping response leads to relaxation.

However, too much stress at once or a great deal of stress that lasts over a long period of time can be harmful. If ineffective coping responses are used, arousal increases, resulting in strain. If stress is unresolved, it leads to burnout. Burnout, in turn, contributes to diagnosable conditions such as depression, anxiety disorders, and substance abuse (Franke, 1999). Harmful effects of stress include increased heart rate and blood pressure and other body changes associated with alarm reaction that can lead to exhaustion and suppression of the immune system. Mental health harm occurs when there is too much emotional arousal and too much demand to cope, such that behavior becomes irrational or unpredictable. In severe cases of stress, psychological and physiological resources are exhausted, and psychological disorganization (e.g., delusions, hallucinations) or personality disintegration can occur. Furthermore, ineffective coping may be a factor in a wide range of mental and physical illnesses with many different causes. See Chapter 8 for details about the changes that occur in the body when a person is subjected to stress.

Sometimes stress occurs suddenly and affects a person's life strongly. For example, the death of someone close, an accident, a divorce, a rape, war, or a natural disaster can have an enormous and sudden impact on a person. *Acute stress disorder* is a term used to describe the numb, detached feeling people have for a few days or a few weeks after the event. If these symptoms persist, and especially if the person continues to mentally reexperience the traumatic event, the term *posttraumatic stress disorder* is typically used.

Anxiety Disorders *Anxiety* is defined as a feeling of apprehension characterized by physical symptoms such as heart palpitations, sweating, and other unpleasant feelings that often are experienced in a stressful situation. It is a particular type of reaction to a stressor. All humans experience anxiety. Under normal circumstances, certain amounts of anxiety are adaptive. They create emotional, physiological, and behavioral responses to recognized external threats (e.g., an intruder, a runaway car) that make people evaluate situations and mobilize their resources to escape or to protect their loved ones or themselves. Without this response, people would not be able to free themselves from danger. However, too much anxiety or anxiety that lasts too long can result in an unpleasant emotional state in which a person evaluates a situation incorrectly and is unable to mobilize his or her resources. Most people have experienced this situation at one time or another—for example, when they are unable to move when scared suddenly or feel the dreadful feelings that arise in times of panic.

Anxiety can have both physical and psychological effects, especially if people are overwhelmed by events. People exhibit different degrees of anxiety; they also differ in their ability to cope with anxiety in general and with specific types of anxiety. Whatever the causes and despite individual differences, when the effects of anxiety are strong and/or prolonged, a person may experience irrational, unrealistic, and disabling fear. This can be characterized as an anxiety disorder. Anxiety disorders are very common. They affect approximately 19 million U.S. adults, but the prevalence of specific anxiety disorders varies considerably between countries and across cultures (Yates, 2005). These disorders vary in degree, but those that are more serious fill people's lives with overwhelming fear. Unlike the relatively mild, brief anxiety caused by a stressful event such as a job interview, making one's first public presentation, or a first date, anxiety disorders can grow progressively worse if not treated.

Anxiety disorders occur when the anxiety system is operating improperly. Numerous physiological and psychological factors contribute to this. For example, research with animals suggests that some anxiety disorders may be associated with the amygdala, a small part of the brain that controls the emotions of fear and anxiety and the development of emotional memories, which may function differently among individuals. Anxiety-related behavior might be influenced by a variation in a gene for a protein involved in transporting the neurotransmitter serotonin around the brain. The serotonin transporter gene has both long and short versions. The short version is less efficient in transport of serotonin (Lin & Madras, 2006).

It is also possible that maternal–infant misatunement in infancy is a cause of, or contributes to, anxiety disorders. This results in permanent dysregulation of the autonomic nervous system, which may contribute to anxiety disorders.

Anxiety may be elevated as a result of physical disorders, such as neurological disorders (e.g., brain trauma), infections, inner ear disorders, cardiovascular disorders (e.g., heart failure, arrhythmias), endocrine disorders (e.g., overactive adrenal or thyroid glands), low blood sugar, middle-ear problems, certain types of tumors, and respiratory disorders (e.g., asthma, chronic obstructive pulmonary disease). Anxiety may be caused by use of drugs, such as alcohol, stimulants, caffeine, cocaine, and many prescription drugs. Also, drug withdrawal is commonly associated with anxiety.

A careful history and physical examination are needed to accurately distinguish anxiety disorders from disorders with purely physical causes. The physical examination should involve a chest X ray, an electrocardiogram (ECG), and a full battery of blood tests—including tests of blood chemistry and thyroid function.

Anxiety disorders also must be distinguished from anxiety that occurs in certain other psychiatric disorders, because they respond to different specific treatments. Treatment should be directed at the primary causes rather than the secondary anxiety symptoms. If anxiety remains after a physical disorder is treated as effectively as possible, or after a causative substance is discontinued long enough for withdrawal symptoms to abate, treatment of anxiety symptoms with appropriate drugs, behavior therapy, or psychotherapy is indicated. (*General sources:* APA, 2000; Bailey & Andrews, 2003; Beers & Berkow, 2005.)

There are numerous types of anxiety disorders. Some of the most common are described next.

Phobias Phobias are fears that are persistent and disproportionate to the actual threat. Specific phobias include fear of things such as snakes, spiders, open water, heights, or being enclosed. Social phobias involve excessive fear of social situations such as feeling embarrassed or fearful in the presence of others. Agoraphobia describes the behavior of people who are fearful of leaving their safe environments. It literally means "fear of open spaces." Phobias differ between genders and age groups and are affected by genetic and environmental factors as well (Hettema et al., 2005).

Panic Disorder Panic disorder is characterized by recurring attacks of sudden, unexpected panic. These are commonly accompanied by feelings of losing control, losing one's mind, fear of dying, increased heart rate, sweating, shortness of breath, dizziness, expecting something terrible to happen, disorientation, or detachment from one's environment. Panic attacks differ from other types of anxiety in that they are of short duration and are very intense. Panic disorders stem primarily from emotional and cognitive factors, but they may be partly related to aspects of biological functioning, including genetics.

Generalized Anxiety Disorder Generalized anxiety disorder is an ongoing state of excessive worry or fear about numerous things. In some cases, this is related to another fear or anxiety, but in other cases it is not. It is characterized by chronic symptoms of physical and emotional arousal. People with generalized anxiety disorder are typically in a state of anxious apprehension, and they try to foresee and deal with future problems but feel unable to do so because they are highly anxious and feel out of control. Such apprehension overtakes logic, even logic that seems quite obvious, and leaves them feeling tense, upset, and discouraged. It sometimes leads to physical and emotional exhaustion.

Obsessive-Compulsive Disorder Obsessive compulsive disorder has two aspects that are very often related. First, obsessiveness is characterized by ideas, worries, and fears that are recurrent and unwanted. These are often accompanied by behaviors that the person feels compelled to do, even if he or she does not want to. Often, these behaviors are repetitive and ritualized. To other people, they may seem silly, weird, nasty, or even horrible, but to the person doing them they often allow an easing of mental tension and anxiety, even if it is only temporary. For example, some people have an obsessive idea that their hands should always be clean and fears that there may be germs on their hands. As a consequence, they wash their hands hundreds of times each day. Obsessive-compulsive disorder affects men, women, and children. Although prevalence rates have been thought to be as high as 2%–3% in adults, one U.S. study reported a 1 year prevalence rate of 0.084% for adults in outpatient settings (Fireman et al., 2001). One U.K. study (Heyman et al., 2003) found a prevalence rate of 0.25% for children ages 5–15.

Attention Deficit/Hyperactivity Disorder Attention deficit/hyperactivity disorder (ADHD) typically emerges in early childhood; its origin remains unclear. This chapter's synopsis is based on Chapter 19 and on the *DSM-IV-TR* (APA, 2000).

Etiological components, or causes, of ADHD may be related to poor attachment (emotional dysregulation in infancy secondary to infant–maternal misattunement), prenatal neurotoxic (teratogenic) effects on the fetus (polybromated diphenyl ethers used as flame retardants are a prime suspect; Mittelstoedt, 2006), genetic factors affecting brain development, or diet. The features of ADHD present along a continuum of degree of expression; at a certain point, the degree of expression may warrant clinical diagnosis in keeping with conventional guidelines. The *DSM-IV-TR*, which sets out the guidelines primarily used for diagnosing this disorder, presents a subtype conceptualization as follows: 1) Attention-Deficit/Hyperactivity Disorder, Combined Type; 2) Attention-Deficit/Hyperactivity Disorder, Predominantly Inattentive Type; and 3) Attention-Deficit/Hyperactivity Disorder, Predominantly Hyperactive-Impulsive Type (APA, 2000, p. 87). Features associated with ADHD include the following:

- Poor sustained attention
- Distractability and inadequate persistence with tasks
- A tendency to talk out of turn, with a blurting-out quality
- General social impulsiveness
- Poorly sustained motivation and initiative for activities
- Poor follow-through on instructions
- Impulsivity and seeking immediate gratification
- Poor organizational and planning skills
- Poor regulation of adaptive level of mental arousal
- Daily forgetfulness
- Compromise in working memory
- Compromise in verbal self-mediation (strategic self-talk that helps to control impulsivity)
- Poor metacognition (awareness and reflection on the quality of one's own learning and thinking style)

In individuals for whom hyperactivity is the predominant feature, there is obvious difficulty with sitting still. These individuals often are fidgety, restless, and excessively physically active with a driven quality; they may also be excessively talkative.

Problems associated with ADHD are quite variable, tending to some degree to be affected by the subjective interest or boredom level that an individual experiences in a given situation and whether the situation provides immediate reward. The symptoms associated with ADHD show some resemblance to mild frontal lobe injury. ADHD is also associated with elevated rates of socioemotional problems in some individuals. Problems are typically expressed most pronouncedly in the context of school. Typically, unaddressed ADHD has a significant negative impact on school performance.

Intervention for ADHD requires a multifaceted approach and might include school accommodations, family therapy, behavioral intervention, medications such as methylphenidate (Ritalin), and parental self-care strategies (e.g., strategies to prevent discipline problems) (see Chapter 19). Evaluating individuals for sensitivities to particular foods (e.g., food additives, refined sugars), allergies, and fatty acid deficiencies should be part of the plan (Schnoll, Burshteyn, & Cea-Aravena, 2003). (*General sources:* APA, 2000; Ben Amor et al., 2005; Biederman & Faraone, 2005; Brown et al., 2005; Bussing et al., 2006; Mittelstoedt, 2006; Pastor & Reuben, 2005; World Health Organization, 1992; Chapter 19.)

Depressive Disorders Unipolar (depressive) and bipolar (manic-depressive) disorders are the most common of a heterogeneous group of illnesses known as mood disorders or affective disorders. Sadness and joy are part of everyday life, but they can be distinguished from clinical depression and unusual elation. Transient depression ("the blues") may result from things such as getting a bad mark at school, or it may occur at certain times such as the premenstrual phase. People are diagnosed with depression when they feel overly sad without sufficient cause, and people are diagnosed with mania when they are considerably more elated than seems appropriate for the situation and to a degree that causes problems. Unipolar major depressive disorder is almost twice as common in women as it is in men; approximately 20% of women and 12% of men, at some point in their lives, experience the effects of this disorder to a degree that may require treatment (Beers & Berkow, 2005). Unipolar disorders typically, but not always, begin when people are in their 20s, 30s, or 40s.

Bipolar disorder, in which episodes of depression alternate with periods of mania, affects 4%–5% of the general population (Beers & Berkow, 2005). This affects the sexes equally, but depressive forms predominate in women whereas manic forms predominate in men. Four different subtypes of bipolar disorder are recognized: bipolar I, bipolar II, cyclothymia, and rapid cycling. Bipolar I is characterized by extreme high periods with relatively moderate forms of depression. Bipolar II is characterized by episodes of severe depression separated by periods of relatively modest mania. In cyclothymia, there are relative moderate episodes of mania and depression. In rapid cycling disorder, there may be up to four periods of great energy and periods of depression within a year. Bipolar disorder used to be diagnosed when people were in their 20s or 30s, but now it is being diagnosed in teens and even in younger children (Kluger & Song, 2002). The diagnosis of bipolar disorder is often confused with ADHD, although up to 15% of children thought to have ADHD may have bipolar disorder. Bipolar disorder tends to be diagnosed more often in higher socioeconomic classes. Genetic factors are thought to play a strong role in bipolar disorder. A child with one parent who has the disorder has a 10%–30% risk of developing the condition. Family, twin, and adoption studies indicate that bipolar disorder has a strong genetic basis, but the involvement of specific genes is not clear (Hayden & Nurnberger, 2006). Approximately 70% of those with bipolar disorder respond favorably to lithium therapy (Young & Newham, 2006).

Bipolar disorder, if not treated, has an approximately 15% risk of death by suicide (Shastry, 2005). One meta-analysis has indicated that the lifetime risk of suicide attempts are substantially higher in bipolar II disorder than in unipolar disorder (Rihmer & Pestality, 1999). Suicide, which is most common in young and elderly men who do not have good social support, tends to occur within 4–5 years of the first clinical episode. (*General sources:* APA, 2000; Beers & Berkow, 2005; Kluger & Song, 2002; Medline Plus Health Information, 2006.)

Eating Disorders Eating disorders are characterized by severe disturbances in eating behavior, and many cases typically first appear in mid-adolescence (Williamson, Martin & Stewart, 2004). Anorexia nervosa, bulimia nervosa, and binge-eating disorder are the most commonly known eating disorders. Pica and certain other conditions related to eating disturbances are lesser known. Each topic is discussed next.

Anorexia Nervosa, Bulimia Nervosa, and Binge-Eating Disorder Eating disorders are commonly divided into three types: anorexia nervosa, bulimia nervosa, and binge-eating disorder. Approximately 90% of individuals affected by these eating disorders are females.

Anorexia nervosa can be a severe, life-threatening disorder in which an individual refuses to maintain a normal weight, is intensely afraid of gaining weight, and exhibits a significant distortion of the perception of the shape or size of the body as well as dissatisfaction with body shape and size. It affects 0.5%–2% of the general population (Beers & Berkow, 2005).

Bulimia nervosa can also be a life-threatening disorder as well. It is characterized by recurrent episodes of binge eating following by self-induced vomiting and other purging methods such as excessive use of laxatives and/or diuretics, excessive exercise, and fasting in an attempt to avoid weight gain. The lifetime prevalence is 3%, and the ratio of female to male patients ranges from 10:1 to 20:1 (Mehler, 2003).

Binge-eating disorder is a newly recognized life threatening disorder characterized by recurrent episodes of compulsive overeating or binge eating. It affects approximately 2% of the population and occurs in approximately 30% of people participating in medically supervised weight loss programs. In this disorder, the purging in an attempt to prevent weight gain characteristic of bulimia nervosa is absent (Weight-Control Information Network, 2004). Binge-eating leads to obesity, a cause of premature death in many people, and predisposes individuals to anorexia and bulimia. A host of medical complications can accompany anorexia and bulimia nervosa. If untreated, the disorder can become life threatening. Approximately 10% of affected individuals succumb to death as the result of starvation, cardiac arrest, or suicide. Individuals who experience an eating disorder may be unaware that they have a problem. If a serious eating disorder is suspected, friends or loved ones should not hesitate to ask for advice about how to help. Treatment for an eating disorder should be comprehensive and involve a variety of approaches and experts, including an internist, a nutritionist, an individual psychotherapist, and a family therapist. Much research is being done in the field of eating disorders. Although various psychological, social, and physiological factors have been found to be associated with different disorders, it is proving difficult to determine which are causes and which are consequences (Klein & Walsh, 2004; Patrick, 2002). (*General sources:* Beers & Berkow, 2005; Mehler, 2003; National Eating Disorders Association, 2002; Weight-Control Information Network, 2004.)

Pica Pica is an eating disorder that may have benign or life-threatening consequences. The word *pica* comes from the Latin word meaning "magpie," a bird of indiscriminate appetite. Pica is typically defined as the persistent eating of nonnutritive substances for a period of at least 1 month at an age in which this behavior is developmentally inappropriate (e.g., beyond the age of 18–24 months). The definition of the disorders sometimes includes the mouthing of nonnutritive substances. People with pica ingest substances ranging from clay, dirt, and pebbles to paint chips, vinyl gloves, light bulbs, needles and thread, and burnt matches (Ellis & Schnoes, 2005). Eating such items sometimes results in serious health problems such as lead poisoning, constipation, intestinal obstruction or perforation, damage to teeth and gums, and infections.

Pica is the most common eating disorder in people with intellectual and/or developmental disabilities, especially autism. Pica also can be a problem in some pregnant women and in some people with epilepsy. It can occur as the result of brain injury. It also can be associated with deficiencies of specific nutrients, such as iron or zinc, malnutrition, dieting, parental neglect, and mental health conditions such as obsessive-compulsive disorder and schizophrenia (Ellis & Schnoes, 2005). Pica can be managed by a number of different approaches depending on the cause. For example, pica secondary to iron deficiency can remit after iron therapy. Other approaches include education about what is acceptable or not acceptable to eat, behavioral intervention to teach a person how to eat more appropriately, prevention of access to nonfood items (e.g., by using safety-locks and high shelving and keeping household chemicals and medications out of reach), medication, as well as screening for and treatment of life-threatening complications of pica. (*General sources:* Ellis & Schnoes, 2005; Gavin & Homeier, 2004; McAdam et al., 2004.)

Other Conditions Related to Eating Disturbances Prader-Willi syndrome is a developmental disability in which an eating disorder resulting from the genetic abnormality is part of the syndrome. In this syndrome, the hypothalamus of the brain is affected; this abnormality results in a constant feeling of hunger that can lead to excessive eating and morbid obesity. A high rate of diabetes is associated with this disorder (see Chapter 15 for further details). Psychosocial dwarfism (sometimes called Psychosocial Short Stature, or PSS) is an eating disorder that is considered to be a reactive attachment disorder, a consequence of child abuse and neglect. This disorder involves food hoarding, binge eating, and bizarre behavior such as eating out of garbage cans (Sirotnak, 2006). Many other conditions, such as depression and anxiety disorders, may be associated with less striking eating problems. (*General sources:* APA, 2000; Beers & Berkow, 2005; National Eating Disorders Association, 2002.)

Personality Disorders Personality is a unique pattern of traits and behaviors that each person develops to interpret and respond to his or her surroundings. Well-functioning people have personalities that allow them to adapt to and cope with the ever-changing conditions, limitations, and opportunities of life. People who are said to have personality disorders have some inflexible, maladaptive personality traits and behaviors that prevent adequate functioning in some aspects of their lives. Personality disorders are usually evident from adolescence. People with personality disorders are often unaware of the social and personal problems they have created, even when they contribute to the deterioration of relationships with others. Personality disorders may affect as many as 13%–14% of the population, including people with intellectual and developmental disabilities (see also Chapters 15 and 42). Research findings and clinical descriptions are available in the following sources; these describe in detail the relationship between specific personality disorders and disability (APA, 2000; Beers & Berkow, 2005; Mayo Foundation for Medical Education and Research, 2004; National Mental Health Association, n.d.). Individuals with personality disorders may show symptoms such as depression or anxiety, or they may show maladaptive behavior such as paranoia, hypochondria, violence, vengefulness, self-defeating or self-destructive behaviors (e.g., alcohol or drug abuse), erratic mood, or rigidness. Behaviors of this type, if carried over into parenthood, can contribute to severe mental health and emotional problems for children. Psychotherapy for personality disorders meets with some success. Selective serotonin reuptake inhibitors (SSRIs) and mood stabilizers can also be effective in the treatment of personality disorders.

Terminology sometimes applied to personality disorders requires clarification. Two terms that are often used to describe abnormal behavior are *neurosis* and *psychosis.* Neurosis is a term that is not included in the *DSM-IV-TR* (APA, 2000) and has diminished in usage. It describes abnormal behavior that is emotionally painful and unwelcome but that does not grossly violate behavioral norms or interfere unduly with thinking, perception, and reality testing. People experiencing neurosis are in distress, but they do not wish to be and realize that they should not be.

Conversely, psychosis is related to more obvious behavior that does violate behavioral norms to a strong degree. It can affect thinking, perception, and reality testing, and it sometimes affects motor functions such as speaking or movement. *Psychosis* is a term that is often used when describing one of several severe mental health disorders known as schizophrenia.

According to the DSM-IV-TR (APA, 2000), there are three broad categories of personality disorders—odd/eccentric, dramatic/erratic, and anxious/inhibited—which are further broken into distinct types.

Odd/Eccentric One disorder in the odd/eccentric personality category is paranoid personality disorder. Individuals with this disorder are suspicious of the intentions of others. They tend to be hypervigilant and easily come to believe that others do not like them, or mean to exploit or manipulate them. They are mistrusting and reluctant to confide in others. They often work independently and are generally focused and driven.

Individuals with schizoid personality disorder are introverted, self-absorbed, and emotionally distant or blunted. They prefer to be alone and do not mix well with others socially. They often seek work that allows them to be isolated. Close relationships are not sought. Generally, they show little interest in any form of interpersonal intimacy. They may be anxious or fearful around others.

Individuals with schizotypal personality disorder appear similar in many ways to individuals who have schizophrenia. They may display very odd beliefs, peculiar ways of thinking that are not logical or rational, and mild delusional or paranoid tendencies. It is not unusual for individuals with this personality disorder to dress very peculiarly. They tend to be socially isolated and lacking in close relationships. People with schizotypal personalities may have a mild variant of schizophrenia (Beers & Berkow, 2005).

Dramatic/Erratic One variant of the dramatic/erratic category is antisocial personality (previously psychopathic or sociopathic) disorder. In developed countries, this condition mostly occurs in males. People with this personality disorder are intentionally insensitive and tend to exploit others. They do not anticipate the repercussions of their actions and often believe that they are justified in their destructive behavior. This disorder is associated with: lack of empathy and interpersonal insensitivity; violent and other forms of antisocial behavior; impulsiveness; attention problems; excessive self-interest and self-serving goals; and lack of insight, remorse, and guilt. Their harmful actions may be obviously criminal or may be "white collar" crimes.

Borderline / Histrionic / Narcissistic Personality Disorders Individuals with borderline personality disorder are unstable in their self-image, mood, behavior, and relationships. In severe cases, they may experience psychotic episodes of paranoia and hallucination. Individuals with borderline personality disorder experience depression, misery, regular failure in their pursuits, self-destructive behavior, feelings of emptiness, fear of abandonment, feelings of entitlement, severe lack of insight, poor reality checking, and easily elicited rage responses. These individuals have no tolerance for constructive criticism. As in all personality disorders, there is also a particular cognitive style associated with borderline personality disorder.

Individuals with histrionic personality disorder (formerly called hysterical personality disorder) are vain, melodramatic attention seekers. Their behaviors often stem from a desire for caring and support. They express emotions superficially and immaturely, which often results in sympathetic or erotic attention from others and fleeting superficial relationships. Affected individuals are often seductive while being sexually unfulfilled or inhibited.

Individuals with narcissistic personality disorder have exaggerated feelings of superiority and entitlement. They are often under the impression that others are envious and can be exploited. They require admiration and are intolerant of criticism. Failure or disappointment results in anger and bouts of depression. Their relationships tend to be shallow and exploitive. They tend to feel empty, unfulfilled, and somewhat lacking in empathy. Often their behaviors are ultimately self-defeating. They have minimal tolerance for criticism and are quick to disassociate themselves from others for minor shortcomings. Their insight into these problems is limited.

Anxious/Inhibited Avoidant personality disorder is the first of the anxious/inhibited category. Individuals with this personality disorder are desperate to avoid rejection and are reluctant to embark on new relationships or experiences for fear that they may fail or be disappointed. Any sign of rejection leads to further withdrawal. People with avoidant personality recognize their desire for care and understanding and are therefore distraught by their difficulties in social interactions and relationships.

Individuals with dependent personality disorder relinquish control in major areas of their lives, then give priority to the needs of those whom they have come to depend upon. They are insecure and feel incapable of caring for themselves and making decisions. Their behavior stems both from a belief that others are more competent, as well as from a fear of offending others with their opinions or perceived demands. Dependency may be masked by other more blatant behavior problems such as histrionic or borderline behaviors.

Individuals with obsessive-compulsive personality disorder develop and abide by structured routines, which they are averse to changing. Their personalities tend to have excessive rigidity. They are self-reliant and have difficulty relinquishing control of their environment and their emotions; this makes spontaneity and relationships a challenge. They are diligent and determined but may lose focus on a task or become anxious and indecisive as they analyze all aspects and consequences of their decisions. Some people who have obsessive-compulsive personalities can apply their perfectionism to advantage, in ways such as excelling at academic study (Beers & Berkow, 2005).

Psychosexual Disorders There is tremendous variation in sexual practices, and attitudes toward those practices, among different cultures of the world. In addition, norms change over time. For example, at the beginning of the 21st century, it seems almost curious to think that masturbation (practiced by approximately 92% of males and 67% of females) was once perceived by Western society as a perversion and something that might cause mental illness (Kinsey, Pomeroy, & Martin, 1948/1998; Kinsey et al., 1953/1998; Langstrom & Hanson, 2006). Today, masturbation is considered a normal sexual practice unless it is done publicly, impairs partner relations, or is done compulsively to the point of distress.

The most common form of psychosexual disorder observed by practitioners is sexual dysfunction. Three other disorder classifications that are common are difficulties balancing sexual activities with other life activities ("sex addiction"), gender identity disorders (identifying with the opposite sex and discomfort with one's biological sex), and paraphilias (*DSM-IV-TR* paraphilias: **fetishism, transvestic fetishism, voyeurism,** exhibitionism, **sexual sadism, sexual masochism, pedophilia,** and frotteurism [rubbing against a nonconsenting person]). Among these, the behaviors that are associated with forms of sexual abuse are most troublesome. Pedophilia (adult preference for a child as a sexual partner), incest (sexual relations between family members), and rape (sexual activity that occurs under threat of coercion or force) are all considered very serious and highly undesirable psychosexual behaviors. Treatments for paraphilias—both serious and less serious—that combine cognitive and behavioral techniques (e.g., aversion therapy, social skills training, and cognitive restructuring) have met with some success. Success has been limited, however, because the reasons for the behaviors in the first place are frequently deeply rooted in the person's personality, because a desire for change is often reluctant or only in response to having been arrested or convicted of a crime, and because the degree to which such methods should be used has been the subject of some controversy. A great deal of work still needs to be done to balance effective treatment methods, public protection, moral and ethical practice, and individual rights.

Since 1973, the APA has not classed homosexuality, both male and female, as a disorder. Rather, it is considered to be a "nonpsychopathological sexual variant." Reports of the prevalence of homosexuality differ from 1%–10% of the population, and reports of bisexual or occasional same-sex behavior also vary widely but appear to be fairly common in most developed countries. On the basis of national data from the United States, the United Kingdom, and France, Sell, Wells, and Wypij (1995) noted that 4.5%–10.7% of males and 2.1%–3.6% of females reported having had sexual contact with another person of the same sex within the past 5 years and that 16.3%–20.8% of males and 8.6%–11.7% of females reported either homosexual behavior or homosexual attraction since age 15.

Sexual orientation is not a choice for many people. It is the result of one or sometimes numerous interrelated factors, both biological and environmental, that lead to a stable inclination for a person to have sexual partners of either the same sex (homosexuality) or of the opposite sex (heterosexuality). Sexual orientation varies by degree, however. For some people this is not strongly pronounced. Human beings have the capacity for a wide variety of sexual responses, some of which change over the adult lifespan in response to changing attitudes and opportunities. Since the 1980s, there has been increasing acceptance of same-sex practices in North America, Europe, Australia, and elsewhere. (*General sources:* APA, 2000; Beers & Berkow, 2005.)

Schizophrenia Schizophrenia is among the top 10 disabilities worldwide in terms of prevalence. It affects approximately 1 in 100 people worldwide. This prevalence of about 1% makes schizophrenia more common than Alzheimer's disease or MS worldwide (Beers & Berkow, 2005). Schizophrenia affects men and women almost equally, although the age of onset is younger in men (Murray et al., 2002): 18 to 25 years in men and 26 to 45 years in women. Onset in childhood, early adolescence, or late life is not uncommon, though. At one time, schizophrenia was thought to be progressive, but there is no compelling evidence that this is the case. It is often a lifelong condition, however, and poses enormous emotional, social, and financial burdens to individuals and their families (Brady & McCain, 2004).

The *DSM IV-TR* (APA, 2000) and *ICD-10* (WHO, 1992) specify criteria that need to be met for its diagnosis. According to the *DSM IV-TR*, there are several subtypes of schizophrenia:

- Paranoid schizophrenia: Characterized by suspicion and grand schemes of persecution; hallucinations, and more frequently delusions, are prominent and common
- Disorganized schizophrenia (*DSM-IV-TR*) or hebephrenic schizophrenia (*ICD-10*): Characterized by verbal incoherence and moods and emotions that are not appropriate to the situation; hallucinations are not usually present
- Catatonic schizophrenia: Characterized by withdrawal, negative affect, isolation, and psychomotor disturbance
- Residual schizophrenia: Characterized by lack of motivation and interest in day-to-day living
- Schizoaffective disorder: Characterized by symptoms of schizophrenia as well as mood disorder (e.g., major depression, bipolar mania, mixed mania)
- Undifferentiated schizophrenia: Meeting the general diagnostic criteria for schizophrenia

To better understand schizophrenia, the concept of clusters of symptoms is often used. Symptom patterns, or syndromes, include positive-syndrome schizophrenia, in which something has been added to the typical pattern of behavior (e.g., delusions, heightened perceptions, excessive or unusual movements, hallucinations, emotional turmoil, angry speech) and negative-syndrome schizophrenia, in which something is lacking from the typical pattern of behavior (e.g., poverty of speech, blunted or flat emotional expression, unresponsiveness to the environment) (Andreasen & Olson, 1982; Tosato & Dazzan, 2005). These two patterns are also sometimes known as Type I and Type II schizophrenia. Within the behavior of individuals, however, there is considerable overlap of these patterns, and most people with schizophrenia cannot be described exclusively by any one type.

Trying to understand the causes of schizophrenia has been the subject of considerable study. Genetic factors are known to be involved in many cases of schizophrenia. Damaging family life, excessive anxiety, and sociocultural stress may contribute to the condition. It may occur secondary to brain injury, dementia, or substance abuse. In many cases, schizophrenia is associated with anomalous neural migration when the brain is first developing. A developmental disorder known as 22q11.2 deletion syndrome (previously known as CATCH 22), resulting from abnormalities of chromosome 22q11.2, is associated with symptoms of schizophrenia (see Chapter 15 for more information about this syndrome). In fact, 22q11.2 deletion syndrome is the highest known risk factor for schizophrenia, and some people with schizophrenia have been found to have this disorder (Bassett et al., 2002). Maternal exposure to famine, influenza in the second trimester of pregnancy, and Rh incompatibility in a second or subsequent pregnancy also are associated with an increased risk of schizophrenia in offspring. Overall, however, the cause of schizophrenia is thought to be complex and multifactorial (Verdoux & Cougnard, 2006). The onset, remission, and recurrence of symptoms of this disorder are thought to result from interaction between vulnerabilities and environmental stressors. Environmental stressors include stressful life events such as ending a relationship.

With schizophrenia, the risk of violent behavior is relatively modest—the level of risk is much less than with substance abuse, for example. At times, people with schizophrenia go to shelters or hospital emergency departments and show somewhat violent behavior when they actually want food, shelter, or medical or psychiatric care.

Schizophrenia is associated with an approximate 10% risk of suicide. Individuals who have paranoid forms with late onset and good premorbid functioning—the very people with the best prognosis for recovery—are also at the greatest risk for suicide (Fenton et al., 1997; Pompili et al., 2005). The reason for this association is not known, but this information helps clinicians to identify affected individuals who are at the highest risk for suicide. (*General sources:* Andreasen & Olson, 1982; APA, 2000; Beers & Berkow, 2005; Maguire, 2002.)

Side Effects of Medication Many medications, including those used to treat mental health disorders, have side effects that affect thinking and emotional control. Side effects may include depression, emotional blunting, obsessiveness, headache, muscular rigidity, cognitive diminishment, reduced creativity, convulsions, impact on libido, diminished mental flexibility, and symptoms associated with psychosis. Mood stabilizers and antidepressant drugs have a history of creating adverse side effects. Side effects of SSRIs, a second-generation family of antidepressants, are reported to be less severe than those of tricyclic antidepressants and monoamine oxidase inhibitors. However, there is some evidence for an increased risk of suicide associated with certain SSRIs in children and adolescents (Whittington, Kendall, & Pilling, 2005) and possibly also in the elderly (Juurlink et al., 2006)—facts that must continue to be made public. For most medications, side effects are more mild than severe and sometimes even go away, so many people choose to continue taking them. Many medications have the potential of interacting with alcohol; hence, the practice of drinking while taking psychotropic medications should be discouraged. Addressing side effects involves understanding whether they are "normal" or the result of an overdose and distinguishing them from serious allergic responses that require immediate intervention. Information about harmful side effects and potential drug interactions are available from pharmacies that supply the medications.

People with intellectual and developmental disabilities often do not tolerate psychotropic medications as well as people in the general population (Bradley et al., 2002). Aging also affects the way one responds to such medicines. One example of a medication with very severe side effects in some people is phenytoin. This drug is commonly used to control seizures. Research has indicated that it should not be used in older people with Down syndrome (Tsiouris et al., 2002). Harmful effects of this drug in older people with Down syndrome include abrupt loss of adaptive daily living skills, drop in performance during cognitive retesting, lethargy, dysarthria, sedation/drowsiness, dizziness, unsteadiness, ataxic gait with muscle hypotonia, bending to one side or the other (e.g., to the right if left-handed), and loss of locomotion. (*General sources:* Beers & Berkow, 2005; Behavioral Health of Greenville, n.d.; Cain et al., 2006; Depression Learning Path, 2006; National Institute of Mental Health [NIMH], 2006; Chapter 9.)

Sleep Disorders Sleep is considered to be a normal, essential behavior, although the functions of sleeping remain largely mysterious. Sleep disorders, therefore, are considered to be forms of abnormal behavior (Sleep Home Pages, n.d.). Sleep disorders include sleep apnea (an interruption or cessation of breathing during sleep), insomnia (inability to sleep), narcolepsy (a disorder with bouts of sleepiness and drowsiness), and restless leg syndrome (a disorder characterized by an irresistible urge to move the legs especially when lying down). These disorders can vary considerably in both frequency of occurrence and intensity. They usually interfere with daily functioning and with the enjoyment of life to some degree, although such interference varies considerably from very mild to severe. Sleep deprivation studies repeatedly show a variable (negative) impact on mood, cognitive performance, learning, behavior, and motor function (Durmer & Dinges, 2005). Sleep disorders in young people affect not only their functions and behaviors but also those of their families and particularly their mothers, who may already suffer from increased levels of stress and poorer mental health. Because people with special needs are reported to have more frequent and persistent sleep problems than their unaffected peers, it is particularly important that they receive appropriate intervention for their sleep problems (Wiggs & France, 2000). (*General sources:* Beers & Berkow, 2005; Sleep Home Pages, n.d.; Chapter 10.)

Somatoform Disorder *Somatoform disorder* is a relatively new term for what is often called psychosomatic disorder. Somatoform disorder is actually a group of psychiatric disorders characterized by physical symptoms that suggest, but are not fully explained by, a physical disorder and that cause significant distress or interfere with social, occupational, or other functioning. To be considered as a somatoform disorder, neither the physical symptoms nor their severity and duration are obviously explained by an underlying physical condition. Hypochondriasis and pain disorder are two of a number of disorders in the somatoform category. (*General sources:* APA, 2000; Beers & Berkow, 2005.)

Substance Abuse Use of alcohol and other drugs, both legal and illegal, brings about effects that many people consider to be positive. These include such feelings as freedom from stress and anxiety, mood elevation, euphoria, enhanced sensory perception, and sense of increased capacity.

However, excessive use of alcohol and drugs can affect people's lives negatively in many ways. When people become dependent on habitual or excessive use, their overall behavior pattern very often becomes more destructive than constructive. When this occurs, the term *substance abuse* is typically used to describe their overreliance on alcohol or other drugs. Dependence is associated with tolerance, whereby an individual must increase the amount of a drug to maintain its original effect and/or whereby the body begins to rely on the substance to the point where symptoms of withdrawal result if it is absent.

There are many harmful effects on individuals resulting from the overuse of alcohol and other drugs. Over time, alcohol can damage the liver and other organs. Chronic use of some street drugs may cause brain damage or permanent changes that affect emotion and cognition. Single use of powerful hallucinogenic drugs, such as lysergic acid diethylamide (LSD) or psilocybin, has the potential to cause emotional and/or cognitive alterations that are permanent and harmful.

Substance abuse is difficult to treat not only because of the dependence but also because its effects are self-reinforcing for many people. Withdrawal from alcohol or drugs, especially in cases of serious dependence, should be treated by an expert because it can result in strong physical and emotional reactions such as loss of appetite, difficulty sleeping, mental confusion, hallucinations, fear, anxiety, body tremors, fever, increased heart rate, perspiration, stomach pain, and chest pain. Referrals for treatment at a substance abuse facility or a doctor with appropriate experience should be made through one's family physician or by another appropriate means, such as the Substance Abuse Facility Locator (Substance Abuse and Mental Health Services Administration, 2006). The literature is sparse about the topic of substance abuse in people with intellectual disabilities (Clarke & Wilson, 1999), but a recent survey suggests that this issue, unfortunately, is alarmingly prevalent (Joszvai et al., in press). (*General sources:* Glanze, 1992; Kalivas, 2004; Chapter 14.)

Suicidal Behavior and Suicide Suicidal behavior includes attempts, completed suicide, and suicide gestures, which are actions that could be interpreted as suicidal even if they are unlikely to lead to completion. In the United States, drug overdose is the most common method of attempted suicide, and firearm use is the most common in completed suicide (National Strategy for Suicide Prevention, 2004). Alcohol use, addiction, and intoxication are implicated in many suicides and suicide attempts.

Risk for suicidal behavior is affected by age and sex and also by sociocultural factors, both within a country and by country. Suicide comprises 10% of deaths among people ages 25 to 34 years, comprises 30% of deaths among university students, and is the second highest cause of adolescent death (Beers & Berkow, 2005). Men are more likely to die as the result of a suicide attempt, but women attempt suicide three times more frequently. Among some Native American tribes and Alaskan natives, the suicide rate is now several times the national average (Beers & Berkow, 2005; Medline Plus Health Information, 2006).

Some conditions—such as behavioral abnormalities, social issues, physical disabilities, and mental disorders (especially depression)—have a somewhat higher association with suicidal behavior than others. Although the majority of people with depression do not die by suicide, approximately 60% of people who commit suicide have been found to have a mood disorder (major depression, bipolar disorder, dysthymia) (National Strategy for Suicide Prevention, 2004). People with epilepsy have a five-fold increased risk of suicide compared to the general population, and those with temporal lobe epilepsy have a twenty-five-fold increased risk (Mazza et al., 2004). Depression is common in children and adolescents with epilepsy, but a connection with epilepsy and suicide is often overlooked. One study suggests that the cause of depression in such individuals is related to a number of factors, including seizure type, high seizure frequency, less than optimal pharmacological management, and lack of occupational and social activity (Grabowska-Grzyb et al., 2006). Identification and treatment of depression need to be high priorities in people with epilepsy.

Recognizing the risk of suicide and respecting the seriousness of suicide attempts are major factors in its prevention. Physicians and other professionals have a responsibility to detect depression and thoughts or actions that might lead to suicidal behavior and to respond to it in a serious and constructive way. When a person threatens suicide, for example, he or she needs to be encouraged to communicate openly by having others listen to and understand the problem, remind him or her of the many people who care, and repeatedly use the person's name to acknowledge him or her as an individual. In addition, support needs to be offered and provided to alleviate immediate problems. In cases of suicide attempts, after receiving any necessary emergency medical aid (e.g., stomach pumping, bandaging), patients require psychiatric assessment and treatment either through a psychiatrist or a professional trained in suicide management. Follow-up is crucial, because 20% individuals who attempt suicide try again within 1 year, and 10% eventually complete it (Beers & Berkow, 2005).

ABNORMAL BEHAVIOR IN THE SCHOOL SYSTEM

Abnormal behavior in the school system includes internalizing behaviors (e.g., anxiety or depression, withdrawal, somatic complaints) and externalizing behaviors (e.g., attention problems, aggressive or delinquent behavior, substance abuse and other rule breaking actions) (McFarlane et al., 2003; Molcho, Harel, & Dina, 2004). Sleep disorders may result in impaired school behavior (Urschitz et al., 2004). Bullying and being bullied are also considered to be abnormal behavior (Juvonen, Graham & Schuster, 2003; Mishna, 2003).

There is increasing evidence that nutritional problems may contribute to abnormal behaviors in certain cases. For example, as explained previously, sensitivities to a variety of food substances may affect the behavior of some people with ADHD (Breakey, 1997; Schnoll et al., 2003). Irritability in some people can be triggered by low blood sugar (Merbis et al., 1996); it can result from having no breakfast or, in the case of a person with diabetes, from too much insulin. In people with celiac disease (affecting as many as 1 in 100 Caucasians and up to 10 times more people with Down syndrome; see Chapter 10), sensitivity to gluten (a protein found in wheat, rye, and other grains) is associated with various neurological and psychiatric disorders including cerebellar ataxia (a movement disorder), peripheral neuropathy, epilepsy, dementia, and depression (Bushara, 2005). Individuals with pervasive developmental disorders (PDDs) including autism show a myriad of behavioral abnormalities. It has been proposed that people with autism may benefit not only from behavioral modification and structured education but also from dietary modification, including removal of milk and other casein dairy products, wheat and other gluten sources, sugar, chocolate, preservatives, and food coloring (Kidd, 2003).

Students who exhibit any of a wide range of behavior disorders or mental health problems are sometimes classified by the school system as having serious emotional disorder (SED) or neurobiological brain disorder (NBD) (Substance Abuse and Mental Health Services Administration, 1996). These terms are not mutually exclusive. *SED* refers to problems resulting from sociological and/or environmental factors (e.g., abuse; neglect; crime; poverty; emotional, neurotic, or life-adjustment issues). This term is among the 13 disability categories specified by the Individuals with Disabilities Education Improvement Act of 2004 (PL 108-446; see Chapter 31 for more information). SEDs can affect students with or without intellectual disabilities. *NBD* refers to a group of brain disorders that cause disturbance in thinking, feeling, or relating and that result in a reduced capacity for coping with the ordinary demands of life. This term originated in the scientific community (Peschel et al., 1992). NBDs can affect individuals of any age and can occur in any family. As already discussed in this chapter, NBDs include syndromes and disorders resulting in intellectual or developmental disability associated with characteristic behaviors such as Down syndrome and fragile X syndrome. They also include schizophrenia, schizoaffective disorder, bipolar disorder, unipolar major depression, obsessive-compulsive disorder, panic disorder, borderline personality disorder, autism or another PDD, Tourette syndrome, ADHD (with or without hyperactivity), and brain damage. A U.S. National Health Interview Survey found that an estimated 8% of children 3–17 years of age had a learning disability and that an estimated 6% of children had ADHD (Dey & Bloom, 2005; see also Chapter 19).

The prevalence of SEDs varies markedly from one school to another, and in some schools it may far exceed that for NBDs. Challenging behaviors in the classroom are thus an enormous problem. They affect the ability of the teacher to maintain discipline and to teach and the abilities of students to be receptive and to learn. Therefore, it is important for parents and teachers to ask what is causing a child's behavior and how may this be most effectively addressed.

In addition to identifying and addressing primary causes of challenging behavior, the value of encouraging students to take part in pleasurable extracurricular activities at the school (e.g., sports; music; drama; field trips to museums and science centers) and extracurricular activities in the community (e.g., Boy Scouts, Girl Guides, 4-H clubs, dancing lessons, music lessons) cannot be overestimated. Participation in such activities promotes healthy development. Furthermore, the bonding that takes place among students during pleasurable extracurricular school activities creates peer pressure for good behavior in the classroom that is independent of influence from teacher or parent.

For further information about challenging behavior and the school system, see the American Academy of Child and Adolescent Psychiatry's web site (http://www.aacap.org), Substance Abuse and Mental Health Services Administration (2006), and Chapters 19 and 42. For strategies on classroom management, see Brylewski and Duggan (2004); Keogh (2003); Koegel and Koegel (2005); Kristal (2005); Mather and Goldstein (2001); and Sigafoos, Arthur, and O'Reilly (2003).

SEEKING HELP

Addressing atypical behavior involves various areas: recognizing when behavior is abnormal, recognizing when abnormal behavior is a form of communication, seeking help and an accurate diagnosis from a professional, and understanding types of treatment.

Recognizing When Behavior Is Abnormal

This chapter has described a wide variety of abnormal behaviors. Abnormal behavior affects people with or without intellectual or developmental disabilities, although it is more common in the former. Support workers, family members, teachers, friends, and neighbors are often the first to notice changes in behavior that may signify abnormal behavior. Help from such people is invaluable because they are familiar with the individual's usual behavior patterns. If a diagnosis is made, however, it should be done by a trained professional.

Parents are often the first to notice a problem in children. Observations of teachers and other family members also may be important. Signs of mental health problems in children include decreased academic performance; anxiety and worry; refusal to go to school; hyperactivity; persistent nightmares; persistent disobedience and aggression; opposition to authority; and frequent, unexplainable temper tantrums. Signs of potential problems in adolescents include change in school performance; abuse of alcohol or drugs; inability to cope with problems and daily activities; marked changes in sleeping and/or eating habits; complaints of physical ailments; violation of the rights of others; opposition to authority; theft or vandalism; intense fear of becoming obese; and depression as revealed by sustained, negative mood and attitude and often accompanied by poor appetite, difficulty sleeping, thoughts of death, and frequent outbursts of anger. Signs of potential problems in adults may include weight change, lethargy, depression, mood changes, and changes in daily living skills. (Refer to Chapter 44 for information about dementia development in adults.)

Recognizing When Abnormal Behavior is a Form of Communication

For some people with intellectual or developmental disabilities, especially those who have limited formal methods of communication, abnormal behavior can function as a form of communication. This has been recognized in people with autism, for example, for whom it has been stated that behavior is communication (Freeman, Perry, & Bebko, 2002). What might otherwise be considered to be abnormal behavior might be a way for a person to communicate that he or she is in pain (see Chapter 41); that he or she is hungry, tired, or thirsty; or that he or she wants or needs something.

Seeking Help and an Accurate Diagnosis from a Professional

If emotional or behavior problems are suspected in a person of any age—or if a teacher, counselor, or other professional suggests that this person should be evaluated—the advice of a professional should be sought. As discussed elsewhere in this text, there are different ways of obtaining a functional diagnosis (e.g., autism) or a primary diagnosis for which the cause of the problem is known (e.g., fetal alcohol syndrome, fragile X syndrome). Research continues to improve diagnostic accuracy. Family doctors will make referrals to qualified professionals (psychologists, psychiatrists, or geneticists), who can conduct evaluations and make a diagnosis. Such individuals are usually located in university-associated hospitals, but they also may practice at other hospitals and institutions or be in private practice. School boards may be able to provide assistance in helping to obtain an accurate classification or primary diagnosis, which is often essential for obtaining the appropriate level of support.

It is important to work with professionals and therapists who will listen and with whom good communication can be established. Issues to consider in choosing a therapist include the therapist's qualifications, the length of treatment, the method of paying for visits, and other people's experiences with the therapist.

Understanding Types of Treatment

Getting an accurate diagnosis is the crucial first step. Once a diagnosis has been made, psychotherapy, behavior therapy, family therapy, medication, other therapies, or a combination of therapies may be recommended. (Descriptions of specific therapies and approaches may be found in other chapters of this book, especially Chapters 21, 23, and 42.) If medication is recommended as an intervention, questions to ask about medication include the following:

- What symptoms might the medication alter?
- When and how should the medication be taken?
- What are the side effects, and are such side effects short term or long term?
- What are the effects of overdoses of the medication?
- Are there strategies to lessen the effects of side effects?

SUMMARY

The purpose of this chapter was to introduce readers to the concepts of normal and abnormal behaviors, to help readers understand how to interpret abnormal behaviors in children and adults with intellectual and developmental disabilities, and to emphasize the need to find out what is causing abnormal behavior in people with intellectual or developmental disability. Is the abnormal behavior the result of the disability, or is it the result of a disorder not related to the disability?

In addition to abnormal behavior resulting from a genetic disorder, there are numerous other causes and conditions of abnormal behavior, including stress and anxiety; attention problems; depressive, eating, psychosexual, and sleeping disorders; suicidal behavior; pain disorders; substance abuse; medication side effects; personality disorders; schizophrenia; neurological conditions; and brain injury. It is usually beneficial to identify and classify abnormal behavior as early as possible in childhood so that the school system can make necessary accommodations and appropriate treatment can be obtained. Abnormal behavior creates marked personal, social, and support problems throughout the life span, and adequate methods of handling and treating them are critical.

FOR FURTHER THOUGHT AND DISCUSSION

1. What types of behavior might be considered abnormal by some people in society but might not really be abnormal?
2. If a 40-year-old female with Down syndrome begins to develop trouble with her short-term memory, can it automatically be assumed that she might be developing Alzheimer's disease? What other conditions might explain her symptoms?
3. Explain the pros and cons of assigning a diagnosis of autism to a child in kindergarten.

REFERENCES

American Psychiatric Association. (2000). *Diagnostic and statistical manual of mental disorders* (4th ed., text rev.) Washington, DC: Author.

Anandan, S., Wigg, C.L., Thomas, C.R., et al. (2004). Psychosurgery for self-injurious behavior in Tourette's disorder. *Journal of Child and Adolescent Psychopharmacology, 14,* 531–538.

Andreasen, N.C., & Olsen, S. (1982). Negative v. positive schizophrenia: Definition and validation. *Archives of General Psychiatry, 39,* 789–794.

Arciniegas, D.B., & Silver, J.M. (2006). Pharmacotherapy of posttraumatic cognitive impairments. *Behavioural Neurology, 17*(1), 25–42.

Bachevalier, J., Malkova, L., & Mishkin, M. (2001). Effects of selective neonatal temporal lobe lesions on socioemotional behavior in infant rhesus monkeys (Macaca mulatta). *Behavioral Neuroscience, 115*(3), 545–559.

Bailey, N.M., & Andrews, T.M. (2003). Diagnostic Criteria for Psychiatric Disorders for Use with Adults with Learning Disabilities/Mental Retardation (DC-LD) and the diagnosis of anxiety disorders: A review. *Journal of Intellectual Disability Research, 47*(Suppl. 1), 50–61.

Bassett, A.S., Chow, E.W., Weksberg, R., et al. (2002). Schizophrenia and genetics: New insights. *Current Psychiatry Reports, 4,* 307–314.

Beers, M.H., & Berkow, R. (Eds.). (2005). *The Merck Manual of Diagnosis and Therapy* (17th ed.). Retrieved July 24, 2005, from http://www.merck.com/mrkshared/mmanual/home.jsp

Behavioral Health of Greenville. (n.d.). *Psychotropic medications overview & general comments.* Retrieved May 30, 2006, from http://www.behavioralhealthofgreeneville.com/psychnurse.html

Ben Amor, L., Grizenko, N., Schwartz, G., et al. (2005). Perinatal complications in children with attention-deficit hyperactivity disorder and their unaffected siblings. *Journal of Psychiatry and Neuroscience, 30,* 120–126.

Biederman, J., & Faraone, S.V. (2005). Attention-deficit hyperactivity disorder. *The Lancet, 366*(9481), 237–248.

Bigler, E.D. (1999). Neuroimaging in pediatric traumatic head injury: Diagnostic considerations and relationships to neurobehavioral outcome. *Journal of Head Trauma Rehabilitation, 14,* 406–423.

Bradley, E.A., Lunsky, Y., Berg, J.M., et al. (2002). Re: Atypical antipsychotic use in treating adolescents and young adults with developmental disabilities. *Canadian Journal of Psychiatry, 47,* 785–786.

Brady, N., & McCain, G.C. (2004). Living with schizophrenia: A family perspective. *Online Journal of Issues in Nursing, 29, 10*(1), 7. Retrieved May 29, 2006, through Medscape from http://www.medscape.com/viewpublication/1151_toc?vol=10&iss=1

Breakey, J. (1997). The role of diet and behaviour in childhood. *Journal of Paediatrics and Child Health, 33,* 190–194.

Brown, R.T., Amler, R.W., Freeman, W.S., et al. (2005). Treatment of attention-deficit/hyperactivity disorder: Overview of the evidence. *Pediatrics, 115,* 749–757.

Bruce, D.A. (1995). Pathophysiological responses of the child's brain following trauma. In S.H. Broman & M.E. Michel (Eds.), *Traumatic head injury in children* (pp. 40–51). Oxford, United Kingdom: Oxford University Press.

Brylewski, J., & Duggan, L. (2004). Antipsychotic medication for challenging behaviour in people with learning disability. *Cochrane Database of Systematic Reviews (Online), 3,* CD000377.

Bushara, K.O. (2005). Neurologic presentation of celiac disease. *Gastroenterology, 128*(4 Suppl. 1), S92–S97.

Bussing, R.E., Koro-Ljungberg, M., Williamson, P., et al. (2006). What "Dr. Mom" ordered: A community-based exploratory study of parental self-care responses to children's ADHD symptoms. *Social Science and Medicine, April 25* [Epub ahead of print].

Cain, N.N., Holt, G., Davidson, P.W., et al. (2006). *Training handbook of mental disorders in individuals with intellectual disability.* Kingston, NY: National Association for the Dually Diagnosed.

Clarke, C., & Moore, A.P. (2004). Parkinson's disease. *Clinical Evidence, 11,* 1736–1754.

Clarke, J.J., & Wilson, D.N. (1999). Alcohol problems and intellectual disability. *Journal of Intellectual Disability Research, 43*(Pt. 2), 135–139.

Cuvo, A.J., May, M.E., & Post, T.M. (2001). Effects of living room, Snoezelen room, and outdoor activities on stereotypic behavior and engagement by adults with profound mental retardation. *Research in Developmental Disabilities, 22,* 183–204.

Deb, S., Matthews, T., Holt, G., et al. (2001). *Consensus practice guidelines for the assessment and diagnosis of mental health problems in people with intellectual disability.* Brighton, United Kingdom: Pavilion Publishing.

Dellinge-Ness, L.A., & Handler, L. (2006). Self-injurious behavior in human and non-human primates. *Clinical Psychology Review,* May 17 [Epub ahead of print].

Depression Learning Path. (2006). *Side effects of antidepressants.* Retrieved May 30, 2006, from http://www.clinical-depression.co.uk/Treating_Depression/side_effects.htm

Dey, A.N., & Bloom, B. (2005). Summary health statistics for U.S. children: National Health Interview Survey, 2003. *Vital and Health Statistics, Series 10. Data from the National Health Survey,* 1–78.

Durmer, J.S., & Dinges, D.F. (2005). Neurocognitive consequences of sleep deprivation. *Seminars in Neurology, 25*(1), 17–29.

Dykens, E.M. (1995). Measuring behavioral phenotypes: Provocations from the "new genetics." *American Journal on Mental Retardation, 99,* 522–532.

Dykens, E.M., Hodapp, R.M., & Finucane, B.M. (2000). *Genetics and mental retardation syndromes: A new look at behavior and interventions.* Baltimore: Paul H. Brookes Publishing Co.

Edelson, S.M. (2005a). *Stereotypical/self-stimulatory behavior.* Retrieved July 24, 2005, from http://www.creative-minds.info/Lorelei/Stimming.htm

Edelson, S.M. (2005b). *Understanding and treating self-injurious behavior.* Retrieved July 24, 2005, from http://www.autism.org/sibpaper.html

Ellis, C.R., & Schnoes, C.J. (2005). *Eating disorder: Pica.* Retrieved July 24, 2005 from http://www.emedicine.com/ped/topic1798.htm

Fenton, W.S., McGlashan, T.H., Victor, B.J., et al. (1997). Symptoms, subtype, and suicidality in patients with schizophrenia spectrum disorders. *American Journal of Psychiatry, 154*(2), 199–204.

Fireman, B., Koran, L.M., Leventhal, J.L., et al. (2001). The prevalence of clinically recognized obsessive-compulsive disorder in a large health maintenance organization. *American Journal of Psychiatry, 158*(11), 1904–1910.

Franke, J. (1999). Stress, burnout, and addiction. *Texas Medicine, 95*(3), 43–52.

Freeman, N.L., Perry, A., & Bebko, J. (2002). Behaviour is communication: Nonverbal communicative behaviour in students with autism and instructors' responsivity. *Journal on Developmental Disability, 9*(2), 145–155.

Friedrich, C.A. (2001). Genotype-phenotype correlation in von Hippel-Lindau syndrome. *Human Molecular Genetics, 10,* 763–767.

Gaetz, M. (2004). The neurophysiology of brain injury. *Clinical Neurophysiology, 115,* 4–18.

Gavin, M.L., & Homeier, B.P. (2004). *Pica.* Retrieved July 24, 2005, from http://www.kidshealth.org/parent/emotions/behavior/pica.html

Gillberg, C., & O'Brien, G. (2000). *Developmental disability and behavior.* London: Mac Keith Press.

Glanze, W.D. (1992). *The Mosby medical encyclopedia.* Novato, CA: The Learning Company.

Gottesman, I.I., & Hanson, D.R. (2005). Human development: Biological and genetic processes. *Annual Review of Psychology, 56,* 263–286.

Grabowska-Grzyb, A., Jedrzejczak, J., Naganska, E., et al. (2006). Risk factors for depression in patients with epilepsy. *Epilepsy and Behavior, 8*(2), 411–417.

Hall, P., Adami, H.O., Trichopoulos, D., et al. (2004). Effect of low doses of ionising radiation in infancy on cognitive function in adulthood: Swedish population based cohort study. *British Medical Journal, 328*(7430), 19.

Hamer, D. (2002). Rethinking behavior genetics. *Science, 298,* 71–72.

Haw, C., Hawton, K., Sutton, L., et al. (2005). Schizophrenia and deliberate self-harm: A systematic review of risk factors. *Suicide & Life Threatening Behavior, 35,* 50–62.

Hayden, E.P., & Nurnberger, J.I., Jr. (2006). Molecular genetics of bipolar disorder. *Genes, Brain and Behavior, 5*(1), 85–95.

Hettema, J.M., Prescott, C.A., Myers, J.M., et al. (2005). The structure of genetic and environmental risk factors for anxiety disorders in men and women. *Archives of General Psychiatry, 62*(2), 182–189.

Heyman, I., Fombonne, E., Simmons, H., et al. (2003). Prevalence of obsessive-compulsive disorder in the British nationwide survey of child mental health. *International Review of Psychiatry, 15*(1–2), 178–184.

Individuals with Disabilities Education Improvement Act of 2004, PL 108-446, 20 U.S.C. §§ 1400 *et seq.*

Jaffe, J. (with Segal, J). (2004). *Self-injury: Types, causes and treatment.* Retrieved July 24, 2005, from http://www.helpguide.org/mental/self_injury.htm

Johnson, H., Wiggs, L., Stores, G., et al. (2005). Psychological disturbance and sleep disorders in children with neurofibromatosis type 1. *Developmental Medicine and Child Neurology, 47*(4), 237–242.

Joszvai, E., et al. (in press). *Journal on Developmental Disabilities.*

Juurlink, D.N., Mamdani, M.M., Kopp, A., et al. (2006). The risk of suicide with selective serotonin reuptake inhibitors in the elderly. *American Journal of Psychiatry, 163*(5), 813–821.

Juvonen, J., Graham, S., & Schuster, M.A. (2003). Bullying among young adolescents: The strong, the weak, and the troubled. *Pediatrics, 112* (6, Pt. 1),1231–1237.

Kalivas, P.W. (2004). Recent understanding in the mechanisms of addiction. *Current Psychiatry Reports, 6,* 347–351.

Karno, M., Golding, J.M., Sorenson, S.B., et al. (1988). The epidemiology of obsessive-compulsive disorder in five US communities. *Archives of General Psychiatry, 45,* 1094–1099.

Keogh, B.K. (2003). *Temperament in the classroom: Understanding individual differences.* Baltimore: Paul H. Brookes Publishing Co.

Kidd, P.M. (2003). An approach to the nutritional management of autism. *Alternative Therapies in Health and Medicine, 9,* 22–31; quiz: 32, 126.

Kinsey, A.C., Pomeroy, W.B., & Martin, C.E. (1948/1998). *Sexual behavior in the human male.* Philadelphia: W.B. Saunders/Bloomington: Indiana University Press.

Kinsey, A.C., Pomeroy, W.B., & Martin, C.E. (1953/1998). *Sexual behavior in the human female.* Philadelphia: W.B. Saunders/Bloomington: Indiana University Press.

Klein, D.A., & Walsh, B.T. (2004). Eating disorders: Clinical features and pathophysiology. *Physiology & Behavior, 81*(2), 359–374.

Kluger, J., & Song, S. (2002). Young and bipolar. *Time, 160* (8), 38–46, 51.

Koegel, R.L., & Koegel, L.K. (2005). *Pivotal Response Treatments for autism: Communication, social, and academic development.* Baltimore: Paul H. Brookes Publishing Co.

Kristal, J. (2005). *The temperament perspective: Working with children's behavioral styles.* Baltimore: Paul H. Brookes Publishing Co.

Langstrom, N., & Hanson, R.K. (2006). High rates of sexual behavior in the general population: Correlates and predictors. *Archives of Sexual Behavior, 35*(1), 37–52.

Levin, H.S., Benton, A.L., & Grossman, R.G. (1982). *Neurobehavioral consequences of closed head injury.* Oxford, United Kingdom: Oxford University Press.

Levin, H.S., Eisenberg, H.M., & Benton, A.L. (1991). *Frontal lobe function and dysfunction.* Oxford, United Kingdom: Oxford University Press.

Lin, Z., & Madras, B.K. (2006). Human genetics and pharmacology of neurotransmitter transporters. *Handbook of Experimental Pharmacology, 175,* 327–371.

Lovell, A. (2004). People with learning difficulties who engage in self-injury. *British Journal of Nursing, 13,* 839–844.

Maguire, C.A. (2002). Comprehensive understanding of schizophrenia and its treatment. *American Journal of Health Systems and Pharmacology, 59*(17, Suppl. 1 5), S4–S11.

Mather, N., & Goldstein, S. (2001). *Learning disabilities and challenging behaviors: A guide to intervention and classroom management.* Baltimore: Paul H. Brookes Publishing Co.

Mayo Foundation for Medical Education and Research. (2004). *Personality disorders.* Retrieved May 26, 2006, from http://www.mayoclinic.com/health/personality-disorders/DS00562

Mazza, M., Orsucci, F., De Risio, S., et al. (2004). Epilepsy and depression: Risk factors for suicide? *La Clinica Terapeutica, 155*(10), 425–427.

Mbarek, O., Marouillat, S., Martineau, J., et al. (1999). Association study of the NF1 gene and autistic disorder. *American Journal of Medical Genetics, 88*(6), 729–732.

McAdam, D.B., Sherman, J.A., Sheldon, J.B., et al. (2004). Behavioral interventions to reduce the pica of persons with developmental disabilities. *Behavior Modification, 28,* 45–72.

McDougle, C.J., Scahill, L., Aman, M.G., et al. (2005). Risperidone for the core symptom domains of autism: Results from the study by the Autism Network of the Research Units on Pediatric Psychopharmacology. *American Journal of Psychiatry, 162,* 1142–1148.

McFarlane, J.M., Groff, J.Y., O'Brien, J.A, et al. (2003). Behaviors of children who are exposed and not exposed to intimate partner violence: An analysis of 330 black, white, and Hispanic children. *Pediatrics, 112*(3, Pt. 1), 202–207.

Medline Plus Health Information. (2006). *Suicide.* Retrieved May 29, 2006, from http://mentalhealth.about.com/library/mlp/blsuicide.htm

Mehler, P.S. (2003). Bulimia nervosa. *New England Journal of Medicine, 349,* 875–881.

Merbis, M.A., Snoek, F.J., Kanc, K., et al. (1996). Hypoglycaemia induces emotional disruption. *Patient Education and Counseling, 29,* 117–122.

Merkens, L.S., Connor, W.E., Linck, L.M., et al. (2004). Effects of dietary cholesterol on plasma lipoproteins in Smith-Lemli-Opitz syndrome. *Pediatric Research, 56,* 726–732.

Mild Traumatic Brain Injury Committee of the Head Injury Interdisciplinary Special Interest Group of the American Congress of Rehabilitation Medicine. (1993). Definition of mild traumatic brain injury. *Journal of Head Trauma Rehabilitation, 8,* 86–86.

Miller, L. (1994, November/December). Unusual head injury syndromes: Clinical, neuropsychological, and forensic considerations. *The Journal of Cognitive Rehabilitation,* 12–22.

Mishna, F. (2003). Learning disabilities and bullying: Double jeopardy. *Journal of Learning Disabilities, 36,* 336–347.

Mittelstoedt, M. (2006, May 30). Ottawa plans to snuff out flame retardants. *The Globe and Mail,* A6.

Molcho, M., Harel, Y., & Dina, L.O. (2004). Substance use and youth violence. A study among 6th to 10th grade Israeli school children. *International Journal of Adolescent Medicine and Health, 16,* 239–251.

Moldavsky, M., Lev, D., & Lerman-Sagie, T. (2001). Behavioral phenotypes of genetic syndromes: A reference guide for psychiatrists. *Journal of the American Academy of Child & Adolescent Psychiatry, 40,* 749–761.

Moss, J., Oliver, C., Hall, S., et al. (2005). The association between environmental events and self-injurious behaviour in Cornelia de Lange syndrome. *Journal of Intellectual Disability Research, 49*(Pt. 4), 269–277.

Murray, R.M., Jones, P.B., Susser, E., et al. (Eds.). (2002). *The epidemiology of schizophrenia.* Cambridge, United Kingdom: Cambridge University Press.

National Eating Disorders Association. (2002). *Home page.* Retrieved May 30, 2006, from http://www.nationaleatingdisorders.org/p.asp?WebPage_ID=337

National Institute of Mental Health. (2006). *Medications.* Retrieved May 29, 2006, from http://www.nimh.nih.gov/publicat/medicate.cfm#ptdep4

National Institute of Neurological Disorders and Stroke. (2005). *Tourette syndrome fact sheet.* Retrieved April 26, 2005 from http://www.ninds.nih.gov/disorders/tourette/detail_tourette.htm

National Institute of Neurological Disorders and Strokes. (2006). *NINDS brain and spinal tumors information page.* Retrieved May 29, 2006, from http://www.ninds.nih.gov/disorders/brainandspinaltumors/brainandspinaltumors.htm

National Mental Health Association. (n.d.). *Personality disorders.* Retrieved May 26, 2006, from http://www.nmha.org/infoctr/factsheets/91.cfm

National Strategy for Suicide Prevention. (2004). *Suicide facts.* Retrieved May 29, 2006, from http://www.mentalhealth.samhsa.gov/suicideprevention/fivews.asp)

O'Brien, G., & Yule, W. (1995). *Behavioral phenotypes.* London: Mac Keith Press.

Parker, R.S. (2001). *Concussive brain trauma: Neurobehavioral impairment and maladaptation.* New York: CRC Press.

Pastor, P.N., & Reuben, C.A. (2005). Racial and ethnic differences in ADHD and LD in young school-age children: Parental reports in the National Health Interview Survey. *Public Health Reports, 120,* 383–392.

Patrick, L. (2002). Eating disorders: A review of the literature with emphasis on medical complications and clinical nutrition. *Alternative Medicine Review, 7*(3), 184–202.

Percy, M., Lewkis, S., Birkan, R., et al. (2003). Abnormal behavior. In I. Brown & M. Percy (Eds.), *Developmental disabilities in Ontario* (2nd ed., pp. 277–309). Toronto: Ontario Association on Developmental Disabilities.

Peschel, E., Peschel, R., Howe, C., et al. (Eds.). (1992). *Neurobiological disorders in children and adolescents.* San Francisco: Jossey-Bess.

Pompili, M., Mancinelli, I., Ruberto, A., et al. (2005). Where schizophrenic patients commit suicide: A review of suicide among inpatients and former inpatients. *International Journal of Psychiatry in Medicine, 35*(2), 171–190.

Povlishock, J.T. (1993). Pathobiology of traumatically induced axonal injury in animals and man. *Annals of Emergency Medicine, 22,* 980–986.

Rihmer, Z., & Pestality, P. (1999). Bipolar II disorder and suicidal behavior. *Psychiatric Clinics of North America, 22*(3), ix–x, 667–673.

Ruggieri, V.L., & Arberas, C.L. (2003). Fenotipos conductuales. Patrones neuropsicologicos biologicamente determinados. [Behavioural phenotypes. Biologically determined neuropsychological patterns]. *Revista de Neurologia, 37,* 239–253.

Rush, J.A., & Frances, A. (Eds.). (2002). Expert consensus guidelines series: Treatment of psychiatric and behavioral problems in mental retardation. *American Journal on Mental Retardation (Special issue), 105,* 159–228.

Rutter, M. (2006). *Genes and behavior: Nature–nurture interplay explained.* Ames, IA: Blackwell Publishing Professional.

Ryan, L.M., & Warden, D.L. (2003). Post concussion syndrome. *International Review of Psychiatry, 15,* 310–316.

Schnoll, R., Burshteyn, D., & Cea-Aravena, J. (2003). Nutrition in the treatment of attention-deficit hyperactivity disorder: A neglected but important aspect. *Applied Psychophysiology and Biofeedback, 28,* 63–75.

Sell, R.L., Wells, J.A., & Wypij, D. (1995). The prevalence of homosexual behavior and attraction in the United States, the United Kingdom and France: Results of national population-based samples. *Archives of Sexual Behavior, 24,* 235–248.

Shastry, B.S. (2005). Bipolar disorder: An update. *Neurochemistry International, 46*(4), 273–279.

Shaywitz, S.E, & Shaywitz, B.A. (2005). Dyslexia (specific reading disability). *Biological Psychiatry, 57,* 1301–1309.

Shea, V. (2004). A perspective on the research literature related to early intensive behavioral intervention (Lovaas) for young children with autism. *Autism, 8,* 349–367.

Sigafoos, J., Arthur, M., & O'Reilly, M. (2003). *Challenging behavior and developmental disability.* Baltimore: Paul H. Brookes Publishing Co.

Sirotnak, A.P. (2006). Child abuse and neglect: Psychosocial dwarfism. In *E-Medicine.* Retrieved May 24, 2006, from http://www.emedicine.com/PED/topic566.htm

Sleep Home Pages. (n.d.). *Basics of sleep behavior.* Retrieved May 30, 2006, from http://www.sleephomepages.org/sleepsyllabus/a.html

Steinhausen, H.C., Von Gontard, A., Spohr, H.L., et al. (2002). Behavioral phenotypes in four mental retardation syndromes: Fetal alcohol syndrome, Prader-Willi syndrome, fragile X syndrome, and tuberosis sclerosis. *American Journal of Medical Genetics, 111,* 381–387.

Substance Abuse and Mental Health Services Administration. (2006). *Substance abuse treatment facility locator.* Retrieved May 29, 2006, from http://findtreatment.samhsa.gov/

Substance Abuse and Mental Health Services Administration, National Mental Health Information Center. (1996). *Your child's mental health. What every family should know.* Retrieved May 29, 2006, from http://www.mentalhealth.samhsa.gov/publications/allpubs/CA-0001/default.asp

Summers, J., Adamson, J., Bradley, E., et al. (2005). The need for more community nursing for adults with intellectual disabilities and mental health problems. *Canadian Journal of Psychiatry, 50,* 187.

Symons, F.J., Clark, R.D., Hatton, D.D., et al. (2003). Self-injurious behavior in young boys with fragile X syndrome. *American Journal of Medical Genetics, Part A, 118,* 115–121.

Thompson, S.M., Arrowsmith, F.E., & Allen, J.R. (2003). Dietary management of galactosemia. *The Southeast Asian Journal of Tropical Medicine and Public Health, 34*(Suppl. 3), 212–214.

Tierney, E., Nwokoro, N.A., & Kelley, R.I. (2000). Behavioral phenotype of RSH/Smith-Lemli-Opitz syndrome. *Mental Retardation and Developmental Disabilities Research Reviews, 6,* 131–134.

Tosato, S., & Dazzan, P. (2005). The psychopathology of schizophrenia and the presence of neurological soft signs: A review. *Current Opinion in Psychiatry, 18*(3), 285–288.

Trestman, R.L., Sevarino, K.A., & Kelly, M. (2004). Management of psychiatric issues in patients with intellectual disability. *Connecticut Medicine, 68,* 495–498.

Tselis, A., & Booss, J. (2003). Behavioral consequences of infections of the central nervous system: with emphasis on viral infections. *The Journal of the American Academy of Psychiatry and the Law, 31,* 289–298.

Tsiouris, J.A., Patti, P.J., Tipu, O., et al. (2002). Adverse effects of phenytoin given for late-onset seizures in adults with Down syndrome. *Neurology, 59,* 779–780.

Tyfield, L., Reichardt, J., Fridovich-Keil, J., et al. (1999). Classical galactosemia and mutations at the galactose-1-phosphate uridyl transferase (GALT) gene. *Human Mutation, 13,* 417–430.

Urschitz, M.S., Eitner, S., Guenther, A., et al. (2004). Habitual snoring, intermittent hypoxia, and impaired behavior in primary school children. *Pediatrics, 114,* 1041–1048.

Verdoux, H., & Cougnard, A. (2006). Schizophrenia: Who is at risk? Who is a case? *International Clinical Psychopharmacology, 21*(Suppl. 2), S17–S19.

Weight-Control Information Network. (2004). *Binge eating disorder* (NIH Publication No. 04-3589). Retrieved May 24, 2006, from http://win.niddk.nih.gov/publications/binge.htm

Weiss, J. (2002). Self-injurious behaviours in autism: A literature review. *Journal on Developmental Disability, 9*(2), 128–143.

Whittington, C.J., Kendall, T., & Pilling, S. (2005). Are the SSRIs and atypical antidepressants safe and effective for children and adolescents? *Current Opinion in Psychiatry, 18*(1), 21–25.

Wiggs, L., & France, K. (2000). Behavioural treatments for sleep problems in children and adolescents with physical illness, psychological problems or intellectual disabilities. *Sleep Medicine Reviews, 4*(3), 299–314.

Williamson, D.A., Martin, C.K., & Stewart, T. (2004). Psychological aspects of eating disorders: Best practice research. *Clinical Gastroenterology, 18,* 1073–1088.

World Health Organization. (1992). *The International Statistical Classification of Diseases and Related Health Problems, 10th Revision (ICD-10).* Geneva: Author.

Yates, W.R. (2005). Anxiety disorders. In *E-medicine.* Retrieved May 24, 2006, from http://www.emedicine.com/med/toopic152.htm

Young, A.H., & Newham, J.I. (2006). Lithium in maintenance therapy for bipolar disorder. *Journal of Psychopharmacology, 20*(2, Suppl.), 17–22.

III

Support and Intervention

21

An Introduction to Assessment, Diagnosis, Intervention, and Services

Ivan Brown and Maire Percy

WHAT YOU WILL LEARN ABOUT IN THIS CHAPTER

- Assessment
- Diagnosis
- Intervention
- Services

To introduce this book's Support and Intervention section, this chapter presents four topics that are very much interrelated in practice: assessment, diagnosis, intervention, and services. The term *assessment* refers to the process of documenting (usually in measurable terms) knowledge, skills, attitudes, and beliefs. In the field of intellectual and developmental disabilities, assessment is used to help determine the support needs of individuals and to suggest the most appropriate types of interventions and services. Assessment is also sometimes used to determine whether a person has an intellectual or developmental disability, and, if so, to describe its nature or type on the basis of its signs, symptoms, and the results of various tests. The conclusion reached from this process is called a *diagnosis*. Making a diagnosis in the intellectual and developmental disabilities field often requires ongoing assessment over a number of years. The word *intervention* refers, in a literal sense, to the act or an instance of interfering or intruding. In the field of intellectual and developmental disabilities, *intervention* means something slightly different. It refers to a group of methods for taking intentional action to help people improve their lives in a variety of positive ways, and it should be based on sound assessment procedures that are ongoing in nature. The term *service* (also sometimes called *support*) refers to the potential for helping others or the act of helping others or of doing work that provides assistance or benefits to someone. Service for people with intellectual and developmental disabilities is multidisciplinary, and it includes direct care, health, education, and a variety of specialist supports. Some service is designed to be specifically for people with disabilities and other service is for broader populations but is also available to people with disabilities. Overall, though, *service* means the presence of formal and informal resources that are available to people with disabilities that can directly help to improve their lives. Interventions, to be effective, very much depend on the availability of services.

This chapter provides an introduction to assessment, diagnosis, intervention, and services because it is critical to stress their importance to the overall support provided to children and adults with intellectual and developmental disabilities. These topics have been addressed through a vast number of books, articles, and practical materials. It is not possible to represent or summarize all of the information that is available in these resources; thus, this chapter serves as an introduction to a much larger area of study. Readers are encouraged to explore, through more specific reading and study, specific diagnostic criteria and guidelines, as well as the large number of specific methods of assessment and intervention strategies for a broad array of purposes that are available in the disability literature. They are also encouraged to become fully familiar with services that are available in their local areas.

ASSESSMENT

The field of intellectual and developmental disabilities—like the fields of education, social work, psychotherapy, psychiatry, and medicine—has a well-developed literature on assessment for both individuals and populations (groups of individuals). This litera-

The authors are very grateful to Yona Lunsky and Adrienne Perry for their helpful comments on portions of this chapter and to Rivka Birkan for the material she researched.

ture places a strong emphasis on individual assessment to identify and address the specific needs of individuals with disabilities and, to a lesser degree, on population assessment to identify and address the needs of groups of people with disabilities. This literature continues to evolve. Yet, its basic premise has remained stable over time—namely, that assessment is crucial to providing information for identifying needs and difficulties that can be addressed by available personnel and other resources and through teaching methods, interventions, services, and other forms of assistance for the specific purpose of helping to maintain or improve people's lives. Depending on the situation, assessment that is carried out for the purpose of helping to maintain or improve people's lives may or may not require formal documentation of intellectual and/or developmental disability and/or a formal diagnosis of its type (see the Diagnosis section).

Ongoing need for intervention and services is the most important reason for assessment, but it also has become important to deliver intervention and services in the most cost-effective and efficient manner that benefits individuals. Most countries, but especially the more economically developed countries, have expanded both their services and the funds to support them quite dramatically since the mid-20th century. Along with this expansion, there has been a shift toward attempting to ensure that these services are cost-effective and efficient (see Chapter 4 for a fuller discussion). One important aspect of cost-effectiveness and efficiency is providing the services that address the needs of people with disabilities in ways that maximize the amount of care provided or the degree of improvement in their lives. This trend has increased the need to assess as accurately as possible the requirements of individuals and groups of individuals so that they can be more directly addressed.

At the same time, broad concepts such as inclusion, quality of life, and self-determination have gained tremendous attention since about 1990, especially because they emphasize the importance of maximizing independence, abilities, and the quality within each person's life. Service has responded to these broad concepts by incorporating many of their core ideas and values into the daily work of frontline workers and by putting into place a stronger emphasis on person-centered approaches to service (see Chapters 4 and 22). Such individual emphasis on individual strengths and abilities and on quality has further increased the need for individual assessment that can accurately identify aspects of life that currently provide quality and thus need to be maintained and enhanced, as well as those aspects of life that are problematic and need to be improved or removed from the person's life (Brown & Brown, 2003).

Overall Approach to Assessment for Service Needs

A large amount of literature details assessment for people with intellectual and developmental disabilities. Numerous texts, detailing assessment methods and strategies that are useful for many purposes and over the life span, are readily available, in such places as university and professional libraries. Here, in keeping with the objectives of this chapter, an overall approach to assessment is outlined.

Individual and Population Assessment Assessment involves gathering information about something and drawing conclusions based on that information. In the field of intellectual and developmental disabilities, that "something" for an individual is most typically the person's characteristics or behavior, the environment in which the person lives, the interaction between the person and that environment, or the interaction between the person and other people. Assessment may occur for a variety of reasons, including teaching and learning, physical and mental health, support in everyday activities, and identifying needed services and supports. Whatever the reason for carrying out a specific individual assessment, its overall purpose is to suggest strategies or interventions that help improve the way an individual does things, the support in an individual's life, or the environment in which an individual lives.

Assessment for populations, or a focus on a group of individuals, is also important in the field of intellectual and developmental disabilities. For example, it may become apparent through population assessment that large numbers of youth with disabilities do not have major daily activities immediately on leaving school and that this situation is problematic for both the youth and their families. Such information, once gathered, can lead to recommendations for interventions, supports, and services that address the need identified and, in the process, help the youth and their families.

Assessment for Specific Reasons and Ongoing Assessment At times, an assessment is carried out for a very specific reason. Frontline support personnel, family members, or others may refer an individual for a formal assessment because they would like opinions or answers to questions that they have identified. At other times, professionals or frontline workers may carry out an assessment themselves to address a specific question or problem that has arisen. For example, educators may want to assess an 8-year-old girl's learning strengths and preferred styles to help determine the most appropriate teaching strategies for her, or parents may want to understand why their 40-year-old son is showing symptoms of depression and is having mood swings.

Not all individual assessment is carried out for a specific reason, at a specific time, or in such a formal way. Rather, assessment may—and should—be conducted in an ongoing way by those who support people with intellectual and developmental disabilities. A simple example is a 5-year-old boy who is crying. His caregiver will probably wonder if he is hurt, frightened, hungry, or tired, or if there is another problem. She will, in all likelihood, try to find out why he is crying and attempt to do something about it. If she determines that he is crying because he is frightened, she will probably try to separate him from the source of his fear and offer him physical and emotional comfort. In doing these things, the caregiver has gathered information about a problem situation, made a decision about the cause of the problem, and taken steps to improve it. Using the same basic approach, effective caregivers, support personnel, and professionals notice numerous small and not-so-small things during the course of a day that they assess for the purpose of improving or maximizing their support or the environment. In this way, individual assessment is integrated into the ongoing daily care, education, and support that are provided to individuals.

Five Basic Assessment Actions Assessments are described and organized in many different ways. They differ quite markedly because the purposes of assessments are different. For example, one would use different methods to assess for hearing loss, vision problems, speech and language ability, communication, motor skills, level of intelligence, daily living skills, need for physical and occupational therapy, ability to be responsible for a pet, capacity for traveling independently on a bus, or friend-making skills. Regardless of the specific assessment methods, they share some basic, overall components. Five actions that describe such common components are to

1. Attend to a situation or problem that has come to one's attention for a specific reason or simply because it is occurring in an individual's life
2. Gather as much information as possible about the situation or problem
3. Analyze which aspects of the situation are working well (strengths) and which aspects are not working well (needs)
4. Understand the factors that help improve the situation, as well as factors that hinder its improvement
5. Decide on plans to maintain or enhance factors that help improve the situation and to decrease or eliminate factors that hinder improvement; such plans, once put into action, are often referred to as *intervention* (Brown & Brown, 2003)

Theoretical Frameworks for Assessment It is often helpful to conceptualize and conduct assessment within a set of procedures that reflect both a theoretical stance and sound professional-ethical practice. Many such sets of procedures are available in assessment texts. One example (see Table 21.1) was put forward by Brown and Brown (2003) who advocated from the theoretical perspective that effective quality of life is an inherent right for all people with disabilities.

Formal Assessment Formal tests are often included in an assessment battery (a group of tools that use a variety of methods—e.g., intelligence tests, tests of adaptive behavior, tests of motor skills, hearing and vision tests). Typically, formal tests are characterized as objective or subjective, and both are often used in testing to provide balance. Objective tests include fixed and well-defined scoring procedures. Often, these tests are "standardized." Being standardized means that the test has been applied to a group of individuals of defined age and sex; thus, test results of a person being tested for a disability are compared with the test results of others of similar age and sex. Subjective tests typically seek the perception or perspective of the person being assessed and other people, and they are often designed to be interpreted by the assessor (e.g., ink blot tests; tests of apperception, or the perception of new experience in relation to past experience). Formal testing is typically used by professionals who make diagnoses or recommendations to others for intervention strategies. Professionals in different countries may use somewhat different points of reference, but it is common in many countries to formally measure intelligence and adaptive behavior (when a need to do so is identified), as well as often a number of other things such as learning ability and style.

Formal assessment typically includes a variety of informal tests as well. For example, an assessor might ask someone to walk across the room, to answer some simple arithmetic questions, or to repeat a sentence that contains two or three ideas. The responses to these and numerous other informal tests can provide valuable information to the assessor about the functioning of the person being assessed.

Should formal testing be required for eligibility to services? Due to fiscal restraints since approximately 1990, it has become more common in many countries for services to require formal testing of individuals before services are offered. There are a number of advantages of requiring formal testing to determine eligibility for services (see Chapters 1 and 31). The most important of these are ensuring that services are available to the individuals for whom they were intended, ensuring that people are not given inappropriate or unnecessary services (e.g., special education, residential services for people with disabilities, long-term care facilities), and being accountable to administrators (and indirectly to taxpayers) for monies spent on ser-

Table 21.1. Steps for blending quality-of-life concepts into assessment and intervention

- Look at the person and his or her environment
  - Person's own life experiences
  - Personal domains common to most people (e.g., family, friends, accommodations, work, leisure)
  - Environmental, social, and historical conditions in which the person lives
  - Environmental domains common to most people (e.g., community resources, public safety)
- Set priorities for action
  - First: Basic necessities
  - Second: Satisfaction with what is important
  - Third: Achieving high levels of fulfillment and meaning in life
- Carry out initial appraisal
  - Determine individual strengths and needs
  - Determine the individual's wishes
  - Determine if short term or long term and if immediate or distant
- Determine how to assess
  - Use objective indicators and standardized instruments
  - Gather personal perceptions of the individual and others
  - Take into account the importance and value to the person of the needs being assessed
  - Shape information toward stated personal goals
- Consider two key aspects
  - Holism/domains: Life is often thought of in parts but works as an integrated whole
  - Changing nature of life over time
- Focus on what to assess and apply
  - What is valued, relevant, and important to the person
  - What the individual perceives as leading to satisfaction and happiness
  - What offers opportunities for improvement
  - What reflects personal choice
  - What enhances self-image
  - What contributes to personal empowerment
- Consider other practice factors
  - Effect on families and close others
  - Professional considerations
  - Ethical issues
  - Policy and management issues
- Look to goals (end points) in five key areas of improvement
  - Well-being
  - Enjoyment/satisfaction
  - Personal meaning
  - Positive self-image
  - Social inclusion

From Brown, I., & Brown, R.I. (2003). *Quality of life and disability: An approach for community practitioners* (p. 117–118). London: Jessica Kingsley Publishers; adapted by permission.

vices (see also discussion in Chapter 1). There is considerable literature available on the difficulties of obtaining reliable test results from some individuals. For example, difficulties with hearing, vision, and speech interfere with formal testing, as do problems with concentrating; distractibility; and hypersensitivity to bright light, background noise, and other environmental factors. Another problem is that services sometimes allocate their available services, at least partially, based on test results, and this is not always appropriate. For example, many services are restricted to people for whom there is evidence of IQ scores not higher than 70, but some of these people require few or no formal services, especially if they live with family members or other caregivers. Conversely, many people who have IQ scores between 70 and 85 (approximately one seventh of the general population in North America) have social and emotional problems that are not addressed well by generic services but are ineligible for intellectual or developmental disability services because they do not have a formal diagnosis or meet other eligibility criteria set by service providers (Tymchuk, Lakin, & Luckasson, 2001; Zetlin & Murtaugh, 1990). Table 21.2 summarizes the components of formal assessment of intellectual and developmental disability.

Trend Toward Multifaceted Assessment Multifaceted (or multidisciplinary) assessment involves assessment by professionals with different areas of expertise (e.g., pediatrics, family medicine, neurology, psychiatry, clinical genetics, education, psychology, social work) and the compilation of information over time from these different sources while observing adaptive and maladaptive behaviors in more than one environment. This type of assessment is considered especially useful in developing individualized plans for supports and services. Multifaceted assessment is typically carried out in environments that reveal needs for early childhood services, educational services, and—in some cases—social services for adults or families that have children with disabilities.

Table 21.2. Components of formal assessment in intellectual or developmental disability

- Formal assessment typically identifies needs and strengths in these areas:
  - Intellectual functioning (an essential component of most formal assessments)
  - Adaptive skills (an essential component of most formal assessments)
  - Learning abilities and learning styles
  - Neurosensory functions (i.e., hearing, vision, and motor skills)
  - Speech and language function
  - Health and medical conditions
  - Dental health
  - Nutrition
  - Neuropsychological issues
  - Life skills
  - Activities of daily living
  - Living environment
  - Available supports

The purposes of multifaceted assessment often differ according to the age-related needs of the individual. For example, a pediatric clinic conducts assessments of young children for diagnostic purposes, an educational team assesses individuals to pinpoint educational strengths and weaknesses during the school years, and agencies assess adult support needs through a process of care management in relation to community living and/or special care.

DIAGNOSIS

In terms of intellectual and developmental disability, a diagnosis is a formal statement of the presence of a condition affecting intellect, development, and/or behavior (i.e., *intellectual disability* and/or *developmental disability* or related terms; see Chapter 1). It is made as a conclusion of assessment—which is sometimes carried out over extended periods of time—regarding a person's characteristics and/or behavior. A diagnosis need not be more specific than identifying a descriptive term such as *intellectual disability, developmental disability, developmental delay, learning disability,* or *mental retardation.* In almost all countries, a diagnosis is made in accordance with widely recognized criteria, typically provided by professional organizations or legislation (e.g., American Association on Mental Retardation [AAMR], 2002, see Chapter 1 for details; Royal College of Psychiatrists, 2004).

For many people, a more specific diagnosis, again in accordance with widely recognized criteria such as those contained within the *Diagnostic and Statistical Manual of Mental Disorders, Fourth Edition, Text Revision* (*DSM-IV-TR;* American Psychiatric Association [APA], 2000), is also made based on known reasons for the disability. There are two main types of such diagnoses: 1) classification diagnosis (e.g., autism, Asperger syndrome, schizophrenia, dementia, behavior problem), which classifies disabilities according to characteristics or behaviors common to groups of people, and 2) primary diagnosis, also sometimes called etiological diagnosis (e.g., Down syndrome, fragile X syndrome, fetal alcohol syndrome), which addresses the cause(s) of the disability (see also Chapter 9).

An aspect of diagnosis that sometimes seems confusing is that these more specific diagnoses may be made for people who have a diagnosis of intellectual or developmental disability, as well as for people who do not have such a diagnosis. For example, it may be helpful to understand in more detail the diagnosis of a person with intellectual disability by having a further diagnosis of cerebral palsy, but people with cerebral palsy do not necessarily have intellectual disability. Similarly, some people with autism, Tourette syndrome, and many other syndromes or disorders may or may not have a significant intellectual and/or developmental disability.

Determining if People Have Disabilities and Need Services

It is important to determine whether a person has an intellectual or developmental disability for two reasons: 1) it helps others understand their characteristics and behavior and 2) it helps others identify services and interventions that will help the person develop and enjoy life. Determining whether a person has a disability is a basic, and somewhat specialized, type of assessment (see Appendix B at the end of the book for a number of articles that discuss this issue). It can be a challenge at times, however, because meanings and definitions of intellectual and developmental disabilities vary somewhat and because determining if an individual has an intellectual or developmental disability is not an exact science (see Chapter 1). In general, determining whether a person has a disability—and is eligible for disability services—is met in one of three ways. Often, combinations of these three ways are used in the same region, or one service uses one way and another service uses another way. In some countries or states, laws or regulations govern which of these three ways is most commonly used.

1. People are deemed by professionals, and sometimes family members, to function in a way that indicates a disability and a need for services. This occurs in many parts of the world. The general practice is to provide whatever services are available to people who have not met explicit assessment criteria and do not have a formal diagnosis but who have exhibited clear need and who have been assumed to have an intellectual or a developmental disability. Typically, both need and disability are identified in a number of reporting procedures from professionals such as teachers, social service workers, or medical practitioners, or they are identified by family members. Practitioners who make decisions about eligibility for services typically emphasize that the individual needs services in order to function better in the environment in which he or she lives rather than meets certain assessment or diagnostic criteria.

2. After undergoing assessment procedures that yield information other than a diagnosis, people are deemed by professionals to have a disability, to need services, and to be eligible for them because the results of the assessment match eligibility criteria that are specified for services (e.g., lower intellectual functioning and adaptive behavior deficits). A formal diagnosis is not necessarily made. (There are many reasons not

to make a formal diagnosis; see especially Chapter 1). Rather, the purpose of assessing a person against criteria is to follow procedures for determining eligibility for services as set out by specific service organizations or service systems.

3. People are deemed by professionals to be eligible for services based on a formal diagnosis of intellectual or developmental disability (or related term) by a duly-designated professional (see Display 21.1). Formal definitions of terms, such as the definition of *mental retardation* by AAMR (see Chapter 1 for more details), are frequently used for making such a diagnosis. Even when formal definitions are used as criteria for services, though, there is typically some flexibility. For making a diagnosis of mental retardation, the AAMR definition stresses the importance of considering both an individual's limitations and strengths, the supports that are required for successful living, and the likely benefits to the person being diagnosed. The benefits to individuals with disabilities should be greater than the drawbacks and should add positive value to the individuals' lives (AAMR, 2002).

Display 21.1

Example of professionals designated to make diagnoses

This is one example of rules within a jurisdiction that determine who can make a diagnosis. There are many such examples throughout the world. The reader is encouraged to seek local information on who is entitled to make diagnoses.

In Ontario, Canada, the Regulated Health Professions Act (1991 S.O. 1991, c. 18) sets out guidelines for specific health professions and professionals regarding scope of practice, qualifications, job titles that can be used only according to specific rules and regulations (e.g., psychologist, massage therapist), and procedures that only members are permitted to perform (e.g., need to be a member of the Ontario College of Physicians and Surgeons to perform surgery).

For diagnosing developmental (and intellectual) disabilities, the Regulated Health Professions Act stipulates that either a psychologist or a physician should communicate a diagnosis to a patient or client. This is to prevent the harm that might come to the patient or client if the explanation is not communicated correctly. There is a possibility that those who are not entitled to communicate a diagnosis might be prosecuted under the Regulated Health Professions Act; therefore, it is their responsibility not to communicate information that might be construed to be a diagnosis.

Making a Diagnosis of Intellectual and/or Developmental Disability

There are numerous aspects of good practice for making a diagnosis, and not all of these can be covered in this chapter. However, the following subsections discuss four of the most important aspects that need to be considered when making a diagnosis.

Understanding the Reason for the Diagnosis
A diagnosis is a formal designation that identifies a specific term describing a condition in a person. Thus, when an individual is diagnosed with an intellectual or developmental disability, he or she is formally identified as a person who has the characteristics of that disability.

A diagnosis that determines the primary reason(s) for the disability is often very helpful because many of the support needs in such conditions already are known from studies of populations with the particular disorder. Thus, practitioners, family members, and people with disabilities can use this information to plan the most appropriate support resources and activities. In spite of this beneficial intent, some individuals, family members, and service providers are somewhat cautious about seeking or making a diagnosis because of the possibility of stigma associated with being labeled, overidentification with specific characteristics, or assumptions that are made both by practitioners and others based on the diagnosis (see Chapter 1). Another reason for caution is that professionals at times provide a diagnosis without making provision for support services (e.g., counseling or information for parents; see Chapter 28 for additional information about genetic counseling), which distresses families. Thus, professionals should make, or not make, a diagnosis following careful thought, and they should be certain that the benefits of making a diagnosis outweigh the drawbacks. Professionals also should bear in mind the possibility of dual diagnosis (see Chapter 42).

Understanding Who Has Responsibility to Make a Diagnosis A diagnosis needs to be made and communicated in a serious and responsible manner. Often, such responsibility is set out in legal documents or formal policy by government bodies, service or educational organizations, or professional organizations (see Display 21.1 for an example).

Allowing for Flexibility in Diagnosis When a diagnosis is made, it may be permanent, with the diagnosis referred to numerous times and for many purposes throughout the person's life. Yet, there is often a need for flexibility of a diagnosis because conditions and skills change over the life span. For example, in order to be eligible for early intensive behavioral intervention services in some jurisdictions, a child must be diagnosed as having "severe autism." Nonetheless, this program is so successful in some instances that the child is able to participate successfully in the general education classroom and enjoy most aspects of family and community life without undue negative effects (Jacobson, Mulick, & Green, 1998; Mudford et al., 2001). In these cases, the label is still relevant, but the support needs are considerably reduced. Thus, it is essential to think of a diagnosis in terms of the present need of the person with a disability and the supports that are indicated.

In this regard, a very useful development was made by AAMR in the ninth edition of its definition and classification system for mental retardation (Luckasson et al, 1992). At that time, AAMR adopted a classification system based on the intensities of needed supports, and the organization reaffirmed this in 2002 (for information on the Supports Intensity Scale, a way to assess needed supports, see AAMR, 2002). This is a flexible classification system, because people's support needs change—often quite considerably—over their lives. Additional flexibility arises from the AAMR's recognizing that results of formal assessment instruments may differ somewhat, may change over time, and should be interpreted within a range of values. These are positive contributions to assessment that reflect the needs of individuals at any one time in their lives, and is carried out for the purpose of providing supports that are helpful in improving quality of life.

Understanding the Limitations of a Point of Reference A diagnosis needs a point of reference (i.e., a set of criteria) upon which it is based. In the United States and elsewhere, definitions of mental retardation described by such organizations as the AAMR (2002), the APA (2000), or the American Psychological Association (Jacobson & Mulick, 1996) provide such points of reference. Other countries, such as Australia and the United Kingdom, have developed their own definitions of intellectual disability for the purpose of diagnosis and classification (also see Chapter 1).

Typically, most professionals in most jurisdictions exercise some flexibility in making a diagnosis of intellectual or developmental disability. For example, they may not make the diagnosis if special education services and special intervention are not required or if education and other support services are not available in the area where the person lives. Conversely, they may make a diagnosis if special education services and interventions are available and would be helpful to the individual.

Sometimes a single point of reference is adopted for a region; at other times, fields of services are free to adopt the point of reference that they see most appropriate to their needs. For example, psychologists within a school system may use one set of criteria for diagnoses and those in an adult living services agency may use another. Even when one point of reference is used, it may be interpreted in different ways. For example, there are rigorous and less formal ways of assigning a diagnosis of autism (see Chapter 12).

Certain aspects of diagnostic criteria are sometimes stressed more than others for particular reasons. Different services—such as residential services, vocational services, mental health services, recreational programs, life-skills development, and schools—may require demonstration of need in a particular area, resulting in its being overstressed for the purpose of getting the needed support. Unfortunately, there are wait lists for services in many countries, and to compete for eligibility for those services, family members and professionals sometimes present the needs (diagnosis) of the person with the disability in ways that minimize ability and maximize disability.

Perhaps the most important limitation to a point of reference is that it is impossible to design a set of criteria that works well for every individual. There are people who match diagnostic criteria well but do not need services, and people who very much need services but do not quite match the diagnostic criteria. There has been considerable debate in the disability literature about how strictly criteria should be interpreted, and there have been many calls for allowing for a degree of flexibility, especially to reflect clinical opinion that people are in need of services.

INTERVENTION

The term *intervention,* as used in this section, refers to action intentionally taken by others to positively affect the life of a person with intellectual or developmental disabilities. Thus, the intent of intervention is to improve the person's life in some way. It should be noted, however, that in practice not all interventions are helpful, and some might even be harmful to a particular person. For example, the administration of psychotropic drugs can frequently be beneficial for behavior disorders (e.g., Tourette syndrome, fragile X syndrome; Berry-Kravis & Potanos, 2004; Bokszanska et al., 2003; Muller-Vahl, 2003; Scahill et al., 2003; Tsiouris & Brown, 2004) or mental health disorders (e.g., major depression, schizophrenia; Hamrin & Scahill, 2005; McGrath & Tempier, 2005; To, Zepf, & Woods, 2005). Yet, people with intellectual and developmental disabilities do not necessarily respond to these drugs as expected. Children and adolescents with developmental disabilities may experience functional impairment and akathisia (involuntary changes in posture), tics (pointless rapid movements or repeated sounds), and other dyskinesias (movement disorders) when administered traditional neuroleptic medications (Brasic et al., 2004). Another example is the response to phenytoin for treatment of epileptic seizures. Although this drug has beneficial effects for many people, it may have life-threatening adverse effects in people with Down syndrome who have developed late onset seizures, especially in those who have dementia of the Alzheimer type (Tsiouris et al., 2002; Chapter 44; see also Chapters 10, 40, and 41).

In this section, informal intervention and numerous more formal interventions are identified or briefly described. The formal interventions mentioned are not intended to represent all that are practiced throughout the world; rather, they are intended to illustrate the richness of interventions that are available in some areas and that might be developed in others.

Importance of Theoretical Perspective

The types of intervention selected, and the way they are implemented, are highly related to the theoretical and ideological perspectives of the professionals who suggest or initiate them. Two increasingly relevant broad categories of such perspectives are person-centered approaches and professional-centered approaches. In general, the former involves participation of the person with disabilities in the selection and evaluation of the intervention, with the intervention itself focusing on objectives that are of that person's preference or choosing. The latter, by contrast, refers to interventions that are selected by professionals who, because of their experience and knowledge, develop and put in place a set of activities that are designed to bring about positive changes for the person.

Within these two broad categories, numerous theoretical approaches influence specific interventions that are put into practice. Theoretical approaches are often key factors in determining how interventions are carried out, and, ultimately, whether or not they are successful. For this reason, it is important for professionals, and, to the extent possible, those benefiting from the interventions, to understand and evaluate the theoretical perspective upon which they are based.

Informal Intervention

Much intervention that occurs for people with intellectual and developmental disabilities is informal in nature. For example, when a receptionist in a service organization stops to chat for a few minutes with a person who has intellectual disabilities whom she knows to be developing expanded social skills, she is carrying out a valuable informal intervention by providing an enjoyable natural opportunity for practice. Informal intervention takes many forms within the natural living environment. It emerges from the numerous actions taken by family members, community members, and others throughout each day to support people with intellectual and developmental disabilities in positive ways. Most paid staff and other professionals who work in the field of disabilities do considerable informal intervention in addition to their formal intervention. Often this goes unnoticed and unrewarded, as they simply do numerous small, casual, and informal—but nevertheless important—things with the people they support.

Formal Interventions

Formal interventions are carried out by a wide variety of professional frontline workers and specialists. Services offer numerous types of intervention; thus, intervention is often an aspect of the services people with disabilities receive, including education, health, and social services. Other intervention, however, may be carried out in more specialized professional settings (e.g., psychotherapy, special medical intervention, special behavioral intervention).

Many interventions are described in other chapters of this book, and readers are encouraged to seek additional information by consulting the many comprehensive texts on intervention that are available in academic and professional libraries. A variety of specific types of interventions and therapies have been particularly important to people with intellectual and developmental disabilities. Some examples are

- *Activity-focused therapies:* art therapy, aquatic therapy, music therapy, pet therapy, play therapy, recreation therapies, sand play therapy
- *Age-related therapies:* intensive early childhood behavioral intervention, transition counseling, grief and loss counseling
- *Communication:* audiology, speech-language therapy
- *Education and training:* academic upgrading (e.g., completion of school or courses; improvement of specific skills such as reading, writing, or working with numbers), special educational programs, vocational programs
- *Health and medicine:* alternative medicine, correction of hearing and vision problems, gene therapy, hormone replacement, nutritional therapy (general and for specific problems—e.g., phenylketonuria), physiotherapy, pharmacotherapy, surgery for heart and gastrointestinal defects, correction of physical deformities
- *Lifestyle and personal support:* assistance animals, assistive technology, helpful specialized techniques

(e.g., special feeding methods, hygiene and toileting assistance, community involvement, training to travel independently, bathing assistance, medicine schedule monitoring, enhancement of social skills)
- *Personal and skills development:* assertiveness training, behavior therapy (see Display 21.2), counseling, family therapy, individual therapy, group therapy, life skills training, money management training, occupational therapy, psychotherapy, promoting friendships for people with developmental disability, sex education, social skills training, and travel training

Display 21.2

Issues in interventions for behavior problems and mental health

Behavior therapy takes various forms, but, in general, it focuses on positive changes to behavior or the environment in which the behavior occurs while recognizing that there often is an accompanying cognitive or emotional aspect (see Chapter 22 for details). Four issues should be considered regarding behavior therapy:

1. It is crucial to distinguish clinical symptoms of problem behavior and/or psychiatric illness from symptoms that might be characteristic of an underlying disability. Although both problems may be treatable, they may require different intervention techniques.
2. In the past, psychotropic drugs tended to be greatly overused in the intellectual disabilities field. This is becoming much less an issue since approximately 1980, although prudence may still be warranted.
3. It is important to ask what standards professionals should use for making decisions about interventions for behavior problems and mental health. Some special consensus statements have been developed to guide professionals. For example, AAMR published a special volume of its journal *American Journal on Mental Retardation* (Rush & Frances, 2000), and the American Academy of Child and Adolescent Psychiatry also published guidelines (1999).
4. Attempts have been made to educate and empower individuals with intellectual and developmental disabilities regarding use of their medication. For example, the Ohio State University's PROJECT MED group published a set of seven booklets intended for individuals with such disabilities. These booklets explain the uses of psychotropic medications and their side effects in an easy to understand manner (Aman et al., 1999).

New Interventions

New interventions, sometimes for particular intellectual or developmental disabilities, are continually being developed and evaluated. Some of these may prove to be effective in the future, and others may not. For this reason, expert opinion should be sought and care should be taken if these are undertaken. At the time of publication, some examples of such interventions that are being investigated in clinical research studies are

- Avoidance of milk and milk products, as well as gluten, for autism (Lucarelli et al., 1995; Millward, Ferriter, Calver, et al., 2004)
- Cholesterol supplementation for Smith-Lemli-Opitz syndrome (Merkens et al., 2004; Chapter 15)
- Deep brain stimulation (placing an electrode in the brain so that the tip of the electrode is in the globus pallidus of the brain; Chapter 8) in Parkinson's disease (Samuel & Voon, 2005) and other movement disorders (Grill, 2005)
- Fetal surgery for spina bifida (Chescheir & D'Alton, 2005)
- In utero blood transfusions for severe hemolytic disease of the newborn (Lydaki et al., 2005)
- Intramuscular botulinus toxin injection for cerebral palsy (Speth et al., 2005)
- Stem and progenitor cell-based therapy for diseases of the central nervous system (Goldman, 2005)
- Surgery, ketogenic diet, and transvagal stimulation for epilepsies resistant to pharmacological intervention (DiMario & Holland, 2002, Holmes, 2002; Wheless, 2004; Chapter 18)
- Transcranial magnetic stimulation for refractory epilepsy with malformations of cortical development (Fregni et al., 2005; Hoffman & Cavus, 2002; Chapter 18) and depression in neurological disorders (Fregni & Pascual-Leone, 2005)

General Guidelines for Effective Intervention

Numerous sets of guidelines for effective intervention are available from a wide variety of sources, and readers are encouraged to seek out some of these (see Appendix B). Some general guidelines are highlighted next to provide an overall context to understanding and using such guidelines. Intervention should

- Address a specific assessed need
- Set clear and achievable objectives that are designed to improve the life of the person with disabilities
- Be based on a sound theoretical or practical rationale

- Use methods that 1) are the choice of the person with disabilities, 2) are agreeable to the person with disabilities, or 3) do not cause the person with disabilities harm
- Use ongoing evaluation to assess the degree to which progress is being made, and, using this information, adjust the methods to move toward the objectives in an more effective way
- Ensure a smooth transition away from the intervention
- Provide for follow-up intervention, if required

SERVICES

It is not known precisely how many children might have a developmental delay and how many adults have intellectual disabilities or developmental disabilities. Those who are known to the education and service systems, and who are accessible by researchers, may differ considerably from actual numbers. In some jurisdictions already strapped for funding, only approximately 25% of people needing particular services are actually getting them (Brown, Raphael, & Renwick, 1997).

Among those who are known, estimated prevalence rates for intellectual disability range from approximately 0.5%–1.5% of the total population. McLaren and Bryson (1987) reviewed prevalence from sources published internationally before 1987 and estimated that 0.3%–0.4% of the total population had severe or mild mental retardation. Larson et al. (2001) reported on estimated prevalence of mental retardation and developmental disability in the United States, as measured by the 1994/1995 National Health Interview Survey, Disability Supplement, and found the following: mental retardation, 0.78% of the population not living in institutions; developmental disability, 1.13%; and mental retardation/developmental disability combined, 1.49%. Fujiura (2003) found a prevalence of 1.27% for mental retardation/intellectual disability from the same source. In a study of 89,534 10-year-old children in Atlanta, Georgia (Unites States), Murphy et al. (1995) found a prevalence rate of 1.2% for mental retardation, of which 0.84% was for mild mental retardation.

In other countries, mild mental retardation was found in 1.44% and severe mental retardation was found in 0.59% of children ages 2–9 screened in Bangladesh (Islam, Durkin, & Zaman, 1993); 0.56% of the population of Ontario, Canada, was estimated to have intellectual disabilities (Nuyen, 1996); and severe and profound mental retardation in a Finnish study was reported to be 0.13% (Arvio & Sillanpaa, 2003). Fernell (1998) noted that 0.37% of European and 0.59% of non-European children in her Swedish study were classified as having severe mental retardation. A large study of 33,332 Chinese residents, ages 15 years or older, found a prevalence rate of 0.85% for severe mental retardation (although it must be noted that the meaning of the word *severe* may differ for China) (Zhang et al., 2003). Intellectual disability was reported among 0.32% of South Asians living in Leicestershire, United Kingdom, and among 0.30% of Caucasians living in the same region (McGrother et al., 2002). In Australia, prevalence of intellectual disability ranged from .4% to 1.86% of the general population (Australia Institute of Health and Welfare, n.d.).

The Nuyen (1996) and McGrother et al. (2002) studies illustrated two of several methodological problems that are inherent in most prevalence reports (also see Leonard & Wen, 2002). The former computed its estimate for those ages 20 years and older only from a database of people who received a government disability pension. The latter was based on data on South Asian and Caucasian adults known only to the Leicestershire Learning Disabilities Registry. Because a main goal of most disability services is to move people away from relying on disability pensions, funding, and services and toward greater independence, interdependence, and reliance on community supports, large numbers of people (especially adults) are probably unknown to service systems. Many children, especially those in their early years, have not yet received a diagnosis, and children in school may not be receiving special education services. Thus, the number of people known to education and service systems may differ considerably from the actual numbers.

Leonard and Wen (2002) and Yu and Atkinson (1993) discussed methodological problems and assessed differences in prevalence rates (see also Roeleveld, Zielhuis, & Gabreels, 1997). Leonard and Wen pointed out that prevalence rates vary according to definitions used, age, gender, ethnicity, and other factors. Yu and Atkinson noted that the percentage of people with intellectual disabilities is often estimated in the literature to be approximately 1% or lower, but they also cited sources that estimated that up to 3% of the population probably has intellectual/developmental or related disabilities. In their analysis of the existing literature, Yu and Atkinson considered what percentage of people might be expected to have intellectual and developmental disabilities and claimed that 2.25% of the general population is a realistic figure. The discrepancy between the figure drawn from their analysis and the prevalence rates that are typically reported is most likely the difference between how many people with intellectual and developmental disabilities there are within the general population and how many of them are known to formal systems—such as social services, education, and health—at any one time.

An important problem that arises from this difference in estimates is that it is difficult for most jurisdictions to plan for how many people might need or want services, either currently or in the future, because they do not really know how many children and adults have such disabilities. Most jurisdictions do not know the number of people with intellectual or developmental disabilities who do not want or need services at the present time, who have not applied for services for a number of reasons, or who have not been identified as needing services. In addition, a great many jurisdictions do not even have reliable figures on the number of people who have already been helped by their service systems but currently do not require services. This is important because these people may need help again in the future. It may be especially important to track child and adults who live in known "at-risk" situations, such as poverty, single-parent families, recent immigrant status, and social isolation (e.g., see Emerson & Hatton, 2004; Fujiura 2003). Even the number of adults who currently receive services from organizations that specialize in intellectual disabilities is not always known. An example was cited by Brown, Percy, and Garcin (2003) who pointed out that in Canada, the Ontario government estimated the number of people who received services to be approximately 50,000 during the 1990s, but a 1995 survey of organizations throughout Ontario reported that just over 26,000 adults received services (Brown et al., 1997). A consequence of all these factors is that estimates of the number of people needing services have often been made from the number of people on waiting lists for services, but this does not account for people who are not known to the service system.

Informal Supports

In almost every part of the world—but to varying degrees—support is available for children and adults with intellectual and developmental disabilities and their families. Much of this support has an informal character.

Informal supports are offered within the natural settings of home and community. They include the countless ways that family members, friends, neighbors, co-workers, community members, and others help those in need. Basic examples of informal support include holding a door open for someone who uses a wheelchair or offering to look after a neighbor's child while the parents go shopping. Much more substantial informal supports include the large commitments that many parents and other family members make to children and adults with disabilities (e.g., see Todd et al., 2004). Relatives, friends, and neighbors often give a great deal of their time and other resources. Volunteers contribute time, energy, and expertise in any number of areas of life. On the whole, the contribution of informal supports to people with intellectual and developmental disabilities is enormous, and without such supports a large number of people would experience a very poor quality of life.

Parent and family organizations, self-advocacy groups, and other advocacy organizations may be considered informal supports in the sense that they typically have few or no paid professionals. Yet, these organizations often exert considerable influence in the development of new trends and social attitudes toward disability, public policy, public awareness, and eligibility for services. Similarly, professional organizations offer a considerable amount of informal support to the field of intellectual and developmental disabilities (see Chapter 6 for listings).

Formal Supports

Formal supports are those that are set up purposely to address the needs of groups of people. Formal supports are usually called *services.* They are typically administered by community service organizations, often called *agencies,* of varying sizes. Some community agencies offer one or two services to a small number of people with disabilities; others offer a wide array of services to thousands of people. Formal services have expanded considerably in most economically developed countries since the 1970s. They are funded and operated in various ways by governments, government-funded organizations, religious organizations, philanthropic organizations, and other groups. Their availability varies markedly from one country to another and among regions within a country.

The types of services that are available to people with intellectual and developmental disabilities vary widely from one jurisdiction to another. The following represent many of the services offered in various countries, although certainly not all of these are available in every country or in every region of a country.

- *Adult living:* Support for finding large or small group residences, support for living within the family home (i.e., support for biological or foster family members), support for independent living, support to attain community accommodations that are geared to income
- *Education and training:* Early childhood education programs, early specialized intervention programs, literacy programs, special education (segregated) classes or pull-out services in school, accommodations for inclusion in general education classrooms, individualized support for students with special needs, co-op programs (work experience), training for teachers and support workers, community living skills development

- *Employment and work:* Job training, on-the-job support (supported employment), help in seeking new opportunities, support for employers who hire individuals with disabilities, work subsidies
- *Family support:* Assessment services, counseling services, direct funding to families for additional expenses, direct funding to families to hire needed support, family support workers, respite care, support for parents who have disabilities, support for older parents, support for siblings
- *Leisure and recreation:* Leisure activities, life skills programs, drop-in centers, social activities, recreation programs, sports programs
- *Life support for community living:* Adaptive devices, case-management/service coordination, individualized community living support, legal support, social and other skill development programs
- *Medical and health services:* Assessment for specific conditions, genetic-related services, psychiatry and other mental health services, specialized dental services, specialized hearing and vision services, specialized medical services, diagnostic services, programs offering instruction about safety issues (e.g., preventing accidents, abuse, and neglect)
- *Therapeutic services:* Assessment services, behavioral support, physical therapy, sex and relationships education, speech and language services, psychotherapy and counseling, programs to deal with major upheavals such as grief

Potential Barriers to Obtaining Services

There are many potential barriers to services (see Ittenbach et al., 1994; Kim, Larson, & Lakin, 1999; see also Chapter 41). These include, among others, the lack of

- Access to available services
- Availability of programs and activities (i.e., services are not set up or are inadequately funded or staffed)
- Expertise among those providing the services
- Public funding to pay for programs
- Personal finances to pay for specific activities
- Personal supports and other assistance to make services successful
- Time, energy, and other resources to advocate for services
- Transportation

In addition, service shortages pose problems to obtaining needed supports. Although service providers usually attempt to be equitable, almost all countries have such shortages. Moreover, the services that are available are not always those that are most useful to families or individuals with disabilities (Brown, Anand, et al., 2003). Consequently, support sometimes goes to those who make their needs and wishes known most clearly. In any case, people needing services (and the professionals who support them) should identify what they most need, become informed about available services, advocate on their own behalf, inform and educate other professionals, and encourage professionals and others to advocate for them.

Contacting general or specific intellectual or developmental disability organizations, as well as contacting parent groups, sometimes results in individuals, families, and support workers starting from a place that builds on the experiences of others. In almost every area of the world, there are other people who have successfully obtained the services they need, and the strategies they used to gain their successes can be very helpful.

Challenges for Providing Services

The most pressing service provision challenge is to provide adequately for individuals who have been identified as having intellectual and developmental disabilities and who have support needs. There is wide variation among countries in how such individuals are supported; this variation results from enormous differences in

- Availability of financial resources to respond to the needs of people with disabilities
- Availability of human resources to respond to the needs of people with disabilities
- Commitment of government and other leaders to improve life for people with disabilities
- Cultural acceptance of human diversity
- Disability as a national or regional priority
- Legislated recognition of rights and entitlements for people with disabilities
- Social attitudes toward disability

Such differences have resulted in systems of service that vary widely in mandate and scope. Some countries' service systems have solid philosophical foundations, have adequate resources, have well-developed infrastructures, and are supported by professionals and family and self-advocacy organizations. Conversely, some other countries have very few services available.

Despite such variation in services, some challenges are common to all service systems. Six such challenges are key to developing useful disability policy and services should be addressed more fully through discussion and research. These are briefly described next.

1. *To what degree is the well-being of people with intellectual and developmental disabilities a public responsibility?* In some parts of the world, responsibility for the lives of people with intellectual and developmental disabilities is not considered to be a public, or societal, concern. Since the end of the 20th century, however, many other countries have moved toward viewing the welfare

and well-being of people with disabilities as a public responsibility. At the same time, policies and practices have been put into place in many of these countries that mitigate public responsibility and instead promote the role of families and communities in assuming greater responsibility for people with disabilities (see Chapters 3 and 4). A challenge for disability policy makers and service providers is to develop an approach to supporting people with intellectual and developmental disabilities that blends public and private responsibility in ways that suit the cultural context and result in effective improvements to welfare and well-being.

2. *How can people be made aware of entitlement to services?* Some people with disabilities and their families are unaware of services that they need and to which they are entitled, even in countries where services are quite readily available (see Chapter 6 for a full discussion of entitlements). A challenge that is often not adequately addressed is how to build knowledge about disability entitlement so that individuals with disabilities may have their needs met.

3. *How can the most effective service methods be put into place?* Services differ greatly in the degree to which they are effective in supporting needs, improving well-being, and fulfilling the objectives of the service organization. Numerous ways to track and report on what are considered to be effective methods have already been put in place in many jurisdictions, but these need to be continuously improved and altered to address changing needs and conditions.

4. *How can standards of quality of care be ensured?* A great many children and adults with intellectual and developmental disabilities require short-term or long-term care. In addition, because of the disability itself, they are not always in a position to ensure that the care they receive is the type and quality that is best suited to their well-being. Of note are the ethics of invasive procedures (e.g., medical, psychotropic, behavioral) that some professionals may consider important to the overall well-being of a person with a disability but must be balanced with the need for informed consent and control over one's own life. The ideal is providing care that is least intrusive. Service agencies need to put into place methods of ensuring that they provide care that meets quality standards and addresses ethical issues in an ongoing way. (See Chapter 40 for additional information.)

5. *How can quality of life be promoted?* Improving the quality of overall life experience of people with intellectual and developmental disabilities needs to be a core goal of all services. Quality can be improved in numerous general ways for groups of people but also in numerous unique ways for individuals (see Brown & Brown, 2003, for a full description of using the quality-of-life approach in practice). Brown and Brown provided a three-level hierarchy for deciding where to start to improve quality in the lives of people with disabilities: Level 1—attaining the basic necessities of life, Level 2—experiencing satisfaction with aspects of life that are important to the person, and Level 3—achieving high levels of personal enjoyment and fulfillment.

6. *How can equity in service accessibility be addressed?* In all countries, many people with intellectual and developmental disabilities need support, and there are not always sufficient services available to respond to their needs. In some countries, there is a chronic and sizeable shortage of services. Few jurisdictions offer support to everyone who needs it or all of the support that all individuals need. More typically, decisions are made about what individuals receive support and

FOR FURTHER THOUGHT AND DISCUSSION

1. Think of a person you know who has an intellectual disability. What types of assessment would be best to ascertain what his or her support needs are? Who would be best suited to carrying out this assessment?
2. When a diagnosis is made, when should it be thought of as long-term, and when should it be thought of as short-term? Illustrate your view by giving examples from people with disabilities. When, if ever, is it appropriate not to give a diagnosis? What diagnostic criteria are used in the region where you live?
3. What kinds of supports can be given to parents when their young child has been diagnosed with an intellectual or developmental disability? Given that advancements for effective interventions, treatments or even prevention are dependent upon research, what action might be taken by grass roots organizations, by families of people with developmental disabilities, by members of the general public, and by researchers and other health professionals to increase the level of funding for research in the human neurodevelopmental and related disabilities? (Hint: lobby the politicians, become involved in fund-raising activities, and participate in the research.)
4. Working in a small group with others, identify the supports and services that are available locally for four individuals of various ages with different types and disabilities. Identify possible barriers to these supports and services being successful, and specific issues arising from these barriers that are important for professionals and advocates to address.

about what types of support are made available. Service systems in all countries need to follow principles that help them determine how to offer the best possible services in the most equitable way.

SUMMARY

Assessment, diagnosis, intervention, and services are closely linked. They must go hand in hand if improvements are to be made to the support for people with intellectual and developmental disabilities, their families, and their care providers. Some people with intellectual and developmental disabilities receive formal assessment and diagnosis, but others do not. Assessment, both formal and informal, should identify needed supports, and diagnosis should identify causes or classification of an individual's disability with the goal of helping provide needed supports. Numerous types of interventions are applicable to improving the lives of people with intellectual and developmental disabilities.

Although assessment and specific interventions are essential for support to people with intellectual and developmental disabilities, services must also be available. Availability of services varies widely among countries of the world for several reasons. Six key ongoing challenges for services include determining the degree to which services are a public responsibility, ensuring awareness of entitlement to services, putting into place effective service methods, ensuring standards of quality care, promoting quality of life, and addressing equity.

REFERENCES

Aman, M.G., Benson, B.A., Campbell, K.M., et al. (1999). *Project Med Booklet series.* Columbus: The Ohio State University.

American Academy of Child and Adolescent Psychiatry. (1999). Practice parameters for the assessment and treatment of children, adolescents, and adults with mental retardation and co-morbid mental disorders. *Journal of Child and Adolescent Psychiatry, 38*(12, Suppl.).

American Association on Mental Retardation. (2002). *Mental retardation: Definition, classification, and systems of supports* (10th ed.). Washington, DC: Author.

American Psychiatric Association. (2000). *Diagnostic and statistical manual of mental disorders* (4th ed., text rev.). Washington, DC: Author.

Arvio, M., & Sillanpaa, M. (2003). Prevalence, etiology and comorbidity of severe and profound intellectual disability in Finland. *Journal of Intellectual Disability Research, 47,* 108–111.

Australia Institute of Health and Welfare. (n.d.). *The definition and prevalence of intellectual disability in Australia.* Retrieved March 16, 2006 from http://www.aihw.gov.au/publications/welfare/dpida/dpida-c00.html

Berry-Kravis, E., & Potanos, K. (2004). Psychopharmacology in fragile X syndrome—present and future. *Mental Retardation and Developmental Disabilities Research Reviews, 10,* 42–48.

Bokszanska, A., Martin, G., Vanstraelen, M., et al. (2003). Risperidone and olanzapine in adults with intellectual disability: A clinical naturalistic study. *International Clinical Psychopharmacology, 18,* 285–291.

Brasic, J.R., Barnett, J.Y., Kowalik, S., et al. (2004). Neurobehavioral assessment of children and adolescents attending a developmental disabilities clinic. *Psychological Reports, 95*(3, Pt. 2), 1079–1086.

Brown, I., Anand, S., Fung, W.L.A., et al. (2003). Family quality of life: Canadian results from an international study. *Journal of Developmental and Physical Disabilities, 15,* 207–230.

Brown, I., & Brown, R.I. (2003). *Quality of life and disability: An approach for community practitioners.* London: Jessica Kingsley Publishers.

Brown, I., Percy, M., & Garcin, N. (2003). Introduction to assessment, interventions and services in Ontario. In I. Brown & M. Percy (Eds.), *Developmental disabilities in Ontario* (2nd ed., pp. 367–389). Toronto: Ontario Association on Developmental Disabilities.

Brown, I., Raphael, D., & Renwick, R. (1997). *Dream or reality? Life for people with developmental disabilities in Ontario: Results from the provincial quality of life study.* Toronto: Centre for Health Promotion, University of Toronto.

Chescheir, N.C., & D'Alton, M. (2005). Evidence-based medicine and fetal treatment: How to get involved. *Obstetrics & Gynecology, 106,* 610–613.

DiMario, F.J., Jr., & Holland, J. (2002). The ketogenic diet: A review of the experience at Connecticut Children's Medical Centre. *Pediatric Neurology, 26,* 288–292.

Emerson, E., & Hatton, C. (2004). Response to McGrother et al. (Journal of Intellectual Disability Research, 46, 299–309) 'The prevalence of intellectual disability among South Asian communities in the UK'. *Journal of Intellectual Disability Research, 48,* 210–202.

Fernell, E. (1998). Aetiological factors and prevalence of severe mental retardation in children in a Swedish municipality: The possible role of consanguinity. *Developmental Medicine & Child Neurology, 40,* 608–611.

Fijiura, G.T. (2003). Continuum of intellectual disability: Demographic evidence for the "forgotten generation." *Mental Retardation, 41,* 420–429.

Fregni, F., & Pascual-Leone, A. (2005). Transcranial magnetic stimulation for the treatment of depression in neurologic disorders. *Current Psychiatry Reports, 7,* 381–390.

Fregni, F., Thome-Souza, S., Bermpohl, F., et al. (2005). Antiepileptic effects of repetitive transcranial magnetic stimulation in patients with cortical malformations: An EEG and clinical study. *Stereotactic and Functional Neurosurgery, 83,* 57–62.

Goldman, S. (2005). Stem and progenitor cell-based therapy of the human central nervous system. *Nature Biotechnology, 23,* 862–871.

Government of Ontario. (1991). *Regulated Health Professions Act* (1991 S.O. 1991, c. 18).

Grill, W.M. (2005). Safety considerations for deep brain stimulation: Review and analysis. *Expert Review of Medical Devices, 2,* 409–420.

Hamrin, V., & Scahill, L. (2005). Selective serotonin reuptake inhibitors for children and adolescents with major depression: Current controversies and recommendations. *Issues in Mental Health Nursing, 4,* 433–450.

Hoffman, R.E., & Cavus, I. (2002). Slow transcranial magnetic stimulation, long-term depotentiation, and brain hyperactivity disorders. *American Journal of Psychiatry, 159,* 1093–1102.

Holmes, G. (2002). Epilepsy surgery in children: When, why, and how. *Neurology, 58*(12 Suppl 7), S13–20.

Islam, S., Durkin, M.S., & Zaman, S.S. (1993). Socio-economic status and the prevalence of mental retardation in Bangladesh. *Mental Retardation, 31,* 412–417.

Ittenbach, R.F., Abery, B.H., Larson, S.A., et al. (1994). Community adjustment of young adults with mental retardation: A developmental perspective. *Palaestra, 9,* 19–24.

Jacobson, J.W., & Mulick, J.A. (Eds.). (1996). *Manual of diagnosis and professional practice in mental retardation.* Washington, DC: American Psychological Association, Division of Mental Retardation and Developmental Disabilities.

Jacobson, J.W., Mulick, J.A., & Green, G. (1998). Cost-benefit estimates for early intensive behavioral intervention for young children with autism—general model and single state case. *Behavioral Interventions, 13,* 201–226.

Katz, G. (2001). Adolescents and young adults with developmental disabilities interface the Internet: Six case reports of dangerous liaisons. *Mental Health Aspects in Developmental Disabilities, 4,* 77–84.

Kim, S., Larson, S.A., & Lakin, K.C. (1999). Behavioral outcomes of deinstitutionalization for people with intellectual disabilities: A review of studies conducted between 1980 and 1999. *Policy Research Brief, 10,* 99–108.

Larson, S.A., Lakin, K.C., Anderson, L., et al. (2001). Prevalence of mental retardation and developmental disabilities: Estimates from the 1994/1995 National Health Interview Survey Disability Supplements. *American Journal on Mental Retardation, 106,* 231–252.

Leonard, H., & Wen, X. (2002). The epidemiology of mental retardation: Challenges and opportunities in the new millennium. *Mental Retardation and Developmental Disabilities Research Reviews, 8,* 117–134.

Lucarelli, S., Frediani, T., Zingone, A.M., et al. (1995). Food allergy and infantile autism. *Panminerva Medicine, 37,* 137–141.

Luckasson, R., Coulter, D.L., Polloway, E.A., et al. (1992). *Mental retardation: Definition, classification, and systems of supports* (9th ed.). Washington, DC: American Association on Mental Retardation.

Lydaki, E., Nikoloudi, I., Kaminopetros, P., et al. (2005). Serial blood donations for intrauterine transfusions of severe hemolytic disease of the newborn with the use of recombinant erythropoietin in a pregnant woman alloimmunized with anti-Ku. *Transfusion, 45,* 1791–1795.

McGrath, B.M., & Tempier, R.P. (2005). *Pharmacopsychiatry, 38*(4),147–157.

McGrother, C.W., Bhaumik, S., Thorp, C.F., et al. (2002). Prevalence, morbidity and service need among South Asian and white adults with intellectual disability in Leicestershire, UK. *Journal of Intellectual Disability Research, 46,* 299–309.

McLaren, J., & Bryson, S.E. (1987). Review of recent epidemiological studies of mental retardation: Prevalence, associated disorders, and etiology. *American Journal on Mental Retardation, 92,* 243–254.

Merkens, L.S., Connor, W.E., Linck, L.M., et al. (2004). Effects of dietary cholesterol on plasma lipoproteins in Smith-Lemli-Opitz syndrome. *Pediatric Research, 56,* 726–732.

Millward, C., Ferriter, M., Calver, S., et al. (2004). Gluten- and casein-free diets for autistic spectrum disorder. *Cochrane Database of Systematic Reviews (Online), 2,* CD003498.

Mudford, O.C., Martin, N.T., Eikeseth, S., et al. (2001). Parent-managed behavioral treatment for preschool children with autism: Some characteristics of UK programs. *Research in Developmental Disabilities, 22,* 173–182.

Muller-Vahl, K.R. (2003). Cannabinoids reduce symptoms of Tourette's syndrome. *Expert Opinion on Pharmacotherapy, 4,* 1717–1725.

Murphy, C.C., Yeargin-Allsopp, M., Decouflé, P., et al. (1995). The administrative prevalence of mental retardation in 10-year-old children in metropolitan Atlanta, 1985 through 1987. *American Journal of Public Health, 85,* 319–323.

Nuyen, M. (1996). *What is the prevalence of Ontarians labeled as having a "developmental disability"?* Paper prepared for the Developmental Services Branch, Ontario Ministry of Community and Social Services.

Regulated Health Professions Act (1991 S.O. 1991, c. 18).

Roeleveld, N., Zielhuis, G.A., & Gabreels, F. (1997). The prevalence of mental retardation: A critical review of recent literature. *Developmental Medicine & Child Neurology, 39,* 125–132.

Royal College of Psychiatrists. (2004). *OP48. DC-LD: Diagnostic criteria for psychiatric disorders for use with adults with learning disabilities/mental retardation.* Retrieved July 26, 2005, from http://64.233.167.104/search?q=cache:rT-gNxTX5NQJ:www.rcpsych.ac.uk/publications/gaskell/op48.htm+diagnostic+criteria+learning+disabilities+United+Kingdom&hl=en

Rush, A.J., & Frances, A. (Eds.). (2000). Expert consensus guideline series: Treatment of psychiatric and behavioral problems in mental retardation [Special issue]. *American Journal on Mental Retardation, 105*(3).

Samuel, M., & Voon, V. (2005). Beyond the holy grail of motor symptoms: Deep brain stimulation for Parkinson's disease. *Journal of Neurology, Neurosurgery and Psychiatry, 76,* 759–760.

Scahill, L., Leckman, J.F., Schultz, R.T., et al. (2003). A placebo-controlled trial of risperidone in Tourette syndrome. *Neurology, 60,* 1130–1135.

Speth, L.A., Leffers, P., Janssen-Potten, Y.J., et al. (2005). Botulinum toxin A and upper limb functional skills in hemiparetic cerebral palsy: A randomized trial in children receiving intensive therapy. *Developmental Medicine and Child Neurology, 47,* 468–473.

To, S.E., Zepf, R.A., & Woods, A.G. (2005). The symptoms, neurobiology, and current pharmacological treatment of depression. *The Journal of Neuroscience Nursing, 37,* 102–107.

Todd, S., Young, P., Shearn, J., et al. (2004). Family quality of life in Wales. In A. Turnbull, I. Brown, & H.R. Turnbull

(Eds.), *Families and people with mental retardation and quality of life: International perspectives* (pp. 101–147). Washington, DC: American Association on Mental Retardation.

Tsiouris, J.A., & Brown, W.T. (2004). Neuropsychiatric symptoms of fragile X syndrome: Pathophysiology and pharmacotherapy. *CNS Drugs, 18,* 687–703.

Tsiouris, J.A., Patti, P.J., Tipu, O., et al. (2002). Adverse effects of phenytoin given for late-onset seizures in adults with Down syndrome. *Neurology, 59,* 779–780.

Tymchuk, A.J., Lakin, K.C., & Luckasson, R. (2001). *The forgotten generation: The status and challenges of adults with mild cognitive limitations.* Baltimore: Paul H. Brookes Publishing Co.

Wheless, J.W. (2004). Nonpharmacologic treatment of the catastrophic epilepsies of childhood. *Epilepsia, 45*(Suppl. 5), 17–22.

Yu, D., & Atkinson, L. (1993). Developmental disability with and without psychiatric involvement: Prevalence estimates for Ontario. *Journal on Developmental Disabilities, 2,* 92–99.

Zetlin, A., & Murtaugh, M. (1990). Whatever happened to those with borderline IQs? *American Journal on Mental Retardation, 94,* 463–469.

Zhang, K., Wang, S., Wei, X., et al. (2003). Identification and treatment of mental disorders in urban and rural area of Fuyang. *Chinese Mental Health Journal, 17,* 197–199.

22

Person-Centered and Family-Centered Support

Ivan Brown, Diane Galambos, Denise J. Poston, and Ann P. Turnbull

WHAT YOU WILL LEARN ABOUT IN THIS CHAPTER

- Person-centered approaches
- Family-centered approaches
- Professional issues regarding person- and family-centered support

In Chapter 1, it was explained that the field of intellectual and developmental disabilities has moved away from using the term "providing services to people with disabilities" and toward using the term "supporting people with disabilities." This may appear to be a small change in terminology, but the change in meaning is significant. *Supporting* infers action by others associated with strengthening the fundamental abilities of a person with a disability. In this chapter, an important aspect of supporting is expanded. Person-centered and family-centered support focuses, respectively, on individuals with disabilities and their families with a view to ensuring that the support given emerges from, and is fully in keeping with, their wishes and decisions.

PERSON-CENTERED APPROACHES

Since the 1980s, there has been an increasing trend toward taking person-centered approaches to providing services and supports to people with intellectual and developmental disabilities. In practice, this means centering attention and resources on the wants and needs of the person with disabilities when planning, delivering, or reviewing services and supports. Simply put, it means respecting the person's opinions and choices. Person-centered approaches are ways of delivering services and providing supports that place the person—rather than the service, organization, or system—at the center of planning. A number of useful resources have been developed to help professionals take person-centered approaches (Hagner, Helm, & Butterworth, 1996; Holburn & Vietze, 2002; see also Appendix B at the end of the book).

Person-centered support encompasses four of the most important aspects of good services and supports:

1. Respect each person with a disability as an individual human being with unique and valued characteristics.
2. Consider the rights and privileges of individual people with disabilities over the rights and privileges of groups of people or service providers, except when there is harm to oneself or others.
3. Develop and provide services and supports that are tailored to the needs and wants of individual people with disabilities and that enhance the quality of their lives.
4. Determine the cost of services and supports for each individual rather than for groups or programs.

Person-centered supports often incorporate other trends. It is often assumed, for example, that for people with intellectual disabilities to have a high quality of life, they should do so in ways that are close to the way the general population lives. This involves living in communities and taking part in the resources and activities that communities have to offer in ways that are best suited to the individual person. Thus, the trend toward person-centered approaches builds on other trends in the fields of intellectual and developmental disabilities and on existing values held by most members of society. At the same time, it represents a shift in values toward people with disabilities as individuals by addressing their unique needs, working toward effective self-determination (Wehmeyer, 2002), and improving quality of life (Schalock, 2004) as it is perceived and experienced by the individual.

Origins of Person-Centered Approaches

The terms *individualized planning* and *person-centered planning* are commonly used in descriptions of a variety of support models. The various models are characterized by different goals and processes, and although each model has gained or lost favor to different degrees over time, one feature has endured and is increasingly gaining predominance—focus on the person's unique needs, wants, and characteristics (see also Gardner, 2002).

Having goals and written plans outlining services and supports to individuals with disabilities was not a predominant feature of services until the mid-1970s in the more affluent countries. Prior to this, the medical model, which dominated most service organizations, sometimes required professionals (often medical professionals) who were responsible for overall care to produce client, or patient, care plans. These may not have been seen by the client or direct care staff, however, and most plans did not include input from these individuals. This practice still exists in many parts of the world.

In developed countries, the medical model was gradually replaced by a more ecological perspective—seeing the person's life and behavior in relation to the resources and challenges of the environments in which he or she lives. This perspective focused on the unique abilities of individuals and on the relationships between those abilities and the requirements of their living and working environments. Such individual focus resulted in the introduction of individualized planning that was known by a number of names and acronyms, such as individual program plan (IPP). This planning was generated by people whose training and perspective focused on promoting full community living. Direct care staff typically participated in developing these plans, and their day-to-day knowledge of individuals was acknowledged as valuable for specifying future personal goals. They were either consulted by those responsible for designing individualized plans or were given this responsibility directly. In addition, family members and others gradually were consulted more frequently in the planning process, especially in the schools. However, involvement of the person with a disability was still uncommon by the 1980s. This was especially the case for people with intellectual and developmental disabilities who were still living in large institutions, where contact with family members was not always strong and involving anyone but paid staff in planning was rare.

From the 1950s to the 1980s in particular, a deficit model had dominated individual planning. Developmental checklists and other formalized assessment methods were used to identify behavioral deficits (and excesses). People were commonly "modified" to suit a perceived standard. Behaviors that were considered to be unacceptable were targeted for decrease or elimination, and missing skills were targeted for training. There was much interest in developing maximum potential, though, especially in developing skills such that the person might function adequately within various environments (e.g., live and work in a community setting). An important lesson from this era was to emphasize efforts to 1) remove barriers to personal growth and development and 2) promote learning and skill acquisition. However, the scope of planning often remained narrowly focused, often involving behavior modification, and did not necessarily emphasize the unique needs and wishes of individuals.

Over time, a number of problems associated with individual planning began to accumulate (Galambos, 2003; Mansell & Beadle-Brown, 2004):

- Individual planning focused primarily on how the needs of the individual might be met by the service. Thus, although it identified individual need, it was still primarily service centered in that it identified parts of the service that could be most useful for the individual's development rather than devising services and supports that could best contribute to the individual's development.
- The plans took on the connotation of "piles of paper" that took up valuable worker time, frequently had no client input, and were rarely seen by individuals.
- There were efforts to standardize and streamline the process so that it would be less time consuming. These shortcuts, by focusing on efficiency, often overlooked the unique needs of individuals. In this sense, these efforts contributed to depersonalization.
- Plan review became an annual event for service staff or governing/funding bodies, and the documents were kept in remote places such as a program director's office or a locked file cabinet.
- The changes outlined in a plan usually referred to how the individual had to change rather than to how the environment, staff, service organization, or governing/funding bodies might need to change.
- The logical sequence of actions designed to achieve goals was often called a "program." As computers and computer language became more mainstream, the idea of "programming people" took on the connotation of an impersonal, technical, and controlling way of interacting with people.
- For many, individualized planning was linked with the idea of training goals. Service organizations whose mandates did not include training, or whose clients were considered "untrainable," often bypassed or rejected the ideas of individualization and planning. Similarly, planning was thought to be unnecessary for individuals who were viewed as being too high functioning, too low functioning, or even too old.
- The idea of understanding and supporting people as individuals was often misunderstood. For some, individualization implied one-to-one staff ratios, which were, in most cases, not feasible or even desirable.

- When the focus was on programs and plans rather than on people, individualized plans were used to judge readiness and as a method for placing individuals along a given continuum of needs. This approach to planning found service organizations and schools exercising power over individuals, and it tended to serve organizations rather than the interests of those with disabilities.

Although the term *individualized planning* has been used for several decades and continues to be used, the meanings attached to it have evolved. There has been a shift toward person-centeredness in individualized planning. This shift moves planning away from focusing on what the services can offer and toward services and supports that are needed to meet the requirements of the person—from his or her point of view. Change in this area is likely to continue, because time will continue to bring with it new circumstances, new challenges, and fresh ideas. Indeed, it should be recognized that person-centered approaches are still developing and that considerable thought and planning are needed to determine if and how it can become broad policy or even policy of specific services and supports (e.g., Felce, 2004). If it is determined to be feasible as policy, procedural changes such as who exercises power, how funding is administered, and how to train staff will have to be addressed (Emerson & Stancliffe, 2004; Mansell & Beadle-Brown, 2004).

Person-Centered Planning

Planning is a normal everyday activity in which all people engage—some with more or less skill and success than others. Most of planning is informal and does not have accompanying documentation. From time to time people, however, engage in more formal planning activities such as career planning, education planning, financial planning, or retirement planning.

One's everyday plans focus on how one wants things to be, what one would like to happen next, and how it should happen. Planning may take place at home, at work, at school, or during leisure activities. Although some plans may be quite comprehensive and might even be thought of as life plans, others are very specific—focusing on only one aspect of a person's life. The nature and scope of planning, therefore, varies.

Over several years, a person usually develops many plans, each one being somewhat different and having unique features. When one considers the complexities related to planning for an individual in a range of settings, for singular or comprehensive purposes, and across the life span, the idea of individualizing becomes paramount. Thus, planning guides should be used *only* as guides. There is no one way to formulate a plan that will work with all people in every setting. This is contrary to the essence of individualization and the values that have come to be associated with person-centered planning.

No one has total control over the events of his or her life, but planning helps to give a compass on life's journey. When people's life circumstances, which may include disabilities, make them vulnerable to control by others, their journeys may be restricted. For them, a person-centered planning approach that implies involvement and control is critical to having a rich and meaningful life.

What Person-Centered Planning Involves One service provider described the person-centered planning process in this way: "An individual, along with his or her support network, develops a tailor-made support plan that identifies specific goals, expected outcomes, and natural and/or specialized support services required to actualize community living, participation, and quality of life" (Galambos, 2003, p. 394). Another description of person-centered planning is that the individual selects others to assist in a process of developing the plan that is the basis of support arrangements, whether they involve informal supports or more formal services. Whatever description is used, person-centered planning is a shift away from planning by others and toward supporting people with disabilities in planning for themselves. Such planning is no longer based on what a service organization has to offer; rather, it is based on the person's wants and needs, as well as his or her dreams and hopes for life—whatever those may be.

Quality of Life: The Goal of Person-Centered Planning Quality of life as a concept and a goal is "close to most of our hearts, both personally and professionally" (Landesman, 1986, p. 141). For the most part, it is something that individual human beings and human civilizations throughout history have sought—and still seek.

Quality of life has become commonly accepted in services for people with intellectual and developmental disabilities as both an overall goal and an effective organizing principle (Brown & Brown, 2003; Butterworth, Steere, & Whitney-Thomas, 1997; Schalock, 1997). As such, this term has been useful for asking two fundamental questions pertaining to the lives of people with intellectual and developmental disabilities:

1. To what degree is life good?
2. How can life be improved?

At an individual level, it is now accepted that many aspects of quality of life are common to all humans (e.g., personal control, safety, self-efficacy, health), whereas other aspects are unique to individuals (e.g., personal tastes, treasured possessions, meaningful experiences, valued activities) (Brown & Brown, 2003).

Quality of life, as an overall concept, is useful for helping to set person-centered planning goals (Schalock, 2004). The two basic questions that people with disabilities should ask themselves are (Renwick, Brown, & Raphael, 1994)

1. What things currently add to the quality of my life that need to be maintained or enhanced?
2. What things detract from the quality of my life that need to be improved, abandoned, or otherwise addressed?

When using quality of life for the purpose of more specific individual goal setting, it is often helpful to use one or more of the conceptual frameworks available to ask the same questions about their domains and subdomains (see Display 22.1 for an example). This framework is the basis of a 54-item quality of life questionnaire (Raphael, Brown, & Renwick, 1999; Raphael et al., 1996), and the individual questionnaire items can also be useful starting points for thinking about person-centered goals.

A great deal has been written about quality of life (e.g., see Brown & Brown, 2003; Schalock & Verdugo, 2002), but the most important ideas for person-centered approaches that affect quality of life are associated with

1. Living and working in environments that promote contentment and belonging
2. Having a wide range of opportunities available from which to choose
3. Exercising personal choice
4. Being able to act on personal choices by having necessary supports available
5. Engaging in activities that reflect personal values and interests and that result in satisfaction
6. Engaging in life experiences that have personal meaning

These six quality of life ideas serve as one good set of principles for achieving desired outcomes from person-centered planning. There are many other useful sets of principles available in various countries (see Display 22.2 for one example).

Display 22.1

Use of quality of life conceptual frameworks for setting person-centered goals

Several conceptualizations of quality of life are available. These provide useful frameworks for identifying sources of quality in a person's life and areas of life in which improvements would be helpful. One such framework is provided here by way of an example. The nine domains of this conceptual framework are organized around three main concepts: Being, Belonging, and Becoming.

Being: Who you are as a person	
Physical being:	Your body and your health
Psychological being:	Your thoughts and feelings
Spiritual being:	Your values and beliefs
Belonging: The people and places in your life	
Physical belonging:	Where you live
Social belonging:	The people in your life
Community belonging:	Your connection with the people, places, and things in your community
Becoming: What you do in life for fulfillment	
Practical becoming:	The practical work you do at home, school or place of employment
Leisure becoming:	What you do for fun and enjoyment
Growth becoming:	What you do to learn, develop, and adjust

From Center for Health Promotion, University of Toronto. (n.d.). *The Quality of Life Model.* Retrieved December 1, 2005, from http://www.utoronto.ca/qol/concepts.htm; adapted by permission.

Other Guidelines for Person-Centered Planning *Remember who is in charge.* The person at the center of planning should ideally "own" and direct his or her plan as well as the process for developing and implementing it. Optimal involvement in and control of planning may, at times, be best achieved with help from unpaid members of a support circle and/or an advocate. All those involved have a responsibility to help ensure that plans developed are personal and individual.

Focus on people, not on disabilities. Being acknowledged as people first has become a prominent personal (and political) goal for people with disabilities. At the personal level, this involves affirmation as a unique individual who happens to have a disability that may require some form of additional support. Consequently, the wants and needs of the person should govern what supports are required and how supports will be provided.

Connect people to natural supports, not just to programs. Connecting people who have disabilities with natural supports is especially important for some individuals, to whom this approach is particularly meaningful. These partnerships and access to community resources have the potential to add positively to quality of life in an ongoing way, as well as to make existing services more effective.

Avoid mindlessness. In paid service provision, attempts to reduce the complexities of the workplace have at times resulted in planning processes and docu-

Display 22.2

Guiding principles for person-centered planning

There are various sets of principles for achieving desired outcomes from person-centered planning. This one was provided by the Ontario Association for Community Living (1995).

Focus on the person.
Invite assistance from the people around the person.
Have funding controlled by the person and/or his or her significant others.
Ensure that supports are unique to the person and not fragmented.
Guide people into the activities and life of the community.
Guide the community's interest toward the lives of people with disabilities.
Provide help to people and families exactly as they need it.

Source: Ontario Association for Community Living (1995).

ments that are used like recipes. Interactions can become routine, hampering positive mindsets and creativity. Mindful staff remain alert to new ideas, especially those that emerge from natural interaction, and they participate in planning in ways that are both innovative and focused on the individual.

Plan for today, not just tomorrow. A problem associated with traditional planning approaches has been the idea that planning must focus on the long term future—on accomplishments that may be realized "some day." As a consequence, some people with disabilities have plans outlining a vision for tomorrow but none for today. It is important to remember that most people make plans for the next hour, day, and week. Plans are not always realized, and they may be interrupted, changed, or even eliminated by welcome or unwelcome events. Yet, people persist in planning, because not to plan is to surrender control to the people and events around them. People without plans and visions of the future are more likely to be passive and depressed than active and joyful. The thrill of spontaneity comes largely from one's power to alter one's own plans and to decide to willingly embrace unexpected events and opportunities.

Make plans that reflect the fact that all people share the same universal needs for security, belonging, recognition, achievement, and control over one's life. These needs touch on the following areas (see also Schwartz, Jacobson, & Holburn, 2000):

- A home
- A safe environment
- Relationships and mutual respect
- A sense of belonging
- Opportunities to grow and develop
- Opportunities to build self-respect
- Opportunities to engage in meaningful life activities
- Opportunities to make decisions and choices
- Freedom to exercise personal rights and to take personal responsibility
- The right to make mistakes and take reasonable risks
- Opportunities to see oneself and to be seen by others as unique and valued

Participants The individual, should be involved as much as possible in developing the plan. The level of involvement may depend on his or her age, ability, and preferences. Anyone who knows and is committed to the individual and/or the family might also be involved. Thus, other members of the support network or planning team may include

- Parents/guardians
- Other family members (e.g., brothers, sisters, grandparents, aunts, uncles, cousins)
- Friends and neighbors
- People from school, work, place of worship, and so forth
- Individual who specializes in planning and who has been asked (or hired) to facilitate the planning process
- Service providers
- Government or funding representative
- Medical staff

The general principle for involving others is that the person himself or herself has the last word in who helps to construct the plan.

Style and Content The plan can be written by the individual, family members, a facilitator, a friend, an advocate, or an experienced consultant. Plans can be simple or elaborate, of varying lengths, and in formats other than that of a formal report. They can include stories, journals, portfolios, photos, drawings, and diagrams—any form of representation or communication favored by the individual.

The written plan is a compilation of materials reflecting endeavors to understand who the person is and how his or her quality of life can be established, maintained, and enhanced. The plan usually includes the following information:

- An outline, or "map," of the person's support network
- Relevant information about the person's background and present circumstances
- A vision for the future

- A description of the person's likes and dislikes, wants and needs, and desires and hopes
- A statement of objectives to be attained
- A description of the support that is required to attain the objectives
- A list of specific ways the objectives will be attained
- A list of the people who will help to attain the objectives
- A description of how the planning team will know when the objectives have been attained

All of the preceding items are often put together and formalized into a document that contains personal and private information. It is always important to remember that not everyone needs to know everything about a person with a disability. Involvement in planning begins with people with disabilities being in control over who knows what about their lives and circumstances. People with disabilities and their written plans become the focal point of a planning process that involves understanding, deciding, doing, and reviewing.

Potential Applications of Person-Centered Planning Person-centered planning has been applied in a wide variety of situations involving both children and adults with intellectual and developmental disabilities. The examples provided here illustrate this broad scope of application:

- Career choice and employment outcome (e.g., Menchetti & Garcia, 2003)
- Individualized funding (e.g., Fortune et al., 2005)
- Later-life planning (e.g., Heller et al., 2000)
- Goals, especially for people with profound and multiple disabilities (e.g., Green, Middleton, & Reid, 2000; Reid, Everson, & Green, 1999)
- Residential settings (e.g., Davis & Faw, 2002; Heller, 2002)
- Sexuality (e.g., Lumley & Scotti, 2001)
- Transition planning in schools (e.g., Hagner et al., 1996; Miner & Bates, 1997)

FAMILY-CENTERED APPROACHES

Family-centered support is very similar to person-centered support with the exception that the family of the individual with a disability is the focus of supports and services.

Origins of Family-Centered Support

Family-centered support, which began to take on special importance in the 1980s in the early childhood and early intervention fields, is a direct result of a shift in the way that disability services are provided. This is characterized by a shift away from "fixing" the child and his or her mother and toward providing supports to key people in the various environments of the child's life. It is also characterized by a shift away from parental involvement, whereby parents (mostly mothers) were expected to be involved in a service system that was the "center of the universe," with family members revolving around it. Family-centered approaches put the family at the center of the universe, with service systems revolving around the family (Turnbull & Summers, 1987).

Family-centered approaches seem to be the prevalent model in early childhood or early intervention services, although they do not appear to be as strong in school age and adult services (Turnbull & Turnbull, 2002). The results of some research also suggest that the family-centered philosophy is stronger than its actual implementation (Bruder, 2000; Katz & Scarpati, 1995).

Family-Centered Support Plans

Family-centered support is a general approach and a service philosophy that sometimes is informal in nature and other times is more formal, with family-centered support plans drawn up. When there is a family-centered support plan, the family member with a disability may have a separate person-centered support plan, supports for the individual may be included in the family-centered plan, or there may be a person-family interdependent plan (Kim & Turnbull, 2004).

Family Quality of Life: The Goal of Family-Centered Planning Like person-centered planning, the goal of family-centered planning is enhanced family quality of life. This is an area of study that has only recently emerged in a formal sense, although there is a vast amount of related literature in several disciplines that looks at family structure and functioning. The domains and the questionnaire items that are emerging in certain family quality of life studies can be very useful places to start considering what aspects of family life could be the focus of family-centered goal-setting. (See Brown & Brown, 2003; Turnbull, Brown, & Turnbull, 2004; see also http://www.beachcenter.org/research/default.asp?strResource=&Type=General%20Topic&act=view&id=4 for published and emerging work in family quality of life.)

Common Characteristics There are many definitions and descriptions of family-centered supports, but they have three common characteristics: family as the unit of support, family choice, and supports based on family strengths (Allen & Petr, 1996).

Family as the Unit of Support The primary component of a family-centered support approach is the focus on the family as a functional social unit, which requires a family systems approach for understanding and supporting all family members (Leal,

1999). Previously, the main focus of services was the person with a disability (and sometimes his or her mother). There has been a growing research and service focus on support for the family as a whole, as well as a corresponding focus on fathers (Ainge, Colvin, & Baker, 1998), siblings (Heller, Gallagher, & Fredrick, 1999; Meyer & Vadasy, 1994) and extended family members (Mifrin-Veitch, Bray, & Watson, 1997). Research points to the importance of the family's role on child development, caregiving, and support, but most policies and programs still view the individual as the beneficiary of supports and services (Schalock & Verdugo, 2002).

Family Choice Just as choice is central to person-centered support, it is a key component of family-centered support. The family-centered support model encourages families to voice their preferences and priorities and professionals to respond to those needs. Family choice may be expressed in different ways, but its essence is that the family is the final decision maker regarding issues related to child or family (Turnbull, Turbiville, & Turnbull, 2000). One way this can be accomplished is to change the power relationship between families and professionals from one of power over—in which professionals have authority over families in decision making—to power-with—in which families make decisions in cooperation with professionals (Labonté, 1996; Turnbull & Turnbull, 2002), thereby leveling the playing field and focusing on the authenticity and authority of parents' experience and knowledge.

Supports Based on Family Strengths The family-centered approach abandons the pathological orientation that focuses on the deficits of individuals and families and instead focuses on their strengths. Every individual and family has strengths, but often the environment around the family is such that their strengths cannot be easily identified or used effectively to address effective living. One role of professionals is to facilitate relationships and environments in which strengths can be enhanced and put to effective use. Another is to focus on and build strengths and resources rather than to emphasize deficits or needs. Building family strengths requires that service systems enhance families' knowledge, skills, and resources.

Service Challenges for a Family-Centered Approach Any change in service approach brings with it some challenges. Three such challenges that professionals and families might encounter when implementing a family-centered approach are described next.

1. Getting to know families well enough to provide effective family-centered supports is essential but requires time and other resources. Families may be reluctant to share details of their family life, or some family members may not be available due to temporary geographic separation, work hours, or other reasons. Service providers need to value their relationships with family members and must be prepared to be flexible yet thorough in getting to know families.

2. Policy and organizational missions and structures have not always changed in keeping with the trend toward a family-centered approach. For example, many organizations do not have a funding mandate to provide supports to anyone other than the individual with a disability; thus, they have to be creative in the way that family-centered supports are structured and implemented. This may be most feasible for organizations providing services to young children, who almost always live with families upon whom they are highly dependent. As children get older and become adults, the tendency for many organizations has been, and still is, to focus more on the individual than the family. This is problematic because a great many adults with intellectual and developmental disabilities—in both the more developed and less developed countries of the world—are encouraged by policy and practice trends (see Chapter 4) to continue to live with their families.

3. Individual family members may have distinct values, preferences, and needs. As a consequence, there may not be one right service that is appropriate for the family as a whole. Service providers may believe that family members may actually need their own person-centered plans, but this is not always feasible in view of high caseloads. Ways need to be developed that help professionals support the needs of families as a whole, as well as the needs of individual family members, in ways that are time and cost efficient.

PROFESSIONAL ISSUES REGARDING PERSON- AND FAMILY-CENTERED SUPPORT

Providing the person-centered or family-centered support that results from planning almost always requires flexibility and creative problem solving. This can lead to numerous interesting and exciting activities. Along the way, however, those who are helping to implement the support plan will invariably face issues requiring decisions that are sometimes difficult and sometimes contrary to the plan. Six of these issues are described next as examples, although readers may think of others—and, indeed, are invited to do so. Furthermore, readers are encouraged to think of each of these six issues as if they occurred in their own communities, then to discuss how to move to an ethical decision (i.e., how to decide on the best course of action to follow in this particular situation). Thus, for each issue that follows, the dilemma is set out, but the solution is not provided precisely because there is no solution that fits all situations. (For more on professional ethics and person-centered planning, see O'Brien, 2002.)

1. *Personal choice versus professional role:* A central idea in providing person- or family-centered support is to listen to the voice, and the choice, of the person with disabilities or the family. At times, though, what the individual or family needs or wants to do may conflict with the perceived role of a professional. In an example cited in Brown and Brown (2003), a man with disabilities was on probation and under court order not to be in any establishment that served liquor. When his support worker passed by and saw the man sitting in the window drinking a beer and beckoning him to come in, the worker was faced with an interesting dilemma. Should he follow what he saw as his professional role and report this man for not obeying the terms of his probation, or should he support the man in doing what it was he wanted to do—enjoy his beer? In providing person-centered support to individuals, professionals must be prepared to face and meet many similar dilemmas.

2. *Personal choice versus professional personal opinion:* People with intellectual and developmental disabilities or their families sometimes make decisions that professional staff who support them find difficult to accept. Decisions may be difficult to accept because the professional has learned from experience that the consequences probably are not in the person's or family's best interest, because the decision is contrary to basic tenets of the professional's experience, or because the professional personally does not condone the decision. For example, Laila (mother of 8-year-old Kiera, who has an intellectual disability) wanted to quit her job, move away from the city where her family and friends lived, and move to another city to live with a man she has known only for a brief time. The family support worker considered this to be an unwise decision, as it removed Kiera from the supports that helped with her challenging behavior at home and at school and it was fraught with other risks. The support worker recognized that this was Laila's personal wish, one that she was certain she wanted to pursue, but the support worker simply did not agree with it. The dilemma she faced was whether to put her personal feelings aside and support Laila in what she wanted to do or to set her value of always supporting a family member's decision aside and counsel Laila to change her mind. Professionals will face many similar dilemmas when putting into practice family- or person-centered supports. These issues are not impossible to solve, but the response is not the same for every situation and professionals need to be prepared to face them.

3. *Personal choice versus family members' choice:* A common issue that arises in person-centered support, especially for people who live with their families or who are closely associated with them, is that the person's choice may differ from the choice of family members. Markus, for example, was quite happy living in the basement of his mother's home. He expressed a wish to continue living there "forever." His mother wanted Markus to be more independent and to learn to live on his own in supported independent living. She thought he should learn to take greater responsibility for his own life, and she felt worn out after many years of helping him. She asked his support worker to convince Markus to look for another place to live. The worker then faced the interesting dilemma of supporting Markus and asking the mother to reconsider or supporting the mother and asking Markus to reconsider.

4. *Personal choice versus resource and funding limitations:* A limitation to the success of person- or family-centered support is that the personal resources are not always available (there is no one available to help carry out the plan) or that the financial resources do not support the activity (there is not enough money available to carry out the plan). One possible solution to this is that the support worker consider it as part of his or her role to advocate for or seek such resources. This is not always feasible, however, especially in situations when individuals with disabilities have little contact with family and friends or in parts of the world where financial resources are limited. If a personal choice cannot be supported, the support worker must consider whether it is advisable to support another personal choice, such as a second or third choice, and whether it is a valuable lesson simply to help the person with a disability understand that the choice cannot be met.

The story of Anita, who was searching for a new place to live, serves as an example. Anita's family was financially well off, and she had grown up in a large house that had many amenities. When it was time for Anita to look for a place of her own, she informed her support worker that she wanted to buy a house in an affluent area. Her parents could easily afford to buy her a small house, although they were not prepared to support her financially. Moreover, Anita had developed no particular skills in maintaining a house, and her disability allowance was much too low to support upkeep of a house. It seemed to the support worker that Anita's personal choice was not going to be supported by her family or her available funds. The worker decided—but not without having her own doubts—to explain to Anita that her choice was not possible and that she would have to make another choice. Other professionals might have responded another way.

5. *Personal choice and service organization standards:* Person- and family-centered support necessarily feature the needs and wishes of the person or family rather than the service provider organization. This leads to a

number of very interesting dilemmas for professionals who work for the organization.

Two are highlighted here, by way of examples. First, most organizations have mandates, or visions of what they consider they should be doing. Needs and wishes, as expressed by individuals with intellectual and developmental disabilities or their families, are not always in accordance with these mandates. In fact, many people with disabilities and their families do not even know what these mandates are. A challenge for such service organizations is to adopt a mandate that is flexible enough to respond to the expressed needs and wishes of individuals and families. Second, the personal choice of an individual with a disability may be contrary to professional or ethical standards and policies that are adhered to by members of the service organization. In some situations and in some jurisdictions, these standards are actually required by law. In more serious cases, the decision may be obvious, but in less serious cases it may not be. Maria, for example, was a support worker at a supported employment organization that had a strict policy: Individuals they supported would be taken off the job if they stole from their employers. When Maria learned that an employee she supported had taken several rolls of tape to pack some boxes at home, she had to decide whether to go by her organization's policy, to counsel the employee to return the rolls of tape, or to ignore the situation.

6. *Personal choice and the need for advocacy or behind-the-scenes planning:* Personal and family choice suggests that the individual with a disability or family is, for the most part, in control of making the decision and deciding how it will be carried out. In many instances, this is indeed possible. In other cases, though, those who are supporting the person with a disability or the family may need to do some advocacy or behind-the-scenes planning for the plan or activity to work out well. By way of a simple example, Juan liked to plan weekend trips by train to visit family and friends who lived in nearby cities. However, he had difficulty understanding that it was important to make sure those meeting him at the train station knew what day and time he would be arriving. He gave explicit instructions to his worker not to telephone ahead; rather, he claimed he would just wait at the station until they arrived, as he had done many times before. It appeared that he did not actually mind waiting for long periods of time, and it also appeared that this arrangement gave Juan a sense of being in control of the situation. His support worker did not think waiting at the station was a good idea, however, and always telephoned to give the arrival time as soon as Juan boarded the train. Such behind-the-scenes planning resulted in less worry for those who cared about Juan, but it was not in keeping with Juan's wishes.

SUMMARY

Person-centered approaches to support emphasize the needs and wishes of the person who has a disability rather than place service organizations or funders at the center of organizational planning, service delivery, and service evaluation. Similarly, family-centered approaches make the family of the individual with a disability the focus of supports and services. These approaches have occurred along with the trends toward more people with disabilities living in community settings and toward consideration of individuals' strengths rather than their deficits. There are many ways to make and implement person-centered and family-centered plans, but they should adhere to valued service principles, enhance quality of life, and reflect the specific characteristics of the individual or family. Inherent in these approaches are a number of new and interesting challenges for support workers and for service organizations. These often require creative solutions.

FOR FURTHER THOUGHT AND DISCUSSION

1. It is important to understand wants and needs as the basis for deciding what services are needed. What are some good ways of understanding what a person or family wants and needs? How can you listen to the person's or family's opinions rather than present your own?
2. Create a person-centered plan for your own life. It is worth mentioning that a difference between planning for yourself and a person with a disability may be the amount of control that you have over all aspects of the plan. Give serious thought to these differences as you note them, and write down the specific lessons you have learned for helping a person with an intellectual or developmental disability to develop a plan.
3. Using your own family as an example, reflect on how person-centered support would differ from family-centered support.
4. If you currently are affiliated with a service organization, what would have to happen in your organization to fully implement family-centered supports? What facilitators or barriers are present in your organization?
5. It is important to understand that you will have to make some tough choices. Select four examples from the six issues described in the Professional Issues Regarding Person- and Family-Centered Support section. Gather opinions from three colleagues about what they would do in each case. Discuss their reasons for their opinions.

REFERENCES

Aigne, D., Colvin, G., & Baker, S., (1998). Analysis of perceptions of parents who have children with intellectual disabilities: Implications for service providers. *Education and Training in Mental Retardation and Developmental Disabilities, 33*(4), 331–341.

Allen, R.I., & Petr, C.G. (1996). Toward developing standards and measurements for family centered practice in family support programs. In G.H.S. Singer & L.E. Powers (Eds.), *Redefining family support: Innovations in public–private partnerships* (pp. 57–86). Baltimore: Paul H. Brookes Publishing Co.

Brown, I., & Brown, R.I. (2003). *Quality of life and disability: An approach for community practitioners.* London: Jessica Kingsley Publishers.

Bruder, M.B. (2000). Family-centered early intervention: Clarifying our values for the new millennium. *Topics in Early Childhood Special Education, 20,* 105–115.

Butterworth, J., Steere, D.E., & Whitney-Thomas, J. (1997). Using person-centered planning to address personal quality of life. In R.L. Schalock (Ed.), *Quality of life: Vol. II. Applications to persons with disabilities* (pp. 5–23). Washington, DC: American Association on Mental Retardation.

Center for Health Promotion, University of Toronto. (n.d.). *The Quality of Life Model.* Retrieved December 1, 2005, from http://www.utoronto.ca/qol/concepts.htm

Davis, P., & Faw, G. (2002). Residential preferences in person-centered planning: Empowerment through the self-identification of preferences and their availability. In S. Holburn & P.M. Vietze (Eds.), *Person-centered planning: Research, practice, and future directions* (pp. 203–221). Baltimore: Paul H. Brookes Publishing Co.

Emerson, E., & Stancliffe, R.J. (2004). Planning and action: Comments on Mansell & Beadle-Brown. *Journal of Applied Research in Intellectual Disabilities, 17,* 23–26.

Felce, D. (2004). Can person-centred planning fulfill a strategic planning role? Comments on Mansell & Beadle-Brown. *Journal of Applied Research in Intellectual Disabilities, 17,* 27–30.

Fortune, J.R., Smith, G.A., Campbell, E.M., et al. (2005). Individual budgets according to individual needs: The Wyoming DOORS system. In R.J. Stancliffe & K.C. Lakin (Eds.), *Costs and outcomes of community services for people with intellectual disabilities* (pp. 241–262). Baltimore: Paul H. Brookes Publishing Co.

Galambos, D. (2003). Individual approaches to support. In I. Brown & M. Percy (Eds.), *Developmental disabilities in Ontario* (2nd ed.). Toronto: Ontario Association on Developmental Disabilities.

Gardner, J.F. (2002). The evolving social context for quality in services and supports. In R.L. Schalock & P.C. Baker (Eds.), *Embarking on a new century: Mental retardation at the end of the 20th century* (pp. 67–80). Washington, DC: American Association on Mental Retardation.

Green, C.W., Middleton, S.G., & Reid, D.H. (2000). Embedded evaluation of preferences samples from person-centered plans for people with profound multiple disabilities. *Journal of Applied Behavior Analysis, 33,* 639–642.

Hagner, D., Helm, D.T., & Butterworth, J. (1996). "This is your meeting": A qualitative study of person-centered planning. *Mental Retardation, 34,* 159–171.

Heller, K.W., Gallagher, P.A., & Fredrick, L.D. (1999). Parents' perceptions of siblings' interactions with their brothers and sisters who are deaf-blind. *Journal of The Association for Persons with Severe Handicaps, 24*(1), 33–43.

Heller, T. (2002). Residential settings and outcomes for individuals with intellectual disabilities. *Current Opinion in Psychiatry, 15,* 503–508.

Heller, T., Miller, A.B., Hsieh, K., et al. (2000). Later-life planning: Promoting knowledge of options and choice-making. *Mental Retardation, 38,* 395–406.

Holburn, S., & Vietze, P.M. (Eds.) (2002). *Person-centered planning: Research, practice, and future directions.* Baltimore: Paul H. Brookes Publishing Co.

Katz, L., & Scarpati, S. (1995). A cultural interpretation of early intervention teams and the IFSP: Parent and professional perceptions of roles and responsibilities. *Infant-Toddler Intervention, 5*(2), 177–192.

Kim, K., & Turnbull, A.P. (2004). Transition to adulthood for students with severe intellectual disabilities: Shifting toward person-family interdependent planning. *Research and Practice for Persons with Severe Disabilities, 29*(1), 53–57.

Labonté, R. (1996). Measurement and practice: Power issues in quality of life, health promotion, and empowerment. In R. Renwick, I. Brown, & M. Nagler (Eds.), *Quality of life in health promotion and rehabilitation: Conceptual approaches, issues, and applications* (pp. 132–145). Thousand Oaks, CA: Sage Publications.

Landesman, S. (1986). Quality of life and personal satisfaction: Definition and measurement issues. *Mental Retardation, 24*(3), 141–143.

Leal, L. (1999). *A family-centered approach to people with mental retardation.* Washington, DC: American Association on Mental Retardation.

Lumley, V.A., & Scotti, J.R. (2001). Supporting the sexuality of adults with mental retardation: Current status and future directions. *Journal of Positive Behavior Interventions, 3,* 109–119.

Mansell, J., & Beadle-Brown, J. (2004). Person-centred planning or person-centred action? Policy and practice in intellectual disability services. *Journal of Applied Research in Intellectual Disabilities, 17,* 1–9.

Menchetti, B.M., & Garcia, L.A. (2003). Personal and employment outcomes of person-centered career planning. *Education and Training in Developmental Disabilities, 38,* 145–156.

Meyer, D.J., & Vadasy, P.F. (1994). *Sibshops: Workshops for siblings of children with special needs.* Baltimore: Paul H. Brookes Publishing Co.

Miner, C.A., & Bates, P.E. (1997). The effect of person centered planning activities on the IEP/transition planning process. *Education and Training in Mental Retardation and Developmental Disabilities, 32,* 105–112.

Mirfin-Veitch, B., Bray, A., & Watson, M. (1997). We're just that sort of family: Intergenerational relationships in families including children with disabilities. *Family Relations, 46*(3), 305–311.

O'Brien, J. (2002). Numbers and faces: The ethics of person-centered planning. In S. Holburn & P.M. Vietze (Eds.), *Person-centered planning: Research, practice, and future directions* (pp. 399–414). Baltimore: Paul H. Brookes Publishing Co.

Ontario Association for Community Living. (1995). *Evolving our service practices toward more person-centred approaches.* Toronto: Author.

Raphael, D., Brown, I., & Renwick, R. (1999). Psychometric properties of the full and short versions of the Quality of Life Instrument Package: Results from the Ontario province-wide study. *International Journal of Disability, Development and Education, 46*(2), 157–168.

Raphael, D., Brown, I., Renwick, R., et al. (1996). Assessing the quality of life of persons with developmental disabilities: Description of a new model, measuring instruments, and initial findings. *International Journal of Disability, Development, and Education, 43*(1), 25–42.

Reid, D.H., Everson, J.M., & Green, C.W. (1999). A systematic evaluation of preferences identified through person-centered planning for people with profound multiple disabilities. *Journal of Applied Behavior Analysis, 32,* 467–477.

Renwick, R., Brown, I., & Raphael, D. (1994). Linking a conceptual approach to service provision. *Journal on Developmental Disabilities, 3*(2), 32–44.

Schalock, R.L. (1997). Preface. In R.L. Schalock (Ed.), *Quality of life: Vol. II. Applications to persons with disabilities* (pp. xi–xiv). Washington, DC: American Association on Mental Retardation.

Schalock, R.L. (2004). Quality of life from a motivational perspective. In H.N. Switzky (Ed.), *Personality and motivational systems in mental retardation: Vol. 28* (pp. 303–319). San Diego: Elsevier Academic Press.

Schalock, R.L., & Verdugo, M.A. (2002). *Handbook on quality of life for human service practitioners.* Washington, DC: American Association on Mental Retardation.

Schwartz, A.A., Jacobson, J.W., & Holburn, S.C. (2000). Defining person centeredness: Results of two consensus methods. *Education and Training in Mental Retardation and Developmental Disabilities, 35,* 235–249.

Turnbull, A.P., Brown, I., & Turnbull, H.R. (2004). *Families and people with mental retardation and quality of life: International perspectives.* Washington, DC: American Association on Mental Retardation.

Turnbull, A.P., & Summers, J.A. (1987). From parent involvement to family support: Evolution to revolution. In S.M. Pueschel, C. Tingey, J.W. Rynders, et al. (Eds.), *New perspectives on Down syndrome* (pp. 289–306). Baltimore: Paul H. Brookes Publishing Co.

Turnbull, A.P., Turbiville, V., & Turnbull, H.R. (2000). Evaluation of family-professional partnership models: Collection empowerment as the model for the early 21st century. In J.P. Shonkoff & S.J. Meisels (Eds.), *Handbook of early childhood intervention* (2nd ed., pp. 630–650). Cambridge, United Kingdom: Cambridge University Press.

Turnbull, A.P., & Turnbull, H.R. (2002). From the old to the new paradigm of disability and families: Research to enhance family quality of life outcomes. In J.L. Paul, C.D. Lavely, A. Cranston-Gingras, et al. (Eds.), *Rethinking professional issues in special education* (pp. 83–117). Westport, CT: Ablex Publishing.

Wehmeyer, M.L. (2002). The confluence of person-centered planning and self-determination. In S. Holburn & P.M. Vietze (Eds.), *Person-centered planning: Research, practice, and future directions* (pp. 51–69). Baltimore: Paul H. Brookes Publishing Co.

Woodill, G., Renwick, R., Brown, I., et al. (1994). Being, belonging, becoming: An approach to the quality of life of persons with developmental disabilities. In D. Goode (Ed.), *Quality of life for persons with disabilities: International perspectives and issues* (pp. 57–74). Cambridge, MA: Brookline Press.

23

Behavioral Intervention and Intellectual Disabilities

Rosemary A. Condillac

WHAT YOU WILL LEARN ABOUT IN THIS CHAPTER

- Why many people with intellectual disabilities need behavioral intervention
- Behaviors that need intervention
- Types of behavioral intervention
- Why behavioral intervention is effective for people with intellectual disabilities
- Best practices regarding interventions for problematic behavior

Behavioral intervention is the term used to describe a wide range of techniques that are based on learning theories. These theories focus on observable environmental events that prompt, increase, maintain, and decrease the occurrence of both appropriate and inappropriate behaviors. Another term used to describe a type of behavioral intervention is *applied behavior analysis (ABA)*. ABA is the use of behavioral methods to solve practical problems, including those of a serious clinical nature.

There are several key tenets in ABA. Conditions that are known to prompt a particular behavior are called *antecedents*. Antecedents precede a behavior and set the stage for it to occur. For example, the smell of freshly baked bread might be an antecedent for entering a bakery. Conditions that increase, decrease, or maintain behaviors are called *consequences*. Consequences are the responses (or lack of responses) that immediately follow an individual's behavior. A consequence that results in an increase in a particular behavior is called *reinforcement*. Reinforcement literally means strengthening. For example, a student who stays up all night to cram for a mid-term exam might be reinforced for her behavior if she receives a good grade. Reinforcement is more certainly the case if the student crams again for her next exam. Reinforcement is a process that results in an increased likelihood that the behavior will recur.

Conversely, a consequence that decreases the likelihood that specific behavior will recur is called *punishment*. The consequence only counts as a punisher if the behavior in question decreases. For example, if a person who regularly leaves a car in a no parking zone returns to the car to find a sizeable parking ticket, and consequently stops parking in such zones, an effective punishment has occurred. What is important to note is that it is not one's intention, but rather the effect of the consequence upon the individual's behavior, that determines if an event is reinforcing or punishing (see Display 23.1). These are some of the basic tenets of ABA that are essential to a clear understanding of behavioral intervention.

WHY MANY PEOPLE WITH INTELLECTUAL DISABILITIES NEED BEHAVIORAL INTERVENTION

North American reports of the prevalence of problematic behavior suggest that between one third and one half of individuals with intellectual disabilities exhibit some form of challenging behavior. A Canadian study conducted in Ontario found that of 948 individuals with intellectual disabilities, problematic behavior was exhibited by more than 50% of children 4–11 years of age and more than 45% of adolescents and adults ages 12 years and older. The most frequently exhibited behaviors were physical aggression, inappropriate verbal behavior, self-injury, and noncompliance (Atkinson et al., 1994). Such problematic behaviors can increase the risk of social isolation and decrease the quality of life experienced by individuals with intellectual disabilities. It is also important to consider that there is an increase in stress and sense of caregiving burden for the caregivers of individuals with intellectual disabilities who exhibit problematic behaviors (Maes et al., 2003). This stress has been found to have a direct impact on the caregivers and on the individuals with disabilities (Baker et al., 2003).

People with intellectual disabilities may be more likely to exhibit problematic behaviors when they have

Display 23.1

Is this an example of reinforcement or punishment?

Zack is a 10-year-old with limited communication and motor skills. During art class, he is asked to cut out shapes and glue them together. After approximately 1 minute, Zack throws the glue on the floor. The teacher, wanting to punish him for this behavior, sends Zack out to the hallway for 5 minutes. When 5 minutes are up, Zack is returned to his table in the classroom and given his project back. He immediately throws the glue again and is sent back to the hallway for 5 minutes. This scenario is repeated three more times in the next 20 minutes.

Did the consequence of being removed from the task have a reinforcing or a punishing effect on Zack's behavior? Because Zack threw glue often, it had a reinforcing effect. Zack's teacher intended the consequence of sending him into the hallway to be a punishment. However, it was not an effective punisher because throwing did not decrease. Instead, Zack's throwing increased as a result of being sent out of the classroom. This is what is known as inadvertent reinforcement of problematic behavior. In other words, Zack was taught to throw the glue to get out of art class, although this was certainly not the teacher's intention.

Source: Condillac (2003).

limited development of communicative, cognitive, social, emotional, and adaptive skills (Feldman & Griffiths, 1997). Those with limited communication skills may exhibit challenging behavior as a result of their inability to make their needs and wants known in more appropriate ways. Others with compromised cognitive skills might demonstrate problem behavior if task demands or curricula are beyond their current skill levels. Some have learned over time that problematic behavior can be an effective way to elicit change in an environment where they may otherwise lack power and freedom of choice. Thus, it is important that behavioral assessment and intervention practices take into account both the individual's developmental ability and the environmental events that might affect their challenging behavior.

Finally, many individuals with intellectual disabilities who do not exhibit problematic behavior require additional supports to learn new skills. Behavioral teaching methods have been demonstrated to be effective methods for increasing communication skills, social skills, activities of daily living, and academic skills in community settings (Repp, Favell, & Munk, 1996). These methods for skill development can be used to develop target skills that have been identified by the individual or by professionals such as speech-language pathologists, occupational therapists, and teachers.

BEHAVIORS THAT NEED INTERVENTION

People with intellectual disabilities can exhibit a wide range of challenging behaviors. Before attempting to change a behavior, it is important to determine why it is problematic (Griffiths, 1989; Martin & Pear, 1999). Some behaviors—such as hitting, spitting, or head banging—can be considered problematic if they cause physical harm to the person or others and/or limit opportunities for learning and community inclusion. Other behaviors—such as screaming, having tantrums, or throwing items—can be problematic if they disrupt routines or limit opportunities for social interaction. (See Display 23.2 for more information.) Another important reason for targeting a specific behavior for

Display 23.2

Questions to ask about the topography of behavior

Topography refers to a precise and detailed description of a landscape. Behavior analysts borrow this term in an effort to provide specific, observable, and measurable descriptions of behaviors that are considered to be problematic. Four key questions to ask that help to put together a topography are listed next. Behaviors that cross boundaries suggested by each of the four question areas—how often, how intense, how long, and wrong situation—may warrant behavioral intervention.

Frequency: Does the behavior occur too often (e.g., hitting others) or not often enough (e.g., initiating social interaction)?

Intensity: Is the behavior too intense (e.g., causing bleeding or broken bones) or not intense enough (e.g., speaking too quietly for others to hear)?

Duration: Does the behavior last too long (e.g., rocking repeatedly) or is it too brief (e.g., sitting and attending for only very short periods)?

Discrimination: Does the behavior occur in the wrong place (e.g., masturbating in public), at the wrong time (e.g., laughing at a funeral), with the wrong people (e.g., hugging strangers)?

Sources: Martin and Pear (1999) and York Behavior Management Services (1997).

change is because the individual him- or herself has expressed a desire to change. In other situations, caregivers may have to assist the individual in understanding why a particular behavior is problematic and why it needs to be changed. It is not considered ethical to target a behavior for change simply because it is "annoying." If this were acceptable, virtually everyone with or without intellectual disabilities would have at least one behavior program.

It is important to note that in addition to behavioral excesses (e.g., hitting, screaming), deficits in behavior can also require intervention. Some typical areas of skill deficits for people with intellectual disabilities include communication skills, social skills, dressing skills, eating skills, and leisure skills. Similar to behavioral excesses, skill deficits can have limiting effects on an individual's quality of life.

TYPES OF BEHAVIORAL INTERVENTION

For decades, behavioral interventions have been used in the education and treatment of individuals with intellectual disabilities. One of the great debates in the treatment of problematic behaviors for such individuals has been the use of intrusive versus nonintrusive procedures (Repp & Singh, 1990). Intrusive procedures include contingent electric shock, time-out in seclusion, physical or mechanical restraint, and various other techniques that emphasize punishment. There are concerns that these intrusive punishment procedures adversely affect the relationship between the participant and the punisher and that they bring about decreases in the problematic behavior only in the presence of the punisher or in the environment where it was used (LaVigna & Donnellan, 1986). Furthermore, the use of such techniques in community settings (e.g., at a restaurant or shopping mall) may have a negative impact on community acceptance and/or treatment of individuals with intellectual disabilities. There is also concern that more intrusive procedures have a negative impact on the dignity and personal freedoms of individuals with intellectual disabilities.

Since the mid-1980s, there has been extensive research into and development of less intrusive behavior analytic techniques, which have come to be known as positive behavior support (PBS; Jackson & Panyan, 2002; Koegel, Koegel, & Dunlap, 1996; see also Display 23.3). Interventions involving PBS have been demonstrated to be effective in treating self-injurious, aggressive, and severely disruptive behavior exhibited by children and adults with intellectual disabilities in community settings (Feldman et al., 2002). An additional aspect of PBS is that it endeavors to affect behavior change in ways that avoid pain and loss of dignity (Jackson & Panyan, 2002). This is accomplished through environmental changes, increased positive reinforcement, skill building, and planned natural consequences. A major emphasis of PBS is the notion of addressing behavior in the context in which it naturally occurs, using natural caregivers as vital participants in the assessment and treatment process. Many of these approaches attempt to decrease problematic behavior by changing antecedents. When successful, these techniques result in reduced rates of problematic behavior through prevention, thus avoiding the need for more intrusive punitive consequences. The emphasis has shifted from cookbook-style applications of behavioral procedures (e.g., if the person is aggressive, use time-out) to the idea of focusing on the comprehensive assessment of medical and environmental patterns and determining the function of the problem behavior for the individual (Feldman & Griffiths, 1997). More intrusive, punishment-based procedures are typically only used as a last resort, when reasonable attempts to use less intrusive/restrictive approaches have failed and the individual with a intellectual disability is at serious risk of harming him- or herself or others (Feldman, 1990). As noted in Display 23.4, there is some controversy between PBS and ABA.

Display 23.3

Positive behavior support (PBS)

A group of researchers (Carr, Horner, & Turnbull, 1999) completed a research synthesis of PBS in 1999 in response to a request from the U.S. Department of Education. They did a comprehensive review of articles published between 1985 and 1996 that evaluated the use of PBS to treat individuals with intellectual disabilities and problem behavior. The major findings of this research included the following:

- PBS is widely applicable for individuals with intellectual disabilities living in community settings and can be implemented by direct care staff and families.
- The major growth in the field is in the area of changing deficient environments and emphasizing antecedent strategies.
- PBS is effective for between one half and two thirds of reported cases of challenging behavior.

There is an almost two-fold improvement in outcome when intervention is based on the results of a functional analysis and implemented by care providers in natural environments.

Source: Condillac (2003).

Display 23.4

The controversy between positive behavior support (PBS) and applied behavior analysis (ABA)

There is considerable debate between some behavior analysts (e.g., Mulick & Butter, 2004) and some proponents of PBS (e.g., Carr, 1997). Early definitions of PBS described these interventions as being deeply rooted in ABA (Koegel, Koegel, & Dunlap, 1996), but later definitions describe PBS as the evolution of ABA to a new science that has surpassed its parent (Carr et al., 2002). Carr and Sidener (2002) carefully reviewed many published definitions of PBS and noted the following consistent features of PBS:

- Person-centered planning
- Functional assessment
- Multifaceted interventions
- Focus on the environment
- Meaningful outcomes
- Focus on social/ecological validity
- Systems-level intervention

The roots of each of these features can be traced back to ABA, which suggests that PBS is compatible (if not indistinguishable) to the competent use of ABA in clinical practice.

This type of controversy becomes a great concern when it has the potential to limit the available supports and services to the individuals the treatments were designed to help. For example, The Arc of the United States (2004) issued a policy statement, which stated that only PBS should be used for individuals with intellectual disabilities who exhibit problematic behavior. There is a growing concern among behavior analysts that this policy will place some individuals with intellectual disabilities at risk of not being able to access effective treatment. For example, this practice could potentially result in an overreliance on medication to suppress or restrain individuals whose dangerous behavior is not successfully addressed by PBS. Individuals with intellectual disabilities have the right to choose to access effective treatment (Van Houten et al., 1988), and it is important that philosophical debates do not limit an individual's personal rights and freedoms.

PBS is an effective application of ABA for treating problem behavior exhibited by individuals with intellectual disabilities. On occasion, the behavior analytic community has accepted the alternative terms to describe the systematic and planful application of particular components of ABA to a specific set of problems. For example, the term *early intensive behavioral intervention (EIBI)* is widely used by behavior analysts to describe the specific use of ABA to teach young children with autism. One could easily argue that the term *positive behavior support (PBS)* could be used to describe the specific use of particular components of ABA to treat challenging behavior in individuals with intellectual disabilities.

WHY BEHAVIORAL INTERVENTION IS EFFECTIVE FOR PEOPLE WITH INTELLECTUAL DISABILITIES

A large North American study that examined treatment effectiveness found that those behavioral interventions that were functionally related to the cause of severely problematic behaviors had the most demonstrated effectiveness for individuals with intellectual disabilities (National Institutes of Health [NIH], 1991). In this study, experts developed a consensus report based on existing scientific evidence. They found that there was scientific evidence to support the use of behavioral interventions that included behavior enhancement strategies (aimed at increasing desirable behavior), behavior reduction strategies (aimed at decreasing undesirable behavior), educational strategies (aimed at teaching adaptive replacement skills), and ecobehavioral strategies (aimed at preventing problem behavior by changing the environment).

The researchers in this study also found that an alarming number of individuals with intellectual disabilities who engaged in serious problematic behavior were treated only with psychotropic medication, despite the absence of scientific evidence for this approach (in isolation) as a treatment for behavior problems. Medication should be used, when appropriate, to treat medical and psychiatric issues that are diagnosed by a qualified practitioner and that can potentially underlie the individual's problematic behavior. As a treatment for challenging behavior, medication should be used

- As a last resort when less intrusive methods have been unsuccessful
- As a temporary crisis intervention measure
- Only when monitored closely by a physician
- In conjunction with a behavioral intervention program.

The final recommendation of this panel was to endorse the use of multi-elemental behavioral interventions as the treatment of choice for individuals with intellectual disabilities who exhibit severe problematic behaviors. Psychopharmacological intervention (use of medication) should usually be prescribed only to treat a psychiatric or medical condition. In some serious cases, short-term use of medication might be warranted to assist in the implementation of behavioral interventions and as a crisis intervention. Finally, the panel's findings serve as a reminder that regardless of the type of intervention used, valid, informed, legal, and voluntary consent must be obtained from the individual and/or the legal guardian (NIH, 1991).

Consistent with this panel's report, a federal law in the United States, the Individuals with Disabilities Education Improvement Act of 2004 (PL 108-446), or IDEA 2004, includes a strong recommendation that PBS be used to support individuals with disabilities who demonstrate problematic behaviors in schools. Furthermore, if an individual with a disability is suspended from school or is offered alternate placement due to problematic behavior, IDEA requires that a functional behavior assessment be completed before (or within 10 days of) the suspension. Per IDEA, the individualized education program team in the school is required to implement a behavior plan based on the functional assessment or to adjust the existing behavior plan accordingly. In other words, U.S. federal law mandates the use of ABA in the treatment of students with disabilities who exhibit serious problematic behavior.

BEST PRACTICES REGARDING INTERVENTIONS FOR PROBLEMATIC BEHAVIOR

Behavioral intervention should be based on two complementary parts: a comprehensive assessment and a written intervention plan. An intervention plan should be guided by the information gleaned from the assessment, and it should be developed using the least intrusive approaches that will be effective for the individual. The intervention plan should flow naturally from the results of the assessment and should include recommendations that stem from a working hypothesis. More intrusive approaches should only be considered for cases in which careful and systematic attempts at using less intrusive approaches have been unsuccessful (Feldman, 1990).

Comprehensive Behavioral Assessment

A comprehensive behavioral assessment should be undertaken by a trained professional, such as a psychologist with training in ABA or a behavior therapist who has received relevant training. The assessment must consider biomedical, environmental/interactional, and functional explanations for the problematic behavior. Any combination of these factors may influence the emergence and maintenance of challenging behavior (NIH, 1991; Ontario Association for Behavior Analysis, 1998).

Biomedical Assessment Biomedical issues often underlie problematic behavior in people with intellectual disabilities (Feldman & Griffiths, 1997). This can be magnified by an individual's inability to communicate his or her symptoms. Medical questions can also arise if the individual is taking medication with potentially adverse side effects. It is essential to uncover any potential biomedical or psychiatric explanations for problematic behavior and to ensure that they are treated or that medical causes are ruled out before treating the problem using a behavioral approach. If the onset of the problematic behavior is recent, or if there has been a sudden increase in problematic behavior, there may be an underlying medical issue. It is unethical to provide behavioral intervention without ruling out an underlying medical cause.

Many individuals with intellectual disabilities may lack the communication skills necessary to make their basic needs known, and they may lack the daily living skills to meet these needs for themselves (Singh, Oswald, & Ellis, 1998). With this in mind, issues such as hunger, thirst, fatigue, and illness, including earaches, toothaches, headaches, and other forms of pain must be considered as potential underlying influences for problematic behavior. It is important to note that even if physical or medical issues have been the initial cause of problematic behavior, environmental factors may be maintaining the behavior even after these issues have been properly addressed (see Display 23.5).

Environmental/Interactional Assessment Routines and interactions in the individual's natural environment may also influence problematic behavior. Sometimes activities are too difficult; other times activities are not adequately challenging. Some activities involve participation with a group, and others require independence. Unfortunately, many people with intellectual disabilities are not given the choice of participating in preferred activities. Many are taught to comply with requests from staff or family members at the expense of personal preference. As a result, some activities may be associated with more problematic behavior because they lack appeal to the individual (Brown et al., 1984). Therefore, it is important to determine which activities and situations are associated with the highest rates of problematic behavior and which situations are associated with the lowest rates or absence of the problematic behavior (Touchette, MacDonald, & Langer, 1985).

With this information, routines can be altered to create a better match between the individual and his or

Display 23.5

Case example of biomedical assessment

Lisa, a 7-year-old with severely limited verbal skills, had been banging her head with increasing frequency over the course of a few weeks. Her behavior increased in the evening, and it was highest when she was lying down on her bed or in the living room.

Given the sudden onset of this behavior, a medical check-up would be recommended to confirm or rule out a possible medical condition. This was done, and Lisa was found to have otitis media, a painful ear infection. Self-injurious behavior, such as head banging, may have served to decrease or distract from the pain brought on by Lisa's medical condition.

Once Lisa's ear infection was successfully treated by her physician, head-banging decreased significantly. It did not go away completely, however, as it was still being maintained by environmental factors.

Source: Condillac (2003).

Display 23.6

Case example of environmental assessment

Jerome is a 53-year-old who lives in a community group home. Staff are concerned about his aggressive behavior. After keeping track of his hitting for 2 weeks, it became evident that the majority of problems occurred just before, or on the way to, evening outings with the other residents.

What possible antecedent change might you suggest? Simply offering Jerome more control over his environment by allowing him to choose between two desirable activities might prevent many incidents of aggression. Of course, it would be important to know other information as well. With whom does he sit in the van? Does he like the places they go? Is there something he would rather be doing at home?

Source: Condillac (2003).

her environment. Wherever possible, it is essential to involve individuals with intellectual disabilities in the creation of any intervention plan and to consider their personal preferences when suggesting alternate activities.

Some potential antecedent events that may prompt problematic behavior can include 1) the end of a preferred activity, 2) task demands that are too difficult or that are incompatible with the person's developmental level, 3) interaction (or lack thereof) with people in the environment, or 4) denial of access to something that the person has requested. This information is used to develop environmental change procedures that can prevent or reduce problematic behavior by reducing or eliminating the occurrence of antecedent events. For example, if a behavior occurs every time an individual is asked to wash the dishes, a prevention strategy might include not asking him to wash the dishes, asking him to wash only one dish or a few dishes, or asking him to choose one of three times when he will begin to wash the dishes. See Display 23.6 for another example.

Functional Assessment All behavior serves a purpose. It may serve to increase attention or to end an unpleasant situation (see Table 23.1 for additional examples). In order to determine the purpose that problematic behavior serves, a functional analysis should be completed (Iwata et al., 1982). Functional analysis is an assessment technique used to determine the sources and types of reinforcement that an individual receives in response to his or her behavior.

Research regarding intervention effectiveness has demonstrated that functional analysis is a better predictor of the success of behavioral intervention than the specific intervention used. That is, interventions that are guided by the results of functional analysis have proven to be more effective than those that do not use this method (Carr et al., 1999; Freeman, 1993).

There are three basic types of functional analysis techniques used by experts: 1) informant rating scales (Durand & Crimmins, 1988), 2) observations in the person's natural environment (O'Neill et al., 1990), and 3) systematic experimental manipulations (Iwata et al., 1982). Regardless of the approach used, the four functional categories that are most commonly used by clinicians include access to escape, attention, tangibles, and sensory stimulation (see Table 23.1). Once the function(s) of the behavior is (are) determined, the individual can be taught to use an appropriate behavior to serve the same purpose(s) as the problematic behavior (Carr & Durand, 1985). It is not unusual for one be-

Table 23.1. The functions of problem behavior

Behavior might serve to provide escape from tasks or people. Time-out (an intended punisher) often provides students with escape from difficult demands or demanding individuals. As a result, it serves to strengthen behavior instead of decreasing it.
Behavior may serve to gain access to increased attention from caregivers. Even seemingly unpleasant interactions, such as reprimands, may positively reinforce (increase) problematic behaviors.
Behavior may result in increased access to tangibles (e.g., activities, items). An individual might be given an item (e.g., a Popsicle) when a care provider notices the individual biting her fingers.
Behavior that serves a sensory function serves to gain access to internal reinforcement, independent of environmental factors (e.g., rocking back and forth for hours when alone).

Source: Iwata, Dorsey, Slifer, et al. (1982).

havior to serve multiple functions or for two behaviors to serve the same function. See Display 23.7 for more information on determining the function of behavior.

Behavioral assessment is typically based on the collection of relevant information from interview and observational methods. Several data collection techniques may be required to carry out a single comprehensive assessment. These can include interviewing the individual and the care providers, keeping track of the specific problem behavior and the context (antecedents and consequences) in which it occurs, and monitoring the frequency, intensity, and duration of a problematic behavior.

Content and Development of Intervention Plans

After the comprehensive behavioral assessment is complete, a treatment plan specific to the individual's needs should be developed. A treatment plan needs to be

- Developed in consultation with a trained professional
- Documented
- Monitored (Feldman et al., 2004)

The intervention plan flows directly from the findings of the behavioral assessment and is based on the data that has been collected. The goal of the plan is to prevent or decrease problematic behavior using the least intrusive procedures while teaching the individual adaptive replacement skills. Sometimes informal behavioral interventions end up being more intrusive than formal plans (see Display 23.8). Regardless of the intrusiveness level of the interventions being used, the intervention plan must be clearly and thoroughly reviewed by the individual with intellectual disabilities and his or her parent or guardian. Their informed and voluntary consent must be obtained before the plan can be implemented (Griffiths, 1989).

Plans to address challenging behavior should be individualized. Nonetheless, all such plans generally touch on these basic areas: prevention, skill promotion, intervention, and evaluation and training. These are discussed next.

Prevention Prevention strategies are developed from the findings of the environmental assessment. The goal of this phase of intervention is to prevent challenging behavior from occurring by making appropriate changes to the antecedents (e.g., routines, interactions) in the environment that prompt the individual's problematic behavior. Another objective is to create the best match possible between the individual with intellectual disabilities and his or her living and learning environments. In some cases, making changes to these systems-level antecedents (e.g., moving to a new home with fewer residents) can result in significant decreases in problematic behavior and increases in quality of life. Prevention strategies create an environment in which the antecedents that pose the highest risk of prompting the problematic behavior are avoided whenever possible. These high-risk activities are replaced by activities that are not typically associated with the problematic behavior. A careful look at the antecedents might suggest, for example, that an individual exhibits more challenging behavior when watching television alone and rarely acts out when helping a staff person make dinner. For this person, watching television alone should be avoided, whereas opportunities to assist staff should be maximized (Touchette et al., 1985). Antecedent changes can result in rapid decreases in problematic behavior without the use of more aversive techniques.

Skill Promotion Once problematic behaviors are successfully being prevented, the stage is set to teach new adaptive behaviors. The goal of the second phase

Display 23.7

Case example of functional assessment

Kevin is a 23-year-old with severe multiple physical and intellectual disabilities. His problematic behavior consists of screaming for periods ranging from 10 to 30 minutes. Staff try to calm him down by talking to him, but the only thing that appears to calm him down is when staff (as a last resort) make him a cup of tea. In fact, he has been getting so much tea to calm him that staff have stopped making Kevin tea at other times.

Because functional analysis focuses on the consequences of an individual's behavior, in this case it was necessary for staff members to ask, "What happens when Kevin screams?" They realize that the answer is that staff talk to him for awhile, then make him a cup of tea. The next question they asked was, "When else do staff give Kevin their undivided attention and a cup of tea?" Unfortunately, the answer is only when he screams. His screaming serves to gain him both increased attention (staff talk to him) and increased access to tangibles (tea).

Kevin needs to learn a way to ask for these things without having to scream. One approach might be for staff to teach Kevin to raise his hand or blow a whistle when he wants their attention. Another option would be to permanently attach a travel mug to Kevin's chair so Kevin could touch the mug to show staff that he would like tea. Once learned, these new skills may serve the same purpose for Kevin as his screaming and thus make screaming unnecessary.

Source: Condillac (2003).

Display 23.8

Formal versus informal behavioral interventions

A study examining the use of behavioral interventions to treat individuals with intellectual disabilities found that more than 50% of the interventions being implemented were informal, undocumented, and not monitored (Feldman et al., 2004). Formal treatment plans that were 1) designed (or supervised) by a qualified professional, 2) written (documented), and 3) evaluated (data are collected and monitored) were found to be more effective and less intrusive than informal strategies that were implemented by caregivers. Informal interventions tend to evolve from dealing with behavior on an incident-by-incident basis. The following example of an informal approach is NOT recommended as a treatment approach:

Terry threw a plate, so the staff members did not allow him to watch television after dinner on Monday. He threw a plate again on Tuesday and was sent to his room to keep him from watching television with his housemates. On Wednesday he threw his plate and was sent to his room to think about what he had done. On Thursday, he threw the plate and was sent to his room. He started screaming, so staff members shut the door. It took two staff members to keep Terry from opening the door and exiting the room.

This type of informal intervention is problematic in several ways. First, it is not based on an assessment, and there is no consideration of the function of Terry's behavior. Second, the removal of television evolved into being sent to his room, then to having the door closed and held shut. In many jurisdictions, it is against the law for paid caregivers to implement this type of procedure without proper documentation and supervision. Third, the behavioral issue became worse, and the informal intervention escalated in intrusiveness, yet Terry (or his consent source) had not agreed to the intervention plan.

Unfortunately, such situations are quite common. Whenever possible, caregivers implementing behavioral interventions should 1) enlist the help of a qualified professional in developing and monitoring the intervention, 2) write down the plan so that all involved are using the same strategies, and 3) have regular reviews of the progress (or lack thereof).

of intervention, skill promotion, is to teach the individual skills that will serve the function that was originally served by the problematic behavior. Naturally, this phase of treatment depends on the results of the functional analysis.

If, for example, the functional analysis reveals that an individual's self-injury and aggression serves to gain escape from difficult tasks, he or she will be taught to obtain escape from task demands by requesting a break. There are several ways to request a break. A few possibilities include using

- A verbal request, such as "Break, please"
- A signed request, such as BREAK or FINISHED
- A picture communication symbol or card, such as touching a picture of a stop sign or handing over a "break" card
- A gesture, such as pointing to the chair that is used for taking a break

This approach is called *functional communication training* (see Carr et al., 1994, & Durand, 1990, for comprehensive coverage of this topic). Display 23.9 presents an example.

It is essential to consider the person's developmental level when selecting an appropriate replacement skill. If a person lacks verbal skills, then perhaps he or she could be taught to use a sign. If the person cannot gesture or identify pictures, then perhaps using actual objects would be a better way to start.

Once the replacement skill has been selected, a systematic teaching program should be implemented. The teaching program should include the methods for prompting and reinforcing the new desired behavior. Another aspect of the teaching program must include strategies for generalization. Generalization refers to a person's ability to apply or transfer skills across people, settings, materials, and responses (Martin & Pear, 1999). For example, an individual who is learning to gain attention more appropriately also needs to know a variety of responses that achieve that outcome, such as raising a hand, calling a person's name, or tapping someone on the shoulder. This allows the individual then to gain attention in many situations with many different people.

Intervention During the implementation of the program, the identified problematic behavior is typically ignored (no eye contact or verbal response) and, if necessary, physically blocked (to prevent injury to others in the environment). The individual is redirected to task using a simple monotone cue (e.g., "shoe on"). This phase of treatment results in the extinction (or gradual elimination) of the problematic behavior. If the behavior is of a serious nature and the individual and/or others are at increased risk, a crisis plan should be developed by a trained professional. This plan should detail the steps in handling problematic behavior if it does occur.

Evaluation and Training The final component should include clear guidelines for monitoring progress

Display 23.9

Sample skill promotion program

At present, Jeanine exhibits aggressive behavior, in the form of pinching, during difficult tasks. To functionally replace this behavior, her caregivers will teach her to sign BREAK to request breaks from difficult tasks. So that Jeanine can learn the meaning of the sign, they will give her 1) increased opportunities to request breaks and 2) brief breaks (even just 1-minute breaks) each time she approximates the sign. Once Jeanine has learned to use the sign to request breaks, her caregivers will teach her to tolerate waiting for her break by systematically increasing the time Jeanine must work before her break is given and by offering social praise for waiting.

Jeanine's caregivers recognize that prior to implanting the program, the reinforcer (i.e., breaks from task) was being delivered in response to problematic behavior. This program will have the same desired consequences delivered in response to a new socially appropriate behavior.

Source: Condillac (2003).

and fine-tuning the program (Martin & Pear, 1999). Data should be collected on both the problematic behavior targeted for change and the skill(s) being taught to replace the problematic behavior. Criteria for success should be identified (e.g., 80% increase in the replacement skill and 80% decrease in the problematic behavior). It is essential to monitor both the desired effects and the potential side effects of the behavioral intervention (Griffiths, 1989). Regularly scheduled reviews by the trained professional can offer opportunities for discussing progress, dealing with setbacks, and troubleshooting for potential difficulties.

It is important to note that unlike other treatment approaches, behavioral interventions typically rely on consistent implementation by care providers in the individual's natural environment. Families, direct care staff, and teachers often require hands-on training in behavioral techniques. Training can include topics such as data collection, effective use of reinforcement, ways to teach skills, and crisis intervention techniques. Training improves the quality of the behavioral intervention and has been demonstrated as essential to the success of treatment.

SUMMARY

Behavioral interventions are important for individuals with intellectual disabilities because they can help increase desirable behaviors and decrease less desirable behaviors. Research suggests that almost half of individuals with intellectual disabilities exhibit some form of problematic behavior. It is essential that care providers seek trained professionals to provide comprehensive assessment and intervention plans. Assessment procedures should consider biomedical, environmental/interactional, and functional explanations for the problem behavior. The assessment should lead to the development of a formal, documented behavioral intervention program that uses PBS. Once a person's problematic behaviors are being successfully prevented, the individual can be taught adaptive skills that functionally replace the previously problematic behavior. Because behavioral interventions are typically implemented by natural care providers with minimal training in ABA, providing additional training in behavioral methods is often essential to the success of the intervention. Staff training must convey an understanding of behavior principles and strategies and techniques for ongoing evaluation.

FOR FURTHER THOUGHT AND DISCUSSION

1. Why do you think problematic behavior is so prevalent among people with intellectual disabilities?
2. Behavioral interventions can increase the control that an individual with intellectual disabilities has on her or his environment. Why is this statement true?
3. Because behavioral intervention focuses on information that can be seen, heard, and counted, why is biomedical assessment so important?
4. Why would using prevention strategies as a first course of treatment be a better choice than simply punishing the behavior until it disappears?
5. Research has found that functional analysis is critical to the effectiveness of behavioral intervention. Why do you think this is the case?

REFERENCES

The Arc of the United States. (2004). *Behavioral supports.* Retrieved September 15, 2006, from http://www.thearc.org/posits/behaviorpos.doc

Atkinson, L., Feldman, M., McNamara, A., et al. (1994). *Survey of aberrant behavior and its treatment in persons with developmental disabilities in Ontario.* Final report to Ontario Mental Health Foundation, Toronto.

Baker, B.L., McIntyre, J., Blacher, J., et al. (2003). Pre-school children with and without developmental delay: Behavior problems and parenting stress over time. *Journal of Intellectual Disability Research, 47,* 217–230.

Brown, L., Shirage, B., York, J., et al. (1984). *A life-space analysis strategy for students with severe handicaps.* Madison: University of Wisconsin and Madison Metropolitan School District.

Carr, E.G. (1997). The evolution of applied behavior analysis into positive behavioral support. *Journal of The Association for Persons with Severe Handicaps, 22,* 208–209.

Carr, E.G., Dunlap, G., Horner, R.H., et al. (2002). Positive behavior support: Evolution of an applied science. *Journal of Positive Behavior Intervention, 4,* 4–16.

Carr, E.G., & Durand, M.V. (1985). Reducing behavior problems through functional communication training. *Journal of Applied Behavioral Analysis, 18,* 111–126.

Carr, E.G., Horner, R.H., & Turnbull, A.P. (1999). *Positive behavior support for people with developmental disabilities: A research synthesis.* Washington, DC: American Association on Mental Retardation.

Carr, E.G., Levin, L., McConnachie, G., et al. (1994). *Communication-based intervention for problem behavior: A user's guide for producing positive change.* Baltimore: Paul H. Brookes Publishing Co.

Carr, J.E., & Sidener, T.M. (2002). On the relation between applied behavior analysis and positive behavioral support. *The Behavior Analyst, 25,* 245–253.

Condillac, R. (2003). Behavioral intervention and developmental disabilities. In I. Brown & M. Percy (Eds.), *Developmental disabilities in Ontario* (pp. 407–419). Toronto: Ontario Association on Developmental Disabilities.

Durand, V.M. (1990). *Severe behavior problems: A functional communication training approach.* New York: The Guilford Press.

Durand, V.M., & Crimmins, D.B. (1988). Identifying the variables maintaining self-injurious behavior. *Journal of Autism and Developmental Disorders, 18,* 99–117.

Feldman, M.A. (1990). Balancing freedom from harm and right to treatment for persons with developmental disabilities. In A.C. Repp & N.N. Singh (Eds.), *Perspectives on the use of nonaversive and aversive interventions for persons with developmental disabilities* (pp. 261–272). Sycamore, IL: Sycamore Publishing Company.

Feldman, M.A., Atkinson, L., Foti-Gervais, L., et al. (2004). Formal versus informal interventions for challenging behavior in persons with intellectual disabilities. *Journal of Intellectual Disability Research, 48,* 60–68.

Feldman, M.A., Condillac, R.A., Tough, S.E., et al. (2002). Effectiveness of community positive behavioral intervention for persons with developmental disabilities and severe behavioral challenges. *Behavior Therapy, 33,* 377–398.

Feldman, M.A., & Griffiths, D. (1997). Comprehensive assessment of severe behavior disorders. In N.N. Singh (Ed.), *Prevention & treatment of severe behavior problems: Models and methods in developmental disabilities* (pp. 23–48). Pacific Grove, CA: Brooks/Cole.

Freeman, N.L. (1993). *Treatment strategies for aberrant behavior in people with developmental disabilities.* Toronto: Ontario Mental Health Foundation.

Griffiths, D. (1989). Quality assurance for behavior interventions. *Habilitative Mental Healthcare Newsletter, 8,* 74–79.

Individuals with Disabilities Education Improvement Act of 2004, PL 108-446, 20 U.S.C. §§ 1400 *et seq.*

Iwata, B.A., Dorsey, M.F., Slifer, K.J., et al. (1982). Toward a functional analysis of self-injury. *Analysis and Intervention in Developmental Disabilities, 2,* 1–20.

LaVigna, G.W., & Donnellan, A.M. (1986). *Alternatives to punishment: Solving behavior problems with non-aversive strategies.* New York: Irvington.

Jackson, L., & Panyan, M.V. (2002). *Positive behavioral support in the classroom: Principles and practices.* Baltimore: Paul H. Brookes Publishing Co.

Koegel, L.K., Koegel, R.L., & Dunlap, G. (Eds.). (1996). *Positive behavioral support: Including people with difficult behavior in the community.* Baltimore: Paul H. Brookes Publishing Co.

Maes, B., Brokeman, T.G., Dosen, A., et al. (2003). Caregiving burden of families looking after persons with intellectual disability and behavioral or psychiatric problems. *Journal of Intellectual Disability Research, 47,* 447–455.

Martin, G., & Pear, J. (1999). *Behavior modification: What it is and how to do it.* Upper Saddle River, NJ: Prentice Hall.

Mulick, J., & Butter, E.M. (2004). Positive behavior support: A paternalistic utopian delusion. In J. Jacobson, J.A. Mulick, & R.M. Foxx (Eds.), *Fads, controversies, and politically correct treatment in developmental disabilities.* Mahwah, NJ: Lawrence Erlbaum Associates.

National Institutes of Health. (1991). *Treatment of destructive behaviors in persons with developmental disabilities.* Consensus Development Conference, September 11–13, 1989. Bethesda, MD: Author.

Ontario Association for Behavior Analysis. (1998). *Draft standards of practice of the Ontario Association for Behavior Analysis.* Toronto: Author.

O'Neill, R.E., Horner, R.H., Albin, R.W., et al. (1990). *Functional analysis of problem behavior: A practical assessment guide.* Pacific Grove, CA: Brooks/Cole.

Repp, A.C., Favell, J., & Munk, D. (1996). Cognitive and vocational interventions for school-age children and adolescents with mental retardation. In J.W. Jacobson & J.A. Mulick (Eds.), *Manual of diagnosis and professional practice in mental retardation* (pp. 265–276). Washington, DC: American Psychological Association.

Repp, A.C., & Singh, N.N. (Eds.). (1990). *Perspectives on the use of nonaversive and aversive interventions for persons with developmental disabilities.* Sycamore, IL: Sycamore Publishing Co.

Singh, N.N., Oswald, D.P., & Ellis, C.R. (1998). Mental retardation. In T.M. Ollendick & M. Hersen (Eds.), *Handbook of child psychopathology* (3rd ed., pp. 91–116). New York: Kluwer Academic/Plenum Publishers.

Touchette, P.E., MacDonald, R.F., & Langer, S.N. (1985). A scatterplot for identifying stimulus control of problem behavior. *Journal of Applied Behavior Analysis, 18,* 343–351.

York Behavior Management Services. (1997). *The options manual: A community based behavioral approach for teachers with students with developmental disabilities.* Richmond Hill, ON, Canada: York Central Hospital Behavior Management Services.

Van Houten, R., Axelrod, S., Bailey, J.S., et al. (1988). The right to effective behavioral treatment. *Journal of Applied Behavior Analysis, 21,* 381–384.

24

A Positive Intervention Model for Understanding, Helping, and Coping with "Challenging" Families

J. Dale Munro

WHAT YOU WILL LEARN ABOUT IN THIS CHAPTER

- Why some families seem so challenging
- Recognizing challenging family patterns
- Challenging System-Family Therapy Model

Most families of people with intellectual and developmental disabilities support their family members with disabilities and the professionals and organizations working with them. In every community agency or school setting, however, there are a few families that might be described as "challenging." These families need professional assistance, but often they do not receive it. In this chapter, the term *challenging family* is described as a group of two or more blood, partnered, or adopted relatives, at least one of whom has a developmental disability, that behaves in a manner that seems particularly self-destructive, intimidating, aggressive, or resistant. It is important to understand that use of the term *challenging* does not refer to family members who are assertive or occasionally give professionals a difficult time when frustrated. For present purposes, *challenging families* refers to relatives of people with disabilities who present serious, ongoing behavior problems.

Challenging families pose one of the greatest dangers to the emotional well-being of people with developmental disabilities and are a constant source of frustration for frontline professionals and agency or school administrators. These families tend to draw attention to themselves and their own needs, inadvertently obstructing service delivery to the person who has a disability. Frontline professionals, agencies and schools need to become familiar with strategies for diffusing the frustrations, anger, and tension that challenging families are experiencing in order to assist these families and to promote good mental health in the person with the disability. This chapter examines probable causes of challenging family behavior, describes specific behavioral patterns manifested by these families, and presents a positive and effective model of family-system intervention.

WHY SOME FAMILIES SEEM SO CHALLENGING

Most parents experience pain and trauma when they first learn that their child has a developmental disability, and some find this to be almost unbearable. The entire family is confronted with new demands that tax relationships both within and outside the family. Most parents and other family members—even in the most "healthy" families—go through a coping/grieving process that is life changing. As shown in Display 24.1, normally this grieving process is thought to be comprised of five phases—starting with initial shock when first learning that the child has a permanent disability. The process proceeds through several phases to eventual spiritual renewal and relative acceptance of the child and the disability. Even years later, healthy families may periodically experience short periods of cyclic or recurrent distress, especially around times of transition or crisis (e.g., graduation, puberty, birthdays, changes in teaching or support staff, major illness, marriage of a sibling, anniversary date of when the disability was diagnosed). Yet, most parents and other family members gradually learn to accept the person and the disability, and they move on emotionally with their lives—often positively transformed and psychologically stronger (Kausar, Jevne, & Sobsey, 2003; Scorgie & Sobsey, 2000; Scorgie et al., 2001; Stainton & Besser, 1998; Taunt & Hastings, 2002).

In contrast, challenging families seem permanently stuck in the three earliest phases of this coping/grieving process. Their intense reaction and nonacceptance of the child and the disability does not diminish with time, resulting in what has been called "chronic sorrow" (Olshansky, 1961; Sanders, 1999). Siblings and

Display 24.1

Family coping/grieving process

In mourning the loss of the dream of the "normal"/"perfect" child, family grieving is multilayered and the pain is experienced on many levels—emotionally, intellectually, physiologically, and spiritually. This is not a simple straight-line, cause-and-effect process with clear-cut stopping and starting points. Instead, it involves dynamic and evolving phases that vary by person and situation. Predicting how long this process will take to work through is highly individualized, and it may happen relatively quickly. Yet, clinical experience suggests that healthier families probably need somewhere between 18 months and up to approximately 6 years.

Challenging families, however, because of complicated grief, seem permanently stuck in the first three "nonacceptance" phases. Coming to terms with the inescapable reality of the disability is necessary if family members are to escape an emotional prison of self-doubt, deep sadness, guilt, shame, anger, and a need to punish themselves or others. Challenging families need increased social support and/or specialized counseling to work through and accept complex feelings and to move toward greater acceptance, psychological wholeness, and general happiness.

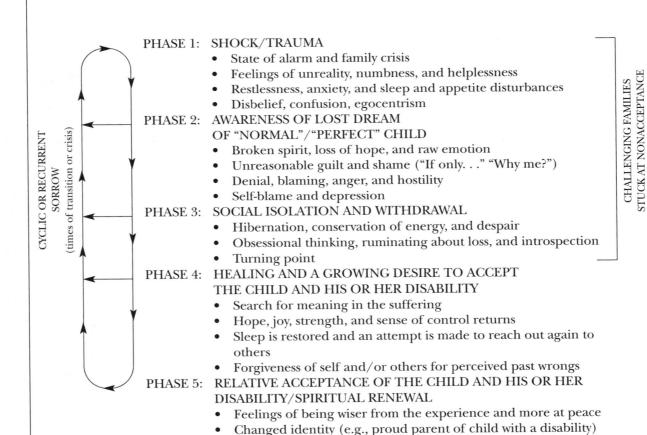

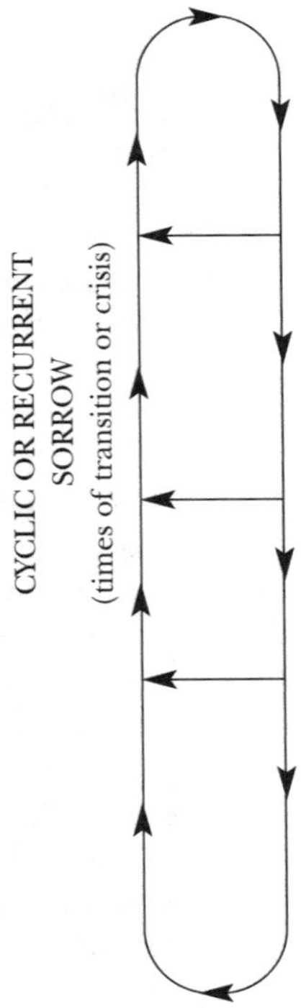

PHASE 1: SHOCK/TRAUMA
- State of alarm and family crisis
- Feelings of unreality, numbness, and helplessness
- Restlessness, anxiety, and sleep and appetite disturbances
- Disbelief, confusion, egocentrism

PHASE 2: AWARENESS OF LOST DREAM OF "NORMAL"/"PERFECT" CHILD
- Broken spirit, loss of hope, and raw emotion
- Unreasonable guilt and shame ("If only. . ." "Why me?")
- Denial, blaming, anger, and hostility
- Self-blame and depression

PHASE 3: SOCIAL ISOLATION AND WITHDRAWAL
- Hibernation, conservation of energy, and despair
- Obsessional thinking, ruminating about loss, and introspection
- Turning point

CHALLENGING FAMILIES STUCK AT NONACCEPTANCE ("chronic sorrow") [Phases 1–3]

PHASE 4: HEALING AND A GROWING DESIRE TO ACCEPT THE CHILD AND HIS OR HER DISABILITY
- Search for meaning in the suffering
- Hope, joy, strength, and sense of control returns
- Sleep is restored and an attempt is made to reach out again to others
- Forgiveness of self and/or others for perceived past wrongs

PHASE 5: RELATIVE ACCEPTANCE OF THE CHILD AND HIS OR HER DISABILITY/SPIRITUAL RENEWAL
- Feelings of being wiser from the experience and more at peace
- Changed identity (e.g., proud parent of child with a disability)

Appreciation is expressed to Keith Anderson for his consultation.

grandparents of the family member who has the disability can become trapped in the parents' cycle of grief, denial, guilt, sadness, and anger (Ashton & Ashton, 1996; Davis, 1987; Moses, 1988; Parks, 1983; Sieffert, 1978; Singer & Powers, 1993). The self-destructive, extremely aggressive, or resistant behavior exhibited by challenging families results from what has been referred to as "complicated grief." Sanders (1999) suggested that complicated grief occurs when the more typical coping/grieving process is confounded by extenuating factors. In the case of families of people with developmental disabilities, six extenuating factors appear to contribute to complicated grief reactions and ultimately challenging behavior:

1. *Personality variables or the basic thinking style* of individual family members can impede a family's coping/grieving process. For example, parents or siblings who typically blame someone or something else about life problems, or persist in blaming themselves, frequently will respond in a similar manner when confronted with the reality of a family member with a permanent disability.
2. *Other unresolved grief or situational factors* may negatively influence personality factors. For instance, the family may experience a serious family crisis (e.g., financial problems, critical illness or injury, marital discord or separation, a recent death), needed services may be unavailable, or service cutbacks may leave parents fearful regarding what the future may hold for their child.
3. *The large, bureaucratic and somewhat impersonal nature of "the system"* of educational, health, correctional, and human service organizations can frustrate otherwise reasonable family members. Complicating this situation is the fact that some overworked professionals and managers experience emotional burnout or behave in a defensive or insensitive manner when confronted by frustrated or hostile family members. Other difficulties may develop when clashes occur with families because of differing socioeconomic, linguistic, religious, or cultural backgrounds (Gabel, 2004; Magana, Seltzer, & Krauss, 2004).
4. *Some challenging family members may have intellectual or communication deficits,* making it difficult to work cooperatively with them.
5. *Power imbalances* may disproportionately favor family members (e.g., a parent sitting on an agency board) or service system managers or staff, creating dysfunctional family–system relations.
6. *Untreated psychiatric difficulties,* such as clinical depression or another mood disorder, severe anxiety or obsessional thinking, alcohol or drug abuse, post-traumatic stress disorder (e.g., from past abuse), schizophrenia, autism spectrum disorders, or personality disorders can cause family members to behave in a manner that makes them appear to be totally unreasonable.

RECOGNIZING CHALLENGING FAMILY PATTERNS

Challenging families often seem overwhelmed with guilt, ambivalence, hostility, and loneliness. They may deny these feelings when confronted directly but show their emotional pain in a variety of overt or passive-aggressive ways. They sometimes try to present an image that everything is okay in their families, or they may mistakenly believe that most of their problems result from having a family member with a disability. In response to tremendous family tension, individuals who have developmental disabilities often begin to exhibit disturbed behavior, inadvertently shifting blame to themselves or making themselves appear responsible for the underlying dysfunction present in the entire family.

As professionals become involved to try to help the families with their "problem" relative, they sometimes encounter tremendous resistance. The homeostasis (balance) in the family may depend on maintaining the member with the disability in the scapegoat or problem role to prevent focusing on the real source of conflict—the parental and family dysfunction. Challenging families of people with developmental disabilities frequently show one or more of the following behavior patterns (Munro, 1995), any one of which signifies the expression of serious needs that require a professional response.

1. *Loud chronic complaining:* These families literally scream and create crises out of minor concerns, even when special and repeated efforts have been made to meet their needs. No matter how much effort professionals show, it is never enough! They seem preoccupied with the way agencies, professionals and school systems "should" and "must" provide quality and expanded services, with little appreciation for large caseloads or limited service resources. Some of these families complicate situations by turning to lawyers, agency or school executives, or the mass media, before first trying to resolve concerns with front-line professionals or managers.

2. *Program or person sabotage:* This is shown by some families who seem to perceive professionals and service providers as adversaries. These families may block attempts to provide interventions, such as psychotropic medication or behavioral approaches that are considered necessary to help reduce self-injurious, suicidal, or aggressive behavior. They may insist on their family member being discharged, against advice, from specialized treatment settings, just as the person is beginning to show progress. They may not show up for

scheduled appointments with professionals. They may also have unrealistically high or overly pessimistic expectations for their family member who has a disability that impede the person's potential for positive change and emotional growth.

3. *Extreme overprotectiveness:* This is demonstrated by some families who seem overwhelmed by guilt, anxiety, and obsessional thinking. These overinvolved families tend to infantilize their family member with the disability (e.g., insist on the person wearing child-like haircuts and clothing, bathe an individual who is physically capable of doing so independently), and they want the person to be protected at all times (e.g., refuse to allow dating or independent use of public transportation). They may be unwilling to go away on vacations without their family member for fear that something awful might happen when they are gone. They may tolerate seemingly intolerable behavior on the part of the person who has a disability (e.g., repeated physical violence or property destruction). Parents may become martyrs, who seem totally devoted to their child but who also secretly resent the lifelong cost of constantly caring for the person (e.g., loss of friends or a career).

4. *False hope/jumping on treatment bandwagons:* This pattern often emerges when long-term denial and unrealistically high expectations are a potent underlying dynamic in the family. Every potential new treatment advance is met with near-religious fervor by these family members. "Shopping around" for specialists to find a miracle (and often expensive) cure for their family member's disability is not uncommon. Some families may discontinue helpful anticonvulsant or psychotropic medication, falsely thinking it is no longer necessary. These families may even demand that physicians perform unnecessary surgery, use improperly tested drugs, or change the person's treatment to some supposed "medical breakthrough" treatment described in sensationalized popular news publications. A few families may sincerely believe that prayer, their religious beliefs, or the right faith healer will cure the disability. Unfortunately, the ongoing zeal of these families to try the latest panacea often gets in the way of initiating more practical, helpful approaches.

5. *Symbiotic (enmeshed) relationships:* These interactions are found when there is a pathologically close tie between the person with the disability and at least one parent and each feels exceptional sensitivity for the other's pain. These relationships stifle independent thought and action on the part of the person who has the disability, and healthy parent–child emotional boundaries are continually violated. More troubled families may have shared delusions of grandeur in which the person who has the disability is idolized beyond realistic dimensions and becomes the recipient of too much family attention and concern.

6. *Open warfare and abuse:* This pattern can be observed in families for whom overt hostility, mind games, sarcastic exchanges, back biting, and violent arguments seem to be a hallmark. Intense sibling rivalry may last into adulthood. Brothers and sisters may vacillate between placing enormous anger onto their sibling with a disability and competing to demonstrate who loves the person most (e.g., by overindulgent gift giving). Shared family secrets (e.g., incest, physical violence, alcohol and drug problems, past mental illness) sometimes create ongoing tension. The person with the disability can be an easy target for the ever-present hostility, as can professionals and school or agency representatives who try to get involved.

7. *Paranoia and evasiveness:* These behaviors are manifested by some families who, because of social isolation or delusions of persecution, begin to believe that professionals, agencies, school systems, neighbors, family, or associates are conspiring against them. These families may leave cryptic or hostile messages on agency or school telephone systems, refuse to meet or fail to show up for scheduled appointments, be hypersensitive to criticism or bear grudges, be preoccupied with unjustified doubts about the loyalty of others, fabricate stories, communicate in a confused manner, or physically threaten outsiders. Serious emotional disturbance and avoidance are the distinguishing characteristics of these exceedingly suspicious families, and communication and support planning with them concerning their family member with a disability can be particularly difficult.

8. *Avoidance of the person:* This is a pattern shown by families who completely terminate contact with the individual who has a disability. Family members may never visit, write, or even acknowledge the person's existence. Such total rejection can destroy the person's self-worth, precipitate severe depression, and leave the individual fantasizing about the family that never comes. Other family members may maintain contact only until money from an inheritance runs dry or make promises that are never kept (e.g., regarding visits or gifts). Sometimes, one parent withdraws totally into work, volunteer, or leisure activities, leaving the other parent to deal almost single-handedly with the child or adult who has the disability.

9. *Psychosocial deprivation:* This is characteristic of some families who live in isolated rural or urban slum areas or in less developed countries around the world. Neglect and harsh discipline may be common, and little attention is paid to the special needs of the person with the disability, because all family members face daily struggles to meet basic needs. The disability may

never even be diagnosed, unless it is severe or a major crisis occurs. These families often distrust professionals, schools, and agencies, because many are frustrated after long-term contact (sometimes involving more than one generation) with other services and government programs.

CHALLENGING SYSTEM-FAMILY THERAPY MODEL

In the developmental disability field, what professionals, managers, and service organizations perceive as challenging families usually are families with dysfunctional backgrounds coming into conflict with rigid, overextended, or unresponsive human service systems. In fact, communication and cooperation problems within formal support systems (health, education, corrections, and social services) can make family problems appear much more serious than they really are.

Because of these difficulties—and based on three decades of work in the developmental disability field—the author of this chapter has developed a family therapy model that combines the best elements of traditional approaches with interventions that recognize the complexity of human service systems. This model of treatment is called the Challenging System-Family Therapy (CSFT) Model. It is particularly helpful in situations in which family and service system cooperation needs to be high. This method of intervention can be likened to a form of systems therapy—an extension of family therapy strategies beyond the family to the system and other concerned people. This is a highly effective, positive, and ethical model that reduces family and professional distress; improves communication and interpersonal relationships among key people; clarifies roles; and improves planning, case management, advocacy, and support for people with disabilities.

Necessity of Being Positive

As a starting point, the CSFT Model emphasizes that a positive or unconditionally constructive attitude on the part of professionals and managers often leads to beneficial results when working with challenging families (Munro, 1997). In fact, family therapists in the developmental disabilities field rarely encounter people whom they would describe as "bad" parents or family members. Yet, they do meet family members with broken spirits who are exhausted, disillusioned, burned out, traumatized, overwhelmed, and frightened about the future. Most of the family members who desperately require support and counseling are trying too hard to do the right things for their relatives who have disabilities—sometimes to the point where their own health is compromised. In this sort of emotional climate, negativity on the part of professionals can breed a self-perpetuating cycle of frustration and hopelessness in family members.

The CSFT Model incorporates many elements of positive psychology and the strengths-based perspective to clinical practice (Early & GlenMaye, 2000; Russo, 1999; Saleeby, 1992; Seligman & Csikszentmihalyi, 2000). This perspective provides a positive foundation from which to build effective working relationships with challenging families. This positive, strengths-based approach is antithetical to the traditional family pathology model, on which many professionals have relied in the past. The professional's sense of humor, insight, and loyalty are often viewed as important ingredients for successful family work. Real problems are not ignored, but this perspective focuses on what is right, rather than what is wrong, with families. Family empowerment, resilience, faith, hope, perseverance, and creativity—as well as the possibility of positive transformation and rebound from personal trauma, abuse, oppression, sickness, and tragedy—are emphasized. This perspective liberates family members to pursue their own personal dreams, and it accepts that people are more motivated to make positive changes when they have genuine decision-making power and when their strengths are respected.

Four Alternative Roles for the Family Therapist

Because there are few family therapists who devote their careers to the field of developmental disabilities, the CSFT Model suggests that professionals specializing in this area must be careful not to overextend themselves. At the time of referral, family therapists must determine the best role to play in order to maximize the range of their influence and the number of families they can assist. Four possible roles exist:

1. The family therapist may play *a consultant role,* offering advice regarding family support strategies to agency or school representatives with the therapist having little or no actual face-to-face involvement with the family. This role usually involves the smallest time commitment.
2. The professional therapist might act as *an outside mediator,* who is brought in as an impartial third party to meet with key people and to help resolve complicated family–system disputes (Munro, 1997).
3. The professional may feel a necessity to work directly with the challenging family—playing *a role similar to that of a traditional family therapist.* If the professional does provide direct family therapy work, a key feature of the CSFT Model is that an agency, school, or service system representative

who knows the individual with the disability well, acts as a co-therapist. This provides an excellent learning opportunity for the co-therapist in effective family work. It also helps to monitor whether any real and positive change is occurring in the way that the family and service system are working together, and it helps to maintain a reliable check-in as to how the individual with the disability is coping.

4. On occasion, the family therapist may provide *individual counseling to the person with a disability* without getting directly involved with the family. This counseling can be helpful in providing emotional support and for developing assertive and coping skills for people who are being rejected, abused, or treated as a scapegoat by family members. Again, it is usually advantageous to include an agency, school, or service system representative who knows the individual well to act as a co-therapist.

Therapeutic Stance

Professionals typically find working with challenging families to be emotionally demanding and sometimes discouraging. Yet, the CSFT Model suggests that frequently there are viable approaches that can be helpful, if the professional is really motivated to assist these people. To a large extent, treatment success depends on the professional's persistence, high energy, optimism, flexibility, knowledge of community resources, persuasiveness, charisma, patience, and ability to be satisfied with small gains.

Interviews and meetings should focus on specific here-and-now strategies to help the individual and the family, because some challenging families tend to dwell on past problems and perceived injustices against them. Professionals should avoid using jargon and, when appropriate, employ humor to reduce tension. They should always be punctual, even if the family is not. Professionals also should carefully document their involvement, just in case the challenging family considers a lawsuit or creates bad publicity—which does occur on occasion.

Professionals must be sensitive to, and empathize with, family feelings of guilt, sorrow, anger, loneliness, confusion, and fear, without blaming or being judgmental. Yet, if required, they must also be capable of "standing up without fighting" when faced with intimidating or hostile family behavior (Bramson, 1981). In addition, professionals must recognize the power of casual small talk, empathic listening, and sharing a coffee together as a low-key starting point in building a positive relationship with the family. The *short-term goal* is always to keep the family's destructive behavior under control, so meaningful supports and services can be maintained or initiated for the person who has the disability. The *long-term goal* is to try to build a positive working relationship with family members, so they feel like collaborative partners on the team delivering services to the individual (Blue-Banning et al., 2004; Munro, 1995).

Maintenance of Objectivity and Perspective

The self-destructiveness, intimidation, sense of chaos, or extreme resistance exhibited by challenging families can elicit strong emotional reactions that can destroy objectivity and cause the professional to behave in a counter-therapeutic manner. The CSFT Model emphasizes that professionals should be particularly vigilant when they find that family members evoke strong reactions in them, such as hostility, repulsion, severe anxiety, rescue fantasies, or overidentification with a particular family member. They should prepare themselves for family antagonism without being provoked into defensiveness or power struggles. Clinical supervision and professional support meetings can be particularly helpful in overcoming these problems and in maintaining professional distance and perspective—so that the family's needs, not the professional's, guide the helping process. Psychotherapy should also be considered as a necessary option for professionals themselves who are particularly distressed or disturbed by family behavior.

Assessment of the Family and the Service System

Before intervening with a challenging family, the CSFT Model recommends that the clinician should first enlist the full support of agency management, or school or service system administration. Without this support, there is a very real danger of the professional being undermined or treated as a scapegoat when intense feelings or other problems surface during the intervention process.

If the family therapist agrees to become involved, he or she—as well as agency, school, or service system representatives—must be particularly sensitive about continually reassuring family members. This reassurance should revolve around four critical but usually unspoken questions relating to the person with the disability. That is, parents or other family members will continuously test professionals and organizations concerning the following questions:

1. Do you really care [about my relative/me]?
2. Is my child/relative really safe?
3. Is my child/relative happy?
4. Am I a good parent/sibling/grandparent?

The assessment process usually begins over the telephone, when arranging for the first interview or meeting. Clues can be picked up regarding family hostility, potential for cooperation, and the nature of the family's previous contact with agencies, schools, or professionals. From the beginning, professionals should show empathy, sensitivity, and honesty and present themselves as people who have knowledge, confidence, hope, and compassion for the family.

Gathering a thorough family history is important. It is usually helpful to review past agency, health, psychological, and school reports regarding the individual with a disability. During interviews, careful attention should be paid to family dynamics (i.e., potent underlying forces) that include the following: verbal and nonverbal communication patterns; family role clarity; problem-solving and decision-making methods; effectiveness of boundary setting; feelings of safety; housing and financial stability; marital discord or other family dysfunction; and the current health of family members, including psychiatric difficulties. Professionals must *listen with a "third ear"*—that is, not only to what is being said but also to what family members are really saying (i.e., meta-communication). Throughout discussions, a sensitivity to the family's religious and cultural background should be maintained.

Many seemingly difficult parents or other family members seem to welcome the opportunity to talk about their past, discuss concerns, and share family photo albums and memorabilia (a useful focal point for discussion). This provides a chance to explore the family's perception of current problems. The professional should note areas of family strength, cohesion, affection, and mutual support, in addition to how well the person with the disability is included in everyday family and community life. At the same time, the professional must meet and get to know the person with the disability and assess the supports he or she already has, paying careful attention to the attitude, accessibility, and availability of needed services. After carefully analyzing the family, the individual, and the support system, professionals can then begin to develop working hypotheses about what appears to contribute to the family's difficult behavior and what might be done to improve the situation.

Intervention with the Family and the Service System

When assessing challenging families, professionals frequently discover that service systems lack coordination, are difficult to gain access to, and often contain poor communication and cooperation among key people. Because of this situation, professionals using the CSFT Model should be skilled at interviewing and group facilitation. They also need to possess clinically refined "reframing" and "cognitive restructuring" skills to reduce destructive or intense emotions, clarify feelings and goals, and help service system and family representatives cope and gain perspective in intense situations (Lustig, 2002; Munro, 1991, 1997). The following interventions, targeting the service system as much as the family, can help to build or reestablish family/system teamwork.

1. *Developing support circles* can greatly improve support for individuals and families, as well as professionals and service providers. This involves person-centered planning or "wrapping services around" the person who has the disability and the family and scheduling regular meetings with the individual, family, and other key people (paid and unpaid) who are involved in the individual's life. These planning meetings—sometimes held at the family's home—help to improve networking, communication, and information sharing; encourage problem solving and brainstorming creative ideas; permit expression of deeply held or troubling feelings; and build mutual support (Munro, 1997; VanDenBerg & Grealish, 1998). Research also suggests that such planning approaches can be helpful with families of culturally diverse backgrounds (Blue-Banning, Turnbull, & Pereira, 2000).

2. *Teaching effective advocacy strategies* to families is very important. Many families of people who have developmental disabilities seem hesitant or unsure about how to gain access to human service systems. When family members learn how to successfully navigate service systems, however, they are empowered by the knowledge that they have had the courage to stand up for their relative with a disability and, indirectly, for others like him or her. The "Step Approach Model" for effective family advocacy is recommended (Munro, 1991).

3. *Bringing in an outside mediator* is often helpful and therapeutic for everyone if communication breaks down and disputes arise among the individual with a disability, the family, and agency or school. An impartial third party mediator can hear all points of view, help disputants cool down and gain perspective, help people find common ground and interests, suggest ways to balance power among all the parties represented, build (or reestablish) good working relationships, and actively strive to resolve conflicts (Munro, 1997).

4. When an individual with a developmental disability becomes involved with a residential or day program, an important rule of thumb is to *identify one contact person* from whom the family can obtain regular and accurate feedback regarding the person's progress. This can greatly reduce confusion and build family confidence in the program.

5. For families struggling to know what to do when spending time with relatives who are potentially violent, have psychiatric problems, or have severe disabilities, agency staff can help by *developing a list of preferred*

activities (e.g., going for car rides, eating special foods, going for walks, attending sporting events, swimming, putting together puzzles). These activities can assist family members in finding meaningful things to do—sometimes with support staff sent along just in case—so that positive visits and experiences can be ensured.

6. *Providing training in techniques for coping with difficult people* (Bramson, 1981; Glass, 1995) can help teachers, agency staff, or managers develop confidence and assertiveness and can help balance power when facing family members who are intimidating, explosive, or manipulative. These techniques—often involving role play and finding one's center of calm—emphasize the need to stand up without fighting, based on the premise that challenging families will never respect people whom they feel they can push around. People can also learn approaches for stopping a meeting or telephone call when there is excessive hostility. Likewise, these same approaches can be shared with family members dealing with difficult (e.g., "pushy") agency or school representatives.

7. Professionals should consider *the strategic use of well-timed and appropriate humor, frankness, cheerleading, and brief inspirational or motivational talks.* These can be important tools for reducing anxiety and building confidence among family and system representatives.

More Traditional Family Therapy Approaches

In many cases, challenging families still need more traditional family therapy intervention to deal with unresolved social, emotional, and grief issues and to help mend their broken spirits. However, these families seem caught in a bind. They desperately need professional support but simultaneously push away potentially helpful outsiders with abusive, chaotic, or socially unacceptable behavior. Nevertheless, the CSFT Model emphasizes that professionals must persist with the goal of building a positive therapeutic relationship with such families. Usually, outside support is gradually accepted, after a family has had time to test out the professional's degree of commitment, knowledge, and concern. With this in mind, the following supportive clinical approaches can be particularly helpful.

1. *Family interviews should be held in private, mutually agreed-on settings.* Sometimes it is useful to meet at the family's home, because this may seem less threatening to family members than office interviews. In some particularly tense situations, however, it is better to meet at a more neutral site, such as a professional office. During interviews, professionals must ensure that people adhere to basic rules of etiquette (e.g., never interrupt the person who is speaking). Sometimes, it is helpful to meet the entire family together. At other times, it is better to meet alone with parents, siblings (often an untapped resource), or the person with the disability to permit free expression of troubling feelings and concerns and eventually to find possible solutions.

2. *All promises or commitments professionals make to the family must be faithfully kept.* In addition, any constructive ideas presented by family members should be supported and carried out. This will gradually encourage desired behavior and gain trust.

3. *Professionals must guard against brushing off the problems raised by chronically complaining families.* Usually, even the most dysfunctional families have some legitimate concerns hidden behind their complaints. Professionals should use active listening, showing empathy and paraphrasing what was said, to ensure that a family member's message has been accurately heard. Being really listened to, as simple as it might seem, is a powerful therapeutic tool that works well, even with the most demanding people. Members of challenging families often have a history of being ignored, put off, or not taken seriously by others. They may have to tell stories about the pain and grief in their lives over and over again until they feel that they are truly being heard and understood. Only then do many families begin to let go of guilt and hostility, accept the reality of their family member's disability, and recognize their own need for outside help.

4. *Negative inquiry is another powerful technique that can be used in conjunction with active listening* (Smith, 1975). Negative inquiry involves actively prompting family members to criticize existing services. This serves the purpose of bringing to light information that might be helpful or exhausting criticism if it is detrimental or manipulative. This process usually guides family members to become more assertive. Negative inquiry works particularly well if the professional writes the family's criticisms down on paper, with the understanding that each concern will be taken seriously and addressed in turn. For example, a professional might say, "You've raised five concerns about how we are dealing with Mary. Is there anything else we should be doing?"

5. *Professionals can give permission to family members to establish more healthy physical and emotional boundaries and take part in activities that otherwise they would not do.* For instance, parents may be encouraged to plan vacations or evenings or weekends away without their children; continue their education; return to work outside the family; join support groups; attend physical exercise programs, wellness seminars, and stress management seminars; use parent respite services; and spend more time with their children who do not have disabilities. Divorced or widowed parents might even be urged to consider dating again.

6. When appropriate, *professionals can suggest to family members that they might benefit from a psychiatric as-*

sessment, psychotropic medication, or specialized counseling. Many family members who at first seem challenging are much less so after receiving proper professional help.

SUMMARY

Challenging families can cause difficulties for frontline professionals and agency or school administrators. These families also may compromise the emotional well-being of people with developmental disabilities because they often draw attention to their own needs, thereby hindering service delivery to the family member with a disability. It is essential that frontline professionals, agencies, and schools familiarize themselves with strategies for addressing the frustrations, anger, and tension that challenging families are experiencing. Doing so can assist these families and promote good mental health in the person with the disability. This chapter noted probable causes of challenging family behavior, explained behavioral patterns shown by these families, and presented a positive and effective model of family-system intervention.

FOR FURTHER THOUGHT AND DISCUSSION

1. Why is the adjective *challenging* in quotation marks when it is introduced in this chapter?
2. What are some specific family behaviors that might be associated with each of the nine behavioral patterns of challenging families described in this chapter? Can you think of any other patterns not listed?
3. Why might professionals find it intimidating or frustrating to deal with challenging families?
4. What can professionals do, both as individuals and as parts of the service system, to build positive working relationships with challenging families?

REFERENCES

Ashton, J., & Ashton, D. (1996). *Loss and grief recovery: Help caring for children with disabilities, chronic or terminal illness.* Amityville, NY: Baywood.

Blue-Banning, M.J., Summers, J.A., Frankland, H.C., et al. (2004). Dimensions of family and professional partnerships: Constructive guidelines for collaboration. *Exceptional Children, 70,* 167–184.

Blue-Banning, M.J., Turnbull, A.P., & Pereira, L. (2000). Group action planning as a support strategy for Hispanic families: Parent and professional perspectives. *Mental Retardation, 38,* 262–275.

Bramson, R.M. (1981). *Coping with difficult people.* New York: Ballantine.

Davis, H.D. (1987). Disability and grief. *Social Casework, 6,* 352–358.

Early, T.J., & GlenMaye, L.F. (2000). Valuing families: Social work practice with families from a strengths perspective. *Social Work, 45,* 118–130.

Gabel, S. (2004). South Asian Indian cultural orientations toward mental retardation. *Mental Retardation, 42,* 12–25.

Glass, L. (1995). *Toxic people: 10 ways of dealing with people who make your life miserable.* New York: St. Martin's Griffin.

Hasting, H.M., & Taunt, H.M. (2002). Positive perceptions in families of children with developmental disabilities. *American Journal on Mental Retardation,107,* 116–127.

Kausar, S., Jevne, R.F., & Sobsey, D. (2003). Hope in families of children with developmental disabilities. *Journal on Developmental Disabilities, 10,* 35–46.

Lustig, D.C. (2002). Family coping in families with a child with a disability. *Education and Training in Mental Retardation and Developmental Disabilities, 37,* 14–22.

Magana, S., Seltzer, M.M., & Krauss, M.W. (2004). Cultural contest of caregiving: Differences in depression between Puerto Rican and Non-Latina white mothers of adults with mental retardation. *Mental Retardation, 42,* 1–11.

Moses, K. (Producer). (1988). *Lost dreams and growth: Parents' concerns* [Videotape]. Evansville, IN: Resource Networks Inc.

Munro, J.D. (1991). Training families in the "Step Approach Model" for effective advocacy. *Canada's Mental Health, 39* (1), 1–6.

Munro, J.D. (1995). Counseling severely dysfunctional families of mentally and physically disabled persons. In F.J. Turner (Ed.), *Differential diagnosis and treatment in social work* (4th ed., pp. 160–172). New York: The Free Press.

Munro, J.D. (1997). Using unconditionally constructive mediation to resolve family-system disputes related to persons with disabilities. *Families in Society, 78*(6), 609–616.

Olshansky, S. (1961). Chronic sorrow: A response to having a mentally defective child. *Social Casework, 43,* 190–193.

Parks, R.M. (1983). Parental reactions to the birth of a handicapped child. In L. Wikler & M.P. Keenan (Eds.), *Developmental disabilities: No longer a private tragedy* (pp. 96–114). Washington, DC: National Association of Social Workers.

Russo, R.J. (1999). Applying a strengths-based practice approach in working with people with developmental disabilities and their families. *Families in Society, 80,* 25–33.

Saleeby, D. (1992). *The strength perspective in social work practice.* New York: Basic Books.

Sanders, C.M. (1999). *Grief: The mourning after: Dealing with adult bereavement.* Hoboken, NJ: John Wiley & Sons.

Scorgie, K., & Sobsey, D. (2000). Transformation outcomes associated with parenting children who have disabilities. *Mental Retardation, 38,* 195–206.

Scorgie, K., Wilgosh, L., Sobsey, D., et al. (2001). Parent life management and transformational outcomes when a child has Down syndrome. *International Journal of Special Education, 16,* 57–68.

Seligman, M.E.P., & Csikszentmihalyi, M. (2000). Positive psychology: An introduction. *American Psychologist, 55,* 5–14.

Sieffert, A. (1978). Parents initial reactions to having a mentally retarded child: A concept and model for social workers. *Clinical Social Work Journal, 6,* 33–43.

Singer, G.H.S., & Powers, L.E. (Eds.). (1993). *Families, disability and empowerment: Active coping skills and strategies for family interventions.* Baltimore: Paul H. Brookes Publishing Co.

Smith, M. (1975). *When I say no, I feel guilty.* New York: Dial Press.

Stainton, T., & Besser, H. (1998). The positive impact of children with an intellectual disability on the family. *Journal of Intellectual & Developmental Disability, 23,* 57–70.

Taunt, H.M., & Hastings, R.P. (2002). Positive impact of children with developmental disabilities on their families: A preliminary study. *Education and Training in Mental Retardation and Developmental Disabilities, 37,* 410–420.

VanDenBerg, J., & Grealish, E.M. (1998). *The wraparound process training manual.* Pittsburgh, PA: The Community Partners Group.

25

Speech and Language Disorders

Ralf W. Schlosser, Jeff Sigafoos,
Nora Rothschild, Maureen Burke, and Leora M. Palace

WHAT YOU WILL LEARN ABOUT IN THIS CHAPTER

- Background on communication
- Background on speech and language
- Background on speech and language disorders
- How speech and language disorders are related to intellectual and developmental disabilities
- How speech and language disorders are related to challenging behaviors
- Sensory factors that contribute to speech and language difficulties
- Who may benefit from speech and language intervention
- Augmentative and alternative communication
- Intervention for people who are deaf and blind

BACKGROUND ON COMMUNICATION

Communication refers to the act or process involved in the mutual sharing of information between at least two people, whereby one person assumes the role of a sender and the other that of a receiver. The National Joint Committee for the Communication Needs of Persons with Severe Disabilities (2003) defined communication as

> Any act by which one person gives to or receives from another person information about that person's needs, desires, perceptions, knowledge or affective states. Communication may be intentional or unintentional, may involve conventional or unconventional signals, may take linguistic or nonlinguistic forms, and may occur through spoken or other modes. (p. 2)

The essence of this definition is the concept of shared meaning. Communication is effective to the extent that there is shared meaning between the sender and receiver. Another important aspect of this definition is the recognition that communication can occur through a variety of behaviors and modes (e.g., gesture mode, graphic mode) other than speech.

Another view of communication comes from the work of B.F. Skinnner (1957). Skinner described a class of verbal behavior that is communicative in the sense that it is effective only indirectly through the mediation of a listener. For example, a person might request a cup of coffee from a waiter, rather than getting a cup directly from the coffee machine. Whether the request works depends on whether there was another person present who heard and understood the request and was willing and able to deliver the requested object.

Because communication allows us to feel a sense of belonging and participate in social activities, it is often regarded as representing the essence of life. Communication impairment can negatively affect a person's quality of life. Indeed, Ferguson (1994) noted that communication is the most important means by which individuals obtain membership in society.

Communication results from a complicated interplay of many sensory and cognitive processes. It includes mastery not only of the verbal component but also mastery of visual, social, and behavior skills (Grizzle & Simms, 2005). In broad terms, there is a distinction between linguistic (verbal) and nonlinguistic (nonverbal) modalities of communication. Linguistic modalities include spoken and written words, certain graphic symbol systems, and sign languages. Nonlinguistic or prelinguistic modalities include facial expressions, body language, use of certain pictures, and gestures.

Prevalence studies indicate that as much as 16% of the U.S. population has some type of communication disorder. Approximately 7.5 million people in the United States have trouble using their voices. Between 6 and 8 million have difficulties with language (National Institute on Deafness and Other Communication Disorders [NIDCD], 2006a). This chapter deals with communication difficulties in speech and language and approaches for addressing them. This topic is very important because there is considerable evidence that children who have impairments in speech and language can make substantial and lasting gains if identification of the problem and intervention occur early. Severe speech and language disorders pose a par-

The volume editors thank Tom Dearie for rendering high-resolution reproductions of the artwork for certain figures in this chapter.

ticular challenge. Because people with severe communication problems may benefit from a form of treatment known as augmentative and alternative communication (AAC), AAC is highlighted later in this chapter.

BACKGROUND ON SPEECH AND LANGUAGE

Communication usually involves listening, speaking, reading, and writing. Of course, there are many ways to communicate that do not involve speech or language. Some people use sign language, communication aids, or other methods to communicate. For example, a young boy might effectively communicate to his father that he wants a drink by pointing to a bottle of juice while vocalizing. This example illustrates the distinction between what the child does to communicate (i.e., form) and the purpose of the communicative act (i.e., function). The main factors affecting verbal communication are speech (including voice, articulation, and fluency) and language. The following sections explain what these factors are and how they are related.

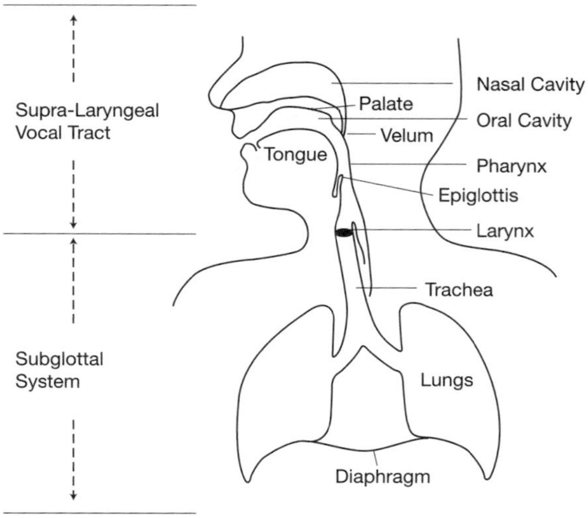

Figure 25.1. The human speech production system. (From Rubin, P., & Vatikiotis-Bateson, E. [n.d.]. *Talking heads: Speech production. Measuring and modeling speech production.* Retrieved November 30, 2006, from http://www.haskins.yale.edu/featured/heads/MMSP/intro.html; reprinted by permission.)

Speech

The term *speech* is sometimes used interchangeably with *language,* but these words do not mean the same thing. Speech is the oral manifestation of language. It is a system of communication that is learned. It depends on the coordinated use of voice, articulation, and language skills. *Voice* is the sound produced by passage of air through vibrating vocal cords. It is defined by its pitch, quality, and intensity. Resonance in the chest, throat, and mouth cavities also contributes to voice. *Articulation* refers to the production of sounds that form the words of language. In articulation, movement of the lips, tongue, jaw, and palate interrupt or shape the airstream after it passes through the vocal cords. The teeth also can produce some particular speech sounds. Rate and fluency also are important aspects of speech. The rate of speaking should not be so rapid or so slow that it interferes with comprehension. *Fluency* of speech refers to the smoothness of the flow. Speech fluency should not be overly choppy or disconnected.

Fundamentals of Speech Production The fundamentals of speech production are explained in Figure 25.1. The human speech organ is called the larynx. This consists of folds of cartilage that have three important functions. These folds protect the airways and prevent material from entering the lungs; they are important for breathing; they are important for talking. When one speaks, the vocal folds in the larynx come close together and vibrate to produce voice. When one breathes, the vocal folds open and allow air flow from the lungs through the mouth and nose and vice versa. Air flow from the lungs is said to be the voice generator. When one stops breathing while swallowing, the vocal folds close to protect the airway and keep food and drink out of the lungs. Sound is produced by vibration of the vocal folds; the vocal folds are sometimes called the vibrator. Sound produced by the vibrator is modified by a three-dimensional cavity called the resonator, which is formed by the individual's oral cavity, nasopharynx, sinuses, and nasal cavity. If someone has a stuffed-up nose, resonance becomes altered and his or her voice is said to be hyponasal. If someone has a cleft palate, there may be excessive nasal resonance and the person's voice is said to be hypernasal. Once the sound is modified by the resonator, it becomes shaped by the articulator, which includes the cheeks, tongue, teeth, and lips. Problems with articulators can result from neurological problems, developmental problems, sensory problems, or growths on the components of the articulator. An individual's generator, vibrator, resonator, and articulator act together to produce the sounds from the human mouth.

Language

Language refers to the code with which one communicates. It is an arbitrary system of symbols used by groups of people to communicate their thoughts and feelings, and it involves thought processes, symbols, grammar, meaning, memory, and words. The reason this system of symbols is called "arbitrary" is because the symbols usually bear no resemblance to their referents. For example, the word *chair* does not look like the object *chair.* Symbols may be spoken, written, or graphic, or they may be gestures and body movements. In spoken language, the skills of articulation are used; in written language, spelling is substituted for articulation. Both auditory and visual skills are important for understanding language and for using it to communicate.

In spoken language, a set of complex, interacting rules governs the ways that individual words are organized and used. Because cognition is the foundation upon which language is built, this area of communication is likely to be affected by cognitive impairments.

Language consists of three components: form, content, and use (Burke-Brassem & Palace, 2003).

Form *Form* refers to the coding of words into meaningful sentences—that is, the grammar or syntax of language. As an individual develops greater language competence, form refers to the way in which the sentences are sequenced and organized to form narratives or discourse production (e.g., instructions on how to get from one place to another). The acquisition of this component of language is usually a function of age. It follows typical developmental patterns and is not highly dependent on personality or stimulation influences.

Content *Content* refers to the content, or the semantics, of language. The development of semantics takes place throughout an individual's life. In a larger sense, this component of language relates to word meanings and more abstract, logical word relationships. Although this component is closely allied to cognition, it may be significantly influenced by stimulation and experience.

Use *Use* refers to the pragmatic use of language—that is, the way in which language is put into practice for different social and communicative functions. It takes conversational rules into account (e.g., taking turns, being able to maintain topics and to introduce topics). It is the component of language that most strongly influences how adaptive an individual is or how well a person functions in his or her environment.

Interaction of the Three Components Form, content, and use are all important for the production of language. However, impairments may occur within one of the three components with little influence on the other two components. For example, people with autism may have good language structure and a well-developed vocabulary, but they may use language in an inappropriate or inadequate manner, resulting in a significant impairment in social functioning. A splintering of language components is also common in Williams syndrome. Individuals with this syndrome develop relatively intact language structure and are seen as highly sociable and interactive (i.e., they have an adequate use of language). Yet, their word choices (semantics) are frequently peculiar, and they are often described as having "cocktail party speech." Frequently, however, language disorder results from more than one component being affected. Individuals with fragile X syndrome, for example, frequently have difficulties with all three components.

Speech and language are not mutually dependent on one another. It is possible to have a fully intact language in the absence of speech, as demonstrated by sign language. Moreover, it is equally possible to have completely intact speech development with major impairments in all components of language (e.g., specific language impairment).

BACKGROUND ON SPEECH AND LANGUAGE DISORDERS

The term *speech and language disorders* refer to particular types of problems in communication resulting from delays and/or problems in speech, language, and/or hearing in accordance with an age-appropriate developmental pattern. These disorders can include problems in related areas such as oral-motor function, and they range from simple sound substitutions to the inability to understand language, use language, or use the oral-motor mechanism for functional speech and feeding. For example, a child's communication is considered delayed when the child is noticeably behind his or her peers in the acquisition of speech and/or language skills. Some warning signs that a child might have a speech/language disorder include difficulty in

- Understanding speech
- Thinking of words and/or finding words
- Putting words together into sentences and use of grammar
- Saying sounds and/or words
- Narrating and sequencing a simple story or event
- Reading and/or writing.

The degree to which the individuals' environments are able to adapt to communication difficulties very often influences the outcome and consequences more than the communication difficulties themselves. For example, an individual with very limited output (one- and two-word utterances) may be empowered in an environment that understands and responds to the intent, as opposed to the structure, of his or her communication. Conversely, an individual who has more complex language but difficulty in recognizing and taking another person's expression of perspective into account may not be understood by others. Such lack of understanding may result in any number of negative emotions and behaviors (Burke-Brassem & Palace, 2003).

Speech Disorders

The term *speech disorders* refers to difficulties producing speech sounds or problems with voice quality. Speech disorders may be characterized by an interruption in the flow or rhythm of speech (e.g., stuttering), which is called dysfluency. Disorders that include problems with the way sounds are formed are called articulation or phonological disorders. Other speech disorders involve problems with the pitch, volume, or quality of the voice. There may be a combination of several problems. People with speech disorders have trouble using some speech sounds, which can also be a symptom of a delay. They may say "see" when they mean *ski,* or they may have trouble using other sounds such as those associated with the letter *l* or *r.* Listeners may have trouble understanding what someone with a speech disorder is trying to say.

A large number of factors affect adequate production of speech (Burke-Brassem & Palace, 2003). The main ones include sensory deficits, structural abnormalities, oral-motor and verbal apraxias, and developmental delays in speech acquisition.

Sensory Deficits In this context, sensory deficits refer specifically to hearing loss. Hearing inconsistently or the inability to hear leads to a distortion in the individual's ability to perceive the individual sounds and sound groups needed for adequate speech production.

Structural Abnormalities Differences in any of the physiological structures that are needed to support speech production (e.g., cleft palate, oral-facial deformities) can result in atypical speech production. In addition, differences in muscle tone may result in speech being characterized by an imprecise production of sounds together with distortions in voice quality, nasality, and timing. People with Down syndrome frequently have low muscle tone. Consequently, their speech may sometimes sound sloppy and unclear. Individuals with cerebral palsy may have a strained, strangled voice quality; hypernasality; a slow rate of speech; and consonant imprecision due to high muscle tone.

Oral-Motor and Verbal Apraxias *Apraxia* refers to the inability to program muscle movements needed for the voluntary production of speech. This occurs in spite of normal musculature. It is believed to be controlled within the cortex of the brain.

Developmental Delays in Speech Acquisition Delays in speech acquisition generally fall into two categories: articulation and phonology. *Articulation* refers to the manner and place in which individual sounds are produced. For example, placing the tongue tip on the palatal ridges immediately behind the upper teeth always produces the letter *s* sound. A typical distortion of this sound may involve sticking the tongue out between the teeth to produce a /th/ sound instead. A phonological delay affects whole sound groups. In this instance, there is a delay or arrest of some of the typical processes that children go through in suppressing error patterns and acquiring accurate speech patterns. For example, the phonological process of "backing" is one in which the individual changes a sound that is made with the front of the tongue to a sound made with the back of the tongue (e.g., *guck/duck, gog/dog*).

Language Disorders

The phrase *language disorders* refers to impairment in the ability to understand and/or use words in context, both verbally and nonverbally. Some characteristics of language disorders include improper use of words and their meanings, inability to express ideas, inappropriate grammatical patterns, reduced vocabulary, and inability to follow directions. One or a combination of these characteristics may occur in children who are affected by language learning disabilities or developmental language delay.

Children may hear or see a word but not be able to understand its meaning. They may have trouble getting others to understand what they are trying to communicate. Sometimes a child will have greater receptive (understanding) than expressive (speaking) language skills, but this is not always the case (National Dissemination Center for Children with Disabilities [NICHCY], 2004). Between the ages of 1 and 3 years, there is a wide variation in the range of typical speech and language development. Receptive language skills usually develop before a child is able to produce understandable words, phrases, and sentences. (Refer to Grizzle and Simms, 2005, for a table of selected language milestones.)

For some children, the development of language skills proceeds in a typical sequence but at a slower pace—a condition referred to as a delay in development. Other children follow an atypical sequence in the development of language skills—a condition referred to as a disorder of development. Disorders of language development may affect expressive abilities alone, or they may affect both expressive and receptive abilities. For children with typical nonverbal cognitive abilities, language problems that are severe and pronounced in the absence of obvious neurological insult or hearing impairment are referred to as specific language impairments (SLIs). Approximately 7% of school-age children are thought to have SLIs, with more males being affected than females (Grizzle & Simms, 2005).

Various issues can interfere with understanding speech (receptive language) and/or using language (expressive language). These include genetic factors that cause different intellectual and/or developmental disabilities; various neurological and neurodegenerative disorders; fetal exposure to alcohol, cocaine, and other drugs; physical impairments such as cleft lip or palate, deafness, blindness, and brain injury; and straining the vocal cords due to vocal abuse or misuse. Frequently, however, the cause is unknown (NICHCY, 2004). Hearing and vision problems also can significantly affect communication. These sensory impairments are explained in a separate section later in this chapter. Table 25.1 summarizes various conditions and disorders that affect speech and language. Some of these conditions are intellectual and/or developmental disabilities; as indicated in the next section, speech and language disorders are more frequent in people with intellectual and developmental disabilities than in the general population.

There is strong evidence that early language development is related to later reading skills. An observation of language delay on the part of a parent or a teacher often is the first indicator to a family doctor or pediatrician that a child will have later reading difficulties. Unlike oral language, access to and use of written language proceeds most effectively in the presence of systematic and explicit instruction. Children who receive adequate instruction, who have typical cognitive function, and who have no history of neurological insult or a sensory impairment and yet continue to struggle in their ability to read are said to have a reading disorder. As many as 10%–20% of the population in the United States have a reading disorder. Although it was once thought that reading disorder affected more males than females, prevalence rates appear to be similar in both sexes (Grizzle & Simms, 2005). The majority (80%) of those with a reading disorder have a condition called dyslexia, in which there is a problem with the decoding of single words.

HOW SPEECH AND LANGUAGE DISORDERS ARE RELATED TO INTELLECTUAL AND DEVELOPMENTAL DISABILITIES

Because communication and cognition are highly related, an intellectual or developmental disability often involves some communication disorder. McQueen et al. (1987) noted that speech disorders were commonly associated with intellectual disability. They estimated that up to 65.5% of children with intellectual disability had speech disorders of varying types and degrees. Approximately 30%–50% of individuals with autism do not have speech (National Research Council, 2001). As shown in Table 25.1, some syndromes associated with intellectual or developmental disability are associated with speech or language problems characteristic of the particular syndrome (e.g., Down syndrome, fragile X syndrome, velocardiofacial syndrome) or with unusual speech or language characteristics (e.g., Williams syndrome). (For further information see the chapters about these particular disorders, Chapter 15, and Appendix B at the end of the book). Given these high prevalence rates, it is understandable that communication intervention is a priority for individuals with intellectual and developmental disabilities. However, the severity of the disability does not always act as a predictor of the extent or type of communication difficulty. Some people with intellectual and/or developmental disabilities experience voice and fluency disorders that are unrelated to their disability and are no more common in this population than in the general population (e.g., stuttering) (McQueen et al., 1987).

Individuals with mild to moderate speech and language disorders may continue to rely on their natural residual speech, which can include delays in the emergence of speech and aspects of language use, such as multiword utterances, syntax, and conversational skills. It is unclear whether the language development of individuals with mild to moderate disabilities is best described as different or delayed (Zigler & Balla, 1982).

A significant percentage of individuals with intellectual and developmental disabilities other than autism also have little or no functional speech, resulting in severe communication impairment. Individuals with such severe communication impairment often acquire a prelinguistic level of communication development characterized by the use of vocalizations, informal gestures, and facial expression. For these people, intervention most likely will need to focus on the use of some AAC strategies and systems in addition to, or instead of, their prelinguistic behaviors.

HOW SPEECH AND LANGUAGE DISORDERS ARE RELATED TO CHALLENGING BEHAVIORS

People with speech and language disorders have long been described as a group at risk for social, emotional, and behavioral difficulties. The most logical and simple explanation for this is that speech and language impairments affect an individual's ability to understand and/or be understood by others. The greater the communicative difficulty, the greater the risk of negative consequences. The range of negative consequences is as great as the range of impairments themselves (Burke-Brassem & Palace, 2003).

Some people may react to communication difficulties by demonstrating externalizing behaviors such as impatience, tantrums, impulsiveness, and aggression. Others may display internalizing behaviors such as withdrawal, avoidance, depression, and dependence. Speech and language impairments also are associated with self-injury and stereotypical behaviors. Individuals with intellectual and developmental disabilities may have learned to use these challenging behaviors to communicate basic wants and needs. For instance, challenging behaviors may allow individuals to communi-

Table 25.1. Some conditions and disorders that affect speech and language

Condition or disorder	Description
Alzheimer's disease	The most common form of dementia among older adults. Central auditory processing impairments (see Auditory processing disorder entry later in this table) may precede diagnosis of this disorder. Dementia of the Alzheimer type often occurs 20–30 years earlier in people with Down syndrome than in the general population.
Amyotrophic lateral sclerosis (ALS; also called Lou Gehrig's disease)	A neurodegenerative disease that affects the voluntary muscles. Initially, this disease prevents the person from talking loudly and clearly; eventually, it prevents them from talking or vocalizing.
Aphasia	A disorder resulting from damage to the language centers of the brain that may affect receptive and expressive language.
Apraxia	A motor speech disorder caused by damage to the parts of the nervous system related to speaking.
Attention-deficit/hyperactivity disorder	A neurobiological condition that affects ability to maintain attention. Effects on speech and language vary from one individual to another.
Auditory processing disorder	A disorder that affects a person's ability to process what is heard and that prevents the individual from understanding what he or she hears. The individual may be able to repeat the words back verbatim without knowing (i.e., without processing) the meaning of the message.
Autism spectrum disorders	Occur in varying forms and degrees of severity. Children with autism have marked problems with communication skills, social relationships, and imagination. As many as 30%–50% have no speech. People with autism whose speech and language are severely affected may benefit from augmentative and alternative communication.
Cancer of head, neck, or larynx	Speech problems may be encountered before surgery as the result of the cancer and after surgery as the result of tissue damage/loss from the cancer and surgery.
Cerebral palsy	Term that describes a group of chronic disorders impairing control of movement that appear in the first few years of life and generally do not worsen over time. This disorder can affect speech.
Cleft lip or palate	Refers to failure of the right and left sides of the lip and/or the roof of the mouth to grow together. This can result in problems with speech production. Velocardiofacial syndrome is one cause of cleft lip or palate.
Dementia	Refers to a cluster of symptoms that includes memory loss and overall cognitive impairment. There are many different causes of dementia, the most frequent being Alzheimer's disease.
Delay in language development	A situation in which the development of language skills proceeds in a normal sequence but at a slower pace than normal.
Developmental speech and language disorders in children	Any disorders in children who are not acquiring spoken and/or written language skills in accordance with an age-appropriate developmental pattern. This group includes children with difficulties in the development of communication interaction, comprehension, and production of language, encompassing the pragmatic/functional aspects of language, articulation, phonology (sound system of a language), fluency, voice, and disorders of swallowing. There may or may not be an identifiable cause. Some of the common identifiable causes for speech and language disorders may be intellectual and/or developmental disability, autism, learning disabilities, hearing loss, cerebral palsy, or brain injury.
Disorder of language development	A condition in which the sequence of development of language skills is atypical. Disorders of language development may affect expressive abilities alone, or both expressive and receptive abilities.
Drug abuse (i.e., prenatal exposure to drugs)	Prenatal exposure to alcohol (fetal alcohol syndrome), cocaine, or other drugs.
Dysarthria	Difficulty with movement of muscles of the mouth, face, and respiratory system resulting from brain injury or stroke.
Dyslexia	A condition in which there is a problem with the decoding of single words. The severity of this condition is highly variable and sometimes affects skill in using numbers. It is not related to intelligence or to general achievement in other areas.

cate that they wish to escape from difficult tasks; for example, an individual who bangs his head against the wall when work demands are placed on him may be granted a break from work. Others may seek to obtain or keep their favorite tangible objects. The behavior of some individuals may be maintained by social attention from communication partners. For instance, each time a student engages in self-injurious behavior, the teacher pays attention to her. Finally, some individuals are motivated by sensory consequences. It should be noted, however, that individuals with intellectual and developmental disabilities may exhibit these behaviors whether they have spoken language or not (Burke-Brassem & Palace, 2003).

Condition or disorder	Description
Dysphagia	Difficulty with swallowing. This can affect speech production.
Hearing loss and deafness	See the section on sensory impairments in the chapter text.
Huntington disease	A neurodegenerative disease associated with communication, swallowing, and cognitive impairment.
Hypernasality	Caused by velopharyngeal incompetence, a condition that makes a person's speech sound as though he or she is talking through his or her nose.
Intellectual and/or developmental disability syndromes (known cause)	Especially Down syndrome, fragile X syndrome, velocardiofacial syndrome, and Williams syndrome. See text of this chapter and Chapters 15 for other examples of specific intellectual and/or developmental disabilities associated with disorders of speech and language.
Intellectual and developmental disability (unknown cause)	See the chapter text.
Language-based learning disability	A disability that interferes with age-appropriate reading, spelling, and writing but does not necessarily compromise intelligence. A well-known example is dyslexia.
Laryngeal papillomatosis	A rare disease caused by human papillomavirus (genital wart virus) infection of the mucous membrane of the larynx.
Orofacial myofunctional disorders	A disorder associated with exaggerated forward movement of the tongue during speech and swallowing.
Paradoxical vocal fold movement	A voice disorder in which the vocal folds occasionally close when they should open, such as when breathing.
Right hemisphere brain damage	Cognitive-communication problems—such as impaired memory, attention problems and poor reasoning—as the result of damage to right hemisphere of the brain.
Selective mutism	Persistent lack of speech in at least one social situation, despite the ability to speak in other situations.
Spasmodic dystonia	A disorder characterized by involuntary movements of one or more muscles of the larynx or voice box.
Specific language impairment	A condition in which nonverbal cognitive abilities have developed typically but in which there are severe and pronounced language problems in the absence of obvious neurological insult or hearing impairment.
Stroke-related problems	Stroke occurs when a clogged or burst artery interrupts blood flow to the brain. This interruption of blood flow deprives the brain of needed oxygen and causes the affected brain cells to die. This may affect speech and language and the ability to understand them.
Stuttering	A disorder of speech fluency that interrupts the forward flow of speech.
Tracheostomy	A surgical opening made in the windpipe (trachea) by cutting the neck below the Adam's apple, below the vocal cords. This opening is used for breathing instead of the nose and mouth. It interferes with speaking.
Traumatic brain injury	Refers to a penetrating closed brain injury.
Usher syndrome	An inherited disorder characterized by moderate to profound hearing impairment and progressive vision loss. It often is evident at birth.
Velocardiofacial syndrome (also known as 22q11.2 deletion syndrome, CATCH 22; see Chapter 15)	A genetic disorder in which the most common features are cleft palate, heart defects, characteristic facial appearance, minor learning problems, and speech and feeding problems.
Ventilators	The connection of a tube from a tracheostomy to a breathing machine (ventilator). Patients on ventilators are able to talk only during expiration.
Vision problems and blindness	See the section on sensory problems in the chapter text.
Vocal fold nodules and polyps	Benign growths on both vocal folds that are caused by vocal abuse.
Vocal fold paralysis	Results from damage to a branch of the vagus nerve that runs from the brainstem to the larynx.

Sources: Auditory Processing Disorder U.K. (2002), MedlinePlus (2006), and National Institute on Deafness and Other Communication Disorders (2006b).

For more information on a specific condition or disorder, refer to the chapter in this book on that topic and/or to Chapter 15.

SENSORY FACTORS THAT CONTRIBUTE TO SPEECH AND LANGUAGE DIFFICULTIES

Sensory impairments such as those related to hearing and vision may contribute to the previously discussed speech and language difficulties. In fact, these sensory issues are so important that "the presence of sensory impairments should always be ruled in or out as contributing factors in cases of communication disability" (Blischak & Wasson, 1997, p. 254). All people with intellectual and/or developmental disabilities should have a hearing assessment and a vision assessment, as well as a speech and language assessment.

Hearing

The human auditory system is very complex (see Figure 10.5 for an illustration of the ear). The ear has three main parts: the outer, middle, and inner ear. The outer ear opens into the ear canal. The eardrum separates the ear canal from the middle ear. Three small bones in the middle ear (the hammer, anvil, and stirrup) help transfer sound to the inner ear. The inner ear contains the auditory (hearing) nerve, which leads to the brain.

Any sound source sends vibrations (sound waves) into the ear. These are channeled through the ear opening and down the ear canal; then, they strike the eardrum, causing it to vibrate. The vibrations are passed to the small bones of the middle ear, which transmit them to the auditory nerve in the inner ear. Here, the vibrations are changed into nerve impulses that go directly to the brain, which then interprets the impulses as sound (e.g., a voice, a fire alarm, music).

Sound waves are produced by pressure changes and vibrations in the air. The process of hearing begins when vibrating air molecules come into contact with the eardrum, causing it to vibrate. The vibrations of the eardrum are relayed to a lever-pulley system of the three middle-ear bones, which amplifies and recodes these incoming signals and transmits them to the inner ear, or cochlea. The detection of sound occurs when the ear's auditory receptors generate neural signals. Actual hearing occurs in the cochlea. The third middle-ear bone is connected to the cochlea. Movement of this bone causes the fluid in the cochlea to move with incoming sound.

The sense of hearing gives one pleasure and connection with one's environment and enables participation in verbal communication. The sense of hearing is fully functional in the second trimester of pregnancy, so a newborn is able to recognize his or her mother's voice at birth. The detection of pure tones at intensities of less than 15 decibels (a unit used to measure sound) is considered to be normal hearing for children. Yet, the detection of pure tones within normal limits does not encompass the entire process of hearing. There are millions of rapid acoustic events that occur during a typical conversation. They require extremely rapid and efficient auditory processing in order for a listener to obtain the full message intended by a speaker. These skills develop by adolescence in a person with typical hearing.

The presence of hearing impairments in children acts as an invisible acoustic filter that has an impact on their auditory processing capacity, their verbal language competency, their behavior, their reading and writing capacity, their academic options, and even their independent functioning. The impact of hearing loss can be exacerbated ten-fold for a child with a developmental disability if left undetected or unaddressed. Thus, early detection and treatment of hearing disorders is critical (Burke-Brassem & Palace, 2003).

Children with intellectual and/or developmental disabilities are often at high risk of hearing loss as a concomitant disability. Burke-Brassem and Palace (2003) estimated that approximately half of all of the people with intellectual and developmental disabilities they support have an undetected ear or hearing disorder.

Attempts are underway in some areas to detect hearing impairments as soon as possible. A newborn hearing test now is done in many hospitals. Whether this should be applied to small groups that are at high risk for hearing loss or to all newborns is being debated (Connolly, Carron, & Roark, 2005). All people with intellectual and/or developmental disabilities should be seen for regular audiology (hearing) services throughout their lives, and impairments should be addressed as quickly as possible. People with intellectual and developmental disabilities come to their audiology appointments with special needs that include their developmental level; their communication ability; their higher than average frequency of hearing loss and middle-ear disease; and, at times, their uncooperative behavior during testing. With adequate support, many hearing impairments can be successfully treated and their negative impact on functioning minimized.

In addition to deafness, hearing impairments include conductive sensorineural or mixed hearing loss and central hearing loss (Burke-Brassem & Palace, 2003). Sensorineural hearing loss (or nerve-related deafness) involves damage to the inner ear caused by aging, prenatal and birth-related problems, viral and bacterial infections, heredity, trauma, exposure to loud noise, fluid backup, or a benign tumor in the inner ear. Almost all sensorineural hearing loss can be effectively treated with hearing aids. Conductive hearing loss involves the outer and middle ear that may be caused by blockage of wax, punctured eardrum, birth defects, ear infection, or heredity. This type of hearing loss often can be effectively treated medically or surgically. Mixed hearing loss refers to a combination of conductive and sensorineural loss and means that a problem occurs in both the outer or middle and the inner ear (Hearing Loss Association of America, 2004). Central hearing loss results from damage or impairment to the nerves or nuclei of the central nervous system, either in the pathways to the brain or in the brain itself. Hearing impairments also can include hyperacusis, an auditory phenomenon characterized by a collapsed tolerance to normal environmental sounds. The cause is theorized to involve a breakdown or dysfunction in the efferent portion of the auditory nerve.

People with different types of developmental disabilities may require different audiological considerations. For example, a person with Down syndrome should undergo regular hearing tests in order to monitor recurrent conductive hearing loss (common in early childhood), mixed hearing loss in early adolescence, and progressive sensorineural hearing loss in early adulthood. These repeated assessments also give the person more experience with audiology procedures, eventually resulting in more reliable and accurate hearing thresholds and usually a complete audiogram (Burke-Brassem & Palace, 2003).

Different tools and services are available to help people who are deaf to function independently. These include assistive devices to enhance face-to-face communication and personal enjoyment of television and radio; devices to improve telephone communication; and technology to provide greater awareness and recognition of environmental sounds and situations. Some of these tools and services can even be customized to meet an individual's specific needs (ABLEDATA, 1999). Hearing ear dogs, specially trained to alert owners to significant sounds, are also available. They are also an excellent source of protection and have been granted legal status equal to that afforded to seeing eye dogs (ABLEDATA, 1999). Cochlear implants may be of benefit to people with severe to profound nerve deafness that is not helped significantly by conventional hearing aids due to damage to the hair cells in the inner ear (ABLEDATA, 1999).

A range of tools is also available for people who are hard of hearing. Various hearing aids, hearing implants, microphone and telephone amplifiers, speech training games and computer software packages, and speech therapy aids help people to carry out their daily activities (ABLEDATA, 1999). Early use of personal frequency modulated (FM) systems with lightweight headsets provides amplification for recurrent, fluctuating hearing loss. An FM system is a good precursor for traditional hearing aid usage. (FM systems work like a small radio transmitter and radio receiver.) Multimemory, programmable hearing aids are good for long-term amplification needs. For people who exhibit hyperacusis, the use of hearing protection devices is helpful in dampening the loudness of incoming sounds. These devices include custom-made and tuned ear plugs, industrial earmuffs, foam earplugs, and electronic noise protectors. An electronic noise protector is a compression hearing aid with the volume control set to minimum, so that loud sounds are attenuated and quiet sounds and speech are amplified (Brassem-Burke & Palace, 2003).

For further details on hearing assessments and interventions for people with intellectual and developmental disabilities, the reader may consult Burke-Brassem and Palace (2003). Other useful sources include the NIDCD web site and NIDCD's (2006a) hearing checklist for babies 3–36 months of age, which parents and others can use to determine if a child may have a hearing problem.

Vision

The eye has a number of individual components that are essential for clear vision (see Figure 25.2). The cornea is the transparent outer layer of the front part of the eye; it is the primary focusing element. The outermost layer of the cornea is called the epithelium; this protects the eye. The epithelial cells of the cornea can regenerate quickly. The inner layers of the cornea also are transparent and allow light to pass. The pupil is the dark opening in the center of the colored iris; this controls the amount of light entering the eye. The iris functions like the iris of a camera; it opens and closes to control the amount of light entering through the pupil. The lens is located just behind the iris; it focuses light rays on the retina. In young people, the lens is soft and pliable; in older people, it is less pliable, resulting in difficulty in focusing on objects near to the eye. The retina is the membrane lining the back of the eye; it contains nerve cells which function as photoreceptors. These nerve cells react to the presence and intensity of light by sending an impulse to the brain via the optic nerve. In the brain, the many nerve impulses received from the photoreceptor cells in the retina are formed into an image.

Vision plays a big role in communication. We watch the facial expressions of other people as they speak and as they listen to what we have to say. Eye contact seems

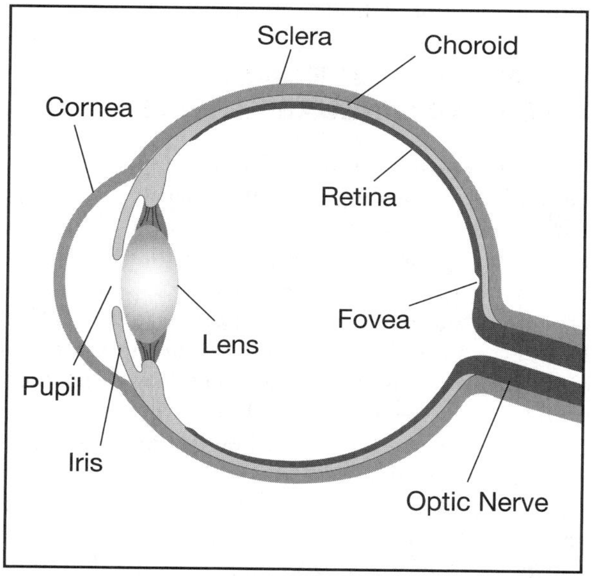

Figure 25.2. Diagram of the human eye. (From *Medical illustration library* [GA2_6008]. [1994]. Philadelphia: Lippincott, Williams & Wilkins; *Adapted illustration*: Copyright © 2007 by Tom Dearie, ThreeSixtyCreative; reprinted by permission.)

to mean a lot. For example, people feel very uncomfortable talking to someone wearing mirrored sunglasses. Also, we often use gestures, such as pointing or shrugging the shoulders, instead of words. The definition of *visual impairment* varies from source to source because there are many types and degrees of visual impairment. Many types and degrees of visual impairments are correctable. In fact, some argue that individuals should be classified as having a visual impairment only if the impairment remains once maximal correction is implemented. For individuals with intellectual and multiple disabilities, visual impairments are 200 times more prevalent than in the general population (Batshaw, 2002).

Similar to hearing impairment, many types and degrees of visual impairment exist, including loss of visual acuity and visual field loss. Also similar to hearing impairment, it is important that visual impairments be detected or ruled out through an adequate visual assessment. If undetected or uncorrected, a visual impairment may seriously thwart social, communication, educational, and vocational opportunities of individuals with intellectual and developmental disabilities. As with the assessment of hearing impairment, visual assessments may require adaptations in order to be functional. Interventions vary from those that are primarily medical (e.g., surgery) to those that are more "low tech" (e.g., using appropriate type size, display style, spacing, contrast, and distance between symbols for someone using AAC; using magnifying glasses or eyeglasses). Regardless of the intervention, with adequate support many vision impairments can be successfully treated and their negative impact on functioning, including communication, minimized.

WHO MAY BENEFIT FROM SPEECH AND LANGUAGE INTERVENTION

Determining whether an individual requires intervention and, if applicable, determining the specific types of intervention needed are complex tasks. These decisions also depend on a number of variables: age, personality, history of adjustments, supports, awareness of difficulties and when to use compensatory strategies, the degree to which a person can be stimulated, and family or living situation. There are many varied communication assessments and treatments available, sometimes commercially marketed, that may serve as treatment options for people with disabilities including autism, pervasive developmental disorder, behavior disorder, attention-deficit/hyperactivity disorder, dyslexia, and auditory processing disorder. Sometimes the intervention serves as a solution for a variety of problems associated with the full spectrum of intellectual and developmental disabilities.

The overall goal of intervention, whether through direct therapy (i.e., working with the client directly) or indirect therapy (i.e., working with communication partners of the client), should recognize, encourage, and respond to appropriate communicative attempts and the underlying function of those attempts. For example, an individual pointing to something outside may be simply trying to join another person, get someone's attention, or engage in some common commentary (verbal or nonverbal) on the identified object.

The approach to intervention that may allow the individual to become a more effective, empowered communicator may not always involve individual, direct, structured therapy. A more appropriate approach to intervention may recognize the individual's social, familial, and work or school milieu; the individual's expectations and functioning within these environments; and ways to facilitate understanding, development, and success within them. Once the proper focus of intervention has been determined, the order, timetable, and type of therapy need to be considered. For example, perhaps a child's specific impairments have not been identified but it turns out that the child has apraxia. Encouraging him or her to speak may be detrimental to further development. In such cases, it may be more appropriate to explore alternative means (e.g., AAC) by which the child can communicate with others. The child's parents and teachers can work together with professionals to foster the child's desire and ability to use an alternate system.

Communication goals will likely vary considerably depending on the nature and severity of a person's communication impairment. Individuals with mild and moderate speech impairments may benefit from early intervention to accelerate the acquisition of vocabulary and the transition from single to multiword utterances. Because delays in expressive speech are typically more obvious than delays in receptive language, it is important to intervene to increase the understanding of speech. In terms of expressive speech intervention, it may be necessary to establish communicative functions such as requesting or commenting that are absent or deficit, and this may vary across different disability conditions (Duker, van Driel, & van de Bercken, 2002). Articulation training may be indicated for individuals with hearing impairment and oral-motor problems.

For individuals with severe communication impairment due to developmental disability, there is often the need to teach functional communication skills that will enable them to communicate basic wants and needs in an efficient manner. To be efficient, others must be able to readily interpret their communication responses. This often means trying to replace existing prelinguistic behaviors with more conventional forms, such as manual signs or the use of a picture-based communication system. Techniques to facilitate early language development with children include the following (Burke-Brassem & Palace, 2003):

- *Expansion:* The child's utterance is expanded into the correct grammatical form.
- *Simple expatiation:* The adult expands on the child's utterance while keeping this expansion relevant.
- *Alternative model:* The adult inquires about the meaning or logic of an utterance, thereby encouraging the child to think of alternative ways to express ideas.
- *Imitation:* The adult provides immediate, corrected imitation of the child's utterance.
- *Completion:* The child completes part of an utterance presented by the adult.
- *Forced alternative:* The adult presents the child with a choice of possibilities of correct utterances or parts thereof.
- *Verbal absurdity:* The adult uses incorrect statements or ridiculous questions to encourage the child to recall lexical items or to correct grammatical structures.

It is important to note that individuals who may benefit from speech and language intervention do not constitute a homogeneous group, even when they share the same diagnosis. The nature and severity of the communication impairment determines the type of intervention that would be most appropriate. The type of intervention that may benefit an individual also depends on his or her age and lifestyle.

For individuals who exhibit challenging behaviors that have been determined to be communicative, functional communication training may be an effective intervention strategy (Durand, 1990). Functional communication training involves the teaching of a replacement behavior that serves the same communicative function as the challenging behavior. In other words, an individual whose behavior is motivated by escape from tasks needs to be shown how to escape through socially more acceptable means, such as asking for a break. The communication status of the individual as well as the needs of his or her environment should taken into account for selecting an appropriate communicative response modality. A person with a sufficient verbal repertoire may be taught to use words to request a break. Individuals with little or no functional speech may need to learn how to use AAC.

AUGMENTATIVE AND ALTERNATIVE COMMUNICATION

Individuals with intellectual and developmental disabilities who have severe communication impairments may be candidates for AAC. As noted, *AAC* refers to approaches that add to (hence, the term *augmentative*) or replace (thus, the word *alternative*) a person's natural speech and/or writing abilities to communicate. Some individuals who cannot make any sounds use AAC to replace natural speech. Others who have some functional speech, however, use AAC to augment their speech attempts. In addition, AAC users often use a variety of modes to communicate. These may consist of vocalizations such as unintentional vocal utterances or vocal patterns as well as gestures such as body movements, facial expressions, or pantomime (Blischak, Loncke, & Waller, 1997). It is not uncommon for an individual to use many different ways of communicating, either together in the same settings or separately in different settings. This is often referred to as multimodal communication.

AAC can be used to share ideas and thoughts using a variety of strategies involving symbols. For example, a child may point to a photograph of a playground in a book or may use a specialized "talking computer" to indicate the message "I want to play." These kinds of strategies are called aided approaches. They include different modes or ways of signaling messages (e.g., communication display, device), as well as various strategies for doing so (Lloyd, Fuller, & Arvidson, 1997).

Other approaches may rely solely on the body. For example, a child may use a manual sign or may use vocalizations and gestures for *playground* to communicate the desire to play. Such communications do not involve any external aids and thus are referred to as unaided approaches. An individual's AAC system may include both aided and unaided approaches. Aided approaches include low-tech and high-tech aids. Low tech refers to a range of nontechnical but potentially powerful communication systems such as pictures, symbols, alphabets, or word displays. High-tech generally refers to specialized electronic or computer-based equipment. High-tech equipment includes various "talking devices," which are called voice output communication aids (VOCAs) or speech generating devices (SGDs); standard or specialized computers; software; and computer components.

In a review of the literature, Mirenda (2003) considered issues related to the use of manual signs versus graphic-based communications systems for individuals with disabilities. Mirenda concluded that both types of systems can be taught and can be functional for the person, provided the communicative partners are familiar with and can interpret the system. Furthermore, there is no reason why only one type of AAC mode needs to be selected. In many cases, it is necessary for an individual to be able to use a variety of forms and modes for communication. AAC intervention can and should include procedures to teach gesture and graphic mode communication.

AAC is often confused with assistive technology. *Assistive technology* refers to devices or services used to help individuals with functions and activities. Although AAC may include assistive technology (e.g., use of a device such as a VOCA), this would be only one part of an AAC system. AAC also involves the use of many methods of communication, such as gestures, manual signs, and vocalizations, which are not considered to be assistive technology.

Components of an Assessment for Augmentative and Alternative Communication

Decision making in assessment and intervention should be based on the principles of evidence-based practice (EBP). Schlosser (2003) defined EBP as "the integration of best and current research evidence with clinical/educational expertise and relevant stakeholder perspectives in order to facilitate decisions about assessment and intervention that are deemed effective and efficient for a given direct stakeholder" (p. 3).

In carrying out an assessment for AAC, it is important to keep in mind that any person with intellectual or developmental disabilities who is nonspeaking, regardless of his or her diagnosis or developmental level, can benefit from AAC strategies. AAC assessment should provide a clear picture of the individual's skills and abilities by addressing a number of questions, including the following:

- What is the individual able to communicate?
- What purposes does the individual's communication serve?
- How competent is the individual in communicating for various purposes?
- What barriers prevent the individual from participating?
- How does the individual communicate that he or she is experiencing barriers?
- What are the individual's receptive and expressive language skills?
- What are the individual's cognitive abilities?
- What are the individual's physical/motor abilities?
- What types of symbols will meet the individual's needs both now and in the future?
- What are the individual's literacy abilities?
- What are the individual's sensory/perceptual abilities, including vision, hearing, and tactile sense?

Observation The first step in an AAC assessment is typically to observe the nonspeaking individual with familiar communication partners. This is ideally carried out in the individual's usual and familiar environments. These observations indicate what the individual is capable of communicating and suggest what his or her future communication needs may be.

Communicative competence depends on a number of things, including the developmental level of the individual. Although some individuals who are nonspeaking may not use speech to communicate, they may still be considered competent communicators if they use AAC strategies to communicate their needs, wants, and ideas functionally and adequately (Blischak et al., 1997). In this way, the communication strengths as well as communication needs will be documented. Standardized tests are generally not a salient part of the assessment, as each nonspeaking individual has a unique set of skills and abilities. Observations also show the general abilities and kinds of strategies that different communication partners are already using and how effective they appear to be. Observation of the environments in which the person carries out life activities is also an important part of the assessment. This should include the opportunities available for participating in environments and the barriers to such participation (Beukelman & Mirenda, 2005).

Determining Needs and Skills From the information gathered through observation, it is possible to project the ideal potential requirements of feature options of the AAC system(s) and AAC strategies. It is also important to identify the preferences of the AAC user, as well as his or her family and other communication partners. A trial should occur to see whether the match is effective or whether changes are required, especially when communicating with different partners.

In determining which of the many available approaches or modes fit best, it is also important to match the AAC system with the individual's environments. Different needs and expectations arise in various settings and from the demands of various tasks, and different strategies and priorities for communication result from them. For example, unaided approaches (e.g., signs, specific gestures) may not be understood in the larger community. Thus, if goals include inclusion, independent communication, and participation in the community at large, manual signs may not be appropriate. In other situations, aided approaches may not be appropriate. For example, the action of a child who is pointing to a graphic symbol to request the teacher's attention only works when the teacher is in close proximity.

Setting Goals The information gathered from the observation and determining skills and needs stages will be helpful in developing communication goals and an intervention plan that follows from it. It is essential for the entire team to set measurable goals so that everyone on the team knows when the goals have been reached. An individual support plan has been found to be a useful tool for setting goals and action plans, as well as monitoring the attainment of goals (Rothschild, McGinnis, & Norris, 1996).

Ongoing Assessment As communication skills change and new situations arise, there is a continuing need for assessment. This is a process that interweaves assessment and intervention in an ongoing way. That is, as an intervention is being implemented, the therapist assesses how the intervention has been working, modifies as necessary, and continues with the intervention.

When Augmentative and Alternative Communication Should Be Considered

It has been said that communication is the "essence of human life" (Article II, Section 1, United States Society for Augmentative and Alternative Communication Bylaws; for further information see http://www.ussaac.org). To the extent that this is true, successful AAC intervention has the potential to improve an individual's quality of life in very substantial ways. AAC may help to create important life possibilities by removing communication barriers. Numerous anecdotes and personal accounts from AAC users describe the potential for AAC to improve quality of life. Justin Clark's legal struggles illustrate this.

On November 26, 1982, Judge John Matheson of the Lanark County Court in Perth, Ontario, Canada, stated, "In a spirit of liberty, the necessity to understand the minds of other men and the remembrance that 'not even a sparrow falls to earth unheeded,' I find and declare Matthew Justin Clark to be mentally competent" (McNaughton, 1982, p. 3). So ended what has been called a landmark case for the rights of people with disabilities—and the first court case in Canadian history in which Blissymbols were used by a witness to give testimony.

Whether individuals with intellectual and/or developmental disabilities use AAC, they are highly overrepresented in cases of physical, sexual, and emotional abuse (Ahlgrim-Delzell & Dudley, 2001; Bottoms et al., 2003; Kvam, 2000; Sullivan & Knutson, 2000; Tang & Lee, 1999; Vig & Kaminer, 2002). Often, they are considered unreliable witnesses by the legal system (Valenti-Hein & Schwartz, 1993). Many people with intellectual and developmental disabilities, however, may be regarded as competent witnesses if they are carefully questioned and if minor adjustments are made in legal proceedings (Perlman et al., 1994). Ericson, Isaacs, and Perlman (2003) provided useful strategies to enhance communication with witnesses who have intellectual and developmental disabilities.

For everyday life activities, AAC may be helpful for people with a variety of intellectual and developmental disabilities, including autism, cerebral palsy, developmental apraxia of speech, developmental delay, specific language disorders, and others (Mirenda & Mathy Laikko, 1989). The need for AAC support may vary in degree and focus across the life span. Often a child is 2–3 years old when his or her parents first seek professional help because the child is not speaking. During early childhood, parents often wish to bring the child's communication skills up to the appropriate age level. The focus of AAC intervention at this time often includes increasing participation in daily routines, expanding the child's communication range, and developing symbolic communication.

During the school-age years, concerns frequently center around friendships, the school curriculum, and literacy. Current trends for school and community inclusion make it necessary for a child to have a way of communicating that is effective with all peers, including those with and without disabilities. Providing opportunities to participate in the curriculum is essential, whether the curriculum is standard or adapted in some way. Participation in early literacy experiences is particularly important if students are to learn the skills necessary for communication, as well as to succeed in school and the workplace. During adulthood, AAC needs often focus on supporting individuals in managing independent living, attendant care, employment, community participation, leisure, and friendships (Collier, 2000). The primary goal of AAC use and intervention is for the individual to become a better or more competent communicator. Zangari and Kangas (1997) provide a list of criteria for establishing AAC goals.

Relationship Between Augmentative and Alternative Communication and Natural Speech Production

Parents, teachers, and therapists often wonder if AAC use will interfere with the acquisition of natural speech. During early childhood years, parents may find it difficult to accept AAC because they fear that using such approaches will delay their child's speech production. However, AAC involves using a variety of modes or ways of communicating, including speech. Thus, children who use AAC to communicate are encouraged not only to use pictures or manual signs but also to do so in conjunction with their speech, if possible. Communication partners are also encouraged to model both speech (by speaking to the individual) and other methods of communication. In addition, auditory feedback from VOCAs can function as speech models. AAC always encourages the use of whatever vocalizations the individual is capable of using, despite other modes of communication that are available to the individual. Children whose vocalizations are understood by partners would not be asked to repeat themselves using their communication boards. Rather, the partners would acknowledge the messages conveyed through the vocalization. There is no evidence that AAC intervention hinders speech production; to the contrary, there is some suggestive preliminary evidence that AAC intervention may actually increase natural speech production (Millar, Light, & Schlosser, in press).

Components of Successful Intervention with Augmentative and Alternative Communication

Often the issue of timing comes up when discussing the need for AAC intervention. Specifically, families ask, "My child doesn't seem ready—should we wait to use AAC?" In the past, some authors considered that there were certain cognitive "prerequisites" that the child needed to master prior to introducing AAC. For example, it was believed that a child needed to understand a cause-and-effect relationship before moving to AAC as a communication method. The difficulty with applying this prerequisite theory is that some people might be kept waiting indefinitely for prerequisites to be learned. Moreover, sufficient research data to support this point of view have not emerged. For these reasons, professionals in the field of AAC have generally accepted that many of these skills may actually be developed by using basic AAC strategies themselves (Kangas & Lloyd, 1988; National Joint Committee for the Communication Needs of Persons with Severe Disabilities, 2003). For instance, if a child who activates a switch that says, "Give me juice, please," is given juice each time, he or she may learn that the action of switch activation results in getting a drink of juice. In general, it is advisable to begin AAC intervention early in life.

AAC interventions should be needs based, documented by goals, and accompanied by appropriate measurement of progress to ensure accountability of everyone involved. One way of ensuring accountability is to monitor when goals are attained. The perspectives of the person receiving service, the family, and other team members—such as the speech-language pathologist, the special educator, the physical therapist, and the occupational therapist (teams are formed based on the client's needs)—are usually used to determine when goals have been attained. Although it is important to know whether these stakeholders perceive changes in the desired direction, more objective measures of accountability are also useful, as perspectives sometimes get influenced by wanting to see the desired effects. Observation in natural settings and recording data of observed behavior provide more objective measures. For example, clinicians and parents may want to record such progress data as the number of symbols used in functional contexts, the number of choices communicated successfully in a given time period, or the number of words or phrases expressed through AAC modes during specified activities. Children with developmental delay require intense, consistent, and systematic intervention during natural activities, especially for the acquisition of the first functional symbols. Table 25.2 lists some commonly used intervention strategies that have proven to be effective.

How to Help Make Communication More Effective for Users of Augmentative and Alternative Communication

As with any form of communication, AAC is not carried out by one person; it always requires a partner. For this reason, AAC interventions often include changing the partner's behaviors in order to elicit desired communication from the AAC user. In other words, communication partners can often offer the most effective intervention strategies to assist nonspeaking individuals to communicate more effectively. Information in Table 25.2 illustrates that communication goals for nonverbal individuals are identified with appropriate partner strategies to facilitate the attainment of goals. It is important to ensure that all partners in the individual's world understand the strategies they can use in all of their interactions. Partners should include parents, siblings, other family members, friends, nannies, teachers, educational assistants, other students, coworkers, caregivers, and mediators. Communication does not happen in a vacuum. It is driven by the activities and settings in which people participate. In addition to partner strategies, the environment (e.g., classroom curriculum) often has a great impact on AAC intervention. Depending on the particular goals targeted, different intervention strategies may be appropriate.

To assist a person in communicating more effectively, partners can create opportunities for communication. Increased opportunities to communication will assist the person in learning and maintaining communication skills. As suggested in Table 25.2, the need for communication can be created in several ways.

Table 25.2. Commonly used intervention strategies that have proven to be effective

AAC user goal	Partner strategies	Description	References
Increase requesting for objects, actions, and assistance.	Provide opportunities by using the missing-item strategy.	Give the person all but one of the items needed to complete or engage in a preferred activity.	Reichle, York, & Sigafoos (1991)
	Provide opportunities by using inadequate portions.	Provide small or inadequate amounts or portions of food during snack time or lunch.	
	Provide opportunities by using the interrupted chain strategy.	Momentarily interrupting the person from completing or continuing an ongoing activity.	
	Provide opportunities by using delayed assistance.	Provide materials that require assistance. After observing that the person needs help, walk over and wait for the him or her to request assistance before providing the help needed.	
Increase commenting.	Provide opportunities by creating absurd situations.	Present absurd or silly situations, and wait for the person to comment.	Zangari & Kangas (1997)
	Provide opportunities through presenting interesting materials and/or tasks.	Use interesting materials and activities, and wait for the person to comment.	
Increase rejecting.	Provide opportunities by using disliked objects.	Use something the person does not like, and wait for him or her to reject it.	Reichle et al. (1991)
Learn to associate symbols with words.	Provide models of AAC use and tell the learner that AAC is acceptable through augmented input.	Model use of the AAC user's system (e.g., point to the appropriate symbols while speaking, sign while speaking).	Goossens', Crain, & Elder (1992); Romski & Sevcik (1996)
Communicate as spontaneously as possible.	Invite communicative responses by using least-to-most prompting.	Provide prompts in a hierarchical fashion according to the degree of intrusiveness of prompts. "Least-to-most" starts with a pause and may end with a full model. Use of pauses between prompt levels is essential.	Reichle et al. (1991)
Increase interaction.	Increase interaction by teaching use of introductory statements.	Use least-to-most prompting to teach the AAC user to introduce him- or herself to a conversation partner.	Light & Binger (1998)
	Partner-focused questions.	Use least-to-most prompting to teach the AAC user to ask questions that are oriented to the interests of the communication.	
	Unforced turns.	Use least-to-most prompting to teach the AAC user to take turns, even though the situation may not necessarily force a turn.	

(continued)

Table 25.2. *(continued)*

AAC user goal	Partner strategies	Description	References
Respond with the least amount of prompting.	Encourage appropriate communicative behavior by using most-to-least prompting.	Use most-to-least prompting, which provides the most intrusive prompt first and then gradually reduces intrusiveness. This is often used when teaching a person to use AAC, instead of challenging behavior, as a form of communication. The use of pauses between prompt levels is essential.	Mirenda (1997); Schlosser (1997)
Communicate appropriately rather than with challenging behavior.	Encourage appropriate communicative behavior by providing functional communication training.	Show the individual how to express the function once served by the challenging behavior through appropriate means (e.g., request favorite objects).	Mirenda (1997); Schlosser (1997)
Use partner feedback to modify messages, if necessary.	Avoid communication breakdown by providing descriptive feedback.	Provide feedback in the form of expanded repetition of the AAC user's message.	Beukelman & Mirenda (2005)
Ensure that gestures are read correctly.	Be consistent in interpreting gestures across situations by relying on a gesture dictionary for interpretation.	Use especially during the early stages of gesture development or for someone with highly idiosyncratic gestures (includes all elements that are part of the person's gesture repertoire—e.g., facial expressions, eye gaze, vocalizations).	Beukelman & Mirenda (2005)
Communicate functionally within routine activities.	Elicit communication by using activity-based intervention.	Use a comprehensive approach that aims at the development of functional and generative skills within the context of child-initiated, planned, or routine transactions using logically occurring events that occasion a specific behavior and consequences that follow the behavior.	Bricker & Cripe (1991)

Source: Schlosser and Rothschild (2003).
Key: AAC = augmentative and alternative communication.

- Temporarily withhold a wanted or needed object until the person communicates a desire for the object.
- Give the person a small amount of a preferred object, thereby creating a need for the person to request more.
- Temporarily block the person from completing an activity, thereby creating a need for the person to communicate.
- Wait a short period of time (e.g., 10 seconds) before giving the person help with a difficult task. This increases the person's motivation to request help.
- Give the person a wrong item, thereby creating a need for the person to repair the communication breakdown.

Augmentative and Alternative Communication Services

Service delivery and philosophy often differ to some extent. Most services are still program centered but are beginning to become more person centered by including people with disabilities and their families as part of service delivery teams. Service users may gain access to any service that includes their needs in their mandate. Mandates may differ, however, by such things as geography, age, diagnosis, need, or enrollment, or they may be all inclusive and statewide. To find out what AAC services are available in one's region, it is a good idea to contact a local speech-language pathologist.

AAC services are usually provided by professionals

with backgrounds in speech-language pathology, occupational therapy, and/or special education. These professionals may have various levels of training or experience in AAC. At the time of this book's publication, there is no generally accepted certification needed to provide AAC services. Areas of AAC expertise commonly acknowledged for these three professional groups include the following:

- Speech-language pathologists focus on speech or other means of communication, strategies used for communication, and functions or use of language including vocabulary and AAC symbols.
- Occupational therapists focus on physical and functional skills, access to communication systems, physical and writing modifications, and sensory issues.
- Special educators focus on literacy and curriculum modification to include students who use AAC as smoothly as possible in the school curriculum.

Many services encourage staff to cross these traditional professional boundaries while working together as a team. Depending on needs, resources, mandates, and philosophies, an AAC user will work with one or a combination of local providers.

INTERVENTION FOR PEOPLE WHO ARE DEAF AND BLIND

Some people have both visual and hearing impairments. Yet, people who are classified as deaf-blind are not necessarily totally deaf or totally blind. The needs of these people are increasingly being recognized, and the range of products that may benefit them is continually expanding. In the past, such individuals have been dependent on braille and other tactile communication methods. At the beginning of the 21st century, they have the opportunity to reap the benefits of emerging technologies for individuals who are deaf and for those who are blind. Among the most common areas where assistive devices can effectively assist individuals who are deaf-blind are communication (both interpersonal and telephone) and environment alert systems for use both indoors and outside (NIDCD, 2006b).

SUMMARY

Communication has been described as the essence of human life. People with intellectual or developmental disabilities often have various speech and language impairments because cognition and communication are very much intertwined. Some people with intellectual or developmental disabilities have speech and/or language difficulties but still are able to rely on their natural speech. Other individuals have severe communication impairments to the extent that they cannot rely on their residual speech. These individuals may benefit from AAC systems and techniques. A third group of individuals with intellectual or developmental disabilities exhibit challenging behaviors in order to communicate their wants and needs. The reader was introduced to each group in terms of its characteristics, common approaches to assessment and intervention, and selected issues of service delivery.

FOR FURTHER THOUGHT AND DISCUSSION

1. Should assessment of communication (speech-language and hearing) be a mandatory part of assessment of a person's capacity and potential?
2. If a person has an undetected communication difficulty (speech-language or hearing), what parts of his or her life could be affected?
3. Working with a group of others, describe one person with communication disabilities. Outline ways to minimize the developmental and environmental effects of that person's communication difficulty.

REFERENCES

ABLEDATA. (1999). *Informed consumer guide to assistive technology for people with hearing disabilities.* Retrieved March 6, 2006, from http://www.abledata.com/abledata_docs/icg_hear.htm

Ahlgrim-Delzell, L., & Dudley, J.R. (2001). Confirmed, unconfirmed, and false allegations of abuse made by adults with mental retardation who are member of a class action lawsuit. *Child Abuse and Neglect, 25,* 1121–1132.

Auditory Processing Disorder U.K. (2002). *What is auditory processing disorder?* Retrieved April 25, 2006, from http://www.apduk.org

Batshaw, M.L. (Ed.). (2002). *Children with disabilities* (5th ed.). Baltimore: Paul H. Brookes Publishing Co.

Beukelman, D.R., & Mirenda, P. (2005). *Augmentative and alternative communication: Supporting children and adults with complex communication needs* (3rd ed.). Baltimore: Paul H. Brookes Publishing Co.

Blischak, D., Loncke, F., & Waller, A. (1997). Intervention for persons with developmental disabilities. In L.L. Lloyd, D. Fuller, & H. Arvidson (Eds.), *Augmentative and alternative communication: A handbook of principles and practices* (pp. 299–339). Boston: Allyn & Bacon.

Blischak, D.M., & Wasson, C.A. (1997). Sensory impairments. In L.L. Lloyd, D. Fuller, & H. Arvidson (Eds.), *Augmentative and alternative communication: A handbook of principles and practices* (pp. 255–279). Boston: Allyn & Bacon.

Bottoms, B.L., Nysse-Carris, K.L., Harris, T., et al. (2003). Jurors perceptions of adolescent sexual assault victims who have intellectual disabilities. *Law and Human Behaviour, 27,* 205–227.

Bricker, D., & Cripe, J. (1991). *An activity-based approach to intervention.* Baltimore: Paul H. Brookes Publishing Co.

Burke-Brassem, M., & Palace, L. (2003). Communication considerations associated with developmental disabilities. In I. Brown & M. Percy (Eds.), *Developmental disabilities in Ontario* (2nd ed., pp. 453–464). Toronto: Ontario Association on Developmental Disabilities.

Collier, B. (Producer). (2000). *Communicating matters: A training guide for personal attendants working with consumers who have enhanced communication needs* [Videotape]. Baltimore: Paul H. Brookes Publishing Co.

Connolly, J.L., Carron, J.D., & Roark, S.D. (2005). Universal newborn hearing screening: Are we achieving the Joint Committee on Infant Hearing (JCIH) objectives? *Laryngoscope, 115(2),* 232–236.

Duker, P.C., van Driel, S., & van de Bercken, J. (2002). Communication profiles of individuals with Down's syndrome, Angelman syndrome and pervasive developmental disorder. *Journal of Intellectual Disability Research, 46,* 35–40.

Durand, V.M. (1990). *Severe behavior problems: A functional communication training approach.* New York: The Guilford Press.

Ericson, K., Isaacs, B., & Perlman, N. (2003). Enhancing communication with persons with developmental disabilities: The special case of interviewing victim-witnesses of sexual abuse. In I. Brown & M. Percy (Eds.), *Developmental disabilities in Ontario* (2nd ed., pp. 465–474). Toronto: Front Porch Publishing.

Ferguson, D.L. (1994). Is communication really the point? Some thoughts on interventions and membership. *Mental Retardation, 32,* 7–18.

Grizzle, K.L., & Simms, M.D. (2005). Early language development and language learning disabilities. *Pediatrics in Review, 26*(8), 274–283.

Grossens, C., & Ericson, K. (1995, May 11). What's going on? The client's understanding of court proceedings and legal terminology. Presentation at the conference *Victims With Developmental Disabilities and the Law,* Toronto.

Goossens', C., Crain, S., & Elder, P. (1992). *Engineering the preschool environment for interactive, symbolic communication.* Birmingham, AL: Southeast Augmentative Communication Publications.

Hearing Loss Association of America. (2004). *Facts on hearing loss.* Retrieved March 6, 2006, from http://www.hearingloss.org/html/hearing_loss_fact_sheets.html

Kangas, K., & Lloyd, L. (1988). Early cognitive skills as prerequisites to augmentative and alternative communication use: What are we waiting for? *Augmentative and Alternative Communication, 4,* 211–221.

Kvam, M.H. (2000). Is sexual abuse of children with disabilities disclosed? A retrospective analysis of child disability and the likelihood of sexual abuse among those attending Norwegian hospitals. *Child Abuse & Neglect, 24,* 1073–1084.

Light, J.C., & Binger, C. (1998). *Building communicative competence with individuals who use augmentative and alternative communication.* Baltimore: Paul H. Brookes Publishing Co.

Lloyd, L., Fuller, D., & Arvidson, H. (1997). *Augmentative and alternative communication: A handbook of principles and practices.* Boston: Allyn & Bacon.

McNaughton, S. (1982). Justin gives to us all. *Communicating Together, 1,* 3–4.

McQueen, P.C., Spence, M.W., Garner, J.B., et al. (1987). Prevalence of major mental retardation and associated disabilities in the Canadian Maritime provinces. *American Journal of Mental Deficiency, 91,* 460–466.

MedlinePlus. (2004). *Speech and language disorders.* Retrieved March 6, 2006, from http://www.nlm.nih.gov/medlineplus/speechandcommunicationdisorders.html

Millar, D., Light, J., & Schlosser, R.W. (in press). The impact of augmentative and alternative communication intervention on the speech production of individuals with developmental disabilities: A research review. *Journal of Speech, Language, and Hearing Research.*

Mirenda, P. (1997). Supporting individuals with challenging behavior through functional communication training and AAC: Research review. *Augmentative and Alternative Communication, 13,* 207–225.

Mirenda, P. (2003). Toward functional augmentative and alternative communication for students with autism: Manual signs, graphic symbols, and voice output communication aids. *Language, Speech, and Hearing Services in Schools, 34,* 203–216.

Mirenda, P., & Mathy Laikko, P. (1989). Augmentative and alternative communication applications for persons with severe congenital communication disorders. *Augmentative and Alternative Communication, 5,* 3–13.

National Research Council. (2001). *Educating children with autism.* Washington, DC: National Academies Press.

National Dissemination Center for Children with Disabilities. (2004). *Speech and language impairments* [NICHCY Fact Sheet 11]. Retrieved March 6, 2006, from http://www.nichcy.org/pubs/factshe/fs11txt.htm

National Institute on Deafness and Other Communication Disorders. (2006a). *Silence isn't always golden.* Retrieved March 6, 2006, http://www.nidcd.nih.gov/health/hearing/silence.asp

National Institute on Deafness and Other Communication Disorders. (2006b). *Velocardiofacial syndrome.* Retrieved from March 6, 2006, http://www.nidcd.nih.gov/health/voice/velocario.asp

National Joint Committee for the Communication Needs of Persons with Severe Disabilities. (2003). Position statement on access to communication services and supports: Concerns regarding the application of restrictive "eligibility" policies. *ASHA Supplement, 23,* 19–20.

Perlman, N., Ericson, K., Esses, V., et al. (1994). Developmentally handicapped witnesses: Competency as a function of question format. *Law and Human Behaviour, 18,* 171–187.

Reichle, J., York, J., & Sigafoos, J. (1991). *Implementing augmentative and alternative communication: Strategies for learners with severe disabilities.* Baltimore: Paul H. Brookes Publishing Co.

Romski, M.A., & Sevcik, R.A. (1996). *Breaking the speech barrier: Language development through augmented means.* Baltimore: Paul H. Brookes Publishing Co.

Rothschild, N., McGinnis, J., & Norris, L. (1996). Outcome measures—tools and processes in AAC: What's driving us? *Journal of Speech-Language Pathology and Audiology, 19,* 257–267.

Schlosser, R., & Rothschild, N. (2003). Augmentative and alternative communication for persons with developmental disabilities. In I. Brown & M. Percy (Eds.), *Developmental disabilities in Ontario* (2nd ed., pp. 435–452). Toronto: Ontario Association on Developmental Disabilities.

Schlosser, R.W. (1997). Communication-based approaches to problem behavior: AAC considerations in intervention development. In L. Lloyd, D. Fuller, & H. Arvidson (Eds.), *Augmentative and alternative communication: A handbook of principles and practices* (pp. 445–473). Boston: Allyn & Bacon.

Schlosser, R.W. (2003). *The efficacy of augmentative and alternative communication: Towards evidence-based practice.* San Diego: Academic Press.

Skinner, B.F. (1957). *Verbal behavior.* Upper Saddle River, NJ: Prentice-Hall.

Sullivan, P.M., & Knutson, J.F. (2000). Maltreatment and disabilities: A population-based epidemiological study. *Child Abuse & Neglect, 24,* 1257–1273.

Tang, C.S., & Lee, Y.K. (1999). Knowledge on sexual abuse and self-protection skills: A study on female Chinese adolescents with mild mental retardation. *Child Abuse & Neglect, 23,* 269–279.

Valenti-Hein, D.C., & Schwartz, L.D. (1993). Witness competency in people with mental retardation: Implications for prosecution of sexual abuse. *Sexuality and Disability, 11,* 287–294.

Vig, S., & Kaminer, R. (2002). Maltreatment and developmental disabilities in children. *Journal of Developmental and Physical Disabilities, 14,* 371–386.

Zangari, C., & Kangas, K. (1997). Intervention principles and procedures. In L. Lloyd, D. Fuller, & H. Arvidson (Eds.), *Augmentative and alternative communication: A handbook of principles and practices* (pp. 235–253). Boston: Allyn & Bacon.

Zigler, E., & Balla, D. (Eds.). (1982). *Mental retardation: The developmental-difference controversy.* Mahwah, NJ: Erlbaum.

26

Role of Diversity in Psychological Assessment and Intervention for Individuals with Developmental Disabilities

Farrokh Sedighdeilami and Shahar Gindi

WHAT YOU WILL LEARN ABOUT IN THIS CHAPTER

- General definitions
- Multicultural issues in assessment
- Culturally sensitive intervention

Diversity and multiculturalism are important issues in the work of any practitioner in the helping professions. This chapter outlines a number of key issues that can help professionals working with individuals who have intellectual or developmental disabilities and are of culturally and ethnically diverse backgrounds.

GENERAL DEFINITIONS

Diversity is a broad term that includes a wide range of attributes such as race, culture, ethnicity, age, gender, language, lifestyle, and social and economic status (Geva, Barsky, & Westernoff, 2000). *Culture* is a more specific term and a key aspect of diversity. People of the same culture often share common attitudes, behavior patterns, beliefs, values, and customs, and professionals need to be aware of these shared elements.

Two extremely important aspects of diversity that go hand in hand with culture are race and language. *Race* refers to "a subgroup of people who possess certain physical characteristics that are genetically determined and that are more or less distinct from other subgroups" (Sue, Kuraski, & Srinivasan, 1999, p. 57). *Language* refers to the verbal communication exchanged among people who may or may not be of a certain ethnic background. Moreover, language often carries with it considerable cultural influences and inherent points of view.

Race has been emphasized as a dominant feature of diversity in North America because of the large populations of African, Asian, and Hispanic Americans in the United States. However, diversity may be manifested differently in different countries around the world. In some countries, diversity involves ethnic groups that speak different languages. In other areas of the world, religious affiliation is dominant in determining differences. In other societies, tribal affiliation most requires the clinician's sensitivity. For the sake of simplicity, this chapter refers to *clients of diverse cultural backgrounds* or to *clients of ethnic/minority backgrounds.* Nonetheless, the reader should note how the complexity of diversity and how language pose limits in even referring to this issue. See Displays 26.1, 26.2, and 26.3 for examples that illustrate the diversity of cultural background.

MULTICULTURAL ISSUES IN ASSESSMENT

This section touches on the various issues involved in effective multicultural assessment.

Required Skills

The assessment of any individual requires the examiner to be culturally competent. For professionals dealing with the assessment of clients with intellectual or developmental disabilities, the importance of understanding their cultural background is critical.

Cultural Competence *Cultural competence* refers to a professional's ability to act in ways that acknowledge diversity. A culturally competent professional is perceived as credible and giving (Sue & Zane, 1987). This means that the professional supporting a client should be both trustworthy and able to deliver a valuable service. Cultural competence includes having a comprehensive base of information about cultural back-

Display 26.1

Case study: Amir

Amir, a 16-year-old with mild cognitive disability who attends a special education class, was referred by his school for psychological intervention because of his high levels of anxiety and anger problems. Amir's parents emigrated from Egypt when he was 10 years old. During the initial screening and consultation interview, Amir's parents told the interviewer, "Amir has difficulty in learning various subjects, especially math and spelling." Amir also noted that he does not fit in with his Canadian classmates. He said that his peers do not like him because he is from Egypt and because he likes Arabic music and food. Sometimes, Amir would come home from school in a very bad mood because his classmates had made jokes about Arab people and their culture.

Source: Sedighdeilami and Gindi (2003).

ground (Rodriguez, 2000). Such information includes familiarity with various cultures, such as their history, traditions, and customs. The professional should also be familiar with ethnographic data, including socioeconomic status, structure, socialization, employment, and literacy.

In addition to these informational aspects, cultural competence should include an understanding of the culture based on personal experiences (i.e., experiential understanding; Copeland, 1983; Dana, 1993). Experiential understanding does not necessarily require the professional to be of the same cultural background as the client. Experiential understanding should first be gained by self-exploration of one's own biases. It can also be gained by role playing and by being attuned and empathic to a culture's narratives.

A third aspect of cultural competence includes a mastery of skills that are compatible with clients from different cultures. As discussed later in this chapter, assessing culturally diverse clients for the possibility of developmental disability requires much more than basic skills in the administration of standardized tests.

Interprofessional Teamwork Geva et al. (2000) stressed the importance of working in an interprofessional team to provide a culturally sensitive assessment. In an interprofessional team, practitioners from different professional backgrounds work together throughout the assessment process. Geva et al. argued that an interprofessional team is a good fit for a culturally competent practice because this framework 1) encourages professionals to consider other people's perspectives, 2) brings a consortium of knowledge (professional and general education) to the assessment, and 3) may bring professionals from diverse personal backgrounds together. An interprofessional assessment team working in the field of developmental disabilities strongly

Display 26.2

Case study: Alhandra

Alhandra was born into a traditional Peruvian family. Alhandra and her family moved from Peru to the United States when she was 4 years old. She was diagnosed as having Williams syndrome, a condition that is recognized to be caused by a microdeletion of chromosome 7. Williams syndrome "is characterized by a recognizable pattern of dysmorphic facial features, connective tissue abnormalities, cardiovascular disease, delayed development, a specific cognitive profile, and a unique personality" (Morris & Mervis, 1999). Although Alhandra attends a special education program with other adolescents with developmental disabilities, she still feels alone and alienated because of her family's background. For example, in one of the therapy sessions, she told the therapist that nobody in her cooking class liked to learn how to make a Hispanic dish. She felt that she was forced to conform and to learn things that were different from what is related to her family situation and what she likes to learn.

Source: Sedighdeilami and Gindi (2003).

Display 26.3

Case study: Mustafa

Mustafa is a 20-year-old young man with spinal-cord injury and mild cognitive deficiency. He was reared in a traditional and rural community in Nigeria. Mustafa and his family lived on a farm during the first 12 years of his life, but when he was injured in an accident, his family moved to a large city in North America to seek medical services for him. He is the only black student in his class and one of the few African students in his school. Mustafa felt mismatched and misunderstood. He felt alienated by his classmates. In addition, he wanted to socialize with other students, but perceived them as being highly competitive, analytical, and aggressive.

Source: Sedighdeilami and Gindi (2003).

benefits from the participation of psychologists, speech-language pathologists, psychiatrists, pediatricians, occupational therapists, clinical audiologists, behavioral geneticists, nurses, and behavior therapists.

The Process

In addition to discussing steps such as referral and culturally based behavioral observations, this section explains how assessing individuals from diverse ethnic backgrounds must involve distinguishing cultural difference from developmental disability and accounting for second language and translation issues. In addition, the section covers the related topics of measurement, social and emotional functioning, and communicating diagnoses to clients and their families.

Referral The importance of considering cultural issues starts when the referral is made. The assessment team must consider the purpose of the assessment in relation to the cultural context. For example, many referrals are made to establish that the person's cognitive functioning is low enough to obtain a disability allowance. However, aspects of diagnoses may be sensitive and complex for clients of diverse cultural backgrounds with developmental disabilities. When considering whether the reason for a referral is appropriate, the assessment team should always strive for a meaningful assessment that is functional, focuses on the person's strengths rather than only on weaknesses, and provides useful recommendations. Display 26.4 provides an example of cultural sensitivity in the stage of the referral.

Culturally Based Behavioral Observations Another important step in the assessment process is making behavioral observations. Behavioral observations provide a distinctive opportunity to assess behavior within a context relevant to the person being assessed. Examiners need to account for different sources of bias when observing a client of a different cultural/ethnic background and to be aware of the cultural context involved in the observed behavior. For example, if a child does not make eye contact with adults, an examiner may conclude that the child lacks social pragmatics. However, a child from India may believe that it is impolite to make eye contact with his or her elders. Examiners also need to be aware of their own biases and values in order to avoid judgments without understanding others' perspectives.

Distinguishing Cultural Difference from Developmental Disability As noted in the preceding example, clinicians need to separate the influence of the ethnic/cultural background from the influences of a developmental disability on a child's achievement in language and cognitive assessments. The first step in assessing the impact of a second language is to obtain information from the family about the language development and preferred language. It is extremely important to know to which languages the child has been exposed, the child's preferred language, and the language spoken at home by other family members. Siblings may provide a "control group" to examine the differential impact of the child's first language. For example, finding that only one child has difficulties whereas the other(s) do not can provide important evidence that language development and cognitive capacity are influenced by a developmental disability rather than second-language issues. Clinicians must remember, however, that it is important to compare the siblings' progression at an equivalent age.

Information about exposure to different languages needs to be obtained sensitively. Families who

Display 26.4

Case study: Chung

Chung is a 10-year-old boy who was referred for an assessment to evaluate his functioning in academic areas. Chung and his family emigrated from China when Chung was 3 years old, and he was diagnosed with autism when he was 6. Chung's parents are hard working and caring. For example, they spend long hours with him and his siblings, helping them with their homework. Like many immigrants from East Asia who move to metropolitan areas, Chung's parents felt that their children have been given a chance for a better life and that the children should use this opportunity by excelling in schoolwork, attending university, and finding lucrative jobs.

Chung's parents were loving and caring people. Although they understood that Chung would not progress academically as far as his siblings, working with Chung on his homework was the only way they knew to help him. When the assessment team received the referral, there was a need to clarify to Chung's parents the purpose of assessment and, later, intervention. The members of the assessment team told the parents that given Chung's diagnosis, it was highly probable that the preferable intervention for him would not address academic areas but rather social skills. When these issues were clarified, the assessment team was able to establish a clear understanding of the purpose of the assessment, which was to provide a profile of Chung's strengths and weaknesses and find effective social skills interventions for his parents to use with him.

Source: Sedighdeilami and Gindi (2003).

have emigrated may strongly believe that exposing a child to their native language will hinder the child's acquisition of their new country's spoken language. This belief has little empirical research support (Geva, 2000), yet parents may feel defensive because of such beliefs. It is important for clinicians to inform parents about the research in the field that shows the benefits of preserving a child's first language (e.g., Cummins, 1984) and to reassure them that their child benefits from promotion of the family's heritage and language. Furthermore, retaining the family's heritage can potentially contribute to the family's cohesiveness, decrease identity confusion, and contribute to other emotional aspects that are important to coping with being in a new country and addressing developmental disabilities.

Second Language and Translation Issues Information gathered about language development and comparison with siblings is often insufficient to determine whether the cause for a child's difficulties is related to a developmental disability or to second-language issues. In such cases, the assessment team should directly address this issue. It is a good practice to conduct some assessment in the child's first language. Nonetheless, this may be difficult to do in a valid way. First, it may be difficult to find psychologists, psychometrists or other professionals who know the language in question. As a result, there may be a need to search for translators. Translators are not always easy to find, and even with their help, some qualitative information may be lost in translation. Second, it may be difficult to find language or psychological assessment materials that are in the client's language, and it may be impossible to find materials that were normed on a comparable population.

There are certain rules about how assessment instruments should be translated. These rules are also helpful to bear in mind when using a translator. For example, the use of metaphors and idioms, which typically are culturally specific, should be avoided as much as possible. In addition, the issue of construct validation should be considered. That is, an examiner must always be alert to the possibility that a construct he or she is using does not exist in the examinee's culture/language or assumes a different function. For example, when administering a measure of receptive language to a child who has recently emigrated from a desert country such as Sudan, asking about an umbrella may be problematic; in Sudan, umbrellas are used mainly to protect from the sun rather than from rain. Thus, when second language seems to be an important issue in impeding the client's achievement, the assessment team may choose to use a dynamic assessment paradigm (discussed in the following section) rather than norm-referenced tests.

Measurement Issues When a person of a different cultural background is thought to have a developmental disability, the assessment team is inevitably faced with issues of measurement. The dominant paradigm in assessment in North America is the norm-referenced paradigm. According to this paradigm, measurement tools are administered in a standardized way to a representative sample of the population. A skilled professional administers these tests individually. Intelligence tests require clinically trained examiners, preferably psychologists holding a master's or doctoral degree. Tests of language competence are best administered and interpreted by speech-language pathologists. The results are analyzed according to the assumption that the scores will follow a normal (bell-shaped) distribution. Norms are then set according to the analyses so that the raw scores will be converted to standard scores, placing the examinee in relation to the larger population.

Many problems arise when using standardized tests with clients of diverse cultural backgrounds and with developmental disabilities. First, people with developmental disabilities have been excluded from the population used in developing many of the test norms. Second, people of diverse cultural backgrounds may not have been included in the norming process of the test. Moreover, the possibility that people of diverse cultural backgrounds with developmental disabilities have been tested for the norming is unlikely. Third, as noted earlier in this chapter, *diversity* is defined differently in different countries (see also Chapter 1). Finally, the development of norms for a specific culture may be criticized for classifying minorities as static entities (Jones & Thorne, 1987)—that is, by not taking into account the fact that various cultural groups are dynamic entities that evolve constantly (e.g., acculturation, or the process of adjusting to a new culture).

Issues of measurement are especially critical when measuring intelligence. Racial/cultural minority spokespersons in the United States have argued fervently against the use of intelligence tests for school placement, even resorting to litigation (e.g., *Larry P. v. Wilson Riles,* 1979). The main argument has been that the norms applied in intelligence tests reflect a Western/Eurocentric worldview. As a result, the use of intelligence testing may well represent a bias against minority groups.

The assessment team is faced with options when faced with intelligence testing of a person of diverse cultural background with a possible developmental disability. These options are discussed next.

Standardized Tests One option is to use traditional norm-referenced intelligence tests, such as the Wechsler tests or a Stanford-Binet scale, without any modifications. This approach is useful because it assists in delivering a diagnosis for developmental disability when one is needed. In addition, using the tests in the way they were standardized is a condition for the scores to be considered meaningful. Unfortunately, this may be necessary, but it does not seem to be sufficient for people of diverse cultural backgrounds. Unless the test is also administered to individuals with developmental disabilities and to people of diverse cultural backgrounds, the scores will lack validity.

The assessment team may tackle the potential bias in traditional norm-referenced intellectual tests by using nonverbal intelligence tests. *Nonverbal testing* has been defined as using assessment procedures to provide more accurate estimate of abilities in populations for which language demands decrease the validity of the assessment results. The assessment team needs to distinguish three aspects of nonverbal testing: 1) nonverbal contents of the test, 2) nonverbal responses by the examinee, and 3) nonverbal administration by the examiner. For example, Raven's Colored and Standard Progressive Matrices (Raven, 1965) is nonverbal in content, but its administration is verbal. By comparison, the Leiter International Performance Scale (Leiter, 1947) and its revised edition (Leiter-R; Roid & Miller, 1997) are nonverbal in administration as well as in content.

Nonverbal tests have the advantage of being normed with relevant populations, thus decreasing the influence of language. For example, *The Fourteenth Mental Measurements Yearbook* (Plake & Impara, 2001) reported that the Test of Nonverbal Intelligence–Third Edition (TONI-3; Brown, Sherbenou, & Johnsen, 1997) was developed to assess aptitude, intelligence, abstract reasoning, and problem solving in a completely language-free format. Other researchers have claimed certain psychological tests to be culture free as well.

Although cultural bias is decreased in nonverbal tests, it is important for professionals to be aware of how cultural preference and language affect any test. For example, matching geometric figures, a task used in the Raven Progressive Matrices, is a skill that is valued and taught in Eurocentric/Western culture but not necessarily in other cultures. In addition, the examiner cannot be expected to be a blank slate in the assessment. The examiner is always influenced by his or her values and beliefs and should be mindful of this potential bias at all times.

Dynamic Assessment Another paradigm that the team may use involves dynamic assessment (Cole, 1996). Dynamic assessment is an approach within the domains of psychology, speech and language, or education that focuses on the ability of the learner to respond to intervention. In this paradigm, the information needed to solve a task is taught to the examinee, and the examinee's ability to maintain and generalize the knowledge is assessed. In this approach, the lack of culturally determined skill or knowledge base is eliminated or minimized as a factor in test outcome. Dynamic assessment usually involves using pretest, coaching, and posttest measures. Teaching can be done in many ways depending on the area that is assessed. For example, if the assessment question concerns a child's readiness for literacy, the examiner may use a phonetic approach and a whole-word approach to actually teach the child some reading in the assessment session. Based on the success of these interventions, the examiner will assess the child's readiness and recommend the appropriate interventions. The extent to which the examinee requires coaching is a measure of his or her ability to perform independently. Dynamic assessment is the method of choice for cases in which second language is affecting the examinee's performance on standardized measures.

Social and Emotional Functioning Another important aspect of a psychological assessment is the examinee's social and emotional functioning. In general, the assessment of emotional functioning has not always been given the attention it deserves in assessments of individuals with developmental disabilities. This has been largely due to the false idea that the cognitive impairment is an overarching attribute that explains all different aspects of the personality.

One common way to assess social and emotional functioning is by using projective measures such as the Thematic Apperception Test (TAT; Bellak, 1975), the Rorschach Inkblot Test (see Exner, 1990), or the Roberts Apperception Test for Children (RATC: McArthur & Roberts, 1982). Although such projective techniques can be useful, several cautions should be taken when applying them. First, it is extremely important that the stimuli be culturally relevant (Dana, 1993). For example, almost all the human figures included in the TAT picture cards appear Caucasian, whereas the RATC includes pictorial representations of visible children from minority backgrounds. Culturally relevant pictures can be added, however, to elicit stories in order to validate the qualitative analysis. The Rorschach is another choice that has relatively little cultural loading. In fact, Rorschach's original studies included individuals with developmental disabilities. Rorschach argued that the inkblot test would be useful for assessing individuals with lower intelligence levels because the results are far less influenced by educational background.

When using such projective techniques to assess social-emotional functioning, it is recommended that examiners rely on qualitative information and analysis of themes rather than on standardized scoring (e.g., the Rorschach Workbook; Exner, 1990). First, there is a dearth of measures that have been standardized on people with developmental disabilities. Second, finding a measure that has been standardized on children with developmental delay of a specific cultural background is practically impossible. Third, people with developmental disabilities typically have fewer resources to cope with stress than people in the general population. Thus, coping strategies or reactions to stress that are appropriate to an individual's developmental level can be misinterpreted as representing psychotic processes.

Communicating Diagnoses to Clients and Their Families Diagnosis is an issue of great concern. People from different cultures may have different worldviews of a given diagnosis. A *worldview* is a set of assumptions about the world shared by people from a common culture. One important aspect of worldview is the understanding of health and illness. In some cultures, a diagnosis may be a source of shame for the family or even a threat to its identity. Before delivering a diagnosis, the assessment team should assess a client's and his or her family's beliefs surrounding the diagnosis, as well as the medical model that is implicit in diagnoses. It is important to consult the literature and experts in the field in order to make informal judgments in this situation. It is then vital to ask the family, in a sensitive way, about its worldviews.

Once the team has obtained an understanding of the client's and family's worldview, it has to convey the diagnosis from within their worldview and not from one that contradicts it. It is important to consider not only the effects of traditional cultural worldview but also the effects of acculturation. For example, Gajjar (2001) found that many clients hold their traditional cultural beliefs and Western medical perspectives concurrently.

Epilepsy is a good example of a disorder that has different cultural connotations (Gajjar, 2001). Epilepsy is important and relevant to the field of developmental disabilities because it is often comorbid with other disabilities (i.e., both existing at the same time; Kawasaki, 1989). It is remarkable to observe the ways in which epilepsy is perceived by different cultures. For example, in Tanzania, epilepsy is attributed to spirits possessing the body (Jilek-Aall, 1999). In China, the entire family of a person with epilepsy is often affected negatively (World Health Organization [WHO], 1997). In India, epilepsy is frequently treated using traditional spiritual techniques (Desai et al., 1998). In a study of a large sample ($N = 1{,}500$) in Denmark (Jensen & Dam, 1992), 70% of the respondents were opposed to allowing their children to be in contact with a person with epilepsy. Results from the WHO survey (1997) indicated that 20% of the respondents in Germany believed that epilepsy is a form of mental illness.

In the field of developmental disabilities, psychologists are sometimes faced with the awkwardness of how to deliver a diagnosis of an intellectual or developmental disability (see Chapters 1 and 21 for more information). *Mental retardation* is still the official term in several important U.S. publications, including the *Diagnostic and Statistical Manual of Mental Disorders, Fourth Edition, Text Revision* (*DSM-IV-TR;* American Psychiatric Association, 2000). At the same time, the term has had negative connotations in many cultural and ethnic groups, as well as in mainstream groups. When delivering a diagnosis to people with diverse cultural backgrounds, using the term *mental retardation* or other terms with negative connotations may be degrading and shameful. Conversely, using ambiguous terms may lead a family to develop an inaccurate understanding of its child's functioning and needs. For example, it has been the chapter authors' experience that the term *delay* is often interpreted to mean something transient and that the person will eventually overcome. Thus, the assessment team should try to deliver the diagnosis in a sensitive but clear manner. Display 26.5 illustrates the complexities that are sometimes involved with delivering a diagnosis.

CULTURALLY SENSITIVE INTERVENTION

Working with culturally diverse clients who have developmental disabilities can be an exciting challenge for professionals. Professionals should be prepared, though, to engage in a time-consuming task. In order to provide a meaningful and culturally sensitive intervention, intervention should be designed to recognize and accommodate for clients' cultural background, level of acculturation, and both past and present personal experiences within the majority culture. These factors have great and direct impact on the way that environment is experienced, on how information is processed, and on the behaviors of clients from diverse cultural backgrounds.

Service providers would do well to be intellectually flexible, to be open to various aspects of different cultures, and to be emotionally ready for the psychological challenges of clients from different cultures. They must also be aware that different variables from the client's culture may enter the therapeutic relationship. According to the American Psychological Association's (1990) guidelines for providing psychological services to ethnically, linguistically, and culturally diverse populations, "psychological service providers need a sociocultural framework to consider diversity of values, interactional styles, and cultural expectations in a systematic fashion." These guidelines also suggest that the psychologist should have appropriate knowledge and skills required for multicultural assessment and intervention including the ability to

Display 26.5

Case study: Teresa

Teresa's mother called a university clinic to seek an assessment for her 11-year-old daughter. She told the intake worker that Teresa had been identified as having a learning disability 1 year ago. However, Teresa's mother found Teresa to be progressing slowly and wanted to find out why. During the parent interview, the assessment team (a psychometrist and a psychologist) learned that the mother was of Filipino-Canadian origin. Although the mother's racial genealogy originated from the Philippines, her cultural background was unique to a cultural group that emigrated from the Philippines to South America, and she herself was born in South America. The father was of South American background. He had only recently acquired English as a second language, and spoke little during the interview. Often, when the father asked for clarification, the mother would translate to Spanish. The first hurdle for the assessment team was to avoid misclassifying the cultural background based on appearance only.

When the assessment team started to compile past reports, it became apparent that Teresa had not been diagnosed with a learning disability in the prior assessment; rather, she had been diagnosed with a mild intellectual disability. The assessment process, which was also complicated by family issues that needed to be addressed, had to account for the worldview of the parents. Specifically, beliefs about developmental disabilities needed to be examined. In consultation with a university psychology professor whose field of research is Latino culture, the assessment team learned that in this culture, developmental disabilities are sometimes seen as a source of shame for the family. The team had to walk a tightrope of delivering a diagnosis with integrity while not offending or alienating the family.

First, the team avoided the use of terms with potentially derogatory connotations, such as *mental retardation.* The team explained that the term *learning disability,* which the mother used with the intake worker, was inaccurate in describing Teresa's condition. The members team explained Teresa's diagnosis of what is called *developmental disability* or a *developmental handicap,* and they talked about realistic expectations for the future.

Source: Sedighdeilami and Gindi (2003).

1) recognize cultural diversity; 2) understand the role that culture and ethnicity/race play in sociopsychological and economic development of ethnic and culturally diverse populations; 3) understand that socioeconomic and political factors significantly impact the psychosocial, political and economic development of ethnic and culturally diverse groups; and 4) help clients to understand/maintain/resolve their own sociocultural identification; and understand the interaction of culture, gender, and sexual orientation on behavior and needs. (American Psychological Association, 1990)

Unfortunately, because of incomplete training, some therapists are unaware or unable to consider cultural issues. Instead, they apply only values and beliefs based on their own training in psychology and psychiatry.

Clients from diverse cultural backgrounds may bring an entirely different set of values and beliefs to the therapy sessions. According to Pinderhughes (1989), the feelings aroused in professionals who work with clients whose culture differs from their own "are more frequently than not negative and driven by anxiety, [and] they can interfere with successful therapeutic outcome" (p. 21). Of course, mental health services providers are not expected to know every aspect of every different culture or to be absolutely free of cultural biases. However, awareness and consideration of cultural issues is an essential variable that will have an important impact on the effectiveness of the treatment.

Acculturation The classical definition of *acculturation* was provided by Redfield and Herskovits (1936). They defined acculturation as a process that "comprehends those phenomena which result when groups of individuals having different cultures come into continuous first-hand contact with subsequent changes in the original culture patterns of either or both groups" (p. 149). According to Berry (1997), acculturation is a strategy that is overtly or inadvertently adopted by individuals when they come into contact with people of different cultures. Berry (1997) noted that acculturation is a reciprocal process whereby both the immigrant culture and the host culture change. From a practical point of view, however, acculturation induces more changes in the immigrants than in the hosts. While working with clients from different cultures, it is important for clinicians to be aware that acculturation is not an isolated phenomenon. It is affected by the social, political, and economic environment in the host society and by the experiences and attitudes of clients.

According to Berry (1997), acculturation can be highly stressful, especially for individuals who try to assimilate by retaining their original culture and rejecting the culture of the host country. Berry (1997) also noted that the process of separation, or adherence to the culture of origin and rejection of culture of settlement, leads to adjustment difficulties. A client who is highly acculturated may not be as influenced by racial factors as a client who is not acculturated. For instance, an American psychologist working with an American-born and raised client from a minority background needs to address different issues than one working with a client from a minority culture who has recently immigrated to the United States. It is important to note that the level of acculturation may vary greatly among different members of a particular ethnic minority and within members of the same family.

"Differentness" and the Mismatch Syndrome Research on children and adolescents with developmental disabilities indicates that the feeling of being different is typical among those who have developmental disabilities. Culturally diverse children and youth may face a double challenge in this regard. Not only are they confronted with the challenges of disabilities but also they must deal with the difficulties of adapting to a new and different culture. The feeling of being culturally different may add to their feelings of alienation and loneliness. They may also feel misunderstood; cultural differences may make children feel mismatched with other people and with the environment. According to Ramirez (1991), the common dynamic in the "differentness syndrome" is mismatch, which may cause loneliness, hopelessness, depression, self-rejection, and rigidity of thinking. Displays 26.1, 26.2, and 26.3 illustrate in more detail how cultural differences may relate to the mismatch syndrome in children and adolescents with developmental disabilities.

Cultural Factors Affecting Assessment and Intervention There are several cultural factors that may affect intervention and its effectiveness. In the following sections, several of the most important factors are discussed.

Communication According to Storti (1994), communication is central to multicultural encounters. *Communication* may be defined as the sending of a message from a source to a receiver with the least possible loss of meaning. Hall (1963) argued that culture itself is communication because culture can be viewed as a continuous process of sending and receiving messages and reinforcing different norms. He emphasized that some aspects of people's activities, of which they may or may not be aware, transmit messages that are easily misunderstood cross culturally. For example, people of Asian, African, and Hispanic backgrounds apply restricted codes in which sentences are shortened without a loss of meaning and nonverbal messages are delivered simultaneously. Among some individuals of Asian and Middle Eastern backgrounds, a hesitant "yes" is a way of politely expressing "no," and gestures and body postures sometimes substitute for words and sentences. In contrast, Anglo-Americans emphasize verbal messages and elaborate codes in which many words are applied to convey a message. Therefore, it is essential for a psychologist working with clients from minority cultures to be aware of and familiar with their communication styles during the process of treatment.

Cultural Norms Cultural norms are the rules that refer to what is usually done and accepted within a specific culture that are unique to that culture. Cultural norms are more than simply nonverbal communications, such as gestures, body language, and manners. Rather, they make human interactions meaningful. For example, in some native cultures, silence is meaningful; in Western culture, it is often considered awkward. Another example of nonverbal behavior in different cultures is crossing legs while sitting in front of another person. Although this is acceptable in Western culture, it would be considered rude in Middle Eastern culture. Unfamiliarity with such cultural norms and not taking cultural differences into account during intervention may result in decreased positive gain for the client or may even be harmful.

Attention to the Environment Aspects of a new environment and culture provide constant sensory information that an individual must filter and categorize. A culturally diverse child with a developmental disability who has cognitive impairments may feel overwhelmed by an unfamiliar and sometimes completely different environment and culture. Because of the child's cognitive capacity, he or she may not be able to absorb all the new aspects of the new culture easily and automatically. Therefore, absorbing the type of information that is processed quite easily within the home culture, such as social norms, may become a major and sometimes exhausting task. In new environments, culturally diverse children and youth with developmental disabilities who do not hear their own language and see little or nothing familiar, who use body language and gestures differently from the majority, who verbalize in unexpected and different ways, or who may expect authority to be exercised differently, may experience feelings of "differentness" that can in turn cause isolation and loneliness.

This experience of differentness will make it harder for professionals to establish a rapport with those clients and to have children's cooperation during the process of intervention. This is particularly true for service providers who are not familiar enough with cultural issues and who do not consider cultural differences to be an important subject in their practice.

Behavioral Norms Each culture has different behavioral norms. In addition to the previous examples, in most Eastern cultures, children are typically expected to be quiet and defer to adults. In Western cultures, however, children and youth are typically encouraged to express themselves and to be independent. Some cultures place great emphasis on family, interdependence, and collectivism (e.g., Middle Eastern or Far East cultures); others emphasize independence from family, self-reliance, and individualism (e.g., North American culture).

All of these behavioral norms affect a client's behavior and influence how an individual behaves toward the therapist or service worker during intervention. For instance, in a society where individualism is encouraged, a therapist may tend to view a child's difficulty as residing within the client rather than in the family or society in large. The therapist may, as a result, use a client-focused strategy to address the problem, with the goal of the intervention focused on changing the child. The client's family may see the importance of the child's contribution to the problem, but they may also put great emphasis on systemic and social factors. If the therapist shares and works with, or at the very least understands, the family's views and perceptions, the intervention will be both more constructive and more successful.

One particularly important nonverbal behavior is eye contact. In a psychologically based intervention, eye contact or the avoidance of eye contact has diagnostic significance. Service providers who do not consider cultural issues in their practices may interpret the lack of eye contact as a sign of shyness, unassertiveness, or even depression. This may lead to misunderstandings when dealing with culturally diverse children and adolescents with developmental disabilities. As mentioned previously, it is not necessary for many people from the Middle and Far East to make eye contact when communicating. In fact, in Middle East cultures, direct eye contact is considered a rude and impolite behavior, especially for children and young adults. Thus, some professionals should be cautioned not to interpret such behaviors as signifying lack of cooperativeness.

Cultural Values and Beliefs One factor that underlies human behaviors involves the values and beliefs that cultures hold. Cultural values about personal relationships affect client–worker interaction (Canino & Spurlock, 2000). A failure to recognize clients' cultural values may potentially contaminate the process of therapy. Pinderhughes (1989) argued that service providers can have a blind spot and may perceive clients from their own culture as being like themselves. A failure to distinguish between their own culture and that of their clients can interfere with treatment and can have a negative impact on the therapeutic environment, as those professionals fail to explore the meaning of particular events for their clients and assume that the clients' issues are similar to their own. As a result, educating culturally diverse clients and their families about the intervention and its process is essential. Culturally diverse clients and their families may have had little or no exposure to these types of intervention and may view them as irrelevant and disconnected from their problems. As a consequence, without adequate understanding of the intervention process, they may simply not return for subsequent appointments. Professionals should therefore allow themselves a longer period of exploration and avoid making interpretations during intervention with clients of diverse cultural/ethnic backgrounds until they have obtained a deep understanding of the clients' worldviews.

Patterns of Thinking It is important for professionals to be aware of the fact that cognitive styles and thinking patterns vary from client to client, especially when the client is from a culture different than their own. For example, it is helpful to know if clients usually think deductively or inductively. Does the child or adolescent consider his or her environment when he or she thinks, or does he or she ignore it?

Some clients typically begin a conversation with concrete facts and then build their ideas based on those facts. Conversely, others may be accustomed to starting with abstract ideas and then moving on to concrete facts. Such patterns of thinking may be developed within individuals because of cultural influences. Information of this kind can be very helpful to the interaction between the professional and the client.

Styles of Communication Different cultures have their own communicative styles. A gesture, a smile, a tone of voice, or a way of shaking hands may add to a message or give special meaning to the reciprocal communication. It is important to note that the addition of an emphasis or meaning to a message varies from one culture to the next. For example, in some cultures, low tone (pitch) of voice is encouraged, whereas other cultural groups may encourage high tone and loud speech. Gesture and body language also differ greatly from culture to culture. For example, people from the Middle East tend to show more emotion, speak slowly, and touch (e.g., a touch on the arm) more than people from the West.

Another factor to be considered is personal space, the distance at which people from different cultures are comfortable when conversing or interacting. This also varies from one culture to another and may have a marked effect on elicited responses.

SUMMARY

Professionals who work with individuals who have developmental disabilities are often confronted with various challenges. When the clients come from diverse cultural backgrounds, the challenge is often compounded. Professionals would do well to move beyond the traditional assessment and intervention approaches, become familiar with multicultural issues related to both assessment and intervention, and design intervention protocols that take into consideration the client's cultural background and personal experiences. They should also be open to various aspects of different cultures, be intellectually flexible, and be able to determine the impact of cultural differences and acculturation issues. At the same time, clinicians should avoid stereotyping and be cautious of overfocusing on a client's cultural/ethnic background. Challenges that clients experience may be related to issues other than their ethnicity. Inability to consider clients' cultural background may contaminate the process and the results of assessment and intervention, causing frustration for both client and clinician.

Although it is not possible for professionals to know every aspect of different cultures, consideration and awareness of cultural issues are essential and will have a considerable effect on working with individuals with developmental disabilities from various cultures. Professionals wishing to enhance their competence should first explore their own cultural identity and their own biases. Research about the cultural backgrounds of clients is good as long as the clinician avoids stereotyping. Professionals may also pursue academic training or workshops. Most important, the basic therapeutic attitude of openness and willingness to learn from each client is the best safeguard for avoiding doing harm to clients, including those from diverse cultural backgrounds.

FOR FURTHER THOUGHT AND DISCUSSION

1. Why is it important for professionals to be aware of cultural issues in working with culturally diverse individuals with developmental disabilities?
2. Define the "mismatch or differentness syndrome" and explain how it can affect an individual you know from a minority group.
3. There are various cultural variables that may affect the process of intervention and its effectiveness. Explain how these variables affect one intervention that you select.
4. Illustrate, by presenting a case example in a creative way, how a client's first language can affect the assessment process and its results.

REFERENCES

American Psychiatric Association. (2000). *Diagnostic and statistical manual of mental disorders* (4th ed., text rev.). Washington, DC: Author.

American Psychological Association. (1990). *APA Guidelines for providers of psychological services to ethnic, linguistic, and culturally diverse populations.* Retrieved July 2, 2003, from http://www.apa.org/pi/oema/guide.html

Bellak, L. (1975). *The Thematic Apperception Test, the Children's Apperception Test, and the Senior Apperception Technique in clinical use.* New York: Grune & Stratton.

Berry, J.W. (1997). Immigration, acculturation, and adaptation. *Applied Psychology: An International Review, 46*(1), 5–68.

Brown, L., Sherbenou, R.J., & Johnsen, S.K. (1997). *Test of Nonverbal Intelligence, Third Edition (TONI-3).* Circle Pines, MN: AGS Publishing.

Canino, I.A., & Spurlock, J. (2000). Diagnostic categories. In I.A. Canino & J. Spurlock (Eds.), *Culturally diverse children and adolescents: Assessment, diagnosis, and treatment* (2nd ed., pp. 103–147). New York: The Guilford Press.

Cole, E. (1996). Immigrant and refugee children and families: Supporting a new road travelled. In M. Luther (Ed.), *Dynamic assessment for instruction: From theory to application* (pp. 35–42). Toronto: Captus University Publication.

Copeland, E.J. (1983). Cross-cultural counseling and psychotherapy: A historical perspective, implications for research and training. *Personnel Guidance Journal, 62*(1), 10–15.

Cummins, J. (1984). Four misconceptions about language proficiency in bilingual education. *The Journal of the National Association for Bilingual Education, 5*(3), 31–45.

Dana, R.H. (1993). *Multicultural assessment perspectives for professional psychology.* Needham, MA: Allyn and Bacon.

Desai, P., Padma, M.V., Jain, S., et al. (1998). Knowledge, attitudes and practice of epilepsy: Experience at a comprehensive rural health services project. *Seizure, 7,* 133–138.

Exner, J.E.J. (1990). *The Rorschach workbook for the comprehensive system.* Bayville, NJ: The Rorschach Workshops.

Gajjar, M.M. (2001). *Developing a rating scale for assessing culture-specific beliefs and attitudes about epilepsy.* Unpublished Doctoral Dissertation, University of Toronto.

Geva, E. (2000). Issues in the assessment of reading disabilities in L2 children: Beliefs and research evidence. *Dyslexia, 6,* 13–28.

Geva, E., Barsky, A., & Westernoff, F. (2000). Interprofessional and diversity informed practice. In E. Geva, A. Barsky, & F. Westernoff (Eds.), *Interprofessional practice with diverse populations: Cases in point* (pp. 1–28). Westport, CT: Auburn House.

Hall, T. (1963). *The silent language.* New York: Anchor Press.

Jensen, R., & Dam, M. (1992). Public attitudes toward epilepsy in Denmark. *Epilepsia, 27,* 316–322.

Jilek-Aall, L. (1999). *Morbus sacer* in Africa: Some religious aspects of epilepsy in traditional cultures. *Epilepsia, 40,* 382–386.

Jones, E.E., & Thorne, A. (1987). Rediscovery of the subject: Intercultural approaches to clinical assessment. *Journal of Consulting & Clinical Psychology, 55,* 488–495.

Kawasaki, Y. (1989). Developmental disorders and epilepsy. *Journal of Mental Health, 35,* 15–23.

Larry P. v. Wilson Riles. (1979). United States District Court, N.D., California.
Leiter, R.G. (1947). *The Leiter International Performance Scale.* Chicago: Stoelting Co.
McArthur, D.S., & Roberts, G.E. (1982). *Roberts Apperception Test for Children manual.* Los Angeles: Western Psychological Services.
Morris, A., & Mervis, B. (1999). Williams syndrome. In S. Goldstein & R. Reynolds (Eds.), *Handbook of neurodevelopmental and genetic disorders in children* (pp. 555–590). New York: The Guilford Press.
Pinderhughes, E. (1989). *Understanding race, ethnicity and power: The key to efficacy in clinical practice.* New York: The Free Press.
Plake, B.S., & Impara, J.C. (Eds.). (2001). *The Fourteenth Mental Measurements Yearbook.* Lincoln: University of Nebraska–Lincoln, Buros Institute of Mental Measurements.
Ramirez, M. (1991). *Psychotherapy and counseling with minorities: A cognitive approach to individual and cultural differences.* New York: Pergamon Press.
Raven, J. (1965). *Raven's Colored and Standard Progressive Matrices.* San Antonio, TX: Harcourt Assessment.
Redfield, R.L., & Herskovits, M. (1936). Memorandum on the study of acculturation. *American Antropologist, 38,* 149–152.
Rodriguez, C. (2000). Culturally sensitive psychological assessment. In I.A. Canino (Ed.), *Culturally diverse children and adolescents: Assessment, diagnosis, and treatment* (2nd ed., pp. 84–102). New York: The Guilford Press.
Roid, G.H., & Miller, L.J. (1997). *The Leiter International Performance Scale–Revised Edition* (Leiter-R). London: NFER Nelson.
Sedighdeilami, F., & Gindi, S. (2003). Multicultural issues in assessment and intervention for individuals with developmental disabilities in Ontario. In I. Brown & M. Percy (Eds.), *Developmental disabilities in Ontario* (2nd ed., pp. 477–489). Toronto: Ontario Association on Developmental Disabilities.
Storti, C. (1994). *Cross-cultural dialogues: 74 brief encounters with cultural difference.* Yarmouth, ME: Intercultural Press.
Sue, S., Kuraski, K.S., & Srinivasan, S. (1999). Ethnicity, gender, and cross-cultural issues in clinical research. In P.C. Kendall, J.N. Butcher, et al. (Eds.), *Handbook of research methods in clinical psychology* (2nd ed., pp. 54–71). Hoboken, NJ: John Wiley & Sons.
Sue, S., & Zane, N. (1987). The role of culture and cultural techniques in psychotherapy: A critique and reformulation. *American Psychologist, 42*(1), 37–45.
World Health Organization. (1997). *Epilepsy: Social consequences and economic aspects* (Fact sheet #166). Geneva: Author.

27

Roles, Education, Training, and Professional Values of Disability Personnel

Roy I. Brown

WHAT YOU WILL LEARN ABOUT IN THIS CHAPTER

- Setting the scene: Context of specific issues
- Disability personnel and their roles
- Education and training of disability personnel
- Philosophy and values of disability personnel

Working with people who have intellectual or developmental disabilities can lead to occupations and life experiences that are challenging, rewarding, and rich with opportunities for personal fulfillment. This is the case for the many different types of paid and unpaid support people who actively work with individuals who have disabilities: paid staff, professionals from a wide variety of fields, family members, friends, volunteers, community members, and many others. In this chapter, the wide range of people whose work involves supporting people with intellectual or developmental disabilities are referred to as *disability personnel* (see Display 27.1).

The work of all disability personnel is essential for people with disabilities to enable them to live in communities in ways that include their lifestyles with others and promote their quality of life. As noted in Display 27.1, many such personnel work in community settings; others work directly within a wide variety of structures, systems, and processes that are usually referred to, collectively, as *service organizations*. Service organizations typically employ disability personnel in the form or managers and supervisors, policy makers, frontline practitioners of various types, and support staff.

Frontline practitioners—those who work most closely with people with intellectual or developmental disabilities—are especially important to ensuring that effective support is provided. The main reasons for this are that frontline practitioners

- Are most knowledgeable about the characteristics and behavior of people with disabilities
- Are key to helping other professionals and policy makers understand the person with disabilities and any difficulties he or she faces
- Are central figures in the multidisciplinary teams needed to support most people with intellectual or developmental disabilities
- Carry out most informal (and sometimes formal) assessment and intervention, and provide needed care and help (see Chapter 21)
- Are in positions of trust, with direct responsibility for supporting personal well-being of those with disabilities

Frontline practitioners do work that is highly varied and personal, because, of necessity, they must respond to the support needs of specific individuals. Some are family members; others are paid workers who are trained and educated at a variety of levels. The latter are described by terms that vary by country and job function but include names such as disability counselors, aides, rehabilitation counselors or practitioners, disability support workers, residential and community support personnel, and options coordinators. A great many frontline practitioners work in or for a wide variety of community-based organizations, both publicly and privately funded, and some work in family homes, whereas others carry out their roles in institutions and hospitals. They are the people who have the closest ongoing contact with the people they support.

This chapter focuses on issues that concern all disability personnel, especially frontline practitioners. Yet, disability personnel carry out their work within a sometimes complex system of disability legislation,

I am grateful to Doreen Croser, Executive Director of the American Association on Mental Retardation, for her helpful comments and suggestions. I thank Patricia M. Brown for reading an early draft of this chapter and providing advice and comments, the editors for their numerous comments and suggestions for improving the text, and Rebecca Zener and Valerie Temple for providing materials for the displays.

Display 27.1

Disability personnel

Disability personnel are professionals and nonprofessionals who have a direct role in the day-to-day care, support, and rehabilitation of people with intellectual and developmental disabilities. These include people who work in residential and group homes, day centers, homes of people with disabilities who live independently with assistance, family homes, places of employment, community service organizations, and institutions of various kinds. This group also includes personnel whose day-to-day work provides support by visiting families in their homes and in the local community and bringing together the necessary resources for the individuals and families they support. Such individuals work under a variety of names: outreach workers, community and rehabilitation practitioners, community counselors, child care workers, early childhood workers, developmental educators, and so forth.

People with intellectual and developmental disabilities, especially those who live in the community, obtain considerable amounts of support from a wide variety of professionals and nonprofessionals. The importance of informal support (see Chapter 21 for more information)—from such people as store employees, bus drivers, neighbors, schoolmates, children in the playground, and even strangers—cannot be overstated. Such support is invaluable to the inclusion of people with disabilities into community life.

More formal support is provided by professionals who assist people with disabilities as a part of their work. Such is the case for a teacher who has one child with Down syndrome in his classroom, a family physician who has three patients who have intellectual disabilities, or a lawyer who dedicates 5% of her practice to assisting people with disabilities. Other examples include, but are not limited to, psychiatrists, psychologists, dentists, general nurses, physiotherapists, homecare workers, occupational therapists, speech-language pathologists, audiologists, behavior therapists, and drama and music therapists. Some of these professionals may have little formal knowledge of disability, and others may have a considerable knowledge.

funding, and services that involves many other professionals and nonprofessionals and operate within broader social environments that have their own values and manifest their own attitudes toward disability. For this reason, the information presented is highly relevant to a broad spectrum of people across the disability field: policy makers whose decisions create the environment within which disability personnel work to provide effective support; professionals and nonprofessionals whose daily work sometimes includes people with disabilities; and society at large, which is ultimately responsible for how people with disabilities are treated as they carry out their lives in their communities.

SETTING THE SCENE: CONTEXT OF SPECIFIC ISSUES

Before addressing the specific issues for disability personnel, it is important to describe the context—or "set the scene"—for these issues. This takes the form of discussion about changes and variations related to disabilities.

Increasing Knowledge of Disability

The last half of the 20th century and the beginning years of the 21st century has been a time of massive increase in knowledge about intellectual and developmental disabilities. The unraveling of the genetic code and the subsequent development of the human genome (see Chapter 7) have led not only to an increasing ability to identify genetic deficiencies but also to an ability to provide, through genetic counseling, advice to prospective parents. Identification of genetic causes of intellectual and developmental disability has or will lead to new treatments and possibly even cures.

These advances have been paralleled by extraordinary changes in understanding of other aspects of life, such as physical health (Chapter 41), psychiatry (Chapter 42), and behavior (Chapters 20 and 23). There also have been advances in knowledge about health and gender differences, and these have been tied to advances in technological skills (Prasher & Janicki, 2002; Walsh & Heller, 2002; see also Chapters 7, 8, 37, and 41).

There has been immense growth in understanding of environmental causes of disabilities (e.g., fetal alcohol spectrum disorder, the leading nongenetic cause of fetal malformations and intellectual disability worldwide; see Chapters 9 and 15). It is increasingly recognized that in many countries, environmental damage related to inadequate food and health services, isolation, and social living conditions cause environmentally induced intellectual and developmental disabilities. For example, children who are born into adverse family and social environments are at risk of developing not only physical diseases and deformity but also mild to severe intellectual disability. To prevent these kinds of disabilities, it is critical for people (particularly infants and children) to receive the basic elements of a healthy life, including clean water, food, and a safe and supportive family environment. Yet, as such improvements occur, countries will see a rise in the number of people with disabilities surviving to greater ages.

Aging, in fact, has become an important area of this increasing knowledge (see Chapter 39). Many people with severe and profound disabilities now survive and require support, care, and training over an increasingly longer life span. Those with more mild disabilities are likely to have even longer life spans and require both generic and specialized services to an advanced age. For example, people with intellectual disabilities may eventually move to homes for people who are aging, although they also require specialized support because of social and possibly behavioral issues (Janicki & Ansello, 2000). One of the most remarkable changes is occuring in people with Down syndrome. At the beginning of the 20th century, they lived on average to approximately 11 years, but now they live on average to more than 55 years in most Western countries (Brown, 2004). People with Prader-Willi syndrome are beginning to show similar changes (James & Brown, 1993).

As a consequence of such factors, disability personnel in the early 21st century work with a wider range of people with intellectual and developmental disabilities about whom increasingly more is known. Adding to this challenge is the fact that this increased knowledge has been accompanied by enormous changes in support methods (Bigby, 2004; Brown & Brown, 2003), including approaches within developing countries and various cultural groups (see Keith & Schalock, 2000; McConkey, O'Toole, & Mariga, 1999).

Changes in Support Methods

The years since the mid-20th century have been a time of fundamental change in how people with disabilities are perceived and how services are delivered. Despite some changing economic conditions over these years, there were ongoing efforts to change the lives of people with disabilities for the better—although these efforts took different forms in different countries. Such efforts have occurred, and are still occurring, within a world context associated with a move from a disablement-based model to one of participation and activity by people with disabilities (see World Health Organization, 1997). The trend is toward supporting and enabling individuals to become more responsible for their own development and key participants in decision making. The philosophical foundation for many of the changes was the principle of normalization (Wolfensberger, 1972) and was later referred to by the same author as social role valorization. This perspective sought to persuade individuals, families, communities, and governments that regular lifestyles in normal circumstances with valued roles for people with intellectual disabilities are not only important and possible but also critically necessary and ethically required. This, and complementary, perspectives have made it apparent that despite a growing awareness of the genetic influence on behavior and the extent of physical impairment, the degree to which people see themselves as "disabled" and the degree to which other members of society see them as "disabled" are strongly influenced by social attitudes and values, most commonly demonstrated by the absence or presence of discrimination (Schalock et al., 2002).

These changes have taken many forms. In most of the more affluent countries, institutional care has been replaced by a wide variety of rehabilitation and support systems based in the community. As a result, most people with intellectual and developmental disabilities remain in their home communities—often with their families—or live in communities of their choice. Even those with severe medical and psychiatric conditions, who were once thought to be extremely difficult to move from institutions successfully, are being provided for in community settings. The thrust for inclusive education, supported by legislation, brought about a decrease in the number of special (segregated) classrooms and schools and an increase in the number of supports within general education classrooms for children with disabilities (see Chapter 31 for fuller details). Various forms of individualized funding (see Chapter 4) are being tried out in many countries. Indeed, individuals, families, and people within service organizations who support those with disabilities are developing and implementing an array of new methods of support for all aspects of life, some of which will prove to be highly beneficial and widely used in the future. These methods are typically based on generally accepted priorities for supports and services, as outlined in Table 27.1, but represent some unique and innovative ways to put them into practice.

Service Variation Among Countries

The services and supports provided by disability personnel in such countries as Australia, Canada, the United Kingdom, and the United States have somewhat different accents. Priorities for services and service development differ, partly because need for services varies markedly from area to area. There are many factors that can influence how priorities for services are put into place. These factors that vary among countries and within countries include: population size and demographics, availability of government and other funding, laws, policies, social customs and traditions, availability of community resources, and education and training of professionals both inside and outside the disability field.

Table 27.1. Generally accepted priorities for supports and services

Support and services should be based on
Broad knowledge of disability's causes and contributing factors
Broad-based knowledge across key domains of life experience
Collaboration between generic and specialized services and resources
Collaboration among all levels of professional personnel and families
Community-based delivery, rather than institutionally based care
Support and services should be
Enabling and enhancing to quality of life
Complete, timely, and efficient
Ethical and respectful
Improving in response to evidence-based research
Proven to be the best way of helping people with their specific problems and concerns (i.e., are in accord with best practice standards)
Integrated
For the life span
Multidisciplinary
Multilayered
Sensitive to culture, religion, family structure, and social circumstances

Services can also be influenced by geography (see Display 27.2). For example, in Australia's "outback," services are widespread, far apart, and situated over difficult terrain, whereas in larger cities like Adelaide or Sydney services are closer at hand. Similarly, in Canada, providing services in Labrador is considerably more difficult (and expensive) than doing so in Vancouver or Toronto. It is often easier to administer and monitor services in urban areas because of proximity and ease of travel, but the complexity of urban life and the larger number of people who need services in cities can make the work more challenging. Services for Indigenous peoples in Australia, Canada, and the United States (and many other countries of the world such as India, Mexico, Japan, the Philippines) sometimes differ greatly from services for non-Indigenous peoples, especially those in urban and socially well-developed areas (Timmons, 1999).

These factors may work together or in opposition, often in complex ways, to facilitate or hamper the development of services. In China, for example, providing effective and comprehensive services for people with disabilities is challenging because of interactions among such factors as large geographical size, terrain diversity, ethnic diversity, regional customs, social attitudes toward disability, a relatively low average personal income in some areas, a particular emphasis on economic development, and, until the 1990s or so, a relatively isolated political and social system. By contrast, providing services in Singapore is much easier because it is small in geography and population and has a strong economy and many international linkages. In impoverished areas, as in some parts of Eastern Europe, Africa, and Asia, the negative factors combine to result in services that generally are backward for even the early 20th century—for example, children malnourished and crammed into residential institutions. Yet, in other countries in similar circumstances, innovative efforts have been made to advance areas such as prevention, early education, physical and occupational therapy, independent living, and community inclusion using advanced social concepts of choice and self-image that reflect the latest conceptualizations of quality of life and self-determination (McConkey et al., 1999).

In general, improved living standards in any country seem to accompany greater attention to disability services by governments, communities, and service organizations. Lessening of wealth, recession, and a perceived need for economic strengthening tend to accompany the withholding of services from people and families where disability occurs; for example, in the United Kingdom and parts of Canada since the 1990s, there has been some withdrawal of individualized funding for families with a member who has intellectual disabilities (see also Chapter 4). Cuts to funding

Display 27.2

Case study: Sanjeev

Sanjeev is 5-year-old boy with cerebral palsy. He lives in Bhaktapur, Nepal, with his family. His mother, Adity, stays at home and takes care of him and her 10-year-old daughter, Pranisha. Sanjeev's father, Padam, works as a waiter in a local family restaurant. Several times per week, Adity, Sanjeev, and Pranisha ride the local bus for 2 hours in order to get to Kanti Children's Hospital, where Sanjeev receives treatment. Kanti is the only hospital of its kind in Nepal. There are no other special facilities or homes for people with developmental disabilities such as Sanjeev's, so Kanti is the only place that provides care for children with cerebral palsy. Adity pays 120 Nepalese rupees for six treatments of physiotherapy at the hospital.

As a result of his disability, Sanjeev is unable to attend school or any other special programming. He enjoys playing with toys and with his older sister. Pranisha treats him like any one of her friends and tries to help him improve his dexterity and movement. Adity works with the occupational therapist and assists in stretching Sanjeev's limbs in order to expand his range of motion.

Source: Rebecca Zener, University of Western Ontario.

for people with disabilities is currently a concern in the United States. In both rich and poor countries, poverty and disability are linked with variables such as nutrition, single-parent families, maltreatment, and behavior challenges (e.g., see Emerson, Robertson, & Wood, 2005; Fudge Shormans & Brown, 2002).

The availability of support and services is not simply a matter of adequate funding. It is also a matter of social values and local attitudes toward people with disabilities, as well as long-term planning that sets government priorities for policy and action. Priorities and values/attitudes work in combination, and results in these areas can be seen, for example, in the following areas: how services address inclusion for people with disabilities once they have completed inclusive schooling, how issues of pregnancy and child care are addressed for mothers who themselves have a disability, and how services provide care and support for individuals with disabilities who are aging. Where attitudes toward children and adults with disabilities remain negative and where government disability priorities are not strong, as is the case especially in economically developing countries, people with disabilities are often still regarded as a source of individual and personal shame.

Points to Remember

The preceding discussion focused on setting the scene or context for the work carried out by disability personnel. It is within this complex picture that the chapter discusses disability personnel and their roles, the education and training that is required to support these roles, and the philosophy and values of disability personnel.

DISABILITY PERSONNEL AND THEIR ROLES

In one sense, disability personnel all do the same thing: They support people with disabilities. They do so, however, in an enormous variety of ways. Many disability personnel still work in specialized units or within services that provide specific disability care. Increasingly, though, disability personnel work in community settings, where the support required for people living with their families, with others, or on their own in the community can cover a wide range of activities. Each of these employment environments has its own knowledge base and methods for obtaining the required support. In addition, disability personnel who work with families and others who support people with disabilities directly must understand the stresses and needs of those people in order to help them provide the best possible support.

The complexity of the roles of disability personnel can seem rather daunting for someone just coming into the field. There are approximately 300 known causes of intellectual and developmental disabilities (see Chapter 7), and knowledge about these, although still quite sparse in some areas, is growing very quickly. Specialized knowledge and skills are increasing rapidly, and support to people with disabilities has extended into areas that were not always provided in past decades (e.g., in mental health and abnormal behavior; see Chapters 20 and 42). In addition, there has been a strong emphasis since approximately 1990 on personal development; quality of life; and living a full, holistic lifestyle (see Brown & Brown, 2003; Schalock et al., 2002). For example, drama, art, and music (Warren, 1988), leisure and recreation (Fidler & Velde, 1999), and spiritual activities (Crompton & Jackson, 2004) are seen to play a role in holistic development, enabling people to be more effective in employment and daily living. It is essential, and will be increasingly necessary, for disability personnel to know about and demonstrate competence in the spectrum of disciplines that address community living, home living, recreation, and employment.

Disability Personnel as Multidisciplinary Specialists

As a result of this growing complexity, disability personnel often specialize in a particular aspect of disability to respond to the ever-increasing knowledge of disabilities and to meet the wide variety of needs that emerge for people with intellectual and developmental disabilities and their families (see Display 27.3 for one example). Specialization allows disability personnel to become experts in specific areas (e.g., autism, HIV infection in children, mobility needs) or interventions (e.g., teaching methods, behavioral strategies, psychotherapy), and such expertise is extremely beneficial to a great many people. It also increases the need for multidisciplinary consultation, however, because teams of specialists often need to be drawn together to provide a full assessment and intervention strategy. Organizations that provide services to people with disabilities, in whole or in part, need to facilitate multidisciplinary consultation by including it as part of the role of disability personnel.

Disability Personnel and Growing Independence

The need for multidisciplinary consultation is particularly important because many disability personnel in the early 21st century work largely on their own—they often do not work in the same environment as their manager or other personnel. Their days may be spent visiting and supporting individuals within the individuals' homes, places of employment, or recreation venues. Some disability personnel work in generic services

Display 27.3

A clinical psychologist's perspective on her role

Although there are many different types of work a psychologist can do, perhaps the most well known to people outside the profession is the role of clinical psychologist. A clinical psychologist is an individual who normally has a doctoral degree in psychology and is licensed by a professional college or association to engage in assessment and treatment.

As a clinical psychologist in Canada, I work with individuals with a variety of difficulties. My practice includes many people with depression, anxiety, autism, dementia, and developmental disabilities, but this varies a great deal depending on where one works. Psychologists are often part of a team of professionals such as speech-language pathologists, behavior therapists, and social workers. The psychologist's contribution to the team usually involves providing information regarding diagnosis and prognosis—what can reasonably be expected in terms of goals and outcomes for a specific client and what types of treatment are likely to be most helpful.

As well as doing core clinical work, many psychologists engage in research and educational activities. I supervise people studying to be psychologists and instruct them in the development of their professional skills. I am also often involved in research projects to evaluate the effectiveness of different treatments or the utility of new scales or methods of diagnosis.

What I love about my job is the diversity. I have the opportunity to help people through difficult times when I do counseling, I can mentor students and watch them develop new skills, and I can provide information through diagnosis that will help individuals with disabilities and families better understand their own situation. I have always found assessment work to be an especially challenging and interesting part of my job. It is like being a detective at times, teasing out complex diagnoses using information from dozens of different sources. Being a psychologist gives me the opportunity to learn and do new things every day and make a different in people's lives.

Source: Valerie Temple, Surrey Place Centre.

where they are the only "expert" on disability. Increasingly, individuals with disabilities have a part in decisions concerning what work should be carried out, where it is carried out, and the people who are involved. A frontline worker is there to provide support and arrange for services to meet individual needs, through his or her own resources or through available specialized and generic services.

This change in function from traditional institutional settings, such as sheltered workshops and rehabilitation centers, results in some new challenges that, if not met, can result in increased stress for personnel. First, there is a reduced ability to monitor services in traditional ways; thus, new methods of assessing the performance of disability personnel are having to be created. Second, community interventions and support also reduce the opportunity of managers to literally see what is happening, and this affects how changes are made to the overall service system. Third, there are frequently reduced opportunities for multidisciplinary consultation. Working on one's own in the community means that disability personnel often must be able to assess and address unexpected situations independently. This increases their need to have broad personal knowledge about disabilities and services that are available. Finally, professional and ethical behavior of personnel who work in communities needs to be adapted to fit the nature and context of the work that is being done (see Brown & Brown, 2003).

Disability Personnel as Links to Generic Services

Increasingly, people with disabilities use generic services, augmented by specialized services, to meet their needs. Disability personnel have an important role to play in connecting people with disabilities to community services that are available to the general population. Part of this role involves identifying the needs of the people with disabilities whom they support, matching those needs with available generic services, assisting people with disabilities to obtain those services, and sharing information and strategies with professionals in generic services so that the work they do will have a stronger likelihood of success.

The use of generic services has advanced in many countries to the point where disability personnel now work within many services that are available to the general population. This is seen especially in some places of employment, many recreation centers, the educational and medical care systems, and increasingly within the mental health systems. Nonetheless, there are many gaps where generic services are not particularly adapted for, or available to, people with intellectual and developmental disabilities. For example, the links between generic services and disability services for older adults is often poor. Such gaps place stress on disability personnel and, more particularly, on older adults with disabilities and those who care for them.

Display 27.4 gives an example of challenges that arise in the field of geriatric care.

Integrating disability and generic services to address the needs of people with intellectual disabilities continues to be a strong aspect of the role of many disability personnel. One aspect of this is to integrate, or at least coordinate, services for people with various types of disabilities and disadvantages. For example, in South Australia, disability personnel work for various units representing different disability groups, such as people with brain injury, intellectual disability, physical disability, and sensory disability. Many of the services required by these groups are similar, because individuals may have multiple disabilities and because different disabilities may give rise to similar challenges (e.g., adapted housing and home appliances, supported employment, personal and family recreation, social and behavior support). Integration and coordination of specialized and generic services is being carried out in many developed countries and takes a wide variety of forms.

Display 27.4

Challenges facing caregivers of aging adults with disabilities

John worked as a frontline service provider for individuals who were aging and had intellectual disabilities. In this role, he was expected to arrange for support for individuals living in their own homes who had a range of disabilities, both physical and behavioral and including mental disturbance. He worked with a couple whose adult son had an intellectual disability and required support.

After discussions with the family members, it was agreed that John would set out to arrange coordinated support services for all members of the family. However, the local services for aging did not provide services for people with intellectual disabilities, so their funds and resources could not be used for the couple's son. Funding problems also arose regarding services for people with intellectual disabilities. The frontline community workers funded from each of these services could establish liaisons, but they could not make the best economic use of funds or services because of the separate policy and financial jurisdictions of the services involved.

Disability Personnel as Support to Families

Increasingly, the role of disability personnel in most countries is to support people with disabilities living in family homes. In this situation, family members, most often parents, are the main caregivers and thus take on the function of frontline worker. There are a number of reasons for this trend (see Chapter 4). Whatever the reason, disability personnel often find themselves working with families and giving support to family members to help them better provide for their family member with the disability.

This trend has led to a realization in the disability field that professionals must understand and recognize the impact of family members on the person with disabilities and the impact of disability on the family (see Turnbull, Brown, & Turnbull, 2004). As reported at a 2005 Roundtable in Quality of Life and Intellectual Disability (an Internal Association for the Scientific Study of Intellectual Disabilities special interest research group) in Vancouver, Canada, one mother stated, "Our family is necessary for our son or daughter with disability, as we influence their quality of life. But the opposite is [also] true—our child and their disability affects our family's quality of life." Frequently, the child with a disability is a primary focus of family activities, particularly the mother's resources (Brown & Renwick, 1998; Todd et al., 2004). This can frequently result in stresses and strains for all members of the family. This suggests that family quality of life needs to be taken into account when providing support in order to enhance family well-being and thus the family's ability to support the individual with the disability.

To enhance family well-being effectively, it is necessary for disability personnel to have a clear understanding of a family's needs and to be in a position to deploy funds and provide resources, including counseling and practical support, to foster family capacity. Families' needs have been made abundantly clear in numerous accounts (e.g., see Brown, 2000). Many require a skilled frontline person with whom they can discuss ideas, funds need to be at least partially controlled by family members, and—if families are asked to take the main responsibility for individuals with disabilities—it is necessary for agencies to use financial and personnel resources to support families as whole. This is particularly important in single-parent families and families facing multiple disabilities or poverty. Reports of family quality-of-life research from various countries underscore these issues. For example, many studies using the Brown, Neikrug, and Brown (2000) Family Quality of Life Survey provided such evidence at the 2005 Roundtable in Quality of Life and Intellectual Disability (e.g., Brown, Shearer, McAdam-Crisp, & Wang—Australia and Canada; Kumja—South Korea; and Iarocci and Wang—Taiwan; reasonably comparable data were presented from Poston and from Turnbull—both from the United States).

The application of resources in ways that meet the family's perceived needs and enhance family well-being will require greater individualization of services and supports. This may seem to add to the role of disability personnel considerably in the short term, but in the longer term, it may reduce family stresses and benefit family adaptation, thereby leading to a better life for both people with disabilities and their families.

Disability Personnel in Urban and Rural Areas

Many disability personnel work in urban areas where the number of needs of the people they support, and the number and types of services and resources that these people need, is very broad. Others work in isolated conditions, where they essentially have to carry out all needed work themselves. The abbreviated commentary shown in Display 27.5—used with permission of Disability, South Australia (David Caudrey, DHS Services Office, Department for Families and Communities), and originally recorded in the Brown report (2000, pp. 7–8)—describes aspects of life for a rural field coordinator of resources and support for people with diverse disabilities.

Disability Personnel as Advocates for Policy Change

Disability personnel have always had—and continue to have—important roles in informing policy makers of needed changes and in holding them accountable to the decisions that are made. This need appears to be more important now than ever, because of the increasing number of roles of disability personnel and the growing complexity of systems of services and supports. There is a need to recognize which services are not available, not accessible, or not appropriate to the specific needs of people with disabilities and their families and then to make this known. Such vigilance needs to be carried out with knowledge of individuals' rights and entitlements (see Chapters 5 and 6). The overall goal of this aspect of the role of disability personnel is to ensure that policy makers are able to set a context in which effective supports are possible and, as a consequence, that those with intellectual and developmental disabilities are able to lead the best life possible.

Display 27.5

Experiences of a rural frontline field coordinator

My front line experience was wonderful and I enjoyed it. The experience with clients was amazing. However, the workload was enormous, and I did not feel qualified to deal with some of the situations. I had a lot of clients with intellectual disabilities who had high needs, and in some families the parents were aging. I had a few clients who were very difficult. I had to deal with the issues concerning a woman who committed suicide and another person who gave up eating because she did not wish to continue living. I was sometimes phoned late at night with serious issues and I was 75 kilometers away. I found it all very interesting, but there were just too many crises.

The number of crises seemed to reduce somewhat over time, although crisis relief does not make problems go away. The families still had to face enormous stress and challenge, and many of the families were exhausted.

I found the training I had was extremely important. I had to make a lot of use of it, but I also learned a lot, particularly from my clients. I have now left my position, but understand from the person who has taken over from me that work is still hectic, although the crisis situations are not as numerous. In rural areas, disability personnel do not go to the city very often, and they really have to rely on their own resources. They work together supporting one another and helping one another with particular needs that arise.

Overall, there are too many crises. The work load is enormous. Respite opportunities have improved and they are wonderful, but they are not the whole answer.

Source: This abbreviated commentary is reproduced with permission of Disability Family Services, South Australia, originally recorded in full in the Brown Report (Brown, 2000, pp. 7–8).

EDUCATION AND TRAINING OF DISABILITY PERSONNEL

The changing needs of individuals with intellectual and multiple disabilities means that diverse, and sometimes complex, supports are required. To help provide these, many disability personnel require a sound professional knowledge of disability, an understanding of the ways in which the needs of people with disabilities are changing, familiarity with the available and needed resources associated with these changes, and a practical knowledge of "what to do" that is learned in training and on the job. Education at a higher educational institution, blended with ongoing training and supervised experience, provides this knowledge. It is important to note that although the chapter refers to examples in the United States, numerous universities and colleges outside of the United States also offer similar courses (see the resources in Appendix B at the end of the book for more information).

Higher Education

Some disability personnel have higher education that relates directly to their field. Throughout the United

States and elsewhere, disability personnel can take specific training through community colleges and universities, which provide 1- and 2-year certificates and diplomas or 3- or 4-year degrees. Many countries (e.g., Australia, Canada, Israel, Singapore, the United Kingdom) have seen increases in the number of people taking diplomas and degrees in disability studies. Some countries that do not have programs of study available in their higher educational institutions send their disability personnel to other countries for such schooling. In Appendix B at the end of the book, some key international resources are noted from which prospective students and professionals can gain information about courses of study.

Other disability professionals may have received higher education from a variety of disciplines, including medicine, sociology, psychology, social work, nursing, education, physiotherapy, occupational therapy, audiology, counseling, and psychotherapy. Having received a first degree or diploma in these fields, however, does not guarantee expertise for the field of intellectual disabilities. In one Australian study (Brown, 2000), the frontline personnel (options coordinators who worked in all areas of disability and were responsible for providing support and integrating services for the individual with a disability) had among them more than 50 different qualifications. In these cases, additional training in intellectual and developmental disability is required.

Regarding personnel recruitment, there is not always coordination between organizations that provide support to people with disabilities and universities and colleges that prepare people for such careers. As a consequence, there are often not enough frontline workers available for service agencies to employ, and incentives to specialize in intellectual and developmental disability are not always provided to potential professionals (e.g., physicians, dentists, lawyers, psychotherapists) who might develop special knowledge and training. Challenges for the field include developing effective methods for engaging institutions of higher learning in planning for the future needs of people with disabilities and engaging a variety of professions in helping to train new specialists who will be able to meet the needs.

Ongoing Training

There is a strong need for ongoing training of disability personnel because of the wide variation in education, the need for broad-based education to meet new developments in the disabilities field, and the increase in individualized and community-based supports and services. There is no guarantee, even in technologically advanced countries with well-developed services, that new entrants to the field will have special knowledge about disabilities. There is also no guarantee that disability personnel who already work in the field will receive ongoing training, although it is needed. The needs of disability personnel, whatever they are, need to be recognized by those who employ them (see Display 27.6).

There are many ways to provide and receive ongoing training. Some of these are formal (e.g., courses that earn credits) and others are less formal. Enrichment courses and workshops of various types are run by service agencies or disability consultants. Numerous national and international conferences, usually sponsored by professional organizations, are held each year. Many of these provide those attending with official letters of attendance, which may be recognized as training credits. Certificate and degree-level part-time programs are available at many local colleges and universities. Some of these are available as extension or electronic courses, and video-communication workshops have become increasingly used since the 1990s. In particular, distance and distributed education is providing opportunities at all levels from interest courses in disabilities through undergraduate and graduate programs. A number of these courses are on line and can be taken through the Internet. An advantage of these courses is that they can involve students from a variety of regions of the world and from a variety of academic backgrounds, who can share their experiences and ideas across disciplines and countries. There are many examples of these in a variety of countries, but two examples follow:

- The College of Direct Support, in collaboration with the University of Minnesota's Research and

Display 27.6

Employers need to understand skills and knowledge of disability personnel

It is essential that employers are well aware of the skill and knowledge requirements for frontline positions. This may seem obvious, but my experience shows that directors of services may have little knowledge or understanding of the demands and skills required of individual disability personnel at the frontline level. For example, I have met directors of services who had little idea of the stresses and challenges faced by such personnel, although other directors recognize this gap in knowledge and made it their job to track and work alongside frontline personnel on a daily basis for a period of time to gain a practical knowledge of the challenges involved.

Training Center on Community Living and the Sertoma Center's My Life Foundation, provides frontline direct support professionals with very practical courses.
- The University of Reno at Nevada has a master's degree program in applied behavioral intervention, which provides education in early intervention for young children with severe autism.

Typically, such courses provide a clear understanding of the role of disability personnel. They are embedded in a clearly stated ethical paradigm and cover a wide range of practical issues such as home care, signs of health and illness, and abuse and neglect. They usually also stress the need for professional standards, effective practice, and advocacy.

Another means of providing ongoing training is through texts and journals, which are widely available in university and college libraries and from publishers that specialize in disability, such as the publisher of this book. Since approximately the early 1990s, various societies for intellectual disabilities, some of which focus on a disability type, also provide formal training packages. For example, in the United Kingdom, the Down Syndrome Educational Trust continues to prepare books for professionals and parents. These books are 25–60 pages in length and address state-of-the-art practice, opportunities and experiences, and the application of research to practice. (For information on these materials, see Down Syndrome Issues and Information Series [birth through 16 years] and Adult Living Series [17 years and older], both available at http://www.downsed.org.) Other groups provide detailed information on line and also include some published articles that can be downloaded from their web sites.

In-service training is often provided by service organizations, especially for their own employees, volunteers, and family members of people they support. These may take many forms, such as workshops, visits, lectures, various presentations, specific skill learning, or involvement in day-to-day work. In-service training often is not mandatory or related to accreditation for practice, but it is sometimes required by service organizations to improve the skill and knowledge levels of disability personnel.

Less formally, most workplaces provide computers with Internet access for looking up needed information. The Internet contains a wealth of information about a variety of disability-related topics (see Appendix B for some examples that disability personnel can readily obtain). In fact, one of the simplest, most cost-effective methods of training is to make computers available and to provide workshops on how to retrieve information from the Internet. However, sites vary in standard, accuracy, and breadth of information.

Supervised Experience

As the preceding sections demonstrated, professional training needs to take place at different levels and at different times. Furthermore, because of ongoing changes in the field of intellectual and developmental disabilities, the need for ongoing training of disability personnel never ceases. Yet, neither of these can substitute for on-the-job experience. All disability personnel, no matter what their formal education and ongoing training, grow enormously in their professional capacity by learning on the job. This is especially the case when practical work is supervised in a way that focuses on building the skills and knowledge of disability personnel. The importance of learning the numerous tricks of the trade cannot be overstated. The following areas of practical learning are among the most important for working with people who have intellectual and developmental disabilities:

- Understanding of current trends and philosophies in disability, as well as ability to apply these to relationships involving people with disabilities
- Knowledge about the causes and characteristics of disabilities
- Facility in communicating effectively with people with disabilities
- Familiarity with resources and other sources of support (professional and nonprofessional)
- Ability to form effective liaisons with family members
- Expertise in managing relationships with people with disabilities in ways that respect their choices and points of view
- Capacity to foster, and work within, a multidisciplinary team

For students who are required to gain practical experience as part of their coursework, and for volunteers who do practical work for personal development, it is essential to select a disability organization that supports their training needs well. Characteristics of such organizations are that they

- Allocate sufficient time to pass on information
- Provide meaningful opportunities to develop skills and knowledge
- Represent current thinking and philosophy, without being overly dogmatic
- Respect people with disabilities and allow for their reasonable self-determination
- Demonstrate numerous practical ways of supporting people with disabilities
- Have the capacity to demonstrate effective programs
- Illustrate, through their practices, professional values and ethics

Challenges for Education and Training

Providing education and training to current and future disability personnel is not without challenges. Five critical challenges are outlined next.

1. *How should disability personnel be educated and trained?* There is a wide variety of educational programs for students and ongoing training courses for professionals. Yet, in many countries, poor funding levels relative to other segments of society result in shortages of both frontline practitioners and other disability professionals who have specific training, at the very time when it is becoming all the more important to have well-trained practitioners. In many regions, the response to this need has been to hire frontline practitioners who have little formal training. The dilemma for service provider organizations is whether to provide personnel who do not have as much training as desired to meet their need for support, or to provide too few trained personnel who cannot meet all the support needs of the people with disabilities.

2. *What is the best way to provide support?* Notwithstanding the problems associated with providing trained disability personnel, approaches to and beliefs about services differ among various countries, even in economically advanced communities. Each engages in innovation and change with increased sophistication and does so in the context of ongoing changes to local health, education, and other services affecting each country's general population. There has not been a consensus on the best ways to provide support, especially vis-à-vis other services.

3. *What is the relationship between knowledge and effective support?* Even if disability personnel are trained adequately, having knowledge of disability does not guarantee effective support or necessary delivery of services. Perhaps the key is to recognize that increased understanding has forced the field to view disabilities in a complex of interacting and changing dynamics, and it is this knowledge—put into practice by frontline professionals and recognized and supported by policy makers—that can ensure effective and comprehensive delivery of optimum services. Thus, the word *multidisciplinary* necessarily takes on wider meaning. These very changes tend to increase the variability of service delivery and support, not only between countries but also within countries. It is necessary to make support services more versatile and wider reaching.

4. *What is the role of disability personnel and other professionals in advocacy?* Some people have questioned whether professionals can be advocates, given that they work for particular organizations and represent specific knowledge and views (Gray & Jackson, 2001). The defense counsel in a trial relating to sterilization of people with intellectual disabilities asked the chapter author if he was essentially an advocate (rather than an unbiased professional). The author's reply was that all effective professionals needed to be advocates for their clients. The important point is not to assume that what one knows and practices is necessarily the best that can be provided. Advocates who represent the views of a client need to be respected whether or not they come from a professional base. All knowledge and concern should emerge from listening respectively to advocates' ideas. However, it is equally essential to recognize that one is serving the individual, the family, or one's service agency. There are occasions where one has to decide where loyalties and interests lie. In such circumstances, it may be necessary to ensure that there are others who represent the views and concerns of interested parties who have a legitimate stake in proceedings. Basic knowledge about advocacy procedures is therefore critical (see Gray & Jackson, 2001).

5. *How can those in the field plan adequately for the future?* Any forecast for service development must recognize ongoing changes in the field of intellectual and developmental disability and predict those that are likely to occur in the future. It is the lack of forward planning that causes concern and worry in many communities—for example, as older parents wonder what will happen to their children with intellectual disabilities (see Jokinen & Brown, 2005). This is a challenge for policy and service development, but the lack of adequately trained frontline personnel puts pressure on the disability system as well as on families, which then taxes the resources of the practitioners who are currently involved.

PHILOSOPHY AND VALUES OF DISABILITY PERSONNEL

A critical aspect of working in the field of disabilities is the development of each employee's professional values. These underlie that nature of the relationships that disability personnel have with individuals with disabilities; in turn, they determine the nature of the work that is done. Professional philosophy changes somewhat over time, but it needs to be laid on solid value foundations that should be discussed during education and training and when disability personnel are interviewed for potential employment. Professional values are closely tied to ethics and professional judgment; thus, in the discussion that follows, readers will note a definite overlap.

Vignettes of Challenging Situations

A clear professional value system is especially important when disability personnel are up against crises or find situations that challenge their own personal values and philosophy (Brown, 1997). The following five vignettes, taken from the work of disability personnel, illustrate some of the issues and concerns personnel face involving their professional values (see Brown & Brown, 2003, for additional examples). These vignettes demonstrate that there are not always simple answers; readers are invited to think what they might do in each of the cases described and to discuss their ideas with colleagues or classmates. Sometimes individual client choices conflict with service rules and regulations. Other times, a professional's response may not support current laws and policies, although it may support strongly held personal views.

Often, disability personnel face the dilemmas described when they work in relative isolation, and they need to make the best judgments possible with little direct supervision. The foundation for making such judgments should be the development of an effective professional values system and professional philosophy, with clear demarcation between professional and private views. This may involve many parties—disability personnel; other professionals; people with disabilities; and advocates, including, as necessary, the public advocate (a formal, paid position within a state or province). In addition, policy makers and those who develop the regulations and rules that guide services must be included. For this reason, ongoing training in professional values and ethics needs to be part of the work of all disability personnel, particularly frontline practitioners.

Vicky and Dan Vicky was a support worker in a center-based day program that encouraged people to obtain work in the community. One person she supported, Dan, wanted to get what he described as "a real man's job." He was 25 years old and had sound social skills. Dan's mother made it clear that she did not wish Dan to be placed in employment. She said that she did not think he could hold down a job and that if he had a full-time job, he would lose his disability allowance. If he failed at work, he would then have to start applying for disability allowance all over again. Vicky believed that Dan had a right to choose but was not sure how to deal with his mother's forceful views.

The questions arising from this story are numerous. Where do Vicky's loyalties lie? Should she accept the mother's views or Dan's wishes? Dan is an adult, and according to legislation in the country in which Dan lives, his mother does not have legal responsibility for him. She has a mother's interests and concern and fears that if things go wrong, she may be left to deal with the resulting financial situation. Now imagine that the manager of the day program says the agency must support the mother at all costs, as the family has given a major donation to the center. What should Vicky do?

Arthur and George Arthur is a community support worker. He has strong religious views about marriage and the need for a wedding before people live together. A young man he supports, George, wants to live with his girlfriend, who also has a disability. George has requested help from Arthur to help to bring this about, as he knows cooperation will be needed between the two agencies from which he and his girlfriend get support. Arthur feels, on religious grounds, that he cannot agree with this partnership.

Arthur has various options. He could decline to assist George, discuss his situation and beliefs with George, consult his manager, or request another support worker to take over. What should Arthur do in this situation?

Ann and Eva Eva, a young woman with an intellectual disability, is pregnant. Ann, a doctor at a medical clinic, does not tell Eva that her unborn child has Down syndrome. Ann believes Eva would request an abortion. Ann is strongly opposed to abortion, which she believes is highly immoral. She wishes to protect Eva from facing a decision involving abortion.

The issues identified in this story, and similar issues, raise the potential difference between personal and professional value systems and personal and professional philosophy. Ann may be breaking national or regional laws or policies but believes that her religious views should take precedence. In other countries or regions, Ann may not be breaking laws or policies and may, in fact, be supporting them. Nonetheless, the question of the right to withhold information is still problematic. The question is how disability personnel can comfortably separate their personal and professional philosophy and value systems, should there be a conflict between the two.

Sometimes, the personal views of a professional may be consistent with those of an organization and the individual with a disability. For example, if Eva herself had strong views against abortion and the organization where she lived and was supported held similar values, everyone's views may well have been consistent. Thus, there would be no dilemma, although withholding information would at least remain a concern on both social and behavioral grounds Suppose, however, that despite prevailing beliefs, Eva did not want to continue the pregnancy. Whose views should prevail?

Disability personnel need to separate personal and professional value systems, and this often takes place on the job. Such separation is becoming even more challenging because field workers do not always have other professionals working closely with them who understand, or are knowledgeable about, the exact circumstances. This is another reason why new personnel need internship periods under supervision of professionals, as these senior and more experienced colleagues can offer modeling.

Two other issues presented by this vignette are 1) the potential for development of self-image through decision making and exercising personal choice based on impartial information and 2) the need for independent advocacy. Apparently, Ann did not consider the possibility of asking for outside assistance through an advocate. In turn, Eva loses an opportunity to learn from her experience, understand that actions have consequences, and further develop her problem-solving skills. How might Ann have handled this situation differently? Remember to consider that people with intellectual and developmental disabilities have different and various skill levels for making and following through on their own decisions.

John and Tyler John has a severe physical disability and a mild intellectual disability. He does not want to work and prefers to wander the streets downtown in his city. He often leaves his group home at night, and in the past has become involved with drugs through the people he meets on the street, where he sometimes sleeps. There have been suggestions that he has been asked to carry drugs, and police have warned him on several occasions. John says it is his right to choose how he lives. The agency says that for John to stay in the group home where he lives, he must abide by the group home rules relating to permission to sleep away from the home and to keep within the law. Yet, John's care worker, Tyler, believes John has the right to choose for himself.

In this situation, John's views and needs, society's requirements, and agency requirements are in conflict. Yet, Tyler is left to try to sort out the conflict. Clearly, Tyler has his own point of view, but he has to answer to other people and agencies. What are Tyler's options? How much time will he have to spend resolving the conflict rather than simply helping John? The answers to such questions are neither simple nor clear at first glance.

Staff Attending a Workshop At a workshop on sexual and personal development of people with intellectual disability, disability personnel were provided with examples of employment experiences and jobs for people with intellectual disabilities. They were also provided with examples of personal activities in relation to partnership and marriage. Disability personnel appeared able to accept people with disabilities working in wide range of skilled and unskilled jobs. When it came to personal and sexual matters, though, they sometimes made remarks such as, "I would not want my son or daughter doing that."

Why did the staff accept employment options for people with intellectual disabilities but not options for family and sexual development? One explanation is that because these disability personnel were well trained in employment activities, they used a professional base for their judgment. When it came to more personal activities, they referred to a personal base because they lacked professional-level experience and knowledge in this area. Emotional and personal experience dominated their thinking.

There is also a possibility that even disability personnel hold long-held prejudices about what people with disabilities should and should not do. Moreover, there are parallel issues that exist in many societies, such as sterilization of people with disabilities, ease of obtaining an abortion, and euthanasia for people with disabilities. New issues are also on the horizon, such as the impact of genetic engineering and the right to give birth to individuals with disabilities. There are other issues that are usually more the day-to-day concerns of advocates, such as the judicial court rulings in relation to doubtful confessions from individuals with intellectual disabilities who are accused of crimes. Thinking more broadly, many of the issues make it necessary to reevaluate the definition of disability and how an ever-changing society should respond to it (see Brown & Brown, 2003).

Self-Analysis of Personal and Professional Values

The preceding vignettes illustrate several instances in which ethical dilemmas arise for disability personnel. It is clearly important that personal and professional value systems must be in place for making judgments in such cases. Yet, it is also clear that personal and professional value systems do not always fit together. It is helpful for disability personnel to undertake self-analysis of their personal and professional views and to determine strategies to follow when there is a conflict or it is not a perfect match. Considering the topics presented in Table 27.2 is one method of undertaking such self-analysis to operationalize (put into practice) and sort these values.

Characteristics of Disability Personnel Who Have Effective Values Systems

Professional values are put into practice through the behavior of disability personnel. Putting such values into practice is easier for some people than it is for others because of their personal and professional characteristics. Disability service organizations might look for favorable characteristics as criteria in hiring new employees. Perhaps more important, however, they should provide ongoing training to help employees develop the characteristics of effective disability personnel.

Table 27.2. Operationalizing and sorting values and philosophy

How do you feel and think—as 1) a private citizen and 2) a professional—in relation to the following:
People with intellectual disabilities in general
The right of people with any disability to be included in society
Discrimination against people with disabilities
Euthanasia for people who are getting very old and who have intellectual disability
Sterilizing a person with an intellectual disability, without his or her consent, 1) when there is no previous aberrant sexual behavior and 2) when there is a record of previous and serious aberrant sexual behavior
Working with people who have intellectual disabilities
The language used to describe persons with disabilities
Being in the company of an individual with profound physical and intellectual disabilities at a party
Having a person with a disability as a friend
Having a person with a disability as a relative
Having your child in a class with someone who has a severe intellectual disability
Having your child in a class with someone who has both an emotional and intellectual disability
Having an adolescent or adult child becoming serious about a partnership with someone who has a disability
Having an adult child with or without an intellectual disability using an escort service

The personal characteristics that are frequently considered helpful, if not necessary, include (Brown & Brown, 2003, p. 214):

- Ability to differentiate personal values and needs from client values and needs
- Creativity
- Emotional energy to change the environment
- Flexibility
- Innovation
- Patience
- Sense of humor
- Stamina
- Strong and positive values related to people in need
- Understanding of own values, attitudes, and beliefs
- Warm and supportive personality

The professional characteristics that are typically considered important include the ability to do the following (Brown & Brown, 2003, pp. 214–215):

- Accept a variety of lifestyles and different options
- Advocate effectively for those they support
- Assess their own professional and personal strengths and abilities and determine when they need to seek outside assistance
- Assume some risks
- Discuss challenges and problems impartially
- Feel comfortable letting others, especially people with disabilities, assume control
- Make decisions regarding difficult ethical issues
- Separate personal choice (i.e., the choices they would make for themselves or within their family) from the choices made by the people they support
- Solve problems in a constructive way
- Work well as a member of a team

Need for Sound Professional Skills

Personal and professional values cannot be operationalized effectively unless an individual has a sound knowledge base and sound professional skills to put the values into place. Table 27.3 outlines some of these knowledge

Table 27.3. Knowledge and skills base

Knowledge base includes, but is not limited to
Clinical knowledge of disabilities
Knowledge about family systems, dynamics, and issues
Knowledge about the development of services
Knowledge of community and environmental factors that contribute to disabling conditions
Knowledge of community services and supports available
Knowledge of language development and common problems associated with language and speech
Knowledge of learning principles
Knowledge of legislation related to disability
Knowledge of life-span development, including early life, transitions, and aging
Knowledge of multicultural concerns
Knowledge of quality-of-life principles
Knowledge of social and emotional development
Knowledge of the main approaches to treatment and intervention
Understanding of the long-term nature of working with people with disabilities
Skills that relate to professional practice strategies include
Ability to judge issues for the best results
Appropriate interviewing skills
Basic knowledge and understanding of policy and management processes
Effective counseling skills based on eclectic counseling theory and practice
Effective interpersonal communication and collaboration skills
Effective observation skills
Effective verbal and writing skills
Effective teaching strategies
Effective time-management skills
Organizational and coordination skills
Skills in understanding the perspective of others
Skills that are supplementary, and in some situations critical, include
Knowledge about local community access and challenges
Knowledge about when to make referrals and suggest alternative methods
Knowledge of possibilities associated with adaptive and technical aids
Specialized knowledge in specific disability areas

From Brown, I., & Brown, R.I. (2003). *Quality of life and disability: An approach for community practitioners* (pp. 212–213). London: Jessica Kingsley Publishers.

and skill requirements; it should be recognized that new knowledge constantly emerges and expands the list. Such skills are often incorporated in formal education courses and into both formal and informal training, although many may need to be expanded.

The disability field is evolving, and it seems likely that both knowledge about disabilities and the ways of effectively supporting people with disabilities will continue to expand quickly. Disability personnel need not only to develop sound professional skills but also to recognize that such skills need to be upgraded continuously. This is important for policy makers, directors of services, professionals who only do part of their work with people who have disabilities, and many others. Yet, it is most important for frontline disability personnel who daily support people with disabilities, for their roles hold an immense amount of influence—and thus responsibility—at the personal level.

SUMMARY

People who work in the field of intellectual and developmental disabilities do a wide variety of work; some directly support people with disabilities while others are in professions that support people with disabilities as part of their work. This chapter collectively refers to such people as *disability personnel.* Of all disability personnel, frontline practitioners have an especially important role, because they work most closely with people who have disabilities.

The work of disability personnel has become more complex since approximately the 1990s, because knowledge of disability is expanding at a fast rate and because the approach to services and supports has changed a great deal. For these and other reasons, formal education, ongoing training, and on-the-job training are all important. Disability personnel may have formal education in any one of numerous disciplines; thus, specific disability training is usually required for new employees.

When carrying out their work, disability personnel encounter a number of challenges, which they often have to face and solve on their own or with little direct supervision. To help guide disability personnel in making wise judgments, professional values and ethics should be part of their education and ongoing training. Clear guidelines for what to do in cases where professional values and personal values conflict, or when professional values and employer policies conflict, need to be in place for disability personnel to function effectively. Professional values are manifested through particular characteristics, which disability service organizations might look for when hiring employees and might provide training for to develop desired skills in existing employees.

FOR FURTHER THOUGHT AND DISCUSSION

1. Critically examine your personal values about people with disabilities, then examine how they might contrast or support your developing professional values and philosophy.
2. Examine your knowledge base and consider what additional knowledge and skills you require to become effective within the disability services field. List the courses and specific training that you require, and see which colleges and universities best respond to your perceived needs.
3. Given your knowledge and experience, consider how you will ensure you maintain up-to-date knowledge and expertise in your chosen field?
4. What strategies and tactics do you need to develop to act as a change agent, encouraging the services with which you have contact to develop and take on board new ideas and systems?
5. Some people do not believe that restricted financial resources alone are the major barriers to advances in support for people with disabilities. Consider which issues are most important when funding is limited. What strategies could be used to advance support for people with disabilities when funding is limited?

REFERENCES

Bigby, C. (2004). *Ageing with a lifelong disability: A guide to practice, program and policy issues for human services professionals.* London: Jessica Kingsley Publishers.

Brown, I., & Brown, R.I. (2003). *Quality of life and disability: An approach for community practitioners.* London: Jessica Kingsley Publishers.

Brown, I., Neikrug, S., & Brown, R.I. (2000). *Family Quality of Life Survey.* Toronto: University of Toronto, Faculty of Social Work.

Brown, I., & Renwick, R. (1998). *The Family Quality of Life Project.* Report to Developmental Services Branch, Ontario Ministry of Community and Social Services. Toronto: University of Toronto, Faculty of Social Work.

Brown, R.I. (Ed.). (1997). Quality of life and professional education. In Roy I. Brown (Ed.), *Quality of life for people with disabilities* (pp. 310–326). Cheltenham, United Kingdom: Stanley Thornes.

Brown, R.I. (2000). *Evaluation of options co-ordination: Report to the Minister for Disability Services from the Committee on the Evaluation of Quality Services for People with Disabilities.* South Australia, Australia: Adelaide.

Brown, R.I. (2004). *Life for adults with Down syndrome: An overview.* In R.I. Brown (Series Ed.), Down Syndrome Issues and Information (DSii) Adult Living series. Portsmouth, United Kingdom: Down Syndrome Educational Trust.

Crompton, M., & Jackson, R. (2004). Spiritual well-being of adults with Down syndrome. *Adult Series: Down Syndrome issues and information.* Portsmouth, United Kingdom: Down Syndrome Educational Trust.

Emerson, E., Robertson, J., & Wood, J. (2005). Emotional and behavioural needs of children and adolescents with intellectual disabilities in an urban conurbation. *Journal of Intellectual Disability Research, 49,* 16–24.

Fidler, G.S., & Velde, B.P. (1999). *Activities: Reality and symbol.* Thorofare, NJ: Slack.

Fudge Shormans, A., & Brown, I. (2002). An investigation into the characteristics of the maltreatment of children with developmental disabilities and the alleged perpetrators of this maltreatment. *Journal on Developmental Disabilities, 9*(1), 1–19.

Gray, B., & Jackson, R. (2001). *Advocacy and intellectual disability.* London: Jessica Kingsley Publishers.

James, T.N., & Brown, R.I. (1993). Prader-Willi syndrome: Quality of life issues in home, school and community. *Australia and New Zealand Journal of Developmental Disabilities, 18*(4), 253–260.

Janicki, M.T., & Ansello, E.F. (Eds.). (2000). *Community supports for aging adults with lifelong disabilities.* Baltimore: Paul H. Brookes Publishing Co.

Jokinen, N., & Brown, R.I. (2005). Family quality of life from the perspective of older parents. *Journal of Intellectual Disability Research, 49*(10), 789–793.

Keith, K.D., & Schalock, R L. (2000). *Cross cultural perspectives on quality of life.* Washington, DC: American Association on Mental Retardation.

McConkey, R., O'Toole, B., & Mariga, L. (1999). Educating teachers in developing countries about disabilities. *Exceptionality Education Canada, 9*(1&2), 15–38.

Prasher, V.P., & Janicki, M.P. (2002). *Physical health of adults with intellectual disabilities.* Oxford, United Kingdom: Blackwell Publishing.

Roundtable in Quality of Life and Intellectual Disability. (2005, April). *IASSID-SIRG roundtable on quality of life.* Vancouver, BC, Canada.

Schalock, R.L., Brown, I., Brown, R.I., et al. (2002). Quality of life: Its conceptualisation, measurement and application. A consensus document. *Mental Retardation, 40,* 457–470.

Timmons, V. (1999). Quality of life of teenagers from Mi'kmaq descent. *Exceptionality Education Canada, 9*(1&2), 5–14.

Todd, S., Young, P., Shearn, J., et al. (2004). Family quality of life in Wales. In A. Turnbull, I. Brown, & H.R. Turnbull (Eds.), *Families and people with mental retardation and quality of life: International perspectives* (pp. 101–147). Washington, DC: American Association on Mental Retardation.

Turnbull, A., Brown, I., & Turnbull, H.R. (2004). *Families and people with mental retardation: International perspectives.* Washington, DC: American Association on Mental Retardation.

Walsh, P.N., & Heller, T. (2002). *Health of women with intellectual disabilities.* Oxford, United Kingdom: Blackwell Publishing.

Warren, B. (1988). *Disability and social performance: Using drama to achieve successful 'acts of being.'* Cambridge, MA: Brookline Books.

Wolfensberger, W. (1972). *Normalization: The principle of normalization in human services.* Toronto: National Institute on Mental Retardation.

World Health Organization. (1997). *ICIDH-2: International Classification of Impairments, Activities, and Participation: A manual of dimensions of disablement and functioning.* Geneva: Author.

IV

Developmental Disabilities Through the Life Span

28

Prenatal and Early Life

KAROLINA MACHALEK, MAIRE PERCY, AND IVAN BROWN

WHAT YOU WILL LEARN ABOUT IN THIS CHAPTER

- Issues in prenatal development
- Issues in early life
- Issues for parents

Three things are crucial to a child's development: health of the parents prior to conception, the neonatal environment, and the first 3 years of the child's life. The purposes of this chapter are to provide an introduction to issues relevant to prenatal and early life and to highlight issues important for parents and families. The information in this chapter is for educational purposes only, and readers should consult professionals for guidance with health issues.

ISSUES IN PRENATAL DEVELOPMENT

Prenatal development issues range from basic health to technology issues. These topics are explored in detail next.

Preconceptual and Prenatal Health

The fetus is very vulnerable to interference in development. Both the parental preconceptual and maternal prenatal nutritional status are thought to be key factors for typical development, as is the diet of the mother during pregnancy. On average, a pregnant woman needs approximately 300 calories per day more than she did prior to pregnancy to support the growth of her fetus and to maintain her own body (International Food Information Council Foundation & March of Dimes, 2003). An enormous variety of factors can result in intellectual or developmental disabilities or low birth weight, which is a risk factor for intellectual and developmental disabilities. Many of these factors are discussed in Chapters 7 and 9 and include the following:

Rivka Birkan and Michael Fung provided some technical information for this chapter; Victoria Duda provided helpful comments. Their contributions are gratefully acknowledged.

- Genetic and environmental factors
- Blood type incompatibility
- Metabolic and/or endocrine disorders in the mother, including hypothyroidism and diabetes
- Prematurity for any reason, including multiple gestation, HIV infection, and other infections such as malaria
- Maternal alcohol or other substance abuse
- Lead or mercury poisoning
- Smoking and indoor air pollution
- Pediatric traumatic brain injury

Fetuses with abnormalities constitute as many as 30% of all pregnancies, but most of these are lost as the result of natural miscarriage. Problems with a mother's immune system may interfere with natural miscarriage and promote the carrying of a fetus with a serious abnormality to term (Ksouri et al., 2003). Standard early and continuous measures can be taken to prevent some abnormalities. In North America, early care before pregnancy includes eating a well-balanced diet and ensuring adequate intake of iron and folic acid, in particular. Table 28.1 outlines the vitamins and minerals whose proper intake is especially important for a healthy pregnancy. This table is by no means exclusive, and it does not include all vitamins and minerals that are important for a well-balanced diet. A vitamins and minerals guide, such as the one by Waasdorp, Winland Brown, and Dunphy (2001), should be consulted for a complete list of vitamins and minerals and their natural sources. In addition, a medical professional or nutritionist should be consulted to ensure proper nutrient intake during pregnancy.

It should be pointed out that different ethnic groups have unique requirements and tolerances for essential nutrients and different protective or adverse responses to foods and dietary substances (Solomons, 2003). For example, people who live in malarial regions actually are protected against malarial infection by having low levels of body iron (Moalem, Weinberg, & Percy, 2004; Oppenheimer, 2001). Nevertheless, during pregnancy, proper and sufficient nutrition should be maintained, with adequate intake of iron and folate being particularly important (Moore & Davies, 2005). (For more information, see the section on nutrition in

Table 28.1. Vitamins and minerals important for a healthy pregnancy

Vitamin or mineral and RDA	Importance	Natural sources
Folic acid RDA: 0.2 mg for children 0.4 mg for adults 0.6 mg for pregnant women	Synthesis of the nucleic acids adenine and thymine; use of the essential amino acid methionine; prevention of elevated levels of the amino acid homocysteine; reduction of risk of birth defects such as neural tube defects, spina bifida, and anencephaly	Fortified cereals, whole wheat breads, dark green vegetables, navy beans, kidney beans, lentils, liver, milk, cheese, beef, chicken, pork, tuna, mushrooms, oranges, barley, brown rice
Iodine RDA: 90 mcg for children 150 mcg for adults 220 mcg for pregnant women	Production of thyroxine, which helps regulate blood cell production, body temperature, growth production, metabolic rate, and nerve and muscle function; prevention of goiter; prevention of iodine deficiency, which causes miscarriages and stillbirths and retards fetal growth and brain development	Bread, iodized salt, lobster, marine fish, milk, oysters (cooked), shrimp, seaweed
Iron RDA: 10 mg for children 18 mg for women 30 mg for pregnant women 10 mg for women age 50 years and older 11 mg for men	Production of hemoglobin and function of red blood cells; function of the immune system; prevention of anemia; prevention of iron deficiency during pregnancy, which contributes to maternal and perinatal mortality	Iron-fortified cereals, green leafy vegetables, beef, soybeans, eggs, fish, liver, whole grains, nuts, avocados, beets, peaches, lentils, raisins, sesame seeds, baked potatoes, clams, pumpkin seeds
Vitamin A RDA: 500 mcg for children 700 mcg for women 900 mcg for men 100,000 mcg is toxic	Proper function of the immune system; prevention of Vitamin A deficiency, which causes blindness in children and night blindness in pregnant women	Fish liver oils, liver, egg yolks, butter, cream, carrots, pumpkin, yams, cantaloupe, mangoes, spinach, tuna, turnip greens, beet greens

Sources: Beers & Berkow (2005); Mitchell (2005); National Institutes of Health (2004); Sethi and Kapil (2004); and Waasdorp et al. (2001).
Key: mcg = microgram; mg = milligram; RDA = recommended dietary allowance.

Chapter 9 and Ramakrishnan, 2004.) Additional preventive measures include avoiding alcohol, cigarettes, and illicit drugs; avoiding X-rays, hot tubs, and saunas, all of which may predispose to neural tube defects as well as infection; limiting caffeine intake; and exercising judiciously (e.g., limiting exercise to the low-impact type), avoiding exercise that might result in trauma to the abdomen or to the elevation of body temperature (ACOG Committee on Obstetric Practice, 2002; Larsson & Lindqvist, 2005; Chapter 9).

Issues for Professionals

Professionals involved in supporting parents through a pregnancy should promote healthy nutrition and a healthy lifestyle, and the avoidance of alcohol and other abusive substances that may have teratogenic effects (see Chapter 9). They should also arrange for regular visits to check fetal and maternal health and to provide information about maternal serum screening and other forms of prenatal testing. If there is a known genetic problem in the family, or if the parents have another child with some type of disability, professionals should inform parents about the availability of genetic counseling. A genetic counselor can inform parents about the risk of the disability occurring again, options for diagnostic testing, and, if the disorder is likely to affect other relatives in the blood line, about appropriate ways to inform other family members and friends.

Prenatal Care

The rationale for providing prenatal care is to screen pregnant women in order to detect early signs of, or risk factors for, abnormal conditions or diseases and to follow this detection with effective and timely intervention.

Suggested General Care The recommended prenatal care programs in developing countries are often the same as those used in developed countries. In developing countries, however, there is wide variation in the proportion of women who receive prenatal care. The World Health Organization (WHO) randomized trial of prenatal care and the WHO systematic review indicated that a model of care that provided fewer prenatal visits could be introduced into clinical practice without causing adverse consequences to the woman or the fetus (Lumbiganon et al., 2004). Follow-up care during pregnancy typically involves the following:

- Determining the mother's blood group
- Testing for anemia and anti-Rh antibodies
- Checking the growth of the uterus
- Listening to the fetal heartbeat
- Checking the urine for protein (testing kidney function)
- Checking the urine for sugar (testing for diabetes)
- Monitoring blood pressure
- Checking for other concerns such as blurred vision, leg cramps, abdominal cramps, and unusual headaches
- Optimizing oral health
- Carrying out genetic testing if warranted

Testing for infections such as hepatitis B virus, rubella, syphilis, and HIV (human immunodeficiency virus) also may be done. HIV is a very serious issue since infection with the virus usually leads to AIDS (acquired immunodeficiency syndrome). Since HIV was first identified in the early 1980s, more than 60 million people worldwide have become affected, and more than 20 million have already died as a result of AIDS. In 2005, an estimated 36.7 to 45.3 million people were affected with HIV, 16.2 to 19.3 million of these being women and 2.1 to 2.8 million being children younger than 15 years of age (United Nations Programme on HIV/AIDS & World Health Organization, 2005). Unfortunately, maternal HIV infection is often spread to babies. In 2005, there were an estimated 0.63 to 0.82 million new cases of HIV in children younger than the age of 15 years. HIV has been referred to as the epidemic of the 21st century, and more outreach and education is needed to prevent the spread of the virus. Some professionals have suggested reevaluating current approaches for managing the epidemic and focusing more attention on strategies to address risky sexual behavior, including the promotion of delayed sexual debut and partner reduction (Genuis & Genuis, 2004). As explained in Chapter 16, HIV can be transmitted from mother to a child while still in the uterus, during the delivery process, and through breast feeding. There is strong evidence that use of antiviral medications during pregnancy can reduce maternal transmission of HIV. Thus, maternal testing for HIV is an extremely important aspect of prenatal health. One U.S. survey indicated that routine HIV testing is a reasonable option for identifying HIV infections in the primary care setting, as this is nondiscriminatory, allows for increased awareness of actual risk for infection, and provides an opportunity for earlier detection of HIV (Simmons et al., 2005). If a father is HIV positive and a mother HIV negative, there is risk of fetal infection if the mother becomes HIV positive. In some European countries, in vitro fertilization with washed sperm is being used to lower such risk (see Chapter 7).

Testing for Down syndrome, trisomy 18, and neural tube defects by ultrasound and maternal serum screening is a routine part of prenatal care in many countries (see the following section and Chapter 7). Midwifery care is an integrated part of some prenatal health care systems. This can provide enormous emotional support for a pregnant woman and a natural approach to birthing. Finally, it has been recommended that nutritionists should be appointed to mother and child clinics, as professional caregivers sometimes are lacking in nutritional knowledge (Endevelt et al., 2003). For more information, see "Helpful Midwifery Links" (Delaware Valley OBGYN & Infertility Group, n.d.) and "Prenatal Care" (MedlinePlus, 2005a).

Types of Prenatal Measures As noted in the previous section, numerous types of screening are recommended. This section provides further details on various measures and tests that may take place prior to conception and birth.

Genetic Counseling Genetic counseling is in growing need, especially for families whose members have been diagnosed with an inherited disorder or are known carriers. Genetic counseling may be sought before and during pregnancy. It is often sought prior to conception if there are known risk factors, such as late maternal age (usually 35 or older) or a family history of a genetic disorder. Genetic counseling may also be sought following conception due to abnormal maternal serum screening or ultrasound results (Nemours Foundation, 2006). Genetic counselors are professionals specifically trained to help individuals and families face the implications of a genetically based diagnosis, or the possibility of a diagnosis, and make decisions on the basis of both medical and nonmedical options. Genetic counselors discuss the chances of a child having a birth defect or genetic condition and the risks and benefits of prenatal testing. The service offered by genetic counselors provides parents and other family members with accurate, full, and unbiased information. It should offer support in the decision-making process and should seek to help families understand the implications of an inherited disorder. Although family physicians typically have some knowledge about inherited genetic disorders, they may not be prepared to offer counseling to their patients. Because of this, genetic counselors should become involved after a need is identified by the family physician and prior to any prenatal diagnostic tests or interventions. (For international perspectives on genetic counseling and prenatal measures, see Aguiar, 2004; Ensenauer, Michels, & Reinke, 2005; George, 1998; Ibarreta et al.,

2004; MedlinePlus, 2005b; MedlinePlus, 2006; Organisation for Economic Co-operation and Development, 2002; Raz, 2004; Tanne, 2004; and Tsianakas & Liamputtong, 2002.) See the Ethical Issues Associated with Genetic Testing section for more information on genetic counseling.

Ultrasound to Monitor Fetal Development Fetal development is now routinely monitored by ultrasound (Filkins & Koos, 2005; Chapter 7). This procedure is considered to be safe, non-invasive, accurate, and cost-effective. Ultrasound is used to help in the assessment of early pregnancy, to check fetal viability in the case of threatened miscarriage, to determine gestational age (the time since conception) and assess fetus size, to check the localization of the placenta, to determine the number of fetuses, and to check for fetal malformation as well as other conditions. Many different structural abnormalities in the fetus, including neural tube defects, congenital cardiac abnormalities, and Down syndrome, can be recognized before 20 weeks of pregnancy. Ultrasound is also used to assist in other diagnostic procedures including amniocentesis, chorionic villus sampling, and percutaneous umbilical cord sampling (see below).

Prenatal Testing for Down Syndrome and Trisomy 18 In many countries, any pregnant woman may choose to have serum tests for Down syndrome and trisomy 18, as well as for open neural tube defects. (In one Canadian study, the detection rate of this test for Down syndrome was found to be 70.6%, with a false-positive rate of 7.2%; for neural tube defects, it was 72.7%, with a false-positive rate of 2.0%; and for trisomy 18, it was 50.0%,with a false-positive rate of 0.2% (Summers et al., 2003). (See the section called Accuracy of Prenatal Testing for more information on false-positive test results.) Women with negative results usually have no further follow-up testing. Women with positive results may arrange to have an ultrasound and diagnostic testing that involves amniocentesis, chorionic villus sampling, and percutaneous umbilical cord sampling to rule out or confirm the results of the serum tests; these procedures are considered to be invasive, as they pose risks to fetal health. Some centers combine maternal serum testing and ultrasound analysis to detect fetal abnormalities (Stenhouse et al., 2004). Before diagnostic testing, however, women should consider what they will do if the diagnostic results are positive. It is important for a woman to receive emotional support from her spouse or partner, family, and/or friends before and after receiving the diagnosis, as a positive diagnosis may be received. Women should also consider talking about the diagnosis with their relatives and friends. They may even want supportive people present at the time of learning about the diagnosis. Women can also seek advice and help from genetic counselors, usually available in hospital settings, to answer any questions about the diagnosis. Follow-up testing is also important to confirm the diagnosis and to rule out a false-positive test result.

Amniocentesis is usually done in mid-trimester. It involves removing a small sample of amniotic fluid from the mother's womb and analyzing the chromosomes in cultured cells of the amniotic fluid. To obtain amniotic fluid, a needle is inserted through the maternal abdomen into the uterus and amniotic sac. Even though it is a relatively common procedure, amniocentesis before 14 weeks of gestation has been associated with an increased risk of postural deformities, and amniocentesis at 14 and 15 weeks has been associated with an increased risk of respiratory disturbances (Cederholm, Haglund, & Axelsson, 2005). Chorionic villus sampling (CVS) may be performed in the first trimester of pregnancy (8–10 weeks after conception). Chorionic villi are actively dividing cells of fetal origin that contain a full complement of chromosomes; the villi are found within the trophoblastic layer. CVS procedures can be transabdominal or transcervical. There now is evidence that transabdominal chorionic villus sampling, which appears to be the gold standard sampling method for genetic investigations between 10 and 15 completed weeks, permits rapid diagnosis in high-risk cases detected by first trimester maternal serum screening for aneuploidies. Sampling efficiency and karyotyping reliability are as high as in mid-trimester amniocentesis but with fewer complications, provided the operator has the required training, skill, and experience (Brambati & Tului, 2005). Because invasive sampling procedures are associated with fetal loss and teratogenicity, although the rates are low, there currently is much interest in developing non-invasive methods for obtaining intact fetal cells from maternal blood. This would allow accurate prenatal diagnosis for aneuploidy and single-gene disorders, without the attendant risks associated with invasive testing, and might increase the use of prenatal diagnosis by women at risk (Guetta et al., 2004; Ho, O'Donoghue, & Choolani, 2003). See Chapter 7 for more information on amniocentesis and CVS.

Prenatal Testing for Other Inherited Disorders If parents know that they are at high risk of having a baby with an inherited genetic condition other than Down syndrome, neural tube defects, or trisomy 18, diagnostic prenatal testing can be arranged. This is also done on amniotic fluid or CVS cells. Percutaneous umbilical blood sampling (PUBS), or cordocentesis, is sometimes performed at 18–27 weeks of pregnancy. The risk of miscarriage associated with PUBS is approximately 2%, which is higher than for amniocentesis or CVS. The PUBS technique is similar to amniocentesis, except that a blood sample is obtained from the fetal circulation via the placental cord. DNA or RNA analysis can be used to identify inherited genetic conditions in the fetal cells and to analyze for the presence or absence or amount of a particular protein. PUBS also is used to check the Rh status of the fetus if a mother is known to make anti-Rh antibodies, or to assess fetal renal function (Preis, Ciach, & Swiatkowska-Freund, 2004). In some places (e.g., Ontario, Canada), if there is no known potential risk to the mother or the fetus, and therefore no medically justified reason for a nonroutine genetic test, requests for invasive testing are not accepted. However, women whose requests for tests are not accepted have the option of being tested for a fee in the United States or elsewhere.

Testing and Prevention of Rhesus Disease One of the simplest, least invasive, and most important tests that parents can have done is a blood test for Rhesus, or Rh factor—a substance present in red cells of some people. It is important that parents obtain proper medical follow-up to ensure that their baby does not develop Rhesus disease. If medical intervention is not sought for Rhesus disease, untreated babies may develop severe brain or nerve damage (including cerebral palsy, hydrops fetalis, and kernicterus) and require lifelong support (Seeho et al., 2005). Individuals who make Rh factor are Rh-positive; those who do not are Rh-negative. If an Rh-negative woman with an Rh-positive partner has an Rh-positive baby, then her fetus is at risk of developing Rhesus disease (Harrod et al., 2003). Fetal red cells can enter a mother's circulation under a number of circumstances: during a spontaneous miscarriage or even during a threatened one, because of an ectopic pregnancy, during chorionic villus sampling or amniocentesis performed for genetic reasons, or as the result of a motor vehicle collision or other accident (Harrod et al., 2003). If a mother is Rh-negative and the fetal cells are Rh-positive, the mother may begin to make antibodies to the fetal Rh-positive cells. If these cross from the mother's circulation to her unborn child during pregnancy, destruction of the fetal red cells (hemolysis) may occur and result in a low blood count in the fetus (anemia) or even fetal death (Brossard, 2001). Because this fetal disorder results from destruction of red cells secondary to anti-Rh-antibodies produced by the mother, it is called *hemolytic disease of the newborn secondary to Rhesus disease,* or *Rhesus disease.* In the United States, the incidence of this disorder is approximately 1 per 1,000 live born infants (University of North Carolina, n.d.; Wagle & Deshpande, 2003). If the resulting fetal anemia is severe, the fetus may require blood transfusions while still in the uterus, via the umbilical cord (Schumacher & Moise, 1996).

Once a mother begins to produce anti-Rh antibodies, the severity of Rhesus disease in her fetus increases with each successive pregnancy. Medication called Rhesus immune globulin (or RhoGAM) is available to prevent Rhesus disease. RhoGAM should be given to all Rh-negative women at 28 weeks of pregnancy and after the delivery of an Rh-positive baby (Fung Kee Fung et al., 2003). Similar medications are not available to prevent fetal hemolytic disease resulting from maternal antibodies produced against factors on fetal red cells that are rarer than Rh factor.

Accuracy of Prenatal Testing Accuracy of prenatal testing depends on a number of factors, including the sensitivity and specificity of the test and its false-negative and false-positive rates. The term *sensitivity* refers to the ability of the test to detect true positives (i.e., individuals who really have the disorder). The term *specificity* refers to the ability of the test to detect true negatives (i.e., individuals who really do not have the disorder). A *false-positive test result* refers to a positive test result in an individual who does not have the disorder. A *false-negative test result* refers to a negative test result in an individual who does have the disorder. When considering prenatal testing, prospective parents should work with a genetic counselor to make sure that they understand the information that the test is likely to yield, as well as the options that are available to them after the testing has been done, particularly if the test results are positive.

Ethical Issues Associated with Genetic Testing As of the early 21st century, guidelines for genetic testing focus on a thorough examination of the psychological, social, and medical implications of a test result for the individual being tested (Robertson & Savulescu, 2001). In research ethics, the autonomy of the individual is of utmost importance. However, genetic information is by its very nature information about families. Detecting a genetic mutation in a person will, in effect, yield information about the risk status of family members who may or may not wish to be informed. Genetic testing done on a research basis sometimes can have unpredictable adverse effects; furthermore, useful guidelines on how to handle genetic information in research are simply not available (Quaid, Jessup, & Meslin, 2004). Discovering that there is a genetic disorder in a family may result in a range of reactions and emotions from partners and relatives including love, affection, obligation, gratitude, jealousy, advice, support, criticism, fear of disapproval, argument, and security or insecurity (Cranley Glass et al., 1996). It is impossible to control and to determine how families will deal with genetic issues. The individuals being tested and the professionals who are guiding them must always think ahead and consider the effects that genetic knowledge might have for other members of the family and for more distant relatives. Especially in families in which there is potential for genetic disorders, genetic counseling and other forms of support should be arranged before genetic testing is initiated.

Genetic testing and genetic counseling can be done prenatally or postnatally at any age. The issue of genetic testing is more complex in children than in adults, because children do not have the freedom to choose whether to be tested, whereas adults can choose for themselves. Generally, genetic testing in children is not done unless it will provide a medical benefit. Testing is usually performed on children when interventions to prevent or treat a disease are available and need to be implemented in childhood (Savulescu, 2001). Testing in children for nonmedical reasons and for conditions without treatment that manifest in adulthood is not advised, although it is sometimes performed (Duncan et al., 2005). A number of policy papers on genetic testing in children have been published internationally (American Society of Human Genetics Board of Directors & American College of Medical Genetics Board of Directors, 1995; Clarke, 1994; European Society of Human Genetics, 2003; Human Genetics Society of Australasia, 2005). These policy papers serve as guidelines for clinicians who are faced with a request to perform genetic testing. Most clinicians agree with the existing guidelines, although they also agree that each test should be considered on an individual basis, because different issues arise depending on the circumstances that surround the test (Duncan et al., 2005). When deciding to test a child for a genetic disorder, it is important to examine the advantages and the disadvantages (Robertson & Savulescu, 2001). Some of these are outlined in Table 28.2.

Neonatal Care and Testing

All infants and toddlers deserve the best possible support to ensure the best quality of life. As discussed in Chapter 8, positive social interactions play a strong role in the proper development of a baby's brain. Medical support includes all aspects of health care, including medications and pharmacological interventions, surgical interventions, dental intervention, and intervention for any vision or hearing problems that might exist. Other forms of support include physiotherapy, speech and language therapy, interventions designated as assistive, infant stimulation programs, early childhood intervention programs, and other types of programs.

Some intellectual disabilities such as Down syndrome, fragile X syndrome, cerebral palsy, and autism have particular needs of which professionals should be aware (see this book's chapters about specific disorders). Thus, it is advantageous to conduct certain types of newborn testing. In most developed countries, newborns are screened for at least congenital hypothyroidism, phenylketonuria, and galactosemia. This testing is done on small blood samples, usually taken from a baby's heel. Other newborn tests may include screening for congenital adrenal hypoplasia, maple syrup urine disease, sickle cell trait and other hemoglobinopathies, biotinidase deficiency, homocystinuria, organic acidemia, and defects in fatty acid oxidation. Treatments for these conditions do exist and are immediately implemented for babies who have them. If a baby is born with a cardiac or gastrointestinal problem, surgical intervention is carried out, if warranted.

It is also important to have a baby's hearing and vision checked as early as possible and to provide remediation if there is a problem. Blocked hearing due to middle ear infection is a common condition that can lead to language difficulty in young children. In many countries, consideration is now being given to implementing routine screening for hearing in newborns (Connolly, Carron, & Roark, 2005). There are many different causes of vision impairment in

Table 28.2. Potential advantages and potential disadvantages of genetic testing in children

Potential advantages
Respect for parental autonomy and decision-making capabilities for their child
Opportunity for child to adapt to genetic knowledge and incorporate it into his or her self-concept
Adequate preparation for the future and more realistic life choices
Better psychosocial adjustment from undergoing testing early on rather than waiting to discover status later in life
Decreased uncertainty about the future leading to decreased parental and child anxiety
Opportunity for earlier treatment and intervention
More openness in the family and in society at large about genetic conditions
Potential disadvantages
Infringement on future autonomy and confidentiality of the child
Psychological harms to the child and his or her family
Low self-esteem and feelings of unworthiness on the part of the child
Altered parent-child bond and negative parental attitudes towards the child
Discrimination and stigmatization affecting future health insurance and employment
Anxiety and depression on the part of the child, the parents, and the child's siblings
Parental guilt and anxiety about disclosing genetic information to the child in the future

Sources: Codori et al. (2003); Duncan (2004); Duncan et al. (2005); Robertson and Savulescu (2001); Savulescu (2001); and Wertz, Fanos, and Reilly (1994).

neonates, the etiology varying from one country to another. Corrective measures should be taken as soon as possible to ensure that children do not become blind as the result of potentially correctable causes, such as cataracts and retinopathy of prematurity (Rudanko & Laatikainen, 2004).

It is estimated that another 15%–18% of children in the United States have some degree of intellectual and developmental or behavioral disability that would benefit from early intervention. An additional 7%–10% experience school failure and drop out before completion of high school. Overall, one in four children have serious psychosocial problems. To ensure that such children are identified as early as possible so that their difficulties are addressed, it has been recommended that pediatricians use screening tools at each health supervision visit (Glascoe, 2000). It is not always possible to perform effective screening for intellectual and developmental disability. In some countries, doctors are reluctant to carry out such testing because they consider that they are not adequately reimbursed. For those doctors willing to perform the screening, young patients are not always compliant, and their families are not always interested.

Disabilities Arising From Birth

Babies who are born too early or babies who do not get enough oxygen during the birthing process are at risk of developing brain damage. Complaints of infection in mothers and babies, especially after a home birth, should always be considered seriously. Developments in medical knowledge and technology can save the lives of many premature babies who would have died prior to the 1990s. However, premature babies whose lives have been saved are at an increased risk of brain damage or even severe disability (Anderson, Doyle, & Victorian Infant Collaborative Study Group, 2003). As it is not possible to predict which babies will have problems of this nature, medical advances in neonatal care are posing challenging ethical dilemmas for which solutions are not obvious.

Family Planning

After prenatal testing or when planning for subsequent children, some parents might consider alternative methods for family planning such as assisted reproductive technology or adoption, in conjunction with the prevention of birth through sterilization and/or contraception. Others might choose to terminate a fetus found to have a condition that is not compatible with their family's situation; abortion may be carried out as early as 3 weeks in the first trimester of pregnancy or as late as the third trimester. It should be noted, however, that having an induced abortion may lead to problems with future pregnancies, and previous induced abortion is associated with an increased risk of premature delivery (Moreau et al., 2005). As discussed in Chapter 9, the more premature or underweight the newborn, the greater the risks of illness (infection, respiratory distress or other problems), cognitive disabilities such as cerebral palsy and learning problems, hearing and vision problems, and death (Haas et al., 2005; McGregor & French, 1997; Monset-Couchard, de Bethmann, & Relier, 1998). In addition, induced abortion may have negative physical and psychological effects on women who choose to terminate their pregnancy. Some publications have observed an association between induced abortion and an increased risk of developing breast cancer (Daling et al., 1994; Ring-Cassidy & Gentles, 2003), as well as subsequent serious mental health problems such as depression, anxiety, suicidal behaviors, and substance abuse (Fergusson, Horwood, & Ridder, 2006; Thorp, Hartmann, & Shadigian, 2003). In particular, the termination of pregnancy due to a genetic defect may cause grief, guilt, and depression (Ring-Cassidy & Gentles, 2003). The links between induced abortion and complications such as pelvic inflammatory disease, ectopic pregnancies, endometriosis, and other infections, as well as cancers of the reproductive tract, have not been firmly established, but some studies point to these associations (Ring-Cassidy & Gentles, 2003). Induced abortion may also have a negative effect on the siblings of the unborn child and on other family members (Coleman, Reardon, & Cougle, 2002; Ring-Cassidy & Gentles, 2003). It is therefore important that pregnant women and their partners be informed about the possible impact of abortion on them and their families; they should also be provided with information on the care of children with disabilities to enable them to make a truly informed decision based on all the available information.

There are also a number of natural family planning methods available, one of the most effective and well-established being the Billings Ovulation Method. The Billings Ovulation Method is a scientifically validated method of natural fertility control, which allows a woman to assess her level of fertility based on observations of her cervical mucus secretions (Scrapa, Dunson, & Colombo, 2005). This method can be used to achieve or to avoid pregnancy. (To learn more about the Billings Ovulation Method, see Billings & Westmore, 1998; Natural Association of the Ovulation Method of Ireland, n.d; WOOMB: World Organization of the Ovulation Method Billings, 2005.)

Assisted Reproductive Technologies Assisted reproductive technology includes procedures known as in vitro fertilization (IVF), intracytoplasmic sperm injection (ICSI), gamete intrafallopian transfer (GIFT), and zygote intrafallopian transfer (ZIFT), the newest technology. IVF involves fertilizing ova with sperm in the laboratory and implanting embryos into the uterus. ICSI involves fertilizing an ovum with a single sperm by injection with a fine needle. GIFT involves the implantation of sperm and ova into the fallopian tube where fertilization occurs in vivo. ZIFT involves the implantation of ova fertilized in vitro into the fallopian tube. The risks of assisted reproductive technology include failure, ectopic pregnancy, multiple pregnancy, drug side effects, and associated complications resulting from anesthesia and surgery. The adoption and implantation of frozen embryos is yet another variation of an assisted reproductive technology used by some couples to have a healthy baby. With multiple pregnancies (for whatever reason) comes the risk of premature birth, which might lead to intellectual and developmental disability in the baby. The costs for assisted reproductive technology are high and beyond the means of some people (The Reproductive Sciences Center, n.d.; Society for Assisted Reproductive Technology & American Society for Reproductive Medicine, 2004).

When assisted reproductive technology is used for conception, some genetic disorders can be identified. This is done by analysis of follicles that are collected after egg retrieval is initiated (i.e., polar body analysis) (Verlinsky et al., 1999) and/or by the analysis of single cells that are harvested from embryos at the eight-cell stage prior to implantation (Kuliev & Verlinsky, 2005; Lashwood, 2005).

Pregnancy Avoidance and Adoption Pregnancy can be avoided by choice, by male or female sterilization, or by the use of contraceptives. Sterilization should be carefully considered before undertaking, as it is not always reversible or 100% effective in preventing pregnancy. The procedure involves blocking the passageway of sperm or the egg by inserting clips or rings, cutting, or cauterizing. Various contraceptive methods are also available. The combined oral contraceptive pill and progesterone-only pill is extremely effective, at approximately the 99% mark. Other methods include emergency contraceptive drugs. Hormonal implants, or injections such as Norplant and Depo-Provera, are ranked at more than 99% effective. Barrier methods such as female and male condoms, cervical caps, and diaphragms also are commonly available methods of contraception. The copper-releasing intrauterine device and progestin-releasing intrauterine device are also options. It should be noted, however, that certain physical side effects and health risks may be associated with the use of contraceptives. These side effects and risks include pain, cramping with menses, abnormal vaginal bleeding, infection, and the risk of perforation of the uterus from the use of the intrauterine device; vomiting, nausea, fatigue, headaches, abdominal pain, and abnormal vaginal bleeding from the use of oral contraceptives; and abnormal vaginal bleeding from the use of hormonal implants (Conard & Gold, 2005; Hickey & d'Arcangues, 2002). The Billings Ovulation Method is an effective and noninvasive form of pregnancy avoidance and natural family planning. This method teaches a woman to interpret her natural signs of fertility throughout the duration of her cycle, based on changes in the cervical mucus. When followed, the method is very effective at preventing pregnancy, and it does not pose any physical side effects and health risks (Attar et al., 2002; Greydanus, Rimsza, & Matytsina, 2005; Johnson, 2005; Natural Association of the Ovulation Method of Ireland, n.d.).

Adoption is considered by people who do not want to pass on a genetic disorder to their offspring as well as by couples not able to conceive and by single individuals as well. Parents considering putting up a child for adoption may benefit from invaluable information available at adoption centers and by communicating with other parents in a similar situation. Parents considering adoption should also contact adoption centers for information on the types of adoption and the adoption process. Like natural-born children, adopted children may or may not have medical and developmental concerns. If growth stunting, abnormal behavior, and delays in motor, speech and language development are identified, intervention protocols that will help the children assimilate into their new family should be developed as soon as possible (Mason & Narad, 2005). Adoptions from international countries have become an option for many U.S. families, with more than 150,000 children being adopted since 1991 (Mason & Narad, 2005). International adoptions are not as feasible in some other countries.

Personal Values Regarding Testing and Related Decisions For many people, having a therapeutic abortion in order to prevent disability, resorting to assisted reproductive technology in order to have a healthy baby, or even taking measures to prevent pregnancy are not options that are morally or ethically acceptable. In addition, some people may not want to partake in prenatal testing because the results will not change the course of the pregnancy in any case. Furthermore, attitudes of different ethnic groups to prenatal testing are different (Singer, Antonucci, & Van Hoewyk, 2004). Thus, decisions about whether or not to perform prenatal testing, and decisions based on their results, should be made on an individual basis, in accordance with personal value systems and beliefs.

ISSUES IN EARLY LIFE

Issues that arise in early life range from first receiving a diagnosis of disability to getting a referral to a specialist. These and related issues are discussed in this section.

Diagnosing Disability in the Preschool Years

Chapters 7, 9, and 15 discussed a number of different ways that intellectual or developmental disability can first be recognized. Observant parents, other family members, friends, family doctors, or other professionals may recognize particular developmental characteristics or realize that a child is not meeting developmental milestones. These principal milestones include sitting at 6 months, crawling at 9 months followed by creeping, walking at 1 year, and talking beginning at approximately age 2 (later for boys) (see also Chapter 7 and Appendix B at the end of the book).

Identifying intellectual and/or developmental disability in a child can be a challenge for doctors and psychologists, especially if the child is nonverbal, has behavior problems, or has a borderline disability. Determining the primary cause of the disability is a process that sometimes takes a number of years. Although certain disorders are screened for or are recognizable at birth, there are also a great many that go unnoticed for months or even years due to their mildness and the lack of observed, delayed milestones necessary for diagnosis. Sometimes the diagnosis is not even made until the child starts school and has trouble keeping up with other children (see Chapter 31 for information on comprehensive preschool systems for children with intellectual and developmental delays).

Although learning about a child's disability within minutes or days of birth may be a shock to parents, experiencing anxiety months or years after a child is born because of suspicion that there might be a problem can be disabling for families. For most parents, it is better to know early so that action to help the child and the family can be taken. Parents' and others' concerns about a child's development should always be taken seriously. Studies have shown that parents play an important role in detecting developmental delay in their children (Chen et al., 2004; Glascoe, 1997). Family doctors can ask parents to provide a report on the child's development (e.g., by taking the Parents' Evaluation of Developmental Status [PEDS] questionnaire; see http://forepath.org), which has been shown to be a very effective and efficient early screening tool for children who require further assessment or referral (Oberklaid & Efron, 2005). Most family physicians are responsive and helpful and readily refer families to specialists, such as developmental pediatricians or developmental psychologists, who have more knowledge of childhood disabilities. At times, though, parents or advocates may need to pursue more formal diagnostic procedures aggressively with their doctors, as some physicians are overly reliant on "clinical judgment," which has been shown in some research studies to detect fewer than 30% of children with intellectual disability (Glascoe, 2005; Glascoe & Dworkin, 1993). A related problem is that many family physicians are not adequately trained in diagnosing disabilities that were not known at birth (see Display 28.1). Disabilities are often included in medical school curricula at universities, but in some schools, intellectual and developmental disabilities are not adequately discussed or experienced. In many countries, the diagnosis of intellectual or developmental disability or specific types of intellectual disability must be done by a specialized physician or a psychologist, so some doctors may not share their suspicions with families. Nonetheless, the process can be initiated by anyone. (See Chapters 7, 9, and 21 for further information about how to obtain a diagnosis of intellectual and developmental disability).

As hinted at in Display 28.1, doctors sometimes underestimate how well parents can take the diagnosis. Some withhold the information for fear of being bearers of bad news. It is likely that parents are more accepting of a physician deliberately holding back diagnostic information if there is a specific benefit for the child. As in the case presented in Display 28.2, a family physician may think it best for parents to bond with their child before the child's disability is revealed to

Display 28.1

Case study: Samantha

When Samantha was 9 months old, her parents started noticing that she had trouble crawling and that her movements were excessively spastic and rigid. They visited their family doctor many times, but he insisted that Samantha was fine and was developing appropriately. By the time Samantha was 12 months old, her parents were convinced something was wrong and decided to seek the advice of other medical professionals at the nearest hospital. When the developmental pediatrician who examined Samantha told her parents that Samantha had cerebral palsy and had developmental delays, she was surprised at how well they accepted the diagnosis. For the parents, it was a relief to have someone finally say what they had feared for so long and to diagnose their daughter's condition. They now felt that they could move forward and do the best for their daughter.

Display 28.2

Case study: Matt

The family doctor finally told Dianne that her son Matt had Down syndrome. The doctor explained that he had suspected this at birth but wanted Matt's parents to learn to love him and know him as a person before they were told. The doctor believed that this bonding process would ensure that they made the right decisions with respect to raising their child. Dianne was surprised that the doctor knew about her son's disability all along and did not say anything to her, but she also appreciated the concern the doctor had for her child and their whole family.

them. Studies have determined that not all mothers experience feelings of love for their baby in the first hours or even days after birth. One U.S. study found that even though 41% of mothers feel love for their baby even before the baby is born, 35% of mothers feel love for the child only after more than a week's time of nurturing and being with the child (MacFarlane et al., 1978, & Pascal, 1989, as cited in Levine, Carey, & Crocker, 1992).

Advice for Parents on Getting the Diagnosis

Parents spend much more time with their child than any professional and are often the first to become aware of a problem. If parents suspect that their child has a disability, it is important to do the following:

- Check a list of warning signs and symptoms provided by the relevant disability organization (see also Chapter 15).
- Visit a local library or search the Internet for additional reading material or information on the disability (not all web sites are credible; see the Understanding the Diagnosis section for more information).
- Ask for a second opinion—some professionals are more knowledgeable about disabilities than others.
- Keep track of the child's progress and possible manifestations of disability, such as missed milestones.

Getting a Referral to a Specialist

Once parents are made aware of a problem, they may be referred by a family doctor, pediatrician, or clinic to a specialist or a diagnostic group. Parents may also self-refer (see Display 28.3).

When parents are not sure what the child's problem is or whether a problem even exists, the search for a specialist can be complicated. It can be helpful to search through a community health care or social service organization. In searching for knowledgeable professionals, parents should remember that a multifaceted team can offer more information and can evaluate the child more comprehensively than a single specialist. This team may consist of such professionals as a pediatrician, a children's education specialist, a physical therapist, an occupational therapist, a speech-language pathologist, an orthopedic surgeon, a psychologist, a psychiatrist, an ophthalmologist, and an audiologist, among others. Teams of specialists are often found at larger hospitals, especially those classified as university teaching hospitals.

Understanding the Diagnosis

Obtaining a diagnosis from a professional or diagnostic group is one step forward. Understanding the meaning of the diagnosis and its immediate and long-term implications are just as important. It is important for professionals to present the diagnosis in simple terms so that the parents are able to fully comprehend it. It is also important for parents to learn as much as possible about their child's disability, so that in time they will become familiar with special terms and other aspects related to the disability.

There has been a dramatic increase and improvement in the quality of information about disabilities that is available on the Internet. For those with access to the Internet, an efficient way to obtain information about a particular disability is to use a search engine to generate many web sites on the desired topic. However, not all web sites portray credible and accurate information. The following questions should be considered when trying to judge the quality of the Internet information:

Display 28.3

Case study: Tommy

Tommy's pediatrician told his parents that he was typically developing. When Tommy's mother insisted that there was a problem, the doctor told her not to worry about Tommy not talking and that he would begin talking when he was ready. When Tommy was 3 years old, his parents took him to see a child psychologist at their local mental health clinic. The psychologist recognized that Tommy showed classic symptoms of autism.

- Who is presenting the information?
- With whom are they affiliated?
- What is their background?
- When was the information last updated?
- Is this web site linked with or sponsored by companies?
- Is there disclosure of sponsorship, advertising policies, and conflicts of interest?
- Where is the information coming from?

Other valuable sources of information come from articles included in PubMed, PsycINFO, and other databases. In order to have free access to full articles in the PubMed and PsycINFO databases, a library card from an organization that subscribes to these facilities is usually required. Another good option is to visit sites associated with recognized organizations for people with disabilities; examples of different types of information sources are included in Appendix B.

Parent–Professional Communication

The importance of communication between parents and professionals cannot be overemphasized. Often, because parents are so highly motivated to become educated and to take constructive action, their knowledge about their child's disorder and available resources may exceed that of the professionals with whom they are interacting. Professionals should be receptive to learning from parents and be respectful of their knowledge, their attitudes and their concerns. Professionals should work in partnership with parents and should strive to empower them. Professionals may accomplish this by assisting parents in finding good sources of information on their child's disability, helping them determine what is reliable, and supporting them in making decisions they feel comfortable with (Davies & Hall, 2005). Occasionally, barriers to communication can lead to difficulties in relationships between professionals and families/caregivers. Strategies for dealing with such difficulties are discussed in detail in Chapter 24.

ISSUES FOR PARENTS

As noted in the preceding section, parents of young children with disabilities must face trying to get (and understand) a diagnosis and communicating with professionals. This section presents other issues that are specific to these parents.

Challenges and Rewards of Having a Child with Developmental Disability

Parenting a child with an intellectual or developmental disability can be very challenging; it also brings rewards and provides opportunities for parents and siblings to learn and experience many new things. In one study (Renwick, Brown, & Raphael, 1997) in which 35 sets of parents were interviewed in depth, parents explained that their lives were enriched by having a child with a disability in a wide variety of ways. Conversely, they readily identified a long list of challenges that they faced as parents. It is essential for new parents of a child with a disability to understand that

- Their lives will be enriched in some ways
- They will face many challenges that they would not face with a typically developing child
- They are not alone—there are many other parents who share their experiences
- Medical and other professionals do not necessarily have expertise on disability
- It is probably best to look for support and practical help from a variety of sources

Grief and Acceptance of Disability

When parents first learn about their child's disability, it is not uncommon for them to feel shocked and numb. Parents may withdraw and be overwhelmed by feelings of denial, rejection, guilt, anger, shame, sadness, suffering, and other emotions (Dickman & Gordon, 1985; Seligman & Darling, 1989). Nearly all parents and other family members of children with disabilities go through periods of grief, even though individuals experience and show their grief in a different way and to a different degree. Mothers may become furious at fathers who seem to be taking the situation calmly, but the fathers may still be upset. It is less common for men to grieve openly—their grief may emerge as unusual quietness (Dickman & Gordon, 1985).

Discovering that a child has a disability may cause parents to cry, shout, scream, or curse. These may well be the best ways to handle the situation—to get the feelings out into the open in order to get on with living. Many couples go through a stage of asking, "Why did it happen to us?" All feelings and thoughts are valid and are neither good nor bad. However, it is important for parents not to become overwhelmed by these feelings or a combination of conflicting emotions. Parents must find the strength to move forward from their grief.

Supportive family and friends are helpful when parents of a child with a disability are overwhelmed by feelings of grief. They have the power to persuade their loved ones to get on with it. Other parents who have a child with a disability and have had similar experiences can offer a special kind of understanding and solace that family, friends, or professionals are unable to provide. Joining such a support group and networking in other ways with parents of children with disabilities may help parents cope, reduce feelings of isolation, and provide relief (Davies & Hall, 2005). (See Appendix B for contact information for such organizations.)

Sometimes, parents are so deeply caught up in despair that they require comfort and help beyond the level that close friends and family can provide. People who cannot cope may benefit enormously from professional counseling. These parents should ask their family doctors to refer them to a counselor or refer themselves by contacting a local clinic.

Programs to Assist in Child Care

Both parents-to-be and new parents are encouraged to take advantage of prenatal education classes, well-baby clinics, and visits from public health nurses. A new birth can be very demanding and families, especially mothers, often need additional help at this time. In many places, there are groups for new mothers that provide them with opportunities for socializing, having adult conversation, and baby sitting. Some new mothers have become inspired to form such groups themselves, if they are not available in the community. Mothers of babies and young children, with or without disabilities, take part in such groups.

The first 3 years are considered the most important for a child's development; therefore, the implementation of home-based programs for a child with special needs should be considered as early as possible. Home-based programs can help families connect with community resources, identify and achieve personal goals, provide up-to-date information on children's growth and development, obtain developmental screening, and provide assistance with transportation to appointments. If a family is particularly strained, short- or long-term respite services may exist to provide caregivers with time to themselves. Family support programs can provide support and information to individuals with intellectual and developmental disabilities and their families so that both personal and family crises can be assisted.

Family support programs can also provide referrals, information about disabilities and genetic counseling, short-term care management, and crisis and stress relief. The general health, safety, and technical advice provided by these programs ranges from feeding, playing, toilet training, addressing hygiene, and taking medication to finding schools, becoming involved in advocacy groups, and facilitating friendships. The support programs are also a source of information about entitlements, guardianship and legal issues, and various types of counseling. Parent matching (or parent-to-parent) groups connect families who have children with the same or similar disorders. Such parent groups frequently provide a lot of information and support. Parents can also seek advice from guides for parents with children with disabilities. One such guide is *One Miracle at a Time: A Guide for Parents of Disabled Children* (Dickman & Gordon, 1985).

Parenting a Child with a Disability

Effective parenting of a child with a disability includes learning as much as possible about the disability and keeping detailed records about the child. Detailed record keeping is essential for monitoring the child's progress. It is also important to provide such information to doctors, psychologists and other professionals involved in the care of the child with a disability. Parents may have a binder or notebook of contacts and telephone numbers. The following are some kinds of information that can be included, as suggested by Dickman and Gordon (1985) in their guide for parents of children with disabilities:

- Emergency telephone numbers: These include numbers for emergency medical attention (ambulance), the fire department, and the police department and for important suppliers and providers, depending on the child's disability.
- The child's and parent's ID numbers: These include social security numbers, health care numbers, and private insurance numbers.
- The child's medical history: If the child was born with the disability, this includes prenatal information about the child and parents, genetic background, and other relevant data. Details about birth and shortly after birth are also relevant. Copies of hospital and medical records should also be included when possible.
- The child's medication record: It is easy to forget the names of drugs or medications, why and when they were prescribed, whether they accomplished the purpose for which they were prescribed. Negative side effects should also be noted.
- Informal notes on conferences, consultations, and conversations (in person or by telephone): Parents can take note of questions asked and answers given during consultations with professionals, the professionals' recommendations, and findings at follow-up. When attending conferences, the purpose, participants, conclusions, and suggestions should be noted. It may be a good idea to tape the conference, when permissible. Notes should also be taken on conversations with agency and school officials. Their names and telephone numbers should be recorded for follow-up purposes.
- Correspondence: This should include any letters to and from government and voluntary agencies, suppliers, school officials, and others who have been contacted about the child's needs and problems.

- The child's educational history: This includes preschool programs and schools attended, infant stimulation and early intervention programs (with dates); names of teachers, therapists, and resource personnel who work with the child; copies of report cards, test results, comments, assessments, individualized education programs (IEPs) or other educational plans, and so forth.
- The parents' observations of the child's behavior: Parents are often experts on their child. Parental observations are helpful and welcomed by physicians, therapists, teachers, and other professionals. These observations are worth keeping; they are proof that the child is making progress. Keeping a record can be therapeutic on its own.

Managing Care for a Child with a Disability

The arrival of a child with a disability can create stresses in a family and can be very challenging. However, the following things are known based on evidence from parents' experiences, as reported by Dickman and Gordon (1985):

- A family with a child who has a disability does not have to be "disabled" in any way.
- A family with a child who has a disability does not have to disintegrate under stress.
- It is not the child's disability that specifically creates family difficulties; rather, these difficulties are caused by the way that family members react to the disability and to one another.
- Finding ways to deal with the additional stresses, to minimize them, and to overcome them together can draw a marriage and a family closer.

When a child with a disability becomes part of the family, tension may begin to mount, and it is not uncommon for some parents to find fault with and to blame one another. Yet, other parents say that the experience of bringing up a child with a disability has brought them closer together, making their marriage stronger. Essential to the well-being of the marriage and the child is communication between the parents. Couples must find a way to talk together about their child. This often means bringing other people, such as the child's siblings, into the discussion. Each family needs to work out an effective communication pattern. For some families, this may mean sitting around the kitchen table once per week. For others, communicating might occur more sporadically. Whatever the case, feelings should be shared, as this will foster an inclusive environment in which all family members feel validated.

Siblings are an important part of the support network that is part of the child's care. The child's brothers and sisters should be informed as much as possible about the nature of the disability, according to each sibling's age and ability to understand and deal with the information. One way to improve sibling adjustment to and understanding of the disability is to join a sibling group or a sibling–parent group (Lobato & Kao, 2002). This understanding will make it easier to reconcile the extra time parents must spend on the care of the child with a disability. Although siblings may understand this at an intellectual level, on an emotional level they may still feel jealous, neglected, or short changed (Fleitas, 2000). In families that have one child with a disability, it is often not possible for parents to spend equal amounts of time with their other children. This can be frustrating for parents who want the best for all of their children. One way to manage this is to set aside special time for every child in the family (Dickman & Gordon, 1985). The length of time is not as important as the fact that special attention and nurturing is given to the siblings. One study noted that children appreciated when parents tried to be equitable about dividing their time, even when parents were often unsuccessful, and that children also appreciated open communication and time spent together (Pit-Ten Cate & Loots, 2000). Often, respite care for the child with the disability provides parents with the time and opportunity to spend time with their other children. Many parents also find it helpful to provide special rewards, such as praise or privileges, to both sons and daughters for helping to care for and look out for their sibling with a disability. Even though some children may find it normal that they help with the care of their brother or sister with a disability, parents should take care to ensure that children do not bear an "undue burden of care," which is often the case with older siblings (especially girls) of children with disabilities (Pit-Ten Cate & Loots, 2000). Siblings can make an extremely important contribution to the development of the child with disabilities, regarding the degree to which he or she is accepted by peers and the stability of family life. This contribution needs to be recognized. When families cannot cope with managing a child with a disability, they should seek professional counseling and help.

Dealing with Family and Friends

New parents of a child with a disability often need guidance and practical assistance to deal positively with family and friends. Two particular studies with parents of children with developmental disabilities point to this need (Brown et al., 2003; Renwick et al., 1997). In these studies, most parents considered care and responsibility for their children with disabilities to be an "in-family" concern and, as a consequence, they relied little on others. Their reasons for doing so were as follows:

- People other than family members do not understand a child with a disability.
- People other than family members do not know how to handle or talk to a child with a disability.
- Parents feel embarrassed about the behavior of their child.
- Parents do not want to burden other people with their child's disability.

However, these parents did not identify acceptance by other people as being a particular problem for them. It appeared from their responses that relatives, friends, and people in the general public are often much more accepting of disability than many parents believe. Still, there are many ways that new parents can help relatives, friends, and others understand and accept their child's disability. First, they need to discuss the disability openly, explaining its nature and what can be expected in the future. Second, they can provide opportunities for others to interact with and care for their child—as they would for a child who does not have a disability. Third, they can include the child in their social activities to the extent that is comfortable—again, as they would do with any other child. Finally, they may need to make extra efforts to instruct others on what they should say, what they should do, and how they should react. It is important to realize that most other people do not have experience with children who have disabilities and simply may not know what to do. Typically, they welcome some helpful pointers from the parents.

As noted, siblings of children with intellectual or developmental disabilities share the experience of disability in their families and often form a special bond with a sister or brother who has a developmental disability (Cicirelli, 1982). However, types of sibling relationships can vary enormously, depending on many factors. Factors that appear to help include setting a positive family atmosphere and interacting with others in positive ways (Greenberg et al., 1999; McPhail, 1996). Yet, parents should be aware that siblings of a child with developmental disabilities often feel an ongoing sense of loss and sometimes experience ridicule from other children (McPhail, 1996). For both parents and siblings, it is important to take initiative in dealing with relatives, friends, and others in positive ways. Because parents and siblings usually do not have experience with this and may be dealing with considerable adjustment themselves, they very often need some help and guidance. Knowledgeable counselors or health, early childhood, or social services professionals can be very helpful in this regard. In Canada, the United States, and many other countries, there are also numerous parent and family support groups (known to local social service organizations; see also Appendix B) that provide invaluable help to new parents of infants with developmental disabilities. Families should get connected to these groups as soon as possible.

SUMMARY

Preconceptual and prenatal health are pivotal for the healthy development of babies. Families can sometimes choose whether to have children with certain types of disabilities or genetic disorders. Such choices may involve the use of genetic counseling, the decision not to continue a pregnancy for which prenatal testing indicates disability in the fetus, and avoidance of pregnancy if parents know there is a risk for having a child with a disability. However, such approaches for prevention are not acceptable to everyone.

The first 3 years of a child's life are considered to be the most influential in their development. General early life issues include good nutrition, good medical care, good parenting methods, and set procedures that ensure the best development setting and quality of life for the child. Early life issues in families of a child with a suspected disability include getting a diagnosis, understanding the diagnosis, communicating a diagnosis to families and friends, coping with grief, establishing a good rapport with health care and other professionals involved in the child's care (sometimes educating professionals), and getting all forms of supports needed for the child and family.

FOR FURTHER THOUGHT AND DISCUSSION

1. Marta has just found out that her 4-year-old son has fragile X syndrome and that she is a carrier of the fragile X mutation. Marta's parents decided to be tested for the fragile X mutation as well. Marta found out that she inherited a fragile X mutation from her mother. Marta and her parents know that Marta's sister, Joy, wants to have a baby and that Joy may have inherited a fragile X mutation from her mother. They do not know if they should tell Joy, as Joy once mentioned that she would never consider genetic counseling for an inherited disorder in the family. How would you handle the situation if you were Marta or her parents?
2. Rose is a single mother of a 5-year-old girl with severe cerebral palsy. She has a job that enabled her to manage financially. Until recently, she had a wonderful live-in caregiver for her daughter. Unfortunately, the caregiver became very ill and Rose had to arrange for nursing care from an agency. Each week, a different nurse comes to the house, and Rose has to spend an enor-

mous amount of time training each new person about her daughter's needs. Rose's employer has become concerned about the amount of time Rose takes off from work. Also, professional nursing assistance is far more expensive than live-in care, and Rose knows that this cannot continue indefinitely. What course of action would you recommend?

3. Riva and Invid have a son with autism whose care requires a great deal of their time. Their other son is engaging in challenging behavior because he feels neglected. What can Riva and Invid do to help both their children and improve their family life?

REFERENCES

Aguiar, M.J. (2004). Genetic services and research in the state of Minas Gerais, Brazil. *Community Genetics, 7,* 117–120.

American Society of Human Genetics Board of Directors & American College of Medical Genetics Board of Directors. (1995). Points to consider: Ethical, legal, and psychosocial implications of genetic testing in children and adolescents. *American Journal of Human Genetics, 57,* 1233–1241.

Anderson, P., Doyle, L.W., & Victorian Infant Collaborative Study Group. (2003). Neurobehavioral outcomes of school-age children born extremely low birth weight or very preterm in the 1990s. *The Journal of the American Medical Association, 289,* 3264–3272.

ACOG Committee on Obstetric Practice. (2002, January). ACOG Committee opinion. Number 267: Exercise during pregnancy and the postpartum period. *Obstetrics and Gynecology, 99*(1), 171–173.

Attar, E., Gokdemirel, S., Serdaroglu, H., et al. (2002). Natural contraception using the Billings ovulation method. *The European Journal of Contraception and Reproductive Health Care, 7,* 96–99.

Beers, M., & Berkow, R. (2005). Section 1: Nutritional disorders. In *The Merck Manual of Diagnosis and Therapy* (17th ed.). Retrieved September 19, 2005, from http://www.merck.com/mrkshared/mmanual/section1/chapter3/3b.jsp

Billings, E., & Westmore, A. (1998). *The Billings method: Controlling fertility without drugs or devices.* Toronto: Life Cycle Books.

Brambati, B., & Tului, L. (2005). Chorionic villus sampling and amniocentesis. *Current Opinion in Obstetrics and Gynecology, 17,* 197–201.

Brossard, Y. (2001). Cytopenies immunes neonatales [Immune cytopenias in newborns]. *Revue du Praticien, 51,* 1571–1576.

Brown, I., Anand, S., Fung, W.L.A., et al. (2003). Family quality of life: Canadian results from an international study. *Journal of Developmental and Physical Disabilities, 15,* 207–230.

Cederholm, M., Haglund, B., & Axelsson, O. (2005). Infant morbidity following amniocentesis and chorionic villus sampling for prenatal karyotyping. *BJOG: An International Journal of Obstetrics and Gynaecology, 112,* 394–402.

Chen, I.C., Lee, H.C., Yeh, G.C., et al. (2004). The relationship between parental concerns and professional assessment in developmental delay in infants and children: A hospital-based study. *Journal of the Chinese Medical Association, 67,* 239–244.

Cicirelli, V.G. (1982). Sibling influence throughout the lifespan. In M.E. Lamb & B. Sutton-Smith (Eds.), *Sibling relationships: Their nature and significance across the lifespan* (pp. 267–284). Hillsdale, NJ: Lawrence Erlbaum Associates.

Clarke, A. (1994). The genetic testing of children. Working party of the Clinical Genetics Society (UK). *Journal of Medical Genetics, 31,* 785–797.

Codori, A.M., Zawacki, K.L., Petersen, G.M., et al. (2003). Genetic testing for hereditary colorectal cancer in children: Long-term psychological effects. *American Journal of Medical Genetics, 116,* 117–128.

Coleman, P.K., Reardon, D.C., & Cougle, J. (2002). The quality of the caregiving environment and child developmental outcomes associated with maternal history of abortion using the NLSY data. *Journal of Child Psychology and Psychiatry, 43,* 743–757.

Conard, L.A., & Gold, M.A. (2005). Emergency contraception. *Adolescent Medical Clinics, 16,* 585–602.

Connolly, J.L., Carron, J.D., & Roark, S.D. (2005). Universal newborn hearing screening: Are we achieving the Joint Committee on Infant Hearing (JCIH) objectives? *Laryngoscope, 115,* 232–236.

Cranley Glass, K., Weijer, C., Palmour, R.M., et al. (1996). Structuring the review of human genetics protocols: Gene localization and identification studies. *IRB: A Review of Human Subjects Research, 18*(4), 1–9.

Daling, J.R., Malone, K.E., Voigt, L.F., et al. (1994). Risk of breast cancer among young women: Relationship to induced abortion. *Journal of the National Cancer Institute, 86,* 1584–1592.

Davies, S., & Hall, D. (2005). "Contact A Family": Professionals and parents in partnership. *Archives of Disease in Childhood, 90,* 1053–1057.

Delaware Valley OBGYN & Infertility Group. (n.d.). *Helpful midwifery links.* Retrieved March 17, 2005, from http://www.delvalobgyn.com/helpful_midwifery_links.htm

Dickman, I.R., & Gordon, S. (1985). *One miracle at a time: A guide for parents of disabled children.* New York: Simon & Schuster.

Duncan, R.E. (2004). Predictive genetic testing in young people: When is it appropriate? *Journal of Paediatrics and Child Health, 40,* 593–595.

Duncan, R.E., Savulescu, J., Gillam, L., et al. (2005). An international survey of predictive genetic testing in children for adult onset conditions. *Genetics in Medicine, 7,* 390–396.

Endevelt, R., Blau, A., Neville, A., et al. (2003). [Mothers know best]. *Harefuah, 142,* 728–733, 808.

Ensenauer, R.E., Michels, V.V., & Reinke, S.S. (2005). Genetic testing: Practical, ethical, and counseling considerations. *Mayo Clinic Proceedings, 80,* 63–73.

European Society of Human Genetics. (2003). Provision of

genetic services in Europe: Current practices and issues. *European Journal of Human Genetics, 11,* S2–S4.

Fergusson, D.M., Horwood, L.J., & Ridder, E.M. (2006). Abortion in young women and subsequent mental health. *Journal of Child Psychology and Psychiatry, 47,* 16–24.

Filkins, K., & Koos, B.J. (2005). Ultrasound and fetal diagnosis. *Current Opinion in Obstetrics and Gynecology, 17,* 185–195.

Fleitas, J. (2000). When Jack fell down . . . Jill came tumbling after: Siblings in the web of illness and disability. *The American Journal of Maternal/Child Nursing, 25,* 267–273.

Fung Kee Fung, K., Eason, E., Crane, J., et al. (2003). Prevention of Rh alloimmunization. *Journal of Obstetrics and Gynaecology Canada, 25,* 716–719.

Genuis, S.J., & Genuis, S.K. (2004). Managing the sexually transmitted disease epidemic: A time for reevaluation. *American Journal of Obstetrics and Gynecology, 191,* 1103–1112.

George, R. (1998). Strengthening genetic services in primary care for Asian Americans and Pacific Islanders. *Community Genetics, 1,* 154–159.

Glascoe, F.P. (1997). Parents' concerns about children's development: Prescreening technique or screening test? *Pediatrics, 99,* 522–528.

Glascoe, F.P. (2000). Early detection of developmental and behavioral problems. *Pediatrics in Review, 21*(8), 272–280.

Glascoe, F.P. (2005). Screening for developmental and behavioral problems. *Mental retardation and developmental disabilities research reviews, 11,* 173–179.

Glascoe, F.P., & Dworkin, P.H. (1993). Obstacles to effective developmental surveillance: Errors in clinical reasoning. *Journal of Developmental and Behavioral Pediatrics, 14,* 344–349.

Greenberg, J.S., Seltzer, M.M., Orsmond, G.I., et al. (1999). Siblings of adults with mental illness or mental retardation: Current involvement and the expectation of future care giving. *Psychiatry Services, 50,* 1214–1219.

Greydanus, D.E., Rimsza, M.E., & Matytsina, L. (2005). Contraception for college students. *Pediatric Clinics of North America, 52,* 135–161.

Guetta, E., Simchen, M.J., Mammon-Daviko, K., et al. (2004). Analysis of fetal blood cells in the maternal circulation: Challenges, ongoing efforts, and potential solutions. *Stem Cells and Development, 13,* 93–99.

Haas, J.S., Fuentes-Afflick, E., Stewart, A.L., et al. (2005). Prepregnancy health status and the risk of preterm delivery. *Archives of Pediatric & Adolescent Medicine, 159,* 58–63.

Harrod, K.S., Hanson, L., VandeVusse, L., et al. (2003). Rh negative status and isoimmunization update: A case-based approach to care. *Journal of Perinatal & Neonatal Nursing, 17,* 166–178.

Hickey, M., & d'Arcangues, C. (2002). Vaginal bleeding disturbances and implantable contraceptives. *Contraception, 65,* 75–84.

Ho, S.S., O'Donoghue, K., & Choolani, M. (2003). Fetal cells in maternal blood: State of the art for non-invasive prenatal diagnosis. *Annals of the Academy of Medicine, Singapore, 32,* 597–603; quiz, 604.

Human Genetics Society of Australasia. (2005). *Predictive testing in children and adolescents (version 2).* Retrieved March 16, 2006, from http://www.hgsa.com.au

Ibarreta, D., Elles, R., Cassiman, J.J., et al. (2004). Towards quality assurance and harmonization of genetic testing services in the European Union. *Nature Biotechnology, 22,* 1230–1235.

International Food Information Council Foundation & March of Dimes. (2003). *Healthy eating during pregnancy.* Retrieved March 11, 2004, from http://www.ific.org/publications/brochures/pregnancybroch.cfm

Johnson, B.A. (2005). Insertion and removal of intrauterine devices. *American Family Physician, 71,* 95–102.

Ksouri, H., Zitouni, M., Achour, W., et al. (2003). Pertes foetales et avortements spontanes a repetition d'origine immunologique [Recurrent pregnancy loss related to immune disorders]. *Annales de Medecine Interne (Paris), 154,* 233–247.

Kuliev, A., & Verlinsky, Y. (2005). Preimplantation diagnosis: A realistic option for assisted reproduction and genetic practice. *Current Opinion in Obstetrics and Gynecology, 17,* 179–183.

Larsson, L., & Lindqvist, P.G. (2005). Low-impact exercise during pregnancy: A study of safety. *Acta Obstetricia et Gynecologica Scandinavica, 84,* 34–38.

Lashwood, A. (2005). Preimplantation genetic diagnosis to prevent disorders in children. *British Journal of Nursing, 14*(2), 64–70.

Levine, M.D., Carey, W.B., & Crocker, A.C. (1992). *Developmental-behavioural pediatrics* (2nd ed.). Philadelphia: W.B. Saunders.

Lobato, D.J., & Kao, B.T. (2002). Integrated sibling-parent group intervention to improve sibling knowledge and adjustment to chronic illness and disability. *Journal of Pediatric Psychology, 27,* 711–716.

Lumbiganon, P., Winiyakul, N., Chongsomchai, C., et al. (2004). From research to practice: The example of antenatal care in Thailand. *Bulletin of the World Health Organization, 82,* 746–749.

Machalek, K., Brown, I., Birkan, R., et al. (2003). Prenatal and early life. In I. Brown & M. Percy (Eds.), *Developmental disabilities in Ontario* (2nd ed., pp. 511–530). Toronto: Ontario Association on Developmental Disabilities.

Mason, P., & Narad, C. (2005). International adoption: A health and developmental prospective. *Seminars in Speech and Language, 26,* 1–9.

McGregor, J.A., & French, J.I. (1997). Preterm birth: The role of infection and inflammation. *Medscape Women's Health, 2,* 1.

McPhail, E. (1996). A parent's perspective: Quality of life in families with a member with disabilities. In R. Renwick, I. Brown, & M. Nagler (Eds.). *Quality of life in health promotion and rehabilitation* (pp. 279–289). Thousand Oaks, CA: Sage Publications.

MedlinePlus. (2005a). *Prenatal care.* Retrieved March 11, 2005, from http://www.nlm.nih.gov/medlineplus/prenatalcare.html

MedlinePlus. (2005b). *Prenatal testing.* Retrieved March 11, 2005, from http://www.nlm.nih.gov/medlineplus/prenataltesting.html

MedlinePlus. (2006). *Genetic counseling.* Retrieved February 24, 2006, from http://www.nlm.nih.gov/medlineplus/geneticcounseling.html

Mitchell, L.E. (2005). Epidemiology of neural tube defects. *American Journal of Medical Genetics. Part C, Seminars in Medical Genetics, 135,* 88–94.

Moalem, S., Weinberg, E.D., & Percy, M.E. (2004). Hemochromatosis and the enigma of misplaced iron: Implications for infectious disease and survival. *Biometals, 17,* 135–139.

Monset-Couchard, M., de Bethmann, O., & Relier, J.P. (1998). Mid-and long-term outcome of 77 triplets and their families. *Journal de gynécologie, obstétrique et biologie de la reproduction (Paris), 27,* 430–437.

Moore, V.M., & Davies, M.J. (2005). Diet during pregnancy, neonatal outcomes and later health. *Reproduction, Fertility, and Development, 17,* 341–348.

Moreau, C., Kaminski, M., Yves Ancel, P., et al. (2005). Previous induced abortions and the risk of very preterm delivery: Results of the EPIPAGE study. *BJOG: An International Journal of Obstetrics and Gynaecology, 112,* 430–437.

National Institutes of Health, Office of Dietary Supplements. (2004). *Nutrient recommendations: Dietary reference intakes (DRI) and recommended dietary allowances (RDA).* Retrieved May 9, 2005, from http://ods.od.nih.gov/health_information/Dietary_Reference_Intakes.aspx

Natural Association of the Ovulation Method of Ireland. (n.d.). *Billings Ovulation Method background: Effectiveness studies.* Retrieved March 18, 2005, from http://www.naomi.ie/effect.htm

Nemours Foundation. (2006). *Genetic counseling.* Retrieved February 24, 2006, from http://kidshealth.org/parent/system/medical/genetic_counseling.html

Oberklaid, F., & Efron, D. (2005). Developmental delay: Identification and management. *Australian Family Physician, 34,* 739–742.

Oppenheimer, S.J. (2001). Iron and its relation to immunity and infectious disease. *The Journal of Nutrition, 131*(2S-2): 616S–633S; discussion, 633S–635S.

Organisation for Economic Co-operation and Development. (2002). *Genetic testing: Policy issues for the new millennium.* Paris: Author.

Pit-Ten Cate, I.M., & Loots, G.M. (2000). Experiences of siblings of children with physical disabilities: An empirical investigation. *Disability and Rehabilitation, 22,* 309–408.

Preis, K., Ciach, K., & Swiatkowska-Freund, M. (2004). Ryzyko wystapienia powiklan po kordocentezie diagnostycznej lub terapeutycznej [The risk of complications of diagnostic and therapeutic cordocentesis]. *Ginekologia Polska, 75,* 765–769.

Quaid, K.A., Jessup, N.M., & Meslin, E.M. (2004). Disclosure of genetic information obtained through research. *Genetic Testing, 8,* 347–355.

Ramakrishnan, U. (2004). Nutrition and low birth weight: From research to practice. *The American Journal of Clinical Nutrition, 79,* 17–21.

Raz, A. (2004). "Important to test, important to support": Attitudes toward disability rights and prenatal diagnosis among leaders of support groups for genetic disorders in Israel. *Social Science and Medicine, 59,* 1857–1866.

Renwick, R., Brown, I., & Raphael, D. (1997). *The family quality of life project: Final report. Report to the Ontario Ministry of Community and Social Services, Developmental Services Branch.* Toronto: Centre for Health Promotion, University of Toronto.

The Reproductive Sciences Center. (n.d.). *Advanced fertility services.* Retrieved March 11, 2005, from http://www.fertile.com/Services/Advanced/index.html

Ring-Cassidy, E., & Gentles, I. (2003). *Women's health after abortion: The medical and psychological evidence* (2nd ed.). Toronto: The deVeber Institute for Bioethics and Social Research.

Robertson, S., & Savulescu, J. (2001). Is there a case in favour of predictive genetic testing in young children? *Bioethics, 15,* 26–49.

Rudanko, S.L., & Laatikainen, L. (2004). Visual impairment in children born at full term from 1972 through 1989 in Finland. *Ophthalmology, 111,* 2307–2312.

Savulescu, J. (2001). Predictive genetic testing in children. *The Medical Journal of Australia, 175,* 379–381.

Schumacher, B., & Moise, K.J., Jr. (1996). Fetal transfusion for red blood cell alloimmunization in pregnancy. *Obstetrics and Gynecology, 88,* 137–150.

Scrapa, B., Dunson, D.B., & Colombo, B. (2005). Cervical mucus secretions on the day of intercourse: An accurate marker of highly fertile days. *European Journal of Obstetrics and Gynecology and Reproductive Biology* [Epub 2005 Sept 7].

Seeho, S.K., Burton, G., Leigh, D., et al. (2005). The role of preimplantation genetic diagnosis in the management of severe rhesus alloimmunization: First unaffected pregnancy: Case report. *Human Reproduction, 20,* 697–701.

Seligman, M., & Darling, R.B. (1989). *Ordinary families, special children: A systems approach to childhood disability.* New York: The Guilford Press.

Sethi, V., & Kapil, U. (2004). Iodine deficiency and development of brain. *Indian Journal of Pediatrics, 71,* 325–329.

Simmons, E.M., Rogers, M.L., Frierson, G.M., et al. (2005). Racial/ethnic attitudes towards HIV testing in the primary care setting. *Journal of the National Medical Association, 97,* 46–52.

Singer, E., Antonucci, T., & Van Hoewyk, J. (2004). Racial and ethnic variations in knowledge and attitudes about genetic testing. *Genetic Testing, 8,* 31–43.

Society for Assisted Reproductive Technology & American Society for Reproductive Medicine. (2004). Assisted reproductive technology in the United States: 2000 results generated from the American Society for Reproductive Medicine/Society for Assisted Reproductive Technology Registry. *Fertility and Sterility, 81*(5), 1207–1220.

Solomons, N.W. (2003). Diet and long-term health: An African Diaspora perspective. *Asia Pacific Journal of Clinical Nutrition, 2,* 313–330.

Stenhouse, E.J., Crossley, J.A., Aitken, D.A., et al. (2004). First-trimester combined ultrasound and biochemical screening for Down syndrome in routine clinical practice. *Prenatal Diagnosis, 24,* 774–780.

Summers, A.M., Farrell, S.A., Huang, T., et al. (2003). Maternal serum screening in Ontario using the triple marker test. *Journal of Medical Screening, 10,* 107–111.

Tanne, J.H. (2004). US experts urge more neonatal screening for genetic disorders. *BMJ (Clinical Research Ed.), 329,* 876.

Thorp, J.M., Jr., Hartmann, K.E., & Shadigian, E. (2003). Long-term physical and psychological health consequences of induced abortion: Review of the evidence. *Obstetrical & Gynecological Survey, 58,* 67–79.

Tsianakas, V., & Liamputtong, P. (2002). Prenatal testing: The perceptions and experiences of Muslim women in Australia. *Journal of Reproductive and Infant Psychology, 20,* 7–24.

United Nations Programme on HIV/AIDS & World Health Organization. (2005). *AIDS epidemic update: December 2005.* Retrieved January 26, 2006, from http://www.unaids.org/epi/2005/doc/EPIupdate2005_pdf_en/epi-update2005_en.pdf

University of North Carolina Department of Obstetrics and Gynecology. (n.d.). *Rh disease.* Retrieved June 1, 2005, from http://www.med.unc.edu/obgyn/MaternalFetalMedicine/RHdisease.html.

Verlinsky, Y., Rechitsky, S., Verlinsky, O., et al. (1999). Prepregnancy testing for single-gene disorders by polar body analysis. *Genetic Testing, 3,* 185–190.

Waasdorp, N., Winland Brown, J., & Dunphy, L. (2001). Vitamins & Minerals. *Quick Study Laminated Reference Guides.* Boca Raton, FL: BarCharts.

Wagle, S., & Deshpande, P.G. (2003). Hemolytic disease of newborn. In *Emedicine.* Retrieved June 1, 2005, from http://www.emedicine.com/ped/topic959.htm

Wertz, D.C., Fanos, J.H., & Reilly, P.R. (1994). Genetic testing for children and adolescents. Who decides? *Journal of the American Medical Association, 272,* 875–881.

WOOMB: World Organisation of the Ovulation Method Billings. (2005). *Billings Ovulation Method.* Retrieved February 26, 2006, from http://www.woomb.org

29

Principles and Practices of Early Intervention

Elaine B. Frankel and Susan Gold

WHAT YOU WILL LEARN ABOUT IN THIS CHAPTER

- Early intervention around the world
- Early intervention in communities
- Early intervention and inclusion
- Providing inclusive programs
- Family involvement in early intervention
- Creating partnerships with families
- Forming collaborative teams

All young children from conception to age 6 require environments and early experiences that support their healthy growth and development. But for young children who are at-risk for developmental delays, early intervention services for them and their families are critical (see Display 29.1). There is now an international focus on the importance of the early years of development and on early intervention services to optimize the potential of young children (Odom et al., 2003). Infants, toddlers, and preschoolers who are at risk for developmental delay and have received high quality early intervention services demonstrate improved developmental outcomes and improved opportunities for lifelong learning and success (Shonkoff & Phillips, 2000). Early intervention does not have one agreed-on meaning but is defined in numerous ways, depending upon the jurisdiction in which services are provided. Thurman, Cornwell, and Gottwald (1997) described early intervention as a process in which the context and settings influence the approaches and programs implemented. Under federal mandates in the United States, the term *early intervention* usually refers to services and supports provided to infants and toddlers who have disabilities or are at risk for developmental delays and their families, whereas services for children ages 3 to 6 years is referred to as *early childhood special education* (Hanson, 2003). In other countries such as Canada (Irwin, Lero, & Brophy, 2000), Australia (Johnston, 2003), and Sweden (Björck-Åkesson, Granlund, & Simeonsson, 2000), the term *early intervention* encompasses services and policies that support the healthy development of vulnerable children and their families from conception to 6 or 7 years of age, when the child enters the formal education system (Kamerman, 2000). This chapter's use of *early intervention* reflects a range of services and approaches to promote the child's development and learning provided in infant development (birth to 3 years of age), early childhood special education (3 to 6 years of age), and community programs.

Early intervention programs are increasingly identifying young children in the community who are at risk for developmental delays at a young age. Early identification and intervention services are essential in minimizing and even eliminating the effects of conditions associated with children at risk for delays in development. Some children may be developmentally at risk because of biological factors such as low birth weight; others are born with established conditions, including chromosomal disorders; and still others face poverty, violence, poor nutrition, and other adverse environmental conditions. Wolery and Bailey (2002, p. 95) described expected outcomes of early intervention as those that have an impact on the child and family, including

1. To promote children's engagement, independence, and mastery
2. To promote children's development in key domains
3. To build children's social competence
4. To promote children's generalized use of skills
5. To prepare children for normalized life experiences in the community and in schools
6. To prevent the emergence of future problems or disabilities
7. To achieve positive family perceptions of the early intervention experience

The authors acknowledge contributions from an earlier version of this chapter authored by Elaine Frankel, Susan Howson, and Ingrid Fish (2003). The chapter authors also thank Katelyn Kiaer for her research assistance.

8. To achieve positive family perceptions of the impact of early intervention on the child and family

Neuroscientific investigations continue to support the importance of providing appropriate early experiences and environments for optimal brain development (Shonkoff & Phillips, 2000). In the early years of a child's development, the brain's rapid growth and ability to self-correct offers a window of opportunity to reverse or minimize the effects of risk conditions such as brain injury, chromosomal anomalies, or environmental stress (Diamond & Hopson, 1999; McCain & Mustard, 1999). Positive effects are enhanced when children are identified and referred to appropriate intervention services early in their development. For children with Down syndrome, studies in Wales, Israel, Australia, and the United States consistently found that intellectual decline can be prevented by comprehensive early intervention starting in the first year of life and continuing for 3–5 years (Guralnick, 2004). Over time, most children at risk for delays, who have received adapted early learning experiences and individualized interventions, present with less severe developmental problems and progress more easily in inclusive school settings (Brown, Odom, & Conroy, 2001). As of 2007, best practices in high-quality early intervention services in the child's natural environments and communities are guided by the principles of inclusion, family-centered care, and collaborative team approaches (see Display 29.2 for more information).

Display 29.1

Case study: Early intervention program

Lachme attends a full day child care program with other children in her community. She is 3 years old and was born with a chromosomal disorder resulting in a visual impairment and mild facial disfigurement. Ashley, her friend, is a child with Down syndrome. She is a very sociable child who exhibits cognitive delays and low muscle tone. Alesandro has a significant speech and language delay and displays frequent, violent outbursts that put him and others in danger. Tuyet has a hearing impairment. Her family speaks only Vietnamese. They are all friends in the preschool room at their neighborhood child care center.

A transdisciplinary team, including the children's parents, met before each child entered the child care center to plan an effective individualized program to support each child's development. Professionals from disciplines related to the child's specific needs participated. For Lachme, this included a vision specialist. For Ashley, the team included a physiotherapist and behavior therapist. For Alesandro, a speech-language pathologist and a child psychologist were included. Because Alesandro's mother expressed feelings of depression, stress, and isolation as a young single mother, a social worker was also included at his team meeting. Tuyet's team included an audiologist, a speech-language pathologist, and a family friend as an interpreter. Each team collaboratively developed individualized educational programs and family service plans to support the child's development and the family's capabilities. Plans were made together to adapt both the classroom and home environment to support each child's growth and development.

Source: Frankel, Howson, and Fish (2003).

EARLY INTERVENTION AROUND THE WORLD

The provision of early intervention services is now a right of children with disabilities. The United Nations' *Convention on the Rights of the Child* (1989) reaffirmed the human right of all children, including those with a disability, to be provided with opportunities to grow and develop within typical communities. In Canada, the Charter of Rights and Freedoms (1982) guarantees children the right to receive services without discrimination due to a disability. This right to equal opportunities for children with disabilities is echoed in the legislation of many countries, including the Commonwealth Disability Discrimination Act (1992) in Australia and the Americans with Disabilities Act (ADA) of 1990 (PL 101-336) in the United States.

In addition to early intervention being viewed as a human right of each child, it is also a legislated right in some countries. For example, in the United States, early intervention services are mandated for preschoolers and their families and permitted for infants and toddlers by federal legislation, the Individuals with Disabilities Education Improvement Act of 2004 (PL 108-446). In other countries such as Canada and Australia, the provision of early intervention services is built into provincial/state and territorial government policies. Funding is available regionally by local, provincial/state, and territorial authorities in countries where there is not a national mandate (Frankel, 2004).

Early intervention services for young children are increasingly being supported in the natural environments and communities where all children and families congregate for child care, education, and recreation. Early interventionists, who are trained in adapting and accommodating learning environments to meet individual developmental needs, deliver services to chil-

Display 29.2

Assumptions and truths about early intervention

Assumption
Early intervention programs and services do little to improve outcomes for young children whose development is at risk.

Truth
Although there are variations in the quality of early intervention programs and services, research indicates that participation in an early intervention program is far better than none for children with special needs (Guralnick, 2004). Child development research and real-life reports demonstrate that early intervention practices are effective in minimizing and even eliminating the effects of conditions that place a child's development at risk for delays (Hester, Baltodano, & Gable, 2003).

Assumption
The early interventionist, not the family, should establish the educational goals to be accomplished by the young child with special needs.

Truth
Positive long term cognitive and social outcomes for children have been demonstrated when early intervention services provide family support and use a collaborative team approach. It is the family's needs and priorities that shape the goals to be achieved through, for example, in the United States, the individualized family service plan and individualized education program (Childress, 2004; Odom, Teferra, & Kaul, 2004). The family takes the lead in this process. In a team approach the role of the professional is to help build the capacity of the family to meet goals and objectives for themselves and their child (Bailey, 2001).

Assumption
Children with special needs require self-contained classrooms with teachers who have the time and training to teach them.

Truth
Inclusive settings are ideal to encourage the development of children with special needs. Each child is challenged in an atmosphere that recognizes their differences while embedding their learning tasks in activities provided for all children. Early childhood educators who understand child development and program planning provide for all children to learn together (Baglieri & Knopf, 2004).

Assumption
Including children with special needs in a regular preschool classroom will hold back those children who do not require early intervention services.

Truth
All children develop at different rates and benefit from an inclusive setting. Children with special needs observe appropriate learning behaviors and strategies from their peers. Typically developing children learn to appreciate individual diversity. Children perform better, as they are aware that they are important role models for their peers with developmental disabilities.

dren and families. These early interventionists provide direct instruction to children with disabilities as well as consult with families and early childhood educators. Early intervention consultants may be known as special education itinerant teachers in the United States, early childhood resource consultants in Canada, and supplementary support service workers (SUPS) in Australia (Frankel, 2004). Although the names change in each country, they fill a similar role of offering technical assistance and providing consultation on appropriate ways to adapt the learning environments to include the child with a disability. Beyond their role to adapt teaching environments for children's healthy development, they promote positive attitudes and support the teachers and families of children with disabilities to be included in early childhood programs in their communities.

EARLY INTERVENTION IN COMMUNITIES

Children and families requiring support and assistance are in all communities. They attend infant development programs, child care centers, family resource centers, library events, and community health clinics. In the United States, these are referred to as the *natural environment for children birth to 3 years of age*. Natural environment has been defined in law to mean settings that are natural or typical for the child's age peers who have no disabilities (U.S.34 C.F.R. 303.18, Federal Register, March 12, 1999). Shelden and Rush defined natural environments as

> Typical places, contexts, activities and experiences that may include the child's home or early care and education settings, and could extend to a visit to the grocery store, going to a park, eating in a restaurant, reading a book at

> the library, going to church or the synagogue, as well as other places and situations identified by the IFSP team. The term natural environment is easily misinterpreted. It does not only mean the place *where* supports and services are provided. Although location is important, it is only one element of quality supports and services. The elements of *why* the service is being provided, *what* the service is, *who* is providing it, *when* it is being provided, and *how* it is being provided are the other essential characteristics. (2001, p. 14)

The first step to successful early intervention in communities requires universal screening programs that identify children at risk for compromised healthy child development. Coordinated community services are needed to reach children and families requiring service. Forming liaisons with community-based medical, health, and educational professionals can assist early interventionists in identifying and referring children at risk for developmental delays and their families (King & Glascoe, 2003). For example, Healthy Babies, Healthy Children was implemented in Ontario, Canada, to screen all newborns and their families for indicators associated with risk and poor child developmental outcomes. Using a blended model of service delivery, both public health nurses and home visitors offer home visits to support infants and families assessed as high risk. By providing support in the family home, forming liaisons with community services, and providing service coordination with an interdisciplinary team of professionals, Healthy Babies, Healthy Children intervenes at an early stage of development to support children's healthy growth. In the United States, early support is provided through programs such as Healthy Start, Healthy Steps, and Early Head Start (Parlakian, 2003). Similarly, Sure Start in the United Kingdom strives to achieve positive developmental outcomes for children by providing coordinated child development and family support services (Glass, 1999). Sure Start services are supported by interministerial policies and developed at the local community level.

The effects of merely identifying children and families are limited if resources are not available in the community. Early intervention services can range in intensity and degree depending on the child and family's strengths and priorities. Early interventionists may support children and families through home visits or consultations in their community child care center. Intense interactions are intended to be transitional responses to family need. They offer a bridge between the family and its community. Outside the home, services may be delivered in inclusive community programs, such as child care centers, as well as in specialized medical clinics and children's mental health centers. In all situations, community programs must be flexible to allow for creative planning and programming solutions based on each child and family's needs, priorities and, cultural values.

The popular media—including newspapers, television, and the Internet—offer parents information about the importance of the early years and healthy child development. This information is alerting parents and professionals to potential concerns in a child's development. For young children with developmental challenges, initiatives in the community offer parents and caregivers the opportunity to screen children for specific developmental challenges such as speech and language delays or cognitive impairments. Local community screening and assessment clinics are available to children from infancy to 5 years of age. Screening programs are usually collaborative ventures between infant development, speech and language, developmental, and behavior specialists for screening and identifying children with special needs. Parents are provided with the opportunity to consult with these professionals about their child's development and to identify developmental issues at an early age when interventions can be most successful.

EARLY INTERVENTION AND INCLUSION

Inclusion for infants and young children with developmental delays is based on the philosophy that all children belong together and can learn together in all aspects of community life, such as going to the park, the neighborhood early childhood program, or the local library. Within inclusive early childhood settings, children may have very different learning needs, learning styles, and rates of learning, yet each child is seen as having unique qualities and gifts that can be nourished, encouraged, and developed to the fullest extent.

Converging evidence suggests that the positive developmental outcomes associated with early intervention can be achieved in inclusive early childhood settings in which children with developmental delay play and learn alongside their typically developing peers (for reviews of the research see Guralnick, 1997; Lamorey & Bricker, 1993; and Odom, 2000). Quality infant-toddler child care programs are also suitable inclusive environments for meeting the individual needs of children (O'Brien, 2001). In inclusive settings, children with developmental delay begin to imitate the more sophisticated play, language, and social interactions of their peer models (Brown, Wilcox, & Sontag, 2004). Children with severe disabilities in inclusive settings are reported to perform better on standardized indicators of development (Cross, Traub, & Hutter-Pishgahi, 2004; Hundert et al., 1998) and on measures of language and social skills development (Rafferty, Piscitelli, & Boettcher, 2003) than those in segregated settings. Greater gains in social-emotional functioning were made in inclusive settings than in self-contained settings by children with moderate social-emotional needs; for children at a lower level of social-emotional growth, gains were equal in inclusive and specialized programs (Holahan & Costenbader, 2000). These empirical findings give support to inclusion, not only as a moral and ethical imperative but also as a strategy to achieve positive developmental and educational outcomes for children. Based on philosophical, theoretical, and empirical understandings of the positive and perceived benefits for children and families, Mackenzie-Keating and Kysela (1997) called early intervention the "least dangerous assumption," (p. 25) which is to say that it is better to intervene at an early age for children at risk for developmental delay than to not intervene (Gomby et al., 1995).

This is not to suggest, however, that a quality early childhood program that offers developmentally appropriate programming for its children is enough to ensure continued gains for children with developmental delay. In other words, mere proximity to typically developing peers does not guarantee developmental advances for the child with a disability. Research shows that to promote successful developmental growth, individualized interventions must be provided to allow children with developmental delays to learn and apply functional behaviors and communication skills (Campbell, 2004).

Successful outcomes for children with disabilities in community child care centers also require quality early childhood programs and professionals who are knowledgeable about inclusive practices. However, research suggests that 80% of all children spend their days in child care centers and family child care homes that are rated as poor to mediocre (Galinsky et al., 1994; Kagan & Cohen, 1997). This crisis in quality child care (Kagan & Cohen, 1997) means that many young children miss the experiences researchers have deemed critical to optimal development and school readiness (Kontos & Wilcox-Herzog, 1997). Although professionals agree on what constitutes a high-quality program, quality is a "complex, value-laden process with objective and subjective components" (Aytch et al., 1999, p. 8). One major challenge in defining *quality* comes with living in a diverse society, in which definitions can change from neighborhood to neighborhood. Thus, the definition of quality takes on another perspective when viewed from a cultural orientation. Some "generally understood universals" (e.g., those called "developmental tasks" and "developmental milestones") are in reality based on Euro-American perspectives of development, which represent an extremely small portion of the world's population (Bhavnagri & Gonzalez-Mena, 1997, p. 3). Therefore, quality must be considered not only from a professional perspective but also from a personal or cultural point of view.

Poor-quality child care is a particularly acute problem for children with disabilities. *Developmentally appropriate practice* refers to a child's experiences during care and includes positive teacher–child interactions and nurturing, which are critical for healthy psychosocial development (Isenberg & Brown, 1997). Families of children with disabilities should look for planned developmental activities that are individualized or occur in small groups. The environment should provide a predictable routine, as well as novelty and stimulation. The lack of safe, healthy, and nurturing environments for all children, but especially for children with disabilities, may seriously compromise their long-term development.

Meeting the needs of children with disabilities and their families presents a continuing challenge for early childhood educators. Training early childhood educators, directors, and resource consultants to understand the exceptional needs of children with disabilities, modifications to programs and environments to meet these needs, and collaborative consultative processes has been recognized as essential to successful inclusion (Craig et al., 2000; Frankel, 1994; Gold et al., 1998). Yet, the lack of training in early intervention and special education in teacher education programs remains a barrier to inclusion.

Beyond educational and ethical rationales for early intervention services, there is a strong economic rationale for providing quality care and education. Research from high-quality preschool projects such as the Perry Preschool project in Ypsilanti, Michigan, the Chicago Child–Parent Center, and the Abecedarian project in North Carolina all demonstrate that for every dollar that was invested in high quality active learning preschool programs, the public is receiving back long term benefits in educational achievement, higher incomes of children, and increased earnings of future generations (Masse & Barnett, 2002; Ramey, Campbell, & Blair 1998; Reynolds et al., 2001; Weikart, 1996). Money spent in early intervention and education will be paid back by adults who become productive contributing members of society and have less need for government services. Although longitudinal studies demonstrating the long-term economic advantage of early intervention have mainly been completed in the United States, McCain and Mustard (1999) noted that Canadian programs for early child development are essential to meet future economic growth.

PROVIDING INCLUSIVE PROGRAMS

The provision of interventions for young children with special needs within inclusive settings requires preparation and planning. Inclusion challenges professionals' ways of thinking and working with young children. It requires them to look at their beliefs and stereotypes of children with developmental delays. Inclusion does not mean that early childhood practitioners must minimize, condense, or eliminate essential components of developmentally, culturally, and linguistically sound practice; rather, they must adapt and modify the learning environment to accommodate children with disabilities and learning delays. Often professionals must overcome conflicting emotions of fear, avoidance, sadness, and guilt that are evoked when children with disabilities enter their classrooms. They must consider where and how to obtain additional training and supports (Frankel, 2004; Gold, 2000). Yet above all, inclusion challenges professionals to view children with developmental disabilities as valued members of society. Inclusive early intervention is based on several underlying beliefs about children and learning:

1. All children can grow, develop, and learn.
2. All children are unique and have gifts to share with others.
3. All children can learn acceptance and appreciate diversity in an inclusive environment.
4. All children have the right to equal access to early childhood programs.
5. Inclusive early childhood programs are not separate or different; rather, they are good-quality programs for all children.

As noted, typically developing children also benefit in inclusive early childhood settings. They become more sensitive toward, tolerant of, and accepting of people with disabilities (Diamond & Carpenter, 2000; Esposito & Reed, 1986; Peck, Carlson, & Helmstetter, 1992). They learn to appreciate and embrace diversity. As they grow to be future leaders, they will have attitudes that are different from many adults today.

Legislation supports the inclusion of young children with disabilities; however, the decision to include a child with developmental disabilities in an early childhood setting requires administrators and staff to change and modify policies and instructional practices (Frankel & McKay, 1997; Sandall, McLean, & Smith 2000). This change is a slow, time-consuming process. Child care providers and directors must be provided with a comprehensive curriculum on inclusion and time to attend training sessions (Gold et al., 1999). Ultimately, the successful inclusion of a child with developmental disabilities is determined by staff values, attitudes, and beliefs about inclusion, by staff perceptions of whether they have the skills to best meet the child's needs, and by the availability of additional resources such as resource teachers and resource consultants to support their efforts (Frankel, 1997). These attitudes and beliefs have been found to be further affected by the experiences center staff and directors have had with inclusion (Irwin et al., 2000). Positive experiences with children with special needs in their programs were found to enhance the staff's commitment and self-confidence in accepting children with greater challenges.

Inclusive practices may vary from program to program depending on staff dynamics, the needs of children in the program, and the number of children with special needs being included. Regardless of how it appears, providing early intervention for children in inclusive environments is considered best practice (Sandall et al., 2000). The following characteristics serve as quality indicators of best practices in inclusive environments:

1. *A philosophy of inclusion:* Inclusion begins with a vision. One of the primary characteristics of a successful inclusive program is a well-articulated philosophy of inclusion (Division for Early Childhood [DEC], 2000; Peck, Furman, & Helmstetter, 1993). It requires that all staff, from the directors and supervisors to the frontline early childhood educators, have a shared philosophy of inclusion. This vision is based on the unconditional acceptance of all children and the belief that it is each child's right to attend the same early childhood program as their siblings and neighborhood peers.

2. *A policy of inclusion:* Boards of directors and supervisors need to be able to articulate clearly the philosophy of inclusion to staff and families. By having a written policy, position, or mission statement affirming inclusion, administrators demonstrate a commitment to ensure that children have access to both equity and quality in all aspects of their early childhood experience. Staff and families should participate in the process of developing inclusive policies in early childhood settings (Craig et al., 2000; Frankel & McKay, 1997).

3. *Inclusion as a planned process:* Although an inclusive philosophy and clear policies are the cornerstones of inclusion, there needs to be a planned process to ensure that the vision is carried out effectively. Administrators, families, early childhood educators, itinerant special education teachers, and early childhood resource consultants have key roles as agents of change and must work together to plan, problem-solve, and determine how to include a child with developmental disabilities within all aspects of the program (Frankel, 1997; Sandall, Schwartz, & Joseph, 2001).

4. *Families as partners:* Inclusive early childhood programs should be based on the premise that the child's family is the central factor in the child's life. Successful inclusive programs depend on the level of involvement family members have in receiving and providing information, collaborating in decisions, and developing trusting relationships with professionals (Erwin et al., 2001). Family-centered practices take into account the lifestyles, culture, values, and priorities of the child's primary caregivers. To ensure family involvement, ac-

commodations may need to occur in methods of communication, time and frequency of team meetings, and the location of meetings.

5. *Reflect prevalence rates:* In North America, 17% of children in the United States (Dunkle, 2005) and 10% of children in Canada (Irwin et al., 2000) are estimated to have developmental delays. The number of children with developmental disabilities in an inclusive early childhood setting should, therefore, reflect these prevalence rates. Children with developmental disabilities should attend early childhood programs with children who are of the same chronological age and stage of development. Multiage groupings in early childhood settings allow this to happen. In these family-like groupings children can model, learn, and practice age-appropriate and individual-appropriate developmental skills.

6. *Intentional relationships:* The promotion of relationships, social competence, and close friendships between children with developmental disabilities and their typically developing peers need to be intentionally encouraged and developed by early childhood educators and caregivers. These intentional interactions provide opportunities for children to learn how to relate to each other as playmates and friends. They also help develop friendships that continue outside the early childhood program.

7. *Staff development:* In an inclusive early childhood program, all staff take responsibility for all children and are involved in all children's learning on a daily basis. It is critical that staff feel comfortable and competent working with all children. Staff development, therefore, is an essential ingredient to the success of an inclusive program. Research has documented the need for staff training to address issues of fear and anxiety, values, skill development, program adaptation, team process, and effective communications (Chang, Early, & Winton, 2005). An ecological approach, in which all staff and administrative personnel partake in all training, has been identified as the most effective training procedure (Miller & Stayton, 2000). Training supports for staff may include attending workshops and having access to recent research, books, ongoing in-service training, and consultative assistance.

8. *Interagency collaboration and communication:* Children with developmental disabilities and their families are often involved with service agencies and organizations other than early intervention programs (e.g., special services at home, respite care). By cooperating, collaborating, and communicating with other service delivery programs, staff in early childhood programs can help to increase the quality of life for the child and family.

9. *Transdisciplinary team approach:* Linder (1993) identified the transdisciplinary team approach as the ideal model for inclusive early childhood settings. As part of a transdisciplinary team, families, early childhood educators, resource teachers, and specialized consultants share roles and cross traditional discipline boundaries and work together to

- Assess a child's learning style
- Determine teaching strategies to facilitate learning
- Determine program goals and objectives
- Determine program adaptations and environmental accommodations
- Evaluate the effectiveness of the program.

Collaborative consultation from specialized services (e.g., speech-language pathology, physical therapy, occupational therapy) occurs among members of the transdisciplinary team. The transdisciplinary team ensures that the *whole child* is supported, resulting in more meaningful assessments, programming, and evaluation (Linder, 1993).

10. *Individualized program planning:* Most early intervention programs in Western countries in North America and Europe require that specialized plans, such as an individualized family service plan (IFSP) or an individualized education program (IEP) in the United States, based on observations and assessments be developed within the first month of the child's enrollment into an early childhood setting and updated regularly (Björck-Åkesson, et al., 2000; Hanson, 2003; Irwin, Lero, & Brophy, 2004). The IFSP or IEP goals and priorities developed by the transdisciplinary team are the basis for the curriculum planned each week. The IEP focuses on strategies for learning (see Figure 29.1 for an example of IEP objectives and strategies). Because children with developmental disabilities are included in a variety of early childhood programs—such as group child care centers, nursery schools, drop-in centers, family resource centers, and private home child care—the way that individualized goals and instructional approaches are implemented may be different from program to program. Recognizing that these differences exist, it is important to ensure that the goals and approaches in the IFSP or IEP account for not only the abilities and needs of the child but also the natural environment in which the program will be implemented and the interactive skills of the caregiver who will implement them (Hopkins, 1995).

11. *Program adaptations:* Staff are responsible for implementing a child's individualized goals within the daily program, but they are also responsible for developing activities that are interesting and promote the involvement of all children (Diamond, Hestenes, & O'Connor, 1994). Activities that embed the expectations for the child within typical classroom learning centers and routines are used by teachers in inclusive settings (Sandall et al., 2001). Discussion of possible adaptations that allow a child with developmental dis-

abilities to participate should occur during the program planning process. Considering the learning objectives of each scheduled activity, Hopkins (1995) suggested that adaptations may occur in the following realms:

- Order sequence of routines or activities (for example, providing indoor active play right after sleep time rather than going outside to accommodate longer sleeping needs of children)
- Location of activities (e.g., moving the water table to an open area to allow for easier access to a child who uses a wheelchair)
- Adult–child groupings (e.g., having several small, short group activities to accommodate younger or less focused children and encourage socialization)
- Developmental variability (e.g., providing single inset puzzles as well as jigsaw puzzles to meet the range of developmental skills of children within the group)
- Number of toys (e.g., ensuring that there are not so many toys that children are overwhelmed, ensuring that the variety of toys is not so limited that children are bored)
- Physical location of toys and activities (e.g., putting toys and activities on lower shelves to ensure that they are accessible to all children)
- Types of materials or equipment used (e.g., providing adapted eating utensils or seat supports to ensure a child's participation in all activities)
- Cues or visual aids (e.g., using labels or symbols to aid in instruction, providing reminders for following directions)
- Teacher interactions and communication strategies (e.g., using verbal, and physical prompts; giving instructions in methods that reflect various learning styles)
- Peer interactions and communication strategies (e.g., teaching children to use sign language, picture exchange systems, or other alternative communication strategies).

12. *Evaluation:* Evaluation can often mean added expense for a program. Regardless, evaluation is critical to the continued improvement and expansion of inclusive early childhood programs (Guralnick, 2004). By using the quality indicators of an inclusive early childhood program, staff, families, resource teachers, resource consultants, and inclusion facilitators can work together to create high-quality programs for all children (Neisworth & Bagnato, 2000). In addition to measuring growth in children in all domains, programs should be encouraged to evaluate all aspects of their programs, including staff development and family satisfaction.

Individualized Education Program

Child: Ashley

Chronological age: 3 years, 3 months

Collaborative team: D. Yager (parent), S. Michael (supervisor), L. Eccles (early childhood educational resource teacher), V. Fraser (early childhood educator [ECE]), C. Combden (behavior therapist), R. Goldman (speech-language pathologist), and R. Tucci (occupational therapist)

6-month objectives and strategies:

Domain	*Implications for instruction*	*Functional/ curriculum targets*	*Action/ strategies*
Social	Ashley engages mostly in parallel play.	Ashley will take turns with another child with adult facilitation.	ECE will engage Ashley and another child in a cooking, dramatic, or creative activity. ECE will encourage turn taking through verbal praise and physical reinforcement. Parent will invite another child to home, park, etc.
Expressive and receptive	Ashley follows through on one-step directions.	Ashley will follow three-step directions independently.	ECE will use verbal and visual cues (e.g., a visual schedule) to prompt Ashley to follow directions in daily routines. Resource teacher will provide play sequencing and memory games. Occupational therapist will provide fingerplays, songs, and motor activities that require following directions.

Figure 29.1. Sample individualized education program. (*Source:* Frankel, Howson, & Fish, 2003.)

FAMILY INVOLVEMENT IN EARLY INTERVENTION

Families reflect diverse cultures, diverse languages, diverse economic backgrounds, and diverse family forms. The current definition of *family* refers to the traditional family—two parents and children—but also includes single parents , same-sex parents, stepparents, grandparents, or other caregivers. In addition, many families are coping with increased stress, whether it is due to a child's known developmental disability such as autism or to conditions such as marital breakdown, poverty, substance abuse, violence, unemployment, or cultural adjustment. To serve the needs of families, parent involvement and family support have become central components of early intervention programs and services (Bailey, 2001; Nunn & McMahan, 2000). Evidence suggests that family participation in early intervention services promotes positive parent attitudes and expectations for the child and changes family processes. These family changes are found to have positive long-term effects on child development outcomes (Conyers, Reynolds, & Ou, 2003).

Parent involvement and family support relate to both the type and nature of interventions that affect child, parent, and family functioning. Professionals assist families in a variety of functions, such as providing access to parent education programs, providing information about disabilities, and supporting family members in acquiring resources for themselves and their child. While providing these services, it is essential that practitioners consider the nature of the help-giving relationship with families. Family-centered approaches that promote mutual trust, open communication, and shared decision making (between professionals and families) have been advocated as building parent competence, confidence, and capabilities (Bailey, 2001).

Inclusive practices ensure that families have access to a broad range of early intervention services that are sensitive to and respectful of diverse cultural, religious, and social values and priorities. Some children with developmental delays and their families experience barriers to participation in inclusive programs in the community. Barriers can include fragile health, age, the availability of child care spaces, cultural preferences, transportation, and parent concerns about sending the child out into the community. A relationship of trust and acceptance between an early interventionist and the family will slowly enable the family to move into the community with confidence. Therefore, a variety of informal and formal services—including speech and language programs, programs that provide intensive behavioral interventions for children with autism spectrum disorders, and family resource drop-in programs for parents—must be available in each community to match with the individualized needs of the child and the preferences of the family (see Display 29.3).

CREATING PARTNERSHIPS WITH FAMILIES

The ecological systemic view of development (Bronfenbrenner, 1979) assists in appreciating the inherent influence of the child's family, community, and society

Display 29.3

Lachme Moves into the Community

When Lachme was born, she was diagnosed with a congenital condition resulting in a severe visual impairment and a mild facial disfigurement. Lachme's parents emigrated from Sri Lanka 8 years ago, lived in a high-rise apartment in a big city with Lachme and her brother, and spoke Tamil at home. Lachme's mother, Gowri, had no formal English instruction, but Lachme's father understood and spoke English. Within a month of her birth, her family was receiving biweekly visits from an infant development consultant specializing in visual impairments and an occupational therapist specializing in feeding issues. These home visits facilitated Lachme's early skill development and supported the bonding process between the parents and their infant daughter.

When Lachme turned 2, plans were made for the transition of services from the early intervention agency to a program serving preschoolers. Lachme's parents were also encouraged to enroll her in a nursery school program, but Gowri was reluctant. She had once taken her daughter to a neighborhood drop-in program and felt very uncomfortable with other parents' questioning stares. In addition, the family had financial constraints and did not have a car to drive Lachme to the nursery school. The early childhood resource consultant from the early intervention program visited the family regularly during the next 2 months, getting to know Lachme and her family, providing suggestions and strategies to promote her development, and helping the family to fill out forms for additional funding. Joint visits were often planned with the visual impairment specialist and occupational therapist. Lachme's parents expressed concern about her speech, and a referral was made for speech and language services. Eventually, when Lachme's father was able to buy a car and a space became available at a local nursery school, her parents decided to enroll Lachme for two mornings per week.

Lachme's parents were concerned about her safety in a new environment, so a special inclusion facilitator was provided at the nursery school. Lachme and her parents gradually became more comfortable with these periods of separation and were more at ease with the safety of the nursery school. To the delight of her parents, Lachme quickly began to acquire new skills. Lachme was soon able to attend a child care center full time, with the resource consultant providing support to the teaching staff. Gowri was finally able to take English lessons at the local school, which were recommended to her by the resource consultant.

on how the child grows and develops. This model provides a framework for the examination of patterns of interaction between a child and the immediate environment and of sources of variation in a person's susceptibility to the effects of environmental conditions (Bronfenbrenner, 1995). At the microsytemic level, the dynamics between the child and the family have a primary impact on successful development. Early intervention practices cannot influence the child's development without at the same time modifying the child's natural social and ecological frameworks. Intervention programs that recognize the importance of the child's family, the social context in which the family operates, and the family's enduring relationship with its child are known as *family-centered programs*. There is a growing body of evidence indicating that interventions that are family centered are more likely to have broad-based positive influences on a number of aspects of child, parent, and family functioning (Turnbull & Turnbull, 2001). Collaborative parent partnerships are acknowledged as critical to early intervention and early school experiences.

There remains, however, tremendous diversity in the ways in which family-oriented programs are designed and delivered. Dunst et al. (1991) proposed a framework for differentiating between four classes of family-oriented program paradigms:

1. *Professionally-centered models* view professionals as experts who determine family needs from their own perspective rather than from the family's perspective.
2. *Family-allied models* see families as agents of professionals whose role it is to implement interventions that the professional has deemed necessary.
3. *Family-focused models* provide professionals with a selection of services for families to choose from (services are determined to be necessary or desirable for the family by the professional).
4. *Family-centered models* view professionals as serving families by helping them to meet their own needs in ways that support and strengthen family functioning.

The orientation of services that professionals provide in their work with families varies according to the different underlying assumptions about the nature of the help-giving relationship and to the established power relationship between the family and professionals. Turnbull, Turbiville, and Turnbull (2000) described how family services in early intervention have evolved from a "power-over" professional as expert model, through a "power-with" partnership between professionals and parents, to a synergistic "power-through" relationship with a group of community partners including parents. In the professionally-centered and family-allied models, professionals lead the intervention process, making decisions based on their own views of the needs of the child and family. In family-centered practice, the relationship between the family and professionals is seen as a partnership that emphasizes the family's power to make decisions based on family choice, family knowledge, and family strengths (Dunst, 2002). Within a family-centered intervention model, the role of the professional has shifted from expert to facilitator of a change process. The professionals support, encourage, and help to create opportunities for families to achieve successes. The professional role is a positive one, helping families to recognize and develop their strengths and to use them most effectively in their lives. The professional assists families in acquiring the services and skills needed to realize their goals. A collective empowerment model, while also assuming the centrality of the family as primary decision maker, creates change within the community ecology through empowering families and professionals to act (Turnbull et al., 2000). Power, resources, and services are shared, and change is created through collaboration within and across all levels of the ecological system.

Early intervention programs for infants and toddlers with disabilities have been most successful in implementing family-centered practices and dispositions, whereas services for preschool children and children in the early elementary grades are still primarily professionally driven and family allied (Dunst, 2002). According to Dunst, Trivette, and Deal (1988), family-centered programs are guided by the following beliefs:

- The family, not the child, is considered the unit of intervention. By strengthening and supporting the family and not just the child, a positive impact will be felt by all members of the family.
- Families should be empowered to become competent and capable rather than dependent on professional help-giving systems. This is accomplished by creating opportunities for families to acquire knowledge and skills to navigate the ongoing challenges that life presents.
- A proactive approach to families involves the acceptance of individual differences, includes the recognition of individual strengths, and encourages the acquisition of skills that will give families increased control and decision-making power.
- Needs and aspirations identified by the family, and not by the professionals, should become the targets for intervention. It should be the role of the family to determine what is in the family's best interests.
- All families have strengths, and these strengths should be recognized and built upon. Focusing on correcting deficits will prevent the development of a meaningful and productive relationship between families and professionals.

- Families often have informal social networks that can provide resources and support that families need. It should be the aim of intervention programs to strengthen and build social networks for families, not to replace them with professional services.
- The relationship between parents and professionals should be considered a partnership in which the individual partners all have capabilities that become enhanced through the sharing of knowledge, skills, and resources.

The collective empowerment model, like the family-centered model, assumes the following: the centrality of the family, family choice as the basis of decision making, and family strengths and capabilities as the focus of intervention. In addition, the collective empowerment model stresses that when professionals and families collaborate to obtain preferred resources, synergistic energy is generated. This energy assists in producing systemic change. The focus of this model includes gaining access to resources from formal and informal support systems, including extended family and professionals, and the changing community ecology (Turnbull et al., 2000).

Early interventionists are responding by demonstrating family-centered practices and forming partnerships with families. These activities require both an ability to relate to families by using flexible and open communications and an ability to use practices that encourage full parent participation (Dunst & Trivette, 1996). Family-driven assessments allow the family to take the lead in articulating the strengths and needs of the child (Boone & Crais, 1999). Sensitive information gathering that is respectful of cultural expectations, family priorities, and family values promotes shared understandings between professionals and parents (Banks, Santos, & Roof, 2003). Families collaborate with the professionals to establish goals and develop intervention plans as part of the IFSP. The IFSP is based on the expressed strengths and requirements of the family with a young child who is at risk for developmental delays (see Figure 29.2 for an example).

Some barriers may exist to optimal parental involvement in the intervention process. These barriers include the presence of overwhelming family stressors, the level of confidence and ability of parents to coordinate their own services, and the family's degree of interest and energy to participate in the process. Families of children with developmental delays generally encounter greater levels of stress than families with typically developing children (Scott, Sexton, & Wood, 1986). Increased stress levels can influence the child's development and the success of interventions. Lessenberry and Rehfeldt (2004) therefore advocated for the assessment of parental stress levels as part of planning appropriate interventions with the family. Professional

Individualized Family Service Plan

Child: Alesandro

Chronological age: 3 years, 6 months

Collaborative team: E. Rodrigues (mother), S. Michael (supervisor), L. Ho (resource consultant), G. Ryan (early childhood educator), T. May (speech-language pathologist), G. Garcia (psychologist), K. Stockton (social worker), and M. Torres (interpreter)

Alesandro lives with his mother, his grandparents, and his teenage uncle. They live in a small apartment in a large city. Alesandro's mother speaks limited English, has few friends, and has little knowledge of community resources. She wishes to continue her education, in hopes of acquiring a better job and, in turn, finding a home for her and Alesandro. Alesandro's teachers have suspected that the uncle resorts to physical abuse when Alesandro misbehaves and have notified child protective services. The mother has expressed the need to work through her own depression and anger at her brother.

Alesandro's current level of functioning

Verbally communicates wants to family members in Spanish
Language skills in English and Spanish are delayed 1 year
Uses three- to four-word utterances in English
Has difficulty showing affection to adults
Lacks social interaction skills with other children
Skills for joining and maintaining play are limited
Separations from mother are very difficult

Family strengths related to enhancing child development

Positive relationship between mother and child
Mother motivated to change and find employment
Grandparents willing to assist in care of Alesandro

Family needs related to enhancing child development

Family's language a barrier to communicating in the community
Mother expresses feelings of depression and loneliness

Goals

Alesandro will choose appropriate ways to express emotions
Alesandro will initiate and maintain play with peers
Alesandro will resolve conflicts by using his words
Mother will obtain job-related skills
Mother will become more proficient in English
Mother will seek and continue in counseling
Family will develop a social network in the Spanish-speaking community
Child care providers will learn basic words in Spanish to use with Alesandro and his family

Early intervention services needed

Alesandro will attend the Superior Child Care Center
Resource consultant, in collaboration with the early childhood educators, will develop an IEP for Alesandro that emphasizes expressive language development and social interaction skills in the regular classroom activities and routines
Mother will enroll in a job training course and attend ESL classes
Social worker will refer mother to counseling services
Family will attend the local Family Resource Program in their neighborhood to expand social network and learn about community resources
Child protection services will provide mother and family with parent education program
Staff will attend a series of workshops to learn Spanish

Figure 29.2. Sample individualized family service plan. (*Source:* Frankel, Howson, & Fish, 2003.)

barriers to family-centered intervention include administrative policies, regulations or procedures that limit family involvement, lack of available resources, and resistance to change established patterns of service delivery (Bailey, 2001). In spite of these barriers, family-centered practices in early intervention achieve a high level of family involvement and family satisfaction.

FORMING COLLABORATIVE TEAMS

Early childhood resource consultants, resource teachers, special education itinerant teachers, special instruction consultant, or SUPS offer critical support in delivering early intervention services to young children with developmental disabilities and delays in community-based early childhood settings (Frankel, 2004). These early interventionists use a collaborative team model to facilitate inclusion. As noted previously, a collaborative team consists of an early interventionist, family members, early childhood educators, and all specialized personnel who are involved with the child and family. For children with extra support needs, a paraprofessional to support the child's interactions in the early childhood setting may join the team as an inclusion facilitator. All members work together to take a transdisciplinary approach to the assessment, problem-solving, program-planning, and decision-making functions of the team. Research suggests that when early interventionists collaborate with families and other professionals to facilitate inclusion, all members develop a common understanding of the issues, take ownership of the problems, and share responsibility for the solutions (Frankel & McKay, 1997).

In using a collaborative team approach, specialized consultants teach, learn, and work with early childhood educators and families within the context of the early childhood setting. One effective way for resource consultants to promote change in teacher practices is to start with the skills and abilities that teachers already demonstrate and then modify them according to the individual needs of the child, the family, and the teachers (Frankel, 1997). Pull-out practices for assessments and therapy are discouraged. Rather, the goal of the specialized consultant is to provide strategies that maximize the child's participation in the general education program by incorporating adaptations into activities and routines presented to all children by the early childhood educators (Winton, 1996). For example, the speech-language pathologist teaches sign language to a group of children during circle time or the physiotherapist participates in group indoor and outdoor games that stretch and strengthen the large muscles of the child with a developmental disability. Instructional strategies and specialized techniques that are modeled by the consultants can then be integrated into the daily activities and routines planned by the early childhood educators.

Successful teams must demonstrate specific characteristics to be collaborative. Six of the most important are described next.

1. *Equality:* Hierarchical power relationships are dismissed in favor of equal partnerships. A collaborative team approach requires that all members of the team are equal partners in the process of providing services to children with developmental disabilities and their families (Friend, Bursuck, & Hutchinson, 1998). The perspectives, priorities, and goals of the family are as equally valued and considered as those of the professionals on the team. Each member of the team has an opportunity to share his or her observations of the child and to suggest critical goals for development.

2. *Communication:* Effective interpersonal communication skills assist all team members in listening and responding to the opinions and perspectives of others on the team (Friend et al., 1998; Frankel, 1997). This requires participants to maintain an open mind, to show empathy to others, and to put aside the priorities of their own discipline to incorporate the views of another when appropriate (see Table 29.1 for more information).

3. *Trust and mutual respect:* An environment of trust is most conducive to the work of a collaborative team. When individuals feel supported and respected, they can, in turn, support and respect the views of others. Creative solutions can flow more freely in an atmosphere of trust and cooperation. Each participant feels freer to express ideas without fear of criticism.

4. *Acceptance of conflict:* Conflict has been seen as an inevitable part of the change process (Frankel & McKay, 1997). It is common for administrators, early childhood educators, families, and specialists to cling to previously held conceptions of practice when including children with developmental disabilities in their classrooms and programs. Yet, conflict can lead to growth and change. Differences of opinions should be viewed as opportunities to consider all perspectives, to be flexible, and to implement new intervention strategies.

5. *Group decision making:* The IEP or IFSP that results from the collaborative team's efforts is based on observations and assessments and guide the interven-

Table 29.1. Communicating with families: Some tips for practice

COMMUNICATE both the child's strengths and needs to parents.
LISTEN to the family's story with empathy while reserving judgment.
LEARN about the family's strengths, resources, values, and priorities.
RESPECT cultural diversity and parental aspirations for success.
SHARE information, resources, and decision making.

Team Meeting Notes

Child: Tuyet

Chronological age: 3 years, 5 months

Collaborative team: W. Ong (parent), S. Michael (supervisor), L. Ho (resource consultant), D. Farr (early childhood educator), T. Kidd (audiologist), R. Goldman (speech-language pathologist), and E. Ng (interpreter)

During the team meeting, Tuyet's mother indicated that she wanted Tuyet to learn both Vietnamese and English. Her family members speak Vietnamese, and she wants to ensure Tuyet is able to communicate with them. The audiologist indicated that hearing aids would increase Tuyet's hearing capacity, but not fully. Tuyet's mother agreed to have Tuyet fitted for hearing aids and to make sure that she wears them daily. The speech-language pathologist expressed concern Tuyet would be confused if taught two languages and wanted to focus on teaching Tuyet only English. Both the consultant and early childhood education staff acknowledged the speech-language pathologist's concerns but expressed their belief that the mother's request for Vietnamese should be respected. The consultant agreed to share with the speech-language pathologist a journal article that demonstrates that children with hearing impairments are able to learn two languages simultaneously. It was agreed that both Vietnamese and English will be included in the communication goals for Tuyet. The interpreter volunteered to come into the child care center and teach Vietnamese to all of the children and staff during one circle time per week. Staff agreed to use Vietnamese words when interacting with Tuyet and to encourage the other children to do so. The speech-language pathologist agreed to collaborate with the teachers in planning strategies to promote speech and language development in the classroom. Tuyet's mother asked the resource consultant for assistance in finding an English as a second language program in her neighborhood. A date was set for the next collaborative team meeting.

Figure 29.3. Sample team meeting notes that illustrate collaborative decision making. (*Source:* Frankel, Howson, & Fish, 2003.)

tion. Group members exchange knowledge, share expertise, and make program recommendations (see Figure 29.3 for an illustration). Decisions derived from group problem solving and decision making are superior to those that can be developed by any one individual alone. Ultimately, though, it is the family—as the consumer—that holds the power to make final decisions related to the IEP or IFSP.

6. *Regeneration:* A collaborative team continually evaluates its efforts. Members leave the team as their expertise is no longer required, and new members may be added as the needs of the child and family change. The collaborative team is dynamic, with participants working together to plan strategies for including children with developmental disabilities in early childhood programs.

SUMMARY

This chapter described early intervention services for young children at-risk for developmental delay. Best practice in early intervention reflects the principles of inclusion, family-centered practice, and collaborative team approaches. Families, early childhood educators, and specialized consultants form the transdisciplinary team. The team has responsibility to assess the abilities and requirements of the child and the family, to seek creative solutions for obtaining goals, and to make mutual decisions about service. Based on the family's priorities, goals, and personal preferences, an IEP, an IFSP, or another relevant plan is formulated. These plans direct services for the family and educational interventions for the child. With the implementation of adapted instructional activities and family services within inclusive early intervention programs, all children like Lachme, Ashley, Alesandro, and Tuyet will have an opportunity to reach their optimal developmental potential.

FOR FURTHER THOUGHT OR DISCUSSION

1. What is the importance of early intervention for children who are at risk for developmental delay?
2. How would you define inclusion for young children with developmental delay?
3. What benefits are derived from including families in the collaborative team?
4. What power differentials exist between professionals and families in family-oriented models of early intervention?
5. With permission, attend a team meeting. What characteristics does the team demonstrate? How would you determine if it is a collaborative team?

REFERENCES

Americans with Disabilities Act (ADA) of 1990, PL 101-336, 42 U.S.C., §§ 12101 *et seq.*

Aytch, L.S., Cryer, D., Bailey, D.B., et al. (1999). Defining and assessing quality in early intervention programs for infants and toddlers with disabilities and their families: Challenges and unresolved issues. *Early Education and Development, 10,* 8–23.

Baglieri, S., & Knopf, J.H. (2004). Normalizing differences in inclusive teaching. *Journal of Learning Disabilities, 37*(6), 525–529.

Bailey, D.B. (2001). Evaluating parent involvement and family support in early intervention and preschool programs: Three levels of accountability. *Journal of Early Intervention, 24,* 1–14.

Banks, R.A., Santos, R.M., & Roof, V. (2003). Discovering family concerns, priorities and resources: Sensitive family information gathering. *Young Exceptional Children, 6*(2), 11–19.

Bhavnagri, N.P., & Gonzalez-Mena, J. (1997). The cultural context of infant caregiving. *Childhood Education, 74*(1), 2–8.

Björck-Åkesson, E., Granlund, M., & Simeonsson, R.J. (2000). Assessment philosophies and practices in Sweden. In M.J. Guralnick (Series Ed.) & M.J. Guralnick (Vol. Ed.), *International issues in early intervention: Interdisciplinary clinical assessment of young children with developmental disabilities* (pp. 391–411). Baltimore: Paul H. Brookes Publishing Co.

Boone, H.A., & Crais, E. (1999). Strategies for achieving family-driven assessment and intervention planning. *Young Exceptional Children, 3*(1), 2–11.

Bronfenbrenner, U. (1979). *The ecology of human development: Experiments by nature and design.* Cambridge: Harvard University Press.

Bronfenbrenner, U. (1995). Developmental ecology through space and time: A future perspective. In P. Moen, G. Elder, Jr., & K. Luscher (Eds.), *Examining lives in context: Perspectives on the ecology of human development* (pp. 619–647). Washington, DC: American Psychological Association.

Brown, L., Wilcox, B., & Sontag, E. (2004). Toward the realization of the least restrictive educational environments for severely handicapped students. *Research and Practice for Persons with Severe Disabilities, 29*(1), 2–8.

Brown, W.H., Odom, H.L., & Conroy, M.A. (2001). An intervention hierarchy for promoting young children's peer interactions in natural environments. *Topics in Early Childhood Special Education, 21*(3), 162–75.

Campbell, P.H. (2004). Participation-based services: Promoting children's participation in natural settings. *Young Exceptional Children, 8,* 20–29.

Canadian Charter of Rights and Freedoms. (1982). Retrieved December 8, 2005, from http://www.efc.ca/pages/law/charter/charter.sect.html

Chang, F., Early, D.M., & Winton, P.J. (2005). Early childhood teacher preparation in special education at 2- and 4-year institutions of higher education. *Journal of Early Intervention. 27,* 110–124.

Childress, D. (2004). Special instruction and natural environments: Best practices in early intervention. *Infants and Young Children, 17*(2), 162–170.

The Commonwealth Disability Discrimination Act. (1992). Retrieved December 8, 2005, from http://www.deakin.edu.au/extern/rdlu/ddaindex.html

Conyers, L.M., Reynolds, A.J., & Ou, S. (2003). The effect of early childhood intervention and subsequent special education services: Findings from the Chicago child–parent centers. *Educational Evaluation and Policy Analysis, 25,* 75–95.

Craig, S., Haggart, A., Gold, S., et al. (2000). Expanding the circle of inclusion: The childcare director's role. *Young Exceptional Children, Natural Environments and Inclusion, 2,* 27–36.

Cross, A.F., Traub, E.K., & Hutter-Pishgahi, L. (2004). Elements of successful inclusion for children with significant disabilities. *Topics in Early Childhood Special Education, 24* (3), 169–183.

Diamond, K.E., & Carpenter, E.S. (2000). Participation in inclusive preschool programs and sensitivity to the needs of others. *Journal of Early Intervention, 23,* 81–91.

Diamond, K.E., Hestenes, L., & O'Connor, C. (1994). Integrating young children with disabilities in preschool: Problems and promise. *Young Children, 49*(2), 68–75.

Diamond, M., & Hopson, J. (1999). *Magic trees of the mind: How to nurture your child's intelligence, creativity, and healthy emotions from birth through adolescence.* New York: Plume.

Division for Early Childhood. (2000). *Position statement on inclusion.* Pittsburgh, PA: Author

Dunkle, M. (2005, March 28). High quality developmental screening. *Developmental Behavioral Pediatrics On-Line.* Retrieved May 2, 2005, from http://dbpeds.org

Dunst, C.J. (2002). Family-centered practices: Birth through high school. *Journal of Special Education, 36,* 139–147.

Dunst, C.J., Johanson, C., Trivette, C.M., et al. (1991). Family-oriented early intervention policies and practices: Family-centered or not? *Exceptional Children, 58,* 115–126.

Dunst, C.J., & Trivette, C.M. (1996). Empowerment, effective helpgiving practices and family-centered care. *Pediatric Nursing, 22,* 334–337, 343.

Dunst, C.J., Trivette, C.M., & Deal, A. (1988). *Enabling and empowering families: Principles and guidelines for practice.* Cambridge, MA: Brookline Books.

Erwin, E.J., Soodak, L.C., Winton, P.J., et al. (2001). "I wish it wouldn't all depend on me": Research on families and early childhood inclusion. In M.J. Guralnick (Ed.), *Early childhood inclusion: Focus on change* (pp. 127–158). Baltimore: Paul H. Brookes Publishing Co.

Esposito, B.G., & Reed, T.M. (1986). The effects of contact with handicapped persons on young children's attitudes. *Exceptional Children, 53,* 224–229.

Frankel, E.B. (1994). Resource teachers in integrated children's centers: Implications for staff development. *International Journal of Early Childhood, 26*(2), 13–20.

Frankel, E.B. (1997). *A naturalistic inquiry into the knowledge, skills, and personal qualities of early childhood resource consultants as agents of change.* Unpublished doctoral dissertation, University of Toronto.

Frankel, E.B. (2004). Supporting inclusive care and education for young children with special needs and their families: An international perspective. *Childhood Education, 80,* 310–316.

Frankel, E.B., Howson, S., & Fish, I. (2003). Early intervention for young children with developmental delays. In I. Brown & M. Percy (Eds.), *Developmental disabilities in Ontario* (2nd ed., pp. 531–549). Toronto: Ontario Association on Developmental Disabilities.

Frankel, E.B., & McKay, D. (1997). Embarking on integration of preschool programs: Creating positive change. *Early Child Development and Care, 138,* 57–70.

Friend, M., Bursuck, W.D., & Hutchinson, N. (1998). *Including exceptional students, Canadian Edition* (Chap. 3, pp. 66–103). Scarborough, ON, Canada: Prentice Hall.

Galinsky, E., Howes, C., Kontos, S., et al. (1994). *The study of children in family child care and relative care.* New York: Families and Work Institute.

Glass, N. (1999). Sure Start: The development of an early intervention programme for young children in the United Kingdom. *Children and Society, 13,* 257–264.

Gold, S.F. (2000). Including young children with special needs in early childhood programs: Where is Florida headed? *Children our Concern, 24*(2), 23–30.

Gold, S.F., Liepack, S., Scott, M., et al. (1998). If you offer inclusion training, they will come! *Children Our Concern, 22* (2), 24–26.

Gold, S.F., Liepack, S., Scott, M., et al. (1999). Creating inclusive classrooms: A report from the field. *Young Exceptional Children, 2*(2), 2–8.

Gomby, D.S., Larner, M., Stevenson, C., et al. (1995). Long-term outcomes of early childhood programs: Analysis and recommendation. *The Future of Children, 6*(3), 6–24.

Guralnick, M.J. (Ed.). (1997). *The effectiveness of early intervention.* Baltimore: Paul H. Brookes Publishing Co.

Guralnick, M.J. (2004). Effectiveness of early intervention for vulnerable children: A developmental perspective. In M.A. Feldman (Ed.), *Early intervention: The essential readings* (pp. 9–50). Oxford, United Kingdom: Blackwell Publishing.

Hanson, M.J. (2003). National legislation for early intervention: United States of America. In M.J. Guralnick (Series Ed.) & S.L. Odom, M.J. Hanson, J.A. Blackman, et al. (Vol. Eds.), *International issues in early intervention: Early intervention practices around the world* (pp. 253–279). Baltimore: Paul H. Brookes Publishing Co.

Hester, P.P., Baltodano, H.M., & Gable, R.A. (2003). Early intervention with children at risk of emotional/behavioral disorders: A critical examination of research methodology and practices. *Education and Treatment of Children, 26* (4), 362–381.

Holahan, A., & Costenbader, V. (2000). A comparison of developmental gains for preschool children with disabilities in inclusive and self-contained classrooms. *Topics in Early Childhood Special Education, 20,* 224–235.

Hopkins, B. (1995). *Inclusion and early intervention: A resource manual for early childhood settings in Ontario.* Hamilton, ON, Canada: St. Matthew's House.

Hundert, J., Mahoney, B., Mundy, F., et al. (1998). A descriptive analysis of developmental and social gains of children with severe disabilities in segregated and inclusive preschools in southern Ontario. *Early Childhood Research Quarterly, 13,* 49–65.

Individuals with Disabilities Education Improvement Act of 2004, PL 108-446, 20 U.S.C. §§ 1400 *et seq.*

Irwin, S.H., Lero, D.S., & Brophy, K. (2000). *A matter of urgency: Including children with special needs in child care in Canada.* Wreck Cove, NS, Canada: Breton Books.

Irwin, S.H., Lero, D.S., & Brophy, K. (2004). *Inclusion: The next generation of child care in Canada.* Wreck Cove, NS, Canada: Breton Books.

Isenberg, J.P., & Brown, D.L. (1997). Development issues affecting children. In J. Isenberg & M. Jalongo (Eds.), *Major trends and issues in early childhood education: Challenges, controversies, and insights* (pp. 29–42). New York: Teachers College Press.

Johnston, C.F. (2003). Formal and informal networks: Australia. In M.J. Guralnick (Series Ed.) & S.L. Odom, M.J. Hanson, J.A. Blackman, et al. (Vol. Eds.), *International issues in early intervention: Early intervention practices around the world* (pp. 281–299). Baltimore: Paul H. Brookes Publishing Co.

Kagan, S.L., & Cohen, N.E. (1997). *Not by chance: Creating an early care and education system for America's children.* New Haven, CT: Yale University, The Bush Center in Child Development and Social Policy.

Kamerman, S.B. (2000). Early childhood intervention policies: An international perspective. In J.P. Shonkoff & S.J. Meisels (Eds.), *Handbook of early childhood intervention* (2nd ed., pp. 613–629). Cambridge, United Kingdom: Cambridge University Press.

King, T.M., & Glascoe, F.P. (2003). Developmental surveillance of infants and young children in pediatric primary care. *Current Opinion in Pediatric, 15*(6), 624–629.

Kontos, S., & Wilcox-Herzog, A. (1997). Influences on children's competence in early childhood classrooms. *Early Childhood Research Quarterly, 12,* 247–262.

Lamorey, S., & Bricker, D.D. (1993). Integrated programs: Effects on young children and their parents. In C.A. Peck, S.L. Odom, & D.D. Bricker (Eds.), *Integrating young children with disabilities into community programs: Ecological perspectives on research and implementation* (pp. 249–270). Baltimore: Paul H. Brookes Publishing Co.

Linder, T.W. (1993). *Transdisciplinary play-based assessment: A functional approach to working with young children* (Rev. ed.). Baltimore: Paul H. Brookes Publishing Co.

Lessenberry, B.M., & Rehfeldt, R.A. (2004). Evaluating stress levels of parents of children with disabilities. *Exceptional Children, 70,* 231–244.

Mackenzie-Keating, S.E., & Kysela, G.M. (1997). Efficacy of early intervention: Fact or fantasy? *Exceptionality Education Canada, 7*(1&2), 21–28.

Masse, L.N., & Barnett, W.S. (2002). *A benefit cost analysis of the Abecedarian early childhood intervention.* New Brunswick, NJ: National Institute for Early Education Research. (ERIC Document Service Reproduction No. ED479989)

McCain, M.N., & Mustard, J.F. (1999). *Reversing the real brain drain: Early years study—Final report.* Toronto: Publications Ontario.

Miller, P.S., & Stayton, V.D. (2000). DEC Recommended practices in personnel preparation. In S. Sandall, M.E. McLean, & B.J. Smith (Eds.), *DEC Recommended practices in early intervention/early childhood special education* (pp. 77–81). Longmont, CO: Sopris West.

Neisworth J.T., & Bagnato, S.J. (2000). Recommended practices in assessment. In S. Sandall, M.E. McLean, & B.J. Smith (Eds.), *DEC recommended practices in early intervention/early childhood special education* (pp. 17–28). Longmont, CO: Sopris West.

Nunn, G., & McMahan, K. (2000). "Ideal" problem solving using a collaborative effort for special needs and at-risk students. *Education, 121*(2), 305–312.

O'Brien, M. (2001). Inclusion child care for infants and toddlers: A natural environment for all children. In M.J. Guralnick (Ed.), *Early childhood inclusion: Focus on change* (pp. 229–251). Baltimore: Paul H. Brookes Publishing Co.

Odom, S.L. (2000). Preschool inclusion: What we know and where we go from here. *Topics in Early Childhood Special Education, 20,* 20–28.

Odom, S.L., Hanson, M.J., Blackman, J.A., et al. (Vol. Eds.). (2003). *International issues in early intervention: Early intervention practices around the world.* Baltimore: Paul H. Brookes Publishing Co.

Odom, S.L., Teferra, T., & Kaul, S.S. (2004). An overview of international approaches to early intervention for young children with special needs and their families. *Young Children, 59*(5), 38–43.

Parlakian, R. (2003). Partnerships for quality infant-toddler child care. *Zero to Three, 23*(4), 4–45.

Peck, C.A., Carlson, P., & Helmstetter, E. (1992). Parent and teacher perceptions of outcomes for nonhandicapped children enrolled in integrated early childhood programs: A statewide study. *Journal of Early Intervention, 16,* 53–63.

Peck, C.A., Furman, G.C., & Helmstetter, E. (1993). Integrated early childhood programs: Research on the implementation of change in organizational contexts. In C.A. Peck, S.L. Odom, & D.D. Bricker (Eds.), *Integrating young children with disabilities into community programs: Ecological perspectives on research and implementation* (pp. 187–205). Baltimore: Paul H. Brookes Publishing Co.

Rafferty, Y., Piscitelli, V., & Boettcher, C. (2003). The impact of inclusion on language development and social competence among preschoolers with disabilities. *Exceptional Children, 69,* 467–479.

Ramey, C.T., Campbell, F.A., & Blair, C. (1998). Enhancing the life course for high-risk children: Results from the Abecedarion Project. In J. Crane (Ed.), *Social programs that really work* (pp. 163–184). New York: Russell Sage.

Reynolds, A.J., Temple, J.A., Robertson, D.L., et al. (2001). Long term effects of an early childhood intervention on educational achievement and juvenile arrest: A 15-year follow-up of low-income children in public schools. *Journal of the American Medical Association, 285,* 2339–2346.

Sandall, S., McLean, M.E., & Smith, B.J. (Eds.). (2000). *DEC Recommended practices in early intervention/early childhood special education.* Longmont, CO: Sopris West.

Sandall, S., Schwartz, I., & Joseph, G. (2001). A building blocks model for effective instruction in inclusive early childhood settings. *Young Exceptional Children, 4*(3), 3–9.

Scott, R., Sexton, D., & Wood, T. (1986, April). *A comparison of marital adjustment and stress of parents of typical and atypical infants.* Paper presented at the meeting of the International Council for Exceptional Children Conference, New Orleans, LA.

Sheldon, M.L., & Rush, D.D. (2001). The ten myths about providing early intervention services in natural environments. *Infants and Young Children, 14*(1), 1–13.

Shonkoff, J.P., & Phillips, D.A. (2000). *From neurons to neighborhoods: The science of early childhood development.* Washington, DC: National Academies Press.

Thurman, S.K., Cornwell, J.R., & Gottwald, S.R. (Eds.). (1997). *Contexts of early intervention: Systems and settings.* Baltimore: Paul H. Brookes Publishing Co.

Turnbull, A.P., Turbiville, V., & Turnbull, H.R. (2000). Evolution of family–professional partnerships: Collective empowerment as the model for the early twenty-first century. In J.P. Shonkoff & S.J. Meisels (Eds.), *Handbook of early childhood intervention* (2nd ed., pp. 630–650). Cambridge, United Kingdom: Cambridge University Press.

Turnbull, A.P., & Turnbull, H.R. (2001). *Families, professionals, and exceptionality: Collaborating for empowerment* (4th ed.). Upper Saddler River, NJ: Prentice Hall.

United Nations. (1989). *Convention on the Rights of the Child.* Retrieved December 8, 2005, from http://www.unhchr.ch/html/menu3/b/k2crc.htm

Weikart, D. (1996). High quality preschool programs found to improve adult status. *Childhood: A Global Journal of Child Research, 3*(1), 117–120.

Winton, P.J. (1996). Family–professional partnerships and integrated services. In R.A. McWilliam (Ed.), *Rethinking pull-out services in early intervention: A professional resource* (pp. 49–69). Baltimore: Paul H. Brookes Publishing Co.

Wolery, M., & Bailey, D.B. (2002). Early childhood special education research. *Journal of Early Intervention, 25,* 88–99.

30

Maltreatment of Children with Developmental Disabilities

Ann Fudge Schormans and Dick Sobsey

> **WHAT YOU WILL LEARN ABOUT IN THIS CHAPTER**
>
> - What is meant by the term *child maltreatment*
> - Historical and current contexts
> - Child maltreatment and developmental disability

The right to live free from fear and from want is a basic human right set out by the United Nations (UN) in the 1948 *International Declaration of Human Rights* (Centre for Human Rights, 1996) and extended to expand protections to people with disabilities in 1971 (*Declaration on the Rights of Mentally Retarded Persons*), 1975 (*Declaration on the Rights of Disabled Persons*), 1982 (*World Program of Actions Concerning Disabled Persons*), and 1994 (*Standard Rules on Equalization of Opportunities for Persons with Disabilities*) (United Nations Enable, 2006). The UN's *Convention on the Rights of the Child* (1989), which was ratified by both developed and developing countries, guarantees every child the right to be free from abuse. Article 23 of the Convention specifically states that children with intellectual and physical disabilities share these rights and that states must make special efforts to meet their special needs. These declarations have prompted many developed and developing nations to begin to design policies, legislation, and practice to ensure these rights. The United States Constitution, the Bill of Rights in the Constitution of South Africa, and the Canadian Charter of Rights and Freedoms are among many national constitutional documents that also promise equal protection of the law for individuals with disabilities. In spite of these fundamental protections, however, child maltreatment remains a major problem for children worldwide and a more severe problem for children with disabilities.

WHAT IS MEANT BY THE TERM *CHILD MALTREATMENT*

As with the term *disability*, the term *child maltreatment* (or *child abuse*) is a socially constructed concept. Consequently, how the term is understood varies across class, culture, geography, gender, and generations. This means that definitions of child maltreatment may differ across, and within, various nations. In fact, even the definition of *child* varies according to laws and customs that set out the ages at which individuals are considered adults.

It is not possible for this chapter to adequately address this multiplicity of meaning, particularly as it pertains to the similarities and contrasts among developed and developing countries. The tremendous social, economic, and political variability prohibits a universal understanding. Colonialist attempts to impose Western European definitions and practices have largely been unsuccessful (Ingstad, 2001). However, child protection history, laws, and practices in the Anglo-American nations (Australia, Canada, New Zealand, the United Kingdom, the United States and others) typically share many major features (Waldfogel, 1998). These countries all have mandated institutions to deal with child protection. Most have laws that define children requiring protection in fairly similar ways. For example, section 72 (1) of the Child and Family Services Amendment Act (1999) of the province of Ontario in Canada, defines a "child in need of protection" as one requiring protection from physical, sexual, and emotional abuse; neglect; and harm (see Display 30.1). Because child welfare, or child protective services, are involved in the majority of reported cases of child maltreatment in these countries, this chapter primarily proceeds from this statutory framework.

HISTORICAL AND CURRENT CONTEXTS

Worldwide, reference to the abuse of children, both with and without developmental disabilities, can be found in some of the earliest historical recordings of children's lives (Chadwick, 1999; Ingstad, 2001; Winzer, 1997). The existence of an organized concern with and response to the maltreatment of children is, however, a relatively recent phenomenon. In 1874, the Society for the Prevention of Cruelty to Animals met in

Display 30.1

Child and Family Services Amendment Act (Child Welfare Reform) (1999) s.37 (2)

A child is deemed in need of protection when:

1. The child has suffered physical harm, inflicted by the person having charge of the child, or caused by, or resulting from that person's:
   i. failure to adequately care for, provide for, supervise or protect the child, or
   ii. pattern of neglect in caring for, providing for, supervising or protecting the child.
2. There is a risk that the child is likely to suffer physical harm inflicted by the person having charge of the child, or caused by, or resulting from that person's:
   i. failure to adequately care for, provide for, supervise or protect the child, or
   ii. pattern of neglect in caring for, providing for, supervising or protecting the child.
3. The child has been sexually molested or sexually exploited, by the person having charge of the child or by another person where the person having charge of the child knows or should know of the possibility of sexual molestation or sexual exploitation and fails to protect the child.
4. There is a risk that the child is likely to be sexually molested or sexually exploited as described in paragraph 3.
5. The child requires medical treatment to cure, prevent or alleviate physical harm or suffering, and the child's parent or the person having charge of the child does not provide, or refuses or is unavailable or unable to consent to the treatment.
6. The child has suffered emotional harm, demonstrated by serious:
   i. anxiety,
   ii. depression,
   iii. withdrawal,
   iv. self-destructive or aggressive behaviour, or
   v. delayed development, and there are reasonable grounds to believe that the emotional harm suffered by the child results from the actions, failure to act or pattern of neglect on the part of the child's parent or the person having charge of the child.
7. The child has suffered emotional harm of the kind described in subparagraph i, ii, iii, iv or v of paragraph 6 and the child's parent or the person having charge of the child does not provide, or refuses or is unavailable or unable to consent to, services or treatment to remedy or alleviate the harm.
8. There is a risk that the child is likely to suffer emotional harm of the kind described in subparagraph i, ii, iii, iv or v of paragraph 6 resulting from the actions, failure to act or pattern of neglect on the part of the child's parent or the person having charge of the child.
9. There is a risk that the child is likely to suffer emotional harm of the kind described in subparagraph i, ii, iii, iv or v of paragraph 6 and that the child's parent or the person having charge of the child does not provide, or refuses or is unavailable or unable to consent to, services or treatment to prevent the harm.
10. The child suffers from a mental, emotional or developmental condition that, if not remedied, could seriously impair the child's development and the child's parent or the person having charge of the child does not provide, or refuses or is unavailable or unable to consent to, treatment to remedy or alleviate the condition.
11. The child has been abandoned, the child's parent has died or is unavailable to exercise his or her custodial rights over the child and has not made adequate provision for the child's care and custody, or the child is in a residential placement and the parent refuses or is unable or unwilling to resume the child's care and custody.
12. The child is less than 12 years old and has killed or seriously injured another person or caused serious damage to another person's property, services or treatment are necessary to prevent a recurrence and the child's parent or the person having charge of the child does not provide, or refuses or is unavailable or unable to consent to, those services or treatment.
13. The child is less than 12 years old and has on more than one occasion injured another person or caused loss or damage to another person's property, with the encouragement of the person having charge of the child or because of that person's failure or inability to supervise the child adequately.

Source: Government of Ontario, Canada (1999).

New York City to discuss the possibility that children could also be protected, and it formed the Society for the Prevention of Cruelty to Children (Bremner, 1971). This movement rapidly spread to Britain (1883), Canada (1891), Australia (1896), and many other countries (Waldfogel, 1998). For example, in Toronto, Canada, in 1887, the Toronto Humane Society was founded with the purpose of the prevention of cruelty to both animals and to children. This led to the passing of the provincial Children's Protection Act (1888), which for the first time made child abuse an indictable offense, and to the organization of Ontario's first Children's Aid Society (CAS) in 1891 (Macintyre, 1993).

In many ways, the development of a systemic response to child abuse parallels the path of service provision to children with developmental disabilities in these countries, with the phenomena of child abuse and developmental disability being inextricably linked. Unfortunately, two ways that services for children with developmental disabilities and services for abused children were similar were that 1) both produced institutional care and 2) institutional care often produced more abuse. For example, by 1898, residential services run by the New York Society for the Prevention of Cruelty to Children were themselves investigated for child abuse and neglect (Bremner, 1971).

Prior to the late 1800s, children were granted few protections from abuse. The laissez-faire ideology of Western governments, combined with the liberal idea of the sanctity of the family (and concomitant view of children as the responsibility and property of their parents), minimized the provision of social supports to children and deterred state intervention in situations involving disability and/or parental abuse of children. Foundling homes, operated by churches, philanthropists, or charitable organizations, provided alternatives to infanticide of unwanted children and temporary refuge for very young children who were orphaned or abandoned (Macintyre, 1993). Yet, the generally deplorable conditions in these homes resulted in reported child mortality rates as high as 50%–80% (Steinhauer, 1991). Almshouses, workhouses, or apprenticeships were the options for older children who were deserted or orphaned or who ran away from abusive families. The risk of maltreatment (see Table 30.1) in these environments was great (Macintyre, 1993; Sobsey, 1994; Steinhauer, 1991) because the children were without rights or recourse; at the mercy of their benefactors; and typically housed with adults exhibiting a host of social, emotional, and psychological problems. It was not until the latter half of the 19th century that all children's needs for protection from abuse, nurturance, and the conditions necessary for healthy growth and development began to be recognized and the state's responsibility in this task acknowledged.

Before industrialization and urbanization, the typical "family" in Western society functioned as a productive unit. With each member (often including members with a disability) contributing to the livelihood of the family as a whole, children were not necessarily distinguished from other family members. The arrival of industrialization found children of families from lower socioeconomic classes working alongside adults in factories. Treated as "little adults," they were exploited (underpaid and overworked) as child laborers and regularly subjected to poor child-rearing practices, lack of protection, and, frequently, severe punishments.

For children with developmental disabilities, a production-based economy created a situation of disadvantage (Macintyre, 1993; Radford, 1994; Steinhauer, 1991). Growing awareness of the impact of these conditions on the health and safety of children combined with the emergence of a strong middle class and the evolution of what is now the traditional patriarchal family model to foster both the notion of childhood as a separate stage of human development and a patriarchal model of helping that has proven tenacious (Macintyre, 1993). In addition, with rising cultural standards of health and welfare, standards of behavior towards children accepted as normal in previous centuries came to be regarded as intolerable (Chadwick, 1999). A growing belief that children with developmental disabilities could be educated, along with recognition of their vulnerability, led to the emergence of an institutional care system intended to provide them with specialized care and training to enable them to take their place in society. However, the growth of institutions was also strongly fuelled by another trend of the times: a strong eugenics movement that used institutions as a means of segregating those of "inferior stock" for life, with little pretense of training to enable children to return to the community (Sobsey, 1994).

Child Saving Movement

Out of the new middle class emerged a social reform movement that was intent on rescuing children from the deplorable conditions that were created, in part, by industrialization and urbanization. Private philanthropic and volunteer efforts—as well as those by people in the animal saving, women's suffragette, abolitionist, and labor movements—played important roles in the child-saving movement, as they advocated a move beyond traditional charitable models of provision for children toward a social welfare model with government legislation for the protection of neglected and maltreated children (Macintyre, 1993; Sobsey, 1994; Waldfogel, 1998). Patriarchal conceptions of family shaped a *parens patriae* model of child protection legislation; *parens patriae* is a Latin term meaning "protector"

Table 30.1. Common indicators of child maltreatment[a]

	Child physical signs	Child behavioral signs	Parent behavioral signs
Physical abuse	Abrasions Bites Bruises Burns and scalds Lacerations Ligature marks Welts Dislocations Broken bones Dental injuries Ear injuries Eye injuries Coma	Atypical attachment Disclosure Fearfulness Learning disabilities Noncompliance Regression Sleep disturbances Withdrawal Acting-out behavior	Lack of empathy for child Unrealistic expectations of child Holding child overly responsible for his or her behavior and blaming child for negative outcomes Interpreting child's behavior negatively and judging misbehavior too harshly Coercive or threatening to child Difficulty managing stress Overly tense, depressed, angry, confused, or impulsive Involved in domestic violence
Emotional abuse/psychological maltreatment	Poor growth	Anxiety and fear Age-inappropriate responsibility (too much or too little expected of child) Decline in cognitive ability Lessened problem-solving capacity Lower educational attainment Poor peer relationships (withdrawn) Poor school attendance Self-abuse	Degrading, hostile, or rejecting Exploitative and/or corrupting Not emotionally responsive to child; detached and uninvolved Denial of services promoting child development and well-being Isolates child Neglectful Comments that shame, insult, or ridicule child Terrorizing and/or threatening behavior Lack of understanding of child's needs and how to meet them Lack of empathy for child
Sexual abuse	Bruises or genital abnormalities Genital discomfort Pregnancy Sexually transmitted disease Signs of physical abuse Torn or missing clothing	Atypical attachment Avoidance of specific adults or settings Development of new fears Depression Dissociation Eating disorder Learning difficulties, deterioration in school performance Low self-esteem Noncompliance Behavioral regression Resists physical examination Self-injurious behavior Sexualized behavior Sleep disturbance Substance abuse Withdrawal or acting-out behavior Excessive fantasy behavior	Antisocial behavior Lack of effective social skills Social anxiety Sociopathology Lack of empathy for child Cognitive distortions that encourage exploitative relationships Impulsivity; lack of inhibitions Seductive or sexually explicit behavior with child in presence of others Overly protective of child Extremely authoritative Criminality, previous conviction for sexual assault Isolating child and family Seeking isolated contact with children

and "father of the country" (Macintyre, 1993, p. 20). Through legislated child welfare agencies, the state acted as a substitute benevolent parent. Within this framework, states had the right, in the best interests of the child, to suspend the authority of the family through their legislative and court systems, to make determinations of good or bad parenting, to define acceptable living conditions for children, to establish services on behalf of children, and to remove from their homes children believed in need of state protection (Macintyre, 1993). For children with developmental disabilities, the "best interests" rationale similarly permitted removal from their homes and institutionalization.

Rescuing children from abusive and neglectful families was not just about protecting children from victimization. State mandated child saving was perceived as the best method to protect society from moral degeneration and social unrest. Adopting an individ-

	Child physical signs	Child behavioral signs	Parent behavioral signs
Neglect	Failure to thrive (i.e., growth falls below satisfactory levels) Illness Malnourishment Poor hygiene	Apathy Avoidance or resistance to attachment Coercive Displays more frustration than typical for age Insecure attachment Isolated at playtime Less effective coping Less positive and more negative Low self-esteem Negative affect Passive behavior Poor problem-solving ability Reduced prosocial behavior Self-centered behavior Withdrawal	Expecting child to fill adult emotional needs Withdrawn, depressed, psychologically unavailable Failure to recognize and attend to child's need for attention Failure to address child's emotional or behavior disorders Exposing child to parent's mental illness or substance abuse or to domestic violence Failure to provide adequate physical care Failure to provide adequate clothing, shelter, or nourishment Failure to provide adequate medical care or treatment Age-inappropriate expectations of child (e.g., very young child expected to feed him- or herself) Lack of appropriate supervision Repeated separations or moves

Sources: Garbarino, Brookhouser, Authier, et al. (1987); Macdonald (2001); and Sobsey (1994); see also Fudge Schormans (2003).

[a]The reader is cautioned to remember that there are no absolute indicators of child maltreatment; maltreatment is the result of a complex interaction of multiple factors and many different responses are possible. Although current research and practice offers some support for the indicators listed, the indicators will not necessarily apply in each and every case.

ual pathology approach, the blame was placed on immoral parents—the optimum solution was to remove "good children" from these "moral imbeciles" (Carlson, 2001, p. 126). This perspective resulted in legislators overlooking, and thus not addressing, the social and economic factors involved in child abuse (Macintyre, 1993; Rutman, 1987; Sobsey, 1994). This same concern with protecting society from moral decay was at the root of moving children with developmental disabilities to segregated institutions (Carlson, 2001; Simmons, 1982).

The child welfare system and the institutional system operated in parallel for the next 60–70 years. Although child protection legislation did not specifically exclude maltreated children with developmental disabilities, the typical response of child welfare services was to transfer the child with a disability and responsibility for the problem to the institutions (Simmons, 1982). Thus, institutions retained control over the investigation and management of abuses occurring in those settings.

Contemporary Context of Developmental Disabilities and Child Protection

The 1950s and 1960s witnessed a renewed interest in the areas of child maltreatment and developmental disability, prompted again by feminist and civil rights movements. The identification of battered child syndrome in 1962 was a key development that led to a medical model approach to child protection focused on physical abuse and rescuing children from physically abusive parents (Waldfogel, 1998). Regarding developmental disability, the primary impetus for change came from a growing movement of parents alarmed by the appalling conditions and abuses within institutions. Rescuing their children from institutional settings and returning them to their home communities became a strong advocacy focus, and gradually deinstitutionalization policies and practices took hold (Radford & Park, 2003; Sobsey, 1994).

In the 1970s and 1980s, as more children with developmental disabilities remained in the community with their families, they were increasingly likely to become involved with child welfare services. Simultaneously, many state and provincial governments began to develop family support services intended to assist families with the care of their child with a disability. The development of these programs was driven both by a philosophical commitment to preserve families and by simple economics, which suggested that relatively modest investments in families could save the high costs of institutionalization.

Paralleling deinstitutionalization and normalization philosophies in developmental disabilities, child protective services also began to shift toward a family preservation model. Respect for parental rights and the integrity of the family were prioritized over children's rights, thus making it more difficult to bring a child into protective care. This response was a reaction to criticism of earlier policies that permitted greater state intrusion into family life and to concerns over the abuse of children in state care and the negative impacts of state care and removal from the family home on a child's well-being. A growing interest in preventing and prosecuting child sexual abuse in the early 1990s resulted in amendments to criminal justice legislation in numerous jurisdictions of the world, modifying investigative and court procedures that made it easier for children to testify (Covell & Howe, 2001).

The recognition in the late 1990s that family preservation policies were no more effective for protecting children from maltreatment than were earlier models coincided with two other developments to return child protective services to a social welfare model. First, acceptance grew for the idea of children's rights, such as the right to protection from abuse and neglect and the right to a stable and healthy childhood. Second, reports of child deaths caused by abuse inflamed concerns that children's needs and rights were inadequately addressed.

Return to a social welfare model has not been without competing interests, however. Both historical and contemporary child protection legislation and practice are rooted in liberal ideologies and a *parens patriae* approach that struggles with the competing demands in most countries to contain child welfare costs, to preserve and not intrude on families, and to protect children. As a result, most legislation remains reactive as opposed to proactive—it is not charged with preventing child maltreatment, only with responding to it once it has occurred (Covell & Howe, 2001; Macintyre, 1993).

CHILD MALTREATMENT AND DEVELOPMENTAL DISABILITY

There is no singular worldwide view of disability (see Chapter 1). Across the vast array of world cultures can be found a similarly vast number of understandings of, and responses to, children and adults labeled "developmentally disabled" (Ghai, 2001; Ingstad, 2001; Stone, 2001). A review of the international literature, however, reveals a strong connection between developmental disability and maltreatment. The available literature does not always distinguish between children and adults, and thus the following discussion makes reference to both.

Prevalence of Child Maltreatment

The risk of abuse for individuals with developmental disabilities may be as much as ten times greater than the risk for people without developmental disabilities (Randall, Parilla, & Sobsey, 2000). As early as 1967, Elmer and Gregg reported that 50% of the abused children they examined had intellectual disabilities. Although there is no epidemiological consensus in the literature, children with developmental disabilities are consistently found to be at a much greater risk for abuse than are their peers without disabilities.

The best evidence available comes from Sullivan and Knutson's (2000) study of a large cohort of more than 40,000 children attending school in Omaha. The cohort design allowed the same definitions of disability to be applied to children with and without histories of maltreatment. Sullivan and Knutson (2000) found that children identified by their schools as requiring special education services were 3.4 times as likely to be maltreated as children who had not been found to need services. This meant that almost one-quarter (22%) of children with a history of maltreatment were identified as needing special education, and almost one third (31%) of children in special education had a confirmed history of child maltreatment. The strongest association between maltreatment and disability was for children with behavior disorders, who were 6.3 times more likely to have a confirmed history of maltreatment than children with no identified disability. Children with intellectual disabilities were 3.7 times more likely to have a confirmed history of neglect, 3.8 times more likely to have a confirmed history of physical abuse, 3.8 times more likely to have a confirmed history of emotional abuse, and 4.0 times more likely to have a history of sexual abuse than children with no identified disability. Among all maltreated children, 24.1% had intellectual disabilities.

It is difficult, if not impossible, to determine the exact scope of this problem for three reasons: reporting issues, variability in research methodology, and lack of clarity in understanding the association. These topics are discussed in detail next.

Reporting Issues Given its multiple causes and manifestations, developmental disability is believed to be underdiagnosed in the general population (Percy & Brown, 2003) and is often neither identified nor noted in the records of child protective services (Sullivan & Knutson, 2000). Child maltreatment itself is believed to be underreported, often because people are not familiar with the indicators of maltreatment. In countries where reporting suspected child abuse is mandatory (see Display 30.2), people may be unaware of their legislated responsibility to report suspected maltreatment or how and to whom to report their suspicions. Even when maltreatment is recognized, there may be a reluctance to report. It is estimated that almost half of all cases of suspected child maltreatment are not reported (Reiniger & Robison, 1995). People may believe that reporting will have negative repercussions for themselves,

> **Display 30.2**
>
> *Responsibility to report a child in need of protection as mandated by the Child and Family Services Amendment Act (Child Welfare Reform), s. 72 (1-8).*
>
> The welfare of children is the responsibility of all members of society. If, however, those people who work closely with children have reasonable grounds to suspect that a child is, or may be, in need of protection, they are legally mandated to report these suspicions to a children's aid society.
>
> Professionals affected include (but are not limited to) the following:
>
> - health care professionals, including physicians, nurses, dentists, pharmacists and psychologists
> - teachers, and school principals
> - social workers and family counselors
> - priests, rabbis and other members of the clergy
> - operators or employees of day nurseries
> - youth and recreation workers (not volunteers)
> - peace officers and coroners
> - solicitors
> - service providers and employees of service providers
> - any other person who performs professional or official duties with respect to a child.
>
> It is an offence not to report the suspicion that a child is in need of protection, and a penalty exists for professionals who fail to do so.
>
> The duty to report overrides any other provincial statute including those that prohibit disclosure of confidential information.
>
> The duty to report is an ongoing one, and any further grounds to suspect abuse would necessitate further reporting.
>
> Unless there is proof that a person who has reported has acted maliciously or without reasonable grounds, the legislation provides protection from liability.
>
> *Source:* Government of Ontario (1999).

the child, and/or the family; that it will cause more harm; or that nothing will be done (Zellman, 1990). Assuming the proportion of reported to unreported cases of abuse is approximately equal, any figure is likely a gross underestimation of the problem (Sobsey, 1994).

Among people with developmental disabilities, abuse is both significantly underdiagnosed and underreported. Children and adults with developmental disabilities are less likely to disclose abuse themselves for several reasons that are typical for people with and without disabilities: fear of reprisal from abuser, feelings of guilt or shame, fear of consequences to self and family (e.g., child separated from family, parent jailed, becoming homeless, losing support network), or the fear of not being believed. Specific to many people with developmental disabilities is the lack of sufficient vocabulary or communication skills needed to make disclosure (Garbarino et al., 1987; Strickler, 2001). As a result, reports most often come from a third party. However, considerable variation exists regarding the competence of caregivers, staff, and professionals to detect abuse (Beail & Warden, 1995). In addition, communication difficulties may prevent or impede a child's ability to verbally disclose maltreatment. The child may instead demonstrate behavioral and emotional signs of having been abused (Ammerman et al., 1989). As these signs are less conclusive than a verbal disclosure, they are often overlooked, misdiagnosed as a symptom of a mental health problem, or improperly labeled as a function of the disability. By attributing the cause of the aberrant behavior or emotional response to the disability, the true cause—child abuse—is overlooked. Because the reporting and substantiation rates for children with and without disabilities may differ, relative rates of confirmed abuse may be misleading.

Variability in Research Methodology Variability in research methodology complicates the ability to get an accurate understanding of the rate of maltreatment in children with developmental disabilities (see Dufour & Chamberland, 2003). Research samples tend to be selective, targeting individuals who have a particular diagnosis (i.e., Down syndrome), thus failing to represent the broad range of diagnoses and abilities captured under the label "developmental disability." Many studies are concerned with only one type of abuse. In addition, incidence studies rarely control for age in comparing children with and without disabilities (Dufour & Chamberland, 2003). Finally, when data are collected from child protective service records, the lower socioeconomic classes and ethnic minorities may be overrepresented in the results (Gorman-Smith & Matson, 1992).

Although children with developmental disabilities reside in a wide variety of settings (i.e., family homes, foster and adoptive homes, group homes, and institutions), samples tend to be drawn from very specific (usually clinical) settings (Perlman & Erikson, 1992; Silverman, Reinherz, & Giaconia, 1996). Estimates drawn from the records of child protective services typically include only cases of intrafamilial abuse, thereby excluding the situations of extrafamilial abuse investigated by the police authorities. For example, drawing on data taken from child protective services records alone, Sullivan and Knutson (2000) determined the incidence of maltreatment among children with developmental disabilities to be 1.7 times greater than for children without developmental disabilities. When they examined data derived by merging a number of sources (i.e., school, police, and child protective services records), children with developmental disabilities were found to be 3.4 times more likely to experience abuse.

This view is supported by Brown (2003) who, in an analysis of data of reported child abuse from all sources in a national Canadian study (Trocmé et al., 2001), concluded that children with developmental disabilities are considerably overrepresented at 8.68% of the children reported for maltreatment; only approximately 3% of the population would be considered to have developmental disabilities, and 1% or fewer are typically known to service systems. Even the figure of 8.68% might be low, Brown suggested, because disability is often not diagnosed in the 20% of the sample who were younger than 6 years old and because the data were gathered from agency files and recording disability was not necessarily required by the service agencies. The need for precise methodology and definitions was further supported by Fudge Schormans and Brown (2002), who noted that overrepresentation of children with developmental disabilities in cases of maltreatment appears to be especially linked to neglect.

Of great concern here is the Eurocentric bias to research. Although approximately 80% of people with disabilities live in developing countries, most available research originates from developed countries, specifically Western Europe and North America (Priestley, 2001). Differential definitions and understanding of the terms *developmental disability* and *abuse* further confound knowledge of prevalence worldwide (Perlman & Erikson, 1992).

Lack of Clarity in Understanding the Association Another concern is that studies relating intellectual disability to maltreatment do not typically clarify the nature of the association. They do not indicate whether children who already have disabilities are at increased risk, whether maltreatment results in the overrepresentation of cases of children with disabilities, or whether some other factors increase the risk for both disabilities and maltreatment.

These three factors suggest that any estimates to date are most likely an underreporting of the true extent of the problem. Despite this, it is still clear that children with developmental disabilities are overrepresented in maltreatment.

Theoretical Perspective for Understanding Maltreatment

Child maltreatment, like all forms of violence, cannot be understood to result from any single determinant. The most accepted theoretical framework in much contemporary research is the integrative ecological model (Macdonald, 2001). From this perspective, child abuse and neglect are the result of the dynamic interplay of genetic, biological, psychological, environmental, and sociological factors that combine to create the conditions necessary for abuse or neglect to occur. Some of these factors act to increase the risk of maltreatment, others to protect the child from harm. Some factors are distal and have a long-lasting or cumulative effect (e.g., attachment disruptions). Current, or recent, factors are termed *proximal factors* (e.g., loss of housing). An understanding of abuse is best accomplished through an assessment of the interplay among the relevant factors over both space (i.e., the individuals involved and the environment) and time (past and present), and across four levels of analysis: the level of the individual (child and caregiver), the family, the community, and society (Macdonald, 2001).

Developmental Disability as a Risk for, and Consequence of, Maltreatment

There is a well-established association between maltreatment and developmental disability. As noted, child maltreatment is implicated in a substantial number of developmental disabilities and children with developmental disabilities are at an increased risk of experiencing maltreatment (Fudge Schormans & Brown, 2002). Sobsey (1994) suggested that 3%–6% of all maltreated children will have some degree of permanent developmental disability as a result of the abuse and that child maltreatment is a factor in 10%–25% of all developmental disabilities. This is, however, not a simple cause-and-effect relationship, and it is neither universal nor inevitable. Yet it can, for some people, create a cycle of maltreatment and disability: childhood maltreatment leading to permanent developmental disability that precipitates lifelong risk and vulnerability to further maltreatment. These two concepts are discussed in detail next.

Child Maltreatment Increases the Risk of Developmental Disability

There are three primary mechanisms by which developmental disability becomes an outcome of child maltreatment: 1) physical trauma, 2) neglect, and 3) the emotional and psychological effects of maltreatment (Garbarino et al., 1987; Hughes & Rycus, 1998; Sobsey, 1994). As more is learned about how emotional and psychological effects produce physiological, and even anatomical, effects in developing children, the line between these primary categories begins to blur.

Physical Trauma Physical trauma leading to neurological damage may result in developmental disability. Permanent brain damage may be a sequela of physical abuse and may be implicated in developmental disability, cerebral palsy, epilepsy, neuromotor disabilities, speech and language deficits, and growth deficits. Shaken-baby syndrome is a well-known example. Women face an increased risk of physical assault during pregnancy. This may be a result of marital stress, sexual frustration, a response to changes in the woman's affect and/or behavior during pregnancy, a conscious or unconscious desire to hurt the fetus, or the woman's decreased capacity to defend herself during pregnancy (Sobsey, 1994). Both the assaults and the stress associated with spousal violence can result in traumatogenic developmental disabilities or low birth weights (also associated with developmental disability) (Teixeira, Fisk, & Glover, 1999). Maternal prenatal substance abuse (e.g., alcohol, street drugs, inhalants), which is associated with violence, also interferes with typical fetal development and may lead to serious, lifelong developmental problems (e.g., fetal alcohol syndrome). The role of violence in pregnancy is relevant both because 1) it is associated with maternal substance abuse, poor nutrition, and poor prenatal care and 2) because prenatal family violence is a risk factor for postnatal child maltreatment. Although there is debate over whether assault to a developing fetus is definable as child maltreatment, the numbers of children born affected after assault warrants inclusion of this category in this discussion (see Covell & Howe, 2001).

Neglect Neglect affects a child's development in several ways. Poor maternal nutrition and prenatal care negatively affects fetal development. Inadequate nutrition, especially in the first 2 years of life, when the brain and central nervous system are growing rapidly, may stunt the child's development. In addition, inadequate supervision of children is implicated in child fatalities, serious injury, and exposure to toxic or poisonous substances. Furthermore, developmental disability may be a consequence of neglect of the child's needs for attention, stimulation, and learning opportunities (Hughes & Rycus, 1998).

Emotional and Psychological Effects of Maltreatment Emotional and psychological effects of maltreatment frequently include delayed or arrested cognitive development. When a child's energies are directed toward surviving and/or trying to cope with extreme stress, learning and adaptive deficits may follow (see Display 30.3). Research also suggests that emotional and psychological trauma can result in changes to the child's developing brain (e.g., atypical brain wave patterns, higher than expected rates of seizure disorder), which affects cognition and learning and possibly increases the risk for future psychiatric disorders (Bremner & Vermetten, 2001; De Bellis & Thomas, 2003; Penza, Heim, & Nemeroff, 2003).

Display 30.3

Case study: Kathryn

Kathryn was born following an uneventful and typical pregnancy. Her mother had a history of psychiatric problems but, with support from the community mental health services, had maintained both employment and housing for several years. Kathryn's early developmental scores were in the average range, and early hospital records reported Kathryn to be developing along normative parameters until approximately 3 years of age. At this time, her mother became involved with a new partner, whom she later married. Over the next 4 years, the family situation steadily deteriorated. Kathryn's mother discontinued her involvement with the community mental health services and, as her behavior became more erratic, she lost her job. The family was frequently homeless or living in shelters. Kathryn was both witness to domestic violence between her mother and stepfather and the victim of repeated incidents of physical and emotional abuse. Kathryn stopped speaking. Following an incident of physical abuse by her mother, which was witnessed by a shelter staff person, Kathryn was brought into the care of child protective services. At Kathryn's admission to care, it appeared that she had developmental disabilities. Kathryn soon started to speak again and disclosed to her foster mother long-standing sexual abuse by her stepfather. Even after several years of intensive support and intervention, as a teenager Kathryn remained several grade levels behind her peers and functioned at a level typical of a much younger child. Her psychologist believed the damage to be permanent.

Source: Fudge Schormans (2003).

Developmental Disability Increases the Risk of Maltreatment

As noted, children born with developmental disabilities and those who acquire developmental disabilities from maltreatment in turn become more vulnerable to further maltreatment. How do we understand this increased risk and vulnerability to maltreatment? Children with disabilities are not substantially different from children without disabilities and therefore share those risk factors common to all children (see Table 30.2). Reflecting a social model of disability, people

Table 30.2. Common risk factors for maltreatment of children with and without disabilities

Risk factors at the level of the child
Childhood
Gender (there are gender differences associated with types of maltreatment; e.g., girls are more likely to experience sexual abuse and boys are more likely to experience physical abuse)
Prematurity/birth anomalies
Exposure to toxins in utero
Chronic or serious illness
Disability (developmental, physical, or learning disability)
Temperament (e.g., fussy, feeding problems, does not readily engage)
Behavior (e.g., activity level, noncompliance)
Childhood trauma
Antisocial peer group
Risk factors at the level of the parent/caregiver
Parental/caregiver psychopathology
Parental/caregiver substance abuse
Parental/caregiver negative affect
Parental/caregiver history of abuse
Low parental/caregiver self-esteem and self-efficacy
Poor child management skills
Unrealistic expectations of child
Poor impulse control
Poor conflict resolution skills
Parental/caregiver illness or disability
Parental/caregiver lack of empathy
Death of parent or sibling
Risk factors at the level of family environment
Conflict between parents
Separation and/or divorce (especially high-conflict divorce)
Negative parent/caregiver–child interactions
Domestic violence
Family disorganization
Harsh or aversive parenting/caregiving style
High levels of family stress
Family size
Risk factors at the level of community environment
Poverty
Homelessness or housing instability
Unemployment
Poor access to medical care and social services
Lack of child care
Community violence
Exposure to discrimination
Exposure to environmental toxins
Poor schools
Social isolation
Single parenthood with lack of support
Societal and cultural risk factors
Societal attitudes and response to violence
Perceptions regarding the sanctity and integrity of the family unit, rights of parents, status of children, and use of physical punishment
Societal attitudes toward the provisions of social supports and educational resources
Societal attitudes and response to minority groups (including disability) and discrimination
Societal mechanisms for identifying and responding to abuse

Sources: Garbarino et al. (1987); Macdonald (2001); and Sobsey (1994); see also Fudge Schormans (2003).

with developmental disabilities are, however, believed to be more vulnerable as a result of a number of factors specific to them as a group. Most of these factors do not apply to everyone with developmental disabilities, nor are they necessarily the result of immutable characteristics of people with disabilities. Instead, they reflect the typical life experiences of many people with disabilities in a society that does not adequately understand, value, or protect them. The relationship between disability and maltreatment is not a causal one—disability alone does not cause maltreatment. To assume a causal relationship serves only to engage in blaming the victim and to obscure the social, political, and economic variables that contribute to both maltreatment and disability.

A number of tenacious myths have sprung up around the abuse of people with developmental disabilities, and these have serious consequences:

- Children and adults with developmental disabilities are never abused.
- The abuse of people with developmental disabilities is not a serious issue because they will neither understand what happened to them nor be affected as severely as would people without disabilities.
- The abuse of people with developmental disabilities is acceptable because it is a natural reaction to the burden of caring for someone with a disability.
- People with developmental disabilities are not sexually desirable—no one would want to sexually abuse them.
- People with developmental disabilities cannot provide a credible account of what happened; therefore, there is no point in dealing with the disclosure.

Acceptance of these myths serves as a rationale for denying the existence of maltreatment among people with developmental disabilities, minimizing the seriousness of the problem, failing to report suspected or disclosed abuse, failing to pursue conviction of the alleged perpetrator, and/or failing to provide appropriate support and interventions to the person who has been abused (Kvam, 2000; Perlman & Erikson, 1992; Tharinger, Burrows Horton, & Millea, 1990).

Some of the most frequently cited risk factors specific to this population are presented next (Gorman-Smith & Matson, 1992; Griffiths, 2003; Kvam, 2000; Mazzucchelli, 2001; Perlman & Erikson, 1992; Randall et al., 2000; Strickler, 2001; Tharinger et al., 1990). It should be noted, however, that this is not an exhaustive list.

1. *For some families living in a society that devalues disability, a developmental disability in their child may be more than they can manage.* Parents may mourn the loss of the "normal" child they had expected. The anger that often accompanies mourning may be directed at the child. Family members' perceptions of the child as being different can impede their ability to form an attachment

or provide appropriate care for their child. It may also precipitate sufficient emotional stress to create a family crisis, thus increasing the child's risk of and vulnerability to abuse. This is exacerbated for families without access to adequate social and professional supports.

2. *Dependence on others increases vulnerability to maltreatment.* Children and adults with developmental disabilities are frequently more dependent on caregivers for their basic needs and for the provision of intimate personal care. In many cases this may be a lifelong dependence. In addition, people with developmental disabilities may have multiple caregivers across a wide variety of situations (e.g., home, school, respite home, therapy center, day program), increasing the risk of maltreatment exponentially.

3. *Compliance training is a common experience for many people with developmental disabilities.* Compliance is often overemphasized at the expense of assertiveness or independence. An unintended consequence is an increased vulnerability, as it places the person in a situation of unusual trust while enhancing the possibility of coercion.

4. *The overuse and/or misuse of specialized interventions or treatments, such as aversive behavioral techniques and pharmacological interventions, creates risk.* Aversive behavioral techniques—especially when administered improperly, by insufficiently trained persons, or in an aggressive or overly punitive manner—can create a situation of risk. Similarly, the misuse or overuse of pharmacological interventions can result in risk of harm.

5. *Social powerlessness stems from power inequities in the settings designed to protect people with developmental disabilities* (e.g., school, foster care, respite care, group homes, institutions). In these settings, children and adults with developmental disabilities generally have little real control and limited influence on decision making.

6. *Limited communication skills can play a role.* These limited skills may affect the ability to report abuse, to have disclosure understood or viewed as credible, to say "no," and/or to call for help. This may lead to some perpetrators identifying persons with developmental disabilities as an "easy mark."

7. *Additional physical or mobility impairments* pose a risk. They may impede the ability to defend oneself, to ward off an attack, or to run away.

8. *The need or desire to "fit in" and to feel accepted can also work to create risk.* Low self-esteem, emotional and social insecurities, and an eagerness to please make one more vulnerable to coercion.

9. *Insufficient education and training regarding sexuality, personal rights, self-protection, and abuse can be a risk factor.* People with developmental disabilities are frequently not equipped to recognize dangerous situations, protect themselves, or report what has happened to them. Some parents and service providers are reluctant to provide this information. They may believe that people with developmental disabilities are asexual, that sexual behavior is not appropriate for people with developmental disabilities, or that providing this information will lead to inappropriate behavior. Most often, training in sexual education is provided only after maltreatment has occurred. (See also Chapter 36.)

10. *A lack of personal privacy also increases vulnerability.* This is most notably a concern for people with developmental disabilities living in large, congregate settings. As the number of residents and staff increases, so may risk.

11. *Social devaluation is a particularly powerful risk factor.* It decreases both internal inhibitions and social restraints against the abuse of people with developmental disabilities. In addition, when societal devaluation is internalized by the person being devalued, it can facilitate an ongoing sense of powerlessness to resist or report abuse.

12. *Segregation and out-of-home care arrangements are more likely for people with developmental disabilities, especially for those with more severe impairments.* Segregated school, therapeutic, and leisure settings and/or residential placement in foster care, group homes, or institutional settings inflate the risk of maltreatment. This is due to increased exposure to potential offenders, fewer available protections, and more limited access to individuals who will act on disclosures. It should be noted, however, that most reported maltreatment occurs in the family home (Fudge Schormans & Brown, 2002; see Display 30.4).

From an ecological perspective, it is necessary to look beyond the personal characteristics of children and adults with developmental disabilities in an attempt to understand why they are maltreated more often than their peers without disabilities. Numerous factors are involved, not the least of which are those related to the aforementioned devaluation and latent assumptions and prejudices about people with developmental disabilities in contemporary culture. See Table 30.3 for Sobsey's (1994) application of an integrated ecological model to abuse of persons with developmental disabilities.

Characteristics of Maltreatment and Developmental Disability

Children with developmental disabilities are subject to the same maltreatment experiences as children without developmental disabilities, yet significant differences also exist. A few of the more significant similarities and differences are outlined next.

Most Common Type of Maltreatment For children with and without developmental disabilities,

Display 30.4

Case study: Nina

Nina was born with a congenital syndrome that resulted in both physical and developmental disabilities. This syndrome was progressive in nature. It was anticipated at her birth that Nina would require increasing levels of care and that she would likely die before reaching adulthood. Nina's parents had no family support to assist with Nina's care. Nina's father was unwilling to accept respite or in-home support services. Feeling unable to cope with her daughter's care needs and impending death, Nina's mother abandoned Nina to her father's care when Nina was 9 years old. Her father began to sexually abuse her once she reached puberty. This continued for more than a year. A neighbor, who had known Nina for several years, suspected that Nina was being abused after observing changes in Nina's behavior with her father. Unable to speak, Nina would close her eyes and turn her head away whenever her father spoke to her or approached her. Previously a friendly child, her apparent sadness also prompted the neighbor's suspicions. When questioned by police and child protective services, Nina's father admitted to abusing his daughter but asserted his belief that he had acted within his rights as Nina's father.

Source: Fudge Schormans (2003).

Table 30.3. Individual, environmental, and cultural aspects of maltreatment of people with developmental disabilities

Potential victim
Impaired physical defenses
Impaired communicative functioning
Lacks critical information
Learned helplessness
Learned compliance
Undeveloped sense of personal space
Dependency
Potential offender
Need for control
Authoritarian
Low self-esteem
Displaced aggression
Exposure to abusive models
Little attachment to victim
Devaluing attitudes
Impulsive behavior
Environment
Emphasizes control
Attracts abusers
Isolated from society
Provides awarded models of aggression
Covers up allegations
Many caregivers
Transient caregivers
Dehumanizes potential victims
Eliminates nonabusers (discourages them from staying and/or reporting maltreatment)
Clusters risks
Discourages attachment
Culture
Devalues victims
Objectifies victims
Teaches compliance
Emphasizes vulnerabilities
Disinhibits aggressions
Denies problems
Discourages attachment
Discourages solutions

From Sobsey, D. (1994). *Violence and abuse in the lives of people with disabilities: The end of silent acceptance?* (p. 163). Baltimore: Paul H. Brookes Publishing Co.; adapted by permission. (See also Fudge Schormans, 2003.)

neglect is the type of maltreatment cited to occur most often (i.e., more frequently than sexual abuse, physical abuse, and emotional maltreatment). In addition, both groups of children are reported to frequently experience multiple forms of maltreatment either simultaneously or at different times or ages. Yet, it is also evident that children with developmental disabilities appear to experience both neglect and multiple categories of maltreatment at a significantly higher rate (Fudge Schormans & Brown, 2002; Sullivan & Knutson, 2000; Verdugo, Bermejo, & Fuertes, 1995). One hypothesis put forth to explain the high incidence of neglect is that the increased care demands of this group of children places them at greater risk (Ammerman et al., 1989), especially if the supports and services they and their families require are not readily available or accessible.

Severity There is strong literature support for the belief that the maltreatment of children and adults with developmental disabilities is more severe than for people without developmental disabilities. This is evident in the area of physical abuse (Brown, 2004), as people with developmental disabilities appear to experience more physical injuries and emotional harm as a result of maltreatment (Ammerman et al., 1989; Tharinger et al., 1990; Trocmé et al., 2001). More severe maltreatment also occurs in sexual abuse, as having a developmental disability increases the likelihood of experiencing contact sexual abuse (e.g., inappropriate touching; oral, anal, or vaginal penetration; attempted penetration) as opposed to noncontact sexual abuse (e.g., indecent exposure, invitation to touch). This means that in addition to being subjected to more severe sexual abuse, people with developmental disabilities are also put at a greater risk of exposure to HIV/AIDS and other sexually transmitted diseases (Ammerman et al., 1989; Beail & Warden, 1995; Sobsey, 1994; Tharinger et al., 1990).

Chronic versus Acute Nature Abuse and neglect for people with developmental disabilities tends also to be chronic. They are much more likely than those in the general population to experience multiple episodes of maltreatment spanning a longer time period (Fudge Schormans & Brown, 2002; Trocmé et al., 2001). Sullivan and Knutson (2000) found that 71% of their sample of children identified as having a developmental disability reported repeated abuse, as opposed to 60.1% of their sample of children without an identified developmental disability. Regarding sexual abuse specifically, this may be even more pronounced for younger children and for children with more significant disabilities (Sobsey, 1994). See Table 30.4 for more information on prevalence.

Degree of Developmental Disability One issue specific to children with developmental disabilities is the degree of disability. In examining this parameter, a common assumption is that people with more severe developmental disabilities are at greater risk of abuse and neglect, primarily as a result of several of the risk factors that were previously identified: increased dependence, the potential for more caregivers, less well-developed communication skills, additional motor impairments, and more involvement with out-of-home care and segregated services. A review of the literature, however, indicates that people with mild or moderate levels of developmental disability appear to be at greater risk. One explanation is that children with more severe disabilities elicit more sympathy than anger, which serves to somehow protect them. A second explanation is that they are less able to engage in behaviors that may trigger an abusive incident (i.e., aggressive or self-stimulating behavior) (Ammerman et al., 1989). Strickler (2001) suggested they are less capable of interacting with others or reacting to a potential abuser in a way that precipitates abuse. Benedict et al. (1990) argued that because caregivers expect less from them, caregiver frustration (leading to abuse) is a less common response.

It must be remembered, however, that maltreatment is far less likely to be verbally disclosed by people with more severe developmental disabilities (largely a result of more limited communication abilities). Also, if abuse is disclosed behaviorally or emotionally, there is less chance it will be correctly identified by others, especially by people unfamiliar with indicators of maltreatment and/or the individual's nonverbal communication methods (Balogh et al., 2001; Kvam, 2000). Sobsey's (1994) finding that people with mild to moderate or severe to profound developmental disabilities are almost equally represented in reported cases of sexual abuse suggests the need to investigate this area further.

Table 30.4. Percentage of children with and without developmental disability who experienced four types of maltreatment

	Developmental status	
Type of maltreatment	No developmental disability	Developmental disability
Any physical abuse	34.8%	34.2%
Inappropriate punishment	22.6%	22.1%
Shaken baby syndrome	0.4%	0.8%
Other physical abuse	12.7%	11.9%
Any sexual abuse	11.4%	12.3%
Sexual activity attempted	2.8%	2.6%
Sexual activity completed	1.8%	2.1%
Touching/fondling genitals	6.1%	7.2%
Exposure of genitals	1.1%	1.2%
Exploitation: pornography/prostitution	0.4%	0.3%
Sexual harassment	0.4%	0.3%
Voyeurism	0.0%	0.0%
Any neglect	49.7%	60.8%[a]
Failure to supervise/protect (physical)	25.1%	24.2%
Failure to supervise/protect (sexual)	3.1%	4.4%
Physical neglect	12.0%	16.5%[a]
Medical neglect	3.4%	10.1%[a]
Failure to provide treatment	0.9%	3.0%[a]
Maladaptive behavior	6.3%	9.9%[a]
Abandonment	3.8%	2.6%
Educational neglect	5.7%	9.6%[a]
Any emotional maltreatment	26.8%	31.4%
Emotional abuse	12.3%	3.7%
Nonorganic failure to thrive	0.1%	0.2%
Emotional neglect	5.0%	11.4%[a]
Exposed to family violence	15.1%	9.6%[a]
Multiple categories	23.1%	34.8%[a]

From Brown, I. (2002). *Abuse and neglect in children with intellectual disabilities: Results from a national study.* Toronto: University of Toronto, Faculty of Social Work; adapted by permission. (See also Fudge Schormans, 2003.)

[a]$p < .01$

Age Two patterns start to emerge when age is examined. First, the maltreatment of children with developmental disabilities tends to begin at a younger age than for children without developmental disabilities. More preschool-age children with developmental disabilities are reported for all types of maltreatment than are their counterparts without developmental disabilities (Benedict et al., 1990; Sullivan & Knutson, 2000).

Investigating children with multiple disabilities in psychiatric hospitals, Ammerman et al. (1989) found that before the age of 2 years, 46% of the children in this sample had been physically abused, 49% had been sexually abused, and 68% had experienced neglect. For both children with and without developmental disabilities, younger children are typically at greater risk for physical abuse and neglect, whereas the risk of sexual abuse increases in adolescence (Ammerman et al., 1989; Beail & Warden, 1995; Gorman-Smith & Matson, 1992; Trocmé et al., 2001).

Second, an inverse relationship between age and maltreatment exists for children without developmental disabilities: As age increases, the rate of maltreatment decreases. As children grow, they typically develop better communication skills and self-protection skills and are physically better able to ward off an attack. With maturity frequently comes an improved capacity to escape or avoid abusive situations (Randall et al., 2000). This is not always the case for children with developmental disabilities (especially those that are more severe) who develop such skills later or not at all. For this group, age is not necessarily a protective factor and vulnerability to maltreatment generally extends across the life span (Gorman-Smith & Matson, 1992; Randall, Sobsey, & Parilla, 2001; Verdugo et al., 1995).

Gender The effect of gender is not equal for children with and without developmental disabilities. Among children without developmental disabilities, Sullivan and Knutson (2000) noted that girls are abused more often (56%) than boys (42%), whereas Trocmé et al. (2001) found an almost equal distribution (49% girls, 51% boys). It is interesting to note that boys with developmental disabilities are overrepresented in all categories of maltreatment: 60.9% of children with developmental disabilities reported for child maltreatment are boys and 39.1% are girls (Fudge Schormans & Brown, 2002).

Does disability status actually increase the risk of abuse for boys? Children with developmental disability are more likely to have paid caregivers and, for boys, these are more likely to be male. As the characteristics "paid caregiver" and "male" are sometimes correlated with perpetrator status, this potentially contributes to this elevated risk of maltreatment for boys with developmental disabilities (Randall et al., 2000). Sullivan and Knutson (2000) offered another explanation, noting that more boys than girls are identified as having developmental disabilities. The greater prevalence of maltreated boys may simply reflect the increased prevalence of boys in the developmental disability population. The differences may be further accounted for by reporting issues. Maltreated boys with developmental disabilities are more likely to act out. That is, they demonstrate behavioral concerns that bring them into contact with professionals, thus potentially increasing the probability of being reported for maltreatment. As a group, their female counterparts tend more towards withdrawal and other emotional and behavioral expressions that do not create the same type of problems for their caregivers as the behaviors exhibited by boys. A consequence is that girls are thus less likely to be diagnosed as being abused (Beail & Warden, 1995). To complicate matters, it is speculated that developmental disability, in addition to maltreatment, is underreported more often for girls than for boys (Randall et al., 2000). Furthermore, although boys seem to be more reluctant to disclose abuse—especially sexual abuse—than do girls, girls are less likely to be believed. This not only affects understanding of the rates of maltreatment but also, more seriously, it results in the threat of continued maltreatment for girls (Beail & Warden, 1995; Randall et al., 2000). In addition, as compared with their peers without a disability, disclosures by people with developmental disabilities are significantly less likely to be believed (Brown, 2002; Kvam, 2000). These factors skew understanding of the intersection between gender, disability, and maltreatment and point to the need for further investigation.

Alleged Perpetrator For all children, irrespective of disability, the alleged perpetrator of maltreatment is usually someone the child knows. "Stranger abuse" is actually a rare event, accounting for less than 1% (Trocmé et al., 2001) to 6.6% (Sobsey, 1994) of child maltreatment. Worldwide, the alleged perpetrator of child maltreatment is most often a family member. For children with disabilities living in India, Ghai (2001) noted that especially for families living in poverty, the family can be a "safe haven" or a "risk" from which they need protection. In Canada, the Canadian Incidence Study (CIS) of Reported Child Abuse and Neglect reported that only 6% of child maltreatment was committed by a nonfamily member such as a teacher, professional, baby sitter, parental girlfriend/boyfriend, peer, or stranger (Trocmé et al., 2001). This figure is perhaps an underestimation, as many instances of non-familial abuse may have been investigated by the police rather than child protective services. For children without a developmental disability, and for many children with this label, immediate family members are believed to be responsible for the majority of neglect, physical, and emotional abuse. Extended family or nonfamily members are implicated in sexual abuse more often than in cases of neglect, physical, or emotional abuse. Mothers and fathers are equally represented as perpetrators of physical abuse, with more mothers reported for neglect and emotional abuse and fathers for sexual abuse. It must be remembered, however, that in Western culture the responsibility for child care often still rests primarily with mothers. In addition, more single-parent families (a risk factor for child maltreatment) are headed by mothers than by fathers (Fudge Schormans & Brown, 2002; Sobsey, 1994; Sullivan & Knutson, 2000; Trocmé et al., 2001).

Debate exists in the literature as to whether people with developmental disabilities are at greater risk of familial or nonfamilial maltreatment. Although some studies report high levels of familial abuse (Ammerman et al., 1989; Beail & Warden, 1995; Tharinger et al., 1990), contradictory findings suggest that maltreatment at the hands of service providers is a greater threat. Sobsey (1994) reported that of those included in his sample, 56% of sexual abuse was perpetrated by service providers, compared with 28% by caregivers. The issue is muddied by the variety, multiplicity, and complexity of living arrangements for this group. Although deinstitutionalization policies have resulted in more people with developmental disabilities living in their family homes, the reality is that a significant number still reside in out-of-home placements. These placements may be permanent (i.e., group homes or institutional settings) or temporary (i.e., respite care). Multiple moves are not uncommon (especially in the foster care system, where children sometimes bounce from one placement to the next). One outcome of such discontinuity of care and involvement with the developmental disability service system is an increased vulnerability to maltreatment by nonfamily members (Balogh et al., 2001). This is not restricted to alternative caregivers or staff persons alone. A consequence of residential and day program settings, in which several people with developmental disabilities are congregated together, is a higher risk of maltreatment by a peer who also has a developmental disability (Balogh et al., 2001).

Potential for Abuse in Institutions Specific to children and adults with developmental disabilities is the notion that the institutionally sanctioned services and procedures may be abusive or neglectful. In some instances, administrative structures, philosophies, and institutional cultures can permit, condone, or even encourage three forms of institutional maltreatment that are then enacted by employees. Institutional child abuse involves the use of physical punishment, aversive behavior management techniques, excessive isolation, denial of freedom, physical or mechanical restraints, or the abuse or misuse of psychotropic drugs. Institutional child neglect refers to failure to provide needed services and negligent attitudes toward the use of punishment, restraints, and medication. Wrongful abrogation of personal rights includes such actions as improper segregation and restrictions on personal choice, decision-making, communications, or socialization preferences (Garbarino et al., 1987).

Impact of Maltreatment on Children and Adults with Developmental Disabilities

The impact of maltreatment on children with developmental disabilities appears to be similar to but more severe than the impact on children without disabilities. Mansell, Sobsey, and Moskall (1998), for example, compared clinical findings among two samples of age- and gender-matched Canadian children served by the same treatment agency: children with developmental disabilities who had been sexually abused and children without disabilities who had been sexually abused. Clinical characteristics were similar, but the children with disabilities exhibited a higher number of clinically significant problems (e.g., increased vulnerability to sexual abuse, withdrawl into fantasy and self-abuse).

Kvam (2000) cautioned that for each individual, the impact is affected by such factors as the seriousness of the abuse, age of onset, single or multiple episodes of maltreatment, characteristics of the individual, family response to disclosure, family situation, and the individual's relationship to the abuser. (Remember, the first five have already been identified as significant factors in the maltreatment of persons with developmental disabilities.) People with developmental disabilities typically experience the same outcomes of maltreatment as do people without developmental disabilities (see Table 30.5). Heeding Kvam's caution, this list is not applicable to everyone who experiences maltreatment, nor is it exhaustive, nor is it likely anyone will experience *all* of these outcomes.

Despite the information presented in Table 30.5, there are effects of maltreatment that are unique to persons with developmental disabilities. These include the following (Gorman-Smith & Matson, 1992; Perlman & Erikson, 1992; Sobsey, 1994; Strickler, 2001; Tharinger et al., 1990):

1. The experience of maltreatment exacerbates the feelings of social isolation and of "being different" that are common to this group.
2. People with developmental disabilities are already stigmatized; further stigmatization may accrue as a result of maltreatment.
3. There is a tendency for these individuals to believe they were abused because they have a developmental disability.
4. Notably higher rates of psychiatric disorder have been correlated with maltreatment of children and adults with developmental disabilities.
5. Because of frequent misdiagnosis of the emotional, social, and behavioral symptomatology of maltreatment, people with developmental disabilities are

Table 30.5. Common effects of maltreatment for people with and without developmental disabilities

Social	
	Difficulty forming or maintaining relationships
	Social isolation
	Social stigmatization
	Less sensitive to social/emotional contexts
	Impaired ability to discriminate between safe situations and potentially abusive situations
	Increased risk of victimization
Personality	
	Negative self-concept
	Low self-esteem
	More egocentric
	Inability to trust
	Increased dependency
	Overly sensitive to approval/threats
	More introspective
	Secretive
	More cautious
	More serious
Behavioral	
	Behavior disturbances
	Eating disorders
	Sleep disturbances
	Sexually inappropriate behavior
	Impaired adaptive functioning
	Overly friendly with strangers
	Antisocial behavior
	Aggressive behavior
	Undercontrolled behavior
	Running away
	Health-risk behaviors (e.g., substance abuse)
	Inability to regulate behavior
Cognitive	
	Impaired cognitive functioning
	Poor school performance
	Neurological consequences to brain development & function
Psychological/emotional	
	Emotional withdrawal
	Emotional distress
	Depression
	Anxiety
	Feelings of helplessness
	Suicidal ideation and attempts
	Impaired ability to discriminate between safe and dangerous
	Diminished coping skills
	Hypervigilance
	Fears/phobias
	Guilt
	Anger
	Shame
	Problems with sexuality, sexual behavior, and sexual relationships
	Unusual thought processes
	Psychopathology
	Posttraumatic stress disorder
	Overly sensitive to approval/threats
	Dissociative disorder
	Attention deficit symptomatology

Sources: Garbarino, Brookhouser, Authier, et al. (1987); Macdonald (2001); and Sobsey (1994); see also Fudge Schormans (2003).

more likely to be mistreated and prescribed intrusive behavior management, inappropriate psychotropic medication, hospitalization, and/or unnecessary placement changes. For example, self-injurious behavior is a common clinical finding among children with and without developmental disabilities who have been abused. Punishment procedures used to eliminate this behavior without understanding why the behavior occurs will likely increase the trauma and do further harm.

6. There is a mistaken belief that people with developmental disabilities are unable to benefit from therapeutic interventions for maltreatment. This is one reason why such services are rarely made available to them. Even if they are available, generic services are frequently unable to accommodate the unique needs of this group. Specialized therapeutic services are limited in number thus more difficult to obtain. This increases the risk that the impact of maltreatment will be more severe and longer lasting and may precipitate emotional, behavioral, or psychological crises.

Investigating Maltreatment of Children and Adults with Developmental Disabilities

Despite investigations, the abuse of people with developmental disabilities is punished less often than might be expected. Alleged perpetrators are rarely criminally charged, tried, and/or convicted (Balogh et al., 2001; Beail & Warden, 1995). As a result, the abuser often continues to live with (or provide care for) the person with the developmental disability. For example, the CIS reported that 11.9% of alleged perpetrators continue to live with the child without a developmental disability, compared with a rate of 34.9% for children with developmental disabilities (Brown, 2003; Trocmé et al., 2001).

In developed countries, criminal law provides some protection for children and adults from physical and sexual abuse and/or deprivation of necessities of life. This legislation is typically the legal basis for prosecution by criminal court systems, which are required to prove beyond a reasonable doubt the guilt of the alleged perpetrator. One consequence of this is that many cases of suspected child abuse are not pursued successfully through criminal law. Obtaining sufficient evidence to establish guilt beyond a reasonable doubt is often more difficult when dealing with child maltreatment.

The second means by which protection is afforded is through child welfare legislation that governs child protection agencies. Applying exclusively to children, this legislation is based on the less demand-

Display 30.5

Case study: Child protection investigation

A social worker received a call from a teacher. The teacher said that a 6-year-old boy and his 5-year-old sister had been sexually abused by their father. Both children had developmental disabilities. The girl was nonverbal, and her disability was more severe. The teacher conveyed the following: the mother forced the father to leave the home after witnessing father in the act of abusing the children; the abuse was ongoing; the boy was anxious, frightened and was threatened by the father not to tell; the mother also had a developmental disability; and the school had ongoing concerns about the children's nutrition, clothing, and hygiene.

The worker completed a standardized tool for assessing risk and discussed the situation with her supervisor. They decided that eligibility criteria for services had been met. According to local government guidelines, the children had to be seen within 12 hours. This would be a joint investigation with police and would take place at the school. To account for the children's disabilities, to minimize trauma, and to maximize information obtained, the social worker tried to arrange for assistance from an expert in developmental disabilities. The social worker wanted the person to accompany her, and a police officer, to the school. No such support person was available that day, so the social worker arranged for the children's classroom aides to be present during the interview. Although the social worker and the police officer knew this had potential to contaminate evidence, they believed it would best facilitate information gathering.

In case the children were later unable to testify in court, the interview was videotaped. During the interview, the boy was anxious, distractible, and unable to give dates, but his aide kept him focused. Consistent details of sexual, physical, and emotional abuse of both children emerged from the boy's report. Despite the presence of her aide, the sister was unable to provide any information.

The mother was called and requested to accompany the children and the worker to the hospital's sexual assault unit, where she was interviewed and the children were examined. The boy complied with being examined. Although no physical evidence could be obtained, the physician noted that his behavior during the exam was consistent with abuse. The physician was unable to complete an exam of the girl, as she was distraught, even with her mother's support. Because the prosecuting attorney would need to prove guilt beyond a reasonable doubt, it became apparent that the lack of physical evidence may compromise prosecution of father. The mother was interviewed and confirmed her son's account of the abuse. However, mother reported that the father had returned home, and she felt unable to protect the children at that time. Because the children were clearly not safe, she agreed with the worker's plan to place the children in foster care until parenting supports could be arranged.

The police found the father at the family home. After questioning him, they decided to charge him despite his denial of wrongdoing and the lack of physical evidence. The boy's disclosure and behavioral indicators warranted this decision. Even if no conviction was obtained, it was hoped this would be a deterrent in the future. The boy was referred to a victim witness program to be prepared for criminal court. His sister would not testify, as her communication was determined to be neither consistent nor reliable. Her brother was deemed competent as a witness because he knew right from wrong and the importance of telling the truth. He testified but, in part because of his cognitive, memory and language difficulties, he was easily confused by the defense attorney and his credibility was damaged. Although behavioral evidence existed, the lack of physical evidence and the boy's difficulties in testifying due to his developmental disabilities meant that the father was found not guilty. The mother refused to testify. Later, it was learned that she has also been the victim of violence at the father's hands. During supervised access visits with the children at the social services agency offices, however, the mother recanted her disclosure and stated her decision to remain with father. The children became wards of the state.

Source: Fudge Schormans (2003).

ing civil law standard of proof of the preponderance of the evidence. The difference in these standards is the purpose of each process. Criminal proceedings are intended primarily to determine guilt and to punish criminal behavior. Child welfare proceedings are intended to determine if a child needs protection and to do what is best for the child.

Child protective services are primarily responsible for investigating reports of child maltreatment when the alleged perpetrator is someone acting in a caregiving capacity (e.g., family member, baby sitter, teacher, child care provider, foster parent, group home staff member). There is typically a joint investigation between the child protective services and the police if the allegation involves sexual abuse, serious physical harm, criminal activity, and/or abandonment. The police are less likely to participate in situations involving neglect or emotional abuse (unless domestic violence is identified as a factor in the emotional abuse). The police maintain responsibility for investigating alleged child maltreatment if the alleged perpetrator is a stranger or nonfamily member. It is not uncommon, however, for the police to include child protective services in such investigations to take advantage of their expertise in interviewing children and linking maltreated children and their families to community supports and services. Adult protective services have been developed in many states and provinces in an attempt to provide a system of similar protection for adults who are vulnerable to maltreatment. These vary substantially from one jurisdiction to another.

The current issues and debates associated with the investigation of maltreatment, for people with and without developmental disabilities, are complex. For people with developmental disabilities, Displays 30.5 and 30.6 present cases that reveal some of the myriad factors that complicate this process and have repercussions for the individual, family, and alleged perpetrator. (The reader is directed to Ericson, Isaacs, & Perlman, 2003; Griffiths & Marini, 2000; and Sobsey, 1994.)

SUMMARY

Historically, societal attitudes about developmental disability are reflected in legislated and practice responses to the maltreatment of people with developmental disabilities. Differential treatment for this group—from social service, child protection, and criminal justice systems—is not uncommon and can serve to perpetuate, condone, or even authorize further maltreatment. Present structures are inadequate to effectively address this problem. Identification as being

Display 30.6

Case study: Police investigation

A 31-year-old woman with developmental disabilities was a frequent customer at a neighborhood variety store down the street from her home. Although nonverbal, she had some alternative communication abilities, and the shop keeper came to know her well. During the day, the woman attended an adult day program funded by the local government.

Over time, the shopkeeper began to notice disturbing changes in the woman's behavior. She appeared overly interested in men in the store but also frightened of them. She openly masturbated in their presence and began to exhibit self-injurious behaviors (e.g., head slapping). Concerned that she had been abused, the shop keeper attempted to engage the woman in conversation and suggested that if she had been abused she should call the police and not let anyone hurt her. The woman was clearly distressed by this conversation. The shopkeeper decided to call the police, who advised her that if the woman could not or would not make a disclosure herself, then the shopkeeper could register a third-party complaint. This was done, and several days later the police met with the shopkeeper. The shopkeeper could provide little information about the woman's family. The police were reluctant to go to the woman's home, fearing this might place her at greater risk. Deciding to meet with the woman at the store, the police were unsuccessful in their attempts to speak with her, but they were convinced by observing her behavior that something had happened to her. As a result, the police decided to speak with the woman's family.

The woman lived alone with her mother. Appearing devastated by the suspicions of abuse, the mother agreed to facilitate a police interview with her daughter. The mother, able to communicate with her daughter using a system of "yes"/"no" responses to questions, elicited from her daughter that she had been sexually touched by staff at the day program. The daughter was then informed of her rights and her options but it was not clear how much she understood. She refused to go to the hospital for an examination, and she did not agree to press charges. Because of her age, the woman was deemed responsible to make her own decisions. The police were unable to proceed without her consent. They reviewed with the mother the option of having her daughter legally declared incompetent so that they could go forward with the investigation. The mother refused, as she saw the risks this posed to her daughter's future ability to make decisions for herself. The police referred the woman and her mother to the local sexual assault center in an effort to assist them to receive information and support.

Source: Fudge Schormans (2003).

both part of the problem and of the solution necessitates stronger collaboration and information sharing among all the parties involved with this issue: child protective services, developmental disability services, police officers, lawyers, judges, school staff, child care providers, health care professionals, therapeutic services professionals, service planners and administrators, governmental administrators and policy makers, and advocates. People with developmental disabilities and their families are a key element to the development of a more responsive system of protection, possessing invaluable insights into the factors contributing to maltreatment and what is required for prevention, protection, and healthy recoveries.

Maltreatment is a reality in the daily lives of many people with developmental disabilities. People with developmental disabilities face a much higher risk of and vulnerability to maltreatment that is both similar to and unique from that experienced by people without disabilities. Yet, maltreatment of these individuals is often unreported and/or undetected and, therefore, untreated. What is missing is recognition and acknowledgement of the magnitude and seriousness of this issue. Also, legislation, policies, and practices are needed that are preventative, as opposed to reactive. Society needs to value people with developmental disabilities, demand active condemnation of the violence perpetrated against them, and challenge the devaluation that lies at the root of such maltreatment.

FOR FURTHER THOUGHT AND DISCUSSION

1. What might be the consequences of conceptualizing maltreatment of children with disabilities in the following ways: an individual pathology issue, a social welfare issue, a public health issue, a public safety issue, or a human rights issue?
2. One thing that people with developmental disabilities share with other oppressed groups is a concern over the language used to describe them. An example from the mental health field demonstrates this point. The current practice for many people labeled as having mental health concerns is to use the term *survivor* as opposed to *victim*. Explain the pros and cons of the use of each term in relation to children and adults with developmental disabilities who experience maltreatment.
3. Discuss the issue of prenatal practices resulting in developmental disabilities (e.g., alcohol or drug use by pregnant women). Should this be defined as child abuse? Do these practices constitute a criminal offense? What role, if any, should child protective services play in cases where an expectant mother is known to be putting her unborn child at risk for developmental disability?
4. The child protection system lacks expertise in the area of developmental disability. The developmental disability service system lacks expertise in the area of child maltreatment. Which service system do you believe is most appropriate to deal with the issue of the maltreatment of children with developmental disabilities and why? What alternatives might be possible?
5. Should people with developmental disabilities be treated as "special cases" within child welfare legislation and/or criminal law in light of their particular vulnerabilities and the systemic issues that have been identified?

REFERENCES

Ammerman, R.T., Van Hasselt, V.B., Hersen, M., et al. (1989). Abuse and neglect in psychiatrically hospitalized multihandicapped children. *Child Abuse and Neglect, 13,* 335–343.

Balogh, R., Bretherton, K., Whibley, S., et al. (2001). Sexual abuse in children and adolescents with intellectual disability. *Journal of Intellectual Disability Research, 45,* 194–201.

Beail, N., & Warden, S. (1995). Sexual abuse of adults with learning disabilities. *Journal of Intellectual Disability Research, 39,* 382–387.

Benedict, M.I., White, R.B., Wulff, L.M., et al. (1990). Reported maltreatment in children with multiple disabilities. *Child Abuse and Neglect, 14,* 207–217.

Bremner, J.D., & Vermetten, E. (2001). Stress and development: Behavioural and biological consequences. *Development and Psychopathology, 13,* 473–489.

Bremner, R.H. (1971). *Children and youth in America: A documentary history: Vol. II. 1866–1932.* Cambridge, MA: Harvard University Press.

Brown, I. (2002). *Abuse and neglect in children with intellectual disabilities: Results from a national study.* Toronto: University of Toronto, Faculty of Social Work.

Brown, I. (2003). Abuse and neglect of disabled and non-disabled children: Establishing a place in quality of life study. In M.J. Sirgy, D. Rahtz, & A.C. Samli (Eds.), *Advances in quality-of-life theory and research* (pp. 129–141). New York: Kluwer Academic/Plenum Publishers.

Brown, I. (2004, June 18). *Physical harm and children with developmental delay.* Paper presented at the 12th IASSID World Congress, Montpellier, France. (Available from the Faculty of Social Work, University of Toronto.)

Carlson, L. (2001). Cognitive ableism and disability studies: Feminist reflections on the history of mental retardation. *Hypatia, 16,* 124–146.

Centre for Human Rights. (1996). *The international bill of human rights, Fact sheet No. 2.* Geneva: Centre for Human Rights, United Nations Office at Geneva.

Chadwick, D.L. (1999). The message. *Child Abuse and Neglect, 23,* 957–961.

Covell, K., & Howe, R.B. (2001). *The challenge of children's rights for Canada.* Waterloo, ON, Canada: Wilfred Laurier University Press.

De Bellis, M.D., & Thomas, L.A. (2003). Biologic findings of post-traumatic stress disorder and child maltreatment. *Current Psychiatry Reports, 5*(2), 108–117.

Dufour, S., & Chamberland, C. (2003). *The effectiveness of child welfare interventions: A systematic review.* Retrieved August 6, 2004, from http://www.cecw-cepb.ca/PubsAll.shtml

Elmer, E., & Gregg, G.S. (1967). Developmental characteristics of abused children. *Pediatrics, 40*(4), 596–602.

Ericson, K., Isaacs, B., & Perlman, N. (2003). Enhancing communication with persons with developmental disabilities: The special case of interviewing victim-witnesses of sexual abuse. In I. Brown & M. Percy (Eds.), *Developmental disabilities in Ontario* (2nd ed., pp. 465–476). Toronto: Ontario Association on Developmental Disabilities.

Fudge Schormans, A., & Brown, I. (2002). An investigation into the characteristics of the maltreatment of children with developmental delays and the alleged perpetrators of this maltreatment. *Journal of Developmental Disabilities, 9*(1), 1–19.

Fudge Schormans, A. (2003). Child maltreatment and developmental disabilities. In I. Brown & M. Percy (Eds.), *Developmental disabilities in Ontario* (pp. 551–582).

Garbarino, J., Brookhouser, P.E., Authier, K., et al. (1987). *Special children, special risk: The maltreatment of children with disabilities.* New York: Aldine De Gruyter.

Ghai, A. (2001). Marginalisation and disability: Experiences from the Third World. In M. Priestley (Ed.), *Disability and the life course: Global perspectives* (pp. 26–37). New York: Cambridge University Press.

Gorman-Smith, D., & Matson, J.L. (1992). Sexual abuse and persons with mental retardation. In W. O'Donohue & J.H. Geer (Eds.), *The sexual abuse of children: Theory and research volume I* (pp. 285–306). Mahwah, NJ: Lawrence Erlbaum Associates.

Government of Ontario, Canada. (1999). *Child and Family Services Amendment Act (Child Welfare Reform).*

Griffiths, D. (2003). Sexuality and people with developmental disabilities: From myth to emerging practices. In E. Brown & M. Percy (Eds.), *Developmental disabilities in Ontario* (2nd ed., pp. 677–698). Toronto: Ontario Association on Developmental Disabilities.

Griffiths, D., & Marini, Z. (2000). Interacting with the legal system regarding a sexual offence: Social and cognitive considerations for persons with developmental disabilities. *Journal on Developmental Disabilities, 7,* 76–121.

Hughes, R.C., & Rycus, J.S. (1998). *Developmental disabilities and child welfare.* Washington, DC: Child Welfare League of America Press.

Ingstad, B. (2001). Disability in the developing world. In G.L. Albrecht, K.D. Seelman, & M. Bury (Eds.), *Handbook of disability studies* (pp. 772–792). Thousand Oaks, CA: Sage Publications.

Kvam, M.H. (2000). Is sexual abuse of children with disabilities disclosed? A retrospective analysis of child disability and the likelihood of sexual abuse among those attending Norwegian hospitals. *Child Abuse and Neglect, 24,* 1073–1084.

Macdonald, G. (2001). *Effective interventions for child abuse and neglect: An evidence-based approach to planning and evaluating interventions.* Hoboken, NJ: John Wiley & Sons.

Macintyre, E. (1993). The historical context of child welfare in Canada. In B. Wharf (Ed.), *Rethinking child welfare in Canada* (pp. 13–36). Toronto: McClelland & Stewart.

Mansell, S., Sobsey, D., & Moskal, R. (1998). Clinical findings among sexually abused children with and without developmental disabilities. *Mental Retardation, 36*(1), 12–22.

Mazzucchelli, T.G. (2001). Feel Safe: A pilot study of a protective behaviours programme for people with intellectual disability. *Journal of Intellectual and Developmental Disability, 26,* 115–126.

Penza, K.M., Heim, C., & Nemeroff, C.B. (2003). Neurobiological effects of childhood abuse: Implications for the pathophysiology of depression and anxiety. *Archives of Women's Mental Health, 6*(1), 15–22.

Percy, M., & Brown, I. (2003). Factors that cause or contribute to developmental disability. In I. Brown & M. Percy (Eds.), *Developmental disabilities in Ontario* (2nd ed., pp. 117–144). Toronto: Ontario Association on Developmental Disabilities.

Perlman, N., & Erikson, C. (1992). Issues related to sexual abuse of persons with developmental disabilities: An overview. *Journal on Developmental Disabilities, 1,* 19–23.

Priestley, M. (2001). Introduction: The global context of disability. In M. Priestley (Ed.), *Disability and the life course: Global perspectives* (pp. 3–14). Cambridge, United Kingdom: Cambridge University Press.

Radford, J.P. (1994). Intellectual disability and the heritage of modernity. In M.H. Rioux & M. Bach (Eds.), *Disability is not measles: New research paradigms in disability* (pp. 9–27). North York, ON, Canada: Roeher Institute.

Radford, J.P., & Park, D.C. (2003). Historical overview of developmental disabilities in Ontario. In I. Brown & M. Percy (Eds.), *Developmental disabilities in Ontario* (2nd ed., pp. 3–18). Toronto: Ontario Association on Developmental Disabilities.

Randall, W., Parilla, R., & Sobsey, D. (2000). Gender, disability status and risk for sexual abuse in children. *Journal on Developmental Disability, 7,* 1–15.

Randall, W., Sobsey, D., & Parilla, R. (2001). Ethnicity, disability and risk for abuse. *Developmental Disabilities Bulletin, 29,* 60–80.

Reiniger, A., & Robison, E. (1995). Mandated training of professionals: A means for improving reporting of suspected child abuse. *Child Abuse and Neglect, 19,* 63–69.

Rutman, L. (1987). J.J. Kelso and the development of child welfare. In A. Moscovitch & J. Albert (Eds.), *The benevolent state: The growth of welfare in Canada* (pp. 68–76). Toronto: Garamond Press.

Silverman, A.B., Reinherz, H.Z., & Giaconia, R.M. (1996). The long-term sequelae of child and adolescent abuse: A longitudinal community study. *Child Abuse and Neglect, 20,* 709–723.

Simmons, H.G. (1982). *From asylum to welfare.* Toronto: National Institute on Mental Retardation.

Sobsey, D. (1994). *Violence and abuse in the lives of people with disabilities: The end of silent acceptance?* Baltimore: Paul H. Brookes Publishing Co.

Steinhauer, P.D. (1991). *The least detrimental alternative: A systematic guide to case planning and decision making for children in care.* Toronto: University of Toronto Press.

Stone, E. (2001). A complicated struggle: Disability, survival and social change in the majority world. In M. Priestley (Ed.), *Disability and the life course: Global perspectives* (pp. 50–63). Cambridge, United Kingdom: Cambridge University Press.

Strickler, H. (2001). Interaction between family violence and mental retardation. *Mental Retardation, 39,* 461–471.

Sullivan, P., & Knutson, J.F. (2000). Maltreatment and disabilities: A population-based epidemiological study. *Child Abuse and Neglect, 24,* 1257–1273.

Teixeira, J.M., Fisk, N.M., & Glover, V. (1999). Association between maternal anxiety in pregnancy and increased uterine artery resistance index: Cohort based study. *British Medical Journal, 318,* 153–157.

Tharinger, D., Burrows Horton, C., & Millea, S. (1990). Sexual abuse and exploitation of children and adults with mental retardation and other handicaps. *Child Abuse and Neglect, 14,* 301–312.

Trocmé, N., MacLaurin, B., Fallon, B., et al. (2001). *Canadian Incidence Study of Reported Child Abuse and Neglect: Final Report.* Ottawa, ON, Canada: Minister of Public Works and Government Services Canada.

United Nations. (1989). *Convention on the Rights of the Child.* Retrieved December 8, 2005, from http://www.unhchr.ch/html/menu3/b/k2crc.htm

United Nations Enable. (2006). *The United Nations focal point on persons with disabilities.* Retrieved January 28, 2006, from http://www.un.org/esa/socdev/enable

Verdugo, M.A., Bermejo, B., & Fuertes, J. (1995). The maltreatment of intellectually handicapped children and adolescents. *Child Abuse and Neglect, 19,* 201–215.

Waldfogel, J. (1998). *The future of child protection.* Cambridge, Massachusetts: Harvard University Press.

Winzer, M.A. (1997). Disability and society before the eighteenth century: Dread and despair. In L.J. Davis (Ed.), *The disability studies reader* (pp. 75–90). New York: Routledge.

Zellman, G.L. (1990). Report decision-making patterns among mandated child abuse reporters. *Child Abuse and Neglect, 14,* 325–336.

31

Education for Individuals with Intellectual and Developmental Disabilities

Ivan Brown, Maire Percy, and Karolina Machalek

> **WHAT YOU WILL LEARN ABOUT IN THIS CHAPTER**
>
> - Description of special education
> - A brief history of special education
> - Legislation governing special education
> - Key aspects of special education
> - Future challenges in special education

It is customary around the world for children to go to school. In most countries, there are laws requiring parents to ensure that their children attend school or receive accredited home schooling. These laws underscore the widely accepted view that education is an exceptionally useful tool not only for individual success but also for the betterment of society as a whole. All children do not attain the same level of education, because motivation, interests, and abilities—as well as available educational opportunities—differ. Thus, being educated is a matter of degree, rather than an absolute. Having a high level of education is not essential for personal happiness, but it certainly helps individuals understand their environment better and adapt to its behavioral expectations.

Laws requiring children's education reflect a trend, especially since the Industrial Revolution, for social institutions—in this case, educational systems—to take on substantial responsibility for helping children develop necessary skills and knowledge. In developed countries especially, it is now widely accepted that all children, including those with intellectual or developmental delays, will attend school throughout their childhood years. In turn, it is widely understood that they will acquire knowledge and skills that assist them to live their childhood years and will help them prepare for their adult years.

This chapter focuses on special education, which is generally understood as education for children with exceptionalities. More specifically, this chapter focuses on that aspect of special education that is specifically tailored to the learning needs of those with intellectual and developmental disabilities. Special education is a field that has attracted a great deal of research and related inquiry, and this has resulted in a very large amount of literature that cannot be adequately captured in one chapter. Thus, this chapter functions as an introduction to special education for students with intellectual and developmental disabilities, highlighting the main trends and issues and some of the important legislation that supports them. There are thousands of excellent resources in special education available from a wide variety of sources. Some of these are provided as examples in Appendix B, but readers are encouraged to search for additional information in libraries at their local universities and colleges, at school board offices, on the Internet, and elsewhere to supplement the information introduced here.

DESCRIPTION OF SPECIAL EDUCATION

The term *special education* has both legal and practical meanings. In the United States, it was legally defined in the Education for All Handicapped Children Act of 1975 (PL 94-142) as "[s]pecially designed instruction, at no cost to the parent, to meet the unique needs of a handicapped child, including classroom instruction, home instruction, and instruction in hospitals and institutions."

In practical terms, *special education* refers to activities that are designed to provide education to children or adults who require, for optimal learning, learning environments and/or teaching methods that differ from those typically used for most people. It can apply to people of any age, although the term is most frequently used in the context of formal educational settings—for children in preschool, elementary school, or secondary school. Special education is not just for "slow learners." It is used to enhance learning for people who have been identified as gifted learners, for those identified as having learning disabilities (as the term is used in North America and elsewhere; see Chapter 1 for information on usage of terms), for people with physical and developmental disabilities, and for those with intellectual disabilities or challenging behaviors.

Special education may occur in a special school, a place outside school (e.g., hospital, group residence, family home), a special classroom within a general education school (public, private, or charter), or a regular classroom where special instruction is provided. Within these various settings, special education takes a wide variety of forms. It may focus on learning that is not carried out by most students—such as sign language, braille, life skills for more successful functioning in daily life, or enrichment activities—or it may focus on alternative ways to approach what most other students learn (e.g., reading, arithmetic). It may involve either extending or reducing what is usually learned by students of the same age. Whatever its form, effective special education involves 1) altered goals and expectations that interest and challenge students but are achievable, 2) curricula and teaching methods that are specially adapted to the abilities and learning styles of the students, and 3) personal supports (e.g., qualified teachers, aides, assistants) and environmental supports (e.g., setting, stimulation, procedures and routines, teaching materials, communication aids, and books, games, teaching aids, computers, and a vast range of other materials) that enhance optimal learning for individual students.

Special education for students with intellectual or developmental disabilities is one subtype of special education. Its primary focus is on promoting optimal learning for children who have lower or different levels of ability than most of their peers, as well as sometimes atypical ways of learning. This subtype encompasses a broad range of abilities and learning styles. For example, some children with developmental delay achieve milestones similar to those of children without disabilities but at slower rates. Other children have strengths or difficulties in particular areas of learning and development such as thinking, attention, motor skills, speech, perception, or memory.

Instructional methods for students with intellectual or developmental disabilities are often individualized or tailored to small groups of children. In the case of intellectual disability, concepts and information are often taught by using more concrete materials, a step-by-step methodology that engages students more actively, or other special adaptations (e.g., adapting the way sports and games are played for children who use wheelchairs). Although there are many similarities in the ways that all children learn, a primary purpose of special education is to ensure a focus on the unique learning needs of each child. For these reasons, many of the educational decisions for students in special education need to be made on a child-by-child basis, and a considerable amount of instruction needs to be individualized for students to achieve to best advantage.

A BRIEF HISTORY OF SPECIAL EDUCATION

The history of special education is rich with detail and is a field of study in its own right. This field not only involves an appreciation of the history of instructional methods and educational institutions but also blends into the history of the disability movement, medicine, neuroscience, the development of assistive technology (mechanical aids that substitute for or enhance the function of some physical or mental ability that is impaired), and political and social evolution. Vast changes in special education occurred in the 20th century. Thus, special education's history is best discussed in the categories of before the 20th century and during the 20th century.

Special Education Before the 20th Century

A recognition of exceptionality has always been a part of every society. Although limited information can be gleaned from historical documents, it is known that people with disabilities, at certain times and in certain societies, were ignored and even demonized by secular, political, and religious leaders. People with disabilities were actively persecuted in numerous ways; they were ostracized; picked on, chained in dungeons; and sometimes killed as infants, children, or adults (see also Brown & Brown, 2003). At other times and in other locations, however, people with disabilities were helped and even considered to be blessed or to be God's messengers (Woodill & Velche, 1994). From this, it can be assumed that a variety of both informal and formal ways to help people with disabilities learn and adjust to their roles in society have existed for centuries.

Special education, as a formal and systematic service, began in the early 18th century, primarily as a result of the growth of egalitarian and humanitarian ideas that swept France, the United States, and, to a lesser degree, other European countries and the countries in their empires. Numerous advances were made in a number of countries, beginning with France and Germany and later moving to England, the United States, and elsewhere. These improvements were led primarily by physicians who were appalled by the lack of care of children who were "idiots" and lived in orphanages, workhouses, asylums, schools for the poor, and other places of care (see Woodill & Velche, 1994, and Chapter 2 for a discussion of historical usage of terms). Despite efforts by religious and philanthropic organizations, conditions for these children often continued to be very poor, and the early pioneers in special education were interested in developing effective educational and training methods primarily for the purpose of equipping children with skills that would enable them to take a better place in society.

Many leaders and followers were instrumental in pioneering and advancing the field of special education, although a few made exceptional contributions (see Display 31.1 for examples of some well-known pioneers in special education). Their work influenced educational methods for all children and is the foundation of educational philosophy even today. Hallahan and Kauffman (2003) identified seven innovations that these early educators put in place that are still used: individual instruction, a carefully sequenced series of educational tasks, emphasis on stimulation and awakening of the child's senses, meticulous arrangement of the child's learning environment, immediate rewards for correct performance, tutoring in functional skills, and a belief that every child should be educated to the greatest extent possible.

The influence of the pioneers of special education, such as those described in Display 31.1, led to the establishment of the residential training school, or asylum, as the dominant model for housing, educating, and caring for children and adults with disabilities. The enormous influence of the asylum era is well documented. Asylums are now mostly thought of as having negative effects on the lives of those who were housed, often for life and without their consent, in structures that were set apart from society. This view needs to be balanced by recognizing that the original intent of the asylums was to provide places for education, health renewal, safety, and rehabilitation and that a great deal of valuable education, training, and other rehabilitation work was carried out within them. Asylums also provided a place of work for educators, physicians, and others interested in helping improve the lives of people with disabilities. Without such places, many of the advances in special education probably would not have occurred at all (Brown & Brown, 2003).

Special Education in the 20th Century

By the beginning of the 20th century, great numbers of asylums, hospitals, special schools, care homes, orphanages, workhouses, and other residences and learning centers had sprung up across Europe, the United States, and countries that were strongly influenced by Europe (e.g., Australia, Canada, New Zealand) (Copeland, 2002; Open Training and Education Network, 1998; Trent, 1994; Winzer, 1993). Such sites had always emphasized education and training, social inclusion, and rehabilitation to an extent, although overcrowding, underfunding, lack of demonstrated success, and other factors detracted from this emphasis (see Brown & Brown, 2003).

In the broader community, some interesting educational innovations were also occurring by this time. In the United States, for example, schools in Chicago attempted to include children who were blind in classrooms with children who could see. New instructional methods, especially braille and sign language, were developed for children who were blind, deaf, or both deaf and blind, and special classes and training centers became available in numerous communities for children who had emotional difficulties or who were "feebleminded" and thus did not attend general education schools. The first college program for training special education teachers opened at New York University in 1906 (Blackhurst & Berdine, 1993), and special education programs within regular school systems gradually increased during the first decades of the 20th century. In addition, many accompanying social services were developed, and these were assisted by the work of psychologists, sociologists, social workers, and professionals in other specialized fields.

Two factors were particularly important in the way special education developed in the first part of the 20th century: 1) intelligence measurement and the development of other psychoeducational assessment tools, and 2) the eugenics movement.

Intelligence Measurement and Other Psychoeducational Assessment Tools Testing people's intelligence is a widely accepted practice today and is carried out for a variety of reasons. In schools, the main reason to test intelligence is to provide information about a pupil's level of functioning within a broader assessment of his or her learning potential and learning style. A number of valid tests for measuring intelligence are in use. These have content differences, and some are more appropriate for certain groups of children than others. The results of intelligence tests should be used with caution and interpreted only by trained and qualified professionals.

It is surprising to many people today to learn that intelligence testing—and the use of numbers to represent relative intelligence—is only approximately 100 years old. In 1904, the French government commissioned psychologist Alfred Binet (1857–1911) to develop a reliable way to identify children who had lower intelligence and who therefore could benefit from instruction that was more specialized than that typically found in schoolrooms. The problem was that children with behavior and mental health problems were being inappropriately placed in special education classrooms and overburdening their resources. As a consequence, Binet and his colleagues, especially Theophile Simon,

Display 31.1

Some well-known pioneers in special education

Pedro Ponce de Leon (1520–1584), a Spanish Benedictine monk, promoted the view that sensory disabilities did not prohibit learning. He demonstrated this belief by teaching boys who were deaf and mute to speak, read, and write. He wrote a book that described his methods, although it has been lost to history. However, another Spaniard who specialized in the same area, J. Pablo Bonet (1560–1620), published teaching methods in his 1620 *Reducción de las letras y arte para enseñar a hablar a los mudos,* the first known book on the topic (Educación Especial, 1991).

John Locke (1632–1704) had many innovative ideas in many fields, including education (Williams, 2006). He was the first to differentiate between intellectual disabilities and emotional difficulties, although this difference was not fully understood until the 20th century.

Jean-Marc-Gaspard Itard (1775–1838) was a French physician who specialized in diseases of the ear. He became known for his development of successful methods for educating children who were deaf. He is most famous for the 5 years he spent teaching a 12-year-old French boy, named Victor, who was deaf and found living wild. Itard described this partial success in his well-known book *The Wild Boy of Aveyron* (Itard, 1801, 1806/1962), and his teaching enabled Victor to live with some degree of dignity in society.

Laurent Clerc (1785–1869) was a deaf teacher whom Thomas Hopkins Gallaudet recruited from The Institution for Deaf-Mutes in Paris; together they founded the American School for the Deaf. Clerc taught for 50 years and was much celebrated as the man who brought deaf education to America. He also adapted the French system of manual signing for his American students, creating a somewhat separate American system of signing (Polley, 2005).

Thomas Hopkins Gallaudet (1787–1851), an American theologian, studied European methods of communicating with and educating people who are deaf. When he returned to the United States, he founded in 1817 the first residential school for children who are deaf in Hartford, Connecticut. This school, later renamed The American School for the Deaf, was modeled after the well-regarded National Institute for the Deaf in Paris. Today, Gallaudet's pioneering work and name are honored by Gallaudet University in Washington, D.C., the only U.S. institution of higher learning for students who are deaf (Hallahan & Kauffman, 2003).

Samuel Gridley Howe (1801–1876) was an American educator, physician, and social reformer for a variety of humanitarian causes, including abolition. In the disability field, he is remembered mostly for his pioneering work in the education of people who were blind and deaf. He helped found the New England Asylum for the Blind (now the Perkins School for the Blind) and was its head for 44 years. Over time, Howe developed methods that he and others used to help a great many people. Helen Keller was a student who later benefited from his pioneering work (TeacherLINK, 2006).

Edouard Séguin (1812–1880) was a student of Jean-Marc-Gaspard Itard in France. He emigrated to the United States in 1848 and became well known for his pioneering work with children who would now be considered to have developmental delays or intellectual disabilities (Kanner, 1960; Stainton, 1994; see Chapter 2 for historic usage of terms). His approach became known as the physiological method and involved motor and sensory physical training, intellectual training (including academic and speech techniques), and socialization (which was considered moral training at the time). He founded an organization that later evolved into the American Association on Mental Retardation (Winzer, 1993).

Jacob Guggenbuhl (1816–1863) was a well-known Swiss educator who opened a residential facility to educate people with intellectual disabilities in Abendberg, Switzerland in 1816. Guggenbuhl is usually considered to be the pioneer in institutional care for people with intellectual disabilities. His work in education, although later discredited, set the scene for many later advances (for details, see Kanner, 1959).

John Langdon Haydon Down (1828–1896) was an English physician who taught medicine and specialized in mental health. He was an early proponent of training for people now described as having intellectual disabilities. Down proposed an early classification system for such people (described in Chapter 2), but is best known for his description of what was once called mongoloidism and is now known as Down syndrome. He made many other contributions to special education and the greater understanding of disability and mental health. During Down's life, he also became well known for his pioneering education and training methods in England, first at Earlswood Asylum for Idiots in Surrey and later at a home called Normansfield (Kanner, 1964; see Chapters 2 and 9 for additional details on Down).

developed the first intelligence test, the Simon-Binet Scale, which was revised in 1908 with the addition of mental age, and revised again in 1911. This test was intended to provide information about a child within a broader assessment of functioning and learning ability. Although a single score for intelligence, the intelligence quotient, was proposed by German psychologist Wilhelm Wundt, this notion was strongly rejected by Binet, who considered intelligence too complex to be described by one score (Whonamedit, n.d.).

Intelligence testing developed quite quickly, particularly in the United States under Henry Goddard, who standardized the Simon-Binet Scale on American children and published the test in 1910, and others at the Vineland Training School in New Jersey. Goddard believed that intelligence was a personal trait that was hereditary, was essentially stable over the lifetime of a person, and could be reliably measured. These views came to be commonly accepted in schools across the United States and in many other countries. Lewis Terman revised the Simon-Binet Scale to what became known as the Stanford-Binet Scale in 1916, and this was widely used for many years in educational systems. In fact, across the following decades, it became standard practice in educational and other systems to test almost all children for intelligence (Winzer, 1993).

The overall score from these intelligence tests, an intelligence quotient that became commonly known as an IQ score, came to be regarded as a predictor of children's learning potential. Goddard developed a system for classifying people by categories—normal, idiot, moron, or imbecile (see Chapter 2 for more details on classification categories)—according to their intelligence test scores, and this was also widely accepted and used. Later, classification terms associated with the broader terms *mental deficiency* and *mental retardation* were updated, but the basic principle was the same: namely, that children could be classified from the results of tests. Today, students are still tested for intelligence for many purposes, including meeting eligibility criteria for publicly funded services.

Intelligence testing and the huge number of psychoeducational tools (including those for adaptive behavior) that were developed across the 20th century provided a powerful way for helping educators to identify children who required special education, and to determine the children's specific learning challenges and abilities. Many of the schools for students with special needs that started out with so much optimism and promise had been floundering because educators simply did not know how to proceed (Brown & Brown, 2003). Intelligence testing and other psychoeducational assessment offered a way to pinpoint an appropriate starting point, to set realistic learning goals, and, later, to specify areas of learning strength and needs. In this sense, the use of testing and assessment tools appears to have represented a substantial move forward in the ability to identify children with special learning needs and to provide them with special education that fit those needs.

Before the 1970s, students who had IQ scores that led to them being diagnosed as "mentally deficient" were typically excluded from education in general education classrooms in almost every advanced country of the world. The principal reason for this was a fairly widespread belief in the futility of providing education for such children. For example, the American Edgar Doll, whose influence in special education was very significant across several decades, described *mental deficiency* in 1941 as "essentially incurable through treatment, and unremediable through training except as treatment and training instill habits, which superficially or temporarily compensate for the limitations of the person so affected" (1941, p. 217).

Such a view seems surprising, but until after the end of World War II there was little or no public recognition of the rights of people with disabilities or of their value to society. The activities and effects of world wars and a serious multiyear economic depression dominated public policy much of the time between 1900 and 1950. Moreover, this was an era when even the most developed countries were still struggling with how to encourage their students with high IQ scores to stay in school. Children with low IQ scores were simply not an educational priority (Doll, 1967; Winzer, 1993).

Eugenics Movement Growth in the belief of the value of intelligence testing was strongly influenced by the broader views of the eugenics movement—that society as a whole could be manipulated and improved by targeted action to discourage procreation among the "feeble-minded." This view was based on the idea that if species could evolve over time (as Darwin has suggested in his 1859 book *On the Origin of Species by Means of Natural Selection*), societies could evolve, too. Furthermore, if the evolution of plants and animals could be manipulated and improved to some degree, as the work of the geneticist Mendel and others demonstrated, then the evolution of societies could also be manipulated and improved. Thus, the goal of the eugenics movement was to help society evolve by intervening in a variety of ways, such as encouraging procreation among the more fit and discouraging it among the less fit.

The term *eugenics* means "well born" and was coined by Sir Francis Galton, a British physician, in 1880. Galton also coined the phrase *nature versus nurture,* and he stressed the importance of hereditary factors in the study of individual differences. It is difficult today to fully understand the strength of the eugenics movement. Simply put, it became the predominant view of leading scientists, educators, psychiatrists, physicians, politicians, judges, and many other professionals in the United States, Europe, and in other areas of the word. Eugenics affected almost every aspect of society. For people who were deemed or feared to be feeble-minded, it led to numerous beliefs and practices that separated them from society and attempted to curb their appetites for reproduction. For example, respected physicians and other professionals equated masturbation with any number of dire consequences, including insanity. Bland diets were often recommended to curtail sexual desire, and the American John Kellogg even developed his well-known corn flakes as a desirable, if bland, breakfast food for the patients in his mental health hospital (Woodill, 1992; see also Chapter 2). Eugenics beliefs led to involuntary institutionalization, sterilizations, and gender separation and a belief in the evils of any sexual activity other than that between (desirable) married couples; it also led to racial discrimination and restrictions on immigration from some countries, as feeble-mindedness was believed to be more common among some nationalities and races than others (Kevles, 1975).

The principles of the eugenics movement began to be blatantly misapplied in the 1930s in Nazi Germany. Yet, such was its strength at the time that it was not until the end of World War II and the shocking discovery of the extermination camps that the eugenics movement came to a rapid close. The subsequent discoveries of the systematic killing of millions of Jews, children with disabilities, people in mental health facilities, and many others who were considered to be undesirable ensured that the main ideas associated with the eugenics movement remained ideas of the past.

Last Half of the 20th Century After World War II ended, the dominant countries of the Western world starting turning their attention toward social equality and human rights. The World Health Organization and the United Nations took leading roles in promoting international agreements that, at least on paper, spoke to the rights of individuals and the equality of all people (see Chapters 5 and 6). Parents of children with disabilities formed groups and began to advocate strongly for educational and social services for their children, especially as there was no legal entitlement to schooling for children with disabilities (Winter, 2003).

At first, such advocacy led to the growth of educational services primarily outside school systems. These services were not always ideal. Access was fairly arbitrary, the quality of instruction was uneven, and some sites were overcrowded and underfunded. As with the residential institutions, some children were left in these services simply because it appeared to be the only option available and not because their learning needs were being served. Similar problems plagued special education programs within school systems. These and other factors helped generate a number of important acts and laws (see the next section) that set out educational rights for all children with disabilities and that have led to the current educational philosophy of inclusion.

LEGISLATION GOVERNING SPECIAL EDUCATION

Because this section covers legislation related to special education, a broad explanation of legislative terms is needed. An act is a product—such as a statute, decree, or enactment—resulting from a decision by a legislative or judicial body (e.g., an Act of Congress). Acts are not enforceable per se. A law is a rule of conduct established and enforced by the authority, legislation, or custom of a given community, state, or nation. Laws are enforceable.

U.S. Legislation

In the United States, there are numerous state and local laws and policies in force. Among the most important national acts and laws are the following:

- Section 504 of the Rehabilitation Act of 1973 (PL 93-112)
- Education for All Handicapped Children Act of 1975 (PL 94-142)
- Handicapped Children's Protection Act of 1986 (PL 99-372)
- Americans with Disabilities Act (ADA) of 1990 (PL 101-336)
- Individuals with Disabilities Education Act Amendments of 1997 (PL 105-17)
- No Child Left Behind Act of 2001 (PL 107-110)
- Individuals with Disabilities Education Improvement Act of 2004 (PL 108-446)

The Rehabilitation Act of 1973 is generally considered to be the first major law in the United States to address the rights of people with disabilities. Although it was limited to programs that received financial assistance from the federal government, it represented a solid beginning point—and one that would be expanded considerably across the 30 years that followed—for addressing discrimination against people with disabilities in a variety of public sites and activities and in places of employment. Section 504 of the Rehabilitation Act of 1973 states,

> No otherwise qualified individual with a disability in the United States, as defined in section 706 (8) of this title, shall, solely by reason of his or her disability, be excluded from participation in, be denied the benefits of, or be subjected to discrimination under any program or activity receiving Federal financial assistance or under any program

or activity conducted by any Executive agency or by the United States Postal Service.

Section 504 did not set out conditions for the broad protection of people with disabilities, nor did it require programs to ensure accessibility. Still, it set a clear policy direction for the future: namely that where public funds are used, disability alone is insufficient reason for exclusion. (See Disability Sports, n.d.)

The Education for All Handicapped Children Act of 1975, which came to be widely known as Public Law (PL) 94-142, was enacted in 1975. This act is perhaps the most important law ever passed for special education for two main reasons. First, its purpose was to move strongly toward a national program of community-based education for all children with disabilities (ages 3–21), including all children with developmental delay (mental retardation, as this was called in the U.S. at the time). This was a bold move, because an enormous number of children and families were affected; new programs needed to be developed; funding needed to be increased or reallocated; and longtime practices needed to be challenged, adapted, or abandoned (e.g., training children in institutions, parents deciding that children with disabilities should stay at home and not attend school). Second, following the enactment of PL 94-142, a very large amount of literature emerged in education and related journals (and is still available through educational database systems) that assessed its scope and impact. The law provided, among other things, for all children with disabilities to receive education in the "least restrictive environment (LRE)," and what this phrase meant had to be debated from educational, practical, and legal points of view. Issues related to methods of providing instruction, training teachers and other education personnel, funding, transportation, and addressing family concerns received a great deal of attention and were the subject of much debate. The overall effect of all this attention was to advance special education in public school systems very substantially and to move quickly toward greatly improved curricula and instruction methods.

Amendments to the Education for All Handicapped Children Act of 1975 were enacted in 1986 (Education of the Handicapped Act Amendments of 1986, PL 99-457). These amendments made funds available to states and territories for early intervention programs (infants and toddlers, birth to age 2), and preschool special education (children ages 3–5). (See also *The Child Find Process in Trumbull Public Law 99-457 Procedures, n.d.,* and Houghton Mifflin Student Resource Center, n.d.)

The Individuals with Disabilities Education Act Amendments of 1997, best known as IDEA '97, was an update of the Education for All Handicapped Children Act of 1975 and other laws that came after it. IDEA '97 applied to children ages 3–21 who had disabilities according to set criteria and who required special education. The specific disabilities covered were autism, deafness, deafness-blindness, hearing impairment, mental retardation, multiple disabilities, orthopedic impairment, other health impairment, emotional disturbance, specific learning disabilities, speech or language impairment, traumatic brain injury, and visual impairment (including blindness).

IDEA '97 required public schools to provide special education for all students with disabilities enrolled in infant programs, elementary school, or secondary school. IDEA '97 highlighted the concept of providing special education in the LRE so that as far as is feasible, students with disabilities could be included with their age peers. The law required that individualized education programs (IEPs) be created for all students with disabilities to specify the following: current level of academic performance, annual goals, educational services to be provided, the starting and ending points for these services, the degree to which the child would be included in general education classroom activities, and procedures for assessing if the goals were being reached.

IDEA '97 also included major provisions to ensure that young children in need of special education had access to appropriate services from birth to the age of school entry. For children younger than 3 years of age, individualized family service plans (IFSPs) were to be developed. In addition, the law required that children with disabilities receive a free appropriate public education (FAPE), as well as participate—along with their parents—in decision making. Procedural safeguards were outlined that protect parents' and students' rights with respect to the provision of a FAPE (see also Lipton, 1999).

The No Child Left Behind Act of 2001 set common standards for schools across the United States in the areas of accountability for student performance (achievement to be rewarded and failure to be sanctioned), focus on what works (funding for effective practice), reduced bureaucracy and increased flexibility (more local control), and empowering parents (more information and more choice if schools perform poorly). IDEA was brought more closely in line with this act by the enactment of the Individuals with Disabilities Education Improvement Act of 2004.

The ADA, enacted in 1990, set out guarantees of the civil rights of all people with disabilities. Although it did not delineate specific supports, its intent was to set a context for enabling people with disabilities to acquire education and training, participate in the work force, and take a full and inclusive role in society. (See also National Dissemination Center for Children with Disabilities, n.d.) Once an individual with disabilities leaves high school and pursues postsecondary education or employment, the ADA becomes the relevant legislation (Reilly & Davis, 2005).

Although these have been the most influential pieces of U.S. legislation, numerous other supporting laws and initiatives are also in effect. For example, the New Freedom Initiative (U.S. Department of Health and Human Services, 2001) set the goal of full inclusion for people with disabilities into all aspects of American life, and the President's Commission on Excellence in Special Education was created to identify all students with special needs and to promote optimal learning (U.S. Department of Education, 2003; see also Vocational and Educational Services for Individuals with Disabilities, n.d., and The White House, 2002).

IDEA and related legislation not only support special education (including the provision of assistive technology) from prekindergarten through secondary school but also different types of Head Start programs. The ADA also supports the right of access to postsecondary education (see Getzel & Wehman, 2005). The key features of U.S. laws in force that govern special education, and thus provide overall policy for special education, are set out in Figure 31.1.

Legislation in Other Countries

Effective special education legislation has been enacted in many countries other than the United States. It is clear, though, that U.S. legislation is very comprehensive and has set trends that have been followed in many other countries (Winzer, 2002). By way of providing some examples, brief descriptions follow regarding the status of special education in Canada and the United Kingdom at the beginning of the 21st century.

Canada In Canada, education is the constitutional responsibility of the 10 provinces and 3 territories. The exception is that education for First Nations Peoples is the responsibility of the federal government; it is regulated by the terms of the federal government's Indian Act. It is somewhat difficult to describe Canada's education system as a whole, because there is no overall coordination at the federal level. What can be said, though, is that all provinces and territories have enacted legislation that guarantees the right to free public education for all children, even if this right takes numerous forms both among and within provinces and territories (Winzer, 2002). Ontario, Canada's most populous province, serves as an example.

Ontario amended its Education Act in 1980 to require all school boards to ensure that all exceptional children are provided with free public education; that exceptional pupils are defined and categorized; and that exceptional pupils are identified and appropriately placed through an Identification, Placement and Review Committee (Ontario Ministry of Education, 2006). Section 1 of the act describes an exceptional pupil as one "whose behavioural, communicational, intellectual, physical or multiple exceptionalities are such that he or she is considered to need placement in a special education program" (Ontario Human Rights Commission, 2002). The other main provisions of the amendment were that special education programs must 1) be based on, and modified by, ongoing assessment and evaluation; 2) provide an Individual Education Plan with specific learning objectives; and 3) specify educational supports that meet the needs of exceptional pupils. The act also established a Special Education Tribunal, whose function was to "provide final and binding arbitration in disagreements between a parent and school board concerning the identification or placement of an exceptional pupil" (Ontario Ministry of Education, 2006).

On the whole, special education in Canada has followed legal and practice developments in the United States (Winzer, 2002). Although there are some differences, there is little doubt that Canada's provinces and territories have all adopted inclusive education politics and practice. Incremental improvements continue to be made by the 13 governments (for specific information, refer to the government web site for the appropriate agency in each province and territory; see http://www.cmec.ca/educmin.en.stm).

United Kingdom The United Kingdom passed a series of laws to provide for the needs of children with learning difficulties and other special needs (see Mittler, 2002). The Education Acts (1993 and 1996) and the Disability Discrimination Act (1995) were updated for special education with the enactment of the Special Educational Needs and Disability Act 2001 (SENDA; see U.K. Centre for Legal Education, 2006; U.K. Office of Public Sector Information, 2001). SENDA applies to England, Wales, and Scotland.

SENDA differs from North American special education legislation in that it proceeds from a human rights perspective. This legislation

> Introduces the right for disabled students not to be discriminated against in education, training and any services provided wholly or mainly for students, and for those enrolled in courses provided by 'responsible bodies', including further and higher education institutions and sixth form colleges. (U.K. Centre for Legal Education, 2006)

In general terms, this means that all students with disabilities, including those in higher education, are given the right not to be treated "less favourably" than students without disabilities, and that it is the responsibility of schools and educational institutions themselves to show that their treatment of individuals with dis-

THREE MAJOR EDUCATION LAWS & HOW THEY RELATE TO STUDENTS WITH DISABILITIES

Responsibilities of K–12[1] and Post-Secondary Institutions[2]

Public Law 105-17 • Public Law 101-336 • Public Law 93-112

LAWS Delivery of services as per intent of laws	**Used by All K-12 Public School Districts** Individuals with Disabilities in Education Act (IDEA), Public Law 105-17	**Used by Post-Secondary Institutions** Americans with Disabilities Act (ADA), Public Law 101-336 & Section 504 of the Rehabilitation Act, Public Law 93-112
Identification of disability	Mandated. Local school district identifies disability	Not mandated. Student provides documentation of disability and verification of need for services/ accommodation(s)
Cost burden of disability evaluation/identification	Provided free by school district	Student's responsibility
Development of plan to ensure school/training success	Mandated. Parent/guardian/school develop individualized education program (IEP)	Student/institution jointly identify disability limitations and determine appropriate accommodation(s)
Provision of specialized disability-related services & accommodations	Mandated. Student entitled to that which is identified on IEP	Mandated. However, provision is based upon disability-caused educational limitations that justify eligibility for reasonable accommodations/services
Accountability	Mandated. District assumes responsibility for IEP implementation	Student responsible for own progress. However, institutions should have in place internal systems to monitor law compliance
Role of advocacy	Mandated. Parent/teacher/student may all assume role as advocates	Not mandated. Student must advocate for self
Changes in curriculum and education/ training procedures to ensure student success	Mandated. Fundamental alterations to educational program/classroom teaching and assessment permitted as identified on IEP	Not mandated and generally not permitted. Accommodations may not alter fundamental nature of course/ training or impose an undue burden on an institution
Provision of personal services (e.g., transportation, personal attendant, nurse, special tutoring)	Mandated	Not mandated
Student Achievement	Mandated right to education	Not assured. Student responsible for own academic/training success
Enforcement	U.S. Department of Education	U.S. Department of Justice

[1]K–12 refers to the years in public school from kindergarten through the end of high school
[2]Includes vocational training schools, colleges and universities

Figure 31.1. Key features of U.S. laws that govern special education and provide overall policy for special education. (From Wilde, J. [2004]. *The disability journey: A bridge from awareness to action.* Lincoln, NE: iUniverse Publishers; © iUniverse Publishers, 2004; adapted by permission.)

abilities is justified. The key features of SENDA include access to public education, the right to inclusive education where possible, the right of students with disabilities not to be substantially disadvantaged, the right of families to be informed, and the right to appeal decisions. It also extends to educational services, such as the use of libraries and resource centers (Special Educational Needs and Disability Act 2001, 2001).

SENDA represents an important step forward for special education and for the rights of individuals with disabilities. It establishes legal rights for all students with disabilities, and it requires educational service providers to anticipate, plan for, and respond to the needs of exceptional students. Finally, it extends the rights of special education students because it applies to educational support services, such as libraries and resource centers, testing and examining procedures, field trips, and employment training placements.

Number of Students Who Benefit from Special Education Legislation

Special education legislation and policies have led to the establishment of numerous programs and services at all levels of education in different countries. These include early childhood and early intervention programs for children with developmental delays or physical or sensory disabilities (e.g., Head Start programs in the United States); special instruction for children with virtually all disabilities at the elementary and secondary levels, both within general education classrooms and in other venues; and some postsecondary and adult learning programs.

Substantial numbers of children with disabilities are receiving special education within formal school systems. The National Center for Education Statistics (2006) in the United States reported that in the academic year 2001–2002, 13.4% of all students were receiving special education services, an increase of 1.8% since 1991–1992. The percentage of students who were classified as having mental retardation or developmental delay remained stable from 1991 to 2001, at approximately 1.3% of all students.

In most other countries, it is more difficult to ascertain the precise number of children who benefit from special education because statistics are not gathered and reported in a systematic way. Winzer (2002) noted that 290 million people worldwide are estimated to have disabilities. The Foundation for People with Learning Disabilities (2000) in the United Kingdom compiled estimates from Europe, North America, and Australia and suggested that approximately 2% of these populations have intellectual disabilities. The Australian Institute of Health and Welfare (2003) reported on the number of people with various types of disabilities in 1998. Although no data were reported for use of special education services, it might be anticipated that almost all children who are identified as having disabilities would receive some form of special education. The percentage of all children who had intellectual disabilities was 0.7% for those from birth through age 4, 4.0% for those ages 5–14, and 2.4% for teens 15–19 years old. For all children from birth through age 14, 7.7% were considered to have physical disabilities or intellectual disabilities. (See also Dempsey, Foreman, & Jenkinson, 2002, for specific information on New South Wales and Victoria.) In Canada, 3.3% of children from birth through age 14 have physical limitations (Statistics Canada, 2003), and an estimated 2.5% of all children have developmental delays (Brown, 2003). Presumably, all of the latter and some of the former receive special education. In 2000, 12.5% of all children in Ontario's school system were receiving special education, although the majority of these had learning disabilities (Roeher Institute, 2000). The Ontario Ministry of Education (2003), using data from five Canadian provinces that was gathered between 2001 and 2004, reported that 1.73%–2.76% of all students had acute or severe special needs.

Children with Disabilities in General Education Classrooms In the United States, it was reported that in the 1988–1989 school year, 31% of students with disabilities spent 80% or more of their school time in general education classrooms, but, by 1998–1999, 47% did so. Across the same time period, children with disabilities not attending a general education school at all dropped slightly (National Center for Education Statistics, 2002). Although statistics are not readily available, it might be expected that similar increases occurred in other countries with special education legislation that follows the U.S. trends in identification and placement and in provision of needed supports to students with special needs.

Students Graduating from Secondary School In spite of higher percentages of students receiving special education, graduation rates for those with intellectual disabilities may still be problematic. According to one report (Katsiyannis, Zhang, & Archwamety, 2002), there has been a decline in the graduation rates of U.S. students identified at the time as having mental retardation. The reasons for such declines are unclear at this time, and more research is needed. International information on secondary school graduation is scarce, but there are some indications that individuals with more severe disabilities are less likely to graduate (e.g., Tramontina et al., 2002).

Students in Postsecondary Education Since around 1980, there has been considerable interest in students with intellectual and developmental disabilities learning within college and university environments or participating in the leisure and recreational activities available in these settings. A number of college programs, in particular, have been developed. In a 2001 review, Neubert et al. noted that evaluation data on postsecondary education programs has been scarce and that attention turned since the 1990s toward preparing students who are already in school for continuing their education in college environments.

KEY ASPECTS OF SPECIAL EDUCATION

A number of aspects are particularly salient in the special education literature and are critical to the way special education is understood and practiced. A great deal of academic and professional information is readily available on each of these aspects, some of which is presented in other chapters of this book. The intent here, therefore, is not to describe these aspects in a comprehensive way. Rather, they are introduced briefly in the following sections with the intent of highlighting for the reader their importance to special education for children with intellectual and developmental disabilities. The information presented applies to special education services in various countries.

Labeling

For many years, there has been considerable debate in the disabilities field about the advantages and disadvantages of using labels, or terms that describe a general classification or specific diagnosis (e.g., *developmental delay, visually impaired, autism, acquired brain injury*). The convention today is that a person's name is used to identify him or her and that labels are only used if there is benefit to the person or the situation, such as clarifying the reason for needed supports (see discussion in Chapter 1). Even when labels are used, people-first language has been the norm for a number of years now. For example, "children with autism" is used instead of "autistic children" and "Pedro, a boy with developmental delay" is preferable to "the delayed boy, Pedro." Such usage is thought to respect the dignity of each person and promotes the view that each human has unique personal and social value.

Labels are used to advantage within almost all school systems. They are helpful to schools for grouping children with similar learning needs, assisting with appropriate placement, and guiding the development of individual education plans that are in keeping with students' abilities. They help ensure that children with special needs are assigned to qualified teachers who use instructional methods that are appropriate to their learning abilities and learning styles (Tilstone et al., 2000). They also help teachers, parents, and other children understand similarities and differences between children who receive special education and those who do not. Finally, legislation often requires that children who receive special education—and the additional funding that accompanies it—are appropriately assessed and clearly classified.

Applying labels is also problematic for schools; thus, labels need to be used with caution. Labels, on their own, do not necessarily lead to better instruction, and they can distort teachers' (and parents') perceptions of student abilities and their expectations of what students can achieve (Fitch, 2002; Kauffman, 2003; Newsom, 2001). For children, labels sometimes can hinder the development of positive self-image and motivation to succeed (Tracey, 2002).

There are problems with grouping children for instruction as well. Many children who are classified, or labeled, in the same way (e.g., developmental delay, intellectual disability, Tourette syndrome, emotional difficulties), have very different instructional needs; thus, grouping them together is not always in their best interests (Freedman, 1999; Winzer, 2002). Perhaps most important, as the noted American educator Ysseldyke pointed out in 1987, the overall learning needs (e.g., reading, writing, oral communication, mathematics, social skills) of students who receive special education do not differ substantially from other children or from one another.

Overall, labels will probably continue to be used in school systems because they have some advantages. However, it is essential that those involved in special education—including school administrators, teachers, teachers' assistants, parents, and students themselves—fully understand the implications of using labels and ensure that appropriate steps are taken to counteract negative effects.

Assessment of Learning and Instructional Needs

Ongoing assessment is an excellent educational practice to determine changing general and specific learning needs of individual students, and thus it is essential to teaching and learning. In addition, though, assessment is set out as a legal requirement in the United States and other countries for students who receive special education. Assessment is a broad area of study that is supported by numerous textbooks, tests, and research reports.

Assessment in special education has two general purposes. First, assessment provides child-specific information that guides school personnel and parents in making decisions to provide individual students with the best learning environment, instructional methods, and supports. Such information may emerge from using some of the many available formal assessment tools, but it also may come from less formal assessment, such as teacher and parent observations, checklists of child behaviors, classroom tests and other documentation of learning achievement, and notes on the effects of the environment (Friend & Bursuck, 2002; see Wodrich, 1997, for a good description of tests and assessment methods). Information that contributes to a special education assessment may be sought from school psychologists, speech-language specialists, physical therapists, medical professionals, social workers, and others.

Second, assessment identifies a child's specific skills and abilities, learning needs, most successful learning methods, and learning progress. In this sense, it is a basic and essential tool of good teaching. Formal assessment tools are sometimes helpful for identifying starting points, but effective teachers need to assess their students less formally in an ongoing way each day, adjusting for specific subject matter and specific skills, as well as for what needs to be taught and the best ways to teach it. With experience, teachers learn to intuitively and continually evaluate children with special needs and to identify routes of learning that are best for a given child.

Individualized Instruction and Individualized Education Programs

Good teachers always have provided individualized instruction to students to help them acquire specific skills and knowledge and have adjusted their content, teaching methods, and expectations to meet individual students' capabilities. This has not changed. Yet, teachers have not always been required to follow plans for students that anticipate the need for individualized instruction and student achievement. Since the 1970s, there has been a general shift to individualize planning and instruction. This has been seen as particularly important in special education, as evidenced by the attention the topic is getting in international special education literature (e.g., Mizutani, Hiruma, & Yanagimoto, 2002). It is also a view that has been strongly supported by legislation (the Education for All Handicapped Children Act of 1975 and many laws) and numerous policy documents by governments and schools districts in many countries.

Individualized education plans or programs are required in several countries or parts of countries. They differ in their legal requirements and makeup, but most specify for each student, following appropriate assessment, what needs to be taught, how it will be taught, what supports are needed, and what evaluation will be used to determine if the progress has been successful.

In the United States, IDEA requires IEPs to be developed for children receiving special education in elementary and secondary schools. Children younger than 3 years of age who have been identified as having disabilities and who are in funded programs must have IFSPs. Although IEPs differ widely among school districts, they are all designed to meet the legal requirements set out by IDEA and to provide child-specific information that will be helpful in providing instruction and achieving educational objectives (see this chapter's preceding description of IDEA). As noted in Figure 31.1, requirements are that a student's needs are assessed, that teachers and school personnel work with parents or guardians in developing an individualized special education program to meet the student's learning needs, that clear goals and objectives be set out, and that progress toward these goals is evaluated. Most plans also describe the methods by which the following will be identified and implemented (see Bateman & Linden, 1998; also see Appendix B at the end of the book for Internet sources of information on IEPs):

1. Specific academic skills to be achieved (e.g., related to reading, mathematics, and written language, but also possibly related to sign language or braille)
2. Particular social skills to be learned (e.g., cooperative play, use of phrases that demonstrate manners)
3. Necessary personnel supports (e.g., teaching assistant, support peer who does not have disabilities, speech-language pathologist, physical therapist)
4. Environmental supports (e.g., quiet work space, assistive technology, equipment, access to community resources)

Placement and Inclusion

One of the most crucial decisions to be made about a child's special education is the place where services will occur. Placement decisions are typically made after a child has been identified as having special learning needs, an assessment has been carried out, and some plans have been developed to meet identified needs (in the United States, IDEA requires the development of the IEP before a placement decision is made). Whenever possible, the placement decision is made by school personnel and parents or guardians and is based on information about which environment can best support the educational goals and objectives of the individual student (see Pitasky, 2002).

Placement has been a controversial area in special education. There have been philosophical differences about which placement is best for students with special needs. Members of the decision committee do not always agree, and such lack of agreement has led to some notable legal battles (Hallahan & Kauffman, 2003). There has been some contradictory evidence about where children with disabilities are best placed. The overall trend that has been evolving across more developed countries, however, is for children with special needs to be placed in general education classrooms in neighborhood schools, unless an alternative is shown to be better.

The term *mainstreaming* was coined in the United States to describe the practice of including students with disabilities and students without disabilities in the same settings for the purpose of teaching and learning. The terms *inclusion* and *mainstreaming* are used as synonyms in some countries (e.g., Canada). *Inclusion* has become the preferred term in the United States, however, because it refers to the overall process of jointly teaching children with and without disabilities and the bringing of support services to children (rather than moving the children to the services). Inclusion also typically represents the method for fulfilling the U.S. requirement for providing education in the least restrictive environment (Friend & Bursuck, 2002). Similar requirements are in place in most provinces and territories of Canada, whereas in the United Kingdom, schools must provide inclusive education unless they can justify alternatives. As a result, students with special needs in most countries may be full-time members of a general education classroom or may join their general education classmates for a part or parts of the day. Such inclusion is considered by most educators and parents to be the preferred placement option.

In school settings, inclusion encompasses a broad acceptance of children with disabilities and recognition by all staff and students of these students' contributions. Specifically, Kochhar, West, and Taymans (2000) described six key components of inclusive schools and classrooms: 1) children with disabilities attend neighborhood schools, 2) schools and classrooms reflect proportions of children with disabilities found in the general population, 3) no student is excluded because of disabilities (the zero-reject philosophy), 4) students with disabilities are placed in classes with same-age peers, 5) students with and without disabilities take part in cooperative learning and peer instruction, and 6) needed special education resources (including personnel) are available within the general education classroom.

An emphasis on inclusion does not mean that separate schools or separate classrooms for special education do not exist. Indeed, they do exist, and, despite the obvious disadvantages related to segregation and exclusion, there are many advantages to teaching some children with intellectual and developmental disabilities in separate venues (Bridle, 2005). In the short term, children with disabilities may even get better instruction, especially if their general education teachers are not fully trained (Ellins & Porter, 2005; Gilmore, Campbell, & Cuskelly, 2003; Jahnukainen & Korhonen, 2003); this is especially the case in some countries, such as Japan, where children with disabilities are only beginning to be accepted (see Tachibana & Watanabe, 2004).

Many advantages of inclusion have been documented (e.g., Peetsma et al., 2001), as well as many ways to enhance inclusion, even for students with more severe disabilities (Fisher & Frey, 2001). The current trend is, whenever possible, to keep open linkages between special and inclusive schools so that teachers, parents, and school administrators can have flexibility in making decisions about full, partial, or no inclusion (e.g., see Cheminais, 2003). For example, a student who attends a special education school might try joining age-peers in a nearby general education school for a limited time each day or each week. Conversely, a special education student who attends a general education school might benefit from taking part in some activities in a special school.

Teachers' Assistants

Teachers' assistants or aides (also sometimes called paraprofessionals) work with, or in support of, children who have special needs. They work under the direction of a teacher and may assist with such things as behavior management, instructional support, preparation of materials, activities of daily living (e.g., toileting, dressing, hygiene), social skills and other types of training, and specific learning tasks. Such people can play extremely important roles in the education of children with special needs. Teachers' assistants are typically seen to be more essential for students with higher support needs (McNally, Cole, & Waugh, 2001).

It has been difficult, however, for educational administrators to obtain financial resources to provide sufficient numbers of teachers' assistants to meet the needs of students with intellectual and developmental disabilities. Providing such personnel can entail a significant expense, especially if an assistant is required full time for only one student. In some regions, this has led to trying to find the balance between what is best for the child's education and how to contain public spending on education.

Curriculum and Curriculum Modifications

The term *curriculum* refers to the particular subject areas and topics that schools and teachers include in their instruction. In its broader sense, it also refers to the methods of instruction and evaluation. Curricula are developed in most countries for each educational level, and typically there is evalution of the degree to which students achieve regarding curriculum standards.

Special education teachers almost always have considerably more flexibility in curriculum than do regular classroom teachers because of individualized planning for students with special learning needs. An IEP is not a curriculum, but it is a framework that directs what should be taught for an individual student. Even when students with special needs are following the general education school curriculum, it is assumed that some modifications may be necessary to the curriculum itself, the methods by which it is taught, or both (Tilstone et al., 2000).

Accommodations and Adaptations Regarding Settings, Routines, and Materials

Teachers of children with special needs must have an ongoing awareness of how the environment affects students with intellectual and developmental disabilities and then adapt it accordingly. This is part of the ongoing assessment that good teachers carry out while they perform their daily work. Some students do not function well when they are isolated, and others do best when working in quiet, undisturbed locations. For some students, being surrounded by colors, pictures, books, and so forth is positively stimulating, and other students find the presence of such things to be stressful and overwhelming. A student may show frustration because his or her wheelchair is uncomfortable, because he or she is not receiving sufficient social interaction, or because he or she is hungry. A student may not understand how to work on a task or who to turn to for help.

Equipment, routines, or presentation of material may need to be made to address these and countless other problems that arise in special education learning situations. Such changes also help ensure equal learning opportunities for students with special needs (Price et al., 2000–2001). Numerous types of accommodations are being used successfully in special education, but Price et al. listed 13 common accommodations in special education:

1. Accessible classroom, location within the classroom, and furniture
2. Advance notice of assignments
3. Alternative ways of completing assignments (e.g., oral presentation versus written paper)
4. Assistive listening devices
5. Assistive technology
6. Auxiliary aids and services (e.g., note takers, lab or library assistants, readers, interpreters)
7. Captions for film and video material
8. Course or program modifications
9. Document conversion (alternative print formats; e.g., braille, large print, tape, electronic, raised lettering)
10. Study skills and strategies training
11. Taped lectures
12. Test modifications
13. Time extensions

There are many other examples of accommodations, but the principle to be followed is the same: The effects of the student's environment, including the way people interact with the child who has a disability, must be assessed in an ongoing way and the appropriate accommodations and adaptations must be made to ensure a supportive environment that maximizes opportunities for learning (see Display 31.2).

Display 31.2

Accommodations for Anthony

Anthony is 10 and has an intellectual disability and attention-deficit/hyperactivity disorder (ADHD). He attends a neighborhood school, where a teacher's assistant supports him in a regular classroom. He joins classmates for group lessons but needs accommodations to succeed. To keep Anthony's attention, the teacher has Anthony sit close by, uses his name, touches him lightly on the shoulder or arm, makes eye contact, or gives him a small job such as turning pages.

For individualized activities, other accommodations are needed. The teacher's assistant directs him to a clutter-free work area, which is slightly apart and angled to help limit distraction from other children's movements or the teacher's voice. The teacher's assistant sits nearby and reviews the lesson in parts. Often, she uses action, facial expression, and interaction to help Anthony understand and remember. Using a quiet, steady voice, she asks questions and solicits responses. She asks him to read instructions and say them in different words. Anthony needs to focus on, and receive praise for, each small task. When he finishes his activities, it is important that he show his classroom teacher for her approval.

Peer Support from Children Without Disabilities

Children who do not have disabilities can be a valuable resource to general education classrooms and special education teachers. The main way they help is simply by acting in ways that are typical of children of their age. In doing so, they model behavior, speech, ways to learn, and many other things to students with disabilities. There are numerous accounts available of how children who do not have disabilities help students with disabilities more directly (e.g., Barfield, Hannigan-Downs, & Lieberman, 1998; Friend & Bursuck, 2002), although specific training may be required (Manetti, Schneider, & Siperstein, 2001). They may act as special friends and help with specific tasks, such as dressing to go outside, engaging in conversations, and walking to and from school. The simple act of helping out can lead to valuable learning experiences and can promote acceptance of disability.

Implementing such roles for children who do not have disabilities needs to be approached and monitored with care. Children are at different stages in their acceptance of, and comfort with, disability. Some children need direct instruction on how to interact with children who have intellectual or developmental disabilities. Above all, teachers must ensure that the interaction of children with and without disabilities is a positive experience. They must take every precaution to ensure that such interactions do not cause the peers without disabilities to feel stress or to think negatively about the children with disabilities.

Postsecondary Education and Lifelong Learning for People with Disabilities

In recent years, an increasing number of students with intellectual and developmental disabilities have been gaining access to postsecondary education. As previously explained, in the United States, the ADA protects the right of access to 2-year colleges, 4-year colleges, and universities or to engage in other types of postsecondary education considered essential for job training (Reilly & Davis, 2005). Such opportunities also are available in other countries. Some educational and community institutions have developed special life skills programs for adults with intellectual and developmental disabilities (e.g., programs that teach enhancing and maintaining daily living skills, cooking, sex education, and parenting).

Developing postsecondary education programs especially for people with intellectual and developmental disabilities is a rather new area, and methods of evaluating the efficacy or success of these programs are still developing. Still, numerous models (e.g., Getzel & Wehman, 2005) and resources are emerging (e.g., Hart, Zimbrich, & Parker, 2005; Levinson, 2004). Benefits of participating in postsecondary education programs include taking part in social and recreational activities in addition to academic ones. (See Table 31.1 for some different types of postsecondary or supplemental educational programs.) People with intellectual or developmental disabilities of any age also may want to attend various types of educational and community programs (e.g., sports events, theater productions, swimming lessons, music appreciation classes) for personal fulfillment.

Table 31.1. Some types of postsecondary or supplemental education programs

Certificate programs

Some careers require people to get certificates that prove that they have trained for a job at an approved school and that they have completed a certain number of hours practicing new skills. Some jobs that may require a certificate include massage therapist, kennel manager, medical assistant, computer technology, and office assistant.

Adult education programs

Adult education programs offer a wide range of courses, including classes in language, cooking, exercise and fitness, computers, history, and many more. Some are 1-day classes; others run for several months, just like typical college courses. Because these courses are for adults, they are usually offered in the evening or on weekends.

Lessons

Some students arrange to take private lessons to develop skills needed for desired jobs or just for personal fulfillment. These lessons include music lessons, singing lessons, and art lessons.

Professional and Continuing Education for Teachers

In almost all jurisdictions, special education teachers are required to have specific training and qualifications that are in addition to those of general education classroom teachers. In accordance with IDEA 2004, as of the 2005–2006 U.S. school year, all special education teachers (whether or not they teach core academic subjects) must hold at least a bachelor's degree and must obtain full state certification in the appropriate area of special education in order to meet the IDEA definition of highly qualified teacher. Depending on the region in which a teacher is working and the subjects that he or she teaches, there is some flexibility in meeting these qualifications. Two ongoing dilemmas are the definition of *special education teacher* and what a special education teacher's specific qualifications should be.

Continuing professional education is very important for teachers in the special education field, yet there appears to be substantial need for broader training (e.g., Dybvik, 2004; Gilmore et al., 2003). There are many opportunities for teachers to obtain learning experiences, and there are renewal programs to support them in helping students enjoy learning and value the education they receive. Such opportunities occur in the form of conferences, workshops, and self-learning experiences, which include learning from different sources (e.g., books, pamphlets, Internet sources).

Parent and Family Involvement

Schools have increasingly recognized the role of family members and others in their social network in influencing and supporting the overall development of children with intellectual and developmental disabilities (e.g., Hiatt-Michael, 2001; Leyser & Kirk, 2004). This has been described quite well in the available literature (e.g., see Chapter 35), and it continues to be an area of focus in disability and special education research. The work of special education and general education teachers is often more effective if families follow similar procedures (e.g., have similar behavior expectations, give praise in the same way for similar actions), and ongoing communication between teachers and parents is necessary to make this work effectively. Conversely, families have lifestyles, skill sets, social and financial needs, and other personal circumstances that influence the support they are able to give their children at home. School personnel need to know and understand these factors when planning and carrying out individual education programs. In general, though, some key areas teachers and parents can cooperatively address for children with intellectual and developmental disabilities are

- Personal care (e.g., dressing, bathing, toileting)
- Safety
- Eating nutritiously
- Household skills (e.g., setting the table, cooking, tidying one's room)
- Social skills (e.g., using manners, knowing the rules of conversation, learning how to take part in group activities, playing cooperatively)
- Academic skills (e.g., reading, listening to stories, writing, applying arithmetic skills)
- Sexuality training
- Knowledge about job possibilities (for teenagers)

Parents and guardians have some legal rights to be involved with their children's education. In the United Kingdom, the United States, and some parts of Canada, schools are required to work cooperatively with parents or guardians, especially around placement. IDEA requires active parent participation, including in the development of children's IEPs, and mandates that schools report progress to parents of children with disabilities as frequently as they report to parents of children without disabilities. The overall goal is to maintain an equal and respectful partnership between schools and families.

In addition to being involved directly with schools in their children's education, family members of children with intellectual and developmental disabilities have a strong history of being involved in a wide range of educational and social services. They participate in any number of school committees; act as volunteers; sit on boards of directors; act as advocates for special needs both within formal advocacy groups and on their own; and present their views to politicians, education administrators, and other policy makers. The importance of this collective action to the development of current special education services has been frequently recognized (e.g., Winter, 2003), and it is likely to be just as important in years to come.

Transition Planning

Transition, in the sense that it is used in educational settings, refers to activities meant to prepare students with disabilities for adult life (see Chapter 32 for additional details on transition work experience while still in school, or setting up linkages with adult service providers such as those who assist with vocational training and placement). Transition activities differ from one student to another, reflecting students' own interests, preferences, skills, and needs. Identifying transition needs and transition planning are policy requirements in some areas (including a requirement of IDEA in the United States), although requirements to follow through on transition activities are not so clear and there is much variation here from one region to another and from one school to another. In addition, transition plans are not required by law in all countries (e.g., see Nadeau, Goupil, & Tassé, 2003).

Numerous print and electronic resources are available to assist with transition planning. These are available from schools, adult disability service providers, and professional and advocacy organizations. For example, Alan Goldberg (2000) prepared a transition checklist for parents called "Transition Timeline." It seems essential that whatever transition planning tools are used, they must fit the individual students' needs as well as the broader social and cultural context (Mizutani & Yanagimoto, 2003; Smythe & McConkey, 2003).

The importance of the family's role in the success of transition planning and in carrying out transition activities is not clear. For example, Kraemer and Blacher (2001) noted that what parents would ideally like for their sons or daughters is not always what even they think is realistic for their children. Moreover, although parent involvement is often essential to successful transition, not all parents are willing to participate or are skilled at assisting with transition plans or activities (see Chapter 32). Display 31.3 provides an example of how transition planning positively supported one student to think ahead about what he might like to do in the future.

FUTURE CHALLENGES IN SPECIAL EDUCATION

Special education for children with intellectual and developmental disabilities has undergone dramatic changes since the early 1970s, and there are many stories of such students succeeding in school systems. Still, there are a number of challenges ahead.

Despite national laws and judicial rulings, special education services are unevenly applied. In an effort to ensure the right of all children to an education, a large number of policies and regulations have been put in place, and understanding how they apply to individual children takes considerable effort. Litigations that stem from disagreements, especially in the United States, hamper progress, yet have resulted in some helpful rulings on how laws must be applied.

The critical problem of applying education rights internationally is only beginning to be recognized and

Display 31.3

Matthew's story

Matt is 15 years old. Because Matt has intellectual disability, he has been receiving special education services since elementary school. These services have helped him tremendously, because they are designed to fit his special learning needs. Last year he started high school. He, his family, and personnel from his school took a good hard look at what he wants to do when secondary school is over. Does he want more education? A job? Does he have the skills he needs to live on his own?

Answering these questions has helped Matt and the school plan for the future. He's always been interested in the outdoors, in plants, and especially in trees. He knows all the tree names and can recognize them by their leaves and bark. So this year he's learning about jobs like forestry, landscaping, and grounds maintenance. Next year he hopes to get a part-time job. He is learning to use public transportation, so he'll be able to get to and from the job. It is harder for Matt to learn new things. He needs things to be very concrete. But he's determined.

He wants to work outside, maybe in the park service or in a greenhouse, and he's getting ready!

From National Dissemination Center for Children with Disabilities. (2004). *Mental retardation fact sheet 8 (FS8).* Retrieved February 28, 2006, from http://www.nichcy.org/pubs/factshe/fs8txt.htm; adapted by permission.

addressed. The United Nations Educational, Scientific and Cultural Organization (UNESCO, n.d.) is one international body that has taken a leading role in identifying this need and has set out an overall plan to make education available to all children by the year 2015. This will be a daunting task; UNESCO itself points out that approximately one third of all children in the world do not attend school for many reasons, despite international documents that say they should (see Chapters 5 and 6). The challenge for making special education available to the world's children is even more daunting, because a great many countries have not yet begun to address the need for it. Developing special education as integral parts of UNESCO's 17 theme areas for the development of general education (Table 31.2) seems to be one reasonable way to ensure that the educational needs of children with intellectual and developmental disabilities start to be addressed in a more uniform way around the world.

Table 31.2. United Nations Education, Scientific and Cultural Organization's *Education for All by 2015* themes

1.	Right to education
2.	Education plans and policies
3.	Early childhood
4.	Primary education
5.	Secondary education
6.	Higher education
7.	Technical and vocational education
8.	Science and technology education
9.	Literacy
10.	Inclusive education
11.	School health and HIV/AIDS
12.	Cultural and linguistic diversity in education
13.	Teacher education
14.	Education in situations of emergency, crises and reconstruction
15.	Physical education and sport
16.	Peace and human rights
17.	Nonviolence education

From United Nations Educational, Scientific and Cultural Organization. (n.d.). *Education for all by 2015.* Retrieved from January 11, 2006, from http://portal.unesco.org/education/en/ev.php-URL_ID=48780&URL_DO=DO_TOPIC&URL_SECTION=201.html

Ongoing Challenges in Special Education for Children with Intellectual and Developmental Disabilities

This section discusses specific ongoing challenges for the special education of children with intellectual and developmental disabilities, where legislation and services are in place.

Increase the Success Rate of Students with Special Needs Outcomes for students in special education are poor in terms of academic progress, and only approximately 25% of them graduate from secondary school (Katsiyannis et al., 2002). The field needs to understand better why this is the case and determine what strategies might be put in place to redress it.

Develop Meaningful and Useful Individualized Education Programs Since their inception, IEPs have been fraught with problems. These result from a lack of adequate teacher training in developing IEPs, poorly developed team processes, compliance with the burdensome paperwork requirements, and excessive demands on teacher time. Additional problems with the IEP requirements are minimal coordination with general education, the failure to link assessment data to instructional goals, and the failure to develop measurable goals and objectives to evaluate student achievement. On the basis of a literature review, Drasgow, Yell, and Robinson (2001) concluded that the IEP process has been replete with such legal errors as failure to report current levels of educational performance; lack of appropriate goals, objectives, and evaluation procedures; absence of key personnel at the IEP meeting; and placement decisions that are not based on the IEP.

Decrease the Number of Minority and Indigenous Children in Special Education A large amount of evidence available indicates that children from minority and indigenous backgrounds are disproportionately represented in special education programs (e.g., National Center for Education Statistics, 2004). The reasons for this appear to be rooted in a complex interaction of socioeconomic factors. These need to be intensively explored, by both researchers and policy makers.

Reduce Teacher Stress and Increase Rewards Teachers involved in special education must not only teach but also tailor lessons, teaching methods, and materials to each student's needs and prepare individual IEPs (Hastings & Brown, 2002). In addition, they must help students prepare for transition to work or postsecondary education, and they provide a certain amount of custodial care. They are incredibly overworked and stressed (Cheminais, 2003). The work is intense, and salaries are not sufficient. Furthermore, it requires dedication, commitment, and hard work to obtain a special education license. Despite some gains, special education programs continue to be underfunded in the United States (Pardini, 2002) and probably elsewhere.

Find Better Ways to Make Inclusion Work Inclusion does not always work well, and, as discussed earlier, some students may benefit more from learning in separate settings. Yet inclusion seems to be the preferred (and perhaps legally required) way in which children will be educated in the future, so efforts to develop better inclusion strategies need to continue. It should be noted, however, that in the United States the LRE does not necessarily mean that a child has to be included in general education classrooms.

Determining the Appropriate Class Size for Inclusion and Classroom Management Including students with intellectual and developmental disabilities in general education classrooms creates additional work for classroom teachers. There has been much debate about the number of children who should be in classrooms so that teachers can carry out inclusive education effectively and manage their classrooms. A number of recommendations for optimal classroom size and suggestions for effective classroom management have been published (e.g., see Kochler et al., 2000), but evaluation needs to continue in this area.

Balance the Cost of Special Education with the Rights of All Children to Education The costs of educating a student with special needs is considerably higher than the cost of educating a student without disabilities. Ways need to be developed to ensure that children with intellectual and developmental disabilities receive high-quality special education services; at the same time, such services need to be provided in cost-effective ways.

SUMMARY

Special education refers to teaching and learning for children and adults who, because of their individual learning characteristics, require methods of instruction other than those provided in general education programs. The 19th and 20th centuries saw substantial growth in special education for children with intellectual and developmental disabilities, but it was not until the 1970s that laws began to be enacted that required schools to provide education for all children with disabilities. The United States, in particular, enacted several laws that progressively ensured education rights. Other countries have followed closely.

This chapter has noted a number of key aspects of special education for students with intellectual and developmental disabilities that stand out in the literature. Special education has undergone a dramatic change since the early 1970s but still faces a number of future challenges. Among these is the daunting challenge of providing special education worldwide, particularly for children who currently receive no education at all.

FOR FURTHER THOUGHT AND DISCUSSION

1. Educational rights for children with intellectual and developmental disabilities have improved dramatically since the early 1970s, especially with the passage of important laws. Select a child you know who has an intellectual or developmental disability. In what ways would this child's life differ if none of the education laws now in place in your country were enacted?
2. Think of the same child identified in the previous question. What rights and entitlements does this student need, in addition to the education laws that are in place in your country, to lead a successful life?
3. Ramos is a 7-year-old boy with a mild intellectual disability and cerebral palsy. His mobility is severely affected, and he uses a wheelchair. Monica has just learned that Ramos will be a student in her class next year. What might Monica do to help prepare herself, her classroom environment, other students in the class, and Ramos' parents so that Ramos will have a successful learning experience?

4. What actions can a school initiate to be more inclusive?
5. What types of transition strategies can schools put in place? For example, what practical suggestions can a school give to employers to help students with intellectual or developmental disabilities succeed in the workplace? How can such suggestions be communicated to places of employment?

REFERENCES

Americans with Disabilities Act (ADA) of 1990, PL 101-336, 42 U.S.C. §§ 12101 *et seq.*

Australian Institute of Health and Welfare. (2003). *Disability prevalence and trends.* Canberra, Australia: Author.

Barfield, J.-P., Hannigan-Downs, S., & Lieberman, L.J. (1998). Implementing a peer tutor program: Strategies for practitioners. *Physical Educator, 55,* 211–221.

Bateman, B.D., & Linden, M.A. (1998). *Better IEPs: How to develop legally correct and educationally useful programs* (3rd ed.). Longmont, CO: Sopris West.

Blackhurst, A.E., & Berdine, W.H. (1993). *An introduction to special education* (3rd ed.). New York: HarperCollins.

Bridle, L. (2005). Why does it have to be so hard?: A mother's reflection on the journey of 'inclusive education'. In C. Newell & T. Parmenter (Eds.), *Disability in education: Context, curriculum and culture* (pp. 1–12). Melbourne, Australia: Australian College of Educators.

Brown, I. (2003). What do we mean by developmental disabilities in Ontario? In I. Brown & M. Percy (Eds.), *Developmental disabilities in Ontario* (2nd ed.; pp. 19–30). Toronto: Ontario Association on Developmental Disabilities.

Brown, I., & Brown, R.I. (2003). *Quality of life and disability: An approach for community practitioners.* London: Jessica Kingsley Publishers.

Cheminais, R. (2003). *Closing the inclusion gap: Special and mainstream schools working in partnership.* London: David Fulton Publishers.

Copeland, I.C. (2002). *Backward pupil over a cycle of a century.* Fengate, Peterborough, United Kingdom: Upfront Publishing.

Darwin, C. (1859). *On the origin of species by means of natural selection.* London: John Murray.

Dempsey, I., Foreman, P., & Jenkinson, J. (2002). Educational enrolment of students with a disability in New South Wales and Victoria. *International Journal of Disability, Development and Education, 49,* 31–46

Disability Discrimination Act. (1995). (c. 50), 1995, Chapter 50.

Disability Sports. (n.d.). *Rehabilitation Act.* Retrieved February 25, 2006, from http://edweb6.educ.msu.edu/kin866/lawrehabact.htm

Doll, E. (1967). Historical review of mental retardation: 1800–1965. *American Journal of Mental Deficiency, 72,* 165–189.

Doll, E.A. (1941). The essentials of an inclusive concept of mental deficiency. *American Journal of Mental Deficiency, 46,* 214–216.

Drasgow, E., Yell, M.L., & Robinson, T.R. (2001). Developing legally correct and educationally appropriate IEPs. *Remedial and Special Education, 22*(6), 359–373.

Dybvik, A.C. (2004). Autism and the inclusion mandate. *Education Next, 4*(1), 42–49.

Educación especial. (1991). Retrieved February 21, 2006, from http://www.mercaba.org/Rialp/E/educacion_especial.htm

Education Act. (1993). (c. 35), 1993, Chapter 35.

Education Act. (1996). (c. 56), 1996, Chapter 56.

Education for All Handicapped Children Act of 1975, PL 94-142, 20 U.S.C. §§ 1400 *et seq.*

Education of the Handicapped Act Amendments of 1986, PL 99-457.

Ellins, J., & Porter, J. (2005). Departmental differences in attitudes to special educational needs in the secondary school. *British Journal of Educational Studies,* 32, 188–195.

Fisher, D., & Frey, N. (2001). Access to the core curriculum: Critical ingredients for student success. *Remedial & Special Education, 22,* 148–157.

Fitch, E.F. (2002). Disability and inclusion: From labeling deviance to social valuing. *Educational Theory, 52,* 463–477.

Foundation for People with Learning Disabilities. (2000). *Statistics on learning disability.* Retrieved February 22, 2006, from http://www.learningdisabilities.org.uk/page.cfm?pagecode=ISBISTMT

Freedman, S. (1999). *Are labels necessary?* Retrieved November 25, 2005, from http://www.nald.ca/PROVINCE/YUKON/lday/newslet/Feb99/page5.htm

Friend, M., & Bursuck, W.D. (2002). *Including students with special needs: A practical guide for classroom teachers* (3rd ed.). Boston: Allyn & Bacon.

Getzel, E.E., & Wehman, P. (Eds.). (2005). *Going to college: Expanding opportunities for people with disabilities.* Baltimore: Paul H. Brookes Publishing Co.

Gilmore, L., Campbell, J., & Cuskelly, M. (2003). Developmental expectations, personality stereotypes, and attitudes towards inclusive education: Community and teacher views of Down syndrome. *International Journal of Disability, Development & Education, 50,* 65–76.

Goldberg, A. (2000). *Transition timeline.* Retrieved December 12, 2005, from http://ndss.org/content.cfm?fuseaction=InfoRes.SchEduarticle&article=225

Hallahan, D.P., & Kauffman, J.M. (2003). *Exceptional learners: Introduction to special education* (9th ed.). Boston: Allyn and Bacon.

Handicapped Children's Protection Act of 1986, PL 99-372, 100 Stat. 796

Hart, D., Zimbrich, K., & Parker, D. (2005). Dual enrollment as a postsecondary education option for students with intellectual disabilities. In E.E. Getzel & P. Wehman (Eds.), *Going to college: Expanding opportunities for people with disabilities* (pp. 253–267). Baltimore: Paul H. Brookes Publishing Co.

Hastings, R.P., & Brown, T. (2002). Coping strategies and the impact of challenging behaviors on special educators' burnout. *Mental Retardation, 40,* 148–156.

Hiatt-Michael, D. (2001). *Preparing teachers to work with parents*

(Report No. EDO-SP-2001-2). Washington, DC: ERIC Clearinghouse on Teaching and Teacher Education. (ERIC Document Reproduction Service Number ED460123)

Houghton Mifflin Student Resource Center. (n.d.). *The Education For All Handicapped Children Act Amendments of 1986 (PL 99-457).* Retrieved February 26, 2006, from http://college.hmco.com/education/resources/res_prof/students/spec_ed/legislation/pl_99-457.html#features

Indian Act (R.S., 1985, c. I-5).

Individuals with Disabilities Education Act Amendments of 1997, PL 105-17, 20 U.S.C. §§ 1400 *et seq.*

Individuals with Disabilities Education Improvement Act of 2004, PL 108-446, 20 U.S.C. §§ 1400 *et seq.*

Itard, J.M.G. (1801,1806/1962). *The wild boy of Aveyron* (G. Humphrey & M. Humphrey, Trans.). New York: Appleton-Century-Crofts. (Original works published 1801 and 1806).

Jahnukainen, M., & Korhonen, A. (2003). Integration of students with severe and profound intellectual disabilities into the comprehensive school system: Teachers' perceptions of the education reform in Finland. *International Journal of Disability, Development and Education, 50,* 169–180.

Kanner, L. (1959). Johann Jakob Guggenbuhl and the Abendberg. *Bulletin of the History of Medicine, 33,* 489–502.

Kanner, L. (1960). Itard, Seguin and Howe: Three pioneers in the education of retarded children. *American Journal of Mental Deficiency, 65,* 2–10.

Kanner, L. (1964). *A history of the care and study of the mentally retarded.* Springfield, IL: Charles C Thomas Publisher.

Katsiyannis, A., Zhang, D., & Archwamety, T. (2002). Placement and exit patterns for students with mental retardation: An analysis of national trends. *Education & Training in Mental Retardation & Developmental Disabilities, 37,* 134–145.

Kauffman, J.M. (2003). Appearances, stigma, and prevention. *Remedial and Special Education, 24,* 195–198.

Kevles, D. (1975). *In the name of eugenics.* Harmondsworth, United Kingdom: Penguin.

Kochlar, C.A., West, L.L., & Taymans, J.M. (2000). *Successful inclusion: Practical strategies for a shared responsibility.* Upper Saddle River, NJ: Prentice Hall.

Kraemer, B.R., & Blacher, J. (2001). Transition for young adults with severe mental retardation: School, preparation, parent expectations, and family involvement. *Mental Retardation, 39,* 423–435.

Lamb, A. (2005). *Information inquiry for teachers.* Retrieved January 31, 2006, from http://eduscapes.com/info/evolve.html.

Lenkowsky, R. (2001, September). Integrated preschool classrooms: Learning together and from one another. *Exceptional Parent,* 38–43.

Levinson, E.M. (2004). *Transition from school to post-school life for individuals with disabilities.* Springfield, IL: Charles C Thomas Publisher.

Leyser, Y., & Kirk, R. (2004). Evaluating inclusion: An examination of parent views and factors influencing their perspectives. *International Journal of Disability, Development and Education, 51,* 271–285.

Lipton, D.J. (1999). *Individuals with Disabilities Education Act Amendments of 1997 and IDEA Regulations of 1999: Summary of changes (with emphasis on IEPs and discipline).* Retrieved from the February 26, 2006, from http://www.dredf.org/idea10.html

Manetti, M., Schneider, B.H., & Siperstein, G. (2001). Social acceptance of children with mental retardation: Testing the contact hypothesis with an Italian sample. *International Journal of Behavioral Development, 25,* 279–286.

McNally, R.D., Cole, P.G., & Waugh, R.F. (2001). Regular teachers' attitudes to the need for additional classroom support for the inclusion of students with intellectual disability. *Journal of Intellectual & Developmental Disability, 26,* 257–273.

Mittler, P. (2002). Educating pupils with intellectual disabilities in England: Thirty years on. *International Journal of Disability, Development and Education, 49,* 145–160.

Mizutani, Y., Hiruma, T., & Yanagimoto, Y. (2002). A nationwide investigation of individualized plans in Japanese special high schools: Implications for the collaborative practices of individualized transition support plans. *Japanese Journal of Special Education, 39,* 41–58.

Mizutani, Y., & Yanagimoto, Y. (2003). Students with intellectual disabilities: A comparison with the ITP process in the United States. *Japanese Journal of Special Education, 40,* 713–722.

Nadeau, A., Goupil, G., & Tassé, M.J. (2003). Entering kindergarten and leaving high school. *Revue de Psychoeducation, 32,* 273–294.

National Center for Education Statistics. (2002). *Digest of education statistics figures and tables.* Retrieved May 14, 2006, from http://nces.ed.gov/programs/digest/d02/dt053.asp

National Center for Education Statistics. (2004). *Children with disabilities.* Retrieved February 26, 2006, from http://nces.ed.gov/programs/coe/2005/charts/chart06.asp

National Center for Education Statistics. (2006). *Digest of education statistics figures and tables 2003.* Retrieved February 22, 2006, from http://nces.ed.gov/programs/digest/d03/tables/dt052.asp

National Dissemination Center for Children with Disabilities. (n.d.). *The education of children and youth with special needs: What do the laws say?* Retrieved March 23, 2006, from http://www.nichcy.org/pubs/outprint/nd15txt.htm#ada

National Dissemination Center for Children with Disabilities. (2004). *Mental retardation fact sheet 8 (FS8).* Retrieved February 28, 2006, from http://www.nichcy.org/pubs/factshe/fs8txt.htm

National Institute for Literacy. (1995). *Adults with learning disabilities: Definitions and issues.* Retrieved January 31, 2006, from http://www.nifl.gov/nifl/ld/archive/definiti.htm

Neubert, D.A., Moon, M.S., Grigal, M., et al. (2001). Postsecondary educational practices for individuals with mental retardation and other significant disabilities: A review of the literature. *Journal of Vocational Rehabilitation, 16,* 155–168.

Newsom, J. (2001). Sanctuary or sanction? *American School Board Journal, 188*(7), 24–28.

No Child Left Behind Act of 2001, PL 107-110, 115 Stat. 1425, 20 U.S.C. §§ 6301 *et seq.*

Ontario Human Rights Commission. (2002). *Report on education.* Retrieved February 22, 2006, from http://www.odacommittee.net/ohrc_education.html

Ontario Ministry of Education. (2003). *Ontario Ministry of*

Education/Ministry of Training, Colleges and Universities: An introduction to special education in Ontario. Retrieved February 28, 2006, from http://www.edu.gov.on.ca/eng/general/elemsec/speced/ontario.html

Ontario Ministry of Education. (2006). *The Education Act on Special Education.* Retrieved May 14, 2006, from http://www.edu.gov.on.ca/eng/general/elemsec/speced/edact.html

Open Training and Education Network. (1998). *Government schools of New South Wales, 1948–1998: 150 years later.* Sydney, Australia: New South Wales Department of Education and Training.

Pardini, P. (2002). Special education: Promises and problems. *Rethinking Schools Online, 16*(3). Retrieved February 26, 2005, from http://www.rethinkingschools.org/archive/16_03/Prom163.shtml

Peetsma, T., Vergeer, M., Roeleveld, J., et al. (2001). Inclusion in education: Comparing pupils' development in special and regular education. *Educational Review, 53,* 125–135.

Pitasky, V.M. (2002). *What do I do when . . . : The answer book on placement under the IDEA and Section 504.* Palm Beach Gardens, FL: LRP Publications.

Polley, B. (2005). *Laurent Clerc.* Retrieved February 21, 2006, from http://www.lifeprint.com/asl101/pages-layout/clerc-laurent.htm

Price, B.J., Mayfield, P.K., McFadden, A.C., et al. (2000–2001). *Collaborative teaching: Special education for inclusive classrooms.* Retrieved March 23, 2006, from http://www.parrotpublishing.com

Rehabilitation Act of 1973, PL 93-112, 29 U.S.C. §§ 701 *et seq.*

Reilly, V.J., & Davis, T. (2005). Understanding the regulatory environment. In E.E. Getzel & P. Wehman (Eds.), *Going to college: Expanding opportunities for people with disabilities* (pp. 25–48). Baltimore: Paul H. Brookes Publishing Co.

Roeher Institute. (2000). *Count us in: A demographic overview of childhood and disability in Canada.* Toronto: Author.

Smythe, M., & McConkey, R. (2003). Future aspirations of students with severe learning disabilities and of their parents on leaving special schooling. *British Journal of Learning Disabilities, 31,* 54–59.

Special Educational Needs and Disability Act 2001 (c. 10), 2001, Chapter 10.

Special Education Needs and Disability Act 2001. (2001). *Special Educational Needs and Disability Act 2001: 2001 Chapter 10.* Retrieved February 22, 2006, from http://www.opsi.gov.uk/acts/acts2001/20010010.htm

Stainton, T. (1994). *Autonomy and social policy: Rights, mental handicap and social care.* London: Avebury.

Statistics Canada. (2003). *Prevalence of disability in Canada.* Retrieved February 22, 2006, from http://www.statcan.ca/english/freepub/89-577-XIE/canada.htm

Tachibana, T., & Watanabe, K. (2004). Attitudes of Japanese adults toward persons with intellectual disability: Comparisons over time and across countries. *Education & Training in Developmental Disabilities, 39,* 227–239.

TeacherLINK. (2006). *Samuel Gridley Howe.* Retrieved February 21, 2006, from http://teacherlink.ed.usu.edu/tlresources/reference/champions/pdf/SamuelHowe.pdf

The Child Find Process in Trumbull Public Law 99-457 Procedures. (n.d.). Retrieved February 26, 2006, from http://www.trumbullps.org/pdf/childfind.pdf

Tilstone, C., Lacey, P., Porter, J., et al. (2000). *Pupils with learning difficulties in mainstream schools.* London: David Fulton Publishers.

Tracey, D.K. (2002). *Self-concepts of preadolescents with mild intellectual disability.* Unpublished thesis, University of Western Sydney, Werrington, New South Wales, Australia.

Tramontina, S., Martins, S., Michalowski, M.B., et al. (2002). Estimated mental retardation and school dropout in a sample of students from state public schools in Porto Alegre, Brazil. *Revista Brasileira de Psiquiatria, 24,* 177–181.

Trent, J.W., Jr. (1994). *Inventing the feeble mind: A history of mental retardation in the United States.* Berkeley: University of California Press.

U.K. Centre for Legal Education. (2006). *SENDA: Special Educational Needs and Disability Act 2001.* Retrieved February 22, 2006, from http://www.ukcle.ac.uk/directions/issue4/senda.html

U.K. Office of Public Sector Information (2001). *Special Educational Needs and Disability Act 2001: Chapter 10.* Retrieved February 22, 2006, from http://www.opsi.gov.uk/acts/acts2001/20010010.htm

United Nations Educational, Scientific and Cultural Organization. (n.d.). *Education for all by 2015.* Retrieved January 11, 2006, from http://portal.unesco.org/education/en/ev.php-URL_ID=15200&URL_DO=DO_TOPIC&URL_SECTION=201.html

United Way of Brazoria County. (2006). *The Arc of the Gulf Coast success story.* Retrieved February 28, 2006, from http://www.uwbc.org/success_stories.htm

U.S. Department of Education. (2003). *President's Commission on Excellence in Special Education (PCESE).* Retrieved February 28, 2006, from http://www.ed.gov/inits/commissionsboards/whspecialeducation/index.html

U.S. Department of Health and Human Services. (2001). *New Freedom Initiative: Fulfilling America's promise to Americans with disabilities.* Retrieved February 28, 2006, from http://www.hhs.gov/newfreedom

Vocational and Educational Services for Individuals with Disabilities (VESID). (n.d.). *Individuals with Disabilities Education Improvement Act of 2004.* Retrieved February 26, 2006, from http://www.vesid.nysed.gov/specialed/idea/home.html

The White House. (2002). *Fact sheet: No Child Left Behind Act.* Retrieved February 26, 2006, from http://www.whitehouse.gov/news/releases/2002/01/20020108.html

Whonamedit. (n.d.). *Alfred Binet.* Retrieved February 21, 2006, from http://www.whonamedit.com/doctor.cfm/1299.html

Wilde, J.W. (2004). *The disability journey: A bridge from awareness to action.* Lincoln, NE: iUniverse Publishers.

Williams, A.N. (2006). Physician, philosopher, and paediatrician: John Locke's practice of child health care. *Archives of Disease in Childhood, 91,* 85–89.

Winter, E. (2003). Developmental disabilities in Ontario's schools. In I. Brown & M. Percy (Eds.), *Developmental disabilities in Ontario* (2nd ed.; pp. 583–601). Toronto: Ontario Association on Developmental Disabilities.

Winzer, M.A. (1993). *The history of special education: From isolation to integration.* Washington, DC: Gaullaudet University Press.

Winzer, M.A. (2002). *Children with exceptionalities in Canadian classrooms* (6th ed.). Toronto: Prentice Hall.

Wodrich, D.L. (1997). *Children's psychological testing: A guide for nonpsychologists* (3rd ed.). Baltimore: Paul H. Brookes Publishing Co.

Woodill, G. (1992). Controlling the sexuality of developmentally disabled persons: Historical perspectives. *Journal on Developmental Disabilities, 1*(1), 1–14.

Woodill, G., & Velche, D. (1994). From charity and exclusion to emerging independence. An introduction to the history of disabilities. *Journal on Developmental Disabilities, 4*(1), 1–11.

Ysseldyke, J.E. (1987). Classification of handicapped students. In M.C. Wang, M.C. Reynolds, & H.J. Walberg (Eds.), *Handbook of special education: Research and practice: Vol. I. Learner characteristics and adaptive education* (pp. 253–272). New York: Pergamon Press.

32

The Transition from School to Adult Life

IVAN BROWN

> **WHAT YOU WILL LEARN ABOUT IN THIS CHAPTER**
>
> - Key support questions
> - Theoretical foundations for support
> - Support to individuals and families
> - Special support to individuals with severe disabilities and their families

All people experience many changes over the span of their lifetimes. Almost all of these changes are small and can be adjusted to relatively easily. There are certain times in most people's lives, however, when the changes are more major—changes that require people to follow patterns of behavior that are quite different from those that had become familiar. People with and without disabilities experience major changes, and most people require assistance at such times. People with intellectual and developmental disabilities, though, may require more, or somewhat specialized, assistance from support personnel, family members, and others.

Thus, in the field of intellectual and developmental disabilities there is a focus on identifying times of life when there is major change for many people with disabilities. Through developing and sharing conceptual, research, and service knowledge, the field is exploring ways to ensure that such times of change result in needed support being available and in individuals' short- and long-term wants and needs being addressed in a quality way. The term *transition* is used in the field to describe times of major change but also to refer to the expanding body of literature and knowledge about such times of major change.

There are a number of key transitions that affect the lives of many people with intellectual and developmental disabilities. Transitions arise from health and biology (e.g., growing up, losing parents, entering a later-life care facility), from social norms (e.g., cohabiting, marrying), from the way society is organized (e.g., entering or leaving school, entering or retiring from employment), and from current demographic trends (e.g., moving, getting separated or divorced) (Brown, 2004). Thus, transitions differ in nature from one country to another, due to social, cultural, and economic differences. They also differ in nature and importance from one individual to another. For example, one person may retire after working for 30 years and experience the transition in a positive way, whereas another person may find this transition to be very problematic.

One transition that affects almost every person with intellectual or developmental disabilities (as well as young people without disabilities) in a fairly major way is the transition from school to adult life. As a consequence, this is the transition that has attracted the most attention and the most research to date in the disabilities field. There are a number of major changes in the lives of most people as they move from school to adult life, particularly those that affect people's places of residence and employment and their social interactions (Blacher, 2001). Wehman (2001) identified seven common changes for youth with disabilities: employment, living arrangements, getting around the community, financial independence, making friends, sexuality and self-esteem, and having fun. Table 32.1 lists the major lifestyle changes that are common and that underlie such transitions. Display 32.1 illustrates how parents of individuals with disabilities experience such transitions.

KEY SUPPORT QUESTIONS

As noted previously, the transition from school to adult life is a period when a number of changes can be expected in the lives of young people and when young

---

Lawrence Spero is a parent of a young adult son with fragile X syndrome. He writes from his extensive experience with school systems and services for adults with disabilities and as an advocate for people with disabilities. He shares his views on transition from school to adult life in Displays 32.1 through 32.8 and in the chapter summary. The author is also grateful to Stewart Brown for providing helpful information for this chapter.

Table 32.1. Issues related to the transition from school to adult life

From	To
Going to school	Going to a job or training or having no occupational activity
Seeing oneself as a student	Seeing oneself as an adult
Living with parents or other family	Living in one's own home or in a shared accommodation
Identifying as a member of parental family	Identifying as an independent adult or as a member of one's own family
Socializing with family and schoolmates	Socializing with work colleagues and community-based friends
Engaging mostly in child and youth leisure	Engaging mostly in adult, community-based leisure and recreation
Relying on parents, siblings, and others	Being responsible for more decisions about oneself

From Brown, R.I. (2004). *Down syndrome issues and information: Adult living series* (R.I. Brown, Ed.). *Life for adults with Down syndrome: New opportunities, new challenges.* Southsea, United Kingdom: The Down Syndrome Educational Trust.

people with intellectual or developmental disabilities may require specialized support. What, then, are the key questions or issues that need to be addressed when preparing for and providing this specialized support?

Display 32.1

A parent's perspective

The chapters that precede and follow this one, on life in the school system and life in the work world, present two very different and separate systems that support people with intellectual and developmental disabilities. The age at which children can leave school differs from country to country and sometimes even within countries, but typically all children are required to be in school until the mid-teen years. Where I live, all children with disabilities are entitled to a public education and, like their peers without disabilities, they may leave school any time after age 16 if they choose; unlike their peers without disabilities, however, if they choose to stay in school past age 16, they are required to leave at the end of the school year in which they turn 21.

From the age of 5, when most children enter school, to when they leave, school dominates life for children and youth. When youth with disabilities leave the school system, they need to be concerned with issues that are important to adult living such as income, housing, employment, and social and recreational activities. Dealing with such issues brings with it many challenges.

- *Theoretical foundations for support:* From what theoretical foundations is work in the transitions area drawn?
- *Support to individuals and families:* Capie, Contardi, and Doehring (2006) set out three helpful support questions: How can families be supported to allow the young person to have increased autonomy? How many risks can be taken? How can young people be best helped to become full participants in society?
- *Special support to individuals with severe disabilities and their families:* Most youth with severe disabilities need additional support. Florian et al. (2000) suggested that the following questions should be asked: What kinds of opportunities for further education are there? Are there other forms of provision? What are they? What options are currently available for young people with profound and complex learning difficulties after the age of 16?

The following three sections do not address these questions fully; rather, they outline much of the progress that has been made to date.

THEORETICAL FOUNDATIONS FOR SUPPORT

Analyses of the transition from school to adult life draw on theory from a number of sources. In a review of the literature, Eisenman (2003) pointed out that the transition literature does not have a strong theoretical foundation. Instead, theory from a number of perspectives informs transition from school to adult roles. Some examples she provided to illustrate this point included the following:

Vocational psychology
- Person–environment fit theories suggest that positive work outcomes result from a good match between worker skills and abilities and the requirements of the job and work environment.
- Career development theories refer to people's awareness of, planning for, and response to work opportunities.

Learning and cognitive psychology
- Learning and sociocognitive theories propose that such things as individuals' cognitive skills, motivation, perceptions, goals, attitudes, and expected rewards are key to successful adjustment.

Quality of life
- Quality of life theory proposes that addressing core quality of life concepts—such as allowing independence; including what is important to the individual; satisfying personal needs and wishes; and providing opportunities, choice, and social connectedness—is key to positive life adjustment outcomes (see also Brown & Brown, 2003; Heal et al., 1999).

Sociology
- Status attainment theories look to social status and cognitive abilities as being most relevant to avail-

ability of opportunities and attainment of life and career options.

- Structuralist theories examine the relationship between major social institutions (e.g., schools, labor markets, health and social services, social policy) and an individual's characteristics.
- Gender- and race-based theories focus on differences and inequities.
- Workplace culture theories emphasize the social patterns and behavioral norms that occur within workplaces.

These examples illustrate the eclectic nature of the theory that informs work in the area of transitions. Drawing from a variety of theoretical sources may add to the richness of this relatively new field of study, which involves virtually all aspects of a person's life, because some aspects of life are more important to individuals than others in times of change. Thus, one theoretical perspective may be more important than others when considering transition for individuals.

Approaches to Transition Arising from Theory

Reflecting the eclectic nature of its theoretical foundations, the practical work associated with successful transition from school to adult life appears to be multifaceted and, consequently, to reflect more than one theoretical approach. Eisenman (2003) summarized the approach most commonly used for work in the area of transition from school to adult life as being not strictly theory based but, rather, as being

> Pragmatically focused on solving culturally and socially determined problems (e.g., employment, graduation) that span multiple environments (educational, vocation, residential, and community) and involve multiple actors, including both individuals (e.g., children, young adults, family members, teachers, employers, social service workers) and corporations (e.g., school systems, community services, businesses, families), whose intrinsic and socially defined characteristics interact across time. (pp. 95–96)

In spite of this multifaceted approach, there are a number of specific ways to look at the transition from school to adult life. Each has its own emphasis on what is considered most important for youth undergoing transition, although they all overlap and all pursue the same ultimate goal—successful adjustment to adult life. Some of the ways to look at transition that are currently in use are as follows (see also Szymanski, 2000):

1. *Developmental life span:* Emphasizes opportunity-seeking skills, involving support groups, and making choices that are suited to the individual's competencies and that will benefit the individual in the long term (e.g., Morningstar, 1997, and Rojewski, Maddy-Bernstein, Meers, Jones, & West, 1996, as cited in Eisenman, 2003, p. 97).
2. *Quality of life:* Emphasizes addressing basic needs, then enhancing the quality of a person's life experiences to promote enjoyment of life and reduce life problems (Kirby, 1997; Kraemer, McIntyre, & Blacher, 2003; see also Brown & Brown, 2003)
3. *Family:* Emphasizes the involvement of the family in transition planning and activities and the effects of transition on both individual family members and the family as a whole (Blacher, 2001; Wehman, 2001)
4. *Social and psychological adjustment:* Emphasizes the stressful nature of the social and psychological changes that face young people as they move from school to adult life (Hepper & Garralda, 2001).
5. *Supports needed:* Emphasizes policy, service, workforce, and family supports needed for successful transition to adult life.

Conceptualizations of Transition Emerging from Theory

A number of conceptual frameworks for transition have been developed since the mid-1990s that are useful for transition planning and putting transition plans into practice. Three such conceptual frameworks are outlined in the following subsections to exemplify three different approaches. Readers are invited to explore the cited sources for full details of these frameworks.

Taxonomy for Transition Programs The Taxonomy for Transition Programs (Kohler, 1996) sets out concepts, subconcepts, and action objectives that are useful for carrying out transition plans and evaluating transition systems. The model comprises five key concepts:

1. Student-focused planning
2. Student development
3. Interagency collaboration
4. Program structure
5. Family involvement

Each of these five concepts has subconcepts that are accompanied by specific action objectives. For example, in the first concept, student-focused planning, one of the subconcepts is student participation. The following action objectives are set out for student participation:

- The planning team includes student, family members, and school and participating agency personnel.
- Assessment information is used as basis for planning.
- Transition-focused planning begins no later than age 14.
- Meeting time is adequate to conduct planning.

- Preparation time is adequate to conduct planning.
- Meeting time and place is conducive to student and family participation.
- Accommodations are made for communication needs (e.g., interpreters).
- Referral to adult service provider(s) occurs prior to student's exit from school.
- A planning team leader identified.

Transition from a Family Perspective Blacher (2001) offered a useful conceptual model that "considers transition from a family perspective, with family well-being as the primary outcome of interest" (p. 173). In Blacher's conceptual model (see Figure 32.1), three interacting types of factors influence transition success:

1. Individual Factors (cognitive level, adaptive behavior, psychiatric status)
2. Environment and Culture (social supports, socioeconomic status, service supports, religious connectedness, cohesion/families, acculturation)
3. Involvement/Detachment (behavioral, cognitive, emotional)

Transition success, in turn, is seen as a major influence on family well-being during the transition period. It is recognized, however, that the three interacting types of factors influence family well-being independently as well. Family well-being is described as both positive and negative indicators of adjustment (individual, dyadic or two-person interactions, and family) considered all together.

Outcomes Measures Synthesis An outcomes measures synthesis was developed by Hughes et al. (1997). This is a helpful method of conceptualizing and categorizing the wide variety of outcome measures that have been used throughout the transition literature to indicate success for youth transitioning from school to adult life. The authors conducted a thorough search of available literature in constructing their 11 major categories and numerous subcategories. In descending order of number of supporting references, these major categories are

> Employment (44), social interaction (39), community adjustment, competence, and independent living (35), psychological well-being and personal satisfaction (31), personal development and fulfillment (25), recreation and leisure (23), social acceptance, social status, and ecological-fit (19), self-determination, autonomy, and personal choice (17), physical and material well-being (17), individual and social demographic indicators (13), and civic responsibility and activity (6). (p. 86)

SUPPORT TO INDIVIDUALS AND FAMILIES

In many countries, but particularly in more developed countries, the point at which young people graduate from school has come to be seen as the true beginning of adult life. It is a significant milestone that is marked

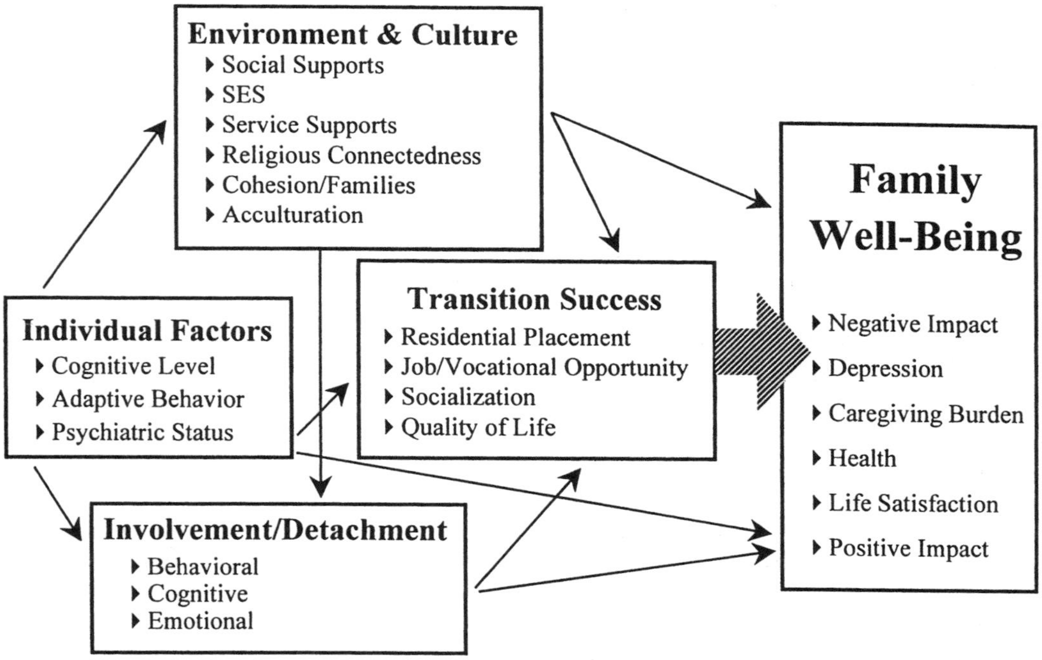

Figure 32.1. Conceptual model of the transition to adulthood. (From Blacher, J. [2001]. Transition to adulthood: Mental retardation, families, and culture. *American Journal on Mental Retardation, 106,* 175; reprinted by permission via Copyright Clearance Center.) (*Key:* SES = socioeconomic status.)

in a number of social ways, such as graduation ceremonies, physical moves, and the beginning of paid work. It is a rite of passage, and, as Ferguson, Ferguson, and Jones (1988) pointed out a number of years ago, it can be a stressful time because of the changes it entails. Yet, it is also a time of heightened expectations and hope for the future (Thorin, Yovanoff, & Irvin, 1996). It is a time to begin new activities, make new friends, live in new places, and learn new skills. Both stress and heightened expectations can create interesting challenges for those who work with individuals and families to support successful transitions. Many of these are related to the overall dilemma inherent in letting go of young adults with intellectual or developmental disabilities and encouraging them to take greater charge of developing their own lives and their own futures in ways that are helpful and safe.

The Dilemmas Inherent in Letting Go

The transition from school to adult life is a period when most parents (of children without disabilities) naturally relinquish most of the control they had over the lives of their sons and daughters. This transition also marks a time when most young people (without disabilities) assume control and independence. They begin setting up their independent lives in the areas of their own accommodation, employment, and finances; making the final decisions about almost everything that affects their lives; and sometimes starting families of their own.

For families that include a transition-age youth who has an intellectual or developmental disability, however, the shift is usually not nearly as straightforward. The problem these families face is that, at the very time when it would be natural for their sons and daughters to be assuming independence and for families (especially parents) to be letting go, the demands on families (especially parents) increase. A number of reasons for this—reasons that vary from family to family, and from country to country—have emerged in the literature and have remained remarkably consistent over the past 20 years (Bramston & Cummins, 1998; Brown & Renwick, 1998; Capie et al., 2006; Lichtenstein & Nisbet, 1992; Richardson, 1989; Ryan, 1997; Smull & Bellamy, 1991; Thorin et al., 1996; Todd et al., 2004; Zetlin & Turner, 2002):

- Some youth with disabilities do not want to leave school because they have become accustomed to a way of life they enjoy.
- Youth with disabilities do not have the life skills to assume control and independence.
- Parents and other family members do not know how to help the person with disabilities plan for or adjust to adult living.
- Parents and other family members feel worn out from many years of providing care and support, and lack hope and energy to address the future.
- Parents' friends (with children who do not have disabilities) are beginning lives free from child-rearing responsibilities.
- Established routines, such as preparing for school, traveling to and from school, and taking part in the daily school schedules, are no longer available and this can be experienced as loss; in addition, there can be a feeling of void if lost routines are not replaced by other routines.
- There are few local options available for youth with disabilities.
- Formal supports (services) are underfunded, with insufficient staff and program alternatives.
- Moving to independent or shared living has a great many challenges that parents recognize, but youth with intellectual disabilities may perceive this as a positive event that lowers stress.
- People with disabilities face unemployment, underemployment, long-term dependency, inappropriate living conditions, inadequate financial resources, restricted opportunities for education and training, limited opportunities for leisure activities, and (in some countries) inadequate health care—all in larger measure than their peers without disabilities.

As a consequence, parents are faced with a number of dilemmas. On the one hand, they want their children with disabilities to become more independent and begin leading their own lives. On the other hand, they want to ensure that their children have both opportunities and support for their lives ahead. Thorin et al. (1996) identified six such dilemmas, and found them to be important to the 103 families they studied for reasons and to degrees that differ among families:

> Dilemma 1: Wanting to create opportunities for independence for the young adult and wanting to assure that health and safety needs are met.
>
> Dilemma 2: Wanting a life separate from the young adult and wanting to do whatever is necessary to assure a good life for him or her.
>
> Dilemma 3: Wanting to provide stability and predictability in the family life and wanting to meet the changing needs of the young adult and family.
>
> Dilemma 4: Wanting to create a separate social life for the young adult and wanting to have less involvement in his or her life.
>
> Dilemma 5: Wanting to avoid burn-out and wanting to do everything possible for the young adult.
>
> Dilemma 6: Wanting to maximize the young adult's growth and potential and wanting to accept the young adult as he or she is. (pp. 118–119)

Two other factors, in particular, complicate what parents want for their sons and daughters with disabilities who are facing young adulthood. First, raising a child with a disability can be stressful, but there are also many positive emotional and practical advantages (Blacher & Hatton, 2001; Brown & Renwick, 1998). For example, many parents enjoy ongoing caregiving, a family member who has disabilities sometimes becomes a valued and central figure in a family, some people with disabilities are helpful in carrying out household chores, and some families rely on disability pensions to support their household income. Many parents are reluctant to give these up. Second, by the time youth reach transition age, most parents have invested a tremendous amount of time and energy in understanding the youth's personal skills, abilities, and personal characteristics, as well as in trying to develop strategies that make the youth's life as successful as possible (Todd et al., 2004; see also Zetlin & Turner, 2002). Quite understandably, many parents see themselves as the experts on their son's or daughter's life. Even though they may wish to have a break from caregiving, they are rather wary of handing the main responsibility for support to paid support workers who are less experienced (Brown & Renwick, 1998). There are several legitimate reasons for this. The most important include the following: some transition age youth choose to turn to those who are closest to them (usually parents or other family members) for additional emotional support in times of change; adult services are not always available; and, if services are available, front line paid support workers often do not know the youth well, are often relatively inexperienced, and typically have limited time to spend with the youth.

Thus, the challenge of "letting go" is not as easy as most family members might wish it to be. The fault, if there is one, lies not in one place, but in many. The framework set out by Ferguson, Ferguson, and Jones (1988)—which identified bureaucracy, family life, and adult status as areas in which transition problems emerge—unfortunately still seems fully relevant today. Problems still emerge from these sources. Equally applicable and equally unfortunate is Wells' (1991) observation that anxieties prevail in families during times of transition because they realize the young person's dependency will not conclude but, rather, will continue into adulthood. Display 32.2 presents a parent's perspective on how these factors often influence the behavior of youth with intellectual or developmental disabilities.

Display 32.2

A parent's perspective: Transition and behavior

Young people react to transition in various ways. They may not realize a change is about to occur, and when it does they may exhibit stress-related changes in their behavior. Conversely, many such youth are glad to leave school. They see their peers leaving, and they see what other young people are doing on television and in other media. They wish to do the same. They are ready to move into the adult phase of their lives. Yet, they may not have the skills to do this independently and become frustrated in their attempts when they set out to live like other young adults who do not have disabilities. Also, their parents may perceive that they do not have these skills, and either curtail their activities or try to provide supports that the youths do not wish to have. Such situations can cause additional problems and can bring on negative behavior.

Legal Independence

One factor that complicates the issues of letting go and accepting responsibility in the transition years is that they occur at about the age when people with disabilities who do not demonstrate incompetence become legally independent of their parents or guardians and, in many countries, are not legally subject to the direction of others at all (e.g., see Millar, 2003). Such legal independence means not only that young people with intellectual or developmental disabilities are entitled to make their own decisions, but also that they are responsible for both making decisions and being accountable for the outcomes of those decisions.

On one hand, legal independence is an assertion of equal rights for people with disabilities (see Chapters 5, 6, and 40) and encourages them to function among others adults in their societies in responsible ways. On the other hand, it sometimes creates stress for family members who feel unsure that their youth with disabilities can make sound decisions and who fear that their youth may be held legally accountable for adverse consequences of unsound decisions (see Display 32.3).

Importance of Planning

A dominant theme of the transitions literature is the importance of planning. Numerous planning principles and methods are available from a number of sources (see Appendix B at the end of the book for a sample). As Capie et al. (2006) cautioned, however, prepared plans may not be helpful for addressing the specific needs of some youth; thus, all should be tailored to the specific needs and circumstances of the individual. Generally accepted principles in transition planning include the following:

- *Self-determination:* Above all, transition planning must reflect the perspective of the youth with a dis-

Display 32.3

A parent's perspective:
The age of majority as a complicating factor

In many countries, youth reach the age of majority at age 18, at which time they become legally responsible for their own decisions unless they have been declared unable to do so. This includes decisions about medication, financial matters, where to live, where to work, and other things.

The age of majority sometimes presents interesting and challenging dilemmas. Legally, it is the 18-year-old who must agree to contracts with agencies, employers, and others. Realistically, it is very often the parents or people in the youth's support circle who make, or at least help to make, arrangements and decisions. When young adults do not have the skills to make decisions fully on their own, those who support them need to be very careful in supporting them to make the decisions they would have made if they did possess such skills. This is challenging for almost all parents, but some find it especially difficult when the decision to be made is not the one the parent would make for himself or herself.

ability and include his or her wishes, dreams, goals for the future, perceptions of themselves as adults, and preferred ways of doing things.

- *Multi-sector participation:* Transition planning should include representatives—who are in a position to effect change—of the person's family, friends, other support group(s), school, adult services, and so forth.
- *Person–planning fit:* Transition planning should be carried out in a way that the person with the disability can understand. For those who express themselves verbally, this may require modifying or adjusting both the process and the content of the plan. For those who do not express themselves verbally, this may require direct experience, such as visiting places and introducing new people and carefully noting nonverbal expressions of likes and dislikes.

Generally accepted methods for helping youth with disabilities and those who support them plan successfully include these approaches:

- Provide the needed human and environmental support to a person with a disability throughout the planning process to allow full participation.
- Prepare the person for his or her roles in future planning.
- Provide the person with opportunities from which to choose.
- Have accurate information about the opportunities that are available.
- Ensure the person has the skills and feels free to express his or her choices independently.
- Expose the person to a variety of experiences to enable him or her to make life-enhancing choices.
- Allow adequate time for planning and for revisiting plans.
- Allow the person to make poor choices and to act on opportunities to learn from those experiences.

Additional information about planning, from the family's point of view, is presented in Display 32.4.

Display 32.4

A parent's perspective:
Planning and being prepared

Family preparedness is an important aspect in the youth's transition from school to adult life. Some parents are very prepared and have set up sources of income, arranged daily activities, and ensured that ongoing social contacts are in place. Other parents have given little thought to what will happen in the future, and are caught off guard when their children finish school. Such youth may move into an unplanned and unstructured life to which they are unaccustomed.

Regardless of the degree of preparedness of the family, the transition from school to community can be very stressful. Most families find that "just letting things happen" is not a good way to manage and that more systematic planning is preferable. To begin, families must think about the options that face their son or daughter. If work placement is not an option, families must consider what else is available (see Chapter 34 for more details of options). Planning can be done informally, through simple family discussion or in a more formal way. Creating a life plan for a young person with an intellectual disability is one more formal way of planning for the future. This can be done in many ways (see Appendix B at the end of the book for some ideas), but, in general, it is a collection of ideas, preferably generated by a circle of supporters with input from the youth. Its first phase does not need to be practical—all that is required are dreams and aspirations. The plan will change as a young person develops, but at least it starts a process that should be beneficial to the youth and to his or her family. For many young people with intellectual and developmental disabilities, having such a structured plan is very empowering and stress relieving.

Other Things that Families Can Do

The most important thing that families can do is to ensure that a transition plan is in place and that someone has taken responsibility for putting it into action. That responsibility may be taken by school or community agency staff, by a family member, or by another person such as a paid consultant. Most transitions work better, however, if parents participate in the process and have an active voice in how it is carried out (Cooney, 2002; Wehman, 2001). This view has been supported by Blacher (2001) and by Mizutani, Hiruma, and Yanagimoto (2003), who recommended that parents keep involved in the transition planning through the school years and when the youth becomes involved in services from community agencies. Display 32.5 illustrates the importance of parents advocating on behalf of their sons and daughters to ensure their needs are being addressed.

One aspect of entering adult life that is often viewed as a family concern, and thus that families can have a strong part in supporting, is addressing sexuality in transition youth, including both procreation and the role of sexuality in social relationships (Hayes Hammer et al., 2000; see also Zetlin & Turner, 2002, and Chapter 36). Although these topics may well have been covered in the school curriculum, families can help by providing additional sex education, offering practical help and advice, and above all being open to ongoing discussions about emerging issues related to sexuality. Some aspects of sexuality continue to be considered from a moral perspective (i.e., specific sexual acts are considered to be right or wrong) within some families and some cultures, and families can be helpful in explaining socially acceptable methods of satisfying adult sexual needs, dealing with the possibility of pregnancy, being a partner in a sexual relationship, and addressing concerns that arise from engaging in sexual activity.

Display 32.5

A parent's perspective: The importance of advocacy

Most parents have a positive attitude about the skills of their young sons or daughters. Parents who advocate strongly for their children and youth are more likely to get needed support, to be well informed about the resources available, and to have realistic aspirations for their children. Proactive parents show up at school meetings and interact with community agencies as needed. Often, they interact with one another and belong to parent or other disability-related groups. Such involvement is time consuming and it can take a toll on personal resources. Yet, some parents find their advocacy work to be a source of strength and satisfaction in their lives.

Some parents simply do not advocate at all. They do not interact with the service system and, in fact, may feel threatened by it. This may occur because they have not come to terms with their child's disability, or because of any number of other social and cultural reasons. While the children of such parents are in the school system, school staff can provide some support, but once they leave, the families are usually on their own. It is essential for schools and community services to be aware of such families so that they can be supported in ways that will be most beneficial to their young adult children during the important transition years.

Other Things that Schools Can Do

Many schools that specialize in disabilities or include students with disabilities in their general education programs throughout the United States, the United Kingdom, Australia, Canada, and other developed countries have aspects of transition in their curricula. A number of specific programs have been developed and described since the late 1990s, and many of these appear to hold considerable promise for supporting successful transition (e.g., Nietupski et al., 2004). However, this is not always the case, and even where transition is included, the quality varies considerably (Bassett & Smith, 1996; Ramcharan, 2003). In a 2004 review, Bouck noted that despite progressive legislation in the United States—including the Education for All Handicapped Children Act of 1975 (PL 94-142) and the Individuals with Disabilities Education Act (IDEA) of 1990 (PL 101-476), its 1997 amendments (PL 105-17), and its 2004 reauthorization (PL 108-446)—there are no specific requirements for transition to be part of the curriculum and it is not always included. However, it is widely assumed—and there is some evidence to support this assumption (e.g., Frank & Sitlington, 2000)—that, if transition planning is in place and carried out effectively, it results in improved outcomes for youth after they graduate from school. As a first step, then, schools can ensure that transition planning and development of skills to support successful transition are part of their curricula.

Transition research has begun to explore skills that are essential to successful transition. Schools can ensure such skills are taught. For example, problem solving, especially in new situations, has been demonstrated to be effective (Crites & Dunn, 2004). Learning how to express points of view and to ensure that those points of view are heard was shown to be important in a U.K. study by Cameron and Murphy (2002). Other recommended skills can be garnered from the previously described or other models for transition, from teaching objectives in transition curricula, and from other practical materials (e.g., Martin et al., 2002). It will be necessary to engage in evaluation research to develop knowledge about which skills are most effective for successful transition.

In the meantime, there are a number of helpful strategies and resources available for teachers (Hughes & Carter, 2000; Wehman, 2001, 2002; Wehman & Walsh, 1999; see also Resources). In general, schools can take a number of direct steps to help ensure successful transition to adult living:

- Advocate with policy makers for ongoing training and adult learning (see Display 32.6).
- Keep transition planning student centered (Miner & Bates, 1997).
- Involve parents and professionals from community agencies in planning for postgraduation activities (Mizutani et al., 2003).
- Involve youth in their own planning to a greater degree (Attanasio, 2003; Braithwaite, 2003; Martin et al., 2002; Mizutani et al., 2003; Ramcharan, 2003; Wehman, 2001; Zhang & Stecker, 2001).
- Provide meaningful work experience for students (Kirby, 1997).
- Provide more accessible information to students to assist with choices (Ramcharan, 2003).
- Refer students to community disability programs that are most likely to meet their needs (Attanasio, 2003).
- Take into full consideration the possibility of attending college (Getzel & Wehman, 2005).
- Well before the students leave school, transfer to community social service agencies information about numbers of students with special needs and descriptions of those needs; doing so will give agencies adequate information and time to plan services (Wehman, 2001; Wells, 1991).
- Undertake continuous improvement of transition planning (Kirby, 1997).

Display 32.6

A parent's perspective: What about college?

For some young people, leaving secondary school may mean going to college vocational programs that are available in some countries. Typically, these programs offer basic level training in life skills or career-specific skills. For some young people with good potential for entering the paid work force, this may be an excellent way to extend the transition period and help prepare for adult social and work life. For other young people, college provides no particular advantage—it simply delays adjusting to adult life.

Other Things that Service Providers Can Do

One of the major problems in transition from school to adult living is that community service organizations very often do not plan for or make themselves available to students who will be graduating from school. This trend has been changing gradually so that schools and community service organizations in many areas of some countries have now developed joint programs to address transition in a systematic way. Many such programs are funded by governments that have identified transition from school to adult living as an important aspect of service to people with disabilities (e.g., see Wehman, 2001). Change has been slow, however, primarily because education and adult social services are typically administered and funded by separate government departments or ministries. In addition, the relatively low level of funding of community services for adults results in waiting lists for services that are sometimes many years long. Where this is the case, it is somewhat understandable that organizations that focus on adult services do not reach out to graduating students who might also need their services.

For those community service organizations that are in a position to take some action, the most important aspects of their role are as follows:

- Take action to coordinate the services that youth with disabilities get while they are in school and the services they will need when they leave school, especially health and social services (Ramcharan, 2003; Wells, 1991).
- Provide comprehensive case management for transition youth with disabilities (Wehman & Walsh, 1999).
- Increase the number of options that are available to youth to engage in meaningful life activity (Braithwaite, 2003).
- Put in place personnel who have training, skill, and experience in helping young adults move from school to adult life (Wells, 1991).
- Ensure that service workers do not give up on youth and stop helping them (Ferguson et al., 1988).
- Train youth in self-development and self-advocacy skills to promote themselves in workplace and other community settings (Martin et al., 2002).
- Invest time and energy in developing relationships with current and potential employers (Luecking, Fabian, & Tilson, 2004).
- Seriously consider self-employment as one option (Griffin & Hammis, 2003).

- Train youth in ways and times to disclose their disabilities to others for helpful purposes (Hagedorn, Bond, & Hatt, 2001).

Other Things that Employers Can Do

In spite of sustained efforts to involve people with intellectual disabilities in paid, community-based employment, Kirby noted in 1997 that large numbers of youth with disabilities continue to be unemployed. This may still be the case, although reliable statistics are not readily available. Information that is available suggests that more than 50% of youth with disabilities are unemployed when they leave school (Wehman & Walsh, 1999), and more than 60% of adults with intellectual disabilities are unemployed (Wehman & Kregel, 1998). This appears to be true in a number of countries. For example, a large study in Canada (Brown, Raphael, & Renwick, 1997) found that, although 71% of people with intellectual and developmental disabilities known to the service system had daily occupational activities, only 17% of such activities were paid jobs or supported community employment. Moreover, this study estimated that only approximately 26% of adults with intellectual or developmental disabilities were actually involved with the service system, and it is unlikely that the employment rate among those not involved would be even as high. In a 1997 survey in Norway, Bollingmo found that there were few paid employment opportunities for people with intellectual disabilities and that vocational program staff were not well qualified to assist people with disabilities to find and hold onto jobs. The question of who needs to assume strong leadership in attempting to redress these long-standing problems (e.g., governments, business, disability organizations, parents and individuals with disabilities) has not yet been resolved. In the absence of such leadership, a great many employers simply take no active role in attempting to include young people with disabilities in their workforces (see Display 32.7).

Display 32.7

A parent's perspective: What graduation means to employers

For most young people who enter the work force, it is important to have a certificate of graduation at some level. Most employers expect that their employees have demonstrated competence in attending and successfully completing whatever school program they enrolled in. In fact, in many countries, a great many jobs are not open to people who do not have a secondary school certificate. Secondary school certificates held by young adults with intellectual and developmental disabilities do not necessarily mean that they are skilled at reading, writing, or mathematics, but they do show that these adults have reliably attended the school program and have met its basic requirements. This is an indication that they may be able to do the same in a job.

For those employers who do take an active role, there are a number of guides readily available to assist employers to better accommodate people with disabilities in their workplaces (e.g., Australian Government, 1998; Conference Board of Canada, 2001; Government of Canada, 2004; U.S. Social Security Administration, n.d.). The Conference Board of Canada guide provides practical advice to employers under three main headings: recruitment, workplace accommodations, and training and education in the workplace. In addition, virtually all larger communities and most smaller ones in the more developed countries have staff in community service organizations who have specialized training in placing youth with disabilities, providing on-the-job support, and assisting employers with training and accommodation. Such guides and personnel provide a great deal of practical help for employers.

Employers, too, must be willing to play their part if youth are to be successfully included. They need to be open to providing a variety of job possibilities within their workplace for which youth might be trained, moving beyond thinking only of the types of work that are repetitive and not mentally challenging (Braithwaite, 2003; Ramcharan, 2003). In addition, they need to be open to providing training for staff without disabilities to be effective in their support for the employees who have disabilities (see Display 32.8).

Other Things that Policy Makers Can Do

Making the transition from school to adult living is a relatively new focus for policy in the field of intellectual and developmental disabilities. Legislation enhancing supported employment has existed in the United States (see Wehman, 2001, for a description of U.S. legislation) and many other countries since the mid-1980s (Kirby, 1997), but a broader policy focus on transition to adult living has not yet emerged. Still, as Eisenman (2003) noted in her review, there have been some helpful policy discussions about how to integrate transition into special education curricula, especially in relation to how this might more positively affect employment and other measures of successful living for youth after they leave school. Some helpful ideas have begun to emerge, and these will no doubt be expanded over the next few years. Policy makers can do the following:

- Address the issue of fair wages for people with disabilities by setting clear rules and guidelines (Kirby, 1997).

- Develop helpful databases for the purposes of evaluating the effectiveness of transitions activities such as making transition plans; putting plans into effect; gaining employment or other meaningful daily activity; acquiring independent accommodation; becoming interconnected with community services, people, and activities; and providing for financial independence (Kirby, 1997).
- Enhance the mandates of government-funded agencies to address transition issues (Kirby, 1997).
- Promote greater independence in early adult life by taking measures to ensure personal safety, financial security, and access to public transportation (Ramcharan, 2003).
- Promote within industry the value of employing workers with disabilities, providing incentives if necessary.
- Put into place programs that link transition planning in the schools to assistance to youth after they leave school. A number of such programs have already been developed. One was described by Mizutani and Yanagimoto (2003), who noted that individualized transition support planning has been in effect in Tokyo since 2001 and that this system ties together the school years and the postschool years. These programs differ in how they are set up and what they do, but they often include staff from service organizations for adults and teachers working together in schools. These individuals cooperate in setting up and carrying out transition plans; providing students opportunities to gain work experience in community settings; setting and amending goals for the future; and putting in place financial, employment, accommodation, and social supports that will be characteristic of a particular youth's adult life.
- Set out policy for training managers and workers in industry who do not have disabilities (Kirby, 1997).

SPECIAL SUPPORT TO INDIVIDUALS WITH SEVERE DISABILITIES AND THEIR FAMILIES

Successful transition to adult life is most challenging for people with severe intellectual, developmental, or behavioral disabilities, yet is so essential to positive life outcomes (Clark & Davis, 2000; Johnson et al., 1997). It might be assumed that lower levels of cognition or other skills might be problematic to putting transition plans into effect. Cooney (2002) noted, however, that students were remarkably articulate about postschool plans; problems appeared to stem primarily from lack of available opportunities. This view is supported by a large study of 3,084 students 14 years of age and older with severe intellectual disability in England and Wales, where students were found to have few opportunities

Display 32.8

A parent's perspective: Transition into the workplace

There are good programs in many areas for helping youth to enter the work force. My son is enrolled in one such program in our city. It assists young adults who are still in school and youth who have recently left school. To be accepted into the program, the family must make a commitment to participate actively in the planning and support process and also bring together a circle of community supporters such as relatives, friends, teachers, religious leaders, and even neighbors. The ultimate goal here is to help family members and others learn how to help ensure that the person with a disability has meaningful daytime activity, not just in the short term but also in the long term. The first task of this group is to create a "career tree," a giant drawing of a tree to which ideas can be added in writing. The tree is a metaphor for the youth's life options, and this metaphor has been demonstrated to be appropriate for all levels of ability. The roots, trunk, and branches represent strengths, interests, and possibilities, and the fruit on the tree are specific examples of jobs. The circle of support forms part of the process of getting specific jobs and may even be involved with support in the workplace. The circle helps make decisions, evaluates progress, and becomes an extended family. Such services may work better for youth who already have a supportive family, but it may also be an important option for youth without large families or for those with single parents.

Even with the help of programs such as these, finding and maintaining a job for a young person with an intellectual disability, whether it is paid or not, can be very difficult. First, the range of available jobs is limited, although, in general, the more skilled the youth, the more job possibilities exist. Second, many employers are hesitant to hire employees who have disabilities. Some programs provide on-the-job training, but finding a workplace that is willing to teach new skills in the manner the worker with disabilities learns best can be a tremendous challenge. For individuals who require close supervision, finding funding for an additional facilitator or job coach is also often difficult and time consuming. Finally, employers, supervisors, and co-workers often consider that they do not have the skills to help an individual with intellectual disabilities. Training for such people appears to be a neglected area in the transition to work life, but it may be one of the most important factors in predicting success.

to participate in the community life of adults (Florian et al., 2000).

Central to the special support needed by individuals with severe disabilities is the inescapable realization that dependency will continue into adulthood. Wells pointed this out in 1991, but it is just as relevant today. This realization may contribute to families, schools, and community service organizations considering fewer options for people with severe disabilities. For example, youth, especially men, with challenging behavior problems are likely in the early transition years to enter residential care (Alborz, 2003). Regarding occupational activity, Kraemer and Blacher (2001) noted that more than half of youth with severe disabilities in their U.S.-based study worked in segregated environments. Similarly, Brown et al. (1997) found that in a random sample of people with (mostly severe) intellectual disabilities who lived in group homes in Canada, 83% attended a major day (segregated) program, but only 9% were in supported employment or other community work. Another important finding of this survey was that 60% of those who lived in group homes and had a major daily activity had no input into the decision to be placed in the program, and another 17% had limited input.

Family involvement may be especially important in broadening opportunities for youth with severe disabilities. One study illustrated that employment seeking that is initiated by schools or community agencies may be most likely to result in sheltered work, whereas employment seeking that is initiated by family members may be linked closer to inclusive options such as continuing education or self-employment (Devlieger & Trach, 1999). Yet, what parents would like to happen does not always match their ability to recognize diverse opportunities (Cooney, 2002) or what they consider to be realistic (Kraemer & Blacher, 2001). Thus, parents' dreams and initiatives appear to be helpful in expanding ideas and opportunities but may not always be able to be realized to the extent that they might wish.

Overall, individuals with severe disabilities typically need to have some specialized support to help them successfully negotiate transition to adult life. For most people with severe disabilities continued success needs to include ongoing personal and professional support. The specific methods for providing such supports are numerous and need to be person specific. However, some general actions that have been described or suggested in the literature and that are helpful to almost all people are to

- Begin with, and integrate throughout the transition process, a full assessment for all youth with severe disabilities (Sax & Thoma, 2002)
- Carry out a thorough assessment of behaviors during transition times to understand the true nature of what people with severe disabilities are responding to and inferring (Clark & Davis, 2000; also see Kern & Vorndran, 2000, for an interesting example)
- Facilitate social interaction in community settings in an ongoing way to help community integration (Souza & Kennedy, 2003)
- Involve families, individuals with disabilities, schools, community agencies, and other support people in the ongoing planning and implementation of transition activities
- Provide a wide variety of community-based experience (Black & Langone, 1997)
- Provide employment support in the form of employment specialists and trained co-workers (Wehman et al., 1998)

SUMMARY

A smooth transition from school to adult life is one of the major keys to the successful inclusion of young adults into community life. Yet, it is important to recognize that no one person, no one family, and no one service organization can provide the full range of services needed by an individual or that individual's family. If the best ways to bring about smooth transitions for youth to adult life are to be found, governments, community services, employers, and families will have to find a way to share and blend their responsibility for doing so.

FOR FURTHER THOUGHT AND DISCUSSION

1. What could be done to better connect the "two solitudes"—the school system for students and the community supports for adults?
2. Consider the case of one youth with disabilities. What factors are most helpful to him or her adjusting to adult life in the community? How many of these factors pertain to most youth with intellectual or developmental disabilities? How many are unique to the person you have selected to describe?
3. Think of a family you know that has a teenager with an intellectual or developmental disability. Now imagine that the parents are not satisfied that a transition plan is being developed in the school. What courses of action might the parents take? Discuss the advantages and disadvantages of each course of action.
4. Many employers are interested in helping people with disabilities, even if they are not required to do so. What can interested employers do to promote opportunities within their workplaces?

5. Not all families connect with community services when their children leave the school system. These families are sometimes described as "falling between the cracks" because their children need services but are not obtaining them. What can policy makers do to ensure that families do not fall between the cracks? What can community service organizations do? What can schools do?

REFERENCES

Alborz, A. (2003). Transitions: Placing a son or daughter with intellectual disability and challenging behaviour in alternative residential provision. *Journal of Applied Research in Intellectual Disabilities, 16,* 75–88.

Attanasio, M.E. (2003). The relationship between locus of control, residential setting, and employment status within a sample of adults with mental retardation. *Dissertation Abstracts International: Section B: The Sciences & Engineering, 64* (6-B), 2904.

Australian Government. (1998). *Practitioner's handbook for public sector employers and employees: Workplace diversity.* Canberra: Commonwealth of Australia, Legislative Services.

Bassett, D.S., & Smith, T.E.C. (1996). Transition in an era of reform. *Journal of Learning Disabilities, 29,* 161–166.

Blacher, J. (2001). Transition to adulthood: Mental retardation, families, and culture. *American Journal on Mental Retardation, 106,* 173–188.

Blacher, J., & Hatton, C. (2001). Current perspectives on family research in mental retardation. *Current Opinion in Psychiatry, 14,* 477–482.

Black, R.S., & Langone, J. (1997). Social awareness and transition to employment for adolescents with mental retardation. *Remedial and Special Education, 18,* 214–222.

Bollingmo, G. (1997). Survey of employment services and vocational outcomes for individuals with mental retardation in Norway. *Journal of Vocational Rehabilitation, 8,* 269–283.

Bouck, E.C. (2004). State of curriculum for secondary students with mild mental retardation. *Education & Training in Developmental Disabilities, 39,* 169–176.

Braithwaite, M. (2003). Transition and changes in the lives of people with intellectual disabilities. *International Journal of Disability, Development & Education, 50,* 225–226.

Bramston, P., & Cummins, R.A. (1998). Stress and the move into community accommodation. *Journal of Intellectual & Developmental Disability, 23,* 295–308.

Brown, I., & Brown, R.I. (2003). *Quality of life and disability: An approach for community practitioners.* London: Jessica Kingsley Publishers.

Brown, I., Raphael, D., & Renwick, R. (1997). *Quality of life: Dream or reality? Life for people with developmental disabilities in Ontario.* Toronto: Centre for Health Promotion.

Brown, I., & Renwick, R. (1998). *Family quality of life: A report to the Ministry of Community and Social Services, Government of Ontario.* Toronto: University of Toronto, Faculty of Social Work.

Brown, R.I. (2004). *Down syndrome issues and information: Adult living series* (R.I. Brown, Ed.). *Life for adults with Down syndrome: New opportunities, new challenges.* Southsea, United Kingdom: The Down Syndrome Educational Trust.

Cameron, L., & Murphy, J. (2002). Enabling young people with a learning disability to make choices at a time of transition. *British Journal of Learning Disabilities, 30,* 105–112.

Capie, A., Contardi, A., & Doehring, D. (2006). *Transition to employment.* In R.I. Brown (Ed.), *Life for adults with Down syndrome: New opportunities, new challenges.* Southsea, United Kingdom: The Down Syndrome Educational Trust.

Clark, H.B., & Davis, M. (Eds.). (2000). *Transition to adulthood: A resource for assisting young people with emotional or behavioral difficulties.* Baltimore: Paul H. Brookes Publishing Co.

Conference Board of Canada. (2001). *Tapping the talents of people with disabilities: A guide for employers.* Retrieved May 16, 2005, from http://www.conferenceboard.ca/documents.asp?rnext=85

Cooney, B.F. (2002). Exploring perspectives on transition of youth with disabilities: Voices of young adults, parents, and professionals. *Mental Retardation, 40,* 425–435.

Crites, S.A., & Dunn, C. (2004). Teaching social problem solving to individuals with mental retardation. *Education & Training in Developmental Disabilities, 39,* 301–309.

Devlieger, P.L., & Trach, J.S. (1999). Mediation as a transition process: The impact on postschool employment outcomes. *Exceptional Children, 65,* 507–523.

Education for All Handicapped Children Act of 1975, PL 94-142, 20 U.S.C. §§ 1400 *et seq.*

Eisenman, L.T. (2003). Theories in practice: School-to-work transitions for youth with mild disabilities. *Exceptionality, 11,* 89–102.

Ferguson, P.M., Ferguson, D.L., & Jones, D. (1988). Generations of hope: Parental perspectives on the transitions of their children with severe retardation from school to adult life. *Journal of The Association for Persons with Severe Handicaps, 13,* 177–187.

Florian, L., Dee, L., Byers, R., et al. (2000). What happens after the age of 14? Mapping transitions for pupils with profound and complex learning difficulties. *British Journal of Special Education, 27*(3), 124–128.

Frank, A.R., & Sitlington, P.L. (2000). Young adults with mental disabilities–does transition planning make a difference? *Education & Training in Mental Retardation & Developmental Disabilities, 35,* 119–134.

Getzel, E.E., & Wehman, P. (Eds.). (2005). *Going to college: Expanding opportunities for people with disabilities.* Baltimore: Paul H. Brookes Publishing Co.

Government of Canada. (2004). *Working together: An employer's resource for workplace accommodation.* Retrieved May 16, 2005, from http://www.hrsdc.gc.ca/en/on/epb/disabilities/pdf/workplace_accommodation.pdf

Griffin, C., & Hammis, D. (2003). *Making self-employment work for people with disabilities.* Baltimore: Paul H. Brookes Publishing Co.

Hagedorn, L., Bond, J., & Hatt, P. (2001). *Learning disabilities: Best practice and innovations.* Retrieved March 18, 2006, from http://www.on.literacy.ca/pubs/best/learndis/insid cov.htm

Hayes Hammer, J., Holloway, J., DePrato, D.K., et al. (2000). Transitioning individuals with mental retardation and developmental disability: The other sister. *Journal of the American Academy of Psychiatry & the Law, 28,* 202–205.

Heal, L.W., Khoju, M., Rusch, F.R., et al. (1999). Predicting quality of life of students who have left special education high school programs. *American Journal on Mental Retardation, 104,* 305–319.

Hepper, F., & Garralda, M.E. (2001). Psychiatric adjustment to leaving school in adolescents with intellectual disability: A pilot study. *Journal of Intellectual Disability Research, 45,* 521–525.

Hughes, C., & Carter, E.W. (2000). *The transition handbook: Strategies high school teachers use that work!* Baltimore: Paul H. Brookes Publishing Co.

Hughes, C., Eisenman, L.T., Hwang, B., et al. (1997). Transition from secondary special education to adult life: A review and analysis of empirical measures. *Education and Training in Mental Retardation & Developmental Disabilities, 32,* 85–104.

Individuals with Disabilities Education Act Amendments of 1997, PL 105-17, 20 U.S.C. §§ 1400 *et seq.*

Individuals with Disabilities Education Act (IDEA) of 1990, PL 101-476, 20 U.S.C. §§ 1400 *et seq.*

Individuals with Disabilities Education Improvement Act of 2004, PL 108-446, 20 U.S.C. §§ 1400 *et seq.*

Johnson, D.R., McGrew, K.S., Bloomberg, L., et al. (1997). Results of a national follow-up study of young adults with severe disabilities. *Journal of Vocational Rehabilitation, 8,* 119–133.

Kern, L., & Vorndran, C.M. (2000). Functional assessment and intervention for transition difficulties. *Journal of The Association for Persons with Severe Handicaps, 25,* 212–216.

Kirby, N. (1997). Employment and mental retardation. In N.W. Bray (Ed.), *International review of research in mental retardation: Vol. 20* (pp. 191–249). San Diego: Academic Press.

Kohler, P.D. (1996). *Taxonomy for transition.* Champaign: University of Illinois. Also available at homepages.wmich .edu/~kohlerp/pdf/Taxonomy.pdf)

Kraemer, B.R., & Blacher, J. (2001). Transition for young adults with severe mental retardation: School, preparation, parent expectations, and family involvement. *Mental Retardation, 39,* 423–435.

Kraemer, B.R., McIntyre, L.L., & Blacher, J. (2003). Quality of life for young adults with mental retardation during transition. *Mental Retardation, 41,* 250–262.

Lichtenstein, S., & Nisbet, J. (1992). *New Hampshire Transition Initiative: From school to adult life. Young adults in transition: A national and state overview.* Durham: University of New Hampshire, Institute on Disability.

Luecking, R.G., Fabian, E.S., & Tilson, G.P. (2004). *Working relationships: Creating career opportunities for job seekers with disabilities through employer partnerships.* Baltimore: Paul H. Brookes Publishing Co.

Martin, J.E., Mithaug, D.E., Oliphint, J.H., et al. (2002). *Self-directed employment: A handbook for transition teachers and employment specialists.* Baltimore: Paul H. Brookes Publishing Co.

Millar, D.S. (2003). Age of majority, transfer of rights and guardianship: Considerations for families and educators. *Education & Training in Developmental Disabilities, 38,* 378–397.

Miner, C.A., & Bates, P.E. (1997). The effect of person centered planning activities on the IEP/transition planning process. *Education & Training in Mental Retardation & Developmental Disabilities, 32,* 105–112.

Mizutani, Y., Hiruma, T., & Yanagimoto, Y. (2003). A nationwide investigation of individualized plans in Japanese special high schools: Implications for the collaborative practices of individualized transition support plans. *Japanese Journal of Special Education, 39,* 41–58.

Mizutani, Y., & Yanagimoto, Y. (2003). Transition support system in Japanese Special High Schools for students with intellectual disabilities: A comparison with the ITP process in the United States. *Japanese Journal of Special Education, 40,* 713–722.

Nietupski, J., McQuillen, T., Berg, D.D., et al. (2004). Iowa's High School High Tech Goes to College Program: Preparing students with mild disabilities for careers in technology. *Journal of Developmental and Physical Disabilities, 16,* 179–192.

Ramcharan, P. (2003). Bridging the divide at transition: What happens for young people with learning difficulties and their families. *Journal of Learning Disabilities, 7,* 283–284.

Richardson, A. (1989). Letting go: A mother's view. *Disability, Handicap & Society, 4,* 81–92.

Ryan, T. (1997). *Making our way: Transition from school to adulthood in the lives of people who have learning difficulties.* London: Values into Action.

Sax, C.L., & Thoma, C.A. (2002). *Transition assessment: Wise practices for quality lives.* Baltimore. Paul H. Brookes Publishing Co.

Smull, M.W., & Bellamy, G.T. (1991). Community services for adults with disabilities: Policy challenges in the emerging support paradigm. In L.H. Meyer, C.A. Peck, & L. Brown (Eds.), *Critical issues in the lives of people with severe disabilities* (pp. 527–536). Baltimore: Paul H. Brookes Publishing Co.

Souza, G., & Kennedy, C.H. (2003). Facilitating social interactions in the community for a transition-age student with severe disabilities. *Journal of Positive Behavior Interventions, 5,* 179–182.

Spero, L. (2003). The transition from school to the community: A parent's perspective. In I. Brown & M. Percy (Eds.), *Developmental disabilities in Ontario* (2nd ed., pp. 603–612). Toronto: Ontario Association on Developmental Disabilities.

Szymanski, E.M. (2000). Disability and vocational behavior. In R.G. Frank & T.R. Elliott (Eds.), *Handbook of rehabilitation psychology* (pp. 499–517). Washington, DC: American Psychological Association.

Thorin, E., Yovanoff, P., & Irvin, L. (1996). Dilemmas faced by families during their young adults' transitions to adulthood: A brief report. *Mental Retardation, 34,* 117–120.

Todd, S., Young, P., Shearn, J., et al. (2004). Family quality of life in Wales. In A. Turnbull, I. Brown, & H.R. Turnbull (Eds.), *Families and people with mental retardation and quality of life: International perspectives* (pp. 101–147). Washington, DC: American Association on Mental Retardation.

U.S. Social Security Administration. (n.d.). *Americans with Disabilities Act: A guide for people with disabilities seeking employment* [Publication Number ADA-0001 ICN 951750]. Retrieved May 16, 2005, from http://www.eeoc.gov/facts/adaguide.html

Wehman, P. (2001). *Life beyond the classroom: Transition strategies for young people with disabilities* (3rd ed.). Baltimore: Paul H. Brookes Publishing Co.

Wehman, P. (2002). *Individual transition plans: The teacher's curriculum guide for helping youth with special needs.* Austin, TX: PRO-ED.

Wehman, P., Gibson, K., Brooke, V., et al. (1998). Transition from school to competitive employment: Illustrations of competence for two young women with severe mental retardation. *Focus on Autism & Other Developmental Disabilities, 13,* 130–143.

Wehman, P., & Kregel, J. (Eds.). (1998). *More than a job: Securing satisfying careers for people with disabilities.* Baltimore: Paul H. Brookes Publishing Co.

Wehman, P., & Walsh, P.N. (1999). Transition from school to adulthood. In P. Retish & S. Reiter (Eds.), *Adults with disabilities: International perspectives in the community* (pp. 3–31). Mahwah, NJ: Lawrence Erlbaum Associates.

Wells, I. (1991). Severe learning difficulties in Northern Ireland: Leaving school. *British Journal of Special Education, 18*(2), 63–66.

Zetlin, A.G., & Turner, J.L. (2002). Transition from adolescence to adulthood: Perspectives of mentally retarded individuals and their families. In J. Blacher & B.L. Baker (Eds.), *The best of AAMR: Families and mental retardation. A collection of notable AAMR journal articles across the 20th century* (pp. 193–201). Washington, DC: American Association on Mental Retardation.

Zhang, D., & Stecker, P.M. (2001). Student involvement in transition planning: Are we there yet? *Education & Training in Mental Retardation & Developmental Disabilities, 36,* 293–303.

33

Work and Employment for People with Intellectual and Developmental Disabilities

Judith Sandys

WHAT YOU WILL LEARN ABOUT IN THIS CHAPTER

- Work and its importance
- Why people with developmental disabilities have been excluded from workforce participation
- A brief historical overview
- The current context
- Program models
- Nonvocational alternatives
- The issue of charity: perceptions and expectations

Because work is so important for everyone, programs for people with intellectual and developmental disabilities have commonly included some focus on work. These programs are often referred to as *vocational services*. This chapter refers to them as *work-related supports and services*. The following sections discuss the importance of work, why people with developmental disabilities are so often excluded, the historical development of such services, and the range of work-related programs currently in operation. Although the author is Canadian and hence most familiar with the Canadian context, the information in this chapter is drawn from a number of sources and includes information from, or about, the United States, the United Kingdom, Australia, and elsewhere.

This transnational focus presents some challenges when it comes to terminology, because different countries use different terms for the same thing (see also Chapter 1). Hence, Canadians tend to use the terms *developmental disabilities* or *intellectual disabilities*. In the United States, the term most frequently used is still *mental retardation* (and in the United States the term *developmental disabilities* has a broader meaning than in Canada and other countries). Those in the United Kingdom use the term *learning difficulties* or *learning disabilities,* the latter of which means something quite different in North America. Similarly, **supported employment** is used to mean different things in different countries; what is called a **sheltered workshop** in Canada may be called "supported employment" or "business services" in Australia. Except in the context of direct quotes, this chapter uses Canadian terminology throughout this chapter. However, Chapter 1 and Appendix B at the end of the book include terms used in other countries as well.

WORK AND ITS IMPORTANCE

When most people talk about going to work, they are referring to engaging in an activity for which they expect to receive pay. Certainly, there are unpaid activities that involve a great deal of effort (perhaps even more than paid work)—caring for children, cooking, taking care of the garden, or cleaning the garage, to name a few. In fact, some people may be paid to do the same things that others do without pay. Almost any activity may be paid work for some people and unpaid for others. Therefore, it is the element of pay, rather than the nature of the activity itself, that defines something as belonging in the work-as-employment category.

Although all people engage in many activities without being paid, most also engage in work for which they are paid. For many people, this work or employment represents a very important facet of their lives. Throughout this chapter, unless otherwise specified, the term *work* is used to connote paid work.

Work as a Central Focus in Life

Employment is a central focus in the lives of most adults. Of course, some people may not work, either because they are unable to find work or because there are other priorities in their lives at a particular mo-

The author extends sincere thanks to Sarah Rooney, Lecturer in the Department of Applied Health and Social Studies at Stockport College, for the excellent information provided about employment programs in the United Kingdom.

ment. They may, for example, be involved in caring for children or other relatives, or they may choose to focus on volunteer community service or particular creative pursuits. It is certainly possible to have a fulfilling life and to make a significant contribution to one's community without engaging in paid work. However, most often in today's society, people expect and are expected to work for much of their adult lives.

When asked, "What is most important to you in the work you do or expect to do?" most people say that they want work that is interesting and challenging, provides opportunities to learn new skills, has good coworkers, and makes a difference. Of course, they say that they want work that pays them enough to meet their needs. Work structures one's days, connects one to the larger society, and influences self-concept and identity. It enables people to see themselves and to be seen as useful contributing members of society.

Needless to say, people work to earn money to buy the things they need and want; paid employment represents the major way that resources are distributed in society. Yet, the need for money is not the only (or sometimes, the most important) reason why people work or why they choose to do a specific kind of work. In addition to the money it generates, work serves a number of other functions. The work that people do, or hope to do, influences how they spend their time, with whom they interact, what they learn, and many other things. Furthermore, work influences greatly how people think of themselves and how others think about them. Most often, work is a central focus of identity. It is not surprising that when people meet for the first time in a social situation, "What do you do?" is usually one of the first questions posed. Society attaches high value to being employed. Unless they have other highly valued characteristics (e.g., wealth), people who are not working are at risk of being seen as being lazy, irresponsible, or incompetent. The societal value accorded to work is internalized at the individual level; people who lose their job often experience a profound sense of loss of identity and status.

As has been noted, not everyone works. Some people with developmental disabilities, like others who do not have disabilities, may engage in other activities that give structure and meaning to their lives. Service providers may be at a loss as to how to involve these individuals in meaningful work. Nevertheless, if work plays such an important role in life, it is logical to assume that it should play an equally important role in the lives of most adults with developmental disabilities. Why would one presume that people with developmental disabilities do not need interesting and challenging work, opportunities to develop relationships, a chance to make a difference, the respect of the broader society, and the resources that work generates?

Characteristics of Good Work

Like everyone else, most people with developmental disabilities need the opportunity to engage in work that reflects their dignity and worth. They need work that

- Is interesting and challenging
- Pays a fair wage
- Is consistent with their interests and skills
- Is valued by society
- Connects them to their community
- Enables them to interact with others
- Provides opportunities to develop relationships
- Encourages ongoing skill development
- Promotes enhanced levels of responsibility

These characteristics seem obvious and straightforward. Yet, most people with developmental disabilities do not have work that can be described in this way.

WHY PEOPLE WITH DEVELOPMENTAL DISABILITIES HAVE BEEN EXCLUDED FROM WORKFORCE PARTICIPATION

People with all kinds of disabilities—and particularly those with developmental disabilities—are often excluded from workforce participation. A study by the Roeher Institute (2002) noted that people with intellectual disabilities are considerably less likely to be employed than people with other disabilities. They are, in general, significantly poorer. When they do work, it most often is in low scale jobs or in work "outside the regular labour market" (p. 14). A U.K. study of one large city, Manchester, found that of 1,179 adults with learning disabilities (i.e., people with developmental disabilities), only 16 people were in paid employment and only 8 of these worked full time (Manchester Learning Disability Partnership Board Employment Strategy, 2003, as cited by S. Rooney, personal communication, April 27, 2004).

Why is this the case? As noted in Sandys (1999a),

> Perceptions of what constitutes work and who is able to work, the meanings attached to work, and the strategies undertaken to encourage workforce participation (for those assumed to be able to work) are all shaped by the perceived needs of a capitalist economy and the values inherent therein. (p. 243)

In simpler times, a good many people, with what are now considered disabilities, may well have been able to contribute through their work. Increased industrialization, more complex technology, and the structure of the labor market—with its ever-increasing emphasis on productivity—have all served to exclude those who do not appear able to "measure up" (e.g., see Rooney, 2002).

At the same time as society has made it more difficult for people with disabilities to gain access to the workforce, the cost of this exclusion, in terms of the impact on people's lives, has become even greater. The very high value placed on productivity means that those who are perceived to be unproductive are treated even more poorly within society. To be *perceived* to be unproductive is to be treated in such a manner as to make it very much more difficult to *become* productive.

The predominant view of developmental (and other) disabilities is to see these as unfortunate, tragic conditions that affect particular individuals who are therefore in need of a host of interventions designed to ameliorate their conditions for more effective participation in the community. This perspective, sometimes referred to as the "individual tragedy" or the "medical" model, locates the "problem" within the individual, who is in need of being "fixed". Today, the medical model is being challenged: It is known that for most people with disabilities, the major source of disadvantage is not the disabling condition itself but the way that society defines and responds to that disability (e.g., see Barnes, Mercer, & Shakespeare, 1999; Chapter 3).

Wolfensberger (1992) contended the societal devaluation of people with disabilities explains their poor treatment within society. Although it is true that some people with developmental disabilities do experience close personal relationships, meaningful activity, economic security, and so forth, there are countless other people whose lives are marked by loneliness, isolation, segregation, inactivity, and poverty. All too often people with developmental disabilities exist in environments where people have low expectations of them and where, as a result, they are denied opportunities for growth and development. All of these factors serve to keep people with developmental disabilities out of the labor force, thereby reinforcing the views of those who see this as inevitable and appropriate.

Without question, some people with developmental disabilities have significant cognitive impairments; they require very high levels of support and the concept of work may not be meaningful for them. Nevertheless, it should not be assumed that this lack of workforce participation is related simply to the nature of the disability itself—that people with developmental disabilities are excluded only because they are not able to work productively. Although there may be limitations on the kinds of work that a person with a developmental disability can do (and, of course, there are limitations on the kinds of work most people can do), there are many examples of people with developmental disabilities—including some with quite significant impairments—who are successfully employed.

A BRIEF HISTORICAL OVERVIEW

In the early and mid-1800s, large institutions for people with developmental disabilities (along with people with psychiatric and other disabilities) were developed across North America and in the U.K. (e.g., see Little, 1993; Noll & Trent, 2004; Race, 2002; Simmons, 1982; Trent, 1994; see also Chapter 2). There were many reasons why people were admitted to these institutions. Sometimes it was because there was no one in the community who could or would provide them with the care they needed. People were also sent to institutions because their behavior was considered delinquent, dangerous, or immoral. There is compelling evidence (e.g., see Noll & Trent, 2004) that conditions in some of these early institutions were abysmal. Nevertheless, and for whatever reason people were sent there, a stated purpose of these early institutions was to educate and train people with developmental disabilities so that they could be returned to the community as productive members. It was commonly believed that the training the institution provided could help some people to learn the skills needed to function in the community.

The earliest work programs for those with developmental disabilities started within these institutions. Sometimes the "inmates" performed various maintenance tasks, farm work, or took care of residents with more severe disabilities. One reason for these work activities was probably to reduce the cost of running the institution. However, work was also believed to be of therapeutic value; it was hoped that these work activities would prepare some people for subsequent employment in the community. It was the desire to provide more training in a wider range of work tasks that led to the development of workshops within institutions.

Work-oriented programs for people with developmental disabilities outside of institutions began to appear in North America in the 1950s and in the late 1960s in the U.K. (Rooney, 2002). In the early 1950s, parents across North America began forming organizations to promote the development of services for their sons and daughters with developmental disabilities. Although some of these organizations did work to promote the development of more (or better) institutions, they also began to focus on services in the community. One of the earliest kind of programs these parent associations implemented were sheltered workshops, where people with developmental disabilities could engage in various kinds of work activities in a protected environment. Beginning in the 1960s (and continuing into the early 21st century), there was increasing pressure to close or phase down institutions. Developing sheltered workshops in the community was seen as a necessary part of this deinstitutionalization thrust.

Sheltered workshops were developed with two goals in mind. One was to train people so that they could acquire the skills needed to work in the community. The other was to provide long term work activities in a protected environment for the people who, it was thought, could not be prepared for community employment. Many sheltered workshops tried to do both of these things at the same time. However, some organizations emphasized one goal over another or had separate programs for each of them. For example, an organization might have a separate place where people would come for a period of time so that they could receive **job training.** At the end of that period, if they were considered employable, people would be helped to find a job. Otherwise, they would go to a sheltered workshop on a long-term basis. In fact, only a small proportion of the people admitted to sheltered workshops moved on to **competitive employment.** Workshops continued to increase in number and size until the mid-1990s.

By the 1970s, some people were already becoming quite critical of workshops. As noted, workshops were not very good at training people for competitive employment. The work activities that people did were most often simple, dull, and repetitive tasks for which they earned very little money. There were efforts during this period to improve workshops. Two people who had a significant impact were Michael Gold (1980) and Tom Bellamy (e.g., see Bellamy, Peterson, & Close, 1975). Both Gold and Bellamy demonstrated that when work activities were broken down into small, manageable steps with systematic teaching strategies, people with major developmental disabilities could learn very complex assembly tasks. John DuRand suggested that introducing a small number of "model workers" (workers without disabilities) into the workshop would improve the behavior of the workers with disabilities and the overall productivity of the workshop. He called these settings *affirmative industries* (DuRand & DuRand, 1978). In other instances, workshops began to disperse by developing **enclaves, work stations,** or mobile work crews, in which a number of workers with disabilities and a supervisor worked in the community or a regular industry. Many more organizations began job placement programs to find employment for the people whom the workshops had trained.

All of these developments had a significant impact across North America and in other countries, where efforts were made to incorporate many of these new elements into existing sheltered workshops. The different components were perceived as part of a continuum through which individuals could progress on their route to competitive employment (DuRand & Neufeldt, 1980). Nevertheless, criticisms of sheltered workshops continued. Despite efforts to develop better ways of training people, there was no evidence that workshops were doing significantly better in terms of preparing people for employment. Perhaps even more important were changing philosophies. An ever-increasing emphasis on community participation and inclusion (e.g., see Taylor, Biklen, & Knoll, 1987) and a heightened appreciation for the need to promote valued roles for people with developmental (and other) disabilities led people to question traditional service models (Osburn, 1998; Wolfensberger, 1980, 1992). As a result, many have come to consider all segregated settings, including sheltered workshops, unacceptable (e.g., see McCallum, 1989; Murphy & Rogan, 1995).

If the theme of the 1970s and early 1980s was trying to make workshops better, the central theme of the mid-1980s and the 1990s was clearly developing work/employment-related alternatives to sheltered workshops. A major development, beginning in the United States in the late 1970s and in Canada in the early 1980s and continuing today, has been the development of supported employment. There have been efforts to enable people with developmental disabilities to become self-employed, either individually, or as part of **co-operatives (co-ops).** As the 20th century drew to a close and the 21st began, some organizations for people with developmental disabilities seemed to be decreasing their emphasis on programs directly related to work and employment and focusing more on the development of nonwork alternatives. The extent to which this is a positive development is still a matter of contention.

THE CURRENT CONTEXT

If one were to read relevant legislative and policy documents from many countries, it would be easy to assume that there was widespread support for enabling people with developmental disabilities to be employed. Of particular note is the Americans with Disabilities Act (ADA) of 1990 (PL 101-336) in the United States, which is perhaps the most comprehensive legislation to address disability discrimination, including discrimination in employment. The legislation provides an enforcement mechanism for dealing with individuals and organizations that engage in discriminatory practices. Similarly, legislation in Ontario, Canada, the Ontarians with Disabilities Act (ODA) of 2001, is designed to prevent disability discrimination in all areas including employment. The ODA is modeled on the ADA but lacks mechanisms to ensure compliance. The ODA speaks to the necessity of addressing the accommodation needs of people with disabilities in order to ensure their full participation. Table 33.1 shows how the legislative focus has changed in Canada. More recently, stronger legislation with mandatory compliance has developed. This new legislation—Accessibility for Ontarians with Disabilities (AODA), which was passed in June 2005—seeks to ensure full accessibility in all areas

Table 33.1. A new approach to disability issues

Old . . .	New . . .
Recipients	Participants
Passive income support	Active measures to promote employment in addition to providing necessary income support
Dependence	Independence
Government responsibility	Shared responsibility
Labelled as "unemployable"	Identification of work skills
Disincentives to leave income support	Incentives to seek employment and volunteer opportunities
Insufficient employment supports	Opportunities to develop skills and experience
Program-centered approach	Person-centered approach
Insufficient portability of benefits and services	Portable benefits and services
Multiple access requirements	Integrated access requirements

Source: Government of Canada (1998).

(including employment) for people with disabilities within 20 years. It has provisions whereby standards will be developed by committees with representation from all sectors of society. The implementation of these standards will take place in each 5-year period until full accessibility has been achieved (see http://www.hrmguide.net/canada/law/ontario-disabilities.htm).

The *Government of Canada Disability Agenda* (2004) espouses "a commitment to work towards the full participation and inclusion of persons with disabilities," and the British document *Valuing People: A New Strategy for Learning Disability for the 21st Century* (U.K. Department of Health, 2001) identifies a number of "key action points" that together are designed "to enable more people with learning disabilities to participate in all forms of employment, wherever possible in paid work and to make a valued contribution to the world of work" (from Rooney, 2002, p. 96). These include, among others, the establishment of targets for increasing workforce participation, increasing employment opportunities within the Public Sector, and the development of skilled "job brokers" (Rooney, 2002). In Australia, the *Employer Incentives Strategy,* which was established in 1997 and reviewed in 2003 (Australian Government, Department of Family and Community Services, 2003), focuses on "improving employment opportunities for people with disabilities" (p. 3) to ensure that they have "the opportunity to be active and productive members of society" (p. 1).

It is important to note that all of these documents, with the exception of Britain's *Valuing People,* are not specific to people with developmental disabilities. As a result, although such documents may be useful in building a climate that supports workforce participation for this group, it is difficult to measure their impact in terms of providing increased opportunities or increased support to people with developmental disabilities.

PROGRAM MODELS

A number of program models are in operation. This section describes some of the more prevalent ones and issues involved in each. Although these programs may be given different names in different countries, their major characteristics remain the same.

Sheltered Workshops

Despite the many new program models that have been developed, it is probably still true that the most common type of work-related program for people with developmental disabilities is the sheltered workshop. As noted, a sheltered workshop is a segregated setting, where people with developmental (and/or other) disabilities come to engage in work and related activities, such as training. The underlying, often unstated, assumption in sheltered workshops is that many people with developmental disabilities are unable to work in the community until they have been "trained"—or perhaps never. (As explained later in this chapter, others have challenged this assumption.) The primary focus of sheltered workshops is (or should be) work.

The most typical kind of work undertaken in workshops has traditionally been packaging and assembly, but workshops have undertaken many different kinds of work, including collating, stuffing envelopes, labeling, mailing, woodworking, printing, janitorial work, clerical work, crafts, ceramics, sewing, and recycling. Most often the work done in sheltered workshops is contract work. Workshops get contracts from regular businesses to do certain jobs. It is often difficult to find contract work that is challenging for the workshop participants and that generates a significant amount of revenue. Some people believe that certain businesses take advantage of sheltered workshops by paying rates that are unrealistically low. The workshops may accept this work because even low-paying work is better than none.

In general, most of the work in sheltered workshops is done on site. However, some may also involve people working in groups outside the workshop. For example, in a mobile work crew, a group, accompanied by a supervisor, may be involved in cleaning bus shelters or doing park maintenance, usually with very little contact with any other workers. People from the workshop may be placed, as a group, in an industry in the community, in what is known as an enclave. Although this setup does provide more opportunities for interaction with other employees, the size of the group and the fact that it is often located apart from the others are definite limiting factors. In both these models, the organization for whom the work is being done typically pays the workshop, on a contract basis, rather than the individuals who are doing the work. See Display 33.1 for an illustration of issues related to workshops.

Because workshops are not considered "real" places of work, workshop participants do not have the legal status of "employee" and usually are not covered by minimum-wage legislation. Most workshops do not generate very much money, and the typical workshop wage is abysmally low. Although the primary focus of sheltered workshops has generally been work, many have also engaged in various kinds of training. This training often, but not always, has some relationship to work, such as providing people with skills that will enhance their work capacity. Some kinds of training include work skills (e.g., operation of a particular kind of machinery), academic skills (e.g., literacy, numeracy), community skills (e.g., use of public transportation), and social/behavioral skills (e.g., communication).

As noted previously, some workshops have seen their role as providing long-term sheltered employment to some, if not all, people who attend. However, some workshops do provide (or attempt to provide) a training environment, either as one component of the workshop or, in some instances, as the only focus. (Sheltered workshops that see their only or major activity as training may identify themselves by such names as employment training centers or adult training centers.) In these settings, people generally engage primarily in work activities, but the expectation is that after a certain period of time, they will leave to go elsewhere. Almost invariably, the goal is that they will be able to get a job. If this is not feasible, then they will be referred to another program—often another kind of training program or a long-term sheltered workshop.

The potential advantage of a training-focused program is that it may enable program supervisors to make decisions based on the training needs of individuals rather than the production needs of the program. It may allow the program to provide more focused, specialized training in particular skills. For some people with disabilities, an environment that is defined as a training environment may be more acceptable than one that is not, because it carries with it the hope of something better at the end. For the most part, though, this "readiness" model has not been effective for people with developmental disabilities. All too often, these programs are characterized by training and work activities that lack intensity and relevance to the real world of work. Many people with developmental and other disabilities move from one segregated training environment to another, never achieving that elusive "real" job.

It is worth noting that some sheltered environments, particularly those that define themselves as training environments, may use community placements for assessment and training purposes. People may be placed in community settings for short (or not so short) periods of time to help determine their interests and abilities or to learn particular skills. Although this has merit, it also has limitations. Employers often do not have the same expectations when people are placed for only a short period of time, so the assessment may not provide an accurate reflection of how the individual will perform in a real job. Furthermore, moving from one work setting to another is likely to be stressful for many people with disabilities. (Most people, with or without disabilities, find adjusting to a new work setting somewhat stressful.) Many people would argue that the staff time spent in supporting people in short-term community work settings would be better spent supporting people in real jobs.

Finally, in some workshops, people are involved in purely recreational activities during part of the regular workshop day, such as going swimming once per week. Although swimming is unequivocally beneficial for health, having such recreation facilities at a workplace is a controversial issue for some.

Although these are very real issues, it is important to remember that as of 2007, a good many people with developmental disabilities still attend sheltered workshops. For many of these people, workshops provide a place to go each day where they can interact with other

Display 33.1

Case study: Robert

Robert has been attending the sheltered workshop for many years. He has many friends there and enjoys the work. The major work activity at this workshop is packaging. The shop has a number of different kinds of heat sealing machines—blister packaging, shrink wrapping, and vacuum packaging. Robert gets great satisfaction out of working on these machines and is known to be a safe and reliable worker. The staff of the workshop are encouraging Robert to get a job through the supported employment program, but Robert does not really want to. Most of his friends who do work in the community only work a few hours a week, and the work they do does not always sound very interesting. Some of them have lost their jobs a number of times, and some say that other people are not very nice to them. Robert has heard that they are going to close this workshop and he is worried about what will happen to him.

people and engage in various kinds of work activities. For most, the workshop is the only place they have ever worked, and it is important to them. They define it as their "work," and they like the opportunity to socialize with their friends. For many families, sheltered workshops represent safe and secure places where their family member is looked after and kept busy. For all of these reasons, it is important that efforts to develop alternatives to workshops are well planned and sensitive to the needs of individuals and families.

Despite their inherent limitations, some are "good"—or at least better—when compared with "bad" ones. The better ones ensure that people with developmental disabilities are treated with dignity and respect. They try to find work that is interesting and challenging and to pay people as much as possible. They continue to look for ways to improve the work environment. They also strive to enable people with developmental disabilities to move out of workshop settings, and are often involved in developing new and better ways of supporting people to work in the community.

Table 33.2 summarizes some main criticisms of workshops. As workshops have very much fallen out of favor, many organizations have closed their sheltered workshops or converted them into other kinds of programs. For those who have long advocated for the closure of sheltered workshops, this would seem to be good news. However, some of the alternatives that have been developed do not always appear to be very different or to be an improvement.

Table 33.2. Ten things that people have often criticized about sheltered workshops

1. The work in sheltered workshops is most often simple, repetitive work (although there are some exceptions).
2. People in workshops almost always receive very little pay.
3. People in workshops have little choice—either about the people with whom they work or about the kind of work they do.
4. In an environment where everyone has a developmental disability, other people are likely to have low expectations.
5. In an environment where there are low expectations, people are less likely to learn.
6. People learn from others around them; segregated environments provide fewer opportunities for learning.
7. People in sheltered workshops learn the skills they need to be a sheltered workshop worker rather than the skills they need to be a worker in the community.
8. Workshops are not effective in enabling people to get jobs.
9. When people with developmental disabilities are kept in sheltered workshops, the community gets the message that they belong there rather than in regular work places in the community.
10. As a result of all of the above, sheltered workshops create and sustain low expectations and reinforce devalued status. They make it more likely that people with developmental disabilities will be treated poorly within society.

Source: Sandys (2002).

Supported Employment

In the early 1970s a new program model, supported employment, arrived on the scene. First developed in the United States, through the work of Wehman and others, supported employment provided a new way of thinking about and responding to the issue of employment for people with developmental disabilities.

Traditionally, workshops have endeavored to train people and, when they are considered "ready," find jobs for them. Supported employment programs work in reverse. They help a person find a job and then they provide the training and support that is necessary to ensure success. Instead of a train-then-place approach, they use a place-then-train-and-support approach. The underlying assumption of supported employment programs is that people with developmental disabilities can work successfully if they are provided with the appropriate amount and type of support. Supported employment is more than simply a new strategy for preparing people for the world of work. It reflects a fundamental change in philosophy. It says that the opportunity to work in the community is a right, not a privilege for which one has to prove one's readiness, and that service providers have an obligation to ensure that the needed supports are provided.

Supported employment programs have enabled people with developmental disabilities to work in a wide variety of settings, including offices, factories, hospitals, restaurants, car dealerships, laboratories, schools, colleges and universities. The jobs are as varied as the settings and include, for example

- Clerical work
- Food preparation and/or service
- Maintenance, janitorial work
- Manufacturing, packaging, and/or assembly
- Laundry
- Mail room and/or internal mail delivery
- Shipping and receiving
- Document assembly
- Assistant in medical laboratory
- Car detailer

As is often the case, the term *supported employment* has been used somewhat differently by different people in different (or sometimes even the same) places. Even aside from the Australians, who use the term to refer to sheltered workshops (and use the term *competitive employment* for what is called *supported employment* in other countries), there are variations in what is or is not included. Thus, some consider enclaves or mobile work crews as a form of supported employment. Some consider situations in which people are paid but receive less than minimum wage as supported employment. Some consider **self-employment** situations (discussed next) as a form of supported employment regardless of how much the individual earns.

In this chapter, supported employment includes paid work in ordinary, inclusive business environments, with regular support provided, as required. Of course, some work environments are large enough to absorb more than one individual with a disability. Although this definition does not preclude more than one person with a disability working in a particular setting, it does exclude situations such as enclaves, where people with disabilities are grouped together on the basis of their disability.

The Supported Employment Process Much has been written about the supported employment process. The following brief overview draws on a number of sources: Callahan and Garner (1997); Hagner and DiLeo (1993); Little (1993); Mcloughlin, Garner, and Callahan (1987); Sandys (2002); Wehman and Moon (1988); and Wehman, Sale, and Parent (1992).

A number of issues must be addressed so that an individual with a developmental disability can succeed in the workplace. In order to find a suitable position, the support worker must have a very thorough understanding of the interests, characteristics, and talents of the individual for whom a job is being sought. Other issues include the following:

- In what kinds of environments will the person be most comfortable?
- How does the individual learn?
- What supports are likely to be required?
- What physical adaptations are likely to be required?

Generally, this means spending a considerable amount of time with the individual and, often, with those who know him or her best.

As well as information about the individual, the support worker needs to be familiar with the kinds of jobs that might be available. Because it is known that many jobs may never be advertised, looking at any personal contacts the individual may have through family or friends is a helpful strategy for identifying potential jobs. A high degree of creativity is required in the job-finding process. Often, support workers collaborate with employers to carve out a job suitable for a particular individual. Although this may involve some redistribution of work tasks within a particular setting, it can result in a job that is tailor made to fit the supported employee's needs at the same time it meets the employer's needs very effectively.

Once a suitable job has been located, the supported employment staff will be available to provide a range of supports to the supported employee and to the work site. In the early days of supported employment, it was assumed that the support worker would provide on-site training and support to the individual, intensively at first, then phasing out his or her involvement as the person learned the required skills and adapted to the workplace. It has since been recognized that success depends, in large measure, on the support that is provided to the individual by the workplace. As much as possible, the goal is for the supported employee to be a regular employee, with supervision, training, and support provided by the employer and co-workers. The term *natural support* (Nisbet, 1992; West et al., 1997) is often used to refer to this kind of support—support that is generated naturally by the work place—as distinguished from the external support provided and paid for by the service agency.

The emphasis on natural support has sometimes been interpreted to mean that support workers did not need to provide much in the way of services. It is now known that the support worker has a key role to play in providing support to the workplace so that it can effectively meet the needs of the supported employee. Employers may need assistance in designing modifications or job adaptations. Supervisors and co-workers may be quite willing to provide direction, mentoring, and other supports to the employee, but they may not always know how to go about doing this. Especially at the outset, but often on an ongoing basis, the support worker can play a critically important role as facilitator, supporter, problem solver, and coach.

Success in the workplace does not only depend on the individual's ability to acquire specific work skills but also on having the skills necessary for daily living. Supported employees may need assistance in learning nonwork routines (e.g., buying lunch at the company cafeteria, learning to use the time clock, traveling to and from work by public transit). They may require assistance regarding appropriate grooming and dress or the development of appropriate behaviors and social skills. Display 33.2 provides an illustration of supported employment.

The support worker must continue to monitor the situation to ensure that the individual is paid equitably for the work done and to deal with any concerns that arise. In addition, the support worker, in collaboration with the employer, must continue to engage in a process of job building to ensure that the supported employee's job continues to grow as the individual acquires competencies. In the ideal situation, the supported employee will have opportunities over time to improve productivity and to participate in a wider range of tasks, with ever-increasing levels of responsibility and complexity. These new job responsibilities will be reflected through longer hours of work and higher rates of pay.

Most people change jobs periodically, usually because they choose to, but sometimes as a result of performance problems or layoffs. The support worker must be available should the supported employee lose his or her job or decide that a change would be desirable.

Pay in Supported Employment Programs Typically, there is an expectation that people in supported employment programs will be paid a "regular" wage. As long as someone is in an employment relationship, the law usually requires that they be paid no less than the legal minimum wage. Nevertheless, some people with developmental disabilities may work at a significantly slower pace, making it unlikely that they will be hired if the employer must pay the full wage. Display 33.2 shows how, as a solution, some disability organizations enter into a contract with the employer so that the employer pays the organization a specified amount for the work done and then the organization pays the worker. (Workshops have been doing this for some time for work stations and mobile work crews.) Since the individual is not an employee of the disability organization, that organization need not pay minimum wage. Another "strategy" that has been used is for an employer to agree to hire a person for a portion of the day at minimum wage standards and then to agree that the person can remain at the work place for additional hours for training purposes. For example, the person may be at the work site for 7 hours a day but only receive pay for 4.

Without a doubt, these approaches are problematic. Some argue that people are better off working in the community than in segregated settings or not at all, even if this does not generate more income. Others argue that there must be mechanisms to ensure that people with developmental disabilities are hired and are paid minimum wage. One such mechanism is that of a wage subsidy. In these instances, arrangements are made to provide a subsidy to employers, compensating them for loss of productivity. Thus, in Australia, the Employer Incentive Strategy (Australian Government, Department of Family and Community Services, 2003) includes a Wage Subsidy Scheme, which "allows for the wages of each worker with a disability to be fully or partially subsidized . . . for 13 weeks, up to a maximum value of $1500" (p. 20). This short-term wage subsidy is intended to promote increased worker competitiveness by enhancing skills and **work experience.**

This same report (Australian Government, Department of Family and Community Services, 2003) indicates that Wage Subsidy Schemes are also in place in Sweden, Denmark, the Netherlands, Austria, and Norway; however, the report notes that the literature on wage subsidies shows mixed results. Also, wage subsidies may "create job opportunities for some people" and help to "address misconceptions that employers may have about employing a person with a disability," but there is the risk that "employment may not last beyond the subsidized period" (p. 14). Display 33.3 presents further information on wage issues in supported employment.

In some instances, employers who have hired people with disabilities have been allowed to pay them below minimum wage if they can provide evidence that the person's productivity is consistently and significantly below the norm for the job. The Supported Wage System currently in place in Australia, under the Employer Incentives Strategy, allows employers to pay supported employees less than the going rate, based on a productivity-based wage assessment. It is interesting to note that such a scheme was available in Ontario, Canada, some years ago. Many people with disabilities and their advocates objected to it, believing that people with disabilities should have the same employment rights as everyone else, that the process was stig-

Display 33.2

Case study: Harry

Harry has been working at a fast food restaurant for 4 years. Typically, he arrives each day at 9:00 A.M. and stays until 2:00 P.M., but sometimes he works extra hours. When he arrives in the morning, he does a series of maintenance tasks, including sweeping and mopping the front lobby, cleaning the bathrooms, and emptying the garbage cans. Then, he fills the dishwasher and scrubs the pots and pans. If there is time, he restocks the napkins, cream, sugar, and condiments on the counter.

The Supported Employment Program found this job for Harry. Harry had said that he wanted to work in a restaurant so that he could learn to cook. Harry was not paid at all for the first month that he worked there. After that he was paid for 2 hours per day, with the rest of the time being considered "training." Over a period of time, the hours for which he was paid increased and now he is paid for all the hours that he works.

For the first 6 weeks, Harry's support worker was at the restaurant all of the time, but over time she started coming less often. Now she visits occasionally, but most often she just checks in by telephone approximately once per month.

Harry likes this job more than the workshop he attended before, but he is getting bored because the job is the same every day. He would like to learn to cook and do more things, to work longer hours, and to be paid more.

Harry likes the people he works with and they say they like him. However, he never sees them outside of work.

matizing, and that it provided a means by which people with disabilities could be exploited. In fact, few employers ever applied for this "handicapped" permit.

Some organizations have supported people to do **unpaid work** in the community. The organizations may refer to this as "volunteer" work. Many people find satisfaction through volunteer work and feel that they are making an important contribution to their communities. Working for a nonprofit organization may well be a positive experience for a person with a developmental disability. It should be noted, however, that most people do not consider volunteer work to be a substitute for paid work. Furthermore, not all unpaid work qualifies as volunteer work. Working for a for-profit company without pay, or at a job that others are being paid to do, does not qualify as volunteer work. It is simply unpaid work. As such, it does not fall within this chapter's definition of supported employment.

Display 33.3

Case study: Mary

Mary works for a large financial services company. She told her support worker that she wanted to work in an office like her sister, and she is very satisfied with her job. She has been working here for 3 years. She works full time and is usually very busy. When she first started, she worked only part time and did mostly cleaning jobs—keeping the coffee room clean and the vending machines stocked. However, she learned those tasks very quickly and would then wander around aimlessly. Her supervisor noticed how carefully and quickly Mary completed her work and began to think about what other kinds of tasks Mary might be given. Over time, and with the support of her co-workers, Mary is doing a wider variety of tasks, including keeping the supply room in order, notifying her supervisor when particular supplies are running low, collecting mail from various departments and bringing it to the mailroom, and shredding documents. When there is a special event, Mary is responsible for compiling the folders for all participants and inserting name cards in their holders. She also does a great deal of photocopying, sometimes making copies of larger or smaller size. Recently, she started answering the telephone when the receptionist is busy.

Mary has developed close relationships with two of her co-workers. When she moved to a new apartment, these two women helped her paint her new place. She is always included in staff events at or after work.

The Growth of Supported Employment Programs There are no reliable data available about the number of people with developmental disabilities involved in supported employment or the rate of growth. Thornton and Lunt (1997) suggested a proliferation of supported employment programs across the European Union. Jenaro et al. (2002) discussed supported employment in the international context and reported that it exists in places as diverse as Peru, Zambia, Spain, Germany, England, and Australia. Wehman, Revell, and Kregel (1998) titled their article "Supported Employment: A Decade of Rapid Growth and Impact." The existence of 38 state chapters of the American Association for Persons in Supported Employment (APSE; with new chapters being continually added since its inception in 1988) and the rich literature on supported employment, primarily from the United States, speak to a continuing lively interest in supported employment in that country.

There have also been articles about supported employment from a variety of countries, including Britain (Stevens & Martin, 1999), Wales (Shearn, Beyer, & Felce, 2000), and Finland (Saloviita, 2000). Nevertheless, although difficult to substantiate, it does appear that after a sustained period of expansion, there has perhaps been a leveling off of interest in this model. A 2004 article by Braddock, Rizzolo, and Hemp was titled, "Most Employment Services Growth in Developmental Disabilities During 1988–2002 Was in Segregated Settings" (p. 317).

Measuring Success A number of studies indicate that successful supported employment programs have made a significant difference in the lives of many people with developmental disabilities (e.g., see for example, Dale, 2002; Mank, Ciotti, & Yovanoff, 2003; Moseley, 1988; Pedlar, Lord, & Van Loon, 1989; Walsh et al., 1999; Wehman & Kregel, 1994). Through supported employment programs, people with developmental disabilities are working in a large variety of settings, doing many different kinds of work. Overall, these people are earning more than they earned in sheltered workshops, sometimes at rates of pay that are well above the legal minimum wage. These studies have indicated that in general, people who are in successful supported employment programs are proud of working in the community, enjoy the work they do, and get along well with their co-workers. They say they prefer working in the community to working in a sheltered workshop.

Employers who have hired people with developmental disabilities usually say that they are good workers: They work hard, learn new skills, are well liked, and are an asset to the workplace. Some employers have observed that when co-workers become involved in supporting a person with a developmental disability, this sometimes carries over to other relationships at work. People may become more supportive of one another—not only supportive of the person with the disability. Finally, many employers take great pride and derive personal satisfaction from having had such a positive impact on the life of a person with a developmental disability (Sandys, 1999b).

Nevertheless, it is clear that supported employment programs have not had the results that many people expected (e.g., see Mank, 1994). Mank et al. (2003) reported on a survey of 14 supported employment programs in the United States. Although they found some evidence of improvement in the "typicalness" of jobs, work rates, work quality, and relationships with co-workers, they reported "little or no increases in wages or hours outcomes for people in jobs acquired later in the 1990s compared to earlier in the 1990s" (p. 193).

When supported employment programs first began, there was a feeling that this new approach would help to find community employment for many people with developmental disabilities and that as a result, many sheltered workshops would be able to close. Sadly, this has not happened. It is hard to know exactly why. Certainly, fluctuating economic conditions has been one factor. During times of economic slowdown, many supported employees lose their jobs, and finding new jobs for people with developmental disabilities is much more difficult.

Another factor is that "good" jobs have not always been found for people with developmental disabilities. Some so-called supported employment jobs do not provide a real wage (or perhaps any pay at all). Some involve people in work activities far worse than what they had done in the sheltered workshop. Some people work in very isolated situations with no opportunities to interact with others with or without disabilities. They may work on only a very part-time basis, perhaps a few hours per week, leaving many empty hours with nothing to do. Even when people do have good jobs and are making a real contribution to the workplace, employers and co-workers may sometimes treat them as though they are children. Sometimes, supported employment programs have not provided enough—or the right kind of—support. Also, well-intentioned employers may not know how to deal with the challenges that individuals with disabilities present. They may become discouraged when positive changes in behavior or productivity are not forthcoming. Noting the isolating effect that supported employment may have, Rooney (2002) emphasized the need to develop mechanisms to ensure that supported employees can maintain the relationships that are important to them.

A number of factors have impeded the success of supported employment initiatives. It is beyond the scope of this chapter to discuss the intricacies of funding, but there is no doubt that funding for supported employment has often been uncertain. All too often, the assumption is made that supported employees should not require a great deal of support or that support should not be provided for very extended periods of time.

A study by Dale (2002) noted that in areas serving primarily people with developmental disabilities (as compared with those serving people with a range of disabilities) there were "lower levels of individuals achieving independence on the job and much higher levels of support needs" (p. 27). This study also noted that people are more likely to maintain their jobs when supports are not limited. The time limitations on the length of time a person may be provided with support is a significant disincentive to involving people with developmental disabilities, because a good many in this group are likely to require support on a continuing rather than on a time-limited basis.

The combination of these factors together has, for at least some people, taken the shine off supported employment. Some organizations and staff who have worked very hard to find jobs for people with developmental disabilities have become discouraged and have begun to question whether supported employment really works. Society has been unprepared for the difficulties related to enabling people—some who have significant degrees of impairment and many who have spent years and years in segregated workshops—to work in the community. Perhaps there has been a tendency to give up too easily when things have not worked out as hoped. It is necessary to remember that even the most positive program model will not work well if it is not implemented properly. Supported employment has the potential to work very well for many people. The challenge is to make it work well for many more.

Self-Employment and Worker Co-ops

Another service model that is receiving a considerable degree of attention is self-employment (Canadian Association for Community Living, 1996; Neufeldt & Albright, 1998; Neufeldt et al., 2000). *Self-employment* refers to a situation in which someone (in this case, a person with a developmental disability) is not an employee but works for him- or herself. This might mean, for example, that the person is an independent contractor, doing specific tasks for someone else in return for pay. Or it might mean that the person actually has his or her own business and that he or she regularly sells a product or service. Co-ops form another type of self-employment that has emerged in Ontario. In co-ops, a group of people jointly own and manage a business. In the United Kingdom, these models come under the rubric of "social firms."

People with developmental disabilities have various types of business. Some examples include the following:

- Refurbishing nuts and bolts
- Catering
- Document processing
- Packaging and assembling
- Cleaning and maintenance
- Recycling and/or salvaging
- Pet grooming and dog walking
- Restaurant operation
- Mailing service

The Appeal of Self-Employment and Co-ops

Self-employment has been on the rise in Western society for some time. A study published by Human Resources Development Canada (2000) suggested that this growth reflects changes in the labor market—that is, it is a response to downsizing, contracting out, layoffs, and other factors. Thus, it is not surprising that it would be considered as a possible model for people with developmental disabilities.

At the same time, it has become obvious that sheltered workshops have very real shortcomings. Along with this are the frustrations that many service providers have encountered in their efforts to implement supported employment programs. If sheltered workshops are outdated and supported employment is just too challenging, what other options are there? Self-employment seems to be an appealing possibility.

It has been hoped that self-employment will provide greater stability, avoiding the ups and downs of the labor market and the insensitivities encountered in some workplaces. Those who promote this model note that within Western society, having one's own business commands some respect and is therefore likely to have a positive impact on an individual's status and self-esteem. They suggest that self-employment maximizes choice and self-determination and enables people to earn more money. Adding to this attractiveness is the fact that self-employment may be perceived to be a relatively low-cost option.

It is possible that this view of self-employment is somewhat romanticized. The previously noted Canadian study (Human Resources Development Canada, 2000) presented a more realistic view of self-employment, drawing on the actual accounts of people who have chosen self-employment. Although this study did not focus on people with disabilities, the findings are nevertheless most certainly relevant. It suggests that self-employment is more likely to have positive outcomes for managers, professionals, and white collar workers and less chance of success with people with fewer skills (and less access to capital). Lack of benefits, isolation, lack of training opportunities, and negative attitudes of others were some of the disadvantages cited. The study does not suggest that self-employment outcomes are always negative, but it does identify some of the challenges inherent in making it successful. These include personality factors, expectations, job requirements (e.g., for niche markets, regarding advanced technologies), skills, and access to needed business training.

Relatively little data are available on the outcomes of self-employment for people with developmental disabilities. There is some evidence that the level of satisfaction of those involved is very high and that people take pride in being self-employed (Sandys, 1999a; Neufeldt et al., 2000). Dale (2002) noted that the few people in the study were somewhat more stable in their employment situations, compared with regular employment. These same studies suggest that people in self-employment tend to work fewer hours and earn less, overall, than those in supported employment.

There are some risks associated with self-employment. When a person runs a business, the amount of money earned depends on the success of the business. The person may earn a great deal, a modest amount, very little, or nothing at all. The person may end up with less money than he or she had to begin. Nothing prevents an entrepreneur from operating at a loss. To date, it seems that people with developmental disabilities who are self-employed tend to generate very limited amounts of income, often only marginally more than they earned in the workshop and certainly less, on average, than those who are working in the community through supported employment programs. Also, because they are generating income through self-employment, they are not covered by minimum-wage legislation.

A number of co-ops have been developed by disability service organizations, which have taken some of the contracts that the sheltered workshop had and turned these over to a small group of workshop participants. Some of these workshops-turned-co-ops have shown an increase in per person earnings, likely because the members of the co-op were selected from among the best workshop workers, with the others being directed to the nonvocational options.

The work people with developmental disabilities do through self-employment is most likely to be similar (or identical) to what they did in the sheltered workshop and/or to involve such things as cleaning and recycling activities. Almost invariably, people either work alone and risk being very isolated, or they work with other people with disabilities in small (or not so small) segregated settings. In many instances, people with developmental disabilities who are self-employed, whether on their own or as part of a co-op, work a very limited number of hours. A pilot study of developing co-ops

(Sandys, 1999a) found that these tend to be very closely tied to sheltered workshops, so that in reality, people have little choice over such things as the nature of the work to be done, the pricing of contracts, the way work is to be done, or the people they worked with. Although there may be an illusion that co-op members are in charge, the range of decisions to be made may be very small as compared with a typical business. See Display 33.4 for an example of a co-op experience.

Starting a business—even a small one—is a challenge for anyone. Although some new businesses prosper, many do not. Few business enterprises can escape the impact of hard economic times. In many jurisdictions, there is no financial support available for setting up a business. Nonetheless, being self-employed is something that many people find appealing, and one would not want to deny this opportunity to people with developmental disabilities. The extent to which this is a realistic option for many people with developmental disabilities remains, at this writing, an open question. This chapter previously discussed the characteristics of a good job. In any self-employment or co-op situation, it is necessary to examine how many of these characteristics are present. How like or unlike a sheltered workshop is a co-op? What would need to happen to generate more positive outcomes for self-employment?

Often there are no reliable sources of funding for the development of self-employment initiatives for people with developmental disabilities. Although some projects are able to obtain development funds, usually the workshop or the larger organization of which the workshop is a part absorbs these costs. In some places, **supported self-employment**—or support to the self-employed person (as distinct from the business development aspect)—may be provided through a supported employment program. Of course, family and friends may provide a great deal of support that is not funded. Indeed, they often play a pivotal role in helping a person establish and sustain self-employment.

Display 33.4

Case study: Joanna

Joanna works in a co-op with nine other people, doing various kinds of packaging and collating. Joanna and the other people in the co-op used to work in a sheltered workshop. The people who ran the workshop told Joanna and the nine others that the workshop was closing and offered them—because they were the best workers—a chance to set up a co-op in which they would do the same kind of work. They would own the business and be the "boss of themselves."

Joanna is very much a leader. She is the president of the co-op. Although the work is very much the same, Joanna feels that she and the others do get to make more decisions. They do not decide what work they do (someone from the organization that ran the workshop brings the contracts to the co-op and sets the prices), but they can decide if they want to work longer or shorter hours. They interviewed several people who used to be workshop staff members to select the person they wanted to hire as the manager. When someone new wants to join the co-op, the other co-op members have to agree that the person can join. If someone is not working or is causing trouble, the others can ask the manager to have that person fired.

The manager is paid the same wages he received in the workshop; the co-op owners make somewhat more than they did in the workshop, but it is far lower than minimum wage. They could earn a bit more if they decided to work longer hours, but they do not want to.

NONVOCATIONAL ALTERNATIVES

A section on program alternatives that do not focus on work and employment perhaps may initially appear misplaced in this chapter. However, given that such programs are being developed at an ever more rapid rate, a brief discussion is required.

There has been a growing trend to developing a range of **nonvocational alternatives** for people with developmental disabilities as an alternative to work. As service providers have felt thwarted in their efforts to promote community employment and self-employment opportunities for people, and as they have felt the effects of funding cutbacks, many organizations have sought to develop other options that provide people with developmental disabilities an opportunity to participate in activities that although not necessarily work related are meaningful for the individual. Some people's disabilities are perceived to be too severe for them to be able to engage in work in a meaningful way, so other activities are developed for these individuals. In other situations, people with developmental disabilities indicate that they do not want to work and service providers believe that this choice must be respected. Still another practice is to involve older adults with developmental disabilities in leisure activities more typical of retirement, even though they may still be in their 40s and 50s. Such programs may also be seen as filling a gap when people are working on a very part-time basis or perhaps during periods of unemployment.

A program that is fairly typical, and that people can have access to as much or as little as they wish, might involve a range of activities—literacy training, cooking classes, computer classes, art and music classes, recreational activities, and community outings. Funding for these programs is often quite low. It may be provided through developmental services, or, in part, through **individualized funding** to which individuals have access.

Pros and Cons

What are the pros and cons of these programs? On the positive side, they provide an opportunity to socialize and perhaps to learn new skills. They provide some structure to a person's life so that there is something to do each day. They ensure that family members are not responsible for providing support all day, every day. They relieve the burden that family members must bear from providing continuous support. Undoubtedly, these are important benefits.

Although some of the individual activities may be age appropriate, many of these programs often seem more like day camps than places that typical, valued adults are likely to attend. Given the importance society attaches to work, why should it be assumed that for some people work is simply not considered an issue? For people who may be able to work, such as those who are between jobs, it is hard to see how this kind of program will enhance their chances of finding employment once again.

As segregated settings, these programs contain all of the disadvantages that were noted in the discussion of sheltered workshops. Segregated programs give society the message that people with developmental disabilities need to be kept separate and cannot be an integral part of the community. There is an irony in sending this message—another part of the same organization may be trying to communicate exactly the opposite message through its supported employment program.

Perhaps the greatest risk with these programs is that they distract from focusing on work and employment for people with developmental disabilities. It is necessary to seek more effective ways of implementing supported employment programs, to assist more people with meaningful self-employment, to develop co-ops that are truly self-managed (and perhaps inclusive), and to advocate for legislation that will provide ongoing employment support for people who need it. Instead, society is content with a renamed and somewhat dressed up segregated day activity program for people with developmental disabilities—and it is called progress. It cannot be forgotten that in the absence of some kind of subsidy, people in these programs are not paid. Welfare or some other form of subsidization is essential for many people with developmental disabilities to get by financially.

The Question of Choice

Under what circumstances should people with developmental disabilities not work? As noted previously, not everyone works, nor should all people with developmental disabilities work. Certainly there are circumstances under which not working is a valid choice. Nevertheless, because work plays such a central role in the lives of most adults in society, it is important to examine the validity of promoting these nonwork alternatives.

People with developmental disabilities should not be forced to work. However, in situations where people indicate that they do not want to work, it is important to question the context in which they are making this choice. Is it a fear of new situations? Perhaps such choices reflect the fact that the work available to people with developmental disabilities often does not meet the criteria of good work? Enabling people to work at good jobs in the community requires an enormous amount of energy and skill on the part of those providing the service. Perhaps people with disabilities are being encouraged to "choose" those options that are easier for service agencies to provide.

On the one hand, demonstrating respect for people with developmental disabilities means honoring their wishes. On the other hand, not encouraging them to develop a work identity and work ethic limits their options for a more satisfying and self-determining life in the future. The challenge is to create the circumstances that encourage people with developmental disabilities to want to work.

THE ISSUE OF CHARITY: PERCEPTIONS AND EXPECTATIONS

Historically, and to this day, people with developmental disabilities have been viewed by society as dependent, as objects of pity, and as recipients of charity. The presumption has been that by and large, people with developmental disabilities are not able to be productive. As a result, they often have not been provided with the opportunities they need to become productive. These perceptions and expectations have certainly had an impact on how work-related services have developed over the years.

Although there has been some change in this regard, seeing people with developmental disabilities as recipients of charity is still very common. Thus, some employers may still consider hiring a person with a developmental disability an act of charity (Sandys, 1999b). Also, in some instances, people may give work to an individual who is self-employed, or to a sheltered workshop, as a charitable act. Under the best of circumstances, something that starts out as an act of charity later proves to be a good economic investment. The employer is surprised at how productive the supported employee really is; the customer is pleased with the quality of the work that is done. In many other situations, however, the perception that this is charity results in little or no pay, low expectations, and limited opportunities.

The charity image is well entrenched and difficult to change. People with developmental disabilities are not helped by being in situations in which others see them simply as the recipients of charity. Whether helping someone to find a job or seeking work for an individual who is self-employed, it is important to emphasize people's strengths (they can be productive) and rights (they must have the same opportunities as everyone else). Where it is not possible to assist people to become employed, it is necessary to do everything possible to enable them to participate in activities that promote valued participation and social inclusion. Growth and development, contribution, and interaction with the broader community are essential.

Certainly, some of the initiatives noted in this chapter do reflect the fact that attitudes toward people with developmental disabilities may be changing. As more people with developmental disabilities are enabled to become involved in positive work situations, more is contributed to the ongoing process of changing society's attitudes.

FOR FURTHER THOUGHT AND DISCUSSION

1. Compare work situations that you have been in with the work situations of some people who have intellectual or developmental disabilities with whom you are familiar. How are they similar or different?
2. Should sheltered workshops be eliminated? Why or why not?
3. Why do you think that the implementation of supported employment programs has proven to be so difficult?
4. Is it okay for a person to work in the community and get less than minimum wage? (After all, he or she would not earn minimum wage in the workshop.)
5. What are the advantages and disadvantages of self-employment and co-ops with sheltered workshops and with supported employment?
6. With regard to employment, do you think that things are getting better or worse for people with intellectual and developmental disabilities? What evidence is there for your position?

SUMMARY

This chapter has examined the nature and importance of work and has discussed the historical development of work-related supports and services. It looked primarily at three service models: sheltered workshops, supported employment, and self-employment. It examined the rationale behind each service model. For each model, it was possible to identify positive outcomes for some people, but it was also noted that each model presented many challenges. The chapter also discussed the development of nonwork day programs and some of the issues surrounding these.

Regardless of setting, all caregivers can contribute to promoting positive work experiences for the people they support. Undoubtedly, much remains to be done in terms of developing strategies that will enable people with developmental disabilities to have opportunities to participate in work that is inclusive, meaningful, challenging, and profitable.

REFERENCES

Accessibility for Ontarians with Disabilities (AODA), 2005.

Americans with Disabilities Act (ADA) of 1990, PL 101-336, 42 U.S.C. §§ 12101 *et seq.*

Australian Government, Department of Family and Community Services. (2003). *Improving employment opportunities for people with a disability: Report of the review of the employer incentives strategy.* Retrieved August 16, 2004, from http://www.facs.gov.au/internet/fascinternet.nsf/content/employerincentives.htm

Barnes, C., Mercer, G., & Shakespeare, T. (1999). *Exploring disability: A sociological introduction.* Cambridge: Policy Press.

Bellamy, T., Peterson, L., & Close, D. (1975). Habilitation of the severely and profoundly handicapped: Illustrations of competence. *Education and Training of the Mentally Retarded, 10,* 174–187.

Braddock, D., Rizzolo, C., & Hemp, R. (2004). Most employment services growth in developmental disabilities during 1988-2002 was in segregated settings. *Mental Retardation 42*(4), 317–320.

Callahan, M.J., & Garner, J.B. (1997). *Keys to the workplace: Skills and supports for people with disabilities.* Baltimore: Paul H. Brookes Publishing Co.

Canadian Association for Community Living. (1996). *Everybody's business: Self employment issues and opportunities for people with a disability.* North York, ON, Canada: Author.

Dale, J. (2002). *Community involvement council: Employment outcomes project.* Tillsonburg, ON, Canada: Community Involvement Council and The Employment Outcomes Steering Committee.

DuRand, J., & DuRand, L. (1978). *The affirmative industry.* St. Paul: Minnesota Diversified Industries.

DuRand, J., & Neufeldt, A. (1980). Comprehensive vocational services. In R. Flynn & K. Nitsch (Eds.), *Normalization, integration and community services* (pp. 283–298). Baltimore: University Park Press.

Gold, M. (1980). *Try another way: Training manual.* Champagne, IL: Research Press.
Government of Canada. (1998). *In unison: A Canadian approach to disability issues.* Retrieved February 6, 2002, from http://socialunion.gc.ca/pwd/unison/unison_e.html
Government of Canada. (2004). *Government of Canada Disability Agenda.* Retrieved August 16, 2004, from http://www.sdc.gc.ca/asp/gateway.asp?hr=en/hip/odi/11_goc.shtml&hs=eya
Hagner, D., & DiLeo, D. (1993). *Working together: Workplace culture, supported employment, and people with disabilities.* Cambridge, MA: Brookline Books.
Human Resources Development Canada. (2000). *Own-account self-employment in Canada: Lessons learned, final report.* Retrieved August 16, 2004, from http://www11.hrdc-drhc.gc.ca/pls/edd/OASEC_148000.htm
Jenaro, C., Mank, D., Bottomley, J., et al. (2002). Supported employment in the international context: An analysis of processes and outcomes. *Journal of Vocational Rehabilitation, 17,* 5–21.
Little, T. (1993). *Streetwise guide to supported employment.* Toronto: Central Marketing Consulting Services.
Lord, J. (1998). *The Nabors experience: Lessons in building community.* Toronto: Green Dragon Press.
Mank, D. (1994). The underachievement of supported employment: A call for reinvestment. *Journal of Disability Policy Studies, 5*(2), 1–24.
Mank, D., Ciotti, A., & Yovanoff, P. (2003). Supported employment outcomes across a decade: Is there evidence of improvement in the quality of implementation? *Mental Retardation 41*(3), 188–197.
McCallum, D. (1989). *Discrimination of the invisible minority.* Paper presented at the 4th Canadian Congress of Rehabilitation, Toronto.
Mcloughlin, C.S., Garner, J.B., & Callahan, M. (1987). *Getting employed, staying employed: Job development and training for persons with severe handicaps.* Baltimore: Paul H. Brookes Publishing Co.
Moseley, C.R. (1988). Job satisfaction research: Implications for supported employment. *Journal of The Association for Persons with Severe Disabilities, 13*(3), 211–219.
Murphy, S.T., & Rogan, P.M. (1995). *Closing the shop: Conversion from sheltered to integrated work.* Baltimore: Paul H. Brookes Publishing Co.
Neufeldt, A., & Albright, A. (1998). *Disability and self-directed employment.* Toronto: Captus Press.
Neufeldt, A., Sandys, J., Fuchs, D., et al. (2000). Supported and self-directed support initiatives in Canada: An overview of issues. *International Journal of Practical Approaches to Disability, 23*(3), 24–36.
Nisbet, J. (Ed.). (1992). *Natural supports in school, at work, and in the community for people with severe disabilities.* Baltimore: Paul H. Brookes Publishing Co.
Noll, S., & Trent, J.W. (Eds.). (2004). *Mental retardation in America: A historical reader.* New York: New York University Press.
Ontarians with Disabilities Act, 2001. SO 2001.
Osburn, J. (1998). An overview of social role valorization theory. *SRV/VRS, 3*(1), 7–12.
Pedlar, A., Lord, J., & Van Loon, M. (1989). *The process of supported employment and quality of life.* Kitchener, ON, Canada: Centre for Research and Education in Human Services.
Race, D. (2002). The historical context. In D. Race (Ed.), *Learning disability: A social approach* (pp. 23–52). London: Routledge.
Rooney, S. (2002). Employment: An opportunity to belong? In D. Race (Ed.), *Learning disability: A social approach* (pp. 85–99). London: Routledge.
Roeher Institute. (2002). *A demographic overview of people with intellectual disabilities in Ontario.* Toronto: Author.
Saloviita, T. (2000). Supported employment as a paradigm shift and a cause of legitimation crisis. *Disability & Society, 15*(1), 87–98.
Sandys, J. (1993). *"It does my heart good": The perceptions of employers who have hired people with intellectual disabilities through supported employment programs.* Unpublished doctoral dissertation, University of Toronto.
Sandys, J. (1999a). "It does my heart good": How employers perceive supported employees. In R. J. Flynn & R. Lemay (Eds.), *A quarter-century of normalization and social role valorization* (pp. 305–316). Ottawa, ON, Canada: University of Ottawa Press.
Sandys, J. (1999b, May). *Worker co-ops for people with intellectual disabilities.* Unpublished paper, presented at the 1999 Annual Conference of the Society for Disability Studies, Washington, DC.
Sandys, J. (2002). *Evaluating your supported employment program.* Baltimore: Author.
Shearn, J., Beyer, S., & Felce, D. (2000). The cost-effectiveness of supported employment for people with severe intellectual disabilities and high support needs: A pilot study. *Journal of Applied Research in Intellectual Disabilities, 13*(1), 29–37.
Simmons, H. (1982). *From asylum to welfare.* Downsview, ON, Canada: National Institute on Mental Retardation.
Stevens, P., & Martin, N. (Eds.). (1999). Supporting individuals with intellectual disability and challenging behaviour in integrated work settings: An overview and a model for service provision. *Journal of Intellectual Disability Research, 43*(1), 19–29.
Taylor, S., Biklen, D., & Knoll, J. (Eds.). (1987). *Community integration for people with severe disabilities.* New York: Teachers College Press.
Thornton, P., & Lunt, N. (1997). *Employment policies for disabled people in eighteen countries: A review.* Retrieved August 9, 2004, from http://www.logos-net.net/ilo/150_base/en/publ/041.htm
Trent, J.W. (1994). *Inventing the feeble mind: A history of mental retardation in the United States.* Berkeley: University of California Press.
U.K. Department of Health. (2001). *Valuing people: A new strategy for learning disability for the 21st century.* Retrieved August 16, 2004, from http://www.archive.official-documents.co.uk/document/cm50/5086/5086.pdf
Walsh, P.N., Mank, D., Beyer, S., et al. (1999). Continuous quality improvements in supported employment: A European perspective. *Journal of Vocational Rehabilitation, 12,* 165–174.

Wehman, P., & Kregel, J. (1994). *At the crossroads: Supported employment ten years later.* Richmond: Virginia Commonwealth University.

Wehman, P., & Moon, M. (Eds.). (1988). *Vocational rehabilitation and supported employment.* Baltimore: Paul H. Brookes Publishing Co.

Wehman, P., Revell, G., & Kregel, J. (1998). Supported employment: A decade of rapid growth and impact. *American Rehabilitation, 24*(1), 31–43.

Wehman, P., Sale, M., & Parent, W. (1992). *Supported employment for persons with severe disabilities: From research to practice.* Andover, MA: Andover Medical Publishers.

West, M.D., Kregel, J., Hernandez, A., et al. (1997). Everybody's doing it: A national study of the use of natural supports in supported employment. *Focus on Autism and Other Developmental Disabilities, 12*(3), 175–181.

Wolfensberger, W. (1980). The definition of normalization: Update, problems, disagreements, and misunderstandings. In R. Flynn & K. Nitsch (Eds.), *Normalization, integration and community services* (pp. 71–115). Baltimore: University Park Press.

Wolfensberger, W. (1992). *A brief introduction to social role valorization as a high order concept for structuring human services* (Rev. ed.). Syracuse, NY: Training Institute for Human Service Planning, Leadership and Change Agentry, Syracuse University.

34

Lifestyles of Adults with Intellectual and Developmental Disabilities

Ivan Brown, M. Katherine Buell, Rivka Birkan, and Maire Percy

WHAT YOU WILL LEARN ABOUT IN THIS CHAPTER

- Historical influences
- Current lifestyles
- Key lifestyle factor: Where people live
- Key lifestyle factor: Inclusion
- Effects of ethnicity and race on service use
- Effects of intellectual disability on health care availability
- Considerations for the future

Lifestyle is a word that has come to refer to the way that people carry out their lives—the places they go, the people with whom they interact, and the many things they do in the course of simply living their lives. In this chapter, *lifestyle* refers specifically to the means and extent of achieving the full range of life activities and fulfilling life needs of adults with intellectual and developmental disabilities. It includes how people spend their days and nights; whether they are employed; where they sleep; with or among whom they sleep; and what support they require for daily activities such as brushing their teeth, using the toilet, dressing, eating, taking medication, cooking, shopping, and spending money. It includes if and how individuals interact with their friends and families, how they participate in their communities, how they spend leisure time, how they experience spirituality, how they get around, how they are entertained, and many other aspects of life that people enjoy.

Lifestyle is different for every human being because everyone is unique, with his or her own characteristics and behaviors. Each person has a distinct set of places to be, a distinct group of people with whom to interact, and a distinct array of things to do in life. Individual lifestyles are often described for people with intellectual and developmental disabilities through such methods as life-story books, journals, file documents, photo albums, and collections of written or verbal narratives. Lifestyles are unique in style and content, and they differ as widely as the individuals to whom they pertain.

It is also possible to describe, in a more general way, how groups of people carry out their lives. Lifestyle is not currently a distinct area of study, but aspects of it can be inferred from the study of the whole lives of people with disabilities. Thus, this chapter looks at some of the aspects of lifestyles of groups of people and identifies two important influences on it: place of residence and inclusion. In doing so, it is essential to keep in mind that what is known about the lifestyles of people with intellectual and developmental disabilities has been gathered primarily from information about people with disabilities who are known to service systems. Much less is known about the lifestyles of those many individuals who live independently, at home with their families, or in other situations not known by the service systems.

HISTORICAL INFLUENCES

The lifestyles of adults who are considered to have intellectual or developmental disabilities in the early 21st century have emerged from a centuries-old history of such people living within the cultures where they happened to find themselves. Usually, this was the very culture into which they were born. Their treatment by others differed widely across the ages and across cultures—from being ostracized or even left to perish to being cherished and thought of as gifts from God (see Chapter 2 for more details). Such differences in treatment arose from corresponding differences in beliefs and values of the populations at large. It can be said in general, though, that their treatment by others always has had substantial impact on their lifestyles—how they lived their lives among their fellow humans.

The authors are very grateful to Karolina Machalek and Mark Shumelda for providing resource information for this chapter and to Oleh Romanchuk, Medical Director, Dzherelo Children's Rehabilitation Centre, Lviv, Ukraine, for supplying a case example.

Some of the important influences on modern lifestyles of adults with disabilities began in the 18th century in Europe and North America. During that century, there developed a growing interest in both education for this group and in humanitarianism. Interest in education for people who were often formerly considered "unteachable" blossomed, incorporating ideas from Condillac's sensationalism (sensations are the basis of mental life) and Reid's faculty psychology (the soul has capacities to carry out reasoning activities). In particular, though, Itard's (1801) demonstration of learning by Victor, the *enfant-sauvage* or "the wild boy of Aveyron," helped precipitate a revolution in thinking about the treatment of people who were different. People saw firsthand that Victor could learn a large number of new skills, when taught in a logical sequence, and that these new skills helped him to behave in ways that were close to the ways in which others around him behaved. Many began to believe that it might be possible for all people to learn new skills if appropriate teaching methods could be discovered and followed.

Related to the growing interest in education in the 18th century was a corresponding growth in humanitarianism. Humanitarianism is a philosophical perspective that views the differences among people in a kindly, sympathetic manner and that treats people with difference in humane ways. The growth of humanitarianism during this period represented a change from previous philosophy that attributed difference to various causes, ranging from God's will to work of the devil.

The Beginning of Institutions

As a result of this humanitarian influence, educational programs (sometimes formalized as schools) and whole lifestyle programs (sometimes formalized as communities or hospitals) were set up in France, Switzerland, the United States, and many other countries to provide good diet, exercise, medical care, and skill development. The idea was that appropriate environment and training could increase a person's competency so that he or she would eventually be able to live in the community.

These programs were, for the most part, conceived, developed, and run by well-meaning people who spent a great deal of creative energy in attempting to develop what they considered to be the best possible environments and training. Some programs were set up in modern, elaborate buildings with extensive grounds that were designed to bring tranquility to those who were to benefit from them. Even at the beginning of the 20th century, many institutions for people with disabilities (often referred to as "feeble-minded" at the time, as the various types of difference, such as lower intelligence, mental illness, and cultural deprivation were not necessarily thought of as separate) were "model" self-supporting communities, providing work, training, social support, and many other advantages. Because this was a lifestyle that was thought by many to be appropriate for feeble-minded people, there was considerable general support for creating institutions that were pleasant and fulfilling.

It is difficult to say how many of the people who would now be considered to have intellectual and developmental disabilities were involved in such programs. No doubt, they formed only a small portion of those who might have been involved. The large majority of people with various types of difference continued to live as they had for centuries—with their families, on the farms, and in the villages and towns that were their homes. Then, as now, little was known of these people who did not become known to the service system, as it existed at that time. They simply lived their lives in the only way they knew, among their families and neighbors. They had lifestyles that are now considered naturally occurring, carrying out the activities that they were able to do in ways that fit with the activities of the others around them and living in environments that offered natural supports. It is somewhat ironic that this is the type of lifestyle that is being promoted for people with disabilities in the early 21st century.

In spite of the apparently good intentions of those who founded and built institutions, over time these places of residence became larger and larger, and more and more people with various disabilities and differences were sent to live in them for longer and longer periods of time. Gradually, they became the overcrowded and underfunded institutions of the 20th century.

Decline of Standards in Institutions

Why was there a decline of standards in institutions? A number of interrelated factors contributed to the change. Among the most important were periods of economic hardship that resulted in reduced support, the growing number of poor working and nonworking people who emerged out of industrialization, and changing social values. Social values were influenced, in particular, by the growth of science and the triumph of rational thought and scientific theories over faith, superstition, and adherence to doctrine (see also Chapter 2).

The growing interest in rational thought helped to fuel overpopulation and underfunding of the institutions. As an example, people became very interested in and accepting of Darwin's theories. Darwin's ideas of survival of the fittest and natural selection produced a more biological view of humanity, and social Darwinism provided a way to explain why all people were not equal. His ideas provided a biological reason for low intellectual functioning and suggested that education might be rather futile because intellectual function was inherited and thus largely predetermined and unchangeable.

One phenomenon that arose from this line of thinking during the overpopulating of institutions was "eugenic alarm" (Meyers & Blacher, 1987), a set of beliefs that feeble-mindedness and criminality were closely related and that both were primarily inherited. Feeble-minded people were thought to be inferior and potentially dangerous; thus, it was thought that they needed to be protected from society within institutions for the good of themselves and others. Furthermore, it was thought important for the general well-being of society to protect itself against such people having children, as, through propagation, they would only add to the "problem" of feeble-mindedness that threatened the vitality of society.

Factors Leading to Deinstitutionalization

The growing urbanization of society that resulted from industrialization also contributed to changing attitudes toward people with difference. Urbanization concentrated larger numbers of people into small geographic locations, and people with difference became highly visible. At the same time, living in towns and cities became more complex and required a higher level of daily living skills than living in rural areas. In addition, greater mobility, the absence of extended family networks, and the dense concentration of people all detracted from informal or natural supports for people who lived in towns and cities. These factors meant, for people with disabilities and other needs, that there was a growing need in urban areas for more formal programs to be developed and maintained.

All of these influences put pressure on programs to educate. The increased numbers of people being admitted to special educational programs resulted in too many demands on the resources available and hence an increasing number of failures. Thus, special schools and special educational programs also came to be regarded as institutional.

The immediate environment of the institution was the predominant (and often the only) influence on the lifestyle of people who lived in them. The view that this was an acceptable, or even the preferred, lifestyle for people with disabilities was not reversed until the 1970s, when the normalization principle first developed by Nirje was popularized by Wolfensberger (1972). This principle was interpreted, somewhat erroneously over the years following its publication, to mean that people with developmental disabilities should live in ways that made them blend into the larger culture and live as closely as possible to the ways that people without disabilities live. Still, the way it was interpreted reflected a growing trend in the field of disabilities to include people with disabilities in community living. Display 34.1 provides information about deinstitutionalization and residency trends in the United States.

Becoming Part of the Community Again

The widespread international adoption of the normalization principle, as it was interpreted, into service policy and procedures had a considerable influence on the lifestyles of people with intellectual and developmental disabilities, both inside and outside institutions. Most jurisdictions began to initiate a series of reforms and advances in services to people with developmental disabilities that changed the lifestyles of people with developmental disabilities to a considerable degree.

In the early 1970s, people began rethinking which services should be made available to people with intellectual and developmental disabilities. It was gradually accepted that there was a need to downsize and eventually close the institutions and to provide considerably more resources to support community-based services. The overall intent of this shift in thinking was that institutional living as a lifestyle should be phased out and that community living as a lifestyle should be encouraged and supported.

This shift in thinking has received support from the governments in some jurisdictions more than others. In Norway, for example, institutions were all closed by 1994, but many still operate in a number of European countries. In North America and the United Kingdom, the trend has been to phase out institutional living on a gradual basis. As of 2007, institutions account for only a small portion of the services to people with disabilities. Government shifts in thinking were accompanied by numerous policy reports that not only articulated the change in thinking but also often set out long-range plans for putting into practice the stronger emphasis on community living.

Such policy documents typically emphasized the need for community, rather than institutional, services for both children and adults with developmental disabilities. They set in motion the establishment of a number of new community programs and services, especially in the 1970s and early 1980s, that substantially broadened the range of services that were available. These new programs provided a wider range of services to those who were involved in community living as a lifestyle than had formerly been the case, and they addressed many, but not all, aspects of lifestyle that were being addressed within the institutions. For example, specialized medical, dental, and psychiatric care, as

Display 34.1

Deinstitutionalization and residency trends in the United States

Deinstitutionalization is the international movement of closing institutions and moving individuals with intellectual and developmental disabilities from institutions to community living. It has been estimated that there are slightly more than 4 million Americans with intellectual or developmental disabilities living outside of institutional settings in the United States. (Larson et al., 2001). In June 1977, an estimated 247,780 people lived in residential programs, and an estimated 207,356 (83.7%) of these individuals lived in institutions of 16 or more people. In June 2003, the number had increased to a reported 273,204 people in residential programs (the actual number was estimated to be 402,281), with only 72,474 (26.5%) living in institutional settings of 16 or more people. Prouty, Smith, and Lakin (2002) reported that in 2001, there were 77,180 individuals with intellectual and developmental disabilities living in public and private facilities and 35,155 individuals living in nursing facilities. In another report, 82.0% of individuals with intellectual or developmental disabilities lived in facilities with 15 or fewer residents; 68.5% lived in places with 6 or fewer residents, and 44.1% lived in places with 3 or fewer residents (Breedlove et al., 2004).

These numbers represent only a fraction of the population with intellectual and developmental disabilities. Approximately one third of such adults (18 years and over), use residential services outside their family homes (Larson et. al., 2001). Although approximately 80% of all individuals with intellectual or developmental disabilities, and about one third of all such adults, live with their families, most social policies and funding for community services are directed at individuals living outside of their homes (Lakin et al., 2004).

Deinstitutionalization and residential trends vary across each state. As of June 30, 2003, the majority of individuals with intellectual and developmental disabilities in 47 states received residential services in settings of a maximum of six residents. In Mississippi, 58.1% received services in settings of 16 or more residents. Most states continue to operate at least one large institution. As of June 2003, only Alaska, the District of Columbia, Hawaii, Maine, New Hampshire, New Mexico, Rhode Island, Vermont, and West Virginia were no longer operating any large state facilities (Breedlove et al., 2004).

There has been a national push toward deinstitutionalization, and national goals have been established to promote inclusion of individuals with disabilities in community life. On February 1, 2001, U.S. President George W. Bush presented the New Freedom Initiative (NFI; U.S. Department of Health and Human Services, 2003b), implementing the Olmstead vs. L.C. decision of 1999 (Cornell University Law School, n.d.). Here, the court ruled that states are required to place people with disabilities in community, rather than institutional, settings when treatment professionals have determined that community placement is appropriate. It also ruled that unjustified placing or keeping people with disabilities in institutions deprives them of community living experiences and thus constitutes a form of discrimination prohibited by Title II of the Americans with Disabilities Act (ADA) of 1990 (PL 101-336; Lakin et al., 2004). Ironically, and in spite of an Executive Order indicating public intentions (U.S. Department of Health and Human Services, 2003a), the NFI has been followed by the least reductions in state institution residents in the past 30 years, both in number and percentage of residents (Lakin et al., 2004).

See Lakin, Prouty, & Coucouvanis (2006) for an update on this topic.

well as recreational and social programs, were often limited in community services.

Moves from institutional to community living have not been without difficulties. These are documented in numerous publications. Not all people with developmental disabilities want to move. Few have been able to exercise any real choice in the location or type of their new homes (Brown, Raphael, & Renwick, 1999), parents sometimes find such moves to be unsettling for them, staff find themselves without jobs, and other resources are displaced. The effect of such moves on the lifestyle of individuals can be very substantial. Very often, these effects are positive, but occasionally they are not (see Display 34.2 for an example).

The shift toward community living represented a move away from disability being viewed as an illness and a deficit that is best dealt with in separate, isolated environments and toward it being viewed as a set of unique characteristics of a portion of society's overall population. This resulted in disability being seen as a much broader social issue—an issue for which society itself had a responsibility—than had been the case pre-

Display 34.2

Case study: Robert

Robert is 35 years old. His mother is not living, and his father is in a nursing home. He has lived in a large care facility for many years and resisted leaving when he was moved to a community home. He ran after the van that took him to the community home, and he was so unhappy—as shown through aggressive behavior—that arrangements were made to move him back to the facility. The day he was set to move back, he packed his suitcase and sat on the steps of the community home hours ahead of the time the van was to come to take him "home." He works in a sheltered workshop within the facility and feels strongly that he does not want to leave again.

From Brown, I., Renwick, R., & Raphael, D. (1999). *The Quality of Life Project: Results from the follow up studies* (p. 68). Toronto: Centre for Health Promotion, University of Toronto; adapted by permission.

viously. In many jurisdictions, legislation added to this change in perception by requiring that special education, and adult living services that covered a wide range of lifestyle issues (especially housing, employment, and physical care) be provided within the community. Finally, these changes were strengthened by improvements to human rights laws and policies (see Chapters 5 and 6 for additional details) in a wide variety of countries and their states and provinces. On the whole, these influences supported the perception that governments, service providers, some parent and other advocacy groups, and to some extent the public at large, were actively seeking to initiate lifestyle changes for people with disabilities. The idea was to move away from institutions being the dominant influence and toward communities being the dominant influence.

One interesting question associated with increasing support for community living lifestyles is whether this lifestyle is actually better for people with intellectual and developmental disabilities. Are they happier? Are they more fulfilled? Is this a better way of life? In large part to address these questions, the concept *quality of life* developed quickly and became accepted during the 1990s, primarily in the United States, Australia, and Canada, and later in a wide range of other countries (see the work of Schalock 1990, 1996b, 1997, in particular). Quality of life works to address lifestyle questions by functioning, for example, as a conceptual framework for policy, research, and practice (e.g., Schalock et al., 2002); as an overall approach to service practice (e.g., Brown & Brown, 2003); as an approach to evaluation (e.g., Schalock, 1996a, 2001); and as a focus for work in physical health and medicine (e.g., see http://www.qolid.org).

CURRENT LIFESTYLES

There are many ways to get a glimpse of the lifestyles of people with intellectual and developmental disabilities. People with disabilities and their families have authored books that describe life from the individuals' perspectives (see Appendix B at the end of the book). Another way is to describe aspects of life of people with disabilities from survey information (e.g., see Anderson, 1993). By way of an illustration, some of the results of one 8-year longitudinal study are presented next.

A Lifestyles Snapshot

This study, carried out in Ontario, Canada, with a sample of 504 adults with intellectual and developmental disabilities, was drawn from an estimated population of 26,000 people receiving government services (Brown, Raphael, & Renwick, 1997; Brown et al., 1999). It looked at people's lives from a whole-person, quality of life perspective, as described by Brown and Brown (2003). The description of this study in the section below (adapted with permission from Brown & Brown, 2003) provides a snapshot of nine aspects of lifestyle. This example is not intended to be representative of all populations, but it shows some of the successes and ongoing challenges of promoting community-based lifestyles.

1. Where People Live

Type of Home

- 10% lived in large care facilities.
- 19% lived in community-based small care residences.
- 25% lived independently in communities, with or without support.
- 46% lived with families.

Where Those Homes Are

- More than 90% of the homes were small care and independent living, and approximately 75% of individuals living with families lived in urban areas.
- Few people lived in communities that were either very well to do or poor.
- The ethnic makeup of people's communities varied, but it was more likely to be described as very homogeneous than as very diverse.
- Most people lived in communities where there were only some or very few other people with special needs.
- Most of those in small care or with family lived in detached or semi-detached houses, whereas those

who lived independently in their communities were most likely to live in buildings with multiple units. The other buildings in their neighborhoods were usually similar to the ones in which they lived.

Choice in Homes

- Almost all people who lived independently in communities chose their own homes and the location of their homes, although they often had help choosing.
- Approximately three quarters of those who lived in small residences had little or no choice about where they lived.
- Almost one half of the adults who lived with families did not perceive that they had yet experienced an opportunity to choose their living arrangement. Of the remainder, surprisingly few considered that they were living with families because of personal choice.

2. What People's Homes Are Like

Table 34.1 lists 20 characteristics of homes of people who live in community settings. It is interesting to compare these characteristics with the characteristics of most people's homes. Note, for example, that it is only in the group of people who live independently that everyone can play the radio at any time—something many people take for granted.

Table 34.1. Percentage of people who answered yes to 20 characteristics of their homes

	Where people live		
Characteristic of home	Small care facility	Independent residence	Family home
Has own bedroom	78	96	94
Has private space	87	97	85
Has own furniture	91	95	85
Has own door key	24	96	49
Has own money to spend	59	94	35
Can come and go any time	25	93	36
Can eat at any time	67	98	78
Can watch television any time	88	99	91
Can play radio any time	89	100	92
Can engage in consensual sex	56	91	6
Can invite guests to home	78	95	71
Has own television	39	94	61
Has own stereo	60	87	68
Has own VCR	20	67	37
Has enhanced TV connection	33	85	44
Has own telephone line	17	85	18
Has pets	13	32	39
Has plants	19	42	22
Has hobbies in home	86	83	79
Receives mail in own name	96	98	84

The reader is encouraged to see additional information on characteristics of homes in Anderson (1993).

3. What People Are Able to Do

- 40% were described as also having some type of physical disability.
- 26% could do most activities of daily living on their own, 35% could do many activities on their own, 22% could do only some life activities on their own, and 17% were able to do few life activities independently.

4. Going to Community Places and Events

Most people got out and did things in their communities—including entertainment and recreational activities—at least once per week, and many of them got out almost every day. By contrast, about two thirds of those who lived in institutions got out and did things in their communities less than once per week. Cost was somewhat more of a barrier to getting out and doing things in one's community for people who lived independently than it was for people who lived in more structured environments. Getting around was a problem for only one third or fewer of people with disabilities, somewhat more so for people who lived in community homes than for people who lived independently or with their families.

Ten things identified as helping people with developmental disabilities to go places and do things in their communities were as follows:

- Accepting people in the community
- Receiving encouragement from friends, family, and volunteers
- Receiving encouragement from staff
- Having places and activities to go to
- Having skills to get around the community
- Having skills to interact with people in the community
- Having transportation readily available
- Living in a small community that is easy to navigate
- Knowing the community and being known in the community
- Wanting to go—showing initiative

5. Occupational Activities

In Western culture, occupational activity—what people do during the day—plays a large role in how they live their lives and how they see themselves fitting in with those around them (see Chapter 33).

Number of People Who Have Occupational Activities

- Of those who lived in communities, 70% had a major occupational activity of some type (attended work, school, or a program regularly at least half days).

What People Did

For those who lived in communities, information is broken down by living arrangement:

- *Small care homes:* Overall, 83% had a major occupational activity. Of these, approximately 40% attended developmental or recreational programs, and approximately 50% worked in sheltered workshops or were in vocational training. The rest (10%) worked in the community or attended school.
- *Independent living:* Overall, 67% had a major occupational activity. Of these, almost 40% worked in the community, and approximately the same percentage worked in sheltered workshops or were in vocational training. Volunteer work was done by 14%, and the remainder engaged in various other activities.
- *With families:* Overall, 83% had a major occupational activity. Of these, fewer than 20% worked in the community, whereas more than 40% worked in sheltered workshops or were in vocational training. Approximately 20% attended a developmental or recreational program and about the same percentage attended school.

Personal Choice

- Approximately 25% chose their occupational activity (some on their own, others with assistance).
- 15% had some limited choice.
- 60% had no part of the decision about what they do during the day.

6. Financial Support

Source of Financial Support

- 93% were supported financially by government pensions.
- 7% earned their own incomes or were supported in other ways (usually by family).
- All but 3% claimed that their current financial resources were sufficient to provide for their basic needs (e.g., shelter, food, clothing).

Control Over Finances

- Other people controlled the finances for 87% of those in small care community homes. This can be partly explained, perhaps, by the low levels of daily living skills of people who lived in these settings.
- Other people controlled the finances of 84% of those who lived with families.
- Even for those who lived independently, only 30% controlled their own finances, whereas 31% had help and 39% had their finances controlled by someone else.

7. Services People Get

The number and types of services received play a major role in defining the way people lead their lives. This is especially so for the one third of adults with disabilities for whom services affect most areas of their lives and even for the one third for whom services affect some or many areas of their lives. Ten general categories of services provide a flavor of the range of services that are most commonly used by adults with intellectual and developmental disabilities (see Table 34.2).

8. Health

Health is a central lifestyle issue, especially because health is being seen more and more in recent years as a resource for daily living (World Health Organization, 1996).

- 13% of the total sample had a serious illness within the past 6 months (almost all, 12%, were hospitalized).
- 17% of the total sample had a formal dual diagnosis (intellectual disability and mental health problem), although twice that number of people were considered informally to have a dual diagnosis. This percentage did not differ significantly among people who lived in institutions, community homes, and independently. Only for those who lived with families was the percentage of dual diagnosis lower.
- Psychotropic medications were used by 47% of people who lived in institutions, 26% of people who lived in community homes, 19% of people who lived independently, and 10% of people who lived with family.

9. Support from Friends, Family, and Other People

Those with whom people interact regularly make up an important part of lifestyles:

- Almost all identified staff or other professional people as people who provided both practical and emotional support.
- Approximately half or fewer of the people who lived outside institutions received support from friends and family, although most of those who lived with their families received support from their parents.
- Approximately one third of those who lived independently received support from a spouse or special person, and approximately one quarter of these same people received support from other people they knew in the community.

Table 34.2. Percentage of adults who used ten categories of services

Occupational programs or work support provided	61
Residences or support in independent living provided	52
Recreation provided or supported	51
Life skills supports	50
Physical health	46
Financial management or support with money	39
Mental health	35
Transportation provided or supported	31
Spiritual aspects of living	18
Other types of service	10

- All other types of support from other people were low.

Summary of Lifestyles Snapshot

The preceding nine aspects of life provide a snapshot of the lifestyles of adults with intellectual and developmental disabilities in one quality of life study. The findings about these aspects raise many questions and issues about the types of support given to people with disabilities. This information neither gives a complete picture of what people's lives are like nor describes what the lives of individuals are like, but it does suggest a range of ways that people with developmental disabilities, as a whole, live their lives.

KEY LIFESTYLE FACTOR: WHERE PEOPLE LIVE

Where people live is probably the most important factor in determining lifestyles of people with intellectual and developmental disabilities. Since the 1970s and early 1980s, when schools began to be required to provide education to all children with disabilities, children with intellectual and developmental disabilities have been increasingly likely to live in their family homes with their parents, often continuing into adulthood. There are several reasons for this, but there are four main reasons:

1. Children are not admitted to large care facilities, or even to small care facilities, in most jurisdictions unless there are specific and justifiable reasons, such as better or more appropriate care.
2. In most more developed countries and in many other countries, children are provided special education in their local schools (see Chapter 31); thus, they are able to continue living in their family homes.
3. The growth of community-based programs has led to an increase in support for parents who have children living at home.
4. Policy shifts by governments of many jurisdictions since the 1990s have increased the responsibility of families (see Chapter 4). This has resulted in a more open expectation that families will contribute, if they can, to the care and support of their children with disabilities. In practice, this means that more children and adults are continuing to live in their family homes, usually with their parents.

For adults who do not live in their family homes, an objective of service providers is to assist them to move toward independence as much as possible (Brown et al., 1999). Many people who lived with families or in small care homes in communities have moved to a wide variety of supported living options that offer more independence. Some community agencies no longer operate group homes but now support people in their own homes, even if they require 24-hour support. Acquiring one's own home may involve renting an apartment (shared or unshared), purchasing a house or condominium (shared or unshared), moving in with a support family, adapting a property to fit specific physical needs, and many other options (see Displays 34.3 and 34.4 for illustrative examples).

KEY LIFESTYLE FACTOR: INCLUSION

Inclusion is now a major issue for adults with intellectual and developmental disabilities. Current use of the term *inclusion* stems from the trends of the last few decades, particularly deinstitutionalization, community living, and integration. The concept of inclusion itself is quite simple, though: People with disabilities need to be included in, rather than excluded from, the general or prevailing culture.

In most parts of the world, both legislation and general policy directions of the past few decades have supported the principle of inclusion, directing and encouraging service providers to support people in being part of the "community"—that part of the general culture represented by the vicinity within which they live. Putting inclusion into practice, in the context of practical everyday living, has proved to be more difficult, however. Part of this difficulty involves supporting individuals in ways that help them live in their communities among other people. This is only a first step toward inclusion. This first step, although necessary, ensures that people are *in* the community, but does not necessarily mean they are *of* the community. Being *of* the community, a major goal of inclusion, means living in it, enjoying it, being accepted and valued by others in it, as well as contributing to it.

Because inclusion is a broad topic, one way of thinking about it in a more manageable way is to consider its various aspects. Three of the most important aspects of inclusion are discussed next: integration, social support, and personal choice.

Integration

In its simplest form, *integration* means that people with disabilities living among other people without disabilities in community settings. It aspires to more than this, though. Its goal is for people with intellectual and developmental disabilities to belong within the larger culture and to form part of it. People with disabilities form a small and diverse cultural group within the broader culture. The larger culture often makes some accommodations (e.g., wheelchair ramps, the use or pictures rather than words on signs), but it is the needs of this smaller culture group that, for the most part, define what has to be supported so that they will be able to live within the larger group. It has sometimes been a for-

Display 34.3

Examples of housing options for individuals with disabilities

Supported living: In supported living environments, the individual with a disability works with professionals, and sometimes with family, to choose the location and style of house or apartment and to decide whether to live alone or select housemates. The degree of professional intervention and professional assistance varies with the severity of the disability. The individual may need 24-hour personal care or none at all.

Small group homes: In small group homes, approximately four to eight individuals (regulations differ among jurisdictions) live together, usually with support by staff. Prouty and Lakin (1997) reported that U.S. small group homes accommodated 3.8 people on average.

Campus-style settings: Housing for people with disabilities is clustered on one site, and residents share central facilities such as a day center, places of worship, and shops (Robertson et. al., 2001).

Supervised home or apartment: In a supervised home or apartment, individuals live either with roommates or alone in semi-independent units or apartments; staff or other caregivers live separately within the same complex (Martinson & Stone, 1993b).

Adult foster care/adult family homes: In adult foster care and adult family homes, one person or more lives with a community family. The family assists individuals in activities of daily living.

Section 8 housing: This is a program run through the U.S. Department of Housing and Urban Development (HUD), which provides vouchers to pay for low-income rent (Martinson & Stone, 1993a).

Section 202 housing: This is another HUD voucher program for aging individuals and individuals with disabilities; it is open to nonprofit agencies with a tax-exempt status from the Internal Revenue Service (IRS). Rent prices are set at a maximum of 30% of the individual's income. The section 202 program is supplemented with Section 8 vouchers (Martinson & Stone, 1993a).

Board-and-care homes: Individuals are supervised and provided with room and board, but the staff neither assist with personal care nor train the residents.

Nursing facilities: Nursing facilities are for individuals with health problems who require extensive daily professional and licensed nursing care and supervision, restorative and rehabilitative care, and help with daily living needs.

Personal care services (PCS) home: PCS homes are available in the United States. The bed capacity in a PCS home is determined by state regulations. Individuals in a PCS home receive medical assistance or support for their activities of daily living but do not receive any formal training (Martinson & Stone, 1993a).

Semi-independent group residential facility: Three to eight individuals, who require little assistance in daily living, cohabitate without live-in staff. Agency staff members oversee the home, as needed. Further support may be provided by family members, service coordinators, or learning-skills program staff.

Residential care facilities: Three or more individuals live within a sheltered facility or neighborhood home, grouped according to the level of assistance required. Residents at Level 1 require room, board, and minimal supervision. The resident does not have behavior problems and can function relatively independently with only reminders from staff. Residents at Level 2 need direct, nonmedical assistance with activities of daily living. Residents at Level 3 need up to 24-hour supervision for activities of daily living, medication, ambulation, behavior management, or other issues.

Demonstration housing: These facilities differ widely, but all are aimed at older individuals (older than 60) and funded by the U.S. Administration on Aging. For example, an ECHO house is a housing module that can be temporarily erected adjacent to the supervising family's permanent home, then removed when no longer necessary (Martinson & Stone, 1993b).

Own home: Individuals with disabilities, like other people in their communities, live in various types of homes (e.g., condominiums, apartments, houses, mobile homes), either on their own or with others such as friends, immediate family members, or other relatives (Martinson & Stone, 1993b).

Specialized residences: Some disorders present particular challenges to families. The MukiBaum Treatment Centres (2005) in Ontario, Canada, are building a residential program to accommodate people with dual diagnosis autism and other complex needs.

Display 34.4

Juanito: Life in a community home

Juanito is a 48-year-old who lives with three other men in a newly constructed single-dwelling home in a small town. Each man has his own bedroom in this rambling bungalow. There are always two paid staff in the home to assist the men with most aspects of their day to day life. Juanito can speak well, but at times it is necessary to encourage him to express his feelings and wishes.

Juanito needs the assistance of staff to manage his meals and routines, his finances, and his medical needs. One staff member is designated as his case manager and advocates for his needs and wants. Juanito has a number of interests, and it is important to him to be active. He especially enjoys playing golf and attending ice hockey games. He also reads the newspaper, especially to follow his favorite teams. Staff assist him in maintaining his interests in bowling and swimming, and often the staff and all four men are involved in activities together on the weekend.

The home has a van, which allows the staff to provide the transportation Juanito requires for his interests as well as to and from his daily education program. This program, which involves a class of his peers with a teacher and a teacher's aide, is very important to him. He is studying numeracy and literacy skills and is making good progress. His program is also focused on building community skills, and the class often goes into the community to learn appropriate social or financial skills or just become familiar with community resources.

Juanito receives a government disability pension, which is managed by his case manager with input from his family. His family members are supportive of him, and visit him—or he visits them—on a regular basis.

Sarah: Life with the family

Sarah is a 40-year-old with Down syndrome who has lived in her family home all her life. Their single-dwelling home is in a middle-class neighborhood in a medium-size city. Her family now consists of just her and her 75-year-old father. Sarah's mother died 2 years ago, and there are no other siblings available to help with the support needs.

Sarah's father helps her with meals, self-maintenance, money needs, and health needs. The only time they are apart is when Sarah goes to her day program. He also usually drives her to this program, although she sometimes takes the bus.

Sarah attends the recreational day program every day. She participates in a rotating schedule of activities with other adults with disabilities. Because she has limited verbal communication abilities, she makes her needs and opinions known through gestures and actions. Some of her actions can be quite intense and often require the support of staff to determine the expressed need or opinion. Sarah enjoys her social contact with others at her day program and is involved in some evening and weekend activities provided by a local service agency.

As both Sarah and her father age, they worry about long-term placement, social and emotional contacts, and continuity of services. One community service agency involved with the family is trying to assist Sarah and her father with these concerns.

Andrea: A family beyond the institution

Andrea is a 78-year-old who has lived with a family for 5 years. Prior to this, Andrea lived in a large care facility. Andrea has a history of mental illness that requires psychiatric intervention intermittently. Because of this, when plans for closing her large care facility were being made, it was originally decided that Andrea would move into a small care home in the community. Instead, Andrea moved into the home of a couple in their 50s who are paid a per diem fee for supporting Andrea. She is very proud of her independence, and she has been accepted into the family's routines and activities—becoming part of the family.

The couple helps her with her medical needs, and monitors her day-to-day decisions and activities. Andrea has no next of kin of her own, and she appreciates the love and support of her new family. It is the couple's intention to have Andrea with them as long as they can, and they are currently planning for this. Andrea also receives case management through the community agency that recruited the family. A case worker is in frequent contact and is responsible for coordinating the supports for Andrea. Andrea's institutional history has left its mark. Andrea smokes, even though she has been advised not to for medical reasons. Unsuspected things or activities can trigger swearing and physical outbursts, but these are occurring less frequently as she adjusts to her new home.

It is important to Andrea to keep in touch with the people she once lived with in the institution. Because she is of retirement age, Andrea attends a seniors program with her old friends. The program, located in a beautifully restored old home close to where she lives, involves activities such as crafts, use of the pool, and trips. All of these activities are supported by a number of staff. Andrea views this program as her job, attends 3 days per week, and is given a stipend by her case manager there on a weekly basis.

Clifford: Being independent

Clifford is a 40-year-old who lives in a semidetached house with one other 30-year-old man in a working class neighborhood in an urban area. He and his roommate share the household tasks, and Clifford maintains responsibility for his room and the designated areas of the house. Cost for his home is subsidized by an organization that is funded by government. He has lived in his home for the past 8 years, at which time he moved from a boarding home where he fended for himself.

Clifford has a volunteer position with the housekeeping staff at an organization, where his duties include assisting with the general upkeep of the offices. He works with a colleague at times but generally goes about his job independently. He views this position as his job and receives a small amount of money at the end of each week. Others would view Clifford's job as a volunteer position, but he is adamant that it is his job. It certainly is what he does during the week, and plays a central role in how he thinks of himself.

Clifford is supported primarily by one case manager who helps him with shopping and general chores around the house. He has regular contact with this support staff a few hours each week but has 24-hour access to help if he needs it. It was with the help of his support staff that Clifford was able to find both his home and his job. Clifford also has the support of a dietician who helps to manage his diabetes through diet and insulin, which he administers himself.

Clifford has several close friends in the community, rides the city bus to get about, and pays for and uses his telephone for contact with his friends. He enjoys fishing, gardening, listening to music, going to garage sales, and using his CB radio. Clifford makes regular visits to his family in a nearby city, generally making the arrangements himself. Clifford is fiercely independent and usually makes his own decisions about his life. At times, however, his case worker considers it necessary to assist Clifford with some of his choices, especially around his diet, but the case worker is careful to help Clifford to make the choice that is in his best interest.

Source: Buell and Brown (2003).

midable challenge to describe accurately what supports are required and how they can best be offered. This challenge remains.

Social Support

Social support means the practical and the emotional ties and reciprocal relationships people have with others—ties that make life both easier to live and more enjoyable (Brown et al., 1997). For people with intellectual and developmental disabilities, social support is an important aspect of inclusion. Social support emerges from having people involved in one's daily life, having people to share personal interests and experiences, and having people who are connected to all the various things one does in the course of carrying out daily life. Social support means feeling accepted by all of these other people, feeling respected, being able to give and receive trust, feeling there is someone who responds respectfully when practical and emotional needs arise, and having people with whom to share close bonds.

Because many people with developmental disabilities have limited social functioning skills, social support is especially important for them and contributes a great deal to their lifestyles. Unfortunately, a great deal of this social support for people who receive services comes from professional staff, or, if they live at home, from their families (Krauss, Seltzer, & Goodman, 1992; Robertson et al., 2001). In keeping with the findings of these authors, almost all people surveyed by Brown et al. (1997), regardless of type of living situation, identified professional staff as sources of practical and emotional support. There were other sources of social support as well—especially from parents of adults with disabilities who lived at home—but the survey results suggested that support is not nearly as strong nor as broadly based as might be hoped. A major ongoing challenge for improving the lifestyles of adults with developmental disabilities is to expand social support networks beyond professional staff into the larger culture. In the meantime, the overreliance on professional staff for social support underscores the need for having knowledgeable, trained, and skilled people as professional staff and for such professionals to act as ambassadors and educators for expanding social support. Display 34.5 illustrates the impact of social support.

Personal Choice

Personal choice involves a person making choices that affect his or her own life activities. The concept of personal choice comprises two subconcepts, each with its own parts (Buell & Brown, 2003). First, *ability to make decisions* is part of personal choice. Ability to make de-

Display 34.5

Case study: Myron

Myron, age 37, has a developmental disability. When he was born, the doctors told his parents that he would have a developmental disability and that "no good will come of him." They advised his parents to abandon him, but they refused. Myron lived with his family, but during his childhood, he did not have a chance to go to preschool or school with children from his neighborhood.

Throughout childhood and adolescence Myron was very lonely. He generally wandered around the streets of his neighborhood alone. He did not have friends, and others often laughed at him and made fun of him. He had nothing to do and was very withdrawn.

When Myron came to the attention of service professionals while in his early 30s, he was so withdrawn that it was practically impossible to communicate with him. He did not respond to greetings or answer questions. His face was always sad and joyless. However, when Myron traveled to a special summer camp, for the first time in his life, he found himself surrounded by people who wanted to talk to him. Here he felt accepted, and he had the courage to open up to people. Then one evening, there was a dance. For the first time in his life, he asked a girl to dance with him. He danced the whole evening, and when the party broke up and the stars were shining in the sky, he said, "Oh, life is really mighty fine."

Myron was able to open up and to see that life is beautiful, but only because he felt that someone saw him as a human being, that someone believed that there was something beautiful hidden away in his heart, that someone wanted to be his friend. Because of this feeling of acceptance, his heart was able to be healed: This is what communities of people with disabilities need. Unfortunately, they often feel lonely, rejected, and alienated. They need friendship, others who believe in them, and others who are just glad to be with them and spend time with them.

Now Myron's life is much happier. Changes in his country meant that many more services became available for people with disabilities. Every day Myron goes to workshops, where he works with wood and produces icons and candles. He gets a small salary and he is very happy with that. He has many friends. On weekends, he attends various activities. Myron is much more accepted in his neighborhood, although sometimes he still becomes object of ridicule by adolescents.

Myron's life is not a typical example of life of people with disabilities worldwide. Unfortunately, many people still are closed up in institutions, where conditions of life are very poor and there is lack of respect and of high-quality services. Other people with disabilities live with their parents and have no day activities, no friends, and little social life. It seems that, for many, television is the only friend they have. Thus, many things still must be done. Many changes are needed to fully include people with disabilities into society and make their lives more human and happy.

Source: Oleh Romanchuk, Medical Director, Dzherelo Children's Rehabilitation Centre, Lviv, Ukraine.

cisions refers to 1) having the skills to select, 2) feeling free and having permission/being encouraged to select, and 3) having sufficient initiative to carry out the selection. Second, *availability of options* is also part of personal choice. Availability of options refers to 1) having two or more options readily available from which selection can be made and 2) having options available that are known to the person who is selecting. The availability of options for personal choice is often limited by these factors:

- *Opportunity:* People with disabilities need to have opportunities to learn which options are available.
- *Ease of access:* Options should be easily accessible so that people with disabilities can select without delay and hardship.
- *Values:* The values that form the basis of the "agenda" of the professionals, service organizations, or even family members who provide support often differ from the values held by the individuals with disabilities. When this is the case, support people may implicitly or explicitly limit or even contradict options, thus limiting personal choice. In addition, although many people believe that it is the right of people with developmental disabilities to experience readily available options, in reality options are often limited by the implicit attitudes and values of a broader culture that may not fully support inclusion.
- *Legislative and bureaucratic policy:* Policies and legislation vary in the degree to which they are supportive of the availability of options for personal choice. Furthermore, they vary in the degree to which there is commitment to implement them. Formal methods of implementing them include identifying available service options, clearly describing what those service options are, and holding those who

administer these service options accountable for fostering inclusion for people with disabilities. More informal methods of implementing supportive policies and legislation include working to conscientiously implement the policies and legislation that are supportive of inclusion and working toward changing public attitudes to be more inclusive.

At the beginning of the 21st century, the challenges for inclusion through exercising personal choice continue. Although many advances have been made, largely through the advocacy of families and people working in the field, ongoing advocacy is required by groups that represent individuals with disabilities, families, and people working in the field of disabilities. Advocacy also is needed to ensure that people with disabilities from various ethnic backgrounds have choices that are similar to other individuals in their countries.

EFFECTS OF ETHNICITY AND RACE ON SERVICE USE

Most studies and discussions regarding community involvement, social networks, and life satisfaction of individuals with developmental disabilities do not acknowledge potential differences among minority individuals with intellectual disability. In comparing individuals with intellectual disabilities in the United States, Kuehn and Imm-Thomas (1993) defined *minority* as racial/ethnic groups that have "an unequal and unrepresentative share of the resources in United States society" (Kuehn & Imm-Thomas, 1993, p. 328). The report, *Meeting the Unique Needs of Minorities with Disabilities* (1993), published by the National Council on Disability, identified concerns, including an increase in the number of minorities with disabilities and minorities being overrepresented in the population with intellectual disabilities. In a study of long-term care residents that was conducted in 2000, 85% of individuals were Caucasian. In comparison with residents who did not have intellectual disabilities, residents with intellectual disabilities were likelier to be African American, Hispanic, or American Indian/Alaska Native (Larson, 2004).

There are discrepancies in intellectual disability service use when comparing minority groups with Caucasians in the United States. Reasons suggested by Lakin et al. (2005) include the following:

1. There are fewer community services available in communities with a high proportion of minority membership.
2. There is less information about community service availability in such communities.
3. Among minority communities, there are fewer people being trained to develop human service agencies.
4. There may be higher levels of distrust of public agencies in minority communities.
5. The cultural approach of in-family and extended family support among members of some minority groups may be incompatible with more out-of-home Western European approaches to service.

A lack of cultural sensitivity within the health care industry is a barrier to service. The format of services may be unsuitable, as well as the language in which the service is provided. Most institutions do not accommodate things such as celebrating various holidays and upholding culturally specific traditions. The style of service, or the style of room and board, also may be unsuitable for potential residents of large and small homes.

Individuals obtaining services may be more comfortable speaking in their native tongue or may not be fluent enough (if at all able) to communicate their service needs to service providers in another language. Even when translators are available, the message may not be properly relayed.

Lack of culturally appropriate care is a consistent form of discrimination for minority individuals with developmental disabilities. Individuals who have experienced discrimination distrust the service system, and past occurrences of discrimination and racial bias among health care providers often dissuades individuals with intellectual disability from seeking services (Kuehn & Imm-Thomas, 1993).

Those individuals who want to obtain services may not have access to them. Available services may be harder to obtain for individuals with less physical access to services, such as American natives, many of whom live in rural regions (Kuehn & Imm-Thomas, 1993). Access to services is also a challenge for older individuals with limited mobility, who may lack the financial resources to assist with transportation (Kuehn & Imm-Thomas, 1993). Insufficient financing is a major barrier to services among minority populations. In the United States, poverty rates are higher among ethnic and racial minority groups than among Caucasians. Such poverty restricts an individual's eligibility for Medicare and other forms of health insurance. Hispanics, especially Puerto Rican Americans and Mexican Americans, are often employed in lower-paying jobs, such as some manual-labor positions, which often do not provide health insurance for their employees.

EFFECTS OF INTELLECTUAL DISABILITY ON HEALTH CARE AVAILABILITY

The previous discussion alluded only briefly to the importance of health care in quality of life. Health maintenance can play a major role in the lifestyles and life satisfaction of many individuals with intellectual disability. Some individuals with intellectual disability may require assistance with establishing, maintaining, and monitoring their health care regime. An individual who lives alone may need a reminder to take her pills, whereas another may need assistance with basic personal care.

Recognizing the discrepancies among the healthcare of individuals with and without intellectual disability, the U.S. initiative Healthy People 2010 targeted areas of discrepancy based on baseline health care data of individuals with and without disabilities (Centers for Disease Control and Prevention [CDC], 2005).

According to the CDC study, individuals with disabilities have 1) high incidences of pressure sores, among those who live in long-term care facilities; 2) high frequencies of hospitalization and emergency room visits for their primary disability; 3) low rates of formal patient education; 4) low treatment rates for mental illness or multiple diagnoses/comorbidities; 5) restricted activities and difficulties with personal care; 6) preventable secondary conditions, such as fractures, amputation, and unemployment; 7) early deaths from their primary disabling condition, such as asthma; and 8) early deaths from comorbidities, such as kidney failure or diabetes related cardiovascular disease.

The CDC study also found that in comparison with Americans without disabilities, those with disabilities have less health insurance coverage and use the health care system less for services such as PAP tests, mammographies, and oral health exams. Those with disabilities have higher rates of such chronic conditions as high blood pressure and blood cholesterol, obesity, depression or sadness, diabetes, and tooth loss. Americans with disabilities also have lower rates of what are recommended as health conscious behaviors, such as quitting smoking, and performing flexibility activities and cardiovascular strengthening exercises (CDC, 2005).

CONSIDERATIONS FOR THE FUTURE

In addition to having access to the same quality of health care as people without disabilities, a number of factors may be important to the lifestyles of adults with intellectual and developmental disabilities in the future. Ten such factors are as follows:

1. *Happiness and satisfaction levels:* Happiness and life satisfaction need to be monitored in an ongoing way to help determine the most suitable lifestyles.
2. *Material resources:* It is difficult for people to lead full and dignified lives if they are financially marginalized.
3. *Personal control:* Many people with disabilities do not exercise personal choice or have control over many aspects of their lives that are feasible for them to control. Most experts link personal control to improved lifestyle (e.g., Brown & Brown, 2003).
4. *Awareness of the general public:* People within the general culture need to remain aware of the experiences of people with disabilities in order to understand how their lifestyles can be improved.
5. *The extent of inclusion:* An important factor for lifestyles is the degree to which inclusion of people with disabilities continues to be a value and a priority within the general culture. Positive lifestyle is greatly affected by inclusive practices. Inclusion should be free of inequalities that are the result of ethnic or racial background, gender, and age.
6. *The role of governments:* Resources need to be provided from clearly identified sources. Leadership from governments in defining those sources is required.
7. *The role of families:* The degree to which families will be called upon to support their sons and daughters, especially as they age, is an important lifestyles issue.
8. *Professional training:* Not all people who work in the field of intellectual and developmental disabilities have formal, or even informal, education, training, or experience (see also Chapter 27). The ways that this lack of opportunity affect lifestyles need to be monitored carefully.
9. *The role of professionals:* The role of professionals has been changing in recent years. Such changes impact the lives of people with developmental disabilities, and the extent of this impact needs to be evaluated (see also Chapter 27).
10. *Evaluation methods:* In many jurisdictions, service organizations themselves monitor and evaluate the support and care they provide. In many parts of the United States and in some other countries, there are more formal evaluation requirements. In general, these have been positive, especially when the key indicators of success are improvements to the lifestyles of people with disabilities.

SUMMARY

Over the years, the lifestyles of people with intellectual and developmental disabilities have been influenced by prevailing philosophies and cultural ideas. As cultures have changed, so have lifestyles for people with disabilities. In developed countries especially, the 20th century saw tremendous change in the approach to intellectual and developmental disabilities: the eugenics movement; increased urbanization that resulted in the decline of informal supports, overexpansion, and underfunding within the institutional system; and a community living movement based on the principles of inclusion and recognition of individual dignity. The current emphasis is on community-based or generic services that support people with disabilities, and often their families, in a lifestyle that promotes being involved in their community in a worthwhile way.

The lifestyles of adults with intellectual and developmental disabilities vary quite markedly. Two key factors in determining lifestyle of individuals are where they live and the degree to which inclusion has been successful. Three important aspects of inclusion include integration, social support, and personal choice. A number of factors that affect the lifestyles of people with intellectual and developmental disabilities need to continue to be addressed in the future. These involve personal characteristics, social values and attitudes, and the roles of families, professionals, and government.

FOR FURTHER THOUGHT AND DISCUSSION

1. Think about how the prevailing philosophies have over time influenced the lifestyles of people with intellectual and developmental disability. Identify the philosophies prevalent in today's society. How are these ideas influencing the lifestyles of people with disabilities?
2. Think of your own home. Answer yes or no to each characteristic on the list in Table 34.1. Put a star beside the items that you consider important to have.
3. What aspects of lifestyle do you think are the most important? What policy and practice recommendations would you make to strengthen those aspects?
4. Think of one person with an intellectual or developmental disability. Describe in detail how you would support that person to improve his or her lifestyle.
5. Focus on one person you know who has a disability. Describe that person's lifestyle in a creative way.

REFERENCES

Americans with Disabilities Act (ADA) of 1990, PL 101-336, 42 U.S.C. §§ 12101 *et seq.*

Anderson, D.J. (1993). Social inclusion of adults with mental retardation. In E. Sutton, A.R. Factor, B.A. Hawkins, et al., (Eds.), *Older adults with developmental disabilities: Optimizing choice and change* (pp. 79–93). Baltimore: Paul H. Brookes Publishing Co.

Breedlove, T., Bruiniks, R., Coucouvanis, K., et al. (2004). *Residential services for persons with developmental disabilities: Status and trends through 2003.* Minneapolis: University of Minnesota, Research and Training Center on Community Living, Institute on Community Integration.

Brown, I., & Brown, R.I. (2003). *Quality of life and disability: An approach for community practitioners.* London: Jessica Kingsley Publishers.

Brown, I., Raphael, D., & Renwick, R. (1997). *Quality of life: Dream or reality? The lives of people with developmental disabilities in Ontario.* Toronto: Centre for Health Promotion, University of Toronto.

Brown, I., Renwick, R., & Raphael, D. (1999). *The Quality of Life Project: Results from the follow up studies.* Toronto: Centre for Health Promotion, University of Toronto.

Buell, M.K., & Brown, I. (2003). Lifestyles of adults with developmental disabilities in Ontario. In I. Brown & M. Percy (Eds.), *Developmental disabilities in Ontario* (2nd ed., pp. 439–661). Toronto: Ontario Association on Developmental Disabilities.

Centers for Disease Control and Prevention. (2005). *Healthy people 2010.* Retrieved March 19, 2006, from http://www.cdc.gov/nchs/hphome.htm

Cornell University Law School. (n.d.). *Supreme court collection: OLMSTEAD V. L.C. (98-536) 527 U.S. 581 (1999).* Retrieved March 19, 2006, from http://supct.law.cornell.edu/supct/html/98-536.ZS.html

Krauss, M.W., Seltzer, M.M., & Goodman, S. (1992). Social support networks for adults with retardation who live at home. *American Journal on Mental Retardation, 96,* 432-441.

Kuehn, M.L., & Imm-Thomas, P. (1993). A multicultural context. In E. Sutton, A.R. Factor, B.A. Hawkins, et al. (Eds.) *Older adults with developmental disabilities: Optimizing choice and change* (pp. 327–343). Baltimore: Paul H. Brookes Publishing Co.

Lakin, K.C., Gardner, J., Larson, S., et al. (2005). Access and support for community lives, homes, and social roles. In K.C. Lakin & A.P. Turnbull (Eds.), *National goals and research for people with intellectual and developmental disabilities* (pp. 179–215). Washington, DC: American Association on Mental Retardation.

Lakin, K.C., Prouty, R., & Coucouvanis, K. (2006). Changing patterns of residential settings for persons with intellectual and developmental disability, 1977–2005. *Mental Retardation, 44*(4), 306–309.

Lakin, K.C., Prouty, R., Polister, B., et al. (2004). States' initial response to the President's New Freedom Initiative: Slowest rates of deinstitutionalization in 30 years. *American Association on Mental Retardation, 42,* 241–244.

Larson, S.A. (2004). *Gender and ethnicity of nursing home residents with and without intellectual or developmental disabilities in 2000.* Minneapolis: Research and Training Center on Community Living, University of Minneapolis.

Larson, S.A., Lakin, K.C., Anderson, L., et al. (2001). Prevalence of mental retardation and developmental disabilities: Estimates from the 1994/1995 National Health Survey-Disability Supplements. *American Journal on Mental Retardation, 106,* 231–252.

Martinson, M.C., & Stone, J.A. (1993a). Federal legislation and long-term funding streams that support community living options. In E. Sutton, A.R. Factor, B.A. Hawkins, et al. (Eds.), *Older adults with developmental disabilities: Opti-*

mizing choice and change (pp. 199–221). Baltimore: Paul H. Brookes Publishing Co.

Martinson, M.C., & Stone, J.A. (1993b). A national survey of community living options. In E. Sutton, A.R. Factor, B.A. Hawkins, et al. (Eds.), *Older adults with developmental disabilities: Optimizing choice and change* (pp. 187–198). Baltimore: Paul H. Brookes Publishing Co.

Meyers, C.E., & Blacher, J. (1987). Historical determinants of residential care. In S. Landesman & P. Vietze (Eds.), *Living environments and mental retardation* (pp. 3–16). Washington, DC: American Association on Mental Retardation.

MukiBaum Treatments Centres for Children and Adults with Complex Disabilities. (2005). *Programs: Residential.* Retrieved November 2006 from http://www.mukibaum.com/Programs/progresidential.html

National Council on Disability. (1993). *Meeting the unique needs of minorities with disabilities: A report to the President and the Congress.* Washington, DC: Author.

Prouty, R., & Lakin, K.C. (1997). *Residential services for persons with developmental disabilities: Status and trends through 1996.* Minneapolis: University of Minnesota, Research and Training Center on Community Living, Institute on Community Integration.

Prouty, R.W., Smith, G., & Lakin, K.C. (Eds.). (2002). *Residential services for persons with developmental disabilities: Status and trends through 2001.* Minneapolis: University of Minnesota, Research and Training Center on Community Living, Institute on Community Integration.

Robertson, J., Emerson, E., Gregory, N., et al. (2001). Social networks of people with mental retardation in residential settings. *Mental Retardation, 39,* 201–214.

Schalock, R.L. (Ed.). (1990). *Quality of life: Perspectives and issues.* Washington, DC: American Association on Mental Retardation.

Schalock, R.L. (1996a). Quality of life and quality assurance. In R. Renwick, I. Brown, & M. Nagler (Eds.), *Quality of life in health promotion and rehabilitation: Conceptual approaches, issues, and applications* (pp. 104–118). Thousand Oaks, CA: Sage Publications.

Schalock, R.L. (Ed.). (1996b). *Quality of life: Vol. I. Conceptualization and measurement.* Washington, DC: American Association on Mental Retardation.

Schalock, R.L. (Ed.). (1997). *Quality of life: Vol. II. Application to persons with disabilities.* Washington, DC: American Association on Mental Retardation.

Schalock, R.L. (2001). *Outcome-based evaluation* (2nd ed.). New York: Kluwer Academic/Plenum Publishers.

Schalock, R.L., Brown, I., Brown, R.I., et al. (2002). Conceptualization, measurement, and application of quality of life for persons with intellectual disabilities: Report of an international panel of experts. *Mental Retardation, 40,* 457–470.

U.S. Department of Health and Human Services. (2003a). *Executive order 13217.* Retrieved March 19, 2006, from http://www.hhs.gov/newfreedom/eo13217.html

U.S. Department of Health and Human Services. (2003b). *New Freedom Initiative: Fulfilling America's promise to Americans with disabilities.* Retrieved March 19, 2006, from http://www.hhs.gov/newfreedom

Wolfensberger, W. (1972). *Normalization.* Toronto: National Institute on Mental Retardation.

World Health Organization. (1996). *Ottawa charter for health promotion.* Geneva: Author.

35

Providing Supports and Services that Enhance a Family's Quality of Life

ANN P. TURNBULL, DENISE J. POSTON, PATRICIA MINNES, AND JEAN ANN SUMMERS

WHAT YOU WILL LEARN ABOUT IN THIS CHAPTER

- Families are dynamic systems
- Families in caregiving and other roles
- Family quality of life

Chapter co-author Denise Poston will illustrate concepts throughout this chapter with stories from her own family. Denise is a single mother raising two sons: 18-year-old AJ, who has autism and very challenging behavior, and 16-year-old Jim, who currently lives with his father. The Poston family has many strengths. It also faces some challenges, including addressing AJ's needs. AJ receives special education services through the school district as well as Medicaid Home and Community-Based Services (HCBS) through the local developmental disability organization. Denise characterizes her experience with the service systems as positive; however, she believes she has to continue to be an advocate for her son to keep things improving, especially in times of budget reductions. She is hopeful for the future of her family as well as for the futures of Jim and AJ individually.

A fundamental role of families that have a member with a disability is to provide caregiving for that member. Based on data from the United States, approximately 60% of individuals with intellectual disabilities across the life span live with their families (Braddock, Hemp, & Rizzolo, 2004). It is likely that this figure is higher in countries that do not have as many residential services as those that are available in the United States. Without question, families are the primary source of caregiving worldwide for individuals with intellectual disabilities across the life span.

In working to provide services and supports that will be beneficial to families, the most important tenet to remember is that each family is *unique*. Just as it is important to recognize, value, and take into account the individual differences of people with disabilities, it is just as important to take this same *individualized perspective* with families.

FAMILIES ARE DYNAMIC SYSTEMS

The caregiving roles of families can best be understood through a family systems perspective. Systems theory, in general, addresses the interrelated parts of an entity in order to understand it as a whole. Family systems theory suggests that it is impossible to understand the caregiving of a child with a disability within the family without an understanding of how the family functions as a whole. A family systems perspective is interested in the well-being of every family member and not just the individual with the disability. Figure 35.1 visually illustrates a family systems framework. This section highlights each of the four components of the family systems framework—characteristics, interaction, functions, life cycle—by briefly highlighting its definition, noting illustrative related research, presenting a perspective from the Poston family, and providing tips for family–professional partnerships in providing services and supports.

Family Characteristics

Definition Family characteristics include the unique elements of each family. These elements can be delineated as follows:

- Characteristics of the family as a whole: family size and form, cultural background, socioeconomic status, and geographic location

The authors gratefully acknowledge the contributions made to this chapter by Jennifer Nachshen and Lynn Woodford.

- Each family member's personal characteristics: health, the particular nature of impairment of the individual with a disability, and coping strategies
- Special challenges not specifically related to family member's intellectual disability: poverty, abuse, illness, disability considerations of other family members, or crises such as hurricanes or floods

A systems perspective suggests that each family has a set of characteristics that provide the *input* into the way that the family interacts and the way the family members carry out their functions.

Illustrative Research Highlights To illustrate family characteristics, this section focuses on the third previously described element—each family member's personal characteristics, specifically the particular nature of impairment of the individual with a disability. Research has shown that family adjustment varies according to the type of disability and the degree of disability (Minnes, 1998). Families of children with Down syndrome report lower stress than families of children with autism or developmental disabilities due to an unknown cause (Konstantareas & Homatidis, 1991). Such differences may be the result of the child's temperament, social responsiveness and behavior, and the availability of support services, especially in the early childhood years. Two characteristics that are often associated with higher levels of family stress are problem behavior of the individual with a disability and complicated caregiving needs (Essex, Seltzer, & Krauss, 1999; Krauss et al., 1996). Although caregiving stress is often proportional to dependency, management needs, and severity of the disability, some researchers have found that parents of children with milder disabilities report more caregiving stress (Minnes, 1988). The behavior and appearance of children with milder disabilities may

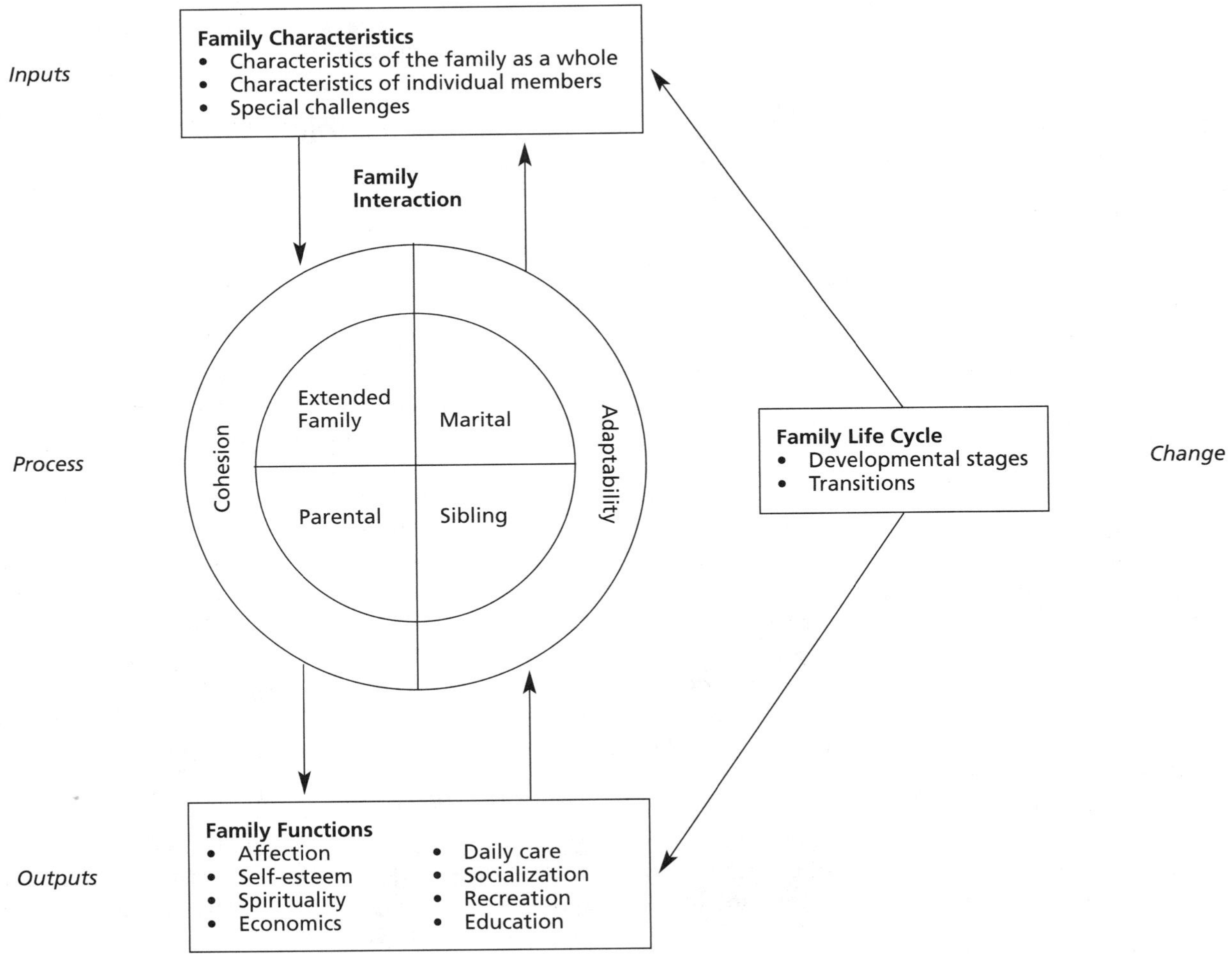

Figure 35.1. Family systems framework. (From Turnbull, A.P., Summers, J.A., & Brotherson, M.J. [1984]. *Working with families with disabled members: A family systems approach* [p. 60]. Lawrence: University of Kansas, Kansas Affiliated Facility; adapted by permission.)

be closer to "normal" and, as a result, parents may develop unrealistic expectations for their child, whereas parents of children with more severe disabilities may be less prone to deny or overlook problems (Turnbull et al., 2006).

Until the late 1980s, research tended to focus on negative outcomes and stress in family research (Glidden, 1993; Summers, Behr, & Turnbull, 1989; Turnbull, Guess, & Turnbull, 1988). Since that time, however, research has demonstrated that families can have positive as well as negative outcomes. Parents frequently report considerable stress, but they also report positive outcomes such as an increased sense of purpose in life and the development of new skills and career opportunities as a result of raising a child with a disability (Hastings & Taunt, 2002).

Perspectives from the Poston Family The most significant impact of AJ's disability on our family comes from his obsessive and often aggressive behavior. I have to watch him always, especially in public places, because of the fear that he might scare or hurt someone. He is fairly independent in terms of self-care, but his behavior is volatile and hard to predict. Jim used to be really afraid of AJ, but now that he is older, it's not as bad. Having to be so hypervigilant all of the time is exhausting.

Implications of Family Characteristics for Providing Supports and Services to Families

- In conversations with families, pay attention to the information that they share related to the characteristics of their family as a unit, the individual characteristics of each member, and any long-term or episodic special challenges that they are facing.
- If families are interested, connect them with other families that have similar characteristics.
- Recognize the unique strengths that each family has and find ways to positively affirm these strengths in your conversations and interactions.

Family Interaction

Definition As depicted in Figure 35.1, family interaction is the *process hub* of the family system and represents different subsystems that constitute family life. These subsystems include parental, extended family, marital, and sibling. Often when caregiving is considered, it is thought about primarily in terms of the parental subsystem (often just the mother–child relationship). It is clear, however, that caregiving is influenced by the dynamics of each subsystem and the dynamics of the system as a whole. This perspective is expressed by a well-known family therapist as follows:

> In a mobile, all the pieces, no matter what size or shape, can be grouped together and balanced by shortening or lengthening the strings attached, or rearranging the distance between the pieces. So it is with the family. None of the family members is identical to any others; they are all different and at different levels of growth. As in a mobile, you can't arrange one without thinking of the other. (Satir, 1972, pp. 119–120)

In considering family interaction, it is important that families be resilient in all of their subsystems—marital (Risdal & Singer, 2004), sibling (Stoneman & Berman, 1993), parental (Turnbull et al., 2006), and extended family (Sandler, 1998).

Illustrative Research Highlights This section focuses on the sibling subsystem in terms of illustrating issues associated with balancing time and attention among all children in the family. Research has addressed the adjustment of siblings ranging from the early years and throughout adulthood. Many parents struggle to meet the needs of other children in the family (Nachshen, 1996). Some families believe that their children without disabilities are forced to grow up too fast. As one parent stated,

> Having a handicapped little brother, at times, has created stress for my daughter and son. He doesn't learn as quickly as a non-handicapped child does. Often he makes messes and gets into mischief. Sometimes the older two are frustrated because we depend on them so much to help us with their little brother. I sometimes feel guilty for robbing them of their childhood. (Nachshen & Minnes, 1997)

Research has shown that these parental concerns are warranted. Often siblings serve in the role as socialization agent and tutor (Gallagher et al., 2000; Tekin & Kircaali-Iftar, 2002). Some siblings benefit from these responsibilities in terms of increased self-esteem, insight, advocacy, and maturity. Conversely, other siblings experience resentment, pressure, embarrassment, and guilt (Damiani, 1999; Fisman et al., 2000; Heller, Gallagher, & Frederick, 1999; Lardieri, Blacher, & Swanson, 2000).

Studies indicate the importance of the roles played by siblings in in-home interactions and activities with older and younger children with disabilities (Stoneman et al., 1991). Relationships between those with and without disabilities are often unequal, with the responsibilities for multiple caregiving tasks and the role of teacher frequently assumed by older siblings, especially sisters. This asymmetry increases with age and with greater language and adaptive skill deficits in the younger sibling with a disability. Similar patterns have been found between younger siblings of older children with intellectual and developmental disabilities, where younger siblings commonly assume the dominant role of teacher and behavior manager normally held by the oldest children in the family.

Perspectives from the Poston Family As AJ's sibling, Jim often felt that I gave AJ more attention or "gave AJ a break" that Jim didn't get. I try to ensure that Jim and I have special time and activities where Jim is the center of attention. Still, Jim sometimes feels resentment. I intend to keep on making a special place for Jim so that in the future, as Jim matures, he will recognize the effort that I made to help him feel as special as AJ.

Implications of Family Interactions for Providing Supports and Services to Families

- Learn from families how they carry out their roles in terms of providing care to all members.
- Find out families' priorities of what they would consider the most useful supports and services that could be provided to them in order to address the needs of all family members.
- Provide supports and services to the individual with a disability that are focused on enabling that individual to make positive contributions to other family members and to other subsystems within the family.
- Encourage families to consider inviting siblings, grandparents, and other family members to the individualized planning meetings if other family members would like to gain information or provide their perspective.

Family Functions

Definition As illustrated in Figure 35.1, family functions are the *outputs* of the interaction system. Thus, based on the unique characteristic of each family (input) and the way that the family members interact with each other (process), functions are the outputs or the way that families address their needs related to affection, self-esteem, spirituality, economics, daily care, socialization, recreation, and education needs. Clearly, one of the purposes of families is to meet the individual and collective needs of members. Individuals with a disability can affect each of the eight types of family functions in positive, neutral, or negative ways (Turnbull et al., 2006).

Illustrative Research Highlights Parents often work with professionals in developing educational plans and in implementing educational programs. Related to the education function, many parents have worked to promote successful inclusion for their son or daughter with an intellectual disability. Based on a review of 17 studies related to the perspectives of parents of children with disabilities toward inclusion, researchers concluded that most parents 1) were generally positive about inclusion, 2) perceived that their child would get better preparation for the real world and have better self-esteem in inclusive placements, and 3) had major concerns that teachers are not qualified to address individual needs and that individualized services are not available (Duhaney & Salend, 2000).

Many families report that they resent the intensive work that they have to invest in promoting the success of inclusion when they see that this is the school's responsibility (Erwin et al., 2001; Soodak & Erwin, 1995). Although some families achieve success—often after years of struggling—many remain unsatisfied, feeling that the schools are "reluctant to integrate and modify programs" (Nachshen & Minnes, 1997).

One parent who felt more strongly about this issue stated that "forced integration [is a] farce—[there's] no such thing" (Nachshen & Minnes, 1997). Another parent whose children were fully included was unsatisfied for a different reason:

> I don't think integration into normal classrooms helps with our kids' social lives. Yes, they are well-liked as a rule, but not invited to things by normal kids. They need opportunities to be with their peers. They seem to make the best friends with people like themselves. (Nachshen & Minnes, 1997)

A consideration to keep in mind is that most families are incredibly busy trying to balance needs across all eight family functions. As families give more time and attention to one function, such as advocating for inclusive education, time and attention has to be withdrawn from other functions. Many parents are especially appreciative of respite care services that enable them to devote their time and attention to other important aspects of their lives.

Perspectives from the Poston Family Our family tries to live by the saying "busy but balanced." I do put a lot of effort into AJ's education—meeting regularly with his teacher and planning for his transition to adulthood. But I also try to maintain a balanced life of a career, family fun activities, travel, hobbies, chores around the home, and social relationships. AJ's personal assistants, provided through the HCBS program, are able to do activities with AJ so that I can enjoy some time with Jim or quiet time at home.

Implications of Family Functions for Providing Supports and Services to Families

- Make sure to provide state-of-art services and supports so that parents will not have to spend their valuable time advocating for service improvements.
- Support the individual to learn skills that can contribute positively to the family meeting all of its functions (doing chores around the house to address needs related to the function of daily care).
- Support the individual with the disability to make friends and to participate in community and school

extracurricular activities that will also serve as giving the family a break from caregiving responsibilities.

Family Life Cycle

Definition The family life cycle can be thought of in terms of life cycle *stages* and life cycle *transitions*. Life cycle stages include the developmental periods of time in which family functions are relatively stable (Carter & McGoldrick, 1999). One way to categorize stages is as follows: birth and early childhood, middle/secondary school years, early adulthood, middle adulthood, and late adulthood. In each of these life stages, families often vary in how they interact with each other and how they meet their needs related to family functions. For example, parents of an infant express affection to their child in different ways than when the child is a teenager.

Family life cycle transitions represent the dynamic changes that occur within the family system as the family encounters both developmental and nondevelopmental changes. Developmental changes include changes expected due to the growth of family members (e.g., moving from elementary school to middle school, leaving home to go to college); nondevelopmental changes represent changes that are not tied to the evolution of time (e.g., moving from one town to another).

Illustrative Research Highlights Research clearly documents that the times that are often the most stressful in families' lives are times of transition when significant changes are occurring (Turnbull et al., 2006). One of the most stressful periods of family life is when individuals with disabilities graduate from high school and face the dilemma of adult life, such as where to work, where to live, and the nature of social relationships and recreation (see Chapter 32). Families vary greatly in their priorities for their son or daughter during adulthood, and these variations are influenced by family characteristics, interaction, and functions (Turnbull & Turnbull, 1996). Many individuals with intellectual disabilities and their families would like to pursue supported employment, which has the goal of developing independent work skills and the ability to earn competitive wages in an inclusive job market (Wehman, Bricout, & Kregel, 2000). The average hourly wage in supported employment is often more than two times the average hourly wage in sheltered employment (Coker, Osgood, & Clouse, 1995). Families need support in knowing how to assist their son or daughter in supported employment initially and in being successfully employed over the long term.

Perspectives from the Poston Family I am keenly aware of the impact that life cycle has on AJ and our family. When AJ was young, his challenging behavior was more manageable because he was smaller and people tend to be more forgiving of young children. Now, as a young adult, AJ's behavior is more dangerous and people have less tolerance. His teacher and I are especially concerned about AJ's behavior at his workplace. Having a job will be an integral part of AJ's adult life, both financially and socially. I am concerned that his obsessive or aggressive behavior may get him fired from his job at the pet store. I am also preparing myself emotionally for how my role as mother will change once AJ and Jim are launched into adult life.

Implications of Life Cycle Issues for Providing Supports and Services to Families

- Support families by identifying the cognitive and behavioral expectations of the next environment and helping to teach skills in advance.
- Develop partnerships with local employers so that students with disabilities can have successful job experience before graduating from high school.
- Support individuals and families to gain information on resources that they may want to consider in the future and how they might go about arranging visits to adult programs/services.
- When individuals with disabilities and their families are in the midst of making major life cycle transitions, talk with them about what kinds of additional supports you might provide that would be helpful to them.

FAMILIES IN CAREGIVING AND OTHER ROLES

Families of individuals with disabilities often take on roles over and above caregiving. This section briefly highlights three of these roles and points out advantages and disadvantages to families assuming these responsibilities. The three roles include parents as therapists, parents as educators of others, and parents as advocates. For more information on the roles of siblings, see Burke (2006) and McPhail (1996). An overview, perspectives from the Poston family, and implications are provided for each role.

Families as Therapists

Overview of Role The role of families as therapists involves mothers, fathers, and often other family members implementing a "treatment intervention." The professional meets with the family several times at the beginning of the intervention to do an assessment, formulate a plan, and teach the family to carry out the intervention in their home. The professional then collects and analyzes the data from the family and provides ongoing feedback. This approach allows more families to be served by a small number of trained professionals and enables professionals to work with many groups simultaneously (Briesmeister & Schaefer, 1998; Feldman & Werner, 2002).

Involving families' expertise and firsthand experience can be indispensable in the assessment and implementation of the intervention. This collaboration between professionals and family members can be a catalyst for empowering families to take action to address their needs.

Alternatively, many parents whose sons and daughters need interventions do not have the time, energy, or personal resources to carry out the role of therapist (Turnbull et al., 2006). The expectation that the family will be able to carry out explicit intervention programs may be setting them up for frustration and even failure. Another problem is that in the therapist model, parents must be highly motivated, consistent, and capable of the dual role of therapist and parent. This dual role can create stressful interactions between parents and children. It can also result in individuals with disabilities perceiving themselves as recipients of perpetual therapy.

Perspectives from the Poston Family I have always tried to keep my primary role as AJ's mom, but often I find myself in other roles as well. These days, my primary focus is on AJ's behavior, and I find myself implementing positive behavior support strategies at home and teaching them to his personal assistants (or PAs, who are provided through the HCBS program). Although I know I should be recording data on AJ's behavior and the interventions, it's hard to do that and still fix dinner at the same time.

Implications of Therapist Role for Providing Supports and Services to Families

- Brainstorm with families about what role is comfortable and possible for them related to serving as therapist for the family member with a disability.
- Be sensitive to the fact that having a parent serving as a therapist can strain relationships with the individual with the disability.
- Look for additional community resources to provide the therapy so that family members will not need to assume this role.

Parents as Educators of Others

Overview of Role Professionals and parents often acknowledge the need for more information about intellectual and developmental disabilities for the general public and for professionals. In particular, many parents spend a significant amount of time informing themselves and then, in turn, sharing that knowledge with others. One of the reasons they adopt this role is that they are better equipped to deal with professionals if they are well informed. A comment from one parent illustrates this: "I have had good success with my doctors. I tell my doctors things they didn't know about Down syndrome" (Nachshen & Minnes, 1997).

Educating others about their child's disability helps many parents increase the knowledge and comfort of others. One parent explained, "Most of the time when I name the syndrome, people have never heard of it, and want to know more about it. So I have had great experiences with explaining her condition. People have really accepted her" (Nachshen & Jamieson, 2000). It is obvious from this parent's perspective that serving as an educator of others can be an empowering experience for some parents. Although parents who educate may feel empowered by helping to educate others, it is also an added responsibility.

Alternatively, other parents do not want the role of educator: "It's nice not to have to explain anything and see our child played with and accepted as he is. Otherwise, I try to be vague on the disability and promote his abilities" (Nachshen & Minnes, 1997). Parents who have this perspective may perceive it burdensome to be the "explainer" and "informer" when it comes to their child's condition. They may choose a much more normalized experience in which they are not serving as a disability expert.

Perspectives from the Poston Family AJ has a lot of therapists, case managers, and support personnel; I am the glue that holds them all together. I have to make sure that the techniques we are working on in speech therapy are carried out at home and with his PAs and that the speech therapist knows what has been successful for the music therapist in terms of managing AJ's behavior during therapy sessions. I guess I see myself more as case manager and service coordinator in addition to a mom, a therapist, and an advocate.

Implications of the Educator Role for Providing Supports and Services to Families

- Have conversations with families about their preferred role related to providing knowledge to others related to disability issues.
- Find out from families how to be helpful in providing resources to them so that they will have the information that they need.
- As a team of professionals and families, consider how community education related to disability can be carried out so that all of the responsibility for this role will not fall on families.

Parents as Advocates for Services and Supports

Overview of Role Parents of individuals with disabilities often experience gaps in the system of supports and services. These gaps may be related to education, health care, recreation, employment, residential options, or other issues. Historically, and still today, parents often assume the role of advocates. Advocacy consists of presenting, supporting, or defending a position in order to obtain a particular result. The role of parents as advocates involves acting on knowledge related to social, economic, and political environments in order to improve the life situation of their families (Nelson, Howard, & McLaughlin, 1993).

All parents advocate for their children in various ways, but parents who have children with developmental delays typically have a considerably greater need for advocacy. In responding to this need, they may advocate in numerous different situations and use a wide range of approaches. They may write letters, make telephone calls, and enlist the help of the media to address specific needs of their children or of all children with disabilities. Parents may act as advocates individually or as part of a group at the community, national, or international level.

A qualitative study examined the role of advocacy in relation to parents' sense of well-being (Nachshen & Jamieson, 2000). The authors found that six factors contributed positively:

1. Parents' sense that advocating was a strategy to achieve change, rather than an extra struggle
2. Parents' belief that their actions would exert a positive effect on their environment
3. Positive responses by professionals to the parents' efforts
4. A clear focus for the advocacy (e.g., for things to come or past injustices)
5. Balancing advocacy with other personal needs (e.g., time, money, relaxation) and creating interpersonal links, rather than destroying them
6. Experiencing positive feelings, such as confidence and empowerment, rather than negative ones, such as depression, guilt, or anxiety

Advocacy can have negative outcomes as well as positive ones. In a different qualitative study, parents of children with disabilities pointed out more drawbacks than benefits in relationship to their advocacy activities (Wang, Mannan, et al., 2004). They particularly emphasized that advocacy can result in parents being involved in adversarial struggles and can cause stress. One parent expressed this perspective as follows:

> You just get to where it gets very difficult to stay joyful and enjoy your life. I've decided this is a lot of work, but I'm not going to not enjoy my children. And I actually have to make a conscious effort to go put all of this behind me. Don't think about how mad I am, don't think about how stressed I am, don't think about how unjust this all is, don't think how tired I am and not miss the little things they (my children) are doing and enjoy them. (Wang, Mannan, et al., 2004, p. 149)

Perspectives from the Poston Family I see the need to advocate on many different levels: advocating on AJ's behalf that will benefit him directly, advocating for change at the local systems level, and advocating for changes in federal and state policy changes. Each type of advocacy takes a different skill and a different level of energy, but they are all important. I am really pleased that AJ's teacher and school are so responsive that advocacy there feels more like a celebration. I know that's not always going to be the case.

Implications of Advocacy Role for Providing Supports and Services to Families

- Ensure that services are offered at such a quality level that it is not necessary for parents to advocate for service deficiencies.
- Work collaboratively among professionals, families, and community citizens to start new programs for individuals with disabilities and ensure that this responsibility does not fall solely to parents.

FAMILY QUALITY OF LIFE

A new way of addressing family support and family outcomes is through an emphasis on family quality of life. Various aspects of this concept are described next.

Definition

Family quality of life as a concept is a relatively new area of study. Most family research focused on family systems, family roles, family stress and coping, and family dysfunction, as previously described. Family quality of life is the embodiment of a paradigm shift in disability services and family support (Poston et al., 2003). It moves the focus from "fixing" to support, from deficit to strengths, and from the child as the focus of intervention and support to the family as the target of supports.

Due to the infancy of this area of study, there are few definitions of family quality of life in the research literature. Many times researchers use the term *family quality of life* but are in fact referring to individual quality of life of the mother, family functioning, or caregiving, or they are applying a quality of life framework that was not developed specifically regarding families (Cummins & Baxter, 1997). Two parallel lines of research on family quality of life have emerged since 2000: one at The University of Kansas' Beach Center on Disability and another among an international group of researchers from Canada, Australia, and Israel. Both lines of research have similar definitions of family quality of life.

The Beach Center defines family quality of life as the conditions in which the family's needs are met, they enjoy spending time together, and members have opportunities to do things that they believe are important (Poston et al., 2003). Similarly, the international team describes family quality of life as both the place where the individual quality of life of each family member mingles, as well as the place where other factors affect the family as a whole (Brown & Brown, 2003). Both of these definitions share the concept that family quality of life concerns individual family members as well as the whole family.

Perspectives from the Poston Family

I sometimes struggle with balancing the needs of AJ, Jim, and me with the well-being of our family as a whole. It requires compromise because sometimes the boys' needs conflict with each other or with the family as a whole; sometimes I feel we have to sacrifice one for the other. For example, AJ and Jim have been fighting a lot, as many brothers do. Jim was not doing well in school and was stressed at home. I felt I was always being the referee between the two boys. Jim's dad and I decided that it might be best for Jim to live with his dad in Texas. I felt I was abandoning our family unity and that I had failed to keep us together peacefully. Jim and AJ's individual quality of life, however, is much better now. Jim and I talk frequently by telephone and see each other every holiday. AJ and Jim enjoy the time they spend together now instead of fighting all the time. I see family boundaries in a different way now, too. Even though we don't live under the same roof, we are family.

Implications for Providing Supports and Services to Families

- Ask family members who they consider to be part of their family.
- Consider how the aspects of the family member's disability may affect both individual family members and the family as a whole.
- Consider how the concept of family quality of life could change the way you provide supports to individuals with disabilities.

Domains of Family Quality of Life

Family quality of life is a holistic, multidimensional concept, intended to represent the totality of family life (Poston et al., 2003; Schalock & Verdugo Alonso, 2002). Its multidimensional nature is often represented by its component parts, typically referred to as *domains.* Considering the domains of family quality of life separately makes it a more practical concept, whereas thinking of these domains as being interrelated retains its holistic nature.

The domains of family quality of life differ somewhat depending on the line of research. The international team offers the following domains: health, financial well-being, family relationships, support from other people, support from services, careers and preparing for careers, spiritual and cultural life, leisure, and community and civic involvement (Brown et al., 2003; see Brown, Brown, & Neikrug, 2005, for an updated conceptualization). The survey developed based on these domains enables families to respond in terms of their *opportunities* for participation, their *initiative* in taking advantage of opportunities, their *attainment* in getting or accomplishing things important to them, and their *satisfaction* with their overall family life (Brown et al., 2003).

The Beach Center framework offers five similar domains: family interaction, parenting, physical/material well-being, emotional well-being, and disability-related support (Wang et al., 2004). Each of these domains is described in more detail next.

- *Family interaction:* The family interaction domain refers to the relationships among and between family members. It includes indicators such as communicating, problem solving, spending time together, and showing love and support.
- *Parenting:* The parenting domain relates to the activities that adults in the family do to help their children grow and develop. The indicators include helping children learn to make good decisions, helping them learn to be independent, helping with schoolwork, knowing who the children's friends are, and having time for the needs of all the children in the family.
- *Emotional well-being:* This domain concerns the emotional aspects of family life. Its indicators include having support to relieve stress, having friends to provide support, having time to pursue interests, and having help from outside the family to care for family members.
- *Physical/material well-being:* The physical/material well-being domain includes the basic physical needs of family members. Some representative indicators include getting medical and dental care, having transportation, taking care of expenses, and feeling safe.
- *Disability-related supports:* The disability-related supports domain refers to the supports needed in the home and community for the family member with a disability. Indicators include having support to make progress at school, work, and home; having support to make friends; and having a good relationship with service providers.

Perspectives from the Poston Family Even given the challenges we have faced, we have a pretty good life. We have a nice home to live in, although it is rented. We have enough money to meet our needs. We have our health and friends, and the supports for AJ are fairly stable and are enabling him to make progress. Our most difficult challenge, however, is our family interaction. AJ and I struggle to spend quality time together. I know he wants me nearby, but he seems to have a compulsive need to repeat the same sentence to me over and over again. If I don't respond just right, he gets mad. This routine is getting in the way of our relationship during fun activities and housework or when I give him directions. We have to get some help for this issue before it escalates into a major behavior problem—it's almost there now. Of all the areas of our family quality of life, this is the one that needs immediate attention. It affects everything we do as a family.

Implications for Providing Supports and Services to Families

- Use family quality of life domains to facilitate conversations with family members about what is happening within their family.
- Consider the impact of one or more of the family quality of life domains on the supports and services you provide.
- Recognize that families may need their basic needs met (housing, transportation, or family relationships) before a disability-related intervention can be effective.

SUMMARY

A family systems perspective is helpful in identifying and understanding family priorities. This perspective includes recognizing the characteristics of families, the way that they interact through subsystems, and the priority that they give to different family functions. Furthermore, family systems change through the life cycle, especially at times of transition.

Family members assume many roles related to serving as a therapist, an educator of others, and an advocate. Professionals can support families to be successful in these roles by understanding their family system and providing services and supports that are tailored to each family's circumstances. The most contemporary way of supporting families is to recognize that their quality of life as a family is critically important and that family–professional partnerships can be helpful in attending to each domain of family quality of life. A permeating theme throughout the chapter is the critical importance of *individualization* in forming and carrying out partnerships that support families to meet their needs, helping them enjoy spending time together, and enabling them to have opportunities to do the things that are important to them.

FOR FURTHER THOUGHT AND DISCUSSION

1. What are your assumptions about the impact of having a person with a disability in the family?
2. How can professionals, paid caregivers, or volunteers be more supportive of families?
3. When working with families of children with developmental delays
   - Are we asking too much of families or too little, given their levels of stress and resources?
   - Are we giving too much or too little?
   - Are our suggestions consistent with the family's priorities? Illustrate with examples to help explain your point of view.
   - Are our priorities consistent with the family's stage in the life cycle? Again, illustrate with examples to help explain your point of view.
4. How can we partner with other professionals to address all of a family's priorities for support in a way that is consistent with a family quality of life perspective?

REFERENCES

Braddock, D., Hemp, R., & Rizzolo, M.C. (2004). State of the states in developmental disabilities: 2004. *Mental Retardation, 42*(5), 356–370.

Briesmeister, J.M., & Schaefer, C.E. (1998). *Handbook of parent training* (2nd ed.). Hoboken, NJ: John Wiley & Sons.

Brown, I., Anand, S., Fung, W.L.A., et al. (2003). Family quality of life: Canadian results from an international study. *Journal of Developmental and Physical Disabilities, 15*, 207–230.

Brown, I., & Brown, R.I. (2003). *Quality of life and disability: An approach for community practitioners.* London: Jessica Kingsley Publishers.

Brown, I., Brown, R.I., & Neikrug, S. (2005). *Family Quality of Life Survey: 2005.* Toronto: Faculty of Social Work, University of Toronto.

Burke, P. (2006). *Brothers and sisters of disabled children.* London: Jessica Kingsley Publishers.

Carter, E.A., & McGoldrick, M. (1999). *Changing family life cycle: Individual, family, and social perspectives* (3rd ed.). Boston: Allyn & Bacon.

Coker, C.C., Osgood, K., & Clouse, K.R. (1995). *A comparison of job satisfaction and economic benefits of four different employment models for persons with disabilities.* Stout, WI: University of Wisconsin, Rehabilitation Research and Training Center on Improving Community-Based Rehabilitation Programs.

Cummins, R.A., & Baxter, C. (1997). The influence of disability and service delivery on quality of life within families. *International Journal of Practical Approaches to Disability, 21*(1), 2–8.

Damiani, V.B. (1999). Responsibility and adjustment in siblings of children with disabilities: Update and review. *Families in Society: The Journal of Contemporary Human Services,* 34–40.

Duhaney, L.M.G., & Salend, S.J. (2000). Parental perceptions of inclusive educational placements. *Remedial and Special Education, 21*(2), 121–128.

Erwin, E.J., Soodak, L.C., Winton, P.J., et al. (2001). "I wish it wouldn't all depend upon me": Research on families and early childhood inclusion. In M.J. Guralnick (Ed.), *Early childhood inclusion: Focus on change* (pp. 127–158). Baltimore: Paul H. Brookes Publishing Co.

Essex, E.L., Seltzer, M.M., & Krauss, M.W. (1999). Differences in coping effectiveness and well-being among aging mothers and fathers of adults with retardation. *American Journal of Mental Retardation, 104*(6), 545–563.

Feldman, M.A., & Werner, S.E. (2002). Collateral effects of behavioral parent training on families of children with developmental disabilities and behavior disorders. *Behavioral Interventions, 17,* 75–83.

Fisman, S., Wolf, L., Ellison, D., et al. (2000). A longitudinal study of siblings of children with chronic disabilities. *The Canadian Journal of Psychiatry, 45,* 369–375.

Gallagher, P.A., Floyd, J.H., Stafford, A.M., et al. (2000). Inclusion of students with moderate or severe disabilities in educational and community settings: Perspectives from parents and siblings. *Education and Training in Mental Retardation and Developmental Disabilities, 35*(2), 135–147.

Glidden, L.M. (1993). What we do not know about families with children who have developmental disabilities: Questionnaire on Resources and Stress as a case study. *American Journal on Mental Retardation, 97,* 481–495.

Hastings, R.P., & Taunt, H.M. (2002). Positive perceptions in families of children with developmental disabilities. *American Journal on Mental Retardation, 107,* 116–127.

Heller, K.W., Gallagher, P.A., & Frederick, L.D. (1999). Parents' perceptions of siblings' interactions with their brothers and sisters who are deaf-blind. *The Journal of The Association for Persons with Severe Handicaps, 24*(1), 33–43.

Konstantareas, M.M., & Homatidis, S. (1991). The developmentally disordered child and the effect of severe dysfunction on parents. *Psychiatric Clinics of North America, 14,* 15–29.

Krauss, M., Mailick-Seltzer, M., Gordon, R., et al. (1996). Binding ties: The roles of adult siblings of persons with mental retardation. *Journal on Mental Retardation, 34*(2), 83–93.

Lardieri, L.A., Blacher, J., & Swanson, H.L. (2000). Sibling relationships and parent stress in families of children with and without learning disabilities. *Learning Disability Quarterly, 23*(2), 105–116.

McPhail, E.R. (1996). A parent's perspective: Quality of life in families with a member with disabilities. In R. Renwick, I. Brown, & M. Nagler (Eds.), *Quality of life in health promotion and rehabilitation: Conceptual approaches, issues, and applications* (pp. 279–289). Thousand Oaks, CA: Sage Publications.

Minnes, P. (1988). Family stress associated with a developmentally handicapped child. In N. Ellis & N. Bray (Eds.), *International review of research in mental retardation: Vol. 15* (pp. 195–226). New York: Academic Press.

Minnes, P. (1998). Mental retardation: The impact upon the family. In J.A. Burack, R.M. Hodapp, & E. Zigler (Eds.), *Handbook of mental retardation and development* (pp. 693–712). Cambridge, United Kingdom: Cambridge University Press.

Nachshen, J.S. (1996). *Parental stress in families of children with developmental disabilities: A pilot study using the Family Stress and Support Questionnaire.* Unpublished Bachelor of Arts Honours thesis, Queen's University, Kingston, ON, Canada.

Nachshen, J.S. & Jamieson, J. (2000, April). *Advocacy, stress, and quality of life in parents of children with developmental disabilities.* Poster presented at the Annual Conference of the Ontario Association on Developmental Disabilities, Research Special Interest Group, Richmond Hill, ON, Canada.

Nachshen, J.S., & Minnes, P. (1997, April). *Parents' feelings about their experiences raising a child with developmental disabilities: Preliminary data from the Family Stress and Support Questionnaire.* Paper presented at the annual meeting of the Ontario Association on Developmental Disabilities, Kitchener, ON, Canada.

Nelson, D., Howard, V.F., & McLaughlin, T.F. (1993). Empowering parents to become advocates for their own children with disabilities. *Journal of Special Education, 17,* 62–72.

Poston, D., Turnbull, A., Park, J., et al. (2003). Family quality of life: A qualitative inquiry. *Mental Retardation, 41*(5), 313–328.

Risdal, D., & Singer, G.H.S. (2004). Marital adjustment in parents of children with disabilities: A historical review and meta-analysis. *Research and Practice for Persons with Severe Disabilities, 29*(2), 95–103.

Sandler, A.G. (1998). Grandparents of children with disabilities: A closer look. *Education and Training in Mental Retardation and Developmental Disabilities, 33*(4), 350–356.

Satir, V. (1972). *Peoplemaking.* Palo Alto, CA: Science and Behavior Books.

Schalock, R.L., & Verdugo Alonso, M.A. (2002). *Handbook on quality of life for human service practitioners.* Washington, DC: American Association on Mental Retardation.

Soodak, L.C., & Erwin, E.J. (1995). I never knew I could stand up to the system: Families' perspectives on pursuing inclusive education. *Journal of The Association for Persons with Severe Handicaps, 20*(2), 136–146.

Stoneman, Z., Brody, G.H., Davis, C.H., et al. (1991). Ascribed role relations between children with mental retardation and their younger siblings. *American Journal on Mental Retardation, 95,* 537–550.

Stoneman, Z., & Berman, P.W. (Eds.). (1993). *The effects of mental retardation, disability, and illness on sibling relationships: Research issues and challenges.* Baltimore: Paul H. Brookes Publishing Co.

Summers, J.A., Behr, S.K., & Turnbull, A.P. (1989). Positive adaptation and coping strengths of families who have children with disabilities. In G.H.S. Singer & L.K. Irvin (Eds.), *Support for caregiving families: Enabling positive adaptation to disability* (pp. 27–40). Baltimore: Paul H. Brookes Publishing Co.

Tekin, E., & Kircaali-Iftar, G. (2002). Comparison of the effectiveness and efficiency of two response prompting procedures delivered by sibling tutors. *Education and Training in Mental Retardation and Developmental Disabilities, 37*(3), 283–299.

Turnbull, A.P., Summers, J.A., & Brotherson, M.J. (1984). *Working with families with disabled members: A family systems approach.* Lawrence: University of Kansas, Kansas Affiliated Facility.

Turnbull, A.P., & Turnbull, H.R. (1996). Self-determination within a culturally responsive family systems perspective: Balancing the family mobile. In L.E. Powers, G.H.S. Singer, & J. Sowers (Eds.), *On the road to autonomy: Promoting self-competence among children and youth with disabilities* (pp. 195–220). Baltimore: Paul H. Brookes Publishing Co.

Turnbull, A.P., Turnbull, H.R., Erwin, E., et al. (2006). *Families, professionals, and exceptionality: Positive outcomes through partnership and trust* (5th ed.). Upper Saddle River, NJ: Prentice Hall.

Turnbull, H.R., Guess, D., & Turnbull, A.P. (1988). Vox populi and Baby Doe. *Mental Retardation, 26*(3), 127–132.

Wang, M., Mannan, H., Poston, D., et al. (2004). Parents' perceptions of advocacy activities and their impact on family quality of life. *Research and Practice for Persons with Severe Disabilities, 29*(2), 144–155.

Wang, M., Turnbull, A.P., Summers, J.A., et al. (2004). Severity of disability and income as predictors of parents' satisfaction with their family quality of life during early childhood years. *Research and Practice for Persons with Severe Disabilities, 29*(2), 82–94.

Wehman, P., Bricout, J., & Kregel, J. (2000). Supported employment in 2000: Changing the locus of control from agency to consumer. In M. Wehmeyer & J.R. Patton (Eds.), *Mental retardation in the 21st century* (pp. 115–150). Austin, TX: PRO-ED.

36

Sexuality and People Who Have Intellectual Disabilities

Dorothy Griffiths

WHAT YOU WILL LEARN ABOUT IN THIS CHAPTER

- Myths and facts
- Changing sexual policy
- Socio-sexual education
- Birth control
- Sexual diversity
- Sexual victimization
- Treatment and counseling

Sexuality is often overlooked in relation to people who have intellectual disabilities. This chapter explores the subject in terms of myths and facts, matters related to changing sexual policy, socio-sexual education, birth control, sexual diversity, sexual victimization, and treatment and counseling.

MYTHS AND FACTS

The topic of sexuality of people with intellectual disabilities conjures up many myths. Even at the beginning of the 21st century, it is surprising that many of the commonly held beliefs from the beginning of the last century still exist. Seven of the most common are listed in Table 36.1. After reading them, it may appear that some of the concepts contradict others. Some myths imply that people who have an intellectual disability are "eternal children"; hence, they need to be protected by society from sexual experiences. Other beliefs depict individuals with intellectual disabilities as sexually impulsive, promiscuous, or even deviant; hence, society needs to be protected from their sexual expression through social control. Both notions are equally false as they relate to people who have a label of intellectual disability. However, both myths achieve the same social effect: They promote the view that the sexuality of people who have an intellectual disability is different and outside the "normal" range. Such myths allow society to continue to deny this aspect of life to people with intellectual disabilities.

Dispelling the Myths

The myth that people with intellectual disabilities are eternal children is based on a misunderstanding that mental age is a predictor of all aspects of the person's life. *Mental age* refers to the age equivalence for the number of questions a person can answer correctly on a test of intelligence. There is considerable research to show, however, that just because a person's mental age is equivalent to that of a child, it does not mean that he or she is childlike in all respects. An adult with a mental age of 7 does not act like a 7-year-old. This person is physically more mature than, is emotionally different from, and has additional years of learning experiences than a 7-year-old. This significantly changes how the person will experience and react to life events and determine his or her life aspirations. With regard to sexuality and disability specifically, Johnson's (1973) view is still highly relevant: "There does not seem to be a high correlation between sex IQ and general IQ" (p. 60).

Most definitions of intellectual and intellectual disability address the point that IQ and mental age should never be used in isolation to make a determination of a person's abilities or potentials. These include the area of sexuality. For example, the term *mental retardation* as defined and described by the American Association on Mental Retardation (2002) involves not only a reference to the person's level of intelligence (IQ score below the normal range) but also considers adaptive functioning as expressed in conceptual, social, and practical adaptive skills to be essential components. In addition, it is assumed that with supports, people so defined will show improvement over time.

Like people without disabilities, people with intellectual disabilities typically show an interest in closeness, affection, and contact with others. However, individuals with various syndromes may have unique influences on their physical, relationship, and intimacy development (see Griffiths, Richards, Fedoroff, et al., 2002), and most individuals with intellectual disabilities experience unique social learning conditions that

Table 36.1. Dispelling seven common myths about the sexuality of people who have intellectual disabilities

Myth	Information that dispels the myth
1. People with intellectual disabilities are eternal children and are asexual.	Most people who have intellectual disabilities develop physical sexual characteristics at about the same rate as people without intellectual disabilities. Individuals may vary in their rate of development, however, especially those with certain genetic or endocrine dysfunctions. Generally, individuals with intellectual disabilities have sexual feelings and responses to the same kinds of things as do people without intellectual disabilities.
2. People with intellectual disabilities need to live in environments that restrict and inhibit their sexuality to protect themselves and others.	People who have intellectual disabilities require environments that provide the types of learning about one's sexuality that are generally taught in one's culture. Like others in the general population, people with intellectual disabilities benefit from an environment that models and teaches personal, moral, social, and legal responsibility regarding sexuality.
3. People with intellectual disabilities should not be provided with sex education, as it will only encourage inappropriate behavior.	Socio-sexual education helps individuals to understand their changing bodies and feelings and provides the knowledge and guidance necessary to learn responsibility about one's sexuality. There appears to be a correlation between socio-sexual education and a reduced frequency of abuse (Hard, 1986 as cited in Roeher Institute, 1988). For people who demonstrate inappropriate sexual behavior, socio-sexual education provides knowledge and skills to replace the inappropriate behavior.
4. People with intellectual disabilities should be sterilized because they will give birth to children who also have intellectual disabilities.	A large percentage of people with intellectual disability acquired their disability later in life, and often the cause is organic but not genetic or cultural-familial (Rioux, 1996). Thus, most people with intellectual disabilities do not have disabilities because of a known genetic abnormality. There is no physical reason for people with intellectual disabilities to give birth to children with disabilities, unless there is a genetic cause for the disability. It should also be noted that the disabling condition for some people with intellectual disabilities, especially those with genetic causes, is such that they can never procreate (Griffiths, Richards, Fedoroff, et al., 2002).
5. People with intellectual disabilities are more likely to develop diverse, unusual, or deviant sexual behavior.	The sexual development of people with intellectual disabilities can be affected by many factors: lack of sexual education, deprivation of peer group interactions, family restrictions on activities, lack of social exposure, and even lack of motor coordination. People with intellectual disabilities do not develop any more sexually inappropriate behavior than the general population if they have normal opportunities to learn about their sexuality.
6. People with intellectual disabilities are over-sexed, promiscuous, sexually indiscriminate, and dangerous; children should not be left unattended with them.	Although it appears that people with intellectual disabilities may be somewhat overrepresented in the population of people who are convicted of sexual offenses, these data may reflect that they are more likely to get caught, confess, and waive their rights, rather than indicating an increased rate of offense. When people with intellectual disabilities act inappropriately in a sexual way (e.g., public masturbation), it is often less serious than offenses committed by people without intellectual disabilities. Some clinicians have suggested that sexual deviance may be less common in this population than among people who do not have intellectual disabilities (Day, 1994). People with intellectual disabilities are more likely to be the victims of sexual offenses, rather than the victimizers.
7. People with intellectual disabilities cannot benefit from sexual counseling or treatment.	There is a growing body of literature that has demonstrated that people who have intellectual disabilities can benefit from treatment or intervention directed at 1) sexual abuse counseling or 2) teaching appropriate socio-sexual behavior to replace sexually inappropriate behavior.

Sources: Griffiths (1991, 2003).

can affect the development of their sexuality. From the moment of birth, both families and the more general society often treat people with intellectual disabilities as asexual. They have historically been denied, through isolation from the general public and especially from people of the opposite sex, the usual cultural experiences through which to learn about, and understand, their sexuality.

Early in the 20th century, institutions for people with intellectual disabilities grew dramatically in size in most more developed countries. The fear of procreation was one of the reasons that society began to segregate and institutionalize such individuals. This way of thinking began to change over time, however, and when Wolfensberger (1972) wrote his classic book *Normalization,* he emphasized the importance of providing the most culturally normative life experiences possible for people with intellectual disabilities. This included experiences relating to socio-sexual needs.

The remainder of this chapter explores some of the key issues revolving around sexuality and the field of intellectual disabilities: sexuality policy, socio-sexual education, birth control, sexual diversity, victimization, counseling, and treatment. For expanded discussions of these and other related topics, the reader is referred especially to *Ethical Dilemmas: Sexuality and Persons with Intellectual Disabilities* (Griffiths, Richards, Federoff, et al., 2002).

CHANGING SEXUAL POLICY

People with intellectual disabilities have the right to be treated in the same way as anyone else, and this includes the realm of sexuality. In some countries, this right is implied in various laws. For example, the Canadian Charter of Rights and Freedoms (1982) guarantees protections against discrimination based on physical and mental disability. The American Bill of Rights and the Rehabilitation Act of 1973 (PL 93-112) protect rights for privacy, choice of marital status, and freedom to procreate and raise a family. Globally, the 1971 United Nations *Declaration on the Rights of Mentally Retarded Persons* proclaimed that people with intellectual disabilities have the right to cohabitate and marry. When it comes to sexuality, however these rights are routinely denied to people with intellectual disabilities.

There has been a growing awareness of the need for community service organizations and other bodies to develop socio-sexual policies to ensure that the rights of people with intellectual disabilities are respected. Policies are vital in ensuring that a consistent and responsible atmosphere in which to learn about culturally appropriate socio-sexual interactions exists. Unless there are clear guidelines for staff in a school or community agency for providing direction on socio-sexual issues, each staff member might come up with his or her individual approach. In essence, each staff member becomes the policy maker. This practice leads to great inconsistencies in what is being taught. Certain behaviors might be at times accepted and at other times punished, depending on which staff member is responding to the situation. This type of inconsistent treatment creates an environment in which it is very difficult for people to learn to take responsibility for their own behavior.

To create a positive atmosphere in which to teach appropriate and responsible socio-sexual behavior, it is recommended that a school, community agency, or other organization commit the following in policy:

- A statement that recognizes the sexuality of people with intellectual disabilities and recognizes related rights
- An educational program to ensure that educators and support staff respond to both appropriate and inappropriate socio-sexual issues in a consistent manner
- Opportunities for people with intellectual disabilities to learn appropriate socio-sexual education and behavior
- Access for people with intellectual disabilities to medical and services and interventions as needed for sexual issues, including abuse counseling and intervention for inappropriate sexual behavior
- A clear policy and set of procedures to prevent abuse and to respond if there is a suspicion of abuse.

Parents have become more outspoken and less conservative about the topic of sexuality of their sons and daughters with disabilities. Research has shown a growing recognition among parents of the importance of sex education for their children because of the concern that without it, their children could be at greater risk of abuse (Johnson & Davies, 1989; see also Chapter 30). Staff attitudes have also become more generally accepting toward sexual behavior between consenting adults in private settings (Adams, Tallon, & Alcorn, 1982), but there are still inconsistent attitudes regarding abortion, sterilization, and homosexuality (Johnson & Davies, 1989). The rigid disapproval that existed in earlier years is now giving way to indecision (Griffiths & Lunsky, 2000). Policy is the only means by which agencies can ensure that the sexuality of people with intellectual disabilities will be responsibly, consistently, and proactively addressed.

SOCIO-SEXUAL EDUCATION

Early sex education programs focused on behavioral control of inappropriate sexual activities, particularly inappropriate masturbation (Mitchell, Doctor, & Butler, 1978), and neglected issues such as dating, relationships, gender security, and exploitation (Rowe & Savage, 1987). By the late 1970s, most facilities reported teaching sex education to some degree, but sexual activity, with the exception of masturbation, continued to be met with disapproval and prohibition (Coleman & Murphy, 1980). Mitchell et al. (1978) conducted research on attitudes of institutional staff and found that educators generally omitted explicit discussion of sexual behavior from sex education reading materials in keeping with the conservative attitudes held by parents and staff.

Pioneer sexuality educators such as Kempton (1975) and Gordon (1971) changed the nature of sex education to focus more on the socio-sexual learning needs of people with intellectual disabilities and less on repressive education. In addition to education about anatomy, birth control, sexual intercourse, hygiene, and venereal disease, these educators began to incorporate into their curriculum an increased emphasis on relationships, social behavior, self-esteem, decision making, sexual lifestyles, and abuse (see Kempton, 1993).

Griffiths and Lunsky (2000) identified a shift in the priorities in socio-sexual education. They suggested that this change reflected four areas of increased understanding in society: the growing awareness of the vulnerability to abuse, attention to intervention for inappropriate sexual expression, the discovery of human immunodeficiency virus/acquired immunodeficiency syndrome (HIV/AIDS), and the interest in preventive health practices.

First, a profound and thoughtful stream of research has emerged demonstrating that people with intellectual disabilities are far more vulnerable to abuse than people without disabilities and that abuse is most likely perpetrated by people known to the victim (see Chapter 30). For children with intellectual delay who live in the family home, this is most frequently the biological parents (Fudge Schormans & Brown, 2002). For those in care, a caregiver has opportunity to abuse through the disability system (Sobsey & Doe, 1991). Hard (as cited in Roeher Institute, 1988) presented correlational data that showed that among people who had been provided with sex education, abuse rates were considerably lower than for those who had not. Sex education, therefore, became identified as a key factor in the reduction of abuse.

Second, it has been recognized that a lack of sexuality education may not only leave people with intellectual disabilities vulnerable to abuse but also may lead to the expression of their sexuality in inappropriate ways (Griffiths, Quinsey, & Hingsburger, 1989). Hingsburger, Griffiths, and Quinsey (1991) presented case examples of people with intellectual disabilities for whom the treatment for certain inappropriate sexual behaviors was sex education alone. Other cases, however, require more clinically complex intervention, in which sex education is often a critical vulnerability for the development of the inappropriate sexual expression and one of the components of effective intervention but is not the only factor (Griffiths, 2002).

Third, the discovery of HIV/AIDS changed society's perspective on sex education. People with intellectual disabilities often have little knowledge about HIV/AIDS or about how to minimize their risk of infection (McGillvray, 1999). Many currently used sexual education programs for people with intellectual disabilities are silent on the topic of HIV/AIDS (Scotti et al., 1997). Jacobs et al. (1989) suggested that HIV education programs for people with intellectual disabilities should include teaching individuals that HIV infection is a personal threat, that it is preventable, and that individuals can manage the changes needed to prevent infection while still achieving sexual satisfaction. However, they further suggested that before a significant reduction in HIV-risk behaviors can be expected, HIV/AIDS programs for people who have intellectual disabilities will need to target the modification of specific risk behaviors. This can be accomplished by providing direct skills training and adequate support for application of those new skills. Schools and community agencies are beginning to recognize the critical importance of evaluating and documenting the effectiveness of their educational programs and the need for accountability regarding the quality of sexuality education.

Fourth, preventive health care is an emerging concern. Since the 1990s, initiatives have focused on preventive health methods, including sexual health, that go beyond simple hygiene (e.g., Lunsky, Armstrong, & Straiko, 1999).

When to Teach Sexuality

Learning about sexuality does not take place in six 1-hour sessions, nor is it restricted to a single period in a person's life. It is a lifelong process. This means that people with intellectual disabilities, just like people without disabilities, will learn about sexuality throughout their lives. People need access to accurate information when it is age appropriate and contextually relevant for them to know it. Parents and staff can capitalize on these moments to teach about different parts of sexuality. Examples of natural "teachable moments" for sexuality education are when children begin to ask questions about their bodies, when they want to know where babies come from, or when they experience body changes during puberty.

Formal Sexuality Programs

In addition to these "teachable moments," people who have intellectual disabilities benefit from formal socio-sexual education programs. There are some excellent programs that are available commercially. One of the most widely used is the Life Horizons I and II program by Kempton (1988). This program is very comprehensive and includes hundreds of slides to aid instruction. Kempton, one of the most important founding educators in this field, suggests that a good socio-sexual education program should include male and female anatomy, human reproduction, birth control, and sexual health (including safer sex practices). However, she also recommends that training should include the moral, social, and legal aspects of sexuality, male and female socio-sexual behavior, dating, parenting, marriage, prevention of and coping with abuse, ways to build self-esteem, and how to establish relationships. A fundamental part of socio-sexual education is teaching that there are responsibilities that come with sexual expression.

Needs in Sexuality Education

Although most professionals agree in 2006 that sex education should be provided for people with intellectual disabilities, there are several major challenges in the manner in which socio-sexual education is provided. It is generally

- Provided sporadically or only in response to a problem
- Based on educational programs that have very little, if any, empirical evidence of effectiveness
- Incomplete and fails to address the full range of topics to allow for a comprehensive understanding of sexuality
- Not evaluated for effectiveness, generalization or transfer of skill to the person's life

Research clearly indicates that there is a need for sexuality education for people with intellectual disabilities (Adams et al., 1982; Whitehouse & McCabe, 1997). Despite the significant consensus in the field about the value of socio-sexual education, the practice of providing sexuality education in programs for people with intellectual disabilities is often limited. McCabe and Schreck (1992) demonstrated that people with mild levels of intellectual disability expressed knowledge about their sexuality that was limited, inaccurate, inconsistent, and even improbable. In two other studies, researchers concluded that individuals who have an intellectual disability have lower levels of sexual knowledge and experience in almost all areas, except menstruation and body part identification (McCabe & Cummins, 1996; Szollos & McCabe, 1995). In addition to a lack of knowledge, people with intellectual disabilities also hold negative feelings in relation to their sexuality and many misconceptions about sexuality, including the belief that sexual intercourse is intended to hurt the female, that women can give birth without being pregnant, that masturbation causes harm, that men have periods, and that in heterosexual intercourse the penis generally goes into the woman's anus (Szollos & McCabe, 1995).

McCabe (1993) found that individuals with a intellectual disability are afforded very little opportunity to learn about sexuality from sources other than the media and formal sex education classes. When individuals are afforded the opportunity for education, however, they typically demonstrate significant and substantial increases in sexual knowledge (e.g., Lindsay et al., 1999).

Watson et al. (2002) recommend five critical dimensions for effective sexuality education:

1. Educational materials should be valid tools that have been field tested and/or researched and that cover a comprehensive range of topics (e.g., anatomy to parenting), present options (e.g., from sexual intercourse to abstinence), and include current issues (e.g., safer sex practices).
2. The materials must be appropriate to a person's age, special needs, sensitivities, culture, and values.
3. Sexuality training should be conducted by people who have the knowledge and skill to do so.
4. Sex education is most effective if it is taught using a variety of instructional methods such as direct instruction, movies or slides, group discussion, group exercises, role playing of social skills, repetition of topics in different ways, and concrete or visual materials.
5. In addition to evaluating training before presenting it, there should be postevaluation of training to assess whether each participant gained the desired knowledge and skill acquisition or if further training is required. Sexuality education should adhere to the same standards placed on other training programs. There should be educational goals, training steps, and outcome evaluation.

BIRTH CONTROL

In the early part of the 1900s, sexuality of people with intellectual disabilities was dominated by the eugenics movement and a concern regarding procreation (see Scheerenberger, 1983). During World War II, approximately 300,000 people with intellectual and other disabilities in Nazi-occupied countries underwent forced sterilization to prevent their procreation. Primarily for the same reason, similar forced sterilization occurred throughout other parts of the world, including North America, until the 1970s. Sterilization of people with intellectual disabilities was based on beliefs that arose from the eugenics movement popular in North America, Europe and elsewhere that "feeble-mindedness" was largely inherited. Intelligence tests were being used to determine if individuals should be institutionalized or sterilized to prevent procreation. Because institutionalization was expensive, people with intellectual disabilities were often sterilized so that they could then be put to work in the community.

The beliefs of the eugenics movement have long been discredited. It has been known for some time that many of the causes of disabling conditions are not linked to heredity (Zigler, 1967). It is estimated that approximately 50% of the individuals who have intellectual disabilities have a nonhereditary cause for their disability, including such conditions such as premature birth, fetal alcohol syndrome, and other "organic but not genetic" causes (Matilainen et al., 1995; Zigler & Hodapp, 1986). Even people who have intellectual disabilities because of a genetic condition will not necessarily pass on the disabilities to the next generation. The nature of some disabilities is such that they make procreation less likely (e.g., the fertility rate in females with Down syndrome is low, males with Down syndrome are typically sterile). However, where procreation is possible, the same genetic probabilities of passing on specific genes apply to individuals with intellectual disabilities, such that recessive genes need to be paired with similar recessive genes and dominant genes have basically a 50% chance of being passed on from one generation to the next. (See Chapter 9 for more detail about primary causes of intellectual disability.)

The right to procreate and parent has stirred heated debate in the field of intellectual disabilities. In Canada during the 1970s, the case of Eve (Rioux & Yarmol, 1987) provided very clear consent guidelines for nontherapeutic sterilization. In Canada and in many U.S. states, a third party (e.g., parent) does not have the right to consent to nontherapeutic sterilization for a person who has intellectual disabilities, whether an adult or a minor. For a person with an intellectual disability to give consent to nontherapeutic sterilization, the nature and consequences of consenting to the procedure must be established.

The right to procreate and raise children does not end with the topic of sterilization. Concern is often expressed as to whether people with intellectual disabilities can be adequate parents. It is common for a parent with an intellectual disability to be subject to considerable scrutiny regarding his or her ability to raise the child free from neglect or harm. Feldman (2002) developed a rich body of empirical research in the area of parents with intellectual disabilities and the challenges they face in parenting. The reader is directed to Chapter 35 of that book for a reference to a specialized program that was been developed to support those parents with disabilities who are able to learn the skills necessary for parenting. Counseling and support is very often vital to help people with disabilities make the right decision for themselves and their future children.

SEXUAL DIVERSITY

People with intellectual disabilities exhibit the same range of sexual expression that occurs in people without disabilities, including heterosexual, homosexual, and bisexual relationships; dating; petting; masturbation; premarital coitus; and marital intimacy. Some individuals with intellectual disabilities are limited in their sexual expression by physical challenges, interest, or opportunity. However, many people with intellectual disabilities are further limited in their sexual expression by the environments in which they live and by the attitudes of caregivers and society. In addition, many people with intellectual disabilities live in sex-segregated environments where it is almost impossible to develop a heterosexual relationship. In some environments, there are severe restrictions on sexual behavior of people with intellectual disabilities, and the rights of association or privacy that would be afforded to people without disabilities are denied. In addition, people with intellectual disabilities have been punished or even abused for their sexuality. There have been instances of people with intellectual disabilities being beaten, drugged, or emotionally berated for engaging in sexual behavior that would be generally considered appropriate if engaged in by a people without intellectual disabilities. As a result inappropriate sexual behavior can develop as a means of adapting to a sexually aberrant living and learning environment.

As with people who do not have disabilities, individuals with intellectual disabilities may choose to express or not express their sexuality in various ways, depending on their learning experiences, family values, or religious background. However, some people with intellectual disabilities have experienced atypical learning experiences with regard to their sexuality. They are often sheltered from sexual knowledge and typical experiences that would assist them in developing a healthy understanding of their sexuality. Inappropriate sexual behavior can sometimes develop as a result of a lack of sexual knowledge and understanding. People with intellectual disabilities do not inherently have more unusual or inappropriate sexual behavior than people without intellectual disabilities, but it is common for them to encounter very different learning experiences about their sexuality. For this reason, they have sometimes learned unusual or inappropriate sexual behaviors through atypical life and learning experiences, such as abuse and institutional living.

SEXUAL VICTIMIZATION

Research has provided evidence that the sexual abuse of people with intellectual disabilities is widespread (Sobsey, 1993; see also Chapter 30). Conservative statistics suggest that people with intellectual disabilities are one and a half times more likely to be sexually abused than people without disabilities (Doucette, 1986). Sobsey (1993) reported that abuse occurs across all levels of disability, with both female (83%) and male (17%) victims. The majority of offenders against people with intellectual disabilities were males who were known to the person. In 43.7% of the cases, the offender's relationship with the person with an intellectual disability was related to the victim's disability. The offenders were often people who held a trusted, caregiving role in the victim's life. The offenses frequently occurred in the natural environments of the person with intellectual disabilities. Often, the abuse experiences were repeated.

The increased vulnerability for abuse of people with intellectual disabilities is not related directly to the nature of the person's disability. Rather, abuse is more likely to occur because of the way society treats and views people with intellectual disabilities and their sexuality, and because of the systems in which people with intellectual disabilities live. In these systems, people with intellectual disabilities have little or no power, choice, or control over many aspects of their lives. Sexual abuse is more than a sexual act: It is an expression of power. People with disabilities often live in environments where their powerlessness creates a disadvantage.

Risk factors for the increased vulnerability for sexual abuse of people with intellectual disabilities have been largely associated with the service delivery system and social attitudes related to people with disabilities (Sobsey & Doe, 1991). These include the isolation of individuals within service environments; the lack of screening of staff and of policy enforcement; the devaluing of people with disabilities, which leaves them desiring acceptance; their training in compliance; limitations in their verbal communication skills; and the use of psychotropic medication (Sobsey & Doe, 1991).

Sexual abuse prevention programs have been developed to address the risk factors individuals face through a lack of knowledge about sexuality as well as ways to overcome learned compliance and communication difficulties (Collins, Schuster, & Nelson, 1992; Haseltine & Miltenberger, 1990; Lumley et al., 1998). However, the systemic issues in the intellectual and social service system, the mental health system, and the judicial systems remain an ongoing challenge.

Theorists believe that there is a need for a multidimensional approach to the reduction of abuse of people with intellectual disabilities (Sobsey, 1994). This approach would include changing systems in terms of policy, screening staff, empowering individuals, addressing attitudes that dehumanize people with disabilities, and providing staff and people with intellectual disabilities with education about healthy boundaries. However, individuals with intellectual disabilities are further disadvantaged in the system following an abusive event. Three distinct disadvantages have been identified in the literature:

1. Abuse of people with intellectual disabilities is less likely to be detected or reported (Sobsey, 1994). Such people may not have the knowledge, communication abilities, or power to report abuse. Nor may they be believed if they do report the abuse. Because the abuse is not identified, individuals can be revictimized by the system or the victimizer. For example, the individual may display symptoms of abuse (e.g., resistance to attend various programs), withdrawn behavior, sleep disturbances, incontinence, and even aggression and self-injury, but sometimes these are not treated as a natural response to abuse. Rather, they may be misunderstood as behavior problems or even mental illness. As such, the victim is then sometimes subjected to behavior or chemical intervention to manage the symptoms, without exploration of the cause. However, a lack of detection or reporting also means that the individual is more likely to remain in the presence of the victimizer and vulnerable to repeated abuse.
2. If abuse is identified, there is a general lack of therapeutic support available in most communities to assist survivors to receive adequate counseling or therapy (Sobsey, 1994). Many communities do not have specialized programs for counseling and therapy for people with intellectual disabilities, nor are all general therapeutic services aware of how to adapt and accommodate generic resources to meet the needs of people with intellectual disabilities.
3. If the abuse is identified and reported, the judiciary system is challenged to accommodate people with intellectual disabilities to ensure the victimizer is charged and prosecuted. Establishing the credibility of people with disabilities to obtain their legal rights with regard to sexual abuse may be difficult (Sobsey, 1994), as are guidelines for clearly establishing an individual's capacity to give consent to sex, given the systemic power differentials within which most people with disabilities live (McCarthy, 1993; Thompson, 1994).

TREATMENT AND COUNSELING

Until the 1980s, it was widely assumed that people with intellectual disabilities would not benefit from counseling or treatment for sexual issues. Traditional insight-oriented therapy was considered inappropriate for people with intellectual disabilities. Since then, these therapies have developed in keeping with the cognitive abilities of people with intellectual disabilities.

The two primary areas of counseling and treatment of sexually-related issues are victim (survivor) counseling and treatment of inappropriate sexual behavior. These are discussed next.

Victim (Survivor) Counseling

Although people with intellectual disabilities have been sexually abused at higher rates than people without disabilities, their access to appropriate supports and counseling services has been largely ignored. An emerging body of literature, however, has helped clinicians who work with sexual abuse survivors to adapt their counseling procedures to support people with intellectual disabilities. Some contributions include the book *Counseling People with Intellectual Disabilities Who Have Been*

Sexually Abused and the training video, *Alone in a Crowd,* both of which were created by two of the leaders in this field (Mansell & Sobsey, 2001a, 2001b).

Treatment of Sexually Inappropriate Behavior

Edgerton (1973) suggested that people with intellectual disabilities do not demonstrate any more sexually inappropriate behavior then people without disabilities if they are provided with a normative learning experience. As noted, however, the sexual learning experience of many people with intellectual disabilities is often anything but normative. Population statistics indicate that individuals with intellectual disabilities are overrepresented in the population of convicted sexual offenders (e.g., Shapiro, 1986). Many researchers suggest that these data may be misleading because the data might imply that people with intellectual disabilities commit more sexual offenses. The high rates of convicted offenders are more likely to represent the fact that when people with intellectual disabilities interact with the judicial system they are disadvantaged: They are more easily caught, they confess more readily, and they are less likely to mount a suitable defense (Santamour & West, 1978). Moreover, the nature of their offences is more likely to be inappropriate behaviors such as public masturbation, exhibitionism, and voyeurism (rather than serious sexual violations) than is the case for people without disabilities (Gilby, Wolf, & Goldberg, 1989).

Paraphilia is rare among people with intellectual disabilities (Day, 1994), but it can occur in males and females of all intellectual levels (Fedoroff, 2000). Paraphilia refers to recurring fantasies, sexual urges, or behaviors that involve objects, suffering or humiliation of oneself or a partner, or children or nonconsenting people; these occur over a period of at least 6 months (American Psychiatric Association [APA], 2000). When paraphilia does occur in people with intellectual disabilities, it is often misdiagnosed. The *Diagnostic and Statistic Manual of Mental Disorders, Fourth Edition, Text Revision* (*DSM-IV-TR*) states that people with intellectual disabilities may present a "decrease in judgment, social skills, or impulse control that, in rare cases, leads to unusual sexual behavior" that should be distinguished from paraphilia (APA, 2000, p. 525). The term *counterfeit deviance* was used in an article by Hingsburger, Griffiths and Quinsey (1991) to illustrate case examples where the sexual misbehavior of people with intellectual disabilities was determined to be the product of experiential, environmental, or medical factors, rather than paraphilia.

The nature of an inappropriate sexual behavior provides no indication regarding the cause of the behavior. For example, a particular sexual behavior could have many different causes. An example behavior is touching one's genitals in public. The typology of this behavior could look like sexual indecency or exhibitionism. However, there are many rival hypotheses for this behavior that have been clinically identified in people with intellectual disabilities (see Table 36.2). In examining years of clinical records, Griffiths (2004) identified a range of biomedical, psychological, and social reasons why this same behavior had presented itself in different individuals with intellectual disabilities. None of the hypotheses listed relate to paraphilia but rather to counterfeit deviance, although many of the behaviors were originally referred as public indecency or exhibitionism.

As demonstrated by Table 36.2, it is vital that a thorough assessment be conducted to determine the factors that influence the behavioral symptom so that appropriate intervention can follow. This distinction often requires a comprehensive biopsychosocial assessment by professionals knowledgeable about individuals with intellectual disabilities. (For more information, see Griffiths, 2002.)

Since the mid-1980s, an increasingly rich body of clinical literature on intervention for sexually inappropriate behavior has emerged in this field (Griffiths, 2002). The treatment focus has shifted toward promotion of the development of adaptive sexual behaviors to replace the behavior of concern rather then a focus on inhibition of the inappropriate expression alone.

Table 36.2. Rival biopsychosocial hypotheses regarding causes of inappropriate sexual behavior such as touching genitals in public

Biomedical hypotheses
Psychiatric (symptom related to posttraumatic stress disorder, mania, obsessive-compulsive disorder, or a tic disorder)
Medical (allergies to soap or material in underwear, various genital and sexually transmitted medical problems)
Medication (with the side effect of inhibited arousal and sexual frustration)
Psychological hypotheses
Lack of appropriate sociosexual knowledge regarding privacy and boundaries
Communication deficits (inability to request a bathroom)
Social hypotheses
Presence of attractive girl (arousing stimuli) in a public area with no access to arousing stimuli available when in an appropriate private area
Lack of access to a private place or time
Social learning (institutional learning regarding a disregard for privacy)
Attention gained or escape or delay/avoidance achieved because of the display of the behavior

From Griffiths, D. (2004). *Sexual aggression and persons with intellectual disabilities.* Invited address at Working Together: Creating Opportunities Conference. Canadian Mental Health, Red Deer, Alberta; adapted by permission.

Griffiths, Richards, Watson, and Fedoroff (2002) suggested that treatment strategies for inappropriate sexual behavior include teaching and reinforcing alternative replacement behaviors, altering the conditions sustaining the behavior, and judiciously using medication or hormonal therapy (if and only if appropriate).

Based on a growing body of clinical experience, specialized treatment providers have reported that sexuality problems of people with intellectual disabilities, particularly people with mild and moderate disability, are surprisingly responsive to intervention (Knopp & Lackey, 1987). The clinical literature provides convincing evidence of effective sexual treatment and counseling strategies that have been developed for people with intellectual disabilities, although there is a lack of empirical research in this area (Griffiths et al., 2004). Specialized treatment for people who are dually diagnosed (i.e., they have both mental health needs and intellectual disabilities) is not available in all areas. It often requires coordination with generic mental health and correctional resources that may be reluctant or ill informed to adapt resources for this population (see Griffiths, Stavrakaki, & Summers, 2002).

SUMMARY

It is important to dispel the myths, described at the beginning of this chapter, associated with the sexuality of people with intellectual disabilities. These myths continue to influence how some people in society treat people with intellectual disabilities with respect to their sexuality and how the social service, medical, mental health, and judicial systems respond to sexual issues regarding people with intellectual disabilities. Available research and clinical evidence contradicts the myths, demonstrating that people with intellectual disabilities are sexual people and, like people without disabilities, need knowledge and a normal learning environment to understand and learn to act responsibly on their natural feelings.

FOR FURTHER THOUGHT AND DISCUSSION

1. Did you believe any of the myths in Table 34.1 before reading this chapter? Do you still believe some? Why? What do you think most people believe?
2. Do you think people with intellectual disabilities have the same sexual rights as people without disabilities? Why do you think these rights are so often denied?
3. Why do you think the sexuality of people with intellectual disabilities makes so many people uncomfortable?
4. Why do you think people with intellectual disabilities are more likely to be sexually abused? What systemic changes could occur to minimize this risk?
5. What would you do if you came across two residents alone and engaged in petting in the family room of a five-person group home? What would the major issues be in this situation? Would their level of cognitive functioning change your response? What if both individuals were consenting? What if one was not consenting? Would your response differ if the couple was a man and a woman or a couple of the same sex? Where is an appropriate place to engage in petting behavior in a group home? What teaching programs might be recommended?

REFERENCES

Adams, G.L., Tallon, R.J., & Alcorn, D.A. (1982). Attitudes toward the sexuality of mentally retarded and nonretarded persons. *Education and Training of the Mentally Retarded, 17,* 307–312.

American Association on Mental Retardation. (2002). *Mental retardation: Definition, classification and systems of supports* (10th ed.). Washington, DC: Author.

American Psychiatric Association. (2000). *Diagnostic and statistical manual of mental disorders* (4th ed., text rev.). Washington, DC: Author.

Canadian Charter of Rights and Freedoms, Constitution Act (1982[1]) Schedule B, Part 1.

Coleman, E.M., & Murphy, W.D. (1980). A survey of sexual attitudes and sex education programs among facilities for the mentally retarded. *Applied Research in Mental Retardation, 1,* 269–276.

Collins, B.V., Schuster, J.W., & Nelson, C.M. (1992). Teaching a generalized response to the lures of strangers to adults with severe handicaps. *Exceptionality, 3,* 67–80.

Day, K. (1994). Male mentally handicapped sex offenders. *British Journal of Psychiatry, 165,* 630–639.

Doucette, J. (1986). *Violent acts against disabled women.* Toronto: DAWN Canada.

Edgerton, R. (1973). Socio-cultural research considerations. In F.F. de la Cruz & G.G. La Veck (Eds.), *Human sexuality and the mentally retarded* (pp. 240–249). New York: Brunner/Mazel.

Fedoroff, P. (2000). Treatment of paraphilias in people with intellectual disabilities. *Journal on Intellectual Disabilities, 7*(1), 50–65.

Feldman, M. (2002). Parents with intellectual disabilities: Impediments and supports. In D.M. Griffiths, D. Richards, P. Fedoroff, et al. (Eds.), *Ethical dilemmas: Sexuality and intellectual disabilities* (pp. 255–293). Kingston, NY: National Association of the Dually Diagnosed.

Fudge Schormans, A., & Brown, I. (2002). An investigation into the characteristics of the maltreatment of children with intellectual disabilities and the alleged perpetrators of this maltreatment. *Journal on Intellectual Disabilities, 9*(1), 1–19.

Gilby, R., Wolf, L., & Goldberg, B. (1989). Mentally retarded adolescent sex offenders: A survey and pilot study. *Canadian Journal of Psychiatry, 34,* 542–548.

Gordon, S. (1971). Missing in special education: Sex. *Journal of Special Education, 5,* 351–354.

Griffiths, D. (1991, May). Myths and facts of sexuality. Part of a panel presentation by L. Walker-Hirsh, W. Kempton, J. Stowell, et. al, *Sexuality and mental retardation: A glance at the present and a view to the future.* American Association on Mental Retardation, Washington DC.

Griffiths, D. (2002). Sexual aggression. In W.I. Gardner (Ed.), *Aggression and persons with intellectual disabilities* (pp. 325–386). Kingston, NY: National Association of the Dually Diagnosed.

Griffiths, D. (2003). Sexuality and people who have developmental disabilities: From myth to emerging practices. In I. Brown & M. Percy (Eds.), *Developmental disabilities in Ontario* (2nd ed., pp. 677–689). Toronto: Ontario Association on Developmental Disabilities.

Griffiths, D. (2004a, February 12). *Behavior disorders or mental illness: A question revisited.* Presentation at the Centre for Addiction and Mental Health Regional Conference on Dual Diagnosis, Red Deer, AB, Canada.

Griffiths, D. (2004b). *Sexual aggression and persons with intellectual disabilities.* Invited address at Working Together: Creating Opportunities Conference. Canadian Mental Health, Red Deer, Alberta.

Griffiths, D., & Lunsky, Y. (2000). Changing attitudes towards the nature of socio-sexual assessment and education for persons with intellectual disabilities: A twenty-year comparison. *Journal of Intellectual Disabilities, 7,* 16–33.

Griffiths, D.M., Quinsey, V.L., & Hingsburger, D. (1989). *Changing inappropriate sexual behavior: A community-based approach for persons with developmental disabilities.* Baltimore: Paul H. Brookes Publishing Co.

Griffiths, D.M., Richards, D., Fedoroff, P., & Watson, S.L. (Eds.). (2002). *Ethical dilemmas: Sexuality and intellectual disabilities.* Kingston, NY: National Association of the Dually Diagnosed.

Griffiths, D., Richards, D., Watson, S., & Fedoroff, P. (2002). Sexuality and mental health issues. In D.M. Griffiths, C. Stavrakaki, & J. Summers (Eds.), *Dual diagnosis: An introduction to the mental health needs of persons with intellectual disabilities* (pp. 419–482). Sudbury, ON, Canada: Habilitative Mental Health Resource Network.

Griffiths, D.M., Stavrakaki, C., & Summers, J. (Eds.). (2002). *Dual diagnosis: An introduction to the mental health needs of persons with intellectual disabilities.* Sudbury, ON, Canada: Habilitative Mental Health Resource Network.

Griffiths, D., Watson, S., Lewis, R., et al. (2004). Research in sexuality and intellectual disability. In E. Emerson, C. Hatton, T. Parmenter, et al. (Eds.), *Handbook of methods of research and evaluation in intellectual disabilities* (pp. 311–334). Hoboken, NJ: John Wiley & Sons.

Haseltine, B., & Miltenberger, R.G. (1990). Teaching self-protection skills to persons with mental retardation. *American Journal on Mental Retardation, 95,* 188–197.

Hingsburger, D., Griffiths, D., & Quinsey, V. (1991). Detecting counterfeit deviance. *The Habilitative Mental Healthcare Newsletter, 10*(9), 51–54.

Jacobs, R., Samowitz, P., Levy, J.M., et al. (1989). Developing an AIDS prevention program for persons with intellectual disabilities. *Mental Retardation, 27,* 233–237.

Johnson, P.R., & Davies, R. (1989). Sexual attitudes of members of staff. *The British Journal of Mental Subnormality, 35,* 17–21.

Johnson, W. (1973). Sex education of the mentally retarded. In F.F. de la Cruz & G.D. LaVeck (Eds.), *Human sexuality and the mentally retarded* (pp. 57–66). New York: Penguin Books.

Kempton, W. (1975). *Sex education for persons with disabilities that hinder learning.* North Scituate, MA: Duxbury Press.

Kempton, W. (1988). *Life Horizons I and II.* Santa Barbara, CA: James Stanfield Publishing.

Kempton, W. (1993). *Sexuality and persons with disabilities that hinder learning.* Santa Barbara, CA: James Stanfield.

Knopp, F.H., & Lackey, L.B. (1987). *Sexual offenders identified as intellectually disabled: A summary of data from 40 treatment providers.* Orwell, VT: Safer Society Press.

Lindsay, W.R., Bellshaw, E., Culross, G., et al. (1999). Increases in knowledge following a course of sex education for people with intellectual disabilities. *Journal of Intellectual Disability Research, 36,* 531–539.

Lumley, V.A., Miltenberger, R.G., Long, E.S., et al. (1998). Evaluation of a sexual abuse prevention program for adults with mental retardation. *Journal of Applied Behavior Analysis, 31,* 91–101.

Lunsky, Y., Armstrong, S., & Straiko, A. (1999, May). *New approaches to the medical care of women with intellectual disabilities: The Nisonger Center UAP women's health groups.* Paper presented at the annual meeting of the American Association on Mental Retardation. New Orleans, LA.

Mansell, S., & Sobsey, D. (2001a). *Alone in a crowd* [training video]. Kingston, NY: National Association of the Dually Diagnosed.

Mansell, S., & Sobsey, D. (2001b). *Counseling people with intellectual disabilities who have been sexually abused.* Kingston, NY: National Association of the Dually Diagnosed.

Matilainen, R., Airaksinen, E., Mononen, T., et al. (1995). A population based study on the causes of severe and profound mental retardation. *Acta Pediatricia, 84,* 261–266.

McCabe, M.P. (1991). Sexual knowledge, experience, feelings and needs scale for people with disabilities. *Sexuality and Disability, 17,* 157–170.

McCabe, M.P. (1993). Sex education program for persons with mental retardation. *Mental Retardation, 31*(6), 377–387.

McCabe, M., & Cummins, R. (1996). The sexual knowledge, experience, feelings and needs of people with mild intellectual disability. *Education and Training in Mental Retardation and Intellectual Disabilities, 31*(1), 13–21.

McCabe, M., & Schreck, A. (1992). Before sex education: An evaluation of the sexual knowledge, experience, feelings and needs of people with mild intellectual disabilities. *Australia and New Zealand Journal of Intellectual Disabilities, 18*(2), 75–82.

McCarthy, M. (1993). Sexual experiences of women with learning difficulties in long-stay hospitals. *Sexuality and Disability, 11,* 277–286.

McGillvray, J.A. (1999). Level of knowledge and risk of contracting HIV/AIDS among young adults with mild/moderate intellectual disability. *Journal of Applied Research in Intellectual Disabilities, 12,* 113–126.

Mitchell, L., Doctor, R.M., & Butler, D.C. (1978). Attitudes of caretakers toward the sexual behavior of mentally retarded persons. *American Journal of Mental Deficiency, 83,* 289–296.

Rehabilitation Act of 1973, PL 93-112, 29 U.S.C. §§ 701 *et seq.*

Rioux, M. (1996, Summer). Reproductive technology: A rights issue. *Entourage,* 5–7.

Rioux, M., & Yarmol, K. (1987, Winter). The right to control one's own body: A look at the "Eve" decision. *Entourage,* 28–30.

Roeher Institute. (1988). *Vulnerable.* Toronto, ON, Canada: Author.

Rowe, W., & Savage, S. (1987). *Sexuality and the intellectually handicapped: A guidebook for health care professionals.* Lewiston, NY: E. Mellen Press.

Santamour, W., & West, B. (1978). *The mentally retarded offender and corrections.* Washington, DC: U.S. Department of Justice.

Scheerenberger, R.C. (1983). *A history of mental retardation.* Baltimore: Paul H. Brookes Publishing Co.

Scotti, J.R., Nangle, D.W., Masia, C.L., et al. (1997). Providing an AIDS education and skills training program to persons with mild intellectual disabilities. *Education and Training in Mental Retardation and Intellectual Disabilities, 32,* 113–128.

Shapiro, S. (1986). Delinquent and disturbed behavior within the field of mental deficiency. In A.V.S. deReuck & R. Porter (Eds.), *The mentally abnormal offender* (pp. 76–90). New York: Grune & Stratton.

Sobsey, D. (1993). Sexual abuse of individuals with intellectual disability. In A. Craft (Ed.), *Practice issues in sexuality and intellectual disability* (pp. 93–115). London: Routledge.

Sobsey, D. (1994). *Violence and abuse in the lives of people with disabilities: The end of silent acceptance?* Baltimore: Paul H. Brookes Publishing Co.

Sobsey, D., & Doe, T. (1991). Patterns of sexual abuse and assault. *Sexuality and Disability, 9*(3), 243–259.

Szollos, A.A., & McCabe, M.P. (1995). The sexuality of people with mild intellectual disability: Perceptions of clients and caregivers. *Australia and New Zealand Journal of Intellectual Disabilities, 20*(3), 205–222.

Thompson, D. (1994). The sexual experiences of men with learning disabilities having sex with men: Issues for HIV prevention. *Sexuality and Disability, 12*(3), 221–242.

United Nations. (1971, December 20). *Declaration on the Rights of Mentally Retarded Persons.* General Assembly Res. 2856 (XXVI).

Watson, S., Griffiths, D., Richards, D., et al. (2002). Sex education. In D.M. Griffiths, D. Richards, P. Fedoroff, et al. (Eds.), *Ethical dilemmas: Sexuality and intellectual disabilities* (pp. 175–226). Kingston, NY: National Association of the Dually Diagnosed.

Whitehouse, M.A., & McCabe, M.P. (1997). Sex education programs for people with intellectual disabilities: How effective are they? *Education and Training in Mental Retardation and Intellectual Disabilities, 32*(3), 229–240.

Wolfensberger, W. (1972). *Normalization.* Toronto: National Institute on Mental Retardation.

Zigler, E. (1967). Familial mental retardation: A continuing dilemma. *Science, 155,* 292–298.

Zigler, E., & Hodapp, R.M. (1986). *Understanding mental retardation.* Cambridge, United Kingdom: Cambridge University Press.

37

A Gendered Approach to Intellectual and Developmental Disabilities

Patricia Noonan Walsh

WHAT YOU WILL LEARN ABOUT IN THIS CHAPTER

- Effects of culture and social roles on women with intellectual and developmental disabilities and their female caregivers
- Sources of evidence regarding the lives of women with disabilities
- Women's work as support providers

Each person's lifelong identity is interwoven with his or her gender. *Gender* refers not only to the inherent biological differences that help to shape human development, but also to the ways that men and women are expected to behave as they live and grow to maturity in the family and wider society. The experiences of young children; school-age children and adolescents; and young, middle-age, and older adults are imbued with their gender roles. In the public domain, gender helps to determine individuals' economic and political status. Typically men earn more than women and are more likely to be elected as representatives in government. Women and men incur different health risks. Gender influences life itself: In most countries, women outlive men. For this reason, global and national policy makers increasingly place the quality of women's longer lives as a matter of central importance. Across the globe, populations will age for some time to come. Yet, longer life expectancy cannot by itself guarantee a better quality of life. Women can expect to live more years of life with lowered quality, often alone, because they are likely to survive longer after the development of disability in adult life (Robine, Romieu, & Cambois, 1999). Health is a core element in quality of life (Schalock & Verdugo, 2002), but poverty, marginalization, limited access to primary health care, and lack of health promotion knowledge compromise health.

It is known that these grave risks shadow the lives of people with intellectual and developmental disabilities (referred to throughout this chapter as *developmental disabilities*), even as they, too, can expect to live longer. Yet, understanding of how gender plays a part in the lives of people with such disabilities has emerged only recently. This chapter addresses what is known about women in this population by exploring, from sources of evidence that are available, how girls and women with developmental disabilities experience life stages and transitions, how women experience key domains of adult life, and some factors related to women's healthy aging. It also focuses on what is often regarded as women's work—giving long-term or perhaps lifelong support and care to people with disabilities.

EFFECTS OF CULTURE AND SOCIAL ROLES ON WOMEN WITH INTELLECTUAL AND DEVELOPMENTAL DISABILITIES AND THEIR FEMALE CAREGIVERS

Culture and its accompanying social roles have the potential to affect the opportunities of both women with intellectual disabilities and their caregivers. Both areas of influence are discussed next.

Culture and Disability

Culture filters the influence of gender on the life experience of people with developmental disabilities. It is known that the very words used to describe people in this group and assign them to categories vary across time and place. In their study of what *disability* means in many cultures worldwide, Whyte and Ingstad warned readers of the "pitfall of cultural juxtaposition: our tendency to look at other cultures in terms of our own problems and thus to fail to grasp the premises upon which other people are operating" (1995, p. 5).

In some cultures, being a woman may attract greater stigma (Hanna & Rogovsky, 1991). The birth of a baby girl may by itself be a cause of dismay, whereas that of a baby with a condition likely to give rise to disability may be a source of family shame. Arguably, disadvantages accrue for girls and women with disabilities growing up in cultures where their gender has already devalued them. Being poor, without a spouse, without employment, without a vote, and perhaps at the mercy of overbearing relatives may potentially exacerbate the impact of having a lifelong disability for women. Cross-cultural study of older mothers caring for adult children with intellectual disabilities in the United States, Ireland, and Northern Ireland found that mothers differed in their perception of their role and in their uptake of social supports according to the country in which they lived (Seltzer et al., 1995).

Social Roles and Disability

Women with developmental disabilities may potentially adopt any social role available to women in the general population: Each is a daughter; many are sisters, aunts, cousins, and friends; and, depending on cultural expectations, some become co-workers, spouses, and parents (Walsh & LeRoy, 2004). Yet, they do not often participate in the same array of social roles as their peers. Historically, single-sex wards in hospitals or large institutions separated women from their male peers and further deprived them of human contact and friendships typical in their societies (Walsh, 2000). Even at the beginning of the 21st century, social roles may be out of step with other aspects of the woman's life and status. Behavior that was appropriate for a compliant 13-year-old daughter may not best serve the needs for autonomy and rich life experiences when the daughter becomes an adult woman in her forties still living in her family home.

Lifelong caregiving alters the social roles of women caregivers and other family members not yet directly involved in giving primary support. Mothers and sisters may find diminished opportunities to take part in a wide array of roles as they support a relative at home for years or even decades. Caregiving may expand to fill all the time there is, moving other relationships, household duties, energy for leisure, or a cherished career to the sidelines (Todd & Shearn, 1996). In their study of Canadian families that have children with developmental disabilities, Brown and colleagues (2003) found mixed views among parents about whether they enjoyed full opportunities to pursue further education and careers. Although most were positive about their options at least in the future, it was notable that one or both parents in 8 of the 34 families surveyed had given up a career or education in order to care for a child full-time.

Women with developmental disabilities will increasingly live their longer lives in the community in countries where government policy endorses this form of living arrangement rather than institutional life. Over the years, an aging or frail mother in her eighties may relinquish her role as primary caregiver in favor of a daughter or other relative. Siblings may step forward to assume caregiving responsibilities and distinctive relationships with their family members. As with any adult brothers and sisters, temperament, custom, proximity, and compatibility play a part. A brother may assume responsibility for a sister's financial matters, whereas an older sister may help the woman with personal care or shopping. Yet, many adults do not have siblings to step into these roles, and in their absence it is not uncommon for cousins or sisters-in-law to find they have "inherited" an adult relative with developmental disabilities. The strength of family cohesion will help to determine how closely the new caregiver will become attached to the woman, who may have little say in choosing her living arrangements or co-residents.

Women provide most personal and instrumental support as caregivers for people who have disabilities, as by far most rely on family care. Does this mean that mothers and sisters have inborn gifts of nurturance and are willing to abandon their own careers to become full-time caregivers? Do all adults with intellectual disabilities relish living in the family home until their own middle- or older-age period? Sweeping statements such as these ignore individual circumstances and the nuances of family relationships. For example, gender influences the relationships between adult siblings when one has developmental disabilities. In one study, sisters reported higher scores in caregiving, companionship, and positive affect when compared with brothers (Orsmond & Seltzer, 2000). Caregiving arrangements may reflect what must be now rather than what might be in the future. Further research embracing the testimony of women and their caregivers will aid in understanding more about the lives that they wish to lead.

Points to Remember

Gender is interwoven with personal and social development throughout the human life course. It is fundamental to the identity of each person, including a person with developmental disabilities, and it helps to determine social roles, expectations, and life opportunities. In addition, gender influences other important life outcomes such as employment, education, and health status. The next section examines sources of evidence about the place of women with developmental disabilities as family members, the key domains of adult life, and the factors related to women's healthy aging.

SOURCES OF EVIDENCE REGARDING THE LIVES OF WOMEN WITH DISABILITIES

What is known about the lives of adults with developmental disabilities draws on different sources of evidence. In more developed countries with formal human service systems, evidence may be available from dedicated databases. In Ireland, for example, there is a national Intellectual Disability Database recording demographic and other anonymous information about the 26,000 children and adults with intellectual disabilities who are reported annually by various service provider agencies (Barron & Mulvany, 2003). Yet, it is important to recall that such special databases reflect administrative information and do not tell us anything about those individuals who are not currently in contact with service systems. Many people with a mild level of intellectual disability, for example, may simply become invisible to social service systems after they finish school or job training.

Other evidence is more comprehensive, as it is drawn from population-based surveys such as the NHIS–Disability Supplement in the United States (Anderson, 2002). Such documents permit comparison of the characteristics of men and women with developmental or other disabilities and, in some cases, comparison of men and women with disabilities with their peers in the general population. Yet, ignorance persists about the daily lives of millions of men and women with intellectual disabilities leading ordinary lives in homes, villages, streets, and remote countryside in the less developed countries of the world—the very regions where most people with disabilities live (McConkey & O'Toole, 2000).

Longitudinal studies, which focus on individuals or groups of people over time, are valuable sources of evidence. They permit investigators to gather the same evidence about the same individuals over weeks, months, or years. An example might be evaluating the impact of an early intervention program targeting families with young children by gathering information before, during, and after the intervention. If the same children later take part in the same study when they have grown to be adolescents or even young adults, it is clear that the information yielded would be very helpful indeed in determining both the short-term and the long-term outcomes of interventions. A drawback is that longitudinal studies are usually complex and costly, and they carry the risk that some participants will move away or choose not to take part in the future.

On the whole, some understanding of women's lives has been captured through portraits and group snapshots rather than full-length films or epic novels. There has been comparatively little longitudinal research on the outcomes over time of growing older, whether as an individual with developmental disabilities or as a caregiving parent or sibling of family members in this group. The many publications reported by Seltzer and Krauss and their colleagues, among others, since the 1980s are a striking exception. These authors have illuminated the life transitions of hundreds of caregiving mothers who provide primary care for adult family members with developmental disabilities. Collaborating with colleagues, they have extended their studies to encompass the experiences of caregiving fathers (Essex, Seltzer, & Krauss, in press), brothers, and sisters and also to focus on individuals who have autism (Seltzer et al., 2000) or mental health difficulties (Greenberg et al., 1999).

By contrast, cross-sectional studies provide valuable evidence about individuals, groups, and families at a given time or place. These studies may be very large in scope, perhaps spanning a geographical region to provide a vital overview of gender and age differences in functioning among thousands of individuals (Porrell & Miltiades, 2002). Yet, they often rely on smaller samples of participants drawn from service settings or regions or assembled for the purpose of a once-off study if it is convenient and useful to do so. For example, Egan and Walsh (2001) explored the factors related to caring for adults with developmental disabilities among adult sibling caregivers living in a particular regional service setting in Ireland.

Finally, a most important and potentially very rich source of evidence is emerging in the voices and narratives of men and women with developmental disabilities who have at last begun to tell their own life stories. Often these are harrowing reminders of personal loss, years endured in bleak institutions, broken family ties, poor health, and poverty. Interest has flourished in women's—and men's—narratives of their own experiences and in the history of how people with disabilities were perceived and treated. The biographical accounts of women themselves can lend insight into their own lives and those of other women with developmental disabilities, then and now. Mabel, a middle-age Englishwoman who had been removed from her unmarried mother's care as an infant, was interviewed in later life (Brigham et al., 2000). Her mother was unmarried and had been deemed unfit at a time when social perceptions of women's competence were blurred with their social, especially reproductive, behavior. She was institutionalized and never saw her daughter again (Brigham et al., 2000; see also Appendix B at the end of the book). Mabel was herself a resident in a huge institution for 20 years. Later in life, a photograph of the now-defunct institution provoked vivid memories:

> Yes, it was (huge). On the female side it was A to H, on the male side it was A to D. There was more females than men. I think it was because the women were sent from the courts, some of them, and in the old days if you had a child and you wasn't married, it was a disgrace so they used to take the child away, put it in a home, and then the mother went into a workhouse. (Brigham et al., 2000, p. 164)

Yet, many voices also testify to the individuals' resilience, and contentment—attributes honed in the teeth of adversity (LeRoy et al., 2004). In their study of 167 older women with intellectual disabilities in 18 countries—including Canada, Taiwan, Argentina, and Ireland—Walsh and LeRoy (2004) presented both quantitative and qualitative findings about the women's personal histories, living arrangements, education and employment, social roles, and relationships. In addition, the women spoke of their fears, dreams, worries, and hopes for the future. Not surprisingly, these women named relationships with family members and others, health, and home as most important in their lives—thus echoing the sentiments of adults in the general population (Bowling, 1995).

Family Members

Whether rich or poor, whether living in a developed or still-developing country, families provide primary support and care for people with developmental disabilities. Family members compose the largest—if not the most vocal—body of caregivers, and most of these caregivers are women. In addition, as Schalock and Verdugo reminded, "A person's quality of life cannot be separated from the care provided or the people providing the care" (2002, p. 177). Family relationships are important for optimal development and well-being of individuals with intellectual disabilities. Although most individuals with intellectual disabilities live with their families, who may incur additional expenditure with little guidance from a formal service system, more is known about the quality of life of people living in group homes or other residential settings.

Seltzer and Krauss (2001) reviewed evidence about the quality of life of adults with intellectual disabilities who live at home with their families. They commented that relatively little research has explored outcomes for adults with intellectual disabilities who remain in the family home although this is by far the dominant mode of residential arrangement. Their review included five domains of quality of life: family relationships, friends and social activity, health and functional abilities of adults, formal services received, and planning for future care. Families, like individuals, follow a predictable life course during which relationships and roles within the family change over time. In families with a member who has intellectual disability, there may be altered stages, as adults may not depart from the family home as young adults (launching) and their relationships with siblings may grow to reflect an expectation of providing care as all adult children reach middle age and even older adulthood. The evidence points to the importance of family relationships for the quality of life of adult family members with intellectual disabilities living at home and the value of making plans for their future life.

Even when adults move out of the family home, they do not depart from the family's "zone of influence" (Seltzer & Krauss, 2001, p. 191). Seltzer and Krauss found that aging mothers of adult offspring with intellectual disabilities in the United States were highly involved in the process of transition to another living situation, reporting frequent contact and continued emotional involvement. Mothers became less worried about the future; adult siblings reported improved relationships with their brother or sister with intellectual disability. The authors concluded that service providers should actively nurture long-term family involvement and recommended that research encompass more diverse families and explore perspectives of the individuals themselves.

Walsh and LeRoy (2004) and their collaborators interviewed 167 older women with intellectual disabilities in 18 countries. The women who took part in their study reported family histories and contexts far more rich and varied than expected. Some women had kept alive for 50 or more years the sights and sounds of the time when they were removed from their parents and placed in institutions. Others had made do all their lives with entry-level employment and adequate living arrangements that provided shelter but which were not exactly as they would wish. Many women living in parts of Southeast Asia where there are scant formal systems of support had married and had thus been sustained throughout their lives by spouses, in-laws, and—for many—adult children. This pattern contrasted with typical arrangements in much of Europe, where older women reported being moved away from their family homes as girls or young women and currently living in single-sex residential units or, for a few, in apartments or houses in the community. Very few of these European women had ever married.

Key Domains of Adult Life

Besides home, other key domains of adult life are relationships and work, and typically these domains overlap.

Adult Relationships Although families nurture and support, they may buffer women with developmental disabilities from fulfilling adult social roles and building social networks that are comparable with those reported by women in the general population. Often, these women have little chance to build reciprocal relationships with mothers, sisters, and other relatives (Walmsley, 1996). Rather, the women may retain some hallmarks of childhood and dependency, even into their own middle age. Their social networks are likely to be smaller and denser than those of other people of their age. Often, women in this group name family members, paid staff members in service settings, and their mothers' friends as their own friends. A study of men and women with intellectual disabilities 15–66 years of age living with their parents in the United States indicated that both men and women had large, active, and diverse social support networks dominated by family members; women were less at risk for social isolation (Krauss, Seltzer, & Goodman, 1992).

Social networks do not only provide vital companionship and care: They are life enhancing, as how people are connected to their society is associated with mortality, health, and many other beneficial outcomes. Adopting a framework of community membership as a valuable outcome for women with developmental disabilities means that social well-being, especially relationships with family and friends, is essential to their quality of life (Bigby, 2002; Egan & Walsh, 2001).

Gradually, something has been learned about the experiences of women with developmental disabilities who become parents. Often their life circumstances are difficult (Parish, 2002). Frequently, women who become parents are poor—as is likely for people with developmental disabilities overall—and poverty brings in its wake additional risks such as violence and limited access to health care. Booth and Booth (2000) interviewed offspring of women with developmental disabilities in the United Kingdom and found that although they had encountered problems in their childhood, many of these had originated outside the home, and most of the informants had maintained a valued relationship with their family and remained close to their mother. In some cultures, notably those without an institutional history of segregated residences or formal systems of support, marriage and parenthood comprise a socially valuable life option for women with developmental disabilities (Walsh & LeRoy, 2004).

Finally, it must be noted that although caregivers often express concern about their adult offspring's sexuality and interest in intimate relationships, knowledge of what women themselves understand and how they wish to live their lives as adults is as yet incomplete (McCarthy, 2002). Adult choices are not without risk: Regrettably not all adult relationships for women with developmental disabilities enhance their lives. On the contrary, they incur risks to their health and safety from others and have a higher risk for various forms of abuse. It is suggested that interventions to promote women's autonomy and at the same time to minimize risk should take into account the cultural environment and living and working conditions as well as the individual's characteristics (Walsh & Murphy, 2002). (See Chapter 36 for more information on socio-sexual issues.)

Work Most adults with developmental disabilities are unemployed. In their analysis of population-based data in the United States, Yamaki and Fujiura (2002) concluded that adults in this group—including those who had jobs—reported incomes near or below the poverty level. Relatively few employment outcome studies analyze findings according to gender. What evidence is available suggests that women with intellectual disabilities in ordinary employment have shown themselves at a disadvantage in terms of job type and income and more likely to work in jobs traditionally stereotyped by gender. In a U.S. study, women with developmental disabilities were found to work fewer hours and to earn less money than men (Olson et al., 2000). (See Chapter 33 for more information on work issues.)

Points to Remember Although evidence has accrued about the adult experiences of women with intellectual disabilities as family members and friends, neighbors, and co-workers, knowledge of the factors related to good life outcomes, much less about the factors related to the goals women themselves wish to achieve, remains slender. It is suggested that multiple sources of evidence—including women's biographical narratives—that are gathered over time and in different cultural settings will best contribute to this understanding.

Healthy Aging

According to the World Health Organization (WHO), "By 2025 there will be more than 800 million older people in the world, two-thirds of them in developing countries, and a majority of them will be women" (1998, p. 101). As gender is a determinant of health, it affects the quality of life of people with intellectual disabilities; women in this group, as other women, have specific health needs as they age (Walsh & Heller, 2002). Poverty, marginal social standing, limited access to primary health care, and ignorance of health promotion strategies exacerbate risks to healthy aging. Even in the richer countries, health resources are finite. It makes sense to understand women's distinctive health needs to inform decisions on allocating health resources. Qualitative findings based on focus groups with women in several countries were reported in an international study of healthy aging of adults with intellectual disabilities carried out in collaboration with WHO (2000). The authors concluded that there are compelling research priorities in the areas of identifying effective health promotion strategies and reproductive and sexual health practices for women in this population.

Living longer brings wider opportunities, a trend toward moving out of the family home, and age-related risks to health (Walsh, 2002). Some groups of women with developmental disabilities have particular vulnerabilities. For example, a prospective study of 92 women with Down syndrome found an earlier-than-expected age at onset of menopause; the presence of hypothyroidism did not influence age of menopause (Seltzer, Schupf, & Wu, 2001). The study suggested that women with Down syndrome are at an increased risk for postmenopausal health disorders.

Reviewing health indicators literature, Eckermann (2000) concluded that there have been few attempts to develop measures to reflect women's experiences of health, well-being, illness, and disability. The author suggested that a gender approach is vital to capture fully the diversity of men's and women's life experiences, and that appropriate indicators should be suited to the level of analysis—whether global, regional, national, special group, or individual. This approach is no less pertinent to the physical and mental health of women with developmental disabilities as they age. Mental health problems may be masked by the presence of developmental or other disabilities and hence elude treatment (Thorpe, Davidson, & Janicki, 2001). Antecedent conditions may include life stressors, limited social networks, and fewer opportunities for social learning. In addition, adverse reactions may be exacerbated among adults with intellectual disabilities due to cognitive impairments, poor self-esteem, and relatively poor social support. Gender is likely to influence the impact of each of these risk factors.

Cohort Differences Sometimes researchers wish to compare the attributes of individuals in different age groups—perhaps comparing the adaptive behavior scores of younger adults with those of older adults with intellectual disabilities. Yet, it is important to recall that today's twenty-somethings are very different from people of their age in earlier decades, when the presence of people with disabilities in community life was attenuated. In addition, these young adults have flourished in an environment influenced by inclusion, human rights, and equal opportunities. They will be rather different sixty-somethings in years to come when compared with today's older people, who may have lived in institutions; who had poor dental care; who had limited education; and who may never have voted, paid taxes, managed a household, or enjoyed an intimate adult relationship. These are cohort differences; researchers endeavor to take account of these when designing studies and interpreting the results.

When considering the lives of older women with intellectual disabilities in 2006, it is important to recognize that they are unique in many ways. Life expectancy for this group has increased markedly since the 1970s. For many of today's older women, it was not expected that they would live into middle or old age, much less that they would live in ordinary homes, enter employment, or make a rightful claim to citizenship. Many spent years of their lives in institutional settings (Trent, 1994; Walsh & LeRoy, 2004), where their individual identity as mature, sexual beings was not always respected. Women in this cohort had little chance to develop a sense of themselves, their gifts, and their capacities. Institutional life left its marks on women in many ways—for example in terms of limited education, segregation, poor nutrition, and negligible oral health care during their growing years.

As people with developmental disabilities grow older, the likelihood of moving out of the family home tends to increase. Braddock et al. (2001) presented an overview of residential patterns in five prosperous countries—Australia, Canada, England, the United States, and Wales. Nearly all children and many adults lived in family homes, but a striking finding was that the likelihood of placement outside the family home rose steadily with adulthood and progressively so as adults aged. In general, these authors reported trends toward smaller, community settings, although many people with intellectual disabilities lived in larger groups than would be found among their peers in the general population. Another important finding was that all countries reported a gap between available housing and increasing needs of individuals in this group for suitable homes.

Points to Remember In summary, health is a core element in quality of life. Promoting healthy aging among the emerging population of older women with intellectual disabilities is a priority for practitioners and policy makers alike. Adopting a health promotion framework means engaging women themselves and their caregivers in helping to identify needs. Acknowledging the distinctive health risks and vulnerabilities of women at different stages of their lives is vital in building optimal supports across the life course.

WOMEN'S WORK AS SUPPORT PROVIDERS

Because they often take on general caregiving roles, women are staunch providers of informal support and care for women and men with developmental disabilities. Previous research in caregiving tended to highlight the perceived burdens and stresses of caregiving, although more recent studies also focus on the contentment and resilience achieved by caregivers and indeed their adult relatives with disabilities. Such studies have explored the more positive aspects of caregiving, such as caregiving satisfaction, and have highlighted the reciprocal nature of the caregiving roles and the contributions that adults with intellectual disability make to their caregivers' quality of life (Heller, Miller, & Factor, 1997). This support can take various forms—decreased loneliness for the caregiver; companionship; help with household tasks; and shared, jointly enjoyed activities—resulting in greater caregiver satisfaction and less perceived burden.

Poverty and disability often go hand in hand, as people with disabilities tend to be poor, and as poverty is associated with many risk factors (e.g., inadequate housing, poor nutrition). Poverty ensnares those who care for people with developmental and other disabilities, most of whom are women. Giving care may be priceless as a virtue—but doing so day after day bears tremendous costs for caregivers, who are likely to lose their own paid employment and earnings and generally to live with lowered standards of living. Evidence suggests that caregivers who have looked after relatives or friends with disabilities for more than 10 years have lower incomes, depend more on welfare, have less invested in pensions, and have less wealthy families (Harbison, 2003).

Older family caregivers, chiefly women, face challenges. Demographic changes in many countries mean that people with developmental disabilities live longer and thus depend for more years on their families for primary support. In the United Kingdom, evidence from one region indicated that family caregivers age 60 years and older were responsible for looking after 44% of all adults living in a family home; the vast majority (89% in this study) of these caregivers were women (Grant, 2000). Overall, approximately 30,000–35,000 caregivers in the United Kingdom ages 60 or older support relatives with developmental disabilities at home (Hogg & Lambe, 1998). In the United States, it has been estimated that most people with developmental disabilities live outside the formal long-term care system with families as the dominant form of support, and a large group live in households headed by aging family members (Fujiura, 1998). In Ireland, a striking proportion of older adults with intellectual disabilities remain in their family homes (Barron & Mulvany, 2003). See Display 37.1 for an illustrative example.

Grant (2000) charted several caregiving trajectories that may be helpful to families over the life course. It is likely that older caregivers would welcome more predictability about what comes next so they can gather their resources to tackle what tasks to undertake next on behalf of their offspring making life transitions—from adolescence to young adulthood, for example. Furthermore, families have distinct stages in the life cycle: young parents with small children become middle-age people with teenage children or adult children leaving the family home. Yet, an adult daughter or son with a developmental disability may stay in this otherwise empty nest for many years more than would be typical for other families. It is important that those charged with lending support to caregiving families should be sensitive to the stage that the individual with disabilities, their caregivers, and the family itself have reached so that they can match supports to needs.

Display 37.1

Case study: Sadie and Margaret

Sadie is 84 and lives in a terraced house in a large town in Ireland with her only daughter, Margaret, age 55. Margaret was always slow to learn, and someone in a clinic told her parents that she had mental handicap and was unlikely to live very long. She spent a few years boarding weekly at a school run by a nearby convent and seemed to enjoy the company there. Since age 20, Margaret has lived at home with her widowed mother. The two women make ends meet fairly well, as Sadie owns her home and as a pension, along with a weekly disability allowance for Margaret, cover most of their needs. They have excellent neighbors and are active in the local parish. Two sons in England send money regularly and visit often. Last winter, Sadie experienced poor health and was hospitalized. Margaret was offered some weeks of home help and managed the household quite well. After all, she has had many years to learn from her mother, who is famous for her fine cooking and impeccable housekeeping. Sadie has become quite frail now, but she resists talk of moving from home and is determined to stay as she is, come what may, particularly as she has Margaret to help her now.

Longer life expectancy for women and men with intellectual disabilities is a laudable achievement but also a challenge for policy makers and practitioners who support families. As people with disabilities and their caregivers expect to live longer lives, new forms of support that are effective and acceptable must be offered. Evidence suggests that families differ in how they sustain themselves as the primary source of support. Most family caregiving remains women's work; both women with disabilities and the women who live with and support them deserve equal consideration.

SUMMARY

Gender is expressed at the intersection of personal and public domains—where the individual's identity becomes visible in the society where she lives and grows to maturity. Yet, a gendered approach has only recently been applied to understanding something of the lives of people with intellectual disabilities as individuals, family members, and social and civic identities. Women with intellectual disabilities, too, have emerged as individuals who are family members and citizens, sharing a cultural context and prey to the same environmental shifts as their peers—whether economic, political, or physical. This chapter has considered briefly some sources of knowledge about women in this population and has charted some areas that are priorities for further study.

We have reflected on the global truth that most women in this group rely on family care and that family caregiving is typically women's work. As women live longer, it becomes even more important to promote healthy aging and to support them in achieving autonomy and satisfying, reciprocal relationships with family members and others. For many caregivers at the beginning of the 21st century, their lives are irrevocably linked, come what may, with the women for whom they care. To ensure a more confident future with richer opportunities, it is necessary to work with women and their families to deepen understanding and build supports on this evidence.

FOR FURTHER THOUGHT AND DISCUSSION

1. What are the implications of encouraging girls and women with developmental disabilities to develop an appropriate gender identity within their cultures?
2. What factors prevent women with developmental disabilities from reaching higher levels of employment?
3. Do women have a special gift for sacrifice and caregiving?
4. Why are front-line, direct support workers—chiefly women—so poorly paid?

REFERENCES

Anderson, D.J. (2002). Women aging with intellectual disabilities: What are the health risks? In P.N. Walsh & T. Heller (Eds.), *Health of women with intellectual disabilities* (pp. 21–56). Oxford, United Kingdom: Blackwell Publishing.

Barron, S., & Mulvany, F. (2003). *Annual report of the National Intellectual Disability Database Committee 2002.* Dublin, Ireland: Health Research Board. Retrieved on September 29, 2004, from http://www.hrb.ie/display_content.php?page_id=72&stream=1&div_id=3

Bigby, C. (2002). Social roles and informal support networks in mid life and beyond. In P.N. Walsh & T. Heller (Eds.), *Health of women with intellectual disabilities* (pp. 121–126). Oxford, United Kingdom: Blackwell Publishing.

Booth, T., & Booth, W. (2000). Growing up with parents who have learning difficulties. *Mental Retardation, 38,* 1–14.

Bowling, A. (1995). What things are important in people's lives? A survey of the public's judgments to inform scales of health related quality of life. *Social Science and Medicine, 41,* 1447–1462.

Braddock, D., Emerson, E., Felce, D., et al. (2001). Living circumstances of children and adults with mental retardation or developmental disabilities in the United States, Canada, England and Wales and Australia. *Mental Retardation and Developmental Disabilities Research Reviews, 7,* 115–121.

Brigham, L., Atkinson, D., Jackson, M., et al. (Eds.). (2000). *Crossing boundaries: Change and continuity in the history of learning disability.* Plymouth, United Kingdom: British Institute of Learning Disabilities.

Brown, I., Anand, S., Isaacs, B., et al. (2003). Family quality of life: Canadian results from an international study. *Journal of Developmental and Physical Disabilities, 15,* 207–230.

Eckermann, L. (2000). Gendering indicators of health and well-being: Is quality of life gender neutral? *Social Indicators Research, 52,* 29–54.

Egan, J., & Walsh, P.N. (2001). Sources of stress among adult siblings of Irish people with intellectual disabilities. *Irish Journal of Psychology, 22,* 28–38.

Essex, E.L., Seltzer, M.M., & Krauss, M.W. (in press). Fathers as caregivers for adult children with mental retardation. In B.J. Kramer & E.H. Thompson (Eds.), *Men as caregivers: Theory, research, and service implications.* New York: Springer.

Fujiura, G.T. (1998). Demography of family households. *American Journal on Mental Retardation, 103,* 225–235.

Grant, G. (2000). Older family carers: Challenges, coping strategies and support. In D. May (Ed.), *Transition and change in the lives of people with intellectual disabilities* (pp. 177–193). London: Jessica Kingsley Publishers.

Greenberg, J.S., Seltzer, M.M., Orsmond, G.I., et al. (1999). Siblings of adults with mental illness or mental retardation: Influences on current involvement and the expectations of future caregiving responsibility. *Psychiatric Services, 50,* 1214–1219.

Hanna, W.J., & Rogovsky, B. (1991). Women with disabilities: Two handicaps plus. *Disability, Handicap and Society, 6,* 49–63.

Harbison, J. (2003). Social policy, poverty and disability: A Northern Ireland perspective. In S. Quin & B. Redmond (Eds.), *Disability and social policy in Ireland* (pp. 155–170). Dublin, Ireland: University College Dublin Press.

Heller, T., Miller, A.B., & Factor, A. (1997). Adults with mental retardation as supports to their parents: Effects on parental caregiving appraisal. *Mental Retardation, 35,* 338–346.

Hogg, J., & Lambe, L. (1998). *Older people with learning disabilities: A review of the literature on residential services and family caregiving.* London: Foundation for People with Learning Disabilities.

Krauss, M.W., Seltzer, M.M., & Goodman, S.J. (1992). Social support networks of adults with mental retardation who live at home. *American Journal on Mental Retardation, 96,* 432–441.

LeRoy, B., Walsh, P.N., Kulik, N., et al. (2004). Retreat and resilience: Life experiences of older women with intellectual disabilities. *American Journal on Mental Retardation, 109,* 429–441.

McCarthy, M. (2002). Sexuality. In P.N. Walsh & T. Heller (Eds.), *Health of women with intellectual disabilities* (pp. 90–102). Oxford, United Kingdom: Blackwell Publishing.

McConkey, R., & O'Toole, B. (2000). Improving the quality of life of people with disabilities in least affluent countries: Insights from Guyana. In K.D. Keith & R.L. Schalock (Eds.), *Cross-cultural perspectives on quality of life* (pp. 281–290). Washington, DC: American Association on Mental Retardation.

Olson, D., Cioffi, A., Yovanoff, P., et al. (2000). Gender differences in supported employment. *Mental Retardation, 38,* 89–96.

Orsmond, G.I., & Seltzer, M.M. (2000). Brothers and sisters of adults with mental retardation: The gendered nature of the sibling relationship. *American Journal on Mental Retardation, 105,* 486–508.

Parish, S.L. (2002). Parenting. In P.N. Walsh & T. Heller (Eds.), *Health of women with intellectual disabilities* (pp. 102–120). Oxford, United Kingdom: Blackwell Publishing.

Porrell, F.W., & Miltiades, H.B. (2002). Regional differences in functional status among the aged. *Social Science & Medicine, 54,* 1181–1198.

Robine, J.-M., Romieu, I., & Cambois, E. (1999). Health expectancy indicators. *Bulletin of the World Health Organization, 77,* 181–185.

Schalock, R.L., & Verdugo, M.-A. (2002). *Handbook of quality of life for human service practitioners.* Washington, DC: American Association on Mental Retardation.

Seltzer, G., Schupf, N., & Wu, H.S. (2001). A prospective study of menopause in women with Down's syndrome. *Journal of Intellectual Disability Research, 45,* 1–7.

Seltzer, M.M., & Krauss, M.W. (2001). Quality of life of adults with mental retardation/developmental disabilities who live with family. *Mental Retardation And Developmental Disabilities Research Reviews, 7,* 105–114.

Seltzer, M.M., Krauss, M.W., Orsmond, G.I., et al. (2000). Families of adolescents and adults with autism: Uncharted territory. In L.M. Glidden (Ed.), *International review of research on mental retardation: Vol. 23.* San Diego: Academic Press.

Seltzer, M.M., Krauss, M.W., Walsh, P.N., et al. (1995). Cross-national comparisons of ageing mothers of adults with intellectual disabilities. *Journal of Intellectual Disability Research, 39*(5), 408–418.

Thorpe, L., Davidson, P., & Janicki, M.P. (2001). Healthy ageing: Adults with intellectual disabilities: Biobehavioural issues. *Journal of Applied Research in Intellectual Disabilities, 14,* 218–228.

Todd, S., & Shearn, J. (1996). Time and the person: The impact of support services on the lives of parents of adults with learning disability. *Journal of Applied Research in Intellectual Disabilities, 9,* 40–60.

Trent, J. (1994). *Inventing the feeble mind: A history of mental retardation in the United States.* Berkeley: University of California Press.

Walmsley, J. (1996). "Doing what Mum wants me to do": Looking at family relationships from the point of view of adults with intellectual disabilities. *Journal of Applied Research in Intellectual Disability, 9,* 324–341.

Walsh, P.N. (2000). Rights of passage: Life course transitions for women with intellectual disabilities. In D. May (Ed.), *Transition and change in the lives of people with intellectual disabilities* (pp. 135–156.). London: Jessica Kingsley Publishers.

Walsh, P.N. (2002). Ageing and mental retardation. *Current Opinion in Psychiatry, 15,* 509–514.

Walsh, P.N., & Heller, T. (Eds.). (2002). *Health of women with intellectual disabilities.* Oxford, United Kingdom: Blackwell Publishing.

Walsh, P.N., & LeRoy, B. (2004). *Women with disabilities aging well: A global view.* Baltimore: Paul H. Brookes Publishing Co.

Walsh, P.N., & Murphy, G.H. (2002). Risk and vulnerability: Dilemmas for women. In P.N. Walsh & T. Heller (Eds.), *Health of women with intellectual disabilities* (pp. 154–169). Oxford, United Kingdom: Blackwell Publishing.

Whyte, S.R., & Ingstad, B. (1995). *Culture and disability.* Berkeley: University of California Press.

World Health Organization. (1998). *The World Health Report 1998: Life in the 21st century—a vision for all.* Geneva: Author.

World Health Organization. (2000). *Aging and intellectual disabilities—improving longevity and promoting healthy aging: Summative report.* Geneva: Author.

Yamaki, K., & Fujiura, G.T. (2002). Employment and income status of adults with developmental disabilities living in the community. *Mental Retardation, 40,* 132–141.

38

Parenting by People with Intellectual Disabilities

Marjorie Aunos and Maurice Feldman

WHAT YOU WILL LEARN ABOUT IN THIS CHAPTER

- Variables influencing parenting
- Parent education programs
- Specialized preschools and child care

Parents with intellectual disabilities make up approximately 1% of the population (Keltner & Tymchuk, 1992; McConnell, Llewellyn, & Ferronato, 2003). These parents are overrepresented in child custody proceedings, and many of them have their children taken away because of concerns about their capacity to raise children (Glaun & Brown, 1999; Hayman, 1990; McConnell, Llewellyn, & Ferronto, 2003; Vogel, 1987). The termination of parenting rights of parents with intellectual disabilities may not always be justified. Few workers have experience supporting these families. Many parents with intellectual disabilities are not given a chance to parent or are not provided adequate supports and resources. Negative stereotypes and misconceptions abound concerning parenting by people with intellectual disabilities. There are general misunderstandings that people with intellectual disabilities 1) simply are incapable of providing adequate child care, 2) cannot benefit from parent training, and 3) always have children with intellectual disabilities (Aunos & Feldman, 2002; Espe-Sherwindt & Kerlin, 1990). Although this is sometimes the case (see Display 38.1), it is now known that in many cases, these presumptions are unwarranted (see Display 38.2).

VARIABLES INFLUENCING PARENTING

Research in the area of parenting by people with intellectual disabilities started in the 1980s following the deinstitutionalization movement and the ban on involuntary sterilization. Since then, many authors have argued that parental IQ level is not a valid or sole predictor of a person's parenting abilities (Feldman, 2002). Some researchers maintain that the problems experienced by parents with intellectual disabilities and their children primarily relate to poverty because most of these families are poor (Budd & Greenspan, 1981; Fotheringham, 1971; Tymchuk, 1992). However, being poor and having a parent with intellectual disabilities may increase risk of childhood problems above that of poverty alone (Feldman & Walton-Allen, 1997; Ramey & Ramey, 1992).

Parenting models have been proposed to identify the host of variables that could affect parenting abilities and child outcomes. Feldman (2002) proposed a model specifically for families headed by parents with intellectual disabilities. Feldman's model is based on ecological (Bronfenbrenner, 1979), transactional (Sameroff & Chandler, 1975), and interactional (Belsky, 1984) family models. These models highlight the complex interactions that occur over time between wider-range variables within and external to the family that influence parenting and child development. Feldman's model, presented in Figure 38.1, identifies variables that can affect parenting abilities, such as the social factors (stigmatization and discrimination), parental developmental history, personal characteristics, socioeconomic status, and health. Table 38.1 provides descriptions of these key variables. Feldman's model also outlines the importance of informal (e.g., family, friends) and formal (services) social support. In addition, the model proposes a reciprocal effect of the child's development and behavior on parental health and practices.

The model assumes accumulated risk. That is, given two sets of parents with the same IQ score, parents who have more impediments (e.g., are stigmatized, have mental health issues, have few supports, have a history of abuse) will not do as well—and their children will be at greater risk for developmental problems—than the parents who have adequate support, no mental health issues, no additional stressors, and one healthy and typically developing child for whom to provide care.

The model can be illustrated by referring to the cases in Displays 38.1 and 38.2. Julie's parenting skills were assessed and were considered inadequate (Display 38.1). She was inconsistent in her interactions with her

Display 38.1

Case study: Julie's situation

Julie, who has intellectual disabilities, is a single mother who lost custody of four of her five children. Her children are in foster care due to concerns about Julie's ability to parent. Her youngest daughter, who still lives with Julie, is 4 years old. The child protective services agency is closely watching Julie and her daughter. Mother and daughter live in a tiny, dirty, two-room apartment. Julie does not work and receives family support allowance (welfare) which gives her less than $10,000 per year, putting her family income below the poverty level. Julie was abused by her mother's partner when she was a child and was physically abused by her ex-husband (who also abused their children). Julie reports being depressed and highly stressed, but she does not take any medication or receive counseling. Her apartment is a mess and she stays in bed much of the day. Although her daughter is only 4 years old, she fends for herself much of the time and also takes care of Julie. Julie has few friends on whom she can count. Some of her "friends" take advantage of her (hang out in her apartment, take her money). Four different workers are involved with Julie and her daughter and provide her with support. Julie does not like to have so many workers involved in her life, and she feels that they are just spies for child protective services. They always tell Julie what she is doing wrong and she tunes them out. Her daughter has mild developmental delays (particularly in language) and sometimes displays both externalized problem behaviors (aggressiveness) and internalized problem behaviors (social problems, depressive mood).

Display 38.2

Case study: Mary and Pierre's situation

Meet Mary and Pierre, whose son is 5 years old and daughter is 12 months old. Both Mary and Pierre were diagnosed with intellectual disabilities when they were in school and continue to be considered as having intellectual disabilities. Pierre works in a grocery store, making minimum wage, and is very supportive in raising their children. Pierre does not drink or use drugs. Mary volunteers at a community center several days each week. Mary and Pierre neither have mental health issues nor feel stressed. Mary and Pierre have a good support network. Apart from her husband, Mary receives daily support from her mother-in-law, who is very encouraging. Mary is satisfied with the help she receives, although she has difficulties asking for it at times. Their son is in kindergarten and has been diagnosed with attention-deficit/hyperactivity disorder, which makes his behavior difficult to manage at times. Their daughter is developing typically and is looked after by Mary's mother when Mary is at the community center. Pierre and Mary are confident that they can raise their children well with the supports that they receive.

daughter, and it was extremely difficult for her to set limits despite interventions and suggestions from workers. Due to her past abuse and her depression, it was difficult for Julie to understand that her daughter was reacting to her own history of abuse when she was aggressive. Julie's apathy (related to her depression) also made her unmotivated to keep the house clean; prepare nutritious meals; and provide supervision, structure, affection, and positive interactions to her daughter. Her poor relationship with her daughter and her daughter's behavior problems added to Julie's stress and depression, thereby exacerbating her difficulties in parenting. Furthermore, the workers who visited her were very negative and no help as far as Julie was concerned. Her friends took advantage of her and she could not think of a single person she could turn to in time of need or for advice and emotional support.

Conversely, Mary and Pierre's parenting skills were acceptable, although they had difficulties displaying positive interactions with their children and managing their son's attention-deficit/hyperactivity disorder (Display 38.2). At the same time, they worked well together as a team and they were very open to suggestions from Mary's mother and their social worker. Mary participated in a parenting skills group that taught her some basic skills. With the support of her social worker, Mary transferred those skills to the home. The fact that the parents neither were overly stressed nor had mental health issues made it easier for them to handle the hard work of parenting two children. Most important, they had a very positive and satisfactory support network. Mary's mother and the social worker were very encouraging and did not put down Mary and Pierre. Mary and Pierre also supported and encouraged each other. Although Mary did most of the child care, Pierre helped and was very appreciative of Mary's hard work. They were content and happy with their lives, and their children did reasonably well.

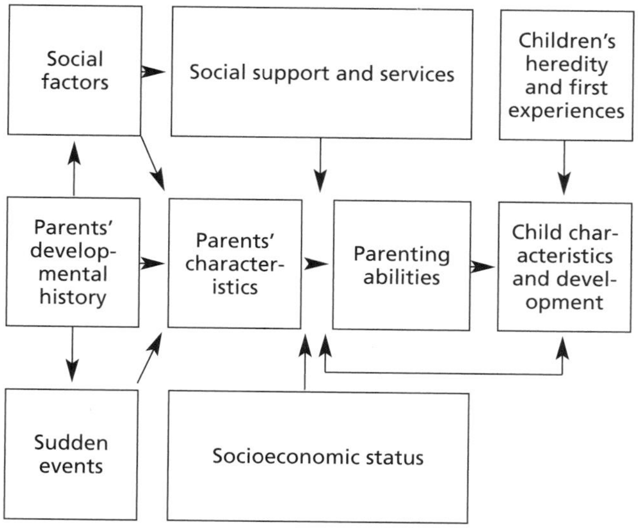

Figure 38.1. A Parenting Interaction Model. (From Feldman, M.A. [2002]. Parents with intellectual disabilities and their children: Impediments and supports. In D. Griffiths & P. Federoff [Eds.], *Ethical dilemmas: Sexuality and developmental disability* [p. 257]. Kingston, NY: National Association of the Dually Diagnosed; adapted by permission.)

Characteristics of Parents with Intellectual Disabilities

Although the characteristics of parents with intellectual disabilities vary on an individual basis, they can be grouped in four basic categories. These are discussed next.

General Abilities Parents with intellectual disabilities have cognitive limitations and deficits in adaptive behaviors. Generally, such parents who are given the chance to parent are able to cope well in the community either independently or with minimal supports. They may have difficulties expressing themselves, reading, budgeting, getting a job, using public transportation, eating well, handling tricky social situations, problem solving, making good decisions, reasoning in abstract ways, making complex judgments, and in retaining and generalizing newly learned skills.

Sociodemographics Many parents with intellectual disabilities are single and often have had their first child before the age of 25. Since 1980–1985, most people with intellectual disabilities were raised by one- or two-parent families, by other family members, or in foster homes. Thus, it is not surprising that many of them want to have families of their own. Many parents with intellectual disabilities have limited resources, often living below the poverty line. Some people are unemployed, with social assistance or a disability allowance as income. They typically live in low-income housing and small, subsidized apartments. Many par-

Table 38.1. Variables that can affect parenting abilities

Social factors
Stigmatization (as a person with intellectual disabilities)
Discrimination
Parents' developmental history
Cognitive limitations and deficits in adaptive behaviors
Past abuse
Institutionalization
Parental role models
Past experiences in raising and taking care of children
Age at the birth of the first child
Sudden events
Currently experiencing abuse and violence
Illnesses
Loss of revenue
Loss of partner or other important person through separation or death
Eviction and homelessness
Social support and services
Supportive partner and family
Satisfaction with social network
Type of support and services and proportion of formal supports (services) versus informal supports (e.g., family members, neighbors, volunteers, friends)
Involvement of child protective services agency
Supports and services needed versus received
Parents' characteristics
Mental health issues, such as depression, anxiety disorder, or substance abuse
Physical health issues, such as asthma, diabetes, or lupus
High stress levels
Vulnerability to exploitation
Parenting abilities
Basic care needs of children
Safe and healthy home environment
Sensitive, responsive, and positive parent–child interactions
Sound judgments (e.g., discipline, limit setting, supervision)
Positive behavior support for children
Effective problem solving
Socioeconomic status
Family income
Employment status
Quality of the neighborhood (e.g., safety, availability of services, transportation, community activities)
Children's heredity and first experiences
Family history of low IQ scores, genetic syndromes, or mental illness
Prenatal, perinatal, and/or postnatal experiences and conditions that could affect development (e.g., prenatal maternal ingestion of alcohol or drugs, maternal hepatitis C or HIV/AIDS, birth complications, prematurity, low birth weight, early postnatal infections)
Children's characteristics and development
Temperament and behavior (e.g., irritable, behavior problems)
Developmental level (e.g., delay)
School status (e.g., special education)
Physical and mental health
Number of children living at home
Age and gender of each child

ents with intellectual disabilities feel isolated, although parents with custody of their children participate more in community activities than parents who do not have custody of their children (Aunos, Goupil, & Feldman, 2004).

Mental and Physical Health Most research in this area has focused on mothers with intellectual disabilities; little is known of fathers with intellectual disabilities. Many mothers with intellectual disabilities are vulnerable to high parenting stress, low self-esteem, and mental health problems (e.g., depression, anxiety disorders) (Aunos et al., 2004; Feldman, Léger & Walton-Allen, 1997; Tymchuk, 1994). Parental distress could be associated with a history of abuse, low income, no partner or a nonsupportive partner, loneliness, few supports, discrimination, exploitation, learned helplessness, or feeling inadequate as a parent. Furthermore, increased parenting stress could be related to trying to raise multiple children, children with disabilities and behavior problems, and school-age children (Feldman, Garrick, & Case, 1997). Mothers with intellectual disabilities also have more physical ailments than women in the general population (Aunos et al., 2004). These conditions may be related to chronic stress, poor nutrition, smoking, and inadequate hygiene and health care.

Parenting Skills Parents with intellectual disabilities are often described as having difficulties responding to basic child needs (Feldman, 1998). Research has suggested that before intervention, parents with intellectual disabilities have difficulties understanding child development, bathing, diapering, cleaning bottles, feeding, scheduling, providing nutritious meals, recognizing and treating common childhood ailments, handling medical emergencies, providing a safe environment, and problem solving. Parents with intellectual disabilities may or may not play with their children, provide reinforcing and affectionate interactions, promote language and social development, or use positive and consistent discipline (Feldman, 1998). According to Feldman's model, these inadequacies are likely due to a host of factors in addition to, or instead of, the parent's cognitive disability. Moreover, research has clearly shown that with specialized and personalized training, parents with intellectual disabilities can improve their skills to levels seen in parents without intellectual disabilities (Feldman, 1994). Table 38.2 lists key elements of the legal definition of effective parenting; see the Parent Education Programs section for more information on intervention for parenting skills. Researchers have argued that a more concrete definition should be developed and that adequate standards should be elaborated (Spencer, 2001; Tymchuk, 1998).

Social and Formal Supports

Not all forms of social support are perceived as beneficial. Supports can either impair or empower parents (Espe-Sherwindt & Kerlin, 1990; Tucker & Johnson, 1989). The quality of the support offered and the parent's satisfaction with it are more important than the number of people and services agencies interacting with these families (Feldman et al., 2002). In offering supports, a support worker's own personal beliefs and values regarding parenting by people with intellectual disabilities may influence the tone and type of interventions provided (Aunos & Feldman, 2002). Support workers who believe that an intellectual disability is a major impediment to parenting may not try to teach the parents to take major responsibility for child care. Such an attitude may lead workers to encourage the parents to give up their children, focus on their mistakes, or do everything for them. On the contrary, some support workers believe that supports and teaching that match needs and learning styles enable parents with intellectual disabilities to adequately care for their children. These workers may be more willing to support and empower the parents.

Likewise, the parents' attitude toward supports affects their willingness to accept them. Although most parents with intellectual disabilities admit they have learning difficulties, some of them reject the intellectual disability label. Some parents disguise their disability and deny that they need help. They are leery of offers of support and especially distrust support workers. Parents with intellectual disabilities are in a double-bind: They fear that an admission of need for assistance may result in their children being taken away by child protection authorities. Conversely, by rejecting offers of support, parents may be perceived as lacking judgment and not understanding how difficult it is to parent. Rapport and trust is necessary before informal and formal supports can be effectively implemented. Table 38.3 presents tips for establishing rapport.

Many research studies have outlined the need for supporting mothers with intellectual disabilities (Feldman & Walton-Allen, 1997; Feldman et al., 2002; Llewellyn, 1995; Llewellyn et al., 1999). The most significant relationships for a mother with an intellectual

Table 38.2. Key elements of effective parenting

Provide love and affection
Perform daily domestic task
Meet the child's physical needs
Cognitively stimulate the child
Protect the child from physical, sexual, and emotional abuse
Prevent neglect

Source: Adapted, in part, from Tymchuk (1998).

Table 38.3. Tips for building rapport

- Be patient and understanding; respect the family's lifestyle and cultural differences.
- Show an interest in the family's life.
- Believe in and empower the parents' learning potential.
- Address each parent's concerns regarding his or her involvement in the services program.
- Clarify the roles of each professional, help the parents coordinate services and informal supports, and minimize the number of different workers who visit the home regularly.
- Use a positive approach when intervening (build and reinforce skills; do not dwell on mistakes).
- If possible, start by teaching skills based on the parents' interests. When rapport is established, other areas of learning can be suggested.
- Be consistent, sincere, and honest.

Source: Case and Gang (2003).

disability are those with her spouse/partner and her own parents (especially her mother). Usually, her partner and own mother are the most involved in her life, so the attitudes of these individuals should be empowering instead of judgmental. Mothers who neglect their children are more likely to be single, have male partners who do not work and are not the biological father of the children, have fewer contacts with their own mothers, and receive less emotional and instrumental supports than mothers who do not neglect their children (Coohey, 1995).

Three different sources of social support have been identified, each based on a combination of formal and informal supports (Llewellyn et al., 1999):

- Type 1 includes a social network that is oriented towards the extended family; few supports come from the community or external agencies.
- Type 2 is the opposite of type 1 in that it includes a social network of few family members but many community or formal agencies.
- Type 3 is a mix between type 1 and type 2 in that the social network is composed of both family members and community agencies.

The most common social support network seems to consist of family members, including their partners and then workers, friends, and neighbors (Aunos et al., 2004). Mothers are usually satisfied with the services they receive, although services are mostly focused on increasing parenting skills and child development and not on the parent's personal growth (e.g., work skills) (Feldman et al., 2002; Walton-Allen & Feldman, 1991).

Services for Parents with Intellectual Disabilities

There are few specialized services for parents with intellectual disabilities and their children. These families are referred to early intervention, family support, public health, and child protective services that often do not have expertise to assist them. In fact, sometimes these services will have negative biases against parents with intellectual disabilities. Services often are fragmented and uncoordinated; as many as six different workers may routinely visit the home. Most community agencies are geared to parents with higher cognitive skills. Important information is often presented in didactic parenting classes, in a restricted amount of time, and in a limited number of sessions. The material may be too complex or presented in writing. These approaches are not very effective for most parents with intellectual disabilities (Feldman, 1994). As described in the Parent Education Programs section, parents with intellectual disabilities do better with concrete instruction of specific skills that are broken down into small steps, with training carried out in the home or in a home-like setting over several sessions (Feldman, 1994, 1998).

As an increasing number of these families are appearing on agency caseloads, a more concerted effort is being made to provide relevant, adapted, and long-term supports. There continues to be a need for specialized, two-generation family-focused programs adapted for families headed by parents with intellectual disabilities. A two-generation program takes into consideration the needs of both parents and children. Some children may have developmental delays or other challenges or may need extra support because their parents may have difficulties with providing adequate stimulation, for example. A two-generation program provides these supports as prevention and when needed. (See Table 38.4 for program characteristics; also see the Specialized Preschools and Child Care section.) Services need to be adapted in view of the specific needs, capacities, and limitations of families with parents who have intellectual disabilities. Here are some suggestions:

1. Have a team (or at least one worker) who has expertise in working with these families.
2. Plan for an assessment of the family's needs and the needs of each family member, including the needs of the parents as individuals.
3. Identify areas of need—use a systemic, interactional approach (Feldman, 2002).
4. Establish trust and rapport with the family (see Table 38.3).
5. Provide evidenced-based intervention and other supports in areas identified as needing improvement (e.g., parental and child health, child development, social support, parenting and related skills).
6. Objectively monitor progress of the parents in learning new skills and the child's health and development.

Table 38.4. Characteristics of effective two-generation programs

Parent/family component
Academic and vocational upgrading
Advocacy
Case management
Competency enhancing and empathic social support network
Crisis support
Financial support
Health and nutrition services and training
Incentives
Job finding and coaching
Other individualized services as needed (e.g., counseling, home visitor)
Parenting education
Transportation
Child component
Close monitoring of child health and development
Enrollment in specialized preschool as soon as possible after birth
Follow-through in school if needed
Healthy, safe, nurturing, and stimulating environments
Other specialized services as needed (e.g., occupational therapy, behavior therapy, tutoring)
Parental involvement in preschool
Placement in a specialized preschool or a general child care program with extra supports to provide stimulation that may be lacking at home
Specially trained baby sitters

7. Establish partnerships and coordinate between various agencies (particularly child protective services if involved).
8. Involve the parents in designing the intervention plan.
9. Have the parents identify and enlist others (informal support: Who could help support the intervention plan?).

Children's Characteristics and Development

Children of parents with intellectual disabilities are at risk of developmental delay (especially in the area of language), school difficulties, and emotional and behavior problems (Feldman et al., 1985; Feldman & Walton-Allen, 1997; Gillberg & Geijer-Karlsson, 1983). Developmental delay is seen in children as young as 6 months old, and cognitive development is more affected than physical and social development (Feldman et al., 1985; McConnell, Llewellyn, Mayes, et al., 2003). Not all child problems can be attributed to growing up in poverty because school-age children living in poverty and raised by parents without intellectual disabilities had higher IQ scores, fewer school difficulties, and fewer behavior problems (Feldman & Walton-Allen, 1997).

These problems continue into adolescence and adulthood. In a study of 30 adult offspring of parents with intellectual disabilities, 50% had learning problems and 23% had emotional or psychiatric problems (Booth & Booth, 1997). They expressed considerable ambivalence toward their parents: "I both love and hate my mentally retarded [sic] mother" (Ronai, 1997). On the one hand, they respected how difficult it was for their parents to raise them given the parent's own abuse history, disability, stigmatization, discrimination, and poverty. On the other hand, they blamed their parents for not taking good care of them and keeping them safe from harm. Ronai, for example, reported that her mother with intellectual disabilities failed to protect her from being abused by her mother's male companion. Another theme described by Ronai and by the offspring interviewed by Booth and Booth was that of the positive impact of other people (e.g., grandmothers, aunts, family friends) who took the children under their wing and protected and nurtured them in ways their parents did not.

PARENT EDUCATION PROGRAMS

Since the 1980s, a few specialized supportive parenting programs have been established for parents with intellectual disabilities (Aunos, 2000; Feldman, 1997; Hur, 1997; Tymchuk, in press). Several evaluation studies and reviews have shown that these programs can increase parenting skills (to levels seen in parents without intellectual disabilities) and increase benefits to children (Feldman, 1994; Feldman, Case, & Sparks, 1992; Feldman, Garrick, & Case, 1997; Feldman, Sparks, & Case, 1993; Llewellyn et al., 2003).

Curriculum

Table 38.5 lists the skills that could be covered in a parenting program for these parents. Note that each parent is different and therefore not all of these areas need to be addressed for every parent. Also, there may not be sufficient time to cover all of these areas, or the agency may lack expertise in certain areas. Topics that will immediately improve the child's health, safety, and development should be covered first.

Training Strategies

Effective programs use behavioral strategies that have been shown to rapidly increase complex skills in people with intellectual disabilities (Feldman, 1994). The general procedure involves task analysis and performance-based teaching methods (e.g., audiovisual materials, modeling, role playing, practice, reinforcement, error correction). There are specific strategies for teaching child-care skills to parents with intellectual disabilities.

Table 38.5. Potential components of a parent education curriculum

Developmental expectations: understanding milestones and their sequence, interpreting child's behaviors, understanding physical limitations, and understanding attachment	
Child care: caring for a newborn, holding, diapering, bathing, clothing, supervising, scheduling, and toilet training	
Nutrition: feeding, burping, preparing formula, selecting wholesome foods, planning menus for nutritious and balanced meals, and shopping for groceries	
Safety: safety issues related to crib, sleep, home, street, playground, park, pool, beach, skating rink, public transportation, and shopping centers	
Health: treating diaper rash, cradle cap, colds, fever, infections, vomiting, and teething; taking temperature; and using medication, sunscreen, and protective clothing	
Emergencies and first aid: responding to cuts, burns, falls, head injuries, poisoning, choking, insect bites, sunburn, heat stroke, and frostbite	
Child development and secure attachment: providing a stimulating home environment and interactions, play, affection, sensitivity, responsiveness, contingent recognition, and consistency; reading to the child; providing conversation and asking questions; telling stories; and going on outings	
Parent–child rapport: paying attention; listening; supervising; providing choices; and demonstrating responsivity, engagement, reciprocity, warmth, sensitivity, and empathy	
Positive behavior support: providing clear rules and instructions, setting limits, reinforcing appropriate behavior, correcting inappropriate behavior, and using noncorporal discipline	
Stress/anger management: identifying own emotions and anger triggers, engaging in relaxation techniques; understanding removal, self-control, and incompatible responses; handling failure; handling stressors; and managing time	
Social skills training: being appropriately assertive, showing empathy, engaging in conversation, asking for help, listening, giving a compliment, responding to criticism, negotiating, apologizing, and dealing with persuasion, group pressure, and embarrassment	
Obtaining community resources: child care/preschool; library; community drop-ins; parent-tot programs, parenting courses, vocational and academic upgrading, counseling services, transit training	
Empowerment training: dealing with "the system," workers, other professionals, and bureaucrats; being appropriately assertive; self-advocating; and participating in support groups	
Problem solving: identifying problems, setting priorities, understanding causes of the problem, identifying possible solutions, implementing the best solution, evaluating outcomes, and generalizing what was learned	

The following list presents components that are generally accepted as contributing to effective parenting programs:

1. Through direct observation, assess how well the parent performs the set child-care skills needed given the child's age.
2. Use validated child-care checklists that break down skills into smaller steps (e.g., see Feldman, 1998; McGaw et al., 2002).
3. Teach skills one at a time.
4. Teach skills in several locations in which the parent will need to learn the skill to promote generalization.
5. Provide simple, concrete verbal explanations and instructions.
6. Provide a picture book illustrating each step of the skill, along with simple text and an audiotape describing each picture (Feldman, 2004). Try these manuals first on their own as self-learning tools before adding more intensive training.
7. Model the skill, step-by-step, focusing on the steps that the parent missed in the assessment.
8. Have the parent practice the skill in real or role-played situations. Role plays also can be conducted in a game format.
9. Use verbal and gestural modeling and physical prompts to guide correct performance as necessary.
10. Provide immediate praise and feedback for correct performance.
11. Give corrective feedback. Try to provide four times as much positive feedback as corrective feedback.
12. Provide tangible rewards (e.g., parenting coupons exchangeable for small gift items contingent on improvements). Fade the tangible rewards after the parent shows generalization and maintenance of the skill (e.g., over a 3-month period).

More details regarding these strategies can be found in Feldman (1998).

The training can be carried out individually in the home or in a small group (preferably in a home-like setting). Home visits usually occur weekly and last 1–2 hours (of which only a portion focuses on training). The home visit starts with an exchange of pleasantries and updates on events since the last visit. Then the parent educator observes previously learned skills (to check for maintenance), skills to be trained soon (baseline), and/or skills currently being trained. Training time itself can vary depending on how long it takes to model and to have the parent perform the task; most single-task training sessions last approximately 10 minutes. Following training, the parent and educator often have a drink or snack and discuss other issues in the family's life (e.g., difficulties with neighbors or with trying to find a job or a child care). The parent educator may offer advice and assistance or recommend other services. If group instruction is used, it is important to conduct home visits and observations to check that the parent has generalized skills learned in the group to the home setting. Before any specific training is conducted, it is recommended that a personalized intervention plan be made in conjunction with all partners involved with the family. These intervention plans are usually elaborated based on a needs assessment of family and following the recommendation of the parents,

Display 38.3

Case study: Julie's intervention plan

Julie's intervention was complicated and multidisciplinary. It started with a formal assessment of her mental health by a psychologist. Julie was diagnosed with major depression. She agreed to take antidepressant medication and attend counseling, both of which helped her improve her mood and energy level. While receiving treatment, her daughter was temporarily placed in a foster home.

In the meantime, a parent educator helped Julie clean and organize the apartment to better suit the needs of her daughter so that weekly supervised visits could start. During those visits, the parent educator worked with Julie on a set of parenting skills that had been identified as weak areas in earlier baseline observations.

In her counseling sessions, Julie learned stronger assertiveness skills and learned how to keep people she did not like from hanging out in her apartment. An agreement was made between Julie, the child protective services agency, and the parent education service to gradually increase the duration of her daughter's visits and decrease the amount of supervision as Julie learned more skills and cleaned up her apartment.

After 6 months, Julie's daughter returned home and started attending a subsidized licensed child care program. Julie's family doctor monitored her mental health; the parent educator continued to teach her more skills; and the child protective services worker gradually faded her visits, as Julie's daughter remained safe and well cared for.

their support worker, and the child care worker. Displays 38.3 and 38.4 continue the previously presented cases with illustrations of parenting programs for each mother.

SPECIALIZED PRESCHOOLS AND CHILD CARE

In addition to, or instead of, providing intervention through parent education, some programs focus on the children by enrolling them in specialized preschools as early as possible (Garber, 1988; Ramey & Ramey, 1992). The rationale is to give the children the stimulation that they may not be getting at home. Results of two studies suggest that this approach can significantly decrease the risk of low IQ scores in children of parents with intellectual disabilities (Garber, 1988; Ramey & Ramey, 1992). Unfortunately, such specialized preschools are rare and costly to maintain. However, even

Display 38.4

Case study: Mary's intervention plan

Mary's intervention plan was fairly easy to put in place. Based on the skills assessment using child-care checklists, she needed to learn to provide more positive interactions to her children. Although Mary was a gentle woman, she found that she had no patience for her son's misbehavior and lack of cooperation. She felt that she was constantly reprimanding him for every little thing and that she could not think of anytime he was well behaved. Mary's baseline use of praise was zero.

At the start of training, the parent educator discussed the importance of positive interactions in promoting her son's social development, appropriate behavior, and a positive relationship between them. The parent educator then showed Mary how to verbally praise her son when he was behaving appropriately during a play activity. Then Mary played with her son, and the educator prompted Mary when to praise and gave Mary positive feedback when she did so. At first, Mary felt awkward giving praise (she said that her parents never praised her), and her praise was not very genuine. After a couple of sessions, however, Mary saw that her son would smile whenever she praised him and that he was cooperating more during play. She found that she had more tolerance for his misbehavior and she did not feel the need to reprimand him as often. With feedback from the parent educator, Mary's praise became frequent, enthusiastic, specific, and genuine. It looked like she had been praising her son for years. Mary was then observed interacting with her son in a variety of settings (e.g., mealtime, bedtime, outside play), and she needed feedback in some of these settings before she generalized praising her son in all settings. She then transferred her skills to her baby daughter without any extra training.

An illustrated poster was hung on the living room wall to remind Mary to play with and praise her children. Mary was so proud of her new, positive way of interacting with her children that she made an audiotape of a play session for the parent educator to hear how well she was remembering the skills she had learned. In this training situation, Mary did not need any tangible rewards to improve her positive interactions because her son's smile when she praised him was such a big reinforcer for her.

putting these children in a quality child care program (without special supports) seems to help the development of these children (Ramey & Ramey, 1992). Further research is needed to determine if the initial effects of out-of-home stimulation have a lasting impact and whether the combination of child- and parent-focused interventions (as recommended in the previously discussed two-generation model) is the most effective intervention.

SUMMARY

Despite progressive changes in many other facets of rights for people with intellectual disabilities, there is still a strong bias against parenting by people with intellectual disabilities. This perception is based on the myth that their low IQ scores preclude them from learning to be competent parents. It is now known that many factors apart from cognitive disability may impede their ability to parent adequately and respond to interventions. One of these obstacles is a prevalent stigmatization and pessimistic attitude that may lead to inappropriate services, competency-inhibiting supports, unfair and discriminatory custody decisions, and denial of parenting rights. As with parents who do not have intellectual disabilities, some parents with intellectual disabilities learn and apply new skills with supports and advice easily and some do not. For some parents with intellectual disabilities to be successful, specialized and intensive supports are needed. It has been shown that with appropriate, personalized services and supports, these parents can learn to be effective parents and raise their children in a safe, nurturing, and loving home.

FOR FURTHER THOUGHT AND DISCUSSION

1. What are the ethical ramifications of allowing or denying the right to parent in people with intellectual disabilities? How can parenting rights be balanced with what is in the best interests of the child?
2. Many studies have documented the need and importance of adequate support in helping parents with intellectual disabilities. There may be a need for intensive and long-standing support. Conversely, many children are removed from the custody of their parents who have intellectual disabilities. Which solution is the most appropriate: offering extensive support or placing children? Which is more humane? Which is the more affordable?
3. Parents with intellectual disabilities face many challenges. In your opinion, what are those challenges? Can parents be offered support in overcoming them?
4. Every country has a somewhat different approach in providing services to people with intellectual disabilities. Based on your country's service approach, how could services be adapted to better meet the needs of parents with intellectual disabilities and their children?
5. A young mother with intellectual disabilities and her baby daughter participate in a specialized arrangement whereby foster parents agree to teach the mother to parent while they look after the child. The foster parents are well off and well respected in their community. They have raised two wonderful teenage children. Over the year, they do not offer much training to the young mother and discourage her from taking care of her daughter. Instead, they treat her like the child's older sister. At the end of the year, they petition to adopt the child. The young mother obtains legal counsel and fights the adoption request in court. What are your opinions about this case? What is in the best interests of the child? Who do you think won?

REFERENCES

Aunos, M. (2000). Les programmes de formation aux habiletés parentales pour des adultes présentant une déficience intellectuelle. *La revue internationale de l'éducation familiale, 4*(2), 59–75.

Aunos, M., & Feldman, M.A. (2002). Attitudes toward sexuality, sterilization, and parenting rights of persons with intellectual disabilities. *Journal of Applied Research in Intellectual Disability, 15,* 285–296.

Aunos, M., Goupil, G., & Feldman, M. (2004). Mothers with intellectual disabilities who do or do not have custody of their children. *Journal of Developmental Disabilities, 10,* 65–80.

Belsky, J. (1984). The determinants of parenting: A process model. *Child Development, 55,* 83–96.

Booth, T., & Booth, W. (1997). *Exceptional childhoods, unexceptional children. Growing up with parents who have learning difficulties.* London: Family Policies Studies Centre.

Bronfenbrenner, U. (1979). Contexts of child rearing: Problems and prospects. *American Psychologist, 34,* 844–850.

Budd, K.S., & Greenspan, S. (1981). Mentally retarded mothers. In A.E. Blechman (Ed.), *Behavior modification with women* (pp. 477–506). New York: The Guilford Press.

Case, L., & Gang, B. (2003). People with developmental disabilities as parents. In I. Brown & M. Percy (Eds.), *Developmental disabilities in Ontario* (2nd ed., pp. 709–716). Toronto: Ontario Association on Developmental Disabilities.

Coohey, C. (1995). Neglectful mothers, their mothers, and partners: The significance of mutual aid. *Child Abuse and Neglect, 19*(8), 885–895.

Espe-Sherwindt, M., & Kerlin, S. (1990). Early intervention with parents with mental retardation: Do we empower or impair? *Infants and Young Children, 2,* 21–28.

Feldman, M.A. (1994). Parenting education for parents with intellectual disabilities: A review of outcome studies. *Research in Developmental Disabilities, 15,* 299–332.

Feldman, M.A. (1997). The effectiveness of early intervention for children whose parents have mental retardation. In M.J. Guralnick (Ed.), *The effectiveness of early intervention* (pp. 171–191). Baltimore: Paul H. Brookes Publishing Co.

Feldman, M.A. (1998). Preventing child neglect: Child-care training for parents with intellectual disabilities. *Infants & Young Children, 11,* 1–11.

Feldman, M.A. (2002). Parents with intellectual disabilities and their children: Impediments and supports. In D. Griffiths & P. Federoff (Eds.), *Ethical dilemmas: Sexuality and developmental disability* (pp. 255–292). Kingston, NY: National Association of the Dually Diagnosed.

Feldman, M.A. (2004). Self-directed learning of child-care skills by parents with intellectual disabilities. *Infants & Young Children, 17,* 17–31.

Feldman, M.A., Case, L., & Sparks, B. (1992). Effectiveness of a child-care training program for parents at-risk for child neglect. *Canadian Journal of Behavioural Science, 24,* 14–28.

Feldman, M.A., Case, L., Towns, F., et al. (1985). Parent Education Project I: The development and nurturance of children of mentally handicapped mothers. *American Journal of Mental Deficiency, 90,* 253–258.

Feldman, M.A., Garrick, M., & Case, L. (1997). The effects of parent training on weight gain of nonorganic-failure-to-thrive children of parents with intellectual disabilities. *Journal on Developmental Disabilities, 5,* 47–61.

Feldman, M.A., Léger, M., & Walton-Allen, N. (1997). Stress in mothers with intellectual disabilities. *Journal of Child and Family Studies, 6,* 471–485.

Feldman, M.A., Sparks, B., & Case, L. (1993). Effectiveness of home-based early intervention on the language development of children of parents with mental retardation. *Research in Developmental Disabilities, 14,* 387–408.

Feldman, M.A., Varghese, J., Ramsay, J., et al. (2002). Relationship between social support, stress and mother–child interactions in mothers with intellectual disabilities. *Journal of Applied Research in Intellectual Disability, 15,* 314–323.

Feldman, M.A., & Walton-Allen, N. (1997). Effects of maternal mental retardation and poverty on intellectual, academic, and behavioral status of school-age children. *American Journal on Mental Retardation, 101,* 352–364.

Fotheringham, J. (1971). The concept of social competence as applied to marriage and child care in those classified as mentally retarded. *Canadian Medical Association Journal, 104,* 813–816.

Garber, H.L. (1988). *The Milwaukee Project. Preventing mental retardation in children at risk.* Washington, DC: American Association on Mental Retardation.

Gillberg, C., & Geijer-Karlsson, M. (1983). Children born to mentally retarded women: A 1–21 year follow-up study of 41 cases. *Psychological Medicine, 13,* 891–894.

Glaun, D.E., & Brown, P.F. (1999). Motherhood, intellectual disability and child protection: Characteristics of a court sample. *Journal of Intellectual and Developmental Disabilities, 24,* 95–105.

Hayman, R.L. (1990). Presumptions of justice: Law, politics and the mentally retarded parent. *Harvard Law Review, 103,* 1201–1274.

Hur, J. (1997). Review of research on parent training for parents with intellectual disability: Methodological issues. *International Journal of Disability, Development and Education, 44*(2), 147–162.

Keltner, B.R., & Tymchuk, A.J. (1992). Reaching out to mothers with mental retardation. *Maternal Child Nursing, 17*(3), 136–140.

Llewellyn, G. (1995). Relationship and social support: Views of parents with mental retardation/intellectual disability. *Mental Retardation, 33*(6), 349–363.

Llewellyn, G., McConnell, D., Cant, R., et al. (1999). Support network of mothers with an intellectual disability: An exploratory study. *Journal of Intellectual and Developmental Disability, 24*(1), 7–26.

Llewellyn, G., McConnell, D., Honey, A., et al. (2003). Promoting health and home safety for children of parents with intellectual disability: A randomized controlled trial. *Research in Developmental Disabilities, 24*(6), 405–431.

McConnell, D., Llewellyn, G., & Ferronato, L. (2003). Prevalence and outcomes for parents with disabilities and their children in an Australian court sample. *Child Abuse and Neglect, 27,* 235–251.

McConnell, D., Llewellyn, G., Mayes, R., et al. (2003). Developmental profiles of children born to mothers with intellectual disability. *Journal of Intellectual & Developmental Disability, 28*(2), 122–134.

McGaw, S., Beckley, K., Connolly, N., et al. (2002). *Parent assessment manual.* United Kingdom: Cornwell Healthcare, National Health Service Trust.

Ramey, C.T., & Ramey, S.L. (1992). Effective early intervention. *Mental Retardation, 30,* 337–345.

Ronai, C.R. (1997). On loving and hating my mentally retarded mother. *Mental Retardation, 35,* 417–432.

Sameroff, A.J., & Chandler, M. (1975). Reproductive risk and the continuum of caretaking causalty. In F. Horowitz (Ed.), *Review of child development research* (pp. 157–243). Chicago: University of Chicago Press.

Spencer, M. (2001, Winter). Proceed with caution: The limitations of current parenting capacity assessments. *Developing Practice,* 16–24.

Tucker, M.B., & Johnson, O. (1989). Competence promoting versus competence inhibiting social support for mentally retarded mothers. *Human Organization, 48,* 95–107.

Tymchuk, A.J. (1992). Predicting adequacy of parenting by people with mental retardation. *Child Abuse and Neglect, 16,* 165–178.

Tymchuk, A.J. (1994). Depression symptomatology in mothers with mild intellectual disability: An exploratory study. *Australia and New Zealand Journal of Developmental Disabilities, 19,* 111–119.

Tymchuck, A.J. (1998). The importance of matching educational interventions to parents needs in child maltreatment: Issues, methods, and recommendations. In J. Lutzker (Ed.),

Handbook of child abuse research and treatment (pp. 421–448). New York: Kluwer Academic/Plenum Publishers.
Tymchuk, A.J. (in press). *The Health and Wellness Program: A parenting curriculum for families at risk.* Baltimore: Paul H. Brookes Publishing Co.
Vogel, P. (1987). The right to parent. *Entourage, 2,* 33–39.
Walton-Allen, N., & Feldman, M.A. (1991). Perceptions of service needs by parents who are mentally retarded and their workers. *Comprehensive Mental Health Care, 1,* 57–67.

39

Aging with an Intellectual Disability

CHRISTINE BIGBY

> **WHAT YOU WILL LEARN ABOUT IN THIS CHAPTER**
>
> - Summary of key population characteristics
> - Perceptions of successful aging
> - Social changes associated with aging
> - Psychological changes associated with aging
> - Physical changes associated with aging
> - Continuities across the life span

The proportion of older people in the populations of Western countries is increasing due to demographic factors such as increased life expectancy and the large baby boom generation (children born 1945–1960, approximately) reaching later life. Demographic changes have been particularly marked for people with intellectual disabilities, as the proportion that reaches later life has increased dramatically. For example, institutional residents with intellectual disability surviving to 50 years increased from 10% to 50% between 1930 and 1980 (Carter & Jancar, 1983), and the average life expectancy for people with Down syndrome almost doubled between 1983 and 1997, increasing by 35 years between 1960 and 1995. In comparison, during this period the average life expectancy of the general population in European countries only increased by 7–8 years (Haveman, 2004; Yang, Rasmussen, & Friedman, 2002). Many people with mild or moderate intellectual disability now have a similar life expectancy to the general population, although some important exceptions exist. People with Down syndrome experience premature aging, and they, together with those with profound or multiple disabilities, have a shortened life expectancy.

Issues of aging were only recognized in the intellectual disabilities field in the 1970s, as more people survived into later life. The current generation of older people with intellectual disabilities are the first to outlive their parents and reach old age in significant numbers. Since the mid-1980s, knowledge about the impact of aging has grown and policy makers have grappled with the implications. However, professional expertise and knowledge about the nature of services and supports required to support successful aging for people with intellectual disabilities are still in the early stages. It is an exciting area in which to work, one that provides opportunities to develop innovative programs to ensure the values and principles embedded in legislation and policy for younger people are applied to the latter part of the life course.

Aging is a process rather than an event that occurs at a fixed point in time, yet "old age" is generally defined by the attainment of a particular chronological age. Traditionally, in Western countries, this has been associated with the age of retirement—65 years (60 for women in some countries), but is becoming more fluid in postmodern societies. Due to the misperception that most people with intellectual disabilities age prematurely, the fact that some do age prematurely and that those in their 40s and 50s are often the oldest service users, a much earlier age tends to be used for this group to denote being an older person. Most commonly this is 55 years, but at times is as young as 40. This definition has meant that perceptions skip from young adults to older people and that middle age has barely been recognized for people with intellectual disabilities. Another tendency has been to associate old age with high support needs and frailty and to include much younger people with complex health needs in programs designed for older people.

This chapter aims to alert readers to some of the issues associated with the social construction of aging—that is, to the psychological, social, and physical changes that might occur and the challenges these present for professionals. The difficult part lies with the practitioner in the application of this knowledge to each individual's unique pattern of aging.

Aging also affects families and the capacity of parents to continue in caregiving roles. Middle-age adults residing with their parents inevitably face the loss of parental support, their parents' death, and the transition to nonparental care. Assisting individuals, parents and families to plan for the future is a complex task that must juggle many competing needs. Parental anxiety and the limited experiences of adults can lead to plans for a safe and secure future. Plans must, however, be flexible to respond to the changing needs of a middle-age adult and provide continuing opportunities for personal growth and development. The literature on issues of planning and the midlife transition for adults of "moving on without parents" is growing (e.g., see Bigby, 2000; Harris, 1998; Heller et al., 2000). One study suggests that people with intellectual disabilities who have always lived at home with their parents make the transition from nonparental care in their early 50s (Bigby, 2000). Space precludes further discussion in this chapter, as its focus is on old age, when people are in their late 50s and beyond, rather than on middle age.

SUMMARY OF KEY POPULATION CHARACTERISTICS

Although the proportion of people with intellectual disabilities surviving until later life has increased dramatically, they are still a very small group. For example, a database in one Australian state shows that the number of clients with an intellectual disability who are 60 years of age increased four-fold in 18 years, from 321 (3%) in 1982 to 1,327 (6.7%) in 2000. Estimates suggest people with intellectual disabilities make up 0.4% of the general population 55 years and older and that older people compose between 6%–12% of all people with intellectual disabilities. Various outreach projects suggest that as many as 25% of people with intellectual disabilities are out of touch with specialist services as they begin to age (Bigby, 2004).

Old age is a significant portion of the life course that can span many years. The conceptualization by Laslett (1989) of the Third and Fourth Ages emphasizes the diversity of people labeled as "old". Laslett sees the Third Age, when people are "the younger old," as a time when they are still healthy and maintain functional skills and the Fourth Age, when people are "old old," as typified by increasing infirmity, frailty, and decreasing ability for self-care.

Older people are a diverse rather than homogenous group, reflecting key differences related to class, gender, ability, race, and ethnicity found in earlier parts of the life course. The way people age is shaped by their own unique combination of genetics, lifestyles, experiences, and health in the earlier part of their life course, as well as by their current social and economic context. The variations are endless, which highlights the dangers of simply labeling people as "old"—that can lead to stereotypical assumptions and expectations based on this one characteristic and can reduce choice and opportunities. Bearing in mind the dangers of stereotyping, older people with intellectual disabilities as a group have the following characteristics:

- They age at a similar rate to the general population but have a slightly reduced life span. Some groups, such as people with Down syndrome, are an exception and experience premature aging and a shortened life span.
- They have less severe disabilities than their younger counterparts and are more skilled in relation to adaptive behavior and functional skills. This is because younger people with more severe disabilities tend not to reach "old age."
- They have rates of age-related health conditions comparable to or higher than the general population.
- They have high risk factors for ill health, particularly related to lifestyle factors such as exercise and diet and to socioeconomic status.
- They have high rates of psychological disturbance, which partly is accounted for by a high rate of dementia of the Alzheimer's type (DAT) among people with Down syndrome.
- They are less likely to be employed, attend a day program, or have opportunities for meaningful leisure than their younger counterparts.
- They are much more likely to live in a shared supported accommodation than in a private home with family or friends.
- They are likely to be relocated to mainstream aged care facilities as they age but to be substantially younger than other residents. Families and other advocates are often not satisfied with the responsiveness or quality of mainstream care facilities, where the emphasis is on care rather than support.
- They have restricted and reduced access to specialist disability services.
- They are less likely to have strong advocates and robust informal social networks than their younger counterparts.
- They are likely to experience disruption of relationships and loss of contact with long- term friends due to residential mobility and retirement from formal day programs.
- They are likely to experience substantial discrimination on the basis of age.

PERCEPTIONS OF SUCCESSFUL AGING

As the preceding list of key characteristics demonstrated, external social and economic factors as well as individual features shape the experience of aging for people with an intellectual disability. Aging is perceived and constructed differently through historic time and by different cultures. In the early 1960s, for example, perceptions of successful aging were the disengagement and withdrawal by older people from the social life of the community (Cummings & Henry, 1961). In the next decade, Lawton and Nahemow (1973) stressed the importance of older people maintaining activity, replacing lost roles with new ones, and continuing their involvement in society and interpersonal relationships. It has since been suggested that successful aging has three components: absence of disease and disability; high cognitive and physical capacity; and active engagement with life, including productive capacity and interpersonal relationships (Rowe & Kahn, 1998). Some of these dimensions appear to exclude people with intellectual disabilities completely. It is argued that the aspirations of older people with intellectual disabilities and the factors that make up their quality of life are not too different from those in the early parts of their life. Central is the achievement of core human rights such as equal citizenship, community inclusion, participation, dignity, and self-determination. Nolan's senses framework, highlights the subjective and perceptual nature of what the achievement of these broad concepts might mean and therefore what might constitute a good life for an older person (Nolan, Davies, & Grant, 2001, p. 175):

- *A sense of security:* freedom from pain or discomfort and attention to physical and psychological needs
- *A sense of continuity:* recognition of an individual's biography and connection to their past
- *A sense of belonging:* opportunity to maintain or develop meaningful relationships with family and friends and to be part of a chosen community or group
- *A sense of purpose:* opportunity to engage in purposeful activity, identify and pursue goals and exercise choice
- *A sense of achievement:* opportunity to meet meaningful goals and make a recognized and valued contribution
- *A sense of significance:* recognition and value as a person of worth

This approach takes account of individual differences and uses each person's own experience as the starting point to consider factors that are important to him or her. It provides a useful set of questions for practitioners to use in relation to each individual's life and its meaning for the individual.

SOCIAL CHANGES ASSOCIATED WITH AGING

Certain social changes accompany aging. Three prominent ones—changes in social attitudes, changes in social roles, and changes in social relationships—are discussed next.

Changes in Social Attitudes

Cultures differ in their attitudes towards aging and older people. In Japan and in North American native cultures, for example, older people often have a valued status in the family and are revered by the community for their wisdom. By contrast, many Western cultures devalue older people and subject them to discrimination on the basis of their age. An Australian journalist suggested the community perceives older people as "useless, toothless, hairless and sexless" ("Images of Ageing," 1998). Such negative stereotypes generate fear and denigration of the aging process, embedding presumptions of incompetence in community attitudes and responses. Bytheway suggested that ageism "legitimates the use of chronological age to mark out classes of people who are systematically denied resources and opportunities that others enjoy" (1995, p. 14). Ageist attitudes are reminiscent of discriminatory and stigmatizing community attitudes toward people with disabilities, suggesting that those who are older will experience a double jeopardy of disadvantage on the basis of both age and disability.

Common stereotypical views about older people with intellectual disabilities include that they all age prematurely, have much higher support needs than younger people and poorer health, have a wish to sit at home and put their feet up, are past learning new skills, have an inability to benefit from and no need of opportunities to develop skills or explore new interests, and are likely to be observers rather than participants in day programs. Such views have led to discriminatory policies and program development and outcomes, such that older people

- Are less likely to be relocated from institutions
- Are less likely to be employed or attend a day program
- Have fewer opportunities for choice and active programs
- Are included with younger people with complex needs (Bigby, 2004)

With the exception of people with Down syndrome, who are at extremely high risk of developing DAT 20–30 years earlier than people with other types of developmental disability (see Chapters 10 and 44), many older people with intellectual disabilities do have a continuing ability to learn, many do not age more rapidly than other people, and many have fewer support needs than younger day program participants (Bigby, 2004). These people are survivors. They tend to be more competent than at any other stage of their life. Compared with people with developmental disability in general, they have less severe disabilities and are more skilled than their younger peers. Such older people obviously do not include those with more severe, complex, or multiple disabilities, many of whom still do not survive into old age.

Changes in Social Roles

The social roles people occupy and their relationships change as they age, influenced by their social environment and the life changes experienced by others in their social network. Retirement—leaving work and losing the role of "worker"—is a major change that can be compensated for by greater involvement in the community as a volunteer or in leisure activities. In the Australian community, older people outnumber younger age groups in voluntary community work (Australian Bureau of Statistics, 1999). Older people may also acquire new roles, such as being a grandparent as their own children age or a great aunt or uncle.

The relevance of retirement to people with intellectual disabilities—who may never have been part of the paid work force but may have attended a day activity center for much of their lives—has been subject to much debate (Hawkins, 1999; Heller, 1999). For this group, retirement has been shown to lead to social isolation and loss of friendships, as older people lose connection with the context in which they have sustained relationships (Bigby, 2000). Retirement also has the potential to be a discriminatory mechanism, providing an arbitrary point for exclusion from specialist disability services or a strategy for managing demand and for creating vacancies for younger clients.

Conversely, it has been argued that older people with intellectual disabilities have the same rights as others to lead a more relaxed lifestyle and that existing day support services are too inflexible to respond to changing needs as people age. It is suggested that "retirement" programs are necessary to meet older people's needs for more support, quieter environments, a reduced emphasis on skill development, less formal programming, greater flexibility of attendance, and a staff skill base that includes knowledge of aging (Bigby, 2004). It is important to note that the limited research that has sought the views of people with intellectual disabilities about later life suggests they value active engagement, choice, continued working, learning, and participation. They are concerned about isolation and loss of networks and are satisfied by—and value—the day services they attend.

A review of the literature found the following to be the overarching goals of day support for older people (Bigby, 2004):

- Provision of choice and person-centered planning
- Maintenance and strengthening of social networks
- Support for participation in the community
- Maintenance of skills
- Opportunities for self-expression and sense of self
- Promotion of health and a healthy lifestyle

Many different program models have the capacity to deliver outcomes of this nature, including more traditional age-integrated day centers, brokerage whereby an individual budget is available to purchase support to participate in activities of choice, and programs specifically targeted at older people. Rigid age-based retirement policies do not account for the diversity among people as they age. There is a danger, too, that age-based retirement programs, by making assumptions based on age alone and restricting continued access to other types of programs, may actually curtail choice. In addition, decisions about retirement and the establishment of retirement programs will be influenced by the nature and the capacity of the service system and its potential to adapt to changing individual preferences, health, and physical capacity. Paramount in decisions about lifestyle, however, should be a consideration of the person's existing daytime occupation and preferences.

Changes in Social Relationships

Relationships with family and friends are vulnerable to disruption when changes to place of residence or day occupation occur. Many middle-age people move out of the family home when their parents die and lose contact with long-term acquaintances in the neighborhood, their parent's friendship network, and the incidental contact that occurred with distant family members who kept in touch with their parents or attended family gatherings. Retirement can mean loss of the social milieu that sustained friendships. Maintenance of friendships in this stage of life requires, first, the recognition that such friendships exist and, second, active support to create opportunities for continuing contact and shared activities. Social relationships are often endangered by family members or residential staff who have a limited awareness of, or fail to acknowledge, such ties.

Although the pattern might change in future generations, most older people with intellectual disabilities in the early 21st century do not have a spouse or children. Once their parents die, siblings are likely to be their closest relatives. Australian research suggests that it is mostly siblings, but sometimes more distant relatives or close family friends, who replace some of the roles previously fulfilled by parents. These are more likely to be "caring about" roles, such as overseeing well-being and monitoring and organizing the provision of formal support services, than direct "caring for" roles that entail providing day-to-day care (Bigby, 2000). Performance of "caring about" roles means that older people have someone outside the service system who is committed to their well-being and is critically important to ensuring the quality and responsiveness of formal services. These roles require a long-term and significant commitment to an older person, although not necessarily geographic proximity. When planning future accommodation support for a middle-age adult living at home, it is important to ensure those who care about the adult with intellectual disability replace parents in this supervisory and monitoring role and are available to negotiate formal service provision. Such planning must be ongoing, however, and over time it should include the younger generation of nieces or nephews. This helps ensure succession, especially if siblings or older family friends predecease the person with intellectual disability.

PSYCHOLOGICAL CHANGES ASSOCIATED WITH AGING

Various psychological changes accompany aging as well. These are seen in the areas of cognitive function and psychological tasks, grief and loss, and Alzheimer's disease.

Cognitive Function and Psychological Tasks

As people age, changes occur to cognitive functioning related to intelligence, memory, and learning ability. Despite assumptions to the contrary, people with intellectual disabilities have the potential for continued development of intellectual and adaptive functioning until their mid-60s or older. Age-related changes to cognitive function do not occur uniformly. Aspects such as speed of response or short-term memory may decline sooner than longer-term memory or the ability to recall stored verbal information.

Maintaining capacity and the realization of continued development are affected, however, by genetics and opportunity. As noted, people with Down syndrome may experience decline in functioning as early as 35–40 years (Zigman, Seltzer, & Silverman, 1994). Although it has not been documented in research studies of people with Down syndrome, anecdotal evidence raises the possibility that cognitive decline may be most marked among people who do not use their abilities, and it may be particularly associated with poor physical or mental health and sensory loss. Theoretically, adaptations to the nature of support and the environment can optimize individual capacity and compensate for cognitive and sensory changes. These include use of more direct lighting, pictorial representations, and color and texture to define the physical environment more clearly.

Little is known about how people with intellectual disabilities make sense of their world or cope with its challenges. Behavioral rather than emotional aspects of their lives have been the main focus of study. Still, psychological theories developed from the general population can be used to aid understanding. For example, Erikson's (1973) stage theory of personality development suggests the final task confronting older people is one of achieving "ego integrity versus despair"—the acceptance that one's life has had meaning. Supporting reminiscence and life review are important ways of helping older people to deal with these tasks. Compilation of a "life story book" is one strategy that has been used to assist people with intellectual disabilities to preserve their life history and support reminiscence. Life story books can be compiled by a caregiver or by the person with the disability with assistance from a caregiver. Such books may include key items as well as pictures and words. In addition to helping an individual maintain a connection to his or her past, such books can provide insight for staff into the person's history and enhance their capacity to support the individual's sense of continuity.

Drawing on mainstream theories, Seltzer (1985) conceptualized the tasks of aging for older people with intellectual disabilities as follows:

- Adjustment to losses and reduced physical capacity
- Restructuring of roles
- Reassessment of self concept
- Interaction with societal prejudices
- Acceptance of mortality

Seltzer (1993) suggested that people with intellectual disabilities are disadvantaged in dealing with these psychological tasks by their limited problem-solving capacity and poor access to external resources. Moss (1999) suggested their disadvantage is further compounded by negative past experiences such as separation in childhood; social stigma; abuse; limited opportunities; and current adverse circumstances, such as loneliness, lack of choice and autonomy, and poor social networks. An indicator of their vulnerability in later life is the high risk of older people with intellectual disability for psychiatric problems. Their rate of mental illness exceeds that of their younger peers and is as much as four times higher than that found in the general population of older people (Torr & Chiu, 2002). As with other aspects of aging, it is clear that a person's earlier life experiences, current social attitudes, and opportunities substantially affect mental well-being in old age.

There is poor identification of mental illness, particularly depression and anxiety, in older people with intellectual disabilities; consequently, there are low levels of active treatment. Because of communication problems, they often find it difficult to convey their feelings and stress, and diagnostic overshadowing ascribes psychiatric symptoms to intellectual disability instead. In addition, symptoms of illness may simply be identified as being associated with aging and therefore not judged as warranting any further investigation (Torr & Chiu, 2002).

Grief and Loss

Older people with intellectual disabilities face the challenges of dealing with the death of family and friends, which are the losses most commonly associated with aging. The strong emotional feelings of grief, the expression of grief, and the meanings associated with loss are influenced by the rituals and traditions of the social/cultural context. Expected behavior during bereavement and the processes of mourning vary considerably across different religions and cultures. Clegg and Lansdall-Welfare (2003) warned against assumptions based on the normalization philosophy; first, that resolution of grief follows uniform stages, and, second, that people with intellectual disabilities respond to loss in a similar way to others. In their view, such assumptions have led to a narrow range of ideas about appropriate types of support—such as the need to attend funerals, view the body, visit the grave, and attend counseling—and to a limited understanding of what such strategies might achieve. A person-centered approach demands such prescriptions are not followed without question and recognizes the complexities involved in supporting bereavement. Issues that arise include confusion of responsibility between staff and family; experience and expression of complex family tensions that require flexible and sensitive negotiation; finding appropriate representation of the lost relationship, which may need to evolve over time; and locating prompts to enable people with intellectual disabilities to express shared experiences and indications of their inner emotional worlds. Clegg and Lansdall-Welfare (2003) suggested that supporting people with intellectual disabilities through grief and loss requires creativity and can raise a minefield of ethical decisions for staff. Adjustment to and accommodation of loss occurs in multiple ways. The challenge for practitioners is to find ways that are meaningful for each individual to express grief in his or her own way and to identify who in the social environment needs what type of support.

Alzheimer's Disease

Alzheimer's disease is one of the most common psychiatric conditions among older people with intellectual disability, particularly those with Down syndrome. It follows a predictable course that involves the progressive deterioration of cognitive and adaptive skills necessary for everyday functioning, eventual total loss of function, and the need for 24-hour nursing care (Janicki & Dalton, 1999). More specifically, its progress includes

- *Amnesia*—memory loss
- *Apraxia*—loss of ability to coordinate learned movements
- *Aphasia*—inability to speak or understand
- *Agnosia*—inability to recognize what is seen (Sloan, 1997, as cited in Janicki, McCallion, & Dalton, 2000, p. 389)

This irreversible progression can span between 3 and 20 years. Progression is generally accelerated to between 1 and 9 years for people with Down syndrome, with their significantly higher risk of this disease at a much earlier age as compared with the general population. For example, 22% of people with Down syndrome older than 40 years and 56% of those older than 60 years have been found to have Alzheimer's disease (Janicki & Dalton, 2000). In comparison, the rate of Alzheimer's disease in the general population is 0.1% between the ages of 30–59 years, 1.4% between the ages of 65–69 years, and 13% in those older than 80 years. It is critical to remember, however, that not all people with Down syndrome develop symptoms of Alzheimer's disease. Almost half of those who survive to age 60 show no symptoms at all.

The early symptoms of Alzheimer's disease mimic those of a number of other conditions that are treatable. Treatable conditions include depression, thyroid dysfunction, urinary tract infections, diabetes, poor diet, and sensory loss. If a person's functional capacity is declining and Alzheimer's disease is suspected, a thorough diagnostic procedure is needed to eliminate all other treatable causes of the symptoms (Janicki, Heller, & Hogg, 1996). Diagnosis should include physical examinations and identification of a pattern of functional decline over time. Clinicians are often very dependent on accurate, reliable accounts of change from those who know the person well. Difficulty of diagnosis is compounded by communication problems and the inappropriateness of standard tests based on population norms. Various diagnostic tools specific for people with intellectual disability have been developed (see Appendix B at the end of the book).

Supporting a person with Alzheimer's disease requires flexibility and continual adjustment to take account of his or her changing needs and to enable participation in everyday life for as long as possible. Loss of motivation and functional capacity can be compensated for by providing more active cues, support, and prompting, as well as adaptation of the social and physical environment. The "Edinburgh Principles" suggest that the right should exist for people to remain in the community with sufficient and appropriate supports and not be subjected to inappropriate or premature institutionalization (Wilkinson & Janicki, 2002). A variety of well-designed resources have been developed that provide comprehensive and sensitive ideas for tackling these difficult tasks (see Appendix B). Refer to Chapter 44 for more detail about Alzheimer's disease.

PHYSICAL CHANGES ASSOCIATED WITH AGING

Age-related changes occur to the structures and organs of the body that result in a gradual decline in the physical capacity and functioning of older people. Changes include less efficient circulation, reduced bone density, and sensory decline such as loss of hearing and eyesight acuity. These changes are gradual and irreversible but vary among individuals and are influenced by lifestyle, social and environmental factors, and genetic differences. Both current and past lifestyles have a critical impact on health and physical capacity in later life. It is estimated, for example, that half the decline in older people is due to physical and mental disuse and lack of exercise rather than to illness or biological change (Australian Bureau of Statistics, 1999). An unhealthy lifestyle in the younger years means embarking on the aging process with poor fitness and higher risk of age-related disease such as diabetes, hypertension, heart disease, stroke, arthritis, and respiratory disease.

People with intellectual disabilities are often disadvantaged by their lifestyles, as a high proportion lead sedentary lives, get little exercise, eat poor diets, and are overweight or obese. In the United States, for example, 50% of adults with intellectual disability are overweight compared with a third of the general population (Janicki et al., 2002). They also have difficulty obtaining quality health care and, as a result, have high rates of undiagnosed and untreated conditions. Insufficient attention to supporting inclusive practices has meant that the majority of general practitioners, who are increasingly providing primary health care for people with intellectual disabilities, feel inadequately trained to provide treatment for this group (Lennox, Diggens, & Ugoni, 1997). Other obstacles to good health are the exclusion of older people with intellectual disabilities from health promotion programs and their poor access to screening programs and health-related information.

Specific syndromes are associated with particular patterns of physical changes or higher risks of diseases. In addition to the high risk of early onset Alzheimer's disease that is characteristic of Down syndrome, fragile X syndrome is associated with an increased risk of mitral valve prolapse and muscoskeletal disorders and Prader-Willi syndrome is associated with an increased risk of diabetes, cardiovascular disease, and obesity (Evenhuis et al., 2001).

Preexisting health conditions or long-term use of medication can increase risk of certain age-related conditions. For example, osteoporosis is increased for women with cerebral palsy and for those with epilepsy who have used medication to control seizures over a long period of time. Chronic medical conditions may be compounded by age-related changes. For example, swallowing problems may be exacerbated by age-related muscle and digestive system changes. As many as a third of people with intellectual disabilities use antipsychotic medication over extended periods of time, which carries long-term risks of constipation and urinary retention, increased infections, weight gain, and heart problems (Emerson, 2002).

Older people have an increased risk of chronic disease and acute health conditions. Incontinence, reduced mobility, hearing impairment, arthritis, hypertension, and cerebrovascular disease are all more common than in younger people. The health of older people with intellectual disabilities is generally poorer compared with the general population of older people, with an increased frequency of thyroid disorders, heart disorders, and sensory impairments. The greatest physical and health-related changes occur after the age of 75 years, but old age is not necessarily synonymous with poor health. For example, two thirds of older people in the general community are free from any condition that makes them depend on assistance. Assumptions should not be made that physical decline or poor health is due simply to aging, as this can leave treatable medical conditions unacknowledged, uninvestigated, and untreated. The challenge for practitioners working with older people with intellectual disabilities is prevention, detection, treatment, and management of health conditions, as well as minimizing their impact on well-being.

CONTINUITIES ACROSS THE LIFE SPAN

Although the study of aging and intellectual disability has focused on changes associated with aging, it is also characterized by many elements of continuity from the earlier stages of the life span. Each individual takes into later life his or her own biography—interests, social relationships, health issues, and lifestyle. A life-span perspective reinforces the significance of earlier life experiences to the aging process and suggests that good health care and support to develop skills, interests, and social relationships in the earlier years provide the foundations for successful aging.

The key principles that inform government policies for younger people with disabilities are equally applicable to older people. Age should neither define access to community facilities and appropriate support nor curtail choice and self-determination. It should not limit opportunities for participation and inclusion. Segregation by age is no more acceptable than by disability. Age should not affect the protection of human rights. Similarly, much of the knowledge and skills practitioners use in working with younger people and their families is applicable to older people, as are the funding mechanisms and program designs. For example, person- and family-centered approaches to planning and support, communication, negotiation and network building skills, and individualized programs/ funding can be applied to work with older people. Issues for practitioners—such as dealing with discriminatory attitudes and inadequate resources, confronting ethical dilemmas, addressing conflicting priorities and the necessity to negotiate conflicting interests and measure individual choice against notions of best interest—occur at all stages of the life course.

Adaptation and Compensation

The frameworks for thinking about broad policy and service development and skills for working with individuals and their families, which are used at earlier stages in the life course, can be applied to the issues that confront older people. It is important to recognize, however, that they will be applied in a different context—namely, the social, physical and psychological changes associated with aging. It also is necessary to account for an additional service network to the disability service system: the care system that is designed to support the general community of older people. Consideration must be given to the appropriateness of these services for older people with intellectual disabilities and how the service agencies might be provided with resources and supported to provide additional options for this group.

A framework that is particularly useful for thinking about responses to age-related changes emerges from the theory of "selective optimization with compensation" developed by Baltes and Baltes (1990). Here, the focus is on the process of aging. Age-related changes are conceptualized as requiring adaptation to minimize the impact of reduced capacity, adaptation to the loss of roles and relationships, and use of remaining capacity to maximize the degree of satisfaction and achievement of individual goals. This framework suggests that adaptation to aging involves selection, compensation, and optimization:

- Greater *selection* of activity as physical capacity is reduced
- *Compensation* for loss of either skill or function by internal and external adjustments
- *Optimization,* or making the most of what one has by engaging in behaviors and activities that maximize reserves and enrich life choices

Emphasizing adaptation and compensation highlights the multiple strategies available to respond to the changes associated with aging and to compensate for losses. As the examples throughout this chapter have illustrated, behavior patterns or activities undertaken may be altered through individual actions or with staff support. The external social or physical environment may be adapted by changing the nature or intensity of individual support or programs offered, altering physical features in the home or other places, and introducing of technology or other supportive devices. These ideas support evolving and dynamic responses to aging, by a continual adaptation to change and a search for ways to support the realization of individual goals. They highlight the importance of focusing on the individual and adapting the social and physical environments.

SUMMARY

Due to an increased life expectancy, more people with intellectual disabilities are outliving their parents and surviving into later life. There are social, psychological, and physical changes associated with aging. Successful aging, though, is associated with continuity from younger years, health, lifestyle, relationships, and personal interests. Inaccurate assumptions about aging sometimes lead to age-based discrimination, in turn reducing opportunities for older people. Many of the frameworks and skills that are considered in designing support for younger people with intellectual disabilities are also applicable to older people. An additional framework for thinking about support to older people is suggested—one that emphasizes the importance of adapting individual behavior, providing support, adapting external physical and social environment to age-related changes, and compensating for age-associated loss.

FOR FURTHER THOUGHT AND DISCUSSION

1. Spend some time with an older person who has an intellectual disability, talking about his or her life story and aspirations. Consider the nature of the person's social relationships, how these have changed over time, and how they might change again as he or she gets older. How might the type of support this person requires to maintain relationships and achieve aspirations change as he or she gets older?
2. Think about your local area and the various aspects of the service system, such as health care, accommodation, day support, and family support. What changes might be necessary to adapt these programs to the needs of people as they age?
3. Assume that you have been given the task of designing a policy on aging for your local service system. On what principles might it be based? What issues might it need to address?

REFERENCES

Australian Bureau of Statistics. (1999). *Older people, Australia: A social report.* Canberra, Australia: Author.

Baltes, P., & Baltes, M. (1990). Psychological perspectives on successful aging: The model of selective optimisation with compensation. In P. Baltes & M. Baltes, *Successful aging: Perspectives from the behavioural sciences.* Cambridge, United Kingdom: Cambridge University Press.

Bigby, C. (2000). *Moving on without parents: Planning, transitions and sources of support for middle-aged and older adults with intellectual disability.* Baltimore: Paul H. Brookes Publishing Co.

Bigby, C. (2004). *Aging with a lifelong disability: Policy, program and practice issues for professionals.* London: Jessica Kingsley Publishers.

Bytheway, B. (1995). *Ageism.* Maidenhead, United Kingdom: Open University Press.

Carter, C., & Jancar, J. (1983). Mortality in the mentally handicapped: A fifty year survey at the Stoke Park Group of Hospitals. *Journal of Mental Deficiency Research, 27,* 143–156.

Clegg, J., & Lansdall-Welfare. (2003). Death, disability and dogma. *Philosophy, Psychiatry and Psychology, 10*(1), 67–79.

Cummings, E., & Henry, W. (1961). *Growing old.* New York: Basic Books.

Emerson, E. (2002, June). *Unhealthy lifestyles.* Paper presented at the inaugural European International Association for the Scientific Study of Intellectual Disabilities conference, Dublin, Ireland.

Erikson, E. (1973). *Childhood and society.* New York: W.W. Norton.

Evenhuis, H., Henderson, C., Beange, H., et al. (2001). Healthy ageing—adults with intellectual disabilities: Physical health issues. *Journal of Applied Research in Intellectual Disabilities, 14*(3), 175–194.

Harris, J. (1998). *Working with older carers: Guidance for service providers in learning disability.* Widderminster, United Kingdom: Bild Publications.

Haveman, M. (2004). Disease epidemiology and aging people with intellectual disabilities. *Journal of Intellectual Disability Policy and Practice, 1*(1), 16–23.

Hawkins, B.A. (1999). Rights, place of residence, and retirement: Lessons from case studies on aging. In S.S. Herr & G. Weber (Eds.), *Aging, rights, and quality of life: Prospects for older people with developmental disabilities* (pp. 93–107). Baltimore: Paul H. Brookes Publishing Co.

Heller, T. (1999). Emerging models. In S.S. Herr & G. Weber (Eds.), *Aging, rights, and quality of life: Prospects for older people with developmental disabilities* (pp. 149–165). Baltimore: Paul H. Brookes Publishing Co.

Heller, T., Miller, A., Hsieh, K., et al. (2000). Later-life planning: Promoting knowledge of options and choice-making. *Mental Retardation, 38*(5), 395–406.

"Images of ageing." (1998). *Good Weekend, Sydney Morning Herald.*

Janicki, M.P., & Dalton, A. (1999). *Dementia, aging and intellectual disabilities.* Philadelphia: Brunner/Mazel.

Janicki, M.P., & Dalton, A. (2000). Prevalence of dementia and impact on intellectual disability services. *Mental Retardation, 38*(3), 276–288.

Janicki, M.P., Davidson, P., Henderson, C., et al. (2002). Health characteristics and health service utilization in older adults with intellectual disability living in community residences. *Journal of Intellectual Disability Research, 46*(4), 287–298.

Janicki, M.P., Heller, T., & Hogg, J. (1996). Practice guidelines for the clinical assessment and care management of Alzheimer's disease and other dementias among adults with intellectual disability. *Journal of Intellectual Disability Research, 40,* 374–382.

Janicki, M.P., McCallion, P., & Dalton, A.J. (2000). Supporting people with dementia in community settings. In M.P. Janicki & E.F. Ansello (Eds.), *Community supports for aging adults with lifelong disabilities* (pp. 387–413). Baltimore: Paul H. Brookes Publishing Co.

Laslett, P. (1989). *A fresh map of life.* London: Weidenfield & Nicholson.

Lawton, M., & Nahemow, L. (1973). Ecology and the aging process. In C. Eidsdorfer & M. Lawton (Eds.), *Psychology of adult development and aging* (pp. 619–674). Washington, DC: American Psychological Association.

Lennox, N., Diggens, J., & Ugoni, A. (1997). Barriers and solutions to general practice care of people with intellectual disability. *Journal of Intellectual Disability Research, 41,* 380–390.

Moss, S. (1999). Mental health: Issues of access and quality of life. In S.S. Herr & G. Weber (Eds.), *Aging, rights, and quality of life: Prospects for older people with developmental disabilities* (pp. 167–187). Baltimore: Paul H. Brookes Publishing Co.

Nolan, M., Davies, S., & Grant, G. (2001). Integrating perspectives. In M. Nolan, S. Davies, & G. Grant (Eds.), *Working with older people and their families* (pp. 160–178). Maidenhead, United Kingdom: Open University Press.

Rowe, J., & Kahn, R. (1998). *Successful aging.* New York: Random House.

Seltzer, G.B. (1985). Selected psychological processes and aging among older developmentally disabled persons. In M.P. Janicki & H.M. Wisniewski (Eds.), *Aging and developmental disabilities: Issues and approaches* (pp. 211–228). Baltimore: Paul H. Brookes Publishing Co.

Seltzer, G.B. (1993). Psychological adjustment in midlife for persons with mental retardation. In E. Sutton, A.R. Factor, B.A. Hawkins, et al. (Eds.), *Older adults with developmental disabilities: Optimizing choice and change* (pp. 157–184). Baltimore: Paul H. Brookes Publishing Co.

Torr, J., & Chiu, E. (2002). The elderly with intellectual disability and mental disorder: A challenge for old age psychiatry. *Current Opinion in Psychiatry, 15,* 383–386.

Yang, Q., Rasmussen, S., & Friedman, J. (2002). Mortality associated with Down's syndrome in the USA from 1983 to 1997: A population based study. *The Lancet, 359,* 1019–1025.

Wilkinson, H., & Janicki, M. (2002). The Edinburgh Principles with accompanying guidelines and recommendations. *Journal of Intellectual Disability Research, 46*(3), 279–284.

Zigman, W., Seltzer, G., & Silverman, W. (1994). Behavioral and mental health changes associated with aging in adults with mental retardation. In M. Seltzer, M. Krauss, & M.P. Janicki (Eds.), *Lifecourse perspectives on adulthood and old age* (pp. 67–92). Washington, DC: American Association on Mental Retardation.

V

Health

40

Ethics of Consent in People with Intellectual and Developmental Disabilities

John Heng and William F. Sullivan

WHAT YOU WILL LEARN ABOUT IN THIS CHAPTER

- The importance and meaning of informed consent
- Components of decision making
- The goal and limits of health care in relation to consent and the judgment of benefits and burdens of treatments in relation to consent

This chapter discusses various clinical and ethical issues for health care professionals surrounding consent to health care by people with intellectual and developmental disabilities. Although the focus of this chapter is on consent to health care, many of the same practical and ethical issues of consent also arise in other areas, such as decisions about living arrangements (Robertson et al., 2001; Struhkamp, 2005), employment, relationships (Murphy & O'Callaghan, 2004), and participation in research (Dye et al., 2004).

THE IMPORTANCE AND MEANING OF INFORMED CONSENT

In the health care field, ensuring that there is prior and ongoing informed consent for a procedure, treatment, or plan of care follows from respecting an individual's intrinsic dignity and participation in the human community. This concern for informed consent goes beyond a health care provider's obligation to be professional or to recognize legally or socially determined rights. When a health care provider solicits consent, this ought to be motivated by a concern for acting ethically in relation to another human being. Failure to respect the dignity and moral worth of a person results in neglect or harm to him or her, even if the health care professional thinks that some desirable consequences could result. Nevertheless, health care professionals should be aware of various vulnerabilities that could diminish a person's capacity for decision making and consent giving. Such vulnerabilities necessitate providing appropriate supports to which the person, who always maintains his or her dignity and membership in the human community, is entitled.

Intrinsic Human Dignity

Some thinkers believe that dignity is an *attribute* that depends on particular qualities and capacities that may be absent, acquired, or lost in a human being—for example, rationality, autonomy and self-consciousness (Singer, 1993). According to this view, people with severe intellectual and developmental disabilities who do not have such capacities have a lower moral status than those who do. Other thinkers hold that every member of the human community has an *intrinsic* dignity that does not diminish through life (Sulmasy, 2002). According to this view, people with intellectual and developmental disabilities are on an equal moral footing with other human beings.

The chapter authors affirm the second view. Each human being is a member of the same biological species and related to other human beings through kinship, friendship, and socialization. Such relationships are based on affection and goodwill and do not only depend on the presence or absence of qualities or capacities such as rationality, autonomy, and self-consciousness.

In the health care field, affirming the intrinsic moral value and human dignity of people with intellectual and developmental disabilities means providing them with adequate and appropriate care based on available resources. It also means ensuring their participation in making decisions about such care, to the extent that they are able. These two goals might seem to be at odds in some circumstances. In publications on ethics and on intellectual and developmental disabilities, it is quite common to encounter ethical problems

This chapter uses the term *health care professionals* for physicians, nurses, psychologists, and others who provide health care services. It refers to individuals with intellectual and developmental disabilities as *people with developmental disabilities.*

posed in terms of a health care provider's conflicting duties between respecting the choice of the patient or of the substitute decision maker, on the one hand, and avoiding a preventable harm to the patient, on the other. In the chapter authors' opinion, such dilemmas can often be resolved ethically through a correct understanding of informed consent and of the proper goals and limits of health care.

Distinguishing Legal and Ethical Approaches to Consent

As of 2007, most legal jurisdictions have laws on consent to health care. Health care professionals should seek to understand the different legal requirements that apply to their particular jurisdictions. It is important, however, to understand the difference between legal and ethical approaches to consent in health care. Although there are areas of overlap between the requirements of various laws on consent and the ethics of consent, there are also noteworthy differences.

First, the law sets down general standards and rules for a society as well as various consequences for failure to abide by them when it is appropriate. There may be provisions for exceptions in laws and criteria for when these exceptions apply, but laws do not anticipate every possible situation that could differ from the norm. By contrast, ethical inquiry is concerned with the basis of decisions to act or to refrain from acting in particular circumstances. Sometimes applying a general legal standard or rule to a specific circumstance, without taking into account relevant exceptional factors, could result in harm being done to an individual. Health care professionals should be aware that laws on consent in health care may not take into account the strengths and vulnerabilities of people with developmental disabilities in particular circumstances.

Second, a legal approach to consent focuses on adhering to the law. In some health care settings, the legally required routines of documenting consent tend to be formalized without due reflection on what is necessary ethically for informed consent. The concern for proper procedures and paperwork then takes priority over the relationship of the health care professional with the person from whom consent is being sought. As a result, the importance of careful listening and communicating in the process of consent giving can be overlooked. Health care professionals should be aware that giving consent is the outcome of a prior process that depends to a large extent on the quality of the relationship and communication between themselves and those who are receiving care.

Third, laws on consent typically consider competence or capacity as an all-or-none attribute. That is, either a person independently meets some standard threshold of capacity or that person does not. If the person does not meet such a standard, then some other person—the next of kin or another legally designated substitute—is authorized to provide consent. The philosophical basis of this approach in the law is a negative understanding of the ethical principle of autonomy as freedom from the interference of others. To the extent that health care professionals operate entirely within this legal and philosophical framework, they may dismiss the possibility of supported decision making. Health care professionals should be aware that people with developmental disabilities who, on their own, do not meet all the legal criteria for competence in making decisions about health care may sometimes be capable of doing so, either partially or fully, with assistance from family and others who provide ongoing care.

Elements of Consent

Most ethicists agree that there are at least four essential elements of informed consent. The person must have sufficient, although not necessarily technically detailed, information on which to base a decision; understand this information; be able to understand the consequences of giving or withholding consent; and be free to give or withhold consent (Evans, 1997). Some ethicists have proposed a fifth element: being able to weigh the benefits and burdens of various options in light of a person's values or what that person judges to be good in life (Grisso, 1986; Sulmasy, 1997). The addition of this fifth element raises the contentious question of whether there is a distinction between being capable of understanding information and being capable of making an ethical judgment. It is the chapter authors' opinion that a person's ability to consider various options in light of his or her values and life circumstances is an integral part of giving consent. Giving consent expresses a person's evaluation that a procedure, treatment, or plan of care is, on the balance, good in that it contributes to that person's overall well-being in his or her circumstances, even if it could be disagreeable in the short term. In other words, such judgments are about values.

COMPONENTS OF DECISION MAKING

Properly understood, giving or withholding consent is the outcome of a process of ethical decision making (American Association on Mental Retardation, 2000). Suto et al. (2005) identified what they regard as an emerging consensus among health care professionals on the distinct but related abilities required in each step of this process. These abilities include

1. Realizing that a decision needs to be made
2. Understanding sufficient information that is relevant to the decision

3. Reasoning with that information to come to a decision
4. Appreciating who is affected by the decision
5. Communicating a choice

The chapter authors add that Abilities 3 and 4 involve apprehending values and weighing the benefits and burdens for oneself of various medical options in light of those values. Ability 5 corresponds to what the law typically means by giving or withholding consent and comes at the end of this decision-making process.

Assessing Decision-Making Capacity

As noted, laws regarding consent to health care differ from jurisdiction to jurisdiction. There is no universally agreed-on set of criteria for assessing the capacity of a person to give or to refuse consent to health care. Because consent is the outcome of a decision-making process, from a clinical perspective, it is more accurate to speak about assessing decision-making capacity rather than consent-giving capacity. Again, there are no universally accepted criteria for such assessments by health care professionals. Nevertheless, the five abilities described by Suto et al. (2005) seem to be a reasonable guide for assessments of decision-making capacity. According to Suto et al., a person is capable of making a decision only if he or she is able to perform adequately all five of the described operations. Research has found that understanding the relevant information and reasoning with this information are the most difficult parts of this process for people with developmental disabilities.

In jurisdictions where the law on consent for health care expressly sets out criteria for assessing capacity to consent, and these are different from the previously outlined criteria, health care professionals should ensure that the legal criteria are fulfilled. They will often find, however, that the legal criteria are fewer and that there is a lower standard for assessing capacity to consent than what has been proposed in this chapter. This is because the law tends to focus more on a person's ability to understand health information than on his or her ability to make ethical judgments. In the chapter authors' opinion, it is ethically acceptable for health care professionals to use further criteria in their assessments than those given in the law in order to identify in which aspects of the decision-making process individuals may need support. In regard to finding a person incapable of giving or refusing consent, however, there is no consensus among ethicists. Some argue, on the basis of commutative justice or fairness, that a person ought not to be found incapable of consent by a higher standard than is set out by the law. Others maintain, on the grounds of social justice, that vulnerable individuals need more vigilance than is generally the case for the sake of ensuring their safety.

Particular Issues in Assessing the Decision-Making Capacity

It follows that assessing a person's capacity to give or withhold consent should involve more than simply testing his or her ability to understand and to recall information, for this is only a part of the decision-making process. There should also be some analysis of the other abilities involved in the process of decision making. For a person with developmental disability, this may entail the use of hypothetical vignettes, described in pictures or stories or a mixture of both, to determine the match between an individual's decision-making abilities and the level of complexity of the actual decision to be made (Morris, Niederbuhl, & Mahr, 1993).

The decision-making capacity of people with developmental disabilities is usually compared with that of individuals in the general population faced with similar decisions. There is, however, a range of decision-making capacities in individuals in the general population as well as in those with intellectual and developmental disabilities. Although, as a group, the latter's decision making is more likely to be impaired when compared with what some researchers call the "very able" decision makers in the general population, this is not always the case. For instance, there are often similarities in the decision-making abilities of people with mild developmental disabilities and the very able in the general population (Gunn et al., 2000). For individuals with moderate developmental disabilities, the standard of capacity to give or to withhold consent need not be the same as for the very able in the general population if the decision involves relatively little risk of harm. In these situations, with the support of family and other regular caregivers, such individuals may be capable of participating partially in some aspect of decision making. They may, however, not be capable of participating at all in making decisions that are complex. In general, it is unlikely that a person whose intellectual and functional abilities are in the severe to profound range of developmental disability (i.e., a person with an IQ score below 40 who needs significant supports in the areas of self-care, health, and safety) is capable of providing consent for most medical procedures (Dinerstein, Herr, & O'Sullivan, 1999). Nevertheless it is important to conduct a proper assessment of capacity, regardless of the level of an individual's functioning.

People with developmental disabilities, whatever their level of function, are usually better able to make decisions about procedures, treatments, or plans of care if they have had some prior experience with making decisions. Some people with developmental disabilities have had a limited range of life experiences and opportunities to make decisions, as many live in a protective family or a highly structured institution; this may often account for their underdeveloped decision-making abilities (Cea & Fisher, 2003). Learned helplessness, acquiescence, and suggestibility can predispose a person with developmental disabilities to be overly compliant with requests from health care professionals, thereby diminishing the voluntary nature of their decisions. In addition, having experienced or witnessed something distressing or harmful in the past can influence a person's judgment and willingness to consent to a procedure, treatment, or plan of care that he or she associates with that negative experience. These difficulties point to the importance of taking extra time and making the effort to involve others who know the person well in the process of obtaining consent. When considering a plan of care or a treatment that lasts over time, it is good to receive periodic feedback from the person.

A further consideration in assessments is that a person's decision-making abilities may change over time. This is particularly important for individuals who have disabilities that result in progressive functional deteriorations, such as dementia in some adults with Down syndrome. Also there may be factors affecting a person's capacity for decision making in some circumstances but not in others. The stress caused by an illness or the presence of a depression, even if it does not meet the criteria for a psychiatric diagnosis, are examples of such factors. Health care professionals should not simply assume that the results of a prior assessment of an individual's capacity to make decisions and to give consent are still valid in the present circumstances.

In addition, it is important to know that some people with intellectual and developmental disabilities are unable to communicate well or at all. Some may use alternative means of communication with which their health care professionals are unfamiliar. In these situations, the health care provider assessing a person's decision-making abilities must use an appropriate level of language or means of communication. Often the involvement of interpreters who know the person well can be very helpful (Morris et al., 1993).

Finally, health care professionals should be aware that a significant number of people with developmental disabilities may also have some form of affective disorder or psychiatric illness (i.e., a dual diagnosis). It is important for health care professionals to obtain an adequate psychosocial history to recognize various mental health factors that might affect decision making and the freedom to give or to withhold consent.

Discerning People's Values

The chapter previously proposed that a person's ability to consider medical options in light of his or her values is a key component in the process of ethical decision making in health care. A question might be raised about whether people with intellectual and developmental disabilities are capable of apprehending and holding values.

Values are apprehended by means of morally attuned feelings. Having some preconceptual notion of what is good and what contributes to one's overall well-being in life is an ability that is distinct from, and does not depend on, one's intellectual abilities (Sullivan, 2005). Health care professionals should not dismiss the possibility that people with developmental disabilities can apprehend and hold values, but they should be attentive to individuals' various strengths and weaknesses in this area. For example, people with developmental disabilities that primarily affect intellectual performance, such as Down syndrome, generally can develop morally attuned feelings that enable them to apprehend values. In comparison, people with other developmental disabilities may have difficulty apprehending values. For example, those with Asperger syndrome can have highly developed intellectual capacities in areas such as mathematics but may have significant affective and social challenges that affect their ability to apprehend some values.

Although many people with developmental disabilities may be capable of apprehending values, they may need assistance in connecting those values to a concrete decision about care. Giving or withholding consent for a particular procedure, treatment, or plan of care sets into motion a series of events that might have an effect contrary to what a person ultimately values and judges to be good in life. For example, a person with an intellectual and developmental disability who requires physiotherapy might not truly want to be immobilized but might refuse consent to the procedures that are necessary to recover some motor function. Health care professionals should not consider a person's expression of consent or refusal to consent without taking the time and making the effort to probe the value basis for this choice. Health care professionals ought to discern as much as possible, through appropriate means of communication and by consulting those who know the individual well, whether a given choice reflects what that person ultimately judges or would judge to be worthwhile. Many people with developmental and intellectual disabilities are unable to understand what is meant by *value* or to relate their apprehension, through feelings, of what is worthwhile in life to this word. What often is needed to discern a person's values is attentive communication with that person, as well as a history of that person's pattern of preferences and choices in health care and in other areas of life (Wong et al., 1999). Such interactions can be conducted in a manner that does not give undue weight to a health care professional's own values but raises questions that might help a person or his or her caregiver to consider what values may have been overlooked.

Uncertainty About a Person's Decision-Making Capacity

When a health care professional is unsure about the ability of an individual with an intellectual and developmental disability to make decisions and to provide consent to a proposed treatment or plan of care, a capacity assessment by another health care professional is necessary. The decision to seek such an assessment should not be based only on a health care professional's or family's disagreement with the person's consent or refusal to consent. There must be reasonable grounds to hold that the person may be having difficulty performing one or more of the skills in the previously described decision-making process.

The capacity assessment should be conducted by someone who has sufficient familiarity with the general as well as the particular strengths and weaknesses of people with intellectual and developmental disabilities. Such assessments should also involve regular caregivers who know the person well. For reasons already stated, however, it must be reiterated that health care professionals should not assume a person to be capable or incapable of making decisions and giving consent based on a single assessment in the past.

Different Types of Decision Making

Decisions can be made in various ways: through supported decision making, substitute decision making, or advance directives. These are discussed next, as are issues to consider for decision making during emergencies.

Supported Decision Making The chapter authors have argued for a notion of partial decision-making capacity and thus urge that the goal of capacity assessments should not simply be to conclude that a person is or is not capable of making decisions and of giving or refusing consent. The primary goal ought to be to identify strengths and weaknesses in particular aspects of the decision-making process in order to determine what supports are needed to enable a person with developmental disabilities to participate in making decisions about health care to the extent that he or she is able. Examples of such support include adapting the format for disclosing information relevant to the decision (Cea & Fisher, 2003), using alternative means or drawing on the help of interpreters to communicate, providing reassurance and counseling to address emotional and psychological challenges, helping a person to identify his or her values and to relate them to the medical options at hand, and involving a member of the person's family or some other caregiver whom the person trusts to give advice if asked.

Substitute Decision Making Sometimes, even with supports, a person with developmental disabilities might not be capable of participating very much or at all in the process of decision making, either in a particular situation or in general. In these cases, it is necessary to find a substitute decision maker. *Representative* or *proxy consent giver* are other terms for a substitute decision maker. This is someone who has the authority to give or to refuse consent on behalf of the person with an intellectual and developmental disability who is incapable of doing so himself or herself.

Substitute decision makers should decide based on a prudential weighing of each medical option's benefits and burdens for the person who is fully incapable of giving consent. This judgment should be informed by the person's known or presumed values in life. Care must be taken to ensure that those who are incapable of participating very much or at all in health care decision making are not undertreated and neglected. Substitute decision makers should be accountable to society for their decisions on behalf of people with intellectual and developmental disabilities.

Most laws concerning consent for health care specify which people are authorized to be substitute decision makers and in what order of priority. Usually, priority is given to the legal guardian, whether a family member or publicly appointed figure, or to someone whom the person has designated in an advance directive.

Advance Directives

An advance directive is a written document or verbal instruction made at a time when a person is capable of making decisions about health care in anticipation of some future possible medical circumstance in which the person may no longer be capable of making such decisions (Friedman, 1998). Advance directives can outline particular procedures or treatments that a person would accept or refuse in various medical situations. Because these situations are not always possible to predict, however, it is usually more prudent for the advance directive to give a general statement of values and to designate a substitute decision maker—someone who knows the person well and whose judgment and goodwill the person trusts. Health care professionals should inform people with intellectual and developmental disabilities and their family or regular caregivers about advance directives, and the importance of communicating about the care they would want to receive, as part of their planning for the future.

Emergencies

In emergency situations, the consequences of delaying decision making could be life threatening. When there are grounds to conclude that the patient is able to participate very little (if at all) in decision making, even with supports, and an authorized substitute decision maker cannot be located despite reasonable efforts to do so, it is ethically acceptable for the health care professional to proceed with treatment based on a prudential judgment of its benefits and burdens for that person. In these situations, health care professionals must be careful to act out of a concern for the individual's overall well-being.

JACK'S STORY

Many of the ethical and clinical issues discussed in this chapter are illustrated in Jack's story. Jack, age 28, had a mild-to-moderate developmental disability. He attended school, found work and had recently moved from his parents' house into a group home. Jack's transition to increased independence and responsibility in adulthood was complicated by limitations that were part of his developmental disability. Two such limitations were his tendency to become constipated, thus limiting his ability to care for himself, and his longstanding fear of medical procedures.

Although Jack was typically in excellent health, his first major encounter with the medical system occurred while he was in his mid-twenties, when he developed abdominal pain and persistent diarrhea. His family physician referred him to a nearby hospital to be assessed. The hospital's emergency physician determined that Jack's diarrhea was due to severe constipation. The physician also became aware of Jack's desire to avoid the proposed medical investigations and treatments for his constipation.

Concerned that Jack's fear of medical procedures was affecting his ability to make decisions in this instance, the emergency physician asked a psychiatrist, who had experience in this area, to assess Jack's capacity to consent. The psychiatrist thought that Jack was unable adequately to understand his medical problem or the consequences for himself of accepting or declining the proposed investigation and treatment. On these grounds, the psychiatrist concluded that Jack was not capable of withholding consent in this situation.

A family member became Jack's substitute decision maker. Based on the family member's understanding of what was in Jack's best medical interest, this person consented on Jack's behalf to the emergency physician's proposed investigations and treatment. Following these interventions, Jack's constipation improved and he was released from the hospital.

Approximately 2 years later, Jack again developed symptoms of constipation. As before, Jack's family physician referred him to the hospital. Jack again refused to consent to the investigation and treatment proposed by the emergency physician. This time, however, the emergency physician thought that Jack was expressing his values validly and did not refer Jack for an assessment of his capacity to consent. Rather, the emergency physician decided to accommodate Jack's wishes not to undergo the proposed investigations and treatments but instead admitted him to hospital to monitor his condition and oral medications.

Over the next 5 days, Jack continued to refuse medical investigations and treatments. Jack's refusal caused escalating tensions between his family and the medical staff. Jack's family wanted him to be treated and argued that Jack could not be responsible for his decision to decline the recommended medical care. They argued that when Jack was experiencing the stress of such an illness and hospitalization, he had even more difficulty than usual understanding or appreciating the possible consequences of his decision.

The medical staff agreed with Jack's family on the medical facts. That is, they agreed on what the problem was that was causing his symptoms and which medical interventions would best address it. The medical staff was hesitant, however, to override Jack's refusal to consent to their proposed investigations and treatment. They argued that because Jack was an adult and exercised autonomous decision making in other areas of his life, they should respect his wishes in the area of health care as well. To go against Jack's wishes, they maintained, would constitute an assault legally.

Jack's abdomen became increasingly distended due to his ongoing constipation. A few days into his hospital stay, Jack's condition suddenly worsened, and his primary health care professional summoned a member of the surgical staff to assess him. The surgeon removed a large amount of stool, and this appeared to improve Jack's distress. This apparent improvement was temporary, however, and 3 hours later Jack suffered a cardiorespiratory arrest and died.

Presumably, Jack had developed a bowel obstruction from being constipated. Before this was known, he was given liquid medication to help relieve his constipation. A person with a bowel obstruction should not be given anything by mouth, however, because food and fluids will accumulate in the patient's stomach, causing vomiting. Jack's aspiration of liquid into his lungs, which may have preceded his manual disimpaction of stool, resulted in respiratory distress and precipitated cardiac arrest.

Discussion of the Case

The ethical starting point for the health care professionals in this case should be respecting Jack's intrinsic dignity. This entails an obligation to provide Jack with adequate and appropriate care and to allow him to participate in making decisions about that care to the extent that he is able.

The case is an illustration of the classic dilemma of conflicting duties for health care professionals to respect a person's autonomy, on the one hand, and to avoid harming the person, on the other. In the chapter authors' view, however, there is a different way in which the case can be approached. Once it is realized that consent is the outcome of a decision-making process and that the capacity to make decisions in regard to one's care is not an all-or-none attribute, other ethical and clinical questions can be raised: What are Jack's strengths and weaknesses in decision making? Is he capable, at least partially and with the appropriate supports, of participating in decision making about his care? What are the values, if any, that Jack holds or can be presumed to hold, and can these be a guide for judging the treatment benefits and burdens for Jack?

One can reasonably judge in this case that Jack was capable of understanding information and acting in response to that information in some contexts in his life, such as at work. He also had undergone the proposed treatment before, and it might be assumed that he understood what was involved and could appreciate the implications of treatment of this kind for himself. Two separate assessments of capacity to consent, however, drew different conclusions about Jack's ability to understand the seriousness of his medical situation and the consequences for him of refusing consent to treatment. This need not be surprising, as a person's decision-making capacity can vary from time to time and from situation to situation. Furthermore, as pointed out previously, there is no universal agreement on the criteria used for assessing a person's capacity to consent and the interpretation of those criteria. The fact that Jack had intellectual and developmental disabilities should be a reason, however, for health care professionals to be attentive to possible vulnerabilities in his decision-making capacity. A strictly legal approach that focuses on understanding health information rather than on reasoning with that information in light of one's values might overlook some of these vulnerabilities.

It would have been ethically acceptable for the health care professionals in Jack's prior visit to the hospital to go along with Jack's refusal to consent, even if they disagreed with it, if Jack were fully capable of making a decision about care in this situation. However, some relevant ethical and clinical questions can be raised to suggest that such a conclusion would have been too hasty and imprudent. Even if Jack was able to understand the seriousness of his medical condition and the consequences of not receiving treatment, was he capable of *judging* the benefits and burdens, for him, of treatment or nontreatment in light of his values? Was the distress of Jack's severe pain and extreme fear of medical procedures a relevant factor to be considered? Was Jack's refusal to consent to treatment consistent with the hopes that he seemed to have for a possible recovery from his symptoms and a return to a life that he values? Had the health care professionals adequately considered possible supports for Jack's decision making within the constraints of the emergency situation? What could have been the role here for Jack's family?

It would have been ethically acceptable for the health care professionals in this case to seek a substitute decision maker for Jack if there were reasonable grounds for finding him fully incapable of making a decision of this sort. However, it may have been possible for Jack to participate to some extent in some aspects of the decision-making process—for example, communicating his values to a substitute decision maker, who then would complete the process of decision making on his behalf. This sort of communication is better done prior to emergency situations in an advance directive. The reality that Jack had recurrent problems with constipation suggests that it would have been prudent for him to have an advance directive to the extent that he was capable of making decisions about care.

The substitute decision maker, in turn, ought to have decided based on Jack's best interests, as informed by his known or presumed values. The goal of health care is to heal and not to harm. Thus, substitute decision makers cannot ethically consent to the withholding or withdrawing of treatment if the intention is to end the life of the person with an intellectual and developmental disability. Such people are sometimes at risk of being undertreated by not being provided simple, nonburdensome, medical interventions such as antibiotics for a pneumonia.

Conversely, there are limits to the ethical duty to preserve the life of a person whose progressive disease cannot be reversed. This is because all human beings are mortal, and the medical means to address diseases and their effects are finite. It should be clear, however, that disability, although possibly arising from a disease process, is not itself a disease. Substitute decision makers can ethically consent to withholding or withdrawing treatment on behalf of a person with an intellectual and developmental disability who is incapable of making this decision, when, in their prudential judgment, the treatment gives little hope of benefit or is excessively burdensome to the person. In this case, however, the likelihood that the treatment could have addressed the cause of Jack's constipation, relieved his pain, and enabled him to recover to return to a life that he valued suggests that the treatment was beneficial for Jack. If Jack had undergone the treatment before without evident harm to him, it would have been reasonable to suppose that the treatment might not be overly burdensome to Jack. Jack might have needed the assistance of his family and perhaps forms of support such as reassurance, encouragement, and counsel to address his fears so that he could look beyond the avoidance of immediate dissatisfaction to the values that he held deeply.

SUMMARY

As noted, weighing a medical option's benefits and burdens for a particular patient is an essential component of the decision-making process in health care. Doing this is a matter not only of understanding medical information but also of apprehending values and relating them to one's personal circumstances. Many people with developmental disabilities can apprehend and hold values, although they might require assistance to express and relate these values to a decision at hand. When a person with developmental disabilities does not have the capacity to weigh the benefits and burdens of various medical options for him- or herself, even with appropriate supports, a substitute decision maker must do this in the person's stead, informed by that person's known or presumed values.

A few points should be made clear concerning the judgment of benefits and burdens of medical options in such situations. Because people with developmental disabilities have the same moral status and intrinsic dignity as all other human beings, their lives ought not to be valued less than other human lives on account of their disabilities. According this view, a substitute decision maker cannot ethically refuse consent to treatment on the grounds that it would be "merciful" to end the life of a person with disabilities. This would be a decision for euthanasia, with the intention of ending "suffering" by hastening death through a culpable omission. In the chapter authors' view, euthanasia contravenes ethically the goal of medicine, which is to do good and avoid harm by promoting health, preventing disease, and caring for people when they are sick.

Conversely, there is a limit to the ethical duty to sustain any human being's life. This is because all human beings are mortal, and the medical means that are available to address the challenges of illness and disability have limits. A substitute decision maker may ethically authorize the withholding or withdrawing of a treatment that prolongs the life of a person with developmental disabilities when that treatment would provide no hope of benefit for the patient or is excessively burdensome for the patient. *Benefit,* however, should not be understood in relation to completely eliminating a person's disability, for otherwise no treatment could be judged beneficial for a person with disabilities. Likewise *burden* ought to refer to the treatment and its effects on a patient's life and not to the burden of being a person with developmental disabilities or caring for one. A substitute decision maker who gives consent to withhold or withdraw a treatment that is excessively burdensome for a person with disabilities, when the natural course of this person's disease cannot be reversed, would not be intending to kill him or her. Such a decision can be distinguished ethically from choosing involuntary passive euthanasia, and it is compatible with recognizing the moral value and intrinsic dignity of people with developmental disabilities (The Arc & American Association on Mental Retardation, 2002).

FOR FURTHER THOUGHT AND DISCUSSION

1. How is an ethical approach to obtaining informed consent similar and different from a legal approach?
2. In your opinion, is the ability of an individual to understand medical information, including the health benefits and risks of a treatment, sufficient evidence of his or her capacity to give or to refuse consent? Ought the individual to show also that he or she can judge the broader personal implications of such a decision?
3. Is capacity to consent only present or absent in an individual? Can an individual have a *partial* capacity to consent such that he or she requires the support of a family member or other regular caregiver for some aspects of the decision-making process?
4. Should the same ethical standard of respecting an individual's informed consent apply to a diagnostic procedure as to a medical treatment? What about a low-risk intervention to which most people would consent?
5. Should a substitute decision maker go along with the expressed wish of a person who is incapable wholly of giving informed consent, or should the substitute decision maker try to judge what would be in the overall best interest of that person? Is it ethical for a substitute decision maker to refuse treatment on behalf of a person who is incapable fully of giving informed consent for the reason that prolonging life with an intellectual and developmental disability is too burdensome?

REFERENCES

American Association on Mental Retardation. (2000). Expert consensus guideline series: Treatment of psychiatric and behavioral problems in mental retardation. Guideline 2: Informed consent. *American Journal on Mental Retardation, 105,* 169.

The Arc & American Association on Mental Retardation. (2002). *Position statement: Health care.* Retrieved October 21, 2005, from http://thearc.org/posits/healthcarepos.doc

Cea, C.D., & Fisher, C.B. (2003). Health care decision-making by adults with mental retardation. *Mental Retardation, 41,* 78–87.

Dinerstein, R.D., Herr, S.S., & O'Sullivan, J.L. (1999). *A guide to consent.* Washington, DC: American Association on Mental Retardation.

Dye, L., Hendy, S., Hare, D.J., et al. (2004). Capacity to consent to participate in research: A recontextualization. *British Journal of Learning Disabilities, 32,* 144–150.

Evans, D.R. (1997). *The law, standards of practice, and ethics in the practice of psychology.* Toronto: Edmond Montgomery Publications.

Friedman, R.I. (1998). Use of advance directives: Facilitating health care decisions by adults with mental retardation and their families. *Mental Retardation, 36,* 444–456.

Grisso, T. (1986). *Evaluating competencies: Forensic assessments and instruments.* New York: Kluwer Academic/Plenum Publishers.

Gunn, M.J., Wong, J.G., Clare, I.C., et al. (2000). Medical research and incompetent adults. *Journal of Mental Health Law, 2,* 60–72.

Morris, C.D., Niederbuhl, J.M., & Mahr, J.M. (1993). Determining the capability of individuals with mental retardation to give informed consent. *American Journal on Mental Retardation, 98,* 263–272.

Murphy, G.H., & O'Callaghan, A. (2004). Capacity of adults with intellectual disabilities to consent to sexual relationships. *Psychological Medicine, 34,* 1347–1357.

Robertson, J., Emerson, E., Hatton, C., et al. (2001). Environmental opportunities and supports for exercising self-determination in community-based residential settings. *Research in Developmental Disabilities, 22,* 487–502.

Singer, P. (1993) *Practical ethics.* New York: Cambridge University Press.

Struhkamp, R.M. (2005). Patient autonomy: A view from the kitchen. *Medicine, Health Care and Philosophy, 8,* 105–114.

Sullivan, W.F. (2005) *Eye of the heart: Knowing the human good in the euthanasia debate.* Toronto: University of Toronto Press.

Sulmasy, D. (1997). Futility and the varieties of medical judgment. *Theoretical Medicine, 18,* 63–78.

Sulmasy, D. (2002). Death, dignity, and the theory of value. *Ethical Perspectives, 9,* 103–18.

Suto, W.M., Clare, I.C., Holland, A.J., et al. (2005). Capacity to make financial decisions among people with mild intellectual disabilities. *Journal of Intellectual Disability Research, 49,* 199–209.

Wong, J.G., Clare, I.H., Gunn, M.J., et al. (1999). Capacity to make health care decisions: Its importance in clinical practice. *Psychological Medicine, 29,* 437–446.

41

Physical Health

Tom Cheetham, John S. Lovering,
Joseph Telch, Frances Telch, and Maire Percy

WHAT YOU WILL LEARN ABOUT IN THIS CHAPTER

- Key considerations in primary care
- Barriers to high-quality care
- Approaches for overcoming barriers
- Tips for successful health care visits
- Special problems and easily overlooked issues
- Prevention

This chapter focuses on primary care, the point of first contact with the health care system. The information emphasizes care of adults with intellectual and developmental disabilities. Historically, pediatric services have included children with such disabilities within their field, but health care for adults has been less well defined. Many of the issues presented here apply equally to care by primary health care providers as to care by specialists. These issues also cut across most settings in which care is delivered, including community clinics, physicians' offices, homes, hospitals, and institutional settings. In the past, physicians and nurses were considered the predominant health care providers. In the early 21st century, it is recognized that individuals from many disciplines can be involved in providing care. There is a great need for establishing intellectual and developmental programs not only for physicians and nurses but also for other professionals in the field.

Historically, children with intellectual and developmental disabilities were seen by pediatricians and adults with intellectual and developmental disabilities were seen by psychiatrists. In North America, such specialists complete at least 4 years of residency following medical school. As noted, primary care physicians have increasingly taken on this role. Such specialists usually complete 2 or 3 years of residency in family medicine following undergraduate medical education. There currently are great opportunities for nurse practitioners to take on an expanded role in providing primary care.

Owing to the complexity of medical problems in some people with intellectual and developmental disabilities and difficulties providing services in particular geographical areas, many other professions may need to collaborate in care (e.g., see Iacono et al., 2004; Sices et al., 2004). Other professions that are important for comprehensive health care include, among others, audiologists, clinical geneticists and genetic counselors, dentists, dietitians, kinesiologists and recreationists, nurses, occupational therapists, optometrists, pharmacists, physiotherapists, psychiatrists, psychologists, speech-language pathologists, and social workers.

KEY CONSIDERATIONS IN PRIMARY CARE

Importance of the Support Person

Before considering what is known about medical care for people with intellectual and developmental disabilities, there is one "professional" who has been neglected in most studies, someone with perhaps the most crucial role in ensuring high quality health care for individuals with disabilities. That person is the family member or front-line staff member, hereafter called the support person. Not professional in the literal sense, support people are knowledgeable, caring, and involved, and are as important as any professional trained in a health profession. They have an advantage no other caregiver does; it is the support person who is with the person with disabilities day in and day out and knows that individual best. Extremely important functions of the support person include identifying a health issue that requires attention, assisting with the medical encounter, providing information for diagnosis, and monitoring subsequent treatment. Sometimes a significant health problem may be evident only from subtle changes in the person; the support person who knows the person well is best positioned to recognize such changes. In addition, the support person can advocate for prevention strategies to help maintain health. One front-line staff person stated it best when

The authors thank Marika Korossy of Surrey Place Centre, who contributed information for this chapter's resources (in Appendix B at the end of the book), and Clive Friedman, University of Western Ontario, for all of his assistance with the Oral Health section.

she described the frustration of having her observations ignored when trying to have a client's medical problem addressed by a health care provider: "We are in the business of observation."

After more than 25 years of experience working in a medical setting with people who have intellectual and developmental disabilities, the chapter authors continue to be surprised at how apparently trivial and nonspecific observations can herald significant medical problems. In many instances, a support person's concern that something was wrong or unusual led to the discovery of an important medical problem that required treatment, when taken seriously and investigated. High-quality medical care for people with disabilities is a collaborative effort for people with disabilities, their support people, and their health care providers.

Understanding Health Needs

A number of studies have explored primary care for people with intellectual and developmental disabilities (e.g., Beange, McElduff, & Baker, 1995; Howells, 1986; Rogers et al., 1992; van Schrojenstein Lantman-de Valk et al., 1997; van Schrojenstein Lantman-De Valk et al., 2000; Webb & Rogers, 1999; Wilson & Haire, 1990). On the whole, these studies have shown that a great many medical problems go undetected and untreated within this population. They suggest that considerably more attention needs to be paid to the health needs of people with intellectual and developmental disabilities.

Several conclusions can be drawn from this body of research about the unmet health needs of people with disabilities. These health issues are often presented as undesirable behaviors because of difficulty with verbally communicating either psychic (psychological) or physical discomfort (Lennox, Diggens, & Ugoni, 1997; Poindexter, 1995; Ziviani et al., 2004). Seven statements reflect the literature on medical care:

1. People with intellectual and developmental disabilities often do not complain; many common problems will be neither reported by the person with a disability nor suspected by his or her support people.
2. Even serious medical problems are often expressed atypically by irritability, inactivity, disturbance in appetite or sleep, deterioration in speech or activities of daily living, or self-injurious behavior.
3. Basic risk factors are often ignored (e.g., Down syndrome is a risk factor for thyroid disease, cardiac disorders, and celiac disease).
4. Medical issues of people with disabilities are under-investigated; more tests are required.
5. Common problems are not always adequately managed (e.g., hearing, vision, or motor problems).
6. Routine screening measures are performed less often than needed (e.g., blood pressure measurements, mammograms, Pap smears, prostate examinations).
7. Careful systematic evaluation will uncover significant medical problems, even in people presenting psychiatric or behavior challenges.

In addition to these basic considerations, it is essential to consider factors that promote access to high-quality care: barriers to such care; approaches for overcoming such barriers; and the role of medical records, the so-called medical database that forms the cornerstone for diagnosis and treatment. Following this information, tips are presented for helping support people to interact effectively with health care providers.

BARRIERS TO HIGH-QUALITY CARE

Several authors have addressed barriers to accessing primary health care (Chambers et al., 1998; Curtis, Curtis, & Vicari, 2004; Gitta & Deagle, 1992a, 1992b; Goodenough & Hole-Goodenough, 1997; Lennox, Diggens, & Ugoni, 1997; Martin & Martin, 2000; Minihan, Dean, & Lyons, 1993; Nehring & Faux, 2004; Phillips, Morrison, & Davis, 2004; Roeher Institute, 1994; Sulkes, 1989; Trumble, 1993; Tyler, & Bourguet, 1997; U.S. Department of Health and Human Services, 2002; Walsh et al. 2000). Barriers include those associated with health care providers, those faced by patients and their caregivers, those connected to systems, and those related the environment.

Health care providers may have the following:

- Lack of knowledge, training, and experience in the field of intellectual and developmental disabilities
- Difficulty communicating with patients and caregivers
- Difficulty taking patient histories
- Difficulty examining patients
- Insufficient time for the encounter
- Difficulty with follow-up due to patient nonadherence
- Difficulty with consent for examination, investigations or treatment
- Difficulties arising from discontinuity of care (e.g., different support people provide information and attend visits)

As a result of the preceding barriers, medical diagnoses and treatments may be made on an inadequate information database.

Patients and caregivers can present barriers as well. They may have the following:

- Inadequate knowledge of the services and resources available
- Difficulty gaining access to the health care system
- Difficulty explaining problems to doctors
- Difficulty due to aversive past health care experiences
- An inability to cooperate with what is required

- Altered pain behavior
- Difficulties arising from discontinuity of care (e.g., different doctors are seen during different visits)

Barriers with systems may affect individuals and groups of individuals. These environmental problems include the following:

- Long waiting lists to obtain medical services
- Lack of available services
- Fragmentation and lack of coordination of services
- Poor remuneration for physicians
- Failure of the health care system to recognize the importance of preventive health care and health promotion
- Failure of the health care system to recognize the importance of research with people with intellectual and developmental disabilities

APPROACHES FOR OVERCOMING BARRIERS

Various approaches can be taken to overcome barriers. These include avoidance of diagnostic overshadowing, improvement of communication with health care providers, development of creative approaches for cooperating with health care providers, and establishment of informative medical records.

Avoidance of Diagnostic Overshadowing

If a health care provider is unfamiliar with disability-related care, the treatment provided may focus on the disability rather than on the underlying health problem (Roeher Institute, 1994). In this regard, many studies have cited the lack of physician preparation during medical school or residency (e.g., Curtis et al., 2004; Lennox et al., 1997). There is a tendency for both primary care physicians and psychiatrists to assume that any behavior problem is the result of the person's intellectual or developmental disability. This should not be assumed to be the case. A person with an intellectual or developmental disability may exhibit not only behaviors characteristic of the disability but also behaviors that are the result of mental health issues or a reflection of underlying physical health issues. A person who has an intellectual or developmental disability plus a diagnosed mental illness is said to have a *dual diagnosis.* The term *diagnostic overshadowing* is usually used to refer to overlooking a mental health issue and attributing behavior solely to the disability (Reiss, 1994), but it also could refer to overlapping physical health problems and attributing behavior problems to mental illness or to the disability.

Improvement of Communication with Health Care Providers

Communication barrier concerns may affect the ability to obtain valuable health information. In general medical settings, patients without intellectual and developmental disabilities typically express 1.2 to 3.9 major health complaints but talk on average only 18 seconds before the doctor interrupts (Buckman, 1992). Health care communication problems can be addressed by having the support person take on an educational role, such as providing information about the person's syndrome and associated medical issues. By presenting the required data in a succinct, efficient manner, communication with health care providers can be improved.

Development of Creative Approaches for Cooperating with Health Care Providers

Further barriers arise when a person with a disability is unwilling or unable to cooperate during an examination. There may be similar problems following through with the treatment plan (Lennox et al., 1997). (See Chapter 40 for ethical issues related to consent for treatment.) With respect to the environment, the setting may be physically inaccessible to people who use wheelchairs or have other mobility problems, it may be difficult to get onto an examination table, and some people may become overstimulated in a crowded or noisy office setting. Support people can raise these issues with health care providers and suggest solutions. For example, trial visits that are not threatening to the person may help to desensitize examinations. Home visits may be appropriate for some individuals. Finding solutions may require creative approaches.

Establishment of Informative Medical Records (the Medical Database)

Establishment of complete medical records (i.e., the medical database) is essential for the provision of quality health care to anyone. Traditionally, the medical database was written on paper and kept in one section of a person's file, with new information being added as new medical issues arise. Increasingly, however, the medical database is created in electronic form. A medical database is often missing in the file of an individual being supported by a social services agency. This is unfortunate, because the medical database is the foundation on which diagnoses are based. Treatment follows from the appropriate diagnosis, so if information is missing or inaccurate, then appropriate treatment is less likely. The medical database is such an important component of thorough health care provision that it is explained at length in the remainder of this section.

There are several factors that can result in a missing or incomplete medical database: lack of awareness that medical history is extremely important for treatment (Cutler, 1985; Sackett, 2000); inexperienced interviewers; and communication difficulties on the part of the interviewer, the patient, or those who know the patient well. For example, a person who reports, "Everything hurts," is as difficult to assess as the person who reports, "Nothing hurts." When the patient has difficulty explaining, the history must be provided by his or her support person. Thus, the support person is crucial in the interview, and the more efficiently he or she can present the required information, the more effective the visit will be. Interviews that are satisfying to all parties involved will be motivational for the continued provision of high-quality health care. In an interview, there should be time not only for history taking but also for a discussion of issues related to the diagnosis, such as treatment options. Some agencies have found that the core database can be effectively completed by a skilled interviewer who is not necessarily a health care worker, thus saving time for nurses and doctors.

This section focuses on the database for a general medical problem. Others have outlined an approach for mental health consultations (Silka & Hurley, 1998; Sovner & Hurley, 1993). The general medical database consists of the history, examination, and investigation. History is the patient's description of the problem, previous problems, and answers to specific questions that the health care provider uses to ensure that no important information has been omitted. The history is followed by a physical examination. Then appropriate investigations such as X rays, blood tests, or other tests take place, and finally a diagnosis is reached. Only when a diagnosis has been made can a treatment plan be established.

History There are a number of aspects to the medical history:

- *Chief complaint:* In a few words, the complaint can be determined by asking, "Why are you here?" This is sometimes called the *presenting problem.*
- *History of present illness:* This is a detailed description of the problem, including features such as when it began; whether any factors make it better or worse; and, if there is discomfort, where it is located, whether it radiates to somewhere else, and what brings this on. It is important to remember that health care providers use the word *pain* to refer to everything from mild discomfort to more severe discomfort. Pain is a key element in many conditions; thus, if there is concern about how the individual feels or expresses pain, this is a very important part of the history to provide. The caregiver may have observed the person's behavior in a situation that likely would have caused pain, such as having a finger caught in a door or getting a burn or a laceration. The caregivers should share the person's reactions in such situation with the health care provider.
- *Past history:* This is sometimes divided into illnesses and times in hospital, which are separated from surgical past history. Yet, the two may be combined and presented as a time line, with medical and surgical past history in chronological order. Past history could involve immunizations, developmental history, and any previous psychiatric or behavioral hospitalizations or treatment.
- *Allergies:* Whenever possible, a true allergic reaction should be distinguished from a side effect. All drugs have the potential to cause side effects, such as vomiting or diarrhea from an antibiotic. Drug allergies are more likely to result in a rash, hives, or swelling.
- *Medications:* This part of the database should start with all current medications being taken, including the strength and frequency of doses. Sometimes it is helpful to know if a person was prescribed a particular drug that did not seem to work. For example, if an antidepressant was used for one week and discontinued, this situation has to be understood in the context of the fact that it may take 4–6 weeks for an antidepressant to become effective. Similarly, if a drug was stopped due to side effects, further details may help a health care professional to decide if the side effects would likely have gone away after the person's body had time to adapt to the medication. It is also necessary to mention over-the-counter medications, vitamins, and herbal preparations being taken in addition to prescription drugs. For example, some herbal products may have side effects and can interfere with prescription drugs.
- *Family history:* Some conditions have an inherited component. Thus, it can be helpful for health care professionals to know that certain disorders have occurred within the family. It is useful to know which disorder was present in the family, as well as who was affected and at what age.
- *Social history/patient profile:* Historically, this component has included the person's occupation, marital status, family status (e.g., if they have children), and relevant risk factors (e.g., smoking, alcohol use, drug use). Since the late 1990s, with the emphasis shifting to patient-centered medicine, there is a need to understand the whole person and the context within which he or she lives (Stewart et al., 1995). For people with intellectual and developmental disabilities, the social history/patient profile is more useful if it describes a day in the person's life, with brief notations about the following: living arrangements, participation in day programs and leisure activities, and community involvement. A brief indication of communication skills (both receptive and expressive abilities) is very helpful as

well. Personal care skills (e.g., eating, toileting, dressing, grooming) should be included, as well as pertinent information about the person's sexual history and any history of physical, emotional, or sexual abuse. Also, did the person live at home or in an institutional setting in the past?

- *Review of systems:* The review of systems is sometimes called *functional inquiry* and consists of a few questions about each body system that might not initially seem related to the presenting problem or chief complaint, but can suggest a possible diagnosis. For example, in the case of a 60-year-old man whose chief complaint is a cough for 3 months, a functional inquiry revealed a 20-pound weight loss in that time without dieting. In addition, the man has a long history of smoking. As a result, the man may have to be considered for lung cancer, as well as other possible conditions.

It has been pointed out that the usual functional inquiry is only helpful when obtained from a caregiver who knows the patient well (Rideau Regional Centre, 1995), because behavior or changes in behavior may be relevant to the medical condition and best recognized by the support person. Although it may be efficient to have some information briefly recorded under the headings presented, a health care professional will likely have further questions. Therefore, someone who knows the person and the details concerning the problem under review must accompany him or her to all health care appointments.

For people with intellectual and developmental disabilities, particularly for those who are nonverbal, there is a greater reliance on what are called *vegetative signs* (Levesque, 1995). These signs assume relatively great importance because they are more observable and objective than a patient's subjective description, which may not even be possible to obtain. It may be helpful to have these listed, noting any abnormality in the following areas prior to the visit:

- Energy level: Increased? Decreased? Any pattern with time of day? Week? Month?
- Appetite: Increased? Decreased? Specific foods avoided?
- Weight changes
- Sleep pattern: Difficulty falling asleep? Awakening during the night? Awakening too early in the morning? Increased need for sleep?
- Bowel function: Constipation? Diarrhea? Incontinence (day, night)?
- Bladder function: Urinary frequency? Difficulty passing urine? Incontinence (day, night)?
- Sexual function
- Menstrual changes
- Seizures

Other items that might be important for some people with disabilities include physical activity, rituals, hygiene, response to stimulation, relationships, and leisure activities (Ryan, 1996).

Physical Examination It is important to conduct a physical examination. Experienced physicians have pointed to the frequent lack of usual physical findings on examination (Rideau Regional Centre, 1995). For example, the person with spastic quadriplegia may often have a rigid abdomen or rigid neck, which could be misinterpreted as signs of serious abdominal or central nervous system pathology. People with intellectual and developmental disabilities may have acute intestinal obstruction, but few physical signs (Jancar, & Speller, 1994). In illnesses or injuries where one would normally have significant pain, the person may exhibit minimal evidence of pain. Chest examinations can be challenging when a person fails to take deep breaths or refuses to breathe. Also hypothermia, rather than fever, may occur in acute infections. Examinations of the breasts, cervix and prostate should be conducted as in the general population.

Investigations Additional laboratory tests and X rays are often required due to a lack of information from the history and physical examination. However, these investigations can be equally challenging. More than one attempt may be necessary before the test is completed; sometimes a period of desensitization to the procedure may be helpful. Creative solutions can work. For example, a person may slowly receive a feeding of his or her favorite pudding in order to remain still for an X ray. At times, sedation can assist; only rarely, after weighing all the risks and benefits, and obtaining appropriate informed consent, would a general anesthetic be necessary. If investigations are avoided because of the difficulty in performing them, serious conditions may be missed. (See Chapter 40 for more information.)

Diagnosis and Treatment Plan A list of possible diagnoses is developed primarily by taking data from history, in addition to findings from the physical examination and the result of investigations. This is called the *differential diagnosis.* The most likely diagnosis is selected from the list and is sometimes called the *working diagnosis.* The clinician brings his or her past experience to bear in the diagnostic process. Treatment often follows directly from the diagnosis. For example, the need for a specific antibiotic to treat a (working) diagnosis of pneumonia will be influenced by the experience of knowing what worked in the past for the individual, the knowledge of current infection trends in the particular geographic area, and the effect of time of year (e.g., influenza is more common during cold months of the year). Guessing which antibiotic might work is no substitute for determining the most effective antibiotic on the basis of laboratory testing when possible.

TIPS FOR SUCCESSFUL HEALTH CARE VISITS

Both caregivers and health care professionals can take actions that make health care visits more successful. These are discussed next.

Tips for Caregivers

There are a number of tips for helping caregivers ensure successful health care visits (e.g., Heaton, 1995). First, a caregiver must always be clear and specific about the reason for the visit. "She needs a check up" does not help to schedule appropriate time. Instead, the caregiver should state, for example, "She has had four episodes where she was just sitting and became sweaty and pale, lasting a half an hour each, and these are happening closer together." Second, the caregiver should identify the patient's special needs. If the person has difficulty waiting or becomes agitated in a crowded room, it may be possible to book the first morning or first afternoon appointment or a house call. Third, the caregiver should come to the visit with information about the medical problems and previous diagnoses. This information needs to include basic facts about the chief complaint. Fourth, appointments are often not on time because doctors have to fit urgent patients into an already busy schedule, may face emergencies or obstetrical deliveries that require their absence from the office, and may take longer than expected to complete appointments for which insufficient information was provided by the patient and/or caregiver. Thus, the caregiver should consider ways to occupy the individual's time while waiting. Options include bringing one of the individual's friends (for company) or favorite objects such as books or games (to occupy his or her time).

Tips for Health Care Professionals

There are several important principles of mental health care for people with intellectual and developmental disabilities that are equally applicable for general medical care (Ryan, 1996):

- When considering a medical problem, it is important to account for a person's particular disability and any changes in his or her usual behavior.
- Common conditions may present themselves in unusual ways (e.g., rubbing the face when a tooth is infected).
- Conditions that are present in the general population may occur more frequently in people with intellectual or developmental disabilities (e.g., dementia of the Alzheimer type in older people with Down syndrome).
- A large number of investigations may be required.
- High pain tolerance may be a clue that the individual has had considerable experience with pain.
- People capable of communication may fear expressing opinions because of how they were treated in the past when they expressed themselves.
- It is a good idea to watch the body part that a person touches or rubs or avoids touching.
- The workup is complete when the person is getting well or is as comfortable as possible.

SPECIAL PROBLEMS AND EASILY OVERLOOKED ISSUES

Special problems and conditions are often easily overlooked by practitioners who have not had significant experience caring for people with intellectual and developmental disabilities. For example, having a patient die of constipation because of the complications that may follow it is beyond the experience of most primary care physicians, but this has occurred to a number of those providing care to people with intellectual and developmental disabilities. Similarly, working with a person who engages in aggression, property destruction, or self-injurious behavior because there is no other way to express a toothache, ear infection, or even the loss of a significant person in his or her life is outside most health care providers' experience. In this section, 11 topics are highlighted as areas with special problems: gastrointestinal system, respiratory system, musculoskeletal system, genitourinary system, central nervous system, head and neck, skin, sudden death, visual and hearing problems, oral health, and nutrition.

Gastrointestinal System

The gastrointestinal system extends from mouth to anus; this encompasses an area where a variety of very significant medical problems occur in people with intellectual or developmental disabilities. Many of these may be unsuspected. These include problems with the following:

- Teeth and gums
- Swallowing
- Chewing and dealing with food
- Esophagus
- Stomach, such as *Helicobacter pylori* infection and gastroesophageal reflux disease (GERD) (Approximately 20% of the U.S. population experiences GERD symptoms once per week [Fass, 2003]; by comparison, a study of 186 people with intellectual

and developmental disabilities found a high prevalence of GERD and complications of this condition but with less specific symptoms [Böhmer et al., 1999], and the authors concluded that nearly 50% of this population had GERD)

- Intestines, such as celiac disease, constipation, diarrhea, hemorrhoids, perianal irritation, and parasites
- Hydration
- Nutrition

It is important to note that treatment to neutralize stomach acid can result in failure of absorption of vitamin B_{12}; in turn, vitamin B_{12} deficiency can appear as dementia. In early stages of B_{12} deficiency, cognitive effects are reversible.

Respiratory System

Respiratory problems are extremely common and account for the majority of deaths among people with intellectual and developmental disabilities (Cole et al., 1994; Durvasula, Beange, & Baker, 2002). Because of a high prevalence of reflux (the backward flow of stomach contents and acid into the esophagus) and aspiration (inhalation of swallowed material into the lungs), there is a corresponding risk of aspiration pneumonia. Asthma also occurs frequently.

Musculoskeletal System

Fractures are common in people with intellectual and developmental disabilities. There are several risk factors for fractures, including lack of weight-bearing exercise, poor calcium intake, low vitamin D intake or low exposure to sunlight, smoking, drugs such as anticonvulsants, and menopause. Interest in the consequences of menopause and other health issues of women with intellectual and developmental disabilities is increasing (Schupf, 1998; Walsh, & LeRoy, 2004). Lohiya, Tan-Figueroa, and Iannucci (2004) called attention to unrecognized osteoporosis in this population. Fractures also result from falls that result from problems with balance (ataxia), challenging behavior exhibited from peers, and other trauma (Glick et al., 2005).

Neuromuscular problems such as spasticity and contractures occur frequently in people with cerebral palsy or severe levels of disability. In addition to physical therapy and occupational therapy, newer treatments for spasticity such as injection with botulinum toxin (Botox) or the delivery of baclofen in innovative ways (e.g., intrathecal injection through a small tube next to the spinal cord) need to be evaluated. There can be a role for surgery with percutaneous tendon release. Mobility disorders increase the risk of skin breakdown, aspiration, and constipation.

Genitourinary System

Severe urinary retention is a serious problem often associated with a lack of symptoms. Hernia may be present but found only upon conducting a thorough examination. Urinary incontinence may have a number of causes, including urinary retention with overflow, a situation analogous to the overflow diarrhea in someone with constipation. There seems to be an increased incidence of neurogenic bladder (dysfunction of the bladder due to a lesion of the central or peripheral nervous system) in people with disabilities, including people in whom this would not be suspected because of their associated medical conditions, such as spina bifida. Other genitourinary problems include enlarged prostate and prostate cancer in men and dysmenorrhea (painful menstrual periods) and premenstrual syndrome in women. The latter two problems may be difficult to diagnose until a careful record is kept of the woman's cycle and associated symptoms. A Pap test to detect cytological abnormalities in the uterine cervix should be a part of physical examinations, as it is for women without intellectual and developmental disabilities.

An area often neglected in the field of intellectual and developmental disability is that of sexual activity, pregnancy, and sexually transmitted infections (STIs), including syphilis, gonorrhea, chlamydia, genital warts caused by papillomavirus infection, and HIV/AIDS (human immunodeficiency virus/acquired immunodeficiency syndrome). It is often presumed that people with intellectual disabilities who live in institutions, group homes, or other types of community settings do not engage in sex, but sexual needs are part of human nature. Pregnancy and infection with STIs, including HIV, can occur as the result of voluntary sexual activity or as the result of sexual exploitation or abuse. One U.S. study identified 45 adults with intellectual disability and advanced AIDS in 44 states (Marchetti et al., 1990), and it is estimated that hundreds of other such cases already exist (Kowalski, 2002). See Display 41.1 for more information on this topic.

Central Nervous System

It is not surprising that in a population with an underlying neurological condition that results in intellectual and developmental disability, other neurological problems are also significant. Two are included here: neuroleptic malignant syndrome and epilepsy.

Neuroleptic Malignant Syndrome Neuroleptic malignant syndrome is a severe and sometimes fatal complication of neuroleptic drug use (Boyd, 1993; Fidler & Hodgetts, 1992). Included here because of the importance of early recognition, it is a fairly rare con-

Display 41.1

Human immunodeficiency virus/acquired immunodeficiency syndrome (HIV/AIDS)

People with intellectual and developmental disabilities may become infected with HIV just as people in the general population. There are three main ways for a person to become infected with HIV:

1. Having unprotected sexual intercourse with an HIV-positive person (the virus may be present in semen, vaginal secretions, or in blood released during sexual activity)
2. Engaging in other activities that transmit HIV from an HIV-positive person, such as sharing needles and syringes to inject drugs, tattooing, ear piercing done in an unsanitary setting, biting and scratching, or sharing personal care items such as razors or scissors that may have blood on them and that could nick the skin
3. Being a baby of an HIV-infected mother; babies whose mothers have HIV may be born with the infection or acquire it during birth or during breast feeding

Materials designed by The Arc of the United States and other organizations are used to teach safer sex and to reinforce appropriate behaviors to people with intellectual and developmental disabilities (Kowalski, 2002). People need to learn about their sexual rights and responsibilities. Sometimes it requires a lot of patience and encouragement for people to learn about using contraception, making safer choices, and changing their habits (Best, 1999).

The only fully "safe" sex is no sex. Safer sex lowers the risk of getting infected with HIV or other sexually transmitted diseases. Safer sex also reduces the risk of unplanned pregnancy. Safer sex involves limiting the number of one's sexual partners, minimizing the exchange of body fluids, and using latex or polyurethane condoms with water-based lubricants that do not break the condom.

Blood tests are available to measure the presence of HIV antibodies. These tests are highly reliable and accurate in people who are producing antibodies to HIV. People who have early HIV infection may not test positive for the virus, so a negative test does not always mean that a person is not infected. HIV antibody testing should not be done without counseling by a trained professional.

All pregnant women should consider getting HIV antibody tests because transmission from an infected mother to her unborn child can be substantially reduced by the proper use of the drug AZT during pregnancy.

See also Chapters 16 and 36.

dition; prevalence estimates range from less than 1% to slightly more than 2% in all people taking neuroleptic medications. Features include unexplained elevated temperature (hyperthermia), severe extrapyramidal side effects (muscle rigidity) and autonomic dysfunction such as hypertension (elevated blood pressure), tachycardia (increased pulse rate), tachypnea (increased respiratory rate), prominent diaphoresis (profuse sweating), and incontinence. There may be clouded consciousness. Because neuroleptic malignant syndrome can mimic a flu-like illness, flu-like symptoms should be considered seriously. A blood test, creatine phosphokinase (CK or CPK), is typically markedly elevated in neuroleptic malignant syndrome.

Epilepsy Epilepsy is sometimes difficult to diagnose in people with intellectual and developmental disabilities, and misdiagnoses can occur (Ahmed et al., 1997; Levesque, 1995). For individuals who present with repeated behavioral disturbances, epilepsy should be considered as a possible diagnosis. Generally, the likelihood of epilepsy increases with the severity of the developmental disability and has been reported to occur in 30%–40% of adults (McDermott et al., 2005).

Although phenytoin is frequently given to ameliorate seizures, this should not be used in people with intellectual and developmental disabilities (Iivanainen, 1998), or given for late-onset seizures in people with Down syndrome, as it causes serious adverse side effects (Tsiouris et al., 2002). Barbiturates similarly should not be prescribed due to their side effects (Alvarez, 1998; Poindexter, 2000).

Head and Neck

Although neither an organ nor a body system, the head and neck area is an anatomic region that is susceptible to a number of serious health issues. Many studies have addressed unsuspected vision and hearing problems. Special techniques may be required in order to perform adequate testing, particularly for individuals with more severe disability. Ear infections and wax buildup are relatively common and must be considered. Dental problems must not be overlooked (see Oral Health section for additional information).

Skin

Skin disorders are seen frequently in people with intellectual disabilities. Fungal infections of the feet and groin are common. Also, fungal infections are often present in fingernails and toenails. Particularly in larger settings, scabies can occur and may be difficult to diagnose. Pruritis ani is uncomfortable itching or irritation of the perianal area. It can be related to poor hygiene; the most lasting treatment is training in better perianal cleaning. Herpetiform dermatitis may co-exist with celiac disease, which tends to be unusually common in people with Down syndrome.

Sudden Death

Like head and neck, this topic does not fit as a body system, but it is important to consider because a number of people with intellectual and developmental disabilities have one of the risk factors identified to date as being associated with sudden death. These include epilepsy (Forsgren et al., 1996; McKee, & Bodfish, 2000; Morgan, Baxter, & Kerr, 2003); tube feeding (Heymsfield, Casper, & Funfar, 1987); and a rare condition called *septo-optic dysplasia,* in which there is visual impairment and abnormal development of the optic nerve (Brodsky et al., 1997).

Among people without disabilities, cardiovascular disorders are common, but these are less common in people with intellectual and developmental disabilities. There are some exceptions, such as the congenital heart problems that tend to accompany Down syndrome. However, one cardiac condition that may be a risk for sudden death is torsade de pointes ("twisting of the points," an electrical conduction abnormality that takes this appearance on an electrocardiogram [EKG/ECG]). Several frequently used drugs, alone or in combination, can predispose to this condition. These drugs include neuroleptics such as phenothiazines, the antibiotic erythromycin, older tricyclic antidepressants, and newer selective serotonin reuptake inhibitors (SSRIs) such as fluoxetine (Prozac).

Sudden death is more common in people with intellectual and developmental disabilities than in those without. In addition to the preceding factors, sudden death may also occur as the result of a serious illness that may have an atypical presentation and not be apparent to the support person. When physicians or support people undergo an experience with sudden death, it is not uncommon for them to feel that they should have been able to do something more to prevent the person's death. Although it is always helpful to consider if anything more could have been done, it must be remembered that sudden, unexpected death does occur in people with and without intellectual and developmental disabilities.

Vision and Hearing

The prevalences of impairments in hearing and vision are higher in people with intellectual and developmental disabilities than in people in the general population (Evenhuis et al., 2001; Evenhuis et al., 2004; Warburg, 2001). Many causes of congenital and acquired childhood hearing and visual impairment are causes of cerebral damage as well. Furthermore, there is a high tendency for impairments in hearing and vision to go unnoticed in people with intellectual and developmental disability. In some people with autism, a false diagnosis of sensory impairment may be made because of failure to respond during testing. Impacted earwax is a common cause of hearing difficulty. Hearing and visual impairments are more common in older people with disabilities, as their prevalences increase with increasing age. In 1997 and 1998, the International Association for the Scientific Study of Intellectual Disabilities Special Interest Research Group on Health Issues, together with a Dutch association of physicians providing care for people with an intellectual disability, convened to develop an international consensus on early identification of hearing and visual impairments in children and adults with intellectual disabilities. Children with Down syndrome, cerebral palsy, or a severe or profound intellectual disability were found to be the largest special risk groups. All infants with intellectual disabilities should be evaluated for vision and hearing problems at as early an age as possible so that remedial action can be taken. Research in this field should be promoted (Evenhuis & Nagtzaam, 1998).

Oral Health

It has been established that a person's oral health and general health are intimately related (Horbelt, 2004). Periodontal (gum) disease, for example, has been associated with a higher incidence of cardiovascular disease and, for women, with the risk of bearing low birth weight babies. Gum disease, tooth decay, and poor oral hygiene are prevalent throughout the general population, but the prevalence is higher in people with intellectual and developmental disabilities. There may be several reasons for this. In some cases, genetic disorders and medications can affect the oral environment. One example is dry mouth, a condition that inhibits salivary flow and leads to gum disease, tooth decay, or other mouth infections that subsequently can lead to nutritional and psychological problems. Another reason for the higher prevalence of gum disease may be that as more people with special needs are living in the community, they or their caregivers may not know where to obtain dental services or how to find a dentist who will provide these services. Many dentists believe that they have inadequate training, experience, or interest to treat people with intellectual and developmental disabilities. Also, a large part of the caregiving day may devoted to addressing acute medical problems, so daily preventive dental care may be overlooked.

Certain oral problems are commonly associated with particular intellectual and developmental disabilities. For example, children with cerebral palsy frequently have gastroesophageal reflux as well as episodes of vomiting. Either problem can lead to dental erosion or loss of tooth structure. These teeth are obviously more prone to decay. Overgrowth of gum tissue (gingival overgrowth), a side effect of taking medications to control seizures, is a frequent problem for children with cerebral palsy. Drooling is another problem in cerebral palsy; this is not due to excessive production of saliva but to a poor and disorganized swallowing pattern. Children with cerebral palsy and other intellectual and developmental disabilities may demonstrate self-injurious behavior including tongue, cheek, and lip biting, finger arm and hand chewing. Protective oral appliances may be useful to combat this. Gum problems are often seen in children with Down syndrome. Children with cleft palates often have congenitally missing teeth and teeth that do not align properly.

A daily oral hygiene regimen (see Display 41.2) helps main healthy teeth and gums and provides the best preventive care. The parent, caregiver, or person with the disability should undertake this responsibility. The American Academy of Pediatric Dentistry recommends that a child's first dentist visit should come within 6 months of the eruption of the first tooth or no later than the child's first birthday. Periodic dental recall appointments are recommended to supervise and evaluate oral hygiene. Recall appointments also allow the dentist to monitor, for example, any gingival overgrowth as well as growth and development of the teeth and orofacial structures. For further information about oral health issues in people with intellectual and developmental disabilities, see D'Oliviera and Ciampiaoni, 2004; Fenton et al., 2003; Otomo-Corgel and Marcus, 2003; and Waldman and Perlman, 2001.

Display 41.2

Home dental care

Home dental care includes brushing; flossing; rinsing the mouth; and eating a healthy, balanced diet.

1. *Brushing:* Brushing removes the food and bacteria which accumulate on the teeth and gums after eating and drinking. The teeth should be brushed two or three times a day, after every meal if possible. As soon as a tooth breaks through the gum, it should be brushed. Brushing the tongue helps prevent halitosis. Children without disabilities do not have the manual dexterity to brush independently until age 8–10 years. Thus, the physical and cognitive abilities of an individual with a disability should be assessed to see if he or she needs assistance with brushing. For those requiring assistance, the caregiver should choose a well-lit location and support the head. If the person with a disability uses a wheelchair, the caregiver can sit or stand behind the person. It is often helpful to have the person with the disability lying down on a bed or sofa. In many cases, an electric toothbrush is very useful.
2. *Flossing:* It is important to floss the food particles out from between the teeth; otherwise, they can cause decay. Daily flossing also promotes gum health.
3. *Rinsing the mouth:* After flossing and brushing, it is helpful to rinse the mouth with a recommended amount of fluoride rinse or prescribed medication. For example, one might rinse with chlorhexidine, an antibacterial oral rinse, for 60 seconds. If there is a concern about swallowing the rinse, it can be applied with a toothbrush.
4. *Eating a healthy, balanced diet:* Balanced meals should be provided, and plenty of healthy snacks should be available. Sugar-laden foods and snacks should be avoided. It is a good idea to brush teeth after taking medications, if possible, as some medications contain a high amount of sugar.

It is important that the person with the disability and his or her family or caregiver work as part of the person's oral health team to maintain good oral health and a positive self-image.

Nutrition

Irrespective of age, people need an adequate and completely balanced diet to achieve their maximum potential. People with intellectual and developmental disabilities are at a higher risk of nutritional problems (Telch & Telch, 2003). Although this principle sounds obvious, in the majority of cases it is a challenge to achieve. The most prominent causes of nutritional deficiency are neuromuscular dysfunction, dysphagia, anatomic defects or mechanical obstruction of the oral-gastrointestinal tract, and behavior problems. Some of the most frequent clinical conditions in which nutritional status is affected are chronic metabolic diseases (e.g., cystic fibrosis, diabetes mellitus, inflammatory bowel disease, celiac disease), sensory neuromotor disorders (e.g., cerebral palsy), and congenital abnormalities (e.g., cleft palate, meningomyelocele, congenital heart disease). In many cases, the medications used to treat people with these disorders may also interfere with their ability or desire to eat or negatively interact with some of the nutrients.

Poor diet during development may make an existing disability worse. It has been documented that inadequate protein, fat, and calorie (energy) intake in infants and children is associated with decreased brain growth and inappropriate nerve functioning (Cravioto, DeLicalde, & Birch, 1966). Adverse mental development and concentration in infants and young children may occur because of a specific mineral deficiency (e.g., iron) (Zlotkin, 2003). It is essential, therefore, to meet the person's nutritional needs and to help caregivers achieve this universal goal.

The ideal situation is to prevent nutritional deficiencies. Nutritional rehabilitation should be attempted in cases of malnourishment. If the gut is functioning and there are no signs of obstruction, malabsorption, or other functional problems, the first choice should be to provide the required nutritional intake by mouth. This is the cheapest and most natural way of providing adequate nutrition. If feeding problems are severe, then nutritional rehabilitation can be done through providing enteral nutrition or parenteral nutrition.

Enteral nutrition refers to nutrition provided through a tube that has been inserted into the gastrointestinal tract. Usually the tube is a fine-bore Silastic or polyurethane tube placed via the nose, the stomach, duodenum, or jejunum. Enteral nutrition is only an option if the person's gut is functioning properly.

Parenteral nutrition refers to providing nutrition via the circulatory system. It involves the intravenous administration of nutrients. The term *total parenteral nutrition (TPN)* involves the intravenous administration of all essential nutrients. TPN may also be used for "bowel rest" if the underlying disease requires it (i.e., inflammatory bowel disease, intestinal fistulas, pancreatitis).

When nutritionally related problems are identified, they must be treated rapidly to prevent further deterioration and avoid irreversible damage. An integral assessment of the family and patient, from emotional and psychological aspects, should be included before, during, and after the procedure is considered and performed. The patient and family will need periodic follow-up and reassessment, the frequency of which depends on the individual's recovery and nutritional rehabilitation. Continuous oral stimulation, if safe, should continue with small amounts of solids and/or liquids so that a person with a feeding tube does not forget to use that route. An attempt to discontinue the feeding tube should be undertaken when it is safe to do so and the patient can handle the oral route with no risk for aspiration.

In most instances, artificial feeding is proposed when patients are perceived to have a poor quality of life, such as coughing and choking with oral feeding. The placement of an artificial feeding method brings a spectrum of ethical concerns, however (Mayo, 1996). The participants in a tube feeding program are the patient (if mentally and legally competent), the patient's family, and the physician (as an individual or as a part of the nutritional team). Pediatric patients are represented by their families or principal caregivers (i.e., those in charge of the children's well-being). Any clinical decision making made among the patient, family, and physician should be consistent with legal and ethical principles. Religious principles also may be important to consider.

The decision to place a feeding tube in the first place centers on the question of the perceived benefits of providing hydration and nutrients to the particular patient. This decision has to be carefully thought out, taking into consideration factors such as the following:

- The morbidity and mortality rates associated with the procedure
- The proposed benefits versus the possible complications
- The patient's functional status
- The risk of aspiration
- The likelihood of developing pressure sores
- The person's life expectancy
- The person's quality of life

In some clinical situations, it is easy to make the decision about placing a feeding tube, as the benefits derived from it are very clear; in others circumstances, such as when a patient has a terminal illness or advanced dementia, considerable controversy exists (Gillick, 2000).

Specific ethical/moral questions to consider include the following:

- Will the artificial provision of nutrients and fluids increase the patient's suffering with no gain?
- Will the artificial provision of nutrients and fluids offer no benefits for the patient, even without increased suffering?
- May the insistence on artificial provision of nutrients and fluids violate the respect owed to the dignity of the individual?
- Will this procedure be of ultimate benefit to the patient?
- Will withholding nutrients and fluids result in a natural death or death by starvation and thirst, which could be compared with active euthanasia?

Several recommendations follow for decision making in this area. First, artificial feeding should be evaluated as any other medical intervention. When the patient's wishes are clearly known, artificial feeding should be provided or withheld in accordance to those wishes. A patient's wishes may be clearly stated either because he or she is mentally competent or had previously made an informed decision or, if the patient is incompetent at the time, there is clear and reliable written or oral testimony of the patient's previous wishes. In addition, artificial feeding should be provided only when it is more beneficial than harmful for the patient, and it never should be provided if it poses more risk than benefit to well-being. Furthermore, when the patient is competent, his or her specific preferences regarding artificial feeding should take precedence over physician or family judgments about the benefits and burdens of this treatment. When the patient's wishes are unknowable, the object of discussion and further investigation is to determine if the treatment proposed is acceptable and beneficial. If there is a disagreement between the family and or the caregiver, additional discussion should focus on what course of action is in the patient's best interest. Finally, an adolescent or a young adult who is competent has the right to decide for him- or herself whether artificial nutrition should be procured and or a feeding tube should be placed. No tube should be placed without informed consent.

For the previously noted reasons, enteral and parenteral nutrition are considered temporary, not definitive, solutions. Refer to Chait et al. (1996); Rimon (2001); and Telch and Telch (2003) for additional details about enteral and parenteral nutrition.

PREVENTION

As of 2006, although there is growing interest in preventive activities for people with intellectual and developmental disabilities, there is yet little evidence to offer guidance (Cheetham, 1997; Turner & Moss, 1996). Early intervention in infants who are at risk or already diagnosed with intellectual and developmental disabilities is key in prevention (Bear, 2004).

Efforts to prevent intellectual and developmental disabilities among children have been classified in terms of primary, secondary, and tertiary activities. Primary prevention activities include genetic counseling; immunization programs; improved prenatal, perinatal, and postnatal health care; and improved legislation regarding service provision. Secondary prevention activities include prenatal diagnosis and newborn screening. Tertiary preventive efforts include special education and comprehensive rehabilitation services (e.g., Chen & Simeonsson, 1993). In most countries, resources for such prevention are not adequate to meet the demand. Furthermore, special emphasis needs to be placed on the integration of existing primary health care systems with early intervention programs, public education and information, personnel preparation, and research and evaluation (Chen & Simeonsson, 1993).

General preventive health care should be made as accessible to people with intellectual and developmental disabilities as to those without (e.g., see the Canadian guide to clinical preventive health care [Canadian Task Force on Preventive Health Care, 2000] and similar guides for other countries). Specific health care guidelines are available for a number of particular developmental disabilities, including Down syndrome (Cohen, 1999; Leshin, 2005); fragile X syndrome (Committee on Genetics, American Academy of Pediatrics, 1996; Hagerman, 1999); Prader-Willi syndrome (Hanchett & Greenswag, 2005), and Williams syndrome (Committee on Genetics, American Academy of Pediatrics, 2001). Some examples of specialized preventive activities include the prevention of obesity and diabetes in people with Down syndrome and Prader-Willi syndrome. There is an urgent need to develop specific information for educating health care professionals about the prevention of medical problems for people with other developmental disabilities. One recent effort in this regard was the Colloquium on Primary Health Care for Adults with Developmental Disabilities (held November 7–11, 2005, in Toronto) to develop consensus guidelines for primary care providers (Sullivan et al., in press).

SUMMARY

To offer effective health care, a health care provider must have knowledge of specific risk factors, have an understanding of the atypical presentation of signs and symptoms, and conduct regular routine screenings for people with developmental disabilities. The most crucial component in providing medical care, however, is the careful observations of support people, who know the person well, have knowledge of health issues related to the person's particular developmental disability, and provide strong advocacy on the person's behalf.

FOR FURTHER THOUGHT AND DISCUSSION

1. What barriers to physical health care have you encountered for a particular person with developmental disabilities? How were they overcome, or how could they be handled in the future?
2. Think of a person with an intellectual or developmental disability whom you know well. Practice summarizing the person's history succinctly—perhaps in five or six sentences—to present to a health care provider.
3. Consider ways to deal with a health care provider who does not seem to recognize the importance of the information provided by a support person.
4. Review the Special Problems and Easily Overlooked Issues section while thinking of a person you support. Can you identify any previously unrecognized medical issues within the different areas discussed?

REFERENCES

Ahmed, Z., O'Brien, G., Betts, T., et al. (1997). Learning disabilities: Moving forward—a focus on epilepsy. *Journal of Intellectual Disability Research, 41,* 355–360.

Alvarez, N. (1998). Barbiturates in the treatment of epilepsy in people with intellectual disability. *Journal of Intellectual Disability Research, 42*(Suppl. 1), 16–23.

Beange, H., McElduff, A., & Baker, W. (1995). Medical disorders of adults with mental retardation: A population study. *American Journal on Mental Retardation, 99,* 595–604.

Bear, L.M. (2004). Early identification of infants at risk for developmental disabilities. *Pediatric Clinics of North America, 51,* 685–701.

Best, K. (1999). Mental disabilities affect method options. *Network, 19*(2), 19–22.

Böhmer, C.J.M., Niezen-de Boer, M.C., Klinkenberg-Knol, E.C., et al. (1999). The prevalence of gastroesophageal reflux disease in institutionalized intellectually disabled individuals. *American Journal of Gastroenterology, 94*(3), 804–810.

Boyd, R. (1993). Neuroleptic malignant syndrome and mental retardation: Review and analysis of 29 cases. *American Journal on Mental Retardation, 98,* 143–155.

Brodsky, M.C., Conte, F.A., Taylor, D., et al. (1997). Sudden death in septo-optic dysplasia. Report of 5 cases. *Archives of Ophthalmology, 115,* 66–70.

Buckman, R. (1992). *How to break bad news: A guide for health care professionals.* Baltimore: The Johns Hopkins University Press.

Canadian Task Force on Preventive Health Care. (2000). *Evidence-based clinical prevention.* Ottawa, ON: Health Canada. Retrieved on January 9, 2005, from http://www.ctfphc.org

Chait, P.G., Weinberg, J., Connolly, B., et al. (1996). Retrograde percutaneous gastrostomy and gastrojejunostomy in 505 children. A 4½-years experience. *Radiology, 201,* 691–695.

Chambers, R., Milsom, G., Evans, N., et al. (1998). The primary care workload and prescribing costs associated with patients with learning disability discharged from long stay care to the community. *British Journal of Learning Disabilities, 26*(1), 9–12.

Cheetham, T. (1997). Prevention. *The University of Western Ontario Clinical Bulletin of the Developmental Disabilities Program, 8*(4), 1–4.

Chen, J., & Simeonsson, R.J. (1993). Prevention of childhood disability in the People's Republic of China. *Child Care Health Development, 19,* 71–88.

Cohen, W.I. (1999). Health care guidelines for individuals with Down syndrome: 1999 revision (Down syndrome preventive medical check list). *Down Syndrome Quarterly, 4*(3), 1–16.

Cole, G., Neal, J.W., Fraser, W.I., et al. (1994). Autopsy findings in patients with mental handicap. *Journal of Intellectual Disability Research, 38,* 9–26.

Committee on Genetics, American Academy of Pediatrics. (1996). Health supervision for children with fragile X syndrome. *Pediatrics, 98,* 297–300.

Committee on Genetics, American Academy of Pediatrics. (2001). Health care supervision for children with Williams syndrome. *Pediatrics, 107,* 1192–1204.

Cravioto, J., DeLicalde, E.R., & Birch, H.G. (1966). Nutrition, growth, and neurointegrative development: An experimental and ecological study. *Pediatrics, 49,* 103–118.

Cutler, P. (1985). *Problem solving in clinical medicine.* Philadelphia: Lippincott, Williams & Wilkins.

Curtis, K., Curtis, R., & Vicari, S. (2004). Do physicians receive adequate training in the health care of persons with mental retardation? A physician survey. *The NADD Bulletin, 7*(5), 83–86.

D'Oliviera, G.R., & Ciampiaoni, A.L. (2004). Prevalence of periodontal disease in the primary dentition of children with cerebral palsy. *Journal of Dentistry for Children, 71,* 27–32.

Durvasula, S., Beange, H., & Baker, W. (2002). Mortality of people with intellectual disability in northern Sydney. *Journal of Intellectual & Developmental Disability, 27*(4), 255–264.

Evenhuis, H., van Splunder, J., Vink, M., et al. (2004). Obstacles in large-scale epidemiological assessment of sensory impairments in a Dutch population with intellectual disabilities. *Journal of Intellectual Disability Research, 48*(8), 708–718.

Evenhuis, H.M., & Nagtzaam, L.M.D. (1998). *IASSID international consensus statement: Early identification of hearing and visual impairment in children and adults with an intellectual disability.* Retrieved on October 21, 2004, from http://www.iassid.org/pdf/sensory-imp-consensus.pdf

Evenhuis, H.M., Theunissen, M., Denkers, I., et al. (2001). Prevalence of visual and hearing impairment in a Dutch institutionalized population with intellectual disability. *Journal of Intellectual Disability Research, 45*(5), 457–464.

Fass, R. (2003). Epidemiology and pathophysiology of symptomatic gastroesophageal reflux disease. *American Journal of Gastroenterology, 98*(Suppl. 3), S2–S7.

Fenton, S.J., Hood, H., Holder, M., et al. (2003). The American Academy of Developmental Medicine and Dentistry: Eliminating health disparities for individuals with mental retardation and other developmental disabilities. *Journal of Dental Education, 67,* 1337–1344.

Fidler, K., & Hodgetts, P.G. (1992). Neuroleptic malignant syndrome in a developmentally handicapped adult. *Canadian Family Physician, 38,* 1491–1493.

Forsgren, L., Edvinsson, S.O., Nystrom, L., et al. (1996). Influence of epilepsy on mortality in mental retardation: An epidemiological study. *Epilepsia, 37*(10), 956–963.

Gillick, M.R. (2000). Rethinking the role of tube feeding in patients with advanced dementia. *New England Journal of Medicine, 342,* 206–210.

Gitta, M., & Deagle, G. (1992a). What family doctors want to know. *The University of Western Ontario Clinical Bulletin of the Developmental Disabilities Program, 3*(1), 1–3.

Gitta, M., & Deagle, G. (1992b). What family doctors want to know: Part II. *The University of Western Ontario Clinical Bulletin of the Developmental Disabilities Program, 3*(3), 1–3.

Glick, N.R., Fischer, M.H., Heisey, D.M., et al. (2005). Epidemiology of fractures in people with severe and profound developmental disabilities. *Osteoporosis International, 16*(4), 389–396.

Goodenough, G.K., & Hole-Goodenough, J. (1997). Training for primary care of mentally handicapped patients in

US family practice residencies. *Journal of the American Board of Family Practice, 10,*(5), 333–336.

Hagerman, R.J. (1999). *Neurodevelopmental disorders: Diagnosis and treatment.* Oxford, United Kingdom: Oxford University Press.

Hanchett, J., & Greenswag, L. (2005). *Health care guidelines for individuals with Prader-Willi syndrome.* Retrieved on January 9, 2005, from http://www.pwsausa.org/postion/HCGuide/HCG.htm

Heaton, C. (1995). Tips for interacting with the doctor. *Healthy Times, 7,* 1–8.

Heymsfield, S.B., Casper, K., & Funfar, J. (1987). Physiologic response and clinical implications of nutrition support. *American Journal of Cardiology, 60,* 75G–81G.

Horbelt, C.V. (2004, October 8). *Systemic manifestations of oral health disorders.* Paper presented at the World Congress & Exposition on Disabilities, Orlando, FL.

Howells, G. (1986). Are the medical needs of mentally handicapped being met? *The Journal of the Royal College of General Practitioners, 36,* 449–453.

Iacono, T., Humphreys, J., Davis, R., et al. (2004). Health care service provision for country people with developmental disability: An Australian perspective. *Research in Developmental Disabilities, 25,* 265–284.

Iivanainen, M. (1998). Phenytoin: Effective but insidious therapy for epilepsy in people with intellectual disability. *Journal of Intellectual Disability Research, 42*(Suppl. 1), 24–31.

Jancar, J., & Speller, C.J. (1994). Fatal intestinal obstruction in the mentally handicapped. *Journal of Intellectual Disability Research, 38*(4), 413–422.

Kowalski, J.N.T. (2002). *HIV/AIDS and mental retardation.* Retrieved on September 27, 2004, from http://www.thearc.org/faqs/hiv.html

Lennox, N.G., Diggens, J.N., & Ugoni, A.M. (1997). The general practice care of people with intellectual disability: Barriers and solutions. *Journal of Intellectual Disability Research, 41,* 380–390.

Leshin, L. (2005). *Down syndrome: Health issues.* Retrieved on January 9, 2005, from http://www.ds-health.com

Levesque, C.A. (1995). Evaluation and treatment of "spells." *Conference Proceedings from the National Association for the Dually Diagnosed (NADD), 12th Annual Conference, Collaboration: The Essential Element.* Kingston, NY: National Association for the Dually Diagnosed.

Lohiya, G.S., Tan-Figueroa, L., & Iannucci, A. (2004). Identification of low bone mass in a developmental center: Finger bone mineral density measurement in 562 residents. *Journal of the American Medical Directors Association, 5,* 371–376.

Marchetti, A.G., Nathanson, R.S., Kastner, T.A., et al. (1990). AIDS and state developmental disability agencies: A national survey. *American Journal of Public Health, 80,* 54–56.

Martin, G.B.H., & Martin, D.M. (2000). A register for patients with learning disabilities in general practice. *Journal of Learning Disabilities, 4*(1), 37–48.

Mayo, T.W. (1996). Forgoing artificial nutrition and hydration: Legal and ethical considerations. *Nutrition in Clinical Practice, 11,* 254–264.

McDermott, S., Moran, R., Platt, T., et al. (2005). Prevalence of epilepsy in adults with mental retardation and related disabilities in primary care. *American Journal on Mental Retardation, 110*(1), 48–56.

McKee, J.R., & Bodfish, J.W. (2000). Sudden unexpected death in epilepsy in adults with mental retardation. *American Journal on Mental Retardation, 105*(4), 229–235.

Minihan, P.M., Dean, D.H., & Lyons, C.M. (1993). Managing the care of patients with mental retardation: A survey of physicians. *Mental Retardation, 31*(4), 239–246.

Morgan, C.L., Baxter, H., & Kerr, M.P. (2003). Prevalence of epilepsy and associated health service utilization and mortality among patients with intellectual disability. *American Journal on Mental Retardation, 108*(5), 293–300.

Nehring, W.M., & Faux, S.A. (2004). Downsizing of developmental centers for persons with intellectual and developmental disabilities affect nurses. *Chart, Journal of Illinois Nursing, 101*(3), 3–4.

Otomo-Corgel, I., & Marcus, R.C. (2003). Periodontal disease and systemic health. What you and your patients need to know. *Oral Health, 93,* 21–26.

Phillips, A., Morrison, J., & Davis, R.W. (2004). General practitioners' educational needs in intellectual disability health. *Journal of Intellectual Disabilities Research, 48*(Pt. 2), 142–149.

Poindexter, A. (1995). Medical aspects of challenging behaviors. In *Proceedings, International Congress II on the dually diagnosed* (pp. 36, 37). Boston: National Association for the Dually Diagnosed.

Poindexter, A. (2000). Phenobarbital, propranolol, and aggression. *Journal of Neuropsychiatry and Clinical Neurosciences, 12*(3), 413.

Reiss, S. (1994). Psychopathology in mental retardation. In N. Bouras (Ed.), *Mental health in mental retardation: Recent advances and practices* (pp. 67–78). Cambridge, United Kingdom: Cambridge University Press.

Rideau Regional Centre Medical Centre. (1995). *A handbook on the medical management of developmentally handicapped persons* (Rev. ed.). Smiths Falls, ON, Canada: Author.

Rimon, E. (2001). The safety and feasibility of percutaneous endoscopic gastrostomy placement by a single physician. *Endoscopy, 33,MO* 241–244.

Roeher Institute. (1994). *Health care planning innovations project literature review.* Toronto: Author.

Rogers, B., Stratton, P., Victor, J., et al. (1992). Chronic regurgitation among persons with mental retardation: A need for combined medical and interdisciplinary strategies. *American Journal on Mental Retardation, 96,* 522–527.

Ryan, R.M. (1996). *Handbook of mental health care for persons with developmental disabilities.* Evergreen, CO: S&B Publishing.

Sackett, D.L. (2000). *How the Internet can help clinicians improve their clinical skills.* Retrieved July 17, 2000, from http://www.medscape.com/viewarticle/408063

Schupf, N. (1998). Menopause and women's health. *Healthy Times, 10,* 7–8.

Sices, L., Feudtner, C., McLaughlin, J., et al. (2004). How do primary care physicians manage children with possible developmental delays? A national survey with an experimental design. *Pediatrics, 113,* 274–282.

Silka, V., & Hurley, A. (1998). How to get the most out of a psychiatric appointment. *Mental Health Aspects of Developmental Disabilities, 1,* 22–27.

Sovner, R., & Hurley, A. (1993). The psychiatric consultation information form for persons with developmental disabilities. *Mental Health Newsletter, 12*(5), 67–81.

Stewart, M., Brown, J.B., Weston, W.W., et al. (1995). *Patient-centred medicine.* Thousand Oaks, CA: Sage Publications.

Sulkes, S.B. (1989). Consultation services to schools and residences. In I.L. Rubin & A.C. Crocker (Eds.), *Developmental disabilities: Delivery of medical care for children and adults* (pp. 34–42). Philadelphia: Leah & Febiger.

Sullivan, W.F., Heng, J., Cameron, D., Lunsky, Y., et al. (in press). Consensus practice guidelines for the primary health care of adults with developmental disabilities. *Canadian Family Physician.*

Telch, J., & Telch, F.E. (2003). Practical aspects of nutrition in the disabled pediatric patient. *Clinical Nutrition, 3,* 1–6.

Tsiouris, J.A., Patti, P.J., Tipu, O., et al. (2002). Adverse effects of phenytoin given for late-onset seizures in adults with Down syndrome. *Neurology, 59,* 779–80.

Trumble, S. (1993). Communicating with people who have intellectual disabilities. *Australian Family Physician, 22,* 1081–1082.

Turner, S., & Moss, S. (1996). The health needs of adults with learning disabilities and the health of the nation strategy. *Journal of Intellectual Disability Research, 40,* 438–450.

Tyler, C.V., & Bourguet, C. (1997). Primary care of adults with mental retardation. *The Journal of Family Practice, 44*(5), 487–494.

U.S. Department of Health and Human Services. (2002). *Closing the gap: A national blueprint for improving the health of individuals with mental retardation. Report of the Surgeon General's Conference on Health Disparities and Mental Retardation.* Retrieved May 3, 2006, from http://www.surgeongeneral.gov/topics/mentalretardation

van Schrojenstein Lantman-DeValk, H., Metsemakers, J.F., Haveman, M.J., et al. (2000). Health problems in people with intellectual disability in general practice: A comparative study. *Family Practice, 17*(5), 405–407.

van Schrojenstein Lantman-de Valk, H.M.J., van den Akker, M., Maaskant, M.A., et al. (1997). Prevalence and incidence of health problems in people with intellectual disability. *Journal of Intellectual Disability Research, 41,* 42–51.

Waldman, H.B., & Perlman, S.P. (2001). Children with both mental retardation and mental illnesses live in our communities and need dental care. *Journal of Dentistry for Children, 68,* 360–365.

Walsh, K.K., Hammerman, S., Josephson, F., et al. (2000). Caring for people with developmental disabilities: Survey of nurses about their education and experience. *Mental Retardation, 38*(1), 33–41.

Walsh, P.N., & LeRoy, B. (2004). *Women with disabilities aging well: A global view.* Baltimore: Paul H. Brookes Publishing Co.

Warburg, M., (2001). Visual impairment in adult people with intellectual disability: Literature review. *Journal of Intellectual Disability Research, 45*(5), 424–438.

Webb, O.J., & Rogers, L. (1999). Health screening for people with intellectual disability: The New Zealand experience. *Journal of Intellectual Disability Research, 43*(6), 497–503.

Wilson, D.N., & Haire, A. (1990). Health care screening for people with mental handicap living in the community. *British Medical Journal, 301,* 1379–1381.

Ziviani, J., Lennox, N., Allison, H., et al. (2004). Meeting in the middle: Improving communication in primary health care consultations with people with an intellectual disability. *Journal of Intellectual & Developmental Disability, 29*(3), 211–225.

Zlotkin, S. (2003). Clinical nutrition: 8. The role of nutrition in the prevention of iron deficiency anemia in infants, children and adolescents. *Canadian Medical Association Journal, 168,* 59–63.

42

Intellectual Disabilities and Behavioral, Emotional, and Psychiatric Disturbances

Elspeth A. Bradley, Jane Summers, Avril V. Brereton, Stewart L. Einfeld, Susan M. Havercamp, Geraldine Holt, Andrew Levitas, and Bruce Tonge

WHAT YOU WILL LEARN ABOUT IN THIS CHAPTER

- Overview of mental health problems
- Assessment and treatment
- International perspectives
- Developing a vision of a mental health service that is sensitive to the needs of people with intellectual disabilities

This chapter provides an international perspective on the assessment and treatment of mental health problems in people with intellectual disabilities. Many of the key issues are generic in nature, and the chapter authors have attempted to reflect best clinical practice irrespective of geographic locality, particularly in the sections on clinical challenges and assessment and treatment principles and approaches. Differences arise, however, in regard to government policies, laws, and legislation as well as how service systems are organized and function in various parts of the world. The chapter builds on the foundation the first two chapter authors developed for their own audience of Ontario, Canada (Bradley & Summers, 2003), by bringing together contributions from researchers and clinicians well known in the field of intellectual disabilities and mental health problems from Australia (Avril Brereton, Stewart Einfeld, and Bruce Tonge), England (Geraldine Holt), and the United States (Susan Havercamp and Andrew Levitas). These contributors were asked to provide a commentary on the issues and highlight challenges and opportunities that are specific to their country and service systems. The chapter uses this broader perspective as the basis for suggestions to overcome some of the difficulties faced when trying to respond to the needs of this heterogeneous and often clinically complex population. Throughout, the chapter uses the term *people with intellectual disabilities.* It is important to bear in mind, however, that worldwide, various terms are used synonymously to refer to this group, including *developmental disabilities* (Canada), *learning disabilities* (United Kingdom), and *mental retardation* (United States) (see Chapter 1 for more information on terms).

The view that people with intellectual disabilities experience the same types of mental health problems that similarly affect the general population was not widely recognized in some countries until the late 1980s. In North America, it is said that these individuals have a dual diagnosis, whereas in the United Kingdom and some other European countries, this term can still cause confusion. For this reason, the authors have chosen to avoid the term *dual diagnosis* in the main body of this chapter and refer instead to *people with intellectual disabilities and mental health problems* (which include psychiatric, emotional, and/or behavioral problems). At the end of the chapter, where country-specific issues are discussed, the preferred terminology of the particular country is used.

OVERVIEW OF MENTAL HEALTH PROBLEMS

The chapter begins with an overview of mental health problems. The following sections discuss the prevalence, types, causes, and clinical challenges of these disorders.

Prevalence

There is mounting evidence that people with intellectual disabilities are at greater risk for developing mental health problems than their peers without disabilities (Dykens, 2000). The first epidemiological study of mental health problems in young people with intellectual disabilities that compared this group with matched controls without intellectual disabilities, showed an in-

The authors thank Nick Bouras for kindly reviewing the chapter and providing helpful comments.

creased rate of disorder of approximately four times that experienced by the matched controls (Rutter, 1971). Subsequent prevalence estimates in studies of both children and adults with intellectual disabilities have varied widely, ranging from approximately 10% to 70% (Corbett, 1979; Einfeld & Tonge, 1996b; Tonge & Einfeld, 2003; for reviews see Borthwick-Duffy, 1994; Campbell & Malone, 1991). These statistics can be confusing but may be understood more easily if one recognizes that this extensive range of prevalence estimates appears to be associated with the following factors:

1. The use of a broad definition of *mental health problems* that includes emotional and behavior disturbances in addition to psychiatric disorders
2. Estimates for psychiatric disorders (as opposed to mental health and behavioral problems) are somewhat uncertain because of a lack of agreed-on diagnostic criteria for the different levels of intellectual functioning
3. The individuals examined are those living in institutional settings or who have been referred for mental health services
4. Groups referred to mental health services may be overrepresented by those more verbal individuals who are better able to communicate their distress—and hence get referred

Within the broader population of people with intellectual disabilities, certain subgroups may be especially prone to disturbance and contribute disproportionately to the overall prevalence rate of psychiatric and behavior disorders. The findings of a Canadian epidemiological study of adolescents and young adults with intellectual disabilities indicate that individuals with autism are three times more likely to have a concurrent psychiatric disorder than those without autism (Bradley, Bolton, & Bryson, 2004; Bradley & Bryson, 1998). Moreover, individuals with autism and severe intellectual disabilities display significantly higher rates of psychiatric and behavior disturbances compared with peers with severe intellectual disabilities alone (Bradley, Summers, et al., 2004; Brereton, Tonge, & Finfeld, 2006). In addition, some genetic syndromes associated with intellectual disabilities (e.g., Williams, fragile X, and Prader-Willi syndromes) may also confer greater risk for psychiatric disorder (Dykens, Hodapp, & Finucane, 2000).

Types

People with intellectual disabilities experience the same kinds of emotional and psychiatric disorders that occur among the general population (Benson, 1985; Rutter, 1971). Some of the more common psychiatric conditions include mood and anxiety disorders, adjustment problems, personality disorders, and attention-deficit/hyperactivity disorder (King et al., 1994; Luckasson et al., 2002). Behavior disturbances, which are often the reason for referral to mental health services, are generally captured under these categories and include verbal and physical aggression, self-injury, hyperactivity, attention problems, and oppositional behavior (e.g., Jacobson, 1982). Some conditions, such as autism, stereotypies, and hyperkinetic syndrome are seen more frequently in people with intellectual disabilities than in the general population (Nordin & Gillberg, 1996; Rutter, 1971; Shah, Holmes, & Wing, 1982; Wing & Gould, 1979).

Causes

Organic, psychosocial, and environmental factors may each and in combination play a major role in the etiology of mental health problems in people with intellectual disabilities. Organic factors—which include genetic influences, brain injury, trauma, disease, or infection—may directly underlie both the intellectual disability and the mental health problem (Jakab, 1982; Rutter, Tizard, & Whitmore, 1970). In terms of environmental and psychosocial influences on mental health problems, many people with intellectual disabilities live in impoverished environments, lack meaningful employment opportunities and strong support systems, do not have control over many aspects of their lives and feel isolated from the mainstream of society (Stark, Kiernan, & Goldbury, 1988). Research suggests that social strain (related to stressful interpersonal interactions) is more strongly associated with mental health problems than are overall low levels of social support for individuals with intellectual disabilities (Lunsky & Benson, 2001; Lunsky & Havercamp, 1999). People with intellectual disabilities may also have poor or inadequate social and coping skills; when these conditions occur on top of the cognitive and communication deficits, feelings of frustration, sense of failure, and an awareness of being "different" can be heightened, contributing further to the mental health vulnerability.

Clinical Challenges

A number of challenges exist in correctly diagnosing mental health disturbances and psychiatric disorders in individuals with intellectual disabilities (see Deb et al., 2001; Royal College of Psychiatrists, 2001). Diagnostic overshadowing refers to the tendency of professionals to underestimate signs of psychiatric or emotional disturbance (Reiss, Levitan, & Szysko, 1982). This occurs when professionals misattribute symptoms of a mental health problem to the person's intellectual disability; hence, these symptoms are less likely to be seen as evidence of possible underlying mental health or psychiatric problems. Another phenomenon that poses a challenge is known as *behavioral highlighting*, whereby severe or intense behavior problems may make the detection of underlying problems more difficult (Sovner & Hurley, 1986). Other diagnostic challenges are related to personal characteristics, such as severe communication and cognitive impairments that make it difficult for people to articulate the nature and sources of their distress (Reid, 1982). In these situations, it is necessary to rely more heavily on information that is provided by caregivers than on self-reports. With increasing disability, it becomes more difficult to detect distinctive clinical patterns to assist with diagnosis, as the behavioral presentation can be nonspecific (e.g., when aggression or self-injury is the main referral problem) or even atypical in individuals with these more severe impairments (Ross & Oliver, 2002, 2003; Tsiouris, 2001).

Comorbidity, which is the coexistence of additional medical or psychiatric problems, can further complicate the clinical picture. For instance, sensory impairments (i.e., vision and hearing problems), seizure disorders, and medical disorders—such as cardiovascular problems, abnormal thyroid functioning, otitis externa (see Cheetham, 2001a), and rib fractures (Cheetham, 2001b)—can be missed because of the atypical clinical presentation.

ASSESSMENT AND TREATMENT

As a group, people with intellectual disabilities are often overmedicated and undertreated (Reiss & Aman, 1998). Cognitive and language impairments often limit their capacity to reflect on their own internal mental and feeling states and to communicate this subjective experience to others. With increasing disability in these areas, they are more reliant on immediate caregivers to be sensitive to the pattern of their daily lives and to understand the impact of daily events, such as changes in daily routines or inappropriate expectations, on their emotional responses and capacity to cope. If caregivers are unfamiliar with the usual responses of the individual or are unaware of particular life events that may have occurred for that person, emotional and psychiatric disorders may be missed and remain untreated. For example, withdrawn behavior and loss of interest may not be noticed or, if observed, may be incorrectly attributed to the person's intellectual disability (diagnostic overshadowing) rather than possible depression.

Those engaging in behaviors that are disruptive or causing damage to themselves or to others may be referred to mental health services or to the emergency medical services. As noted, service providers (e.g., physicians, nurses) unfamiliar with the needs of people with intellectual disabilities may also attribute this disturbed or unusual behavior to the intellectual disability; thus, the behavior may be managed with medication or other behavioral interventions, leaving the underlying problems undiagnosed and untreated (Bradley & Lofchy, 2005). Emotional upsets, difficulties in coping with situations, frustrations with daily circumstances, physical illnesses, and psychiatric disorders most frequently present to emergency and mental health services as nonspecific behavior disturbance.

The challenge for these service providers is therefore to understand what these disturbed or unusual behaviors really mean (i.e., what these behaviors are communicating) and to determine whether they fit into a pattern of functional changes (e.g., in sleep, appetite, or mood) that is diagnostic of a psychiatric disorder. Teasing these issues apart requires coordinated teamwork involving the client, his or her immediate caregivers, and access to specialists who have experience working the fields of mental health and intellectual disabilities and who are aware of the medical and mental health vulnerabilities of this population. In England, for instance, there are teams of professionals in each health locality (called Community Learning Disability Teams) that provide specialist support to people with intellectual disabilities. Such teams may include mental health professionals with specialist training in the mental health needs of people with intellectual disabilities or else have close links with such professionals. Formal training of mental health professionals in these teams is provided through university and college programs. In the United States, formal training in intellectual disabilities is provided through University Centers for Excellence in Developmental Disability (UCEDD). Each U.S. state has a UCEDD that is affiliated with a university and has the mandate to conduct research, provide services, and to train students to work with this population. A handful of these programs offer specialized training in mental health issues in people with intellectual disabilities. In Canada, the training of mental health professionals in intellectual disabilities has been greatly neglected (Lunsky & Bradley, 2001). Services and systems have evolved somewhat differently, and specialized support (if such is available) tends to develop around each individual only after recurrent failures of the generic services to provide appropriate care (see example in Display 42.1). In general, in Canada, there are few formal training programs available for mental health professionals in the area of health and intellectual disabilities, and access to generic medical and particularly psychiatric services is problematic because service providers may consider they do not have the expertise to deal with the individual with intellectual disability.

An international perspective and more comprehensive description of service issues and challenges

Display 42.1

Case study: Michelle

Michelle, age 29, was referred because of severe self injurious behavior (SIB), which had been present from an early age. Michelle was mostly nonverbal, and her functional skills were at approximately a 18–24 month level. During her life, in response to severe escalations of the SIB, she had been seen by many specialists, including those in the medical, neurological, behavioral, and psychological fields. She was diagnosed as having "autistic behaviors" and was being treated for an underactive thyroid. Various interventions were tried, including high doses of medication and behavioral strategies, but with limited success. At the time of referral, she had been in the same group home for a number of years, with a stable group of caregivers committed to ensuring optimum quality of life. The caregivers were experienced in supporting people with intellectual disabilities and had an excellent working relationship with a consulting behavior therapist; together they were able to provide Michelle with an environment that was geared to her developmental level, was emotionally nurturing, and had appropriate expectations of her both in her day and residential settings. However, there continued to be concern about the level of medication Michelle was taking. (Later in life, Michelle developed sudden abdominal obstruction, which was likely related to this long-term use of medication as an intervention for her SIB, and a piece of her bowel had to be removed.) Caregivers had managed to secure a psychiatric consultation and a medication change was recommended, but no psychiatric follow-up was available. This medication change was monitored carefully by the family doctor and caregivers, but Michelle's behavior started to escalate and she was taken to the local emergency room where she was immediately reinstated on the original medication but at higher doses.

SIB arises out of many circumstances but can only begin to be adequately assessed in a continuous and stable setting where caregivers and involved health care staff share an understanding of the behaviors and emotional responses of the person with intellectual disability (particularly when the person is distressed or medically ill) and have a shared vision of possible outcomes. Michelle's care was continuous and stable as long as she remained within her day and residential settings and as long as she had no medical problems or behavioral escalations requiring emergency medical or psychiatric intervention. The assessment of SIB often requires trials of interventions some of which may cause behavioral escalations. Therefore, it is necessary from the outset to map out responses to crises that may arise to ensure continuity of assessment and treatment between inpatient and outpatient settings. In Michelle's case, the following local services became partners in Michelle's care over the ensuing 2 years: Michelle's immediate care team (residential and day counselors, supervisors, and managers); a consulting behavior therapist; representatives from family, hospital services, impatient psychiatric services, specialty medical services (including neurology, endocrinology, and surgery), and community nursing. In addition, as Michelle was unable to consent to her treatment (because of the extent of her cognitive impairment) and had no family, there was a representative from the Office of the Public Guardian. Regular meetings occurred to review Michelle's progress and to ensure that all partners in her care were informed as required. The anxiety was taken out of the crises: There was no longer the fear that Michelle's medication would be changed without adequate consultation with caregivers, and inpatient services staff no longer feared that Michelle would become a long-term patient. As the crises abated for Michelle and for the systems for support, Michelle's behavior stabilized and a pattern of cyclical behavior emerged. She was treated with a mood stabilizing medication, and her antipsychotic medication was successfully reduced. Since these interventions there has been significant improvement in her quality of life and SIB now rarely occurs.

Source: Bradley and Summers (2003).

in each of the different countries follows later in this chapter.

Assessment Process

Although the clinical presentation of psychiatric disorder in people with mild intellectual disabilities is similar in many ways to the general population, with increasing intellectual disability, behavior disturbance is often the hallmark of psychiatric disorder. When identifying whether behavioral disturbance is due to a psychiatric disorder, it is necessary to explore systematically all those areas that may give rise to behavior disturbance. A brief outline of this process is provided in Figure 42.1 and Table 42.1 (see also Bradley & Hollins, 2006).

In many instances, nonspecific behavior disturbance may be the final outcome of more than one related or unrelated cause, such as disruptive behavior associated with a mood disorder but made worse by toothache. People with mild or moderate intellectual disabilities usually are able to assist in this exploration and often are able to share some of their inner discomforts, although time is usually required for them to feel comfortable with the interviewers and for both to understand how the other communicates. Independent information from someone who knows the person well (an informant) should also be sought, as the individual may not fully appreciate the larger context within which he or she feels distressed (e.g., the distress may be associated with an external event such as bereavement). For an individual with little or no language, the assessment rests primarily in understanding the behavior changes and in making inferences about internal feeling states from the characteristics and patterns of these changes in behavior. Here, informants who know the individual well are key to a good assessment in terms of providing information on how the person usually communicates frustration, emotion, physical pain, and so forth. It is always helpful to meet with the referred people in settings where they normally live and spend their work and leisure time. Knowing and observing whether the behaviors of concern change in different settings provides clues to their underlying cause.

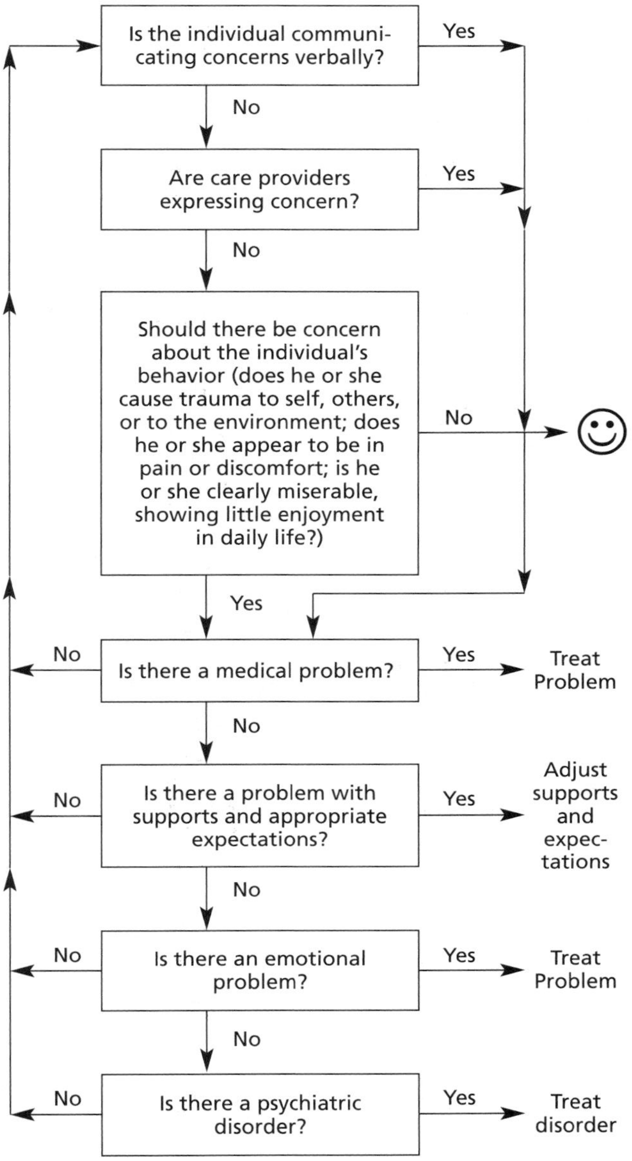

Figure 42.1. Mental health assessment decision tree. (*Source:* Bradley & Summers, 2003.)

Circumstances Giving Rise to Behavior Disturbance

As indicated in Figure 42.1, a variety of circumstances can lead to behavior disturbance. These are discussed next.

Physical Health and Medical Issues Individuals with mild intellectual disabilities may be less able than their peers without disabilities to articulate or comment on their physical discomfort and pain and often do not do so spontaneously. If a problem is suspected, it may be necessary to ask specific questions and to help the individual communicate his or her discomfort and to pinpoint where the pain is located. Individuals with more severe disability may be totally unable to communicate a pain or localize a discomfort verbally or even by gesture. Discomfort from chronic disorders (e.g., constipation), fluctuating pain (e.g., toothaches), or side effects of medication may present to caregivers and clinicians as disruptive or irritable behaviors.

As a group, people with intellectual disabilities have a higher prevalence of other disabilities (e.g., visual and hearing impairments) and medical conditions (e.g., diabetes, neurological impairments including seizures and cerebral palsy). In one U.S. study, adults with intellectual disabilities were found to lead more sedentary lifestyles and to have the same or greater risk of the following health conditions as adults without disabilities: diabetes, high blood pressure, cardiovascular disease, and chronic pain (Havercamp, Scandlin, & Roth, 2004). Individuals with identifiable genetic or metabolic disorders, which may occur in up to 45% of those with severe intellectual disabilities (for reviews, see Curry et al., 1997; Raynham et al., 1996; Rondal et al., 2004), frequently have associated physi-

Table 42.1. Psychiatric assessment and treatment formulation

Concerns[a]

What are the concerns, who is concerned, and why the concern?

History of concerns

What has been tried, for how long, what worked, what did not work, and who was involved?

When was client last at his or her best, how was a typical day spent then, how is the day spent now, and what has changed?

Background information: client[a]

Developmental level: Reports of psychological and adaptive functioning, communication assessments, school reports, and developmental/pediatric assessments[b]

Communication skills: Verbal and nonverbal, including how the person communicates pain, bodily discomfort, and emotional distress[b]

Social circumstances in past: Family and social supports, institutional care, losses, major life events, trauma, abuse, school, work, occupation, and leisure

Recent changes/life events: Consider whether recent changes are linked to the onset of concern

Medical: Hearing or visual impairments, cerebral palsy, seizures, biological cause of developmental disability, presence of a syndrome, other medical disorders, and medications past and present

Family history: Medical conditions, developmental disability, psychiatric disorders, and responses to treatments

Emotional and coping responses: Life events and past response to stressors

Psychiatric history and preexisting behaviors: Baseline behaviors (e.g., tics, self-injury, obsessions) that were present before concerns began

Background information: supports

The caregivers' understanding of the developmental disability

Social, emotional, physical (environmental), residential, and day supports

The structures and organization within which caregivers and staff work

The appropriateness of services and expectations on clients

Support for caregivers and staff

Examination

Client

Physical (e.g., determine if there is a medical condition or a syndrome)

Interview to determine mental state

Review of behavioral data

Support system

Determination of whether the physical and emotional environments are optimally supportive

Determination of whether attitudes and expectations are appropriate

Formulation

What is the problem?

Where is the problem located?

- Individual (e.g., psychiatric or physical illness)
- Caregivers (e.g., inappropriate expectations or staffing structure)
- Support system (e.g., lack of appropriate services)
- Philosophy of care (e.g., insistence on chronological, rather than developmental, age-appropriate behaviors)

What further information or data is required?

What further investigations (e.g., medical) are required?

What intervention or treatment is needed for the individual? For caregivers? For the system?

Source: Bradley and Summers (2003).

[a]Before gathering information, identify a reliable and knowledgeable informant

[b]Prior to, and since, onset of concerns

cal and medical disorders that can give rise to painful conditions (e.g., arthritis in adults with Down syndrome). Other problems—such as orthopedic, gastrointestinal, nutritional, feeding, pulmonary, cardiac, endocrine, urological, gynecological, dermatological, and dental problems—may also give rise to pain and distress. Some syndromes (e.g., Down, Williams, Prader-Willi) are associated with particular medical conditions and specific psychological and behavior patterns (Dykens et al., 2000). Identifying such syndromes—and, when possible, the cause of the intellectual disabilities—is an important part of assessment, as this may direct attention to medical disorders and painful conditions that might otherwise remain hidden.

Expectations and Support Needs Intellectual disabilities encompass significant impairments in cognitive and adaptive functioning. The latter involves deficits in conceptual, social, and practical skills (Luckasson et al., 2002). Each person with an intellectual disability is unique in his or her blend of adaptive abilities and skills, and he or she may demonstrate considerable strengths in some areas and considerable weaknesses in others. Some strengths may hide or mask weakness in other areas and give rise to unreasonable expectations of the individual, which in turn can lead to emotional and psychiatric disturbance. For instance, good conversational and social skills may mask severe difficulties in understanding (as in Williams syndrome). Assessment of behavior disturbance therefore includes an assessment of the person's psychological profile, including adaptive functioning, and an assessment of the environment supporting that person, including the expectations of caregivers (and including teachers if the individual is still in school).

Emotional Disorders People with intellectual disabilities develop along a different developmental pathway because of atypical juxtaposition of developmental and social milestones, caused by the interaction of the intellectual disabilities and the habilitative system set up to deal with it (Levitas & Gilson 1994). They often experience circumstances that might be expected to predispose or give rise to emotional disturbances. In fact, adults with intellectual disabilities are seven times more likely to report inadequate emotional support compared with adults without disabilities (Havercamp et al., 2004). Any associated disability—such as a language and communication disorder, sensory impairment, seizures, neurological impairment (including cerebral palsy), or pain and discomfort from physical disorders—has to be managed and accommodated. Early experiences may have interfered with early bonding and personality development, adversely affecting the person's response to stress, coping strategies, and capacities to develop social supports and friendships. People with intellectual disabilities are generally at risk for stigmatization, rejection, and teasing by peers. They often develop poor self-esteem and self-image in societies that value achievement, independence, and conformity. Opportunities for satisfactory work and leisure pursuits and for intimate relationships are often greatly limited. Most people with intellectual disabilities have experienced disadvantaged environments, and some have lived in abusive situations. It is not surprising that behavior disturbance associated with emotional problems is often as severe as that associated with serious mental illness. Distinguishing between these two underlying causes, however, is often difficult, as they frequently coexist. As for the general population, there is increasing awareness of gender issues across the life span (Bradley, Lunsky, & Korossy, 2005).

Identification of Psychiatric Disorders

In areas where there is no network of specialist psychiatric services for people with intellectual disabilities, family doctors or local emergency services are most frequently involved when psychiatric disturbances occur. At these times, an appropriate immediate response is often to stabilize the situation with medication. However, medication should be reviewed at the earliest opportunity and a more comprehensive assessment begun to identify whether a psychiatric disorder is indeed present or whether the problems are related to the other considerations outlined in the previous sections (i.e., physical health and medical issues, expectations and support needs, and emotional responses) (Bradley & Lofchy, 2005; Summers, Boyd, & Morgan, 2004). A decrease in behavior disturbance in response to medications (most often antipsychotics) that are used at a time of crisis does not imply that a psychiatric disorder is present. Indeed, such medications are known to mask some conditions (for a review, see Crabbe, 1989), many contribute further to the intellectual disability by impairing or slowing down the person's ability to focus and think clearly, and many have side effects. In people who already have difficulties communicating bodily discomforts, these side effects may give rise to further behavior disturbance. It is prudent, therefore, to distinguish clearly between managing the behavior disturbance and treating the underlying cause giving rise to this disturbance (see Figure 42.2).

Some syndromes are associated with a vulnerability to particular disorders. For example, dementia of the Alzheimer type and depression are associated with Down syndrome, attention problems and overactivity with fragile X syndrome, and anxiety disorders with Williams syndrome (Dykens et al., 2000). Comorbid psychiatric disorders—such as attention-deficit/hyperactivity disorder (ADHD), stereotypies, anxiety, obsessive-compulsive disorder (OCD), phobias and fears, and tics—should be systematically identified when present (see Caron & Rutter, 1991). The clinical presentation of new onset disorders, such as mood and psychotic disorders, may be distorted by these preexisting disorders, and, unless the latter are identified as background behaviors, misdiagnoses may be made. For example, an increase in "bizarre" self-talk in someone with autism can easily be mistaken for schizophrenia, or, an escalation of behavior disturbance in someone with ADHD and limited verbal skills, can be mistaken for mania. A good psychiatric assessment, therefore, requires a detailed description of baseline (usual) behaviors prior to the onset of the new disturbance (see Bradley & Bolton, 2006).

Changes in behavior are examined to identify whether they meet standard diagnostic criteria, using standard classification systems such as the *Diagnostic and Statistical Manual of Mental Health, Fourth Edition, Text Revision* (*DSM-IV-TR;* American Psychiatric Association, 2000) and the *International Classification of Diseases-10* (*ICD-10;* World Health Organization [WHO], 1992) for psychiatric disorders. From the standpoint of these classification systems, people with intellectual disabilities constitute a subculture; thus, criteria must be modified to account for the differences in opportunity to display symptoms in a life structured by others, differences in how symptoms may be articulated at different levels of cognitive functioning, or ways that symptoms may be reported or observed by caregivers rather than by self-report (see Levitas, Hurley, & Pary, 2001; Levitas & Silka, 2001; Pary, Levitas, & Hurley, 1999; Sovner, 1986). For example, the common experience of self-talk can easily be mistaken by inexperienced clinicians for hallucinations. Classification systems and diagnostic approaches that have been modified to be more appropriate for people with intellectual disabilities are now available (Deb et al., 2001; Royal College of Psychiatrists, 2001; WHO, 1996).

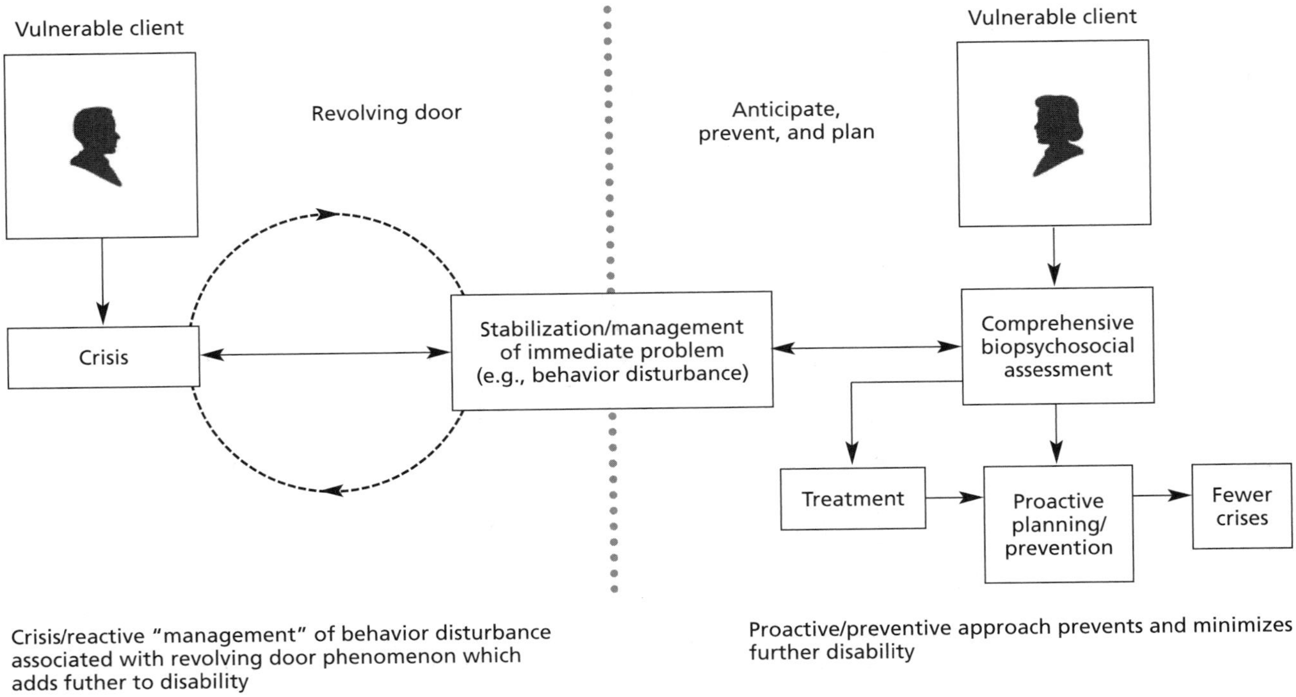

Figure 42.2. Reactive versus proactive responses to psychiatric/behavior disturbance in vulnerable individuals. (*Source:* Bradley & Summers, 2003.)

Changes in behavior can be used as markers (or target behaviors) for monitoring the effectiveness of the treatment offered. However, suppression of unwanted behaviors should never be mistaken for adequate treatment of an underlying psychiatric disorder. For example, an antipsychotic medication can suppress irritability and associated aggression but do nothing to treat the depression causing these symptoms.

The goal of the psychiatric assessment is to identify and diagnose any psychiatric disorder and to treat it—optimally, without adding either to the intellectual disability or to any physical problem. A further goal is to identify stressors and other circumstances that contribute to, or precipitate, the psychiatric or behavior disturbance so that future crises and relapses can be prevented or minimized.

Because of the complexity in diagnosing psychiatric disorders among people with intellectual disabilities, there is often uncertainty as to the precise diagnosis. When this occurs, the steps to follow are

1. Generate the best diagnostic hypothesis using information currently available
2. Collect data to confirm or refute this hypothesis
3. Review these data along with the results of the assessments in other areas (e.g., psychological, communication, environmental, expectations)

By following this approach, it should be possible to minimize the potential for inappropriate treatment, particularly with psychotropic medication (see the clinical scenario in Display 42.2).

The comprehensive psychiatric assessment of the person with intellectual disability is usually an ongoing and dynamic process that may take several months. It requires a coordinated approach across all of the settings where the individual spends time, including inpatient and outpatient settings if hospital admission is required (Bradley & Hollins, 2006).

Assessing and correctly diagnosing psychiatric disorders in this population requires an understanding and experience of intellectual disabilities and of psychiatric disorders. Assessment is best done within an interdisciplinary team context, working closely with caregivers who know the individual best. During the assessment process, specialist input may be required from many perspectives, including medicine (developmental pediatrics, genetics, psychiatry, neurology, family medicine, audiology, ophthalmology), nursing, psychology, speech-language pathology, behavior therapy, and occupational therapy and/or physiotherapy. Review of old records can be invaluable, as can information from family members.

An effective team develops a systematic approach to assessment and treatment and uses valid and reliable instruments and procedures. Team members are experienced in working with individuals with intellectual disabilities and are able to adapt their usual clinical ap-

Display 42.2

Case Study: Dave

Dave, age 22, was referred to the Community Dual Diagnosis Team by his community psychiatrist, who felt "out of his depth." Despite knowing Dave for many years and helping him through two periods of distress during adolescence, the underlying diagnosis remained unclear and Dave was not responding to conventional treatment approaches.

Dave was the middle child of an academic family; he was identified as having mild intellectual disability at an early age, but this had largely been ignored within the family. Dave himself had internalized expectations of academic success and was unable to enjoy some successes in other aspects of his life. Feelings of worth and self-esteem were closely tied to academic achievement. High school was a very difficult time for Dave; he struggled to keep up. He identified with the students heading toward university and felt very rejected when he was not accepted into their friendship groups. Dave succeeded in graduating from a modified high school program through hard work, good attendance, and an understanding school principal. He enrolled in college but had to leave because it was too stressful. Two years after graduating from high school, Dave started to hear voices. He described people calling him "retard"; he was tearful, agitated, and lethargic; and he said he did not want to live. At this time, Dave had also experienced a number of recent life events, including a rejection from a girlfriend and his friends going off and living together and he was not included. Physical examination and routine laboratory investigations were normal. An initial diagnostic hypothesis of depressive illness was made and he was started on an antidepressant and supportive psychotherapy. His mood improved, but the voices remained. An antipsychotic was started, resulting in fewer experiences of hearing voices. Any attempt to reduce the antipsychotic medication resulted in a return of the voices, however, requiring that the medication be reinstated at higher doses. Even with the antipsychotic medication, Dave continued to hear voices at times of high anxiety (e.g., when his program was too stressful, when he was out in crowds, when he was seeking the attention of peers). The voices were always derogatory, and he believed they came from people present (although some distance away) in his immediate environment.

The underlying disorder giving rise to Dave's behavior and mental experiences was not clear initially. His intellectual disability and concreteness limited his capacity to share, or to see the relevance of sharing, these experiences with his psychiatrist. Furthermore, when hearing the voices, he became hostile and paranoid and refused to discuss them (perhaps because of cognitive confusion and fear). More detail about these experiences would have been helpful; from the information available, Dave's new therapist considered a number of psychiatric disorders: psychotic disorder, including schizophrenia; major depressive disorder; anxiety disorder, including social phobia; and posttraumatic stress disorder (in the form of flashbacks from experiences in school). Working from a biopsychosocial perspective and acknowledging the impact of Dave's intellectual disability on his clinical presentation, the therapist generated a diagnostic hypothesis (rather than making a more definitive diagnosis based on less-than-adequate information). From this she was able to formulate an intervention plan, including a procedure to identify and collect further information that would support (or refute) the working diagnosis. The intervention plan included a process to review the working diagnosis to determine whether this needed to be modified, given the further information available and given Dave's response to the intervention.

Source: Bradley and Summers (2003).

proaches appropriately to the broad spectrum of functioning levels seen in this group. Such a team should be able to focus the assessment in appropriate areas, be able to coordinate the assessment findings in a meaningful manner, and be able to provide a balanced formulation on which treatment recommendations should be based. Fragmented or incomplete assessments and those conducted by professionals who are unfamiliar with the emotional responses of people with intellectual disabilities unfortunately contribute to misdiagnoses and inappropriate—and sometimes harmful—treatments.

Treatment and Intervention

Initially, treatment may be more focused on the *management* of the behavior disturbance until a clearer understanding of its cause is available. A comprehensive assessment will indicate the presence (or absence) of a psychiatric disorder and will provide information not only on circumstances that may be underlying the behavior disturbance but also on circumstances that exacerbate or maintain these and other behaviors (even after the initial cause is no longer present). During the assessment period, various crisis interventions (most often medication or behavioral) may be implemented to manage serious or dangerous behaviors. The individual's responses to these interventions should be monitored and documented carefully, as they may provide further insights into the underlying cause of the disturbance and may be relevant to future treatment recommendations (e.g., it is important to note how the patient responded to being restrained). As a clearer understanding of the underlying disorder becomes available, treatment becomes more focused and individualized (see Tables 42.2 and 42.3).

Just as assessment follows a biopsychosocial approach, so do the interventions (Table 42.2). After a diagnosis, medication is required only to the extent that it is recommended for the optimal treatment of a clearly defined psychiatric disorder or disorders (e.g., a person with autism might also have bipolar disorder and panic disorder). Effective treatment involves educating the patient and caregivers about the disorder(s), treatment options, and strategies to minimize relapses and promote mental well-being. It is important to map out a proactive response to crisis or relapse, with a clear outline of the involvement of community, emergency, and inpatient services. This will stabilize the system supporting the individual and consolidate the treatment plan, minimize anxiety and the escalation of distress in both the person with intellectual disability and his or her caregivers, and, most importantly, ensure continuity of care and specialized treatment (an example of this approach is outlined in Display 42.1).

With counseling or psychotherapy, individuals can be helped to develop alternative coping strategies, learn to modulate their emotional responses, and manage frustration and stress more effectively. Caregivers have a key role in managing the amount of stress in the individual's environment (e.g., stress from a noisy work environment when the person has a hearing impairment, stress from inappropriate expectations given the individual's developmental level) and in helping them to gain access to lifestyles that promote physical and emotional well-being (e.g., attention to physical health and medical disorders, friendships, inclusion in work and recreational activities; see Table 42.3).

Research into the psychological and behavioral aspects of various syndromes has gained prominence (for a review of syndromes and behavioral phenotypes, see Dykens et al., 2000; O'Brien & Yule, 1996; Rondal et al., 2004), giving rise to the concept of a behavioral phenotype; this refers to behavioral traits and patterns of psychiatric disorder particular to specific intellectual disability syndromes (Dykens, 1995; Levitas & Hurley, 2001). Coupled with autobiographical accounts by some individuals with these syndromes (e.g., see Kingsley & Levitz, 1994, for Down syndrome; Lenhoff et al., 1997, for Williams syndrome; Grandin & Scariano, 1986, and Williams, 1992, 1994, for autism), this new knowledge offers an opportunity to design environments and supports that are more sensitive to the challenges experienced by these individuals. People with autism, for example, appear to be at greater risk for psychiatric disorder than people with intellectual disabilities without autism, and they may present with severe behavior disturbance. A broader understanding of the experience of individuals with autism and of the disabilities associated with autism allows a greater appreciation for the confusion and stress in their daily pattern of social life. These broader perspectives encourage the development of services that can optimally support individuals with autism and minimize the stress they experience.

Table 42.2. Treatment principles

Principle	Conditions that address principle
Decrease organic/biological contribution (to mental health disturbances) to prevent the occurrence of secondary disorders and disabilities	Attention to sensory impairments Attention to physical impairments Treatment of seizures Treatment of other medical disorders Treatment of psychiatric disorders and/or symptoms that respond to psychotropic medications
Decrease stress	Appropriate environments Appropriate expectations Appropriate supports to match the level of functioning and adaptive skills
Increase competence	Increased coping skills Increased self-esteem Increased social supports and promotion of systems of support
Develop a coordinated system of supports around the person	Continuity of care (e.g., when moving from inpatient to outpatient status) Identification of generic and specialist supports (e.g., physicians, nurses, behavior support specialist, case manager) and how and when to obtain these Development of proactive crises management protocols

Source: Bradley and Summers (2003).

Table 42.3. Treatment approaches

- Communication assistance
- Behavior support and skills development
- Environmental alteration
- Education for the client, family, and caregivers about intellectual disability and mental health
- Caregiver and staff support
- System interventions
- Counseling
- Psychotherapy (e.g., individual, family, group, cognitive)
- Psychopharmacology

Source: Bradley and Summers (2003).

People with intellectual disabilities and psychiatric disorders require regular follow-up and careful monitoring of their medication. Shared care involving a psychiatrist, nurse, and family doctor with access to specialist services (e.g., psychology, behavior management, counseling/psychotherapy) can work well. In some areas (e.g., England and parts of the United States), community psychiatric nurses are core members of the treatment team and play a crucial role in ensuring that the person has access to appropriate health care. In Canada, however, the nursing role in supporting individuals with intellectual disabilities and mental health problems remains largely unrecognized, and few nurses are trained to practice in this area. In some localities, generic (or nonspecialized) community nurses may become involved with specific people for a limited time. Generally speaking, the relative roles of the nurse, psychiatrist, and family doctor at any time during treatment are determined by the needs of the individual, the service context within which each of these professionals works, and the comfort level of each in working with people with intellectual disabilities.

Barriers

Although people with intellectual disabilities in Australia, Canada, England, and the United States have, in principle, access to the full spectrum of services available to all citizens, in many situations there are still significant barriers that impede access to and benefits from these services. For this population it is therefore relevant to differentiate between access in principle and access in practice (sometimes referred to as *equity of access*).

In many countries, people with intellectual disabilities and mental health needs are described as tending to fall through the gaps in and between services. This is often due to the relatively separate operation of mental health and developmental service sectors. In places where there has been comparatively little joint planning and activity between the two sectors, professionals and caregivers receive little or no training or experience with crossover issues. Some additional factors that affect the provision of mental health services include the following:

- Services have exclusionary criteria, which result in many people with intellectual disabilities being denied access to generic services.
- There is a need to utilize the expertise offered by different disciplines (e.g., psychiatry, family medicine, psychology, behavior therapy, speech-language pathology, neurology, developmental pediatrics, genetics, occupational therapy, physiotherapy, nursing) in complex cases; this may be difficult to arrange due to a lack of professionals with relevant training and experience, and problems coordinating this type of input.
- There is a need for professional staff to modify traditional procedures and approaches due to differences among people with intellectual disabilities in cognitive and communicative functioning. For example, it takes longer to assess and treat an individual with an intellectual disability and a mental health problem than it does for a person without an intellectual disability. The existing generic system is not easily able to accommodate this additional time requirement.
- Reimbursement schedules often do not permit physicians and other health care providers to be appropriately compensated for the amount of time that the clinical care may require.
- Individuals with intellectual disabilities do not always behave as "typical" patients, which can leave staff feeling bewildered, unskilled, and sometimes angry and terrified if their best treatments and intentions only result in further escalation of disruptive behaviors. Professionals may feel out of their depth due to lack of training or experience. This can lead to negative stereotyping of people with intellectual disabilities and avoidance of getting involved with them in the future.
- Budget cuts threaten existing services and place individuals with developmental disabilities at even further disadvantage in trying to gain access to appropriate services.
- There is a lack of infrastructure and clear lines of responsibility and accountability within which to address gaps in the provision and coordination of services.

INTERNATIONAL PERSPECTIVES

As noted, intellectual disabilities and behavioral, emotional, and psychiatric disturbances may be addressed or referred to differently according to country. This section presents perspectives from Australia, Canada, England, and the United States.

Australia

Three specific issues for Australia are prevalence, service context, and training. Each is discussed next.

Prevalence Comprehensive information is available from a longitudinal study of an epidemiological sample of young people with intellectual disability (Einfeld & Tonge, 1996a, 1996b; Tonge & Einfeld, 2003). The sample was gathered in 1991 and has been systematically followed up every 3–4 years since, with an ongoing participation rate of more than 80%. The initial sample comprised 597 young people with intellectual disabilities ages 4–18 years who were receiving any health, education, or welfare services in five census regions in the states of New South Wales and Victoria. These regions are representative of the full range of Australian urban, rural, ethnic, and social class communities, containing approximately 179,000 young people. The sample comprised virtually all young people with moderate or more severe levels of intellectual disabilities, but as with other studies, those with mild intellectual disabilities were underrepresented because all do not all receive identified services; they merge with the general community and it is not possible to conduct cognitive assessments of the entire population.

A range of biopsychosocial information was gathered by questionnaire at each follow-up, including education, daily activities, child temperament, living circumstances, life events, social networks, parental mental health, and family function. There were also separately obtained groups of young people with Down syndrome (n = 74), fragile X syndrome (n = 61), Prader-Willi syndrome (n = 50), Williams syndrome (n = 66), and autistic disorder (n =111).

The main measure of psychopathology was the *Developmental Behavior Checklist* (DBC; Einfeld & Tonge, 2002). This is a reliable and valid 96-item questionnaire completed by parents or caregivers (DBC–P) or teachers (DBC–T) that assesses the broad range of emotional and behavior disturbance associated with intellectual disabilities. It produces a total score which reflects the overall level of psychopathology, including "psychiatric caseness"—a cutoff score above which an experienced clinician would agree that the young person had emotional and behavior problems of sufficient severity to justify psychiatric treatment. The DBC also has five factorially derived subscales that define syndromes of disruptive/antisocial, communication disturbance, self absorbed, social relating, and anxiety problems. This study has found that the prevalence of clinically significant psychopathology in 4- to 18-year-old young people with intellectual disabilities is approximately 47% (Tonge & Einfeld, 2003). Of concern, only 10% of these young people were receiving any specific mental health service. Young people with autism, Prader-Willi syndrome, or Williams syndrome had higher levels of psychopathology than the epidemiological sample. Those with Down syndrome had lower levels of disturbance, but even for these individuals, approximately 30% were "psychiatric cases" and specifically had problems with disruptive and oppositional behavior. These findings reflect the likelihood that biological factors, such as the expression of a behavioral phenotype, contribute to the causes of psychopathology in these vulnerable populations (Einfeld et al., 1999). Clearly, the significantly higher levels of mental health problems in people with intellectual disabilities are due to a complex interaction of biopsychosocial factors. In this study, the level of intellectual disability was not a predictor of psychopathology apart from those with profound intellectual disability who have relatively low levels of disturbance—perhaps because of their limited capacity to interact with others. People with greater intellectual disability had more problems with self-absorbed behaviors and those with mild intellectual disabilities were more likely to have disruptive and antisocial behavior problems (Tonge & Einfeld, 2003).

Difficult childhood temperamental characteristics of emotionality and overactivity were predictors of psychopathology. Poor parental mental health was both a consequence and a predictor of emotional and behavioral problems in these young people over time. A limited social network was a predictor of subsequent mental health problems. This is an important finding because it points to the probability that early intervention, which increases the range of social contact for children with intellectual disabilities and their families, might promote mental health. Well-controlled epilepsy was not associated with poor mental health, but the risk of psychopathology tripled if epilepsy was not effectively treated (Lewis et al., 2000).

Over time, as the young people are moving into adult life, the prevalence of psychopathology significantly reduces to approximately 35% (Tonge & Einfeld, 2003). This level of serious mental health problems is still at least twice that of the general population. Problems with disruptive and attention-deficit hyperactive symptoms significantly decrease from childhood into adult life, as is the case for the general population. Symptoms of depressive illness rise during adolescence, emphasizing the adverse consequences for adults with intellectual disabilities when affective disorder is undiagnosed and untreated. Fortunately, the level of psychopathology, particularly anxiety, falls significantly as individuals with Williams syndrome become adults. Young adults with Prader-Willi syndrome face a 30% risk of developing a schizophreniform psychosis, particularly those with the XXX form of the syndrome, and already approximately 20% of the original group have died, many from obesity-related conditions (Einfeld et al., 1999).

Service Context Australia is a commonwealth of states in which each state has responsibility for health, education, and welfare services for people with intellectual disabilities. There is generally a degree of uniformity among these services. Specific services for individuals with intellectual disabilities are not usually provided until a child enters primary school at age 6. Prior to this early intervention, preschool, and maternal and child health services are available to young children with developmental delay. Eligibility criteria for the receipt of intellectual disabilities services are similar to those in the *ICD-10* (WHO, 1992) and the *Diagnostic and Statistical Manual of Mental Disorders, Fourth Edition* (*DSM-IV;* American Psychiatric Association, 1994), including both a cognitive assessment of subaverage intellectual functioning and impairments in adaptive functioning beginning during childhood. The range of specific services includes case management, respite care, family support, disability pensions, special education, education aide funding, workplace support, special employment or day programs, and community residential unit placement or support accommodation.

Most states have a disability services Act of Parliament, which legislates services and includes a services review tribunal that acts to protect the rights of a person with an intellectual disability. The legislature and bureaucracy that provides for mental health services is separate. Therefore, an individual with an intellectual disability who also has a mental illness may fall between mental health and intellectual disability services, with neither side accepting responsibility. Some states such as Victoria have made an attempt to address this issue by establishing an intellectual disabilities and mental health consultation service, but these only receive enough funding to address the most obvious and problematic cases.

On the positive side, Australia has a universal system of health services delivery (Medicare), which enables people with intellectual disabilities to obtain general and specialist medical services. The high level of medical and mental health needs in people with intellectual disabilities has been well researched and identified in Australia, and the standards of medical care are improving (Lennox & Beange, 1999; Lennox & Diggens, 1999). The challenge of providing services to isolated rural areas are well identified; all medical schools have departments of rural health, and all medical students spend part of their training in rural settings. Indigenous Australians face poor health, unemployment, dispossession, and substance abuse and have a life expectancy no better than the poorest regions of developing countries (Australian Bureau of Statistics [ABS], 2001, 2002, 2003). The desperate national challenge to deliver basic health services to indigenous Australians totally overshadows attention on the mental health need of these marginalized groups. There is a lack of adequate data and understanding of intellectual disability in indigenous Australians, and this—together with the need to effectively respond to their mental health needs—is an urgent national health priority.

Training The training of professionals in intellectual disability and mental health issues is relatively haphazard. There are no formal training requirements for the poorly paid education aides and residential care staff, although an increasing number of courses are available in colleges of technical and further education. Intellectual disability nursing is no longer a special branch of nursing, but individuals pursuing generic nursing undergraduate degrees at universities learn a valuable degree of information about intellectual disabilities in their courses. Specific disability studies and undergraduate and postgraduate degree courses, usually in association with departments of psychology, are now available at a few universities. There are centers of disability health associated with university medical schools in Queensland, New South Wales, and Victoria, which provide teaching in medical and psychology courses and particularly focus on general medical practitioner training. There is no specific specialist training in intellectual disabilities and mental health for psychiatrists, although the training regulations for the Royal Australian and New Zealand College of Psychiatrists recognize the need for this topic to be covered in general psychiatry training. However, only a handful of psychiatrists in Australia are recognized as specialists in this field of dual disability. The Third National Mental Health Policy makes only passing reference to the unmet mental health needs of individuals with intellectual disabilities, which is a numerically bigger problem than schizophrenia (Tonge & Einfeld, 2003).

Canada

As with Australia, issues of particular relevance in Canada include prevalence, service context, and training. Perspectives on each topic follow.

Prevalence Two epidemiological studies have been conducted in Canada. The first study was set in Nova Scotia. It reported the prevalence of autism (in children ages 6–14 years) to be at least 10 per 10,000, with a male:female ratio of 2.5:1; approximately 75% of this population with autism had intellectual disability (Bryson, Clarke, & Smith, 1988). The second study was set in the Niagara Region of Ontario (Bradley, Thompson, & Bryson, 2002). It reported a prevalence of autism in at least 25% of people with intellectual disabilities in the population of 14- to 20-year-olds (Bryson & Bradley, 2006). In this study, those with autism were matched on age, gender, and nonverbal IQ scores to those without autism; it revealed that the former had experienced significantly more episodes of psychiatric illness (Bradley, Bolton, & Bryson, 2004). These episodes were primarily related to depression and adjustment disorders and less frequently bipolar disorder. A small but significant number of individuals (again, more in the autism group) suffered unclassifiable disorders that were characterized by particularly severe and complex symptomatology and deterioration in functioning, from which they had not recovered (Bradley & Bolton, 2006). A comparison of the autism and non-autism groups with severe intellectual disability showed significantly greater disturbance in the autism group, as measured by a mental health screening tool with specific vulnerabilities to anxiety, mood, sleep, organic syndromes, and stereotypies/tics (Bradley, Summers, et al., 2004); across the range of functioning there were differences between autism and non-autism groups in attention, hyperactive and impulsive behaviors (Bradley & Isaacs, 2006).

Service Context Canada lags behind other nations (cf. Australia: Beange, Lennox, & Parmenter, 1999, & Lennox & Diggins, 1999; the United Kingdom: U.K. Department of Health, 2001; and the United States: U.S. Department of Health and Human Services, 2002a, 2002b) in developing a national agenda that recognizes, and sets standards of care to address, the health care needs of people with intellectual disabilities. This situation may be related in part to issues involving logistics and critical mass. Canada is a vast country (it has a land mass of 9 million square kilometers and is divided into 10 provinces and 3 territories) with a small population base (30 million people in 2001). There are several unifying themes to health and social care across Canada: Canada provides free, universal health care and has a charter of rights and freedoms, both of which shape human services nationally. The Ministries of Health and Social Services are funded jointly by federal and provincial governments. This administrative arrangement can work as a barrier to local initiatives; for example, a proposal for a national plan to increase teaching and professional capacity in intellectual disabilities, accompanied by letters of intent from 15 of the 16 university departments of psychiatry across the country, was unsuccessful in securing federal funding, as support from each province and territory had not first been negotiated (McCreary, 1998).

Historically, the province of Ontario (which is the third largest province) has spearheaded change and innovation in the field of intellectual disabilities. Possible reasons for this include its large population base (as of 2007, approximately 11 million people, representing one third of Canada's total population) and the fact that the nation's capital (Ottawa) and most populous city (Toronto) are located there, creating a critical capacity and necessary momentum for change. Although details may differ among the different provinces and territories, the historical context and current service challenges in providing appropriate health care to those with intellectual disabilities (Ouellette-Kuntz et al., 2004), and in particular those with dual diagnosis (Lunsky & Bradley, 2001), appear to be similar across the country.

As institutions were being closed, it was assumed that people with intellectual disabilities would successfully gain access to generic health services. In Ontario, for example, the closure of 13 of its 16 institutions since the 1970s (representing 6,000 beds), without accompanying policies to build community capacity, has resulted in significant loss of knowledgeable and skilled professional and support staff. Furthermore, when these changes also involved transfer of lead agency from health to social services (as happened in Ontario in 1974), there has been an erosion of understanding of the specialist health needs of this group. By contrast, the province of British Columbia on the west coast of Canada closed all its institutions for people with intellectual disabilities as of 1996. The money freed up with these closures was transferred from the social services agency to the health agency and now supports specialized mental health support teams for people with intellectual disabilities in all five health authorities.

Since the mid-1990s, greater awareness that people with intellectual disabilities have an increased prevalence of behavioral and psychiatric disturbance has, across Canada, lead to discussions, pilot projects, and policy guidelines for people with dual diagnosis; Alberta, British Columbia, Ontario, and Saskatchewan are among several provinces with policy documents on dual diagnosis and/or challenging behaviors. Unfortunately, this concept of dual diagnosis is somewhat narrow in scope, focusing on established disturbances and ignoring the proactive preventive approaches that should be available to all members of the group given their greater vulnerability to mental health disorders. Canada has benefited from mental health advocacy organizations in the United States (e.g., National Association for the Dually Diagnosed [NADD]), and some provinces have formed associations, such as the Ontario chapter of NADD, the Ontario Association on Developmental Disabilities (OADD), and British Columbia Association for Mental Health in Developmental Disability (BC AMHiDD). With joint support from the

Ontario Ministries of Health and Social Services, for instance, the Ontario chapter of NADD was able to lead a project to develop a provincial dual diagnosis training curriculum (Griffiths, Stavrakaki, & Summers, 2002). However, family members and service providers continue to describe many frustrations with current services, which in part perhaps reflects the continued lack of central (federal and provincial) leadership in recognizing and articulating the unique health needs of this population.

Training Professional training in intellectual disabilities in Canada has also struggled at many different levels. Some of the underlying reasons include 1) lack of federal recognition of the needs of this population; 2) absence of national standards of care that could drive the accreditation and certification processes at the professional colleges level; and 3) absence of academic programs and secure career paths at the local level to ensure that the necessary infrastructure to support and encourage good clinical practice is developed, maintained, and sustained (see Bradley et al., 2005).

There are two chairs in intellectual disabilities in Canada, both in Ontario (at the University of Western Ontario [UWO] and Queen's University), and both funded by the provincial Social Services Ministry. For a number of years, the Developmental Disabilities Division at UWO has published *Clinical Bulletin* and hosted a web site that provides information and updates on current practice in the field of intellectual disabilities, including mental health issues (http://www.psychiatry.med.uwo.ca/ddp). There has been interest in the profile of people with dual diagnosis who use tertiary mental health services (Lunsky et al., 2003) and in the role of this system in meeting some of these people's needs (Cochrane et al., 2000; Goering et al., 1998). There is clearly a continued interest and commitment from practitioners and researchers in the field across the country, as demonstrated by participation at conferences in Ontario (McCreary et al., 2001) and British Columbia (Lunsky, Bradley, & Korrosy, 2002). As a result of these sustained activities over the years, a recognized network across Canada of concerned clinicians, researchers and consumers has been established with the support of the Canadian Institute of Health Research (HEIDI program—http://www.heidiresearch.ca). This network is now providing a national forum for discussion, national meetings and conferences, and opportunities for collaborative education and research activities (e.g., see http://www.autismtraining.ca). For the first time, a national survey of services for people with dual diagnosis has been completed (http://www.heidiresearch.ca), as has the business plan for a Canadian Association for Research and Education in Intellectual Disabilities (CARE-ID/ACREDI; http://www.care-id.com).

England

Issues relevant to England include prevalence, policy/legislation, service context, training, and challenges and opportunities. The following sections present details on each.

Prevalence There is evidence to suggest that people with learning disabilities in the United Kingdom are at least as likely, and indeed are probably more likely, to develop mental health problems than the general population (Deb et al., 2001). Research has examined risk factors associated with the presence of psychopathology in people with learning disability (Cowley et al., 2004). In this study, data were collected from 742 people who had been referred to a specialist mental health service for people with learning disabilities. The presence of certain features in the person's history was associated with a diagnosis of a mental disorder (i.e., older age, mild learning disabilities, previous admission to a psychiatric unit, referral from generic mental health services, and previous detention under mental health legislation). Other features were associated with a lower prevalence of mental health disorder (i.e., severe learning disabilities, epilepsy, living in the family home).

Policy/Legislation The White Paper (a statement of what the Government recommends, rather than a law) *Valuing People* (U.K. Department of Health, 2001) sets out the vision of how services in England for people with learning disabilities should be shaped. It promotes deinstitutionalization, which in 2006 is almost complete and is underpinned by four key principles: rights, independence, choice, and inclusion. It emphasizes that whenever possible, people with learning disabilities should use general health services, including mental health services. The National Service Framework (NSF) for Mental Health (U.K. Department of Health, 1999) gives an overview of how mental health services should be developed and improved. It sets out seven standards that are applicable to all adults of working age, including people with learning disabilities. Local Implementation Teams are responsible for monitoring the implementation of the NSF and are expected to link with the local Partnership Boards responsible for implementing *Valuing People.* The Mental Health Act (1983) is the legal framework that is concerned with the care and treatment of those with mental health problems in England and Wales. It is currently being ammeded. The Mental Capacity Act (2005), The Human Rights Act (2000), and the Disability Discrimination Act (1995) are other pieces of legislation that are particularly relevant to people with learning disabilities.

Service Context In England, community learning disability teams support people with learning disabilities. These teams are multiprofessional and may be led by health or social services agencies. They provide a range of inputs, including physical and mental health care, resettlement, and social care. *Valuing People* (U.K. Department of Health, 2001) proposes that these teams refocus to enable access to general services as much as possible. This will result in general mental health services being increasingly required to care for people with learning disabilities and mental health problems, although it is recognized that some will need specialist provision. Guidance has been published (U.K. Department of Health, 2004) to facilitate the production of protocols between generic and specialist mental health services to ensure that this happens in a planned and coordinated way. There continues to be a debate as to the most appropriate service model, especially with the lack of an adequate evidence base on which to base decisions (Bouras & Holt, in press).

Training In the United Kingdom, doctors must complete approved psychiatric training for a minimum of 6 years' duration and pass the Membership of the Royal College of Psychiatrists exams before becoming a National Health Service (NHS) consultant psychiatrist. All trainees have clinical placements in general adult psychiatry in addition to rotational clinical experience in a range of recognized specialties. Completion of a 6-month attachment in either child and adolescent or learning disabilities psychiatry (or a combination of the two) is necessary before going on to higher training so that everyone has experience in developmental psychiatry. Higher training can be in a number of specialties, including the psychiatry of learning disability.

Clinical psychologists undertake a postgraduate 3-year university course leading to a doctoral degree in clinical psychology, which is approved by the British Psychological Society. The academic program includes lectures on learning disability, and trainees may opt to complete a 6-month clinical placement in learning disability services. Nurses who work with people with learning disabilities and mental health problems may be registered mental nurses (RMNs) or registered learning disability nurses (RNLDs) following a 3-year diploma course. Both receive lectures on the needs of people with learning disabilities and mental health problems, but not all have the opportunity for clinical placement in this area.

Challenges and Opportunities People with learning disabilities are at risk of being placed out of district when local services are unable to meet their needs (Jaydeokar & Piachaud, 2004). This is particularly so for those with mental health problems and/or challenging behavior (Mitra & Alexander, 2003). Effective collaboration between specialist and generic mental health services is needed to improve the competence and capacity of local services. Clear service pathways are required so that no one falls between services. Service boundaries are sometimes disputed, for example, for people with learning disabilities who have mental health problems in association with autism spectrum disorders and those who have committed offenses or are perceived at being at high risk of doing so. In the United Kingdom, the tradition of training in the psychiatry of learning disabilities for those working in the mental health field, as well as for those wishing to specialize in this area, should help resolve these issues so that the mental health needs of this vulnerable group are appropriately met.

United States

Although historical details differ, the outcome of exclusion of people with intellectual disabilities from mental health services in the United States is virtually identical to that in Ontario, Canada. Prevalence data do not differ; the studies usually cited are the same on both sides of the border. Thus, the main issue to discuss is that of policy/legislation.

Policy/Legislation Mental Retardation Facilities and Community Mental Health Centers Construction Act of 1963 (PL 88-164) untangled what had been an indiscriminate institutional residential system into discrete systems for people with mental health problems and intellectual disabilities and created the bases for systems of community-based mental health treatment and intellectual disabilities habilitation. Implementation was left to the states, creating minor differences in practices but major differences in funding and outcome. Although separation of the two systems accomplished much, the separation of the funding streams, professional systems, and skills resulted in the creation of two competing, rather than cooperating, systems. As political and economic support for public health declined, people with both intellectual disabilities and mental health problems became caught between two increasingly overburdened systems. The distance between the systems was also widened as, on the intellectual disabilities side, the application of the doctrine of normalization interpreted mental health interventions as restrictive and, on the mental health side, the fear grew that as institutions were emptied and more individuals received care in the community, any behavior problem could be "dumped" on the mental health system as a psychiatric disorder. Funding for medical and mental health services for both populations typically is in the form of Medicaid, the state/federal medical insurance program for those living in poverty, adding poor reimbursement rates to the mix of reasons that intellectual disability became an exclusionary criterion for admission to many, if not most, psychiatric inpatient services.

The situation is further exacerbated by the fact that in the United States, "psychiatry of learning disabilities" (as it is known in the United Kingdom) is not a formal specialty or subspecialty. Typically, only child psychiatry trainees are required to have any exposure to people with intellectual disabilities; the vast majority of adult psychiatrists have no such experience, and very few psychiatrists in the course of training have any exposure to adults with intellectual disabilities. Few fellowships in psychiatry and intellectual disabilities have been proposed and fewer funded. Unfortunately, this situation overlaps with the rise of the use of psychiatric medications in all populations, leaving those with both an intellectual disability and a psychiatric disorder for the most part in inexpert hands.

The services that exist are for the most part the product of dedicated individuals and local conditions. Coordination of inpatient psychiatric services; outpatient psychiatric services; and intellectual disabilities residential, vocational, and educational services is, with few exceptions, ad hoc. The separated funding streams and other manifestations of systemic separation remain almost insuperable.

Both the American Psychiatric Association and the American Academy of Child and Adolescent Psychiatry have sections on mental retardation, and the American Association on Mental Retardation (AAMR) has a section on psychiatry; none of these groups has been able to mount an independent conference or special journal issue on the subject. The American Psychological Association has a division on mental retardation and developmental disabilities, and the Association for the Advancement of Behavior Therapy has a special interest group on developmental disabilities.

In 1994, the American Psychiatric Association Caucus for Psychiatrists Treating Persons With Mental Retardation/Developmental Disabilities did propose guidelines for fellowships in developmental disabilities psychiatry. Because no consensus or experimental verification exists concerning diagnostic criteria for psychiatric disorders in people with intellectual disability, the majority of extant literature on psychopharmacologic treatment ties drug use to behaviors. Among the few exceptions are *Psychotropic Medications and Developmental Disabilities: The International Consensus Handbook* (Reiss & Aman, 1998), co-published by AAMR and the Arc, and a special issue of AAMR's *American Journal on Mental Retardation* on psychopharmacologic and behavioral treatment (Rush & Frances, 2000).

In 1982, NADD was founded in Kingston, New York (one of the few places with an integrated mental health and intellectual disabilities service), by Robert Fletcher. At about the same time, Robert Sovner and Anne Hurley started the *Mental Health/Mental Retardation Newsletter.* The intent of both was to serve as sources and forums for information about approaches to the population of people who are dually diagnosed. NADD now holds international conferences; the newsletter has become *Mental Health Aspects of Developmental Disabilities,* a peer-reviewed quarterly. Both are dedicated to the ideas that 1) people with intellectual disabilities are subject to the same psychiatric disorders and mental health problems as others; 2) medications treat psychiatric disorders or symptoms of psychiatric disorders, not behaviors; 3) diagnostic criteria for psychiatric disorders must be modified for this population to take into account differences in development, life possibilities, communication ability, and differences unique to some intellectual disabilities syndromes.

NADD, in conjunction with the American Psychiatric Association, is developing *Diagnostic Manual for Persons with Intellectual Disabilities (Provisional Title).* Consensus modifications of *DSM-IV-TR* diagnostic criteria (the criteria most widely used in the United States for psychiatric diagnosis) will be proposed as a first step toward experimental verification. It is hoped that the availability of such diagnostic criteria will spread the expertise necessary to general psychiatrists, who are those most often faced with patients who have intellectual disabilities and psychiatric disorders. In addition, it is hoped that these criteria will make possible clinical studies of medications for psychiatric disorders similar to those in the literature available on people without intellectual disability, thereby leading to data-based approaches to the question of diagnosis-based versus behavior-based pharmacology and more informed psychopharmacologic treatment than now exists. Despite these potential changes, the systemic barriers to a comprehensive mental health approach to this population in the United States most likely awaits fundamental change to the entire health care system.

DEVELOPING A VISION OF A MENTAL HEALTH SERVICE THAT IS SENSITIVE TO THE NEEDS OF PEOPLE WITH INTELLECTUAL DISABILITIES

In reviewing the literature on service development and provision in this area (Bouras, 1995, 1999; Dosen, 1993, 1995; Jacobson & Mulick, 1996), certain requirements stand out as being particularly pertinent in the planning and delivery of mental health services sensitive to the needs of people with intellectual disabilities. These include the following:

- It is necessary to recognize the greater prevalence of mental health-related problems experienced by people with intellectual disabilities so that 1) resources can be targeted to those most at risk and 2) problems can be anticipated and prevented.

- There needs to be a sustained commitment to, and support for, developing a more integrated mental health system for people with intellectual disabilities.
- There should be workable protocols between different ministries or departments (e.g., health, social, education) and service sectors (e.g., housing, social, recreational supports).
- It is necessary to develop a spectrum of mental health and health-related services that are organized into a coordinated and cohesive network, including primary (e.g., family medicine), secondary (e.g., crisis and emergency services, community psychiatric services and access to general psychiatric inpatient services), and tertiary level services (e.g., consultation, assessment, and treatment of more complex problems, access to professionals with special expertise in intellectual disabilities and mental health problems); at each level, staff are needed who are experienced and comfortable working with people with intellectual disabilities.
- It is important to develop a life-span approach and coordinated services to facilitate life-span transitions (e.g., from services for children to services for adults).
- There is a need to integrate broad-based resources (e.g., case management, respite, home-based services, employment options, social and leisure supports, education, housing) into the mental health service system to address people's needs from a holistic perspective.
- There is a need to promote clinical and service excellence and innovation by partnering with universities and colleges to develop training, education, and research activities that focus on the needs of people with intellectual disabilities.
- There is a need to develop a process to bring together service providers from relevant service systems to identify common issues and promote joint "ownership" through collaborative problem-solving efforts.
- An appreciation of the concept of critical mass also appears to be crucial to the successful and effective development and delivery of mental health services for people with intellectual disabilities and for training professionals. Relative to their peers without disabilities, individuals with intellectual disabilities are few in number but have significantly greater health care needs. Health care professionals need to be exposed to a sufficiently large number of people with intellectual disabilities in order to develop knowledge, understanding, and expertise in the assessment and treatment of psychiatric and behavior disturbance.

People with intellectual disabilities and mental health problems present service challenges that can only be embraced by a truly biopsychosocial approach. Their needs span traditional administrative boundaries of health, social services, and education. Policies and initiatives that span traditional boundaries and combine funding and expertise provide the solid bedrock on which integrated services develop.

SUMMARY

This chapter has presented key issues in the assessment and treatment of mental health problems in people with intellectual disabilities and in the ways that service systems affect optimal assessment, treatment, and mental health support. There has been an explosion of knowledge in the biological and neurosciences and in clinical genetics. This knowledge already has relevance for further understanding of intellectual disabilities and for understanding (and therefore the assessment and treatment) of individuals who have intellectual disabilities and additional emotional problems, behavior disturbances, or psychiatric disorders. If individuals with intellectual disabilities are to benefit from this explosion of knowledge in a timely manner, it is imperative that effective research, academic (education and training), and clinical links are developed alongside the service systems responsible for the care and support of this vulnerable population (see Moss et al., 1997, for further exploration of these issues).

FOR FURTHER THOUGHT AND DISCUSSION

1. A friend has recently moved into your neighborhood. She is worried about her teenage daughter Sophie, who has started to stay up late at night and has become oppositional and stubborn. Sophie has Down syndrome. What might be going on, what assistance is required, and how would you help your friend obtain appropriate services in your area?
2. Consider the origins of negative attitudes toward people with intellectual disabilities. How do such attitudes affect access to good health care?
3. What is meant by a "proactive/preventive" and "crisis/reactive" health care services? Why is a proactive/preventive approach preferable to a crisis/reactive approach in the support of people with intellectual disabilities?

REFERENCES

American Psychiatric Association. (1994). *Diagnostic and statistical manual: Mental disorders* (4th ed.). Washington, DC: Author.

American Psychiatric Association. (2000). *Diagnostic and statistical manual: Mental disorders* (4th ed., text rev.). Washington, DC: Author.

Australian Bureau of Statistics. (2001). *Population characteristics, Aboriginal and Torres Strait Islander Australians* (No. 4713.0). Canberra, Australian Capital Territory: Author.

Australian Bureau of Statistics. (2002). *National Aboriginal and Torres Strait Islander Social Survey* (No. 4714.0). Canberra, Australian Capital Territory: Author.

Australian Bureau of Statistics. (2003). *The health and welfare of Australia's Aboriginal and Torres Strait Islander Peoples* (No. 4704.0). Canberra, Australian Capital Territory: Author.

Beange, H., Lennox, N., & Parmenter, T.R. (1999). Health targets for people with an intellectual disability. *Journal of Intellectual & Developmental Disability, 24,* 283–297.

Benson, B.A. (1985). Behavior disorders and mental retardation: Associations with age, sex and level of functioning in an outpatient clinic sample. *Applied Research in Mental Retardation, 6,* 79–85.

Borthwick-Duffy, S.A. (1994). Epidemiology and prevalence of psychopathology in people with mental retardation. *Journal of Consulting and Clinical Psychology, 62,* 17–27.

Bouras, N. (1995). The Frank Menolascino lecture: Dual diagnosis towards the year 2000. *The NADD Newsletter, 12,* 1–4.

Bouras, N. (Ed.). (1999). *Psychiatric and behavioral disorders in developmental disabilities and mental retardation.* Cambridge, United Kingdom: Cambridge University Press.

Bouras, N., & Holt, G. (Eds.). (in press). *Psychiatric and behavioral disorders in intellectual and developmental disabilities* (2nd ed.). Cambridge, United Kingdom: Cambridge University Press.

Bradley, E.A., & Bolton, P.F. (2006, October). Episodic psychiatric disorders in teenagers with learning disabilities with and without autism. *British Journal of Psychiatry.*

Bradley, E.A., Bolton, P.F., & Bryson, S.E. (2004). Psychiatric co morbidity in persons with intellectual disabilities with and without autism. *Journal of Intellectual Disability Research, 48,* 296.

Bradley, E.A., & Bryson, S. (1998). *Psychiatric illness in mentally handicapped adolescents (and young adults) with autistic disability.* Report to the National Health Research and Development Program. Ottawa, ON: Health Canada.

Bradley, E.A., Cain, N., Costello, H., et al. (in press). Professional training for those working with people with intellectual disabilities. In N. Bouras & G. Holt (Eds.), *Psychiatric and behavioral disorders in intellectual and developmental disabilities* (2nd ed.). Cambridge, United Kingdom: Cambridge University Press.

Bradley, E.A., & Hollins, S. (2006). Assessment of persons with intellectual disabilities. In D. Goldbloom (Ed.), *Psychiatric clinical skills* (pp. 235–253). New York: Elsevier.

Bradley, E.A., & Isaacs, B.J. (2006). Inattention, hyperactivity and impulsivity in teenagers with intellectual disabilities, with and without autism. *Journal of Psychiatry, 51*(9), 598–606.

Bradley, E.A., & Lofchy, J. (2005). Assessment of psychiatric and/or behavioral disturbance in persons with learning disability in the A&E department. *Advances in Psychiatric Treatment, 11,* 45–57.

Bradley, E.A., Lunsky, Y., & Korossy, M. (2005). Living with intellectual disability. In S. Romans & M. Seemens (Eds.), *Women's mental health: A life cycle approach* (pp. 237–253). Philadelphia: Lippincott, Williams & Wilkins.

Bradley, E., & Summers, J. (2003). Developmental disability and behavioral, emotional and psychiatric disturbances. In I. Brown & M. Percy (Eds.), *Developmental disability in Ontario* (2nd ed., pp. 751–774). Toronto: Ontario Association on Developmental Disability.

Bradley, E.A., Summers, J.A., Wood, H.L., et al. (2004). Comparing rates of psychiatric and behavior disorders in adolescents and young adults with severe intellectual disability with and without autism. *Journal of Autism and Developmental Disorders, 34,* 151–161.

Bradley, E.A., Thompson, A., & Bryson, S.E. (2002). Mental retardation in teenagers: Prevalence data from the Niagara Region, Ontario. *Canadian Journal of Psychiatry, 47,* 652–659.

Brereton, A.V., Tonge, B.T., & Einfeld, S.L. (2006, August). Psychopathology in children and adolescents with autism compared to young people with intellectual disability. *Journal of Autism and Developmental Disorders.*

Bryson, S.E., & Bradley, E.A. (2006). *Prevalence of autism among adolescents with intellectual disability.* Manuscript under review.

Bryson, S.E., Clark, B.S., & Smith, I.M. (1988). First report of a Canadian epidemiological study of autistic syndromes. *Journal of Child Psychology and Psychiatry and Allied Disciplines, 29,* 433–445.

Campbell, M., & Malone, R.P. (1991). Mental retardation and psychiatric disorders. *Hospital and Community Psychiatry, 42,* 374–379.

Caron, C., & Rutter, M. (1991). Comorbidity in child psychopathology: Concepts, issues and research strategies. *Journal of Child Psychology and Psychiatry, 32,* 1063–1080.

Cheetham, T. (2001a). Challenges in medical care for persons with developmental disabilities: An illustrative case, "Jane." *Clinical Bulletin of the Developmental Disabilities Program, 12,* 1–3.

Cheetham, T. (2001b). Challenges in medical care for persons with developmental disabilities: An illustrative case, "Ray." *Clinical Bulletin of the Developmental Disabilities Program, 12,* 1–3.

Cochrane, J., Goering, P., Durbin, J., et al. (2000). Tertiary mental health services: II—Subpopulations and best practices for service delivery. *Canadian Journal of Psychiatry, 45,* 185–190.

Corbett, J. (1979). Psychiatric morbidity and mental retardation. In F.E. James & R.P. Snaith (Eds.), *Psychiatric illness and mental handicaps* (pp. 11–25). London: Gaskell.

Cowley, A., Holt, G., Bouras, N., et al. (2004). Descriptive psychopathology in people with mental retardation. *Journal of Nervous and Mental Disease, 192,* 232–237.

Crabbe, H.F. (1989). *A guidebook for the use of psychotropic medication in persons with mental illness and mental retardation.* Hartford: State of Connecticut Department of Mental Retardation.

Curry, C.J., Stevenson, R.E., Aughton, D., et al. (1997). Evaluation of mental retardation: Recommendations of a consensus conference. *American Journal of Medical Genetics, 72,* 468–477.

Deb, S., Matthews, T., Holt, G., et al. (2001). *Practice guidelines for the assessment and diagnosis of mental health problems in adults with intellectual disability.* Brighton, United Kingdom: Pavilion.

Disability Discrimination Act. (1995). Retrieved January 20, 2006, from http://www.opsi.gov.uk/acts/acts1995/1995050.htm

Dosen, A. (1993). Development for mental health care for persons with handicaps in Europe. *The NADD Newsletter, 10*(6), 1–4.

Dosen, A. (1995). Mental health in mental retardation: A path to normalisation. *The NADD Newsletter, 12*(6), 1–4.

Dykens, E.M. (1995). Measuring behavioral phenotypes: Provocations from the "new genetics." *American Journal on Mental Retardation, 99,* 522–532.

Dykens, E.M. (2000). Annotation: Psychopathology in children with intellectual disability. *Journal of Child Psychology and Psychiatry, 41,* 407–417.

Dykens, E.M., Hodapp, R.M., & Finucane, B.M. (2000). *Genetics and mental retardation syndromes: A new look at behavioral interventions.* Baltimore: Paul H. Brookes Publishing Co.

Einfeld, S.L., & Tonge, B.J. (1996a). Population prevalence of behavioral and emotional disturbance in children and adolescents with mental retardation: I. Rationale and methods. *Journal of Intellectual Disability Research, 40,* 91–98.

Einfeld, S.L., & Tonge, B.J. (1996b). Population prevalence of behavioral and emotional disturbance in children and adolescents with mental retardation: II. Epidemiological findings. *Journal of Intellectual Disability Research, 40,* 99–109.

Einfeld, S.L., & Tonge, B.J. (2002). *Manual for the developmental behavior checklist* (2nd ed.). Melbourne, Australia: Monash University Centre for Developmental Psychiatry and Psychology.

Einfeld, S.L., Tonge, B.J., Turner, G., et al. (1999). Longitudinal course of behavioral and emotional problems of young persons with Prader-Willi, Fragile X, Williams and Down Syndromes. *Journal of Intellectual & Developmental Disability, 24,* 349–354.

Goering, P., Butterill, D., Cochrane, J., et al. (1998). *Towards a reformed system of mental health care in Southwest Ontario: The role of tertiary care.* Toronto: Health Systems Research and Consulting Unit, Centre for Addiction and Mental Health.

Grandin, T., & Scariano, M. (1986). *Emergence: Labeled autistic.* Navato, CA: Arena Press.

Griffiths, D.M., Stavrakaki, C., & Summers, J. (Eds.). (2002). *An introduction to the mental health needs of persons with developmental disabilities.* Sudbury, ON, Canada: Habilitative Mental Health Resource Network.

Havercamp, S.M., Scandlin, D., & Roth, M. (2004). Health disparities among adults with developmental disabilities, adults with other disabilities, and adults not reporting disability in North Carolina. *Public Health Reports, 119,* 418–426.

Human Rights Act. (2000). Retrieved October 5, 2004, from http://www.obv.org.uk/education/humanrightsact.html

Jacobson, J.W., (1982). Problem behavior and psychiatric impairment within a developmentally disabled population I: Behavior frequency. *Applied Research in Mental Retardation, 3,* 121–139.

Jacobson, J.W., & Mulick, J.A. (Eds.). (1996). *Manual of diagnosis and professional practice in mental retardation.* Washington, DC: American Psychological Association.

Jakab, I. (1982). Psychiatric disorders in mental retardation. In I. Jakab (Ed.), *Mental retardation* (pp. 270–326). Basel, Switzerland: Karger.

Jaydeokar, S., & Piachaud, J. (2004). Out-of-borough placements for people with learning disabilities. *Advances in Psychiatric Treatment, 10,* 116–123.

King, B.H., DeAntonio, C., McCracken, J.T., et al. (1994). Psychiatric consultation in severe and profound mental retardation. *American Journal of Psychiatry, 151,* 1802–1808.

Kingsley, J., & Levitz, M. (1994). *Count us in: Growing up with Down syndrome.* New York: Harcourt Brace & Co.

Lenhoff, H.M., Wang, P.P., Greenberg, F., et al. (1997). Williams syndrome and the brain. *Scientific American,* 277, 68–73.

Lennox, N., & Beange, H. (1999). Aged care. In N. Lennox & J. Diggens, (Eds.), *Management guidelines: People with developmental and intellectual disabilities* (pp. 47–60). Melbourne, Australia: Therapeutic Guidelines.

Lennox, N., & Diggens, J. (Eds.). (1999). *Management guidelines. People with developmental and intellectual disabilities.* Melbourne, Australia: Therapeutic Guidelines.

Levitas, A., & Gilson, S.F. (1994). Psychosocial development of children and adolescents with mild and moderate mental retardation. In N. Bouras (Ed.), *Mental health in mental retardation: Recent advances and practices* (pp 34–45). Cambridge, United Kingdom: Cambridge University Press.

Levitas, A., & Hurley, A.D. (2001). Behavioral and psychiatric phenotypes. *Mental Health Aspects of Developmental Disabilities, 4,* 161–165.

Levitas, A., Hurley, A.D., & Pary, R. (2001). The mental status examination in patients with mental retardation and developmental disabilities. *Mental Health Aspects of Developmental Disabilities, 4,* 2–16.

Levitas, A., & Silka, V.R. (2001). Mental health clinical assessment of persons with mental retardation and developmental disabilities. *Mental Health Aspects of Developmental Disabilities, 4,* 31–42.

Lewis, J.N., Tonge, B.J., Mowat, D.R., et al. (2000). Epilepsy and associated psychopathology in young people with intellectual disability. *Journal of Paediatrics and Child Health, 36,* 172–175.

Luckasson, R., Borthwick-Duffy, S., Buntinx, W.H.E., et al. (2002). *Mental retardation: Definition, classification, and systems of support* (10th ed.). Washington, DC: American Association on Mental Retardation.

Lunsky, Y., & Benson, B.A. (2001). Association between perceived social support and strain, and positive and negative outcome for adults with mild intellectual disability. *Journal of Intellectual Disability Research, 45,* 106–114.

Lunsky, Y., & Bradley, E.A. (2001). Developmental disability training in Canadian psychiatry residency programs. *Canadian Journal of Psychiatry, 46,* 63–67.

Lunsky, Y., Bradley, E., Durbin, J., et al. (2003). *Dual diagnosis in provincial psychiatric hospitals: A Population-based study—year one summary report.* Retrieved October 5, 2004, from http://www.camh.net/pdf/dualdiagnosis_provpsychhosp_1styr2003.pdf

Lunsky, Y., Bradley, E., & Korrosy, M. (2002, April). *Developmental disability psychiatry: An analysis of residents' feedback.* Plenary address given at State of the HART: Habilitative Achievements in Research and Treatment for Mental Health in Developmental Disabilities, Vancover, BC, Canada.

Lunsky, Y., & Havercamp, S.M. (1999). Distinguishing low levels of social support and social strain: Implications for dual diagnosis. *American Journal on Mental Retardation, 104,* 200–204.

McCreary, B.D. (1998). *Educating Canadian psychiatrists for professional responsibilities in the field of developmental disabilities.* Discussion paper prepared for the Educational Council of the Canadian Psychiatric Association, Department of Psychiatry, Queen's University. Kingston, ON, Canada: Queen's University.

McCreary, B.D., Peppin, P., Stanton, B., et al. (2001). *Catalysts for university education in developmental disabilities.* Kingston, ON, Canada: Developmental Consulting Program, Queen's University.

Mental Capacity Act 2005. Retrieved September 25, 2006, from http://www.opsi.gov.uk/acts/acts2005/20050009.htm

Mental Health Act. (1983). Retrieved October 5, 2004, from http://www.markwalton.net/guidemha/index.asp

Mental Retardation Facilities and Community Mental Health Centers Construction Act of 1963, PL 88-164, 42 U.S.C. §§ 2670 *et seq.*

Mitra, I., & Alexander, R. (2003). Out-of-area placements: Implications of psychiatric services in learning disability. *Psychiatric Bulletin, 27,* 382–385.

Moss, S., Emerson, E., Bouras, N., et al. (1997). Mental disorders and problematic behaviors in people with intellectual disability: Future direction for research. *Journal of Intellectual Disability Research, 41,* 440–447.

Nordin, V., & Gillberg, C. (1996). Autism spectrum disorders in children with physical or mental disability or both: II, Screening aspects. *Developmental Medicine and Child Neurology, 38,* 314–324.

O'Brien, G., & Yule, W. (Eds.). (1996). *Behavioral phenotypes: Clinics in developmental medicine* (No. 138). Cambridge, United Kingdom: Mac Keith Press.

Ouellette-Kuntz, H., Garcin, N., Lewis, M.E.S., et al. (2004). *Addressing health disparities through promoting equity for individuals with intellectual disability.* Retrieved January 21, 2006, from http://www.igh.ualberta.ca/RHD/synthesis.htm

Pary, R.J., Levitas, A., & Hurley, A.D. (1999). Diagnosis of bipolar disorder in persons with developmental disabilities. *Mental Health Aspects of Developmental Disabilities, 2,* 37–49.

Raynham, H., Gibbons, R., Flint, J., et al. (1996). The genetic basis for mental retardation. *Quarterly Journal of Medicine, 89,* 169–175.

Reid, A.H. (1982). *The psychiatry of mental handicap.* London: Blackwell Scientific Publications.

Reiss, S., & Aman, M.G. (Eds.). (1998). *Psychotropic medication and developmental disabilities: The international consensus handbook.* Columbus: The Ohio State University, Nisonger Center.

Reiss, S., Levitan, G.W., & Szysko, J. (1982). Emotional disturbance and mental retardation: Diagnostic overshadowing. *American Journal of Mental Deficiency, 86,* 567–574.

Rondal, J.A., Hodapp, R.M., Soresi, S., et al. (2004). *Intellectual disabilities: Genetics, behavior and inclusion.* Philadelphia: Whurr Publishers.

Ross, E., & Oliver, C. (2002). The relationship between levels of mood, interest and pleasure and 'challenging behavior' in adults with severe and profound intellectual disability. *Journal of Intellectual Disability Research, 46,* 191–197.

Ross, E., & Oliver, C. (2003). The assessment of mood in adults who have severe or profound mental retardation. *Clinical Psychology Review, 23,* 225–245.

Royal College of Psychiatrists. (2001). *DC-LD: Diagnostic criteria for psychiatric disorders for use with adults with learning disabilities/mental retardation* [Occasional Paper No. 48, Royal College of Psychiatrists]. London: Gaskell.

Rush, J.A., & Frances, A. (2000). Expert consensus guidelines series: Treatment of psychiatric and behavioral problems in mental retardation. *American Journal on Mental Retardation, 105*(3), 159–228.

Rutter, M. (1971). Psychiatric disorder and intellectual retardation in childhood. In J. Wortis (Ed.), *Mental retardation: Vol. III. An annual review.* New York: Grune & Stratton.

Rutter, M., Tizard, J., & Whitmore, K. (1970). *Education, health and behavior.* New York: Longman.

Shah, A., Holmes, N., & Wing, L. (1982). Prevalence of autism and related conditions in adults in a mental handicap hospital. *Applied Research in Mental Retardation, 3,* 303–317.

Sovner, R. (1986). Limiting factors in the use of DSM-III with mentally ill/mentally retarded persons. *Psychopharmacology Bulletin, 22,* 1055–1059.

Sovner, R., & Hurley, A.D. (1986). Managing aggressive behavior: A psychiatric approach. *Psychiatric Aspects of Mental Retardation Reviews, 5,* 16–21.

Stark, J.A., Kiernan, W.E., & Goldbury, T. (1988). In J.A. Stark, F.J. Menolascino, M.H. Albarelli, et al. (Eds.), *Mental retardation and mental health: Classification, diagnosis, treatment and services* (pp. 300–312). New York: Springer-Verlag.

Summers, J., Boyd, K., & Morgan, J. (2004). Evaluating patients with intellectual disabilities and comorbid mental health problems. *Psychiatric Annals, 34,* 214–220.

Tonge, B.J., & Einfeld, S.L. (2003). Psychopathology and intellectual disability: The Australian child to adult longitudinal study. *International Review of Research in Mental Retardation, 27,* 61–91.

Tsiouris, J.A. (2001). Diagnosis of depression in people with severe/profound intellectual disability. *Journal of Intellectual Disability Research, 45,* 115–120.

U.K. Department of Health. (1999). *The mental health national service framework.* Retrieved October 5, 2004, from http://www.nelh.nhs.uk/nsf

U.K. Department of Health. (2001). *Valuing people: A new strategy for learning disability in the 21st Century.* Retrieved October 5, 2004, from http://www.archive.official-documents.co.uk/document/cm50/5086.html

U.K. Department of Health. (2004). *Green light for mental health: A service improvement toolkit.* Retrieved October 5,

2004, from http://www.learningdisabilities.org.uk/page.cfm?pagecode=PUBOHE

U.S. Department of Health and Human Services. (2002a). *Closing the gap: A national blueprint for improving the health of individuals with mental retardation.* Retrieved October 5, 2004, from http://www.surgeongeneral.gov/topics/mentalretardation/retardation.pdf

U.S. Department of Health and Human Services. (2002b). *The Report of the Surgeon General's Conference on Health Disparities and Mental Retardation.* Retrieved October 5, 2004, from http://www.surgeongeneral.gov/topics/mentalretardation/retardation.pdf

Williams, D. (1992). *Nobody nowhere: The extraordinary autobiography of an autistic.* New York: Avon Books.

Williams, D. (1994). *Somebody somewhere: Breaking free from the world of autism.* New York: Random House.

Wing, L., & Gould, J. (1979). Severe impairments of social interaction and associated abnormalities in children: Epidemiology and classification. *Journal of Autism and Developmental Disorders, 9,* 11–29.

World Health Organization. (1992). *The ICD-10 classification of mental and behavioral disorders: Clinical descriptions and diagnostic guidelines.* Geneva: Author.

World Health Organization. (1996). *ICD-10 guide for mental retardation.* Geneva: Author.

43

Nutritional Considerations in Children with Intellectual and Developmental Disabilities

DIANA MAGER AND PAUL B. PENCHARZ

WHAT YOU WILL LEARN ABOUT IN THIS CHAPTER

- Common causes of malnutrition
- Nutrition assessment of children
- Assessment of growth in children
- Assessment of energy requirements
- Nutritional management
- Functional capacity
- Obesity

The most common nutritional concern in children with intellectual and developmental disability is growth failure caused by feeding difficulties. Among children with such disabilities, 30%–35% have feeding problems that result in slow growth, inadequate weight gain, developmental delay, psychosocial problems, **anemia,** and vitamin/mineral deficiencies (Palmer, Thompson, & Linscheid, 1975; Telch & Telch, 2003). Overnutrition leading to obesity is also common in this population. This usually results from dietary intake in excess of energy requirements and diminished physical activity/mobility. In this chapter, the terms *developmental disability(ies)* and *developmental delay* area used to denote intellectual and/or developmental disabilities.

Proper nutrition is an important issue for children with developmental disabilities. A comprehensive approach to nutrition support in this population can result in improved rates of growth, improvement in development, and enhanced quality of life. Assessment of feeding difficulties should include an interdisciplinary approach involving at least a physician, nurse, and registered dietitian. The team also could include a speech-language pathologist, occupational therapist, physiotherapist, radiologist/interventional radiologist (to diagnose the etiology of the swallowing disorder and to conduct the appropriate diagnostic studies), dentist and dental hygienist, psychiatrist, social worker, teacher, and pharmacist. Some countries have laws mandating that infants and children at risk for developmental disability are entitled to nutritional assessment and treatment within the context of a family-centered approach (see Telch & Telch, 2003).

This chapter presents key concepts in nutrition concerns for children with developmental disabilities. These are summarized in Table 43.1, and many are discussed in detail in the following sections.

COMMON CAUSES OF MALNUTRITON

Malnutrition in children with developmental disabilities may be caused by several factors. These include the presence of significant swallowing and gastrointestinal dysfunction, medication, development, and behavioral issues. **Dysphagia** is very common in children with developmental delay (Palmer et al., 1975; Reilly, Skuse, & Poblete, 1996; Zemel & Stallings, 1997). The most common causes of dysphagia in this population include neurological impairment and structural abnormalities (e.g., cleft palate) of the oral and pharyngeal cavities (Rudolph, 1994). Dysphagia can lead to poor food intake, impaired feeding efficiency (length of time to finish a meal), choking, regurgitation, and aspiration of food contents into the lung. Severity and duration of swallowing impairment has also been linked to a lag in the developmental progress in children with neurological impairment (Cloud, 1993; Zemel & Stallings, 1997). Significant improvement in nutritional status in children with developmental disabilities who have dysphagia can occur following assessment of nutritional requirements, dietary intake, type and severity of swallowing dysfunction, and functional capacity to self-feed (Reilly et al., 1996; Rudolph, 1994; Zemel & Stallings, 1997).

Common causes of gastrointestinal dysfunction in children with developmental disabilities may include delayed gastric emptying, impaired intestinal motility (movement through the intestine), and **gastroesophageal reflux disease (GERD).** Severe and persistent GERD can cause esophagitis (inflamed mucosa of the esophagus), vomiting, failure to thrive, or lung disease from aspiration (Sondheimer & Morris, 1979). GERD

Table 43.1. Nutritional considerations at a glance

Feeding Issues

Factors that affect food intake

- Acute and chronic illness (e.g., gastrointestinal dysfunction, neurological impairment)
- Psychosocial variables (e.g., depression, poverty, drug abuse)
- Side effects of drug therapy (e.g., anorexia, nausea, vomiting, diarrhea)
- Functional capacity
- Dysphagia (inability to swallow or dysfunctional swallow): There is a need to differentiate between normal versus abnormal dysphagia and to define issues regarding functional capacity. Impairment of fine and gross motor skills and the presence of dysphagia can affect functional capacity or the ability to self-feed.

Signs of oral/pharyngeal dysphagia

- Drooling
- Slow eating (low feeding efficiency or extended time to finish one meal)
- Altered posturing of head and neck during swallow
- Large food residual in mouth following a swallow
- Coughing during and after the swallow
- Choking with significant shortness of breath
- Voice quality changes
- Expectoration of food and/or saliva

Signs of impairment of fine and gross motor skills

Causes may be neurological or structural (outlined as follows):

- Ataxia (failure of muscle coordination, resulting in poorly judged movements)
- Dysarthria (imperfect articulation of speech due to disturbances in muscle control)
- Abnormal reflexes (e.g., tongue thrusting in an infant)
- Apraxia (inability to plan and execute a skilled movement in the absence of sensory and motor deficits)

Compensatory feeding strategies

- Changes in food bolus consistency (e.g., puréed versus soft textures, thin versus thickened liquids)
- Postural change (head should be in upright position, not over on one side)
- Verbal cues (gentle reminders or cues to redirect attention to eating)
- Controlled intake (pacing of intake, portion size, outside distracters such as noise)
- Adaptive equipment (adaptive utensils, wrist or hand splints)
- Other therapies (effortful swallow, supraglottic versus supersupraglottic swallow)

Food intake assessment techniques

- Food frequency
- Intake records or diary
- 24-hour recall
- Food preferences (likes versus dislikes)
- Direct observation
- Diet history: This includes a review of current and past food intake and food preferences. It also usually includes a review of issues related to food intake (dental health, psychosocial factors such as depression, socioeconomic status, occupation, physical health, age, allergies, and medication) and functional capacity (ability to self-feed, prepare food, have access to food, and so forth).

Food frequency assessment techniques

- Determination of food portion size
- Determination of food type/food group
- Determination of food frequency and number of servings per day versus per week versus per month
- Single food type versus multiple food types (e.g., cheese slice versus cheese casserole regarding estimation of portion size/nutrient composition)

Strategies to aid with food identification and estimation of food portion size

- Pictures of foods or food labels
- Food models (especially plastic food models)
- Commercial product containers and labels to identify food types, food products, and food ingredients (especially important in cases of food allergy/intolerance)
- Food utensils (e.g., commercial product containers, measuring cups, cups, bowls, plates, cutlery) to approximately measure food portion size
- Hand measures or rulers to identify thickness or dimensions of foods
- Kitchen scales to precisely measure food portions

Factors affecting accuracy of food intake assessment

- Recollection or memory of the interviewee about issues regarding duration or length of time of particular food intake—the usual intake, versus the most recent intake versus seasonal intake versus holiday or special occasion (e.g., birthday) intake
- Seasonal variations in food intake
- Food preparation techniques (e.g., baking versus frying to estimate fat content)
- Methods used to estimate portion sizes
- Method or type of interview
- Order of presentation of food groups (bias may be introduced)
- Socioeconomic factors

Screening Issues

Purpose of nutrition screening

- Identification of individuals with inadequate nutritional status
- Identification of risk factors for malnutrition
- Prevention of inadequate/suboptimal nutritional status

Nutritional risk factors

- Inadequate oral intake
- Significant or recent weight loss (i.e., ideal body weight, percent of recent weight change)
- Psychosocial variables (e.g., depression, poverty, drug abuse)
- Chronic or acute illness
- Side effects of drug therapy (e.g., drug–nutrient interactions, anorexia, nausea)
- Altered functional capacity (due to changes in mobility, muscle strength)

Anthropometrics

- Body mass index (BMI): body weight in kg/height in m squared
- Percent ideal body weight (IBW), percent usual body weight (UBW)
- Percent recent weight change =

$$\frac{\text{usual weight} - \text{current weight} * 100\%}{\text{usual weight}}$$

- Significant weight loss (weight loss associated with an increased risk of adverse sequelae):
  - >1%–2% over 1 week
  - >5% over 1 month
  - >7.5% over 3 months
  - >10% over 6 months

Biochemical measurements of blood samples

- Hemoglobin: to detect iron-deficiency anemia
- Triglyceride/cholesterol: to detect hyperlipidemia
- Albumin: to estimate visceral protein status when hepatic, renal, gastrointestinal functions and hydration status are normal

Diet history

- Suboptimal intake for more than 3 days
- Abnormal eating pattern
- Nutrition-related problems present (dentition, gastrointestinal upset [acute and chronic], dysphagia, food intolerance, anorexia)

Screening tools

- *Canada's Guide to Healthy Eating and Physical Activity* (see http://www.phac-aspc.gc.ca/guide/index_e.html)
- Computer nutrient database (e.g., Food Smart; see http://www.food-smart.com)
- Food frequency questionnaires
- Nutrition screening checklists (include information about past medical history, food consumption patterns, socioeconomic status, multiple medications, weight history, mobility, and so forth)

Labs at admission (first set of biochemical analyses obtained from a client at the time of admission to the hospital)[a]

- Albumin (serum): normal, 33g/L–58 g/L; 31g/L is indicative of decreased visceral protein stores or inflammation in gut
- Erythrocyte sedimentation rate (ESR): normal, 1–10; elevated in collagen vascular disease, inflammatory states, acute phase reactions
- Electrolytes (serum): measures of ions such as sodium, potassium, calcium, and magnesium
- Platelets: normal, 150–450; 617 or above is a nonspecific gut inflammatory marker (e.g., Crohn's disease)
- Hemoglobin: normal, 120–160; 76 or below is indicative of blood loss, microcytic anemia
- Mean corpuscular (red cell) volume (MCV): normal, 80–94; 63 or below is indicative of microcytic, hypochromic anemia
- Mean corpuscular (red cell) hemoglobin (MCH): normal, 24–31; 20 or below is indicative of microcytic anemia
- Serum iron: normal, 9–27 mmoles/L; 8 or below is abnormal
- Ferritin (serum): normal, 18–300 ng/mL
- Transferrin (serum): normal, 24–48 mmoles/L; 14.6 or below is abnormal
- Transferrin saturation is a marker of iron supply to the tissues; low values are indicative that iron stores are inadequate for erythropoiesis
- Transferrin saturation: normal, 20%; 6% or below is abnormal
- Transferrin saturation = serum iron/2 × serum transferrin

Sources: Mager and Pencharz (2003); [a]Traub (1996).

Key: kg = kilogram; m = meter; g = gram; L = liter; ng = nanogram; mL = milliliter; mmole = milllimole.

and delayed gastric and/or intestinal motility are usually treated with medications that promote motility and block acid production in the gut. Treatment of GERD and delayed gastric emptying with these medications can promote increased dietary intake and improved weight gain (DiLorenzo et al., 1991). Impaired intestinal motility can also cause constipation leading to vomiting, decreased food intake, and weight loss. Improvement in the frequency of bowel motions can lead to significant improvement in dietary intake (DiLorenzo et al., 1991; Sullivan, 1997). Treatment of constipation in children includes the use of motility agents, stool softening agents, suppository or fleet enemas, and assessment of fluid and fiber intake to ensure that adequate amounts are present in the diet.

Patients with persistent GERD and delayed gastric emptying may develop feeding aversions (DiLorenzo et al., 1991). Feeding aversions may include partial or total food refusal and selectivity of food choices (picky eating) and food texture (e.g., refusal to eat solids or liquids) (Cloud, 1993; Rodas-Arts & Benoit, 1998). Behaviors, such as tantrums associated with requests to eat or changes in food texture and delay in self-feeding, may also result in impairment of feeding efficiency. These problems can be exacerbated by dysphagia. Treatment and management of behavior problems associated with feeding is complex (Cloud,1993; Rodas-Arts & Benoit, 1998). Assessment of behavioral feeding problems should include a review of functional (e.g., posture) and physiological (e.g., swallowing function, gastrointestinal function) aspects of feeding.

The use of medications in children with developmental disabilities may have a significant impact on nutritional status. These include potential drug–nutrient interactions or side effects such as nausea, vomiting, diarrhea, or poor appetite. For example, anticonvulsant medications (e.g., phenytoin) used for children with seizure disorders may interfere with the absorption and utilization of vitamin D and calcium, leading to increased risk for bone fracture (Lifschitz & Maclaren, 1975). Use of antibiotics may produce gastrointestinal symptoms (e.g., diarrhea), and psychotropics may cause depressed appetite (Roe, 1982). In addition, many children with developmental disabilities take multiple medications (prescription and over the counter) that potentially may interact and cause adverse reactions for appetite and feeding (specifically swallowing) issues (Roe, 1982).

NUTRITION ASSESSMENT OF CHILDREN

Nutrition assessment in children includes the assessment of growth, body composition, dietary intake (past and present), and current health status. Assessment of growth includes examining weight and height growth to determine the adequacy of nutritional status. Deficits in growth and reductions in fat and lean body mass are the most common indicators of malnutrition (Cloud, 1993; Zemel & Stallings, 1997). Assessment of body composition is also necessary to establish severity of obesity in overnutrition. Assessment of dietary intake is important for identifying causative factors in over- and undernutrition. This assessment includes a review of current and past intake; preferences; food frequency; use of caloric, vitamin, and mineral supplementation; food availability; and feeding patterns (Cloud, 1993; Rudolph, 1994; Zemel & Stallings, 1997). The review of feeding patterns can include timing of meals, behavioral patterns associated with feeding, and difficulties with feeding. A review of current health status may include a review of medical history (acute and chronic) and current medications (drug–nutrient interactions) in order to identify potential factors affecting current nutritional status. The history includes a review of body systems, with an emphasis on the child's ability to chew, swallow, and digest food to identify potential causes (e.g., nausea, vomiting, malabsorption, reflux, diarrhea) for under- or overnutrition (Cloud, 1993; Reilly et al., 1996; Rudolph, 1994; Zemel & Stallings, 1997).

Blood tests are also done in a nutritional assessment to screen for vitamin and mineral deficiency. These blood values should be assessed along with a child's medical, growth, and nutritional history to ensure completeness of assessment. The most common blood parameters used in nutrition assessment are measurements of **serum albumin** and a complete blood count (CBC). Serum albumin is a good indicator of adequacy of **visceral protein status** over the previous month in the absence of kidney and liver disease (half-life, or the length of time it takes for the body to replace 50% of the body pool of albumin, is 18–20 days) (Hopkins, 1993). Other markers of visceral protein status include **transferrin,** thyroxine-binding pre-albumin (transthyretin), and retinol-binding protein. Evaluation of the CBC (hemoglobin, hematocrit, and red cell indices) is a useful screening tool for the detection of nutrition-related anemias (Hopkins, 1993). A more complete analysis of iron status includes assessment of **ferritin, serum** iron, transferrin, and iron-binding capacity (Cloud, 1993; Zemel & Stallings, 1997).

ASSESSMENT OF GROWTH IN CHILDREN

Assessment of growth in children is an important part of nutritional assessment. A complete assessment here includes measurement of height (lying or standing), weight, and skinfolds (Cloud, 1993; Zemel & Stallings, 1997). Height and weight of a child should be plotted using standard growth curves (Hamil et al., 1979). Children grow at different rates over time. The highest rates of growth occur in utero, during early infancy, and around puberty. Differences in growth may occur annually, with faster rates during the spring and summer and slower rates in the fall and winter months in some countries (Goldbloom, 1997). Growth measurements should be recorded at regular intervals to account for these changes in growth patterns. Assessment of growth can be done by comparing height and weight percentiles, channel differences (one channel is representative of the distance between two percentile curves), or velocity curves. Children usually maintain their heights and weights in the same channels during the preschool and early childhood years (Guo et al., 1991). However, growth in any particular channel may not be defined until after 2 years of age (Guo et al., 1991; Roche & Himes, 1980). Genetic inheritance also plays a large role in growth in infancy and early childhood. Adjustment of stature of length measurements using mid-parental stature charts is a technique that may be used to correct for differences in genetic potential for linear growth (Himes et al., 1985).

For children with neurological impairment, growth may be impeded by dysphagia, chronic illness, and the presence of skeletal disorders. Weight loss or lack of weight gain, in particular, may place these children at significant risk for malnutrition. Obesity can also be a problem in these children. This can hamper their mobility and can result in additional complications, including increased risk for cardiovascular disease.

Assessment of Specific Indicators of Growth

Specific indicators of growth include height, height velocity, and weight. Each is discussed next.

Height Measurement of height is an important tool in the assessment of a child's nutritional status. Linear growth is an excellent marker of a child's nutritional history and helps in distinguishing between short- and long-term nutritional problems (i.e., height reflects longer-term nutritional issues). Recumbent lengths (lying down) are used for infants and children younger than 2 years of age or for children older than 3 years of age who are unable to stand. Recumbent length is not identical to standing height and must be measured using a device called a *length board* (Goldbloom, 1997; Roche & Davila, 1974). Plotting of height on reference growth curves should be done at sequential intervals for assessment of growth (see Figures 43.1 and 43.2 for examples) (College of Family Physicians of Canada & Community Health Nurses Association of Canada, 2004; Hamil et al., 1979; Himes & Roche,

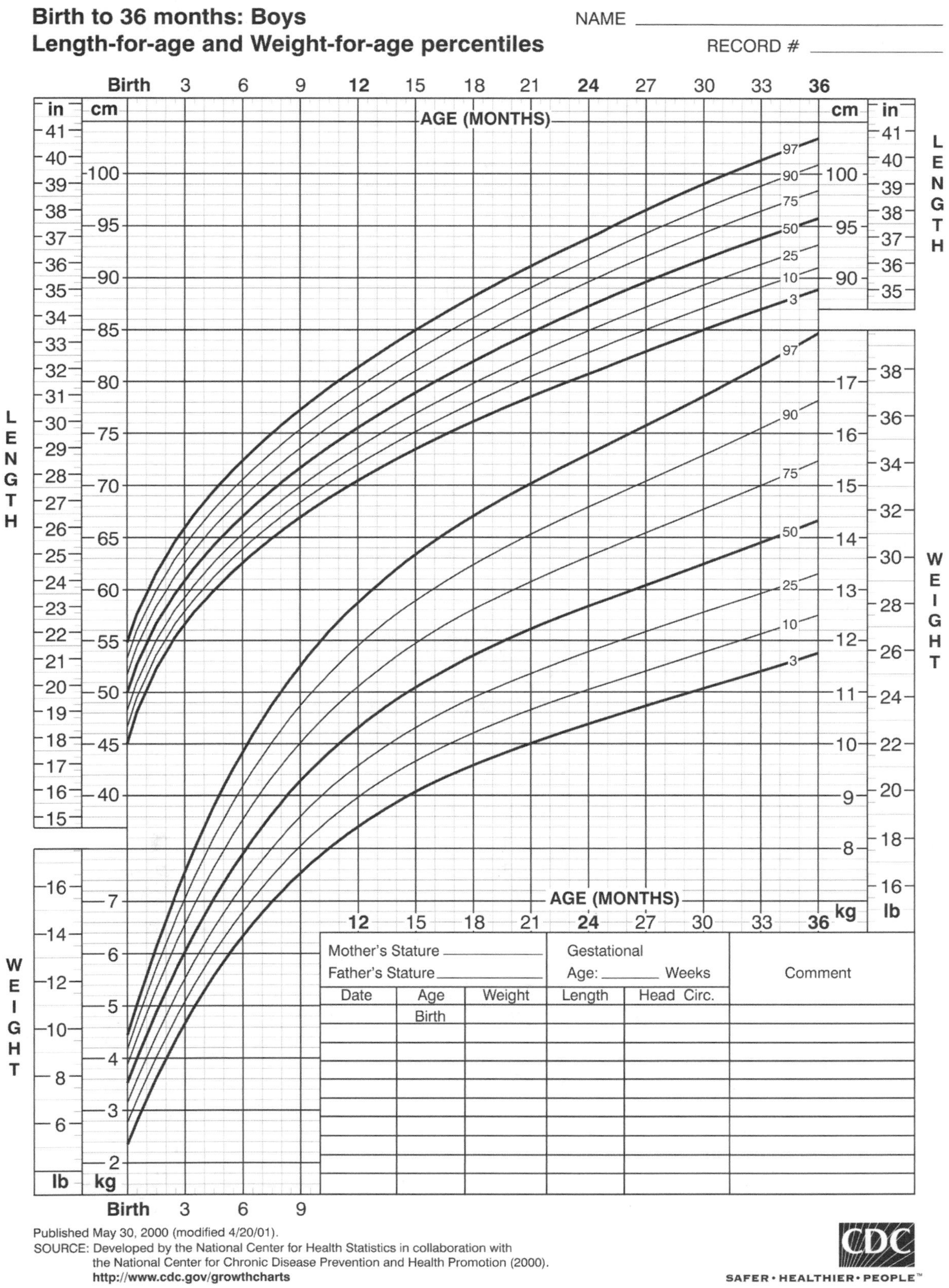

Figure 43.1. Length-for-age and weight-for-age percentiles for boys, birth to 36 months. (From Centers for Disease Control and Prevention & National Center for Health Statistics. [2004]. *CDC growth charts: United States.* Retrieved August 12, 2004, from http://www.cdc.gov/growthcharts)

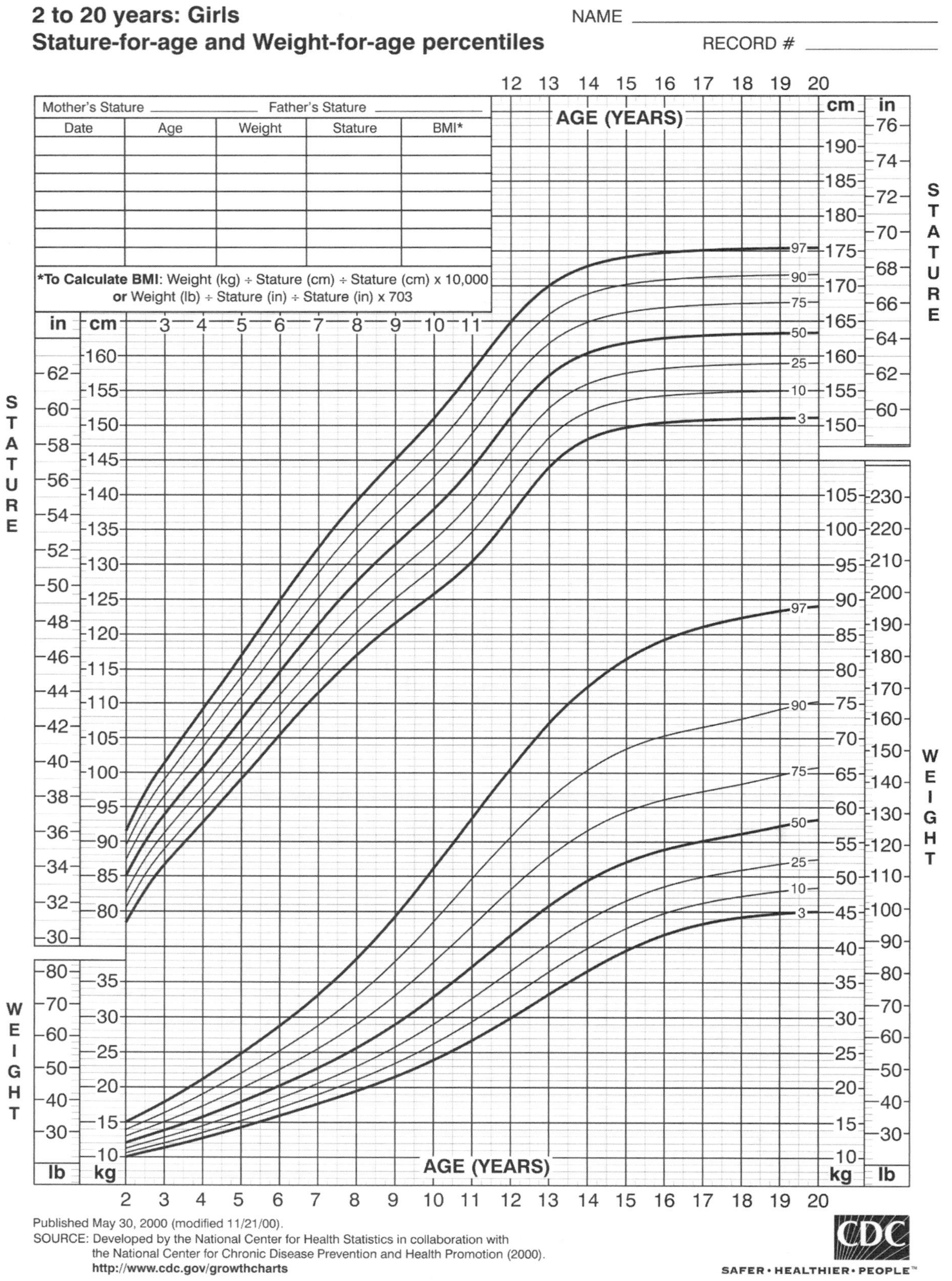

Figure 43.2. Stature-for-age and weight-for-age percentiles for girls, 2 to 20 years. (From Centers for Disease Control and Prevention & National Center for Health Statistics. [2004]. *CDC growth charts: United States.* Retrieved August 12, 2004, from http://www.cdc.gov/growthcharts)

1985). The Centers for Disease Control and Prevention (CDC) (2004) growth charts consist of charts for infants from birth to age 3 for weight, recumbent length, head circumference, and weight-for-recumbent length; growth charts for children and adolescents from ages 2 to 20 include charts for weight, height, and body mass index. The charts are available in two forms: clinical and individual. The clinical charts were designed for use by health care provides (College of Family Physicians of Canada & Community Health Nurses Association of Canada, 2004). The World Health Organization, in collaboration with the United Nations Children Fund, is developing new international growth curves (birth to 5 years) that will be representative of an ethnically diverse population (Garza & de Onis, 1999; Grummer-Strawn, Garza, & Johnson, 2002). Use of these curves to evaluate growth in children with developmental disabilities will need to be evaluated when these charts are released. These curves will be used for assessment of growth in children. The main benefit of these curves is that the population from which the data was drawn will be more heterogenous and hence reflect the cultural and ethnic populations of North America.

Measurement of recumbent or standing height may be inappropriate for children with spinal curvature or contractures because proper positioning for these measurements may not be possible (Goldbloom, 1997). The use of arm span—or upper, lower and segmental arm length—measures may be more appropriate. Comparison with reference standard tables should be used to compare growth when using these measures (Schenker & Ward, 1999; Spender et al., 1989). Sometimes severe physical disabilities make even these measurements difficult. For example, the presence of severe contracture or spinal curvature may make it difficult to measure arm span or upper and lower arm lengths accurately. Assessment of height using arm span lengths is also not appropriate in children with bony skeletal disorders, such as achrondroplasia, as lower bone growth may be significantly different from upper bone growth, leading to overestimates of stature (Goldbloom, 1997; Zemel & Stallings, 1997). The use of upper and lower arm lengths for assessment of linear stature is the most appropriate method to use when recumbent and when standing lengths are not possible (Schenker & Ward, 1999; Zemel & Stallings, 1997). Repeated measures on the same side of the body with the least involvement and comparison of both upper and lower measure should be done to minimize error and to ensure accuracy of height estimates (Goldbloom, 1997; Zemel & Stallings, 1997).

Height Velocity Assessment of height velocity (how height changes over time) should be used to assess rates of linear growth. Calculation of height velocity should be done at 1 year intervals to account for seasonal variations in growth. Comparison with reference curves may be done to assess rates of linear growth (Roche & Himes, 1980). The use of these curves for the assessment of linear growth in children with skeletal impairment may be of limited value because growth patterns may be significantly different due to impairment of bone growth (see Figures 43.1 and 43.2 for examples).

Weight Infants and children should wear little or no outer clothing and be placed on the same scale used for prior measurements to ensure accuracy in weight measurements. Weight should be measured to the nearest 0.1 kilogram (kg) for older children and to the nearest 0.01 kg for infants (Goldbloom, 1997; Zemel & Stallings, 1997). The scale should be zeroed between measurements to ensure precision of the weight measurement. Factors that affect accuracy of weight measurements in children include the presence of **edema, organomegaly,** and measurement technique. It is important to distinguish between these variables when assessing weight in terms of a child's nutritional status. Plotting of weight on reference growth curves should be done at sequential intervals for assessment of growth (Guo et al., 1991; Hamil et al., 1979) (see Figures 43.1 and 43.2 for examples).

Head Circumference Below-normal head circumference in children and infants is often associated with developmental delay (Goldbloom, 1997). Hence, head circumference is not a useful marker of nutritional status in children with central nervous system impairment. Another cause of poor cranial growth includes premature fusion of cranial sutures (**premature synostosis**). Premature synostosis can lead to increased intracranial pressure and abnormal cranial skeletal development (Goldbloom, 1997). Head circumference that is larger than normal is usually familial (known as familial megalencephaly). Head circumference should be serially monitored on clinical charts as an integral part of assessment of neurological development in children (see Figure 43.3 for an example).

Nutritional Status Using Weight as a Percentage of Ideal Body Weight Evaluation of the nutritional status of children includes assessment of growth parameters. Plotting the height and weight of a child on standard growth curves over time is critical when assessing height and weight growth failure. Growth failure may include lack of height or weight growth or both. Lack of weight gain or loss of weight over several months may be indicative of the presence of severe undernutrition, disease, or psychosocial disturbance (Goldbloom, 1997). Excessive weight gain may be in-

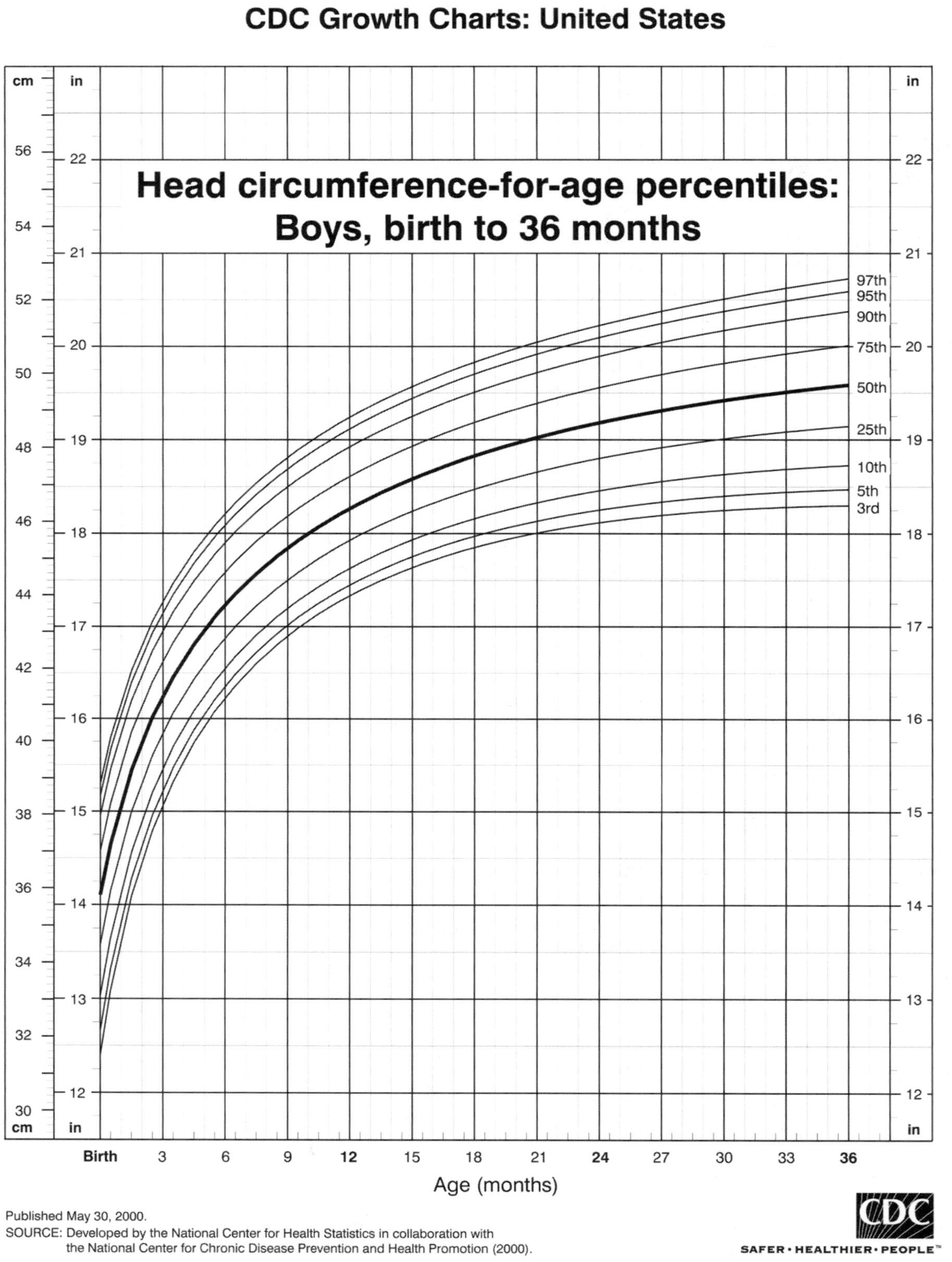

Figure 43.3. Head circumference-for-age percentiles for boys, birth to 36 months. (From Centers for Disease Control and Prevention & National Center for Health Statistics. [2004]. *CDC growth charts: United States.* Retrieved August 12, 2004, from http://www.cdc.gov/growthcharts)

dicative of excessive energy intake, edema, or organomegaly. Disturbances of linear growth may also be due to the presence of chronic under- or overnutrition, chronic disease, and/or endocrine abnormalities (Goldbloom, 1997; Zemel & Stallings, 1997). Assessment of weight as a percentage of **ideal body weight** assists the clinician in identifying the risk and severity of either under- or overnutrition (McLaren & Read, 1972; see Table 43.2). Calculation of ideal body weight should be done using the 50th percentile weight for chronological age or by determining the child's height percentile and finding the corresponding weight for that percentile. Calculation of the ratio between the child's actual weight and ideal body weight is used to identify the risk for **protein–energy malnutrition (PEM).** Table 43.2 presents the way in which such ratios are used to classify the risk for PEM.

Plotting growth (height and weight) patterns of children on standard growth curves (CDC 2000 clinical curves; CDC, 2004) may not be appropriate in children with quadriplegia, as linear growth retardation is common in this population (Tanner, Whitehouse, & Takaishi, 1966). Use of other growth curves developed for children with endocrine and/or neurodevelopmental delay may be more appropriate (Cronk et al., 1988). Growth studies in children with cerebral palsy indicate that growth is severely depressed (Krick et al., 1996). Growth retardation has been attributed to nutritional and nonnutritional factors among children who have cerebral palsy with quadriplegia. One reason for this is a lack of weight-bearing exercise, which plays a direct role in the growth of long bones (Krick et al., 1996). Depressed weight gain is likely due to the prevalence of oral-motor dysfunction, decreased feeding efficiency, dysphagia, and/or gastroesophageal reflux.

Skinfold Measures Skinfold measures may be used to assess subcutaneous fat and lean body mass stores in the body. Tricep and subscapular skinfold measures are good indicators of whole body fat stores (Goldbloom, 1997; Zemel & Stallings, 1997). Calculation of **mid-arm muscle circumference (MAMC)** using **mid-arm circumference (MAC)** and **tricep skinfold measures** may be used to assess lean body stores. Decreased MAMC measures reflect skeletal muscle wasting due to denervation and/or malnutrition, whereas decreased tricep skinfold measures reflect wasting secondary to malnutrition only (Nutrition Committee, 1994). Comparison of MAMC and tricep skinfold measures with reference standards may be done to assess the adequacy of lean body mass and fat stores (Canadian Bureau of Nutritional Sciences, 1983; Cronk & Roche, 1982; Spender et al., 1988). Assessment of body composition using these measures is most useful with sequential measurements.

Table 43.2. Classification of the risk for protein–energy malnutrition (PEM)

Ratio of actual weight to ideal body weight	Risk of PEM
90%–110%	Normal
85%–90%	Mild PEM
75%–85%	Moderate PEM
<75%	Severe PEM

McLaren, D.S., & Read, W.C. (1972). Classification of nutritional status in early childhood. *The Lancet, 2,* 146; reprinted with permission from Elsevier.

There are limitations to the use of these measures (Spender et al., 1988). Use of single-site skinfold measurements may lead to inaccurate assessments of body composition because fat deposition in the body may be site dependent. Measurement technique may also affect the accuracy and precision of information derived from use of this approach. Individuals responsible for measurement of skinfolds should be trained in this method and measurements should be done in triplicate to minimize errors due to technique. A repeat measure by the same individual over time ensures that the values obtained from these measurements are consistent. Measurement of skinfolds should also be done using the same calipers to reduce the potential for instrument error. Hence, standardizing the method of measurement of skinfolds and mid-arm circumference is important to reduce the potential for error in assessment of body composition.

ASSESSMENT OF ENERGY REQUIREMENTS

Assessment of energy requirements is an essential component of nutrition assessment. Under- and overnutrition in children with developmental disabilities may be caused by deficits or surpluses of dietary intake over current energy requirements. Total energy requirements (total amount of energy expenditure in 24 hours) may be divided into the following components: basal requirements (energy expended at rest, shortly after awakening, after a 12–14 hour fast), energy requirements secondary to activity, thermic effect of food, and disease-related losses (e.g., fever, burns) (Zemel & Stallings, 1997). **Resting energy expenditure (REE)** refers to the amount of energy expended under conditions of rest, 12–14 hours after eating.

Several methods may be used to determine energy requirements in children with developmental disabilities. These include measurement of resting energy requirements using such techniques as indirect calorimetry, doubly labeled water techniques, reference equations, or recommended nutrient intake data (Spender et al., 1988). The use of recommended nutrient data is not appropriate for children with developmental disabilities, as it does not reflect the differences in activity, body composition, and body size that are prevalent in this group (Canadian Bureau of Nutritional Sciences, 1983). The use of the doubly-labeled water technique is most appropriate in research settings due to its high costs and demands for technical support. Use of indirect calorimetry is appropriate for assessment of resting energy requirements in this population, but it requires the availability of a skilled technician for use in a clinical setting.

The most convenient tool to assess energy requirements of children with developmental disabilities in clinical settings are the World Health Organization (1985) formulas. These formulas allow individualized assessment of resting energy requirements based on the age and weight of the child. Assessment of total energy requirements may be accomplished by adjustment for activity and disease factors. For healthy children, this translates into total energy requirements. Total energy requirements is equal to REE (based on WHO standards) multiplied by a factor of 1.5–1.7. For children with spastic quadriplegic cerebral palsy, however, estimates of total energy requirements should be based on REE (based on WHO standards) multiplied by a factor of 1.1 (Azcue et al., 1996; Bandini et al., 1991; Fried & Pencharz, 1991; Johnson et al., 1995). It is necessary to adjust REE (based on World Health Organization standards) to account for estimations of total energy requirements that also consider current neuromuscular function. For example, children with cerebral palsy with significant athetosis (continuous, involuntary motion) or who are ambulatory have increased energy needs that may require adjustment of the REE values (Johnson et al., 1995). Hence, adjustments to estimates of resting energy requirements based on the WHO standards should consider neuromuscular status in children with spastic quadriplegic cerebral palsy to ensure that accurate assessments of total energy requirements are made (Azcue et al., 1996; Bandini et al., 1991; Johnson et al., 1995). Display 43.1 demonstrates how a nutritional assessment resulted in improved growth and quality of life for a child with spastic quadriplegia.

NUTRITIONAL MANAGEMENT

Feeding difficulties that result from dysphagia can be managed as follows (Cloud, 1993; Palmer et al., 1975; Reilly et al., 1996; Telch & Telch, 2003; Zemel & Stallings, 1997):

- Altering food textures to ensure safety of swallowing
- Increasing the energy density of the diet
- Using proper positioning during feeding
- Selecting appropriate feeding utensils
- Assessing the route of feeding

Alteration in food texture to minimize the risk of aspiration of food contents into the lungs is the most common compensatory strategy for children with dysphagia. Food texture alterations may include the use of minced, puréed or thickened textures. Choice of food texture(s) is based on feeding efficiency and on the ability to swallow a food texture safely. Limitations in food texture choices and selections may result in decreased food intake and weight loss. Energy intake may be enhanced by the addition of protein, carbohydrate, and/or fat modules to foods or by the addition of high-energy/high-protein oral supplements to the diet. This chapter focuses on nutritional issues, but it should be remembered that evaluation of the need for adaptive feeding utensils, positioning, and route of feeding are all important parts of a comprehensive feeding assessment.

Persistent undernutrition can lead to the necessity of enteral support to meet nutritional and hydration requirements (Cloud, 1993; Zemel & Stallings, 1997). Enteral support involves the insertion of **enterostomy devices** such as nasogastric (short-term) or gastrostomy (long-term) feeding tubes (Grunow et al., 1994; Nutrition Committee, 1994; Telch & Telch, 2003). These tubes are used to deliver nutrition and hydration to children whose requirements cannot be met orally. Feeding with these devices is usually supplemental. However, when the risk of aspiration from oral feeding is significant or when oral intake is severely limited, the insertion of enterostomy devices may be necessary to meet total nutritional and hydration needs of the child (Reilly et al., 1996). Careful monitoring of tolerance to tube feeding regimens, oral intake, and enterostomy devices can make this mode of nutrition support successful. Transition from tube to oral feeding should be a primary goal in supplemental tube feeding. The weaning process should be directed toward supporting optimal nutrition, growth, and development during transition to oral feeding, with feeding interventions directed toward the child's developmental state (Grunow et al., 1994; Nutrition Committee, 1994). Assessment of nutritional status, swallowing function, and feeding behaviors (willingness to eat) should be done throughout this process to ensure a successful transition to oral feeding. Tube feeding should be discontinued when more than 75% of total energy needs can be met through oral intake (Nutrition Committee, 1994; Schauster & Dwyer, 1996), although devices must remain in place long enough to ensure that a patient can continue to maintain his or her nutritional status on oral feeds alone. Removal of gastrostomy devices should occur after 8–12 weeks of discontinuing nutri-

Display 43.1

Case study: Mary

Mary, age 8, has spastic quadriplegia and a history of many recent hospital admissions for pneumonia. It was thought that this was related to the aspiration of food in the lungs. A gastrostomy tube had been inserted at the age of 3 years because Mary was malnourished. Through the gastrostomy tube, she received overnight feeds that provided 500 kilocalories (kcal) per day, including 15 grams of protein. Assessment yielded the following findings.

Height and weight

- Current height (estimated): 110 centimeters (cm; third percentile)
- Current weight: 15 kilograms (kg; third percentile)

Current issues

- Mary exhibited failure to thrive.
- There appeared to be intolerance to overnight gastrostomy feeds. Mary was experiencing vomiting with these feeds. This was thought to be due to gastroesophageal reflux.
- Diet history indicated an energy intake of 200 kcal–300 kcal per day and difficulty with chewing meats and raw vegetables. There was no history of choking on liquids. Mary was now vomiting after each meal. Mealtimes were associated with a lot of stress associated with feeding. Her caregivers were very anxious about her food intake.
- Diagnostic tests, such as a gastric emptying study and a pH probe, indicated delayed gastric emptying and gastroesophageal reflux. A feeding study indicated feeding difficulty with solids. Soft foods were tolerated.

Assessment

- Ideal body weight: 19.5 kg
- Current percent ideal body weight: 77%: This indicated a moderate protein–energy malnutrition or a need for more nutrition.
- Total energy requirements (based on WHO formula: REE × 1.1) = 950 kcal per day: Mary's total energy intake (by gastrostomy tube plus oral intake) was not sufficient to meet these needs. Her current intake was providing only 75% of total energy requirements.

On the basis of the preceding findings, the following interventions were recommended:

- Provide increased energy diet with soft textures that are more easily tolerated. Document intake with the goal of meeting total energy intake via oral intake and gastrostomy feeds. Gastrostomy tube feeds should be kept at the present level, with the goal to adjust regimen in accordance with Mary's tolerance and rate of weight gain. The goal should be to promote oral intake and supplement with feeds via the gastrostomy tube. Monitor weight monthly in an outpatient setting.
- Focus on normalizing the feeding environment by promoting self-feeding. Initiate an occupational therapy referral regarding positioning and feeding utensils to facilitate self-feeding. Meal times should be limited to 20–30 minutes.
- Start giving Mary gastric motility agents and/or proton pump inhibitors for treatment of delayed gastric emptying and gastroesophageal reflux.

Outcome

Mary started to gain weight. She gained 1 kg (2.2 pounds) over the next 8 weeks. Her oral food intake started to increase. Her mother believed that this was due to the medications, as her vomiting had stopped. Mary still did not want to feed herself but was more willing to take food from her mother.

Source: Mager and Pencharz (2003).

tion support through these devices and when oral intake and rate of weight gain has become consistent (Nutrition Committee, 1994; Schauster & Dwyer, 1996). Complex ethical issues arise in the case of tube-feeding a person with intellectual or developmental disability (Telch & Telch, 2003); see also Chapter 41.

FUNCTIONAL CAPACITY

Assessment of the functional capacity to self-feed is also very important in children with neurological impairment (Cloud, 1993; Reilly et al., 1996). Significant impairment in gross and fine motor skills may lead to a loss of independence to self-feed by limitations of food access, inability to participate in food preparation, and loss of fine motor skills that are required to self-feed. Adaptive feeding devices and assistance with positioning may be useful in increasing independence and safety in feeding. Functional impairments may include ataxia (failure of muscle coordination, resulting in poorly judged movements), apraxia (inability to plan and execute a skilled movement in the absence of sensory and motor defects), and skeletal-muscular limitations (e.g., upper limb contracture). When possible, individuals should be comfortably positioned in an upright position during a meal to facilitate ease and safety of feeding. Assistance with feeding by caregivers should promote independence with feeding. Pace of feeding, volume of the food bolus (how much food is being chewed at one time) and alterations in food textures can promote a self-feeding environment for children with neurological impairments. Length of meal times should be limited to approximately 30 minutes to ensure optimal feeding efficiency (Cloud, 1993; Reilly et al., 1996).

Intervention by a behavioral feeding specialist can also assist in identifying and treating feeding problems in children with developmental disabilities. There is a focus on the child–feeder interaction in addition to oral-motor skills and functional capacity to assist in normalizing the feeding environment (Rodas-Arts & Benoit, 1998). This usually includes mealtime observation for assessment of caregiver responses to adaptive and maladaptive feeding behaviors and intervention to promote appropriate eating behaviors (Rodas-Arts & Benoit, 1998).

OBESITY

The most common causes of obesity in children with developmental delay include dietary intake in excess of energy requirements and lack of mobility. A few children with spastic quadriplegic cerebral palsy have been shown to have decreased REE (Azcue et al., 1996; Fried & Pencharz, 1991). Caregiver overestimation of energy requirements can lead to overfeeding and excessive weight gain in this population. Obesity is also common in children with Prader-Willi syndrome and trisomy 21 (Down syndrome).

Assessment of obesity in children with developmental disabilities may be difficult due to limitations in the ability to measure height, weight, and skinfold measures. This limits the use of the body mass index (BMI) to quantify or serial track the onset and severity of obesity in this population. Waist circumference measures have been used to provide information regarding the severity of obesity in children (Rudolf et al., 2004). Measurement of waist circumference is a simple and easy tool that can be used to provide additional information regarding the severity of obesity in this population.

Dietary treatment of obesity in children with developmental disabilities involves modification of energy intake. Dietary intake should include all food groups to prevent macro- and micronutrient deficiency with energy restriction. Pediatric enteral formulas should be used for children fed via enterostomy devices. These formulas contain higher nutrient–energy ratios, which decrease the risk of micronutrient deficiency with energy restriction (Azcue et al., 1996; Fried & Pencharz, 1991). Dietary counseling of caregivers by a registered dietitian regarding food portion size and food selection is an essential component to the successful dietary treatment of obesity in this population. A weight management program that has been used with considerable success by many people with Prader-Willi syndrome is called the Red-Yellow-Green Weight Control Program. This is based on the traffic light color system. Green means "Go!", yellow means "Caution—be careful, go slow," and red means "Stop!" (The Children's Institute, 2004). The program requires a dietitian skilled in its administration to support its application.

SUMMARY

Under- and overnutrition are common concerns of children with developmental delay. Under- and overnutrition are the deficit or surplus of dietary intake over total nutritional needs. The common causes of malnutrition in children with developmental delay include poor dietary intake and diminished feeding efficiency that result from swallowing and gastrointestinal dysfunction. Feeding problems and functional impairments to self-feeding may compound this. Assessment of nutritional status should include assessment of growth parameters, body composition, diet and medical history, and energy requirements to identify risk for under- and overnutrition. Management of nutritional disorders in children with developmental disabilities is complex and should include a multidisciplinary approach.

FOR FURTHER THOUGHT AND DISCUSSION

1. Consider both the children and adults with developmental disabilities that you have known. How common do you think malnutrition might be in this population?
2. Think of a child you know who might benefit from a nutrition assessment. What steps would you take to ensure that a full multidisciplinary assessment occurs?
3. In a group with three others, identify four children with developmental disabilities who have feeding difficulties of various kinds. What are some practical ways that each could be helped in ways that promote his or her independence?

REFERENCES

Azcue, M.P., Zello, G.A., Levy, L.D., et al. (1996). Energy expenditure and body composition in children with spastic quadriplegic cerebral palsy. *Journal of Pediatrics, 129,* 870–876.

Bandini, L.G., Scholler, D.A., Gukagawa, N.K., et al. (1991). Body composition and energy expenditure in adolescents with cerebral palsy or myelodysplasia. *Pediatric Research, 29,* 70–77.

Canadian Bureau of Nutritional Sciences. (1983). *Recommended nutrient intakes for Canadians.* Ottawa, ON, Canada: Health and Welfare Canada, Canadian Government Publication Centre.

Centers for Disease Control and Prevention & National Center for Health Statistics. (2004). *CDC growth charts: United States.* Retrieved August 12, 2004, from http://www.cdc.gov/growthcharts

The Children's Institute. (2004). *What the Red-Yellow-Green Weight Control Program is all about.* Retrieved August 24, 2004, from http://amazingkids.org/red_yellow_green.asp

Chumlea, W.C., & Cronk, C.E. (1981). Overweight among children with trisomy 21. *Journal of Mental Deficiency Research, 25,* 275–280.

Cloud, H. (1993). Feeding problems of the child with special health care needs. In S.W. Ekvall (Ed.), *Pediatric nutrition in chronic diseases and developmental disorder* (pp. 203–217). Oxford, United Kingdom: Oxford University Press.

College of Family Physicians of Canada & Community Health Nurses Association of Canada. (2004). Which growth charts to use for assessing and monitoring growth in Canadian infants and children. *Canadian Journal of Dietetic Practice and Research, 65,* 22–32. (Available at http://www.dietitians.ca/news/highlights_positions.asp)

Cronk, C., Crocker, A.C., Pueschel, S.M., et al. (1988). Growth charts for children with Down syndrome: 1 month to 18 years of age. *Pediatrics, 81,* 102–110.

Cronk, C.E., & Roche, A.E. (1982). Race- and sex-specific reference data for triceps and subscapular skinfolds and weight/stature. *American Journal of Clinical Nutrition, 35* (2), 347–354.

DiLorenzo, C., Piepz, A., Ham, H., et al. (1991). Gastric emptying with gastroesophageal reflux. *Archives of Disabled Children, 62,* 499–453.

Fried, M.D., & Pencharz, P.B. (1991). Energy and nutrient intakes of children with spastic quadriplegia. *Journal of Pediatrics, 119,* 947–949.

Garza, C., & de Onis, M. (1999). A new international growth reference for young children. *American Journal of Clinical Nutrition, 70*(Suppl. 1), 169–172.

Goldbloom, R.B. (1997). Assessment of physical growth and nutrition. In R.B. Goldbloom, *Pediatric clinical skills* (2nd ed., pp. 23–48). New York: Churchill Livingston.

Grummer-Strawn, L.M., Garza, C., & Johnson, C.L. (2002). Childhood growth charts. *Pediatrics, 109,* 141–142.

Grunow, J., Chait, P., Savoie, S., et al. (1994). Recent advances in gastrostomy feeding. In T.J. David (Ed.), *Recent advances in paediatrics* (12th ed., pp. 23–29). New York: Churchill Livingston.

Guo, S., Roche, A.F., Fomon , S.F., et al. (1991). Reference data on gains in weight and length during the first two years of life. *Journal of Pediatrics, 119,* 355–362.

Hamil, P.V., Drizd, T.A., Johnson, C.L., et al. (1979). Physical growth: National Center for Health Statistics (NCHS) percentiles. *American Journal Clinical Nutrition, 36,* 607–629.

Himes, J.G., Roche, A.F., Thissen, D., et al. (1985). Parent-specific adjustments for evaluation of recumbent length and stature of children. *Pediatrics, 75,* 304–313.

Hopkins, B. (1993). Assessment of nutritional status. In M.M. Gottschlich, L.E. Matarese, & E.P. Shronts (Eds.), *Nutrition support dietetics core curriculum* (2nd ed., pp. 15–63). Silver Spring, MD: American Society of Parenteral and Enteral Nutrition.

Johnson, R.K., Goran, M.I., Ferrara, M.S., et al. (1995). Athetosis increases resting metabolic rate in adults with cerebral palsy. *Journal of the American Dietetic Association, 95,* 145–148.

Krick, J., Murphy-Miller, P., Zeger, S., et al. (1996). Pattern of growth in children with cerebral palsy. *Journal of the American Dietetic Association, 96,* 680–685.

Lifschitz, F., & Maclaren, N.K. (1975). Vitamin D-dependent rickets in institutionalized, mentally retarded children receiving long-term anticonvulsant therapy: A survey of 288 patients. *Journal of Pediatrics, 56,* 52–57.

Mager, D., & Pencharz, P. (2003). Nutritional considerations in children with developmental disabilities. In I. Brown & M. Percy (Eds.), *Developmental disabilities in Ontario* (2nd ed., pp. 775–792). Toronto: Ontario Association on Developmental Disabilities.

McLaren, D.S., & Read, W.C. (1972). Classification of nutritional status in early childhood. *The Lancet, 2,* 146.

Nutrition Committee, Canadian Paediatric Society. (1994). Clinical practice guidelines: Undernutrition in children with a neurodevelopmental disability. *Canadian Medical Association Journal, 151,* 759.

Palmer, S., Thompson, R.J., & Linscheid, T.R. (1975). Applied behavior analysis in the treatment of childhood feeding problems. *Developmental Medicine and Child Neurology, 17,* 333–339.

Reilly, S., Skuse, D., & Poblete, X. (1996). Prevalence of feeding problems and oral motor dysfunction in children with cerebral palsy: A community survey. *Journal of Pediatrics, 129,* 877–882.

Roche, A.F., & Davila, G.H. (1974). Differences between recumbent length and stature within individuals. *Growth, 38,* 313.

Roche, A.F., & Himes, J.H. (1980). Incremental growth charts. *American Journal of Clinical Nutrition, 33,* 2041–2052.

Rodas-Arts, D., & Benoit, D. (1998). Feeding problems in infancy and early childhood: Identification and management. *Paediatric Child Health, 3,* 21–27.

Roe, A. (1982). *Handbook: Interactions of selected drugs and nutrients in patients* (3rd ed.). Chicago: American Dietetic Association.

Rudolf, M.C.J., Greenwood, D.C., Cole, T.J., et al. (2004). Rising obesity and expanding waistlines in school children: A cohort study. *Archives of Diseases of Childhood, 89,* 235–237.

Rudolph, C.D. (1994). Feeding disorders in infants and children. *Journal of Pediatrics, 125,* S116–S124.

Schauster, H., & Dwyer, J. (1996). Transition from tube feedings to feedings by mouth in children: Preventing eating dysfunction. *Journal of the American Dietetic Association, 96,* 277–281.

Schenker, J., & Ward, R. (1999). Development and application of a pediatric anthropometric evaluation system. *Canadian Journal of Dietetic Practice and Research, 60,* 20–26.

Sondheimer, J.M., & Morris, B.A. (1979). Gastroesophageal reflux among severely retarded children. *Journal of Pediatrics, 94,* 710–714.

Spender, Q.W., Cronk, C.E., Charney, E.B., et al. (1989). Assessment of linear growth of children with cerebral palsy: Use of alternative measures to height or length. *Developmental Medicine and Child Neurology, 31,* 206–214.

Spender, Q.W., Hediger, M.L., Cronk, C.E., et al. (1988). Fat distribution in children with cerebral palsy. *Annals of Human Biology, 15,* 191–196.

Sullivan, P.B. (1997). Gastrointestinal problems in the neurologically impaired child. *Baillieres Clinical Gastroenterology, 11,* 529–556.

Tanner, J.M., Whitehouse, R.H., & Takaishi, M. (1966). Standards from birth to maturity for height, weight, height velocity and weight velocity: British children 1965, I and II. *Archives of Disease in Childhood, 41,* 454–471, 613–615.

Telch, J., & Telch, F.E. (2003). Practical aspects of nutrition in the disabled pediatric patient. *Clinical Nutrition, 3,* 1–6.

Traub, S.L. (Ed.). (1996). *Basic skills in interpreting laboratory data* (2nd ed.). Bethesda, MD: American Society of Health-System Pharmacists.

World Health Organization. (1985). *Energy and protein requirements* [Technical report series # 724]. Geneva: Author.

Zemel, B., & Stallings, V.A. (1997). Energy requirements and nutritional assessment in developmental disabilities. In W.A. Walker & J.B. Watkins (Eds.), *Nutrition in pediatrics* (pp. 169–177). London: Decker.

44

Implications of Alzheimer's Disease for People with Down Syndrome and Other Intellectual Disabilities

Vee Prasher, Maire Percy, Emoke Jozsvai, John S. Lovering, and Joseph M. Berg

WHAT YOU WILL LEARN ABOUT IN THIS CHAPTER

- Alzheimer's disease in the general population
- Dementia of the Alzheimer's type (DAT) in people with Down syndrome
- Dementia and Alzheimer's disease in people with intellectual disabilities other than Down syndrome
- Multidisciplinary approach to managing Alzheimer's disease, DAT, and dementia

In 1907, Alois Alzheimer, a German neuropathologist, reported clinical and postmortem neuropathological findings in a 56-year-old woman who had developed progressive severe loss of memory, disorientation, disturbance of language, and paranoid ideas across the last 5 years of her life (Alzheimer, 1907). At autopsy, her brain tissue was treated with a newly developed silver stain and examined microscopically. It was found to be riddled with numerous diffuse deposits and intensely staining fibrils that now are called amyloid plaques and neurofibrillary tangles, respectively. This disease process, which was characterized by clinical dementia and unique changes in the brain, apparently was first named Alzheimer's disease by Kraepelin in 1910, a tribute that has become the general designation for the condition since then.

Alzheimer's disease can affect any adult as age advances. Understanding of this disorder in people with preceding intellectual disability has lagged behind knowledge of the disease in the general population, with many clinical and biological issues still unresolved. In view of overall improvements in life expectancy, often dramatic in people with Down syndrome and other types of intellectual disability, aging issues (including Alzheimer's disease) in people with intellectual disabilities are bound to receive increasing attention, leading to prospects of better care for this often ignored section of society. This chapter provides an outline of Alzheimer's disease and considers its implications for people with Down syndrome and other types of intellectual disability. The chapter takes a research-to-practice approach, and its goal is to provide an overview of fundamentals. It focuses on core issues and approaches, identified from reviews of the current literature and from many excellent web sites (listed in Appendix B at the end of the book) and thereby drawing on the vast experiences of the authors in the field.

ALZHEIMER'S DISEASE IN THE GENERAL POPULATION

For the purpose of providing background, the chapter begins with an explanation of Alzheimer's disease in the general population. Topics discussed include abnormal brain features, prevalence, underlying causes and protective factors, changes associated with normal aging and with dementia, clinical manifestations, the need for a diagnosis, and the diagnostic process.

Abnormal Brain Features

Neuropathologically, Alzheimer's disease is a disease process characterized by the appearance of numerous amyloid plaques and neurofibrillary tangles, principally in the outer part of the brain (cortex) but with some changes also in deeper regions (Wilcock & Esiri, 1982). Amyloid plaques (also called senile plaques or neuritic plaques) are areas of degeneration associated with a central core containing a protein often referred to as β-*amyloid,* itself formed from another larger protein called amyloid precursor protein (APP), the gene for which is located on chromosome 21. In a healthy brain,

The chapter authors thank Peter Barber, Senior Lecturer in Pathology, University of Birmingham, United Kingdom, for the prints of the amyloid plaques and neurofibrillary tangles.

β-amyloid fragments either are not formed or are broken down and eliminated. In Alzheimer's disease, the fragments accumulate to form hard insoluble plaques. It is thought that the generation of β-amyloid from APP leads to a type of immune reaction, with the formation of debris and inflammation around the central amyloid core (Butterfield, et al., 2002). Because amyloid binds the metal ions zinc, copper, and iron, some researchers believe that amyloid plaques play a role in defending the brain against metal ion toxicity (Castellani et al., 2004; Todorich & Connor, 2004).

Neurofibrillary tangles are found within the nerve cells (neurons) and are paired helical filaments that disrupt cell function. They are insoluble twisted fibers that are formed inside of neurons. They primarily consist of a protein called tau, which forms part of a structure called a microtubule. The microtubules help transport nutrients and other important substances from one part of the neuron to another. In Alzheimer's disease, the tau is abnormal (it carries too many phosphate groups) and the microtubule structures collapse. Because neurofibrillary tangles bind the metal ions iron and aluminum, some researchers believe that neurofibrillary tangles also play a role in defending the brain against metal ion toxicity (Shin et al., 2003).

Plaques and tangles are not specific to Alzheimer's disease. They are found in other brain diseases such as Parkinson's disease (although in that disease the brain regions involved differ from those affected in Alzheimer's disease). They are also found in the brains of up to approximately 30% of older people with typical cognitive functioning. However, in adults who have been diagnosed with Alzheimer's disease on the basis of their clinical symptoms, the numbers of plaques and tangles in particular regions of the brain are markedly increased above the normal limits expected in people of the same age without dementia. Thus, to reach a diagnosis of Alzheimer's disease after death on the basis of a brain autopsy, attention is necessary not just to the presence of plaques and tangles but also to how many there are and in which brain regions they are located (Khachaturian, 1985; Wilcock & Esiri, 1982). A brain imaging technique has been developed to visualize amyloid deposits in living brains. This approach is expected to help with the early diagnosis of Alzheimer's disease (Klunk et al., 2004). The two characteristic features of the Alzheimer brain are shown in Figure 44.1a and Figure 44.1b. Along with plaques and tangles, which are microscopic abnormalities only seen with special staining techniques or with high-powered microscopes, other brain changes associated with Alzheimer's disease also occur as listed in Table 44.1.

Approximately 40 years after Alzheimer's initial account, an association between Alzheimer's disease and Down syndrome was established. It was recognized that the brains of virtually all people with Down syndrome older than the age of approximately 40 years had features resembling those characteristic of Alzheimer's disease (Figure 44.2), although not all of those aging people with Down syndrome developed clinical manifestations of Alzheimer's disease. During the rest of the 20th century and beyond, there have been numerous reports concerning clinical, pathological, and genetic links between Alzheimer's disease and Down syndrome (Berg, Karlinsky, & Holland, 1993), although investigations of Alzheimer's disease in rela-

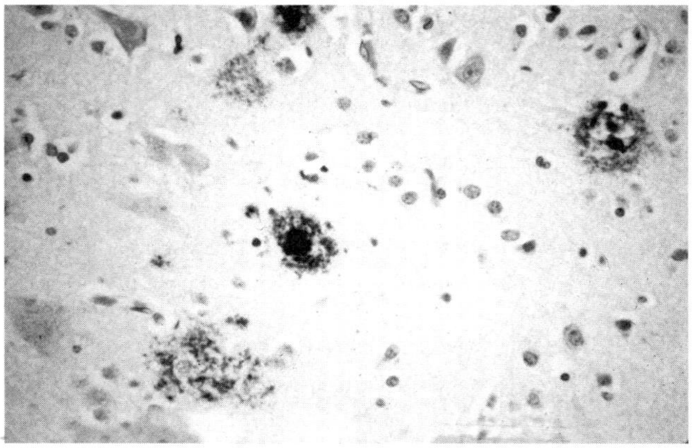

a)

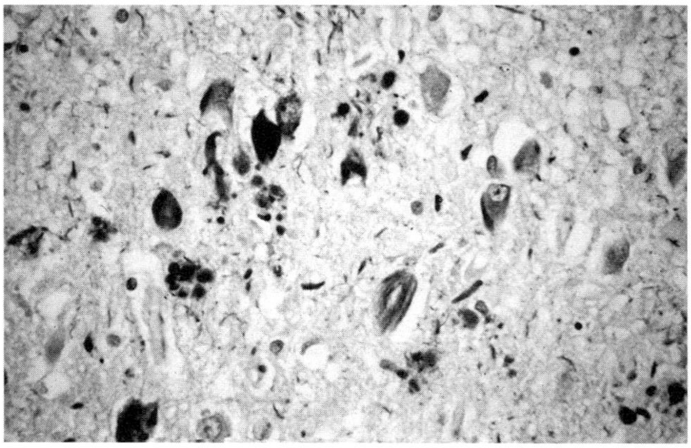

b)

Figure 44.1. a) Characteristic amyloid plaques of Alzheimer's disease. The brain of all individuals with Alzheimer's disease is riddled with amyloid plaques. Brain tissue from the cortex of an individual with Alzheimer's disease stained with antibody (Dako M872) that recognizes β-amyloid, a breakdown product of amyloid precursor protein. The large, dense, roundish deposits in this section are amyloid plaques that have been stained with this antibody. b) Characteristic neurofibrillary tangles of Alzheimer's disease. The brain of all individuals with Alzheimer's disease is also riddled with neurofibrillary tangles. Brain tissue from the cortex of an individual with Alzheimer's disease stained with antibody (Sigma T5530) that recognizes tau protein in neurofibrillary tangles. The densely staining deposits that are present inside some of the neurons (triangular cells with a large, oval nucleus) are neurofibrillary tangles that have been stained with this antibody. (Copyright © 2006 Peter Barber; the authors thank Peter Barber, Senior Lecturer in Pathology, University of Birmingham, U.K., for prints of the amyloid plaques and neurofibrillary tangles.)

Table 44.1. Quantitative brain changes in Alzheimer's disease

Type of change	Reduction
Brain weight	7.5%–18%
Weight of cerebral cortex	20%–58%
Thickness of cortex	10%–15%
Hemispheral volume	13%–18%
Number of nerve cells	22%–60%

Source: Prasher and Percy (2003).

tion to intellectual disabilities other than Down syndrome have been much more limited.

It is not surprising that the widespread changes in the brains of people with Alzheimer's disease result in disturbance of brain function. Chemicals called *neurotransmitters,* which usually maintain communication between nerve cells and normal brain function (see Chapter 7), are progressively reduced as pathological changes increase. This results in the characteristic clinical picture of Alzheimer's disease (see Clinical Manifestations section).

Prevalence

The reported prevalence of Alzheimer's disease (i.e., the number of affected people in a population at a given time) in the general population varies in different studies and among different ethnic groups, but the striking age dependence of the disease is always evident. In North America, the prevalence of Alzheimer's disease doubles every 5 years beyond age 65. Approximately 1 in 13 people older than age of 65, and approximately 1 in 4 people older than age of 85, develop the disease. Approximately two thirds of people diagnosed clinically are women. Approximately 40% of aging people who were not recognized to have dementia before they died are found at autopsy to show the neuropathological changes of Alzheimer's disease, indicating that the disease develops (perhaps many years) prior to the presentation of clinical symptoms (Picard, 2004).

U.S. studies by Evans (1990) and Hebert et al. (2003) indicate the very large numbers of people in the general population affected with Alzheimer's disease and the future prospect of even much greater numbers in the absence of effectively applied preventive measures. Evans' estimate suggested that 2.88 million people age 65 years or older in the United States had probable Alzheimer's disease in 1980, with the number reaching 10.3 million in the year 2050. Hebert et al. estimated higher numbers of affected individuals in that country—that is, 4.5 million in 2000 and 13.2 million 50 years later. These figures are inevitably imprecise and will differ to some extent in different countries, depending on factors such as life expectancy, ethnicity, education level, diet, and diagnostic criteria. However, it is evident that Alzheimer's disease is an increasingly major worldwide concern for affected people, their caregivers, and society as a whole.

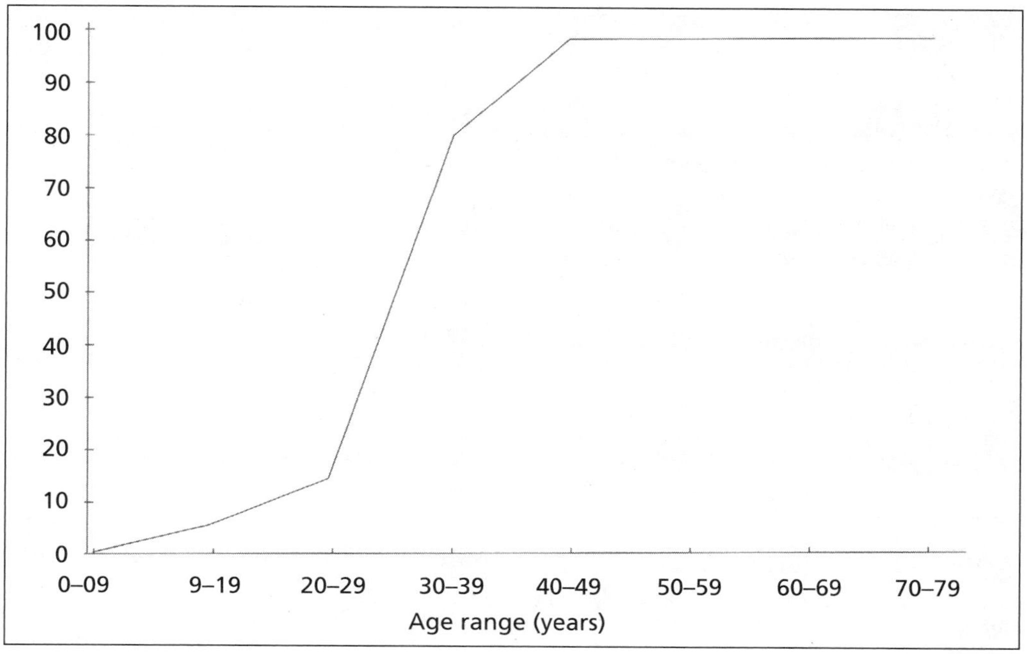

Figure 44.2. Cumulative frequency of senile plaques and neurofibrillary tangles in people with Down syndrome. (*Source:* Prasher and Percy, 2003).

Underlying Causes and Protective Factors

There is no single known cause of Alzheimer's disease and no known cure. However, it is generally accepted that Alzheimer's disease is the end product of a number of different pathways eventually leading to the formation of plaques and tangles and resulting in clinical dementia. Table 44.2 lists some risk factors for Alzheimer's disease. Advancing age of adults is the most obvious risk factor in all populations. The relevance of socioeconomic determinants of health is emerging, particularly from new research on identical and fraternal twins (Karp et al., 2004; Picard, 2004).

Individuals with a first-degree relative (e.g., parent, sibling) with Alzheimer's disease are believed to have a greater chance of developing the disease. In approximately 95% of people with Alzheimer's disease, however, the condition occurs sporadically (without any affected relative being apparent) for reasons that are not well understood. Studies of twins suggest that sporadic Alzheimer's disease generally results from the combination of a genetic predisposition and environmental triggers. A report from Sweden stated that if one identical twin developed Alzheimer's disease, there was a 59% chance that the other twin would do so as well; among fraternal twins, there was a 32% chance of such concordance for the disease (Gatz et al., 2005). However, in the limited number of other studies thus far undertaken, concordance rates for Alzheimer's disease among both identical and fraternal twins have differed substantially (Räihä et al., 1997).

A gene that produces a protein called apolipoprotein E (ApoE) has been recognized to be involved in sporadic Alzheimer's disease. ApoE occurs in three major forms: E2, E3, and E4. Every person inherits one ApoE gene from each parent. Evidence suggests that the E4 form of the protein leads to earlier development of Alzheimer's disease in Caucasians (Khachaturian et al., 2004; see Chapter 7 for more information about ApoE). People with two copies of E4 tend to develop Alzheimer's disease several years earlier than those with one E4. However, not everyone with one or two E4s develops Alzheimer's disease. Research has led to the proposition that different forms of ApoE affect a person's susceptibility to certain types of infection. For instance, the E2 form of ApoE may predispose to early infection with malaria. Also, the herpes simplex virus type 1 (HSV1), when present in brain, acts together with the E4 allele of ApoE to confer a much stronger risk of Alzheimer's disease than E4 alone; in carriers of the other two main alleles of the gene, the virus does not confer a risk (Itzhaki et al., 2004). It has been shown as well that the outcome of infection in the case of five diseases known to be caused by viruses is determined by the ApoE type. It is hoped that the discovery of the involvement of HSV1 in Alzheimer's disease will lead to future antiviral therapy and possibly to immunization against the virus in infancy (Wozniak, Riley, & Itzhaki, 2004).

Table 44.2. Some etiological factors that have strong and possible associations with Alzheimer's disease

Strong association	Possible association
Age	Head trauma
Family history of Alzheimer disease	Excessive aluminium
	History of thyroid disease
Down syndrome	Depression
Apolipoprotein E status	Family history of Down syndrome
Stress	
Low socioeconomic status, including poor education	Mutations in genes (APP, PS1, PS2)

Source: Prasher and Percy (2003).

Key: APP = amyloid precursor protein; PS1 = presenilin type 1; PS2 = presenilin type 2.

Alzheimer's disease can recur in families in an inherited form known as *familial autosomal dominant Alzheimer's disease* that can be passed on from one generation to the next, although recurrence in relatives of an affected person is not inevitable. This inherited form of Alzheimer's disease accounts for approximately 5%–10% of all cases of the disease and usually occurs in people younger than age 65, sometimes even in people who are in their 40s. Rare mutations in one of three genes—APP and presenilins 1 and 2 (PS1 and PS2)—are known to be crucial for the development of Alzheimer's disease in some families with familial autosomal dominant Alzheimer's disease (Percy, 1999). Such mutations should be distinguished from common variants of these three genes, which may affect the risk of getting Alzheimer's disease or its age of onset but not actually cause it.

Because some identical twins develop Alzheimer's disease and others do not, and because the age of onset of the disease is not exactly the same in identical twins who both develop it, it has been postulated that Alzheimer's disease may be warded off to some extent by adopting better lifestyles (Haan & Wallace, 2004; Jansson, 2005; Victoroff, 2002). This includes reducing risk factors for cardiovascular disease such as stress, obesity, high blood pressure, and high cholesterol; increasing physical and mental activity; avoiding polluted air; eating a diet rich in green vegetables that contain folic acid and antioxidants such as spinach and broccoli; and drinking safe water (Jansson, 2005; Picard, 2004).

As of 2007, one research focus involves testing the hypothesis that having an excessive amount of one or more heavy metals in the body contributes to Alzheimer's disease. One reason for this area of interest is that laboratory studies have shown that the β-amyloid found in brain plaques of people with Alzheimer's disease physically binds copper, zinc, and iron and that the neurofibrillary tangles of degenerating neurons in the Alzheimer's disease brain bind iron and aluminum. Although aluminum's involvement in Alzheimer's disease remains controversial, there continues to be interest in it for several reasons:

- Some studies have found the brain levels of aluminum to be higher in people with Alzheimer's disease than in healthy older adults (McLachlan et al., 1996).
- Other studies have reported an association between elevated levels of aluminum in drinking water and an increased risk of Alzheimer's disease (McLachlan et al., 1996).
- Intramuscular injection of desferrioxamine (Desferol), a drug that binds aluminum and iron and removes them from the body, has been found to slow down deterioration of daily living skills in people with moderate Alzheimer's disease by more than 50% (Crapper-McLachlan et al., 1991).

These findings do not provide justification for discarding aluminum cookware. However, it seems judicious to avoid cooking acidic food in aluminum pots (because the acid leaches aluminum from such pots into the food) and to avoid using deodorants, cosmetics, and antacids that contain aluminum.

Additional foci of current research include vitamin deficiencies and the importance of nutrition. There is considerable evidence that older people in general and people with Alzheimer's disease in particular have deficiencies of vitamins B_{12}, B_6, and folate (Miller, 2003), as well as vitamins E and C (Zandi et al., 2004). A clinical trial showed that oral supplementation with high-dose vitamin E substantially slowed down the development of Alzheimer's disease (Sano et al., 1997). Later studies have concern about supplementation with very high amounts of vitamin E, however ("High Doses of Vitamin E," 2005). Furthermore, there is evidence that eating fish at least once per week may help to ward off Alzheimer's disease (Morris et al., 2003), as will physical exercise (Podewils et al., 2005). Table 44.3 lists some factors that might protect against Alzheimer's disease.

Table 44.3. Some factors that might protect against Alzheimer's disease

Factors	Examples
Getting adequate levels of antioxidants	Vitamin E, vitamin C, seligiline (deprenyl)
Getting adequate levels of vitamins that regulate folate and homocysteine metabolism	Folate, vitamin B_6, vitamin B_{12}
Taking cholesterol-lowering drugs	Statins
Taking nonsteroidal anti-inflammatory drugs	Ibuprofen
Engaging in conditions that result in increased blood flow to the brain	Mental and physical activity
Reaching higher educational levels	Each year of education reduces risk of developing Alzheimer's disease
Eating a good diet	Fish as part of the diet at least once per week

Changes Associated with Normal Aging and with Dementia

Mental and physical decline of varying extent is a general phenomenon among all people aging into late life. Most people, including many with intellectual disability, maintain their cognitive abilities and adaptive behavior skills fairly well throughout their adult lives. However, normal aging is associated with declines in some areas of cognitive functioning. Different cognitive abilities decline at different rates with advancing age. Abstract reasoning and verbal skills (expressive and receptive language ability) tend to remain relatively intact, whereas perceptual and motor skills decrease more substantially and earlier (Zec, 1993). As people age, they generally show some reduction in their capacity to learn and recall new information, their reaction time increases, and their motor movements become slower. There are many causes of age-related changes in cognitive functioning. The most prominent factors thought to affect cognitive functioning in old age include sensory deficits (particularly reduced hearing and vision), general health status, and diminished motivation (Lifshitz & Merrick, 2004).

Dementia

Beyond normal aging and extending into the realm of disease, *dementia* is a term used to designate the development, generally in adults, of serious cognitive and associated disorders, often with a detectable pathological basis. More precisely in a diagnostic sense, Wherrett described the term as being applied "to persons in whom cognitive decline sufficient to impair personal, social, or occupational adaptation is the main presenting symptom, is persisting and progressive, and is associated with a chronic diffuse or multifocal brain disorder" (1999, p. 91). Aside from Alzheimer's disease, there are many actual or potential causes of dementia (see Table 44.4), with various designations to indicate particular specific types with distinctive characteristics—for example, multi-infarct dementia, vascular dementia, and dementia pugilistica. Nonetheless, the most common cause of dementia in aging people is Alzheimer's disease, often referred to as dementia of the Alzheimer's type (DAT).

Table 44.4. Common causes of dementia other than Alzheimer's disease

- Alcohol abuse
- Bacterial, fungal, and protozoan infections
- Brain tumor
- Depression
- Drugs
- Head trauma
- Heavy metal exposure
- Human immunodeficiency virus (HIV) infection
- Huntington disease
- Hypothyroidism
- Multiple sclerosis
- Normal pressure hydrocephalus
- Parkinson disease
- Pick disease
- Vascular dementia
- Vitamin deficiencies (folate; vitamins B_{12}, C, and E)

Source: Prasher and Percy (2003).

Clinical Manifestations

Symptoms of Alzheimer's disease range from early mild ones, which may go unnoticed and have little detrimental effect, to severe ones at the end stages of the disease process that can cause considerable stress to caregivers and lead to the need for nursing care. The disorder can be divided into three clinical stages (Table 44.5).

The onset of Alzheimer's disease is slow and gradual, with the precise age of onset often difficult to determine. The clinical symptoms of the disorder tend to develop gradually over a number of years. Those close to affected individuals frequently do not recognize that there is deterioration until it has become quite pronounced. As the disease progresses, it becomes increasingly apparent that there is progressive and significant decline in memory and other mental functions, in ways that are sometimes associated with severe depression. There is a gradual loss of self-care skills and growing additional problems with day-to-day living. Onset of seizures may be the first indication of need for medical attention. The later stage of Alzheimer's disease is marked by intellectual and physical deterioration. Total dependency and inactivity, with increased need for nursing care becomes evident. Pneumonia or urinary tract infection is often the immediate cause of death.

Alzheimer's disease manifestations vary among individuals. Some have a rapid, short illness, whereas others experience a longer, more gradual decline in health. Affected people are unlikely to experience all of the symptoms and signs listed in Table 44.5 or to decline precisely as outlined in the table, which should be used only as a guide. For a confident diagnosis of Alzheimer's disease, the decline of memory and other cognitive functions must be irreversible and present for at least 1 year. In Alzheimer's disease, deterioration of cognitive functioning is typically accompanied by personality, mood, and behavior changes.

Table 44.5. Main stages of Alzheimer's disease

Stage I: Early (duration 1–3 years)
- Memory loss (particularly short-term memory)
- Changes in personality
- Difficulties with language
- Disorientated in time
- Lost in familiar places
- Loss of motivation
- Signs of depression and aggression
- Loss of interest

Stage II: Middle (duration 2–5 years)
- Very forgetful
- Loss of self-care skills
- Greater dependency on others
- Increased speech difficulties
- Wandering
- Seizures
- Reduced mobility
- Behavior problems
- Hallucinations

Stage III: Late (duration 4–8 years)
- Marked intellectual deterioration
- Inability to recognize family, friends, and caregivers
- Dependence on others for dressing, washing, feeding, and toileting
- Immobility
- Bladder and bowel incontinence
- More severe seizures
- Limb rigidity and flexed postures
- Marked physical deterioration

Source: Prasher and Percy (2003).

The Need for a Diagnosis

For the general population, there are reliable clinical diagnostic tests for Alzheimer's disease that are based on signs and symptoms, although certain diagnosis can only be made with direct neuoropathological brain examination. In 1984, McKhann and colleagues published criteria for the diagnosis of possible, probable, and definite Alzheimer's disease. Particularly in settings that specialize in Alzheimer's disease and related disorders, these rigid diagnostic criteria enable an accurate clinical diagnosis to be made in 70% to 80% of individuals.

There are several important reasons for a diagnosis of Alzheimer's disease to be made.

This diagnosis enables

- Families and caregivers to understand what is happening to the person concerned
- Families and caregivers to plan for the future
- Families and caregivers to make provisions, with support if necessary, for appropriate care
- The exclusion of other, often treatable, causes of intellectual decline
- Consideration of appropriate medication

Table 44.6. Components of diagnosing Alzheimer's disease

- Interview of family members/caregivers for evidence of mental deterioration and of a possible differential diagnosis
- Formal assessment of mental condition, including detailed psychological assessment of memory and other intellectual functions[a]
- Comprehensive physical examination—including sensory testing, blood tests, and urinalysis—to exclude treatable conditions
- Electroencephalography, brain scan (computerized tomography, magnetic resonance imaging, single photon emission computed tomography)[a]
- Review of information and provisional diagnosis
- Follow-up, including further regular assessments to confirm diagnosis

Source: Prasher and Percy (2003).
[a]Dependent on availability of resources

The Diagnostic Process

A clinical diagnosis of Alzheimer's disease is principally based on initially identifying the presence of dementia and then excluding other possible treatable causes of the dementia. Over time, the characteristic deterioration of Alzheimer's disease (see clinical manifestations in Table 44.5) often becomes evident. Diagnosis is generally made as shown in Table 44.6. There are indications that the diagnosis of Alzheimer's disease may be aided by sensitive brain imaging techniques (e.g., computed or positron emission tomography, magnetic resonance imaging) or by measuring the amounts of particular substances in peripheral blood and other bodily fluids and tissues (e.g., amyloid or tau protein levels; Khachaturian, 1985).

DEMENTIA OF THE ALZHEIMER TYPE IN PEOPLE WITH DOWN SYNDROME

As noted, there is an association between Down syndrome and DAT. This topic is explored in terms of frequency, risk factors, and diagnosis.

Frequency

Interest in Alzheimer's disease in people with intellectual disabilities has focused primarily on the association between Down syndrome and Alzheimer's disease. It has long been known that virtually all adults with Down syndrome older than 40 years of age have a considerable amount of β-amyloid in their brains (see Figure 44.2). Furthermore, people with Down syndrome are at risk of developing dementia, and some do so 20–30 years earlier than is usually the case in the general population. This chapter uses DAT to refer to dementia that develops in older people with Down syndrome.

The high frequency of DAT in Down syndrome became increasingly apparent as people with Down syndrome lived longer, largely due to improved health care, nutrition, and housing conditions. In the 1920s, the life expectancy for Caucasians with Down syndrome was approximately 9 years, but by the 1980s it had reached approximately 35 years (Thase, 1982). In North America at the beginning of the 21st century, the expected life span of a 1-year-old Caucasian with Down syndrome and mild-to-moderate intellectual disability is 55 years and is approximately 45 years in such a child with profound cognitive impairment (Strauss & Eyman, 1996). In addition, in an extensive U.S. population-based study, Yang, Rasmussen, and Friedman (2002) found that the median age at death of people with Down syndrome increased from 25 years in 1983 to 49 years in 1997.

The life expectancy for females with Down syndrome appears to be less than that for males (Glasson et al., 2003), although the reverse is the case for people in the general population and for those with intellectual disability other than Down syndrome. Furthermore, in general and for whatever reasons—including, as Yang et al. (2002), noted, possible factors such as access, use of, or quality of health care—the life expectancy of non-Caucasians with Down syndrome has often been considerably less than for Caucasians with the syndrome. Because people with Down syndrome generally are living longer, more of them experience normal, although perhaps precocious, aging (Devenny et al., 1996) and the changes (e.g., sensory impairments, diminished interests) that often affect older adults in general. Nevertheless, the frequency of clinical manifestations of dementia in Down syndrome also increases with increasing age, and the frequency of these manifestations is greater at any age in people with Down syndrome than in the general population or in people with intellectual disabilities other than Down syndrome (Berg et al., 1993; Prasher & Krishnan, 1993).

The frequency of clinical features of possible Alzheimer's disease in people with Down syndrome increases from approximately 8% in those age 35–40 years to approximately 75% in those older than 60 years of age (Lai & Williams, 1989; Wisniewski, Silverman, & Wegiel, 1994). In individuals with Down syndrome who have a mild-to-moderate level of disability, the average age of onset of dementia is approximately 55 years, but early signs of dementia may appear before the age of 50 in some people. Higher functioning individuals with Down syndrome tend to remain free of symptoms longer than lower functioning individuals (Temple et al., 2001). Caregivers must be alerted to this possibility and be knowledgeable about how to cope with it.

Risk Factors

It is thought that people with Down syndrome tend to develop dementia much earlier than people in the general population because those with Down syndrome have an extra chromosome 21 and the gene for APP is located on the long arm of that chromosome. Having three APP genes, rather than the normal two, leads to overproduction of APP and subsequently to an excessive accumulation of the breakdown product β-amyloid in the brain. However, not all people with Down syndrome develop clinical symptoms of dementia. Furthermore, in many of them, the early stage of dementia is often overlooked and is attributed to the underlying intellectual disability, evident physical problems, or to a normal process of aging. Manifestations are modified by the genotype, the education level, the underlying degree of intellectual impairment, visual and/or auditory problems, and difficulty in communication and possibly also may be affected by other concurrent medical problems relatively that are common in people with Down syndrome (e.g., cardiovascular abnormalities, hypothyroid autoimmune thyroiditis, latent or chronic hepatitis B virus infection, celiac disease).

Understanding of genetic and environmental predisposing factors for DAT in Down syndrome is not as advanced as for Alzheimer's disease in the general population (Bush & Beail, 2004). However, progress is being made in understanding factors that predispose to DAT in Down syndrome, and indeed, is providing clues that are relevant to understanding Alzheimer's disease in the general population. As indicated in the Underlying Causes and Protective Factors section, the E4 allele of ApoE is a confirmed risk factor for Alzheimer's disease in Caucasians in the general population and it also results in an earlier age of onset of Alzheimer's disease. Its involvement in DAT in Down syndrome is less clear. A meta-analysis has suggested that the E4 allele of ApoE is somewhat overrepresented in people with Down syndrome who are affected with dementia compared with people with Down syndrome not so unaffected (Prasher et al., 1997). Schupf and Sergievsky (2002) noted that males with the E4 allele developed dementia several years earlier than those who did not carry that allele. Because the E4 allele is underrepresented in older people with Down syndrome compared with people of similar age without Down syndrome, having an E4 allele in Down syndrome may be associated with early mortality (Cosgrave et al., 1996). As in the general population, the E2 allele appears to be significantly protective against Alzheimer dementia in people with Down syndrome (Lai et al., 1999; Tyrrell et al., 1998). Percy et al. (2003) found E4 to be significantly overrepresented in females with Down syndrome who were being treated with thyroid hormone to reduce elevated thyroid stimulating hormone (an indicator of hypothyroidism), compared with similarly aged females with Down syndrome who had normal thyroid function, thus raising the possibility of an association between hypothyroidism and dementia in this population. It has been reported that a common variant of the prion gene (see Chapter 7) affects early cognitive decline in people with Down syndrome (Del Bo et al., 2004), as it does in the general population (Berr et al., 1998), and that a common variant of amyloid precursor protein gene significantly affects the age of onset of dementia in Down syndrome (Margallo-Lana et al., 2004). High body levels of iron have been noted in people with dementia and Down syndrome (Prasher, Gosling, & Blair, 1998). Furthermore, as in the general population, there is some evidence that herpes simplex virus type 1 infection may play a role in the development of DAT in people with Down syndrome (Cheon et al., 2001). In one study, DAT in people with Down syndrome was found to be associated with epilepsy, myoclonus (frequent small jerks of the body), and head injury (Tyrrell et al., 2001). Finally, among females with Down syndrome, there is a correlation between age of menopause and age of onset of dementia, suggesting that estrogen deficiency might result in an earlier age of onset of DAT (Cosgrave et al., 1999; Schupf et al., 2003).

Diagnosis

Several elements play a role in diagnosing DAT. These include the histopathological features of Alzheimer's disease in people with Down syndrome, problems distinguishing DAT from underlying cognitive disability, conditions that can mimic DAT, and longitudinal neuropsychological assessment.

Histopathological Features of Alzheimer's Disease in People with Down Syndrome Mrak and Griffin (2004) reported that in fetuses with Down syndrome, neurons fail to show normal dendritic development, yielding a "tree in winter" appearance. This developmental failure is thought to result in the intellectual disability associated with the syndrome. In older people with Down syndrome, there are changes in the histopathological appearance of the brain that resemble those in Alzheimer's disease. However, a high proportion of larger, more amorphous plaque cores with less compact amyloid fibrils, especially within the amygdala and entorhinal cortex, has been noted in older people with Down syndrome. See Mann (in press) for a review of this topic.

Problems Distinguishing Dementia of the Alzheimer Type from Underlying Cognitive Disability The clinical diagnosis of DAT remains problematic in people with Down syndrome and other types of intellectual disability. Clinicians have had difficulty in distinguishing symptoms of dementia from cognitive deficits resulting from the preceding intellectual disability. Because there is a wide variation in the degree of cognitive impairment among people with Down syndrome and people with intellectual disability in general, some tests that are used in dementia screening are too easy for some or too difficult for others. Also, there are a number of medical conditions that can mask as DAT (see next section). An approach has been developed for the diagnosis of dementia in Down syndrome that is based on the World Health Organization's International Classification of Diseases (ICD-10) guidelines (Aylward et al., 1997). Also, a number of tests designed for people with intellectual disability and cognitive deficits are now available to aid diagnosis (Burt & Aylward, 2000; Gedye, 1995, 1998; Prasher, Farooq, & Holder, 2004; Strydom & Hassiotis, 2003; see next section). For people with Down syndrome, information regarding which cluster of symptoms and signs best correlates with DAT remains to be fully determined in differentiating decline due to the normal aging process and that due to the disease process of DAT and other conditions.

When onset of dementia is suspected in a person with Down syndrome, it is vital to determine as early as possible if there is a treatable cause. Such causes in people with Down syndrome that can be effectively treated include early vitamin B_6, vitamine B_{12}, or folate deficiency, and early hypothyroidism, as well as severe depression and anxiety states.

Early signs of possible DAT in people with Down syndrome who have relatively higher levels of functional ability may include changes in personality (e.g., uncharacteristic irritability, mood swings) and reduced verbal communication. Initial symptoms often include problems in learning new things, changes in behavior, and memory loss (Prasher & Filer, 1995). For these people, early indicators of memory loss may be forgetting the location of commonly used objects, such as keys, spectacles, bus tickets, or a lunch bag. As the disease progresses, activities of daily living are further impaired. For example, performance at work may gradually deteriorate, capacity to follow an instruction may decline, ability to use a telephone or to write may dissipate, and loss of language skills (especially word-finding abilities) may occur. At a more advanced stage, seizures frequently develop. The seizures, including myoclonic ones, often appear after 2 years of evidence of dementia, but they usually occur somewhat later in higher functioning individuals with Down syndrome. Mobility typically becomes limited, and there may be bowel and bladder incontinence. Hallucinations and delusions may also develop. In addition, weight loss is common in people with Down syndrome and Alzheimer's disease (Prasher, Metseagharun, & Haque, 2004).

For lower functioning abilities and Down syndrome, the first indicators of possible Alzheimer's disease may be diminished social interaction, loss of interest in hobbies and previously enjoyed activities, or loss of self-care skills (Gedye, 1998). As the disease progresses, memory deficits become more prominent and signs of spatial disorientation appear. The affected person may get lost in familiar surroundings and become unable to travel independently on previously familiar routes. Supervisors at a workshop may begin noticing decreased work performance, with the need for increased supervision. Biological (diurnal) rhythms are sometimes disturbed, with frequent confusion between day and night. Motor functions slow down, and gait disturbances (problems with walking) may appear. The ability to perform the sequence of previously mastered complex tasks, such as toileting, dressing, or setting the table, diminishes. Bladder or bowel incontinence may begin to develop. Individuals without a previous history of epilepsy may commence having seizures.

As the disease progresses further, affected individuals are unable to recall the names of, or even recognize, close relatives and friends. The ability to communicate awareness of recent life experiences diminishes. Symptoms differ in sequence and degree from one person to another, but some include loss of purposeful activity, quiet resignation, delusional behavior, visual and auditory hallucinations, and myoclonus. At the late stages of their dementia, all verbal abilities and the ability to walk are typically lost, although not in a predictable sequence. Assistance with toileting and feeding is required. Death is frequently caused by infectious disease such as aspiration pneumonia, urinary tract infection, and infected bedsores, and it sometimes simply results from a loss of basic life functions, such as the ability to swallow solid food and even liquids.

Onset of symptoms of DAT in people with Down syndrome usually occurs in the early to mid-50s. The duration of the illness, leading ultimately to death, is on average 8 years. Longitudinal assessment over a period of time is often necessary before a diagnosis can be made. Caregivers are an essential source of information, but if a caregiver has known the person only briefly, sufficient details of the person's past and current functioning need to be ascertained elsewhere, if possible. Because the course of the disease may involve rapidly developing dementia or substantial periods of stability, a single assessment may be difficult to interpret accurately. Neurological and mental status examinations are critical to the evaluation. Many standardized psychological tests are problematic because they have not been standardized for a population of individuals who have a preceding cognitive disability. However, neuropsychological evaluation can be very helpful for both diagnosis and ongoing follow-up.

Some diagnostic tests that are frequently beneficial in detecting or excluding various conditions that occur in Down syndrome include neuroimaging and electroencephalography. Neuroimaging can identify atrophy (progressive loss of neuronal cells), in several specific areas of the brain, that is frequently associated with enlargement of the ventricles (spaces within the brain that serve as reservoirs for cerebrospinal fluid). Atrophy is progressive and often rapid. Changes in neuroimaging tend to be correlated with clinical deterioration (Kantarci & Jack, 2003; Wolf et al., 2003). Electroencephalography can identify an increase in slow wave activity in the brain. Although this is neither specific to Alzheimer's disease nor necessarily related to severity of the illness or the length of time dementia has been present, this abnormality can support a diagnosis of Alzheimer's disease (Rosen, 1997).

Conditions that Can Mimic Dementia of the Alzheimer Type Various physical conditions can diminish cognitive function in older people, including those with Down syndrome, and thus be mistaken for early evidence of Alzheimer's disease. Hypothyroidism, which affects approximately 40% of people with Down syndrome (Dinani & Carpenter, 1990; Percy et al., 1990; Percy & Prasher, in press), may precipitate decline by causing weight gain, apathy, mental slowing, and diminished energy levels. Depression related to grief from loss of friends or relatives or changes in residence and support workers may lead to withdrawal or loss of daily living skills, and may it be associated with the onset of incontinence, irritability, and insomnia (Cohen-Mansfield, Marx, & Werner, 1992; Collacott, 1992; Day & Jancar, 1994; Devenny et al., 1996; Pary, 1992).

Hearing loss and visual impairment may also contribute to deterioration of mental function. A large proportion of adults with Down syndrome (approximately one half to three quarters) experience hearing loss, and approximately one half develop cataracts (Keiser et al., 1981). Impaired hearing and vision lead to withdrawal, apathy, and reduced interest in one's environment, mimicking early symptoms of Alzheimer's disease.

Degenerative changes in the upper part of the cervical spine and joint problems in the hip and knee may cause pain and impair functioning in daily living (Tangerud et al., 1990). Vitamin B_{12} or folate deficiency and infectious diseases (e.g., pneumonia) may cause weight loss, tiredness, and, consequently, decreased activity levels. Excessive daytime sleepiness, chronic fatigue, and irritability can also result from sleep apnea, a disorder characterized by frequent, brief respiratory pauses while asleep (Telakivi et al., 1987). Prescribed drugs (e.g., seizure medications, tranquillizers) can interfere with cognitive functioning as well. In particular, there is published evidence (Tsiouris et al., 2002) that phenytoin should not be used to control late onset seizures in adults with Down syndrome, especially in those who already have evidence of dementia. Cardiac disease and diabetes may produce functional decline in the general population and may have similar effects in people with Down syndrome (Launer, 2005; Roman, 2004). In addition, celiac disease is associated with various neurological problems (e.g., cerebellar ataxia, epilepsy, myoclonic ataxia, chronic neuropathies, dementia) in people in the general population (Zelnik et al., 2004) and may have similar effects in people with Down syndrome (Chapter 10; Licastro et al., 2001).

It is important to identify all medical conditions that co-occur with deterioration of cognitive function in older people with Down syndrome, because with medical attention and treatment, cognitive functioning and skills of daily living often return to previous levels. (See Wallace & Dalton, 2006, for a review of medical conditions common in older people with Down syndrome.) It is therefore crucial that all people with Down syndrome suspected of developing DAT should undergo a thorough physical examination. This typically involves assessment of hearing and vision, screenings for thyroid dysfunction and infectious diseases, blood work to identify vitamin B_{12} or folate deficiency, and psychiatric evaluation for depression or anxiety. In addition, a neurological examination and brain imaging are recommended to identify other causes of dementia such as brain tumors or strokes.

Longitudinal Neuropsychological Assessment The diagnosis of DAT can be greatly aided by longitudinal neuropsychological assessment. Such assessment includes tests of memory, language functions, visual–spatial abilities, and adaptive behavior skills. Interviews with various caregivers (e.g., relatives, supervisors at the workplace, support workers in group homes) are an essential part of a neuropsychological assessment, as such people are usually the first to notice signs of cognitive decline and to initiate referrals. A speech-language pathologist is another key member of the assessment team. When individuals have low functioning or are nonverbal and cannot be assessed with formal test instruments, the Adaptive Behaviour Scale and/or the Dementia Scale for Down Syndrome may be administered to caregivers to elicit information about changes in functioning (Gedye, 1995, 1998). In the general population, dementia is diagnosed by comparing performance on cognitive tests with established standards (norms) for the person's age group. In people with Down syndrome, however, dementia is generally superimposed on already reduced cognitive functioning. Furthermore, there are significant individual differences in the abilities of people with Down syndrome who do not have dementia. Some have strengths in the verbal domain but weaknesses in visual–spatial or motor abilities, and the opposite pattern occurs in other people.

To facilitate early diagnosis of DAT, it is recommended that all adults with Down syndrome be evaluated at least once in early adulthood (by age 25 years) to establish a record of baseline cognitive functioning. When DAT is suspected, such earlier baseline data are useful for comparison with current test data to ascertain the nature and magnitude of changes in various areas of functioning. A baseline assessment includes testing functions that are known to decline with dementia, such as memory, orientation, visual–spatial skills, motor functions, and skills of daily living. A review of the literature and resources indicate that different centers have different approaches for screening for and diagnosing dementia. Assessments should be multidisciplinary and should include blood tests, a physical examination, hearing and vision tests, speech-language and neuropsychological evaluations, medical and psychiatric reviews, behavior management, occupational therapy and case coordination. These measures may be available in hospital clinics that specialize in Alzheimer's disease and related disorders, as well as in some settings serving adults with Down syndrome and other intellectual disabilities.

A protocol that could be used in a baseline assessment and adapted for annual screening in a clinical setting has been developed for a Multicenter International Clinical Trial of Vitamin E in Aging Persons with Down syndrome (Aisen et al., 2005; see Table 44.7 for a brief outline). The key outcome measure in the Vitamin E Trial is the Brief Praxis Test. This is a simple memory and praxis test first developed by Dalton et al. (1999). The term *praxis* comes from the Greek work *practice.* The test involves orally asking the participant to carry out a number of different directives, such as touch your head with your right hand, stand on your left foot, open the jar, pick up the quarters, and so forth. Approximately 20 different sites in several different countries are taking part in the Vitamin E Study. Further information about the protocol shown in Table 44.7 is available from any of the site directors of the Vitamin E Study (Aisen et al., 2005).

Table 44.7. Elements of the vitamin E clinical trial protocol for dementia screening

- Blood tests to identify or exclude treatable conditions such as thyroid dysfunction, vitamin B_{12} and folate deficiency, and electrolyte imbalances
- Vital signs
- Symptoms checklist and documentation of symptoms
- Brief Praxis Test (Dalton, Mehta, Fedor, & Patti, 1999)
- Orientation test
- Vocabulary test
- Fuld object memory test
- New dot test
- Behavior and function evaluation
- Dementia diagnosis on the basis of criteria from the *Diagnostic and Statistical Manual of Mental Disorders, Fourth Edition, Text Revision* (*DSM-IV-TR*; American Psychiatric Association, 2000)
- Dementia diagnosis on the basis of criteria from the *International Classification of Diseases* (*ICD-10*; World Health Organization, 1992), with evaluation for Hachinski signs (the Hachinski scoring test is widely used to distinguish Alzheimer's disease from multi-infarct dementia; a score of 0–4 suggests Alzheimer's disease, and a score of 7 suggests that the clinical symptoms are resulting from ischemia, or lack of oxygen in the brain [Patient Plus, 2004])
- Clinical Global Impression of Change

The case report of K.D. (see Display 44.1) illustrates clinical manifestations and progression of DAT often observed in someone with Down syndrome. Readers are also referred to the paper by Devenny et al. (2005) that follows the course of decline of a woman with Down syndrome and DAT over an 11-year-period until her death at age 57:

> This case illustrates features of premature aging that are typically associated with Down syndrome, and the progressive changes in memory and cognition that are usually associated with DAT. Although the subject's cardiovascular condition and thyroid disorder were treated, they may have contributed to the decline of her memory. This case shows the difficulty in diagnosing dementia in an individual with mental retardation who suffered comorbid episodes of depression and psychosis. (p. 1)

Histopathological findings revealed upon brain autopsy are included in this report by Devenney et al. The report also shows the invaluable contribution that a detailed study of only one individual can make to the field and the key role that caregivers can make by collaborating with researchers and by facilitating the donation of their loved one's brain tissue to a "brain bank."

DEMENTIA AND ALZHEIMER'S DISEASE IN PEOPLE WITH INTELLECTUAL DISABILITIES OTHER THAN DOWN SYNDROME

As increasing numbers of people with intellectual disabilities survive into middle age and beyond, psychiatric symptomatology in this adult population has been receiving increasing attention. Within that wide framework, the recognition of dementia and its characteristics is a crucial prerequisite in assessing whether that dementia is due to Alzheimer's disease or to some other, often reversible, condition. Because the subject has long been linked with Down syndrome, in view of the remarkable relationship of that syndrome with Alzheimer's disease (Berg et al., 1993), a great deal of data on this association has accumulated, as exemplified in this chapter.

Although relevant information is expanding (e.g., see the substantial and extensively referenced handbook edited by Janicki & Dalton, 1999), considerably less well documented are the issues of dementia and

Display 44.1

Case study: K.D.

K.D. is a 59-year-old man with Down syndrome. Two years after he had received a baseline evaluation and 1½ years after he had received a neurological assessment, he was referred for an assessment of cognitive functioning. The referral was made by group home staff who had concerns about deterioration in his behavior. K.D. was reported to have episodes of confusion, and his caregivers questioned his ability to distinguish fantasy from reality.

When K.D.'s neurological assessment took place 2 years prior, test results showed mild-to-moderate decline in verbal learning and memory for verbal material, as well as a deterioration in fine motor control in his hands. Cognitive deterioration was coupled with the onset of seizures, so a neurologist prescribed seizure medication. In the meantime, staff from the group home where K.D. lived made referrals to screen for thyroid functions, as well as visual and hearing impairments. K.D.'s physician requested blood tests to screen for possible vitamin B_{12} and folate deficiency. A psychiatric examination showed no overt signs of depression.

At the latest examination for cognitive functioning, K.D. seemed frail and walked slowly with assistance. He was unable to follow test instructions. Consequently, formal testing could not be implemented. Instead, information was gathered from caregivers regarding K.D.'s current difficulties. Interviews with staff at K.D.'s residence revealed significant deterioration in his cognitive functioning and skills of adaptive behavior over the last 2 years. According to reports from residential support workers, K.D. frequently misplaced objects, forgot the names of people he knew, and partly lost track of familiar routines. Over the past 2 years, his speech had slowed and had become difficult to understand. K.D. got lost several times while alone in the community; more recently, he experienced difficulty finding his own bedroom. He was no longer able to dress or bathe himself and required assistance with feeding. He was regularly incontinent of feces and urine if he was not prompted to use the toilet. Certain incidents suggested that he experienced hallucinations and paranoid ideas. At times, K.D. complained of imaginary people wanting to beat him up, putting him into a closet, or attacking him. Sometimes he got angry for no apparent reason, banging his head into the walls or kicking them.

Concerns about the deterioration of K.D.'s functioning prompted initiation of the process to have him transferred to a long-term care facility. In the meantime, K.D.'s supervision at the group home was intensified and he was given assistance with bathing, feeding, and walking. The safety of his current environment was assessed by an occupational therapist, and modifications were made to prevent injury. In addition, in case K.D. got lost in the community again, he was issued a MedicAlert identification bracelet and was registered with the national Alzheimer organization.

Source: Jozsvai (2003).

concomitant Alzheimer's disease in adults with intellectual disability conditions other than Down syndrome. In some respects, elucidation of these issues is more complex than is the case with Down syndrome because, unlike that relatively circumscribed specific syndrome, other intellectual disabilities constitute a wide range of entities with diverse etiology and symptomatology. Hence, generalizations about dementia and Alzheimer's disease in this markedly heterogeneous population, even when fairly uniform sections are made for study, should be cautiously interpreted. Further extensive investigation of this population in this regard (among others) is important in determining service needs because, as noted by an international epidemiology workgroup concerning dementia and Alzheimer's disease, older adults with intellectual disability without Down syndrome will by far outnumber those with Down syndrome (Zigman et al., 1997). While bearing the preceding considerations in mind, however, some notable findings are worth mentioning. Although the findings are not always consistent, they offer documentation of significant implications.

There have been discrepancies in the limited studies of the frequency with which dementia occurs in older adults with intellectual disabilities other than Down syndrome. Evenhuis (1997) investigated a group of 144 such adults, who lived in institutions and were 60 years or older, and noted that the age-related frequency (and natural history) of dementia in this group was comparable to that in the general population. In a subsequent extensive study, Zigman et al. (2004) found that the rates of dementia in 126 adults older than age 64 years who had intellectual disability but not Down syndrome were equivalent to or lower than would be expected compared with general population rates.

Cooper's (1997) study offered a contrast. Among the 134 adults with intellectual disabilities whom she studied, most of whom did not have Down syndrome,

29 adults (21.6%) had received a diagnosis of dementia (5 had Down syndrome, of whom 3 apparently also had dementia), compared with an expected dementia rate of 5.7% for a group of people older than 64 years in the general population. The rate of dementia in successive cohorts of the series studied increased as follows: 15.6%, 23.5%, and 70% at ages 65–74, 75–84, and 85–94 years, respectively. Cooper also listed other clinical studies containing observations on prevalence of dementia in people with intellectual disabilities; among such people older than 64 years, the prevalence ranged from approximately 11%–22%. Discrepant findings in these regards are not surprising in view of such factors as relatively small sample sizes from different sources, with variable etiologies (most unknown), intellectual levels, age distributions, and dementia diagnostic criteria—all of this in circumstances where preceding cognitive, behavior and chronic physical health problems (e.g., sensory and motor impairments) can seriously hamper accurate diagnosis of dementia.

Difficult though it may be to clinically diagnose dementia with certainty in many adults with intellectual disabilities, it seems even more difficult to conclusively recognize Alzheimer's disease during life in such people. Although Alzheimer's disease is a common cause of dementia in older people in general, and particularly in those with Down syndrome, data as to its prevalence in adults with intellectual disabilities other than Down syndrome are scarce; indeed, it has hardly been documented in relation to specific intellectual disability syndromes or entities other than Down syndrome. In the previously referenced studies, there is some mention of a diagnosis of Alzheimer's disease in a number of people in the groups investigated, but the information available is not sufficiently extensive for firm generalizations.

Nevertheless, there have been reports (albeit scanty in number) of postmortem brain examinations focused on Alzheimer's disease neuropathology in groups of adults with intellectual disabilities who did not have Down syndrome. In 70 such adults, ranging in age from 65 to older than 80 years at the time of death, Barcikowska et al. (1989) found neuropathology consistent with a diagnosis of Alzheimer's disease in 22 (31%), a prevalence that they considered comparable to that in the general population at similar ages. In a subsequent larger study of the brains of 385 people with intellectual disability who did not have Down syndrome, ranging in age from 23 to 90 years at death, Popovitch et al. (1990) reported that the proportion of individuals with at least some neurofibrillary tangles and/or neuritic plaque formation ranged from 33% in the age group younger than 45 years to 78% in those older than 65 years—a range in keeping with that in a number of comparably age population groups of people without cognitive disabilities or dementia. From the retrospective clinical data available in each study, it was uncertain to what extent the neuropathology noted was associated with dementia.

Reasonably precise findings on features such as prevalence of dementia and the links with Alzheimer's disease are less clearly documented in adults with intellectual disabilities who do not have Down syndrome than is the case in adults with Down syndrome and in the general population. It can be anticipated that further exploration and clarification of these issues will lead to improved therapeutic, quality of life, and even preventive prospects for those actually or potentially affected. These considerations become increasingly important as people live longer.

Regarding people with intellectual disabilities who do not have Down syndrome, virtually no published information exists about factors that predispose them to or protect them from dementia. Approaches for the diagnosis of dementia in this group are the same as for those who have Down syndrome. As is done for people with Down syndrome, multidisciplinary assessment is strongly recommended for all older people with intellectual disability.

MULTIDISCIPLINARY APPROACH TO MANAGING ALZHEIMER'S DISEASE, DAT, AND DEMENTIA

There is no cure for Alzheimer's disease. However, appropriate management of the disease in people with or without intellectual disability improves the quality of life of those affected and their caregivers. Such management involves a multidisciplinary approach combining medication, psychological therapies, environmental changes, focus on daily activities, and support for caregivers. Treatment may involve trying to minimize the disease process as such, addressing specific symptoms, and assisting caregivers to cope in the best way possible (Janicki et al., 1996). In the general population, clinical trials of proposed medication for Alzheimer's disease are common. Until the late 1990s, such trials usually excluded people with intellectual disability. However, these people are increasingly becoming the focus of attention. For example, an international multisite trial of high dose vitamin E in aging people with Down syndrome was funded by the National Institutes of Health of the United States (see Aisen et al., 2005). In this last major section of the chapter, strategies for managing Alzheimer's disease are presented; these also are applicable to DAT in Down syndrome and sometimes to the management of dementia in the absence of a specific diagnosis.

Medication

Medication is used to treat both Alzheimer's disease and its symptoms. Each is discussed next.

Treatment of Alzheimer's Disease Various drugs—including stimulants, vasodilators, and metabolic enhancers—have had limited success in the treatment of Alzheimer's disease. As of 2006, most approved drugs are intended to increase availability of neurotransmitters (especially acetylcholine). Aricept (donepezil), Exelon (rivastigmine), and Reminyl (galantamine hydrobromide) are three relatively new introduced drugs that prevent the breakdown of acetylcholine and appear to temporarily slow down the clinical progression of Alzheimer's disease in some people (Clegg et al., 2002). Although such drugs offer some protection, their effects, unfortunately, are temporary ("Common Alzheimer's Drug Flunks Test," 2004). A fourth drug, memantine, that blocks effects of excessive glutamic acid, was approved by the U.S. Food and Drug Administration in 2003. These drugs are also being tested in people with Down syndrome (e.g., see Prasher, 2004). None of these drugs can "cure" Alzheimer's disease or DAT.

Although high dose vitamin E is still being evaluated in clinical trials, it is often being given in lower doses along with the acetylcholine-boosting drugs. Statins, which are drugs that reduce circulating levels of cholesterol (Zamrini, McGwin, & Roseman, 2004), and drugs that remove excessive iron, copper, and zinc from the body (Todorich & Connor, 2004) are among a number of other medicines under experimental evaluation. Needless to say, there is an urgent need for the development of drugs and approaches that tackle the primary cause of Alzheimer's disease and can prevent it.

Treatment of Specific Symptoms Medications to alleviate specific distressing symptoms that can occur in Alzheimer's disease and DAT should be used cautiously, with regular review and usually only on a temporary basis to minimize side effects and drug interactions. Such medications include

- Hypnotics for night sedation
- Low dose neuroleptics for aggression, restlessness, and paranoid behavior
- Antidepressants for low mood
- Anticonvulsants for seizures
- Antibiotics for concurrent infections

Psychological Therapies

Psychological therapies such as reality orientation and reminiscence therapy may be used to slow the loss of abilities, whereas behavior therapy strives to strengthen remaining skills and to ameliorate difficult behaviors in people with Alzheimer's disease, DAT, or dementia. Each is described next.

Reality Orientation and Reminiscence Therapy Reality orientation and reminiscence therapy aim to prevent, halt, or reverse intellectual impairment and to maximize remaining abilities. Reality orientation tries to keep the affected person oriented in time and place as much as possible by having caregivers provide appropriate clues (e.g., saying "It's noon—time to use the toilet" or "It's one o'clock—time for your lunch"). The environment may be modified by the use of signs and colors (e.g., blue doors for bathrooms). Reminiscence therapy uses prompts (e.g., objects, photographs) to help people with Alzheimer's disease, DAT, or dementia relive past memories and thereby enable them to remain stimulated and to adjust to recent changes (Woods et al., 2005).

Behavior Therapy Behavior therapy can enhance maintenance of preexisting skills such as dressing, washing, feeding, and communication. It also can reduce difficult behaviors including restlessness, agitation, and aggression. Suitable behaviors are targeted and encouraged by providing positive consequences. Conversely, undesirable behaviors are discouraged by adapting the setting to avoid the situations that cause them and thereby exclude excluding confrontations. It is important to establish and maintain routines, avoid confrontations, keep tasks simple, speak clearly and in short sentences, and maintain existing abilities. Support that emphasizes action (behavior) often works better than support based on verbal exchange (conversation and reasoning) for people with Alzheimer's disease, DAT, or dementia especially after their understanding of words has deteriorated (Bayles & Kim, 2003; Mace, 1990; Mace & Rabins, 1991.)

Environmental Changes

The home must be made safe to prevent serious accidents. Safety assessments are valuable in providing guidelines for preventing accidents in the kitchen, in the bathroom, on the stairs, and in other places. Hutchings and Olsen (2004) noted some simple, low-cost physical arrangements that enhance safety and independence in family and group homes or in supervised apartments with resident aging people who have intellectual disabilities. These arrangements include having even external walkways and steps, easily grasped and sturdy railings, adequate lighting, accessible closets and cabinets for day-to-day objects, and minimal clutter. Wandering can be reduced by use of enclosed areas, door alarms, and safety gates. "Wandering registries" and MedicAlert identification bracelets, which can be obtained at a nominal cost, are also beneficial.

Incontinence is a major cause of burnout in caregivers. Therefore, advice should be readily available to caregivers regarding incontinence management. This includes the use of a waterproof mattress, a commode, and/or a bedpan or bed bottle.

Group homes often allow people with dementia or Alzheimer's disease, DAT, or dementia to remain residents as long as possible. However, nursing home placement may be required if a high level of nursing care becomes necessary and the individual becomes completely dependent. Major causes of death include aspiration pneumonia, urinary tract infections, and infected bedsores, so nursing care is critical in avoiding these complications.

Focus on Daily Activities

Meaningful activity that promotes health and uses and strengthens remaining daily living skills and abilities prevents these qualities from deteriorating. Such activity also provides a sense of accomplishment, improves mood, and increases overall physical fitness. Exercise can be beneficial by serving as a means for other social, memory, and language stimulation activities. Local day programs specifically developed for people with Alzheimer's disease provide opportunities for such activities and reduce continuous pressure on caregivers (Jarrott et al., 1998; Warren et al., 2003).

Support for Caregivers

For caregivers of individuals with Alzheimer's disease, DAT, or dementia, particularly long-standing caregivers who are family members, support is essential. Such support includes emotional solace, information, advice, practical aids, and help with future planning. The many aspects of care, which vary as the disease progresses, require maintaining the affected person's dignity, retaining a sense of humor and understanding, and making sure that the home is safe. This process includes encouraging those who are affected to attend to such needs as dressing, washing, and eating for themselves. For example, the caregiver may select clothes that are easy to put on and lay them out in order in which they should be donned to allow the affected individuals to dress independently with little or no distress.

Caregivers and family members need guidance over time in coping with new negative emotions that can result from their experiences with someone who has Alzheimer's disease, DAT, or dementia. These emotions can involve feelings of loss, guilt, frustration, unrealistic hope, bitterness, sadness, and depression. It is important for others to recognize the challenges that caregivers and family members face, particularly as the behavior of a person with dementia distressingly changes from previously familiar patterns.

Typically, support for primary caregivers is essential, in some cases including financial support. Generally, there is a need for caregivers and family members to learn more about the nature of Alzheimer's disease, its manifestations, and the necessary practical changes to facilitate effective coping. Caregiving help is almost always required, including practical in-house support from home-care workers and emotional backing from relatives, friends, and various professionals. A local Alzheimer support group can be a beneficial source of guidance. Joining such a group makes it possible to meet others who are facing similar issues and enables the sharing of information, feelings, and practical suggestions for coping and for helping a person with Alzheimer's disease to enjoy life as fully as possible (Brodaty et al., 2005; Garand et al., 2005; Lee & Cameron, 2004; Janicki, 1996; Jenkins, Hildreth, & Hildreth, 1993; Maaskant et al., 1996; McConaghy & Caltabiano, 2005; Roberto & Nelson, 1989; Thompson & Briggs, 2000).

Services and Resources Needed by People with Alzheimer's Disease or Dementia and Their Caregivers Early detection of Alzheimer's disease or DAT facilitates prompt attention by family and other caregivers to learn about the nature of the condition, to establish a support network, and to plan for the possibility of alternative living arrangements in the future. Table 44.8 lists services and other resources that are needed for people with Alzheimer's disease, DAT, or dementia, whether those with or without preceding intellectual disability. The availability of such attention varies substantially, however, even among communities in the same country.

Some social services systems have implemented person-centered long-term planning to provide individualized services. This involves comprehensive examination of residential, financial, and legal issues (among others) requiring individual resolution. Planning for guardianship and residential changes benefit

Table 44.8. Needs of people with Alzheimer's disease, DAT, or dementia and of their caregivers

Services
- Differential diagnosis (to distinguish reversible and treatable forms of dementia from Alzheimer's disease)
- Counseling
- Advocacy
- Case management and coordination
- Adult day care programs
- Home care
- Help with home chores
- Home safety assessment by an occupational therapist
- Meal delivery
- Respite care for temporary caregiver relief
- Nursing assistance
- Nursing homes
- "Wandering person" registries
- Support groups

Education
- Brochures, guides, manuals, and videotapes
- Internet information
- Conferences, workshops, forums, and symposia
- Courses and study programs
- Help lines
- Legal and financial assistance

Research
- Proposed therapeutic interventions
- Longitudinal studies of the development of dementia
- Donation of brain tissue for research

Source: Prasher and Percy (2003).

from an interdisciplinary approach, with the affected person's needs and desires being taken into account. High-standard nursing is an aspect of dementia care that is essential for a reasonable quality of life, because people with dementia have complex medical and other needs. Supporting such people in small group-home settings or in their family residences as long as possible tends to respectfully enhance their dignity even in difficult times. Also, an effective support system is needed to assist those concerned with the emotionally draining process of dealing with terminal illness and death.

Gaining Access to Support Services and Community Resources Even in the early stages of Alzheimer's disease, increased supervision of the affected person in his or her home is necessary, with consideration of various compensatory cognitive and environmental strategies to lessen the impact of the disease. Residential support staff are usually very cooperative in applying such strategies, but nursing home placement may be necessary if care requirements become too demanding. Information about available services and community resources can be elicited from multiple sources, including Alzheimer societies, family support groups, social service agencies that provide dementia screening, Alzheimer's disease and related disorder clinics, religious organizations, the Internet, and home care and safety agencies.

Intervention strategies that can be used by caregivers have been outlined by, among others, Bourgeois, Sultz, and Burgio (1996), Hussian and Davis (1985), Mace (1990), and Reisberg et al. (1987). Guides for programming activities for people with Alzheimer's disease have been published by Zgola (1987) and Sheridan (1987).

The Edinburgh Principles In 2001, a panel of experts met in Edinburgh, United Kingdom, to produce set of principles that outline the rights and needs of people with intellectual disability and dementia and that define service practices that enhance the supports available to them. Seven statements, now referred to as "the Edinburgh Principles," were produced (Wilkinson & Janicki, 2002). These form a foundation for the design and support of services to people with intellectual disability and their caregivers. There are four key points in the Edinburgh Principles:

1. Adopting a workable philosophy of care
2. Adapting practices at the point of service delivery
3. Working out the coordination of diverse systems
4. Promoting relevant research.

It is anticipated that the Edinburgh Principles will be adopted by service organizations worldwide and will provide a practical baseline from which further discussions, research efforts, and practice development can progress.

SUMMARY

Alzheimer's disease is the most common form of dementia. This disease is characterized by the presence of large quantities of amyloid plaques and neurofibrillary tangles in particular areas of the brain. The first clinical evidence of Alzheimer's disease tends to be memory loss, but other areas of intellectual functioning are progressively affected, leading to loss of self-care and social skills and marked deterioration of physical health. The prevalence of Alzheimer's disease rises with increasing age in the general population and in people with intellectual disabilities. When older people begin to show signs of developing dementia, it is important that a differential diagnosis be undertaken promptly, because there are various reversible causes of dementia.

DAT is more common, (although not inevitable) in middle-age and older adults with Down syndrome than in similar-age adults in the general population or with intellectual disabilities not due to Down syndrome. The association of DAT with Down syndrome is thought to be principally due to the trisomy 21 aspect of Down syndrome, resulting in three copies of the amyloid precursor protein gene instead of the normal two. People with Down syndrome are at risk of developing DAT at a much earlier age than is the case in the general population. Because they are now living longer, more will be affected by this disorder than heretofore. The diagnosis of DAT in people with Down syndrome and other intellectual disabilities is more difficult than in the general population because dementia must be distinguished from the previously existing cognitive

FOR FURTHER THOUGHT AND DISCUSSION

1. To what degree do people with intellectual disabilities lose cognitive and behavioral skills as they get older?
2. If you are a caregiver of a person approximately 40 years of age or older who has Down syndrome, what do you need to know about Alzheimer's disease and dementia?
3. If you notice evidence of seeming dementia in a person under your care, what steps should you take to gather more information and pursue the matter further?
4. Should recent drug therapies advocated for the general population be used for people with intellectual disabilities? Why or why not?
5. What services are available in your area to help support people with Alzheimer's disease and their families?

impairment. Diagnosis may require a multidisciplinary longitudinal assessment. A baseline assessment at approximately 25 years of age is an advantageous reference in identifying later changes in function. Dementia has not been extensively studied in people with intellectual disability other than that in Down syndrome; it is not clear if some of them are at higher or lower risk than people in the general population of developing Alzheimer's disease.

New drug treatments are now available to slow down the Alzheimer's disease process, but they are not curative. Despite absence of a cure for Alzheimer's disease, diagnosing and managing it effectively improves the quality of life of those who are affected and their caregivers. Family and caregiver support is an essential part of care management. People with dementia and their caregivers play a key role in better understanding dementia by collaborating with researchers and contributing tissue for research.

REFERENCES

Aisen, P.S., Dalton, A.J., Sano, M., et al. (2005). Design and implementation of a multicenter trial of vitamin E in aging individuals with Down syndrome. *Policy and Practice in Intellectual Disabilities, 2,* 86–93.

Alzheimer, A. (1907). Über eine eigenartige Erkrankung der Hirnrinde. *Allgemeine Zeitschrift für Psychiatrie und Psychisch-Gerichtliche Medizin, Berlin, 64,* 146–148.

American Psychiatric Association. (2000). *Diagnostic and Statistical Manual of Mental Disorders* (4th ed., text rev.). Washington, DC: Author.

Aylward, E.H., Burt, D., Thorpe, L.U., et al. (1997). Diagnosis of dementia in individuals with intellectual disability: Report of the task force for development of criteria for diagnosis of dementia in individuals with mental retardation. *Journal of Intellectual Disability Research, 41,* 152–164.

Barcikowska, M., Silverman, W., Zigman, W., et al. (1989). Alzheimer-type neuropathology and clinical symptoms of dementia in mentally retarded people without Down syndrome. *American Journal on Mental Retardation, 93,* 551–557.

Bayles, K.A., & Kim, E. (2003). Improving the functioning of individuals with Alzheimer's disease: Emergence of behavioral interventions. *Journal of Communication Disorders, 36,* 327–343.

Berg, J.M., Karlinsky, H., & Holland, A.J. (1993). *Alzheimer's disease, Down syndrome, and their relationship.* Oxford, United Kingdom: Oxford University Press.

Berr, C., Richard, F., Dufouil, C., et al. (1998). Polymorphism of the prion protein is associated with cognitive impairment in the elderly: The EVA study. *Neurology, 51,* 734–737.

Bourgeois, M.S., Sultz, R., & Burgio, L. (1996). Interventions for caregivers of patients with Alzheimer's disease: A review and analysis of content, process, and outcomes. *International Journal on Aging and Human Development, 43,* 35–92.

Brodaty, H., Thomson, C., Thompson, C., et al. (2005). Why caregivers of people with dementia and memory loss don't use services. *International Journal of Geriatric Psychiatry, 20,* 537–546.

Burt, D.B., & Aylward, E.H. (2000). Test battery for the diagnosis of dementia in individuals with intellectual disabilities. *Journal of Intellectual Disability Research, 44,* 175–180.

Bush, A., & Beail, N. (2004). Risk factors for dementia in people with Down syndrome: Issues in assessment and diagnosis. *American Journal on Mental Retardation, 109,* 83–97.

Butterfield, D.A., Griffin, S., Munch, G., et al. (2002). Amyloid beta-peptide and amyloid pathology are central to the oxidative stress and inflammatory cascades under which Alzheimer's disease brain exists. *Journal of Alzheimer's Disease, 4,* 193–201.

Castellani, R.J., Honda, K., Zhu, X., et al. (2004). Contribution of redox-active iron and copper to oxidative damage in Alzheimer's disease. *Ageing Research Reviews, 3,* 319–326.

Cheon, M.S., Bajo, M., Gulesserian, T., et al. (2001). Evidence for the relation of herpes simplex virus type 1 to Down syndrome and Alzheimer's disease. *Electrophoresis, 22,* 445–448.

Clegg, A., Bryant, J., Nicholson, T., et al. (2002). Clinical and cost-effectiveness of donepezil, rivastigmine and galantamine for Alzheimer's disease. A systematic review. *International Journal of Technology Assessment in Health Care, 18,* 497–507.

Cohen-Mansfield, J., Marx, M.S., & Werner, P. (1992). Agitation in elderly persons: An integrative report of findings in a nursing home. *International Psychogeriatrics, 4,* 221–240.

Collacott, R.A. (1992). The effect of age, and residential placement on adaptive behaviour of adults with Down's syndrome. *British Journal of Psychiatry, 161,* 675–679.

Common Alzheimer's drug flunks test of effectiveness: Initial improvements in cognitive ability made by cholinesterase inhibitors soon disappear. (2004). *Health News, 10*(10), 11.

Cooper, S.-A. (1997). High prevalence of dementia among people with learning disabilities not attributable to Down's syndrome. *Psychological Medicine, 27,* 609–616.

Cosgrave, M., Tyrrell, J., Dreja, H., et al. (1996). Lower frequency of apolipoprotein E4 allele in an "elderly" Down's syndrome population. *Biological Psychiatry, 40,* 811–813.

Cosgrave, M.P., Tyrrell, J., McCarron, M., et al. (1999). Age at onset of dementia and age of menopause in women with Down's syndrome. *Journal of Intellectual Disabilities Research, 43*(Pt 6), 461–465.

Crapper-McLachlan, D.R., Dalton, A.J., Kruck, T.P.A., et al. (1991). Intramuscular desferrioxamine in patients with Alzheimer's disease. *The Lancet, 337,* 1304–1308.

Dalton, A.J., Mehta, P.D., Fedor, B.L., et al. (1999). Cognitive changes in memory precede those in praxis in aging persons with Down syndrome. *Journal of Intellectual and Developmental Disability, 24,* 169–187.

Day, K., & Jancar, J. (1994). Mental and physical health of aging in mental handicap: A review. *Journal of Intellectual Disability Research, 38,* 241–256.

Del Bo, R., Comi, G. P., Giorda, R., et al. (2004). The 129 codon polymorphism of the prion protein gene influences earlier cognitive performance in Down syndrome subjects. *Journal of Neurology, 250,* 688–692.

Devenny, D.A., Silverman, W.P., Hill, A.L., et al. (1996). Normal ageing in adults with Down's syndrome: A longitudinal study. *Journal of Intellectual Disability Research, 40,* 208–221.

Devenny, D.A., Wegiel, J., Schupf, N., et al. (2005, April). Dementia of the Alzheimer's type and accelerated aging in down syndrome. *Science of Aging Knowledge Environment: SAGE KE* [electronic resource], 14, dn1.

Dinani, S., & Carpenter, S. (1990). Down syndrome and thyroid disorder. *Journal of Mental Deficiency Research, 34,* 187–193.

Evans, D.A. (1990). Estimated prevalence of Alzheimer's disease in the United States. *Milbank Quarterly, 68,* 267–289.

Evenhuis, H.M. (1997). The natural history of dementia in ageing people with intellectual disability. *Journal of Intellectual Disability Research, 41,* 92–96.

Garand, L., Amanda Dew, M., Eazor, L.R., et al. (2005). Caregiving burden and psychiatric morbidity in spouses of persons with mild cognitive impairment. *International Journal of Geriatric Psychiatry, 20,* 512–522.

Gatz, M., Fratiglioni, L., Johansson, B., et al. (2005). Complete ascertainment of dementia in the Swedish Twin Registry: The HARMONY study. *Neurobiology of Aging, 26,* 439–447.

Gedye, A. (1995). *Dementia Scale for Down Syndrome: Manual.* Vancouver, BC, Canada: Gedye Research and Consulting.

Gedye, A. (1998). *Behavioural diagnostic guide for developmental disabilities.* Vancouver, BC, Canada: Diagnostic Books.

Glasson, E.J., Sullivan, S.G., Hussain, R., et al. (2003). Comparative survival advantage of males with Down syndrome. *American Journal of Human Biology, 15,* 192–195.

Haan, M.N., & Wallace, R. (2004). Can dementia be prevented? Brain aging in a population-based context. *Annual Review of Public Health, 25,* 1–24.

Hebert, L.E., Scherr, P.A., Bienias, J.L., et al. (2003). Alzheimer's disease in the US population: Prevalence estimates using the 2000 census. *Archives of Neurology, 60,* 119–1121.

High doses of vitamin E may increase risk of death. Talk to your doctor before taking supplements containing more than 200 IUs. (2005). *Health News, 11*(4), 12–13.

Hussian, R.A., & Davis, R.L. (1985). *Responsive care: Behavioral interventions with elderly persons.* Champaign, IL: Research Press.

Hutchings, B.L., & Olsen, R.O. (2004). Home modifications to support ageing in places with an intellectual disability. *Journal of Intellectual Disability Research, 48,* 425.

Itzhaki, R.F., Dobson, C.B., Shipley, S.J., et al. (2004). The role of viruses and of APOE in dementia. *Annals of the New York Academy of Sciences, 1019,* 15–18.

Janicki, M.P. (1996). Aging and persons with mental handicap and developmental disabilities. *Journal of Practical Approaches to Developmental Handicap, 12*(2), 9–13.

Janicki, M.P., & Dalton, A.J. (Eds.). (1999). *Dementia, aging, and intellectual disabilities: A handbook.* Philadelphia: Taylor & Francis.

Janicki, M.P., Heller, T., Seltzer, G.B., et al. (1996). Practice guidelines for the clinical assessment and care management of Alzheimer's disease among adults with intellectual disability. *Journal of Intellectual Disability Research, 40,* 374–382.

Jansson, E.T. (2005). Alzheimer's disease is substantially preventable in the United States—review of risk factors, therapy, and the prospects for an expert software system. *Medical Hypotheses, 64,* 960–967.

Jarrott, S.E., Zarit, S.H., Berg, S., et al. (1998). Adult day care for dementia: A comparison of programs in Sweden and the United States. *Journal of Cross Cultural Gerontology, 13,* 99–108.

Jenkins, E.L., Hildreth, B.L., & Hildreth, G. (1993). Elderly persons with mental retardation: An exceptional population with special needs. *International Journal of Aging and Human Development, 37,* 69–80.

Jozsvai, E. (2003). Alzheimer disease and Down syndrome. In I. Brown and M. Percy (Eds.), *Developmental disabilities in Ontario* (2nd ed., pp. 809–817). Toronto: Ontario Association on Developmental Disabilities.

Kantarci, K., & Jack, C.R., Jr. (2003). Neuroimaging in Alzheimer's disease: An evidence-based review. *Neuroimaging Clinics of North America, 13,* 197–209.

Karp, A., Kareholt, I., Qiu, C., et al. (2004). Relation of education and occupation-based socioeconomic status to incident Alzheimer's disease. *American Journal of Epidemiology, 159,* 175–183.

Keiser, H., Montague, J., Wold, D., et al. (1981). Hearing loss of Down syndrome adults. *American Journal of Mental Deficiency, 85,* 467–472.

Khachaturian, A.S., Corcoran, C.D., Mayer, L.S., et al. (2004). Cache County Study Investigators. Apolipoprotein E epsilon4 count affects age at onset of Alzheimer's disease, but not lifetime susceptibility: The Cache County Study. *Archives of General Psychiatry, 61,* 518–524.

Khachaturian, Z.S. (1985). Diagnosis of Alzheimer's disease. *Archives of Neurology, 42,* 1097–1104.

Klunk, W.E., Engler, H., Nordberg, A., et al. (2004). Imaging brain amyloid in Alzheimer's disease with Pittsburgh Compound-B. *Annals of Neurology, 55,* 306–319.

Lai, F., Kammann, E., Rebeck, G.W., et al. (1999). APOE genotype and gender effects on Alzheimer's disease in 100 adults with Down syndrome. *Neurology, 53,* 331–336.

Lai, F., & Williams, R.S. (1989). A prospective study of Alzheimer's disease in Down syndrome. *Archives of Neurology, 46,* 849–853.

Launer, L.J. (2005). Diabetes and brain aging: Epidemiologic evidence. *Current Diabetes Reports, 5,* 59–63.

Lee, H., & Cameron, M. (2004). Respite care for people with dementia and their carers. *Cochrane Database Systematic Reviews, 2004*(2), CD004396.

Licastro, F., Mariani, R.A., Faldella, G., et al. (2001). Immune-endocrine status and coeliac disease in children with Down's syndrome: Relationships with zinc and cognitive efficiency. *Brain Research Bulletin, 55,* 313–317.

Lifshitz, H., & Merrick, J. (2004). Aging among persons with intellectual disability in Israel in relation to type of residence, age, and etiology. *Research in Developmental Disabilities, 25,* 193–205.

Maaskant, M.A., van den Akker, M., Kessels, A.G.H., et al. (1996). Care dependence and activities of daily living in relation to aging: Results of a longitudinal study. *Journal of Intellectual Disability Research, 40,* 535–543.

Mace, N.L. (1990). The management of problem behaviors. In N.L. Mace (Ed.), *Dementia care: Patient, family, and community.* Baltimore: The John Hopkins University Press.

Mace, N.L., & Rabins, P.V. (1991). *The 36-hour day: A family guide to caring for persons with Alzheimer's disease, related dementing illnesses, and memory loss in later life.* Baltimore: The John Hopkins University Press.

Mann, D.M.A. (in press). Neuropathological changes of Alzheimer's disease in Down syndrome population. In V.P. Prasher (Ed.), *Dementia and Down syndrome.* London: Jessica Kingsley Publishers.

Margallo-Lana, M., Morris, C.M., Gibson, A.M., et al. (2004). Influence of the amyloid precursor protein locus on dementia in Down syndrome. *Neurology, 62,* 1996–1998.

McConaghy, R., & Caltabiano, M.L. (2005). Caring for a person with dementia: Exploring relationships between perceived burden, depression, coping and well-being. *Nursing Health Sciences, 7,* 81–91.

McKhann, G., Drachman, D., Folstein, M., et al. (1984). Clinical diagnosis of Alzheimer's disease: Report of the NINCDS-ADRDA Work Group under the auspices of Department of Health and Human Services Task Force on Alzheimer's disease. *Neurology, 34,* 939–944.

McLachlan, D.R., Bergeron, C., Smith, J.E., et al. (1996). Risk for neuropathologically confirmed Alzheimer's disease and residual aluminum in municipal drinking water employing weighted residential histories. *Neurology, 46,* 401–440.

Miller, A.L. (2003). The methionine-homocysteine cycle and its effects on cognitive diseases. *Alternative Medicine Reviews, 8,* 7–19.

Morris, M.C., Evans, D.A., Bienias, J.L., et al. (2003). Consumption of fish and n-3 fatty acids and risk of incident Alzheimer's disease. *Archives of Neurology, 60,* 940–946.

Mrak, R.E., & Griffin, W.S. (2004). Trisomy 21 and the brain. *Journal of Neuropathology and Experimental Neurology, 63,* 679–685.

Pary, R. (1992). Differential diagnosis of functional decline in Down's syndrome. *The Habilitative Mental Healthcare Newsletter, 11,* 37–41.

Patient Plus. (2004). *Hachinski Scale.* Retrieved June 5, 2005, from http://www.patient.co.uk/showdoc/40002258

Percy, M.E. (1999). Risk factors and biological consequences. In M.P. Janicki & A.J. Dalton (Eds.), *Dementia, aging and intellectual disabilities: A handbook* (pp. 55–89). Philadelphia: Taylor & Francis.

Percy, M.E., Dalton, A.J., Markovic, V.D., et al. (1990). Autoimmune thyroiditis associated with mild "subclinical" hypothyroidism in adults with Down syndrome: A comparison of patients with and without manifestations of Alzheimer's disease. *American Journal of Medical Genetics, 36,* 148–154.

Percy, M.E., Potyomkina, Z., Dalton, A.J., et al. (2003). Relation between apolipoprotein E genotype, hepatitis B virus status, and thyroid status in a sample of older persons with Down syndrome. *American Journal of Medical Genetics, 120A,* 191–198.

Percy, M.E., & Prasher, V.P. (in press). Thyroid function, dementia and Down syndrome. In V.P. Prasher (Ed.), *Dementia and Down syndrome.* London: Jessica Kingsley Publishers.

Picard, A. (2004, July 22). Developing Alzheimer's linked to lifestyle more than genetics. *The Globe and Mail Newspaper,* A13.

Podewils, L.J., Guallar, E., Kuller, L.H., et al. (2005). Physical activity, APOE genotype, and dementia risk: findings from the Cardiovascular Health Cognition Study. *American Journal of Epidemiology, 161,* 639–651.

Popovitch, E.R., Wisniewski, H.M., Barcikowska, M., et al. (1990). Alzheimer neuropathology in non-Down's syndrome mentally retarded adults. *Acta Neuropathologica, 80,* 362–367.

Prasher, V., & Percy, M. (2003). Alzheimer disease. In I. Brown and M. Percy (Eds.), *Developmental disabilities in Ontario* (2nd ed., pp. 793–807). Toronto: Ontario Association on Developmental Disabilities.

Prasher, V.P. (2004). Review of donepezil, rivastigmine, galantamine and memantine for the treatment of dementia in Alzheimer's disease in adults with Down syndrome: Implications for the intellectual disability population. *International Journal of Geriatric Psychiatry, 19,* 509–515.

Prasher, V.P., Chowdhury, T.A., Rowe, B.R., et al. (1997). ApoE4 and Alzheimer's disease in adults with Down syndrome. Effects of ApoE genotype on age of onset and longevity: Meta-analysis. *American Journal on Mental Retardation, 102,* 103–110.

Prasher, V.P., Farooq, A., & Holder, R. (2004). The Adaptive Behaviour Dementia Questionnaire (ABDQ): Screening questionnaire for dementia in Alzheimer's disease in adults with Down syndrome. *Research in Developmental Disabilities, 25,* 385–397.

Prasher, V.P., & Filer, A. (1995). Behavioural disturbance in people with Down's syndrome and dementia. *Journal of Intellectual Disability Research, 39,* 432–436.

Prasher, V.P., Gosling, P., & Blair, J. (1998). Role of iron in Alzheimer-type dementia in Down syndrome. *International Journal of Geriatric Psychiatry, 13,* 818–819.

Prasher, V.P., & Krishnan, V.H.R. (1993). Age of onset and duration of dementia in people with Down syndrome. A study of 98 reported cases. *International Journal of Geriatric Psychiatry, 8,* 915–922.

Prasher, V.P., Metseagharun, T., & Haque, S. (2004). Weight loss in adults with Down syndrome and with dementia in Alzheimer's disease. *Research on Developmental Disabilities, 25,* 1–7.

Räihä, I., Kaprio, J., Koskenvuo, M., et al. (1997). Alzheimer's disease in twins. *Biomedicine and Pharmacotherapy, 51,* 101–104.

Reisberg, B., Borenstein, J., Salob, S.P., et al. (1987). Behavioral symptoms in Alzheimer's disease: Phenomenology and treatment. *Journal of Clinical Psychiatry, 48,* 9–15.

Roberto, K.A., & Nelson, R.E. (1989). The developmentally disabled elderly: Concerns of service providers. *Journal of Applied Gerontology, 8,* 175–182.

Roman, G.C. (2004). Vascular dementia: Advances in nosology, diagnosis, treatment and prevention. *Panminerva Medicine, 46,* 207–215.

Rosen, I. (1997). Electroencephalography as a diagnostic tool in dementia. *Dementia and Geriatric Cognitive Disorders, 8,* 110–116.

Sano, M., Ernesto, C., Thomas, R.G., et al. (1997). A controlled trial of selegiline, alpha-tocopherol, or both as treatment for Alzheimer's disease. The Alzheimer's Disease Cooperative Study. *The New England Journal of Medicine, 336,* 1216–1222.

Schupf, N., Pang, D., Patel, B.N., et al. (2003). Onset of dementia is associated with age at menopause in women with Down's syndrome. *Annals of Neurology, 54,* 433–438.

Schupf, N., & Sergievsky, G.H. (2002). Genetic and host factors for dementia in Down's syndrome. *British Journal of Psychiatry, 180,* 405–410. (Review.)

Sheridan, C. (1987). *Failure-free activities for Alzheimer's patients: A guidebook for caregivers.* San Francisco: Cottage Books.

Shin, R.W., Kruck, T.P., Murayama, H., et al. (2003). A novel trivalent cation chelator Feralex dissociates binding of aluminum and iron associated with hyperphosphorylated tau of Alzheimer's disease. *Brain Research, 961,* 139–146.

Strauss, D., & Eyman, R.K. (1996). Mortality of people with mental retardation in California with and without Down syndrome, 1886–1991. *American Journal on Mental Retardation, 100,* 643–653.

Strydom, A., & Hassiotis, A. (2003). Diagnostic instruments for dementia in older people with intellectual disability in clinical practice. *Aging and Mental Health, 7,* 431–437.

Tangerud, A., Hestnes, A., Sand, T., et al. (1990). Degenerative changes in the cervical spine in Down's syndrome. *Journal of Mental Deficiency Research, 34,* 179–185.

Telakivi, T., Partinen, M., Leinonen, L., et al. (1987). Nocturnal periodic breathing in adults with Down's syndrome. *Journal of Mental Deficiency Research, 31,* 31–39.

Temple, V., Jozsvai, E., Konstantareos, M.M., et al. (2001). Alzheimer dementia in Down syndrome: The relevance of cognitive ability. *Journal of Intellectual Disability Research, 45,* 47–55.

Thase, M.E. (1982). Longevity and mortality in Down's syndrome. *Journal of Mental Deficiency Research, 16,* 177–192.

Thompson, C., & Briggs, M. (2000). Support for carers of people with Alzheimer's type dementia. *Cochrane Database Systematic Review, 2000*(2), CD000454.

Todorich, B.M., & Connor, J.R. (2004). Redox metals in Alzheimer's disease. *Annals of the New York Academy of Sciences, 1012,* 171–178.

Tsiouris, J.A., Patti, P.J., Tipu, O., et al. (2002). Adverse effects of phenytoin given for late-onset seizures in adults with Down syndrome. *Neurology, 59,* 779–780.

Tyrrell, J., Cosgrave, M., Hawi, Z., et al. (1998). A protective effect of apolipoprotein E e2 allele on dementia in Down's syndrome. *Biological Psychiatry, 43,* 397–400.

Tyrrell, J., Cosgrave, M., McCarron, M., et al. (2001). Dementia in people with Down's syndrome. *International Journal of Geriatric Psychiatry, 16,* 1168–1174.

Victoroff, J. (2002). *Saving your brain.* New York: Bantam Doubleday Dell.

Vitamin E in aging persons with Down syndrome. (2005). Retrieved June 5, 2005, from http://www.clinicaltrials.gov/show/NCT00056329

Wallace, R.A., & Dalton, A.J. (2006). Clinicians' guide to physical health problems of older adults with Down syndrome. *Journal on Developmental Disability.*

Warren, S., Kerr, J.R., Smith, D., et al. (2003). The impact of adult day programs on family caregivers of elderly relatives. *Journal of Community Health Nursing, 20,* 209–221.

Wherrett, J.R. (1999). Neurological aspects. In M.P. Janicki & A.J. Dalton (Eds.), *Dementia, aging and intellectual disabilities: A handbook* (pp. 90–102). Philadelphia: Taylor & Francis.

Wilcock, G.K., & Esiri, M.M. (1982). Plaques, tangles and dementia: A quantitative study. *Journal of the Neurological Sciences, 56,* 343–356.

Wilkinson, H., & Janicki, M.P. (2002). Edinburgh Working Group on Dementia Care Practices (EWGDCP): The Edinburgh Principles with accompanying guidelines and recommendations. *Journal of Intellectual Disabilities Research, 46*(Pt. 3), 279–284.

Wisniewski, H.M., Silverman, W., & Wegiel, J. (1994). Aging, Alzheimer's disease and mental retardation. *Journal of Intellectual Disability Research, 38,* 233–239.

Wolf, H., Jelic, V., Gertz, H.J., et al. (2003). A critical discussion of the role of neuroimaging in mild cognitive impairment. *Acta Neurologica Scandinavica, 179*(Suppl.), 52–76.

Woods, B., Spector, A., Jones, C., et al. (2005). Reminiscence therapy for dementia. *Cochrane Database of Systematic Reviews, April 18*(2), CD001120.

World Health Organization. (1992). *The ICD-10 classification of mental and behavioral disorders: Clinical descriptions and diagnostic guidelines.* Geneva: Author.

Wozniak, M.A., Riley, E.M., & Itzhaki, R.F. (2004). Apolipoprotein E polymorphisms and risk of malaria. *Journal of Medical Genetics, 41,* 145–146.

Yang, Q., Rasmussen, S.A., & Friedman, J.M. (2002). Mortality associated with Down's syndrome in the USA from 1983 to 1997: A population-based study. *The Lancet, 359,* 1019–1025.

Zamrini, E., McGwin, G., & Roseman, J.M. (2004). Association between statin use and Alzheimer's disease. *Neuroepidemiology, 23,* 94–98.

Zandi, P.P., Anthony, J.C., Khachaturian, A.S., et al. (2004). Reduced risk of Alzheimer's disease in users of antioxidant vitamin supplements: The Cache County Study. *Archives of Neurology, 61,* 82–88.

Zec, R.F. (1993). Neuropsychological functioning in Alzheimer's Disease. In R.W. Parks, R.F. Zec, & R.S. Wilson (Eds.), *Neuropsychology of Alzheimer's disease and other dementias* (pp. 3–80). Oxford, United Kingdom: Oxford University Press.

Zelnik, N., Pacht, A., Obeid, R., et al. (2004). Range of neurologic disorders in patients with celiac disease. *Pediatrics, 113,* 1672–1676.

Zgola, J.M. (1987). *Doing things: A guide to programming activities for persons with Alzheimer's disease.* Baltimore: The Johns Hopkins University Press.

Zigman, W.B., Schupf, N., Devenny, D.A., et al. (2004). Incidence and prevalence of dementia in elderly adults with mental retardation without Down syndrome. *American Journal on Mental Retardation, 109,* 126–141.

Zigman, W., Schupf, N., Haveman, M., et al. (1997). The epidemiology of Alzheimer's disease in intellectual disability: Results and recommendations from an international conference. *Journal of Intellectual Disability Research, 41,* 76–80.

VI

Future

45

Current Advances and a Vision for the Future

Ivan Brown, Robert L. Schalock, Maire Percy, and Marcia H. Rioux

WHAT YOU WILL LEARN ABOUT IN THIS CHAPTER

- Significant recent changes in the field of intellectual and developmental disabilities
- Factors that influence and support changes in core areas of the field
- Possible changes in the future
- A vision for the future

It has been the common experience of the chapter authors that we pick up and use a book because of where it takes us. It is our hope that using this book has taken the reader to a new and broader level of understanding of the lives of people who are described as having intellectual and developmental disabilities. Authors of the preceding chapters have presented a comprehensive range of information that is critical in the disabilities community, and they have summarized well the current status of the field of intellectual and developmental disabilities. The information in this chapter provides an overall view of some of the changes that are taking place in our field and a vision of where we would like to take our field in the future. To facilitate this process, this final chapter has four purposes: first, to identify and briefly describe significant recent changes in the field of intellectual and developmental disabilities; second, to outline some of the important factors that contribute to these changes; third, to identify some of the changes that might be expected in the future; and fourth, to present a future vision for intellectual and developmental disabilities.

The authors are grateful to the following people for supplying ideas that helped to shape this chapter: Mark Shumelda; Rivka Birkan; Karolina Machalek; Trevor Parmenter; H. Rutherford Turnbull, III; and Matthew J. Stowe.

SIGNIFICANT RECENT CHANGES IN THE FIELD OF INTELLECTUAL AND DEVELOPMENTAL DISABILITIES

Most readers of this book will come away with the feeling that the field of intellectual and developmental disabilities is changing rapidly throughout the world. Knowledge and professional skills have increased dramatically during the past few decades and continue to change. Applying such changes in ways that help to improve the lives of people with disabilities and their caregivers is somewhat uneven and not without challenges, however, among the various countries of the world and within regions of those countries. A number of significant challenges still must be overcome regarding public policy, service provision, community attitudes, inclusion, and personal fulfillment.

There have been significant changes in four core areas of the field: the conceptualization of disability (how we think about disability), the etiology of disability (what we know about the causes of disability), disability-related public policy (what laws and procedures we put in place to regulate public behavior toward disability), and our service paradigm (how we support people with disabilities in a formal way). Descriptions of changes in these four core areas are outlined briefly next, and, in the next section, some of the important, specific factors that influence and support them are highlighted.

Shift in the Concept of Disability

The concept of disability that has increasingly emerged as the primary guide to thinking in the field of intellectual and developmental disabilities is that

- Disability forms a legitimate part of every society and should be recognized as having a valued place in every society.
- Consequently, people with disabilities not only have rights and responsibilities as do people without disabilities, but they also merit the necessary personal

and societal supports to enable them to exercise their rights and responsibilities.

- Consequently, public policy and social practices that affect the lives of people with disabilities should be governed by principles of equality, inclusion, positive support, fairness, personal rights and entitlements, self-determination, and quality of life.

Adopting this concept has meant that the field has moved toward stressing inclusion and positive life experience and away from thinking of disability in terms of deficiency and separation of people with disabilities. In doing so, it has moved away from relying solely on the value of the so-called "medical model" of disability, which identified disability as a problem that warranted the attention of those who could help alleviate or eliminate the problem: medically (e.g., through medical procedures and treatment), socially (e.g., providing special services in communities and in institutions), educationally (e.g., special schools, training centers, and programs), and financially (e.g., disability pensions). The medical model supports positive aspects of life that are still used and will continue to be used—helpful medical interventions, special education, access to needed services, and financial supports. Yet, even in these areas, efforts to support people with disabilities are increasingly guided by principles related to equality, social acceptance and inclusion, personal determination, and happiness, rather than by an interest in addressing the deficiencies of disability.

This conceptual shift has been influenced by similar shifts in a variety of related fields (e.g., social work, gerontology, early childhood development) toward more ecological and human rights perspectives. These perspectives recognize that human differences—in this case, disability—are a feature of all social orders. They stress that because disability is one aspect of all societies, it is the responsibility of the social environment to ensure that all citizens, no matter what their differences may be, are able to participate in community life and pursue their life courses in satisfactory ways. Personal competence is encouraged by making the environment more accessible and more suitable, and social competence is encouraged by adopting public policy and common practices that include people with disabilities in all aspects of human life. (For more in-depth information on using the ecological framework see Ouellette-Kuntz et al., 2005; Ruddick, 2005; Schalock, 2004; and Tuffrey-Wijne, 2003.)

Broader Understanding of the Causes of Disability

Historically, the etiology of intellectual and developmental disabilities (the study of its causes or origins) has been described in two broad categories: biological origin and psychosocial disadvantage. The tremendous growth in our understanding of the etiology of intellectual and developmental disabilities, since the 1980s, has meant that this concept has become much broader. It is now understood that, although some intellectual and developmental disabilities result from single causes (e.g., fragile X syndrome results from an expanded trinucleotide region in the FMR1 gene), others result from two or more factors that may not be interrelated or may be interrelated in ways that are sometimes quite complex.

One aspect of this complexity is that etiological factors interact, at times, across time and generations (Luckasson et al., 2002). For example, in certain communities, there is an association among fetal alcohol syndrome (FAS) or fetal alcohol spectrum disorder (FASD), breakdown of families, placing of children in foster care, unemployment, poverty, poor education, poor nutrition, poor physical or mental health, and sexual and emotional abuse that continues across generations (Fudge Schormans & Brown, 2002). Interactions among such factors and their duration over time often exacerbate the disability resulting from FAS/FASD, unless mitigated by helpful interventions. This example is one of many that illustrates the importance of paying close attention to etiological factors and their effects on people's lives.

Changes in Public Policy

Throughout the world, there have been significant changes in public policy regarding people with intellectual and developmental disabilities that have paralleled shifts in the field's conceptualization of disability. The United Nations' World Programme of Action Concerning Disabled People 1982 (United Nations Enable, 2006b) was one of many landmark public policy documents that acts as a reference point and guide for future advances. The fundamental change in thinking at the public policy level has been that people with disabilities have rights and entitlements that are equal to those of all other people, and that both legal systems and societal practices need to be proactive in promoting these. In other words, public policy has moved away from its historic systemic exclusion of people with disabilities and has moved toward recognizing the necessity of its role in enhancing inclusion and equality.

Over the years, these changes in public policy are reflected—explicitly and sometimes implicitly—in the language of the numerous international, national, and local laws, conventions, sets of procedures, and other policy documents that have been put into effect (see also Chapters 5 and 6). An analysis of major public policy documents in the United States indicated that the following core concepts form the basis of disability public policy (Turnbull et al., 2001): antidiscrimination, multidisciplinary assessment, service coordination and collaboration, empowerment and participatory decision making, individualized and appropriate services, protection from harm, autonomy and integration, privacy and confidentiality, productivity and contribution, family-centered integrity and unity, accountability, cultural responsiveness, and prevention and amelioration. Similar core concepts are typical of public policy documents in other countries.

Public policy sets legal and/or procedural guidelines for practice. Consequently, changes in the core concepts of public policy documents have resulted in positive advancements in early intervention services, inclusive education initiatives, supported employment and living programs, and many other helpful supports that have been detailed throughout this book. Progress in these areas has not always matched the intent of public policy statements, however, because national and regional commitment, funding, the availability of professionals and other support personnel, and the availability of needed supports and services have not been adequate. Still, a great deal of progress has been made.

Transition to a Person-Centered Paradigm

A consistent theme through the preceding chapters, and a feature of Chapter 22, is the transition in thinking within our field from a program-based service paradigm to a person-centered supports paradigm. A person-centered supports paradigm is an approach that moves away from a focus on the needs of groups of people with disabilities as perceived primarily by others and addressed through structured systems and toward attending to the unique needs of each person as perceived primarily by the person or close caregivers in ways that are most helpful and that may be unique. In doing so, this approach encompasses the principles and practices associated with self-determination, personal and family supports, positive behavior support (see Chapter 23), and community building (Schalock, Baker, & Croser, 2002). The goal here is to provide needed and wanted supports, in ways that are directed by and helpful to the person with a disability or by his or her close caregivers, and that contribute to quality of life, well-being, and community participation.

FACTORS THAT INFLUENCE AND SUPPORT CHANGES IN CORE AREAS OF THE FIELD

Many factors influence change of any kind, and these may be interrelated in complex ways. Changes in the field of intellectual and developmental disabilities are no exception. For the sake of simplicity, a number of other changes that have influenced and supported changes in the four core areas of the field are listed next.

Increasing Acceptance of Equality and Human Rights

Increasingly around the world, but in some countries more than others, there is an acceptance of the equality of all people and of the necessity to recognize human rights (for details, see Chapters 5 and 6 especially). This more general social trend has been accompanied by the growing and widespread acceptance of the valued place of people with intellectual and developmental disabilities in typical social and cultural life (Roeher Institute, 1996).

Development of Self-Advocacy

Although addressed directly in only Chapter 6 of this text, one striking recent change in the field has been the appearance and influence of the self-advocacy movement at the national and international levels. This movement is having at least two significant impacts: 1) providing supports based on individual needs, equity, self-determination, and societal inclusion; and 2) the demand for quality services and quality outcomes (Hayden & Nelis, 2002).

Recognizing the Need for Reconciliation

The self-advocacy movement and other shifts in thinking have led to an understanding that exclusionary and discriminatory practices of the past have resulted in harm to some people with intellectual and developmental disabilities (e.g., see Worth, n.d.). The process of reconciliation hears and recognizes the harm that was done; allows those who have caused harm to regret their actions and in some cases to be forgiven; suggests a conceptual reframing and affirming, where a better future path is envisioned; and brings people with and without disabilities together in a new relationship and sets out a new path for this relationship in the future (Blackstock et al., 2006). It should be emphasized that there does not appear to be a universal need for reconciliation in our field but, rather, there is a need for this process to enable some individuals to move forward to experience positive lives.

Explosion of Genetic and Scientific Knowledge

Perhaps the most striking feature of recent decades is the explosion of genetic and neuroscientific knowledge. New knowledge is emerging that is reshaping our field. Three examples of exciting areas of development include the sequencing of the human genome and the ongoing identification of new genes and their functions, brain functioning, and the roles that proteins play in how people behave. It is not possible to predict precisely how the current explosion of genetic and neuroscience information will affect people with intellectual and developmental disabilities. It seems very probable, however, that the effects will be significant and that this is an area in which our field will need to have a watchful eye and a strong voice (see Parmenter, 2003; Stowe, Turnbull, Schrandt, et al., in press). Ethics—the best thing to do given the circumstances and current knowledge—will be essential to guide the application of new genetic and neuroscience knowledge to the field of intellectual and developmental disabilities.

Recognition of the Roles of Professions Supporting Disability

Many chapters in this book recognize the important role played by the many professionals whose work supports people with intellectual and developmental disabilities. These professionals have contributed significantly to the positive changes in our field, through reassessing the values and principles that guide our work and through changing their support practices to fit evolving values and principles. An increasing variety of professionals are working with people with intellectual and developmental disabilities along with people who do not have disabilities (e.g., teachers, social workers, lawyers, psychologists, physicians and other health care professionals). A goal for the future is to ensure that all professionals demonstrate the value of inclusion to members of the broader community.

Just as important for many children and adults with intellectual and developmental disabilities is the large amount of extra support provided by parents and other family members, friends, acquaintances, and volunteers. The unpaid work of these people fosters community inclusion by serving as examples to others how people with disabilities can live successfully in communities and contribute to their social environment. They also are very often active in advocacy organizations that have supported disability rights and quality of life principles, and they have spoken out for quality services and adequate funding.

The role of academics, intellectual leaders, and researchers in the field of intellectual and developmental disabilities has not been expressed explicitly in this book, and, indeed, is often overlooked in texts. Yet, those who carry out and report on research, who write and speak, and who teach future professionals in the field, are key players in developing new ideas and transferring acquired knowledge to new professionals. In addition, numerous academic and professional organizations have been extremely helpful in developing new laws, policies, service structures, methods of knowledge exchange, and other supports for positive changes in our field.

Those who provide direct care are the most essential support to people with intellectual and developmental disabilities. Reported problems with stability of support staff and developing competence through training (Biersdorff, 2002; Larson, Hewitt, & Lakin, 2004; Larson, Lakin, & Hewitt, 2002; Taylor, Bradley, & Warren, 1996) suggest that it may be wise, and fully in keeping with current philosophical perspectives, to reconceptualize the role of support workers to ensure that they have more transferable skills such as understanding of the human care needs and social inclusion in a more general sense. At the same time, it will be important to address systemic changes so that we allow considerably more flexibility among the many support services that are available in any country and so that we break down the barriers that now keep services for people with intellectual and developmental disabilities quite separate.

Growing Importance of Knowledge Exchange

Increasingly, it is being recognized in many fields that research, policy, service, and education need to be more closely connected to one another than was previously the case. A number of terms have been used since 2000 to describe ways of communicating among these areas, but *knowledge exchange* is the term that is most widely used at the time of this book's publication.

Knowledge exchange refers to expressing the essential findings from research in ways that policy makers and practitioners can readily understand and can put to practical use. It also refers to expressing the needs and challenges that policy and practice identify in ways that interest researchers and research funders. Often, these needs and challenges are ones that are not traditionally areas of study in a field but perhaps need to be in the future (e.g., human rights, successful community living), or they suggest alternate ways to do research or sources of information (e.g., understanding the life experiences of indigenous people who have children with disabilities). The art, or process, of knowledge exchange is only beginning to emerge, and in the future it will without doubt be an important area of focus, as well as an area of study in its own right. For the time being, however, the emphasis appears to be primarily in two areas: 1) producing research knowledge in forms that are accessible to nonacademics and that directly or indirectly address their needs; and 2) developing strong working relationships among researchers, policy makers, and practitioners to help facilitate the exchange of knowledge (e.g., service organizations becoming affiliated with universities or other research centers, establishment of centers of excellence in specific areas).

Development of Individual Funding Models and Mechanisms

In many countries, there is a perception that there is insufficient public money to support the growing expectations to support people with disabilities (also see Chapter 4). In response, many funding bodies have been concluding that the only reasonable solution is to redefine the public's obligations in ways that make better use of available resources while being more responsive to the expressed needs and desires of consumers (Brown, 1999; Gettings, 2002). As discussed by Gettings (p. 18), the five cornerstones of this approach are

- Developing individualized support systems
- Delivering services and supports in the community
- Empowering the individual and his/her family to develop individualized goals and determining how public dollars can best be deployed to achieve them
- Fostering the development and use of informal support networks, as well as strong ties to the community
- Limiting paid supports to those aspects of an individualized service/support plan that are either deemed necessary to the achievement of one's goals and/or cannot be accomplished by the person's informal support network.

Embedded in this approach are two related phenomena: 1) the realignment of intergovernmental responsibilities, such as devolution from federal/national to state/local levels of responsibility, and 2) the restructuring of service delivery systems to focus on person-centered services and supports and to help resolve issues related to waiting lists, fiscal resources, individualized support networks, human resource development, and continuous program improvement (Gettings, 2002; Schalock & Bonham, 2003).

The perception that our field faces a problem arising from the necessity of balancing rising consumer demands with available public funding may continue for some time. If so, future individual funding models and mechanisms may be developed that attempt to make better use of available resources and are more responsive to the expressed needs and desires of consumers. Although these models and mechanisms will be different across countries, research suggests that they

- Will not be based on traditional models of social welfare spending (Braddock & Fujiura, 1991; Parish, 2002)
- Will most probably be based on individualized goals because it has been shown across a number of evaluation studies that if people gain control of their own funding, their lives improve and costs do not increase (Head & Conroy, 2005)
- Will involve a wide variety of residential, employment, and habilitation options (Butterworth, 2002)

Such changes, should they occur, are not necessarily in keeping with other changes described in the preceding sections and may not result on their own in positive outcomes either for people with disabilities and their families or for the societies in which they live. Other more inclusive models that consider overall environmental, social, and economical costs and benefits are already emerging and will need to be developed in the future.

Recognizing the Benefits of Assistive Technology

Assistive technology has been developing rapidly and is helping some individuals with disabilities to lead considerably enhanced lives. Assistive technologies include mobility and communication devices, home modifications, and an enormous range of other techniques for maintaining and improving a wide variety of functions. Use of computers, e-mail, and the Internet is particularly important not only for professionals and caregivers but also for people with intellectual and developmental disabilities, as these modes provide a window for learning, for acquiring essential resources, and for gaining access to entertainment (see Chapter 31 for more details about assistive technology).

When setting-specific demands and individual-specific characteristics do not match, adaptations typically become necessary in order for the person to perform those tasks. Bryant, Seay, and Bryant (1999) suggested that during the process of making the adaptation to the person's needs, the following best evaluation criteria should be used: ease of use (setup, operation, and maintenance); amount of training required for the person with intellectual and developmental disabilities; cost to purchase, maintain, and repair; technical features; performance reliability and durability; usability across environments and tasks; promotion of personal independence; and the knowledge level required for proper use.

Generating a Sense of Community

The trend throughout the world, although applied in different ways in different countries, has been for current policy and practices to generate a sense of community by promoting the acceptance and inclusion of people with intellectual and developmental disabilities into their communities. This trend is based on the premise that people want and have a right to full community membership. Generating a sense of community is being accomplished by simultaneous action at several levels, including public laws and other policies, individualized supports provided by individuals' support networks, and the social capital that is available in most communities, as well as the attitudes of community members towards people with intellectual and developmental disabilities. Such attitudes influence the actions of community members and thereby determine opportunities, supports, and valued outcomes for people with intellectual and developmental disabilities. A helpful classification of community attitudes was provided by Myers et al. (1998):

1. A preparedness to engage with people as consumers, neighbors, and friends. This attitude needs to be supported and reinforced.
2. A lack of awareness about individuals with intellectual and developmental disabilities. This attitude needs to be addressed by providing information about the positiveness and potential of these individuals.
3. A wariness or even hostility regarding the idea of community inclusion. This attitude can best be changed by identifying people in the community who can be agents of positive change. As Reinders reminded us, "Without the influence of people who have sufficient moral character to care, rights can do little to sustain the mentally disabled and their families" (1999, p. 383).

The change required in the third item may be the most difficult and challenging because it requires fundamental shifts in the way people individually and collectively view individuals with intellectual and developmental disabilities. To support such shifts, it is necessary to use enhancing language, develop realistic but substantial expectations, envision and assign roles that contain value, and designate importance to the lives of people with intellectual and developmental disabilities. It is also important to continue to foster a community and policy philosophy that is based on the premise that the quality of personal life is grounded in social relationships and is embodied in the political art of integrating the various kinds of self-concerns into an awareness of mutual interdependency (Turnbull & Brunk, 1997).

Evaluating Valued Outcomes

Achieving valued outcomes is a concept that has garnered considerable interest in the field of intellectual and developmental disabilities, although we are still developing the concept and creating useful applications. In the future, it will be necessary to address the considerable confusion in the literature about terms such as *program processes, program outputs, short-term outcomes,* and *long-term outcomes.* However, some clarification of these key concepts has already occurred (Andrews, 2004; Schalock & Bonham, 2003):

- *Program processes:* Activities related to individualized services and supports (e.g., individual program plan, individual service/support plan, person-centered planning)
- *Program outputs:* Results of program efforts, including factors such as number of program participants, kinds of activities performed/offered, time spent in the program, and efficiency measures (outputs relative to inputs)
- *Short-term outcomes:* Measures of subjective well-being such as happiness or satisfaction
- *Long-term outcomes:* Objectively based personal experiences and circumstances; examples include developmental outcomes, community participation, relationships, lifestyle outcomes, and quality of life indicators (Emerson et al., 2005; Schalock & Verdugo, 2002; Stancliffe et al., 2005)

A related challenge is the evaluation of costs and outcomes. This area—one that clearly needs to be addressed in more depth in the future—will need to address costing models with clearly conceptualized and operationally defined and measured valued outcomes. As stated by Stancliffe and Lakin (2005),

> High-quality research information on outcomes and costs will be essential as stakeholders continue to struggle with the issue of how best to allocate available funding. In addition, state funding arrangements will need to be scrutinized carefully to assess whether they meet basic tests of fairness and consistency. (p. 333)

POSSIBLE CHANGES IN THE FUTURE

Futurists are in general agreement that nothing about the future is inevitable except change and that the wise exploit the inevitable (Snyder, 2004). The implication for the field of intellectual and developmental disabilities is that we will have the best outcomes if we understand the trends of the future and adapt to them in ways that are in keeping with our values.

The preceding chapters of this book presented many different advances and also needed changes that relate directly to our work in the field of intellectual and developmental disabilities. Future changes are expected in a great many of these areas, because they have already been accorded importance and some change has already begun. Areas that stand out include the following:

- Addressing the specific needs of Indigenous people and minority groups
- Applying rights and entitlements in universal ways
- Decreasing barriers to resources and services
- Developing ways to provide ethical, medical, and health treatment
- Encouraging increased research support

- Encouraging qualified professionals and frontline staff to enter and remain in the field
- Enhancing communication between medical and psychosocial professionals and among researchers, practitioners, and policy makers
- Finding helpful ways of obtaining and assigning a diagnosis
- Fostering community inclusion in new and additional ways
- Identifying and redressing gaps in the services and supports provided across the life span
- Improving supports for people with intellectual and developmental disabilities in educational systems
- Preventing disabilities (preventing biomedical, environmental, attitudinal, and social conditions that lead directly and indirectly to exclusionary lifestyles)
- Tackling underfunding at all levels in the field

A VISION FOR THE FUTURE

The previous sections of this chapter have outlined significant recent and expected changes in the field of intellectual and developmental disabilities. Readers will no doubt identify other changes in the course of their work and studies. The effects of current and future changes to our field need to be measured against a set of principles. This section sets out a vision of 10 principles for this purpose.

Our vision for the future is international in scope, recognizing that disability is part of every society. It is also universal in design, beginning with the belief that whatever a society has to offer should be offered to *all* of its citizens—laws, rights and privileges, freedoms, opportunities, education and services, and many more. The 10 principles in our vision support the view of a world where social orders extend their assets to people with intellectual and developmental disabilities as they do to people without disabilities and where the strengths of the world are used in positive ways for people with intellectual and developmental disabilities, their families, and those who support them in other ways. Our vision is detailed next and a summary is provided in Table 45.1.

Table 45.1. A vision for the future of people with intellectual and developmental disabilities

For social orders to extend their assets fully to people with intellectual and developmental disabilities, we envision a world where

1. The rights of people with intellectual and developmental disabilities are respected and acted upon
2. People with intellectual and developmental disabilities live among us with dignity and respect
3. People with intellectual and developmental disabilities have the education and supports they require
4. People with intellectual and developmental disabilities contribute to their societies in positive ways
5. People with intellectual and developmental disabilities enjoy the quality of life of their own determination

For the strengths of the world to be used in positive ways to help the field of intellectual and developmental disabilities, we envision a world where

6. National and international leadership in intellectual and developmental disabilities and other disabilities flourishes
7. Poor environmental conditions that contribute to intellectual and developmental disabilities and other disabilities are overcome
8. Medical and related knowledge is used to prevent intellectual and developmental disabilities and to enable people with intellectual and developmental disabilities
9. Emerging technology is used to assist, rather than segregate, people with intellectual and developmental disabilities
10. The professions and families that support people with intellectual and developmental disabilities are respected and honored in society

1. The rights of people with intellectual and developmental disabilities are respected and acted upon

We envision a world where disability is no impediment to the full realization of the rights and entitlements that are available to all people of a society. For this to occur, it is recognized that special provisions, rights, and entitlements are required at several levels simultaneously. At the international level, a variety of conventions and agreements are already in place (see Chapters 5 and 6), and as of the date of publication of this book, a United Nations Convention on the Rights and Dignity of Persons with Disabilities is being developed. Some special groups of people with disabilities also have specific rights, such as refugees who have disabilities (United Nations Enable, 2006a). Within countries, but varying considerably from one country to another, constitutions, laws, and other policy documents set out the rights of people with disabilities, and often stipulate methods by which those rights should be acted upon. At the service system and individual levels, entitlement related to a wide variety of needs and ways to put them into practice are set out under a variety of funding agreements and service mandates for such things as residential care, employment support, inclusive education, adaptive devices, medications, and many other supports and services (see Herr & Weber, 1999).

2. People with intellectual and developmental disabilities live among us with dignity and respect

We envision a world where people with intellectual and developmental disabilities live freely among their family members, relatives, friends, neighbors, and acquaintances. For children, such freedom is supported or limited somewhat by the influences of the family home, neighborhood, and school. For adults, it entails a degree of self-determination, following a variety of life experiences regarding the choice of living environment, personal habits, friends, family, daily activities, leisure activities, learning options, and life goals.

Whatever the life situations of children and adults may be, they will be fully recognized only if their human lives are accorded respect by others and if each person with a disability is treated by others in a dignified way that reflects the value of unique personalities within the larger social group. For the field of intellectual and developmental disabilities, it will be essential to continue to build on the foundations already in place for according respect and dignity to people with disabilities (see Display 45.1) and to provide leadership to the broader society for doing so.

Display 45.1

A wish for dignity and respect

I hope that when a child with a disability is born in Ukraine, he or she is greeted and welcomed into this world. I hope no parents will receive advice to abandon their child and hear bad things about their child. I also hope that early intervention programs will be available everywhere in my country, and that families will get the necessary support and intervention. I hope that the educational system will change in Ukraine, and that it will be possible for disabled children to be integrated into regular schools and preschools. I hope that attitudes of people towards persons with disabilities will change, so that persons with disabilities will have no experience with stigmatization, but will experience acceptance, friendship, and recognition of their gifts and talents. I hope in their adulthood, people with disabilities will have lots of possibilities to lead normal lives, with opportunities for realizing their human needs and their potential. I hope in their old age, people with disabilities can be in an environment that makes the experience of their aging and dying as human as it should be.

Source: Oleh Romanchuk, Dzherelo Children's Rehabilitation Centre in Lviv, Ukraine; used by permission.

3. People with intellectual and developmental disabilities have the education and supports they require

We envision a world where society acts on its responsibility for accommodating, including, and promoting people with disabilities by providing them with stimulating learning opportunities and the supports that enable them to take part in and enjoy life throughout their life spans. Stimulating learning opportunities include access to high-quality, close-to-home education throughout the childhood years that reflects individualized planning and instruction, and access to lifelong learning and training opportunities. Enabling supports include adequately trained and/or experienced personnel who help people with disabilities shape the overall direction and daily activities of their own lives in positive ways, as well as access to the resources (e.g., funding, community programs, human resources) and the services (e.g., housing, personal support, employment support) that make this possible.

4. People with intellectual and developmental disabilities contribute to their societies in positive ways

We envision a world where people with intellectual and developmental disabilities can accomplish their dreams and contribute to society in ways that are recognized and valued by all members of society. To achieve this, the field of intellectual and developmental disabilities will have to assume a considerable amount of responsibility for encouraging affected individuals to participate fully in society, for developing methods to assist them in delivering their contributions, and, perhaps most important, for taking leadership in helping people without disabilities to understand the value of these contributions and the importance to all humans for demonstrating that such contributions are valued. As shown by Philip's story (see Community Living Guelph Wellington, n.d.), these aspects of Vision Item 4 are indeed possible. We owe it to Philip and others like him to set examples and to provide confidence that such a vision can be attained.

5. People with intellectual and developmental disabilities enjoy the quality of life of their own determination

We envision a world where people with intellectual and developmental disabilities can determine and enjoy their own lives. To help achieve this, we need to begin by recognizing that people with intellectual and developmental disabilities, like people without disabilities, are best positioned to define and act on (within a range of opportunities available to them) the people, places, and things that add quality to their lives. Using such self-determination as a guide, our field's responsibility is then to try to enable quality of life improvement to occur. A critical aspect of providing such enablement is to remove physical, policy, practice, and attitudinal barriers, especially by providing a strong and credible alternative to the view that limits to social worth and personal happiness are intrinsic to disability. This alternative will emphasize individualized definitions of quality that are recognized and valued by others and will provide ways for people with intellectual and developmental disabilities to move toward them.

6. National and international leadership in intellectual and developmental disabilities and other disabilities flourishes

We envision a world where the existing national and international leadership in intellectual and developmental disabilities joins with leaders in the broader disability field to take a prominent role in the direction of human affairs. People who are identified with disabilities make up between 10% and 25% of the general population (selection criteria differ somewhat among countries). For example, in the United States, 12% of working-age adults were reported as having a disability (Rehabilitation Research and Training Center on Disability Demographics and Statistics, 2004), and 23% of adults in Wales were reported to have a disability (National Statistics, 2006b). The United Kingdom reported that approximately 18% of children and youth younger than 20 years of age were identified as having a disability (National Statistics, 2006a). These prevalence rates represent such a significant proportion of the population of countries that virtually all human activities must accommodate disability. Strong national and international leadership is required to ensure that this occurs.

7. Poor environmental conditions that contribute to intellectual and developmental disabilities are overcome

We envision a world where the world's resources are used to enable people and to address problems that arise from the poor environmental conditions that contribute to intellectual and developmental disabilities. In all regions of the world, but to varying degrees, a great many people have intellectual and developmental disabilities that result from preventable causes such as malnutrition, deficiencies of certain minerals (e.g., iodine, iron), deficiencies of vitamins (e.g., folate), infections (e.g., measles) that can be prevented by immunization, and environmental hazards, including inadvertent exposure to teratogens and lead or mercury poisoning (Chapter 9). In addition, lack of good water, poor sanitation, and lack of medical care, including insufficient attention to HIV/AIDS (see Display 45.2), not only increase the prevalence of intellectual and developmental disabilities but also pose barriers to rehabilitation efforts. Finally, lack of physical activity, poor social and cognitive stimulation, and physical and emotional neglect contribute significantly to disability. Unfortunately, many of these problems are more prevalent within minority or indigenous populations (see Display 45.3). The resources of the world should be actively channeled to address these issues.

Display 45.2

Disability and HIV/AIDS

Human immunodeficiency virus/acquired immunodeficiency syndrome (HIV/AIDS) is a serious problem everywhere and is an enormous problem in some parts of the world. In the intellectual and developmental disabilities literature, there is still insufficient attention to the risk of HIV infection and AIDS in people with intellectual and developmental disabilities (Groce, 2004). People with intellectual and developmental disabilities are sexually active and require education concerning risk of infection.

HIV infection adds to the intellectual and developmental disabilities rate. In vitro infection with HIV or postnatal HIV infection in children can result in significant intellectual and/or developmental disability, and HIV infection in adults is associated with cognitive impairment.

Practicing safer sex, safer handling of bodily fluids, and other precautions are important to containing and reducing the rate of HIV infection. Some treatments for HIV infection are now available, but prevention is still an uphill battle. Our vision for a future includes developing strategies for harnessing the increasing rate of HIV infection and the severity of HIV infection.

8. Medical and related knowledge is used to enable people with intellectual and developmental disabilities

We envision a world where medical advances prevent intellectual and developmental disabilities where possible, and, where not possible, to enable people with intellectual and developmental disabilities to live in greater dignity and to attain higher levels of personal happiness. Knowledge is increasing about how to prevent intellectual and developmental disabilities, although methods of putting prevention knowledge into practice need to be strengthened. Since 1990, more has been learned about the brain and its relation to development and behavior than in all previous decades and even centuries. Brain imaging methods are particularly exciting, because they enable scientists to study the brain under different conditions. Information is

Display 45.3

Disability and indigenous peoples

Some countries have citizens whose ancestors were indigenous to the lands that now form those countries. Some examples include the Aborigines in Australia, the Native Americans in the United States, First Nations peoples in Canada, the Maori of New Zealand, the Sami people living north of the Scandinavian border (Norway, Sweden, Finland, and Russia), and the Bedouins in Israel. India, Japan, the Philippines, and many other countries also have indigenous populations.

In spite of many positive steps forward for indigenous people since the 1990s in many countries (e.g., New Zealand, Australia, Canada, United States), these citizens often do not receive the same health, education, or social services as non-indigenous citizens. For children and adults with intellectual or developmental disabilities and their families, in particular, this is an important issue that needs ongoing redress.

exploding in the field of genetics, largely due to an extraordinary degree of international cooperation and collaboration among members of the scientific and medical communities who are contributing to the Human Genome Project.

We envision a world where there is similar international cooperation and collaboration among scientists who share the vision of preventing disabilities and enabling people with disabilities. In doing so, they might focus especially on emerging knowledge that is helping us to do the following (adapted with permission from the Association of University Centers on Disabilities, 2005):

- Prevent many types of intellectual and developmental disabilities by treating maternal infections and viruses transmitted to infants.
- Use brain imaging and genetic methods to better understand the causes of specific disabilities and suggest strategies for treatment.
- Develop gene therapies to prevent or reverse some of the symptoms of specific disabilities.
- Better understand the process of brain cell development and enrichment through studying the interplay of the brain's own chemistry with the child's experiences.
- Capitalize on the brain's natural "plasticity" to optimize brain development in children born with developmental disabilities through early intervention or by extending the period of brain development.
- Develop culturally competent psychological and medical assessment and treatment procedures for children born into families from minority backgrounds.
- Prevent and treat atypical behavior among children and adults with disabilities who are especially prone to such difficulties, such as children with autism, fragile X syndrome, and Rett syndrome.
- Design learning environments so children have improved academic outcomes.
- Assist families in preparing their adult sons and daughters with disabilities for successful lives of their own.
- Prepare older people with disabilities for coping with the normal processes of aging.

9. Emerging technology is used to assist, rather than segregate, people with intellectual and developmental disabilities

We envision a world where current and future technology will be used to help people with intellectual and developmental disabilities lead successful lives. Two types of technology are particularly important for people with intellectual and developmental disabilities: assistive technology, and electronic and information technology. Assistive technology is any device that can increase, maintain, or improve functional capacities of individuals with disabilities.

Electronic and information technologies include such things as computers (to use for videoconferencing, looking at web sites, receiving e-mail, and so forth), telephones, bank machines, television and related technology, and the numerous fast-changing electronic devices for practical use and entertainment. Applications of these technologies include helping people with communication, mobility, management of their homes, activities of daily living, education, employment, and sports and recreation. However, not all people with disabilities can use technology in its current form, and already the term *e-divide* is used to describe the separation between those who use ever-changing electronic technology and those who do not. Cost, ongoing training, and ease of use are important challenges that need to be addressed for electronic and information technology to be helpful, not segregating. Social segregation resulting from technology that is too complex is a real and serious future danger for people with intellectual and developmental disabilities (Parmenter, 2003).

There is an enormous amount of technological expertise throughout the world, and we envision a world where this expertise focuses as much on ease of application as on innovation. The challenge is to make emerging technology as easy to use as turning on the lights or getting a radio to play music. If this challenge can be met, society will have gone a long way toward including people with intellectual and developmental disabilities, as it has an obligation to do.

10. The professions and families that support people with intellectual and developmental disabilities are respected and honored in society

We envision a world where the professionals and family members who support people with intellectual and developmental disabilities are valued for the work they do. There is still a shortage of frontline workers and of knowledgeable professionals in many areas related to intellectual and developmental disabilities (see Chapter 27). The reasons for this are complex but are fairly well understood, and numerous strategies are available for addressing this problem (Larson et al., 1998). Primarily, though, the challenge for the field is to help ensure that the work of its professionals, paraprofessionals, other support personnel, and students is clearly understood by the wider society as essential and valued. To achieve this fully, leaders within the field will have to promote this view, both directly—by clearly stating the contribution of the field's work and providing accompanying training—and indirectly—by advancing the other nine aspects of this vision.

SUMMARY

Significant changes have occurred in four core areas of the field of intellectual and developmental disabilities. There has been: 1) a shift in the concept of disability, 2) a broader understanding about the causes of disability, 3) change in public policy, and 4) a transition to a supports paradigm. Several other changes are also occurring, and all changes have some impact on others. It is not possible to predict precisely what changes may occur in the future, but we expect many changes—and these will help shape the nature of our field in the future.

Finally, our future vision is a world where people with intellectual and developmental disabilities are fully recognized as having rights that are respected and acted on, live among us with dignity and respect, have the education and supports they require, contribute to their societies in positive ways, and enjoy the quality of life of their own determination. We envision the strengths of the world being used in positive ways so that national and international leadership in disabilities flourishes, poor environmental conditions that contribute to disabilities are overcome, medical and related knowledge is used to prevent and enable people with disabilities, emerging technology is used to assist rather than segregate people with disabilities, and professions and families that support people with disabilities are respected and honored in society.

FOR FURTHER THOUGHT AND DISCUSSION

1. Identify two important policy changes and two important practice changes that have occurred in your geographic region during the past few years. Provide a rationale for why you consider each to be important.
2. Change occurs, but not without contributing factors. Some contributing factors are beyond your control and influence, but others are within your control and can be influenced. Think of three factors related to the field of intellectual and developmental disabilities that you and your colleagues might control or influence. For each, identify three or four specific actions that you might take to help exert control or influence, and discuss how you might ensure that these actions are successful.
3. Select 1 of the 10 areas of the vision provided in the final section of this chapter. List specific methods of making this part of the vision become a reality. For each method, consider which people should be involved, what they should do, and what success indicators should be used (i.e., how you will know that the goal has been achieved).
4. Talk with a person you know who has an intellectual or developmental disability. What is his or her personal vision for the future?

REFERENCES

American Association on Mental Retardation. (1998). *A provider's guide to quality community services: Shaping our destiny. For people with developmental disabilities and their families.* http://www.open.org/~people1/articles/shaping_destiny_provider.htm

Andrews, A.B. (2004). Start at the end: Empowerment evaluation product planning. *Evaluation and Program Planning, 27,* 275–285.

Association of University Centers on Disabilities. (2005). *Developmental Disabilities Research Centers: Future directions.* Retrieved March 9, 2006, from http://www.aucd.org/ddrc/future.html

Biersdorff, K.K. (2002). Meeting the challenges of challenging behavior. *Rehabilitation Review, 13*(2). Retrieved March 9, 2006, from http://www.vrri.org/rhb0202.htm

Blackstock, C., Cross, T., George, J., et al. (2006). *Reconciliation in child welfare: Touchstones of hope for Aboriginal children, youth and families.* Portland, OR: National Indian Child Welfare Association.

Braddock, D., & Fujiura, G. (1991). Politics, public policy and the development of community mental retardation services in the United States. *American Journal on Mental Retardation, 95,* 369–387.

Braddock, D., & Parish, S.L. (2002). An institutional history of disability. In D. Braddock (Ed.), *Disability at the dawn of the 21st century and the state of the states* (pp. 3–59). Washington, DC: American Association on Mental Retardation.

Brown, I. (1999). Embracing quality of life in times of spending restraint. *Journal of Intellectual and Developmental Disability, 24*(4), 299–308.

Bryant, B.R., Seay, P.C., & Bryant, D.P. (1999). Assistive technology and adaptive behavior. In R.L. Schalock (Ed.), *Adaptive behavior and its measurement: Implications for the field of mental retardation* (pp. 81–98). Washington, DC: American Association on Mental Retardation.

Butterworth, J. (2002). From programs to supports. In R.L. Schalock, P.C. Baker, & M.D. Croser (Eds.), *Embarking on a new century: Mental retardation at the end of the 20th century* (pp. 83–100). Washington, DC: American Association on Mental Retardation.

Cetron, M.J., & Davies, O. (2003, March/April). Trends shaping the future: Technological, workplace, management, and institutional trends. *The Futurist,* 30–43.

Community Living Guelph Wellington. (n.d.). *Community Living stories: Philip's story.* Retrieved March 10, 2006, from http://www.gwacl.on.ca/Stories_Philip.htm

Down Syndrome Educational Trust. (2006). *The Down Syndrome Educational Trust online.* Retrieved May 17, 2006, from http://www.downsed.org

Emerson, E., Robertson, J., Hatton, C., et al. (2005). Costs and outcomes of community residential supports in England. In R.J. Stancliffe & K.C. Lakin (Eds.), *Costs and outcomes of community services for people with intellectual disabilities* (pp. 151–174). Baltimore: Paul H. Brookes Publishing Co.

Fitzgerald, M.A. (n.d.) *Primary, secondary, and tertiary prevention. Important in certification and practice.* Retrieved March 9, 2006, from http://www.fhea.com/CertificationCols/level_prevention.htm

Fudge Schormans, A., & Brown, I. (2002). An investigation into the characteristics of the maltreatment of children with developmental delays and the alleged perpetrators of this maltreatment. *Journal on Developmental Disabilities, 9* (1), 1–19.

Gettings, R.M. (2002). Public policy challenges in the new millennium. In R.L. Schalock, P.C. Baker, & M.D. Croser (Eds.), *Embarking on a new century: Mental retardation at the end of the 20th century* (pp. 17–26). Washington, DC: American Association on Mental Retardation.

Groce, N. (2004). *The World Bank/Yale University Global Survey on HIV/AIDS and Disability.* Retrieved from http://cc.msnscache.com/cache.aspx?q=2843625729763&lang=en-US&mkt=en-US&FORM=CVRE

Hayden, M.F., & Nelis, T. (2002). Self-advocacy. In R.L. Schalock, P.C. Baker, & M.D. Croser (Eds.), *Embarking on a new century: Mental retardation at the end of the 20th century* (pp. 221–234). Washington, DC: American Association on Mental Retardation.

Head, M.J., & Conroy, J.W. (2005). Outcomes of self-determination in Michigan: Quality and costs. In R.J. Stancliffe & K.C. Lakin (Eds.), *Costs and outcomes of community services for people with intellectual disabilities* (pp. 219–240). Baltimore: Paul H. Brookes Publishing Co.

Herr, S.S., & Weber, G. (Eds.). (1999). *Aging, rights, and quality of life: Prospects for older people with developmental disabilities.* Baltimore: Paul H. Brookes Publishing Co.

Larson, S.A., Hewitt, A.S., & Lakin, K.C. (2004). Multiperspective analysis of workforce challenges and their effects on consumer and family quality of life. *American Journal on Mental Retardation, 109,* 481–500.

Larson, S.A., Lakin, K.C., Bruiniks, R.H., et al. (1998). *Staff recruitment and retention: Study results and intervention strategies.* Washington, DC: American Association on Mental Retardation.

Larson, S.A., Lakin, K.C., & Hewitt, A.S. (2002). Direct support professionals: 1975–2000. In R.L. Schalock, P.C. Baker, & M.D. Croser (Eds.), *Embarking on a new century: Mental retardation at the end of the 20th century* (pp. 203–220). Washington, DC: American Association on Mental Retardation.

Luckasson, R., Borthwick-Duffy, S., Buntinx, W.H.E., et al. (2002). *Mental retardation: Diagnosis, classification, and systems of supports.* Washington, DC: American Association on Mental Retardation.

Myers, F., Ager, A., Kerr, P., et al. (1998). Outside looking in?: Studies of the community integration of people with learning disabilities. *Disability and Society, 13,* 389–413.

National Statistics. (2006a). *Children and youth with disabilities.* Retrieved January 17, 2006, from http://www.statistics.gov.uk/CCI/Nscl.asp?ID=6485&Pos=1&ColRank=1&Rank=64

National Statistics. (2006b). *Wales: Its people.* Retrieved January 17, 2006, from http://www.statistics.gov.uk/CCI/nugget.asp?ID=453

Ouellette-Kuntz, H., Garcin, N., Lewis, M.E., et al. (2005). Addressing health disparities through promoting equity for individuals with intellectual disability. *Canadian Journal of Public Health, 96,* S8–S22.

Parish, S.L. (2002). Forces shaping developmental disabilities services in the United States: A comparative study. In D. Braddock (Ed.), *Disability at the dawn of the 21st century and the state of the states* (pp. 353–475). Washington, DC: American Association on Mental Retardation.

Parmenter, T.R. (2003, September 21–24). *Are we engineering ourselves out of existence?* Inaugural Trevor Parmenter Lecture presented to the First Life Activities International Conference on Disability, Creative Community Initiatives for People with Disability, Newcastle, Australia.

Rehabilitation Research and Training Center on Disability Demographics and Statistics. (2004). *2004 Disability Status Reports United States.* http://www.ilr.cornell.edu/ped/disabilitystatistics/StatusReports/2004-pdf/2004-StatusReport_US.pdf?CFID=3982222&CFTOKEN=46857962

Reinders, H. (1999). The ethics of normalization. *Cambridge Quarterly of Health Care Ethics, 6,* 381–489.

Robertson, J., Emerson, E., Pinkney, L., et al. (2005). Treatment and management of challenging behaviours in congregate and noncongregate community-based supported accommodation. *Journal of Intellectual Disability Research, 49* (Pt. 1), 63–72.

Roeher Institute. (1996). *Disability, community and society: Exploring the links.* Toronto: Author.

Ruddick, L. (2005). Health of people with intellectual disabilities: A review of factors influencing access to health care. *British Journal of Health Psychology, 10*(Pt. 4), 559–570.

Scale, toll of gene birth defects vast, study finds. (2006, January 31). *Los Angeles Times.* Retrieved September 16, 2005, from http://www.latimes.com/news/science/la-sci-birthdefect31jan31,0,6356077.story?coll=la-news-science

Schalock, R.L. (2001). *Outcome-based evaluation* (2nd ed.). New York: Kluwer Academic/Plenum.

Schalock, R.L. (2004). The emerging disability paradigm and its implications for policy and practice. *Journal of Disability Policy Studies, 14,* 204–215.

Schalock, R.L., Baker, P.C., & Croser, M.D. (2002). Trends and issues. In R.L. Schalock, P.C. Baker, & M.D. Croser (Eds.), *Embarking on a new century: Mental retardation at the end of the 20th century* (pp. 255–262). Washington, DC: American Association on Mental Retardation.

Schalock, R.L., & Bonham, G.S. (2003). Measuring outcomes and managing for results. *Evaluation and Program Planning, 26,* 229–235.

Schalock, R.L., & Luckasson, R. (2004). American Association on Mental Retardation's classification and systems of supports and its relation to international trends and issues in the field of intellectual disabilities. *Journal of Policy and Practice in Intellectual Disabilities, 1*(Pts. 3 & 4), 136–146.

Schalock, R.L., & Luckasson, R. (2005). *Clinical judgment.* Washington, DC: American Association on Mental Retardation.

Schalock, R.L., & Verdugo, M.A. (2002). *Handbook on quality of life for human service practitioners.* Washington, DC: American Association on Mental Retardation.

Snyder, D.P. (2004, July/August). Five meta-trends changing the world. *The Futurist,* 22–27.

Stancliffe, R.J. (2005). Semi-independent living and group homes in Australia. In R.J. Stancliffe & K.C. Lakin (Eds.), *Costs and outcomes of community services for people with intellectual disabilities* (pp. 129–150). Baltimore: Paul H. Brookes Publishing Co.

Stancliffe, R.J., & Lakin, K.C. (Eds.). (2005). *Costs and outcomes of community services for people with intellectual disabilities.* Baltimore: Paul H. Brookes Publishing Co.

Stancliffe, R.J., Lakin, K.C., Shea, J.R., et al. (2005). The economics of deinstitutionalization. In R.J. Stancliffe & K.C. Lakin (Eds.), *Costs and outcomes of community services for people with intellectual disabilities* (pp. 289–312). Baltimore: Paul H. Brookes Publishing Co.

Stowe, M.J., Turnbull, H.R., III, Schrandt, S., et al. (in press). Looking to the future: Intellectual and developmental disabilities in the genetics era. *Journal on Developmental Disabilities.*

Switzky, H., & Greenspan, S. (2003). *What is mental retardation?* Washington DC: American Association on Mental Retardation.

Taylor, M., Bradley, V., & Warren, R., Jr. (1996). *The community support skills standards: Tools for managing change and achieving outcomes.* Cambridge, MA: Human Services Research Institute.

Tuffrey-Wijne, I. (2003). The palliative care needs of people with intellectual disabilities: A literature review. *Palliative Medicine, 17,* 55–62.

Turnbull, H.R., III, & Brunk, G.L. (1997). Quality of life and public policy. In R.L. Schalock (Ed.), *Quality of life: Vol. II. Application to persons with disabilities* (pp. 201–210). Washington, DC: American Association on Mental Retardation.

Turnbull, H.R., III, Wilcox, B.L., Stowe, M.J., et al. (2001). Matrix of federal statutes and federal and state court decisions reflecting the core concepts of disability policy. *Journal of Disability Policy Studies, 12,* 144–176.

United Nations Enable. (2006a). *Disability and the United Nations.* Retrieved March 9, 2006, from http://www.un.org/esa/socdev/enable/disunandpwd.htm

United Nations Enable. (2006b). *World programme of action concerning disabled persons.* Retrieved May 23, 2006, from http://www.un.org/esa/socdev/enable/diswpa00.htm

University of Minnesota, College of Education and Human Development. (2006). *Resources for political activism by persons with disabilities.* Retrieved February 9, 2006, from http://ici.umn.edu/products/impact/172/res3.html

U.S. Preventive Services Task Force. (1996). *Guide to clinical preventive services* (2nd ed.). Baltimore: Author.

World Health Organization. (2001). *International Classification of Functioning, Disability, and Health (ICF).* Geneva: Author.

Worth, P. (n.d.). *The self-advocacy movement: 1980s–present.* Retrieved January 26, 2006, from http://www.mncdd.org/parallels/seven/7d2/1.html

APPENDIX A

GLOSSARY

Aarskog-Scott syndrome An inherited autosomal dominant syndrome affecting the face, digits (fingers/toes), and genitals.

abruptio placentae Means "placental abruption." Refers to separation of the normally located placenta after the 20th week of gestation and prior to birth.

absence seizures Nonconvulsive seizures that consist only of a few seconds of blank staring and immobility. The three per second spike and wave activity is seen in the electroencephalographic (EEG) readings of people with absence seizures. (formerly called *petit mal seizures*).

acculturation The process of learning a second culture.

acetaldehyde The major metabolite of alcohol in the body; many toxic effects of excessive alcohol consumption are actually caused by acetaldehyde.

adaptive behavior An individual's effectiveness in meeting the standards of maturation, learning, personal independence, and social responsibility expected for his or her age level and cultural group.

adrenoleukodystrophy An X-linked inborn error of metabolism that results in the accumulation of saturated, very long chain fatty acids in several target organs. The most common form affects boys between 4 and 8 years old.

alcohol Any of a series of hydroxyl compounds, the simplest of which are derived from saturated hydrocarbons, have the general formula C_nH_{2n}+1OH, and include ethanol and methanol. Ethanol is the alcohol present in alcoholic beverages. Methanol is poisonous.

aldehyde dehydrogenase An enzyme (protein) in the body which converts aldehyde into a less toxic substance.

allele One of two or more different forms of a gene at a given locus.

alpha-fetoprotein (AFP) A protein secreted by the fetal liver that enters the mother's blood. In the AFP test, which is generally used to screen for neural tube defects like spina bifida and anencephaly, a blood sample is drawn from the mother to check the levels of AFP. The test can also indicate abdominal wall defects, esophageal and duodenal atresia, some renal and urinary tract anomalies, Turner syndrome, some low birth weight fetuses, placental complications, and Down syndrome. AFP is one of three substances in the blood of pregnant women that is used to screen for Down syndrome and neural tube defects; three other substances that are often measured along with AFP are human chorionic gonadotropin, unconjugated estriol, and inhibin-A (see entries). The AFP test is most sensitive between the 15th and 17th weeks of pregnancy; however, false-positive and false-negative results are associated with the AFP and other screening tests.

amino acid The fundamental building block of proteins.

amniocentesis A procedure that involves sampling the amniotic fluid (the fluid surrounding a fetus in the uterus). The test is mostly done between the 15th and 18th weeks of pregnancy to screen for genetic or chromosomal abnormalities, such as Down syndrome. Other reasons for having amniocentesis include checking to see if the baby has Rh sensitization (a condition in which the mother's and baby's blood are incompatible), to determine if a baby's lungs are mature enough for an early delivery, or to diagnose or rule out a uterine infection if the membranes have ruptured prematurely or if an infection is suspected for another reason. Not all women choose to have this test because it carries a small risk of miscarriage.

amnion The innermost membrane that encloses and protects the embryo of a reptile, bird, or mammal.

amnionic Pertaining to the amnion.

anemia A below-normal reduction of the number of red cells per unit of blood, the quantity of hemoglobin, or the volume of packed red cells per unit of blood, when the equilibrium between blood loss and blood production is disturbed.

anencephaly A congenital malformation characterized by the total or partial absence of the cranial vault and the covering skin, as well as the absence of the brain or its reduction to a small mass.

Angelman syndrome Initially described in 1965 by Harry Angelman. It was reported only infrequently until 1987, when a small deletion of the long arm of chromosome 15 was recognized. Up to 80% of individuals with the syndrome have a deletion of maternal chromosome 15, with a small number having two copies of the paternal chromosome 15 (uniparental disomy).

anisotrop(h)y The property of being anisotropic means having a different value when measured in different directions. In the ventricles of the brain, water diffuses freely in all directions. In contrast, in nerves, white matter of the spinal cord, and white matter of the cortex, the motion of water is restricted and it diffuses along the length of the nerve fibers. The technique of magnetic resonance diffusion imaging is sensitive to the motion of water and can reveal abnormalities in the diffusion of water that are caused by abnormalities in the brain's microstructure.

antipsychotic medication Medication used to treat psychoses (e.g., hallucinations, paranoia).

aortic regurgitation The backflow of blood from the aorta into the left ventricle, owing to imperfect functioning of the aortic semilunar valve.

Apgar score A numbered rating—based on heart rate, skin color, breathing, response to stimulus, and muscle tone—that reflects the health of a newborn. A score of 10 means that the infant is robust.

apraxia A neurological impairment involving the inability to execute a voluntary motor movement despite being able to demonstrate normal muscle function. Apraxia is not related to lack of understanding or to any kind of physical paralysis but is caused by a problem in the cortex of the brain.

arginosuccinic aciduria An error of metabolism called hyperammonemia. This particular condition is caused by a defective urea cycle enzyme called arginosuccinate lyase.

asphyxia A condition in which there is anoxia (lack of oxygen) and increased carbon dioxide tension in the blood and tissues.

astrocytes A category of glial cells in the brain that have a star-like shape. They play an active role in the brain and central nervous system.

ataxia Loss of full control of body movements, especially the ability to coordinate voluntary movements of the muscles. The word *ataxia* comes from the Greek word *ataxis,* meaning "without order" or "incoordination." However, ataxia is also used to refer to a group of disorders that display the symptom as a dominant feature. Ataxia can be a symptom of many disorders, including those associated with infections, injuries, or degenerative changes in the central nervous system.

attention-deficit/hyperactivity disorder (ADHD) A developmental disorder characterized by difficulty in concentration and hyperactive behavior.

autonomic instability Instability of the autonomic nervous system. The autonomic nervous system is the portion of the nervous system concerned with regulation of the activity of heart muscle, smooth muscles, and glands.

autosomal Pertaining to chromosomes 1 to 22 (i.e., autosomes) and excluding the sex chromosomes (X and Y).

blastula An animal embryo at an early stage of development, when it is a hollow ball of cells.

Bloom syndrome An inherited autosomal recessive condition characterized by short stature, immune deficiency, and a greatly increased frequency of many types of cancers; this is due to mutation in a DNA-unwinding enzyme called *helicase,* which is encoded on chromosome 15.

bolus A mass of food ready to be swallowed or a mass passing along the intestines, or portion of food that is swallowed at any particular time.

bovine spongiform encephalopathy (BSE) A spongiform brain disease of cattle first identified in Britain in 1986.

cerebral dysgenesis Abnormal development of the cerebral cortex.

choreoathetotic movements Constant, slow, involuntary movements of the hands, fingers, toes, and feet.

chorionic villus sampling (CVS) Prenatal test that involves taking a tiny tissue sample from outside the sac where the fetus develops. The tissue is tested to diagnose or rule out certain birth defects. The test generally is performed between 10 and 12 weeks after a woman's last menstrual period. CVS may be offered when there is an increased risk of chromosomal or genetic birth defects and parents want to know as early in pregnancy as possible. Amniocentesis can diagnose the same birth defects but is performed later in pregnancy.

chromatid Either of two threadlike strands into which a chromosome divides longitudinally during cell division.

chromosomes The cellular structures in the cell's nucleus that carry the genetic information in the form of long strands of DNA bound to proteins. Chromosomes are constant in number in each species. The normal number in humans is 46: 22 pairs of autosomes and 2 sex chromosomes (XX or XY).

cleavage division The first sets of mitotic divisions following fertilization. These give rise to cells called *blastomeres.*

clone 1) A group of genetically identical individuals descended from the same parent by asexual reproduction. Many plants show this by producing suckers, tubers, or bulbs to colonize the area around the parent. 2) A group of genetically identical cells produced by mitotic division from an original cell. This occurs when the cell creates a new set of chromosomes and splits into two daughter cells. This is how replacement cells are produced in the human body when the old ones wear out. 3) A group of DNA molecules from an original length of DNA sequences produced by a bacterium or a virus using molecular biology techniques. This is often called *molecular cloning* or *DNA cloning.* 4) The production of genetically identical animals by embryo splitting. This can occur naturally at the two-cell stage to give identical twins. In cattle, when individual cells from 4- and 8-cell embryos are implanted in different foster mothers, they can develop normally into calves; this technique has been used routinely within cattle breeding schemes since the 1990s. 5) The creation of one or more genetically identical animals by transferring the nucleus of a body cell into an egg from which the nucleus has been removed. This is also known as nuclear transfer (NT) or cell nuclear replacement (CNR) and is how the sheep Dolly was produced.

comorbid Occurring together (often used to denote the simultaneous existence of two conditions).

competitive employment Situation in which an individual works in a regular setting in the community and is paid a regular salary at or above the legal minimum wage. In Australia, the term *competitive employment* is often used to denote situations in which an individual who is paid a competitive wage is receiving ongoing support from a specialized organization. In North America, these situations fall within the definition of *supported employment.*

complementary base pair sequence A linear array of nucleotide base pairs in double-stranded DNA or RNA, the sequence of which is determined by the order of nucleotides in one of the strands. In DNA, the sequence is determined by hydrogen bonding between adenosine and thymine (A-T) and guanine and cytosine (G-C). There are two hydrogen bonds in A-T pairs, and three hydrogen bonds in G-C pairs. In RNA, the sequence is determined by hydrogen bonding between adenosine and uracil (A-U) and (G-C).

complex partial seizures Seizures in which epileptic spiking is often seen on both sides of the individual's brain in the temporal lobe areas. The patient does not convulse and does not lose consciousness but is out of contact with his or her environment. Consciousness is said to be impaired. (formerly called temporal lobe seizures or psychomotor seizures.)

computed tomography (CT) A series of detailed pictures of areas inside the body taken from different angles; the pictures are created by a computer linked to an X-ray machine.

computerized axial tomography (CAT) scan A process in which an X-ray scanner makes many sweeps of the body and the results are processed by computer to give a cross-sectional image.

conduct disorder A group of behavioral and emotional problems in children who have great difficulty following rules and behaving in a socially acceptable way.

congenital Existing from birth but not necessarily inherited.

co-operatives (co-ops) A number of people jointly own the business in which they all work. They make joint decisions and share in the profits or losses of the business, at least in theory. In the United Kingdom, these are called *social firms.*

craniofacial Pertaining to the structural appearance of the head and face.

Creutzfeldt-Jakob disease (CJD) A rare prion disorder (spongiform encephalopathy) affecting human beings. It is characterized by progressive dementia and affects approximately 1 person in 1 million.

cri-du-chat syndrome A disorder caused by a defect on chromosome 5 that is associated with microcephaly, epicanthic folds, and a high-pitched cry. It is an example of a syndrome with mental retardation in which a cryptic chromosomal abnormality has been defined.

cytomegalovirus (CMV) One group of herpes viruses that infect humans. It usually produces very mild symptoms in most infected people but may cause neurological damage and a variety of clinical symptoms—including deafness or hearing impairment and intellectual disability—in people with weakened immune systems and in newborns (infection may occur before or after birth). Effective vaccination is a prospect for the future.

deletion An absence of a segment of DNA that may be as small as a single base or large enough to encompass one or more entire genes. Large deletions involving a whole segment of a chromosome may be detected by routine examination of the chromosomes; intermediate deletions involving a few genes may be detected by using fluorescent in situ hybridization (FISH); smaller deletions involving a portion of a gene may only be detected by analyzing the DNA.

dendrite Nerve fiber leading to the cell body of a neuron.

dendritic arborization The degree of branching of a dendrite.

diploid number Having two complete sets of chromosomes per cell (i.e., from the mother and the father). In humans, the diploid chromosome number is 46.

DNA Deoxyribnucleic acid. Present in chromosomes, it contains genetic information.

dominant Refers to a situation in which the expression of a particular gene is the same whether it is present in two copies or in one copy.

Dubowitz syndrome A dysmorphism syndrome with developmental delay, transient short stature, hyperactive behavior, and eczema.

Duchenne muscular dystrophy An X-linked lethal recessive disorder that severely affects males. It is the most common type of muscular dystrophy. Nonprogressive intellectual disability occurs in some patients. Serum levels of creatine kinase are grossly elevated in presymptomatic and early stages of the disorder. Many different mutations of the dystrophin gene causing this disorder have been identified.

duodenal lumen The duodenum is the first part of the small intestine; the lumen is the inner, open region of the duodenum.

duplication Occurs when an error in DNA replication leads to the duplication of a region of DNA containing a (generally functional) gene.

dysphagia Abnormal swallowing or inability to swallow.

dystonia A state of abnormal muscle tone, especially in relation to a postural disorder marked by spasm of the trunk, neck, shoulders, or limbs and due to disease of the basal ganglia of the brain.

echocardiogram (ECHO) A record produced by echocardiography, the use of ultrasound waves, to investigate the action of the heart.

edema Condition characterized by an excess of watery fluid collecting in the cavities or tissues of the body.

electrocardiogram (EKG) A record produced by an electrocardiograph, used in the diagnosis of heart disease. The electrocardiograph is an instrument that displays the electric activity of the heart by means of electrodes attached to the skin.

electroencephalography A method of measuring electrical activity of the brain by recording from electrodes placed on the scalp, or sometimes subdurally or in the cerebral cortex. The resulting traces are called electroencephalograms (EEGs) and represent an electrical signal (postsynaptic potentials) from a large number of neurons.

embryo A human offspring in the first 8 weeks from conception.

encephalitis Inflammation of the brain.

encephalopathy Disease of the brain.

enclave A small group of people with disabilities working as a group within a larger work environment in the community. Most often the individuals involved are paid through the sheltered workshop or vocational program rather than directly by the organization for whom the work is performed. An enclave may also be called a work station. (*Note:* Some consider enclaves and work stations to be a form of supported employment.)

endocrine A term applied to body organs whose function is to secret into the blood or lymph a substance that has an effect on another organ, body part, or cell.

endogenous Produced from within the body.

enterostomy devices A tube or feeding device that is placed in the gastrointestinal tract. Devices include tubes placed in the stomach (gastrostomy tube) or small intestine (jejunostomy or gastrojejunal tubes) via a stoma (an outside opening on the skin) or through the mouth or nose.

enuresis nocturna Urination during sleep.

enzyme A protein produced by living cells that functions as a catalyst in a specific biochemical reaction.

epicanthal fold A fold of skin extending from the eyelid over the inner, and sometimes outer, corner of one eye.

epilepsies A group of neurological disorders, characterized by spontaneous, recurrent seizures.

eugenics The practice of controlling breeding for desirable inherited characteristics.

exhibitionism The compulsive desire to expose one's genitals.

extrapyramidal Involving the nerves concerned with motor activity that descends from the cortex of the brain to the spine (i.e., the basal ganglia).

fatal familial insomnia A form of familial Creutzfeldt-Jakob disease that presents initially as persistent insomnia indicative of disease.

ferritin A protein that helps to compartmentalize iron inside of cells. Serum ferritin is the biochemical marker used to assess total body iron.

fetal hydantoin syndrome Syndrome caused by the use of diphenylhydantoin (also known as phenytoin or Dilantin), a drug that is used to treat epilepsy. Diphenylhydantoin has toxic effects on fetal development.

fetishism In psychology, an erotic attachment to an inanimate object or a nongenital body part whose real or imagined presence is necessary for sexual gratification.

fetus The unborn offspring of a mammal from the stage of development at which the main features of the adult can be recognized (e.g., for a human, from 8 weeks after conception).

fragile X carrier A genetic term used to refer to males and females who have an FMR1 gene mutation. This can be either the premutation or full mutation, so carrier status alone does not indicate likely effects or the lack thereof.

fragile X mental retardation (FMR1) gene The gene on the X chromosome that causes fragile X syndrome. Everyone has a copy of the FMR1 gene, but people with fragile X syndrome have a mutant FMR1 gene that is larger than the normal FMR1 gene. The normal FMR1 gene has an unusual DNA sequence. Instead of the usual mixture of A, T, C, and G, there is a segment of repeated CGGs (triplet repeats): ATGTCGATCT CGG CGG CGG CGG CGG CGG CGG CGG CTTAGTGATG. In contrast to most genes, which show no change when passed from one generation to the next, the number of CGG repeats in the FMR1 gene changes when transmitted from parents to offspring, and the number of repeats exceeds the normal range. Normal versions of the gene have 6–54 CGGs; males and females with fragile X syndrome have more than 200 CGGs (full mutation). Unaffected male and female carriers have 55 to approximately 200 repeats (premutation). There is also a grey zone (40–54 repeats), in which the number of repeats is intermediate. It is thought that some grey zone alleles have a propensity to be somewhat unstable and that over many generations, some of these may become fragile X premutations.

fragile X syndrome A common X-linked, inherited form of intellectual disability that sometimes is associated with emotional and/or behavioral difficulties. Most cases are caused by an unstable mutation on the X-chromosome, causing a ragged-looking or broken region on the X-chromosome in cells when they are cultured under particular conditions (hence the term *fragile X*). The most common form of fragile X is caused by a large amplification of the CGG trinucleotide repeat region of the fragile X mental retardation gene-1 (FMR1). The most common inherited form of intellectual disability.

fragile XE syndrome (FRAXE) An intellectual disability resulting from expansions of a polymorphic (CGG) repeat in the FMR2 gene. This is associated with a phenotype of mild mental impairment and severe language delay. FRAXE does not have a distinct dysmorphology, so clinical diagnosis is difficult. Females with FMR2 expansions usually have typical development.

free radicals Reactive molecules that contain an unpaired electron. They are particularly damaging to fatty acids, which are important for the integrity of membranes of cells. Free iron that is released from damaged cells generates free radicals if it comes into contact with oxygen.

Friedrich ataxia A genetic disorder related to a problem in the number 9 chromosome. It is marked by various symptoms of dysfunction of the cerebellum.

functional magnetic resonance imaging (fMRI) A type of MRI used to visualize brain function, by visualizing changes in chemical composition of brain areas or changes in the flow of fluids that occur over short time periods (seconds to minutes) when a person is talking or engaged in various tasks. This method can also be used to study other organs—for example, blood flow to diseased organs, thus helping with the understanding of disease processes. The principle behind functional MRI is that when cells are active, blood flows to them, and the MRI scanner registers increased oxygen in the area. fRMI can detect the difference between hydrogen atoms in oxygenated blood and deoxygenated blood.

GABA Gamma-aminobutyric acid, a major neurotransmitter in the brain. It is considered to be involved in muscle relaxation, sleep, diminished emotional reaction, and sedation.

galactosemia Refers to the presence of galactose in the blood; galactose and its metabolites build up in the tissue and adversely affect carbohydrate energy metabolism.

GALK The enzyme galactose-1-phosphate uridyl transferase. This enzyme is deficient in some cases of galactosemia (an inborn error of galactose metabolism).

GALT The enzyme galactokinase. This enzyme is deficient in some cases of galactosemia.

gametes Haploid cells that give rise to ova (eggs) and sperm. Also called *germ cells.*

ganglioside A complex molecule that contains both lipids (fats) and carbohydrates (sugars) and is found in the plasma (outer) membrane of many kinds of cells. Several different types of gangliosides have been identified.

gastroesophageal reflux disease (GERD) Refluxing of the contents of the stomach into the esophagus (the musculomembranous passage extending from the back of the mouth to the stomach).

gene A unit of heredity that is comprised of DNA or RNA and forms part of a chromosome that determines a particular characteristic of an individual.

genetic metabolic disorders Metabolic disorders in which clinical, biochemical, and pathological manifestations are the consequences of a genetically determined deficiency of a specific enzyme.

genetic recombination The process by which crossing over occurs between maternal and paternal chromatids during meiosis.

genome The total genetic material in the cell nucleus of an individual.

genomic imprinting Genetic process involving inactivation of particular genes in chromosomes. Homologous chromosomes inherited from the mother or father sometimes carry different numbers of active genes as the result of genomic imprinting.

genotype The particular genetic constitution, either at one specific locus of a chromosome or for an entire cell or organism.

Gerstmann-Straussler syndrome A rare familial human prion disorder (spongiform encephalopathy) characterized by cerebellar ataxia, progressive dementia, and absent reflexes in the legs.

gestation The process of carrying or being carried in the womb between conception and birth.

glial cell Nonneuronal cells that provide support and nutrition, maintain homeostasis, form myelin, and participate in signal transmission in the nervous system. These specialized cells surround neurons, providing mechanical and physical support and electrical insulation between neurons.

gray matter Areas of the brain that are dominated by cell bodies and have no myelin covering.

group B *Streptococcus* Bacterial infection associated particularly with preterm birth, septicemia (blood poisoning), meningitis (inflammation of the meninges of the brain or spinal cord due to infection by viruses or bacteria), mental retardation, deafness, blindness, epilepsy, and death.

habituation The gradual adaptation to a stimulus or to the environment.

haploid cell Cells that have only one complete set of chromosomes, usually germ cells. In humans the haploid number is 23.

helix An object coiled either in a spiral curve around an axis (e.g., a corkscrew) or in a one-lane curve (e.g., a watch spring).

hemoglobin The oxygen-carrying pigment of red blood cells.

herpes simplex virus Viruses that cause lesions in the genital area as well as cause cold sores of the mouth. The virus remains permanently in the nerves and can be dormant for months or years. Newborns may get herpes during birth, resulting in central nervous system damage (e.g., mental retardation, tetraplegia, hemiplegia, delayed speech development, learning disorder, opthalmological abnormalities, progressive or recurrent encephalitis) or death. Caesarean delivery is advised for babies of infected mothers.

histidinemia An aminoaciduria (type of error of metabolism). The enzyme affected in this case is histidase. The amino acid that is metabolized by histidase is histidine.

homocystinuria An aminoaciduria (type of error of metabolism). Three different enzymes may be affected—most commonly, cystathionine synthase. People with cystathionine synthase deficiency respond to treatment with vitamin B_6 and dietary restriction of methionine.

homologous Chromosomes that pair during meiosis. These have identical appearance and contain genes that govern the same functions.

HPRT The enzyme hypoxanthine-guanine phosphoribosyltransferase, which is involved in the purine salvage pathway. It is almost completely deficient in Lesch-Nyhan syndrome.

human chorionic gonadotropin (hCG) A hormone produced early in pregnancy by trophoblastic tissue that becomes the placenta. It can be detected in the plasma 6 days after conception and in the urine 2 days after conception. This has led to the development of pregnancy tests based on measurement of hCG in the urine. Levels of hCG are higher than normal when a woman is carrying a baby with Down syndrome.

Huntington disease Chorea—nervous system disorder characterized by jerky involuntary movements affecting especially the shoulders, hips, and face—that is accompanied by progressive dementia.

hypertension A dangerous condition in which the blood pressure is significantly higher than normal. People with untreated hypertension are at risk for heart attack, stroke, and/or kidney failure.

hypoplasia Underdevelopment of an organ or tissue because of loss of cells.

hypotonia Reduced muscle tone or resistance to passive movement.

hypsarrythmia An abnormal electroencephalogram pattern of excessive slow activity and multiple areas of epieptiform activity associated with infantile spasms.

ideal body weight Located on standard weight-for-height measures. Ideal body weight is located on the same percentile curve as the height percentile, or it can be considered to be the weight at the 50th percentile for age. (Comparison for 50th percentile weight for age, however, does not take into consideration genetic, race, or other factors that might be relevant for assessment of ideal body weight.)

in utero While in the mother's uterus.

inborn errors of metabolism Metabolic disorders in which clinical, biochemical, and pathological manifestations are the consequence of a genetically determined deficiency of a particular enzyme. Such a mutation leads to a buildup of metabolites immediately preceding a block. Inborn errors associated with intellectual disability have been identified in virtually all major pathways of metabolism.

individualized funding Funding that is provided to the individual rather than to the program. The individual, often with the support of family and/or relatives and friends, determines his or her goals and uses these funds to purchase needed supports. Such funds may be used to address a variety of support needs including, but not limited to, employment support.

inhibin-A A hormone made by the placenta. Its level is sometimes measured in the blood of pregnant women in the quad test to screen for Down syndrome and neural tube defects.

intractable seizures Seizures that resist control by anticonvulsant drugs.

inversion A chromosomal defect in which one segment of

a chromosome breaks away and reattaches in the reverse direction.

ischemia A reduction of the blood supply to part of the body.

job training program A program designed to prepare people for competitive employment. It may be conducted within a sheltered workshop, as a stand-alone segregated program, or within a community environment.

karyotype An organized profile of a person's chromosomes. In a karyotype, chromosomes are arranged and numbered by size, from largest to smallest. This arrangement helps scientists quickly identify chromosomal alterations that may result in a genetic disorder. In karyotyping, or the process of constructing a karyotype, scientists take a picture of someone's chromosomes, cut them out, and match them up using size, banding pattern, and the position of the centromere.

ketogenic diet A high-fat diet with adequate protein and very limited carbohydrate.

Klinefelter syndrome The first human sex chromosome abnormality to be reported. Those with the syndrome are tall and thin, with relatively long legs. They have a typical physical appearance until puberty, when signs of hypogonadism become evident.

kuru A human prion disease (spongiform encephalopathy) resulting from cannibalism.

Leber's hereditary optic neuropathy A rare condition resulting from a mutation in mitochondrial DNA that results in loss of central vision. It commonly affects men, usually in the late 20s or early 30s, but can occur at any age and also affects women.

Lesch-Nyhan syndrome An X-linked metabolic genetic disorder characterized by severe behavior disturbance and self-injury. It is caused by near absence of the enzyme hypoxanthine guanine phosphoribosyltransferase (HPRT).

linkage Genes on the same chromosome show linkage if they have a tendency to be transmitted together through meiosis.

linkage analysis A statistical method used in human and medical genetics to aid in identifying, mapping, and diagnosing the genes responsible for inherited diseases and disorders.

Listeria monocytogenes A microorganism causing developmental disability.

long-term potentiation Changes in brain neurons that are thought to be important for memory.

low birth weight Birth weight of less than 2.5 kilograms or 5.5 pounds.

lyonization The process by which all X chromosomes in excess of one are made genetically inactive. In the female, the decision as to which X (maternal or paternal) is inactivated is made independently for each cell, early in development, and is permanent for all descendants of that cell. Also called the *Lyon hypothesis.*

lysosomal hydroxylase Enzyme that degrades mucopolysaccharides.

magnetic resonance imaging (MRI) A medical imaging method that uses radiofrequency waves and a strong magnetic field, rather than X-rays, to provide clear and detailed pictures of internal organs and tissues. The MRI machine aligns all of the protons that are in hydrogen atoms in the water of the body. The magnetic fields of slightly more than half of the protons are aligned with the external field, and those of the rest are aligned against it. Once the protons are lined up, they "precess" around the direction of the field, like a child's spinning top does when it begins to fall over. When under precession, protons may relax back and emit rather low-frequency radio waves with the energy that was previously acquired by the proton precession. A receiver antenna picks up these emissions which differ in strength and location.

maladaptation Faulty or inadequate adaptive behavior.

maple syrup urine disease An inborn error of metabolism involving branched chain amino acids. The enzyme that is affected is a branched chain ketoacid decarboxylase. The expression is variable.

meiosis A process occurring in the germ cells by which gametes, containing the haploid number of chromosomes, are produced from diploid cells.

meninges The three membranes that line the skull and vertebral canal and enclose the brain and spinal cord.

meningitis Meningitis is an infection that causes inflammation of the membranes covering the brain and spinal cord. Nonbacterial meningitis is often referred to as *aseptic meningitis.* Bacterial meningitis may be referred to as *purulent meningitis.* The most common causes of meningitis are viral infections that usually resolve without treatment. However, bacterial infections of the meninges are extremely serious illnesses and may result in death or brain damage even if treated. Meningitis is also caused by fungi, chemical irritation, drug allergies, and tumors.

meta-analysis A long-established statistical method summarizing studies that do not necessarily show the same results.

metabolism All of the chemical processes that occur within a living organism to result in energy production.

metabolite Chemical by-product produced in the body.

methylation Addition of a methyl (-CH3) moiety to a base in a DNA molecule, usually cytosine. Methylated cytosine mimics thymine and becomes a potential site for mutation. Methylation likely has a role in gene regulation and may be involved in the imprinting process.

microcephaly Small head size for age and gender.

micrognathia Unusual smallness of the lower jaw with recession of the chin.

mid-arm circumference (MAC) Composite measure of muscle, fat, and bone on the arm. MAC is measured by measuring the diameter of the arm. The measurement should be taken at the halfway point between the acromion process (shoulder) and the elbow. MAC is sensitive to current nutritional status and can be used in combination with the triceps skinfold thickness measure to estimate muscle area and arm fat area.

mid-arm muscle circumference (MAMC) Used to assess body composition; reflects the muscle mass. It can be calculated using the following equation: MAC – 3.14 × (triceps skinfold) / 10.

mitochondria Organelles in cells that each contain a number of copies of a small circular molecule, the mitochondrial chromosome. Mitochondrial DNA encodes 13 key structural genes as well as a number of structural ribonucleic acid RNA molecules. Mitochondria are a major source of energy production in cells.

mitochondrial inheritance Transmission of a mutation that is present in the mitochondrial DNA. Males and females are equally frequently and severely affected. Because mitochondrial DNA is transmitted to offspring only by mothers, mothers transmit the mutant mitochondrial chromosomes to all of their offspring, whereas affected fathers transmit the mutation to none of their offspring.

mitochondrial myopathy A disorder in which there is a defect in one or more components of the respiratory chain that produces energy (ATP) in mitochondria. Prognosis is often poor.

mitosis Somatic cell division resulting in the formation of two cells, each with the same chromosome complement as the parent cell.

mitral valve prolapse Billowing of one or both mitral valve leaflets into the left atrium at the end of each active contraction of the heart.

mobile work crews Small groups of people with disabilities who, generally with a supervisor, work in the community. Unlike a work station or enclave, there may not be workers without disabilities in the same work environment when the work is being done. Most often the individuals involved are paid through a sheltered workshop or vocational program rather than directly by the organization for whom the work is performed. (*Note:* Some people consider this a form of supported employment.)

Moro reflex An infantile startle response that usually disappears a few months after birth. It may be demonstrated by placing an infant face up on a soft, padded surface. The head is gently lifted with enough traction to just begin to remove the body weight (not the body) from the pad. The head is then released suddenly, allowed to fall backward momentarily, but quickly supported again (not allowed to bang on the padding). The infant may have a startled look, and his or her arms should fling out sideways with the palms up and the thumbs flexed. As the reflex ends, the infant draws the arms back to the body with elbows flexed and then relaxes.

morphology Structural appearance.

mosaic An individual or tissue with two or more cell lines of different genetic or chromosomal constitution, derived from the same zygote.

motor immaturity Immaturity of muscle, nerve(s), or center(s) that bring about or produce movement.

mucopolysaccharide Any of a group of polysaccharides (complex sugars) whose molecules contain sugar residues and are often found as components of connective tissues.

mucopolysaccharidoses (MPS) Disorders of the metabolism of mucopolysaccharide. MPS I is known as Hurler syndrome; MPS IIA and IIB are variants of Hunter syndrome; and MPS III is known as Sanfilippo syndrome (variants A and B).

multifactorial Determination of a phenotype by genetic and environmental factors. (*Polygenic* is used to refer just to multiple genetic factors.)

muscular dystrophy Hereditary progressive weakening and wasting of the muscles.

mutations Genetic changes, which when transmitted to offspring give rise to heritable variations. In missense mutations, there is a substitution or replacement of one nucleotide for another that results in a different codon and hence amino acid being incorporated into the protein chain. In frameshift mutations, an insertion or a deletion results in the shift in reading frame of the gene and possible production of different proteins.

myelination The formation of myelin sheaths (a white substance) around certain nerve fibers. This process allows neurons to conduct signals more efficiently and protects the axon. Myelination is a long process. Some areas of the brain myelinate before birth and many others during early childhood. Yet, the areas responsible for decision making and judgment do not complete myelination until late adolescence.

myoclonus Jerking, involuntary movements of the arms and legs; may occur normally during sleep.

myotonic dystrophy An autosomal dominant disorder sometimes associated with nonprogressive mental impairment. It is caused by a trinucleotide repeat expansion.

negative affective response Negative expression of feelings or emotions of an infant towards his or her parent(s).

neural tube defect Any of a range of congenital abnormalities, including spina bifida, resulting from incomplete fusion of the neural tube (a hollow structure from which the brain and spinal cord develop).

neurofibromatosis A dominant hereditary disorder that affects the brain and nervous system. Affected people may have birthmarks called café-au-lait spots, which look like coffee stains. They also have larger tumors derived from nerves in any organ, including the brain. Expression of this disorder is quite variable.

neuroimmunological Involving the immune system and the central and/or peripheral nervous systems.

neuromuscular Involving the motor unit (a single motor neuron and all of the corresponding muscle fibers it innervates).

neurooncological Pertaining to the broad field of neurooncology, which includes primary brain tumors, metastatic and nonmetastatic effects of systemic cancer on the central and peripheral nervous systems, neurotoxicity due to cancer treatment, and related issues of quality of life.

neurootological Pertaining to neurootology, a field of medicine dedicated to the study of the ear and related nerve structures, and to the treatment of hearing disorders, facial nerve disorders, and tumors that occur near the ear.

NMDA antagonist Substance that interferes with N-methyl-D-aspartate (NMDA)'s selective activation of ionotropic receptors for glutamate, a major exitatory neurotransmitter.

nondisjunction The failure of two members of a chromosome pair to disjoin during meiosis I, or of two chromatids of a chromosome to disjoin during meiosis II or mitosis, so that both pass to one daughter cell and the other daughter cell receives neither.

nonvocational alternatives A catch-all term for a variety of day activity programs for people who are perceived as not wanting, or not being able, to engage in work activities. These activities/day programs may take place in inclusive or segregated environments.

Noonan syndrome A syndrome of mental retardation, short stature, and craniofacial and other abnormalities with a locus on chromosome 12.

nucleus A large, dense organelle of eukaryotic cells containing the genetic material.

Opitz syndrome An inherited defect of mid-line development with one locus on the X chromosome and another on chromosome 22.

organomegaly Enlarged organ.

oxidative phosphorylation Process occurring in the cell that produces energy and synthesizes ATP (an energy carrier of the body).

palpebral fissure Distance between the outer corners of the eyes (horizontal) or between the upper and lower eyelids when the eye is open (vertical). The horizontal palpebral fissures are reduced in fetal alcohol syndrome.

parachute reflex A reflex that occurs in older infants. It is elicited by holding the child upright then rotating the body quickly face forward (as if falling). The arms are reflexively extended as if to break a fall, even though this reflex appears long before walking.

Parkinson's disease A progressive disease of the nervous system that produces tremors, muscular rigidity, and slowness and imprecision of movements. It is caused by damage to the substantia nigra area of the brain, where dopamine is produced.

parvovirus B19 A single stranded DNA virus that causes erythema infectiosum, a viral illness in which both cheeks appear bright red as though they had been slapped.

pedophilia A sexual behavior disorder that involves sexual activity by an adult with a prepubescent child. The sexual activity ranges from looking at the child to more direct physical acts.

phenotype The outward observable characteristics of a cell or organism.

phenylketonuria (PKU) A disorder resulting from an inability to metabolize the amino acid phenylalanine (Phe) that can cause developmental delay. Diets that are low in Phe prevent developmental delay in persons with PKU. If the blood level of Phe is not kept sufficiently low in pregnant women with PKU, the fetus develops a condition called maternal PKU (mPKU), which is associated with developmental delay.

philtrum The vertical groove in the median position of the face above the upper lip.

polymerase chain reaction (PCR) A molecular technique for rapidly creating many extra copies of a sequence of DNA.

polymorphism The quality or state of existing in or assuming different forms, such as the existence of a gene in several allelic forms.

positron emission tomography (PET) imaging or scan A medical imaging method that involves the collection of images based on the detection of radiation from the emission of positrons. Positrons are very small particles emitted from a radioactive substance given to the patient. The radioactive substance is usually attached to glucose or another natural body substance. The radioactivity localizes in particular areas of the body. Gamma rays are given off at the site where a positron emitted from the radioactive substance collides with an electron in the tissue, and are detected by the PET scanner. Different degrees of brightness on a PET image represent different levels of function of a tissue or organ.

Prader-Willi syndrome A genetic cause of mental retardation resulting from aberrations of genomic imprinting. Fifty percent of individuals with this syndrome have a paternal deletion of chromosome 15. The remainder have two copies of maternal chromosome 15 (uniparental disomy).

preeclampsia A problem (sometimes called *toxemia*) that occurs in some women during pregnancy. Signs of preeclampsia include high blood pressure and the presence of large amounts of protein in the urine. Preeclampsia can prevent the placenta from getting enough blood and result in low birth weight and other problems for the fetus. The condition is called *preeclampsia,* because rarely it can go on to cause eclampsia. The term *eclampsia* is derived from the Greek, meaning "bolt from the blue," and describes the convulsions that sometimes result from preeclampsia.

premature synostosis Premature joining of the bony plates in the skull.

prevalence The number of cases of a disease or disorder in existence at a certain time in a designated area.

prion An infectious protein particle.

prostaglandin A fatty acid that can affect biologic activities in every organ system.

protein–energy malnutrition (PEM) Condition in which the ratio of actual body weight to ideal body weight is 90% or less.

psychotropic drugs Mind-altering drugs such as antidepressants, antipsychotics, or sedatives.

purine nucleotide A double-ringed nitrogen-containing organic base from which is derived adenine, guanine (found in DNA and RNA), and the metabolite uric acid.

recessive A characteristic of a phenotypic trait that is expressed only when the responsible gene is present in two copies. Recessive genetic disorders require the same defect on two homologous chromosomes.

resting energy expenditure (REE) Amount of energy expended under conditions of rest 2 hours after eating. REE is measured using indirect or direct calorimetry methods. Indirect calorimetry involves the use of equipment that measures and collects an individual's inspired and expired air. Indirect calorimetry bases estimates of energy expenditure on oxygen consumption and carbon dioxide production.

ribosomal RNA (rRNA) One of the structural components of the ribosome.

ribosomes Cytoplasmic organelles composed of ribosomal RNA and protein on which polypeptide synthesis from messenger RNA occurs.

rubella German measles. Since introduction of the rubella vaccine, congenital rubella infections have rarely occurred in Canada or the United States. The current prevalence rate is less than 1 per 100,000.

scrapie A progressive brain disease of sheep that frequently causes itching so intense that the animals scrape off their wool seeking relief.

seizures Periods of self-sustained neural hyperexcitation, whereby the neurons in the brain cease their normal activities and fire in massive, synchronized bursts. In some cases, the intervention approach is brain surgery designed to improve seizure control. In adults, seizure surgery commonly involves removal of the part of the brain that contains the focus, most often the anterior part of one of the temporal lobes.

self-employment Situation in which an individual does not work for an employer but works as an independent contractor or has his or her own business.

serum The clear liquid part of blood that remains after blood cells and clotting proteins have been removed.

serum albumin The main protein in blood plasma. Low levels occur in people with malnutrition, inflammation, and serious liver and kidney diseases.

sex chromosomes Chromosomes responsible for sex determination; in humans, these are the X and Y chromosomes. Females have two X chromosomes; males have one X chromosome and one Y chromosome.

sexual sadism The act of deriving sexual pleasure from mistreating others. Severe sexual sadism activities include burning, beating, stabbing, raping, and killing.

sheltered workshop A segregated work program for people with disabilities. May provide job training and/or long-term sheltered employment. In Australia, sheltered workshops are often referred to as *supported employment* or *business services.*

simple partial seizures Seizures in which spiking is limited to one part of the individual's brain. The clinical symptoms depend on the brain area activated by the epileptic discharge and vary greatly. Consciousness is retained. (formerly called *cortical focal seizures*)

single nucleotide polymorphisms (SNPs) A natural genetic variability occurring at high density in the human genome. An SNP represents an alternate nucleotide in a given and defined genetic location at a frequency exceeding 1% in a given population. This definition does not include other types of genetic variability such as insertions and deletions or variability in copy number of repeated sequences. SNPs are considered to be the major genetic source to phenotypic variability that differentiate individuals within a given species. SNPs may occur in noncoding regions as well as in coding regions.

SNRPN Small nuclear ribonucleoprotein particle-associated polypeptide N. One of a gene family that encode proteins involved in pre-mRNA splicing. SNRPN maps to the smallest deletion region within chromosome 15q11-q13 in Prader-Willi syndrome.

somatic cells All cells in the body except for ova (eggs) and sperm.

Southern blotting A technique used to search for a specific DNA fragment. The process is as follows: 1) The DNA fragments are separated by electrophoresis in a gel. 2) The pH of the gel is changed to basic, allowing disruption of H-bonds. 3) The gel is blotted with nitrocellulose paper. 4) The paper is heated to bind the DNA fragments to the paper. 5) The paper is treated with probe (labeled mRNA or cDNA). 6) The paper is washed. 7) Complementary mRNAs or cDNAs will hybridize to DNA fragments on the paper.

spasms Sudden, involuntary muscle contractions.

spasticity Extra stiffness in the muscles.

spina bifida A family of congenital malformation defects in the closure of the spinal column, characterized by herniation or exposure of the spinal cord and/or meninges through an incompletely closed spine.

spinobulbar muscular atrophy A gradually progressive neuromuscular disorder in which degeneration of lower motor neurons results in proximal muscle weakness, muscle atrophy, and contractions. All males with this disorder have expansion of a CAG trinucleotide repeat in the androgen receptor (AR) gene. Its inheritence is X-linked.

spinocerebellar ataxia A form of hereditary ataxia—a special group of inherited diseases that cause degeneration of the cerebellum of the brain or its pathways. These disorders are characterized by a progressive incoordination of walking. In addition they are often associated with poor coordination of hand movements, eye movements, and speech. With some exceptions, the onset of symptoms usually occurs after the age of 18 ("adult onset"). The disorder is slowly progressive, which means that symptoms of the condition gradually worsen over time. Some types can progress more rapidly than others. At this time, there is no cure or treatment that can prevent or slow the progression of symptoms or atrophy of the cerebellum.

stem cells Cells that have the ability to divide for indefinite periods in culture and to give risk to specialized cells. Pluripotent stem cells can give rise to most tissues of an organism. Totipotent stem cells have unlimited capability.

stereotypies Repetition of meaningless movements.

supported employment Situation in which an individual works in a regular setting in the community and is paid by his or her employer. The vocational program provides a support worker or job coach who is available to provide training and support to the individual. The support worker/job coach may also work with the employer and co-workers so that they can provide the supported employee with the required supports. In theory, supported employees are paid at least minimum wage. In Australia, this situation considered competitive employment. The term *supported employment* is used to refer to what are called *sheltered workshops* in North America.

supported self-employment Same as self-employment, with support provided by a support worker/job coach.

synaptogenesis Synaptogenesis is the formation of synapses, or connections between neurons. Synapse formation is a lifelong process that begins prenatally. Synapse formation during the prenatal and early childhood periods appears to be biologically driven, not based on specific experiences. Synapses are "overgenerated" in the early years, meaning that the brain generates many more synapses than needed.

syndrome A combination of traits or characteristics resulting from a single cause. For example, fragile X syndrome, arising from triplet repeat expansion in the FMR1 gene, results in a combination of learning disabilities, joint flexibility, and physical characteristics such as large ears.

syntax The grammar, structure, or order of the elements in a language statement.

syphilis A contagious venereal disease caused by the microorganism *Treponema pallidum.* Approximately one third of children with congenital syphilis have serious neurological damage, including intellectual disability. This condition can be treated prenatally and neonatally to prevent such consequences. The prevalence of congenital syphilis was about 0.39 per 1,000 live births in the United States in 1995.

Tay-Sachs disease An inherited autosomal recessive metabolic disorder associated with progressive mental degeneration in which certain lipids accumulate in the brain, causing spasticity and death in childhood. Lack of the enzyme hexosaminidase results in the accumulation of sphingolipids.

tonic-clonic seizures Type of seizure characterized by sudden loss of consciousness, stiffening of the whole body (tonus), and then jerking of the body musculature (clonus) that may last for up to a few minutes. After a tonic-clonic seizure, a patient may exhibit various behaviors, such as regaining consciousness, feeling confusion or disorientation, lacking memory of the immediate events, and having further seizures. (formerly called *grand mal seizures*)

transfer RNA (tRNA) Small RNA that has a very specific secondary and tertiary structure such that it can bind an amino acid at one end and mRNA at the other end. It acts as an adaptor to carry the amino acid elements of a protein to the appropriate place as coded for by mRNA.

transferrin A protein used to assess iron-binding capacity. Serum transferrin receptor, in conjunction with serum iron, is used to assess total iron-binding capacity.

translocation A genetic abnormality in which part of a chromosome is transferred to another chromosome or in which two chromosomes trade pieces with each other.

transvestic fetishism Recurrent intense sexual urges and sexually arousing fantasies that involve dressing in clothing associated with members of the opposite sex. This term, usually practiced by males, is sometimes called cross-dressing; people who frequently engage this practice are sometimes called transvestites.

triceps skinfold measure Measure taken at the midway point between the acrominion process and the elbow, on the triceps skinfold. A triceps skinfold measure reflects the fat composition in the body.

trinucleotide repeat region A sequence of the same three nucleotides repeated over and over again.

toxicity The quality of being poisonous.

toxoplasmosis An infectious disease caused by a microscopic parasite, *Toxoplasma gondii,* found in infected, undercooked meat; soil; and the feces of cats.

tuberous sclerosis One of several neurocutaneous syndromes, also known as *phakomatoses* or *ectodermal dysplasias.* These autosomal dominant disorders present with sclerosis (an abnormal hardening of body tissue) as lesions both of the skin and central nervous system. There may also be associated ocular and visceral abnormalities. Tuberous sclerosis is referred to as a complex disorder because it involves all tissues. In addition to the brain and retina, the skin, kidneys, heart, and lungs are most frequently involved.

Turner syndrome A disorder in females resulting from the absence of one X chromosome. Characteristics include short stature, premature ovarian failure in utero, and a neuropsychological profile that shows a spatial deficit.

UBE3A Ubiquitin protein ligase E3A. Some cases of Angelman syndrome are caused by mutations in this gene.

umbilical cord The membranous duct connecting the fetus with the placenta.

unconjugated estriol One of the substances measured in the maternal triple or quad screen test. It is normally produced at low levels by the ovaries. It is elevated in pregnancy, as it is produced by the placenta from precursors supplied by the fetal adrenal glands and fetal liver. Levels of unconjugated estriol typically increase throughout pregnancy. Levels in maternal serum decrease when the baby has Down syndrome or trisomy 18.

unpaid work Work without pay. What is unpaid work for some people with disabilities may be paid work for others in the same environment. When this is a short-term situation, it comes under the definition of work experience. At other times, it may be inaccurately referred to as volunteer work, although it does not resemble work that is typically done on a volunteer basis.

vagus nerve stimulation (VNS) Intervention for epilepsy that involves the implantation of an electrical stimulator that stimulates an individual's vagal nerve. (Also called vagal stimulation.)

varicella-zoster virus Virus that causes chicken pox.

vCJD A new form of Creutzfeldt-Jakob disease believed to be transmitted by eating the tissue of cattle infected with bovine spongiform encephalopathy.

velocardiofacial syndrome A genetic condition characterized by structural or functional abnormalities of the palate, heart defects, unique facial characteristics, hypernasal speech, learning difficulties, loss of muscle tone, developmental delay, and learning disabilities. The majority of individuals with this syndrome have a small region missing in the DNA of chromosome 11.

ventricles Cavities in the brain or heart. Those within the brain contain the cerebrospinal fluid.

visceral protein status Reflection of lean body mass stores (primarily skeletal muscle mass).

voyeurism Deriving sexual satisfaction by secretly watching others undress or engage in sexual activity. People who engage in voyeurism are sometimes called peeping Toms.

white matter The shiny layer underneath the cortex that consists mostly of axons with white myelin sheaths.

Williams syndrome A genetic syndrome associated with a distinct behavioral phenotype, caused by an abnormality on chromosome 7. People with Williams syndrome tend to be loquacious and unusually musical.

work experience Situation in which an individual with a disability works in the community to gain some knowledge about community work and/or to get an assessment of his or her work skills. This is often part of a job training program. Typically the person is not paid for the work.

work station *See* enclave.

X-linked Pertaining to disorder caused by the X chromosome, the sex chromosome of which the number in female cells is twice that in male cells.

yolk sac One of four extrambryonic membranes that supports embryonic development. The first site of blood cells and circulatory system function.

zygote A fertilized egg, the result of fused gametes.

APPENDIX B

ADDITIONAL RESOURCES

RESOURCES ON ASSESSMENT, INTERVENTION, AND SERVICES

Behavioral Intervention

Recommended Reading

Crone, D.A., & Horner, R.H. (2003). *Building positive behavior support systems in schools: Functional behavioral assessment.* New York: The Guilford Press.

Demchak, M., & Bossert, K. (1996). Assessing problem behaviors. *Innovations, 4.* Washington, DC: American Association on Mental Retardation.

Horner, R. (1997). Behavior analysis in developmental disabilities 1968–1995. *Journal of Applied Behavior Analysis, 30,* 591–594.

Jackson, L., & Panyan, M.V. (2002). *Positive behavioral support in the classroom: Principles and practices.* Baltimore: Paul H. Brookes Publishing Co.

Koegel, L.K., Koegel, R.L., & Dunlap, G. (Eds.). (1996). *Positive behavioral support: Including people with difficult behavior in the community.* Baltimore: Paul H. Brookes Publishing Co.

Luiselli, J.K., & Cameron, M.J. (Eds.). (1998). *Antecedent control: Innovative approaches to behavioral support.* Baltimore: Paul H. Brookes Publishing Co.

Lucyshyn, J.M., Dunlap, G., & Albin, R.W. (2002). Families and positive behavioral support: Addressing problem behaviors in family contexts. *American Journal on Mental Retardation, 109*(3), 264–265.

Singh, N. (1997). *Prevention & treatment of severe behavior problems: Models and methods in developmental disabilities.* Pacific Grove, CA: Brooks/Cole.

Witt, J.C., Daly, E.M., & Noell, G. (2000). *Functional assessments: A step-by-step guide to solving academic and behavior problems.* Longmont, CO: Sopris West.

Journals

The Behavior Analyst
http://www.abainternational.org/journals/behavior_analyst.asp

Behavior Therapy
http://www.aabt.org/publication/BT/bt.html

The Behavior Therapist
http://www.aabt.org/publication/tbt/the_behavior_therapist.html

Behavioral Interventions
http://www3.interscience.wiley.com/cgi-bin/jhome/24375?CRETRY=1&SRETRY=0

Journal of Applied Behavior Analysis
http://seab.envmed.rochester.edu/jaba

Journal of Positive Behavior Interventions
http://www.education.ucsb.edu/autism/jpbi.html

Helpful Internet Information

Office of Special Education, Technical Assistance Center on Positive Behavioral Interventions and Supports
http://www.pbis.org/english/default.htm

University of South Florida: Behavior Analysis Resources
http://www.coedu.usf.edu/behavior/bares.htm

Key Organizations

Association for Behavior Analysis International (ABA)
http://www.abainternational.org

The Association for Behavioral and Cognitive Therapies (ABCT; formerly the Association for the Advancement of Behavior Therapy [AABT])
http://www.abct.org

Challenging Families

Recommended Reading

Buscaglia, L. (1983). *The disabled and their parents: A counseling challenge.* Toronto: Holt, Rinehart and Winston.

Forward, S. (1989). *Toxic parents: Overcoming their hurtful legacy and reclaiming your life.* New York: Bantam Books.

Leal, L. (1999). *Innovations: A family-centered approach to people with mental retardation.* Washington, DC: American Association on Mental Retardation.

Nichols, M.P., & Schwartz, R.C. (2004). *Family therapy: Concepts and methods* (6th ed.). Boston: Allyn & Bacon.

Seligman, M., & Darling, R.B. (1997). *Ordinary families, special children: A systems approach to childhood disability* (2nd ed.). New York: The Guilford Press.

Siegel, B., & Silverstein, S. (1994). *What about me? Growing up with a developmentally disabled sibling.* New York: Insight Books.

Diversity and Psychological Intervention

Helpful Internet Information

Citizenship and Immigration Canada: Cultural Profiles Project
http://www.settlement.org/cp/english/index.html

EU Monitoring and Advocacy Program of the Open Society Institute
http://www.eumap.org

Key Organizations

American Psychological Association
http://www.apa.org

British Institute of Learning Disabilities
http://www.bild.org.uk

Canadian Ethnocultural Council (CEC)
http://www.ethnocultural.ca

National Center for Latinos with Disabilities
http://homepage.interaccess.com/~ncld

National Multicultural Institute
http://www.nmci.org

Early Intervention

Recommended Reading

Accardo, P.J. (Ed.). (in press). *Capute and Accardo's neurodevelopmental disabilities in infancy and childhood* (3rd ed.). Baltimore: Paul H. Brookes Publishing Co.

Early Childhood Resource Teacher Network of Ontario. (1997). *Checklist for quality inclusive education: A self-assessment tool and manual for early childhood settings.* Barrie, ON, Canada: Early Childhood Resource Teacher Network of Ontario.

Helpful Internet Information

Circle of Inclusion
http://circleofinclusion.org

Early Childhood Resource Teacher Network of Ontario (ECRTNO)
http://www.ecrtno.com

Infant Mental Health Promotion Project
http://www.sickkids.on.ca/imp

Invest in Kids
http://www.investinkids.ca

SpeciaLink
http://specialinkcanada.org

Key Organizations

Division for Early Childhood (DEC) of the Council for Exceptional Children
http://www.dec-sped.org

National Association for the Education of Young Children (NAEYC)
http://www.naeyc.org

ZERO TO THREE
http://www.zerotothree.org

Education

Recommended Reading

Berger, E.H. (2004). *Parents as partners in education* (6th ed.). Upper Saddle River, NJ: Merrill Prentice Hall.

Hallahan, D.P., & Kauffman, J.M. (2005). *Exceptional learners: Introduction to special education* (10th ed.). Boston: Allyn & Bacon.

Helpful Internet Information: General

10 Tips: How to Use IDEA 2004 to Improve Your Child's Special Education
http://www.wrightslaw.com/idea/art/10.tips.steedman.htm

AAMR Fact Sheet: Self-Advocacy
http://www.aamr.org/Policies/faq_movement.shtml

Central England People First: PeopleFirst and Other Self Advocacy Links
http://www.peoplefirst.org.uk/pflinks.htm

Developing Legally Correct and Educationally Appropriate IEPs
http://www.ldonline.org/ld_indepth/iep/legally_correct_ieps.html

Division of International Special Education and Services, Council for Exceptional Children
http://www.cec.sped.org/intl/index.html

Educating Children with FAS/FAE
http://www.taconic.net/seminars/fas-c.html

Elementary School Age Children with Fragile X Syndrome
http://www.fragilex.org/html/textelementary.htm

Educating the Child with Prader-Willi Syndrome: A Guide for Teachers, Educational Care Assistants and Others Concerned with the Education of a Child with PWS
http://www.pwsa-uk.demon.co.uk/educatn.htm

A Guide to Individualized Education Plans
http://www.ed.gov/parents/needs/speced/iepguide/index.html

IDEA's Requirements for Paraprofessionals
http://www.wrightslaw.com/law/code_regs/20USC1412.html

National Association of Protection and Advocacy Systems (NAPAS)
http://www.napas.org

A Needs Assessment for Students Age 17–21 with Significant Disabilities
http://www.education.umd.edu/oco/training/oco_training_modules/start.html

Paul H. Brookes Publishing Co.: Special Education Books
http://www.brookespublishing.com/store/specialeducation.htm

IDEA Reauthorized Statute: Highly Qualified Teachers
http://www.ed.gov/policy/speced/guid/idea/tb-qual-teachers.pdf

Individual Supports to Increase Access to an Inclusive College Experience for Students with Intellectual Disabilities
http://www.education.umd.edu/oco/training/oco_training_modules/IndividualSupports/start.html

National Resource Center for Paraprofessionals
http://www.nrcpara.org/resources/stateoftheart

Rights and Responsibilities of Parents of Children With Disabilities
http://www.kidsource.com/kidsource/content2/Parents_of_Children.html

Special Education Inclusion
http://www.weac.org/resource/june96/speced.htm

U.S. Department of Health and Human Services,
Administration for Children and Families,
Head Start Bureau
http://www.acf.hhs.gov/programs/hsb/hsweb/index.jsp

U.S. Department of Health and Human Services,
Office for Civil Rights
http://www.hhs.gov/ocr/newfaq.html

Information About Special Education Around the World

Australia

Australian Education International
http://aei.dest.gov.au/Aei/Default.aspx

Canada

Highlights of Regulation 181/98 (IPRC)
http://www.edu.gov.on.ca/eng/general/elemsec/speced/hilites.html

China

China Through a Lens: Special Education and Vocational Education
http://www.china.org.cn/english/features/38282.htm

Finland

Kivirauma, J. (2004). Scientific revolutions in special education in Finland. *European Journal of Special Needs Education, 19,* 123–143.

Japan

Japan OECD International Workshop on Special Education
www.nise.go.jp/PDF/JSEAP-7.pdf

Jamaica

History of Special Education in Jamaica
http://www.moec.gov.jm/divisions/ed/specialeducation/history.htm

New Zealand

Ministry of Education, Special Education
http://www.minedu.govt.nz/index.cfm?indexID=6871&layout=index

United Kingdom

Every Child Matters
http://www.everychildmatters.gov.uk

General Information

Recommended Reading

American Psychiatric Association. (2000). *Diagnostic and statistical manual of mental disorders* (4th ed., text rev.). Washington, DC: Author.

Beail, N., & Edwards, W.J. (2004). Rigidity and flexibility in diagnosing mental retardation in capital cases. *Mental Retardation, 42,* 480–483.

Bergen, D.C. (1998). Preventable neurological diseases worldwide. *Neuroepidemiology, 17,* 67–73.

Bodensteiner, J.B., & Schaefer, G.B. (1995). Evaluation of the patient with idiopathic mental retardation. *Journal of Neuropsychiatry, 7,* 361–370.

Ceci, S.J., Scullin, M., & Kanaya, T. (2003). The difficulty of basing death penalty eligibility on IQ cutoff scores for mental retardation. *Ethics & Behavior, 13,* 11–17.

Curry, C.J., Stevenson, R.E., Aughton, D., et al. (1997). Evaluation of mental retardation: Recommendations of a consensus conference. *American Journal of Medical Genetics, 72,* 468–477

Harris, J.C. (1995). *Developmental neuropsychiatry: Vol. II. Assessment, diagnosis and treatment of developmental disorders.* Oxford, United Kingdom: Oxford University Press.

Jacobson, J.W., & Mulick, J.A. (Eds.). (1996). *Manual of diagnosis and professional practice in mental retardation.* Washington, DC: American Psychological Association, Division of Mental Retardation and Developmental Disabilities.

Wilska, M.L., & Kaski, M.K. (2001). Why and how to assess the aetiological diagnosis of children with intellectual disability/mental retardation and other neurodevelopmental disorders: Description of the Finnish approach. *European Journal of Pediatric Neurology, 5,* 7–13.

Helpful Internet Information

Disabilities WebLinks
http://www.disabilityweblinks.ca

Fetal surgery for spina bifida
http://www.fetal-surgery.com

Online Mendelian Inheritance in Man (OMIM)
http://www.ncbi.nlm.nih.gov/entrez/query.fcgi?db=OMIM

Quality of Life for People with Developmental Disabilities
http://www.utoronto.ca/qol/pwdd.htm

Regulated Health Professionals Act
http://www.e-laws.gov.on.ca/DBLaws/Statutes/English/91r18_e.htm

World Health Organization's *International Statistical Classification of Diseases and Related Health Problems, 10th Revision, Version for 2006*
http://www.who.int/classifications/apps/icd/icd10online

Key Organizations

American Association on Mental Retardation (AAMR)
(in 2007, organizational name change to American Association on Intellectual and Developmental Disabilities)
http://www.aamr.org

American Psychiatric Association
http://www.psych.org

American Psychological Association
http://www.apa.org

Birth Defect Research for Children
http://www.birthdefects.org

National Easter Seal Society
http://www.easterseals.com

Person- and Family-Centered Support

Recommended Reading

Person-Centered Approaches

Allen, W.T. (1989). *Read my lips: It's my choice.* St. Paul, MN: Minnesota Governor's Planning Council on Developmental Disabilities.

Amado, A.N. (Ed.). (1993). *Friendships and community connections between people with and without developmental disabilities.* Baltimore: Paul H. Brookes Publishing Co.

Bradley, V.J., Ashbaugh, J.W., & Blaney, B. (Eds.). (1994). *Creating individual supports for people with developmental disabilities: A mandate for change at many levels.* Baltimore: Paul H. Brookes Publishing Co.

Gardner, J.F. (2002). The evolving social context for quality in services and supports. In R.L. Schalock, P.C. Baker, & M.D. Croser (Eds.), *Embarking on a new century: Mental retardation at the end of the 20th century* (pp. 67–80). Washington, DC: American Association on Mental Retardation.

Goode, D.A. (Ed.). (1994). *Quality of life for persons with disabilities: International perspectives and issues.* Cambridge, MA: Brookline Press.

Hagner, D., Helm, D.T., & Butterworth, J. (1996). "This is your meeting": A qualitative study of person-centered planning. *Mental Retardation, 34,* 159–171.

Holburn, S., & Vietze, P.M. (Eds.). (2002). *Person-centered planning: Research, practice, and future directions.* Baltimore: Paul H. Brookes Publishing Co.

Jeffreys, M., & Sproul, P. (1993). *Making choices for community living: A guide for self-planning.* Windsor, ON, Canada: Windsor Community Living Support Services.

Mansell, J., & Beadle-Brown, J. (2004). Person-centred planning or person-centred action? Policy and practice in intellectual disability services. *Journal of Applied Research in Intellectual Disabilities, 17*(1), 1–9.

Menchetti, B.M., & Garcia, L.A. (2003). Personal and employment outcomes of person-centered career planning. *Education and Training in Developmental Disabilities, 38,* 145–156.

Mount, B., & Zwernik, K. (1990). *Making futures happen: A manual for facilitators of personal futures planning.* St. Paul, MN: Metropolitan Council.

O'Brien, J. (1987). A guide to life-style planning: Using *The Activities Catalog* to integrate services and natural support systems. In B. Wilcox & G. Thomas Bellamy, *A comprehensive guide to the activities catalog: An alternative curriculum for youth and adults with severe disabilities* (pp. 175–189). Baltimore: Paul H. Brookes Publishing Co.

Pearpoint, J., O'Brien, J., & Forest, M. (1993). *PATH (Planning Alternative Tomorrows with Hope): A workbook for planning positive possible futures.* Toronto: Inclusion Press.

Perske, R. (1988). *Circles of friends: People with disabilities and their friends enrich the lives of one another.* Nashville, TN: Abingdon Press.

Roberts, C., Smith, B., & Ross, R. (1994). Drawing forth personal vision. In P.M. Senge, C. Roberts, R.B. Ross, et al. (Eds.), *The fifth discipline fieldbook: Strategies and tools for building a learning organization* (pp. 201–207). New York: Doubleday.

Schwartz, A.A., Jacobson, J.W., & Holburn, S.C. (2000). Defining person centeredness: Results of two consensus methods. *Education and Training in Mental Retardation and Developmental Disabilities, 35,* 235–249.

Snow, J.A. (1994). *What's really worth doing and how to do it: A book for people who love someone disabled.* Toronto: Inclusion Press.

Stainback, S., Stainback, W., & Forest, M. (Eds.). (1989). *Educating all students in the mainstream of regular education.* Baltimore: Paul H. Brookes Publishing Co.

Taylor, S.J., & Bogdan, R. (1990). Quality of life and the individual's perspective. In R.L. Schalock (Ed.), *Quality of life: Perspectives and issues* (pp. 27–40). Washington, DC: American Association on Mental Retardation.

Taylor, S.J., Bogdan, R., & Racino, J.A. (Eds.). (1991). *Life in the community: Case studies of organizations supporting people with disabilities.* Baltimore: Paul H. Brookes Publishing Co.

Family-Centered Approaches

Bailey, D.B., Jr., & McWilliam, P.J. (1993). The search for quality indicators. In P.J. McWilliam & D.B. Bailey, Jr. (Eds.), *Working together with children and families: Case studies in early intervention* (pp. 3–20). Baltimore: Paul H. Brookes Publishing Co.

Birenbaum, A., & Cohen, H.J. (2002). On the importance of helping families: Policy implications from a national study. In J. Blacher & B.L. Baker (Eds.), *The best of AAMR: Families and mental retardation: A collection of notable AAMR journal articles across the 20th century* (pp. 351–357). Washington, DC: American Association on Mental Retardation.

McWilliam, R.A., Lang, L., Vandiviere, P., et al. (1995). Satisfaction and struggles: Family perceptions of early intervention services. *Journal of Early Intervention, 19*(1), 43–60.

Murphy, D.L., Lee, I.M., Turnbull, A.P., et al. (1995). The family-centered program rating scale: An instrument for program evaluation and change. *Journal of Early Intervention, 19*(1), 24–42.

Saleeby, D. (1996). The strengths perspective in social work practice: Extensions and cautions. *Social Work, 41*(3), 296–306.

Singer, G.H.S., Powers, L.E., & Olson, A.L. (1996). *Redefining family support: Innovations in public-private partnerships.* Baltimore: Paul H. Brookes Publishing Co.

Trivette, C.M., Dunst, C.J., Boyd, K., et al. (1995). Family-oriented program models, helpgiving practices, and parental control appraisals. *Exceptional Children, 62,* 237–248.

Turnbull, A.P., & Turnbull, H.R. (2005). *Families, professionals, and exceptionality: Collaborating for empowerment* (5th ed.). Upper Saddle River, NJ: Prentice Hall.

Helpful Internet Information

Fact Sheet: Person-Centered Planning
http://www.aamr.org/Policies/faq_planning.shtml

QualityMall: Person-Centered Planning
http://www.qualitymall.org/directory/dept1.asp?deptid=23

Personnel Issues

Recommended Reading

International Journal of Practical Approaches to Disability. (2000). Post secondary models in disability studies and community rehabilitation [Special issue]. *International Journal of Practical Approaches to Disability, 24,* 1–37.

McConkey, R. (1996). Down syndrome in developing countries. In B. Stratford & P. Gunn (Eds.), *New approaches to Down syndrome* (pp. 451–469). London: Cassell.

Neufeldt, A.H. (Guest Ed.). (1992). Personnel training [Special issue]. *Journal of Practical Approaches to Developmental Handicap, 16*(1/2), 5–46.

Roeher Institute. (1995). *Harm's way: The many faces of violence and abuse against persons with disabilities.* Toronto: Author.

Roeher Institute. (1996). *Disability, community and society: Exploring the links.* Toronto: Author.

Rondal, J.A., Perera, J., & Nadel, L. (1999). In J. Rondal, J. Perera, & L. Nadel (Eds.), *Down syndrome: A review of current knowledge* (pp. 238–240). London: Whurr.

Stewart, M., Brown, J.B., Weston, W.W., et al. (1995). *Patient-centered medicine: Transforming the clinical method.* Newbury Park, CA: Sage Publications.

Thomas, D., & Woods, H. (2003). *Working with people with learning disabilities: Theory and practice.* London: Jessica Kingsley Publishers.

Uditsky, B. (1994). Advocacy perspectives: Family support and inclusive education initiatives of the Alberta Association for Community Living. *Journal of Practical Approaches to Developmental Handicap, 18,* 26–27.

Wight Felske, A. (1988). Rehabilitation practitioners: Making a difference in the quality of life for disabled persons. In R.I. Brown (Ed.), *Quality of life for handicapped people* (pp. 267–293). London: Croom Helm.

Helpful Internet Information

Beach Center on Disability
http://www.beachcenter.org

College of Direct Support: An Internet-Based College for Direct Support Professionals
http://collegeofdirectsupport.com

eLearners.com: Graduate Certificates in Education
http://www.elearners.com/campus/level/g-certificates/subject/13.1006.htm

Roeher Institute
http://www.roeher.ca

Speech and Language Disorders

Recommended Reading

American Academy of Pediatrics. (n.d.). *Children's health topics: Vision and hearing.* Retrieved March 7, 2006, from http://www.aap.org/healthtopics/visionhearing.cfm

Atlantic Provinces Special Educational Authority. (2003). *Handbook for teachers serving students who are deafblind, deaf or hard of hearing with additional disabilities and blind or visually impaired with additional disabilities.* Retrieved March 25, 2006, from http://www.ed.gov.nl.ca/edu/dept/pdf/DeafblindHandbook.pdf

Brice, A. (2001). *Children with communication disorders: Update 2001.* Retrieved March 7, 2006, from http://ericec.org/digests/e617.html

Buchanan, L.H. (1990). Early onset of presbycusis in Down syndrome. *Scandinavian Audiology, 19,* 103–110.

Dahle, A.J., & McCollister, F.P. (1986). Hearing and otologic disorders in children with Down syndrome. *American Journal of Mental Deficiency, 90,* 636–642.

Grizzle, K.L., & Simms, M.D. (2005). Early language development and language learning disabilities. *Pediatrics in Review, 26*(8), 274–283.

Hauser, M.D., Chomsky, N., & Fitch, W.T. (2002). The faculty of language: What is it, who has it, and how did it evolve? *Science, 298*(5598), 1569–1579.

Khadem, F., McKenzie, F., Smith, R.L., et al. (2005). Identification of FOXP2 truncation as a novel cause of developmental speech and language deficits. *American Journal of Human Genetics, 76*(6), 1074–1080.

MacDermot, K.D., Bonora, E., Sykes, N., et al. (1997). Language as a psychological adaptation. *Ciba Foundation Symposium, 208,* 162–172; discussion 172–180.

Marcell, M.M., & Cohen, S. (1992). Hearing abilities of Down syndrome and other mentally handicapped adolescents. *Research in Developmental Disabilities, 13,* 533–551.

Plomin, R. (2001). Genetic factors contributing to learning and language delays and disabilities. *Child and Adolescent Psychiatric Clinics of North America, 10*(2), viii, 259–277.

Plomin, R., & Kovas, Y. (2005). Generalist genes and learning disabilities. *Psychology Bulletin, 131*(4), 592–617.

Pober, B., & Dykens, E. (1996). Williams syndrome: An overview of medical, cognitive, and behavioral features. *Mental Retardation, 5,* 929–942.

Shanker, S., & Greenspan, S.I. (2004). *The first idea: How symbols, language, and intelligence evolved from our primate ancestors to modern humans.* Cambridge, MA: Da Capo Press.

Shaywitz, S.E., & Shaywitz, B.A. (2005). Dyslexia (specific reading disability). *Biological Psychiatry, 57*(11), 301–309.

Van Borsel, J., Curfs, L.M.G., & Fryns, J.P. (1997). Hyperacusis in Williams syndrome: A sample survey study. *Genetic Counselling, 8,* 121–126.

Whitehurst, G.J., & Fischel, J.E. (1994). Practitioner review: Early developmental language delay. What, if anything, should the clinician do about it? *Journal of Child Psychology and Psychiatry, and Allied Disciplines, 35,* 613–648.

Helpful Internet Information

ACE Centre
http://www.ace-centre.org.uk/html/publications/publicat.html

Augmentative and Alternative Communication Connecting Young Kids (YAACK)
http://aac.unl.edu/yaack/index.html

Augmentative and Alternative Communication Intervention Ideas
http://www.aacintervention.com

Augmentative Communication Community Partnerships–Canada
http://www.accpc.ca

Augmentative Communication, Inc.
http://www.AugComInc.com

Augmentative Communication On-line User's Group (ACOLUG)
http://www.temple.edu/instituteondisabilities/programs/assistive/acolug/index.htm

Blissymbolics
http://www.blissymbolics.org

Center for Literacy and Disability Studies
http://www.med.unc.edu/ahs/clds

Closing the Gap
http://www.closingthegap.com

Creative Communicating
http://creativecommunicating.com

Picture Communication Symbols (PCS)
by Mayer Johnson Company
http://www.mayer-johnson.com

Picture Exchange Communication System (PECS)
http://www.pecs.com

Rehabilitation Engineering Research Center
on Communication Enhancement
http://www.aac-rerc.com

Special Education Technology-British Columbia (SET-BC)
http://www.setbc.org

Talking Overboard Symbols
http://www.gusinc.com/Overboard/index.html

Technology Integration in Education
http://www.lburkhart.com

University of Nebraska-Lincoln, Barkley Center
http://aac.unl.edu

University of Washington, Seattle
http://depts.washington.edu/augcomm

Widgit Rebus Symbols
http://www.widgit.com

Key Organizations

American Speech-Language-Hearing Association
http://www.asha.org

International Society for Augmentative and Alternative Communication (ISAAC)
http://www.isaac-online.org

National Dissemination Center for Children with Disabilities (NICHCY)
http://www.nichcy.org/index.html

National Institute on Deafness and Other Communication Disorders (NIDCD)
http://www.nidcd.nih.gov

Transition Issues

Recommended Reading

Berkell, D.E. (1989). *Transition from school to work for persons with disabilities.* New York: Longman.

MacMillan, D.L. (1982). *Mental retardation in school and society.* Glenview, IL: Scott Foresman and Company.

Rusch, F.R. (1992). *Transition from school to adult life: Models, linkages, and policy.* Sycamore, IL: Sycamore Publishing.

Wehman, P. (2006). *Life Beyond the Classroom* (4th ed.). Baltimore: Paul H. Brookes Publishing Co.

Helpful Internet Information

10 Essentials to Get that Job
http://www.hrsdc.gc.ca/asp/gateway.asp?hr=en/on/work/10_essentials.shtml&hs=on0

AAMR Fact Sheet: Transition
http://www.aamr.org/Policies/faq_transition.shtml

Career development for adolescents and young adults with mental retardation
http://www.worksupport.com/Topics/transition.asp

Disability Employment Opportunities
http://disability-resource.com/employ.html

Employment Strategy for Persons with Disabilities
http://www.mhr.gov.bc.ca/PUBLICAT/DB/EmployStrat.htm

Getting and Keeping a Job When You Have a Disability
http://www.canberra.edu.au/special-ed/papers/shaddock2001c.html

The Individuals with Disabilities Education Act: Transition from School to Work and Community Life
http://www.thearc.org/faqs/qa-idea-transition.html

Parent's Role in the Transition to Adult Life
http://www.cise.missouri.edu/publications/proltran.html

Parents' Guide to Transition: What Happens After High School?
http://www.pluk.org/trans.html#2

Tapping the Talents of People with Disabilities: A Guide for Employers
http://www.conferenceboard.ca/documents.asp?rnext=85

Transition
http://www.scddc.state.sc.us/transit.htm

Transition and Post-School Outcomes for Youth with Disabilities: Closing the Gaps to Post-Secondary Education and Employment
http://www.ncd.gov/newsroom/publications/2000/transition_11-01-00.htm

Transition from School to Adult Life
http://www.doe.mass.edu/sped/links/transition.html
http://www.iidc.indiana.edu/cclc/transition1.htm

Transition Planning: Preparing for Postsecondary Employment for Students with Learning Disabilities and/or Attention Disorders
http://www.ldonline.org/ld_indepth/transition/lda_trans_planning.html

Transition to Adult Life for Student with Disabilities
http://www.psrn.org/Sp%20Ed%20transition.html

Transition to the Next Steps After High School
http://www.pacer.org/legislation/idea/transitionNextSteps.htm

Where Do We Go from Here?
http://www.transitionmap.org

Working Together: An Employer's Resource for Workplace Accommodation
http://www.hrsdc.gc.ca/asp/gateway.asp?hr=en/on/epb/disabilities/onworking.shtml&hs=pyp

Youth and Transition Issues
http://www.dhs.state.mn.us/main/groups/disabilities/documents/pub/dhs_id_004733.hcsp

Key Organizations
Division on Career Development and Transition, Council on Exceptional Children
http://www.dcdt.org

National Center on Secondary Education and Transition
http://www.ncset.org

RESOURCES ON ETIOLOGY AND CONDITIONS

Abnormal Behavior

Helpful Internet Information
BrainInjury.com
http://www.braininjury.com

Clinical Best Practices for Serving People with Developmental Disability and Mental Illness
http://www.ohiomimrdd.org/about_ccoe.htm

The National Association for the Dually Diagnosed (NADD) Store
http://www.thenadd.org/content/products/home.shtml

National Institute of Neurological Disorders and Stroke (NINDS) Attention Deficit-Hyperactivity Disorder Information Page
http://www.ninds.nih.gov/disorders/adhd/adhd.htm

Key Organizations
National Eating Disorders Association
http://www.nationaleatingdisorders.org

Alzheimer's Disease and Dementia

Helpful Internet Information
ADEAR Alzheimer Disease Education and Referral Center
http://www.alzheimers.org/trials/index.html

The Dementia Services Development Centre, University of Stirling
http://www.dementia.stir.ac.uk

Down's Syndrome Scotland: Ageing
http://www.dsscotland.org.uk/ageing

Intellectual Disabilities and Dementia
http://www.albany.edu/aging/IDD

Research and Rehabilitation Training Center on Aging with Developmental Disabilities, University of Chicago at Illinois
http://www.uic.edu/orgs/rrtcamr/aboutus.htm

Vitamin E in Aging Persons with Down Syndrome
http://www.clinicaltrials.gov/show/NCT00056329

Key Organizations
Alzheimer Society of Canada
http://www.alzheimer.ca

Alzheimer Society of Ireland
http://www.alzheimer.ie

Alzheimer's Association
http://www.alz.org

Alzheimer's Australia
http://www.alzheimers.org.au

Alzheimer's Society
http://www.alzheimers.org.uk

Asperger Syndrome

Recommended Reading
Attwood, T. (1998). *Asperger's syndrome.* London: Jessica Kingsley Publishers.
Cumine, V., Leach, J., & Stevenson, G. (1998). *Asperger syndrome: A practical guide for teachers.* London: David Fulton Publishers.
Fling, E.R. (2000). *Eating an artichoke: A mother's perspective on Asperger syndrome.* London: Jessica Kingsley Publishers.
Jackson, L. (2002). *Freaks, geeks and Asperger syndrome: A user guide to adolescence.* London: Jessica Kingsley Publishers.
Klin, A., Volkmar, F.R., & Sparrow, S.S. (Eds.). (2000). *Asperger syndrome.* New York: The Guilford Press.
Myles, B.S., & Simpson, R.L. (1998). *Asperger syndrome: A guide for educators and parents.* Austin, TX: PRO-ED.
Stoddart, K.P. (Ed.). (2004). *Asperger syndrome in children, youth and adults: Integrating multiple perspectives.* London: Jessica Kingsley Publishers.
Willey, L.H. (1999). *Pretending to be normal: Living with Asperger's syndrome.* London: Jessica Kingsley Publishers.

Helpful Internet Information
Aspen Asperger Syndrome Education Network
http://www.aspennj.org

Asperger and Autism Information by MAAP Services
http://www.asperger.org

Asperger Syndrome Australian Information Centre
http://members.ozemail.com.au/~rbmitch/Asperger.htm

Independent Living on the Autistic Spectrum
http://www.inlv.demon.nl

National Institute of Neurological Disorders and Stroke (NINDS) Asperger Syndrome Information Page
http://www.ninds.nih.gov/disorders/asperger/asperger.htm

Online Asperger Syndrome Information and Support (O.A.S.I.S.)
http://www.udel.edu/bkirby/asperger

Key Organizations
Asperger's Society of Ontario
http://www.aspergers.ca

U.S. Autism and Asperger's Association
http://www.usautism.org

Attention-Deficit/Hyperactivity Disorder

Helpful Internet Information

Attention-Deficit/Hyperactivity Disorder
http://www.nimh.nih.gov/publicat/adhd.cfm

Learning Disabilities Online
http://www.ldonline.org

Learning Disabilities Worldwide
http://www.ldam.org

What is ADHD?
http://www.kidshealth.org/parent/emotions/behavior/adhd.html

Key Organizations

British Institute of Learning Disabilities (BILD)
http://www.bild.org.uk

Attention Deficit Disorder Association (ADDA)
http://www.add.org

Australian Learning Disability Association (ALDA)
http://student.admin.utas.edu.au/services/alda

Children and Adults with Attention-Deficit/Hyperactivity Disorder (CHADD)
http://www.chadd.org

CHADD Canada
http://www.chaddcanada.org

Learning Disabilities Association of America (LDA)
http://www.ldanatl.org

Learning Disabilities Association of Canada (LDAC)
http://www.ldac-taac.ca

Autism

Recommended Reading

Cohen, D.J., & Volkmar, F. (Eds.). (1997). *Handbook of autism and pervasive developmental disorders* (2nd ed.). Hoboken, NJ: John Wiley & Sons.

Gillberg, C., & Coleman, M. (2000). *The biology of the autistic syndromes* (3rd ed.). London: Mac Keith Press.

Howlin, P. (1997). *Autism: Preparing for adulthood.* London: Routledge.

Koegel, R.L., & Koegel, L.K. (Eds.). (1995). *Teaching children with autism: Strategies for initiating positive interactions and improving learning opportunities.* Baltimore: Paul H. Brookes Publishing Co.

Maurice, C., Green, G., & Foxx, R.M. (Eds.). (2001). *Making a difference: Behavioral intervention for autism.* Austin, TX: PRO-ED.

Maurice, C., Green, G., & Luce, S.C. (Eds.). (1996). *Behavioral intervention for young children with autism: A manual for parents and professionals.* Austin, TX: PRO-ED.

Neisworth, J.T., & Wolfe, P.S. (Eds.). (2005). *The autism encyclopedia.* Baltimore: Paul H. Brookes Publishing Co.

Quill, K.A. (Ed.). (1995). *Teaching children with autism: Strategies to enhance communication and socialization.* New York: Delmar.

Siegel, B. (1996). *The world of the autistic child: Understanding and treating autistic spectrum disorders.* Oxford, United Kingdom: Oxford University Press.

Smith, M.D. (1990). *Autism and life in the community: Successful interventions for behavioral challenges.* Baltimore: Paul H. Brookes Publishing Co.

Sperry, V.W. (2001). *Fragile success: Ten autistic children, childhood to adulthood* (2nd ed.). Baltimore: Paul H. Brookes Publishing Co.

Volkmar, F.R. (Ed.). (1998). *Autism and pervasive developmental disorders.* Cambridge, United Kingdom: Cambridge University Press.

Wetherby, A.M., & Prizant, B.M. (Vol. Eds.). (2000). *Autism spectrum disorders: A transactional developmental perspective: Communication and Language Intervention Series, Vol. 9.* Baltimore: Paul H. Brookes Publishing Co.

Wing, L. (1996). *The autistic spectrum: A guide for parents and professionals.* London: Constable.

Journals

Autism: International Journal of Research and Practice
http://www.sagepub.co.uk/journalsProdDesc.nav?prodId=Journal200822

Focus on Autism and Other Developmental Disabilities
http://www.proedinc.com/Scripts/prodView.asp?idProduct=1649

Journal of Autism and Developmental Disorders
http://www.springerlink.com/content/1573–3432/

Helpful Internet Information

Autism Information Center
http://www.cdc.gov/ncbddd/dd/ddautism.htm

Autism Research at the National Institute of Child Health and Human Development
http://www.nichd.nih.gov/autism

Autism Resources
http://www.autism-resources.com

Key Organizations

Autism Society of America
http://www.autism-society.org

Autism Society Canada
http://autismsocietycanada.ca

Autism Speaks
http://www.autismspeaks.org

Center for the Study of Autism
http://www.autism.org

Families for Early Autism Treatment
http://www.feat.org

Geneva Centre for Autism
http://www.autism.net

National Autistic Society
http://www.nas.org.uk

Cerebral Palsy

Recommended Reading

Dormans, J.P., & Pellegrino, L. (Eds.). (1998). *Caring for children with cerebral palsy: A team approach.* Baltimore: Paul H. Brookes Publishing Co.

Levitt, S. (2004). *Treatment of cerebral palsy and motor delay* (4th ed.). Oxford, United Kingdom: Blackwell Publishing.

Miller, F., & Bachrach, S.J. (1995). *Cerebral palsy: A complete guide for caregiving.* Baltimore: The Johns Hopkins University Press.

Molnar, G.E., & Alexander, M.A. (1999). *Pediatric rehabilitation* (3rd ed.). Philadelphia: Hanley & Belfus.

Scherzer, A.L. (Ed.). (2001). *Early diagnosis and interventional therapy in cerebral palsy: An interdisciplinary age-focused approach* (3rd ed.). New York: Marcel Dekker.

Stanley, F., Blair, E., & Alberman, E. (2000). *Cerebral palsies: Epidemiology and causal pathways.* London: Mac Keith Press.

Journals

Developmental Medicine & Child Neurology
http://journals.cambridge.org/action/displayJournal?jid=DMC

Helpful Internet Information

CanChild Centre for Childhood Disability Research
http://www.fhs.mcmaster.ca/canchild

HemiHelp Newsletter
http://www.hemihelp.org.uk

Movement Disorder Virtual University
http://www.mdvu.org

Scope: Cerebral Palsy Organisations in England and Wales
http://www.scope.org.uk

Key Organizations

American Academy for Cerebral Palsy and Developmental Medicine
http://www.aacpdm.org/index?service=page/Home

United Cerebral Palsy
http://www.ucp.org/main.cfm/1

Down Syndrome

Recommended Reading

Appendix II: More resources relevant to health issues in adults with Down syndrome. (2005). *Journal on Developmental Disabilities, 12*(2, Suppl.). Retrieved from http://www.oadd.org/publications/journal/issues.htm

Cohen, W.I. (1999). Health care guidelines for individuals with Down syndrome: 1999 revision. *Down Syndrome Quarterly, 4*(3). Retrieved October 20, 2006, from http://www.denison.edu/collaborations/dsq/health99.html

Cohen, W.I., Nadel, L., & Madnick, M.E. (2002). *Down syndrome: Visions for the 21st century.* Hoboken, NJ: John Wiley & Sons.

Pueschel, S.M. (2001). *A parent's guide to Down syndrome: Toward a brighter future* (Rev. ed.). Baltimore: Paul H. Brookes Publishing Co.

Pueschel, S.M. (2006). *Adults with Down syndrome.* Baltimore: Paul H. Brookes Publishing Co.

Helpful Internet Information

Birth Disorder Information Directory: Down Syndrome Related Books
http://www.bdid.com/downsyndromebooks.htm

Celiac Disease and Down Syndrome
http://www.ds-health.com/celiac.htm

Directory of Down Syndrome Sites (United States and International)
http://www.downsyndrome.com

Down Syndrome: For New Parents
http://www.downsyn.com

Down Syndrome: Health Issues (News and Information for Parents and Professionals)
http://www.ds-health.com

Down Syndrome: Understanding the Gift of Life
http://www.nas.com/downsyn

Down Syndrome Quarterly
http://www.denison.edu/collaborations/dsq

Education by Design
http://www.edbydesign.com/parentres.html

For Aunts, Uncles and Other Relatives
http://www.downsyn.com/relatives.html

Lemon & Allspice Cookery
http://www.commongroundco-op.ca

Recommended Down Syndrome Sites on the Internet
http://www.ds-health.com/ds_sites.htm

Riverbend Down Syndrome Parent Support Group
http://www.altonweb.com/cs/downsyndrome/index.html

Speech Delay.com
http://www.speechdelay.com/testrosebooks.htm

The Thyroid and Down Syndrome
http://www.ds-health.com/thyroid.htm

Key Organizations

Down Syndrome Association of Victoria (Australia)
http://www.dsav.asn.au

Down Syndrome International
http://www.down-syndrome-int.org

Down Syndrome Research Foundation (Canada)
http://www.dsrf.org

Down's Syndrome Association (United Kingdom)
http://www.downs-syndrome.org.uk

Kiwanis Down Syndrome Foundation
http://www.kdsf.org.my/html/links.html#

National Down Syndrome Congress
http://www.ndsccenter.org

National Down Syndrome Society (United States)
http://www.ndss.org

Epilepsy

Recommended Reading

Burnham, W.M. (1998). Antiseizure drugs. In H. Kalant & W. Roschlau (Eds.), *Principles of medical pharmacology* (pp. 250–261). Oxford, United Kingdom: Oxford University Press.

Burnham, W.M. (2002). Epilepsy. In L. Nadel (Ed.), *Encyclopedia of cognitive neuroscience.* London: Nature Publishing Group.

Burnham, W.M., Carlen, P.L., & Hwang, P.A. (Eds.). (2002). *Intractable seizures: Diagnosis, treatment and prevention.* New York: Kluwer Academic/Plenum Publishers.

Dodson, W.E., & Pellock, J.M. (Eds.). (1993). *Pediatric epilepsy diagnosis and therapy.* New York: Demos Publications.

Engel, J., & Pedley, T.A. (Eds.). (1997). *Epilepsy: A comprehensive textbook.* Philadelphia: Lippincott, Williams & Wilkins.

Levy, R.H., Mattson, R.H., Meldrum, B.S., et al. (2002). *Antiepileptic drugs* (5th ed.). Philadelphia: Lippincott, Williams & Wilkins.

Luders, H.O. (Ed.). (1992). *Epilepsy surgery.* New York: Raven Press.

McLachlan, R. (1997). Vagus nerve stimulation for intractable epilepsy: A review. *Journal of Clinical Neurophysiology, 14,* 358–368.

Persaud, V., Thompson, M.D., & Percy, M.E. (2003). Epilepsy and developmental disability, part I: Developmental disorders in which epilepsy may be comorbid. *Journal on Developmental Disabilities, 10*(2), 123-152.

Rowan, A.J., & Ramsay, E.E. (1997). *Seizures and epilepsy in the elderly.* Boston: Butterworth-Heineman.

Wallace, S. (Ed.). (1996). *Epilepsy in children.* New York: Chapman and Hall Medical.

Key Organizations

Epilepsy Canada
http://www.epilepsy.ca

Epilepsy Foundation
http://www.epilepsyfoundation.org

Fetal Alcohol Spectrum Disorders

Recommended Reading

Abel, E.L. (Ed.). (1996). *Fetal alcohol syndrome: From mechanism to prevention.* Boca Raton, FL: CRC Press.

Abel, E.L. (1998). *Fetal alcohol abuse syndrome.* New York: Kluwer Academic/Plenum Publishers.

Buxton, B. (2004). *Damaged angels: A mother discovers the terrible cost of alcohol in pregnancy.* New York: Alfred A. Knopf.

Institute of Medicine. (1996). *Fetal alcohol syndrome: Diagnosis, epidemiology, prevention, and treatment.* Washington, DC: National Academies Press.

Spohr, H.L., & Steinhausen, H.C. (Eds.). (1996). *Alcohol, pregnancy and the developing child.* Cambridge, United Kingdom: Cambridge University Press.

Streissguth, A. (1997). *Fetal alcohol syndrome: A guide for families and communities.* Baltimore: Paul H. Brookes Publishing Co.

University of Washington School of Medicine, Department of Psychiatry and Behavioral Sciences. (1996). *Understanding the occurrence of secondary disabilities in clients with fetal alcohol syndrome (FAS) and fetal alcohol effects (FAE): Final report.* Seattle: Author.

Journals

Alcohol Research and Health
http://www.niaaa.nih.gov/Publications/AlcoholResearch

Alcoholism Clinical and Experimental Research
http://www.blackwellpublishing.com/journal.asp?ref=0145-6008

Child Development
http://www.blackwellpublishing.com/journal.asp?ref=0009-3920

Developmental Brain Research
http://www.elsevier.com/wps/find/journaldescription.cws_home/506051/description#description

Developmental Neuropsychology
http://www.leaonline.com/loi/dn?cookieSet=1

Drug and Alcohol Review Journal
http://www.tandf.co.uk/journals/titles/09595236.asp

Journal of Studies on Alcohol
http://alcoholstudies.rutgers.edu/journal

Journal of Substance Abuse Treatment
http://www.elsevier.com/wps/find/journaldescription.cws_home/525475/description#description

Neuroscience
http://www.neuroscience-ibro.com

Neurotoxicology and Teratology
http://www.elsevier.com/wps/find/journaldescription.cws_home/525481/description#description

Helpful Internet Information and Hot Lines

Canadian Centre on Substance Abuse: Fetal Alcohol Spectrum Disorder (FASD) Information Service
http://www.ccsa.ca/CCSA/EN/Topics/Populations/FASDInformationService.htm

FAS Community Resource Center
http://www.come-over.to/FASCRC

FASlink: Fetal Alcohol Disorders Society
http://www.acbr.com/fas/index.htm

FASworld
http://www.fasworld.com

Motherisk Alcohol and Substance Abuse Help Line
1-877-FAS-INFO (1-877-327-4636)

Office for National Statistics (UK)
http://www.statistics.gov.uk

Substance Abuse and Mental Health Services Administration (SAMHSA): Substance Abuse Treatment Facility Locator
http://dasis3.samhsa.gov

University of Washington, Fetal Alcohol and Drug Unit
http://depts.washington.edu/fadu

Key Organizations

Alcoholics Anonymous
http://www.aa.org

Centers for Disease Control and Prevention (CDC)
http://www.cdc.gov/ncbddd/fas

National Institute on Alcohol Abuse and Alcoholism
http://www.niaaa.nih.gov

National Organization on Fetal Alcohol Syndrome
http://www.nofas.org

Fragile X Syndrome

Recommended Reading

Braden, M., Head, K., Inz, A., et al. (2004). *Curriculum guide for individuals with fragile X syndrome.* San Francisco: National Fragile X Foundation.

Spiridigliozzi, C.A., Lachiewica, A.M., MacMurdo, A.D., et al. (1994). *Educating boys with fragile X syndrome: A guide for parents and professionals.* Durham, NC: Duke University Medical Center, Child Development Unit.

Helpful Internet Information

Carolina Fragile X Project
http://www.fpg.unc.edu/~fx/index.htm

Conquer Fragile X
http://www.conquerfragilex.org

FMR1 and the Fragile X Syndrome
http://www.cdc.gov/genomics/hugenet/factsheets/FS_FragileX.htm

Fragile X Syndrome: Diagnostic and Carrier Testing
http://genetics.faseb.org/genetics/acmg/pol-16.htm

Fragile X Syndrome
http://www.genomelink.org/fragile

Math Skills Development Project, Kennedy Krieger Institute
http://www.msdp.kennedykrieger.org

Waisman Center, University of Wisconsin
http://www.waisman.wisc.edu/index.htmlx

Key Organizations

Fragile X Association of Australia
http://www.fragilex.org.au

Fragile X Research Foundation of Canada
http://www.fragile-x.ca/default2.htm

FRAXA Research Foundation
http://www.fraxa.org

National Fragile X Foundation (United States)
http://www.fragilex.org

Genetic and Environmental Variables that Cause Disabilities

Recommended Reading

Bear, M.F., Connors, B.W., & Paradiso, M.A. (2001). *Neuroscience: Exploring the brain* (2nd ed.). Philadelphia: Lippincott, Williams & Wilkins.

Carlson, B.M. (2001). *Human embryology and developmental biology* (2nd ed.). St. Louis: Mosby.

Larsen, W.J. (2001). *Human embryology* (3rd ed.). New York: Churchill Livingston.

Matthews, G.G. (2001). *Neurobiology: Molecules, cells and systems* (2nd ed.). Cambridge, United Kingdom: Blackwell Science.

Moore, K.L., & Persaud, T.V.N. (1989). *Before we are born. Basic embryology and birth defects.* Philadelphia: W.B. Saunders.

Moore, K.L., & Persaud, T.V.N. (1998) *The developing human: Clinically oriented embryology* (6th ed.). Philadelphia: W.B. Saunders.

Sadler, T.W. (2004). *Langman's medical embryology* (9th ed.). Philadelphia: Lippincott, Williams & Wilkins.

Helpful Internet Information

Electronic Atlas of the Developing Human Brain (EADHB)
http://www.ncl.ac.uk/ihg/EADHB

Environmental Contaminants and Their Relation to Learning, Behavioral, and Developmental Disorders
http://www.niehs.nih.gov/oc/factsheets/ceh/contamin.htm

Environmental Contaminants and Their Relation to Learning, Behavioral, and Developmental Disorders
http://www.niehs.nih.gov/oc/factsheets/ceh/contamin.htm

Human Genome Project Information
http://www.genome.gov
http://www.ornl.gov/sci/techresources/Human_Genome/home.shtml

Malnutrition Overview
http://www.sustaintech.org/world.htm

Motherisk Program, Hospital for Sick Children, Toronto
http://www.obgyn.net/women/articles/motherisk.htm

National Institute of Environmental Health Sciences, Children's Environmental Health and Disease Prevention Research Centers
http://www.niehs.nih.gov/oc/factsheets/ceh/centers.htm

The National Toxicology Program (NTP), Center for the Evaluation of Risks to Human Reproduction (CERHR)
http://cerhr.niehs.nih.gov

Nutrient Recommendations: Dietary Reference Intakes (DRI) and Recommended Dietary Allowances (RDA)
http://ods.od.nih.gov/health_information/Dietary_Reference_Intakes.aspx

Online Mendelian Inheritance in Man (OMIM)
http://www.ncbi.nlm.nih.gov/entrez/query.fcgi?db=OMIM

Protein Calorie (Energy) Malnutrition
http://www.pediatriconcall.com/fordoctor/DiseasesandCondition/Protein.asp

Thyroid Disease Manager
http://www.thyroidmanager.org

World Health Organization: Nutrition
http://www.who.int/nut

Key Organizations

The International Council for the Control of Iodine Deficiency Disorders (ICCIDD)
http://www.iccidd.org

National Center on Birth Defects and Developmental Disabilities (NCBDDD), Centers for Disease Control and Prevention (CDC)
http://www.cdc.gov/ncbddd

HIV/AIDS

Recommended Reading for General Audiences

Atlantic First Nations AIDS Task Force. (1996). *Healing our nations: 4th Canadian Aboriginal conference on HIV/AIDS and related issues.* Ottawa, ON, Canada: Indian and Northern Affairs Canada.

De Matteo, D., & Roberts, J. (2001). *Disclosing HIV/AIDS to children: The paths we take.* Calgary, AB, Canada: Detselig Enterprises.

Ethno-cultural Diversity Committee of the Canadian AIDS Society (ECDC-CAS). (1995). *Education and support within the context of ethno-cultural diversity.* Ottawa, ON, Canada: Canadian AIDS Society.

Jacobs, R., Samowitz, P., Levy, J.M., et al. (1989). Developing an AIDS prevention program for persons with intellectual disabilities. *Mental Retardation, 27,* 233–237.

Pizzo, P.A., & Wilfert, C.A. (Eds.). (1998). *Pediatric AIDS: The challenge of HIV infection in infants, children, and adolescents* (3rd ed.). Philadelphia: Lippincott, Williams & Wilkins.

Scotti, J.R., Nangle, D.W., Masia, C.L., et al. (1997). Providing an AIDS education and skills training program to persons with mild intellectual disabilities. *Education and Training in Mental Retardation and Intellectual Disabilities, 32,* 113–128.

Recommended Reading for Children

The Group of Five. (2002). *Bye-bye secrets: A book about children living with HIV or AIDS in their family.* Toronto: The Teresa Group and The Hospital for Sick Children.

Merrifield, M. (1990). *Come sit by me.* Toronto: Women's Press.

Merrifield, M., & Collins, H. (1995). *Morning light: An educational storybook for children and their caregivers about HIV/AIDS and saying goodbye.* Toronto: Stoddard.

Weiner, L., Best, A., & Pizzo, P. (1994). *Be a friend: Children who live with HIV speak.* Morton Grove, IL: Albert Whitman.

Helpful Internet Information

The Body: An AIDS and HIV Information Resource
http://www.thebody.com/index.shtml

Canadian Aboriginal AIDS Network
http://www.caan.ca

Canadian Public Health Association
http://www.cpha.ca/CPHA/ch/ch.html

Centers for Disease Control and Prevention (CDC)
http://www.cdc.gov

Children with AIDS Project
http://www.aidskids.org

Children's Animated Television (CAT) HIV/AIDS Information Site
http://www.qcfurball.com/cat/aids.html

The Community AIDS Treatment Information Exchange (CATIE)
http://www.catie.ca

Health Topics: HIV Infections
http://www.who.int/health_topics/hiv_infections/en/

HIV/AIDS and Disability Global Survey
http://circa.med.yale.edu/globalsurvey

How HIV Infection Is Transmitted
http://www.niaid.nih.gov/vrc/clinitrials/clin_transmission.htm

Infoseek Health Channel: AIDS and HIV
http://www.infoseek.com/health/sexual_health/disease/AIDS_and_HIV

The Integrated Network of Disability Information and Education
http://indie.ca

Mother-to-Infant HIV Infection Transmission
http://www2.niaid.nih.gov/newsroom/simple/perinatal.htm

National Institutes of Health
http://www.nih.gov

National Prevention Information Network
http://www.cdcnpin.org

National Pediatric and Family HIV Resource Center
http://www.pedaids.org

The Teresa Group Child and Family Aid
http://www.teresagroup.ca

UNAIDS: The Joint United Nations Program on HIV/AIDS
http://www.unaids.org

Nervous Systems

Recommended Reading

Noback, C.R., Strominger, N.L., Demarest, R.J., et al. (Eds.). (2005). *The human nervous system: Structure and function* (6th ed.). Totowa, NJ: Humana Press.

Paxinos, G., & Mai, J.K. (2003). *The human nervous system* (2nd ed.). Burlington, MA: Elsevier.

Helpful Internet Information

Kimball's Biology Pages: Central and Peripheral Nervous Systems
http://users.rcn.com/jkimball.ma.ultranet/BiologyPages/C/CNS.html
http://users.rcn.com/jkimball.ma.ultranet/BiologyPages/P/PNS.html

Other Syndromes and Conditions

Recommended Reading

Accardo, P.J., & Whitman, B.Y. (with Behr, S.K., Farrell, A., Magenis, E., et al.) (2002). *Dictionary of developmental disabilities terminology* (2nd ed.). Baltimore: Paul H. Brookes Publishing Co.

American Psychiatric Association. (2000). *Diagnostic and statistical manual of mental disorders* (4th ed., text rev.). Washington, DC: Author.

Baraitser, M., & Winter, R.M. (1996). *Color atlas of congenital malformation syndromes.* London: Mosby-Wolfe.

Batshaw, M.L. (Ed.). (2001). *When your child has a disability: A complete sourcebook of daily and medical care* (Rev. ed.). Baltimore: Paul H. Brookes Publishing Co.

Batshaw, M.L., Pellegrino, L., & Roizen, N.J. (Eds.). (in press). *Children with disabilities* (6th ed.) Baltimore: Paul H. Brookes Publishing Co.

Capute, A.J., & Accardo, P.J. (Eds.). (1996). *Developmental disabilities in infancy and childhood* (2nd ed.). Baltimore: Paul H. Brookes Publishing Co.

Deb, S. (1998). Self-injurious behaviour as part of genetic syndromes. *British Journal of Psychiatry, 172,* 385–388.

Dykens, E. (1995). Measuring behavioral phenotypes: Provocations from the new genetics. *American Journal of Mental Retardation, 99,* 522–532.

Dykens, E. (1996). DNA meets DSM: The growing importance of genetic syndromes in dual diagnosis. *Mental Retardation, 34,* 125–127.

Harris, J.C. (1995). *Developmental neuropsychiatry: Assessment, diagnosis, and treatment of developmental disorders, Vol. II.* Oxford, United Kingdom: Oxford University Press.

Hodapp, R.M. (1997). Direct and indirect behavioral effects of different genetic disorders in mental retardation. *American Journal on Mental Retardation, 102,* 67–79.

Jones, K.L., Smith, D.W., & Fletcher, J. (Eds.). (1997). *Smith's recognizable patterns of human malformation* (5th ed.). Philadelphia: W.B. Saunders Company.

Jung, J.H., Gagne, J.-P., Godden, A.L., et al. (1989). *Genetic syndromes in communication disorders.* Austin, TX: PRO-ED.

Kurtz, M.B., & Berman, W. (1996). Medical issues in residential placement. In A.J. Capute & P.J. Accardo (Eds.), *Developmental disabilities in infancy and childhood, Vol. I: Neurodevelopmental diagnosis and treatment* (2nd ed., pp. 485–510). Baltimore: Paul H. Brookes Publishing Co.

Nickel, R.E., & Desch, L.W. (2000). *The physician's guide to caring for children with disabilities and chronic conditions.* Baltimore: Paul H. Brookes Publishing Co.

Ryan, R.M. (1996). *Handbook of mental health care for persons with developmental disabilities.* Evergreen, CO: S&B Publishing.

Sunada, K. (1995). Syndromes: Do they make a difference? *The National Association for the Dually Diagnosed (NADD) Newsletter, 12*(1), 5–10.

Symons, F.J., & Thompson, T. (1997). Self-injurious behavior and pain. In N.W. Bray (Ed.), *International Review of Research in Mental Retardation: Vol. 21* (pp. 78–83). Toronto, ON: Academic Press.

U.S. National Library of Medicine & the National Institutes of Health. (2003). *Medical dictionary.* Retrieved June 25, 2005, from http://www.nlm.nih.gov/medlineplus/mplusdictionary.html

Wain, H.M., Bruford, E.A., Lovering, R.C., et al. (2002). Guidelines for human gene nomenclature. *Genomics, 79 (4),* 464–470.

Zimmerman, A.W., Jinnah, H.A., & Lockhart, P.J. (1998). Behavioral neuropharmacology. *Mental Retardation and Developmental Disabilities Research Reviews, 4,* 26–35.

Helpful Internet Information

Developmental Disabilities: Resources for Healthcare Providers
http://www.ddhealthinfo.org

Developmental Disabilities Division, University of Western Ontario
http://www.psychiatry.med.uwo.ca/ddp

Disease Directory.net: Genetic Disorders
http://www.diseasedirectory.net/Genetic_Disorders/default.aspx

GeneTests
http://www.geneclinics.org/servlet/access?id=8888891&key=l4PhYLqC9VkbI&fcn=y&fw=XQzz&filename=

The MAGIC Foundation
http://www.magicfoundation.org

National Center for Biotechnology Information, National Library of Medicine, National Institutes of Health
http://www.ncbi.nlm.nih.gov

Online Mendelian Inheritance in Man (OMIM)
http://www.ncbi.nlm.nih.gov/entrez/query.fcgi?db=OMIM

Paul H. Brookes Publishing Co.
http://www.brookespublishing.com

PsycINFO
http://www.apa.org/psycinfo

PubMed
http://www.ncbi.nlm.nih.gov/entrez/query.fcgi

Specific Disabilities and Syndromes
http://ani.autistics.org/other_specific.html

Whonamedit
http://www.whonamedit.com

RESOURCES ON HEALTH AND WELLNESS

General Physical Health

Recommended Reading

Bezchlibnyk-Butler, K.Z., & Jeffries, J.J. (2002). *Clinical handbook of psychotropic drugs* (12th ed.). Toronto: Hogrefe & Huber Publishers.

Blackman, J.A. (1997). *Medical aspects of developmental disabilities in children birth to three* (3rd ed.). Gaithersburg, MD: Aspen Publishers.

Cassidy, S.B., & Allanson, J.E. (2001). *Management of genetic syndromes.* Hoboken, NJ: John Wiley & Sons.

Dykens, E.M., Hodapp, R.M., & Finucane, B.M. (Eds.). (2000). *Genetics and mental retardation syndromes: A new look at behavior and interventions.* Baltimore: Paul H. Brookes Publishing Co.

Fenton, S.T., Perlman, S., & Turner, H. (Eds.). (2003). *Oral health care for people with special needs: Guidelines for comprehensive care.* Englewood Cliffs, NJ: Exceptional Parent Library.

Goldstein, S., & Reynolds, C.R. (1999). *Handbook of neurodevelopmental and genetic disorders in children.* New York: The Guilford Press.
Lennox, N. (Ed.). (2005). *Management guidelines: People with developmental and intellectual disabilities* (Version 2). Melbourne, Australia: Therapeutic Guidelines.
Lewis, C.W., Grossman, D.C., Domoto, P.K., et al. (2000). The role of the pediatrician in the oral health of children: A national survey. *Pediatrics, 106*(6), E84.
National Institute of Dental and Craniofacial Research. (2004). *Practical oral health for people with developmental disabilities.* Retrieved on January 9, 2005, from http://www.nohic.nidcr.nih.gov/poc/Index.aspx
Reiss, S., & Aman, M.G. (Eds.). (1998). *Psychotropic medication and developmental disabilities: The international consensus handbook.* Columbus: The Ohio State University Nisonger Center.
Rubin, I.L., & Crocker, A.C. (Eds.). (2006). *Medical care for children and adults with developmental disabilities* (2nd ed.). Baltimore: Paul H. Brookes Publishing Co.
Surabian, S.R. (2001). Developmental disabilities: Epilepsy, cerebral palsy and autism. *Journal of the California Dental Association, 29,* 424–432.
Tymchuk, A.J. (2006). *The Health and Wellness Program: A parenting curriculum for families at risk.* Baltimore: Paul H. Brookes Publishing Co.
University of Western Ontario. (2005). *Developmental Disabilities Division.* Retrieved December 27, 2005, from http://www.psychiatry.med.uwo.ca/ddp
Wilson, G., & Cooley, W.C. (2000). *Preventative management for children with congenital anomalies and syndromes.* Cambridge, United Kingdom: Cambridge University Press.

Nutrition

Helpful Internet Information

2000 CDC Growth Charts: United States
http://www.cdc.gov/growthcharts

Food Stamp Nutrition Connection: Nutrition and Disability Resources
http://www.nal.usda.gov/foodstamp/Topics/disab1.html

North American Society for Pediatric Gastroenterology, Hepatology and Nutrition
http://www.naspghan.org

Red-Yellow-Green Weight Control System
http://amazingkids.org/red_yellow_green.asp

Psychiatric and Behavioral/Emotional Disturbances

Recommended Reading

Bouras, N. (Ed.). (1999). *Psychiatric and behavioral disorders in developmental disabilities and mental retardation.* Cambridge, United Kingdom: Cambridge University Press.
Brown, I., & Percy, M. (Eds.). (2003). *Developmental disabilities in Ontario* (2nd ed.). Toronto: Ontario Association on Developmental Disabilities.
Fletcher, R.J. (Ed.). (2000). *Therapy approaches for persons with mental retardation.* Kingston, NY: National Association of the Dually Diagnosed.
Fraser, W., & Kerr, M. (Eds.). (2003). *Seminars in the psychiatry of learning disabilities* (2nd ed.). London: The Royal College of Psychiatrists, Gaskell.
Griffiths, D.M., & King, R. (Eds.). (2004). *Demystifying syndromes: Clinical and educational implications of common syndromes associated with persons with intellectual disabilities.* Kingston, NY: National Association of the Dually Diagnosed.
Griffiths, D.M., Stavrakaki, C., & Summers, J. (Eds.). (2002). *An introduction to the mental health needs of persons with developmental disabilities.* Sudbury, ON, Canada: Habilitative Mental Health Resource Network.
Jacobson, J.W., Holburn, S., & Mulick, J.A. (2002). *Contemporary dual diagnosis-MH/MR: Service models Volume II: Partial and supportive services.* Kingston, NY: National Association of the Dually Diagnosed.
Lennox, N., & Diggens, J. (Eds.). (1999). *Management guidelines. People with developmental and intellectual disabilities.* Melbourne, Australia: Therapeutic Guidelines.
Reiss, S., & Aman, M.G. (Eds.). (1998). *Psychotropic medication and developmental disabilities: The international consensus handbook.* Columbus: The Ohio State University, Nisonger Center.

Helpful Internet Information

Centre for Developmental Disability Health, Monash University
http://cddh.med.monash.edu.au/index.html

Centre for Developmental Psychiatry and Psychology, Monash University
http://www.med.monash.edu.au/psychmed/units/devpsych/index.html

Developmental Disabilities Division, University of Western Ontario
http://www.psychiatry.med.uwo.ca/ddp

Learning About Intellectual Disabilities and Health
http://www.intellectualdisability.info

Mental Health Aspects of Developmental Disabilities
http://www.mhaspectsofdd.com

Online Mendelian Inheritance in Man (OMIM)
http://www.ncbi.nlm.nih.gov/omim

Key Organizations

National Association for the Dually Diagnosed (NADD)
http://www.thenadd.org

Society for the Study of Behavioural Phenotypes
http://www.ssbp.co.uk

Sexuality

Recommended Reading and Viewing

Champagne, M.P., & Walker-Hirsch, L. (1993). *Circles: Intimacy and relationships.* Santa Barbara, CA: James Stanfield Publishing.

Feldman, M. (2002). Parents with intellectual disabilities: Impediments and supports. In D.M. Griffiths, D. Richards, P. Fedoroff, et al. (Eds.), *Ethical dilemmas: Sexuality and intellectual disabilities* (pp. 255–293). Kingston, NY: National Association of the Dually Diagnosed.

Griffiths, D. (2002). Sexual aggression. In W.I. Gardner (Ed.), *Aggression and other disruptive behavioral challenges: Biomedical and psychosocial assessment and treatment* (pp. 325–397). Kingston, NY: National Association of the Dually Diagnosed.

Griffiths, D., & Lunsky, Y. (2003). *Sociosexual Knowledge and Attitude Assessment Tool-Revised.* Wood Dale, IL: Stoelting Co.

Griffiths, D., Owen, F., & Arbus-Nevestuk, K. (2002). Sexual policies in agencies supporting persons who have intellectual disabilities: Practice and implementation issues. In D.M. Griffiths, D. Richards, P. Fedoroff, et al. (Eds.), *Ethical dilemmas: Sexuality and intellectual disabilities* (pp. 78–132). Kingston, NY: National Association of the Dually Diagnosed.

Griffiths, D., Richards, D., Watson, S., et al. (2002). Sexuality and mental health issues. In D.M. Griffiths, C. Stavrakaki, & J. Summers (Eds.), *Dual diagnosis: An introduction to the mental health needs of persons with intellectual disabilities* (pp. 419–482). Sudbury, ON, Canada: Habilitative Mental Health Resource Network.

Griffiths, D.M., Quinsey, V.L., & Hingsburger, D. (1989). *Changing inappropriate sexual behavior: A community-based approach for persons with developmental disabilities.* Baltimore: Paul H. Brookes Publishing Co.

Griffiths, D.M., Richards, D., Fedoroff, P., et al. (2002). *Ethical dilemmas: Sexuality and intellectual disabilities.* Kingston, NY: National Association for the Dually Diagnosed.

Haaven, J., Little, R., & Petre-Miller, D. (1990). *Treating intellectually disabled sex offenders.* Orwell, VT: Safer Society.

Hingsburger, D. (1993). *I openers: Parents ask questions about sexuality and children with intellectual disabilities.* Vancouver, BC, Canada: Family Supports Institute Press.

Jacobs, R., Samowitz, P., Levy, P.H., et al. (1992). Young Adult Institute's comprehensive AIDS staff training program. In A.C. Crocker, H.J. Cohen, & T.A. Kastner (Eds.), *HIV infection and intellectual disabilities: A resource for service providers* (pp. 161–169). Baltimore: Paul H. Brookes Publishing Co.

Kastner, T., DeLotto, P., Scagnelli, B., et al. (1990). Proposed guidelines for agencies serving persons with intellectual disabilities and HIV infection. *Mental Retardation, 28,* 139–145.

Kempton, W. (1988). *Life Horizons I and II.* Santa Barbara, CA: James Stanfield Publishing.

Kempton, W. (1993). *Sexuality and persons with disabilities that hinder learning: A comprehensive guide for teachers and professionals.* Santa Barbara, CA: James Stanfield Publishing.

Mansell, S., & Sobsey, D. (2001). *Alone in a crowd* [Training video]. Kingston, NY: National Association of the Dually Diagnosed.

Mansell, S., & Sobsey, D. (2001). *Counseling people with intellectual disabilities who have been sexually abused.* Kingston, NY: National Association of the Dually Diagnosed.

Owen, F., Griffiths, D., & Arbus-Nevestuk, K. (2002). Sexual policies in agencies supporting persons who have intellectual disabilities: Ethical and organizational issues. In D.M. Griffiths, D. Richards, P. Fedoroff, et al. (Eds.), *Ethical dilemmas: Sexuality and intellectual disabilities* (pp. 53–77). Kingston, NY: National Association of the Dually Diagnosed.

Rowe, W., & Savage, S. (1987). *Sexuality and the intellectually handicapped: A guidebook for health care professionals.* Lewiston, NY: E. Mellen Press.

Roeher Institute. (1988). *Vulnerable.* Toronto: Author.

Ward, K.M., Heffern, S.J., Wilcox, D., et al. (1992). *Managing inappropriate sexual behavior: Supporting individuals with intellectual disabilities in the community.* Anchorage: Alaska Specialized Education and Training Services.

Watson, S., Griffiths, D., Richards, D., et al. (Eds.), *Ethical dilemmas: Sexuality and intellectual disabilities* (pp. 175–226). Kingston, NY: National Association of the Dually Diagnosed.

Women's Issues

Recommended Reading

Brigham, L., Atkinson, D., Jackson, M., et al. (Eds.). (2000). *Crossing boundaries: Change and continuity in the history of learning disability.* Plymouth, United Kingdom: British Institute of Learning Disabilities.

Fray, P. (2000). *Caring for Kathleen: A sister's story.* Plymouth, United Kingdom: British Institute of Learning Disabilities.

U.S. Department of Health and Human Services. (2002). *Closing the gap: A national blueprint to improve the health of persons with mental retardation* [Report of the Surgeon General's Conference on Health Disparities and Mental Retardation]. Rockville MD: Office of the Surgeon General.

World Health Organization. (2001). *Gender and women's mental health: Gender disparities and mental health.* Retrieved September 29, 2004, from http://www.who.int/mental_health/prevention/genderwomen/en/

RESOURCES ON HISTORY, TRENDS, AND PERSPECTIVES

Definitions of Disability

Recommended Reading

Accardo, P.J., & Whitman, B.Y. (Eds.). (2002). *Dictionary of developmental disabilities terminology* (2nd ed.). Baltimore: Paul H. Brookes Publishing Co.

Albrecht, G.L., Seelman, K.D., & Bury, M. (Eds.). (2001). *Handbook of disability studies.* Thousand Oaks, CA: Sage Publications.

Helpful Internet Information

The Definition and Prevalence of Intellectual Disability in Australia
http://www.aihw.gov.au/publications/welfare/dpida/dpida-c00.html

Definition of "Disability" in Iran (and Other Countries)
http://www.unescap.org/stat/meet/widsm1/widsm1%5Fnenad3.asp

Developmental Disabilities
http://www.pitt.edu/~ginie/disability/dvp_delay.html

Disability Organizations
http://www.theagapecenter.com/Organizations/Disabilities

Hebrew-Language Site Dedicated to Intellectual Disabilities
http://www.pigur.co.il/main/main.htm

Revising the United Nations Census Recommendations on Disability
http://www.cdc.gov/nchs/about/otheract/citygroup/products/me_mbogoni1.htm

Future Challenges

Recommended Reading

American Association on Mental Retardation. (2005). *Fact sheet: Person-centered planning.* Retrieved March 13, 2006, from http://www.aamr.org/Policies/faq_planning.shtml

The Arc of the United States. (2005). *Technology for people with intellectual disabilities.* Retrieved March 13, 2006, from http://www.thearc.org/faqs/assistivetechnology.doc

Hammel, J., Lai, J.-S., & Heller, T. (2002). The impact of assistive technology and environmental interventions on function and living situation status with people who are ageing with developmental disabilities. *Disability and Rehabilitation: An International Multidisciplinary Journal, 24,* 93–105.

Ouellette-Kuntz, H., Garcin, N., Lewis, M.E., et al. (2005). Addressing health disparities through promoting equity for individuals with intellectual disability. *Canadian Journal of Public Health, 96,* S8–S22.

Pennsylvania Department of Public Welfare. (2004). *Reframing the future.* Retrieved March 13, 2006, from http://www.dpw.state.pa.us/General/FormsPub/MentalRetardationPublications/003670119.htm

Ruddick, L. (2005). Health of people with intellectual disabilities: A review of factors influencing access to health care. *British Journal of Health Psychology, 10,* 559–70.

Samuel Gridley Howe Library. (2001). *Bibliographies: Person-centered planning.* Retrieved March 13, 2006, from http://www.brandeis.edu/lemberg/SGHL/Subpages/Collections/bibs/Percenpl.pdf#search='personcentered%20planning

Social Work Program at Metropolitan State College of Denver. (2005). *Assessing strengths and stresses with families with children with special needs: An ecological perspective.* Retrieved March 13, 2006, from http://www.developmentaldisability.org/assessing_strengths_and_stresses.htm

Tuffrey-Wijne, I. (2003). The palliative care needs of people with intellectual disabilities: A literature review. *Palliative Medicine, 17,* 55–62.

U.S. Department of Health and Human Services, Administration for Children and Families. (2006). *National Network of University Centers for Excellence in Developmental Disabilities Education, Research, and Service.* Retrieved March 13, 2006, from http://www.acf.dhhs.gov/programs/add/states/ucedds.html

U.S. Department of Health and Human Services, Administration for Children and Families. (2006). *Assistive technology and information.* Retrieved March 13, 2006, from http://www.acf.hhs.gov/programs/pcpid/2004_rpt_pres/2004_rpt_pg9.htm

Wehmeyer, M.L., Smith, S.J., Palmer, S.B., et al. (2004). Technology use and people with mental retardation. *International Review of Research in Mental Retardation, 29,* 291–337.

Helpful Internet Information

AAMR Special Interest Group on Technology and Mental Retardation
http://www.aamr.org/Groups/si/TE

ConnectABILITY, Community Living Toronto
http://www.communitylivingtoronto.ca/TACLWeb/ConnectAbility

Key Organizations

American Association of People with Disabilities (AAPD)
http://www.aapd.com

American Association on Mental Retardation (AAMR)
http://www.aamr.org

The Arc of the United States
http://thearc.org

Association of University Centers on Disabilities (AUCD)
http://www.aucd.org

Down Syndrome International
http://www.down-syndrome-int.org

Inclusion International
http://www.inclusion-international.org

InterRAI
http://www.interrai.org/section/view

National Association for the Dually Diagnosed
http://www.thenadd.org

Ontario Association on Developmental Disabilities (OADD)
http://www.oadd.org

World Association of Persons with disAbilities
http://www.wapd.org

History of Disabilities

Recommended Reading

Braddock, D. (Ed.). (2002). *Disability at the dawn of the 21st century and the state of the states.* Washington, DC: American Association on Mental Retardation.

Braddock, D.L., & Parish, S.L. (2001). An institutional history of disability. In G.L. Albrecht, K.D. Seelman, & M. Bury (Eds.), *Handbook of disability studies* (pp. 11–68). Thousand Oaks, CA: Sage Publications.

Clark, A.M., & Clarke, A.D.B. (1975). *Mental deficiency: The changing outlook.* London: Methuen.

Laws, G., & Radford, J. (1998). Place, identity and disability: Narratives of intellectually disabled people in Toronto. In R.A. Kearns & W.M. Gesler (Eds.), *Putting health into place: Landscape, identity and well-being* (pp. 77–101). Syracuse, NY: Syracuse University Press.

Longmore, P.K., & Umansky, L. (Eds.). (2001). *The new dis-*

ability history: American perspectives. New York: New York University Press.
McLaren, A. (1990). *Our own master race: Eugenics in Canada.* Toronto: McClelland and Stewart.
Mithen, S. (1996). *The prehistory of the mind.* London: Phoenix.
Neugebauer, R. (1979). Medieval and early modern theories of mental illness. *Archives of General Psychiatry, 36,* 477–483.
Oliver, M. (1990). *The politics of disablement.* London: Macmillan.
Park, D.C. (1995). *An imprisoned text: Reading the Canadian Mental Handicap Asylum.* Unpublished Doctoral Dissertation, York University, Toronto.
Radford, J.P., & Park, D.C. (1993). 'A convenient means of riddance': Institutionalization of people diagnosed as 'mentally deficient' in Ontario, 1876–1934. *Health and Canadian Society, 1,* 369–392.
Rapley, M. (2004). *The social construction of intellectual disability.* Cambridge, United Kingdom: Cambridge University Press.
Rosen, M., Clark, G.R., & Kivitz, M.S. (Eds.). (1976). *The history of mental retardation: Collected papers.* Baltimore: University Park Press.
Sloan, W., & Stevens, H.A. (1976). *A century of concern: A history of the American Association on Mental Deficiency, 1876–1976.* Washington, DC: American Association on Mental Retardation.
Tyler, L.T., & Bell, L.V. (1984). *Caring for the retarded in America.* Westport, CN: Greenwood Press.

Helpful Internet Information

1824 Law Establishing County Poorhouses in New York
http://www.poorhousestory.com/1824_law.htm

Anencephaly
http://www.angelfire.com/mn/michaelashope/anencephalyfact.html

Asylums History: United States
http://search.yahoo.com/search?fr=slv1–&p=+asylums+history+united+states

Bibliography of the Histories of Idiocy
http://www.personal.dundee.ac.uk/~mksimpso/histories.htm

Disability History Museum
http://www.disabilitymuseum.org

Historic Asylums
http://www.rootsweb.com/~asylums/index.html#il

Impact of Infectious Diseases on Development of Human Societies
http://www.cas.muohio.edu/~stevenjr/mbi111/impact111.html

Index of English and Welsh Lunatic Asylums and Mental Hospitals
http://www.mdx.ac.uk/www/study/4_13_TA.htm#AsylumsIndex

Mental Health History Timeline
http://www.shef.ac.uk/~nmhuk/mhnurs/timline/mhtimeline.html

Museum of disABILITY History
http://www.people-inc.org/museum/mission.asp

NINDS Microcephaly Information Page
http://www.ninds.nih.gov/disorders/microcephaly/microcephaly.htm

Parallels in Time: A History of Developmental Disabilities
http://www.mncdd.org/parallels/menu.html

A Timeline of Learning Disability Nursing
http://www.shef.ac.uk/~nmhuk/ldnurs/timline/ldtimeline.html

Perspectives on Disabilities

Recommended Reading

Clinical Bulletin
http://www.psychiatry.med.uwo.ca/ddp/index.htm
Inclusion International. (1994). *Just technology? From principles to practice in bio-ethical issues.* Toronto: Roeher Institute.
Ingstad, B., & Whyte, S.R. (Eds.). (2001). *Disability and culture.* Berkeley: University of California Press.
Journal on Developmental Disabilities
http://www.oadd.org
Renwick, R., Brown, I., & Nagler, M. (1996). *Quality of life in health promotion and rehabilitation: Conceptual approaches, issues, and applications.* Thousand Oaks, CA: Sage Publications.
Rioux, M., & Bach, M. (1994). *Disability is not measles: New research paradigms in disability.* Toronto: Roeher Institute.
Roeher Institute. (1991). *Changing Canadian schools: Perspectives on disability and inclusion.* Toronto: Author.
Roeher Institute. (1992). *On target? Canada's employment-related programs for persons with disabilities.* Toronto: Author.
Roeher Institute. (1993). *Social well-being: A paradigm for reform.* Toronto: Author.
Roeher Institute. (1997). *Disability, community and society: Exploring the links.* Toronto: Author.
Taylor, S.J., Bogdan, R., & Lutfiyya, Z.M. (Eds.). (1995). *The variety of community experience: Qualitative studies of family and community life.* Baltimore: Paul H. Brookes Publishing Co.
United Nations. (1988). *Human rights: A compilation of international instruments.* New York: Author.

Trends and Issues in Disabilities

Recommended Reading

Braddock, D. (Ed.). (2002). *Disability at the dawn of the 21st century and the state of the states.* Washington, DC: American Association on Mental Retardation.
Brown, I. (1998). *How to develop an individual funding plan.* Toronto: University of Toronto, Faculty of Social Work.
Governor's Commission on Mental Retardation. (2000). *The road ahead: Trends in mental retardation services at the beginning of the 21st century.* Boston: Author.

Helpful Internet Information

Developmental Disabilities Resources
http://www.nornet.on.ca/~dbiddle/devdis.htm

Disability Resources-Developmental Disabilities
http://www.independentliving.org/links/links-developmental-disabilities.html

SelfAdvocateNet.com
http://www.selfadvocatenet.com/links

RESOURCES ON LEGAL AND HUMAN RIGHTS ISSUES

Human Rights

Recommended Reading

The Council on Quality and Leadership. (2004). *All about rights: A guide to supporting the rights of people with intellectual disabilities.* Available from http://www.accredcouncil.org/publications/gettingready.html#rights

Office of the High Commissioner for Human Rights. (1998). *Basic human rights instruments.* Geneva, Office of the High Commission for Human Rights.

Quinn, G., & Degener, T. (Eds.). (2002). *Human rights and disability: The current use and future potential of United Nations human rights instruments in the context of disability.* Retrieved October 28, 2005, from http://193.194.138.190/disability/study.htm

Rioux, M. (Ed.). (2001). *Let the world know: Report of a seminar on human rights and disability.* Retrieved October 28, 2005, from http://www.un.org/esa/socdev/enable/stockholmnov2000.htm

Helpful Internet Information

Disability Rights Promotion International (DRPI)
http://www.yorku.ca/drpi

Office of the High Commission for Human Rights: Disability
http://www.ohchr.org/english/issues/disability/index.htm

United Nations Enable (UN Enable)
http://www.un.org/esa/socdev/enable

Key Organizations

International Disability Alliance (IDA)
http://www.internationaldisabilityalliance.org

Legal Entitlements

Recommending Reading

The Arc of New Mexico. (2004). *Self-determination and self-advocacy.* Retrieved March 14, 2006, from http://www.arcnm.org/index.php/selfdet_selfadvoc

Carty, E.M. (1998). Disability and childbirth: Meeting the challenges. *Canadian Medical Association Journal, 159,* 363–369.

Cooper, J. (2000). *Law, rights, and disability.* London: Jessica Kingsley Publishers.

Council of Canadians with Disabilities. (n.d.). *Consumers with disabilities speak out on health issues.* Retrieved March 14, 2006, from http://www.ccdonline.ca/publications/Health%20Issues/healthissues.htm

Council of Canadians with Disabilities. (1999). *A work in progress: A national strategy for persons with disabilities-the community definition.* Retrieved March 14, 2006, from http://www.ccdonline.ca/law-reform/analysis/natstategy.htm

Comhairle. (2005). *Entitlements for people with disabilities* (11th ed.) Retrieved March 14, 2006, from http://www.comhairle.ie/publications/entitlements/downloads/Disabilities.pdf

Griffiths, D., Owen, F., Gosse, L., et al. (2003). Human rights and persons with intellectual disabilities: An action-research approach for community-based organizational self-evaluation. *Journal on Developmental Disabilities, 10*(2), 25–42.

Hakimian, R. (2002). Patients' rights and emergency medical treatment: An emerging right to emergency care? *European Journal of Emergency Medicine, 9,* 87–90.

Hammum, H. (Ed.). (1992). *Guide to international human rights practice* (2nd ed.). New York: Transnational Publishers.

Hendriks, A. (1995). Disabled persons and their right to equal treatment: Allowing differentiation while ending discrimination. *Health and Human Rights, 1,* 152–173.

Hernandez, B., Keys, C., Balcazar, F., et al. (1998). Construction and validation of the Disability Rights Attitude Scale: Assessing attitudes toward the Americans with Disabilities Act (ADA). *Rehabilitation Psychology, 43,* 203–218.

Herr, S. (1995). A humanist's legacy: Burton Blatt and the origins of the disability rights movement. *Mental Retardation, 33,* 328–331.

Mandelstam, M. (2005). *Community care practice and the law* (3rd ed.). London: Jessica Kingsley Publishers.

Manderson, L. (2004). Disability, global legislation and human rights. *Development, 47*(2), 29–35.

Mechanic, D. (1998). Public trust and initiatives for new health care partnerships. *The Milbank Quarterly, 76,* 281–302.

Parens, E., & Asch, A. (2003). Disability rights critique of prenatal genetic testing: Reflections and recommendations. *Mental Retardation and Developmental Disabilities Research Reviews, 9,* 40–47.

Racino, J.A. (1999). *Policy, program evaluation, and research in disability: Community support for all.* New York: Haworth Press.

Raz, A. (2004). Important to test, import to support: Attitudes toward disability rights and prenatal diagnosis among leaders of support groups for genetic disorders in Israel. *Social Science & Medicine, 59,* 1857–1866.

Rioux, M., & Carbert, A. (2003). Human rights and disability: The international context. *Journal on Developmental Disabilities, 10*(2), 1–13.

United Nations, Ad Hoc Committee on a Comprehensive and Integral International Convention on Protection and Promotion of the Rights and Dignity of Persons with Disabilities. (2003, June 16–27). *Issues and emerging trends related to advancement of persons with disabilities: Report of the Secretary-General.* Retrieved March 14, 2006, from http://www.un.org/esa/socdev/enable/rights/a_ac265_2003_1e.htm

Van Houten, D., & Bellemakers, C. (2002). Equal citizenship for all: Disability policy in the Netherlands: Empowerment of marginals. *Disability & Society, 17,* 171–185.

Walsh, P.N. (1997). Old world-new territory: European perspectives on intellectual disability. *Journal of Intellectual Disability Research, 41,* 112–128.

Young, D.A., & Quibell, R. (2000). Why rights are never enough: Rights, intellectual disability and understanding. *Disability & Society, 15,* 747–764.

Helpful Internet Information

DND Press Disability Research Library
http://www.dndpress.com/index.htm

Independent Living
http://www.jik.com/ilcs.html

RESOURCES ON LIFESPAN ISSUES

Key Organizations

General

Inclusion International
http://www.inclusion-international.org

Institute on Disability (University Center for Excellence on Disability)
http://iod.unh.edu

International Association for the Scientific Study of Intellectual Disabilities (IASSID)
http://www.iassid.org

People First
http://www.peoplefirst.org.uk

Special Olympics
http://www.specialolympics.com/Special+Olympics+Public+Website/default.htm

By Country or Region

Canada
Canadian Association for Community Living
http://www.cacl.ca

Europe
European Association of Service Providers for Persons with Disabilities
http://www.easpd.org

Finland
Finnish Association on Mental Retardation
http://www.famr.fi/frontpage

India
National Institute for Mentally Handicapped
http://www.nimhindia.org

Ireland
National Disability Authority
http://www.nda.ie

Netherlands
Landelijk Kennis Netwerk Gehandicaptenzorg [National Knowledge Network on Disabilities]
http://www.lkng.nl

Singapore
Association for Persons with Special Needs
http://www.apsn.org.sg

Spain
Confederación Española de Federaciones de Asociaciones en favor de las Personas con Retraso Mental
http://www.feaps.org

Uganda
National Union of Disabled Persons of Uganda
http://www.disability.dk/site/countryindex.php?section_id=4

United Kingdom
British Institute of Learning Disabilities
http://www.bild.org.uk

United States
American Association on Mental Retardation (AAMR)
http://www.aamr.org

The Arc of the United States
http://thearc.org

Aging with Disabilities

Recommended Reading

Bigby, C. (2000). *Moving on without parents: Planning, transitions and sources of support for middle-aged and older adults with intellectual disability.* Baltimore: Paul H. Brookes Publishing Co.

Bigby, C. (2004). *Aging with a lifelong disability: Policy, program and practice issues for professionals.* London: Jessica Kingsley Publishers.

Davidson, P., Prasher, V., & Janicki, M.P. (Eds.). (2003). *Mental health, intellectual disabilities and the ageing process.* Oxford, United Kingdom: Blackwell Publishing.

Dodd, K., Turk, V., & Christmas, M. (2002). *Resource pack for carers of adults with Down syndrome and dementia.* Kidderminster, United Kingdom: British Institute of Learning Disabilities.

Janicki, M.P., & Ansello, E.F. (Eds.). (2000). *Community supports for aging adults with lifelong disabilities.* Baltimore: Paul H. Brookes Publishing Co.

Janicki, M.P., & Dalton, A. (Eds.). (1999). *Dementia, aging and intellectual disabilities.* Philadelphia: Brunner/Mazel.

Janicki, M.P., Heller, T., Seltzer, G., et al. (1996). Practice guidelines for the clinical assessment and care management of Alzheimer's disease and other dementias among adults with intellectual disability. *Journal of Intellectual Disability Research, 40,* 374–382.

Prasher, V., & Janicki, M. (Eds.). (2003). *Physical health of adults with intellectual disabilities.* Oxford, United Kingdom: Blackwell Publishing.

Special Interest Research Group on Aging and Intellectual Disability, Inclusion International, & World Health Organization. (2001). Ageing and intellectual disability: Improving longevity and promoting healthy ageing. *Journal of Applied Research in Intellectual Disabilities, 14*(3), 171–275.

Walsh, P.N., & Heller, T. (Eds.). (2002). *Health of women with intellectual disabilities.* Oxford, United Kingdom: Blackwell Publishing.

Helpful Internet Information

The Arc: Aging with Mental Retardation
http://www.thearc.org/aging.html

International Association for the Scientific Study of Intellectual Disabilities (IASSID): Aging Special Interest Research Group
http://www.iassid.org

Rehabilitation and Research Training Center on Aging with Developmental Disabilities, University of Illinois at Chicago
http://www.uic.edu/orgs/rrtcamr

Child Maltreatment

Recommended Reading

Arnaldo, C.A. (Ed.). (2001). *Child abuse on the Internet: Ending the silence.* New York: UNESCO Publishing/Berghahn Books.

Covell, K., & Howe, R.B. (2001). *The challenge of children's rights for Canada.* Waterloo, ON, Canada: Wilfred Laurier University Press.

Ericson, K., Isaacs, B., & Perlman, N. (2003). Enhancing communication with persons with developmental disabilities: The special case of interviewing victim-witnesses of sexual abuse. In I. Brown & M. Percy (Eds.), *Developmental disabilities in Ontario* (2nd ed., pp. 465–476). Toronto: Ontario Association on Developmental Disabilities.

Garbarino, J., Brookhouser, P.E., Authier, K., et al. (1987). *Special children, special risks: The maltreatment of children with disabilities.* New York: Aldine De Gruyter.

Griffiths, D., & Marini, Z. (2000). Interacting with the legal system regarding a sexual offence: Social and cognitive considerations for persons with developmental disabilities. *Journal on Developmental Disabilities, 7,* 76–121.

Macdonald, G. (2001). *Effective interventions for child abuse and neglect: An evidence-based approach to planning and evaluating interventions.* Hoboken, NJ: John Wiley & Sons.

Sobsey, D. (1994). *Violence and abuse in the lives of people with disabilities: The end of silent acceptance?* Baltimore: Paul H. Brookes Publishing Co.

Trocmé, N., MacLaurin, B., Fallon, B., et al. (2001). *Canadian incidence study of reported child abuse and neglect: Final report.* Ottawa, ON, Canada: Minister of Public Works and Government Services Canada.

Helpful Internet Information

American Academy of Pediatrics Policy Statement on Assessment of Maltreatment of Children with Disabilities
http://aappolicy.aappublications.org/cgi/content/full/pediatrics%3b108/2/508

American Academy of Pediatrics Statement on Sexual Abuse, the Need for Sex Education, and Developmental Disabilities
http://aappolicy.aappublications.org/cgi/content/abstract/pediatrics;97/2/275

CAN Do: Child Abuse and Neglect Disability Outreach Project
http://disability-abuse.com/cando/index.html

Centers for Disease Control and Prevention, Division of Violence Prevention: Selected Publications
http://www.cdc.gov/ncipc/dvp/SelectedPubsViolence%20Prevention.htm

Disability and Victimization Resources
http://www.vaonline.org/dbty.html

DisabilityResources.org: Resources on Abuse of People with Disabilities
http://www.disabilityresources.org/ABUSE.html

Family Violence and People with Intellectual Disabilities
http://www.hc-sc.gc.ca/hppb/familyviolence/html/fvintellectu_e.html

People with Mental Retardation and Sexual Abuse
http://www.thearc.org/faqs/Sexabuse.html

Violence, Abuse and Disability
http://www.ualberta.ca/~jpdasddc/abuse

Lifestyle Issues of Adults with Disabilities

Recommended Reading and Viewing

Brock, W. (Producer). (1998). *If I can't do it* [Videorecording]. Harriman, NY: Walter Brock Productions.

Brown, I., & Renwick, R. (1997). Understanding what we mean by quality of life [editorial]. *Journal on Developmental Disabilities, 5*(2), i–vii.

Carter, E.W. (in press). *Including people with disabilities in faith communities: A guide for service providers, families, and congregations.* Baltimore: Paul H. Brookes Publishing Co.

McLaughlin, J.F., & Bjornson, K.F. (1998). Quality of life and developmental disabilities [editorial]. *Developmental Medicine and Child Neurology, 40,* 435.

New York State Developmental Disabilities Planning Council. (1990). *When people with developmental disabilities age* [Videorecording]. Albany: Author.

Walker-Hirsch, L. (Ed.). (2007). *The facts of life . . . and more: Sexuality and intimacy for people with intellectual disabilities.* Baltimore: Paul H. Brookes Publishing Co.

Helpful Internet Information

Community Living and Family Issues Resources and Sites
http://www.psychiatry.med.uwo.ca/ddp/resources&sites/communityliving&familyissues/communityliving&familyissues.htm

Disability Action Hall
http://disability.activist.ca

Institute for Health Research, Lancaster University: Residential Supports
http://www.lancs.ac.uk/fss/ihr/research/learning/publications/residential.htm

Residential Services and Trends for Persons with Developmental Disabilities: Status and Trends Through 2003
http://rtc.umn.edu/risp03/risp03.pdf

Roeher Institute's *Portraits of Our Lives* book series
http://www.roeher.ca/comersus/subject.htm

You're Able.com
http://www.youreable.com

Parenting by People with Intellectual Disabilities

Recommended Reading

Booth, T., & Booth, W. (1998). *Growing up with parents who have learning difficulties.* London: Routledge.

Feldman, M.A. (1997). The effectiveness of early intervention for children of parents with mental retardation. In M.J. Guralnick (Ed.), *The effectiveness of early intervention* (pp. 171–191). Baltimore: Paul H. Brookes Publishing Co.

Feldman, M.A. (1998). Parents with intellectual disabilities: Implications and interventions. In J. Lutzker (Ed.), *Child abuse: A handbook of theory, research and treatment* (pp. 401–419). New York: Kluwer Academic/Plenum Publishers.

Feldman, M.A. (2002). Parents with intellectual disabilities and their children: Impediments and supports. In. D. Griffiths & P. Federoff (Eds.), *Ethical dilemmas: Sexuality and developmental disability* (pp. 255–292). Kingston, NY: National Association of the Dually Diagnosed.

Feldman, M.A. (2004). *The Family Game: Enhancing parent-child cooperation and rapport to parents with learning problems.* St. Catharines, ON, Canada: Department of Child and Youth Studies, Brock University.

Feldman, M.A., & Case, L. (1997). *Step by step child care: Teaching aids for parents, child-care workers, and babysitters.* St. Catharines, ON, Canada: Department of Child and Youth Studies, Brock University.

Heighway, S. (1992). *Helping parents parent: A practice guide for supporting families headed by parents with cognitive limitations. Supported Parenting Project.* Madison: Wisconsin Council of Developmental Disabilities.

Jewell, P. (1998). *Out of the mainstream: A parenting group for parents with an intellectual disability and their children.* Melbourne, Victoria: Disability Services Division, Victoria Government Department of Human Services.

Jones, A. (1996). *Parents with an intellectual disability: A worker's manual.* Melbourne, Victoria, Australia: Disability Services Division, Victoria Government Department of Human Services.

Llewellyn, G., McConnell, D., Grace-Dunn, R., et al. (1999). *Parents with intellectual disability and older children: Strategies for support workers.* Melbourne, Victoria, Australia: Disability Services Division, Victoria Government Department of Human Services.

McCusker, B., & Irwin, B. (2001). *Building foundations: A curriculum guide for supported parenting.* Baltimore: PACT.

Tymchuk, A.J. (1998). *Parents with "functional or categorical" disabilities: Risk assessment, case management and techniques for improving parenting skills. A training manual for caseworkers.* Los Angeles: Inter-University Consortium on Child Welfare.

Tymchuk, A. (2006). *The Health and Wellness Program: A parenting curriculum for families at risk.* Baltimore: Paul H. Brookes Publishing Co.

Tymchuk, A.J., Andron, L., Bavolek, S.J., et al. (1992). *Nurturing program for parents with special learning needs and their children: Activities manual for parents.* Los Angeles: University of California-Los Angeles.

International Reports

Australia

McConnell, D., Llewellyn, G. & Ferronato, L. (2000). *Parents with a disability and the NSW children's court: Report to the Law Foundation of NSW. University of Sydney.* Lindcombe, Australia: University of Sydney.

Canada

Aunos, M., Goupil, G., & Feldman, M. (2004). *Les mères présentant une déficience intellectuelle au Québec: Rapport préliminaire concernant 50 mères et leurs enfants. Centre de Réadaptation de l'Ouest de Montréal. Dépôt légal Bibliothèque Nationale du Canada, Bibliothèque Nationale du Québec* [Mothers with intellectual disabilities: Preliminary report regarding 50 mothers and their children]. Lachine, Quebec, Canada: Research Department, West Montreal Readaptation Center.

France

Coppin, B., Dubus, A., & Hedoux, J. (2003). *Enquete sur la deficience intellectuelle et la parentalite: rapport intermediaire* [Survey on intellectual disabilities and parenthood: Preliminary report]. Lille, France: Laboratoire de récherche Parents avec Déficience Intellectuelle (PADI).

Helpful Internet Information

Australia

Disability Services Division, Victoria Government Department of Human Services
http://www.dhs.vic.gov.au/disability

Family Support and Services Project, School of Occupational and Leisure Sciences, University of Sydney
http://www3.fhs.usyd.edu.au/fssp/parents/index.htm

United Kingdom

Learning About Intellectual Disabilities and Health
http://www.intellectualdisability.info/lifestages/ds_parent.htm

Supported Parenting for Mothers and Fathers with Learning Difficulties
http://www.supported-parenting.com

United States

Children's Services Practice Notes
http://www.practicenotes.org

Quality Mall Supported Parenting Series
http://www.qualitymall.org

Wisconsin Council on Developmental Disabilities
http://wcdd.org/Publications/publications.cfm

Prenatal and Early Life Issues

Helpful Internet Information

Canadian Abilities Foundation
http://www.abilities.ca

CanChild Centre for Childhood Disability Research at McMaster University
http://www.fhs.mcmaster.ca/canchild

Contact a Family
http://www.cafamily.org.uk

Disability World
http://www.disabilityworld.org

Dzherelo Children's Rehabilitation Centre
http://www.dzherelocentre.org.ua

International Center for Disability Resources on the Internet (ICDRI)
http://www.icdri.org

Internet Resources for Special Children (IRSC)
http://www.irsc.org

Jim Lubin's disABILITY Information and Resources
http://www.makoa.org

Mobility International USA (MIUSA)
http://www.miusa.org

Parents Helping Parents (PHP)
http://www.php.com

PsycINFO
http://www.apa.org/psycinfo

PubMed
http://www.ncbi.nlm.nih.gov/entrez/query.fcgi

World Health Organization: Disability, Including Prevention, Management and Rehabilitation
http://www.who.int/ncd/disability

World Institute on Disability (WID)
http://www.wid.org

Quality of Life Issues

Recommended Reading and Viewing

Bailey, D.B., McWilliam, R.A., Darkes, L.A., et al. (1998). Family outcomes in early intervention: A framework for program evaluation and efficacy research. *Exceptional Children, 64*(3), 313–328.

Harry, B. (2002). Trends and issues in serving culturally diverse families of children with disabilities. *Journal of Special Education, 36*(3), 131–138.

Ouellette-Kuntz, H., & Burge, P. (Producers). (1998). *Learning from each other: Physicians and parents of persons with developmental disabilities* [Videotape]. Kingston, ON, Canada: Queen's University.

Schiefelbusch, R.L., & Schroeder, S.S. (Eds.). (2006). *Doing science and doing good: A history of the Bureau of Child Research and the Schiefelbusch Institute for Life Span Studies at the University of Kansas.* Baltimore: Paul H. Brookes Publishing Co.

Singer, G.H.S. (2002). Suggestions for a pragmatic program of research on families and disability. *Journal of Special Education, 36*(3), 148–154.

Helpful Internet Information

Birth Defect Research for Children
http://www.birthdefects.org

Consortium on Appropriate Dispute Resolution in Special Education (CADRE)
http://www.directionservice.org/cadre/index.cfm

Contact a Family
http://www.cafamily.org.uk

Family Village
http://familyvillage.wisc.edu

Federation of Families for Children's Mental Health
http://www.ffcmh.org

Mothers United for Moral Support (MUMS)
http://www.netnet.net/mums

Parent Advocacy Coalition for Educational Rights (PACER) Center
http://www.pacer.org

Quality Mall
http://www.qualitymall.org

Quality of Life Research Unit
http://www.utoronto.ca/qol

Roeher Institute
http://www.roeher.ca

Work and Employment

Recommended Reading

Griffin, C., & Hammis, D. (2003). *Making self-employment work for people with disabilities.* Baltimore: Paul H. Brookes Publishing Co.

Wehman, P., Inge, K.J. Revell, Jr., W.G., et al. (Eds.). (2007). *Real work for real pay: Inclusive employment for people with disabilities.* Baltimore: Paul H. Brookes Publishing Co.

Journals

Education and Training in Mental Retardation
http://www.dddcec.org/publications.htm

Journal of Rehabilitation
http://www.nationalrehab.org/website/pubs/index.html

Journal of Vocational Rehabilitation
http://www.iospress.nl/loadtop/load.php?isbn=10522263

Helpful Internet Information

Australian Government, Department of Family and Community Services
http://www.facs.gov.au

Canadian Centre for Disability Studies
http://www.disabilitystudies.ca

The Center on Human Policy, Syracuse University
http://soeweb.syr.edu/thechp/index.html

Human Resources and Skills Development Canada
http://www.hrdc-drhc.gc.ca

Research and Training Center (RRTC), Virginia Commonwealth University
http://www.vcu.edu/rrtcweb

Roeher Institute
http://www.roeher.ca

Social Firms UK
http://www.socialfirms.co.uk

Index

Page numbers followed by *d, f,* and *t* indicate displays, figures, and tables, respectively.